D1365742

ENCYCLOPEDIA OF

COLLEGE

BASKETBALL

ENCYCLOPEDIA OF

COLLEGE

BASKETBALL

MIKE DOUCHANT

FOREWORD: HOOP HEAVEN, BY DICK VITALE

Gale Research Inc.

An International Thomson Publishing Company

I(T)P

NEW YORK • LONDON • BONN • BOSTON • DETROIT • MADRID
MELBOURNE • MEXICO CITY • PARIS • SINGAPORE • TOKYO
TORONTO • WASHINGTON • ALBANY NY • BELMONT CA • CINCINNATI OH

Gale Research Inc. Staff

Lawrence W. Baker, *Managing Editor*
Marie Ellavich, Jolen Gedridge, Jane Hoehner, Camille Killens, Allison McNeill, Kelle Sisung, *Contributing Editors*

David E. Salamie, *Acquisitions Editor*

Mary Beth Trimper, *Production Director*
Evi Seoud, *Assistant Production Manager*
Shanna P. Heilveil, *Production Assistant*

Cynthia Baldwin, *Product Design Manager*
Mark C. Howell, *Cover and Page Designer*

Barbara J. Yarrow, *Graphic Services Supervisor*
Todd Nessel, *Macintosh Artist*
C. J. Jonik, *Desktop Publisher*
Willie Mathis, *Camera Operator*

Front cover photograph: AP/Wide World Photos
Back cover photograph: Cliff McBride, *College Sports Magazine*
Front cover graphics: Somberg Design
Typesetting: Marco Di Vita at the Graphix Group—the ultimate clutch player in the game of page layout. Neither natural fires, nor broken-down motor homes, nor inactive cellular phones, nor thunderstorms keep this guy down for long.

Library of Congress Cataloging-in-Publication Data

Douchant, Mike, 1951–
    Encyclopedia of college basketball / Mike Douchant.
    p.   cm.
    Includes bibliographical references and index.
    ISBN 0-8103-9640-8
    1. Basketball—United States—History. 2. College sports—United States—History. I. Title.
GV885.7.D68 1994
796.323'0973   94-35209
                                                                                                                                    CIP

 ™ This book is printed on acid-free paper that meets the minimum requirements of American National Standard for Information Sciences—Permanence Paper for Printed Library Materials, ANSI Z39.48-1984.

 This book is printed on recycled paper that meets Environmental Protection Agency standards.

ISBN 0-8103-9640-8
Printed in the United States of America by Gale Research Inc.
Published simultaneously in the United Kingdom by Gale Research International Limited
(An affiliated company of Gale Research Inc.)

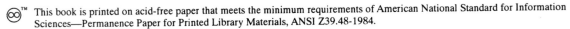

The trademark **ITP** is used under license.

I'm fortunate to be surrounded by the finest "Final Four" of all—
Linda, Keith, Rebekah, and Laura

CONTENTS

Post-Game Festivities

HOOP HEAVEN
by Dick Vitale

It's hoop heaven every time I walk into an arena. The color, the spontaneity, the pageantry, and excitement all make the game I love an unbelievable thrill. Every game is different, bringing something entirely new to the picnic. Doesn't something that leaves you with so many special feelings deserve an innovative lingo all its own? Unless you've been living under a rock, you know that I'm a basketball junkie with a wild vocabulary. Don't ask me to explain it, but I just live and breathe the game and am consumed with learning and sharing Vital(e) facts.

As an out-and-out hoop addict, I speak a different language with lots of wacko phrases and words and all sorts of combinations of abbreviations. For instance, I call a basketball "the rock." A Rolls Roycer is a player or coach among the best. Brick City is when a player or team shoots poorly. A Diaper Dandy is a dazzling freshman. N.C. stands for no contest. P.T. is playing time. P.T.P.er is prime time player. W's and L's are wins and losses, respectively. Yes, Dick's Dictionary is unbelievable, baby, and needs to be updated annually. The unique terms represent my emotional attachment to an out-of-this-world sport I've always loved.

In a galaxy far far away and otherwise known as New Jersey, I had a full head of hair and loved playing and watching basketball. You better believe I can stroke the open J (jumper). Get me the rock, baby! I'll take on anyone in a free-throw shooting contest. I can flat-out hit the 15-footer, but move me beyond the free-throw line and it's Brick City, USA.

I loved coaching and watching basketball. Back then I wore thick glasses and K-Mart special outfits that now inspire good-natured razzing when someone looks at my old photos. If ESPN had existed during my coaching days, I probably would have been recognized as the wackiest coach to ever patrol a sideline.

I love announcing while watching basketball as an analyst for ESPN and ABC. And I've seen a lot for a guy with only one good eye. I've also been fond of reading everything I can get my hands on about hoops. If conservative talk-show host Rush Limbaugh is the "Doctor of Democracy," then I guess I can conservatively be called the "Doctor of Dynamite Data." I flat-out devour various newspapers and specialty publications and constantly am on the telephone with contacts to stay informed.

I'm no different than anyone else in getting caught up in the emotion of the moment. Occasionally, we lose our historical perspective in rating teams and players. We see an exciting move by a youngster and immediately think he has the potential to be a Magic, Michael, Bird, or Oscar. But then reality sinks in and we realize how unfair it is to be compared to the All-Rolls Roycers. That is one of the reasons we need a PTB (prime-time book) like *Encyclopedia of College Basketball* to help keep things in proper context.

As if I need to repeat myself, let me reiterate that basketball is the finest of all sports. I love the game with my mind, my heart, and my soul. There is nothing like the jubilation of the NCAA Tournament, which I like to call the Big Dance.

Give me the pizazz of the college game on campus. It's awesome, baby! It's rock and roll time! I love an atmosphere filled with spirit and enthusiasm. If college hoops doesn't exhilarate you, then you better check your pulse. Defying description at times, college hoops provides never-ending images of last-second decisive shots, bubbly cheerleaders, Tina Turner-like dance routines, dynamite dunks, overtimes and tears, unlikely heroes and unlikelier upsets, pom poms and band music, endless color and deafening noise.

It seems as if I've always resided in hoop heaven. Growing up in Jersey, I was about halfway between the meccas of the game—Madison Square Garden in New York and the Palestra in Philadelphia. I'll always remember Joe Lapchick coaching at St. John's when Louie Carnesecca was his assistant and Frank McGuire brought in his New York-dominated club from North Carolina. That was the genesis of my fantasy to become a coach. The Palestra was sold out one night when a bunch of my buddies and I wheeled and dealed with the ticket-taker at the old barn off Chestnut Street so we could somehow sneak in to watch Princeton All-American Bill Bradley. I was a total freak for the game.

One of my heroes back then was Oscar Robertson. Since I wasn't skilled enough to make the varsity team as a student at Seton Hall, I was in the stands one night in 1958 when the Pirates were playing Cincinnati in the Garden. The Big O outscored the Pirates by himself with 56 points in a 118-54 M&Mer (mismatch). He may have been the greatest all-around player ever. Of course, he's on my Solid Gold all-time college team with fellow guard Jerry West, center Kareem Abdul-Jabbar (UCLA) and forwards Larry Bird (Indiana State) and David Thompson (North Carolina State). My all-time coach is a very easy selection. John Wooden (UCLA) is the only possible pick. You can talk about any of the great coaches and managers for dynasties in other sports, but the greatest coach of all time, in any sport, has to be Wooden for winning 10 national titles and doing it with different personnel.

Parity has set in since the Wooden Era. How can anybody not be totally turned on by the variety and unpredictability of college hoops? There's nothing more stimulating than seeing the joy on the faces of coaches, players, and fans of a Cinderella team in the winner's circle.

The college game is just something that can't be duplicated anywhere. Some of my favorite campuses to visit are Duke, Syracuse, Indiana, Kentucky, Kansas, Arkansas, and North Carolina. Even when a game I attend isn't at one of these hot spots, I cherish my relationship with all of the young people connected with the college game. Fans, players—wackos all.

College hoops has captured the imagination of the general public, especially March Madness during the NCAA Tournament and NIT. Selection Sunday, when the NCAA Division I Basketball Committee announces the bracket, is anything but a peaceful Sabbath for devotees of possible at-large teams all across the country. The nerve-wracking tension doesn't end there as the craving for pressurized basketball in a one-loss-and-you're-out format ascends to an unbelievable level at the NCAA semifinals otherwise known as the "Final Four," a two-word icon of American sports.

If I would have stayed longer than just four seasons in college head coaching, I know I would have been obsessed with reaching the Final Four. But I couldn't stand it physically and was diagnosed with a bleeding ulcer on three occasions. You think I'm wacko now, you should have seen me as a coach! I'm still on medication.

Back in 1977, when I was head coach at the University of Detroit, it was the best medicine of all to receive a phone call from the Division I Committee notifying us that the Titans were invited to the NCAA Tournament. It made all the Dow Joneser days (ups and downs) worth it. I'll never forget wondering what Wooden thought of our program while the Wizard of Westwood worked as a television analyst for the Titans' Mideast Regional semifinal game against top-ranked Michigan in Lexington, Kentucky. It was Heartbreak Hotel for us when we lost in the last minute to the mighty Wolverines.

I like being undefeated as an analyst. All my opinions about what player or team is best generate a reaction. That doesn't mean I'm right or wrong. Sometimes I'm very disappointed that people get so upset and can't respect an opinion without getting personal and attacking the analyst. I plan on using the *Encyclopedia of College Basketball* as an ace in the hole to support some of my commentary.

I'm eternally grateful to the beautiful people at ESPN and ABC for allowing me a forum to share my views with the fantastic fans. It has been a 16-year winning streak for me. Please don't tell my bosses, but I would probably do this for nothing. I sit in the best seat in the house and get paid for this. Are you serious? It's a basketball junkie's delight.

If there is one thing I've learned in television, it's to be prepared. You can't fool the public for long. I'm very proud of my longevity. All the razzle dazzle wouldn't matter if I wasn't prepared. Get to know as much as possible. As I learned from my buddy Jim Simpson, we should treat every game like it is the NCAA championship because that night is the most important game in someone's career.

I try not to be surprised by anything that happens, so I attempt to arrive at every telecast equipped to know about the coaches, the players, the numbers, strategy, and any factor that might be involved. I try to make the game interesting, exciting, and fun. And in my analysis I try to be authoritative, too. The bottom line is that there is a balance between entertainment and educating the fans with X's and O's. You better believe I'll get a T.O. (timeout), baby, whenever it's necessary to sink my teeth into the *Encyclopedia of College Basketball* and refresh my memory or unearth a relevant fact.

My zany schedule allows me to be like a kid in an ice cream shop—every game has a fabulous flavor of its own. It's rejuvenating. The same metaphor can be used for the more leisurely-paced activity of reliving moments in college hoops history with this book.

I know what basketball has done for me in my life. As I look back over the last few decades, my memories are filled with the opportunities I have had to meet so many beautiful people. Questions and answers on talk shows and with the media, rapping with the fans, getting into friendly arguments about teams and players and coaches—I love all of it.

In my years of broadcasting games on television I've seen enough dribbles and dunks to last several normal lifetimes. But you think I've ever had enough? Never in a million years! Similarly, I don't think you'll get enough of this encyclopedia, either. Whether it's the early years, player and coaching records, year-by-year rundowns, small-college hoops, women's basketball, conference and school directories, national awards, the Olympics and much more, you'll find it here. In a way, it's almost like me—perhaps an occasional tendency to give you too much analysis but always dependable because of a passion for the sport of basketball.

All in all, if I was forced to describe the *Encyclopedia of College Basketball* in just a few words, I believe you can guess what they would be. It's awesome, baby! With a capital A!

INTRODUCTION

The idea for *Encyclopedia of College Basketball* came while browsing through periodicals at a book store, when I again noticed longstanding respected encyclopedias covering major league baseball, the NFL, and NBA. At the same time, I found it irksome that a similar comprehensive volume on college basketball wasn't available. If no one else would tackle the project, I'd be willing to take it on. After all, "Final Four" has ascended to a spotlight previously reserved for marquee events such as the Super Bowl, World Series, Indianapolis 500, Kentucky Derby, and major New Year's Day football bowl games.

Naturally, the majority of a much-needed scholarly source on college hoops needs to accentuate major college basketball and the incredibly popular NCAA Division I Tournament. I also envisioned that an enterprising edition would be more authoritative by including pertinent material on other significant levels of competition such as the NIT, small colleges (junior colleges, Divisions II and III, and NAIA) women's basketball, and the Olympics.

I was enamored by the diverse approaches by which the history of college hoops could be portrayed if the information was packaged properly. Thus, in the pages that follow I've tried to deliver a variety of highly readable points to ponder plus relevant statistics and facts that a college basketball fan requires in order to be properly illuminated about the sport.

What's in the Book

Encyclopedia of College Basketball contains 18 chapters of historical facts, individual and team profiles, relevant statistics, enlightening trivia, and other pertinent information.

- **Chapter 1: The early years (1891–1937)**—The game's evolution, pioneering individuals, and trend-setting schools.

- **Chapters 2–6: Decade-by-decade, year-by-year summaries**—Textual summaries of each year, regular-season highlights and statistics, polls and rankings, and recaps of the NCAA Tournament since its debut in 1938. An "At-a-Glance" fact box for each season provides a brief, visual capsule.

- **Chapter 7: The National Invitational Tournament (NIT)**—Once college basketball's premiere event.

- **Chapters 8 and 9: Player and coach directories**—Highlights and statistics from hundreds of college basketball's stars, both on and off the court.

- **Chapter 10: Celebrity hoopsters**—Short profiles of businessmen, actors, politicians, and athletes who dribbled the ball in college.

- **Chapter 11: Women's basketball**—Historical facts and figures on a part of college basketball that continues to grow in popularity.

- **Chapter 12: Small colleges**—Background on the "Don't Forget about Us!" fringe of hoopdom.

- **Chapter 13: Olympics**—U.S. results from the Berlin games to the Dream Team.

- **Chapters 14 and 15: School and conference directories**—Contact information, all-time leading scorers stats, tournament numbers, logos, and more.

- **Chapter 16: NCAA records**—The most and the highest in such individual and team categories as field goals, free throws, rebounds, assists, steals, and more.

- **Chapter 17: Award winners**—Players- and coaches-of-the-year as picked by wire services (AP, UPI) and other sports writers and organizations.

- **Chapter 18: Statistical odds & ends**—For the basketball lover who loves to pore over the fine print on the sports page.

- **Index**—A detailed section that allows instant accessibility to names, organizations, leagues, and teams.

Encyclopedia of College Basketball also contains hundreds of photos, a multitude of statistical tables, and a smattering of sidebar features on rules and famous games.

Acknowledgments

This treasure trove of facts and statistics is unique only because it catalogs the matchless performances of uncommon participants. It couldn't have been achieved without securing input from a variety of basketball aficionados. Therefore, I offer hearty thank-yous and high fives to the following contributors for their mix of clean prose and pertinent stats:

John Duxbury—His painstaking research enlightened year-by-year reviews and made player/coaching records more comprehensive. A glance at the "They Played the Game, Too" section confirms the notion that he is the nation's premier sports historian. Dux was, is, and always will be "The Answer Man."

Andy Geerken and Gary Johnson—Their work on the coaches register was especially efficient. Here is how I think Dick Vitale would describe Andy, the director of communications for the National Association of Basketball Coaches, and Gary, a statistics coordinator for the NCAA: "They're the 3-R Men, baby! They're Reputable, Reliable, and Resourceful."

Roland Lazenby—As with any subject delving into archival material, this book is dependent on precise and relevant analysis on the pioneers of the sport. He capitalized on his extensive experience as a sports book author to supply an incisive look at "The Early Years."

Walt Meyer—I value his keen insight and still can't believe some of the salient statistical research he conducted for the "Statistical Odds and Ends" chapter.

Wendy Parker—She has honed a witty and well-informed writing style that is the principal reason why I'm starting to shed my male basketball chauvinism. In her whirlwind way, "Windy" is to women's basketball at this stage what *Sports Illustrated* legend Frank Deford is to sports writing in general.

Patrick Premo—A Naismith Memorial Basketball Hall of Fame recommendation proved accurate as he supplied invaluable perspective with pre-wire service national polls.

Mike Shank—He adroitly handled the thankless but vital task of collating no-nonsense statistics and tournament box scores. I think his aligning with the Big South Conference is just the start of a promising sports career.

I'm also appreciative to Orville Paller from Salt Lake City for reconstructing lost statistics of Utah's 1944 NCAA championship team. Finally, I'm indebted to college sports information directors from across the country and USA Basketball for providing the vast majority of the photographs and title team statistics.

Of course, Larry Baker and the folks at Gale Research and Visible Ink have my genuine respect for allowing creativity to deviate somewhat from traditional encyclopedias yet providing a necessary focus to keep me from going off on too many tangents. I believe the end result is an exceptional reader-friendly product.

Mike Douchant

ENCYCLOPEDIA OF

COLLEGE
BASKETBALL

1

THE EARLY YEARS:

1891–1937

As the well-worn legend goes, James Naismith, a young physical education instructor at the YMCA's School for Christian Workers in Springfield, Massachusetts, invented the game of basketball in 1891 to relieve boredom in his winter gym classes.

The school in Springfield trained its students to become managers in the YMCA's network of health clubs around the world. Every winter, the students grew weary of the routine of gymnastics and calisthenics used in their "physical training." They often complained bitterly. In the fall of 1891, the mood seemed nastier than usual, and two instructors had quit rather than deal with the headache. Naismith announced at a faculty meeting that he would take on the problem. He said the students needed an indoors game, one they could learn easily and play in the gym by artificial light.

At first Naismith tried a combination of soccer, lacrosse, and football, but it was too rough. He turned to other options but none worked. "I tried all games that seemed to offer any hope, and studied each one," he later explained in a letter to a friend, "but kept the idea of lacrosse always in mind."

Then, Naismith recalled a childhood game, "Duck on a Rock," where the players attempted to knock a larger, melon-sized rock off a boulder by throwing smaller rocks at it. There seemed to be something to that concept. Plus, he remembered how a rugby team he once played on spent winter days indoors throwing rugby balls into a box.

So he tinkered with a new idea. In late December of 1891 he gave the idea a try, and posted the rules on a bulletin board outside the gym. He first envisioned a game where the players would attempt to throw a soccer ball into a box suspended above the gym floor. But the school janitor, Pops Stebbins, couldn't find any boxes, so he brought Naismith two peach baskets. The railing around the school gym happened to be 10 feet off the floor, so the baskets were set at that height. And because his class held 18 students, Naismith divided them into nine on a side.

"The first words were not very encouraging, when one of the class made the remark, 'Humph, a new game,'" Naismith recalled. "I asked the boys to try it once as a favor to me.

They started, and after the ball was first thrown up there was no need of further coaxing."

Naismith's Game Is a Hit

The elements meshed together rather loosely, but all in all the effort was a rousing success. The first hoopsters had been bitten by the bug. One student even suggested that the instructor label the new game "Naismith ball," which Naismith rejected. The student, Frank Mahon, then offered another suggestion—"basket ball."

It wasn't long before lunchtime crowds began gathering to watch the frenetic action of "basket ball" in Naismith's class. It was an awkward game with two teams of nine students attempting to heave a soccer ball into peach baskets suspended 10 feet above the gym floor. But even in its rudimentary stage, it held a peculiar magic. It was fun to play and, almost as important, fun to watch. Basketball rather quickly became a spectator sport. Aided by the YMCA's missionary nature and its network of centers, Naismith's invention soon spread.

James Naismith: The father of basketball.

On February 12, 1892, the central and Armory Hill branches of the Springfield YMCA staged a boys game that drew a crowd of 100 or so and resulted in a 2-2 tie. "The game is a very pretty one to watch," reported the *Springfield Daily Republican*.

By March 12, Naismith's idea was refined enough to weather another public display. The school's faculty took on the students in a game

that drew 200 spectators. The students won, 5-1, and Amos Alonzo Stagg, who would go on to fame coaching college football, scored the faculty's only goal. "The most conspicuous figure on the floor was Stagg in the blue Yale uniform, who managed to have a hand in every scrimmage," the *Republican* reported. "His football training hampered him and he was perpetually making fouls by shoving his opponents."

Later that same month, Naismith took a team on a tour of exhibition games in Troy, Albany, and

Schenectady, New York, and Newport and Providence, Rhode Island. In April, the Brooklyn YMCA was playing games against other New York branches.

Something of a fad, the game was on its way to rapid distribution. Its popularity among YMCA members and high school athletes grew from there. By the winter of 1893–94, the YMCA in Hartford, Connecticut, had organized a five-team league. The public was invited in to see the games. No admission was charged, except 10 cents for reserved seats. By the end of the winter, more than 10,000 spectators had come to watch the action and the YMCA had collected a $250 profit.

Soon, athletic clubs and high schools took up basketball; then the colleges followed. Women, too, were soon won over by the new game's charm. And before long, "professionals" were attempting to make a few dollars on weekends playing on courts enclosed by wire cages (thus, early basketballers were called "cagers"). By the turn of the century, barnstorming pro teams playing in small Northeastern cities were drawing a few hundred paying fans.

THE FIRST RULES   On January 15, 1892, James Naismith's "basket ball" rules were printed in the Springfield (Mass.) YMCA School for Christian Workers newspaper, the *Triangle*. They read as follows:

1. The ball may be thrown in any direction with one or both hands.

2. The ball may be batted in any direction with one or both hands (never with the fist).

3. A player cannot run with the ball. The player must throw it from the spot on which he catches it; allowance to be made for a man who catches the ball when running at a good speed.

4. The ball must be held in or between the hands; the arms or body must not be used for holding it.

5. No shouldering, holding, pushing, tripping or striking, in any way the person of an opponent shall be allowed; the first infringement of this rule by any person shall count as a foul, the second shall disqualify him until the next goal is made; or, if there was evident intent to injure the person for the whole of the game, no substitute shall be allowed.

6. A foul is striking at the ball with the fist, violation of Rules 3, 4, and such as described in Rule 5.

7. If either side makes three consecutive fouls, it shall count a goal for the opponents. (Consecutive means without the opponents in the meantime making a foul.)

8. A goal shall be made when the ball is thrown or batted from the ground into the basket and stays there, providing those defending the goal do not touch or disturb the goal. If the ball rests on the edge and the opponent moves the basket, it shall count as a goal.

9. When the ball goes out of bounds, it shall be thrown into the field and played by the person first touching it. In case of a dispute, the umpire shall throw it straight into the field. The thrower-in is allowed five seconds. If he holds it longer, it shall go to the opponent. If any side persists in delaying the game, the umpire shall call a foul on them.

10. The umpire shall be the judge of the men and shall note the fouls and notify the referee when three consecutive fouls have been made. He shall have power to disqualify men according to Rule 5.

11. The referee shall be the judge of the ball and shall decide when the ball is in play, in bounds, to which side it belongs, and shall keep the time. He shall decide when a goal has been made, and keep account of the goals, with any other duties that are usually performed by a referee.

12. The time shall be two fifteen minute halves, with five minutes rest between.

13. The side making the most goals in that time shall be declared the winners. In case of a draw, the game may, by agreement of the captains, be continued until another goal is made.

But the real growth in popularity came with the college sport. The early 20th century brought a refinement of rules, and by the 1920s, promoters found they could earn a tidy profit staging college games, the only problem being that the crowds demanded more action and less stalling and fouling and free-throw shooting. The rules makers eventually complied, and the sport bounced along toward a new level of popularity. In 1938 and 1939, with the founding of the National Invitation and the National Collegiate Athletic Association tournaments, basketball found a format that would open the way to mass appeal.

Yet much of the success of the modern game can be traced to the sport's early decades, a fascinating time, complete with strange stories, hot competition, and constantly changing rules.

The New Century

Basketball was born in a time of bicycles and penny arcades and Sunday school picnics. Women wore corsets and full skirts; men sported straw hats, slightly tilted. Community brass bands were a favorite. "There'll Be a Hot Time in the Old Town Tonight" was the hit song. Yet all around there were signs of change in 1891. The newly invented wonders of the world were the trolley car and electric elevator. Ragtime music marked America's quickening, nervous rhythm.

To fill leisure time brought on by industrialization, people hungered for more diversion, and sports provided cheap, quick alternatives. In the spring and summer, they had baseball, and in the fall they had the newfangled game of football. But winters were the dark ages, until quite suddenly in 1891, Naismith introduced some light.

Seemingly overnight, basketball was being played in every YMCA in America.

"It is doubtful if the history of competitive games contains an example of more rapid growth than that shown by basket ball during the first two or three years of its existence," wrote Dr. Joseph E. Raycroft, the coach of the University of Chicago's great early teams. "Even the remarkable spread of baseball in the years immediately following the Civil War was second to this."

Basketball fit just the need for a rigorous indoor game, plus it had the evangelistic fervor of "muscular Christianity" on its side. From Nai-

RULES CHANGES DURING THE EARLY YEARS

1895: The free-throw line is moved from 20 feet to 15.

1896: A field goal changes from three to two points, and free throws from three points to one point.

1897: Backboards are first installed.

1901: A dribbler cannot shoot for a field goal and may dribble only once, and then with two hands.

1909: A dribbler is permitted to shoot. The double dribble is made illegal.

1911: Players are disqualified upon committing their fourth personal foul. No coaching is permitted during the progress of a game by anybody connected with their team. A warning is given for the first violation and a free throw is awarded after that.

1914: The bottom of the net is left open.

1915: College, YMCA, and AAU rules are made the same for the first time.

1921: A player is permitted to reenter the game once. Previously, a player could not reenter for the remainder of the game if he exited the contest. Backboards are moved two feet from the wall of the court. Previously, players would "climb" up the padded wall to sink baskets.

1922: Running with the ball changes from a foul to a violation.

1924: A fouled player must shoot his own free throws. Previously, one person usually shot all of his team's foul shots.

1929: The charging foul is introduced.

1931: A "held ball" can be assessed when a closely guarded player is keeping the ball from play for five seconds. The result will be a jump ball.

1933: The 10-second center line is introduced to de-emphasize stalling.

1934: A player is permitted to reenter a game twice.

1936: No offensive player can remain in the free-throw lane, with or without the ball, for longer than three seconds. Following a successful free throw, the team scored upon shall put the ball in play at the end of the court where the goal was scored.

smith's first class, one student introduced the game in India; another took it to China, and another to Japan. Everywhere the YMCA reached, basketball touched the population. And through students who belonged to YMCAs, the sport eventually worked its way into the colleges. In 1893, W. O. Black left the YMCA's school in Springfield and took the game to Stanford University. A classmate, W. H. Anderson, introduced basketball at Yale. Another Springfield alumnus, Charles Bemus, reportedly started a team at little Geneva College in Pennsylvania as early as 1892. The University of Toronto and Vanderbilt University also reportedly had teams as early as 1893. That same year Amos Alonzo Stagg left Springfield and went to the

University of Chicago, where he founded a team in 1894 that played a seven-game schedule against local athletic clubs. Early written accounts indicate that during 1894 students at Yale and Cornell formed teams to play against New England athletic clubs. Temple University, Ohio State University, and Haverford College all started teams shortly thereafter.

The First College Game?

In February of 1895, a team from the Minnesota School of Agriculture and Mining beat Hamline College, 9-3, in what is generally considered the first game between two college teams. Each side, however, played nine players at a time. A month later, a Haverford College team beat Temple, 6-4. In 1896, Stagg's Chicago team defeated a YMCA team composed of University of Iowa students, 15-12, in a game that featured five men on a side. But Penn athletic director Ralph Morgan claimed the first real intercollegiate game occurred when Yale defeated Penn, 32-10, in 1897.

As it had for early football, Yale played a large role in the development of basketball. It was there that the five-man game found its footing, and there that the dribble gained popularity as both a defensive and offensive weapon.

"Yale continued to put a team on the floor in 1898, 1899 and 1900," Morgan wrote, "but no college team was again met until 1899, when Yale played and defeated Cornell in Poughkeepsie, N.Y., by the score of 49-7. In 1900, Yale took a Western trip and played, among other teams, Ohio State and Wisconsin."

Morgan's opinion that Yale and Penn played the first intercollegiate game may reflect an Eastern bias because historians have found it difficult to determine exactly who played the first game. After a time, it mattered little anyway. Each passing season brought more schools into the fold. After all, basketball was the new game for the new age. Its rapid pace appealed to the young.

"In playing it comes the joy of a quickened pulse and fast-working lungs, the health-giving exercise to all our muscles, the forgetting of all troubles," wrote an elated Southerner in 1902. "There is no game which requires more wind or endurance nor which needs greater agility and deftness."

Despite the game's appeal, a large number of colleges still had no team, leaving basketball to those schools that had gymnasiums. Other colleges, eager to begin the sport, played their games outdoors. Hiram College won an exhibition tournament played outdoors at the 1904 Olympic games in St. Louis. Some colleges continued outdoor competition well into the next decade, and international competition would retain that format even longer.

Some traditionally strong football teams, such as Harvard and Princeton, couldn't seem to get the knack of the new game. Others found almost instant success. The University of Nebraska started a team and created an early dynasty of sorts by closing out the century with 19 wins in a row from 1898–1900. Notre Dame, the most recognized football power in college history, has an unusual historical footnote involving its first basketball captain, John Shillington. Most people know that the sinking of the *Maine* led to the United States' involvement in the Spanish-American War. Few, however, know that Shillington was among those who went down with the ship in the Havana harbor on February 15, 1898. A monument to him—a mounted shell taken from the sunken ship—was erected in front of Brownson Hall, his last home on Notre Dame's campus.

Rules Made to Order

The more colleges became involved in basketball, the more they wanted to have a say in the rules, a situation that grew increasingly awkward early in the new century. The YMCA and the Athletic Amateur Union (AAU) had run the rules committee together, but this arrangement didn't last long. The AAU forbade Yale to play during the 1904–5 season because it was an "unregistered" team, but the school persisted anyway. The AAU then told Penn that it, too, would lose official sanction if it played a scheduled game against Yale. Penn athletic director Ralph Morgan, then still an undergraduate, was angered by the AAU's position and called a series of meetings in 1905, leading to the formation of the Intercollegiate Athletic Association, the forerunner of the NCAA, and the establishing of a separate set of college rules. Soon afterward, college and AAU officials made peace and began meeting to discuss the rules of their respective games, but they would not merge as a joint rules organization until 1915.

This organizing of the college game helped bring a surge of growth. In 1905, there were an estimated 88 colleges engaged in basketball, with the bulk of them in Pennsylvania, New York, and Ohio. By 1914, these ranks had swelled to 366, with substantial growth in Illinois, Indiana, Iowa, Kansas, Michigan, Minnesota, Missouri, Virginia, and Wisconsin.

This overwhelming acceptance left basketball's earliest promoters both amazed and proud. "More men and boys are playing Basket Ball than are playing any organized sport in America, with the exception of baseball," declared the YMCA's Dr. Luther Gulick in the 1908–9 issue of *Spalding's Guide,* the sport's early yearbook. "It has become the American indoor game."

But, as *Spalding's* editors explained, there simply weren't enough qualified and seasoned officials to keep up with the pace of expansion. Other difficulties stemmed from the evolution of the rules. Drastic changes were made yearly, requiring officials to have the skills of a lawyer to keep pace.

"During 1908, 1909 and 1910, considerable criticism of the game was made, principally from New England, where President (Charles) Eliot of Harvard was a particular foe," wrote Ralph Morgan in 1914. One player acquired 15 fouls in a game against Harvard, which hastened Eliot's complaints. The criticism was answered with a series of revisions, but not to Eliot's liking. Declaring that "basket ball has become even more brutal than football," Eliot barred the sport at Harvard in 1909. In its official reasoning, the university stated, "The games more closely resembled free fights than friendly athletic contests between amateur teams."

Opponents of Harvard's action suggested the school was merely frustrated by a poor record. But such criticism hastened the sport away from unnecessary roughness. There was little question that Eastern basketball had developed a reputation for forwards who powered and shoved their way near the goal for a score. There was no three-second violation in those days, which left the floor open to sumo-style struggles underneath the hoop.

To counteract the criticism, the rules committee in 1909–10 rescinded its 1908 five-foul rule. Instead, players would be disqualified after four fouls, which reduced the violence somewhat. Some areas of the country even saw the addition of a second referee in 1910.

Playing style was another factor in moving basketball away from brutishness. Observers were already noting the different styles Western teams played. The Mississippi Valley style focused on solid defense, fast-breaking offense and one-handed shots, wrote E. P. O'Neill in the 1906–7 *Spalding's Guide.* "Long, swift passes replace excessive footwork, and the forwards depend on backward one-foot pivots and one-handed throws for shots at goal rather than numerous passes to obtain an unguarded throw. A one-handed shot is more inaccurate than a two-handed shot, but it is not to be guarded without a foul."

Another help in alleviating the inside struggle was the development of the outside shooter. The early game featured forwards and centers as the big scorers, until players such as 5-4 guard Barney Sedran came along. He led City College of New York in scoring from 1909 to 1911. The first of the great set shooters, Sedran would heave 20- and 30-footers into goals without backboards, a skill that carried him on to a celebrated professional career.

Bucknell's John Anderson, the only player to score 50 or more points in a game until George Mikan in 1945, had 80 vs. Philadelphia College of Pharmacy in 1903. No team averaged at least 80 points in a season until 1952.

East Meets West

Perhaps the most important development in the college game was the founding of leagues or conferences. That brought organization and scheduling to the competition. More important, the leagues began setting up training classes for officials.

In May 1901, several schools, including Yale, Harvard, Trinity, Holy Cross, Amherst, and Williams, formed the New England Intercollegiate Basketball League. However, Yale and Harvard dropped out later that year to join the newly formed Eastern Intercollegiate League, the forerunner of the Ivy League. The New England League lasted just one season before folding.

The formation of leagues added a new element of competitiveness to college basketball, setting up the potential for intersectional rivalries. This potential was realized in 1905 when teams from the universities of Wisconsin and Minnesota barnstormed east to take on Columbia, the undefeated champion of the Eastern League.

Emmett Angell coached Wisconsin; his team featured Christian Steinmetz, the first college player to score one thousand points (1903–5), and Bob Zuppke, who would go on to fame as a college football coach. Steinmetz had gained notoriety by scoring what then was the incredible total of 44 points in an 80-10 win over Beloit. In 1905, he would score 50 points in another game. But even his firepower didn't help on the Eastern road trip. The Badgers "played a number of minor games on their trip from the West," reported the 1905–6 edition of *Spalding's*, "and consequently were in excellent condition when they met the Columbia University Five in New York City. As had been predicted by the Eastern critics, the Westerners could not cope with the accurate

passing and shooting, or the speedy play of the Blue and White Five, and were handily defeated by the respective scores of 21-15 and 27-15. The victories in these two contests and the winning of the championship of the Eastern colleges gives Columbia the undisputed title of 'Intercollegiate Champions of the United States.'"

If nothing else, the games reflected just how differently the regions approached the game. "Western" teams were used to closely called games, while the Eastern players were glad to mix it up.

"The Minnesota and Wisconsin men played in the style prevalent among most of the girl colleges in the East, that is, the 'no contact' game," sneered Yale's W. C. Hyatt.

Such pettiness aside, Steinmetz was named to the Naismith Memorial Basketball Hall of Fame in 1961. He scored 462 points in a single season, an amazing total in the early years. Harry Fisher, Columbia's leading scorer between 1902 and 1905, was elected to the Hall of Fame in 1973. He scored 13 field goals in a game in 1905, a collegiate record that stood for 45 years. After college, Fisher went on to an esteemed coaching career at Columbia and Army.

Early Conferences

In the 1905–6 season, the big schools of the Midwest met in Chicago to form the "Western Conference," the forerunner of the Big Ten. Members included the universities of Chicago, Minnesota, Wisconsin, Illinois, and Purdue. Similar alliances appeared around the country. The Southern Intercollegiate Athletic Association, featuring Georgia Tech, Auburn, Howard College, Tulane, Vanderbilt, and the University of Georgia, formed for the 1905–6 season and entertained Yale's Southern tour.

The 1908–9 season brought two more major conferences plus the expansion of the Western with Indiana, Iowa, and Northwestern joining the league. The Missouri Valley Conference formed two divisions, with Kansas, Missouri, and Washington College in the Southern and

Nebraska, Ames (Iowa State), and Drake in the Northern.

The Northwest College Conference formed that same season (1908–9) with Oregon Agricultural (Oregon State), Whitman College, Washington State, and the University of Idaho. The next season, the universities of Washington and Oregon also joined the group.

The top program in basketball during the era was the University of Chicago, which compiled a 78-12 record from 1900 to 1909. Chicago's best player was 6-3 center John Schommer, who led the Western League in scoring for three years, averaging just over 10 points per game. A three-time Helms Foundation All-American, he was selected national player of the year in 1909 and would become known in later life for inventing the modern backboard.

"Head and shoulders above all players in the league" is how Wisconsin great Chris Steinmetz described Schommer, who, according to *Spalding's,* had all the assets of a great center—speed, strength, reach, and size. Plus, he could shoot and never loafed on defense, Steinmetz said.

In the backcourt, Chicago had H. O. "Pat" Page, a quick guard and two-time All-American who went on to coaching fame at both Chicago and Butler. Page was named national player of the year in 1910.

Chicago was also one of the first colleges to have a paid coach, Dr. Joseph E. Raycroft. The combination of a paid coach, quick guard, and star center carried Chicago to a 21-2 record and the "national" championship in 1908. But before claiming national honors, Chicago had to battle the University of Wisconsin in Madison before a crowd of 1,500 for the Western title. Chicago won on a last-minute shot by Page, 18-16. The prize was a berth in a two-game playoff with the Eastern champion, Penn. At 8-0, Penn was projected by basketball's Eastern establishment to be the favorite.

But Chicago beat Penn in a two-game series. Although his team lost, Penn's all-conference forward Charles Keinath dazzled a *Spalding's*

writer, who reported "his dribbling electrified the crowd, many of whom before had never seen such fancy footwork."

Other conferences, particularly the resuscitated New England League, scoffed that a playoff between two leagues hardly amounted to a national championship. With college leagues springing up in every region of the country, schools were tiring of the Eastern bias. With the help of the New York newspapers, the Eastern League pretentiously announced an "All-America" team each year featuring only Eastern players.

Still, the college game was young and already thirsting to declare a national champion. "The 1908 series had a very good effect on basket ball," declared *Spalding's,* "and the contending teams showed tremendous crowds in Philadelphia and Chicago what a good, wholesome, sportsmanlike game basket ball is."

Chicago finished the 1908–9 season undefeated at 12-0, but despite a clamoring for a championship match against Columbia, the Eastern champion, none could be scheduled. Instead, *Spalding's* listed the various regional league champions, including Georgetown in the Southern, Kansas in the Middle West, Oregon Agriculture in the Northwest, and Williams in New England. The no-championship stalemate would remain for many seasons. Chicago won the Western and Columbia the Eastern again in 1910, but no national championship series between the two leagues could be scheduled.

"The question of intercollegiate supremacy arose, bringing in its wake volumes of idle words, footless arguments and bootless discussions," wrote Oswald Tower, a member of the rules committee, in 1910, "and when all was said and done, no impartial critic could say with any certainty that the best team of this section was better than the best team of any other section."

Great Teams Emerge

The first decade of the new century brought a stunning evolution in basketball. Several teams emerged as powerhouses. Joining the ranks of prominent winners were Dayton, Oregon State, Michigan State, Montana, and Wisconsin. Minnesota won a whopping 107 games during the period.

The next 10 years brought the rise of the Naval Academy with a record of 109-9 from 1910–19, a .924 winning percentage. The University of Texas won 102 games during that period, including a 44-game winning streak beginning in 1913. Other big winners included Virginia, Creighton, California, Virginia Polytechnic, Wisconsin, Illinois, Texas A&M, Kansas State, Syracuse, and numerous other schools.

Despite the flowering of these regional college basketball cultures, the establishment of an annual national champion was further complicated by the difficulties of travel and changes in rules and equipment. Some teams played outdoors. Some used old rules, some new. The official joining of the YMCA, NCAA, and AAU in a rules committee in 1915 helped, but the question of a national champion remained cloudy. Some teams took turns trumpeting their greatness through friendly newspaper editors. Other college teams entered the national AAU competition, hoping that the national title there would stand as evidence that they were the best.

Allen and the Rise of Coaches

The 1908–10 seasons marked a major turning point for the college game. Glass backboards were allowed; out-of-bounds rules were firmed up to eliminate the mad scrambles for the ball out of play; traveling rules were tightened to allow the ball handler only one step; and the double dribble was eliminated.

Despite complaints about roughness, the game was opening up. James Naismith, who had since obtained his degree in medicine and retreated to the faculty at the University of Kansas where he coached that school's team for nine seasons, was particularly pleased with the effect dribbling had on the game.

"The restoration of the dribble has made the game more enjoyable from the standpoint of the spectators as well as the players," he observed. "It has done away with some of the negative features and helped make the game cleaner. This is especially true on large floors, for the chief cause of the roughness was the attempt of the guard to prevent the player with the ball from getting a good, clean throw, and as the player was unable to move, he was unmercifully crowded, and this individual crowding was so evident to the spectators that it made it appear as if the game was exceedingly rough. But with the dribble, if there is no one to whom a player can pass, he can get away from the crowding. The dribble gives the opportunity for the exhibition of skill of the highest order, and spectators show their appreciation of this by bursts of applause that greet the performance of some favorite expert."

With its early success, the college game was beginning to show tinges of commerce. Many programs found they could be self-supporting, even profitable, from ticket sales alone. Dr. Raycroft, Chicago's paid coach, created a stir when he accepted a similar job at Princeton because that school, eager for a winning, big-time program, made him a better offer.

From the game's earliest days, Naismith had believed coaches were unnecessary. "The game isn't meant to be coached; it's meant to be played," he said. But experience proved him wrong. Naismith coached with a philosophy of letting his players play. To this date, he is the only coach in Kansas history with a losing career record.

As schools became more competitive, they wanted men who could make them winners. Yale hired its first professional coach in 1907. About that time Naismith learned what effect a good coach could have. An undergraduate named Forrest "Phog" Allen coached Baker University to an undefeated season, including wins over Kansas and Missouri. Naismith agreed to turn the Kansas coaching job over to Allen for 1907–8. That season Allen coached both Baker and Kansas, and the following season, 1908–9, he added the coaching job at Haskell Institute to his duties. Over two busy seasons, Allen won

116 games. Kansas alone went to a 26-3 record under the young coach in 1908–9 and won the Missouri Valley Conference championship.

Allen earned his medical degree over the next four years at the Kansas City School of Osteopathy, then returned to coaching at Warrensburg Teachers College, where he ran up a 107-7 record and won seven Missouri College Conference championships in seven years. He then returned to Kansas and compiled a career record of 771-233, a .768 winning percentage, good enough for fourth on the all-time list of winningest college coaches.

An autocratic man, Allen pushed college basketball toward the concepts of recruiting and professionalism. Naismith, of course, opposed these things, believing instead in the supremacy of amateurism. He supported the notion of basketball for the fun of it. He and Allen often disagreed over rule changes, but the two men worked together amicably on the Kansas campus for a number of years.

Something of a self-promoter, Allen fancied himself as a "father of basketball coaches." His innovations included a blending of man-to-man and zone defenses, what he called a man defense "with zone principle." His teams ran the standard pattern offense, but Allen believed deeply that the formula for victory in basketball was coaching strategy. His record suggests that he knew what he was talking about.

There were several other excellent coaches in college basketball's formative era. Among them were:

Doc Meanwell: He never played basketball but became one of the early game's most innovative coaches. Meanwell received his medical degree from the University of Maryland in 1909, and became interested in the game while teaching it to children in Baltimore's slums. He became the coach at the University of Wisconsin in 1911 and earned a doctorate in public health there in 1915. In 20 years at Wisconsin and two at the University of Missouri, he won 290 games and six conference titles. He also helped direct the development of the valve-free, hidden-lace ball. As a coach, he believed fiercely that, using the short pass in a pattern offense, a team could work for the right shot. His teams were patient and ran up a 44-1 record in his first three years at Wisconsin. He disdained the dribble and taught tight, tight defense.

Cam Henderson: He coached at two West Virginia colleges, Davis & Elkins first, then at Marshall. From about 1916 to 1930, the standing zone was the defense that ruled college basketball. Henderson's teams played it so well that other coaches copied his innovations. His 611 career victories still rank him among the all-time winningest college coaches.

Doc Carlson: He earned his medical degree at the University of Pittsburgh in 1920, then became basketball coach there in 1922. Carlson invented the "Figure 8" offense and directed two Pitt teams (1928 and 1930) to the mythical national championship. He won 371 games in 31 years at Pitt. Known as one of early basketball's more colorful figures, he was never too consumed with a game to carry on with spectators. A fan in Morgantown, West Virginia, once dumped a bucket of water on Carlson, after the coach continually complained of bad officiating by saying, "This burns me up."

The Fans Arrive

The college game got a glimpse at its future in 1920 when 10,000 fans packed the 168th Street Regimental Armory in New York to see a tournament featuring City College of New York and New York University. The rival New York teams were off to big seasons, and just like that, entrepreneurs saw where the money was. Instead of the usual 1,500 to 2,000 spectators (NYU didn't have a gym and played some games on a Hudson River barge), the game was standing room only. Led by star (and future college coaching legend) Howard Cann, NYU won 39-21 and went on to capture the national AAU title in Atlanta later in the year.

The game helped show college basketball its future—big crowds. The 1920s brought the construction of numerous arenas, many of them in the Midwest. The University of Iowa, for example, built a 16,000-seat facility.

The decade brought more good teams. Montana State led the charge, winning 213 games against 44 defeats between 1920 and 1929. Army, Navy, North Carolina, Cal, Creighton, Oklahoma, Penn State, and CCNY all produced excellent teams.

At Kansas, Phog Allen won six Missouri Valley conference championships in the 1920s, leading Kansas partisans to claim at least two national championships. In 1928, Pittsburgh went 21-0. The Panthers were led by forward Chuck Hyatt and guard Sykes Reed. Hyatt, a three-time college All-American, led the nation in scoring his senior year, 1929–30, and Pitt again earned top rankings with a 23-2 season. During his career, Pitt rang up a 60-7 record. He went on to become an AAU All-American, playing nine seasons for the Phillips 66 Oilers.

Other great players of the 1920s included:

Paul Endacott: Named Helms Foundation Player of the Year in 1923, Endacott was the heart of Phog Allen's undefeated 1923 Kansas team. In 1924, Dr. Naismith declared Endacott the best ever at Kansas. A quarter century later, the appraisals were still high. Allen named him to the national All-Time College Team.

Victor A. Hanson: A three-time All-American for Syracuse, 1925–27, Hanson led the Orangemen to a 48-7 record during his college career and the 1925-26 national championship. He was named national player of the year in 1927, and Grantland Rice named him to the All-Time All-American team in 1952. Hanson played pro basketball with the Cleveland Rosenblums and organized baseball in the New York Yankees' organization. He even coached football at Syracuse from 1930 to 1936 (see Chapter 9).

Branch McCracken: Led Indiana to basketball prominence in the late 1920s. An All-Big Ten selection three years running, he set the conference scoring record his senior year and was named All-American. He later coached the

Hoosiers to national championships in 1940 and 1953.

John Roosma: A key player on the great Passaic (N.J.) High School "Wonder Team," Roosma went on to play at the U.S. Military Academy, where he led the Cadets to 33 consecutive wins and an undefeated season. Over three years, he carried Army to a 70-3 record. Later he achieved the rank of colonel in the Army.

Charles Murphy: He led his high school team to the Indiana state title in 1926, then went on to two-time All-American honors at Purdue.

Forrest S. DeBernardi: He scored 50 points in a game for Westminster College in 1920, then went on to become an AAU All-American in 1921, 1922, and 1923. He played three different positions and earned All-American honors at each of them.

John A. "Cat" Thompson: The player largely responsible for Montana State's great success in the 1920s, Thompson was named Helms Foundation player of the year in 1929. During his career, Montana State compiled a 72-4 record. Thompson scored 1,539 points in three years of college play, astronomical numbers for the era.

Harold "Bud" Foster: One of Doc Meanwell's key charges at Wisconsin, Foster led the Badgers to the Western Conference championship in 1929 and was named All-American in 1930.

Early Integration and African-American Teams

African Americans took up basketball shortly after the game's invention, and by the turn of the century were beginning to gain limited prominence. By 1906, black athletic clubs in Brooklyn, New Jersey, and New York had begun sponsoring teams. Soon college programs followed. By 1910, Lincoln University, Howard University, Hampton Institute, and Union University entered the competition.

The 1920s brought limited integration of some college teams. At Columbia, sophomore

George Gregory gained notoriety as the All-Eastern Conference center for 1928–29. Described in *Spalding's* as "the tall colored boy who played center" and as "the graceful Columbia center," Gregory ranked fourth in the conference in scoring and second in free throws made.

Penn athletic director Ralph Morgan wrote, "Gregory had height; he got the tap; he was fast and could shoot. The coaches were clearly right when they selected him (to the all-conference team)."

That same season Western Illinois State Teacher's College had two black players, one of whom, a guard named Page, was selected all-conference. For 1928–29, Southern Cal, the Brooklyn College of Pharmacy, and the Columbia College of Pharmacy teams all had an African-American player.

High school and junior high teams in Pennsylvania showed extensive integration in 1928–29. Elsewhere, from Yankton, South Dakota to Peoria, Illinois, to Warwick, New York, incidents of integration were isolated. But they eventually helped break down the sturdy racial barriers in the college game. In the 1920s, 1930s, and 1940s, noted African-American players began to appear, including Paul Robeson (the future actor and pro football player) at Rutgers, Wilbur Woods at Nebraska, Sadat Singh at Syracuse, and Dolly King at Long Island University.

The Last Great Dribble Debate

Basketball seemed to be heading briskly toward its future in the late 1920s, but it paused in 1927 and flirted briefly with the past. Urged on by Wisconsin's Doc Meanwell, who loved the notion of moving the ball only with the short pass, the Joint Rules Committee voted 9-8 to eliminate the dribble. The committee then adjourned to watch the Original Celtics use the passing game to whip the Cleveland Rosenblums for the professional championship. After the game, the committee reconvened, and Meanwell further praised the passing game. But Nat Holman, a member of the Celtics who also coached at CCNY, urged a reconsideration. College players, he argued passionately, were not pros and needed the dribble to maneuver. Upon hearing Holman, the committee voted to keep the dribble in college basketball.

Surviving this threat, the college game was up and running—or off and bouncing—with its big games drawing big crowds. Unknown to many, its greatest legend was already afoot. John Wooden, a quietly determined young guard, had entered Purdue after playing on a high school state championship team in Martinsville, Indiana.

The City Game and the Wonder Five

The moment that college basketball hit the big time isn't exactly clear, but there is little doubt as to the location. The game had kept New York City in its grip since Naismith invented it. Basketball was just the sport to suit Gotham's aggressive nature; it spread quickly across the boroughs, through the YMCAs and athletic clubs. Goals and dirt courts soon appeared on playgrounds around the city, and the neighborhoods came alive with this new competition. Basketball hadn't been born to New Yorkers, but they adopted it as their own.

These feelings only deepened with time. As the game moved into the colleges, the whole city seemed to burn with interest. First came Columbia's big success in 1905. Then dawned the age of "professional" coaches, and New York got its share. Nat Holman, the playmaker for New York's Original Celtics, started at City College of New York in 1919 while still playing pro ball. Ed Kelleher took the coaching job at Fordham in 1922, and Howard Cann went to work at NYU a year later. St. John's hired Buck Freeman, and Lew Andreas took over at upstate Syracuse. Each of these coaches built winning programs, and that in turn built excitement. Within a matter of years, games in small college gyms were packed with 1,500 fans craning their necks for a view of the floor.

The more crowded the games, the more obvious it became that the sport was bursting at the seams. On January 1, 1927, the Palestra opened in Philadelphia, and soon 10,000 spectators crowded inside to see Penn play Princeton. "The Palestra (built for the princely sum of $750,000) was constructed for basketball," wrote Penn's Ralph Morgan.

College basketball, the business, was waiting to be born. All it needed was someone to slap it on the fanny and make it breathe. That someone was a Penn undergraduate, Ned Irish, who witnessed the Palestra phenomenon first hand. A New Yorker, Irish had been working as a part-time sportswriter since high school, making as much as $100 a week from the local papers. When he headed off to college, the New York papers hired him to cover the Philadelphia sports scene. He also worked full time for the *Philadelphia Record*.

Irish returned to New York in 1929 as a sportswriter for the *World-Telegram* and soon made that paper the leader in college basketball coverage (most New York papers virtually ignored

Star Purdue guard and future UCLA coaching legend John Wooden.

the game). For Irish and basketball, the timing couldn't have been better, although the first quake of the Great Depression had already struck. Clair Bee was coaching little Rider College to an 18-3 record, and Freeman had assembled "The Wonder Five" at St. John's. Maturing together for four years, from freshmen to seniors, the "Wonder Five" included 6-5 center Matty Begovich and forward Mack Posnack. The three guards were 5-8 dribble king Mac Kinsbrunner, quick-shooting Allie Schuckman, and defensive specialist Rip Gerson. Freeman

packed them into a nifty, Celtics-style post game and let 'em go. In their sophomore season, 1928–29, they ran off an 18-game winning streak on their way to a 23-2 record. They opened the next season, 1929–30, with a 13-game streak, lost a few games, then closed with another run of victories.

Early in the 1930–31 season, the string had grown to 20-something games. The Redmen had grown immensely popular but still played most nights in a packed gym before 1,200 fans. Then, early in 1931, the "Wonder Five" beat CCNY at the 106th Infantry Armory with a record New York crowd of 12,000 watching. Within weeks, Mayor Jimmy Walker was calling on sportswriters to help promote a tripleheader at Madison Square Garden to benefit the Unemployment Relief Fund. Columbia, Fordham, CCNY, Manhattan, St. John's, and NYU were the draw. All had good teams and good records, and 15,000 fans paid to see them play. The Wonder Five beat CCNY again that night to push their win streak to 22. They went on to win 27 in a row and compile a four-year record of 86-8. From there, they toured two years independently, then played five years as the Jewels in the old American League. But the Wonder Five's biggest impact on basketball was the excitement they brought to the city. They had given Irish a hint of things to come.

In 1933, Mayor Walker again set up a basketball benefit, a seven-game extravaganza that attracted 20,000 fans to the Garden, which gave Irish more pause to think. According to some accounts, Irish first hatched the idea of staging big-time games one night as he tore his pants while crawling through a window of a little gym in Riverdale to cover a sold-out Manhattan College game. The next season, 1933–34, found the 28-year-old sportswriter plotting to promote a game between NYU and CCNY. He had hoped to play the game at the Garden but a conflict with a boxing match killed the deal. Still, Irish decided to move ahead with his promotional plans. He lined up six dates at the Garden for the following season.

Irish's frantic planning conflicted with his job, and he left the *World-Telegram* a month before the first event. He staked his future on a December 29 doubleheader at the Garden featuring St. John's vs. Westminster and NYU vs. Notre Dame. A sell-out crowd of 16,000 watched, and college basketball, the business, was on its way. Irish's next seven doubleheaders drew 100,000 fans, and he became a rich young man.

From New York, he branched out to Philadelphia, then Buffalo, then other venues. He made vast sums promoting college games.

Soon, other promoters picked up his lead with big games from Atlanta to Boston to Chicago.

Bee's Blackbirds vs. Hank's One-Hander

In his writing, author Clair Bee created an ideal athlete, the fictional character Chip Hilton who had it all. Intelligence. Diligence. Honesty. And a nose for victory.

Bee sought to instill those same qualities in the college basketball teams he coached. For the most part, he was overwhelmingly successful. His teams lost just seven games in his seven years of coaching at Rider College. From there, he established a powerhouse at Long Island University from 1931 to 1951. Over those 18 years (Bee missed two seasons while in the service during World War II), his teams won 95 percent of their games, including two NIT titles. LIU's record consisted of winning streaks of 43, 38, 28, and 26 games.

Bee, a small, intense man, was a gentle, scholarly sort, but he could seize on opponents' weaknesses like a mongoose. A thinking man's coach, he held five degrees and authored 44 books, including 23 Chip Hilton volumes. He created the 1-3-1 zone defense and even played a role in bringing the 24-second shot clock to pro basketball (he coached the Baltimore Bullets after leaving LIU in 1951). A native of Grafton, West Virginia, Bee overcame tuberculosis as a child, and his rehabilitation led to an intense involvement with sports.

In his third year at LIU, 1933–34, the Blackbirds finished 27-1, losing only to St. John's and scoring 1,000 points, a benchmark in those days of center jumps after each basket. The next season they ran up a 24-2 record, and suddenly Bee was the toast of New York. In 1935–36, his Blackbirds finished 26-0 with a lineup that featured Marius Russo (who later pitched for the Yankees), Willie Schwartz, Art Hillhouse, Leo Merson, and Jules Bender. Their one close call on the schedule came against Duquesne in the Garden. Down five points with four minutes to play, the

Blackbirds survived on Russo's bucket at the buzzer.

LIU opened the next season on the same note, stretching their winning streak to 43 straight before running into the college game's newest sensation. He was a West Coast player, Stanford's Hank Luisetti, whose polished, running, one-handed shooting style created a stir in those days of set-shooters. Luisetti was 6-3 and handsome, which made him a hero to youngsters on the West Coast. On the East Coast, however, he was virtually unknown until Irish lured Stanford to the Garden.

An invitation from Irish to play at the Garden quickly became a status symbol in 1930s college basketball, and Stanford was definitely among the elite. Luisetti's freshman team went undefeated in 1934–35, and the next year he led Stanford to the Pacific Coast Conference championship. Luisetti's team came East in December of 1936. First, Stanford stopped off in Philadelphia to beat Temple. Then, on December 29, the Indians (called Cardinal now) met Bee's top-ranked LIU team in the Garden. Plump with confidence from their 43-game streak, the Blackbirds were the darlings of the 17,623 spectators. Luisetti didn't open the game with a flashy show of play, but it wasn't long before he wooed the crowd.

Early on, while being guarded by LIU All-American Art Hillhouse, Luisetti fired up his one-hander on the run. "I'll never forget that look on Hillhouse's face," he said years later. "He'd never seen a shot like that. When it hit, I could just see him saying, 'Boy, is this guy lucky.'"

Luisetti went on to score 15, but it was his floor game, passing, and defense that made the difference. Stanford ended LIU's streak that night, 45-31, and the Garden crowd gave Luisetti a standing ovation when he left the floor. "It seemed Luisetti could do nothing wrong," the *New York Times* reported the next morning. "Some of his shots would have been deemed foolhardy if attempted by somebody else, but

Stanford star Hank Luisetti was best known for his one-handed shooting style.

with Luisetti shooting, these were accepted by the crowd as a matter of course."

The subsequent media attention made Luisetti the darling of college basketball over the remainder of the season and the following year. Stanford traveled about the country, drawing large crowds wherever Luisetti played. And although their coaches frowned on it, schoolboys everywhere began trying to heave up Hank's one-hander.

Stanford returned to New York later that season for a game against CCNY. "I'll quit coaching if I have to teach the one-handed shot to win," declared CCNY coach Nat Holman. "Nobody can convince me that a shot predicated on a prayer is smart basketball."

If Luisetti's shots were prayers, they seemed to get answers. At one point, he popped in 13 consecutive points, and Stanford won, 45-42. The

New York newspapers again trumpeted his greatness. Yet Luisetti remained an unselfish player, until finally against Duquesne in Cleveland in 1938, his teammates refused to take shots, feeding his own passes back to him. Luisetti scored 50 that night as Stanford won, 92-27.

Luisetti was twice named national player of the year and led Stanford to three consecutive Pacific titles. He left Stanford in 1938 and was offered a Hollywood deal to make a film, *Campus Confessions,* with Betty Grable. It bombed, and worse, the AAU suspended his amateur status for a season, ruling that he had profited from basketball. Luisetti returned from suspension and went on to star in AAU basketball, but he never followed up his college success with a pro career. He played service ball while in the Navy during World War II and contracted meningitis. Although he won an AAU national championship in 1951 as a coach, the illness shortened his playing career.

One of the schoolboys affected by Luisetti's example was Jim Pollard, who played at Stanford and later starred with the Minneapolis Lakers. Pollard greatly admired Luisetti: "He was a great guy to watch. He had that charisma about him that everybody liked. Because he was such a graceful ball player and such a great one everybody tried to copy the greatness he had. But Hank was not primarily a scorer. He was a great defensive ball player and an excellent passer. Everybody gives him credit for popularizing the one-hander, which he did. I admit I freely copied it because he was my hero when I was a kid.

"I got to see Hank play a number of times and even played against him frequently in the service for a couple of years. Then when I got out of the service we were going to play together in the Oakland area. I was dying to play with him. He had been hurt during the war when he got spinal meningitis. We scrimmaged about 10 minutes one day. Hank and I took the next three best ball players and just wiped them. Hank was marvelous. But he walked off the floor just like he was drunk. He was weaving; he'd lost his sense of balance. I don't think he ever got on the court again to play."

Tournament Time

Off and on since 1897, the AAU had run a national basketball tournament. The event attracted big interest in Atlanta in 1920, then settled into Kansas City for 1921 and stayed there the next 14 years. But no tournament was held in 1936, and the event moved to Denver.

Angered at the loss of the tournament, Kansas City civic leaders enlisted the help of Dr. Naismith (who was still on the faculty at Kansas) in founding a "national" tournament. The first event in Kansas City in 1937 was actually an eight-team playoff of Midwest conference champions. This tournament organization later flowered into the National Association of Intercollegiate Athletics. As such, the NAIA is credited with staging the first national collegiate tournament. Its initial champion in March 1937 was Warrensburg (later to become Central Missouri), a 45-30 winner over Washburn College. The trophy was named for Naismith's wife, Maude.

But, as usual, the "big time" was in New York. Doubleheaders in the larger arenas meant that money was pouring into college basketball. That, in turn, meant that college teams could afford to travel. Figuring there should be a national tournament, the Metropolitan Basketball Writer's Association, a New York sportswriters group, organized the National Invitation Tournament (NIT) to close the 1937–38 season. They hoped to attract the big-name teams and players. Little did they realize they were opening college basketball's billion-dollar future.

PREMO POWER POLL The first wire-service national poll wasn't conducted until the 1948–49 season by the Associated Press. In an attempt to recognize some of the premier teams in the history of men's college basketball before that time, Patrick M. Premo, a professor of accounting at St. Bonaventure, analyzed every season since 1892–93. Not only did Premo look at each team's opponents and the final scores of each game, but he also reviewed as many of those opponents' games as possible in an attempt to derive a "strength of schedule" for each team.

In the early years, there were often no common opponents, making the evaluations of teams from different regions of the country very difficult. In addition, obtaining information on some schools in the early years was impossible in a number of cases; this accounts for why only a smattering of teams were rankable in the early years. Consequently, some subjectivity was necessary to complete Premo's analysis in reviewing the early years of the sport. Once teams began to oppose clubs outside of their geographic regions, the task of comparing squads became somewhat easier.

In order to avoid confusion, the current name for each school is cited in practically all cases. Premo does not claim that his polls are definitive. They are simply his opinion. But the Premo Power Polls provide a nostalgic trip through the early history of men's college basketball! (See the end of each season's regular-season account in Chapter 2 for the Premo Power Polls in the late 1930s and 1940s. A Premo Power Poll for best teams of each decade is also included at the end of Chapters 1 through 6.)

1892–93

RANKING	TEAM
1	Iowa (2-0-1)
2	Geneva (1-0)

1893–94

RANKING	TEAM
1	Hiram (Ohio) (1-0)

1894–95

RANKING	TEAM
1	Temple (8-3)

1895–96

RANKING	TEAM
1	Temple (15-7)
2	Yale (8-5)
3	Chicago (5-2)
4	Minnesota (3-2)
5	Bucknell (1-3)

1896–97

RANKING	TEAM
1	Yale (11-5-1)
2	Temple (10-11)
3	Chicago (5-2)
4	Bucknell (4-1)
5	Wabash (1-0)

1897–98

RANKING	TEAM
1	Mount Union (8-1)
2	Yale (12-9)
3	Westminster (Penn.) (4-2)
4	Temple (20-5)
5	Hiram (Ohio) (3-2)

1898–99

RANKING	TEAM
1	Yale (9-1)
2	Allegheny (8-1)
3	Nebraska (4-0)
4	Temple (18-6)
5	Minnesota (7-2)
6	Ohio St. (12-4)
7	Wabash (2-0)
8	Hiram (Ohio) (4-1)
9	Kansas (7-4)
10	Syracuse (1-0-1)

1899–1900

RANKING	TEAM
1	Yale (9-6)
2	Dartmouth (22-4-1)
3	Allegheny (10-4)
4	Nebraska (5-0)
5	Penn St. (7-1)
6	Geneva (8-3)
7	Illinois St. (5-0)
8	Hiram (Ohio) (7-1)
9	Bucknell (6-3)
10	Temple (13-9)

1900–1

RANKING	TEAM
1	Bucknell (12-1)
2	Purdue (12-0)
3	Penn St. (5-1)
4	Yale (10-6)
5	Amherst (4-0)
6	Allegheny (14-2)
7	Minnesota (11-1)
8	Hiram (Ohio) (9-1)
9	Williams (9-2)
10	Dartmouth (11-8)
11	Geneva (10-2)
12	Western Reserve (5-2)
13	Princeton (7-5)
14	Harvard (11-8)
15	Lafayette (4-3)
16	Mount Union (10-6)
17	Syracuse (2-1)
18	Wisc.-Superior (8-2)
19	Michigan St. (3-0)
20	Illinois St. (4-1)

1901–2

RANKING	TEAM
1	Minnesota (15-0)
2	Purdue (11-3)
3	Allegheny (12-1)
4	Amherst (8-0)
5	Iowa (10-2)
6	Williams (12-3)
7	Bucknell (12-2)
8	Wisconsin (7-3)
9	Dartmouth (11-5)
10	Yale (13-8)
11	Penn St. (9-2)
12	Washington (7-0)
13	Colgate (7-2)
14	Harvard (9-5)
15	Pennsylvania (7-2-1)
16	Mount Union (10-2)
17	Lehigh (9-5)
18	Grove City (13-3)
19	Michigan St. (5-0)
20	St. Francis (13-1)

1902–3

RANKING	TEAM
1	Minnesota (13-0)
2	Yale (15-1)
3	Purdue (8-0)
4	Bucknell (10-0)
5	Colgate (7-1)
6	Grove City (13-1)
7	Geneva (10-1)
8	Allegheny (10-2-1)
9	Williams (18-2)
10	Ohio St. (5-2)
11	Columbia (10-6)
12	Princeton (9-6)
13	Wabash (12-3)
14	Hiram (Ohio) (4-1)
15	Wisconsin (5-2)
16	Lehigh (4-2-1)
17	Michigan St. (6-0)
18	Latter Day Sts. (15-1)
19	Wheaton (Ill.) (8-1)
20	Vanderbilt (6-0)

PREMO POWER POLL (CONTD.)

1903–4

RANKING	TEAM
1	Columbia (17-1)
2	Minnesota (11-2)
3	Allegheny (12-2)
4	Purdue (11-2)
5	Holy Cross (10-2)
6	Pennsylvania (10-4)
7	Princeton (10-5)
8	Ohio St. (10-4)
9	Hiram (Ohio) (9-3)
10	Wisconsin (11-4)
11	Williams (15-7)
12	Colgate (12-5)
13	Chicago (7-0)
14	Wheaton (Ill.) (10-3-1)
15	Iowa (6-2)
16	Lehigh (5-2)
17	Washington (5-1)
18	Oregon St. (7-3)
19	Maine (8-2)
20	Illinois St. (7-1)

1904–5

RANKING	TEAM
1	Columbia (19-1)
2	Williams (20-2)
3	Ohio St. (12-2)
4	Allegheny (10-2)
5	Syracuse (16-7)
6	Brown (12-6)
7	Harvard (11-5)
8	Wabash (8-1)
9	Dartmouth (20-10-1)
10	Chicago (9-2)
11	Holy Cross (6-4)
12	Princeton (8-5)
13	Colgate (10-7)
14	Yale (22-13)
15	Butler (6-1)
16	Augustana (Ill.) (9-0)
17	Nebraska (11-5)
18	Penn St. (6-2)
19	Cincinnati (6-3)
20	Dayton (6-1)

1905–6

RANKING	TEAM
1	Wabash (17-1)
2	Dartmouth (16-2)
3	Minnesota (13-2)
4	Wisconsin (12-2)
5	Westminster (Pa.) (12-2)
6	Williams (14-3-1)
7	Pennsylvania (16-4)
8	Bucknell (10-2)
9	Allegheny (13-4)
10	Ohio St. (9-1)
11	Columbia (12-4)
12	Nebraska (12-3)
13	Syracuse (9-3)
14	Harvard (12-4)
15	Holy Cross (12-3)
16	Michigan St. (11-2)
17	Western Reserve (13-3)
18	Wooster (7-3)
19	Oregon St. (10-0)
20	Denison (Ohio) (12-2)

1906–7

RANKING	TEAM
1	Chicago (20-2)
2	Williams (15-1)
3	Wabash (17-2)
4	Columbia (14-4)
5	Allegheny (10-1)
6	Yale (30-6-1)
7	Dartmouth (13-4)
8	Minnesota (10-2)
9	Wisconsin (11-3)
10	Oregon St. (17-1)
11	Westminster (Pa.) (7-1)
12	Bucknell (10-1)
13	Michigan St. (14-2)
14	Dayton (14-0)
15	Grinnell (9-2)
16	Akron (5-2)
17	Lehigh (9-2)
18	CCNY (8-1)
19	Buffalo (6-2)
20	Vanderbilt (6-1)

1907–8

RANKING	TEAM
1	Wabash (24-0)
2	Chicago (21-2)
3	Pennsylvania (23-4)
4	Allegheny (12-0)
5	Wisconsin (10-2)
6	Bucknell (12-0)
7	Grinnell (14-3)
8	Notre Dame (12-4)
9	Syracuse (11-2)
10	Michigan St. (15-5)
11	Dartmouth (11-4)
12	CCNY (9-2)
13	Penn St. (10-4)
14	St. Lawrence (9-2)
15	Lehigh (6-1)
16	Georgetown (5-1)
17	Haskell (24-11)
18	Mount Union (17-3)
19	Washington St. (12-3)
20	Cincinnati (9-0)

1908–9

RANKING	TEAM
1	Chicago (12-0)
2	Swarthmore (12-0)
3	NYU (13-0)
4	Williams (13-1)
5	Columbia (16-1)
6	Ohio St. (11-1)
7	Notre Dame (33-7)
8	Allegheny (11-2)
9	Army (9-2)
10	Grinnell (12-1)
11	Wooster (10-2)
12	Bucknell (9-3)
13	Oregon St. (10-1)
14	Vanderbilt (11-4)
15	Kansas (25-3)
16	Georgia (6-2)
17	Washington (9-1)
18	Dayton (12-2)
19	Illinois St. (9-0)
20	MIT (10-6)

1909–10

RANKING	TEAM
1	Williams (11-0)
2	Columbia (11-1)
3	Army (14-1)
4	Kansas (18-1)
5	VPI (11-0)
6	Cotner (Neb.) (11-0)
7	Centre (Ky.) (20-3)
8	Minnesota (10-3)
9	Kansas St. (11-2-1)
10	Chicago (9-3)
11	Navy (10-1)
12	Ohio St. (11-1)
13	Grinnell (12-1)
14	Iowa (11-3)
15	Allegheny (9-3)
16	NYU (13-4)
17	Swarthmore (9-3)
18	Niagara (13-3)
19	Oberlin (10-3)
20	Oklahoma (8-0)

1910–11

RANKING	TEAM
1	St. John's (14-0)
2	Columbia (13-1)
3	Navy (10-1)
4	Dayton (10-0)
5	Wabash (10-1)
6	Ohio St. (7-2)
7	VPI (11-1)
8	Notre Dame (7-3)
9	Allegheny (9-2)
10	Wesleyan (Conn.) (10-3)
11	Army (9-3)
12	Oberlin (10-2)
13	Washington (11-1)
14	N. Central College (14-2)
15	Grinnell (13-1)
16	Williams (8-2)
17	Wooster (16-4)
18	Oregon (9-3)
19	CCNY (7-2)
20	Union (7-2)

1911–12

RANKING	TEAM
1	Wisconsin (15-0)
2	Purdue (12-0)
3	Grove City (13-0)
4	Allegheny (11-1)
5	Swarthmore (11-1)
6	Wesleyan (Conn.) (13-0)
7	Notre Dame (15-2)
8	Navy (7-1)
9	Beloit (6-2)
10	Columbia (10-2)
11	Dayton (13-0)
12	Oregon St. (16-3)
13	Washington (12-4)
14	Nebraska (14-1)
15	Oregon (9-3)
16	Kentucky (9-0)
17	Syracuse (11-3)
18	St. Lawrence (12-3)
19	Mississippi St. (9-0)
20	Mississippi (10-2)

PREMO POWER POLL (CONTD.)

1912–13

RANKING	TEAM
1	Navy (9-0)
2	Denison (Ohio) (13-1)
3	Dayton (11-0)
4	Wisconsin (14-1)
5	Detroit Mercy (13-0)
6	Georgia (10-1)
7	Akron (7-1)
8	Grinnell (11-0)
9	Army (11-2)
10	Nebraska (17-2)
11	Wesleyan (Conn.) (14-2)
12	Notre Dame (13-2)
13	Catholic (14-3)
14	Penn St. (8-3)
15	Lehigh (12-2)
16	Allegheny (9-2)
17	Virginia (12-3)
18	Utah (21-3)
19	Springfield (6-1)
20	Mississippi St. (11-1)

1913–14

RANKING	TEAM
1	Wisconsin (15-0)
2	Denison (Ohio) (15-1)
3	Navy (10-0)
4	Syracuse (12-0)
5	Cornell (14-2)
6	Lehigh (12-2)
7	St. Mary's (Cal.) (15-0)
8	Nebraska (15-3)
9	Virginia (12-1-1)
10	Grinnell (10-1)
11	Georgia (9-1)
12	Kansas (17-1)
13	Oberlin (7-3)
14	Kentucky (12-2)
15	Duquesne (7-2)
16	Washington (12-2)
17	Catholic (13-4)
18	Tennessee (15-2)
19	Utah (12-2)
20	BYU (10-1)

1914–15

RANKING	TEAM
1	Illinois (16-0)
2	Army (11-2)
3	Navy (9-2)
4	Virginia (17-0)
5	Yale (14-3)
6	Syracuse (10-1)
7	Chicago (9-3)
8	Notre Dame (15-2)
9	Cornell (12-4)
10	Allegheny (10-1)
11	Wabash (7-2)
12	Penn St. (10-3)
13	Seton Hall (15-2)
14	Kansas (16-1)
15	Denison (Ohio) (12-2)
16	Washington (17-2)
17	Whittier (17-3)
18	Texas (14-0)
19	Wisconsin (13-4)
20	Duquesne (12-2)

1915–16

RANKING	TEAM
1	Wisconsin (20-1)
2	Allegheny (10-1)
3	Pittsburgh (16-2)
4	Illinois (13-3)
5	Princeton (16-4)
6	Swarthmore (10-2)
7	Navy (12-2)
8	Nebraska (13-1)
9	Utah (10-0)
10	Missouri (13-3)
11	Kansas St. (13-3)
12	Texas (12-0)
13	Wabash (17-4)
14	Washington St. (18-3)
15	Virginia (11-2)
16	Texas A&M (11-2)
17	Catholic (10-4)
18	Tennessee (12-0)
19	Ripon (15-3)
20	Montana St. (10-1)

1916–17

RANKING	TEAM
1	Washington St. (25-1)
2	California (15-1)
3	Wabash (19-2)
4	Minnesota (15-2)
5	Illinois (13-3)
6	Wisconsin (15-3)
7	Kansas St. (15-2)
8	Navy (11-0)
9	CCNY (15-3)
10	Purdue (11-3)
11	Yale (19-5)
12	Lehigh (15-4)
13	Penn St. (12-2)
14	Syracuse (13-3)
15	Montana St. (19-1)
16	Washington & Lee (13-0)
17	Central Missouri St. (13-2)
18	Georgia (8-1)
19	VPI (17-2)
20	Case Tech (12-1)

1917–18

RANKING	TEAM
1	Syracuse (16-1)
2	Oregon St. (15-0)
3	Penn St. (12-1)
4	Pennsylvania (18-2)
5	Geneva (13-2)
6	Navy (14-2)
7	Princeton (12-3)
8	Stevens (14-0)
9	Wash. & Jefferson (10-2)
10	Union (14-1)
11	Idaho (11-1)
12	Missouri (17-1)
13	Wisconsin (14-3)
14	Springfield (13-3)
15	Virginia (7-1)
16	Centre (10-1)
17	Utah St. (9-0)
18	LSU (12-1)
19	Kentucky (9-2-1)
20	North Carolina St. (12-2)

1918–19

RANKING	TEAM
1	Navy (16-0)
2	Minnesota (13-0)
3	Pennsylvania (15-1)
4	Georgetown (9-1)
5	Penn St. (11-2)
6	Wabash (13-3)
7	Cornell (11-3)
8	Oregon (13-3)
9	Yale (7-2)
10	Idaho (13-2)
11	VPI (18-4)
12	Kansas St. (17-2)
13	Santa Clara (14-1)
14	Missouri (14-3)
15	Bucknell (13-3)
16	Delaware (8-2)
17	Chicago (10-2)
18	Oklahoma (12-0)
19	Washington & Lee (10-3)
20	Texas (17-3)

1918–19 TOP SERVICE TEAMS

RANKING	TEAM
1	Great Lakes NTS (23-7)
2	Camp Dodge (10-1)

1919–20

RANKING	TEAM
1	Pennsylvania (22-1)
2	Missouri (17-1)
3	Penn St. (12-1)
4	NYU (16-1)
5	Georgetown (13-1)
6	Purdue (16-4)
7	Delaware (13-2)
8	Wisconsin (15-1)
9	Navy (14-3)
10	Chicago (11-4)
11	Army (12-2)
12	Westminster (Mo.) (17-0)
13	Texas A&M (19-0)
14	Nebraska (22-2)
15	Syracuse (15-3)
16	Montana St. (13-0)
17	Millikin (22-1)
18	CCNY (13-3)
19	Ripon (11-2)
20	Wyoming (10-1)

1920–21

RANKING	TEAM
1	Missouri (17-1)
2	Pennsylvania (21-2)
3	Navy (18-1)
4	NYU (12-1)
5	Penn St. (14-2)
6	Grove City (15-0)
7	VMI (16-1)
8	Stanford (15-3)
9	Nebraska (12-3)
10	Arizona (7-0)
11	Virginia (11-3)
12	Wisconsin (13-4)
13	Ohio Northern (21-3)
14	Michigan (16-4)
15	Central Mo. St. (22-2)
16	Wabash (21-4)
17	Denison (Ohio) (14-3)
18	Ohio University (16-2)
19	DePauw (12-3)
20	Oberlin (11-1)

PREMO POWER POLL (CONTD.)

1921–22

RANKING	TEAM
1	Missouri (16-1)
2	Kansas (16-2)
3	Army (17-2)
4	Idaho (19-1)
5	Oregon St. (21-2)
6	Wabash (21-3)
7	Holy Cross (14-3)
8	Purdue (15-3)
9	Michigan (15-4)
10	CCNY (10-2)
11	Butler (23-4)
12	Princeton (20-5)
13	Illinois (14-5)
14	Wisconsin (14-5)
15	Pennsylvania (24-3)
16	Texas A&M (18-3)
17	Navy (15-3)
18	Wooster (14-1)
19	Beloit (12-0)
20	Texas (20-4)

1922–23

RANKING	TEAM
1	Army (17-0)
2	Kansas (17-1)
3	Missouri (15-3)
4	Springfield (15-1)
5	Butler (16-4)
6	Iowa (13-2)
7	Penn St. (13-1)
8	N. Texas St. (13-1)
9	Hardin-Simmons (13-1)
10	Marquette (19-2)
11	Grove City (15-2)
12	Idaho (14-3)
13	Wisconsin (12-3)
14	Texas A&M (16-4)
15	West Texas St. (12-4)
16	Navy (14-4)
17	Colgate (14-4)
18	Akron (12-1)
19	Washington (13-3)
20	Denison (Ohio) (12-1)

1923–24

RANKING	TEAM
1	North Carolina (26-0)
2	Kansas (16-3)
3	Navy (15-3)
4	Penn St. (13-2)
5	Texas (23-0)
6	Oklahoma (15-3)
7	Columbia (15-4)
8	Cornell (13-3)
9	Vermont (15-2)
10	USC (15-4)
11	Tulane (22-1)
12	Army (16-2)
13	CCNY (12-1)
14	Beloit (14-0)
15	Creighton (13-2)
16	California (7-3)
17	Alabama (12-4)
18	RPI (11-1)
19	Springfield (13-3)
20	Washington (12-4)

1924–25

RANKING	TEAM
1	Princeton (21-2)
2	Wabash (18-1)
3	Ohio St. (14-2)
4	Kansas (17-1)
5	Syracuse (15-2)
6	Fordham (15-1)
7	Butler (20-4)
8	Oklahoma St. (15-3)
9	Army (12-3)
10	Washburn (15-0)
11	Penn St. (12-2)
12	Creighton (13-2)
13	CCNY (12-2)
14	Dartmouth (12-5)
15	Grove City (15-2)
16	Pennsylvania (17-5)
17	Harvard (11-2)
18	Evansville (11-2)
19	TCU (14-5)
20	Navy (18-5)

1925–26

RANKING	TEAM
1	Syracuse (19-1)
2	Notre Dame (19-1)
3	Kansas (16-2)
4	Columbia (16-2)
5	California (14-0)
6	Oklahoma (11-4)
7	Purdue (13-4)
8	Michigan (12-5)
9	Indiana (12-5)
10	Iowa (12-5)
11	Cincinnati (17-2)
12	Maryland (14-3)
13	Butler (16-5)
14	Oregon (18-4)
15	UCLA (14-2)
16	Lehigh (13-1)
17	North Carolina (20-5)
18	Navy (12-5)
19	Arkansas (15-1)
20	Mississippi (16-2)

1926–27

RANKING	TEAM
1	Notre Dame (19-1)
2	California (13-0)
3	Michigan (14-3)
4	Fordham (18-2)
5	Indiana (13-4)
6	Evansville (16-4)
7	Butler (17-4)
8	Kansas (15-2)
9	Navy (15-2)
10	Oregon (24-4)
11	Vanderbilt (20-4)
12	Syracuse (15-4)
13	West Texas St. (23-3)
14	Western Michigan (16-2)
15	Furman (16-4)
16	Montana St. (30-7)
17	Loyola (Ill.) (15-4)
18	Washington (15-4)
19	Creighton (14-5)
20	Xavier (Ohio) (11-3)

1927–28

RANKING	TEAM
1	Pittsburgh (21-0)
2	Montana St. (36-2)
3	Indiana (15-2)
4	Purdue (15-2)
5	Butler (19-3)
6	Notre Dame (18-4)
7	Arkansas (19-1)
8	Oklahoma (18-0)
9	Fordham (12-1)
10	Springfield (18-2)
11	Georgetown (12-1)
12	Auburn (20-2)
13	Pennsylvania (22-5)
14	USC (22-4)
15	Westminster (Pa.) (17-3)
16	Evansville (14-3)
17	St. John's (18-4)
18	LSU (14-4)
19	Oregon (18-3)
20	Wayne St. (18-1)

1928–29

RANKING	TEAM
1	Montana St. (36-2)
2	San Francisco (21-2)
3	Arkansas (16-1)
4	Michigan (13-3)
5	Butler (17-2)
6	Oklahoma (13-2)
7	Texas (18-2)
8	California (16-4)
9	Wisconsin (15-2)
10	Purdue (13-4)
11	Washington (18-2)
12	Fordham (18-1)
13	West Texas St. (16-2)
14	Loyola (Ill.) (16-0)
15	Notre Dame (15-5)
16	Northwestern (15-2)
17	Pittsburgh (16-5)
18	Westminster (Pa.) (15-2)
19	Washington & Lee (15-1)
20	Creighton (13-4)

1929–30

RANKING	TEAM
1	Alabama (20-0)
2	Syracuse (18-2)
3	Pittsburgh (23-2)
4	Wisconsin (15-2)
5	Duke (18-2)
6	Purdue (13-2)
7	Missouri (15-3)
8	St. John's (23-1)
9	Furman (16-1)
10	USC (15-5)
11	NYU (13-3)
12	Kansas (14-4)
13	Michigan St. (12-4)
14	Western Michigan (17-0)
15	Washington (21-7)
16	Kentucky (16-3)
17	Notre Dame (14-6)
18	Columbia (17-5)
19	CCNY (10-3)
20	Temple (18-3)

PREMO POWER POLL (CONTD.)

1930–31

RANKING	TEAM
1	Northwestern (16-1)
2	St. John's (21-1)
3	Washington (25-3)
4	Columbia (21-2)
5	Georgia (23-2)
6	Pittsburgh (20-4)
7	Syracuse (16-4)
8	Michigan (13-4)
9	Minnesota (13-4)
10	Purdue (12-5)
11	Illinois (12-5)
12	Manhattan (17-2)
13	Furman (15-2)
14	Michigan St. (16-1)
15	Kansas (15-3)
16	Butler (17-2)
17	West Texas St. (17-3)
18	Williams (12-3)
19	Army (12-3)
20	Santa Clara (16-3)

1931–32

RANKING	TEAM
1	Purdue (17-1)
2	Notre Dame (18-2)
3	Minnesota (15-3)
4	Kentucky (15-2)
5	CCNY (16-1)
6	Santa Clara (15-4)
7	St. John's (22-4)
8	Princeton (18-4)
9	Washington St. (22-5)
10	Butler (14-5)
11	Wyoming (18-2)
12	Northwestern (12-5)
13	Creighton (17-4)
14	Arizona (18-2)
15	Providence (19-5)
16	North Carolina (16-5)
17	Michigan St. (12-5)
18	West Texas St. (20-3)
19	Westminster (Pa.) (16-2)
20	Mount Union (16-1)

1932–33

RANKING	TEAM
1	Texas (22-1)
2	South Carolina (21-2)
3	Ohio St. (17-3)
4	Kentucky (20-3)
5	Princeton (19-3)
6	Yale (19-3)
7	Navy (14-2)
8	Syracuse (14-2)
9	Iowa (15-5)
10	St. John's (23-4)
11	Marquette (14-3)
12	TCU (16-4)
13	Northwestern (15-4)
14	Duquesne (15-1)
15	Butler (16-5)
16	Notre Dame (16-6)
17	Creighton (12-5)
18	West Texas St. (20-4)
19	CCNY (13-1)
20	Morgan (28-1)

1933–34

RANKING	TEAM
1	South Carolina (18-1)
2	Kentucky (16-1)
3	Duquesne (19-2)
4	NYU (16-0)
5	Wyoming (26-3)
6	Purdue (17-3)
7	Notre Dame (20-4)
8	Pittsburgh (18-4)
9	Alabama (16-2)
10	Pennsylvania (16-3)
11	DePaul (17-0)
12	Syracuse (15-2)
13	CCNY (14-1)
14	Navy (11-2)
15	LIU-Brooklyn (26-1)
16	Westminster (Pa.) (22-4)
17	North Carolina (18-4)
18	St. John's (16-3)
19	Kansas (16-1)
20	Marquette (15-4)

1934–35

RANKING	TEAM
1	Richmond (20-0)
2	NYU (19-1)
3	Duquesne (18-1)
4	Kentucky (19-2)
5	North Carolina (23-2)
6	Purdue (17-3)
7	LSU (14-1)
8	LIU-Brooklyn (24-2)
9	DePaul (15-1)
10	USC (20-6)
11	Pittsburgh (18-6)
12	Navy (11-3)
13	Pennsylvania (16-4)
14	SMU (14-3)
15	Syracuse (15-2)
16	Illinois (15-5)
17	Wisconsin (15-5)
18	Ohio Wesleyan (17-2)
19	Rutgers (13-3)
20	Westminster (Pa.) (19-3)

1935–36

RANKING	TEAM
1	LIU-Brooklyn (25-0)
2	Notre Dame (22-2-1)
3	Kansas (21-2)
4	Indiana (18-2)
5	Arkansas (24-3)
6	Washington (25-7)
7	DePaul (18-4)
8	Manhattan (17-2)
9	Washington & Lee (18-2)
10	NYU (15-4)
11	Stanford (22-7)
12	St. John's (18-4)
13	Purdue (16-4)
14	Columbia (19-3)
15	George Washington (16-3)
16	Northwestern (13-6-1)
17	Western Kentucky (26-4)
18	Temple (18-6)
19	Duquesne (14-3)
20	Murray St. (23-2)

1936–37

RANKING	TEAM
1	Stanford (25-2)
2	Notre Dame (20-3)
3	LIU-Brooklyn (28-3)
4	Michigan (16-4)
5	Purdue (15-5)
6	Pennsylvania (17-3)
7	Illinois (14-4)
8	George Washington (16-4)
9	USC (19-6)
10	Western Kentucky (21-2)
11	Temple (17-6)
12	Kentucky (17-5)
13	Rhode Island (18-3)
14	Hardin-Simmons (16-1)
15	Oklahoma St. (20-3)
16	Springfield (18-3)
17	Washington St. (24-8)
18	Loyola (Ill.) (16-3)
19	Murray St. (22-3)
20	Ohio Univ. (18-3)

PREMO POWER POLL: BEST TEAMS BY DECADE

1890–99

RANKING	SEASON	TEAM
1	1898–99	Yale (9-1)
2	1898–99	Allegheny (Pa.) (8-1)
3	1898–99	Nebraska (4-0)
4	1897–98	Mt. Union (Ohio) (8-1)
5	1898–99	Temple (18-6)
6	1896–97	Yale (11-5-1)
7	1898–99	Minnesota (7-2)
8	1897–98	Yale (12-9)
9	1897–98	Westminster (Pa.) (4-2)
10	1894–95	Temple (8-3)

1900–9

RANKING	SEASON	TEAM
1	1907–8	Wabash (Ind.) (24-0)
2	1902–3	Minnesota (13-0)
3	1907–8	Chicago (21-2)
4	1901–2	Minnesota (15-0)
5	1906–7	Chicago (20-2)
6	1904–5	Columbia (19-1)
7	1908–9	Chicago (12-0)
8	1902–3	Yale (15-1)
9	1905–6	Wabash (Ind.) (17-1)
10	1903–4	Columbia (17-1)
11	1908–9	Swarthmore (Pa.) (12-0)
12	1906–7	Williams (Mass.) (15-1)
13	1904–5	Williams (Mass.) (20-2)
14	1907–8	Pennsylvania (23-4)
15	1907–8	Allegheny (Pa.) (12-0)
16	1908–9	New York Univ. (13-0)
17	1902–3	Purdue (8-0)
18	1906–7	Wabash (Ind.) (17-2)
19	1904–5	Ohio St. (12-2)
20	1906–7	Columbia (14-4)

PREMO POWER POLL (CONTD.)

1910–19

RANKING	SEASON	TEAM
1	1918–19	Navy (16-0)
2	1912–13	Navy (9-0)
3	1911–12	Wisconsin (15-0)
4	1913–14	Wisconsin (15-0)
5	1918–19	Minnesota (13-0)
6	1914–15	Illinois (16-0)
7	1910–11	St. John's (14-0)
8	1916–17	Washington St. (25-1)
9	1911–12	Purdue (12-0)
10	1913–14	Denison (Ohio) (15-1)
11	1912–13	Denison (Ohio) (13-1)
12	1909–10	Williams (Mass.) (11-0)
13	1915–16	Wisconsin (20-1)
14	1916–17	California (15-1)
15	1913–14	Navy (10-0)
16	1917–18	Syracuse (16-1)
17	1910–11	Columbia (13-1)
18	1911–12	Grove City (Pa.) (13-0)
19	1918–19	Pennsylvania (15-1)
20	1916–17	Wabash (Ind.) (19-2)

1920–29

RANKING	SEASON	TEAM
1	1928–29	Montana St. (36-2)
2	1927–28	Pittsburgh (21-0)
3	1922–23	Army (17-0)
4	1919–20	Pennsylvania (22-1)
5	1925–26	Syracuse (19-1)
6	1927–28	Montana St. (36-2)
7	1923–24	North Carolina (26-0)
8	1926–27	Notre Dame (19-1)
9	1920–21	Missouri (17-1)
10	1925–26	Notre Dame (19-1)
11	1922–23	Kansas (17-1)
12	1919–20	Missouri (17-1)
13	1928–29	San Francisco (21-2)
14	1924–25	Princeton (21-2)
15	1921–22	Missouri (16-1)
16	1919–20	Penn St. (12-1)
17	1920–21	Pennsylvania (21-2)
18	1921–22	Kansas (16-2)
19	1928–29	Arkansas (16-1)
20	1927–28	Indiana (15-2)

1930–39

RANKING	SEASON	TEAM
1	1938–39	LIU-Brooklyn# (23-0)
2	1936–37	Stanford (25-2)
3	1935–36	LIU-Brooklyn (25-0)
4	1931–32	Purdue (17-1)
5	1937–38	Temple# (23-2)
6	1934–35	Richmond (20-0)
7	1929–30	Alabama (20-0)
8	1932–33	Texas (22-1)
9	1935–36	Notre Dame (22-2-1)
10	1936–37	Notre Dame (20-3)
11	1933–34	South Carolina (18-1)
12	1930–31	Northwestern (16-1)
13	1934–35	NYU (19-1)
14	1931–32	Notre Dame (18-2)
15	1937–38	Stanford (21-3)
16	1938–39	Bradley (19-3)
17	1930–31	St. John's (21-1)
18	1933–34	Kentucky (16-1)
19	1932–33	South Carolina (21-2)
20	1934–35	Duquesne (18-1)
	1935–36	Kansas (21-2)

#–NIT Champion

EARLY AWARD WINNERS

NCAA CONSENSUS FIRST-TEAM ALL-AMERICANS FROM 1929 TO 1937

1928–29: Thomas Churchill, Oklahoma; Vern Corbin, California; Chuck Hyatt, Pittsburgh; Charles Murphy, Purdue; Joe Schaaf, Pennsylvania; John Thompson, Montana State

1929–30: Chuck Hyatt, Pittsburgh; Charles Murphy, Purdue; Branch McCracken, Indiana; John Thompson, Montana State; Frank Ward, Montana State; John Wooden, Purdue

1930–31: Wes Fesler, Ohio State; George Gregory, Columbia; Joe Reiff, Northwestern; Elwood Romney, Brigham Young; John Wooden, Purdue

1931–32: Louis Berger, Maryland; Ed Krause, Notre Dame; Forest Sale, Kentucky; Les Witte, Wyoming; John Wooden, Purdue

1932–33: Ed Krause, Notre Dame; Elliott Loughlin, Navy; Jerry Nemer, Southern Cal; Joe Reiff, Northwestern; Forest Sale, Kentucky; Don Smith, Pittsburgh

1933–34: Norman Cottom, Purdue; Claire Cribbs, Pittsburgh; Ed Krause, Notre Dame; Hal Lee, Washington; Les Witte, Wyoming

1934–35: Bud Browning, Oklahoma; Claire Cribbs, Pittsburgh; Leroy Edwards, Kentucky; Jack Gray, Texas; Lee Guttero, Southern Cal

1935–36: Vern Huffman, Indiana; Bob Kessler, Purdue; Bill Kinner, Utah; Hank Luisetti, Stanford; John Moir, Notre Dame; Paul Nowak, Notre Dame; Ike Poole, Arkansas

1936–37: Jules Bender, Long Island; Hank Luisetti, Stanford; John Moir, Notre Dame; Paul Nowak, Notre Dame; Jewell Young, Purdue

HELMS FOUNDATION CHAMPIONS FROM 1901 TO 1937

The Helms Foundation of Los Angeles, under the guidance of founder Bill Schroeder, chose national college champions from 1942 to 1982 and researched retroactive No. 1 selections from 1901 to 1941. There are four years when the Helms picks differ from the actual champion since the NIT commenced in 1938–39 (Helms selected LIU), 1940 (Southern Cal), 1944 (Army), and 1954 (Kentucky). Army had a policy against postseason play until accepting a bid to the 1961 NIT. Kentucky rejected a bid to the 1954 NCAA Tournament after the NCAA declared three seniors ineligible.

Multiple Helms national championships from 1901 to 1937 include Chicago (3), Columbia (3), Wisconsin (3), Kansas (2), Minnesota (2), Notre Dame (2), Penn (2), Pittsburgh (2), Syracuse (2), and Yale (2). Only two of these 10 schools won an NCAA Tournament since it started in 1939—Wisconsin (1941) and Kansas (1952 and 1988).

YEAR	CHAMPION (RECORD)	HEAD COACH	TOP PLAYER, POS.
1901	Yale (10-6)	No coach	G. M. Clark, F
1902	Minnesota (15-0)	Louis Cooke	W. C. Deering, F
1903	Yale (15-1)	W. H. Murphy	R. B. Hyatt, F
1904	Columbia (17-1)	No coach	Harry Fisher, F
1905	Columbia (19-1)	No coach	Harry Fisher, F
1906	Dartmouth (16-2)	No coach	George Grebenstein, F
1907	Chicago (22-2)	Joseph Raycroft	John Schammer, C
1908	Chicago (21-2)	Joseph Raycroft	John Schammer, C
1909	Chicago (12-0)	Joseph Raycroft	John Schammer, C
1910	Columbia (11-1)	Harry Fisher	Ted Kiendl, F
1911	St. John's (14-0)	Claude Allen	John Keenan, F-C
1912	Wisconsin (15-0)	Doc Meanwell	Otto Stangel, F
1913	Navy (9-0)	Louis Wenzel	Laurence Wild, F
1914	Wisconsin (15-0)	Doc Meanwell	Gene Van Gent, C
1915	Illinois (16-0)	Ralph Jones	Ray Woods, G
1916	Wisconsin (20-1)	Doc Meanwell	George Lewis, F
1917	Washington State (25-1)	Doc Bohler	Ray Bohler, G
1918	Syracuse (16-1)	Edmund Dollard	Joe Schwarzer, G
1919	Minnesota (13-0)	Louis Cooke	Arnold Oss, F
1920	Penn (22-1)	Lon Jourdet	George Sweeney, F
1921	Penn (21-2)	Edward McNichol	Danny McNichol, G
1922	Kansas (16-2)	Phog Allen	Paul Endacott, G
1923	Kansas (17-1)	Phog Allen	Paul Endacott, G
1924	North Carolina (26-0)	Bo Shepard	Jack Cobb, F
1925	Princeton (21-2)	Al Wittmer	Art Loeb, G
1926	Syracuse (19-1)	Lew Andreas	Vic Hanson, F
1927	Notre Dame (19-1)	George Keagan	John Nykas, C
1928	Pittsburgh (21-0)	Doc Carlson	Chuck Hyatt, F
1929	Montana State (36-2)	Schubert Dyche	John Thompson, F
1930	Pittsburgh (23-2)	Doc Carlson	Chuck Hyatt, F
1931	Northwestern (16-1)	Dutch Lonborg	Joe Reiff, C
1932	Purdue (17-1)	Piggy Lambert	John Wooden, G
1933	Kentucky (20-3)	Adolph Rupp	Forest Sale, F
1934	Wyoming (26-3)	Willard Witte	Les Witte, G
1935	NYU (19-1)	Howard Cann	Sid Gross, F
1936	Notre Dame (22-2-1)	George Keogan	John Moir, F
1937	Stanford (25-2)	John Bunn	Hank Luisetti, F

2

START OF THE NCAA TOURNAMENT:

1938–49

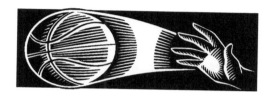

The NCAA's prize product, the Division I Men's Basketball Tournament, wasn't the NCAA's idea and was literally dumped into the governing body's lap by the National Association of Basketball Coaches (NABC). A group of New York sportswriters staged the first major college tournament, the National Invitation Tournament, in 1938 in New York. But a coalition of NABC members, particularly coaches from the Midwest, felt if there was to be a national tourney, it should be sponsored by a collegiate organization and not scribes, especially those possessing what they perceived to be a "biased" Eastern influence.

Harold Olsen, a former Wisconsin player and Ohio State coach, is accorded much of the credit for unveiling the NCAA Tournament to the American sports scene. The first NCAA Tournament was conducted in 1939, sponsored not by the NCAA but by the NABC. Oddly, Olsen's Ohio State team reached the final of the eight-team event (one from each district) before losing to Oregon, 46-33.

Total attendance for the inaugural NCAA playoff was a meager 15,025, and the venture produced $2,531 worth of red ink. Because the NABC was out of funds, it asked the NCAA to assume responsibility.

"We were darn lucky to get out of debt," said former Wisconsin coach Harold (Bud) Foster, a past president of the NABC. "When the NCAA bailed us out, they provided tickets for all our members.

"It was interesting that Wisconsin played a major role in pulling the basketball tournament out of debt. We had the NCAA boxing tournament in Madison in '39 and drew packed houses. The university turned over $18,000 to the NCAA, and that was the biggest amount the NCAA had received from any source up to that time."

A more vital fighting led to numerous players having their college playing careers interrupted by World War II. For instance, all 11 regulars on Pittsburgh's 1941 Final Four team served in World War II, and one of them, guard Bob Artman, was killed in action. Seven two-time first- and second-team NCAA consensus All-Americans had their college careers interrupted while serving in the U.S. military. In the Air Force was Charles Black (Kansas); Army soldiers were

LUISETTI EXPLODES FOR 50 POINTS Stanford's star player Hank Luisetti ushered in 1938 with a bang. On New Year's Day, Stanford trounced Duquesne, 92-27, in Cleveland, thanks to Luisetti's 50-point outburst. Luisetti was best known for his running one-handed shot.

STANFORD (92)	FG	FT	PTS.
Lafaille	1	0	2
P. Zonne	7	1	15
Huff	1	0	2
Luisetti	23	4	50
Stoefen	5	3	13
Calderwood	1	0	2
Lyon	0	2	2
Lee	0	0	0
Burnett	3	0	6
B. Zonne	0	0	0
Rapp	0	0	0
Heath	0	0	0
TOTALS	**41**	**10**	**92**

DUQUESNE (27)	FG	FT	PTS.
Cristofack	0	1	1
Weitzel	3	1	7
Fortney	3	0	6
Yankitis	2	0	4
Scarry	0	0	0
O'Malley	0	1	1
Neiderberger	0	0	0
Kreilling	1	2	4
Adams	2	0	4
TOTALS	**11**	**5**	**27**
Halftime: Stanford 55-12.			

Vince Boryla (Notre Dame/Denver), Arnie Ferrin (Utah), Alex Groza (Kentucky), and Gerry Tucker (Oklahoma); the Marine Corps counted Andy Phillip (Illinois) as one of its own; and the Navy included Leo Klier (Notre Dame).

Conflict on the basketball court in the mid-1940s focused on an argument regarding which of the first two imposing big men was best: Oklahoma A&M's Bob Kurland (7-0) or DePaul's George Mikan (6-10). There has been an infatuation with tall players ever since.

Similarly, the NCAA Tournament struggled with the NIT over which national postseason tournament was best. The NCAA began to make substantial inroads to stealing some of the NIT's thunder after the first Eastern school (Holy Cross) won the NCAA in 1947.

There was also a beginning of separating the haves from the have-nots in 1948, the first year of official classification of schools when 160 universities were designated as major colleges.

1937-38

AT A GLANCE

NIT Champion: Temple (23-2).

New Conference: New England (forerunner of Yankee disbanded in 1976).

New Rule: Center jump after every basket is rescinded.

NCAA Consensus First-Team All-Americans: Meyer "Mike" Bloom, C, Sr., Temple; Hank Luisetti, F, Sr., Stanford; John Moir, F, Sr., Notre Dame; Paul Nowak, C, Sr., Notre Dame; Fred Pralle, G, Sr., Kansas; Jewell Young, F, Sr., Purdue.

Perhaps no player had more of an effect on basketball than Stanford's Hank Luisetti. A couple of decades ahead of his time, he is credited with revolutionizing basketball by introducing his running one-handed shot. Luisetti led Stanford to three consecutive Pacific Coast Conference championships and to a 46-5 record in his final two seasons. Regrettably, it wasn't until the year after his graduation that the NCAA staged its first tourney. Luisetti (50 points vs. Duquesne; see accompanying box score) and Brown sophomore Harry Platt (48 vs. Northeastern) established what are still single-game school scoring records. Luisetti almost doubled Duquesne's output in a 92-27 victory, contributing to the Dukes' only losing season (6-11) in a 37-year span from 1921 to 1957.

Joe Hagan's 48-foot shot with 12 seconds remaining enabled Kentucky to edge Marquette, 35-33. Showing the state's obsession with hoops success after the game, Gov. Happy Chandler pounded a nail into the floor to mark the spot of the decisive shot. Hagan went to Kentucky to play football, tried out for the basketball team uninvited by coach Adolph Rupp, and was captain of the Wildcats' 1937 football squad.

New York's Madison Square Garden was the mecca of college basketball at the time, however. Long Island University was featured in six of the 12 doubleheaders played in the Garden.

In the Big Ten, Illinois junior forward Lou Boudreau was declared ineligible for further intercollegiate competition in early February because his mother had been given monthly payments by baseball's Cleveland Indians. John Kundla, who later coached the NBA's Minneapolis Lakers to six league titles, was the second-leading scorer for a Minnesota squad that finished second in the Big Ten. Michigan's John Townsend was named to the first five on the Converse All-American team. Fifty-six seasons later (1993–94), his grandson, North Carolina center Eric Montross, would be selected to the first five on the National Association of Basketball Coaches All-American team.

Oklahoma A&M lost its Missouri Valley opener to Grinnell before winning 13 consecutive league games en route to a conference crown.

Phog Allen guided Kansas to its seventh title in the 10-year history of the Big Six Conference.

Gail Goodrich of Southern California finished sixth in scoring in the Pacific Coast Conference Southern Division. His son, Gail Goodrich Jr., became an All-American for UCLA in the mid-1960s.

Four starters for New Mexico A&M (now New Mexico State) were named to the first five on the All-Border Conference team after their school went undefeated (18-0) in league competition.

1937–38 PREMO POWER POLL

RANKING	SCHOOL
1	Temple# (23-2)
2	Stanford (21-3)
3	Purdue (18-2)
4	Notre Dame (20-3)
5	Oklahoma St. (25-3)
6	Bradley (18-2)
7	Western Kentucky (30-3)
8	Minnesota (16-4)
9	Kansas (18-2)
10	LIU-Brooklyn (23-5)
11	Central Missouri St.+ (24-3)
12	Roanoke (19-2)
13	Rhode Island (19-2)
14	Murray St. (27-4)
15	New Mexico St. (22-3)
16	Oregon (25-8)
17	Arkansas (19-3)
18	Villanova (25-5)
19	Marshall (28-4)
20	Centenary (13-1)

–NIT champion
+ –NAIA champion

1938–39

AT A GLANCE

NCAA Champion: Oregon (29-5).

NIT Champion: Long Island (23-0).

New Rules: Ball thrown in from out of bounds at midcourt by the team shooting a free throw following a technical foul. Previously, the ball was put into play with a center jump following a technical. The circumference of the ball is established as 30 inches.

NCAA Consensus First-Team All-Americans: Ernie Andres, G, Sr., Indiana; Jimmy Hull, F, Sr., Ohio State; Chet Jaworski, G, Sr., Rhode Island; Irving Torgoff, F, Sr., Long Island; Urgel "Slim" Wintermute, C, Sr., Oregon.

UCLA, the most successful school in NCAA Tournament history, was a playoff pretender instead of contender the first year of the national tourney. The Bruins finished last in the Pacific Coast Conference's Southern Division with an 0-12 record.

Texas toppled Manhattan, 54-32, at Madison Square Garden in front of 18,000 fans, the largest crowd to see a basketball game up to that point. It was the worst defeat dealt to a New York school in the Garden to that time.

Intercollegiate doubleheaders, with Loyola and DePaul serving as hosts, made their debut in Chicago with five twinbills at the 132nd Infantry Armory on West Madison Street (capacity 6,000).

Clemson won the Southern Conference championship although the Tigers never led at halftime in any of their four games.

Wally Johansen Slim Wintermute Bob Anet Howard Hobson Laddie Gale John Dick
Bob Hardy Carol M. Neeley Jay Langston Ford Mullen Matt Pavalunas Bob Officer Ted Sarpola Earl Sandness

The 1938–39 champion Oregon Ducks were dubbed "The Tall Firs" due to their size.

Emphasis on foreigners isn't a recent phenomenon. Francisco "Kiko" Martinez, a member of the 1936 Mexican Olympic team, was the leading scorer for New Mexico A&M (now New Mexico State), which finished with a 20-4 record after losing to NIT champion-to-be LIU in the opening round.

Panzer College of East Orange, New Jersey, compiled a 20-1 record, losing only to unbeaten LIU (41-35) early in the season. NIT champion LIU played only one game outside New York (vs. La Salle in Philadelphia).

Penn State's Max Corbin hit a shot from three quarters length of the floor against West Virginia to send their game into overtime. Penn State won, 46-43, in triple overtime.

Junior college transfer Jesse "Cab" Renick, a full-blooded Choctaw Indian, played guard, center, and forward for Missouri Valley co-champion Oklahoma A&M. He was named to the first five on the all-conference team and finished third in the league in scoring. Renick also lettered for the Aggies football squad. In 1948, while playing for the Phillips 66 Oilers, he was a member of the gold-medal winning U.S. Olympic basketball team.

The seven-year old Eastern Intercollegiate Basketball Conference agreed to dissolve at the end of the season. AP described the league as "one of the best in the nation." Geographical problems had made scheduling difficult for the six members—Carnegie Tech, Georgetown, Penn State, Pittsburgh, Temple, and West Virginia.

1938–39 PREMO POWER POLL

RANKING	SCHOOL
1	LIU-Brooklyn# (23-0)
2	Bradley (19-3)
3	Loyola (Ill.) (21-1)
4	Oregon* (29-5)
5	St. John's (18-4)
6	Indiana (17-3)
7	USC (20-5)
8	New Mexico St. (20-4)
9	Kentucky (16-4)
10	Ohio St. (16-7)
11	California (24-8)
12	Army (13-2)
13	Duquesne (14-4)
14	Villanova (20-5)
15	Marquette (12-5)
16	Washington (20-5)
17	Colorado (14-4)
18	Notre Dame (15-6)
19	Western Kentucky (22-3)
20	Roanoke (21-3)

#–NIT champion
*–NCAA champion

1939 NCAA Tournament

Summary: Different brands of play and refereeing dominated an era when college basketball was basically a regional game. Intersectional games were rare, although Oregon scheduled games in eight Eastern and Midwest cities (New York, Philadelphia, Buffalo, Cleveland, Detroit, Chicago, Peoria, Ill., and Des Moines). Oregon's slate might have made the Ducks more prepared for the inaugural NCAA Tournament. Another factor was Oregon's height. The Ducks, nicknamed "The Tall Firs" by a sportswriter because they had a 6-8 center and a pair of 6-4½ forwards, boasted more size than most teams.

One and Only: John Dick is the only leading scorer in an NCAA Tournament final (15 points as a junior forward for champion Oregon in 1939 against Ohio State) to subsequently serve as an admiral in the U.S. Navy. Dick commanded the aircraft carrier *Saratoga* for two years and served as chief of staff for all carrier forces in the Western Pacific.

Numbers Game: Only two players scored at least 20 points in the eight tourney games.

Putting Things in Perspective: Oregon State, which compiled a 6-10 record in the PCC, defeated Oregon, 50-31.

1938–39 NCAA CHAMPION: OREGON

SEASON STATISTICS OF OREGON REGULARS

PLAYER	POS.	CL.	G	PPG
Laddie Gale	F	Sr.	34	12.0
Slim Wintermute	C	Sr.	31	10.0
John Dick	F	Jr.	34	6.7
Wally Johansen	G	Sr.	34	5.7
Bobby Anet	G	Sr.	33	5.4
Bob Hardy	F	Jr.	30	3.8
Ted Sarpola	F	Jr.	27	3.4
Matt Pavalunas	G	Jr.	33	2.7
Ford Mullen	G	Jr.	29	1.2
TEAM TOTALS			**34**	**49.5**

1939 CHAMPIONSHIP GAME

EVANSTON, IL

OREGON (46)	FG	FT-A	PF	PTS.
Gale	2	4-5	1	8
Dick	5	5-5	3	15
Wintermute	2	0-1	1	4
Anet	4	2-3	3	10
Johansen	4	1-2	1	9
Mullen	0	0-0	0	0
Pavalunas	0	0-0	0	0
TOTALS	**17**	**12-16**	**9**	**46**
FT%: .750.				

OHIO STATE (33)	FG	FT-A	PF	PTS.
Hull	5	2-2	2	12
Baker	0	0-1	0	0
Schick	1	0-0	1	2
Dawson	1	0-0	4	2
Lynch	3	1-3	3	7
Maag	0	0-0	0	0
Scott	0	1-1	1	1
Boughner	1	0-0	0	2
Sattler	3	1-2	0	7
Mickelson	0	0-0	2	0
Stafford	0	0-0	0	0
TOTALS	**14**	**5-9**	**13**	**33**
FT%: .556.				
Halftime: Oregon 21-16.				

MOST OUTSTANDING PLAYER
None selected.

1939 CHAMPIONSHIP BRACKET

Regional Semifinals	Regional Finals	National Championship

WESTERN REGIONALS

Oregon
March 20
Texas

Oregon 56-41

San Francisco, CA
March 21

Oregon 55-37

Oklahoma
March 20
Utah St.

Oklahoma 50-39

Evanston, IL
March 27

Oregon 46-33

NATIONAL CHAMPION

EASTERN REGIONALS

Villanova
March 17
Brown

Villanova 42-30

Philadelphia, PA
March 18

Ohio State 53-36

Wake Forest
March 17
Ohio St.

Ohio St. 64-52

Regional Third Place
March 21
at San Francisco, CA
Utah St. 51, Texas 49

1939–40

AT A GLANCE

NCAA Champion: Indiana (20-3).

NIT Champion: Colorado (17-4).

New Rules: Teams have the choice of whether to shoot a free throw or take the ball out-of-bounds at midcourt. If two or more free throws are awarded, the option applies to the final free throw. The backboards move from two to four feet from the end line to permit more movement under the goal.

NCAA Consensus First-Team All-Americans: Gus Broberg, G-F, Jr., Dartmouth; John Dick, F, Sr., Oregon; George Glamack, C, Jr., North Carolina; Bill Hapac, F, Sr., Illinois; Ralph Vaughn, F, Sr., Southern California.

Dr. James Naismith, the inventor of basketball, died at his home in Lawrence, Kansas, at the age of 78. The previous season, Naismith had criticized the use of zone defense in a talk before New York writers, saying: "I have no sympathy with it. The defensive team is stalling which lays back and waits for the offense to come to it. If a soccer team hung back and grouped itself in front of the goal, what could the other team do? The zone is much like that."

Clair Bee, the director of LIU's Department of Physical Education, coached the school's football, basketball, and baseball teams. A *New York Times* article announcing the resumption of football at LIU pointed out that "Bee prefers football to basketball." On Thanksgiving Day, LIU's Dolly King started at center for the basketball team in a 59-41 victory over the alumni after starting at end for the football squad and catching a touchdown pass that afternoon at Ebbets Field in a 35-14 defeat to Catholic University.

North Carolina All-American George Glamack was an inspiration to those fond of individuals overcoming adversity. *The Spalding Guide* noted that "Glamack, who is ambidextrous when on the court, is also so nearsighted that the ball is merely a dim object, but apparently he never looked where he was shooting, depending upon his sense of distance and direction." The secret of "The Blind Bomber" was looking at the black lines on the court. By doing that he knew where he was in reference to the basket and could measure his shot.

The first basketball game telecast was on February 28, 1940, when WXBS carried a doubleheader from Madison Square Garden (Pittsburgh vs. Fordham and NYU vs. Georgetown).

Duke became the 12th different school to win the Southern Conference championship in the first 19 years of the league.

Future NBA coaching legend Arnold "Red" Auerbach was George Washington's leading scorer, averaging 8.5 points per game.

Navy's streak of consecutive non-losing seasons ended at 33.

Tennessee sophomore Bernie Mehen, described by Kentucky coach Adolph Rupp as "one of the greatest first-year men of all-time," earned a berth as a forward on the SEC All-Tournament team.

1939–40 PREMO POWER POLL

RANKING	SCHOOL
1	Indiana* (20-3)
2	USC (20-3)

3	Colorado# (17-4)		
4	Duquesne (20-3)		
5	Oklahoma St. (26-3)		
6	Purdue (16-4)		
7	NYU (18-1)		
8	Rice (25-4)		
9	Kansas (19-6)		
10	DePaul (22-6)		
11	LIU-Brooklyn (19-4)		
12	Seton Hall (19-0)		
13	Utah (18-4)		
14	St. John's (15-5)		
15	Western Kentucky (24-6)		
16	Villanova (17-2)		
17	Marshall (25-4)		
18	Santa Clara (17-3)		
19	Rhode Island (19-3)		
20	Toledo (24-6)		

#–NIT champion
*–NCAA champion

1940 NCAA Tournament

Summary: Indiana's "Hurryin' Hoosiers" were noted for their fast break, which emphasized quick ball movement because coach Branch McCracken detested dribbling. The Hoosiers' 60-42 victory over Kansas in the NCAA final marked the highest output for the winner in the championship game until 1950.

Outcome for Defending Champion: Oregon (19-12) finished second in the North Division of the Pacific Coast Conference.

Biggest Upset: Heavily favored Southern Cal blew a six-point lead in the closing minutes of a 43-42 setback against Kansas.

One and Only: McCracken is the only NCAA consensus first-team All-American (1930) to later coach his alma mater to an NCAA championship.

Numbers Game: Bob Allen is the only player to lead an NCAA championship game in scoring while playing for his father. Phog Allen was coach of the Kansas squad that lost the championship game to Indiana (60-42) despite his son's game-high total of 13 points.... Winning teams usually shot about 30 percent from the floor, but Springfield's 12.7 percent shooting (8 for 63) in a 48-24 opening-round loss to Indiana was particularly paltry.

What If: Indiana would not have participated in the tourney if Big Ten champion Purdue had chosen to participate in the event instead of stay home because coach Piggy Lambert wasn't fond of postseason play.

1939–40 NCAA CHAMPION: INDIANA

SEASON STATISTICS OF INDIANA REGULARS

PLAYER	POS.	CL.	G	PPG
Curly Armstrong	F	Jr.	23	8.9
Herman Schaefer	G-F	Jr.	23	8.0
Bill Menke	C	Jr.	23	7.7
Bob Dro	F-G	Jr.	23	6.3
Jay McCreary	F	Jr.	21	4.5
Marv Huffman	G	Sr.	23	4.3
Andy Zimmer	C	So.	18	1.8
Chet Francis	F	Jr.	14	1.4
Bob Menke	C-F	Jr.	18	1.4
Ralph Dorsey	F	Sr.	20	1.2
James Gridley	G	Jr.	18	1.1
Bill Torphy	G	So.	12	1.0
TEAM TOTALS			**23**	**45.6**

1940 CHAMPIONSHIP GAME

KANSAS CITY, MO

INDIANA (60)	FG	FT-A	PF	PTS.
Schaefer	4	1-1	1	9
McCreary	6	0-0	2	12
W. Menke	2	1-2	3	5
Huffman	5	2-3	4	12
Dro	3	1-1	4	7
Armstrong	4	2-3	3	10
Gridley	0	0-0	0	0
R. Menke	0	0-0	0	0
Zimmer	2	1-1	1	5
Dorsey	0	0-0	0	0
Francis	0	0-0	1	0
TOTALS	**26**	**8-11**	**19**	**60**
FT%: .723.				

KANSAS (42)	FG	FT-A	PF	PTS.
Ebling	1	2-5	0	4
Engleman	5	2-3	3	12
Allen	5	3-4	3	13
Miller	0	2-2	4	2
Harp	2	1-3	1	5
Hunter	0	1-1	0	1
Hogben	2	0-0	0	4
Kline	0	0-0	0	0
Voran	0	1-2	0	1
Sands	0	0-0	0	0
Johnson	0	0-0	0	0
TOTALS	**15**	**12-20**	**11**	**42**
FT%: .600.				

Halftime: Indiana 32-19.

ALL-TOURNAMENT TEAM
Bob Allen, C, Jr., Kansas
Howard Engleman, F, Jr., Kansas
Marvin Huffman, G-F, Sr., Indiana*
Jay McCreary, G-F, Jr., Indiana
Bill Menke, C, Jr., Indiana
*—Most Outstanding Tournament Player

1940 CHAMPIONSHIP BRACKET

Regional Semifinals	Regional Finals	National Championship

EASTERN REGIONALS

Indiana
March 20 — Indiana 48-24
Springfield

Indianapolis, IN
March 21 — Indiana 39-30

Duquesne
March 20 — Duquesne 30-29
Western Ky.

Kansas City, MO
March 30 — Indiana 60-42

WESTERN REGIONALS

Southern Cal
March 20 — Southern Cal 38-32
Colorado

Kansas City, MO
March 21 — Kansas 43-42

Rice
March 20 — Kansas 50-44
Kansas

NATIONAL CHAMPION

Regional Third Place
March 21
at Kansas City, MO
Rice 60, Colorado 56 (ot)

1940-41

AT A GLANCE

NCAA Champion: Wisconsin (20-3).

NIT Champion: Long Island (25-2).

New Rule: Fan-shaped backboards are legalized.

NCAA Consensus First-Team All-Americans: John Adams, F, Sr., Arkansas; Gus Broberg, G-F, Sr., Dartmouth; Howard Engleman, F, Sr., Kansas; Gene Englund, C, Sr., Wisconsin; George Glamack, C, Sr., North Carolina.

Postseason conference tournaments haven't always filled big-time league coffers. According to the *Official Basketball Guide,* "[the SEC Tournament] for the first time in history was a complete financial success, paying the entire expenses of all twelve schools and leaving a substantial amount in the conference treasury. The gross gate was slightly over $15,000."

Dartmouth's Gus Broberg became the first of five players in Ivy League history to win three consecutive scoring championships (the conference was known at the time as the Eastern Intercollegiate League).

Duke opened its season with a 43-39 defeat to Lincoln Memorial and had a 6-9 record after 15 games. The Blue Devils, however, won their last seven games, including two victories over Southern Conference regular-season champion North Carolina, and captured the league tournament.

St. Louis, winless in seven games before meeting Oklahoma A&M, upset the defending Missouri Valley Conference champion, 32-29, in perhaps the biggest upset of the season.

Florida's second-place finish in the SEC was the Gators' highest in the league until 1966–67.

1940-41 PREMO POWER POLL

RANKING	SCHOOL
1	LIU-Brooklyn# (25-2)
2	Wisconsin* (20-3)
3	Washington St. (26-6)
4	Indiana (17-3)
5	Stanford (21-5)
6	Ohio Univ. (18-4)
7	Arkansas (20-3)
8	Duquesne (17-3)
9	Westminster (Pa.) (20-2)
10	Western Kentucky (22-4)
11	Toledo (21-3)
12	Dartmouth (19-5)
13	CCNY (17-5)
14	Washington & Jefferson (15-3)
15	San Diego St. (24-7)
16	Murray St. (25-5)
17	Seton Hall (20-2)
18	Penn St. (15-5)
19	Oregon St. (19-9)
20	Xavier (La.) (29-0)

\#–NIT champion
*–NCAA champion

1941 NCAA Tournament

Summary: Wisconsin, capitalizing on a home court advantage to overcome halftime deficits in the first two rounds of the tourney, captured the crown in a fairy tale script resembling the hit movie *Hoosiers*. In 1940, Wisconsin finished a dismal ninth in the Big Ten and the Badgers' overall record of 5-15 represented their worst mark since joining the Big Ten in 1906. They became the only school to finish more than two games below .500 one season and win the national championship the next year.

Outcome for Defending Champion: Indiana (17-3), an eight-point loser to Wisconsin, finished runner-up to the Badgers in the Big Ten.

Star Gazing: Washington State center Paul Lindeman (6-7, 230 lbs.) was limited to three points by Wisconsin in the final after he averaged 20 points in the Cougars' first two games.

One and Only: Howard "Red" Hickey is the only individual to appear in the Final Four before playing and coaching in the NFL at least five seasons apiece. Hickey, a first-team All-Southwest Conference forward for Arkansas, was sufficiently skilled as a tackle in football to make the Razorbacks' all-decade team. Hickey, a lineman for six seasons in the NFL with two different franchises from 1941 through 1948, coached the San Francisco 49ers for five years from 1959 through 1963, compiling a 27-27-1 record.

Numbers Game: The only player to score more than 30 points in a playoff game the first 11 years of the event was North Carolina's George Glamack, who supplied 31 points in a 60-59 loss to Dartmouth in the East Regional third-place game after the Tar Heels succumbed to Pittsburgh, 26-20, in the opening round.

Putting Things in Perspective: Amazingly, Wisconsin lost its conference opener by 17 points at Minnesota when the Badgers failed to make a single field goal in the second half before going undefeated through the remainder of their league schedule and the playoffs.

1941 CHAMPIONSHIP BRACKET

1940–41 NCAA CHAMPION: WISCONSIN

SEASON STATISTICS OF WISCONSIN REGULARS

PLAYER	POS.	CL.	G	PPG
Gene Englund	C	Sr.	23	13.2
John Kotz	F	So.	23	9.0
Ted Strain	G	Sr.	23	4.8
Charlie Epperson	F	Jr.	22	4.5
Fred Rehm	G	So.	21	3.7
Bob Alwin	G	Jr.	21	2.7
Don Timmerman	C	Sr.	22	1.9
Ed Scheiwe	G	Jr.	17	1.4
TEAM TOTALS			**23**	**43.7**

1941 CHAMPIONSHIP GAME

KANSAS CITY, MO

WISCONSIN (39)	FG	FT-A	PF	PTS.
Epperson	2	0-0	3	4
Schrage	0	0-0	1	0
Kotz	5	2-3	2	12
Englund	5	3-4	2	13
Timmerman	1	0-0	1	2
Rehm	2	0-1	2	4
Strain	0	2-2	1	2
Alwin	1	0-0	0	2
TOTALS	**16**	**7-10**	**12**	**39**
FG%: .254; FT%: .700.				

WASHINGTON STATE (34)	FG	FT-A	PF	PTS.
Gentry	0	1-2	1	1
Gilberg	1	0-2	1	2
Butts	1	1-1	1	3
Lindeman	0	3-4	1	3
Zimmerman	0	0-0	0	0
Gebert	10	1-2	1	21
Hunt	0	0-0	0	0
Sundquist	2	0-1	3	4
Hooper	0	0-0	0	0
TOTALS	**14**	**6-12**	**8**	**34**
FG%: .215; FT%: .500.				
Halftime: Wisconsin 21-17.				

MOST OUTSTANDING PLAYER
John Kotz, F, Soph., Wisconsin

1941–42

AT A GLANCE

NCAA Champion: Stanford (27-4).

NIT Champion: West Virginia (19-4).

NCAA Consensus First-Team All-Americans: Price Brookfield, C, Sr., West Texas State; Bob Davies, G, Sr., Seton Hall; Bob Kinney, C, Sr., Rice; John Kotz, F, Jr., Wisconsin; Andy Phillip, F, Soph., Illinois.

Everett Dean was Stanford's basketball coach from 1938 to 1951 and baseball coach from 1950 to 1955.

Long Island's Clair Bee was the cream of the crop in the coaching profession, improving his career winning percentage to an astonishing 87.7 (291-41 record) when the Blackbirds compiled a 25-3 mark.

Tennessee held LIU to nine points in the second half in a 36-33 victory in the Sugar Bowl Tournament, snapping LIU's 23-game winning streak.

UCLA continued to struggle, compiling a losing league record for the 15th time in as many seasons as a member of the Pacific Coast Conference. Southern Cal defeated UCLA four times, extending the Trojans' winning streak against the Bruins to 40 games.

Bob Faught, a 6-5 sophomore center, joined Notre Dame's basketball team in an effort to keep in shape for tennis. He proceeded to lead the Irish in scoring with 9.5 points per game, including 26 in a 55-43 victory over NYU at Madison Square Garden.

Rhode Island defeated New Hampshire, 127-50, in a game where the Rhode Island regulars played just the first 16 minutes.

Penn's Lou Jourdet coached the son (Larry Davis) of a player (Lardie Davis) he had on his Penn roster in 1918 and 1919.

Kansas' Ralph Miller, who would later be elected to the Naismith Memorial Basketball Hall of Fame after winning 657 games in 38 seasons at three major universities, led the Big Six Conference in scoring. Kansas was eliminated in the NCAA Tournament by Colorado, a school that had four starters who grew up in Kansas.

1941–42 PREMO POWER POLL

RANKING	SCHOOL
1	Stanford* (28-4)
2	LIU-Brooklyn (25-3)
3	Rice (22-5)
4	Colorado (16-2)
5	West Virginia# (19-4)
6	Dartmouth (22-4)
7	Western Kentucky (29-5)
8	Penn State (18-3)
9	West Texas St. (28-3)
10	Duke (22-2)
11	Tennessee (19-3)
12	BYU (17-3)
13	Toledo (23-5)
14	Kentucky (19-6)
15	Kansas (17-5)
16	Arkansas (19-4)
17	Illinois (18-5)
18	Creighton (18-5)
19	CCNY (16-3)
20	Mount Union (17-1)

#–NIT champion
*–NCAA champion

1942 NCAA Tournament

Summary: Stanford overcame the title game absence of flu-ridden standout Jim Pollard, who scored 43.4 percent of his team's points in its first two tourney contests. Was it worth it? Stanford took home a meager check for $93.75 to cover its stay in Kansas City.

Outcome for Defending Champion: Wisconsin (14-7) finished in a three-way tie for second place in the Big Ten.

Star Gazing: Three Stanford starters—co-captains Don Burness and Bill Cowden and sophomore Howie Dallmar—attended the same high school in San Francisco.

One and Only: Dallmar, a 6-5 guard, became the only Final Four Most Outstanding Player to complete his collegiate playing career attending another university (NCAA consensus first-team All-American with Penn in 1945). Sent to Philadelphia by the Navy toward the end of World War II to attend pre-flight training school, Dallmar enrolled at Penn to complete his undergraduate work and to use his final season of sports eligibility (NCAA consensus first-team All-American in 1945). He is also the only Most Outstanding Player to guide a school other than his alma mater to the playoffs. Dallmar posted a 1-1 tourney record with Penn in 1953 before coaching Stanford for 21 years without directing his alma mater to the NCAA playoffs. The principal culprit in denying Dallmar an NCAA appearance with the Cardinal was UCLA's dynasty under John Wooden. Both coaches retired at the end of the 1974–75 season. One of the three defeats for the NCAA champion Bruins that year was at Stanford. Dallmar, an All-NBA first-team selection in 1947–48 when he led the league in assists with the defending champion Philadelphia Warriors, moonlighted in sports the next season in a way practically never done. He played professionally for the Warriors while compiling a 15-8 record in his rookie campaign as coach of Penn.

Numbers Game: Everett Dean, compiling a 3-0 tournament record with champion Stanford, is the only unbeaten coach in NCAA playoff history. He is also the only NCAA basketball championship coach to win a College World Series baseball game for the same school (1953).

1942 NCAA CHAMPION: STANFORD

SEASON STATISTICS OF STANFORD REGULARS

PLAYER	POS.	CL.	G	PPG
Jim Pollard	F	Jr.	23	10.5
Ed Voss	C	Jr.	29	8.7
Don Burness	F	Sr.	26	8.5
Howie Dallmar	G	So.	31	7.3
Bill Cowden	G	Sr.	31	5.5
Jack Dana	F	Jr.	27	3.7
Freddie Linari	F	Jr.	25	2.0
Leo McCaffrey	G	Jr.	22	1.0
TEAM TOTALS			**31**	**39.8**

1942 CHAMPIONSHIP GAME

KANSAS CITY, MO

STANFORD (53)	MIN.	FG	FT-A	PF	PTS.
Dana	40	7	0-0	0	14
Burness	9	0	0-0	0	0
Linari	31	3	0-0	0	6
Voss	40	6	1-1	2	13
Cowden	40	2	1-2	3	5
Dallmar	40	6	3-5	0	15
TOTALS	**200**	**24**	**5-8**	**5**	**53**
FT%: .625.					

DARTMOUTH (38)	MIN.	FG	FT-A	PF	PTS.
Myers	29	4	0-1	1	8
Parmer	11	1	0-0	0	2
Munroe	40	5	2-2	1	12
Olsen	40	4	0-1	0	8
Pearson	40	2	2-2	3	6
Skaug	40	1	0-0	2	2
TOTALS	**200**	**17**	**4-6**	**7**	**38**
FT%: .667.					

Halftime: Stanford 24-22.

MOST OUTSTANDING PLAYER
Howie Dallmar, G, Soph., Stanford

1942 CHAMPIONSHIP BRACKET

Regional Semifinals	Regional Finals	National Championship

EASTERN REGIONALS

Dartmouth
March 20
Penn St.
— Dartmouth 44-39

New Orleans, LA
March 21
— Dartmouth 47-28

Kentucky
March 20
Illinois
— Kentucky 46-44

WESTERN REGIONALS

Stanford
March 20
Rice
— Stanford 53-47

Kansas City, MO
March 21
— Stanford 46-35

Colorado
March 20
Kansas
— Colorado 46-44

Kansas City, MO
March 28
— Stanford 53-38
NATIONAL CHAMPION

Regional Third Place
March 21
at New Orleans, LA
Penn St. 41, Illinois 34
at Kansas City, MO
Kansas 55, Rice 53

Wyoming head coach Ev Shelton.

1942–43

AT A GLANCE

NCAA Champion: Wyoming (31-2).

NIT Champion: St. John's (21-3).

New Conference: Metropolitan New York (disbanded after 1962–63 season).

New Rule: Any player eligible to start an overtime period is allowed an extra personal foul, increasing the total for disqualification to five fouls.

NCAA Consensus First-Team All-Americans: Ed Beisser, C, Sr., Creighton; Charles Black, F, Soph., Kansas; Harry Boykoff, C, Soph., St. John's; Bill Closs, C, Sr., Rice; Andy Phillip, F, Jr., Illinois; George Senesky, F, Sr., St. Joseph's.

Illinois, undefeated in Big Ten competition (12-0) after having four sophomore starters on a league championship squad dubbed "The Whiz Kids" the previous season, placed four players on the first five of the all-conference team—forward Andy Phillip, center Art Mathisen, and guards Gene Vance and Jack Smiley. The fifth Illini starter was named to the second five—forward Ken Menke. Illinois didn't participate in a postseason tournament although it ranked first in the final Dunkel Ratings. The school's athletic director declined a bid because he thought it would be unfair to his players to keep them away from their classes for three weeks. Something more pressing broke up the team at the end of the season when all five starters headed to active duty in the armed forces.

Western Kentucky became the first school to compile 10 consecutive 20-win seasons.

Notre Dame coach George Keogan died of a heart attack on February 17, 1943. In 24 seasons as a college coach (20 with the Irish), he never had a losing record.

Center Ed Beisser, forward Ralph Langer, and guard Dick Nolan finished their three-year varsity careers at Creighton with two Missouri Valley Conference undisputed championships and one co-championship.

Valparaiso, compiling a 17-4 record, claimed to possess the tallest team in the country with a starting lineup averaging 6-6.

Manhattan, boasting eight freshmen among its first 10 players, registered an 18-3 record, including a 42-38 victory over eventual NIT champion St. John's.

Among the top service teams during the 1942–43 "season" in World War II were Great Lakes NTS (34-3), Camp Grant (Ill.) (31-2), Norfolk NTS (35-1), Corpus Christi NAS, and Manhattan Beach CG.

1942–43 PREMO POWER POLL

RANKING	SCHOOL
1	Illinois (17-1)
2	Wyoming* (31-2)
3	Notre Dame (18-2)
4	St. John's# (21-3)
5	Indiana (18-2)
6	Georgetown (22-5)
7	DePaul (19-5)
8	Creighton (19-2)
9	Dartmouth (20-3)
10	Western Kentucky (24-3)
11	Toledo (22-4)
12	Kentucky (17-6)
13	Manhattan (18-3)
14	Penn St. (15-4)
15	Arizona (22-2)
16	Washington & Jefferson (18-5)
17	Kansas (22-6)
18	Detroit (15-5)
19	Fordham (17-6)
20	Tennessee (14-5)

#–NIT champion
*–NCAA champion

1943 NCAA Tournament

Summary: Virtually every university anticipated having players enter the military in the aftermath of the tourney. Wyoming would have become the only champion to trail at halftime in every tournament game had the Cowboys not scored the last three baskets of the first half in the national final to lead Georgetown at intermission (18-16). Wyoming's Everett Shelton later became the only coach to guide teams to the championship game in both the Division I and

RED CROSS GAMES   For three consecutive years during World War II, the NCAA and NIT champions met in a benefit game at Madison Square Garden in New York to raise money for the Red Cross. The NCAA champions won all three games.

YEAR	OUTCOME
1943	Wyoming (NCAA) 52, St. John's (NIT) 47
1944	Utah (NCAA) 43, St. John's (NIT) 36
1945	Oklahoma A&M (NCAA) 52, DePaul (NIT) 44

1942–43 NCAA CHAMPION: WYOMING

SEASON STATISTICS OF WYOMING REGULARS

PLAYER	POS.	CL.	G	PPG
Milo Komenich	C	Jr.	33	16.7
Kenny Sailors	F	Jr.	33	15.0
Jim Weir	F	Jr.	33	10.1
Floyd Volker	F-G	Jr.	33	6.4
Jimmie Reese	F	So.	23	4.3
Lew Roney	G	Jr.	30	2.7
Jim Collins	G	So.	31	2.5
Antone Katana	C	So.	24	1.5
Earl Ray	G	Jr.	19	0.8
TEAM TOTALS			33	59.4

1943 CHAMPIONSHIP GAME

NEW YORK, NY

WYOMING (46)	FG	FT-A	PF	PTS.
Sailors	6	4-5	2	16
Collins	4	0-0	1	8
Weir	2	1-3	2	5
Waite	0	0-0	0	0
Komenich	4	1-4	2	9
Volker	2	1-2	3	5
Roney	0	1-2	1	1
Reese	1	0-0	0	2
TOTALS	**19**	**8-16**	**11**	**46**
FT%: .500.				

GEORGETOWN (40)	FG	FT-A	PF	PTS.
Reilly	1	0-0	0	2
Potolicchio	1	2-3	1	4
Gabbianelli	1	2-3	3	4
Hyde	0	0-0	0	0
Mahnken	2	2-3	2	6
Hassett	3	0-3	4	6
Finnerty	0	0-0	0	0
Kraus	2	0-1	3	4
Feeney	4	0-0	1	8
Duffey	0	0-0	0	0
TOTALS	**14**	**6-13**	**14**	**34**
FT%: .462.				

Halftime: Wyoming 18-16.

MOST OUTSTANDING PLAYER
Kenny Sailors, F, Jr., Wyoming

Division II Tournaments. Shelton directed Sacramento State to a second-place finish in the 1962 Division II Tournament.

Outcome for Defending Champion: Stanford (10-11) became one of only two defending champions to compile a losing record.

Star Gazing: Indiana's Marvin Huffman was named Final Four Most Outstanding Player despite his lowly 4.3-point scoring average for the season.

Biggest Upset: Wyoming went to New York and defeated homestanding St. John's in a benefit game for the American Red Cross between the NCAA and NIT champions.

One and Only: Sam Mele is the only individual to lead the American League in doubles as a player and manage an A.L. team to a pennant (Minnesota Twins in 1965) after leading a school in scoring in an NCAA Tournament (total of 18 points for NYU in two losses).

Numbers Game: The only team to fail to have at least one player score in double figures in the championship game was Georgetown, a 46-34 loser against Wyoming.

1943 CHAMPIONSHIP BRACKET

Regional Semifinals	Regional Finals	National Championship

EASTERN REGIONALS

Georgetown
March 24
New York U.
— Georgetown 55-36

New York, NY
March 25
— Georgetown 53-49

DePaul
March 24
Dartmouth
— DePaul 46-35

WESTERN REGIONALS

Texas
March 26
Washington
— Texas 59-55

Kansas City, MO
March 27
— Wyoming 58-54

Wyoming
March 26
Oklahoma
— Wyoming 53-50

New York, NY
March 30
— Wyoming 46-34
NATIONAL CHAMPION

Regional Third Place
March 25
at New York, NY
Dartmouth 51, New York U. 49
March 27
at Kansas City, MO
Oklahoma 48, Washington 43

1943-44

AT A GLANCE

NCAA Champion: Utah (22-4).

NIT Champion: St. John's (18-5).

NCAA Consensus First-Team All-Americans: Bob Brannum, C, Fr., Kentucky; Audley Brindley, C, Jr., Dartmouth; Otto Graham, F, Sr., Northwestern/Colgate; Leo Klier, F, Jr., Notre Dame; Bob Kurland, C, Soph., Oklahoma A&M; George Mikan, C, Soph., DePaul; Allie Paine, G, Jr., Oklahoma.

NCAA champion-to-be Utah was invited to the NCAA playoffs following Arkansas' withdrawal after two of its best players were injured in a horrific automobile accident. The SWC champion declined to participate because of the auto mishap involving the Razorbacks' five starters. Their station wagon, driven by physical education instructor Eugene Norris, had a flat left rear tire about 20 miles outside Fayetteville, Arkansas, while returning from a tune-up game against a military team in Fort Smith. Norris stopped in the right lane on U.S. 71 because the shoulder was too narrow. Norris and two of the starters—Deno Nichols and Ben Jones—were putting the flat in the back of the wagon when a car driven by a local undertaker plowed into the vehicle at full speed. The 28-year-old Norris, escorting the team for the first time, was pronounced dead of internal injuries and extreme shock after arriving at a nearby hospital. Nichols' right leg was broken in two places and both of Jones' legs were broken and his back fractured. Nichols' leg became gangrenous and was amputated just two months after he was married. Jones spent the next two years in various casts and braces.

Another end-of-the-season incident at Arkansas demonstrated how times were different in 1944, and also contributed to the Razorbacks' withdrawal from the tournament. All-SWC guard "Parson" Bill Flynt dropped out of school to become a full-time minister at a Baptist

The 1944 NCAA champion Utah Utes, with star freshman and Final Four Most Outstanding Player Arnie Ferrin in back row center (#22).

church in Perryville, Arkansas—just before the NCAA Tournament.

St. John's guard Dick McGuire became the first freshman to win the award given by the New York Basketball Writers Association to the outstanding college player in the metropolitan area. McGuire finished the season playing for Dartmouth, where he underwent military training.

Rhode Island State's Ernie Calverley averaged 26.7 points per game, a mark that remained a national record until 1951 and still is a school standard. He was the first player to score at least 45 points twice in a single season (48 vs. Northwestern and 45 vs. Maine).

Rhode Island State (New England) and Dartmouth (Ivy League) each captured its seventh consecutive conference championship.

The University of Havana became the first foreign team to play at Madison Square Garden, losing to LIU, 40-37. Havana displayed "the most spectacular ball handling seen in New York in many years," according to the *Official Basketball Guide*.

Army, under first-year coach Ed Kelleher, compiled a 15-0 record with three starters (Dale Hall, Edgar Kenna, and John Hennessey) who had lettered for the school's football squad. The final Converse-Dunkel Ratings for the season had Army in first, followed by Utah, Kentucky, DePaul, and Western Michigan.

Great Lakes NTS (32-4), Norfolk NTS (31-2), San Diego Marines (35-0), Camp Grant (27-4), Mitchell Field (34-3), and St. Mary's PF (15-0) were top service teams during the 1943–44 season.

1943–44 PREMO POWER POLL

RANKING	SCHOOL
1	Army (15-0)
2	Utah* (21-4)
3	Kentucky (19-2)
4	DePaul (22-4)
5	Dartmouth (19-2)
6	St. John's# (18-5)
7	Oklahoma St. (27-6)
8	Bowling Green (22-4)
9	Rice (15-5)
10	Ohio St. (14-7)
11	Western Michigan (15-4)
12	Iowa St. (14-4)
13	Gonzaga (22-4)
14	Washington (26-6)
15	Muhlenberg (20-5)
16	Denison (18-2)
17	Northwestern (12-7)
18	Illinois (11-9)
19	Miami (Ohio) (10-2)
20	Navy (10-4)

#–NIT champion
*–NCAA champion

1944 NCAA Tournament

Summary: With so many upperclassmen enlisting or being drafted during World War II, Utah had to rely almost entirely on freshmen and sophomores. Utah entered the NCAA Tournament through the back door after losing to Kentucky in the first round of the NIT, but won the NCAA championship game against Dartmouth in overtime (42-40) on freshman Herb Wilkinson's basket from far beyond the top of the key. Freshman Arnie Ferrin scored 22 points in the title game to become Final Four Most Outstanding Player. Two nights later in a benefit game at Madison Square Garden for the American Red Cross, the Utes defeated yet another favorite, beating NIT titlist St. John's (43-36). St. John's had edged Utah's first postseason opponent, Kentucky, in the NIT semifinals. Utah's players, all raised within 35 miles of the campus, had an average age of 18 years, six months. Among the four freshman starters was Wat Misaka, a spirited Japanese-American whose country was at war with the homeland of his ancestors.

Outcome for Defending Champion: Wyoming did not field a team because of the war. In 1944–45, Wyoming posted a 10-18 record.

Star Gazing: Ferrin, Misaka, and Fred Sheffield were the only three of this group to earn any more letters with the Utes, which lost both of their NCAA playoff games in 1945. Fer-

1943–44 NCAA CHAMPION: UTAH

SEASON STATISTICS OF UTAH REGULARS

PLAYER	POS.	CL.	G	PPG
Arnie Ferrin	F	Fr.	21	13.2
Fred Sheffield	C	So.	21	10.4
Herb Wilkinson	G-F	Fr.	21	7.9
Wat Misaka	G	Fr.	20	6.9
Bob Lewis	G	Fr.	20	5.5
Dick Smuin	F-G	Fr.	19	3.7
Bill Kastelic	F	Fr.	14	2.8

TEAM TOTALS   26   52.8
Note: Statistics are unavailable for Utah's first four games of the season.

1944 CHAMPIONSHIP GAME

NEW YORK, NY

UTAH (42)	MIN.	FG	FT-A	PF	PTS.
Ferrin	45	8	6-7	0	22
Smuin	45	0	0-0	2	0
Sheffield	4	1	0-0	1	2
Misaka	41	2	0-0	1	4
Wilkinson	45	3	1-4	0	7
B. Lewis	45	2	3-3	2	7
TOTALS	**225**	**16**	**10-14**	**6**	**42**

FT%: .714.

DARTMOUTH (40)	MIN.	FG	FT-A	PF	PTS.
Gale	37	5	0-2	1	10
Mercer	19	0	1-1	3	1
Leggat	34	4	0-0	1	8
Nordstrom	8	0	0-0	0	0
Brindley	39	5	1-1	3	11
McGuire	38	3	0-1	3	6
Murphy	17	0	0-0	0	0
Vancisin	19	2	0-0	3	4
Goering	14	0	0-0	0	0
TOTALS	**225**	**19**	**2-5**	**14**	**40**

FT%: .400.
Halftime: Dartmouth 18-17. **Regulation:** Tied 36-36.

MOST OUTSTANDING PLAYER
Arnie Ferrin, F, Fr., Utah

rin was a second-team consensus All-American in 1947, when Utah won the NIT as the 5-8 Misaka restricted unanimous first-team All-American Ralph Beard to two points in a 49-45 triumph over Kentucky in the championship game. Wilkinson played the next three seasons for Iowa, where he was an NCAA consensus second-team All-American in 1945. Bob Lewis transferred to Stanford, where he was a three-year letterman from 1947 to 1949.

One and Only: Sheffield, Utah's starting center, is the only Final Four player to finish among the top two high jumpers in four NCAA national track meets. Sheffield, the first athlete to place in the NCAA high jump four consecutive years, was first in 1943 with a best jump of 6-8, second in 1944, tied for first in 1945, and tied for second in 1946.

Numbers Game: Utah is the only championship team to have as many as four freshman starters. Lyman Condie, a second-year medical student, was an original starter for the team. Condie was invited by coach Vadal Peterson to try out for the squad because of a manpower shortage stemming from the war. Condie had a free block of time in the afternoons to practice during the fall quarter. However, when winter quarter started, his afternoons were no longer free and he had to make a choice between bas-

All-American center George Mikan of DePaul.

ketball or medical school. He chose medical school and left the team. His place as a starter was taken by Dick Smuin.

1944 CHAMPIONSHIP BRACKET

Regional Semifinals	Regional Finals	National Championship
EASTERN REGIONALS		
Dartmouth	Dartmouth 63-38	
March 24		
Catholic		Dartmouth 60-53
	New York, NY March 25	
Ohio St.	Ohio St. 57-47	
March 24		
Temple		**New York, NY** March 28
	WESTERN REGIONALS	Utah 42-40 (ot)
Iowa St.	Iowa St. 44-39	**NATIONAL CHAMPION**
March 24		
Pepperdine		Utah 40-31
	Kansas City, MO March 25	
Utah	Utah 45-35	
March 24		
Missouri		

Regional Third Place
March 25
at New York, NY
Temple 55, Catholic 35
at Kansas City, MO
Missouri 61, Pepperdine 46

1944–45

AT A GLANCE

NCAA Champion: Oklahoma A&M (27-4).

NIT Champion: DePaul (21-3).

New Rules: Defensive goaltending is banned, five personal fouls now disqualifies a player (had been four since 1910), an extra foul is not allowed in overtime games, and unlimited substitution is introduced.

NCAA Consensus First-Team All-Americans: Howie Dallmar, G, Sr., Penn; Arnie Ferrin, F, Soph., Utah; Wyndol Gray, F, Soph., Bowling Green; Billy Hassett, G, Jr., Notre Dame; Bill Henry, C, Sr., Rice; Walt Kirk, G, Jr., Illinois; Bob Kurland, C, Jr., Oklahoma A&M; George Mikan, C, Jr., DePaul.

NCAA champion Oklahoma A&M defeated NIT kingpin DePaul, 52-44, at Madison Square Garden in an American Red Cross War Fund benefit game featuring the nation's two premier pivotmen—DePaul's George Mikan and A&M's Bob Kurland. Mikan fouled out of the contest after 14 minutes with the Blue Demons leading, 21-14. Cecil Hankins, the leading pass receiver for A&M's Cotton Bowl winner, scored a game-high 20 points and Kurland contributed 14.

Mikan set a school record with 53 points against Rhode Island State in the NIT semifinals.

In a gigantic mismatch, Kentucky overwhelmed Arkansas State, 75-6, although Alex Groza, the Wildcats' standout freshman center, did not play in the game. Groza led Kentucky to an 11-0 start with an average of 16.5 points per game before he was inducted into the Army.

Iowa's Dick Culberson became the first African American to play for a Big Ten Conference team. The league champion Hawkeyes compiled their best winning percentage in school history with a 17-1 overall record but declined an invitation to the NCAA Tournament. NCAA consensus second-team All-American Max Morris of Northwestern led the Big Ten in scoring in league games (15.8 points per game) after earning MVP honors for the Wildcats' football squad the previous fall as an end.

In the season's marathon match, Temple outlasted Penn State, 63-60, in five overtimes.

Rensselaer Polytechnic Institute was the only undefeated college team during the regular season, compiling a 13-0 record before losing to Bowling Green, 60-45, in the opening round of the NIT.

The top five World War II service teams were Norfolk NAS (23-4), Bainbridge NTC (28-5), Great Lakes NTS (32-5), Norfolk NTS (26-8), and Memphis NATTC (31-1).

1944–45 PREMO POWER POLL

RANKING	SCHOOL
1	Iowa (17-1)
2	Oklahoma St.* (27-4)
3	DePaul# (21-3)
4	Rice (20-1)
5	Army (14-1)
6	Ohio St. (15-5)
7	Navy (12-2)
8	Kentucky (22-4)
9	Notre Dame (15-5)
10	Bowling Green (24-4)
11	St. John's (21-3)
12	NYU (16-8)
13	Akron (21-2)
14	Muhlenberg (24-4)
15	Rhode Island (20-5)
16	Arkansas (17-9)
17	South Carolina (19-3)
18	Hamline (20-4)
19	Tennessee (18-5)
20	RPI (13-1)

#–NIT champion
*–NCAA champion

1944–45 NCAA CHAMPION: OKLA. A&M

SEASON STATISTICS OF OKLAHOMA A&M REGULARS

PLAYER	POS.	CL.	G	PPG
Bob Kurland	C	Jr.	31	17.1
Cecil Hankins*	F	Sr.	23	13.3
Weldon Kern	F	Jr.	31	9.8
Doyle Parrack	G	Sr.	19	7.6
J. L. Parks	F	Fr.	31	4.0
Blake Williams	G	Fr.	31	3.8
John Wylie	G	Fr.	28	1.8
Joe Halbert	C	Fr.	20	0.6
TEAM TOTALS			**31**	**54.1**

*First-semester senior.

1945 CHAMPIONSHIP GAME

NEW YORK, NY

OKLAHOMA A&M (49)	FG	FT-A	PF	PTS.
Hankins	6	3-6	3	15
Parks	0	0-0	3	0
Kern	3	0-4	3	6
Wylie	0	0-0	0	0
Kurland	10	2-3	3	22
Parrack	2	0-1	3	4
Williams	1	0-1	1	2
TOTALS	**22**	**5-15**	**16**	**49**

FT%: .333.

NEW YORK UNIV. (45)	FG	FT-A	PF	PTS.
Grenert	5	2-3	3	12
Forman	5	1-2	1	11
Goldstein	0	2-2	2	2
Schayes	2	2-6	2	6
Walsh	0	0-0	2	0
Tanenbaum	2	0-0	2	4
Mangiapane	2	2-4	3	6
Most	1	2-3	2	4
TOTALS	**17**	**11-20**	**17**	**45**

FT%: .550.
Halftime: Oklahoma A&M 26-21.

MOST OUTSTANDING PLAYER
Bob Kurland, C, Jr., Oklahoma A&M

1945 NCAA Tournament

Summary: The era of the big man arrived. Bob Kurland, continuing his vast improvment in just a couple of years since showing up at Oklahoma A&M as the stereotyped awkward seven-footer, led the Aggies to the NCAA title with 17.1 points per game. They won although Kurland was their only returning letterman.

Outcome for Defending Champion: Utah (17-4) was eliminated in the opening round, 62-37, when Kurland scored 28 points.

Biggest Upset: New York University, featuring just one senior on its roster, erased a 10-point deficit in the final two minutes of regulation on its way to frustrating Ohio State, 70-65, in overtime in the national semifinals.

Numbers Game: Dolph Schayes became the Doogie Howser of Final Four players. He is believed to be the youngest Hall of Famer to appear in an NCAA championship game, joining NYU's varsity lineup in midseason as a 16-year-old freshman and helping the Violets reach the NCAA final against Oklahoma A&M two months before his 17th birthday.

Putting Things in Perspective: Arkansas' 79-76 victory over Oregon in the opening round shattered the previous two-team tourney scoring record by 36 points.

1945 CHAMPIONSHIP BRACKET

1945-46

AT A GLANCE

NCAA Champion: Oklahoma A&M (31-2).

NIT Champion: Kentucky (28-2).

NCAA Consensus First-Team All-Americans: Leo Klier, F, Sr., Notre Dame; Bob Kurland, C, Sr., Oklahoma A&M; George Mikan, C, Sr., DePaul; Max Morris, F-C, Sr., Northwestern; Sid Tannenbaum, G, Jr., NYU.

Clarence "Nibs" Price completed a unique Rose Bowl-NCAA Tournament double when his California basketball team finished in fourth place in the NCAA playoffs. On January 1, 1929, Price had coached the Cal football squad in its 8-7 defeat to Georgia Tech in the Rose Bowl game that is famous for Roy Riegels' wrong-way run for the Bears.

Purdue's Ward "Piggy" Lambert ended his 29-year coaching career with a 371-152 record. Lambert directed the Boilermakers to six Big Ten titles and five co-championships and holds the conference record for longevity.

George Ratterman, a quarterback for Notre Dame's football team, scored the last 11 points for the Irish in a 56-47 upset of a Kentucky squad that eventually won the NIT.

Oklahoma A&M's Bob Kurland poured in a school-record 58 points in an 86-33 rout of St. Louis.

A then college-record crowd of 22,822 watched Ohio State defeat Northwestern, 53-46, and DePaul upend Notre Dame, 63-47, in a doubleheader at Chicago Stadium.

Elmore Morgernthaler, a 7-1 center for New Mexico School of Mines, was called the "tallest player in the world" by the *Converse Basketball Yearbook.* He scored 12 field goals in an 84-61 victory over Drury (Mo.) in an exhibition game with 12-foot baskets at Kansas City. Field goals counted for three points in the contest.

With the end of the war came the end of service teams. The top five teams for the 1945–46 season were Philadelphia Naval Base, Little Creek NAB, Camp Lejeune, Wright Field, and Miramar Marines.

1945–46 PREMO POWER POLL

RANKING	SCHOOL
1	Oklahoma St.* (31-2)
2	Kentucky# (28-2)
3	North Carolina (30-5)
4	Indiana (18-3)
5	DePaul (19-5)
6	Rhode Island (21-3)
7	Ohio St. (16-5)
8	Notre Dame (17-4)
9	West Virginia (24-3)
10	Bowling Green (27-5)
11	NYU (19-3)
12	Kansas (19-2)
13	Illinois (14-7)
14	Wyoming (22-4)
15	Northwestern (15-5)
16	Baylor (25-5)
17	Iowa (14-4)
18	California (30-6)
19	Tennessee St. (26-2)
20	Yale (14-1)

#–NIT champion
*–NCAA champion

1946 NCAA Tournament

Summary: Bob Kurland was the only player for repeat champion Oklahoma A&M to score in double figures in any of the Aggies' three playoff games. Twenty-six different players appeared in A&M's 33 games, but only three scored more than five points in either of the two Final Four frays.

Star Gazing: Sam Aubrey, who had been seriously wounded in the war, came back to be a regular for A&M although there had been some doubt as to whether he would ever walk again.

One and Only: Kurland became the only player to score more than half of a championship team's points in a single tournament when his 72 points accounted for 51.8 percent of Oklahoma State's output in three games.

Numbers Game: Bones McKinney, who averaged 9.8 points per game as a junior center for NCAA runner-up North Carolina, is the only one of the five individuals to play for and coach a team in the Final Four to average more than 5.5 points per game in the season his alma mater reached the national semifinals. McKinney, who averaged 9.8 points per game for Carolina, coached Wake Forest to the 1962 Final Four.

What If: Ohio State captured the Big Ten Conference crown but was edged by national runnerup-to-be North Carolina (60-57 in over-

1945–46 NCAA CHAMPION: OKLAHOMA A&M

SEASON STATISTICS OF OKLAHOMA A&M REGULARS

PLAYER	POS.	CL.	G	PPG
Bob Kurland	C	Sr.	33	19.5
Weldon Kern	F	Jr.	25	8.2
J. L. Parks	G	So.	33	5.7
Blake Williams	G	So.	33	4.5
A. L. Bennett	F	So.	22	3.8
Joe Bradley	G	Fr.	30	3.4
Sam Aubrey	F	Sr.	33	3.3
Joe Pitts	F	Fr.	25	1.9
Joe Halbert	C	So.	27	1.3
Paul Geymann	F	Sr.	21	1.0
TEAM TOTALS			**33**	**50.4**

1946 CHAMPIONSHIP GAME

NEW YORK, NY

OKLAHOMA A&M (43)	FG	FT-A	PF	PTS.
Aubrey	0	1-2	1	1
Bennett	3	0-0	4	6
Kern	3	1-3	2	7
Bradley	1	1-2	1	3
Kurland	9	5-9	5	23
Halbert	0	0-0	0	0
Williams	0	2-4	2	2
Bell	0	1-1	1	1
Parks	0	0-0	2	0
TOTALS	**16**	**11-21**	**18**	**43**

FT%: .524.

NORTH CAROLINA (40)	FG	FT-A	PF	PTS.
Dillon	5	6-6	5	16
Anderson	3	2-3	3	8
Paxton	2	0-0	4	4
McKinney	2	1-3	5	5
White	0	1-1	0	1
Thorne	1	0-0	2	2
Jordan	0	4-8	3	4
TOTALS	**13**	**14-21**	**22**	**40**

FT%: .667.
Halftime: Oklahoma A&M 23-17.

MOST OUTSTANDING PLAYER
Bob Kurland, C, Sr., Oklahoma A&M

time) in the East Regional final to finish the season with a 16-5 record. The Buckeyes might have had sufficient firepower to prevent Oklahoma A&M from repeating as NCAA champion had their top two scorers from Final Four teams the previous two years still been around. But Don Grate, a two-time NCAA consensus second-team All-American forward, signed a pro baseball contract as a pitcher with the Philadelphia Phillies prior to his senior year, and center Arnie Risen played just six games in the first semester before becoming academically ineligible and ending the season with a pro franchise in Indianapolis. Risen led the NBA in field-goal percentage three years later when he was the Rochester Royals' top scorer and an All-NBA second-team selection.

1946 CHAMPIONSHIP BRACKET

1946-47

AT A GLANCE

NCAA Champion: Holy Cross (27-3).

NIT Champion: Utah (19-5).

New Conference: Mid-American.

New Rule: Transparent backboards are authorized.

NCAA Consensus First-Team All-Americans: Ralph Beard, G, Soph., Kentucky; Alex Groza, C, Soph., Kentucky; Ralph Hamilton, F, Sr., Indiana; Sid Tannenbaum, G, Sr., NYU; Gerry Tucker, C, Sr., Oklahoma.

Which enterprise was deemed Bob Davies' second job when he pulled off one of the most amazing feats in college basketball history? Davies coached Seton Hall, his alma mater, to a 24-3 record the same season he also earned National Basketball League Most Valuable Player honors (averaged 14.3 points in 43 regular-season and playoff games with the Rochester Royals).

Kentucky standout center Alex Groza saw limited action in the SEC Tournament because of a back injury, but the Wildcats cruised to victories over Vanderbilt (98-29), Auburn (84-18), Georgia Tech (75-53), and Tulane (55-38). The all-tourney team (considered the all-league team that season) included five Wildcats on the first five—forwards Jack Tingle and Joe Holland, center Wallace "Wah Wah" Jones, and guards Ken Rollins and Ralph Beard.

Wisconsin won its last Big Ten Conference championship.

Oklahoma center Gerry Tucker became an NCAA consensus first-team All-American after having his career interrupted for three years while serving in the U.S. Army. He later became coach of the 1956 U.S. Olympic team.

Texas compiled a 25-2 record, with both of its defeats coming by one point (40-39 to defending NCAA champion Oklahoma A&M and 55-54 in the NCAA Tournament).

UCLA's Don Barksdale, a second-team selection, became the first African American named to an NCAA consensus All-American squad. Washington's Hec Edmundson ended his 29-year coaching career with a 508-204 record.

The top major-college single-game output of the season was a 54-point effort by St. John's Harry Boykoff against St. Francis (N.Y.).

RANKING	SCHOOL
1	Kentucky (34-3)
2	Holy Cross* (27-3)
3	Texas (26-2)
4	Duquesne (20-2)
5	Utah# (19-5)
6	Oklahoma (24-7)
7	Western Kentucky (25-4)
8	Notre Dame (20-4)
9	Navy (16-3)
10	Oregon St. (28-5)
11	N. Carolina St. (26-5)
12	Oklahoma St. (24-8)
13	West Virginia (19-3)
14	Arizona (21-3)
15	CCNY (17-6)
16	Wyoming (22-6)
17	LIU-Brooklyn (17-5)
18	Seton Hall (24-3)
19	Wisconsin (16-6)
20	Santa Clara (21-4)

#–NIT champion
*–NCAA champion

Holy Cross coach Alvin F. (Doggie) Julian.

1947 NCAA Tournament

Summary: Holy Cross, entering the tourney with 20 consecutive victories, fell behind early in all three tourney contests before rallying to win the title.

Outcome for Defending Champion: Oklahoma A&M compiled a 24-8 record.

Star Gazing: The lowest team-leading scoring average for an individual in the season who was named Final Four Most Outstanding Player was compiled by George Kaftan, a forward-center with an 11.1-point average for Holy Cross' NCAA champion, after becoming the first play-

1946–47 NCAA CHAMPION: HOLY CROSS

SEASON STATISTICS OF HOLY CROSS REGULARS

PLAYER	POS.	CL.	G	PPG
George Kaftan	F-C	So.	28	11.1
Dermie O'Connell	F	So.	29	9.0
Bob Cousy	G-F	Fr.	30	7.6
Ken Haggerty	G	Sr.	29	5.7
Andy Laska	G-F	Fr.	30	5.6
Joe Mullaney	G	So.	30	5.0
Frank Oftring	C-F	Fr.	29	4.6
Bob Curran	F-C	Jr.	30	4.4
Charlie Bollinger	C	So.	26	4.0
Bobbie McMullen	G-F	Fr.	29	3.8
TEAM TOTALS			**30**	**60.9**

1947 CHAMPIONSHIP GAME

NEW YORK, NY

HOLY CROSS (58)	FG	FT-A	PF	PTS.
Kaftan	7	4-9	4	18
O'Connell	7	2-4	3	16
Oftring	6	2-3	5	14
Mullaney	0	0-0	2	0
Haggerty	0	0-0	0	0
Laska	0	0-0	0	0
Curran	0	0-1	2	0
Riley	0	0-0	1	0
McMullen	2	4-4	0	8
Cousy	0	2-2	1	2
Bollinger	0	0-0	0	0
Graver	0	0-0	0	0
TOTALS	**22**	**14-23**	**18**	**58**

FT%: .609.

OKLAHOMA (47)	FG	FT-A	PF	PTS.
Reich	3	2-2	3	8
Courty	3	2-3	4	8
Tucker	6	10-12	3	22
Paine	2	2-2	0	6
Landon	1	0-1	4	2
Waters	0	0-0	0	0
Day	0	0-0	0	0
Pryor	0	1-1	2	1
Merchant	0	0-0	1	0
TOTALS	**15**	**17-21**	**17**	**47**

FT%: .810.
Halftime: Oklahoma 31-28.

MOST OUTSTANDING PLAYER
George Kaftan, F-C, Soph., Holy Cross

er to score 30 points in a Final Four game (30 in a 60-45 victory over CCNY in East Regional final before tossing in a team-high 18 in a 58-47 triumph over Oklahoma in the national final).

One and Only: Alvin (Doggie) Julian is the only coach of a championship team to subsequently coach another university and compile a winning NCAA playoff record at his last major college job. Julian captured a national title in the middle of his three seasons as coach at Holy Cross before compiling a 4-3 playoff record in three tournament appearances with Dartmouth from 1956 to 1959.

Putting Things in Perspective: Holy Cross suffered its three defeats in successive early-season games. The Crusaders' first two setbacks were by a total of 26 points.

1947 CHAMPIONSHIP BRACKET

1947–48

AT A GLANCE

NCAA Champion: Kentucky (36-3).

NIT Champion: St. Louis (24-3).

New Rule: Clock stopped on every dead ball the last three minutes of the second half and of every overtime period. This includes every time a basket is scored because the ball is considered dead until put into play again (rule was abolished in 1951).

NCAA Consensus First-Team All-Americans: Ralph Beard, G, Jr., Kentucky; Ed Macauley, C-F, Jr., St. Louis; Jim McIntyre, C, Jr., Minnesota; Kevin O'Shea, G, Soph., Notre Dame; Murray Wier, G, Sr., Iowa.

Long before multi-sport standouts Bo Jackson and Deion Sanders were hailed as jacks of all trades, there was three-sport whiz Dike Eddleman, possibly the most amazing all-around athlete to participate in the Final Four. Eddleman, a 6-3, 180-pound guard-forward for Illinois, was named the Big Ten MVP by the *Chicago Tribune* in 1949 when he was the leading scorer for the national third-place finisher in basketball. In football, he played both offense and defense, punted and returned kicks, and played in the 1947 Rose Bowl for a team that overwhelmed UCLA, 45-14. He set school season records in 1948 for highest punting average (43 yards per kick) and punt return average (32.8). Eddleman, interrupting his collegiate career by joining the U.S. Army Air Corps during World War II, earned an amazing 11 varsity letters at Illinois. He won three Big Ten high jump titles. But his greatest athletic achievement might have been winning a silver medal in the high jump in the 1948 Olympics. This climaxed an outstanding academic school year for him. He won the NCAA high jump crown and led Illinois' football and basketball teams in scoring.

Iowa's Murray Wier is acknowledged as the shortest player (5-9) to lead the nation in scoring (21 ppg) although Norm Hankins of Lawrence Tech in Detroit was designated as the major-college scoring leader (22.5 ppg) that season.

1947–48 INDIVIDUAL LEADERS

SCORING

PLAYER	PTS.	AVG.
Hankins, Lawrence Tech	630	22.5
Wier, Iowa	399	21.0
Lavelli, Yale	554	20.5
Kudelka, St. Mary's	489	20.4
Vandeweghe, Colgate	385	20.3
Haskins, Hamline	605	19.5
Kok, Arkansas	469	19.5
McIntyre, Minnesota	360	18.9
Hatchett, Rutgers	201	18.3
Berce, Marquette	390	17.7

FIELD GOAL PERCENTAGE

PLAYER	FGM	FGA	PCT.
Petersen, Oregon St.	89	187	.476
Mackin, Muhlenberg	158	338	.467
Coleman, Louisville	136	292	.466
Compton, Louisville	109	241	.452
Karpiak, Colorado A&M	77	176	.438
Mann, Bradley	87	199	.437
Brown, Miami (Ohio)	178	417	.427
Walker, Akron	135	316	.427
Dobler, Colorado A&M	106	251	.422
Richter, Cincinnati	122	294	.415
Harman, Kansas St.	76	183	.415

FREE THROW PERCENTAGE

PLAYER	FTM	FTA	PCT.
Urzetta, St. Bonaventure	59	64	.922
Sterling, West Virginia	40	45	.889
Shannon, Kansas St.	55	66	.879
Sharman, USC	38	44	.864
Wylie, Ohio U.	88	102	.863
L. Malamed, CCNY	55	66	.833
Line, Kentucky	48	58	.828
McMullen, Mississippi	70	86	.814
Woodcock, Bucknell	39	48	.813
Nelson, Brigham Young	111	138	.804

1947–48 TEAM LEADERS

SCORING OFFENSE

SCHOOL	PTS.	AVG.
Rhode Island St.	1755	76.3
North Carolina St.	2409	75.3
Bowling Green	2327	70.5
Lawrence Tech	1961	70.0
Bradley	2157	69.6

SCORING DEFENSE

SCHOOL	PTS.	AVG.
Oklahoma A&M	1006	32.5
Alabama	1070	39.6
Creighton	925	40.2
Wyoming	1101	40.8
Siena	1161	41.5

FREE THROW PERCENTAGE

SCHOOL	FTM	FTA	PCT.
Texas	351	481	.730
Michigan	280	411	.681
St. Bonaventure	286	421	.679
DePaul	468	698	.670
New York University	433	646	.670

FIELD GOAL PERCENTAGE

SCHOOL	FGM	FGA	PCT.
Oregon St.	668	1818	.367
Muhlenberg	655	1822	.359
Akron	571	1617	.353
Louisville	709	2028	.350
Bowling Green	918	2639	.348

1947–48 NCAA CHAMPION: KENTUCKY

SEASON STATISTICS OF KENTUCKY REGULARS

PLAYER	POS.	CL.	G	FG%	FT%	PPG
Alex Groza	C	Jr.	39	.377	.629	12.5
Ralph Beard	G	Jr.	38	.362	.591	12.5
Wallace Jones	F-C	Jr.	36	.311	.670	9.3
James Line	F	So.	38	.361	.823	7.0
Ken Rollins	G	Sr.	39	.279	.728	6.6
Cliff Barker	F	Jr.	38	.309	.559	6.5
Dale Barnstable	F	So.	38	.271	.571	4.6
Joe Holland	F	Jr.	38	.280	.511	3.7
Jack Parkinson	G	Sr.	29	.201	.455	3.3
Walt Hirsch	F-G	Fr.	13	.291	.556	2.8
Albert Cummins	G	So.	17	.351	.667	1.9
Jim Jordan	F	So.	30	.148	.720	1.5
Garland Townes	G	Fr.	13	.318	.455	1.5
Roger Day	F	Fr.	11	.278	.778	1.5
Albert Campbell	C	Sr.	15	.222	.571	1.1
Johnny Stough	G	So.	23	.211	.500	0.9
TEAM TOTALS			39	.312	.626	70.0

Note: Statistics include three games in Olympic Trials after the NCAA Tournament.

1948 CHAMPIONSHIP GAME

NEW YORK, NY

KENTUCKY (58)	FG	FT-A	PF	PTS.
Jones	4	1-1	3	9
Barker	2	1-3	4	5
Groza	6	2-4	4	14
Beard	4	4-4	1	12
Rollins	3	3-5	3	9
Line	3	1-1	3	7
Holland	1	0-0	1	2
Barnstable	0	0-1	0	0
TOTALS	23	12-19	19	58

FT%: .632.

BAYLOR (42)	FG	FT-A	PF	PTS.
Owens	2	1-2	0	5
DeWitt	3	2-4	3	8
Heathington	3	2-4	5	8
Johnson	3	4-7	5	10
Robinson	3	2-4	4	8
Pulley	0	1-1	0	1
Hickman	1	0-0	0	2
Preston	0	0-2	2	0
Srack	0	0-0	0	0
TOTALS	15	12-24	19	42

FT%: .500.
Halftime: Kentucky 29-16.

MOST OUTSTANDING PLAYER

Alex Groza, C, Jr., Kentucky

North Carolina State, runner-up to Rhode Island State in team offense with 75.3 points per game, became the first school other than the Rhodies ever to average more than 75. The Wolfpack, undefeated in Southern Conference competition (12-0), finished the season with a 29-3 mark when its leading scorer, sophomore Dick Dickey, was sidelined with the mumps in an NIT opening-round defeat to DePaul.

St. Bonaventure's Sam Urzetta (92.2 percent) became the only player to convert over 90 percent of his free throws in a one season until 1962.

Notre Dame (17-7) beat two teams ranked No. 1 in the country in the final month of the regular season—NCAA champion-to-be Kentucky and NIT runner-up NYU. But Notre Dame's school-record homecourt winning streak was snapped at 38 by eventual NIT kingpin St. Louis.

Arkansas became the first school to compile 25 consecutive winning seasons.

1947–48 PREMO POWER POLL

RANKING	SCHOOL
1	Kentucky* (36-3)
2	St. Louis# (24-3)
3	Holy Cross (26-4)
4	Western Kentucky (28-2)
5	N. Carolina St. (29-3)
6	NYU (22-4)
7	DePaul (22-8)
8	West Virginia (17-3)
9	Michigan (16-6)
10	Oklahoma St. (27-4)
11	Baylor (24-8)
12	Tennessee (20-5)
13	Bowling Green (27-6)
14	Tulane (23-3)
15	Bradley (28-3)
16	Iowa (15-4)
17	Texas (20-5)
18	Illinois (15-5)
19	CCNY (18-3)
20	Columbia (21-3)

#–NIT champion
*–NCAA champion

Kansas State ended its streak of 21 consecutive non-winning conference records by capturing the Big Seven title with a 9-3 league mark. It was the Wildcats' first conference crown in 29 seasons.

Washington's Jack Nichols finished his fifth season of varsity competition in the Pacific Coast Conference (three with the Huskies and two as a military trainee during World War II with Southern California).

Duquesne's Chick Davies ended a 21-year coaching career with a 314-106 record.

1948 NCAA Tournament

Summary: Ken Rollins, the lone senior among coach Adolph Rupp's "Fabulous Five," held standout guard Bob Cousy, the leading scorer for defending champion Holy Cross, to just five points in the semifinals. Kentucky had an excessive amount of maturity since Rollins, Alex Groza, Dale Barnstable, Jim Line, and Cliff Barker were World War II service veterans. Barker, a defensive specialist, was in a German prisoner-of-war camp for 16 months after the crewman's B-17 was shot down in Europe.

Outcome for Defending Champion: Holy Cross finished with a 26-4 record when Kentucky ended the Crusaders' 19-game winning streak.

Numbers Game: Columbia entered the playoffs with just one defeat (in overtime), but Kentucky's Wallace Jones (21), Groza (17), and Beard (15) combined to equal their entire output as the Wildcats prevailed, 76-53, in the first round.

1948 CHAMPIONSHIP BRACKET

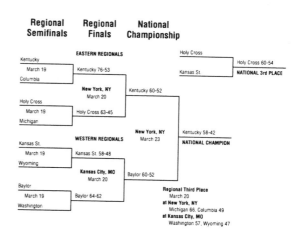

1948-49

AT A GLANCE

NCAA Champion: Kentucky (32-2).

NIT Champion: San Francisco (25-5).

New Conference: Ohio Valley.

New Rules: Coaches allowed to converse while mingling with players during a timeout. NIT field expands from eight teams to 12.

NCAA Consensus First-Team All-Americans: Ralph Beard, G, Sr., Kentucky; Vince Boryla, F, Sr., Denver; Alex Groza, C, Sr., Kentucky; Tony Lavelli, G, Sr., Yale; Ed Macauley, C-F, Sr., St. Louis.

A weekly ritual began when the Associated Press announced the results of the first weekly basketball poll on January 18, 1949. St. Louis was ranked first in the initial poll, followed by Kentucky, Western Kentucky, Minnesota, Oklahoma A&M, San Francisco, Illinois, Hamline, Villanova, and Utah.

Jim Lacy of Loyola (Md.) became the first player to finish his career cracking the 2,000-point plateau.

Villanova's Paul Arizin erupted for 85 points against Philadelphia NAMC. But the only player to score at least 40 points in two games was Yale's Tony Lavelli. A 52-point uprising by Lavelli against Williams remains a school record.

Colgate's Ernie Vandeweghe finished among the nation's top five scorers for the third consecutive season. His son, Kiki, became a standout at UCLA and averaged more than 20 points per game seven consecutive seasons in the NBA from 1981–82 through 1987–88.

West Virginia's homecourt winning streak ended at 57 games with a 34-32 overtime loss to Pittsburgh in the closing contest on the Mountaineers' schedule.

Kentucky, which went unbeaten in SEC competition for the third consecutive season, finished sixth nationally in both team offense and defense. The season's most shocking defeat was the Wildcats' 67-56 setback against Loyola of Chicago in the opening round of the NIT. The defending NCAA champions entered the game ranked No. 1 in the nation in the AP poll. Two years later, it was disclosed that the Kentucky-Loyola game was one in which UK players allegedly were bribed by gamblers to keep the winning margin under 10 points.

Texas' Slater Martin set a school record (subsequently tied) with 49 points against TCU.

John Wooden began his coaching career at UCLA with a 22-7 record, breaking the Bruins' previous single-season mark of 18 victories.

1948-49 FINAL NATIONAL POLL

AP	SCHOOL
1	Kentucky
2	Oklahoma St.
3	St. Louis
4	Illinois
5	Western Kentucky
6	Minnesota
7	Bradley
8	San Francisco
9	Tulane
10	Bowling Green St.

1949 NCAA Tournament

Summary: Despite returning seven of his top eight scorers from an NCAA titlist, Kentucky coach Adolph Rupp experimented with the Wildcats' lineup until he achieved the chemistry he sought. Cliff Barker was moved from forward to guard and forward Dale Barnstable also played some guard. After an early-season defeat to St. Louis on a last-second tip-in, Kentucky won all of its games until bowing in the NIT to eventual finalist Loyola of Chicago. A couple of years later, Alex Groza, Ralph Beard, and Barnstable admitted in sworn testimony that they accepted $1,500 in bribes to throw the NIT game against Loyola. They also testified they accepted money from gamblers to shave points in other contests.

Star Gazing: Alex Groza was the brother of football Hall of Famer Lou Groza.

1948–49 INDIVIDUAL LEADERS

SCORING

PLAYER	PTS.	AVG.
Lavelli, Yale	671	22.4
Arizin, Villanova	594	22.0
Giermak, William & Mary	740	21.8
Senesky, St. Joseph's	483	21.0
Vandeweghe, Colgate	397	20.9
Groza, Kentucky	698	20.5
Goodwin, Rhode Island	433	19.7
Noertker, Virginia	442	19.2
Boryla, Denver	624	18.9
Schaus, West Virginia	442	18.4

FIELD GOAL PERCENTAGE

PLAYER	FGM	FGA	PCT.
Macauley, St. Louis	144	275	.524
Goodwin, Rhode Island	145	291	.498
Brawley, Maryland	78	161	.484
Leverte, Seton Hall	101	210	.481
Boven, Western Michigan	123	257	.479
Share, Bowling Green	193	410	.471
Coleman, Louisville	188	404	.465
Kerris, Loyola (Ill.)	175	382	.458
White, Texas	83	185	.449
Grover, Bradley	98	212	.462

FREE THROW PERCENTAGE

PLAYER	FTM	FTA	PCT.
Schroer, Valparaiso	59	68	.868
Line, Kentucky	43	51	.843
Oftring, Holy Cross	47	56	.839
Dolnics, TCU	99	119	.832
Goodwin, Rhode Island	143	172	.831
Lavelli, Yale	215	261	.824
Palcheff, Washington (Mo.)	65	80	.813
Alston, Xavier	52	64	.813
Cheek, Davidson	75	94	.798
Westerfeld, Cincinnati	50	63	.794

1948–49 TEAM LEADERS

SCORING OFFENSE

SCHOOL	PTS.	AVG.
Rhode Island St.	1575	71.6
Western Kentucky	2028	69.9
Yale	2089	69.6
Bowling Green	2139	69.0
Colgate	1297	68.3

SCORING DEFENSE

SCHOOL	PTS.	AVG.
Oklahoma A&M	985	35.2
Siena	1215	41.9
Wyoming	1509	43.1
Minnesota	912	43.4
St. Bonaventure	1137	43.7

FIELD GOAL PERCENTAGE

SCHOOL	FGM	FGA	PCT.
Muhlenberg	593	1512	.392
Wyoming	674	1777	.379
Loyola (Ill.)	720	1918	.375
Seton Hall	566	1509	.375
Bradley	889	2372	.375

FREE THROW PERCENTAGE

SCHOOL	FTM	FTA	PCT.
Davidson	347	489	.710
Kentucky	514	728	.706
Utah	489	704	.695
Denver	505	730	.692
Valparaiso	340	496	.687

SCORING MARGIN

SCHOOL	OWN	OPP.	MAR.
Kentucky	68.2	43.9	24.3
Tulane	65.6	48.8	16.8
Rhode Island St.	71.6	56.0	15.6
Loyola (Ill.)	61.3	45.7	15.5
Western Kentucky	69.9	54.4	15.5

1948–49 NCAA CHAMPION: KENTUCKY

SEASON STATISTICS OF KENTUCKY REGULARS

PLAYER	POS.	CL.	G	FG%	FT%	PPG
Alex Groza	C	Sr.	34	.423	.726	20.5
Ralph Beard	G	Sr.	34	.299	.713	10.9
Wallace Jones	F-C	Sr.	32	.295	.653	9.7
Cliff Barker	G-F	Sr.	34	.298	.682	7.3
Dale Barnstable	F-G	Jr.	34	.272	.719	6.1
Jim Line	F	Jr.	32	.359	.843	5.7
Walt Hirsch	F-G	So.	34	.321	.688	4.6
Roger Day	F	So.	19	.538	.529	2.7
Garland Townes	G	So.	16	.208	.550	1.9
Johnny Stough	G	Jr.	25	.232	.857	1.5
TEAM TOTALS			34	.328	.706	68.2

1949 CHAMPIONSHIP GAME

SEATTLE, WA

KENTUCKY (46)	FG	FT-A	PF	PTS.
Jones	1	1-3	3	3
Line	2	1-2	3	5
Groza	9	7-8	5	25
Beard	1	1-2	4	3
Barker	1	3-3	4	5
Barnstable	1	1-1	1	3
Hirsch	1	0-0	1	2
TOTALS	16	14-19	21	46
FT%: .737.				

OKLAHOMA A&M (36)	FG	FT-A	PF	PTS.
Yates	1	0-0	1	2
Shelton	3	6-7	4	12
Harris	3	1-1	5	7
Bradley	0	3-6	3	3
Parks	2	3-4	5	7
Jaquet	0	1-2	0	1
McArthur	0	2-2	1	2
Pilgrim	0	2-2	1	2
Smith	0	0-0	1	0
TOTALS	9	18-24	21	36
FT%: .750.				

Halftime: Kentucky 25-20.

MOST OUTSTANDING PLAYER

Alex Groza, C, Sr., Kentucky

One and Only: Groza, the Final Four Most Outstanding Player in 1948 and 1949, is the only player to appear at a minimum of two Final Fours and be the game-high scorer in every Final Four contest in which he played.

Numbers Game: Groza and Villanova's Paul Arizin each scored 30 points when Kentucky defeated Villanova, 85-72. It was the only playoff game in which two players scored at least 30 in the same game until 1953.

1940–49 PREMO POWER POLL: BEST TEAMS BY DECADE

RANK	SEASON	TEAM
1	1947–48	Kentucky* (36-3)
2	1948–49	Kentucky* (32-2)
3	1945–46	Oklahoma St.* (31-2)
4	1942–43	Illinois (17-1)
5	1943–44	Army (15-0)
6	1946–47	Kentucky (34-3)
7	1939–40	Indiana* (20-3)
8	1944–45	Iowa (17-1)
9	1940–41	LIU-Brooklyn# (25-2)
10	1942–43	Wyoming* (31-2)
11	1946–47	Holy Cross* (27-3)
12	1941–42	Stanford* (28-4)
13	1945–46	Kentucky# (28-2)
14	1947–48	St. Louis# (24-3)
15	1944–45	Oklahoma St.* (27-4)
16	1940–41	Wisconsin* (20-3)
17	1943–44	Utah* (21-4)
18	1948–49	Oklahoma St. (23-5)
19	1946–47	Texas (26-2)
20	1942–43	Notre Dame (18-2)
	1944–45	DePaul# (21-3)
	1947–48	Holy Cross (26-4)
	1945–46	North Carolina (30-5)

#–NIT Champion
*–NCAA Tournament Champion

1949 CHAMPIONSHIP BRACKET

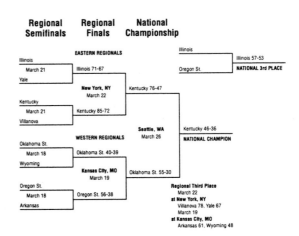

3

THE "GREAT PLAYERS" ERA:
THE 1950s

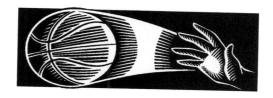

Kentucky, closing out the 1940s with back-to-back NCAA crowns, continued to excel but represented the best and worst of the 1950s. The Wildcats were virtually invincible on the court, winning at least 20 games every season they competed in the decade. On the other hand, they were party to a widespread gambling-related scandal that barred them from participating one season.

The '50s also marked the emergence of dominating African-American players such as Elgin Baylor, Wilt Chamberlain, Oscar Robertson, and Bill Russell. The athleticism of big men Chamberlain and Russell was stunning. Chamberlain became the only seven-foot center to lead a Final Four in scoring (55 points in two games for 1957 runner-up Kansas) and win a conference high jump title in the same year (Big Eight outdoor meet at a height of 6'5"). Russell, 6-10, did more than lead San Francisco to back-to-back NCAA basketball championships. He was ranked as the world's No. 7 high jumper in the *Track and Field News* rankings for 1956 after winning titles in the West Coast Relays, Pacific AAU meet, and Central California AAU meet.

1949–50

AT A GLANCE

NCAA/NIT Champion: CCNY (24-5).

NCAA Consensus First-Team All-Americans: Paul Arizin, F, Sr., Villanova; Bob Cousy, G, Sr., Holy Cross; Dick Schnittker, F, Sr., Ohio State; Bill Sharman, G, Sr., Southern California; Paul Unruh, F, Sr., Bradley.

Paul Arizin, who couldn't earn a spot on his high school squad and didn't bother to try out as a Villanova freshman, led the nation in scoring average (25.3 ppg). Arizin's outbursts helped Villanova end Rhode Island State's streak of 14 consecutive seasons leading the nation in offense. The Wildcats averaged 72.8 points per game.

Bob Zawoluk's school-record 65 points for St. John's against St. Peter's was the top one-game barrage during the season.

Butler's Ralph "Buckshot" O'Brien, a 5-9, 150-pound guard, averaged 25.3 points per game in seven games against Big Nine teams.

1949–50 INDIVIDUAL LEADERS

SCORING

PLAYER	PTS.	AVG.
Arizin, Villanova	735	25.3
Senesky, St. Joseph's	537	22.4
White, Long Island	551	22.0
Lovellette, Kansas	545	21.8
Lavoy, Western Kentucky	671	21.6
Schnittker, Ohio St.	469	21.3
Giermak, William & Mary	646	20.8
Handlan, Washington & Lee	406	20.3
Zawoluk, St. John's	588	20.3
Noertker, Virginia	503	20.1

FIELD GOAL PERCENTAGE

PLAYER	FGM	FGA	PCT.
Moran, Niagara	98	185	.530
Toft, Denver	146	281	.520
McDonald, Toledo	102	200	.510
Arizin, Villanova	260	527	.493
Skendrovich, Duquesne	108	220	.491
Mann, Bradley	135	291	.464
Share, Bowling Green	204	444	.459
Meineke, Dayton	194	424	.458
Beck, Bowling Green	84	186	.452
Pilch, Wyoming	143	317	.451

FREE THROW PERCENTAGE

PLAYER	FTM	FTA	PCT.
Urzetta, St. Bonaventure	54	61	.885
Morrill, Michigan	41	48	.854
Ballots, Temple	73	86	.849
Popp, Baldwin-Wallace	69	83	.831
Sermersheim, Georgia Tech	68	82	.829
Gardiner, St. Louis	53	64	.828
Brawner, Auburn	49	60	.817
Turner, Western Kentucky	84	103	.816
Davis, Pennsylvania	44	54	.815
Norris, Colgate	79	97	.814

1949–50 TEAM LEADERS

SCORING OFFENSE

SCHOOL	PTS.	AVG.
Villanova	2111	72.8
Holy Cross	2251	72.6
St. John's	2093	72.2
Muhlenberg	1651	71.8
Western Kentucky	2216	71.5

SCORING DEFENSE

SCHOOL	PTS.	AVG.
Oklahoma A&M	1059	39.2
Wyoming	1491	41.4
Tulsa	1027	44.7
Washington (Mo.)	1066	46.3
San Francisco	1237	47.6

FIELD GOAL PERCENTAGE

SCHOOL	FGM	FGA	PCT.
Texas Christian	476	1191	.400
Bowling Green	808	2070	.390
Toledo	633	1631	.388
Bradley	999	2588	.386
Akron	676	1752	.386
Wyoming	629	1631	.386

FREE THROW PERCENTAGE

SCHOOL	FTM	FTA	PCT.
Temple	342	483	.708
Colorado	395	576	.686
Auburn	390	574	.679
Duquesne	418	616	.679
Washington St.	456	673	.678

SCORING MARGIN

SCHOOL	OWN	OPP.	MAR.
Holy Cross	72.6	55.4	17.2
Villanova	72.8	55.7	17.1
St. John's	72.2	56.7	15.5
La Salle	69.8	54.8	15.0
North Carolina St.	65.3	51.7	13.7

St. Bonaventure's Sam Urzetta led the nation in free-throw accuracy for the second time in three seasons. Urzetta also went on to win the U.S. Amateur golf title.

Ohio State forward Dick Schnittker earned consensus All-American honors after starting as an end for Ohio State's conference co-championship football squad that defeated California, 17-14, in the Rose Bowl.

Two future teammates with the Boston Celtics for four seasons led the Pacific Coast Conference in scoring. Washington State's Gene Conley paced the Northern Division with 13.8 points per game while Southern Cal's Bill Sharman led the Southern Division with a 19.8 mark. Both Conley and Sharman also played professional baseball.

TCU became the first major-college team to hit 40 percent of its field-goal attempts in a single season.

Nebraska registered the largest ever winning margin in an overtime game with an 85-67 triumph over Iowa State.

Kentucky claimed its seventh consecutive SEC Tournament title.

1949–50 FINAL NATIONAL POLL

AP	SCHOOL
1	Bradley
2	Ohio State
3	Kentucky
4	Holy Cross
5	North Carolina St.
6	Duquesne
7	UCLA
8	Western Kentucky
9	St. John's
10	La Salle
11	Villanova
12	San Francisco
13	Long Island
14	Kansas St.
15	Arizona
16	Wisconsin
17	San Jose St.
18	Washington St.
19	Kansas
20	Indiana

1949–50 NCAA CHAMPION: CCNY

SEASON STATISTICS OF CCNY REGULARS

PLAYER	POS.	CL.	G.	FG%	FT%	PPG
Ed Roman	C	So.	29	.416	.642	16.4
Ed Warner	F	So.	29	.430	.567	14.8
Irwin Dambrot	F	Sr.	29	.371	.580	10.2
Floyd Layne	G	So.	29	.280	.606	6.9
Al Roth	G	So.	29	.288	.515	6.4
Herb Cohen	G	So.	24	.410	.526	5.4
Norm Mager	F	Sr.	29	.353	.629	3.6
Ronald Nadell	G	Jr.	19	.386	.650	2.5
Mike Wittlin	G	Sr.	22	.314	.600	1.7
Joe Galiber	C	Sr.	24	.239	.522	1.4
TEAM TOTALS			29	.363	.577	68.7

1950 CHAMPIONSHIP GAME

NEW YORK, NY

CCNY (71)	FG-A	FT-A	A	PF	PTS.
Dambrot	7-14	1-2	2	0	15
Roman	6-17	0-2	1	5	12
Warner	4-9	6-14	3	2	14
Roth	2-7	1-5	3	2	5
Mager	4-10	6-6	2	3	14
Galiber	0-0	0-0	0	1	0
Layne	3-7	5-6	4	3	11
Nadell	0-0	0-0	1	1	0
TOTALS	**26-64**	**19-35**	**16**	**17**	**71**

FG%: .406. FT%: .543.

BRADLEY (68)	FG-A	FT-A	A	PF	PTS.
Grover	0-10	2-3	3	3	2
Schlictman	0-3	0-0	0	2	0
Unruh	4-9	0-0	2	5	8
Behnke	3-10	3-3	2	4	9
Kelly	0-1	0-2	0	0	0
Mann	2-7	5-5	1	5	9
Preece	6-11	0-0	0	5	12
D. Melchiorre	0-0	0-0	0	0	0
G. Melchiorre	7-16	2-4	5	4	16
Chianakas	5-7	1-3	1	4	11
Stowell	0-0	1-1	0	0	1
TOTALS	**27-74**	**14-21**	**14**	**32**	**68**

FG%: .365. FT%: .667.
Halftime: CCNY 39-32.

MOST OUTSTANDING PLAYER
Irwin Dambrot, F, Sr., CCNY

1950 NCAA Tournament

Summary: CCNY became the only school to win the NCAA playoffs and NIT in the same year. It is also the only former major college to compile a winning playoff record in the NCAA Division I Tournament. The ultimate "Cinderella" squad won the NCAA crown by defeating three teams ranked in the AP top five (second-ranked Ohio State, fifth-ranked North Carolina State, and top-ranked Bradley) although five of CCNY's six leading scorers were sophomores. CCNY, coached by Nat Holman, also defeated 12th-ranked San Francisco, third-ranked Kentucky, sixth-ranked Duquesne, and Bradley a second time the same year on its way to the NIT title.

Outcome for Defending Champion: Kentucky (25-5) was embarrassed by CCNY, 89-50, in its NIT opener.

Star Gazing: CCNY was the first NCAA champion to have black players in its starting lineup—Floyd Layne, Joe Galiber, and Ed Warner. Alas, midnight struck for the Beavers following their storybook season when four CCNY regulars and other New York-based players were indicted in a point-shaving scandal rocking the sport the following year. After the investigation revealed scholastic records were falsified to allow several recruits admission to CCNY, the school de-emphasized its program in 1953.

One and Only: The worst winning percentage for a Final Four team was compiled by Baylor, which finished with a 14-13 record (.519) after losing both of its Final Four games (to Bradley and North Carolina State).

Numbers Game: UCLA, making its playoff debut under coach John Wooden, led mighty Bradley by seven points with five minutes remaining before the Braves went on a 23-2 spurt to end the game.

What If: Bob Cousy and Frank Oftring, members of Holy Cross' 1947 NCAA titlist as freshmen, were senior co-captains when the Crusaders won their first 26 games to temporarily earn AP's No. 1 ranking. But they lost four of their last five contests, including both outings in the NCAA playoffs when Cousy went 17 for 61 from the floor (27.9 percent).

Putting Things in Perspective: Would CCNY have been able to become the only school

1950 CHAMPIONSHIP BRACKET

Regional Semifinals	Regional Finals	National Championship		
	EASTERN REGIONALS		North Carolina St.	
CCNY				North Carolina St. 53-41
March 23	CCNY 56-55		Baylor	**NATIONAL 3rd PLACE**
Ohio St.				
	New York, NY March 25	CCNY 78-73		
North Carolina St.				
March 24	North Carolina 87-74			
Holy Cross				
		New York, NY March 28	CCNY 71-68	
	WESTERN REGIONALS		**NATIONAL CHAMPION**	
Baylor				
March 23	Baylor 56-55			
Brigham Young				
	Kansas City, MO March 25	Bradley 68-66		
Bradley			**Regional Third Place** March 25 at New York, NY Ohio St. 72, Holy Cross 52 at Kansas City, MO Brigham Young 83, UCLA 62	
March 24	Bradley 73-59			
UCLA				

to win the NIT and NCAA playoffs in the same season had both of the national postseason tournaments not been staged in New York? Most observers thought CCNY was out of the playoff picture after the Beavers lost three of five games late in the season.

1950–51

AT A GLANCE

NCAA Champion: Kentucky (32-2).

NIT Champion: Brigham Young (28-9).

New Rule: NCAA Tournament field expands from eight to 16 teams, with 10 conference champions qualifying automatically for the first time (Big Seven, Big Ten, Border, Ivy, Missouri Valley, Pacific Coast, Skyline, Southeastern, Southern, and Southwest).

NCAA Consensus First-Team All-Americans: Clyde Lovellette, C, Jr., Kansas; Gene Melchiorre, G, Sr., Bradley; Bill Mlkvy, F, Jr., Temple; Sam Ranzino, F, Sr., North Carolina State; Bill Spivey, C, Jr., Kentucky.

Long Island University's Clair Bee ended his 21-year college coaching career with a 412-87 record when LIU dropped its program in the

wake of a fixing scandal. Star center Sherman White and two other Blackbird regulars were implicated and later prosecuted. In all, by the time the investigation was completed, some 32 players at seven schools were found to be involved.

"In the first half of the century, Bee was basketball," said Bob Knight, who was befriended by Bee when Knight was at Army and Bee at a local military school. "There wasn't a thing he did that didn't affect the game, and there wasn't a thing that affected the game that he didn't do. He was one of the most singularly brilliant minds ever involved with athletics, and one of the greatest analytical basketball minds we've ever had. He had such a clear, brilliant grasp of what had to be done. He was a coach in the truest sense of the word."

LIU was undefeated at home in its last 13 seasons, compiling an overall 225-3 record at the 800-seat Brooklyn College of Pharmacy. Bee refused to employ a zone defense at home because he thought it would give his team an unfair advantage on a court that was 24 feet shorter than regulation, putting the 10-second line at the rear free-throw line instead of at midcourt. LIU's average record in its last 16 seasons under Bee was 21-4.

Temple's Bill Mlkvy concluded the season with a school-record 73 points against Wilkes College to finish with a national-leading 29.2 average. Mlkvy was also national runner-up in rebounding (18.9) and assists (7.0). Washington & Lee's Jay Handlan, runner-up to Mlkvy in scoring, set an NCAA record with 71 field-goal attempts (30 made) in a game against Furman on February 17, 1951.

Duke assembled the greatest comeback in NCAA history by erasing a 32-point deficit in a 74-72 victory over Tulane on December 30, 1950. The Blue Devils trailed by 29 points at halftime (56-27).

Arizona established an NCAA record for highest rebound margin, grabbing 84 more rebounds (102-18) than Northern Arizona on January 6, 1951. The Wildcats captured their

1950–51 INDIVIDUAL LEADERS

SCORING

PLAYER	PTS.	AVG.
Mlkvy, Temple	731	29.2
Handlan, Washington & Lee	656	26.2
Workman, West Virginia	705	26.1
Groat, Duke	831	25.2
Lovellette, Kansas	548	22.8
Slaughter, South Carolina	569	22.8
Hennessey, Villanova	703	22.0
Ove, Valparaiso	469	21.3
Zawoluk, St. John's	654	21.1
Ranzino, N.C. St.	706	20.8

REBOUNDING

PLAYER	REB.	AVG.
Beck, Pennsylvania	556	20.6
Mlkvy, Temple	472	18.9
Christ, Fordham	493	18.4
Payton, Tulane	426	17.8
Darling, Iowa	387	17.6
Nolen, Texas Tech	492	17.6
Deasy, North Carolina	399	17.3

Spivey, Kentucky	567	17.2
Slaughter, South Carolina	413	16.5
Corizzi, Rutgers	339	16.1

ASSISTS

PLAYER	AST.	AVG.
Walker, Toledo	210	7.2
Mlkvy, Temple	176	7.0
Birch, Niagara	193	6.9
Chadwick, Cornell	170	6.8
Regan, Seton Hall	158	5.6
Markham, Wisconsin	99	5.5
Becker, New York	87	5.4
Baird, Holy Cross	114	5.4
Stratton, Colgate	119	5.4
Cox, South Carolina	135	5.4

FIELD GOAL PERCENTAGE

PLAYER	FGM	FGA	PCT.
Meineke, Dayton	240	469	.512
Maguire, Villanova	86	170	.506
Workman, West Virginia	273	558	.489

Rogers, Texas Western	154	317	.486
Slaughter, South Carolina	222	458	.485
Jennerich, Manhattan	76	157	.484
Chambers, William & Mary	199	413	.482
Koffenberger, Maryland	97	202	.480
Sullivan, Alabama	136	284	.479
Jones, Virginia Tech	184	388	.474

FREE THROW PERCENTAGE

PLAYER	FTM	FTA	PCT.
Handlan, Washington & Lee	158	184	.859
McMurray, Wichita	81	95	.853
Preece, Bradley	62	73	.849
Gordon, Temple	53	63	.841
Skoog, Minnesota	52	63	.825
Davis, Pennsylvania	61	74	.824
Matthews, Hardin-Simmons	60	73	.822
Sayre, Virginia Tech	128	156	.821
Travis, Texas Western	84	103	.816
Stange, Iowa St.	66	81	.815

1949–50 TEAM LEADERS

SCORING OFFENSE

SCHOOL	PTS.	AVG.
Cincinnati	1694	77.0
North Carolina St.	2748	76.3
Kentucky	2540	74.7
Virginia Tech	2149	74.1
Gettysburg	1623	73.8

SCORING DEFENSE

SCHOOL	PTS.	AVG.
Texas A&M	1275	44.0
Arkansas	1101	45.9
Oklahoma A&M	1616	46.2
Texas	1256	46.5
Oklahoma City	1423	47.4

FIELD GOAL PERCENTAGE

SCHOOL	FGM	FGA	PCT.
Maryland	481	1210	.398
Virginia Tech	805	2029	.397
Washington & Lee	639	1613	.396
Toledo	725	1852	.391
Bradley	941	2427	.388

FREE THROW PERCENTAGE

SCHOOL	FTM	FTA	PCT.
Minnesota	287	401	.716
Virginia Tech	539	756	.713
Oklahoma	383	547	.700
Duke	619	888	.697
Baylor	371	533	.696

SCORING MARGIN

SCHOOL	OWN	OPP.	MAR.
Kentucky	74.7	52.5	22.3
Columbia	72.9	52.7	20.1
Cincinnati	77.0	58.1	18.9
Arizona	69.5	55.4	14.1
Kansas St.	68.8	55.1	13.8

sixth consecutive Border Conference championship.

Columbia became the first team in the 50-year history of the Eastern Intercollegiate League to finish its season without a defeat (22-0), but the Lions lost to Illinois, 79-71, in the opening round of the NCAA Tournament. Columbia's leading scorer was 6-4½ sophomore Jack Molinas (14.4 points per game), who later would be implicated in college basketball fix scandals, barred from the NBA for betting on his own team, and murdered at his home in California.

Eastern schools supplied 18 consecutive national team scoring leaders until Cincinnati moved atop the list with a 77-point average.

Connecticut's Bill Corley set a school record with 51 points against New Hampshire.

Eleven players fouled out of a first-round NIT game in which St. Bonaventure outlasted Cincinnati, 70-67, in double overtime. NIT champion Brigham Young attempted to duplicate CCNY's feat the previous year of winning both the NIT and NCAA, but BYU was eliminated by Kansas State, 64-54, in the finals of the NCAA Western Regional.

So many players fouled out of a game against Tennessee Tech that Morehead State had only three men on the court in the final minutes. Morehead coach Ellis Johnson chose to play the remaining few minutes after referees let him

1950–51 NCAA CHAMPION: KENTUCKY

SEASON STATISTICS OF KENTUCKY REGULARS

PLAYER	POS.	CL.	G.	FG%	FT%	PPG	RPG
Bill Spivey	C	Jr.	33	.399	.621	19.2	17.2
Shelby Linville	F	Jr.	34	.389	.757	10.4	9.1
Bobby Watson	G	Jr.	34	.328	.750	10.4	2.5
Frank Ramsey	G	So.	34	.327	.610	10.1	12.8
Cliff Hagan	F-C	So.	20	.367	.738	9.2	8.5
Walt Hirsch*	F	Sr.	30	.285	.706	9.1	8.0
Skip Whitaker	G	Jr.	31	.342	.600	5.2	2.0
Lou Tsioropoulos	F-C	So.	27	.311	.533	3.4	4.8
Dwight Price	F	So.	20	.277	.444	1.7	2.2
C. M. Newton	G	Jr.	18	.229	.454	1.2	0.7
TEAM TOTALS			34	.342	.648	74.7	62.0

*Ineligible for NCAA Tournament as a fourth-year varsity player.

1951 CHAMPIONSHIP GAME

MINNEAPOLIS, MN

KENTUCKY (68)	FG-A	FT-A	REB.	PF	PTS.
Whitaker	4-5	1-1	2	2	9
Linville	2-7	4-8	8	5	8
Spivey	9-29	4-6	21	2	22
Ramsey	4-10	1-3	4	5	9
Watson	3-8	2-4	3	3	8
Hagan	5-6	0-2	4	5	10
Tsioropoulos	1-4	0-0	3	1	2
Newton	0-0	0-0	0	0	0
TOTALS	**28-69**	**12-24**	**45**	**23**	**68**

FG%: .406. FT%: .500.

KANSAS STATE (58)	FG-A	FT-A	REB.	PF	PTS.
Head	3-11	2-2	3	2	8
Stone	3-8	6-8	6	2	12
Hitch	6-15	1-1	9	3	13
Barrett	2-12	0-2	3	1	4
Iverson	3-12	1-2	0	3	7
Rousey	2-10	0-0	2	3	4
Gibson	0-2	1-1	1	5	1
Upson	0-1	0-0	2	1	0
Knostman	1-4	1-2	3	1	3
Peck	2-3	0-1	0	0	4
Schuyler	1-2	0-1	1	2	2
TOTALS	**23-80**	**12-20**	**30**	**23**	**58**

FG%: .288. FT%: .600.
Halftime: Kansas State 29-27.

MOST OUTSTANDING PLAYER
None selected.

participate only after he had conceded the contest. "What bothered me most," said Johnson after his club lost 90-88, "was that my players wouldn't pass the ball to me."

1950–51 FINAL NATIONAL POLLS

AP	UPI	SCHOOL
1	1	Kentucky
2	2	Oklahoma St.
3	5	Columbia
4	3	Kansas St.
5	4	Illinois
6	6	Bradley
7	8	Indiana
8	7	North Carolina St.
9	9	St. John's
10	11	St. Louis
11	10	Brigham Young
12	12	Arizona
13	18	Dayton
14	–	Toledo
15	13	Washington
16	–	Murray St.
17	17	Cincinnati
18	–	Siena
19	–	Southern Cal
20	14	Villanova
–	14	Beloit
–	16	UCLA
–	18	St. Bonaventure
–	18	Seton Hall
–	18	Texas A&M

1951 NCAA Tournament

Summary: The scandal surrounding college basketball had not yet focused intensely on Kentucky when the Wildcats captured their third NCAA title in four years.

Star Gazing: Columbia, undefeated entering the tourney (21-0), blew a seven-point, halftime lead and lost in the first round of the East Regional against eventual national third-place finisher Illinois (79-71). The Lions' John Azary was outscored by the Illini's Don Sunderlage (25-13) in a battle of All-American candidates.

Biggest Upset: Oklahoma A&M, entering the tourney with a No. 2 national ranking, fell behind 37-14 at intermission when it was eliminated by Kansas State, 68-44.

Numbers Game: Four teammates outrebounded Kentucky center Bill Spivey in the Wildcats' 79-68 opening-game victory over Louisville before he averaged 16 rebounds per game in their last three tourney contests.

Putting Things in Perspective: North Carolina State, returning the nucleus of a national third-place team, had a 29-4 record after winning the Southern Conference Tournament. But with three standouts (Sam Ranzino, Paul Horvath, and Vic Bubas) ineligible for the NCAA playoffs

1951 CHAMPIONSHIP BRACKET

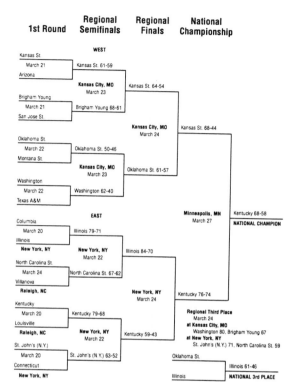

1st Round	Regional Semifinals	Regional Finals	National Championship

WEST

Kansas St.
March 21
Arizona
— Kansas St. 61-59
— Kansas City, MO March 23
Brigham Young
March 21
San Jose St.
— Brigham Young 68-61
— Kansas St. 64-54

Oklahoma St.
March 22
Montana St.
— Oklahoma St. 50-46
— Kansas City, MO March 23
Washington
March 22
Texas A&M
— Washington 62-40
— Oklahoma St. 61-57
— Kansas City, MO March 24
— Kansas St. 68-44

EAST

Columbia
March 20
Illinois
— Illinois 79-71
— New York, NY March 22
North Carolina St.
March 24
Villanova
— North Carolina St. 67-62
— Illinois 84-70

Kentucky
March 20
Louisville
— Kentucky 79-68
— New York, NY March 22
St. John's (N.Y.)
March 20
Connecticut
— St. John's (N.Y.) 63-52
— Kentucky 59-43
— New York, NY March 24
— Kentucky 76-74

Raleigh, NC
Kentucky
Raleigh, NC
New York, NY

Minneapolis, MN March 27 — Kentucky 68-58
NATIONAL CHAMPION

Regional Third Place
March 24
at Kansas City, MO
Washington 80, Brigham Young 67
at New York, NY
St. John's (N.Y.) 71, North Carolina St. 59

Oklahoma St.
— Illinois 61-46
Illinois — **NATIONAL 3rd PLACE**

because they were in their fourth year of varsity competition, N.C. State was eliminated in the second round by Illinois (84-70).

1951–52

AT A GLANCE

NCAA Champion: Kansas (26-2).

NIT Champion: La Salle (25-7).

New Rules: Games are played in four 10-minute quarters. Previously, games were played in two 20-minute halves.

NCAA Consensus First-Team All-Americans: Chuck Darling, C, Sr., Iowa; Rod Fletcher, G, Sr., Illinois; Dick Groat, G, Sr., Duke; Cliff Hagan, F, Jr., Kentucky; Clyde Lovellette, C, Sr., Kansas.

Freshmen made an impact long before the early 1970s when they permanently gained eligibility. Freshman Tom Gola led NIT champion La Salle in scoring (17.2 ppg) and rebounding (16.5 rpg). He was allowed to play varsity ball because La Salle's enrollment was below 1,000. Another standout freshman was Wichita State's Cleo Littleton, who was named to the first five on the All-Missouri Valley Conference team.

Kansas' Clyde Lovellette became the only Big Eight Conference player ever to lead the nation in scoring (28.4 ppg). Defending scoring champion Bill Mlkvy of Temple plummeted to 42nd (17.4 ppg).

Duke's Dick Groat, who would later become a star shortstop in the majors, was national runner-up in scoring and assists.

LSU's Bob Pettit recorded the biggest one-game output of the season with 50 points against Georgia.

Seattle's 5-8 Johnny O'Brien became the first college player to score 1,000 or more points in a season when he amassed 1,051 points in 37 games for a 28.4 average. He had 43 points in a shocking 84-81 victory over the Harlem Globetrotters in a special game played to raise money for the U.S. Olympic Games Fund. The mighty Globetrotters, in an era before they went exclusively to entertainment, usually opened a big lead before going into their crowd-pleasing antics. But they were without ballhandling wizard Marques Haynes against Seattle because he had to appear at his draft board. O'Brien scored most of his points against Globetrotters great Goose Tatum.

Army's Bill Hannon became the shortest player (6-3) to ever lead the nation in rebounding. He averaged 20.9 rebounds per game.

Colgate's Al Antinelli fouled out of 15 of 22 games.

Field-goal accuracy was only 33.7 percent per game despite an all-time high 140.64 field-goal attempts per outing for both teams.

1951–52 FINAL NATIONAL POLLS

AP	UPI	SCHOOL
1	1	Kentucky
2	2	Illinois
3	6	Kansas St.
4	4	Duquesne
5	7	St. Louis
6	5	Washington
7	8	Iowa
8	3	Kansas
9	14	West Virginia
10	9	St. John's
11	18	Dayton
12	–	Duke
13	15	Holy Cross
14	12	Seton Hall
15	11	St. Bonaventure
16	10	Wyoming
17	19	Louisville
18	–	Seattle
19	20	UCLA
20	–	SW Texas St.
–	13	Texas Christian
–	16	Western Kentucky
–	17	La Salle
–	20	Indiana

Kentucky, the first school to lead the nation in scoring with an average of more than 80 points per game (82.3), claimed its ninth consecutive SEC regular-season title. Tennessee's Herb Neff set an SEC record with 36 rebounds against Georgia Tech.

Arizona's 81-game homecourt winning streak, which started in 1945, was snapped by Kansas State, 76-57.

Idaho State won its eighth consecutive Rocky Mountain Conference crown and North Carolina State captured its sixth consecutive Southern Conference Tournament championship.

1952 NCAA Tournament

Summary: Legendary coach Phog Allen, running out of time in which to capture an elu-

1951–52 INDIVIDUAL LEADERS

SCORING

PLAYER	PTS.	AVG.
Lovellette, Kansas	795	28.4
Groat, Duke	780	26.0
Pettit, Louisiana St.	612	25.5
Darling, Iowa	561	25.5
Selvy, Furman	591	24.6
Workman, West Virginia	577	23.1
Retherford, Baldwin-Wallace	457	21.8
Hemric, Wake Forest	629	21.7
Hagan, Kentucky	692	21.6
Clune, Navy	487	21.2

REBOUNDING

PLAYER	REB.	AVG.
Hannon, Army	355	20.9
Dukes, Seton Hall	513	19.7
Beck, Pennsylvania	551	19.0
Tuttle, Creighton	396	18.9
Chamber, William & Mary	509	18.2
Molinas, Columbia	234	18.0
Hemric, Wake Forest	510	17.5

Workman, West Virginia	437	17.5
Gola, La Salle	497	17.1
Peterson, Oregon	465	16.6

ASSISTS

PLAYER	AST.	AVG.
O'Toole, Boston College	213	7.9
Groat, Duke	229	7.6
McLean, Davidson	187	7.5
Friedman, Muhlenberg	168	7.3
Chadwick, Cornell	171	6.9
Simms, Xavier	150	6.3
Holmes, West Virginia	160	6.2
Heim, Xavier	145	6.0
Burch, Pittsburgh	131	6.0
Rhodes, Western Kentucky	182	5.9

FIELD GOAL PERCENTAGE

PLAYER	FGM	FGA	PCT.
Spoelstra, Western Kentucky	178	345	.516
Rogers, Texas Western	136	270	.504
Swanson, Detroit	172	342	.503

Klinar, Virginia Military	98	199	.492
Marshall, Western Kentucky	189	385	.491
Workman, West Virginia	207	430	.481
Lovellette, Kansas	315	660	.477
Patton, Denver	93	198	.470
Daukas, Boston College	136	290	.469
Preston, Hardin-Simmons	117	250	.468

FREE THROW PERCENTAGE

PLAYER	FTM	FTA	PCT.
Chadroff, Miami (Fla.)	99	123	.805
Kenney, Kansas	110	137	.803
Turner, St. Mary's	81	101	.802
Bartlett, Tennessee	93	116	.802
Rerucha, Colorado A&M	76	95	.800
Moore, West Virginia	68	85	.800
Tuttle, New Mexico	87	110	.791
Meineke, Dayton	194	246	.789
Bunt, New York Univ.	85	108	.787
Feiereisel, DePaul	113	144	.785

1951–52 TEAM LEADERS

SCORING OFFENSE

SCHOOL	PTS.	AVG.
Kentucky	2635	82.3
West Virginia	2172	80.4
Louisville	2080	80.0
Duke	2320	77.3
Western Kentucky	2388	77.0

SCORING DEFENSE

SCHOOL	PTS.	AVG.
Oklahoma A&M	1228	45.5
Oklahoma City	1287	47.7

Texas A&M	1159	48.3
New Mexico A&M	1514	48.8
Texas Christian	1395	49.8

FIELD GOAL PERCENTAGE

SCHOOL	FGM	FGA	PCT.
Boston College	787	1893	.416
Western Kentucky	959	2339	.410
Seton Hall	783	1941	.403
Stanford	743	1889	.393
Kansas	748	1906	.392
Furman	691	1761	.392

FREE THROW PERCENTAGE

SCHOOL	FTM	FTA	PCT.
Kansas	491	707	.6944
Pennsylvania	454	654	.6941
Kansas St.	473	684	.692
South Carolina	400	582	.687
Syracuse	430	626	.687

1951–52 NCAA CHAMPION: KANSAS

SEASON STATISTICS OF KANSAS REGULARS

PLAYER	POS.	CL.	G.	FG%	FT%	PPG	RPG
Clyde Lovellette	C	Sr.	31	.474	.728	28.6	13.2
Bob Kenney	F	Sr.	30	.360	.789	13.1	3.8
Bill Hougland	G	Sr.	30	.391	.742	6.8	5.6
Dean Kelley	G	Jr.	31	.397	.605	6.5	3.3
Bill Lienhard	F	Sr.	29	.303	.700	5.8	3.3
Charlie Hoag	F-G	Jr.	21	.303	.564	5.2	3.0
John Keller	F-G	Sr.	27	.388	.767	2.3	2.7
B. H. Born	C	So.	27	.304	.613	1.7	1.2
Bill Heitholt	G-F	Fr.	28	.237	.454	1.5	1.9
Dean Smith	G	Jr.	19	.455	.500	1.5	0.6
Larry Davenport	F	Fr.	22	.324	.700	1.4	1.0
TEAM TOTALS			31	.390	.692	71.3	37.8

Note: Statistics include three games in Olympic Trials after NCAA Tournament.

1951 CHAMPIONSHIP GAME

MINNEAPOLIS, MN

KENTUCKY (68)	FG-A	FT-A	REB.	PF	PTS.
Whitaker	4-5	1-1	2	2	9
Linville	2-7	4-8	8	5	8
Spivey	9-29	4-6	21	2	22
Ramsey	4-10	1-3	4	5	9
Watson	3-8	2-4	3	3	8
Hagan	5-6	0-2	4	5	10
Tsioropoulos	1-4	0-0	3	1	2
Newton	0-0	0-0	0	0	0
TOTALS	**28-69**	**12-24**	**45**	**23**	**68**

FG%: .406. FT%: .500.

KANSAS STATE (58)	FG-A	FT-A	REB.	PF	PTS.
Head	3-11	2-2	3	2	8
Stone	3-8	6-8	6	2	12
Hitch	6-15	1-1	9	3	13
Barrett	2-12	0-2	3	1	4
Iverson	3-12	1-2	0	3	7
Rousey	2-10	0-0	2	3	4
Gibson	0-2	1-1	1	5	1
Upson	0-1	0-0	2	1	0
Knostman	1-4	1-2	3	1	3
Peck	2-3	0-1	0	0	4
Schuyler	1-2	0-1	1	2	2
TOTALS	**23-80**	**12-20**	**30**	**23**	**58**

FG%: .288. FT%: .600.
Halftime: Kansas State 29-27.

ALL-TOURNAMENT TEAM

Dean Kelley, G, Jr., Kansas
John Kerr, C, Soph., Illinois
Clyde Lovellette, C, Sr., Kansas*
Ron MacGilvray, G, Sr., St. John's
Bob Zawoluk, C, Sr., St. John's
*–Most Outstanding Tournament Player

sive national championship, achieved his goal thanks in large part to Clyde Lovellette. Lovellette is the only player to crack the 30-point plateau in the national semifinals and final in the same season (33 points against both Santa Clara in the semifinals and St. John's in the final).

Biggest Upset: St. John's gained sweet revenge against the nation's top-ranked team. Defending NCAA champion Kentucky humili-

1952 CHAMPIONSHIP BRACKET

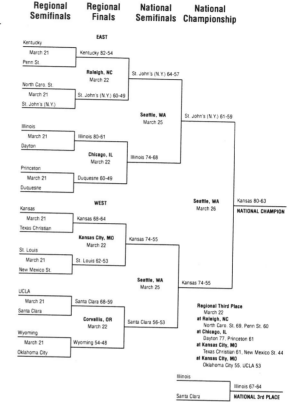

ated the Redmen by 41 points (81-40) early in the season. But St. John's, sparked by center Bob Zawoluk's 32 points, avenged the rout by eliminating the Wildcats (64-57) in the East Regional, ending their 23-game winning streak.

One and Only: Lovellette is the only player to lead the nation in scoring average (28.4 ppg) while playing for a team reaching the NCAA Tournament championship game.

What If: Kansas State finished runner-up in the Big Seven Conference to NCAA champion-to-be Kansas, a team the Wildcats defeated at home in Manhattan by 17 points. K-State, ranked 3rd by AP and 6th by UPI after finishing as national runner-up to Kentucky the previous year, lost another matchup against the Jayhawks on a neutral court in overtime.

1952-53

AT A GLANCE

NCAA Champion: Indiana (23-3).

NIT Champion: Seton Hall (31-2).

New Conference: California Basketball Association (forerunner of West Coast).

New Rules: Teams no longer waive free throws in favor of taking the ball out of bounds. The one-and-one free-throw rule is introduced although the bonus is used only if the first shot misfires. The rule will be in effect the entire game except the last three minutes, when every foul is two shots. The NCAA Tournament bracket expands from 16 teams to 22 and fluctuates between 22 and 25 until 1974.

NCAA Probation: Bradley, Kentucky.

NCAA Consensus First-Team All-Americans: Ernie Beck, F, Sr., Penn; Walter Dukes, C, Jr., Seton Hall; Tom Gola, C-F, Soph., La Salle; Bob Houbregs, C, Sr., Washington; Johnny O'Brien, G, Sr., Seattle.

College basketball's record book was overhauled when intercollegiate competition was interpreted as being between varsity teams of four-year, degree-granting universities. In effect, the ruling negated games against AAU, service, junior college, alumni, and freshman teams. The decision stemmed from 100-point plus outings by Rio Grande's Clarence "Bevo" Francis and Los Angeles State's John Barber. In response to Francis' 113-point performance, Los Angeles State coach Sax Elliott scheduled a game for his team with the Chapman junior varsity and had his players concentrate on feeding Barber, a 6-6 center. Los Angeles State won, 206-82, as Barber scored 188 points.

Furman became the first school to average more than 90 points per game (90.2). Furman's Frank Selvy supplied the season's top scoring effort with 63 points against Mercer.

1952-53 INDIVIDUAL LEADERS

SCORING

PLAYER	PTS.	AVG.
Selvy, Furman	738	29.5
Hennessey, Villanova	438	29.2
J. O'Brien, Seattle	884	28.5
Dukes, Seton Hall	861	26.1
Beck, Pennsylvania	673	25.9
Houbregs, Washington	800	25.8
Schlundt, Indiana	661	25.4
Hemric, Wake Forest	623	24.9
Dalton, John Carroll	669	24.8
Pettit, Louisiana St.	519	24.7

REBOUNDING

PLAYER	REB.	AVG.
Conlin, Fordham	612	23.5
Dukes, Seton Hall	734	22.2

Chambers, William & Mary	480	21.8
Quimby, Connecticut	430	20.5
Virostek, Pittsburgh	424	20.2
Estergard, Bradley	540	20.0
Hannon, Army	365	19.2
Holup, George Washington	396	18.0
Lange, Navy	374	17.8
Tuttle, Creighton	438	17.5

FIELD GOAL PERCENTAGE

PLAYER	FGM	FGA	PCT.
Stokes, St. Francis (NY)	147	247	.595
Houbregs, Washington	306	564	.543
E. O'Brien, Seattle	176	325	.542
J. O'Brien, Seattle	276	518	.533
Hoxie, Niagara	125	235	.532
Spoelstra, W. Kentucky	188	356	.528
Gordon, Furman	249	483	.516

Holup, G. Washington	154	301	.512
Nathanic, Seton Hall	111	222	.500
Glowaski, Seattle	199	405	.491

FREE THROW PERCENTAGE

PLAYER	FTM	FTA	PCT.
Weber, Yale	117	141	.830
Dohner, Virginia	96	117	.821
Sharp, Wyoming	163	200	.815
Sheets, Oklahoma A&M	87	107	.813
Matheny, California	101	125	.808
J. O'Brien, Seattle	332	411	.808
Schlundt, Indiana	249	310	.803
Perry, Holy Cross	101	126	.802
Ollrich, Drake	137	171	.801
Beck, Pennsylvania	183	229	.799

1952-53 TEAM LEADERS

SCORING OFFENSE

SCHOOL	PTS.	AVG.
Furman	2435	90.2
Seattle	2818	88.1
George Washington	1890	85.9
Duke	2093	83.7
Miami (Ohio)	1916	83.3

SCORING DEFENSE

SCHOOL	PTS.	AVG.
Oklahoma A&M	1614	53.8
Maryland	1256	54.6

Oklahoma City	1338	55.8
Wyoming	1676	55.9
San Jose St.	1293	56.2

FIELD GOAL PERCENTAGE

SCHOOL	FGM	FGA	PCT.
Furman	936	2106	.444
Niagara	718	1640	.438
Seattle	1019	2350	.434
Seton Hall	914	2129	.429
William & Mary	603	1410	.428

FREE THROW PERCENTAGE

SCHOOL	FTM	FTA	PCT.
George Washington	502	696	.721
Pennsylvania	502	702	.715
Oklahoma City	548	771	.711
Loyola (Ill.)	525	743	.707
Fordham	493	699	.705

1952–53 NCAA CHAMPION: INDIANA

SEASON STATISTICS OF INDIANA REGULARS

PLAYER	POS.	CL.	G.	FG%	FT%	PPG	RPG
Don Schlundt	C	So.	26	.432	.803	25.4	8.5
Bob Leonard	G	Jr.	26	.326	.667	16.3	...
Dick Farley	F	Jr.	26	.443	.694	10.1	...
Burke Scott	G	So.	26	.369	.647	8.0	...
Charles Kraak	F	Jr.	26	.356	.588	7.2	...
Dick White	F	So.	22	.313	.741	5.6	...
Phil Byers	G	So.	23	.347	.542	2.7	...
James DeaKyne	G	Jr.	20	.230	.417	2.3	...
TEAM TOTALS			26	.365	.701	81.2	...

1953 CHAMPIONSHIP GAME

KANSAS CITY, MO

INDIANA (69)	FG-A	FT-A	PF	PTS.
Kraak	5-8	7-10	5	17
DeaKyne	0-0	0-0	1	0
Farley	1-8	0-0	5	2
Schlundt	11-26	8-11	3	30
White	1-5	0-0	2	2
Leonard	5-15	2-4	2	12
Poff	0-1	0-0	0	0
Scott	2-4	2-3	3	6
Byers	0-2	0-0	1	0
TOTALS	**25-69**	**19-28**	**22**	**69**

FG%: .362. FT%: .679.

KANSAS (68)	FG-A	FT-A	PF	PTS.
Patterson	1-3	7-8	3	9
A. Kelley	7-20	6-8	3	20
Davenport	0-1	0-0	0	0
Born	8-27	10-12	5	26
Smith	0-0	1-1	1	1
Alberts	0-1	0-0	1	0
D. Kelley	3-4	2-4	2	8
Reich	2-9	0-0	2	4
TOTALS	**21-65**	**26-33**	**17**	**68**

FG%: .323. FT%: .788.
Halftime: Tied 41-41.

ALL-TOURNAMENT TEAM

B. H. Born, C, Jr., Kansas
Bob Houbregs, C, Sr., Washington
Dean Kelley, G, Sr., Kansas
Bob Leonard, G, Jr., Indiana
Don Schlundt, C, Soph., Indiana
*Named Most Outstanding Player

A couple of major rebounding records were established. William & Mary's Bill Chambers grabbed an NCAA record 51 rebounds in a game against Virginia. Seton Hall's Walter Dukes set an NCAA single-season record by retrieving a total of 734 missed shots.

Niagara outlasted Siena, 88-81, in a six-overtime game. Niagara's Ed Fleming played all 70 minutes and teammate Larry Costello played all but 20 seconds before fouling out. As a result, Fleming had his uniform number changed to 70 and Costello's was changed to 69. Oddly, one of the referees in the game was Max Tabbachi, who had officiated a five-overtime NBA game between Rochester and Indianapolis two seasons earlier.

The University of Chicago, a former powerhouse, ended its losing streak at 45 games with a 65-52 victory over Illinois-Navy Pier.

Seattle's Johnny O'Brien finished among the top six in both field-goal shooting (53.3 percent) and free-throw accuracy (80.8).

Western Kentucky's Art Spoelstra, who led the nation in field-goal marksmanship (51.6 percent) the previous season, improved to 52.8 percent, yet finished sixth.

Washington's Bob Houbregs (49 points against Idaho) and Penn's Ernie Beck (47 against Duke) set school single-game scoring records.

Northern Arizona set an NCAA record by attempting 79 free throws (46 made) in a game against Arizona on January 26, 1953. A new free-throw rule increased attempts from the charity stripe to a staggering 65.8 per game for both teams.

The season marked the greatest increase in points per game from one year to the next (126.6 to 138.1).

Oklahoma A&M captured its 14th team defense title in 19 seasons although it was the first time a Hank Iba-coached squad allowed as many as 50 points per game (53.8).

Wake Forest ended North Carolina State's streak of six consecutive Southern Conference Tournament championships.

Dayton, struggling to stay above .500, pulled off the biggest upset of the season when the Flyers toppled top-ranked Seton Hall, 71-65. The Pirates, who would go on to capture the NIT, entered the game with a 25-0 record.

Pete Mullins, the sixth-place finisher in the 1948 Olympic decathlon while competing for Australia, finished as Washington State's leading scorer with 13.3 points per game. He had been the Cougars' second-leading scorer as a sophomore and third-leading scorer as a junior.

Utah's Vadal Peterson ended his 26-year coaching career with a 386-223 record.

1952–53 FINAL NATIONAL POLLS

AP	UPI	SCHOOL
1	1	Indiana
2	2	Seton Hall
3	5	Kansas
4	3	Washington
5	6	Louisiana St.
6	4	La Salle
7	–	St. John's
8	7	Oklahoma St.
9	20	Duquesne
10	13	Notre Dame
11	10	Illinois
12	9	Kansas St.
13	17	Holy Cross
14	–	Seattle
15	–	Wake Forest
16	–	Santa Clara
17	11	Western Kentucky
18	8	North Carolina St.
19	14	DePaul
20	–	S.W. Missouri St.
–	12	California
–	14	Wyoming
–	16	St. Louis
–	18	Oklahoma City
–	19	Brigham Young

1953 NCAA Tournament

Summary: Junior guard Bob Leonard supplied the decisive point by hitting one of two free throws with 27 seconds remaining to give Indiana a 69-68 victory over defending champion Kansas in the final. Don Schlundt, averaging 25.4 points per game for Indiana as a sophomore center, is the only player to never appear in the NBA or ABA after averaging more than 20 points per game for a team reaching the NCAA championship game. Schlundt, a 1955 draft choice of the Syracuse Nationals, became successful in the insurance business after rejecting their contract offer of $6,000.

Star Gazing: B. H. Born, the only Kansas starter taller than 6-1, scored more points in two Final Four games (51) for the national runner-up Jayhawks than he did the entire previous season when he averaged just 1.7 points per game as a sophomore backup to Clyde Lovellette, who was named Most Outstanding Player in powering KU to the 1952 title.

Biggest Upset: George (Rinso) Marquette, the first-year coach at Lebanon Valley (Pa.), guided the Flying Dutchmen to the NCAA Tournament when they received an invitation after La Salle and Seton Hall chose to go to the NIT. Lebanon Valley's "Seven Dwarfs"—no player was taller than 6-1—won the Middle Atlantic Conference and led the nation in field-goal shooting (47.2 percent). They flogged Fordham, 80-67, in the first round of the East Regional before bowing to a Bob Pettit-led LSU, an eventual Final Four team. Lebanon Valley, with a current enrollment of 900 after having 425 students in 1953, remains the smallest school ever to play in the tournament. The leading scorer for Lebanon Valley was Howie Landa, who went on to coach nationally-ranked Mercer County (N.J.) Community College and then serve as an assistant to both the men's and women's teams at UNLV.

One and Only: Kansas' Dean Kelley became the only player to have season scoring averages of fewer than 10 points per game in back-to-back years in which he was named to the All-NCAA Tournament team. He and fellow guard Allen Kelley are the only set of brothers to play together in two NCAA playoff title games.

Numbers Game: Of the nearly 50 coaches reaching the national semifinals at least twice, Indiana's Branch McCracken is the only one to compile an undefeated Final Four record. He also won the championship in 1940. . . . Seattle's Johnny O'Brien, a 5-8 unanimous first team All-American, became the only player to score more than 40 points in his first playoff game. He had 42 in an 88-77 victory over Idaho State.

What If: Mighty Kentucky was barred from playing a competitive schedule.

Putting Things in Perspective: Indiana almost finished undefeated, losing three games during the regular season by a total of five points on field goals scored with fewer than five seconds remaining.

1953 CHAMPIONSHIP BRACKET

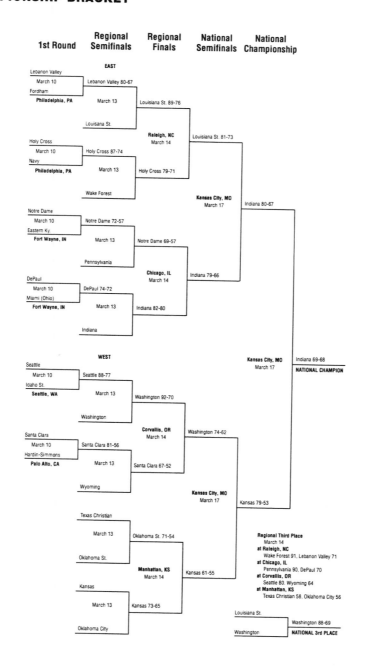

1st Round	Regional Semifinals	Regional Finals	National Semifinals	National Championship

EAST

Lebanon Valley
March 10
Fordham
Philadelphia, PA

Lebanon Valley 80-67
March 13

Louisana St.

Louisiana St. 89-76

Raleigh, NC
March 14

Holy Cross
March 10
Navy
Philadelphia, PA

Holy Cross 87-74
March 13

Wake Forest

Holy Cross 79-71

Louisiana St. 81-73

Kansas City, MO
March 17

Indiana 80-67

Notre Dame
March 10
Eastern Ky.
Fort Wayne, IN

Notre Dame 72-57
March 13

Pennsylvania

Notre Dame 69-57

Chicago, IL
March 14

DePaul
March 10
Miami (Ohio)
Fort Wayne, IN

DePaul 74-72
March 13

Indiana

Indiana 82-80

Indiana 79-66

Kansas City, MO
March 17

Indiana 69-68
NATIONAL CHAMPION

WEST

Seattle
March 10
Idaho St.
Seattle, WA

Seattle 88-77
March 13

Washington

Washington 92-70

Corvallis, OR
March 14

Santa Clara
March 10
Hardin-Simmons
Palo Alto, CA

Santa Clara 81-56
March 13

Wyoming

Santa Clara 67-52

Washington 74-62

Kansas City, MO
March 17

Kansas 79-53

Texas Christian
March 13
Oklahoma St.

Oklahoma St. 71-54

Manhattan, KS
March 14

Kansas
March 13
Oklahoma City

Kansas 73-65

Kansas 61-55

Regional Third Place
March 14
at Raleigh, NC
Wake Forest 91, Lebanon Valley 71
at Chicago, IL
Pennsylvania 90, DePaul 70
at Corvallis, OR
Seattle 80, Wyoming 64
at Manhattan, KS
Texas Christian 58, Oklahoma City 56

Louisiana St.

Washington

Washington 88-69
NATIONAL 3rd PLACE

1953-54

AT A GLANCE

NCAA Champion: La Salle (26-4).

NIT Champion: Holy Cross (26-2).

New Conference: ACC.

New Rule: The Tuesday-Wednesday format for the NCAA Tournament semifinals and final changes to Friday-Saturday.

NCAA Probation: Arizona State.

NCAA Consensus First-Team All-Americans: Tom Gola, C-F, Jr., La Salle; Cliff Hagan, F, Sr., Kentucky; Bob Pettit, C, Sr., Louisiana State; Don Schlundt, C, Jr., Indiana; Frank Selvy, F, Sr., Furman.

Furman forward Frank Selvy scored 100 points vs. Newberry on his way to becoming the first three-year player to reach 2,000 points, finishing with 2,538. (See accompanying box for more details.) Selvy (41.7 ppg) and Darrell Floyd (24.3)

combined for 66 points per game during the season and are the highest-scoring duo in major-college history. Selvy scored 50 or more in seven games. Despite Selvy's explosions, scoring decreased nationally for the first time in 19 years, from 138.1 the previous season to 137.9.

Teammates Joe Holup (57.2 percent) and Elliott Karver (56.1) finished one-two in the country in field-goal accuracy to help George Washington lead the nation in that category.

Kentucky finished among the top 10 in team offense for the eighth consecutive season in which it participated (barred from playing in 1952–53 as the result of an NCAA ruling regarding improper payments to players).

Western Kentucky's Ed Diddle became the first coach to reach the 600-win plateau.

Virginia guard Buzz Wilkinson set ACC Tournament records for most field-goal attempts (13 of 44) and free-throw attempts (16 of 22) when he scored 42 points in a 76-68 first-round defeat against Duke. The ACC's inaugural season

SELVY SCORES RECORD 100 POINTS On February 13, 1954, Furman forward Frank Selvy scored 100 points vs. Newberry on his way to becoming the first three-year player to reach 2,000 points. (He wound up with a career total of 2,538.) Making Selvy's 100-point outburst even more amazing was the fact that his mother, watching her son play for the first time, was among several hundred fans from his hometown of Corbin, Kentucky, who made the trip to Furman, located in Greenville, South Carolina, to watch the game. An early indication that something special was in the offing came less than three minutes into the game when the Newberry player (Bobby Bailey) assigned to defend Selvy fouled out.

Selvy's last three field goals came in the game's closing 30 seconds, and the crowning moment was his final basket. "It (the 100-point game) was something that was just meant to be," Selvy said. "My last basket was from past halfcourt just before the final buzzer." Selvy hit 41 of 66 shots from the floor and 18 of 22 from the free-throw line. He played every minute of every game that season.

FURMAN (149)	FG	FT-A	PTS.	NEWBERRY (95)	FG	FT-A	PTS.
Bennett	0	1-1	1	Boland	0	0-0	0
Floyd	12	1-1	25	Warner	2	0-4	4
Fraley	3	0-2	6	Leitner	6	4-7	16
Poole	0	0-0	0	Bailey	0	1-2	1
Thomas	5	1-1	11	Blanko	14	7-10	35
Kyber	0	0-2	0	Cone	1	0-0	2
Roth	0	0-0	0	Roth	0	3-4	3
Gordon	0	0-0	0	McKlven	1	0-0	2
Selvy	41	18-22	100	Davis	13	6-7	32
Deardorff	1	1-1	3	**TOTALS**	**37**	**21-34**	**95**
Wright	0	0-0	0				
Jones	0	1-1	1				
Gilreath	1	0-0	2				
TOTALS	**63**	**23-31**	**149**				

Halftime: Furman 77-44.

marked the only time North Carolina finished fifth or worse in the league standings.

Wade "Swede" Halbrook, a 7-3, 245-pound sophomore, averaged 21.2 points and 11.9 rebounds per game for Oregon State. He was called "the largest man in basketball history" by the *NCAA Basketball Guide*.

1953–54 FINAL NATIONAL POLLS

AP	UPI	SCHOOL
1	2	Kentucky
2	11	La Salle
3	9	Holy Cross
4	1	Indiana
5	3	Duquesne
6	5	Notre Dame
7	–	Bradley
8	6	Western Kentucky
9	–	Penn St.
10	4	Oklahoma St.
11	14	Southern Cal
12	–	George Wash.
13	10	Iowa
14	8	Louisiana St.
15	20	Duke
16	–	Niagara
17	17	Seattle
18	7	Kansas
19	12	Illinois
20	–	Maryland
–	13	Colorado St.
–	14	North Carolina St.
–	16	Oregon St.
–	17	Dayton
–	19	Rice

Furman's Frank Selvy shoots for 2, on his way to 100 points vs. Newberry.

1954 NCAA Tournament

Summary: After a one-year schedule boycott, Kentucky's undefeated squad declined a bid to the NCAA playoffs because its three fifth-year (postgraduate) stars—Cliff Hagan, Frank Ramsey, and Lou Tsioropoulos—were ineligible. The Wildcats defeated national champion-to-be La Salle by 13 points in the UK Invitation Tournament final on their way to being ranked 1st by AP and 2nd by UPI. UK had just two games tighter than a 12-point decision (77-71 over Xavier and 63-56 over LSU). Sandwiched between those two contests were 16 victories by an average margin of 33.7 points. Without UK, La Salle's achievement lost some of its significance.

Outcome for Defending Champion: Big Ten champion Indiana (20-4) lost its tourney opener to Notre Dame, 65-64.

Star Gazing: Tom Gola is the only individual to be named both NCAA Final Four Most Outstanding Player and NIT Most Valuable Player in his career. Gola led La Salle to the 1954 NCAA crown with a 23-point average. Two years earlier as a freshman when the Explorers won the NIT, he shared the MVP award with teammate Norm Grekin.

Biggest Upset: Penn State, supposedly the final team selected for the NCAA playoffs, reached the Final Four by winning its first three tourney games by at least eight points—knocking off Toledo and a Bob Pettit-led LSU before snapping Notre Dame's 18-game winning streak.

One and Only: The worst composite winning percentage when four teams arrived at the national semifinals was this year as La Salle (24-4), Bradley (18-12), Penn State (17-5), and South-

La Salle's Tom Gola.

Junior center Jesse Arnelle led Cinderella-story Penn State to the NCAA Final Four.

ern California (19-12) combined for a 78-33 record (.703). Southern Cal lost both of its Final Four games (against Bradley and Penn State) to become the only national semifinalist with as many as 14 defeats. Bradley lost the championship game against La Salle to become one of only three Final Four squads to finish a season with more than a dozen defeats.

Numbers Game: Of the more than 40 different players to score more than 225 points in the playoffs and/or average over 25 points per tournament game (minimum of six games), LSU's Bob Pettit is the only one to score more than 22 points in every postseason contest (six games in 1953 and 1954). He is the only player from that select group to have a single-digit differential between his high game (36 points) and his low game (27).

Putting Things in Perspective: Niagara (24-6) defeated La Salle twice by a total of 27 points before finishing in third place in the NIT.

1953-54 INDIVIDUAL LEADERS

SCORING

PLAYER	PTS.	AVG.
Selvy, Furman	1209	41.7
Pettit, Louisiana St.	785	31.4
Wilkinson, Virginia	814	30.1
Short, Oklahoma City	696	27.8
Schafer, Villanova	836	27.0
Walowac, Marshall	548	26.1
Marshall, W. Kentucky	829	25.9
Kerr, Illinois	556	25.3
Bianchi, Bowling Green	600	25.0
Palazzi, Holy Cross	670	24.8

Gola, La Salle	652	21.7
Sundstrom, Rutgers	494	20.6
Koch, St. Louis	502	20.1
Tuttle, Creighton	601	20.0
Russell, San Francisco	403	19.2
Holup, George Washington	484	18.6
Conlin, Fordham	417	17.4
Hannon, Army	381	17.3

REBOUNDING

PLAYER	REB.	AVG.
Quimby, Connecticut	588	22.6
Slack, Marshall	466	22.2

FIELD GOAL PERCENTAGE

PLAYER	FGM	FGA	PCT.
Holup, G. Wash.	179	313	.572
Karver, G. Wash.	124	221	.561
Mattick, Okla. A&M	199	358	.556
Hoxie, Niagara	115	211	.545
Spoelstra, W. Kentucky	202	381	.530
Carpenter, Texas Tech	110	214	.514
Shue, Maryland	237	469	.505
Hemric, Wake Forest	225	446	.504
Heim, Xavier	139	277	.502
Schlundt, Indiana	177	354	.500

FREE THROW PERCENTAGE

PLAYER	FTM	FTA	PCT.
Daugherty, Arizona St.	75	86	.872
Kelley, Kansas	75	87	.862
Powell, Florida	166	195	.851
Dalton, John Carroll	189	225	.840
Nystedt, New Mexico	98	118	.831
Short, Oklahoma City	232	282	.823
Costello, Niagara	125	152	.822
Lamkin, DePaul	105	128	.820
Williams, San Jose St.	184	225	.818
Devlin, G. Wash.	115	141	.816

1953-54 TEAM LEADERS

SCORING OFFENSE

SCHOOL	PTS.	AVG.
Furman	2658	91.7
Kentucky	2187	87.5
W. Kentucky	2730	85.3
Duke	2250	83.3
Holy Cross	2329	83.2

SCORING DEFENSE

SCHOOL	PTS.	AVG.
Oklahoma A&M	1539	53.1

Duquesne	1551	53.5
Wyoming	1522	54.4
Oregon State	1585	54.7
Oklahoma City	1370	54.8

FIELD GOAL PERCENTAGE

SCHOOL	FGM	FGA	PCT.
George Washington	744	1632	.456
Holy Cross	871	2018	.432
Niagara	778	1817	.428
Maryland	669	1564	.428
Furman	990	2370	.418

FREE THROW PERCENTAGE

SCHOOL	FTM	FTA	PCT.
Wake Forest	734	1010	.727
Florida	540	746	.724
Tulane	422	583	.724
New Mexico	444	614	.723
Niagara	667	929	.718

1953-54 NCAA CHAMPION: LA SALLE

SEASON STATISTICS OF LA SALLE REGULARS

PLAYER	POS.	CL.	G.	FG%	FT%	PPG	RPG
Tom Gola	C-G	Jr.	30	.407	.732	23.0	21.7
Charlie Singley	F	So.	30	.382	.654	10.7	5.1
Frank Blatcher	F	So.	27	.374	.640	10.4	4.6
Frank O'Hara	G	Sr.	30	.406	.708	9.6	3.7
Fran O'Malley	G-F	So.	30	.345	.697	7.4	4.6
Bob Maples	C-F	So.	30	.404	.554	6.9	4.7
Charles Greenberg	F-G	So.	26	.311	.545	4.7	3.0
John Yodsnukis	C	So.	18	.304	.625	4.6	5.7
Bob Ames	F	So.	14	.300	.769	2.0	0.9
Manuel Gomez	C	So.	16	.167	.462	0.6	0.8
TEAM TOTALS			30	.378	.667	75.4	51.1

1954 CHAMPIONSHIP GAME

KANSAS CITY, MO

LA SALLE (92)	FG	FT-A	PF	PTS.
Singley	8	7-10	4	23
Greenberg	2	1-2	1	5
Maples	2	0-0	4	4
Blatcher	11	1-2	4	23
Gola	7	5-5	5	19
O'Malley	5	1-1	4	11
Yodsnukis	0	0-0	5	0
O'Hara	2	2-3	1	7
TOTALS	37	18-24	28	92

FT%: .750.

BRADLEY (76)	FG	FT-A	PF	PTS.
Petersen	4	2-2	2	10
Babetch	0	0-0	0	0
King	3	6-7	4	12
Gower	0	1-2	1	1
Estergard	3	11-12	1	17
Carney	3	11-17	4	17
Utt	0	0-0	1	0
Kent	8	0-2	2	16
Riley	1	1-2	1	3
TOTALS	22	32-44	16	76

FT%: .727.
Halftime: Bradley 43-42.

ALL-TOURNAMENT TEAM

Jesse Arnelle, C, Jr., Penn State
Bob Carney, G, Sr., Bradley
Tom Gola, C-F, Jr., La Salle*
Roy Irvin, C, Jr., Southern Cal
Chuck Singley, F, Soph., La Salle
*Named Most Outstanding Player

1954 CHAMPIONSHIP BRACKET

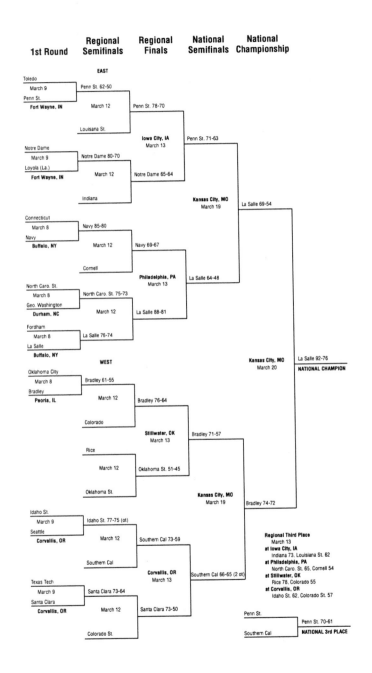

1st Round	Regional Semifinals	Regional Finals	National Semifinals	National Championship

EAST

Toledo
March 9
Penn St.
Fort Wayne, IN

Penn St. 62-50
March 12

Louisana St.

Penn St. 78-70

Notre Dame
March 9
Loyola (La.)
Fort Wayne, IN

Notre Dame 80-70
March 12

Indiana

Notre Dame 65-64

Iowa City, IA
March 13

Penn St. 71-63

Connecticut
March 8
Navy
Buffalo, NY

Navy 85-80
March 12

Cornell

Navy 69-67

North Caro. St.
March 8
Geo. Washington
Durham, NC

North Caro. St. 75-73
March 12

La Salle 88-81

Philadelphia, PA
March 13

La Salle 64-48

Fordham
March 8
La Salle
Buffalo, NY

La Salle 75-74

Kansas City, MO
March 19

La Salle 69-54

WEST

Oklahoma City
March 8
Bradley
Peoria, IL

Bradley 61-55
March 12

Colorado

Bradley 76-64

Rice
March 12
Oklahoma St.

Oklahoma St. 51-45

Stillwater, OK
March 13

Bradley 71-57

Idaho St.
March 9
Seattle
Corvallis, OR

Idaho St. 77-75 (ot)
March 12

Southern Cal

Southern Cal 73-59

Texas Tech
March 9
Santa Clara
Corvallis, OR

Santa Clara 73-64
March 12

Colorado St.

Santa Clara 73-50

Corvallis, OR
March 13

Southern Cal 66-65 (2 ot)

Kansas City, MO
March 19

Bradley 74-72

Kansas City, MO
March 20

La Salle 92-76
NATIONAL CHAMPION

Regional Third Place
March 13
at Iowa City, IA
  Indiana 73, Louisiana St. 62
at Philadelphia, PA
  North Caro. St. 65, Cornell 54
at Stillwater, OK
  Rice 78, Colorado 55
at Corvallis, OR
  Idaho St. 62, Colorado St. 57

Penn St.

Southern Cal

Penn St. 70-61
NATIONAL 3rd PLACE

1954–55

AT A GLANCE

NCAA Champion: San Francisco (28-1).

NIT Champion: Duquesne (22-4).

New Rules: Games changed back to two 20-minute halves. The one-and-one free-throw is altered so that the bonus shot is given only if the first shot is converted.

NCAA Probation: Miami (Fla.), North Carolina State.

NCAA Consensus First-Team All-Americans: Dick Garmaker, F, Sr., Minnesota; Tom Gola, C-F, Sr., La Salle; Si Green, G, Jr., Duquesne; Dick Ricketts, F-C, Sr., Duquesne; Bill Russell, C, Jr., San Francisco.

David slew Goliath twice in a 23-day period. Kentucky's NCAA-record 129-game home-court winning streak was snapped by Georgia Tech, 59-58, on January 8. Tech's triumph on Joe Helms' one-handed, 12-footer with 11 seconds remaining also ended the Wildcats' 54-game regular-season winning streak and 16-year unbeaten streak in the SEC. The Jackets, 2-22 the previous season and 22-73 the previous four years, had lost to Sewanee, 67-66, one game prior to venturing to Lexington. Later that month, Tech became the first team to defeat Kentucky coach Adolph Rupp twice in the same season, leading the Wildcats all the way in a 65-59 decision.

Despite the pair of setbacks to a team that finished with a losing record (12-13), Rupp improved his career mark to 520-86 (85.8 winning percentage) as the Wildcats went 23-3.

Alabama's George Linn grabbed a rebound in the closing seconds of the first half of a game against North Carolina, turned, and made an overhand throw to the basket at the opposite end of the court and made the shot, which was measured at 84 feet, 11 inches.

Brown's Ed Tooley established an NCAA record for most free-throw attempts in a game with 36 against Amherst (23 made).

Marshall's Charlie Slack set an NCAA single-season record for highest rebounding average with 25.6 boards per game.

La Salle's Tom Gola finished his career with 2,462 points and 2,201 rebounds. His total of points and rebounds (4,663) is the highest in NCAA history.

Connecticut set an NCAA single-season record for highest rebounding average with 70 per game.

Minnesota defeated Purdue, 59-56, in six overtimes in the longest game in Big Ten history. Each team used only six players.

Virginia guard Buzz Wilkinson set an ACC single-season scoring average record by averaging 32.1 points per game. Wake Forest's Dickie Hemric set an ACC record by grabbing 36 rebounds against Clemson.

TCU's Dick O'Neil set a school record with 49 points against Rice.

Texas sophomore Raymond Downs averaged 26.1 points per game in Southwest Conference competition, but failed to earn a spot among the first five on the all-league team.

Kansas dedicated Allen Fieldhouse on March 1 with a 77-66 victory over Kansas State before a crowd of 17,228. The Jayhawks had previously played their home games at Hoch Auditorium, which had a seating capacity of 3,800 for basketball.

Hank Iba absorbed his first losing record (12-13) in 21 seasons as coach at Oklahoma A&M/State.

Oregon's Jim Loscutoff established what remains a Pacific-10 Conference record by averaging 17.2 rebounds per game and Oregon State's Swede Halbrook set a league mark with 36 rebounds in a game against Idaho.

Manhattan's Ed O'Connor became the first player to lead the nation in field-goal shooting with a mark above 60 percent (60.5).

Furman led the nation in scoring for the third consecutive season.

1954–55 INDIVIDUAL LEADERS

SCORING

PLAYER	PTS.	AVG.
Floyd, Furman	897	35.9
Wilkinson, Virginia	898	32.1
Freeman, Ohio St.	409	31.5
Yarbrough, Clemson	651	28.3
O'Neal, Texas Christian	676	28.2
Hemric, Wake Forest	746	27.6
Patterson, Tulsa	773	27.6
Mahoney, William & Mary	656	27.3
Brackeen, Mississippi	599	27.2
Arnelle, Penn St.	731	26.1

REBOUNDING

PLAYER	REB.	PCT.
Slack, Marshall	538	.264
Russell, San Francisco	594	.258

Conlin, Fordham	578	.241
Boldebuck, Houston	453	.221
Sparrow, Detroit	489	.218
Harper, Alabama	456	.205
Holup, G. Wash.	546	.203
Gola, La Salle	618	.203
Quimby, Connecticut	611	.196
McCarvill, Iona	422	.189

FIELD GOAL PERCENTAGE

PLAYER	FGM	FGA	PCT.
O'Connor, Manhattan	147	243	.605
Holup, G. Wash.	223	373	.598
Glowaski, Seattle	144	245	.588
Francis, Dartmouth	117	204	.574
Carpenter, Texas Tech	129	227	.568
Crosthwaite, W. Ky.	156	285	.547
Russell, San Fran.	229	423	.541

Young, Lafayette	143	266	.538
Devlin, G. Wash.	263	490	.537
McCarty, Virginia	236	444	.532

FREE THROW PERCENTAGE

PLAYER	FTM	FTA	PCT.
Scott, W. Texas St.	153	171	.895
Walczak, Marquette	104	118	.881
Barnes, SMU	83	97	.856
Williams, San Jose St.	181	214	.846
Forte, Columbia	187	222	.842
Ryan, Hardin-Simmons	105	125	.840
Blackshear, Texas Tech	83	99	.838
Sears, Santa Clara	197	235	.838
Murdock, Wake Forest	101	121	.835
Stewart, Missouri	88	106	.830

1954–55 TEAM LEADERS

SCORING OFFENSE

SCHOOL	PTS.	AVG.
Furman	2572	95.3
Connecticut	2252	90.1
Virginia	2605	89.8
North Carolina St.	2839	88.7
Marshall	1834	87.3

SCORING DEFENSE

SCHOOL	PTS.	AVG.
San Francisco	1511	52.1
Oklahoma A&M	1333	53.3
Oregon State	1660	55.3
Duquesne	1512	58.2
Santa Clara	1427	59.5

FIELD GOAL PERCENTAGE

SCHOOL	FGM	FGA	PCT.
George Washington	867	1822	.476
Wake Forest	803	1745	.460
Lafayette	760	1700	.447
Manhattan	604	1351	.447
Virginia	935	2115	.442

FREE THROW PERCENTAGE

SCHOOL	FTM	FTA	PCT.
Wake Forest	709	938	.756
Arizona State	832	627	.754
George Washington	615	819	.751
Missouri	550	747	.736
Richmond	641	879	.729

REBOUNDING

SCHOOL	TOTAL REB.	REB.	PCT.
Niagara	2417	1507	.624
St. Louis	1512	2499	.605
Seattle	1336	2219	.602
Kentucky	1680	2800	.600
North Carolina St.	1864	2688	.597

1954–55 FINAL NATIONAL POLLS

AP	UPI	SCHOOL
1	1	San Francisco
2	2	Kentucky
3	3	La Salle
4	6	North Carolina St.
5	5	Iowa
6	7	Duquesne
7	4	Utah
8	9	Marquette
9	10	Dayton
10	8	Oregon St.
11	13	Minnesota
12	–	Alabama
13	12	UCLA
14	15	George Washington
15	11	Colorado
16	14	Tulsa
17	–	Vanderbilt
18	16	Illinois
19	–	West Virginia
20	18	St. Louis
–	17	Niagara
–	19	Holy Cross
–	20	Cincinnati

1955 NCAA Tournament

Summary: Bill Russell retrieved 25 missed shots in the final while defensive specialist K. C. Jones, 6-1, held La Salle's three-time consensus first-team All-American Tom Gola, 6-6, without a basket during one 21-minute stretch and outscored him, 24-16, in San Francisco's 77-63 triumph.

Star Gazing: La Salle won its first three tourney games by an average of 32 points.

Biggest Upset: Kentucky, ranked second in the country entering the tourney, lost its opener to Marquette, 79-71.

One and Only: Bradley is the only school to win at least one playoff game in a year it entered the tournament with a losing record. The Braves were the only team to enter the playoffs with a

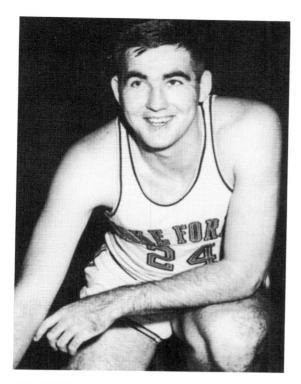

1954 ACC Player-of-the-Year Dickie Hemric of Wake Forest.

record of more than 10 games under the .500 mark (7-19).

Numbers Game: Utah, which defeated Seattle (108-85) in the West Regional third-place game, was the only school to reach triple figures in scoring in the first 20 tournaments.

What If: ACC regular-season and tournament champion North Carolina State, which defeated eventual national runner-up La Salle, was ineligible to participate in the NCAA Tournament because it was on probation.

Putting Things in Perspective: The first of San Francisco's back-to-back champions survived a scare in a West Regional and won by one point at Oregon State (57-56). The Beavers would have avenged a 26-point defeat earlier in the season against the Dons had they not missed a last-second shot. A 60-34 verdict over Oregon State was the first of USF's 60 consecutive victories, the longest winning streak in major-college history until UCLA won 88 games in a row from 1971 to 1974.

1954–55 NCAA CHAMPION: SAN FRANCISCO

SEASON STATISTICS OF SAN FRANCISCO REGULARS

PLAYER	POS.	CL.	G.	FG%	FT%	PPG	RPG
Bill Russell	C	Jr.	29	.541	.590	21.4	20.5
Jerry Mullen	F	Sr.	27	.379	.729	13.6	7.1
K. C. Jones	G	Jr.	29	.358	.674	10.6	5.1
Hal Perry	G	Jr.	29	.372	.750	6.9	1.9
Stan Buchanan	F	Sr.	29	.302	.711	5.2	3.2
Bob Wiebusch	F	Sr.	28	.322	.714	3.6	2.1
Rudy Zannini	G	Sr.	27	.300	.724	1.9	0.4
Dick Lawless	F	Sr.	26	.270	.600	1.8	1.1
Warren Baxter	G	Jr.	19	.524	.706	1.8	0.5
Bill Bush	G	Jr.	25	.333	.556	1.6	1.0
Jack King	F	So.	16	.333	.700	0.9	0.4
Gordon Kirby	C	Sr.	20	.200	.200	0.4	0.7
TEAM TOTALS			29	.396	.657	67.3	45.7

1955 CHAMPIONSHIP GAME

KANSAS CITY, MO

SAN FRANCISCO (77)	FG	FT-A	PF	PTS.
Mullen	4	2-5	5	10
Buchanan	3	2-2	1	8
Russell	9	5-7	1	23
Jones	10	4-4	2	24
Perry	1	2-2	4	4
Wiebusch	2	0-0	0	4
Zannini	1	0-0	0	2
Lawless	1	0-0	0	2
Kirby	0	0-0	1	0
TOTALS	**31**	**15-20**	**14**	**77**

FG%: .373. FT%: .750.

LA SALLE (63)	FG	FT-A	PF	PTS.
O'Malley	4	2-3	1	10
Singley	8	4-4	1	20
Gola	6	4-5	4	16
Lewis	1	4-9	1	6
Greenberg	1	1-2	4	3
Blatcher	4	0-0	1	8
Maples	0	0-0	0	0
Fredricks	0	0-0	0	0
TOTALS	**24**	**15-23**	**12**	**63**

FG%: .353. FT%: .652.
Halftime: San Francisco 35-24.

ALL-TOURNAMENT TEAM
Carl Cain, F, Jr., Iowa
Tom Gola, C, Sr., La Salle
K. C. Jones, G, Jr., San Francisco
Jim Ranglos, F, Jr., Colorado
Bill Russell, C, Jr., San Francisco
    *Named Most Outstanding Player

1955 CHAMPIONSHIP BRACKET

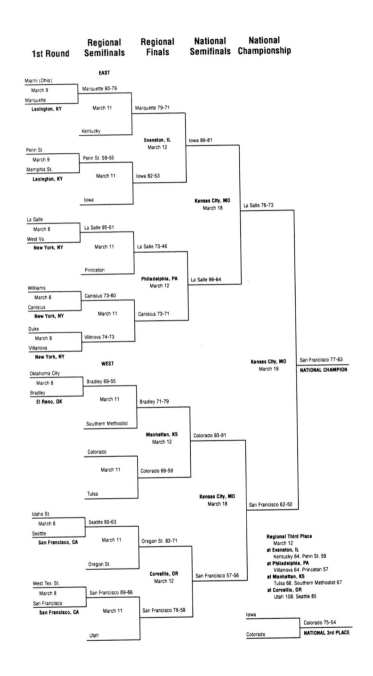

1st Round	Regional Semifinals	Regional Finals	National Semifinals	National Championship

EAST

Miami (Ohio)
March 9
Marquette
Lexington, KY

Marquette 90-79
March 11

Kentucky

Marquette 79-71

Evanston, IL
March 12

Iowa 86-81

Penn St.
March 9
Memphis St.
Lexington, KY

Penn St. 59-55
March 11

Iowa

Iowa 82-53

Kansas City, MO
March 18

La Salle 76-73

La Salle
March 8
West Va.
New York, NY

La Salle 95-61
March 11

Princeton

La Salle 73-46

Philadelphia, PA
March 12

La Salle 99-64

Williams
March 8
Canisius
New York, NY

Canisius 73-60
March 11

Canisius 73-71

Duke
March 8
Villanova
New York, NY

Villnova 74-73

Kansas City, MO
March 19

San Francisco 77-63
NATIONAL CHAMPION

WEST

Oklahoma City
March 8
Bradley
El Reno, OK

Bradley 69-55
March 11

Southern Methodist

Bradley 71-79

Manhattan, KS
March 12

Colorado 93-81

Colorado
March 11
Tulsa

Colorado 69-59

Kansas City, MO
March 18

San Francisco 62-50

Idaho St.
March 8
Seattle
San Francisco, CA

Seattle 80-63
March 11

Oregon St.

Oregon St. 83-71

Corvallis, OR
March 12

San Francisco 57-56

West Tex. St.
March 8
San Francisco
San Francisco, CA

San Francisco 89-66
March 11

Utah

San Francisco 78-59

Regional Third Place
March 12
at Evanston, IL
Kentucky 84, Penn St. 59
at Philadelphia, PA
Villanova 64, Princeton 57
at Manhattan, KS
Tulsa 68, Southern Methodist 67
at Corvallis, OR
Utah 108, Seattle 85

Iowa

Colorado

Colorado 75-54
NATIONAL 3rd PLACE

1955–56

AT A GLANCE

NCAA Champion: San Francisco (29-0).

NIT Champion: Louisville (26-3).

New Rules: The two-shot penalty in the last three minutes of a game is eliminated. The one-and-one is now in effect the entire game. The NCAA Tournament goes from two regionals to four.

NCAA Probation: Cincinnati.

NCAA Consensus First-Team All-Americans: Robin Freeman, G, Sr., Ohio State; Si Green, G, Sr., Duquesne; Tom Heinsohn, F, Sr., Holy Cross; Bill Russell, C, Sr., San Francisco; Ron Shavlik, C, Sr., North Carolina State.

Alabama was ranked 5th by AP and UPI but didn't participate in the NCAA Tournament because of a rules technicality stemming from varsity participation as freshmen by some of the "Rocket Eight" star players in 1953.

Alabama's squad, dominated by Midwest recruits who didn't survive tryouts to receive scholarships from Notre Dame, became the first squad to score 100 points against Kentucky. The 20-6 Wildcats, the league's representative to the NCAA Tournament, were whipped by 24 points (101-77) as 'Bama finished the season with 16 consecutive victories. The Crimson Tide's defeats—at North Carolina and St. John's and against Notre Dame on a neutral court—were in a span of four games.

As incredible as it might seem today, Johnny Dee left Alabama after such a splendid season to coach an amateur team sponsored by the Denver-Chicago Trucking Company. The school wound up failing to participate in the NCAA Tournament for the first time until 1975. Dee later coached at Notre Dame for seven seasons.

Jerry Harper set a conference record by averaging 21.5 rebounds per game to help Alabama become the last team to go undefeated in SEC competition. Alabama's last loss was against Notre Dame (86-80) in the semifinals of

the Sugar Bowl Tournament at New Orleans. The Irish defeated Utah, a Top 20 team most of the season, the next evening. The Sugar Bowl was the high point of the campaign for Notre Dame, which absorbed its first losing record (9-15) in 33 years.

Ohio State guard Robin Freeman's only sub-20 point game all season (12 against Illinois) cost him the national scoring title in a battle with Furman's Darrell Floyd (33.8 points per game). Freeman, who finished at 32.9, was 34.3 in all contests except the mediocre contests against the Illini. Floyd poured in a national-high 62 points against The Citadel.

On the bright side for The Citadel, however, was the fact that their NCAA-record 37-game losing streak was snapped when they defeated Charleston.

In perhaps the biggest upset of the season, Big Ten runner-up Illinois bowed to Northwestern, 83-82, in the closing game of the season for both teams. Northwestern finished with a 2-20 record.

The Air Force Academy competed in its first season of basketball, compiling an 11-9 record against freshman teams as Bob Beckel led the way with a 28.1-point scoring average.

Wyoming's Joe Capua (51 points against Montana), Texas' Raymond Downs (tied with 49 against Baylor), and George Washington's Joe Holup (49 against Furman) set school single-game scoring records.

Marshall's Charlie Slack, 6-5, finished his career as the only major-college player to average more than 22 rebounds per game in three consecutive seasons. Marshall became the first major college to have at least three players average more than 20 points per game—Slack (22.5), Cebe Price (21.2), and Paul Underwood (20.2).

Meanwhile, Al Inniss of St. Francis (N.Y.) set an NIT and Madison Square Garden college record with 37 rebounds in an NIT first-round game vs. Lafayette.

Norm Stewart, finishing 15th in the nation in scoring, averaged 24.1 points per game for

1955–56 INDIVIDUAL LEADERS

SCORING LEADERS

PLAYER	PTS.	AVG.
Floyd, Furman	946	33.8
Freeman, Ohio St.	723	32.9
Swartz, Morehead St.	828	28.6
Heinsohn, Holy Cross	740	27.4
McCoy, Michigan St.	600	27.3
Rosenbluth, North Carolina	614	26.7
Hundley, West Virginia	798	26.6
Downs, Texas	580	26.4
Ray, Toledo	563	25.6
Sigler, Louisiana St.	501	25.1

REBOUNDING

PLAYER	REB.	PCT.
Holup, G. Wash.	604	.256
Tyra, Louisville	645	.235

Harper, Alabama	517	.232
Russell, San Francisco	609	.231
Slack, Marshall	520	.215
Inniss, St. Francis (NY)	465	.196
Shavlik, North Carolina St.	545	.193
Heinsohn, Holy Cross	549	.188
Sobieszczyk, DePaul	316	.182
McLaughlin, St. Louis	455	.181

FIELD GOAL PERCENTAGE

PLAYER	FGM	FGA	PCT.
Holup, G. Wash.	200	309	.647
Greer, Marshall	128	213	.601
Johnson, St. Mary's	134	238	.563
Downs, Texas	167	309	.540
Lombardo, Manhattan	172	322	.534
Roberson, Cornell	117	224	.522
Ellis, Niagara	133	255	.522

O'Shea, Alabama	112	218	.514
Russell, San Francisco	246	480	.513
Choice, Indiana	148	290	.510

FREE THROW PERCENTAGE

PLAYER	FTM	FTA	PCT.
Von Weyhe, Rhode Island	180	208	.865
Murdock, Wake Forest	203	237	.857
Molodet, N. Carolina St.	167	196	.852
Miami, Miami (Fla.)	139	166	.837
McCarty, Virginia	163	196	.832
Petcavich, G. Wash.	138	166	.881
Gaudin, Loyola (La.)	130	157	.828
Plump, Butler	94	114	.825
Downs, Texas	246	290	.823
Forte, Columbia	114	139	.820

1955–56 TEAM LEADERS

SCORING OFFENSE

SCHOOL	PTS.	AVG.
Morehead St.	2782	95.9
Marshall	2145	93.3
Illinois	1996	90.7
Furman	2492	89.0
Memphis St.	2385	88.3

SCORING DEFENSE

SCHOOL	PTS.	AVG.
San Francisco	1514	52.2
Oklahoma A&M	1428	52.9
New Mexico A&M	1358	59.0
Tulsa	1537	59.1
San Jose St.	1485	59.4

FIELD GOAL PERCENTAGE

SCHOOL	FGM	FGA	PCT.
George Washington	725	1451	.500
Manhattan	698	1519	.460
DePaul	659	1456	.453
Niagara	739	1653	.447
Wake Forest	777	1754	.443

FREE THROW PERCENTAGE

SCHOOL	FTM	FTA	PCT.
Southern Methodist	701	917	.764
Murray State	590	791	.746
Texas Western	517	698	.741
Illinois	534	725	.737
North Carolina St.	639	869	.735

REBOUNDING

SCHOOL	TOTAL REB.	REB.	PCT.
George Washington	2356	1451	.616
Niagara	2008	1198	.597
San Francisco	2642	1573	.595
St. Louis	2529	1503	.594
Rice	2181	1294	.593

Missouri. He would later become his alma mater's all-time winningest coach. At another Big Eight school, Kansas coach Phog Allen retired after 48 seasons with a 746-264 record. His final varsity squad lost a preseason game to the school's freshman team when Philadelphia native Wilt Chamberlain collected 42 points and 29 rebounds for the frosh.

George Washington led the nation in field-goal shooting for the third consecutive season.

Yale's Howard Hobson, who guided Oregon to a title in the first NCAA Tournament in 1939, retired after a 23-year coaching career with a 400-257 record.

1955–56 FINAL NATIONAL POLLS

AP	UPI	SCHOOL
1	1	San Francisco
2	2	North Carolina St.
3	3	Dayton
4	4	Iowa
5	5	Alabama
6	7	Louisville
7	6	SMU
8	9	UCLA
9	12	Kentucky
10	8	Illinois
11	–	Oklahoma City
12	10	Vanderbilt
13	11	North Carolina
14	15	Holy Cross
15	14	Temple
16	–	Wake Forest
17	18	Duke
18	13	Utah
19	16	Oklahoma St.
20	–	West Virginia
–	16	St. Louis
–	18	Canisius
–	18	Seattle

1956 NCAA Tournament

Summary: National champion San Francisco averaged 14-point victories after winning all but two of its regular-season games by double-digit margins. Marquette, 13-11 that season, came closest to USF in a 65-58 decision on a neutral court in the DePaul Invitational. Unanimous first-team All-American Bill Russell averaged 22.8 points in four tournament games as the Dons won each of them by more than 10 points. K. C. Jones was ineligible for the playoffs because he had played one game two years earlier before an appendectomy ended his season, but USF still became the first undefeated champion in NCAA history when Russell grabbed a Final Four-record 27 rebounds in the championship game against Iowa.

Star Gazing: Temple mighty mites Hal Lear (5-11) combined with backcourtmate Guy Rodgers (6-0) to score 73.5 percent of the Owls' points in two Final Four games. Lear manufactured 61.5 percent of Temple's offense by scoring 40 points in the Owls' 65-59 victory against Connecticut in the East Regional semifinals.

Biggest Upset: North Carolina State, ranked No. 2 in the nation entering the tourney, was stunned in four overtimes in the first round by Canisius, 79-78.

One and Only: San Francisco center Bill Russell became the only player to grab more than 41 rebounds at a Final Four (50) and more than 21 in a championship game (27 against Iowa).

Numbers Game: The record for most rebounds in a playoff game was set by Temple's Fred Cohen with 34 in a 65-59 victory against Connecticut in the East Regional semifinals. Cohen grabbed just five rebounds in the Owls' next contest, a 60-58 win over Canisius.

1955–56 NCAA CHAMPION: SAN FRANCISCO

SEASON STATISTICS OF SAN FRANCISCO REGULARS

PLAYER	POS.	CL.	G.	FG%	FT%	PPG	RPG
Bill Russell	C	Sr.	29	.513	.495	20.6	21.0
K. C. Jones*	G	Sr.	25	.365	.655	9.8	5.2
Hal Perry	G	Sr.	29	.365	.729	9.1	2.0
Carl Boldt	F	Jr.	28	.326	.783	8.6	5.0
Mike Farmer	F	So.	28	.371	.548	8.4	7.8
Gene Brown	G	So.	29	.377	.641	7.1	4.4
Mike Preseau	F	So.	29	.366	.609	4.1	3.1
Warren Baxter	G	Sr.	26	.301	.667	2.2	0.7
Bill Bush	G	Sr.	22	.208	.625	0.9	0.8
Jack King	F	Jr.	22	.162	.462	0.8	1.0
TEAM TOTALS			29	.388	.604	72.2	54.2

*Ineligible for NCAA Tournament as a fifth-year player.

1956 FINAL FOUR CHAMPIONSHIP GAME

EVANSTON, IL

SAN FRANCISCO (83)	FG	FT-A	PF	PTS.
Boldt	7	2-2	4	16
Farmer	0	0-0	2	0
Preseau	3	1-2	3	7
Russell	11	4-5	2	26
Nelson	0	0-0	0	0
Perry	6	2-2	2	14
Brown	6	4-4	0	16
Baxter	2	0-0	0	4
TOTALS	35	13-15	13	83

FG%: .402. **FT%:** .867. **Rebounds:** 60 (Russell 27).

IOWA (71)	FG	FT-A	PF	PTS.
Cain	7	3-4	1	17
Schoof	5	4-4	3	14
Logan	5	2-2	3	12
George	0	0-0	0	0
Scheuerman	4	3-4	2	11
Seaberg	5	7-10	1	17
Martel	0	0-0	0	0
McConnell	0	0-0	0	0
TOTALS	26	19-24	10	71

FG%: .325. **FT%:** .792. **Rebounds:** 48 (Logan 15).
Halftime: San Francisco 38-33.

NATIONAL SEMIFINALS

IOWA (83): Cain 8 4 20, Schoof 5 8 18, Logan 13 10 36, Seaberg 1 0 2, Scheuerman 1 2 4, Martel 1 1 3. Team 29 25 83.

TEMPLE (76): Reinfeld 1 0 2, Norman 1 0 2, Fleming 2 0 4, Cohen 3 0 6, Van Patton 1 0 2, Rodgers 12 4 28, Lear 15 2 32. Team 35 6 76.

Halftime: Iowa 39-36.

SAN FRANCISCO (86): Boldt 3 1 7, Farmer 11 4 26, Preseau 1 0 2, King 0 0 0, Russell 8 1 17, Perry 6 2 14, Brown 5 2 12, Baxter 4 0 8. Team 38 10 86.

SOUTHERN METHODIST (68): Showalter 4 0 8, Krog 3 0 6, McGregor 1 1 3, Krebs 10 4 24, Miller 1 0 2, Miller 1 9 11, Morris 4 2 10, Herrscher 1 2 4. Team 25 18 68.

Halftime: San Francisco 44-32.

ALL-TOURNAMENT TEAM
Carl Cain, F, Sr., Iowa
Hal Lear, G, Sr., Temple
Bill Logan, C, Sr., Iowa
Hal Perry, G, Sr., San Francisco
Bill Russell, C, Sr., San Francisco
    *Named Most Outstanding Player

1956 CHAMPIONSHIP BRACKET

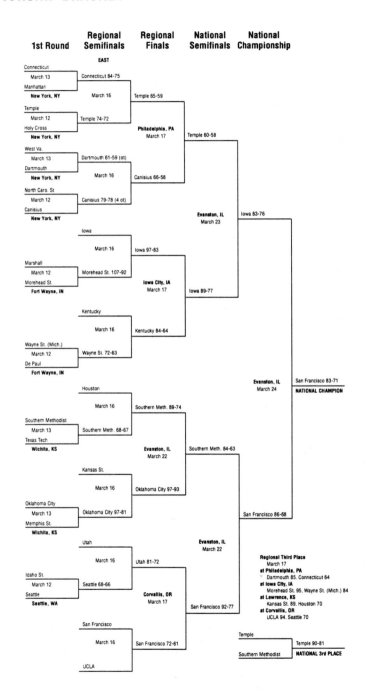

	1st Round	Regional Semifinals	Regional Finals	National Semifinals	National Championship

EAST

Connecticut
March 13
Manhattan
New York, NY

Connecticut 84-75
March 16

Temple
March 12
Holy Cross
New York, NY

Temple 74-72

Temple 65-59

West Va.
March 13
Dartmouth
New York, NY

Dartmouth 61-59 (ot)
March 16

North Caro. St
March 12
Canisius
New York, NY

Canisius 79-78 (4 ot)

Canisius 66-58

Philadelphia, PA
March 17

Temple 60-58

Evanston, IL
March 23

Iowa 83-76

Iowa
March 16

Marshall
March 12
Morehead St.
Fort Wayne, IN

Morehead St. 107-92

Iowa 97-83

Kentucky
March 16

Wayne St. (Mich.)
March 12
De Paul
Fort Wayne, IN

Wayne St. 72-63

Kentucky 84-64

Iowa City, IA
March 17

Iowa 89-77

Houston
March 16

Southern Methodist
March 13
Texas Tech
Wichita, KS

Southern Meth. 68-67

Southern Meth. 89-74

Kansas St.
March 16

Oklahoma City
March 13
Memphis St.
Wichita, KS

Oklahoma City 97-81

Oklahoma City 97-93

Evanston, IL
March 22

Southern Meth. 84-63

Evanston, IL
March 24

San Francisco 83-71
NATIONAL CHAMPION

San Francisco 86-68

Utah
March 16

Idaho St.
March 12
Seattle
Seattle, WA

Seattle 68-66

Utah 81-72

San Francisco
March 16

UCLA

San Francisco 72-61

Corvallis, OR
March 17

San Francisco 92-77

Evanston, IL
March 22

Regional Third Place
March 17
at Philadelphia, PA
Dartmouth 85, Connecticut 64
at Iowa City, IA
Morehead St. 95, Wayne St. (Mich.) 84
at Lawrence, KS
Kansas St. 89, Houston 70
at Corvallis, OR
UCLA 94, Seattle 70

Temple

Southern Methodist

Temple 90-81
NATIONAL 3rd PLACE

1956–57

AT A GLANCE

NCAA Champion: North Carolina (32-0).

NIT Champion: Bradley (22-7).

New Rules: The free-throw lane is increased from six feet to 12 feet. On the lineup for a free throw, the two spaces adjacent to the end line must be occupied by opponents of the free thrower. Previously, one space was marked "H" for a home team player to occupy, and across the lane the first space was marked "V" for a visiting team player to stand in. Grasping the goal is now classified as a technical foul under unsportsmanlike tactics.

NCAA Probation: Auburn, Florida, Louisville, North Carolina State, Ohio State, Southern Cal, Texas A&M, UCLA, and Washington.

NCAA Consensus First-Team All-Americans: Wilt Chamberlain, C, Soph., Kansas; Chet Forte, G, Sr., Columbia; Rod Hundley, G-F, Sr., West Virginia, Jim Krebs, C, Sr., Southern Methodist; Lennie Rosenbluth, F, Sr., North Carolina; Charlie Tyra, C, Sr., Louisville.

West Virginia All-American guard-forward Hot Rod Hundley.

Wilt Chamberlain debuted at Kansas with a school-record 52 points against Northwestern. Chamberlain, who averaged 29.6 points per game, would have had a good chance at leading the nation in scoring except for three games against Iowa State, which limited him to 16 points per game.

South Carolina's Grady Wallace became the only ACC player to ever lead the nation in scoring (31.2 ppg). It was the fifth consecutive season the scoring title remained in the Palmetto State. Wallace's predecessors were Furman's Frank Selvy and Darrell Floyd. Oddly, none of the three were South Carolina natives. Selvy and Wallace were from Kentucky while Floyd was from North Carolina.

The top eight scorers in the country were separated by fewer than 3½ points. The national runner-up in scoring was Mississippi's Joe Gibbon (30), who later pitched in the majors. A couple of other prominent hoopsters who would end up in the majors were Ohio State's Frank Howard and Morehead State's Steve Hamilton.

Howard was one of the nation's premier rebounders with 15.3 boards per game. Hamilton led the Eagles in scoring and rebounding. Hamilton became the only athlete to play in a World Series (New York Yankees in 1963 and 1964) and an NBA Finals (Minneapolis Lakers rookie in 1959 when they were swept by the Boston Celtics). Hamilton's board work helped Morehead State set an NCAA single-season record for rebounding margin with an average of 25 more caroms per game than its opponents.

Illinois ended San Francisco's 60-game winning streak, 62-33.

Columbia's 5-9 Chet Forte became the first Ivy League player to score more than 400 points in a conference campaign as he totaled 403 points in 14 games (28.8 per league contest).

West Virginia's Hot Rod Hundley set a school record with 54 points against Furman.

Kansas star Wilt Chamberlain.

Kansas coaching greats Dick Harp (left) and Phog Allen.

Pitt's Don Hennon set a school record with 45 points against Duke.

Mississippi State's Jim Ashmore (28.3) and Bailey Howell (25.9) became the first set of teammates in NCAA history to average more than 25 points per game in a single season. Howell (37) and Ashmore (24) combined for 61 points in the Bulldogs' first victory over Kentucky in 33 years (89-81).

Wake Forest teammates Ernie Wiggins and Jackie Murdock, deadlocked for the national lead in free-throw shooting entering the postseason, finished 1-2 in the country. Wiggins won by hitting all four of his tournament tosses. North Carolina's Lennie Rosenbluth scored an ACC Tournament-record 45 points in a quarterfinal victory over Clemson.

Seattle coach John Castellani was hung in effigy on the school's campus after the Elgin Bay-

1956–57 FINAL NATIONAL POLLS

AP	UPI	SCHOOL
1	1	North Carolina
2	2	Kansas
3	3	Kentucky
4	4	SMU
5	5	Seattle
6	8	Louisville
7	11	West Virginia
8	16	Vanderbilt
9	16	Oklahoma City
10	10	St. Louis
11	7	Michigan St.
12	–	Memphis St.
13	6	California
14	9	UCLA
15	–	Mississippi St.
16	–	Idaho St.
17	19	Notre Dame
18	–	Wake Forest
19	–	Canisius
19	–	Oklahoma St.
–	12	Dayton
–	13	Bradley
–	14	Brigham Young
–	15	Indiana
–	16	Xavier
–	20	Kansas St.

SCORING

PLAYER	PTS.	AVG.
Wallace, South Carolina	906	31.2
Gibbon, Mississippi	631	30.0
Baylor, Seattle	743	29.7
Chamberlain, Kansas	800	29.6
Forte, Columbia	694	28.9
Ashmore, Mississippi St.	708	28.3
Rosenbluth, North Carolina	895	28.0
Ebben, Detroit	724	27.8
Howell, Mississippi St.	647	25.9
Dees, Indiana	550	25.0

REBOUNDING

PLAYER	REB.	PCT.
Baylor, Seattle	508	.235
Ellis, Niagara	502	.234

Tyra, Louisville	520	.229
Chamberlain, Kansas	510	.227
Guarilia, G. Wash.	447	.218
Howell, Mississippi St.	492	.212
Ramsey, New York	372	.202
Howard, Ohio State	336	.201
Freeman, Xavier	526	.195
Hamilton, Morehead St.	543	.194

FIELD GOAL PERCENTAGE

PLAYER	FGM	FGA	PCT.
Howell, Mississippi St.	217	382	.568
Inniss, St. Francis (NY)	189	337	.561
Roth, Muhlenberg	162	298	.544
Holtsma, William & Mary	117	216	.542
Ellis, Niagara	209	389	.537
Crosthwaite, Western Ky.	185	349	.530
Francis, Dartmouth	127	243	.523

Downs, Texas	155	298	.520
Richter, N.C. St.	136	262	.519
Nymeyer, Arizona	153	298	.513
Embry, Miami (Ohio)	224	437	.513

FREE THROW PERCENTAGE

PLAYER	FTM	FTA	PCT.
Wiggins, Wake Forest	93	108	.877
Murdock, Wake Forest	161	184	.875
Seitz, N.C. St.	95	109	.872
Ricketts, Duquesne	150	174	.862
Plump, Butler	160	186	.860
Forte, Columbia	224	263	.852
Novalesi, St. Francis (Pa.)	90	106	.849
Simmons, Idaho	101	119	.849
Steinke, Brigham Young	105	124	.847
Dees, Indiana	176	209	.842

1956-57 TEAM LEADERS

SCORING OFFENSE

SCHOOL	PTS.	AVG.
Connecticut	2183	87.3
Ohio	2004	87.1
Marshall	2070	86.3
Memphis St.	2562	85.4
Morehead St.	2301	85.2

SCORING DEFENSE

SCHOOL	PTS.	AVG.
Oklahoma A&M	1420	54.6
San Francisco	1560	55.7
California	1484	57.1
Santa Clara	1260	57.3
Kansas	1583	58.6

FIELD GOAL PERCENTAGE

SCHOOL	FGM	FGA	PCT.
Manhattan	679	1489	.456
Seattle	742	1644	.451
Western Kentucky	802	1788	.449
Lafayette	776	1736	.447
Niagara	756	1693	.447

FREE THROW PERCENTAGE

SCHOOL	FTM	FTA	PCT.
Oklahoma A&M	569	752	.757
Auburn	479	648	.739
Tulane	459	622	.738
Wake Forest	610	827	.738
Memphis St.	714	971	.735
Louisville	513	698	.735

REBOUNDING

SCHOOL	TOT. REB.	REB.	PCT.
Morehead St.	2796	1735	.621
Seattle	2165	1307	.604
Dartmouth	2381	1414	.594
Louisville	2270	1327	.585
Dayton	2871	1676	.584

lor-led Chieftains, seeded first in the NIT, lost its postseason opener to St. Bonaventure, 85-68.

In one of the strangest games in NIT history, Bradley erased a 21-point deficit to defeat Xavier, 116-81. The Braves outscored Xavier, 72-29, in the second half, setting NIT and Madison Square Garden college records for most points in a half.

1957 NCAA Tournament

Summary: A championship game frequently misconstrued as an enormous upset was North Carolina's 54-53 triple-overtime victory against the Wilt Chamberlain-led Kansas. After all, Carolina was undefeated that season (32-0), winning 22 games by at least nine points, and the Tar Heels' top three scorers wound up playing in the NBA, albeit briefly—forwards Lennie

Rosenbluth and Pete Brennan and guard Tommy Kearns. Junior center Joe Quigg sank two free throws with six seconds remaining in the third overtime to tie the score and provide the decisive point as North Carolina nipped Kansas, 54-53. Carolina won the national championship by an average of 8.4 points after winning five of its last 11 games against ACC competition by five points or less. The Tar Heels didn't outscore their opponents in both halves of any of their five playoff victories, but Rosenbluth bailed them out by scoring at least 20 points in every game. Rosenbluth was Carolina's leading scorer in 27 of their 32 contests, although the Tar Heels won the triple-overtime final after he fouled out with 1:45 remaining in regulation.

Outcome for Defending Champion: San

1956–57 NCAA CHAMPION: N. CAROLINA

SEASON STATISTICS OF NORTH CAROLINA REGULARS

PLAYER	POS.	CL.	G.	FG%	FT%	PPG	RPG
Lennie Rosenbluth	F	Sr.	32	.483	.758	28.0	8.8
Pete Brennan	F	Jr.	32	.394	.706	14.7	10.4
Tommy Kearns	G	Jr.	32	.434	.711	12.8	3.1
Joe Quigg	C	Jr.	31	.434	.719	10.3	8.6
Bob Cunningham	G	Jr.	32	.393	.598	7.2	6.7
Tony Radovich	G	Sr.	16	.525	.769	3.9	1.8
Bill Hathaway	C	So.	15	.333	.417	2.8	5.0
Stan Groll	G	So.	12	.370	.556	2.1	1.5
Bob Young	C	Sr.	15	.256	.538	1.9	2.1
Ken Rosemond	G	Jr.	15	.400	.556	1.1	0.6
Danny Lotz	F	So.	24	.350	.391	1.0	1.6
TEAM TOTALS			32	.431	.701	79.3	46.7

1957 FINAL FOUR CHAMPIONSHIP GAME

KANSAS CITY, MO

NORTH CAROLINA (54)	FG-A	FT-A	REB.	PF	PTS.
Rosenbluth	8-15	4-4	5	5	20
Cunningham	0-3	0-1	5	4	0
Brennan	4-8	3-7	11	3	11
Kearns	4-8	3-7	1	4	11
Quigg	4-10	2-3	9	4	10
Lotz	0-0	0-0	2	0	0
Young	1-1	0-0	3	1	2
Team			6		
TOTALS	**21-45**	**12-22**	**42**	**21**	**54**

FG%: .467. FT%: .545.

KANSAS (53)	FG-A	FT-A	REB.	PF	PTS.
Chamberlain	6-13	11-16	14	3	23
King	3-12	5-6	4	4	11
Elstun	4-12	3-6	4	2	11
Parker	2-4	0-0	0	0	4
Loneski	0-5	2-3	3	2	2
L. Johnson	0-1	2-2	0	1	2
Billings	0-0	0-0	0	2	0
Team			3		
TOTALS	**15-47**	**23-33**	**28**	**14**	**53**

FG%: .319. FT%: .697.
Halftime: North Carolina 29-22. **Regulation:** Tied 46-46. **First Overtime:** Tied 48-48. **Second Overtime:** Tied 48-48.

NATIONAL SEMIFINALS

NORTH CAROLINA (74): Rosenbluth 11-42 7-9 29, Cunningham 9-18 3-5 21, Brennan 6-16 2-4 14, Kearns 1-8 4-5 6, Quigg 0-1 2-3 2, Lotz 0-1 0-0 0, Young 1-3 0-1 2, Searcy 0-0 0-0 0. Team 28-89 (.315) 18-27 (.667) 74.

MICHIGAN STATE (70): Quiggle 6-21 8-10 20, Green 4-12 3-6 11, Ferguson 4-8 2-3 10, Hedden 4-20 6-7 14, Wilson 0-3 2-2 2, Anderdg 2-7 3-6 7, Bencie 1-6 0-0 2, Scott 2-3 0-2 4. Team 23-80 (.288) 24-36 (.667) 70.

Halftime: Tied 29-29. **Regulation:** Tied 58-58. **First Overtime:** Tied 64-64. **Second Overtime:** Tied 66-66.

KANSAS (80): M. King 6-8 1-1 13, Elstun 8-12 0-0 16, Chamberlain 12-22 8-11 32, Parker 1-1 0-0 2, Loneski 2-6 3-4 7, L. Johnson 1-3 0-0 2, Billings 0-1 0-0 0, Hollinger 1-1 0-1 2, Dater 1-1 0-0 2, Green 1-1 0-0 2, Kindred 0-0 0-0 0, M. Johnson 1-1 0-0 2. Team 34-57 (.597) 12-19 (.632) 80.

SAN FRANCISCO (56): Day 3-14 3-8 9, Dunbar 2-8 0-0 4, Brown 5-14 0-0 10, Farmer 6-15 2-2 14, Preaseau 5-8 2-2 12, Mallen 0-2 0-0 0, Lillevand 1-3 0-0 2, Koljian 0-1 3-4 3, J. King 0-3 0-0 0, Russell 0-0 0-0 0, Radanovich 0-1 0-0 0, Mancasola 1-2 0-0 2. Team 23-71 (.324) 10-16 (.625) 56.

Halftime: Kansas 38-34.

ALL-TOURNAMENT TEAM

Pete Brennan, F, Jr., North Carolina
Gene Brown, G, Jr., San Francisco
Wilt Chamberlain, C, Soph., Kansas
Johnny Green, C, Soph., Michigan State
Lennie Rosenbluth, F, Sr., North Carolina
  *Named Most Outstanding Player

Francisco (22-7) was clobbered by Kansas, 80-56, in the national semifinals.

Star Gazing: Carolina coach Frank McGuire became the first coach to take two different schools to the NCAA championship game. He guided St. John's to a second-place finish in 1952.

Biggest Upset: Kentucky, ranked No. 3 entering the tourney, blew a 12-point halftime lead in an 80-68 setback to Michigan State in the Mideast Regional final.

One and Only: North Carolina became the only school to play in back-to-back triple-over-time games in the playoffs.

Numbers Game: Dick Harp became the only individual to play in an NCAA Tournament championship game (with Kansas in 1940 when the Jayhawks lost to Indiana) and later coach his alma mater to a final (KU lost to North Carolina).

Putting Things in Perspective: Kansas was fortunate SMU shot just 32.1 percent from the floor in their Midwest Regional opener at Dallas. Long before Georgetown tried to minimize distractions, the Jayhawks stayed 30 miles out of town, but some bigots still burned a cross in a yard across from their lodging quarters. And narrow-minded fans at the game punctuated the contest with racial slurs.

1957 CHAMPIONSHIP BRACKET

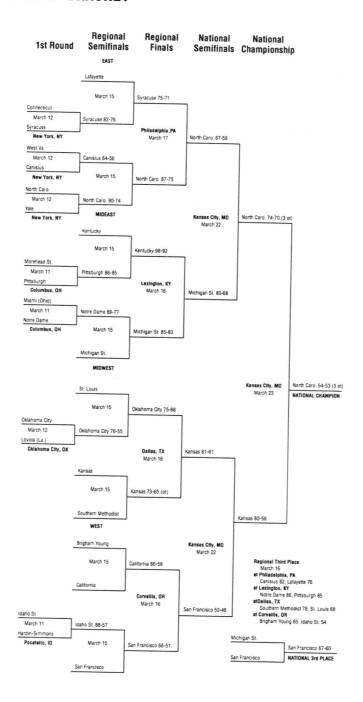

| 1st Round | Regional Semifinals | Regional Finals | National Semifinals | National Championship |

EAST

Lafayette
March 15 — Syracuse 75-71
Connecticut
March 12
Syracuse — Syracuse 82-76
New York, NY

West Va.
March 12 — Canisius 64-56
Canisius
New York, NY
March 15 — North Caro. 87-75
North Caro.
March 12 — North Caro. 90-74
Yale
New York, NY

Philadelphia, PA
March 17 — North Caro. 67-58

MIDEAST

Kentucky
March 15 — Kentucky 98-92
Morehead St.
March 11
Pittsburgh — Pittsburgh 86-85
Columbus, OH

Miami (Ohio)
March 11 — Notre Dame 89-77
Notre Dame
Columbus, OH
March 15 — Michigan St. 85-83
Michigan St.

Lexington, KY
March 16 — Michigan St. 80-68

MIDWEST

Kansas City, MO
March 22 — North Caro. 74-70 (3 ot)

St. Louis
March 15 — Oklahoma City 75-66
Oklahoma City
March 12
Loyola (La.) — Oklahoma City 76-55
Oklahoma City, OK

Kansas
March 15 — Kansas 73-65 (ot)
Southern Methodist

Dallas, TX
March 16 — Kansas 81-61

WEST

Kansas City, MO
March 23 — North Caro. 54-53 (3 ot)
NATIONAL CHAMPION

Kansas City, MO
March 22 — Kansas 80-56

Brigham Young
March 15 — California 86-59
California

Corvallis, OR
March 16 — San Francisco 50-46

Idaho St.
March 11
Hardin-Simmons — Idaho St. 68-57
Pocatello, ID
March 15 — San Francisco 66-51
San Francisco

Regional Third Place
March 16
at Philadelphia, PA
 Canisius 82, Lafayette 76
at Lexington, KY
 Notre Dame 86, Pittsburgh 85
at Dallas, TX
 Southern Methodist 78, St. Louis 68
at Corvallis, OR
 Brigham Young 65, Idaho St. 54

Michigan St.
San Francisco — San Francisco 67-60
NATIONAL 3rd PLACE

1957–58

AT A GLANCE

NCAA Champion: Kentucky (23-6).

NIT Champion: Xavier (19-11).

New Rules: Offensive goaltending is banned. One free throw for each common foul is taken the first six personal fouls by one team in each half, and the one-and-one is employed thereafter. Uniform numbers "1," "2," and any digit greater than "5" are prohibited.

NCAA Probation: Auburn, Florida, Louisville, Memphis State, Montana State, North Carolina State, UCLA, Washington.

NCAA Consensus First-Team All-Americans: Elgin Baylor, F-C, Jr., Seattle; Bob Boozer, F, Jr., Kansas State; Wilt Chamberlain, C, Jr., Kansas; Don Hennon, G, Jr., Pittsburgh; Oscar Robertson, F, Soph., Cincinnati; Guy Rodgers, G, Sr., Temple.

The three major-college players to average more than 30 points per game this season—Cincinnati's Oscar Robertson (35.1), Seattle's Elgin Baylor (32.5), and Kansas' Wilt Chamberlain (30.1)—each went on to become an All-NBA selection at least 10 times.

Baylor and Robertson both had four games with at least 47 points. Robertson, Baylor, and Chamberlain all averaged more than 15 rebounds per game. Chamberlain set a Big Eight Conference record with 36 rebounds against Iowa State. Robertson is one of only two players in NCAA history to be named national player of the year in his first season of varsity competition.

Chamberlain's final college season included one of the most amazing turnarounds in NCAA history. Nebraska, in the midst of 15 consecutive losing seasons, was clobbered at Kansas by 56 points (102-46) before upsetting the Jayhawks (43-41) four games later in Omaha when backup guard Jim Kubacki hit a 15-foot basket with two seconds remaining (see accompanying box score). In the Cornhuskers' next outing, they defeated top-ranked Kansas State (55-48), a team that had overwhelmed them by a total of 46 points in two previous matchups.

West Virginia ended North Carolina's 37-game winning streak, 75-64.

Drake's Red Murrell set a school record with 51 points against Houston.

Dartmouth's Rudy LaRusso grabbed an Ivy League-record 32 rebounds in a game with Columbia.

Xavier upset the top three seeds on its way to the NIT title—No. 2 Bradley (72-62), No. 3 St. Bonaventure (72-53), and top-seeded Dayton (78-74 in overtime). It was the fifth time in eight seasons that Dayton reached the NIT final and lost. The championship game marked one of only two NIT finals matching two schools from the same state (Indiana-Purdue in 1979 was the other).

NYU's Howard Cann ended his 35-year coaching career with a 409-232 record.

HUSKERS AVENGE 56-POINT DEFEAT   Was it a magic potion? The sad-sack Nebraska Cornhuskers, suffering through another losing season, had been walloped by the Kansas Jayhawks four games earlier, 102-46. But playing in front of their home crowd on February 22, 1958, the Huskers upset the Jayhawks, 43-41. Maybe they had something against the state of Kansas—in their next game, they beat up on No. 1-ranked Kansas State, 55-48.

KANSAS (41)	FG	FT-A	PTS.
Chamberlain	7	4-8	18
Cleland	0	0-0	0
Donaghue	4	1-2	9
Hickman	0	0-0	0
J. Johnson	1	1-1	3
Kindred	1	0-0	2
Loneski	3	3-6	9
Thompson	0	0-0	0
TOTALS	**16**	**9-17**	**41**

NEBRASKA (43)	FG	FT-A	PTS.
Arwood	0	0-1	0
Fitzpatrick	3	1-1	7
Harry	1	0-3	2
Kubacki	1	0-0	2
Reimers	4	6-8	14
Smidt	1	4-4	6
Turner	4	4-7	12
TOTALS	**14**	**15-24**	**43**

Halftime: Nebraska 27-21.

1957-58 INDIVIDUAL LEADERS

SCORING

PLAYER	PTS.	AVG.
Robertson, Cincinnati	984	35.1
Baylor, Seattle	943	32.5
Chamberlain, Kansas	633	30.1
Howell, Mississippi St.	695	27.8
Murrell, Drake	668	26.7
Coleman, Ky. Wesleyan	639	26.6
Hennon, Pittsburgh	651	26.0
Reed, Oklahoma City	666	25.6
Dees, Indiana	613	25.5
Flora, Washington & Lee	634	25.4

REBOUNDING

PLAYER	REB.	PCT.
Ellis, Niagara	536	.262
Inniss, St. Francis (NY)	477	.248

Baylor, Seattle	559	.235
Chamberlain, Kansas	367	.216
Cincebox, Syracuse	345	.206
McCadney, Fordham	351	.205
Embry, Miami (Ohio)	488	.202
Green, Michigan St.	392	.199
Howell, Mississippi St.	406	.198
Hamilton, Morehead St.	440	.195

FIELD GOAL PERCENTAGE

PLAYER	FGM	FGA	PCT.
Crosthwaite, W. Ky.	202	331	.610
Robertson, Cincinnati	352	617	.571
Brunone, Manhattan	100	178	.562
Goodall, Tulsa	108	194	.557
Greer, Marshall	236	432	.546
Clark, Oklahoma St.	171	317	.539
Mantz, Lafayette	190	354	.537

Aston, St. Francis (Pa.)	120	226	.531
Cunningham, Fordham	176	332	.530
McDonald, G. Wash.	165	314	.525

FREE THROW PERCENTAGE

PLAYER	FTM	FTA	PCT.
Mintz, Davidson	105	119	.882
Myers, Texas Tech	107	123	.870
Clark, Oklahoma St.	160	185	.865
Hobbs, Florida	98	114	.860
Reed, Oklahoma City	206	242	.851
Sidwell, Tennessee Tech	100	118	.847
McCarthy, Notre Dame	132	156	.846
Kennedy, Temple	112	133	.842
Walsh, Detroit	99	118	.839
Adair, Oklahoma St.	97	116	.836
Hennon, Pittsburgh	117	140	.836

1957-58 TEAM LEADERS

SCORING OFFENSE

SCHOOL	PTS.	AVG.
Marshall	2113	88.0
West Virginia	2433	86.9
Cincinnati	2422	86.5
Kentucky Wesleyan	1993	83.0
Notre Dame	2374	81.9

SCORING DEFENSE

SCHOOL	PTS.	AVG.
San Francisco	1363	50.5
Oklahoma St.	1500	51.7
Kansas	1273	55.3
Providence	1332	55.5
Oregon St.	1449	55.7

FIELD GOAL PERCENTAGE

SCHOOL	FGM	FGA	PCT.
Fordham	693	1440	.481
Cincinnati	910	1895	.480
Marshall	817	1740	.470
Seattle	938	2014	.466
Oklahoma St.	620	1346	.461

FREE THROW PERCENTAGE

SCHOOL	FTM	FTA	PCT.
Oklahoma St.	488	617	.791
Marshall	479	608	.788
Oklahoma City	503	667	.754
Stanford	448	603	.743
Kentucky	502	680	.738

REBOUNDING

SCHOOL	TOTAL REB.	REB.	PCT.
Manhattan	2430	1437	.591
Morehead St.	2262	1331	.588
Seattle	2380	1400	.588
Texas Christian	2162	1253	.580
Muhlenberg	2143	1239	.578

1957-58 FINAL NATIONAL POLLS

AP	UPI	SCHOOL
1	1	West Virginia
2	2	Cincinnati
3	4	Kansas St.
4	3	San Francisco
5	5	Temple
6	6	Maryland
7	8	Kansas
8	7	Notre Dame
9	14	Kentucky
10	13	Duke
11	9	Dayton
12	10	Indiana
13	12	North Carolina
14	11	Bradley
15	–	Mississippi St.
16	–	Auburn
17	19	Michigan St.
18	19	Seattle
19	15	Oklahoma St.
20	16	North Carolina St.
–	16	Oregon St.
–	18	St. Bonaventure
–	19	Wyoming

1958 NCAA Tournament

Summary: Would Kentucky's storied "Fiddlin' Five," a team equaling the most defeats (six) of any Wildcats squad in the previous 15 seasons, have snared the title if it hadn't enjoyed a home-state edge throughout the playoffs (Mideast Regional at Lexington and Final Four at Louisville)? Didn't a highly partisan crowd give them an emotional lift in the national semifinals when they trailed Temple by four points and the Owls had the ball with less than a minute and half remaining? UK benefitted from a sub-par performance by Seattle's Elgin Baylor in the national final, where he went 9 for 32 from the floor. Baylor was still named Final Four Most Outstanding Player.

Outcome for Defending Champion: North Carolina (19-7) tied for second place in the ACC.

1957–58 NCAA CHAMPION: KENTUCKY

SEASON STATISTICS OF KENTUCKY REGULARS

PLAYER	POS.	CL.	G.	FG%	FT%	PPG	RPG
Vern Hatton	G	Sr.	29	.419	.778	17.1	5.0
Johnny Cox	F	Jr.	29	.367	.748	14.9	12.6
John Crigler	F	Sr.	28	.405	.707	13.6	9.9
Adrian Smith	G	Sr.	29	.371	.765	12.4	3.5
Ed Beck	C	Sr.	29	.283	.722	5.6	11.6
Earl Adkins	G	Sr.	19	.453	.742	5.3	1.5
Don Mills	C	So.	20	.253	.625	3.5	5.0
Phil Johnson	F-C	Jr.	22	.306	.517	3.4	5.7
TEAM TOTALS			29	.373	.738	74.7	53.9

1958 FINAL FOUR CHAMPIONSHIP GAME

LOUISVILLE, KY

KENTUCKY (84)	FG-A	FT-A	REB.	PF	PTS.
Cox	10-23	4-4	16	3	24
Crigler	5-12	4-7	14	4	14
Beck	0-1	0-1	3	4	0
Mills	4-9	1-4	5	3	9
Hatton	9-20	12-15	3	3	30
Smith	2-8	3-5	6	4	7
Team			8		
TOTALS	**30-73**	**24-36**	**55**	**21**	**84**

FG%: .411. FT%: .667.

SEATTLE (72)	FG-A	FT-A	REB.	PF	PTS.
Frizzell	4-6	8-11	5	3	16
Ogorek	4-7	2-2	11	5	10
Baylor	9-32	7-9	19	4	25
Harney	2-5	0-1	1	1	4
Brown	6-17	5-7	5	5	17
Saunders	0-2	0-0	2	3	0

Piasecki	0-0	0-0	0	0	0
Team			3		
TOTALS	**25-69**	**22-30**	**46**	**21**	**72**

FG%: .362. FT%: .733.
Halftime: Seattle 39-36.

NATIONAL SEMIFINALS

KENTUCKY (61): Crigler 3-11 0-2 6, Cox 6-17 10-11 22, Collinsworth 0-0 0-0 0, Beck 3-9 2-2 8, Hatton 5-16 3-4 13, Smith 2-10 8-9 12. Team 19-63 (.302) 23-28 (.821) 61.

TEMPLE (60): Norman 7-17 2-3 16, Brodsky 2-5 0-2 4, Van Patton 1-1 1-2 3, Fleming 3-7 3-6 9, Rodgers 9-24 4-6 22, Kennedy 3-7 0-1 6. Team 25-61 (.410) 10-20 (.500) 60.

Halftime: Tied 31-31.

SEATTLE (73): Ogorek 3-9 1-2 7, Frizzell 2-4 6-7 10, Petrie 0-0 0-0 0, Baylor 9-21 5-7 23, Humphries 0-0 0-0 0, Harney 0-4 0-0 0, Brown 5-6 4-5 14, Saunders 5-11 2-3 12, Piasecki 1-1 3-4 5, Kootnekoff 1-1 0-0 2. Team 26-57 (.456) 21-28 (.750) 73.

KANSAS STATE (51): Boozer 6-15 3-5 15, Frank 6-12 3-4 12, Abbott 0-4 0-0 0, Long 2-6 0-1 4, Fischer 0-1 0-0 0, Parr 2-11 0-1 4, Matuszak 3-8 1-3 7, DeWitz 2-7 2-3 6, Holwerda 0-2 0-0 0. Team 21-66 (.318) 9-17 (.529) 51.

Halftime: Seattle 37-32.

ALL-TOURNAMENT TEAM
Elgin Baylor, C, Jr., Seattle*
Charley Brown, G, Jr., Seattle
Johnny Cox, F, Jr., Kentucky
Vernon Hatton, G, Sr., Kentucky
Guy Rodgers, G, Sr., Temple
Named Most Outstanding Player

Biggest Upset: West Virginia, ranked No. 1 in the country at the end of the regular season, was upset by Manhattan in the first round of the East Regional at New York. Jack Powers, the current executive director of the NIT, collected 29 points and 15 rebounds to carry Manhattan (16-10) to an 89-84 victory. Jerry West scored just 10 points in his first NCAA Tournament game for West Virginia (26-2).

What If: West Virginia captain Don Vincent, averaging 12.8 points per game, broke his left leg in the Southern Conference Tournament. The Mountaineers had won by seven points against NCAA champion-to-be Kentucky, handing the Wildcats just their fifth homecourt defeat in 15 years.

1958 CHAMPIONSHIP BRACKET

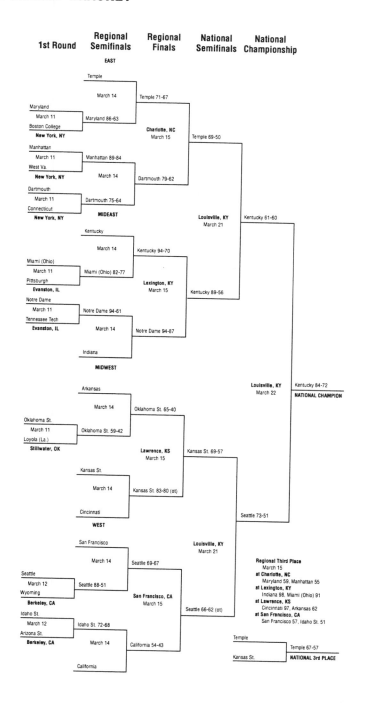

1st Round	Regional Semifinals	Regional Finals	National Semifinals	National Championship

EAST

Temple
March 14 — Temple 71-67
Maryland
March 11 — Maryland 86-63
Boston College
New York, NY
Charlotte, NC March 15 — Temple 69-50
Manhattan
March 11 — Manhattan 89-84
West Va.
New York, NY
March 14 — Dartmouth 79-62
Dartmouth
March 11 — Dartmouth 75-64
Connecticut
New York, NY

MIDEAST

Louisville, KY March 21 — Kentucky 61-60

Kentucky
March 14 — Kentucky 94-70
Miami (Ohio)
March 11 — Miami (Ohio) 82-77
Pittsburgh
Evanston, IL
Lexington, KY March 15 — Kentucky 89-56
Notre Dame
March 11 — Notre Dame 94-61
Tennessee Tech
Evanston, IL
March 14 — Notre Dame 94-87
Indiana

MIDWEST

Louisville, KY March 22 — Kentucky 84-72
NATIONAL CHAMPION

Arkansas
March 14 — Oklahoma St. 65-40
Oklahoma St.
March 11 — Oklahoma St. 59-42
Loyola (La.)
Stillwater, OK
Lawrence, KS March 15 — Kansas St. 69-57
Kansas St.
March 14 — Kansas St. 83-80 (ot)
Cincinnati

WEST

Louisville, KY March 21 — Seattle 73-51

San Francisco
March 14 — Seattle 69-67
Seattle
March 12 — Seattle 88-51
Wyoming
Berkeley, CA
San Francisco, CA March 15 — Seattle 66-62 (ot)
Idaho St.
March 12 — Idaho St. 72-68
Arizona St.
Berkeley, CA
March 14 — California 54-43
California

Regional Third Place
March 15
at **Charlotte, NC**
Maryland 59, Manhattan 55
at **Lexington, KY**
Indiana 98, Miami (Ohio) 91
at **Lawrence, KS**
Cincinnati 97, Arkansas 62
at **San Francisco, CA**
San Francisco 57, Idaho St. 51

Temple
Temple 67-57
Kansas St.
NATIONAL 3rd PLACE

1958–59

AT A GLANCE

NCAA Champion: California (25-4).

NIT Champion: St. John's (20-6).

New Conference: Middle Atlantic (disbanded in 1974 when ECC is formed).

NCAA Probation: Auburn, Memphis State, North Carolina State, Seattle, Southern Cal, UCLA.

NCAA Consensus First-Team All-Americans: Bob Boozer, F, Sr., Kansas State; Johnny Cox, F, Sr., Kentucky; Bailey Howell, F, Sr., Mississippi State; Oscar Robertson, F, Jr., Cincinnati; Jerry West, F, Jr., West Virginia.

Mississippi State's Bailey Howell set a school record with 47 points against Union. Mississippi State won its first SEC title with a 13-1 record and finished 24-1 overall, but was forced to bypass the NCAA Tournament because of the opposition of several state officials to interracial games.

Cincinnati's Oscar Robertson became the first player to lead the nation's scorers in both his sophomore and junior seasons. Robertson's brilliance wasn't enough to prevent the Bearcats from losing against California (64-58) in the national semifinals. Guard Mike Mendenhall, the team's co-captain and third-leading scorer (13.5-point average) as one of the nation's top 15 field-goal shooters (51.3 percent), was declared ineligible for the playoffs by the NCAA because he played briefly in the 1955–56 season before missing the remainder of the year nursing a kidney ailment.

The season's highest single-game output was 50 points by Air Force's Bob Beckel and Rhode Island's Tom Harrington.

Oklahoma State's Arlen Clark set an NCAA record for most successful free throws in a game without a miss when he sank all 24 of his foul shots in a 42-point outburst against Colorado.

West Virginia went unbeaten in Southern Conference competition for the third consecutive season.

Auburn was the only school to rank among the top 35 in both offense and defense.

Villanova's George Raveling, who would go on to become one of the nation's most visible coaches, ranked among the top 25 players in the country in field-goal shooting (50.6 percent) and rebounding (15.5 per game).

North Carolina State coach Everett Case, compiling a 320-81 record through 13 seasons, had more victories than any coach in history from his second year through his 13th.

1958-59 FINAL NATIONAL POLLS

AP	UPI	SCHOOL
1	1	Kansas St.
2	2	Kentucky
3	6	Mississippi St.
4	8	Bradley
5	4	Cincinnati
6	5	North Carolina St.
7	3	Michigan St.
8	10	Auburn
9	6	North Carolina
10	11	West Virginia
11	9	California
12	13	St. Louis
13	–	Seattle
14	20	St. Joseph's
15	18	St. Mary's
16	12	Texas Christian
17	–	Oklahoma City
18	14	Utah
19	–	St. Bonaventure
20	15	Marquette
–	16	Tennessee Tech
–	17	St. John's
–	18	Navy

1959 NCAA Tournament

Summary: Two-time first-team All-American swingman Jerry West was denied an NCAA championship ring when Cal junior center Darrall Imhoff, West's teammate with the Los Angeles Lakers for four seasons in the mid-1960s, tipped in a basket with 17 seconds remaining to give California a 71-70 victory over West Virginia in the NCAA final.

Outcome for Defending Champion: Second-ranked Kentucky (24-3) hit less than one-third of its field-goal attempts in blowing a 15-point lead and absorbing a 76-61 setback against Louisville (19-12).

Star Gazing: West, the Final Four Most Outstanding Player, collected a total of 66 points and

Cincinnati's national scoring leader Oscar Robertson comes down with a rebound.

26 rebounds for West Virginia in the national semifinals and final.

Biggest Upset: Kansas State, an 85-75 loser against Cincinnati in the Midwest Regional final, is one of only two teams ranked No. 1 by both AP and UPI entering the tourney to lose by a double-digit margin before the Final Four.

One and Only: Pete Newell became the only U.S. Olympic basketball coach to win the NCAA and NIT titles with different schools. Newell was the 1960 U.S. Olympic basketball coach after capturing national titles with San Francisco (NIT in 1949) and California.

What If: ACC regular-season co-champion and tournament kingpin North Carolina State, which defeated Final Four teams Louisville and Cincinnati, was ineligible for the tourney because of NCAA probation.

Putting Things in Perspective: Oregon, which compiled a 3-13 record in the PCC and 9-16 overall, defeated California, 59-57.

1950–59 PREMO POWER POLL: BEST TEAMS BY DECADE

RANK	SEASON	SCHOOL
1	1955–56	San Francisco* (29-0)
2	1953–54	Kentucky (25-0)
3	1956–57	North Carolina* (32-0)
4	1954–55	San Francisco* (28-1)
5	1950–51	Kentucky* (32-2)
6	1958–59	Kansas St. (25-2)
7	1951–52	Kentucky (29-3)
8	1957–58	Cincinnati (25-3)
9	1952–53	Indiana* (23-3)
10	1956–57	Kansas (24-3)
11	1953–54	Holy Cross# (26-2)
12	1957–58	West Virginia (26-2)
13	1951–52	Kansas* (28-3)
14	1958–59	California* (25-4)
15	1949–50	CCNY#* (24-5)
16	1952–53	Seton Hall# (31-2)
17	1950–51	Illinois (22-5)
18	1957–58	San Francisco (25-2)
19	1953–54	Duquesne (26-3)
20	1950–51	Indiana (19-3)
	1958–59	Cincinnati (26-4)

#–NIT Champion
*–NCAA Tournament Champion

North Carolina State coach Everett Case and his Wolfpack were on NCAA probation in 1958–59.

1958–59 INDIVIDUAL LEADERS

SCORING

PLAYER	PTS.	AVG.
Robertson, Cincinnati	978	32.6
Byrd, Marshall	704	29.3
Hagan, Tennessee Tech	720	28.8
Howell, Mississippi St.	688	27.5
West, West Virginia	903	26.6
Ayersman, Virginia Tech	556	26.5
Hennon, Pittsburgh	617	25.7
Boozer, Kansas St.	691	25.6
Windis, Wyoming	463	24.4
Hawkins, Notre Dame	514	23.4

REBOUNDING

PLAYER	REB.	PCT.
Wright, Pacific	652	.238

Howell, Mississippi St.	379	.220
Smith, Virginia Tech	429	.202
Mealy, Manhattan	240	.201
Cohen, William & Mary	413	.200
Tormohlen, Tennessee	372	.192
Cincebox, Syracuse	365	.188
Danzig, Bucknell	386	.184
Washington, Boston	382	.183

FIELD GOAL PERCENTAGE

PLAYER	FGM	FGA	PCT.
Crosthwaite, W. Ky.	191	296	.645
Carter, Iona	137	225	.609
Kessler, Muhlenberg	153	271	.565
Herdelin, La Salle	144	256	.563
Sanders, New York	131	236	.555
Stith, St. Bonaventure	162	295	.549

Wilson, Furman	157	289	.543
McCraw, Oklahoma City	119	220	.541
Moses, Oklahoma City	158	293	.539
Price, New Mexico St.	209	401	.521

FREE THROW PERCENTAGE

PLAYER	FTM	FTA	PCT.
Clark, Oklahoma St.	201	236	.852
Burgess, Gonzaga	151	178	.848
Neumann, Stanford	127	150	.847
Kaiser, Georgia Tech	106	127	.835
Wendel, Tulsa	185	222	.833
Kennedy, Temple	184	221	.833
Guarilia, G. Wash.	99	119	.832
Siegfried, Ohio St.	136	164	.829
Hagan, Tennessee Tech	212	256	.828
Mills, Kentucky	101	122	.828

1958–59 TEAM LEADERS

SCORING OFFENSE

SCHOOL	PTS.	AVG.
Miami (Fla.)	2190	87.6
West Virginia	2884	84.8
Cincinnati	2519	84.0
Virginia Tech	1758	83.7
Illinois	1815	82.5

SCORING DEFENSE

SCHOOL	PTS.	AVG.
California	1480	51.0
Oklahoma St.	1319	52.8
Idaho St.	1504	53.7
San Jose St.	1352	56.3
Maryland	1296	56.4

FIELD GOAL PERCENTAGE

SCHOOL	FGM	FGA	PCT.
Auburn	593	1216	.488
Cincinnati	970	2062	.470
Oklahoma City	769	1680	.458
St. Bonaventure	724	1584	.457
West Virginia	1075	2355	.456
Mississippi St.	663	1453	.456

FREE THROW PERCENTAGE

SCHOOL	FTM	FTA	PCT.
Tulsa	446	586	.761
Mississippi St.	532	700	.760
George Washington	402	534	.753
Kentucky	570	758	.752
Marshall	472	631	.748

REBOUND PERCENTAGE

SCHOOL	TOT. REB.	REB.	PCT.
Mississippi St.	1719	1012	.589
Iona	1087	1856	.586
Michigan St.	2597	1508	.581
Eastern Kentucky	2346	1361	.580
Gonzaga	2473	1426	.577

1958–59 NCAA CHAMPION: CALIFORNIA

SEASON STATISTICS OF CALIFORNIA REGULARS

PLAYER	POS.	CL.	G.	FG%	FT%	PPG	RPG
Denny Fitzpatrick	G	Sr.	29	.456	.854	13.3	2.8
Darrall Imhoff	C	Jr.	29	.424	.535	11.3	11.0
Al Buch	G	Sr.	29	.358	.646	9.2	2.8
Bill McClintock	F	So.	28	.416	.561	7.8	7.3
Bob Dalton	F	Sr.	29	.367	.663	7.3	4.6
Jack Grout	F	Sr.	28	.464	.639	5.5	3.7
Dick Doughty	C	Jr.	29	.423	.581	3.4	2.6
Jim Langley	F	Sr.	27	.427	.333	2.6	1.5
Bernie Simpson	G	Sr.	28	.295	.688	2.1	1.3
TEAM TOTALS			29	.406	.634	63.9	45.1

1959 FINAL FOUR CHAMPIONSHIP GAME

LOUISVILLE, KY

WEST VIRGINIA (70)	FG-A	FT-A	REB.	PF	PTS.
West	10-21	8-12	11	4	28
Akers	5-8	0-1	6	0	10
Clousson	4-7	2-3	4	4	10
Smith	2-5	1-1	2	3	5
Bolyard	1-4	4-4	3	4	6
Retton	0-0	2-2	0	0	2
Ritchie	1-4	2-2	4	0	4
Patrone	2-6	1-2	4	1	5
Team			7		
TOTALS	25-55	20-27	41	16	70

FG%: .455. FT%: .741.

CALIFORNIA (71)	FG-A	FT-A	REB.	PF	PTS.
McClintock	4-13	0-1	10	1	8
Dalton	6-11	3-4	2	4	15
Imhoff	4-13	2-2	9	3	10
Buch	0-4	2-2	2	3	2
Fitzpatrick	8-13	4-7	2	1	20
Simpson	0-1	0-0	2	2	0
Grout	4-5	2-2	3	1	10
Doughty	3-6	0-0	1	3	6
Team			7		
TOTALS	29-66	13-18	38	18	71

FG%: .439. FT%: .722.
Halftime: California 39-33.

NATIONAL SEMIFINALS

CALIFORNIA (64): McClintock 2-11 2-4 6, Dalton 2-4 3-4 7, Imhoff 10-25 2-5 22, Fitzpatrick 2-9 0-0 4, Buch 7-15 4-6 18, Grout 2-7 1-2 5, Simpson 1-2 0-0 2. Team 26-73 (.356) 12-21 (.571) 64.

CINCINNATI (58): Robertson 5-16 9-11 19, Wiesenhahn 5-11 0-0 10, Tenwick 2-6 1-1 5, Davis 6-15 1-2 13, Whitaker 4-7 0-2 8, Landfried 0-1 3-5 3, Bouldin 0-0 0-1 0. Team 22-56 (.393) 14-22 (.636) 58.

Halftime: Cincinnati 33-29.

WEST VIRGINIA (94): West 12-21 14-20 38, Akers 2-5 1-2 5, Clousson 5-5 2-2 12, Smith 5-9 2-4 12, Bolyard 4-10 5-7 13, Ritchie 2-6 0-2 4, Patrone 1-4 0-0 2, Retton 3-4 0-0 6, Schertzniger 0-0 0-0 0, Posch 1-2 0-0 0-0 0, Visnic 0-0 0-0 0. Team 35-66 (.530) 24-37 (.649) 94.

LOUISVILLE (79): Goldstein 6-10 9-9 21, Turner 8-16 2-5 18, Sawyer 2-6 3-4 7, Tieman 1-7 1-1 3, Andrews 9-15 1-1 19, Kitchen 3-7 0-0 6, Leathers 2-8 1-1 5, Geiling 0-0 0-0 0, Stacey 0-0 0-0 0. Team 31-69 (.449) 17-21 (.810) 79.

Halftime: West Virginia 48-32.

ALL-TOURNAMENT TEAM

Denny Fitzpatrick, G, Sr., California
Don Goldstein, F, Sr., Louisville
Darrall Imhoff, C, Jr., California
Oscar Robertson, F, Jr., Cincinnati
Jerry West, F, Jr., West Virginia*
     *Named Most Outstanding Player

West Virginia's Jerry West whizzes past Louisville's John Turner in the 1959 NCAA Tournament semifinals.

1959 CHAMPIONSHIP BRACKET

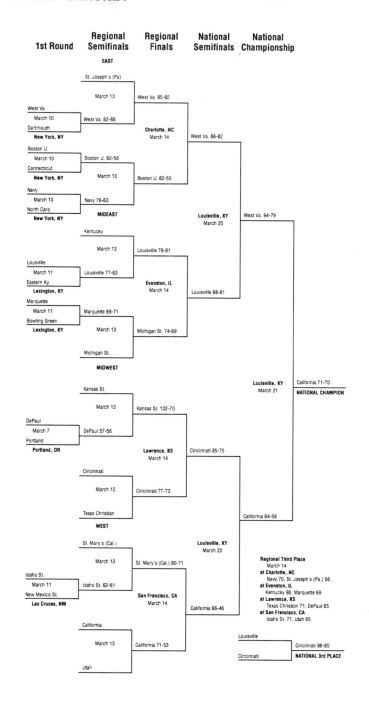

	Regional	Regional	National	National
1st Round	Semifinals	Finals	Semifinals	Championship

EAST

St. Joseph's (Pa)
   March 13   West Va. 95-92
West Va.
   March 10   West Va. 82-68
Dartmouth
New York, NY   **Charlotte, NC**   West Va. 86-82
    March 14
Boston U.
   March 10   Boston U. 60-58
Connecticut
New York, NY   March 13   Boston U. 62-55
Navy
   March 10   Navy 76-63
North Caro.
New York, NY

MIDEAST

    Louisville, KY   West Va. 94-79
    March 20

Kentucky
   March 13   Louisville 76-61
Lousville
   March 11   Louisville 77-63
Eastern Ky.
Lexington, KY   **Evanston, IL**
    March 14   Louisville 88-81
Marquette
   March 11   Marquette 89-71
Bowling Green
Lexington, KY   March 13   Michigan St. 74-69
Michigan St.

MIDWEST

    Louisville, KY   California 71-70
    March 21   **NATIONAL CHAMPION**

Kansas St.
   March 13   Kansas St. 102-70
DePaul
   March 7   DePaul 57-56
Portland
Portland, OR   **Lawrence, KS**   Cincinnati 85-75
    March 14
Cincinnati
   March 12   Cincinnati 77-73
Texas Christian

WEST

    California 64-58

    Louisville, KY
    March 20

St. Mary's (Cal.)
   March 13   St. Mary's (Cal.) 80-71
Idaho St.
   March 11   Idaho St. 62-61
New Mexico St.
Las Cruces, NM   **San Francisco, CA**
    March 14   California 66-46
California
   March 13   California 71-53
Utah

Regional Third Place
March 14
at Charlotte, NC
  Navy 70, St. Joseph's (Pa.) 56
at Evanston, IL
  Kentucky 98, Marquette 69
at Lawrence, KS
  Texas Christian 71, DePaul 65
at San Francisco, CA
  Idaho St. 71, Utah 65

Louisville
    Cincinnati 98-85
Cincinnati
    NATIONAL 3rd PLACE

4

THE UCLA DYNASTY:
THE 1960s

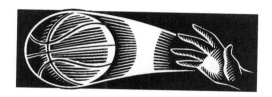

The 1960s marked the beginning of perhaps the greatest dynasty in the history of sports as UCLA began its march toward 10 NCAA championships in a 12-year span. The South was behind the times but African Americans were finally allowed to play in the ACC, SEC, and SWC. The end of the decade supplied the marvelous showmanship of the M Boys—Pete Maravich, Rick Mount, and Calvin Murphy. The combination of these influences dictated that college hoops would never be the same again.

1959–60

AT A GLANCE

NCAA Champion: Ohio State (25-3).

NIT Champion: Bradley (27-2).

NCAA Probation: Arizona State, Auburn, Montana State, North Carolina State, Seattle.

NCAA Consensus First-Team All-Americans: Darrall Imhoff, C, Sr., California; Jerry Lucas, C, Soph., Ohio State; Oscar Robertson, F, Sr., Cincinnati; Tom Stith, F, Jr., St. Bonaventure; Jerry West, F, Sr., West Virginia.

Tom and Sam Stith combined to average 52 points per game, an NCAA single-season record for brothers on the same team. Tom Stith, runner-up in scoring nationally to Cincinnati's Oscar Robertson, improved from ranking 71st in the country the previous year.

Tom Stith averaged more points per game than Robertson over the last two-thirds of the campaign, but the Big O hung on for the title after averaging over 40 points per game through his senior season's first 10 contests. The season's single-game scoring high was Robertson's school-record 62 against North Texas State.

Ohio State's Jerry Lucas had the largest-ever margin over the national runner-up in field-goal shooting. Lucas hit 63.7 percent of his shots compared to 57.6 percent for Cincinnati's Paul Hogue.

West Virginia's Jerry West finished his career as the shortest player (6-3) to score more than 2,300 points and grab more than 1,200 rebounds. West, the Mountaineers' all-time leading rebounder (1,240), tied a school record when he retrieved 31 missed shots in a game against George Washington.

Auburn became the first school to lead the nation in field-goal shooting by hitting more than half of its shots (52.1 percent). The Tigers also paced the country in free-throw accuracy (77.2 percent) en route to their only SEC regular-season championship.

Arizona's Ernie McCray set a school record with 46 points against Los Angeles State.

Future basketball telecaster Billy Packer was 6 for 35 from the floor for Wake Forest in three ACC Tournament games.

Kentucky's streak of 20-win seasons ended at 14 when the Wildcats compiled an 18-7 record.

Hofstra (23-1) compiled the best record of any team, but failed to win the Middle Atlantic Conference College Division-North because its only defeat came to first-place Wagner.

Connecticut captured its 10th consecutive Yankee Conference championship.

Idaho State won its eighth consecutive Rocky Mountain Conference championship in the final season of the league.

CCNY's Nat Holman ended his 37-year coaching career early in the season with a 423-190 record.

Pete Newell, who coached San Francisco, Michigan State, and California, retired after a 14-year coaching career with a 234-123 record.

Wake Forest's team captain Dave Budd (left) and Billy Packer.

1959–60 FINAL NATIONAL POLLS

AP	UPI	SCHOOL
1	2	Cincinnati
2	1	California
3	3	Ohio State
4	4	Bradley
5	6	West Virginia
6	5	Utah
7	10	Indiana
8	7	Utah State
9	11	St. Bonaventure
10	–	Miami (Fla.)
11	17	Auburn
12	12	NYU
13	8	Georgia Tech
14	18	Providence
15	19	St. Louis
16	–	Holy Cross
17	9	Villanova
18	15	Duke
19	–	Wake Forest
20	–	St. John's
–	13	Texas
–	14	North Carolina
–	16	Kansas State
–	20	Dayton

1960 NCAA Tournament

Summary: Ohio State became the only titlist to win all of its tournament games by more than 15 points. Center Jerry Lucas, a first-team All-American as a sophomore, averaged 24 points and 16 rebounds in four playoff contests for the Buckeyes. He collected 36 points and 25 rebounds to help them erase a six-point halftime deficit in their Mideast Regional opener against Western Kentucky. Ohio State, playing in the Bay Area (San Francisco) against the nation's top defensive team (California), hit a sizzling 84.2 percent of its first-half field-goal attempts (16-19) en route to a 75-55 victory over the defending champion Bears. Ohio State's five starters—sophomores Lucas, John Havlicek, and Mel Nowell, senior Joe Roberts, and junior Larry Siegfried—were all high school centers. They each scored in double figures in the NCAA final

1959-60 INDIVIDUAL LEADERS

SCORING

PLAYER	PTS.	AVG.
Robertson, Cincinnati	1011	33.7
T. Stith, St. Bonaventure	819	31.5
Darrow, Bowling Green	705	29.4
West, West Virginia	908	29.3
Burgess, Gonzaga	751	28.9
Butler, Niagara	714	28.6
Dischinger, Purdue	605	26.3
Lucas, Ohio St.	710	26.3
DeBusschere, Detroit	691	25.6
Mudd, N. Texas St.	605	25.2

REBOUNDING

PLAYER	REB.	PCT.
Wright, Pacific	380	.234
DeBusschere, Detroit	540	.198

Mortell, Virginia	350	.194
Cohen, William & Mary	471	.194
Smith, Virginia Tech	495	.190
Jones, Niagara	383	.190
Hadnot, Providence	473	.186
Kojis, Marquette	384	.186
Farley, Cornell	466	.185
Jolliff, Ohio	445	.180

FIELD GOAL PERCENTAGE

PLAYER	FGM	FGA	PCT.
Lucas, Ohio St.	283	444	.637
Hogue, Cincinnati	152	264	.576
Gunter, Seton Hall	128	224	.571
Walker, Bradley	244	436	.560
Nordmann, St. Louis	173	310	.558
Dischinger, Purdue	201	368	.546
Hughes, Texas	111	205	.541

Johnson, Minnesota	186	346	.538
Fibbe, Auburn	108	201	.537
Hart, Auburn	108	201	.537

FREE THROW PERCENTAGE

PLAYER	FTM	FTA	PCT.
Waters, Mississippi	103	118	.873
Larese, N. Carolina	131	151	.868
Kaiser, Georgia Tech	164	190	.863
Carl, DePaul	135	158	.854
Smith, Middle Tenn.	144	170	.847
Butler, Niagara	158	187	.845
Pipczynski, Connecticut	102	122	.836
Names, Washington	90	108	.833
Clarke, St. Joseph's	100	121	.826
Adkins, Virginia	109	132	.826

1959-60 TEAM LEADERS

SCORING OFFENSE

SCHOOL	PTS.	AVG.
Ohio St.	2532	90.4
Miami (Fla.)	2427	89.9
West Virginia	2775	89.5
Cincinnati	2602	86.7
Arizona St.	1930	83.9

SCORING DEFENSE

SCHOOL	PTS.	AVG.
California	1486	49.5
Oklahoma St.	1304	52.2
Stanford	1376	55.0
Oregon St.	1458	56.1
Providence	1632	56.3

FIELD GOAL PERCENTAGE

SCHOOL	FGM	FGA	PCT.
Auburn	532	1022	.521
Cincinnati	1035	2025	.511
Ohio St.	1044	2101	.497
Texas	713	1503	.474
Bradley	921	1969	.468

FREE THROW PERCENTAGE

SCHOOL	FTM	FTA	PCT.
Auburn	424	549	.772
Tulane	438	573	.764
North Carolina	542	715	.758
Mississippi	451	600	.752
East Tennessee St.	438	585	.749

REBOUNDING

SCHOOL	TOTAL REB.	REB.	PCT.
Iona	1736	1054	.607
Cornell	2522	1492	.592
Ohio St.	2447	1415	.578
St. Francis (Pa.)	2472	1429	.578
Loyola (Calif.)	2355	1359	.577

before eventually playing at least two seasons in the NBA, ABA, or both.

Star Gazing: Oscar Robertson generated glittering averages of 32.6 points per game and 33.7 in leading Cincinnati to the national semifinals in 1959 and 1960, respectively, before the Bearcats were beaten both years by California. The Bears restricted the Big O to a total of 37 points in the two Final Four games as he was just nine of 32 from the floor.

Biggest Upset: Oregon, which lost seven of its last 12 regular-season games, defeated Utah, 65-54, in the West Regional semifinals. Utah, ranked No. 5 by UPI and No. 6 by AP entering the tourney, didn't have a player score more than 10 points against the Ducks.

One and Only: Idaho State became the only school to make as many as eight consecutive NCAA Tournament appearances from the year it participated in the event for the first time (since 1953 under three different coaches).... Ohio State's Fred Taylor became the only coach of an NCAA titlist to previously play major league baseball (first baseman for the Washington Senators in parts of three seasons from 1950 through 1952).

Numbers Game: Ohio State, the only team to lead the nation in scoring offense and win the NCAA championship in the same is also the only champion to win all of its tournament games by more than 15 points.... Lucas scored his playoff career-high 36 points in his tournament debut (98-79 victory over Western Kentucky in Mideast Regional semifinal).... West Virginia swingman Jerry West became the only

1959-60 NCAA CHAMPION: OHIO STATE

SEASON STATISTICS OF OHIO STATE REGULARS

PLAYER	POS.	CL.	G.	FG%	FT%	PPG	RPG
Jerry Lucas	C	So.	27	.637	.770	26.3	16.4
Larry Siegfried	G	Jr.	28	.466	.750	13.3	3.8
Mel Nowell	G	So.	28	.473	.767	13.1	2.6
John Havlicek	F	So.	28	.462	.716	12.2	7.3
Joe Roberts	F	Sr.	28	.480	.679	11.0	6.9
Richard Furry	F	Sr.	28	.455	.606	5.1	3.3
Bob Knight	F-G	So.	21	.405	.630	3.7	2.0
Howard Nourse	C	Sr.	17	.511	1.000	3.1	2.7
Gary Gearhart	G	So.	19	.404	.438	2.6	1.2
Richie Hoyt	G	Sr.	23	.423	.778	2.5	0.8
David Barker	G	Sr.	16	.407	.167	1.4	0.8
TEAM TOTALS			28	.497	.717	90.4	50.5

1960 FINAL FOUR CHAMPIONSHIP GAME

KANSAS CITY, MO

OHIO STATE (75)	FG-A	FT-A	REB.	PF	PTS.
Havlicek	4-8	4-5	6	2	12
Roberts	5-6	0-1	5	1	10
Lucas	7-9	2-2	10	2	16
Nowell	6-7	3-3	4	2	15
Siegfried	5-6	3-6	1	2	13
Gearhart	0-1	0-0	1	0	0
Cedargren	0-0	1-2	1	1	1
Furry	2-4	0-0	3	1	4
Hoyt	0-1	0-0	0	0	0
Barker	0-0	0-0	0	0	0
Knight	0-1	0-0	0	1	0
Nourse	2-3	0-0	3	1	4
Team			1		
TOTALS	31-46	13-19	35	13	75

FG%: .674. FT%: .684.

CALIFORNIA (55)	FG-A	FT-A	REB.	PF	PTS.
McClintock	4-15	2-3	3	3	10
Gillis	4-9	0-0	1	1	8
Imhoff	3-9	2-2	5	2	8
Wendell	0-6	4-4	0	2	4
Shultz	2-8	2-2	4	4	6
Mann	3-5	1-1	0	0	7
Doughty	4-5	3-3	6	1	11
Stafford	0-1	1-2	0	1	1
Morrison	0-0	0-0	1	1	0
Averbuck	0-0	0-1	1	0	0
Pearson	0-1	0-0	0	0	0
Alexander	0-0	0-0	0	0	0
Team			7		
TOTALS	20-59	15-18	28	15	55

FG%: .339. FT%: .833.
Halftime: Ohio State 37-19.

NATIONAL SEMIFINALS

CALIFORNIA (64): McClintock 2-11 2-4 6, Dalton 2-4 3-4 7, Imhoff 10-25 2-5 22, Fitzpatrick 2-9 0-0 4, Buch 7-15 4-6 18, Grout 2-7 1-2 5, Simpson 1-2 0-0 2. Team 26-73 (.356) 12-21 (.571) 64.

CINCINNATI (58): Robertson 5-16 9-11 19, Wiesenhahn 5-11 0-0 10, Tenwick 2-6 1-5, Davis 6-15 1-2 13, Whitaker 4-7 0-2 8, Landfried 0-1 3-5 3, Bouldin 0-0 0-1 0. Team 22-56 (.393) 14-22 (.636) 58.

Halftime: Cincinnati 33-29.

WEST VIRGINIA (94): West 12-21 14-20 38, Akers 2-5 1-2 5, Clousson 5-5 2-2 12, Smith 5-9 2-4 12, Bolyard 4-10 5-7 13, Ritchie 2-6 0-2 4, Patrone 1-4 0-0 2, Retton 3-4 0-0 6, Schertzniger 0-0 0-0 0, Posch 1-2 0-0 2, Goode 0-0 0-0 0, Visnic 0-0 0-0 0. Team 35-66 (.530) 24-37 (.649) 94.

LOUISVILLE (79): Goldstein 6-10 9-9 21, Turner 8-16 2-5 18, Sawyer 2-6 3-4 7, Tieman 1-7 1-1 3, Andrews 9-15 1-1 19, Kitchen 3-7 0-0 6, Leathers 2-8 1-1 5, Geiling 0-0 0-0 0, Stacey 0-0 0-0 0. Team 31-69 (.449) 17-21 (.810) 79.

Halftime: West Virginia 48-32.

ALL-TOURNAMENT TEAM

Darrall Imhoff, C, Sr., California
Jerry Lucas, C, Soph., Ohio State*
Mel Nowell, G, Soph., Ohio State
Oscar Robertson, F, Sr., Cincinnati
Tom Sanders, C, Sr., New York University
*Named Most Outstanding Player

player to score at least 25 points in eight consecutive tournament games (1959 and 1960). West is also the only player to rank among the top five in scoring average in both the NCAA Tournament (30.6 points per game) and NBA playoffs (29.1 ppg).

1960 CHAMPIONSHIP BRACKET

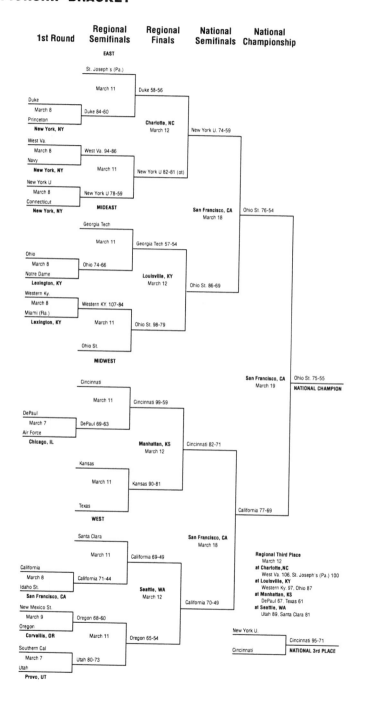

1st Round	Regional Semifinals	Regional Finals	National Semifinals	National Championship

EAST

St. Joseph's (Pa.)
March 11
Duke 58-56

Duke
March 8
Princeton
New York, NY
Duke 84-60

West Va.
March 8
Navy
New York, NY
West Va. 94-86

New York U
March 8
Connecticut
New York, NY
New York U 78-59

Charlotte, NC
March 12

New York U 82-81 (ot)

New York U. 74-59

MIDEAST

Georgia Tech
March 11
Georgia Tech 57-54

Ohio
March 8
Notre Dame
Lexington, KY
Ohio 74-66

Western Ky.
March 8
Miami (Fla.)
Lexington, KY
Western KY. 107-84

Ohio St.

March 11
Ohio St. 98-79

Louisville, KY
March 12

Ohio St. 86-69

MIDWEST

San Francisco, CA
March 18

Ohio St. 76-54

Cincinnati
March 11
Cincinnati 99-59

DePaul
March 7
Air Force
Chicago, IL
DePaul 69-63

Kansas
March 11
Kansas 90-81

Texas

Manhattan, KS
March 12

Cincinnati 82-71

WEST

San Francisco, CA
March 19

Ohio St. 75-55
NATIONAL CHAMPION

Cincinnati 82-71

California 77-69

Santa Clara
March 11
California 69-49

California
March 8
Idaho St.
San Francisco, CA
California 71-44

New Mexico St.
March 9
Oregon
Corvallis, OR
Oregon 68-60

Southern Cal
March 7
Utah
Provo, UT
Utah 80-73

Oregon 65-54

Seattle, WA
March 12

California 70-49

San Francisco, CA
March 18

Regional Third Place
March 12
at Charlotte,NC
West Va. 106, St. Joseph's (Pa.) 100
at Louisville, KY
Western Ky. 97, Ohio 87
at Manhattan, KS
DePaul 67, Texas 61
at Seattle, WA
Utah 89, Santa Clara 81

New York U.

Cincinnati

Cincinnati 95-71
NATIONAL 3rd PLACE

1960-61

AT A GLANCE

NCAA Champion: Cincinnati (27-3).

NIT Champion: Providence (24-5).

NCAA Probation: Auburn, Indiana, Kansas, Loyola (La.), Montana State, North Carolina.

NCAA Consensus First-Team All-Americans: Terry Dischinger, F, Jr., Purdue; Roger Kaiser, G, Sr., Georgia Tech; Jerry Lucas, C, Jr., Ohio State; Tom Stith, F, Sr., St. Bonaventure; Chet Walker, F, Jr., Bradley.

Georgia Tech All-American Roger Kaiser.

Scandal reared its ugly head again. The only player to score 40 or more points in a Final Four contest and not eventually play in the NBA was St. Joseph's forward Jack Egan, who scored 42 points in a four-overtime, 127-120 triumph against Utah in the national third-place game. Egan became a third-round draft choice of Philadelphia but forfeited the opportunity to play in the pros when he was implicated in a game-fixing scandal. Egan was susceptible to such shenanigans inasmuch as he was the father of two children and his wife had suffered a miscarriage just before the season started.

Indiana's Walt Bellamy set a Big Ten Conference record with 33 rebounds in a game against Michigan.

Gonzaga's Frank Burgess closed his season with a 37-point outburst to win the scoring title with a 32.38 average, edging East Tennessee State's Tom Chilton, who was second with a 32.13 average.

Oklahoma State didn't finish among the top three in national defense rankings for the first time in 26 years. The top four defensive teams were all from the San Francisco Bay Area—Santa Clara (48.7), San Jose State (50.3), San Francisco (51.4), and California (54.2).

Sylvester Blye, a 6-5, 220-pound sophomore forward, collected 23 points and 11 rebounds for Seattle in his debut and farewell game, an 86-81 loss to Memphis State. The following day it was discovered that he had played briefly the previous season with the New York Clowns, a touring pro team, and he was declared ineligible for further college competition.

Rutgers (11-10) registered its first winning record in 12 seasons.

1960-61 INDIVIDUAL LEADERS

SCORING

PLAYER	PTS.	AVG.
Burgess, Gonzaga	842	32.4
Chilton, E. Tennessee St.	771	32.1
Stith, St. Bonaventure	830	29.6
Dischinger, Purdue	648	28.2
McGill, Utah	862	27.8
Chappell, Wake Forest	745	26.6
Foley, Holy Cross	688	26.5
Walker, Bradley	656	25.2
Heyman, Duke	629	25.2
Warner, Gettysburg	623	24.9
Lucas, Ohio St.	671	24.9

REBOUNDING

PLAYER	REB.	PCT.
Lucas, Ohio St.	470	.198

Thurmond, Bowling Green	449	.196
Cohen, William & Mary	424	.185
DeBusschere, Detroit	514	.180
Hadnot, Providence	475	.178
Chilton, E. Tennessee St.	403	.175
Bellamy, Indiana	428	.171
Ardon, Tulane	392	.168
Kojis, Marquette	462	.167
Smith, Virginia Tech	362	.164

FIELD GOAL PERCENTAGE

PLAYER	FGM	FGA	PCT.
Lucas, Ohio St.	256	411	.623
Gunter, Seton Hall	200	325	.615
Youngkin, Duke	146	253	.577
Dischinger, Purdue	215	373	.576
Lundy, Lafayette	174	303	.574
Havlicek, Ohio St.	183	321	.570

Ward, Boston College	115	202	.569
Walker, Bradley	238	423	.563
Weiss, Rhode Island	111	199	.558
Hull, Wake Forest	114	206	.553

FREE THROW PERCENTAGE

PLAYER	FTM	FTA	PCT.
Sherard, Army	135	154	.877
Carl, DePaul	161	184	.875
Kaiser, Georgia Tech	176	203	.867
Thompson, Morehead St.	180	208	.865
Carlton, Arkansas	101	117	.863
Siegfried, Ohio St.	123	143	.860
Strickland, Oregon	90	106	.849
Patterson, Clemson	146	173	.844
Zeller, Miami (Ohio)	172	205	.839
Pursiful, Kentucky	99	118	.839

1960-61 TEAM LEADERS

SCORING OFFENSE

SCHOOL	PTS.	AVG.
St. Bonaventure	2479	88.5
Loyola (Ill.)	1989	86.5
West Virginia	2325	86.1
Virginia Tech	1874	85.2
Ohio St.	2383	85.1

SCORING DEFENSE

SCHOOL	PTS.	AVG.
Santa Clara	1314	48.7
San Jose St.	1254	50.2
San Francisco	1440	51.4
California	1192	54.2
Portland	1415	56.6

FIELD GOAL PERCENTAGE

SCHOOL	FGM	FGA	PCT.
Ohio St.	939	1886	.498
St. Bonaventure	1010	2041	.495
Bradley	798	1622	.492
Auburn	500	1018	.491
Utah	1008	2069	.487

FREE THROW PERCENTAGE

SCHOOL	FTM	FTA	PCT.
Tulane	459	604	.760
Ohio St.	505	671	.753
West Texas St.	421	561	.750
W. Kentucky	554	742	.747
Arkansas	428	574	.746

REBOUNDING

SCHOOL	TOTAL REB.	REB.	PCT.
Bradley	2247	1330	.592
Memphis St.	2332	1366	.586
Niagara	1796	1048	.584
Cornell	2406	1384	.575
Cincinnati	2706	1553	.574

St. Bonaventure's 99-game homecourt winning streak, which started in 1948, was snapped

1960-61 FINAL NATIONAL POLLS

AP	UPI	SCHOOL
1	1	Ohio St.
2	2	Cincinnati
3	3	St. Bonaventure
4	4	Kansas St.
5	6	North Carolina
6	7	Bradley
7	5	Southern Cal
8	10	Iowa
9	12	West Virginia
10	9	Duke
11	13	Utah
12	18	Texas Tech
13	–	Niagara
14	20	Memphis St.
15	10	Wake Forest
16	8	St. John's
17	16	St. Joseph's
18	–	Drake
19	–	Holy Cross
20	18	Kentucky
–	14	St. Louis
–	15	Louisville
–	17	Dayton

by Niagara, 87-77. Drake stopped Bradley's 46-game homecourt winning streak, 86-76.

George Washington ended West Virginia's streak of six consecutive Southern Conference Tournament championships. GWU entered the tourney with a 6-16 record. Jon Feldman, 5-10, scored 45 points for the Colonials in the championship game against William & Mary.

William & Mary's Jeff Cohen (49 points against Richmond), Missouri's Joe Scott (46 against Nebraska), and Tulane's Jim Kerwin (45 against Southeastern Louisiana) set school single-game scoring records.

1961 NCAA Tournament

Summary: Paul Hogue, a 6-9 center who hit just 51.8 percent of his free-throw attempts during the season, sank only two of 10 foul shots in

1960–61 NCAA CHAMPION: CINCINNATI

SEASON STATISTICS OF CINCINNATI REGULARS

PLAYER	POS.	CL.	G.	FG%	FT%	PPG	RPG
Bob Wiesenhahn	F	Sr.	30	.481	.678	17.1	10.0
Paul Hogue	C	Jr.	30	.532	.518	16.8	12.5
Tom Thacker	G-F	So.	30	.396	.684	12.3	9.5
Carl Bouldin	G	Sr.	30	.428	.800	11.7	2.8
Tony Yates	G	So.	30	.486	.602	7.4	3.5
Dale Heidotting	F-C	So.	26	.429	.652	3.6	3.7
Fred Dierking	F-C	Jr.	25	.483	.467	2.6	2.2
Jim Calhoun	G	Jr.	17	.378	.538	2.1	0.5
Tom Sizer	G	Jr.	24	.375	.750	2.0	1.0
Larry Shingleton	G	So.	20	.292	.400	0.9	0.6
Mark Altenau	F	So.	18	.429	.444	0.9	0.6
TEAM TOTALS			30	.457	.633	75.0	51.8

1961 FINAL FOUR CHAMPIONSHIP GAME

KANSAS CITY, MO

CINCINNATI (70)	FG-A	FT-A	REB.	PF	PTS.
Wiesenhahn	8-15	1-1	9	3	17
Thacker	7-21	1-4	7	0	15
Hogue	3-8	3-6	7	3	9
Yates	4-8	5-5	2	3	13
Bouldin	7-12	2-3	4	4	16
Sizer	0-0	0-0	1	0	0
Heidotting	0-0	0-0	0	0	0
Team			6		
TOTALS	29-64	12-19	36	13	70

FG%: .453. FT%: .632.

OHIO STATE (65)	FG-A	FT-A	REB.	PF	PTS.
Havlicek	1-5	2-2	4	2	4
Hoyt	3-5	1-1	1	3	7
Lucas	10-17	7-7	12	4	27
Nowell	3-9	3-3	3	1	9
Siegfried	6-10	2-3	3	2	14
Knight	1-3	0-0	1	1	2
Gearhart	1-1	0-0	0	1	2
Team			8		
TOTALS	25-50	15-16	32	14	65

FG%: .500. FT%: .938.
Halftime: Ohio State 39-38. Regulation: Tied 61-61.

NATIONAL SEMIFINALS

CINCINNATI (82): Wiesenhahn 5-7 4-6 14, Thacker 1-7 5-6 7, Hogue 9-16 0-4 18, Bouldin 7-14 7-8 21, Yates 4-6 5-7 13, Heidotting 3-8 1-1 7, Sizer 1-1 0-0 2, Dierking 0-0 0-0 0, Altenau 0-0 0-0 0, Shingleton 0-0 0-0 0, Calhoun 0-0 0-0 0. Team 30-59 (.508) 22-32 (.688) 82.

UTAH (67): Ruffell 6-11 2-2 14, Rhead 2-5 4-6 8, McGill 11-31 3-4 25, Morton 3-9 1-1 7, Rowe 1-3 0-0 2, Crain 2-5 0-1 4, Aufderheide 2-3 2-2 6, Cozby 0-0 0-0 0, Thomas 0-0 1-2 1, Jenson 0-0 0-0 0. Team 27-67 (.403) 13-18 (.722) 67.

Halftime: Cincinnati 35-20.

OHIO STATE (95): Nowell 7-11 1-1 15, Havlicek 5-6 1-2 11, Lucas 10-11 9-10 29, Hoyt 2-6 0-0 4, Siegfried 8-11 5-7 21, Knight 2-5 1-2 5, McDonald 1-4 0-0 2, Gearhart 0-2 2-2 2, Reasbeck 0-1 0-1 0, Lee 1-1 0-0 2, Landes 2-2 0-0 4. Team 38-60 (.633) 19-25 (.760) 95.

ST. JOSEPH'S (69): Lynam 2-5 3-4 7, Hoy 6-17 1-1 13, Majewski 4-12 5-7 13, Egan 3-11 2-3 8, Kempton 5-9 8-8 18, Wynne 1-9 2-2 4, Booth 0-3 2-2 2, Gormley 1-5 2-2 4, Westhead 0-1 0-1 0, Bugey 0-0 0-0 0, Dickey 0-0 0-0 0. Team 22-76 (.289) 25-30 (.833) 69.

Halftime: Ohio State 45-28.

ALL-TOURNAMENT TEAM

Carl Bouldin, G, Sr., Cincinnati
John Egan, F, Sr., St. Joseph's
Jerry Lucas, C, Jr., Ohio State*
Larry Siegfried, G, Sr., Ohio State
Bob Wiesenhahn, F, Sr., Cincinnati
   *Named Most Outstanding Player

his two previous games before putting Cincinnati ahead to stay with a pair of pivotal free throws in overtime in a 70-65 championship game victory. Ohio State, undefeated entering the tourney, lost the national final against Cincinnati (70-65 in overtime) after almost getting upset in its opening playoff game at Louisville. Cincinnati's Ed Jucker became the only individual to win an NCAA title in his first full season as head coach at a school.

Outcome for Defending Champion: Ohio State entered the playoffs undefeated, but needed to overcome a five-point deficit with less than three minutes remaining to escape with a 56-55 triumph at Louisville in the Mideast Regional semifinals.

Star Gazing: Three-time unanimous first-team All-American Jerry Lucas registered game highs of 27 points and 12 rebounds for the Buckeyes in the championship contest while teammate John Havlicek was limited to four points.

Biggest Upset: Tom Stith's 29 points weren't enough to keep third-ranked St. Bonaventure from bowing to Wake Forest, 78-73, in the East Regional semifinals.

One and Only: Guard Carl Bouldin became the only athlete to lead his championship team in scoring at the Final Four and play major league baseball in the same year. He helped Cincinnati win the NCAA title with a total of 37 points in two games at Kansas City before pitching in two games later that year for the Washington Senators.

Numbers Game: St. Joseph's Jack Ramsay became the only coach to win an NBA championship (Portland Trail Blazers '77) after directing a college squad to the Final Four.... Wake Forest became the only team to ever trail by as many as 10 points at halftime of a tournament game (46-36) and then win the contest by more than 20. The Demon Deacons were behind at intermission (46-36) in the first round of the East Regional before rallying to defeat St. John's (97-74).

What If: ACC regular-season champion North Carolina, which defeated NCAA representative Wake Forest twice by a total of 24 points, was ineligible for postseason competition because of an NCAA probation.... Utah, coming off a 26-3 season and with twin towers Billy "The Hill" McGill and Allen Holmes slated to return, were a strong candidate to win it all. The Utes reached the Final Four although Holmes, the 1959 NJCAA Tournament MVP, didn't play after nearly losing his right leg in a summer auto accident.

Putting Things in Perspective: Cincinnati lost three times by a total of 44 points in a five-game stretch early in the season, including the Bearcats' first two Missouri Valley Conference contests.

St. Joseph's (Pa.) coach Jack Ramsay instructs his players.

1961 CHAMPIONSHIP BRACKET

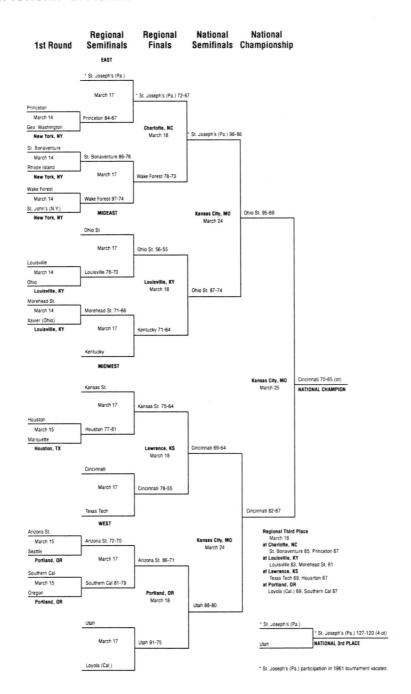

1st Round	Regional Semifinals	Regional Finals	National Semifinals	National Championship

EAST

* St. Joseph's (Pa.)
March 17
* St. Joseph's (Pa.) 72-67

Princeton
March 14
Geo. Washington
New York, NY
Princeton 84-67

Charlotte, NC
March 18
* St. Joseph's (Pa.) 96-86

St. Bonaventure
March 14
Rhode Island
New York, NY
St. Bonaventure 86-76
March 17
Wake Forest 78-73

Wake Forest
March 14
St. John's (N.Y.)
New York, NY
Wake Forest 97-74

Kansas City, MO
March 24
Ohio St. 95-69

MIDEAST

Ohio St
March 17
Ohio St. 56-55

Louisville
March 14
Ohio
Louisville, KY
Louisville 76-70

Louisville, KY
March 18
Ohio St. 87-74

Morehead St.
March 14
Xavier (Ohio)
Louisville, KY
Morehead St. 71-66
March 17
Kentucky 71-64

Kentucky

Kansas City, MO
March 25
Cincinnati 70-65 (ot)
NATIONAL CHAMPION

MIDWEST

Kansas St.
March 17
Kansas St. 75-64

Houston
March 15
Marquette
Houston, TX
Houston 77-61

Lawrence, KS
March 18
Cincinnati 69-64

Cincinnati
March 17
Cincinnati 78-55

Texas Tech

Kansas City, MO
March 24
Cincinnati 82-67

WEST

Arizona St.
March 15
Seattle
Portland, OR
Arizona St. 72-70
March 17
Arizona St. 86-71

Southern Cal
March 15
Oregon
Portland, OR
Southern Cal 81-79

Portland, OR
March 18
Utah 88-80

Utah
March 17
Utah 91-75

Loyola (Cal.)

Regional Third Place
March 18
at Charlotte, NC
St. Bonaventure 85, Princeton 67
at Louisville, KY
Louisville 83, Morehead St. 61
at Lawrence, KS
Texas Tech 69, Housrton 67
at Portland, OR
Loyola (Cal.) 69, Southern Cal 67

* St. Joseph's (Pa.)
* St. Joseph's (Pa.) 127-120 (4 ot)
Utah
NATIONAL 3rd PLACE

* St. Joseph's (Pa.) participation in 1961 tournament vacated.

1961–62

AT A GLANCE

NCAA Champion: Cincinnati (29-2).

NIT Champion: Dayton (24-6).

NCAA Probation: Indiana, Kansas, Tennessee Tech, Utah.

NCAA Consensus First-Team All-Americans: Len Chappell, C, Sr., Wake Forest; Terry Dischinger, F, Sr., Purdue; Jerry Lucas, C, Sr., Ohio State; Billy McGill, C, Sr., Utah; Chet Walker, F, Sr., Bradley.

Ohio State's Jerry Lucas finished his career with the three best single-season rebounding totals in Big Ten Conference history. They were still the top three through the 1993–94 campaign. Lucas became the first player to ever gain five individual national statistical titles in a career (two for rebounding and three for shooting).

The only Ohio State regular-season defeat in the last two years of the Lucas/John Havlicek era after they won the 1960 NCAA title was at Wisconsin (86-67), ending the Buckeyes' 47-game regular-season winning streak.

National scoring leader Billy McGill (38.8 points per game) accounted for 45.8 percent of Utah's output. That figure was especially impressive because the Utes were sixth in the country in team offense. McGill's season included 12 of the 19 games in school history of more than 40 points and all four contests of at least 50, including a school record 60 against Brigham Young.

A deadeye duo—Arkansas' Tommy Boyer (93.3 percent) and Jerry Carlton (88.1)—became the only set of teammates to rank one-two in free-throw accuracy. Boyer's margin of victory in free-throw shooting was the largest in NCAA history.

One of the nation's premier field-goal shooters was Iowa's Don Nelson (55.5 percent), who would go on to play and coach in the NBA.

Davidson, in its second season under coach Lefty Driesell, posted its first winning record (14-11) since 1948–49.

Wake Forest captured its only undisputed ACC regular-season championship with a 12-2 league record. Wake Forest's Len Chappell scored 30 points or more in an ACC-record eight consecutive games, including an ACC game mark of 50 against Virginia. A sell-out crowd watching a non-league game between Wake and another top 10 ACC rival, Duke, was enthralled by the Blue Devils' flashy new uniforms as they became the first college team to have player names on the back of the jerseys. Chappell's 37 points weren't enough to prevent a 75-73 loss to Duke, which received 33 points from Art Heyman.

The two highest-scoring teams in the nation were separated by a single basket of compiling duplicate records. Loyola of Chicago and Arizona State both posted 23-4 records, but Loyola scored two more points than the Sun Devils (2,436 to 2,434).

Purdue's Terry Dischinger finished his three-year varsity career with a 28.3-point average, but he is the only one of more than 50 two-time consensus first-team All-Americans since 1946 to never participate in the NCAA Tournament or the NIT.

Indiana guard Jimmy Rayl, after averaging a modest four points per game the previous season as a sophomore, exploded for a 29.8-point average to finish sixth in the country. He scored a school-record 56 points in two different Big Ten outings (against Michigan State and Minnesota).

Syracuse finished with a 2-22 record, the worst mark in university history.

Penn State's Gene Harris set a school record with 46 points against Holy Cross.

The San Francisco Bay Area supplied the leader in team defense for the seventh time in eight years—Santa Clara (52.1).

Creighton's Paul Silas grabbed a school-record 38 rebounds in a game with Centenary.

Wichita State ended defending champion Cincinnati's 27-game winning streak, 52-51, on Lanny Van Eman's jumper with three seconds remaining.

Purdue forward Terry Dischinger.

1961-62 INDIVIDUAL LEADERS

SCORING

PLAYER	PTS.	AVG.
McGill, Utah	1009	38.8
Foley, Holy Cross	866	33.3
Werkman, Seton Hall	793	33.0
Dischinger, Purdue	726	30.3
Chappell, Wake Forest	932	30.1
Rayl, Indiana	714	29.8
Smith, Furman	728	27.0
DeBusschere, Detroit	696	26.8
Duffy, Colgate	611	26.6
Walker, Bradley	687	26.4

REBOUNDING

PLAYER	REB.	PCT.
Lucas, Ohio St.	499	.2112
Silas, Creighton	563	.2108

Glur, Furman	488	.209
Lundy, Lafayette	437	.200
DeBusschere, Detroit	498	.189
Ellis, St. John's	430	.187
Jennings, Murray St.	431	.181
Luyk, Florida	352	.179
Thompson, DePaul	354	.178
Thurmond, Bowling Green	394	.176

FIELD GOAL PERCENTAGE

PLAYER	FGM	FGA	PCT.
Lucas, Ohio St.	237	388	.611
Johns, Auburn	129	221	.584
Green, Colorado St.	203	348	.583
Swain, Florida St.	157	274	.573
Beckman, Memphis St.	206	361	.571
Harger, Houston	145	258	.562
Russell, Nebraska	136	243	.560

McGill, Utah	394	705	.559
Cerkvenik, Arizona St.	101	181	.558
Hadnot, Providence	198	357	.555
Nelson, Iowa	193	348	.555

FREE THROW PERCENTAGE

PLAYER	FTM	FTA	PCT.
Boyer, Arkansas	125	134	.933
Carlton, Arkansas	140	159	.881
Chappelle, Maine	132	151	.874
Foley, Holy Cross	222	256	.867
Williams, Morehead St.	138	160	.863
Sherard, Army	112	130	.862
Komives, Bowling Green	134	156	.859
Loudermilk, SMU	203	239	.849
Reynolds, TCU	100	118	.847
Stroud, Mississippi St.	116	137	.847

1961-62 TEAM LEADERS

SCORING OFFENSE

SCHOOL	PTS.	AVG.
Loyola (Ill.)	2436	90.2
Arizona St.	2434	90.1
Seton Hall	2115	88.1
Indiana	2089	87.0
West Virginia	2562	85.4

SCORING DEFENSE

SCHOOL	PTS.	AVG.
Santa Clara	1302	52.1
Auburn	1254	52.3
San Jose St.	1262	52.6
Cincinnati	1707	55.1
Texas Western	1343	56.0

FIELD GOAL PERCENTAGE

SCHOOL	FGM	FGA	PCT.
Florida St.	709	1386	.512
Utah	883	1812	.487
Ohio St.	952	1961	.485
Memphis St.	736	1530	.481
Bradley	887	1849	.480

FREE THROW PERCENTAGE

SCHOOL	FTM	FTA	PCT.
Arkansas	502	647	.776
Southern Methodist	552	718	.769
Holy Cross	497	650	.765
Memphis St.	367	482	.761
Western Kentucky	538	713	.755

REBOUNDING

SCHOOL	TOTAL REB.	REB.	PCT.
Cornell	2481	1463	.590
Ohio St.	2362	1391	.589
Creighton	2791	1640	.588
DePaul	1989	1161	.584
Delaware	2077	1204	.580

North Carolina's Dean Smith kicked off his illustrious head coaching career with an inauspicious 8-9 record.

1961-62 FINAL NATIONAL POLLS

AP	UPI	SCHOOL
1	1	Ohio St.
2	2	Cincinnati
3	3	Kentucky
4	4	Mississippi St.
5	6	Bradley
6	5	Kansas St.
7	10	Utah
8	9	Bowling Green St.
9	8	Colorado
10	13	Duke
11	13	Loyola (Ill.)
12	12	St. John's
13	7	Wake Forest
14	11	Oregon St.
15	16	West Virginia
16	15	Arizona St.
17	18	Duquesne
18	19	Utah St.
19	17	UCLA
20	20	Villanova

1962 NCAA Tournament

Summary: Ohio State All-American center Jerry Lucas wrenched his left knee in the national semifinals against Wake Forest, limiting his effectiveness against Cincinnati counterpart Paul Hogue in the Bearcats' 71-59 triumph in the final. In the 1962 national semifinals against UCLA, Hogue scored 14 consecutive points for the Bearcats down the stretch to finish with 36 before Thacker's desperation long-range basket, his only points of the game, gave them a 72-70 triumph.

Star Gazing: Tom Thacker, a 6-2 swingman who averaged nine rebounds per game for Cincinnati's back-to-back titlists, is the only individual to play for an NCAA champion, NBA champion (Boston Celtics '68), and ABA champion (Indiana Pacers '70).

One and Only: Dave DeBusschere became

1961–62 NCAA CHAMPION: CINCINNATI

SEASON STATISTICS OF CINCINNATI REGULARS

PLAYER	POS.	CL.	G.	FG%	FT%	PPG	RPG
Paul Hogue	C	Sr.	31	.498	.566	16.8	12.4
Ron Bonham	F	So.	31	.455	.760	14.3	5.0
Tom Thacker	G-F	Jr.	31	.405	.612	11.0	8.6
George Wilson	F-C	So.	31	.505	.663	9.2	8.0
Tony Yates	G	Jr.	31	.383	.670	8.2	3.0
Fred Dierking	F	Sr.	28	.433	.588	4.1	2.9
Larry Shingleton	G	Jr.	25	.416	.560	3.9	1.4
Dale Heidotting	F	Jr.	22	.511	.571	3.1	2.3
Tom Sizer	G	Sr.	25	.456	.625	2.7	1.3
Jim Calhoun	G	Sr.	18	.368	.667	1.7	0.4
TEAM TOTALS			**31**	**.447**	**.632**	**72.2**	**49.5**

1962 FINAL FOUR CHAMPIONSHIP GAME

LOUISVILLE, KY

OHIO STATE (59)	FG-A	FT-A	REB.	PF	PTS.
Havlicek	5-14	1-2	9	1	11
McDonald	0-1	3-3	1	2	3
Lucas	5-17	1-2	16	3	11
Reasbeck	4-6	0-0	0	4	8
Nowell	4-16	1-1	6	2	9
Doughty	0-1	0-0	2	2	0
Gearhart	1-4	0-0	4	3	0
Bradds	5-7	5-6	4	2	15
TOTALS	**24-66**	**11-14**	**42**	**19**	**59**

FG%: .364. FT%: .786. Turnovers: 9.

CINCINNATI (71)	FG-A	FT-A	REB.	PF	PTS.
Bonham	3-12	4-4	6	3	10
Wilson	1-6	4-4	11	2	6
Hogue	11-18	0-2	19	2	22
Thacker	6-14	9-11	6	2	21
Yates	4-8	4-7	1	1	12
Sizer	0-0	0-0	0	0	0
TOTALS	**25-58**	**21-28**	**43**	**10**	**71**

FG%: .431. FT%: .750. Turnovers: 8.
Halftime: Cincinnati 37-29.

NATIONAL SEMIFINALS

WAKE FOREST (68): Chappell 10-24 7-11 27, Christie 0-2 1-1 1, Woollard 1-3 1-2 3, Wiedeman 5-16 3-6 13, Packer 8-14 1-2 17, Hull 0-2 0-0 0, McCoy 0-1 2-2 2, Carmichael 0-0 0-0 0, Hassell 1-2 0-0 2, Zawacki 0-1 0-1 3 1, Koehler 0-1 0-0 0, Brooks 0-1 2-2 2. Team 25-66 (.379) 18-29 (.621) 68.

OHIO STATE (84): Havlicek 9-19 7-9 25, McDonald 5-10 1-2 11, Lucas 8-16 3-4 19, Nowell 2-11 0-0 4, Reasbeck 5-7 0-0 10, Gearhart 2-5 0-0 4, Doughty 2-4 4-4 8, Bradds 0-0 0-1 0, Knight 0-2 0-0 0, Flatt 0-1 2-1 2, Taylor 0-0 0-0 0, Frazier 1-1 0-0 2. Team 34-75 (.453) 16-22 (.727) 84.

Halftime: Ohio State 46-34.

UCLA (70): Blackman 2-3 0-0 4, Cunningham 8-14 3-3 19, Slaughter 1-4 0-0 2, Green 9-16 9-11 27, Hazzard 5-10 2-3 12, Waxman 2-3 2-3 6, Stewart 0-0 0-0 0. Team 27-50 (.540) 16-20 (.800) 70.

CINCINNATI (72): Bonham 8-14 3-6 19, Wilson 1-6 1-2 3, Hogue 12-18 12-17 36, Thacker 1-7 0-0 2, Yates 4-10 2-3 10, Sizer 1-3 0-0 2. Team 27-58 (.466) 18-28 (.643) 72.

Halftime: Tied 37-37.

ALL-TOURNAMENT TEAM

Len Chappell, F-C, Sr., Wake Forest
John Havlicek, F, Sr., Ohio State
Paul Hogue, C, Sr., Cincinnati*
Jerry Lucas, C, Sr., Ohio State
Tom Thacker, F-G, Jr., Cincinnati
*Named Most Outstanding Player

the only player to post the highest-scoring game in a single tournament the same year he played major league baseball. DeBusschere scored a tourney-high 38 points for Detroit in a 90-81 defeat against Western Kentucky in the first round of the Mideast Regional. He pitched that summer for the Chicago White Sox.

Numbers Game: Utah State's Cornell Green became the only athlete to compile one of the top five scoring averages in an NCAA Tournament before playing for an NFL champion. Green, a five-time Pro Bowl defensive back during his 13-year career with the Dallas Cowboys from 1962 through 1973, tied for fourth in scoring average in the '62 playoffs (24.3 points per game in three games). But the Aggies were eliminated by coach John Wooden's first Final Four team at UCLA despite Green's game-high 26 points (73-62 in West Regional semifinals).... Wooden's initial Final Four squad (18-11 record) was the only national semifinalist in 20 years from 1960 through 1979 to finish a season with double-digit defeats.... Ohio State became the only school to reach the Final Four three consecutive years on two separate occasions (1944 through 1946 and 1960 through 1962).

What If: Utah was on NCAA probation after winning by nine points at UCLA, an eventual Final Four team.... Kansas State, ranked 5th by UPI and 6th by AP the year after being eliminated from the NCAA Tournament by eventual national champion Cincinnati, finished runner-up in the Big Eight Conference to Colorado. The Wildcats' three defeats were in road games against Colorado, Kentucky, and Oklahoma State.

Putting Things in Perspective: Cincinnati would have been undefeated if not for two setbacks by a total of three points in Missouri Valley Conference road games (at Wichita State and Bradley).

1962 CHAMPIONSHIP BRACKET

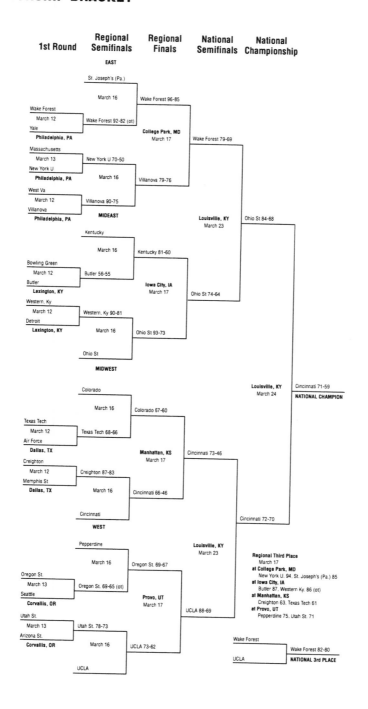

1st Round	Regional Semifinals	Regional Finals	National Semifinals	National Championship

EAST

St. Joseph's (Pa.)
March 16
Wake Forest 96-85
Wake Forest
March 12
Wake Forest 92-82 (ot)
Yale
Philadelphia, PA
College Park, MD
March 17
Wake Forest 79-69
Massachusetts
March 13
New York U 70-50
New York U
Philadelphia, PA
March 16
Villanova 79-76
West Va
March 12
Villanova 90-75
Villanova
Philadelphia, PA

MIDEAST

Kentucky
March 16
Kentucky 81-60
Bowling Green
March 12
Butler 56-55
Butler
Lexington, KY
Iowa City, IA
March 17
Ohio St 74-64
Western. Ky
March 12
Western. Ky 90-81
Detroit
Lexington, KY
March 16
Ohio St 93-73
Ohio St

Louisville, KY
March 23
Ohio St 84-68

MIDWEST

Colorado
March 16
Colorado 67-60
Texas Tech
March 12
Texas Tech 68-66
Air Force
Dallas, TX
Manhattan, KS
March 17
Cincinnati 73-46
Creighton
March 12
Creighton 87-83
Memphis St
Dallas, TX
March 16
Cincinnati 66-46
Cincinnati

Louisville, KY
March 24
Cincinnati 71-59
NATIONAL CHAMPION

WEST

Louisville, KY
March 23
Cincinnati 72-70

Pepperdine
March 16
Oregon St. 69-67
Oregon St.
March 13
Oregon St. 69-65 (ot)
Seattle
Corvallis, OR
Provo, UT
March 17
UCLA 88-69
Utah St.
March 13
Utah St. 78-73
Arizona St.
Corvallis, OR
March 16
UCLA 73-62
UCLA

Regional Third Place
March 17
at College Park, MD
New York U. 94. St. Joseph's (Pa.) 85
at Iowa City, IA
Butler 87. Western Ky. 86 (ot)
at Manhattan, KS
Creighton 63. Texas Tech 61
at Provo, UT
Pepperdine 75. Utah St. 71

Wake Forest
Wake Forest 82-80
UCLA
NATIONAL 3rd PLACE

1962–63

NCAA Champion: Loyola, Ill. (29-2).

NIT Champion: Providence (24-4).

New Conference: Western Athletic.

NCAA Probation: Dayton, Indiana, New Mexico State.

NCAA Consensus First-Team All-Americans: Ron Bonham, F, Jr., Cincinnati; Jerry Harkness, F, Sr., Loyola (Ill.); Art Heyman, F, Sr., Duke; Barry Kramer, F, Jr., NYU; Tom Thacker, F-G, Sr., Cincinnati.

Wichita State's Dave Stallworth.

Mississippi State became the first school other than Kentucky to win outright or share three consecutive SEC championships. But Mississippi State coach Babe McCarthy had to sneak out of town in the middle of the night to participate in the NCAA playoffs. He left before he was served injunction papers stemming from two segregationist state legislators seeking to prohibit the team from leaving Mississippi and using state funds to travel to the tournament.

Billy Mitts, one of the "Jim Crow" state senators, was a former Mississippi State student body president, but his influence waned when a county sheriff apparently sympathetic to the players' plight graciously left an airport in time for them to board their plane and evade an unpleasant scene.

Mississippi State, an all-white school at the time, had captured SEC championships under McCarthy in 1959, 1961, and 1962. But the Bulldogs—then more popularly known as the Maroons—declined automatic bids to play in the NCAA Tournament those three years because of an unwritten bigoted policy forbidding Mississippi State or Ole Miss athletes to compete in racially integrated contests. Eventual champion Loyola of Chicago, featuring four black starters, fell behind Mississippi State 7-0, but wound up winning the Mideast Regional semifinal game (61-51) in East Lansing, Michigan. Incidentally,

the next time Mississippi State appeared in the NCAA playoffs was 1991, when the Bulldogs' 13-man roster had 10 blacks.

Three of the country's top five point producers were from the East as Seton Hall's Nick Werk-

1962–63 INDIVIDUAL LEADERS

SCORING

PLAYER	PTS.	AVG.
Werkman, Seton Hall	650	29.5
Kramer, New York Univ.	675	29.3
Green, Colorado St.	649	28.2
Bradds, Ohio St.	672	28.0
Bradley, Princeton	682	27.3
Robinson, Wyoming	682	26.2
Miles, Seattle	697	25.8
Rayl, Indiana	608	25.3
Heyman, Duke	747	24.9
Crump, Idaho St.	595	24.8
Pokley, Morehead St.	323	17.0
Petersen, Rutgers	389	16.9
Sahm, Notre Dame	438	16.8
Thurmond, Bowling Green	452	16.7
Barnes, Texas Western	428	16.5
Pelkington, Xavier	454	16.2
Jennings, Murray St.	339	16.1
Cunningham, N. Carolina	339	16.1

REBOUNDING

PLAYER	REB.	AVG.
Silas, Creighton	557	20.6
Johnson, Idaho	466	20.3

FIELD GOAL PERCENTAGE

PLAYER	FGM	FGA	PCT.
Harger, Houston	193	294	.656
Raftery, St. Francis (N.Y.)	115	186	.615
Buckley, Duke	130	217	.599
Green, Colorado St.	215	371	.580
Johnson, San Francisco	178	314	.567
Johns, Auburn	119	210	.567
Blackwell, Auburn	123	219	.562
Becker, Arizona St.	225	404	.557
Mullins, Duke	256	466	.549
Cerkvanik, Arizona St.	123	225	.547

FREE THROW PERCENTAGE

PLAYER	FTM	FTA	PCT.
Boyer, Arkansas	147	161	.913
Bradley, Princeton	258	289	.893
Bonham, Cincinnati	173	194	.892
Batchelor, BYU	104	119	.874
Rayl, Indiana	178	204	.873
Stroud, Miss. St.	120	138	.870
Hyland, Princeton	112	129	.868
Ward, South Carolina	118	136	.868
Vadset, Washington St.	119	138	.862
Smith, Furman	204	238	.857

1962–63 TEAM LEADERS

SCORING OFFENSE

SCHOOL	PTS.	AVG.
Loyola (Ill.)	2847	91.8
Miami (Fla.)	2509	89.6
Indiana	2032	84.7
Illinois	2201	84.7
Duke	2496	83.2

SCORING DEFENSE

SCHOOL	PTS.	AVG.
Cincinnati	1480	52.9
Oklahoma St.	1328	53.1
Texas Western	1419	54.6
San Jose St.	1383	57.6
New Mexico	1447	57.9

FIELD GOAL PERCENTAGE

SCHOOL	FGM	FGA	PCT.
Duke	984	1926	.511
Auburn	601	1188	.506
St. Francis (N.Y.)	553	1109	.499
Memphis St.	773	1553	.498
Colorado St.	593	1193	.497

FREE THROW PERCENTAGE

SCHOOL	FTM	FTA	PCT.
Tulane	390	492	.793
Furman	539	708	.761
Princeton	531	699	.760
Cornell	378	498	.759
Florida	533	703	.758

REBOUNDING

SCHOOL	TOTAL REB.	OWN	PCT.
Texas Western	1975	1167	.591
Auburn	1737	1018	.586
Delaware	2116	1239	.586
Davidson	2171	1254	.578
Regis (Colo.)	2089	1205	.577

man became the first Easterner in 13 years to lead the nation in scoring (29.5 points per game).

One-eyed Tommy Boyer of Arkansas became the first player to win two consecutive free-throw shooting titles.

Wichita State ended Cincinnati's 37-game winning streak, 65-64, when Dave Stallworth poured in 46 points for the Shockers. Cincinnati, however, still captured its sixth Missouri Valley Conference championship in as many years as a member of the league.

Texas, the epitamy of a balanced attack, lost just one SWC game although it didn't have one of the top 10 scorers in the league. Seven Longhorn players averaged seven or more points per game in SWC competition and three other teammates had at least one game of 10 points or more.

Indiana guard Jimmy Rayl scored a national high 56 points against Michigan State.

Illinois' Dave Downey (53 points at Indiana) and Texas Western's Jim Barnes (51 against Western New Mexico) set school single-game scoring records. Jimmy Rayl's 53 points against Michigan State were national highs.

Kansas finished in the second division of the Big Eight, but managed a four-overtime victory against regular-season co-champion Kansas State in the Big Eight Holiday Tournament.

St. John's (9-15) endured its worst winning percentage since going winless in 1918–19.

West Virginia captured its eighth Southern Conference championship in nine years.

Connecticut's Hugh Greer ended a 17-year coaching career with a 286-112 record.

1962–63 NCAA CHAMPION: LOYOLA

SEASON STATISTICS OF LOYOLA OF CHICAGO REGULARS

PLAYER	POS.	CL.	G.	FG%	FT%	PPG	RPG
Jerry Harkness	F	Sr.	31	.504	.725	21.4	7.6
Les Hunter	C	Jr.	31	.530	.731	17.0	11.4
John Egan	G	Jr.	31	.361	.789	13.7	3.6
Vic Rouse	F	Jr.	31	.404	.730	13.5	12.1
Ron Miller	G	Jr.	31	.406	.696	13.3	5.4
Jim Reardon	F	Sr.	14	.321	.813	2.2	2.1
Dan Connaughton	G	So.	17	.424	.625	1.9	1.1
Chuck Wood	F-G	Jr.	17	.393	.714	1.9	1.9
Rich Rochelle	C	Jr.	14	.360	.375	1.5	1.4
TEAM TOTALS			**31**	**.439**	**.722**	**91.8**	**57.7**

1963 FINAL FOUR CHAMPIONSHIP GAME

LOUISVILLE, KY

LOYOLA (ILL.) (60)	MIN.	FG-A	FT-A	REB.	A	PF	PTS.
Harkness	45	5-18	4-8	6	0	4	14
Rouse	45	6-22	3-4	12	0	4	15
Hunter	45	6-22	4-4	11	1	3	16
Egan	45	3-8	3-5	3	0	3	9
Miller	45	3-14	0-0	2	0	3	6
Team				11			
TOTALS	**225**	**23-84**	**14-21**	**45**	**1**	**17**	**60**

FG%: .274. FT%: .667. Turnovers: 3.

CINCINNATI (58)	MIN.	FG-A	FT-A	REB.	A	PF	PTS.
Bonham	45	8-16	6-6	4	0	3	22
Thacker	45	5-12	3-4	15	3	4	13
Wilson	41	4-8	2-3	13	0	4	10
Yates	45	4-6	1-4	8	1	4	9
Shingleton	45	1-3	2-3	4	0	0	4
Heidotting	4	0-0	0-0	1	0	2	0
Team				7			
TOTALS	**225**	**22-45**	**14-20**	**52**	**4**	**17**	**58**

FG%: .489. FT%: .700. Turnovers: 16 (Thacker 7).
Halftime: Cincinnati 29-21. Regulation: Tied 54-54.

1962–63 FINAL NATIONAL POLLS

AP	UPI	SCHOOL
1	1	Cincinnati
2	2	Duke
3	4	Loyola (Ill.)
4	3	Arizona St.
5	6	Wichita St.
6	7	Mississippi St.
7	8	Ohio St.
8	5	Illinois
9	11	NYU
10	9	Colorado
–	10	Stanford
–	12	Texas
–	13	Providence
–	14	Oregon St.
–	15	UCLA
–	16	St. Joseph's
–	16	West Virginia
–	18	Bowling Green St.
–	19	Kansas St.
–	19	Seattle

NATIONAL SEMIFINALS

CINCINNATI (80): Bonham 3-12 8-9 14, Thacker 5-8 4-8 14, Wilson 8-9 8-12 24, Yates 5-9 2-3 12, Shingleton 1-2 0-0 2, Heidotting 0-0 1-2 1, Cunningham 2-3 0-0 4, Meyer 1-1 1-2 3, Smith 1-3 0-2 2, Elasser 1-2 0-1 2, Abernethy 1-2 0-0 2. Team 28-51 (.549) 24-39 (.615) 80.

OREGON STATE (46): Pauly 2-8 0-1 4, Kraus 1-6 1-1 3, Counts 8-14 4-4 20, Peters 1-5 2-2 4, Baker 0-9 0-1 0, Jarvis 1-6 3-4 5, Rossi 1-3 0-0 2, Campbell 0-2 1-1 1, Torgerson 1-2 0-0 2, Hayward 0-2 1-1 1, Benner 2-2 0-0 4. Team 17-59 (.288) 12-15 (.800) 46.

Halftime: Cincinnati 30-27.

LOYOLA OF CHICAGO (94): Harkness 7-18 6-9 20, Rouse 6-12 1-2 13, Hunter 11-20 7-9 29, Egan 4-9 6-7 14, Miller 8-11 2-2 18, Wood 0-1 0-0 0, Rochelle 0-0 0-0 0, Reardon 0-0 0-0 0, Cannaughton 0-0 0-0 0. Team 36-71 (.5-7) 22-29 (.759) 94.

DUKE (75): Heyman 11-30 7-9 29, Mullins 10-20 1-3 21, Buckley 4-10 2-4 10, Schmidt 0-2 0-0 0, Harrison 0-3 2-3 2, Herbster 0-2 0-0 0, Ferguson 1-2 0-0 2, Jamieson 0-0 0-0 0, Cox 0-0 0-0 0, Mann 0-1 0-0 0, Tison 5-12 1-3 11. Team 31-82 (.378) 13-22 (.591) 75.

Halftime: Loyola of Chicago 44-31.

ALL-TOURNAMENT TEAM

Ron Bonham, F, Jr., Cincinnati
Art Heyman, F, Sr., Duke*
Les Hunter, C, Jr., Loyola of Chicago
Tom Thacker, F-G, Sr., Cincinnati
George Wilson, C, Jr., Cincinnati
    ***Named Most Outstanding Player**

1963 NCAA Tournament

Summary: Even some teams outside the South adhered to an accepted standard of "start no more than two blacks at home, or three on the road." When Loyola, featuring four African-American starters, upset Cincinnati and the Bearcats' three black starters in the championship game, it was the first time a majority of African-American players participated in the title game. Junior forward Vic Rouse leaped high to redirect center Les Hunter's shot from the free-throw line into the basket to climax the Ramblers' first year in the playoffs. Loyola of Chicago, overcoming 27.4 percent field-goal shooting by committing just three turnovers, won the 1963 final against Cincinnati, 60-58 in overtime, after trailing at halftime by eight points (29-21). No team has won the NCAA championship by overcoming a double-digit halftime deficit in the title game. Cincinnati coach Ed Jucker won his first 11 NCAA Tournament games before bowing in the final to finish his career with an all-time best playoff winning percentage (.917 in minimum of 10 games).

One and Only: Oregon State's Terry Baker became the only football Heisman Trophy winner to play in the basketball Final Four. Baker, a quarterback on Oregon State's football squad that defeated Villanova (6-0) in the 1962 Liberty Bowl on his school-record 99-yard run from scrimmage, was the second-leading scorer for the Beavers' basketball team that finished fourth in the national tourney the same academic school year. Teammate Steve Pauly, Oregon State's second-leading rebounder and third-leading scorer, was the only Final Four player to become AAU national champion in the decathlon the same year.

Numbers Game: Loyola of Chicago, using its starting lineup the entire final, is the only school to deploy just five players in a championship game. The Ramblers are the only team to overcome a halftime deficit of as many as eight points (29-21) to win a title game. Loyola of Chicago became the only team to defeat an opponent by at least 50 points in a tournament game (111-42 over Tennessee Tech in the first round of Mideast Regional).

Idaho's Gus Johnson in action.

1963 CHAMPIONSHIP BRACKET

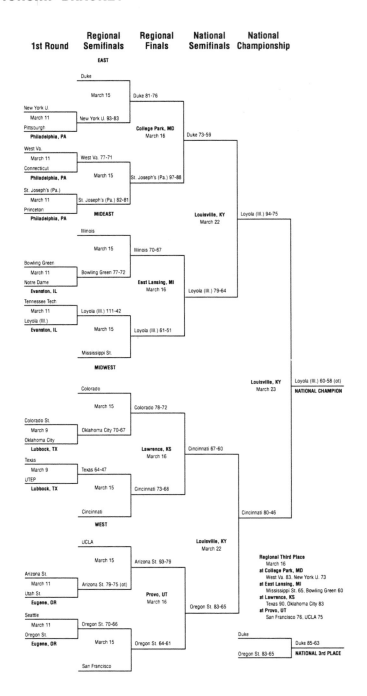

1st Round	Regional Semifinals	Regional Finals	National Semifinals	National Championship

EAST

Duke
March 15 — Duke 81-76
New York U.
March 11 — New York U. 93-83
Pittsburgh
Philadelphia, PA

College Park, MD
March 16 — Duke 73-59

West Va.
March 11 — West Va. 77-71
Connecticut
Philadelphia, PA
March 15 — St. Joseph's (Pa.) 97-88
St. Joseph's (Pa.)
March 11 — St. Joseph's (Pa.) 82-81
Princeton
Philadelphia, PA

MIDEAST

Illinois
March 15 — Illinois 70-67
Bowling Green
March 11 — Bowling Green 77-72
Notre Dame
Evanston, IL

East Lansing, MI
March 16 — Loyola (Ill.) 79-64

Tennessee Tech
March 11 — Loyola (Ill.) 111-42
Loyola (Ill.)
Evanston, IL
March 15 — Loyola (Ill.) 61-51
Mississippi St.

Louisville, KY
March 22 — Loyola (Ill.) 94-75

MIDWEST

Colorado
March 15 — Colorado 78-72
Colorado St.
March 9 — Oklahoma City 70-67
Oklahoma City
Lubbock, TX

Lawrence, KS
March 16 — Cincinnati 67-60

Texas
March 9 — Texas 64-47
UTEP
Lubbock, TX
March 15 — Cincinnati 73-68
Cincinnati

WEST

UCLA
March 15 — Arizona St. 93-79
Arizona St.
March 11 — Arizona St. 79-75 (ot)
Utah St.
Eugene, OR

Provo, UT
March 16 — Oregon St. 83-65

Seattle
March 11 — Oregon St. 70-66
Oregon St.
Eugene, OR
March 15 — Oregon St. 64-61
San Francisco

Louisville, KY
March 22 — Cincinnati 80-46

Louisville, KY
March 23 — Loyola (Ill.) 60-58 (ot)
NATIONAL CHAMPION

Regional Third Place
March 16
at College Park, MD
West Va. 83, New York U. 73
at East Lansing, MI
Mississippi St. 65, Bowling Green 60
at Lawrence, KS
Texas 90, Oklahoma City 83
at Provo, UT
San Francisco 76, UCLA 75

Duke — Duke 85-63
Oregon St. 83-65 — **NATIONAL 3rd PLACE**

1963-64

NCAA Champion: UCLA (30-0).

NIT Champion: Bradley (23-6).

New Conference: Big Sky.

NCAA Probation: Dayton, Indiana, New Mexico State.

NCAA Consensus First-Team All-Americans: Gary Bradds, C, Sr., Ohio State; Bill Bradley, F, Jr., Princeton; Walt Hazzard, G, Sr., UCLA; Cotton Nash, F, Sr., Kentucky; Dave Stallworth, F, Jr., Wichita State.

UCLA won its first of 10 NCAA titles in 12 years, a stretch of dominance that many believe ranks among the greatest achievements in the history of competitive sports.

Kentucky set an NCAA single-game record with 108 rebounds against Mississippi.

Cincinnati's 86-game homecourt winning streak, which started in 1957, was snapped by Kansas, 51-47.

Kansas State finished first or second in the Big Eight Conference standings for the ninth consecutive season.

Defending national scoring champion Nick Werkman of Seton Hall scored almost four points per game more than he did the previous season (from 29.5 to 33.2), but finished runner-up to Bowling Green's Howard Komives, a 6-1 guard who averaged 36.7 points per game after hitting 50 consecutive free throws in his last five games. Komives finished 45th in the country in scoring the previous year with a 20.2 norm. Werkman and Komives were among five players to score more than 32 points per game. Werkman's 52 points against Scranton is still a school record.

Oklahoma State's Hank Iba posted the 700th victory of his college coaching career with an 80-47 triumph over Oklahoma in State's final game of the season.

Texas A&M's Bennie Lennox set a Southwest Conference record with a national single-game high of 53 points against Wyoming. He was one of 10 different players to score 50 or more in a single game during the season.

Setting school single-game scoring records were Xavier's Steve Thomas (50 points against Detroit), Ohio State's Gary Bradds (49 against Illinois), Boston College's John Austin (49 against Georgetown), and Northwestern's Rich Falk (49 against Iowa).

Senior Terry Holland's nation-leading 63.1 percent field-goal shooting helped Davidson pace the country at 54.4 percent. Holland, who would coach Virginia to the Final Four in 1981 and 1984, is the only Final Four coach to previously lead the nation in a statistical category as a major-college player.

Another player who would become a prominent coach was Providence center John Thompson, who ranked among the nation's top 20 in scoring (26.2 ppg), rebounding (14.5 rpg), and field-goal shooting (58.8 percent).

1963-64 FINAL NATIONAL POLLS

AP	UPI	SCHOOL
1	1	UCLA
2	2	Michigan
3	4	Duke
4	3	Kentucky
5	6	Wichita St.
6	5	Oregon St.
7	7	Villanova
8	8	Loyola (Ill.)
9	11	DePaul
10	10	Davidson
–	9	Texas-El Paso
–	12	Kansas St.
–	13	Drake
–	13	San Francisco
–	15	Utah St.
–	16	New Mexico
–	16	Ohio St.
–	18	Texas A&M
–	19	Arizona St.
–	19	Providence

Defending NCAA champion Loyola (Ill.), eliminated in the second round of the national Tournament by Michigan, became the only team in the era of three-year eligibility to have four teammates finish their careers at the same time

1963–64 INDIVIDUAL LEADERS

SCORING

PLAYER	PTS.	AVG.
Komives, Bowling Green	844	36.7
Werkman, Seton Hall	830	33.2
Newsome, W. Michigan	653	32.7
Bradley, Princeton	936	32.3
Barry, Miami (Fla.)	870	32.2
Bradds, Ohio St.	735	30.6
Thomas, Xavier	779	30.0
Austin, Boston College	614	29.2
Barnes, Texas Western	816	29.1
Estes, Utah St.	821	28.3

REBOUNDING

PLAYER	REB.	AVG.
Pelkington, Xavier	567	21.80
Silas, Creighton	631	21.75

Dzik, Detroit	521	20.8
Isaac, Iona	403	20.2
Barnes, Texas Western	537	19.2
Reed, Notre Dame	318	17.7
Sahm, Notre Dame	315	17.5
Kimball, Connecticut	466	17.3
Counts, Oregon St.	489	16.9
Johnson, San Francisco	467	16.7

FIELD GOAL PERCENTAGE

PLAYER	FGM	FGA	PCT.
Holland, Davidson	135	214	.631
DeBerardinis, St. Fr. (Pa.)	112	181	.619
Fisher, Texas	136	222	.613
Nightingale, Rhode I.	139	229	.607
Johnson, San Francisco	206	346	.595
Buckley, Duke	160	271	.590
Thompson, Providence	260	442	.588

Pierce, W. Texas St.	123	210	.586
Bustion, Colorado St.	110	188	.585
Richards, Syracuse	177	305	.580

FREE THROW PERCENTAGE

PLAYER	FTM	FTA	PCT.
Park, Tulsa	121	134	.903
Schultz, Tennessee	101	113	.894
Lee, San Francisco	108	121	.893
Izor, Dayton	95	107	.888
Bailey, N. Texas St.	136	156	.872
Murphy, DePaul	93	107	.869
Geiger, Xavier	119	137	.869
Newsome, W. Michigan	129	149	.866
Vrankovich, Santa Clara	165	191	.864
Perry, Alabama	87	101	.861

1963–64 TEAM LEADERS

SCORING OFFENSE

SCHOOL	PTS.	AVG.
Detroit	2402	96.1
Miami (Fla.)	2575	95.4
Michigan St.	2211	92.1
Weber St.	2288	91.5
Loyola (Ill.)	2556	91.3

SCORING DEFENSE

SCHOOL	PTS.	AVG.
San Jose St.	1307	54.5
Texas Western	1548	55.3
Gettysburg (Pa.)	1363	56.8
New Mexico	1660	57.2
Oklahoma St.	1449	58.0

FIELD GOAL PERCENTAGE

SCHOOL	FGM	FGA	PCT.
Davidson	894	1644	.544
West Texas St.	681	1356	.502
Rhode Island	910	1854	.491
Wichita St.	817	1688	.484
San Francisco	764	1581	.483

FREE THROW PERCENTAGE

SCHOOL	FTM	FTA	PCT.
Miami (Fla.)	593	780	.760
Bowling Green	430	571	.753
Utah	578	769	.752
Kentucky	454	605	.750
Lafayette	454	608	.747

REBOUNDING

SCHOOL	TOTAL REB.	OWN	PCT.
Iona	1673	1071	.640
San Francisco	2343	1410	.602
Cornell	2674	1580	.591
Texas Western	2386	1407	.590
New Mexico	2188	1284	.587

with more than 1,000 points—center Les Hunter (1,472), guards John Egan (1,315) and Ron Miller (1,299), and forward Vic Rouse (1,169).

Western Kentucky's Ed Diddle retired after a 42-year coaching career with a 759-302 record. Oregon State's Slats Gills ended his 36-year coaching career with a 599-392 record.

1964 NCAA Tournament

Summary: UCLA's Kenny Washington was instrumental in helping venerable coach John Wooden capture his first NCAA Tournament championship. Washington, the only player with a single-digit season scoring average (6.1) to tally more than 25 points in a championship game, scored 26 points in a 98-83 triumph over Duke in the final. Washington became the only player to score 25 or more points in a final and

not be named to the All-Tournament team. The Bruins won the national championship by an average of 7.5 points after gifted guards Gail Goodrich and Walt Hazzard sparked them to 12 double-digit margin victories in their last 13 regular-season games. Goodrich (21.5 points per game) and Hazzard (18.6 ppg) represent the only backcourt twosome to be the top two scorers on the season for an NCAA championship team. Despite shooting a meager 40.3 percent from the floor and 52.9 percent from the free-throw line, UCLA overcame a 13-point deficit to end San Francisco's 19-game winning streak (76-72) in the West Regional final. Eight of their 30 victories were by seven points or less, including a 58-56 triumph at California.

Star Gazing: Hazzard, the second-leading scorer over the entire season for UCLA's first championship team in 1964 with an average of 18.6 points per game, was named Most Outstanding Player although he was the Bruins' fourth-leading scorer at the Final Four that year. "I never had a better man on the fast break than Walt Hazzard," UCLA coach John Wooden said. Hazzard had a two-game total of 30 points, finishing behind the scoring aggregates compiled by teammates Goodrich (41), Washington (39) and Keith Erickson (36).

Biggest Upset: Kentucky, ranked No. 3 by UPI and No. 4 by AP entering the tourney, dropped its opener to Ohio, 85-69, when the Wildcats fell behind by 16 points at intermission.

One and Only: Goodrich, a 6-1 junior, became the shortest undergraduate to average more than 20 points per game for an NCAA titlist (21.5 ppg) .... UCLA's Washington became the only championship team player to have a season scoring average of less than six points per game entering a Final Four but accumulate at least 30 points in the national semifinals and final. Washington had a season scoring average of 5.2 points per game entering the Final Four before erupting for a total of 39 points in victories over Kansas State and Duke to help the Bruins capture their first national championship. He is the only player with a single-digit season scoring average to score more than 25 points in a championship game (26 against Duke to finish the year with a 6.1-point average). Goodrich scored 27 in the final as he and Washington combined to become the only teammate duo to each score more than 25 in an NCAA final.

UCLA's Walt Hazzard dishes one off to a teammate.

Numbers Game: Of the individuals to both play and coach in the NCAA Tournament, Jeff Mullins leads that group in both scoring and rebounding totals. Mullins, who later guided UNC Charlotte to the tourney, garnered 200 points and 63 rebounds in eight playoff games to help Duke twice reach the Final Four.... Jim "Bad News" Barnes accounted for 61.8 percent of Texas Western's offense by scoring 42 points in the Miners' 68-62 victory against Texas A&M in the first round of the Midwest Regional. In the Miners' next game, Barnes was whistled for three

1963–64 NCAA CHAMPION: UCLA

SEASON STATISTICS OF UCLA REGULARS

PLAYER	POS.	CL.	G.	FG%	FT%	PPG	RPG
Gail Goodrich	G	Jr.	30	.458	.711	21.5	5.2
Walt Hazzard	G	Sr.	30	.445	.718	18.6	4.7
Jack Hirsch	F	Sr.	30	.528	.664	14.0	7.6
Keith Erickson	F	Jr.	30	.403	.623	10.7	9.1
Fred Slaughter	C	Sr.	30	.466	.484	7.9	8.1
Kenny Washington	F-G	So.	30	.458	.627	6.1	4.2
Doug McIntosh	C	So.	30	.519	.500	3.6	4.4
Kim Stewart	F	Sr.	23	.393	.467	2.2	2.0
Rich Levin	F	Jr.	19	.372	.500	2.0	0.6
Mike Huggins	G	Sr.	23	.382	.478	1.6	1.0
Chuck Darrow	G	So.	23	.379	.583	1.6	1.2
Vaughn Hoffman	C	So.	21	.476	.500	1.2	1.3
TEAM TOTALS			30	.455	.644	88.9	55.7

1964 FINAL FOUR CHAMPIONSHIP GAME

KANSAS CITY, MO

UCLA (98)	FG-A	FT-A	REB.	A	PF	PTS.
Goodrich	9-18	9-9	3	1	1	27
Slaughter	0-1	0-0	1	2	0	0
Hazzard	4-10	3-5	3	8	5	11
Hirsch	5-9	3-5	6	6	3	13
Erickson	2-7	4-4	5	1	5	8
McIntosh	4-9	0-0	11	1	2	8
Washington	11-16	4-4	12	1	4	26
Darrow	0-1	3-4	1	0	2	3
Stewart	0-1	0-0	0	0	1	0
Huggins	0-1	0-1	1	2	2	0
Hoffman	1-2	0-0	0	0	0	2
Levin	0-1	0-0	0	0	0	0
TOTALS	**36-76**	**26-32**	**43**	**22**	**25**	**98**

FG%: .474. FT%: .813. Turnovers: 19.

DUKE (83)	FG-A	FT-A	REB.	A	PF	PTS.
Ferguson	2-6	0-1	1	4	3	4
Buckley	5-8	8-12	9	0	4	18
Tison	3-8	1-1	1	2	2	7
Harrison	1-1	0-0	1	1	2	2
Mullins	9-21	4-4	4	1	5	22
Marin	8-16	0-1	10	1	3	16
Vacendak	2-7	3-3	6	0	4	7
Herbster	1-4	0-2	0	0	0	2
Kitching	1-1	0-0	1	0	0	2
Mann	0-0	3-4	2	0	1	3
Harscher	0-0	0-0	0	0	0	0
Cox	0-0	0-0	0	0	0	0
TOTALS	**32-72**	**19-28**	**35**	**9**	**24**	**83**

FG%: .444. FT%: .679. Turnovers: 24.
Halftime: UCLA 50-38.

NATIONAL SEMIFINALS

UCLA (90): Goodrich 7-18 0-0 14, Slaughter 2-6 0-0 4, Hazzard 7-10 5-7 19, Hirsch 2-11 0-0 4, Erickson 10-21 8-9 28, McIntosh 3-5 2-3 8, Washington 5-11 3-4 13. Team 36-82 (.439) 18-23 (.783) 90.

KANSAS STATE (84): Moss 3-9 1-1 7, Robinson 2-7 0-1 4, Simons 10-17 4-6 24, Suttner 3-9 0-5 6, Murrell 13-22 3-5 29, Paradis 5-9 0-0 10, Williams 1-1 2-3 4, Nelson 0-1 0-0 0, Gottfrid 0-0 0-0 0, Barnard 0-1 0-0 0. Team 37-76 (.487) 10-21 (.476) 84.

Halftime: UCLA 43-41.

DUKE (91): Ferguson 6-11 0-1 12, Buckley 11-16 3-5 25, Tison 3-10 6-10 12, Harrison 6-15 2-3 14, Mullins 8-19 5-6 21, Marin 1-2 0-0 2, Vacendak 2-5 1-2 5, Herbster 0-0 0-0 0. Team 37-78 (.474) 17-27 (.630) 91.

Halftime: Duke 48-39.

MICHIGAN (80): Buntin 8-18 3-3 19, Cantrell 6-10 0-0 12, Russell 13-19 5-6 31, Tregoning 3-11 2-2 8, Darden 2-6 1-1 5, Myers 2-5 0-0 4, Pomey 0-1 1-2 1, Herner 0-1 0-0 0. Team 34-71 (.479) 12-14 (.857) 80.

ALL-TOURNAMENT TEAM

Bill Buntin, C, Jr., Michigan
Gail Goodrich, G, Jr., UCLA
Walt Hazzard, G, Sr., UCLA*
Jeff Mullins, F, Sr., Duke
Willie Murrell, F, Sr., Kansas State
Named Most Outstanding Player

quick personal fouls in the opening minutes against Kansas State and spent almost the entire first half on the bench. He was assessed fouls No. 4 and No. 5 early in the second half and fouled out with four points in their 64-60 defeat....

Michigan became the only Final Four team ever to have a duo each average more than 23 points per game—guard Cazzie Russell (24.8) and center Bill Buntin (23.2).... UCLA had seven players average more than four rebounds per game.

1964 CHAMPIONSHIP BRACKET

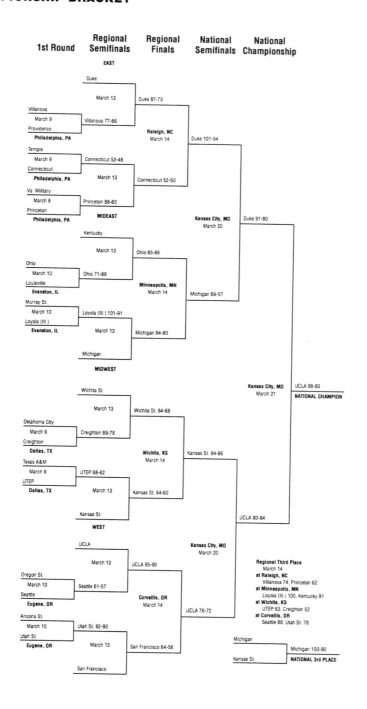

1st Round	Regional Semifinals	Regional Finals	National Semifinals	National Championship

EAST

Duke
March 13 — Duke 87-73
Villanova
March 9 — Villanova 77-66
Providence
Philadelphia, PA

Raleigh, NC March 14 — Duke 101-54

Temple
March 9 — Connecticut 53-48
Connecticut
Philadelphia, PA
March 13 — Connecticut 52-50

Va. Military
March 9 — Princeton 86-60
Princeton
Philadelphia, PA

MIDEAST

Kansas City, MO March 20 — Duke 91-80

Kentucky
March 13 — Ohio 85-69
Ohio
March 10 — Ohio 71-69
Louisville
Evanston, IL

Minneapolis, MN March 14 — Michigan 69-57

Murray St.
March 10 — Loyola (Ill.) 101-91
Loyola (Ill.)
Evanston, IL
March 13 — Michigan 84-80

Michigan

MIDWEST

Kansas City, MO March 21 — UCLA 98-83 **NATIONAL CHAMPION**

Wichita St.
March 13 — Wichita St. 84-68
Oklahoma City
March 9 — Creighton 89-78
Creighton
Dallas, TX

Wichita, KS March 14 — Kansas St. 94-86

Texas A&M
March 9 — UTEP 68-62
UTEP
Dallas, TX
March 13 — Kansas St. 64-60

Kansas St.

WEST

UCLA 90-84

UCLA
March 13 — UCLA 95-90
Oregon St.
March 10 — Seattle 61-57
Seattle
Eugene, OR

Corvallis, OR March 14 — UCLA 76-72

Kansas City, MO March 20

Arizona St.
March 10 — Utah St. 92-90
Utah St.
Eugene, OR
March 13 — San Francisco 64-58

San Francisco

Regional Third Place
March 14
at Raleigh, NC
Villanova 74, Princeton 62
at Minneapolis, MN
Loyola (Ill.) 100, Kentucky 91
at Wichita, KS
UTEP 63, Creighton 52
at Corvallis, OR
Seattle 88, Utah St. 78

Michigan
Michigan 100-90
Kansas St.
NATIONAL 3rd PLACE

1964–65

AT A GLANCE

NCAA Champion: UCLA (28-2).

NIT Champion: St. John's (21-8).

New Rules: Coaches must remain seated on the bench except while the clock is stopped or to direct or encourage players on the court. This rule was to try to help prevent coaches from inciting undesirable crowd behavior toward the referees. NIT field expands from 12 to 14 teams.

NCAA Probation: Miami (Fla.).

NCAA Consensus First-Team All-Americans: Rick Barry, F, Sr., Miami (Fla.); Bill Bradley, F, Sr., Princeton; Gail Goodrich, G, Sr., UCLA; Fred Hetzel, F-C, Sr., Davidson; Cazzie Russell, G, Jr., Michigan.

Miami of Florida's Rick Barry led the country in scoring in 1964–65.

Wayne Estes, runner-up to Rick Barry of Miami (Fla.) for the national scoring championship, was electrocuted in a freak accident the evening of February 8, 1965. The tragedy occurred less than three hours after Estes scored 48 points against Denver to become Utah State's first player to reach the 2,000-point plateau in his career.

En route back and forth to his off-campus apartment and then a restaurant, Estes was with teammate Delano Lyons and another friend when they passed three times the scene of an auto accident that had killed a Utah State student. The group stopped and inspected the scene briefly. They were returning to their car when Lyons, who is 6-2, noticed a live high-voltage wire dangling in front of him after being dislodged when the victim's car hit a utility pole. Lyons ducked and hollered "Watch it" to the 6-6 Estes, who was walking behind him. But Estes didn't react quickly enough and the wire carrying 2,700 volts of electricity brushed against his forehead, killing him instantly.

Miami's Barry was able to stay ahead of Estes by amassing six 50-point games.

Princeton's Bill Bradley, who would become a U.S. senator (D-N.J.), led the country in free-throw shooting.

In one of the most memorable college games in Madison Square Garden history, Princeton lost to the Cazzie Russell-led Michigan Wolverines, 80-78, in the semifinals of the Holiday Festival. Bradley fouled out with with 4½ minutes remaining with 41 points and Princeton leading, 76-63. Russell led Michigan's comeback and hit the game-winning basket from 15 feet away with three seconds left to finish with 27 points.

Western Kentucky's Clem Haskins (55 points against Middle Tennessee State), Rice's Doug McKendrick (47 against Georgia Tech), Georgetown's Jim Barry (46 against Fairleigh Dickinson), and Wisconsin's Ken Barnes (42 against Indiana) established school single-game scoring records.

Tennessee (55.64), Oklahoma State (55.66), and New Mexico (55.70) finished one-two-three in team defense in the closest race ever in point prevention. The tight defense helped Oklahoma State capture its only undisputed Big Eight regular-season championship.

North Carolina State's Everett Case retired because of illness early in the 19th season of his coaching career with a 377-134 record. His successor was Press Maravich, the father of future All-American Pete Maravich. N.C. State reserve forward Larry Worsley entered the ACC Tournament with a modest 5.2 scoring average. In three tourney games, all of which he entered as a substitute, he scored 12, 15, and 30 points to pace the Wolfpack to the title and earn the Outstanding Player Award. He hit 14 of 19 field-goal attempts in a 91-85 championship game victory over Duke.

Florida defeated Kentucky, 84-68, for the Gators' first victory over the Wildcats since 1934. Florida had lost 18 games to Kentucky in that span.

West Virginia (14-15) posted its first losing record since 1943–44.

Utah's Jack Gardner had a team finish in last place for the first time in his 29 seasons of coaching. The Utes were in the basement of the six-team WAC with a 3-7 record, although they finished with a 17-9 overall mark.

St. John's Joe Lapchick ended his 20-year coaching career with a 335-129 record. Indiana's Branch McCracken, who previously had coached Ball State, retired after a 32-year coaching career with a 450-231 record.

1964–65 INDIVIDUAL LEADERS

SCORING

PLAYER	PTS.	AVG.
Barry, Miami (Fla.)	973	37.4
Estes, Utah St.	641	33.7
Bradley, Princeton	885	30.5
Schellhase, Purdue	704	29.3
Thomas, Xavier	405	28.9
Robinson, Wyoming	701	27.0
Austin, Boston College	673	26.9
Hetzel, Davidson	689	26.5
Beasley, Texas A&M	619	25.8
Russell, Michigan	694	25.7

REBOUNDING

PLAYER	REB.	AVG.
Kimball, Connecticut	483	21.0
Isaac, Iona	480	20.9

Woods, E. Tennessee St.	450	19.6
Barry, Miami (Fla.)	475	18.3
Swagerty, Pacific	473	18.2
Sahm, Notre Dame	393	16.4
Johnson, San Francisco	469	16.2
Branch, Fairfield	208	16.0
Washington, Villanova	442	15.8
Anderson, St. Joseph's	450	15.5

FIELD GOAL PERCENTAGE

PLAYER	FGM	FGA	PCT.
Kehoe, St. Peter's	138	209	.660
Finkel, Dayton	293	450	.651
McKendrick, Rice	152	250	.608
Newton, Auburn	126	208	.606
Johnson, San Francisco	242	405	.598
Hetzel, Davidson	273	471	.580
Kimball, Connecticut	177	311	.569

Chambers, Utah	199	355	.561
Thoren, Illinois	219	391	.560
Stallworth, Wichita St.	153	275	.556
Ritch, Army	140	252	.556

FREE THROW PERCENTAGE

PLAYER	FTM	FTA	PCT.
Bradley, Princeton	272	308	.886
Banko, UC Santa Barbara	156	177	.881
Park, Tulsa	145	165	.879
Estes, Utah St.	137	156	.878
K. McIntyre, St. John's	144	164	.878
Lloyd, Rutgers	127	145	.876
Neuman, Penn	112	129	.868
Barry, Georgetown	110	127	.866
Anderson, W. Michigan	158	183	.863
Barry, Miami (Fla.)	293	341	.859

1964–65 TEAM LEADERS

SCORING OFFENSE

SCHOOL	PTS.	AVG.
Miami (Fla.)	2558	98.4
Brigham Young	2639	94.3
Duke	2310	92.4
Illinois	2213	92.2
Indiana	2200	91.7

SCORING DEFENSE

SCHOOL	PTS.	AVG.
Tennessee	1391	55.64
Oklahoma St.	1503	55.66
New Mexico	1504	55.7
Texas Western	1468	56.5
Oregon St.	1525	58.7

FIELD GOAL PERCENTAGE

SCHOOL	FGM	FGA	PCT.
St. Peter's	579	1089	.532
Davidson	908	1784	.509
San Francisco	931	1893	.492
Duke	942	1921	.490
Manhattan	677	1382	.490

FREE THROW PERCENTAGE

SCHOOL	FTM	FTA	PCT.
Miami (Fla.)	642	807	.796
Morehead St.	487	620	.785
Indiana 464	604		.768
Kentucky	517	675	.766
UC Santa Barbara	482	633	.761

REBOUNDING

SCHOOL	TOTAL REB.	OWN	PCT.
Iona	1896	1191	.628
Tennessee	1997	1207	.604
Florida	1749	1041	.595
Connecticut	2439	1432	.587
New Mexico	2286	1342	.587

1964–65 NCAA CHAMPION: UCLA

SEASON STATISTICS OF UCLA REGULARS

PLAYER	POS.	CL.	G.	FG%	FT%	PPG	RPG
Gail Goodrich	G	Sr.	30	.525	.717	24.8	5.3
Keith Erickson	F	Sr.	29	.443	.725	12.9	8.8
Fred Goss	G	Jr.	30	.442	.729	12.2	3.3
Edgar Lacey	F	So.	30	.469	.579	11.6	10.2
Kenny Washington	F	Jr.	30	.425	.653	9.2	5.0
Mike Lynn	C	So.	30	.503	.581	6.7	5.1
Doug McIntosh	C	Jr.	30	.429	.737	6.5	5.6
TEAM TOTALS			30	.463	.665	86.3	52.0

1965 FINAL FOUR CHAMPIONSHIP GAME

PORTLAND, OR

UCLA (91)	FG-A	FT-A	REB.	PF	PTS.
Erickson	1-1	1-2	1	1	3
Lacey	5-7	1-2	7	3	11
McIntosh	1-2	1-2	0	2	3
Goodrich	12-22	18-20	4	4	42
Goss	4-12	0-0	3	1	8
Washington	7-9	3-4	5	2	17
Lynn	2-3	1-2	6	1	5
Lyons	0-0	0-0	0	1	0
Galbraith	0-0	0-0	0	0	0
Hoffman	1-1	0-0	1	0	2
Levin	0-1	0-0	1	0	0
Chambers	0-0	0-1	0	0	0
Team			6		
TOTALS	33-58	25-33	34	15	91

FG%: .569. **FT%:** .758. **Assists:** 4.

MICHIGAN (80)	FG-A	FT-A	REB.	PF	PTS.
Darden	8-10	1-1	4	5	17
Pomey	2-5	0-0	2	2	4
Buntin	6-14	2-4	6	5	14
Russell	10-16	8-10	5	2	28
Tregoning	2-7	1-1	5	5	5
Myers	0-4	0-0	3	2	0
Brown	0-0	0-0	0	0	0

	FG-A	FT-A	REB.	PF	PTS.
Ludwig	1-2	0-0	0	0	2
Thompson	0-0	0-0	0	0	0
Bankey	0-0	0-0	0	0	0
Clawson	3-4	0-0	0	2	6
Dill	1-2	2-2	1	1	4
Team			7		
TOTALS	33-64	14-18	33	24	80

FG%: .516. **FT%:** .778. **Assists:** 2.
Halftime: UCLA 47-34.

NATIONAL SEMIFINALS

MICHIGAN (93): Tregoning 6-9 1-1 13, Darden 6-13 1-3 13, Buntin 7-13 8-10 22, Russell 10-21 8-9 28, Pomey 2-8 2-2 6, Myers 1-4 0-0 2, Thompson 0-1 2-2 2, Dill 0-0 3-4 3, Ludwig 0-0 0-0 0, Clawson 2-2 0-1 4. Team 34-71 (.479) 25-32 (.781) 93.

PRINCETON (76): Bradley 12-25 5-5 29, Haarlow 4-10 1-4 9, Brown 2-6 0-0 4, Walters 5-10 1-2 11, Rodenbach 2-5 2-2 6, Hummer 10-4-5 12, Koch 1-4 1-2 3, Kingston 0-1 2-2 2. Team 30-71 (.423) 16-22 (.727) 76.

Halftime: Michigan 40-36.

WICHITA STATE (89): Smith 4-11 0-1 8, Thompson 13-19 10-11 36, Leach 6-14 0-1 12, Pete 6-11 5-5 17, Criss 4-13 0-0 8, Reed 2-3 1-1 5, Davis 1-2 0-0 2, Trope 0-1 0-0 0, Nosich 0-0 1-3 1, Reimond 0-1 0-0 0. Team 36-75 (.480) 17-22 (.773) 89.

UCLA (108): Lacey 9-13 6-10 24, Erickson 1-6 0-0 2, McIntosh 4-5 3-4 11, Goodrich 11-21 6-8 28, Goss 8-13 3-3 19, Chambers 0-5 0-0 0, Lyons 2-3 0-0 4, Levin 0-1 0-0 0, Lynn 5-9 0-0 10, Galbraith 0-0-0 0, Hoffman 0-0 0-0 0. Team 44-89 (.494) 20-29 (.690) 108.

Halftime: UCLA 65-38.

ALL-TOURNAMENT TEAM

Bill Bradley, F, Sr., Princeton*
Gail Goodrich, G, Sr., UCLA
Edgar Lacey, F, Soph., UCLA
Cazzie Russell, G, Jr., Michigan
Kenny Washington, F, Jr., UCLA
*****Named Most Outstanding Player**

1964–65 FINAL NATIONAL POLLS

AP	UPI	SCHOOL
1	1	Michigan
2	2	UCLA
3	3	St. Joseph's
4	4	Providence
5	5	Vanderbilt
6	7	Davidson
7	8	Minnesota
8	11	Villanova
9	6	Brigham Young
10	9	Duke
–	10	San Francisco
–	12	North Carolina St.
–	13	Oklahoma St.
–	14	Wichita St.
–	15	Connecticut
–	16	Illinois
–	17	Tennessee
–	18	Indiana .
–	19	Miami (Fla.)
–	20	Dayton

1965 NCAA Tournament

Summary: UCLA was overwhelmed at Illinois early in the season, 110-83, but the Bruins finished the campaign with a victory over another Big Ten team, Michigan, in the NCAA final.

Star Gazing: Princeton's Bill Bradley holds the career playoff record for highest free-throw percentage (minimum of 50 attempts). He was 89 of 96 from the foul line (90.6 percent) from 1963 through 1965. In five of his nine playoff games, Bradley made at least 10 free throws while missing no more than one attempt from the charity stripe. He made 16 of 16 free throws against St. Joseph's in the first round of the 1963 East Regional and 13 of 13 foul shots against Providence in the 1965 East Regional final to become the only player to twice convert more than 12 free throws without a miss in a playoff game. Bradley also holds the record for most points in a single Final Four game (58 against Wichita State in national third-place game). He scored 39 points in the second half of the consolation game. The Rhodes Scholar was the only player to have a double-digit season scoring average (30.5 points per game) for Princeton's Final Four team.

One and Only: UCLA's Gail Goodrich became the only guard to score more than 35 points in an NCAA final, erupting for 42 points on 12 of 22 field-goal shooting and 18 of 20 free-throw shooting in a 91-80 triumph over Michigan.

Numbers Game: Princeton's Butch van Breda Kolff went on to become the only coach to direct teams to the NCAA Final Four and the NBA Finals (Los Angeles Lakers in 1968 and 1969) and compile a winning NCAA playoff career record (7-5).... Wichita State's Gary Thompson became perhaps the first-year coach overcoming the biggest obstacle to reach the national semifinals. The Shockers' roster was depleted in the second half of Thompson's inaugural season after the departures of both of their high NBA draft picks—All-American forward Dave (The Rave) Stallworth and first-round draft choice center Nate Bowman. Stallworth completed his eligibility after the first 16 games and Bowman was declared ineligible for the second semester. Nonetheless, the Missouri Valley Conference champion's roster of primarily local players emerged victorious out of a relatively feeble Midwest Regional field.... Michigan's Cazzie Russell became the only player to score more than 25 points in Final Four defeats in back-to-back years.

What If: Rick Barry-led Miami (Fla.) defeated NCAA playoff first-round winners Houston and Oklahoma City by a total of 35 points, but the Hurricanes were ineligible because of NCAA probation.

UCLA All-American and All-Tournament guard Gail Goodrich shoots over a defender.

1965 CHAMPIONSHIP BRACKET

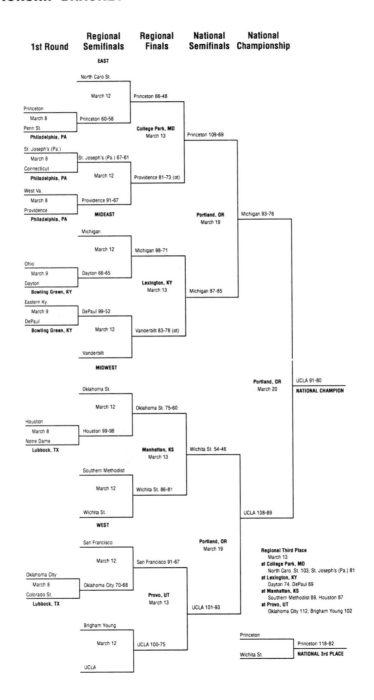

1st Round	Regional Semifinals	Regional Finals	National Semifinals	National Championship

EAST

North Caro St.

March 12 — Princeton 66-48

Princeton
March 8 — Princeton 60-58
Penn St.
Philadelphia, PA

College Park, MD
March 13 — Princeton 109-69

St. Joseph's (Pa.)
March 8 — St. Joseph's (Pa.) 67-61
Connecticut
Philadelphia, PA

March 12 — Providence 81-73 (ot)

West Va.
March 8 — Providence 91-67
Providence
Philadelphia, PA

MIDEAST

Michigan
March 12 — Michigan 98-71

Ohio
March 9 — Dayton 66-65
Dayton
Bowling Green, KY

Lexington, KY
March 13 — Michigan 87-85

Eastern Ky.
March 9 — DePaul 99-52
DePaul
Bowling Green, KY

March 12 — Vanderbilt 83-78 (ot)

Vanderbilt

Portland, OR
March 19 — Michigan 93-76

MIDWEST

Oklahoma St.
March 12 — Oklahoma St. 75-60

Houston
March 8 — Houston 99-98
Notre Dame
Lubbock, TX

Manhattan, KS
March 13 — Wichita St. 54-46

Southern Methodist
March 12 — Wichita St. 86-81

Wichita St.

WEST

San Francisco
March 12 — San Francisco 91-67

Oklahoma City
March 8 — Oklahoma City 70-68
Colorado St.
Lubbock, TX

Provo, UT
March 13 — UCLA 101-93

Brigham Young
March 12 — UCLA 100-75

UCLA

Portland, OR
March 19 — UCLA 108-89

Portland, OR
March 20 — UCLA 91-80
NATIONAL CHAMPION

Regional Third Place
March 13
at College Park, MD
North Caro. St. 103, St. Joseph's (Pa.) 81
at Lexington, KY
Dayton 74, DePaul 69
at Manhattan, KS
Southern Methodist 89, Houston 87
at Provo, UT
Oklahoma City 112, Brigham Young 102

Princeton
Princeton 118-82

Wichita St.
NATIONAL 3rd PLACE

1965–66

NCAA Champion: Texas Western (28-1).

NIT Champion: Brigham Young (20-5).

New Conference: Metropolitan Collegiate (disbanded four years later).

NCAA Consensus First-Team All-Americans: Dave Bing, G, Sr., Syracuse; Clyde Lee, C, Sr., Vanderbilt; Cazzie Russell, G, Sr., Michigan; Dave Schellhase, F, Sr., Purdue; Jimmy Walker, G, Jr., Providence.

UCLA's Lew Alcindor goes high for a rebound.

The best team in the country might have been UCLA's freshman squad. The Bruins' frosh, led by 7-1 Lew Alcindor's 31 points and 21 rebounds, defeated the two-time NCAA champion UCLA varsity, 75-60. The yearlings compiled a 21-0 record, outscoring their opponents 113.2 points per game to 56.6. Starters for what is considered by some as the best freshman team in NCAA history included Alcindor (33.1 ppg and 21.5 rpg), forwards Lynn Shackelford (20.9 ppg and 9.3 rpg) and Kent Taylor (7.2 ppg), and guards Lucius Allen (22.4 ppg and 7.8 rpg) and Kenny Heitz (14.3 ppg).

It was a version of Dave's World for the national scoring championship. Purdue forward Dave Schellhase (32.54) edged Idaho State guard Dave Wagnon (32.50) in the closest race in major-college history. Wagnon, who averaged a modest 14.6 points per game the previous season as a junior, averaged 36.4 the second half of his senior campaign before falling one basket short of overhauling Schellhase. Purdue posted an 8-16 record, leaving Schellhase on the worst team ever for an NCAA consensus first-team All-American.

Establishing school single-game scoring records were Texas Tech's Dub Malaise (50 points against Texas), North Carolina's Bob Lewis (49 against Florida State), and Southern Cal's John Block (45 against Washington).

Syracuse, after failing to finish among the top 30 in the previous 12 scoring races, won its first scoring title.

Ron Widby punted for Tennessee's football squad in the afternoon in its 27-6 triumph over Tulsa in the Bluebonnet Bowl and then flew to Shreveport, Louisiana, where he scored 18 points that evening for the Volunteers' basketball team in a 49-43 victory over Centenary in the championship game of the Gulf South Classic. Tennessee handed Kentucky its only regular-season defeat (69-62).

Bob Knight ushered in his acclaimed coaching career with an 18-8 record at Army, leading the Cadets to the NIT for the first of four times under him through 1970. Another head coaching newcomer with an 18-8 record was Lou Carnesecca at St. John's.

Maryland guard Billy Jones became the first African American to compete in the ACC.

Steve Vacendak was named ACC player of the year despite being voted second team all-

1965–66 INDIVIDUAL LEADERS

SCORING

PLAYER	PTS.	AVG.
Schellhase, Purdue	781	32.54
Wagnon, Idaho St.	845	32.50
Russell, Michigan	800	30.8
Chambers, Utah	892	28.8
Bing, Syracuse	794	28.4
Kerwin, Centenary	726	27.9
Freeman, Illinois	668	27.8
Beasley, Texas A&M	668	27.8
Melchionni, Villanova	801	27.6
Lewis, North Carolina	740	27.4

REBOUNDING

PLAYER	REB.	AVG.
Ware, Oklahoma City	607	20.9
Unseld, Louisville	505	19.4

Swagerty, Pacific	514	18.4
Woods, East Tennessee St.	361	17.2
Hayes, Houston	490	16.9
Murrey, Detroit	416	16.6
Wolters, Boston College	431	16.6
Lee, Vanderbilt	412	15.8
Cunningham, Murray St.	390	15.6
Williams, Temple	421	15.0

FIELD GOAL PERCENTAGE

PLAYER	FGM	FGA	PCT.
Hammond, Tulsa	172	261	.659
McKendrick, Rice	168	265	.634
Finkel, Dayton	248	397	.625
Lewis, Duke	161	271	.594
Stephenson, Rhode I.	128	216	.593
Lechman, Gonzaga	145	246	.589
Williams, Temple	195	336	.580

Murrey, Detroit	195	341	.572
Dean, Syracuse	125	219	.571
Hayes, Houston	323	570	.567

FREE THROW PERCENTAGE

PLAYER	FTM	FTA	PCT.
Blair, Providence	101	112	.902
Morawski, Seton Hall	136	153	.889
Lloyd, Rutgers	161	183	.880
Jones, Miami (Fla.)	134	153	.876
Long, Wake Forest	153	176	.869
Beasley, SMU	137	158	.867
Baumann, The Citadel	91	105	.867
Wetzel, Virginia Tech	123	142	.866
Butler, Memphis St.	114	132	.864
Heroman, LSU	132	153	.863

1965–66 TEAM LEADERS

SCORING OFFENSE

SCHOOL	PTS.	AVG.
Syracuse	2773	99.0
Houston	2845	98.1
Oklahoma City	2829	97.6
Loyola (Ill.)	2438	97.5
Brigham Young	2388	95.5

SCORING DEFENSE

SCHOOL	PTS.	AVG.
Oregon St.	1527	54.5
Tennessee	1499	57.7
Oklahoma St.	1523	60.9
Princeton	1425	62.0
Texas Western	1817	62.7

Kansas	1692	62.7
Pennsylvania	1568	62.7

FIELD GOAL PERCENTAGE

SCHOOL	FGM	FGA	PCT.
North Carolina	838	1620	.517
Davidson	877	1713	.512
Syracuse	1132	2271	.498
Brigham Young	946	1898	.498
Seattle	849	1722	.493

FREE THROW PERCENTAGE

SCHOOL	FTM	FTA	PCT.
Auburn	476	601	.792
Austin Peay St.	463	591	.783

Rhode Island	596	770	.774
Murray St.	488	640	.763
Davidson	563	739	.762

REBOUNDING

SCHOOL	TOTAL REB.	OWN	PCT.
Texas Western	2480	1430	.577
Duke	2598	1490	.574
Tennessee	2193	1255	.572
Detroit	2384	1356	.569

league. Vacendak finished ninth in the All-ACC balloting after averaging 13.3 points and four

1965–66 FINAL NATIONAL POLLS

AP	UPI	SCHOOL
1	1	Kentucky
2	2	Duke
3	3	Texas-El Paso
4	4	Kansas
5	6	St. Joseph's
6	5	Loyola (Ill.)
7	9	Cincinnati
8	8	Vanderbilt
9	7	Michigan
10	–	Western Kentucky
–	10	Providence
–	11	Nebraska
–	12	Utah
–	13	Oklahoma City
–	14	Houston
–	15	Oregon St.
–	16	Syracuse
–	17	Pacific
–	18	Davidson
–	19	Brigham Young
–	19	Dayton

rebounds per game for Duke's 26-4 squad.

North Carolina attempted a slowdown game in an effort to upend heavily-favored Duke in the ACC Tournament semifinals but lost, 21-20. Entering the tourney, Duke was ranked No. 3 in the AP poll and No. 2 by UPI. No other ACC team was in the top 20.

1966 NCAA Tournament

Summary: Texas Western, now called Texas-El Paso, put the finishing touches on dismantling the prejudiced myth that black athletes couldn't play disciplined basketball by capturing the 1966 title. The Miners' Don Haskins was a demanding coach who wouldn't let forward-center Nevil Shed ride back to the hotel with the team after Shed was thrown out in the first half of their 78-76 overtime victory against Cincin-

1965–66 NCAA CHAMPION: TEXAS WESTERN

SEASON STATISTICS OF TEXAS WESTERN REGULARS

PLAYER	POS.	CL.	G.	FG%	FT%	PPG	RPG
Bobby Joe Hill	G	Jr.	28	.411	.610	15.0	3.0
David Lattin	C	So.	29	.495	.703	14.0	8.6
Orsten Artis	G	Sr.	28	.470	.867	12.6	3.5
Nevil Shed	F-C	Jr.	29	.494	.755	10.6	7.9
Harry Flournoy	F	Sr.	29	.500	.649	8.3	10.7
Willie Worsley	G	So.	29	.403	.719	8.0	2.3
Willie Cager	F	So.	27	.410	.680	6.6	4.0
Louis Baudoin	F	Jr.	16	.386	.200	2.2	1.3
Jerry Armstrong	F	Sr.	24	.279	.875	1.9	1.4
TEAM TOTALS			**29**	**.445**	**.700**	**77.9**	**49.3**

1966 FINAL FOUR CHAMPIONSHIP GAME

COLLEGE PARK, MD

KENTUCKY (65)	FG-A	FT-A	REB.	PF	PTS.
Dampier	7-18	5-5	9	4	19
Kron	3-6	0-0	7	2	6
Conley	4-9	2-2	8	5	10
Riley	8-22	3-4	4	4	19
Jaracz	3-8	1-2	5	5	7
Berger	2-3	0-0	0	0	4
Gamble	0-0	0-0	0	1	0
LeMaster	0-1	0-0	0	1	0
Tallent	0-3	0-0	0	1	0
TOTALS	**27-70**	**11-13**	**33**	**23**	**65**

FG%: .386. FT%: .846.

TEXAS WESTERN (72)	FG-A	FT-A	REB.	PF	PTS.
Hill	7-17	6-9	3	3	20
Artis	5-13	5-5	8	1	15
Shed	1-1	1-1	3	1	3
Lattin	5-10	6-6	9	4	16
Cager	1-3	6-7	6	3	8
Flournoy	1-1	0-0	2	0	2
Worsley	2-4	4-6	4	0	8
TOTALS	**22-49**	**28-34**	**35**	**12**	**72**

FG%: .449. FT%: .824.
Halftime: Texas Western 34-31.

NATIONAL SEMIFINALS

DUKE (79): Marin 11-18 7-10 29, Riedy 2-7 2-2 6, Lewis 9-13 3-3 21, Verga 2-7 0-0 4, Vacendak 7-16 3-3 17, Wendelin 1-4 0-1 2, Liccardo 0-1 0-0 0, Barone 0-0 0-0 0. Team 32-66 (.485) 15-19 (.789) 79.

KENTUCKY (83): Conley 3-5 4-4 10, Riley 8-17 3-4 19, Jaracz 3-5 2-3 8, Dampier 11-20 1-2 23, Kron 5-13 2-2 12, Tallent 1-2 2-2 4, Berger 1-4 5-6 7, Gamble 0-0 0-0 0. Team 32-66 (.485) 19-24 (.792) 83.

Halftime: Duke 42-41.

TEXAS WESTERN (85): Hill 5-20 8-10 18, Artis 10-20 2-3 22, Shed 2-3 5-6 9, Lattin 5-7 1-1 11, Flournoy 3-6 2-2 8, Cager 2-5 1-1 5, Worsley 5-8 2-3 12, Armstrong 0-2 0-1 0. Team 32-71 (.451) 21-27 (.778) 85.

UTAH (78): Tate 0-4 1-3 1, Jackson 3-9 2-2 8, MacKay 4-10 6-9 14, Ockel 1-1 3-3 5, Chambers 14-31 10-12 38, Black 3-8 2-4 8, Lake 1-1 0-0 2, Day 1-2 0-0 2. Team 27-66 (.409) 24-33 (.727) 78.

Halftime: Texas Western 42-39.

ALL-TOURNAMENT TEAM

Jerry Chambers, F, Sr., Utah*
Louie Dampier, G, Jr., Kentucky
Bobby Joe Hill, G, Jr., Texas Western
Jack Marin, F, Sr., Duke
Pat Riley, F, Jr., Kentucky
*Named Most Outstanding Player

nati in the second round. Texas Western, featuring an all-black starting lineup with three players 6-1 or shorter in the NCAA final, stunned top-ranked and all-white Kentucky (72-65). Junior college transfer Bobby Joe Hill, one of the Miners' tiny trio, converted steals into layups on consecutive trips down the floor by flustered Kentucky guards to give them a lead they never relinquished. In the wake of Texas Western's sterling performance, major Southern schools started modifying their unwritten directives by recruiting more African-American players.

Outcome for Defending Champion: UCLA (18-8) finished second in the AAWU, failing to win the conference title for the only time in an 18-year span.

Star Gazing: Utah forward Jerry Chambers became the only Final Four Most Outstanding Player to play for a national fourth-place team.

One and Only: Texas Western's Hill, at 5-10, is the shortest player to lead an NCAA champion in scoring average (15 points per game). Hill's 20.2-point average in five tournament games in 1966 doubled the regular-season mark in his career.... Utah, the only Western Athletic Conference school ever to reach the Final Four, lost in the national semifinals to future WAC member Texas-El Paso.

Numbers Game: Jack Gardner became the only coach to direct two different schools to the Final Four at least twice apiece—Kansas State (4th in 1948 and 2nd in 1951) and Utah (4th in 1961 and 4th in 1966).

1966 CHAMPIONSHIP BRACKET

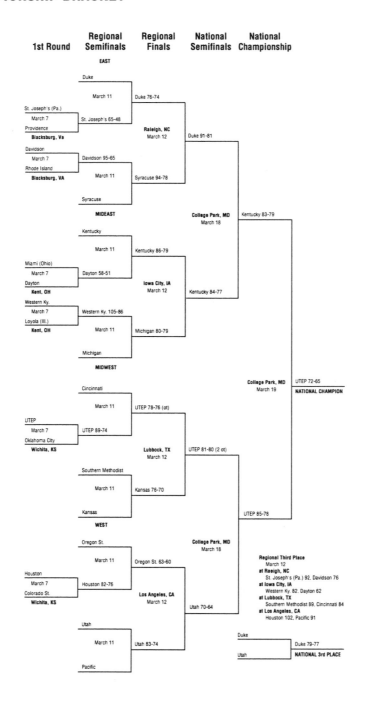

	1st Round	Regional Semifinals	Regional Finals	National Semifinals	National Championship

EAST

Duke

March 11 — Duke 76-74

St. Joseph's (Pa.)
March 7 — St. Joseph's 65-48
Providence
Blacksburg, Va

Raleigh, NC
March 12

Davidson
March 7 — Davidson 95-65
Rhode Island
Blacksburg, VA

March 11 — Syracuse 94-78

Syracuse

Duke 91-81

MIDEAST

Kentucky

March 11 — Kentucky 86-79

Miami (Ohio)
March 7 — Dayton 58-51
Dayton
Kent, OH

Iowa City, IA
March 12

Western Ky.
March 7 — Western Ky. 105-86
Loyola (Ill.)
Kent, OH

March 11 — Michigan 80-79

Michigan

Kentucky 84-77

College Park, MD
March 18

Kentucky 83-79

MIDWEST

Cincinnati

March 11 — UTEP 78-76 (ot)

UTEP
March 7 — UTEP 89-74
Oklahoma City
Wichita, KS

Lubbock, TX
March 12

Southern Methodist
March 11 — Kansas 76-70
Kansas

UTEP 81-80 (2 ot)

WEST

Oregon St.

March 11 — Oregon St. 63-60

Houston
March 7 — Houston 82-76
Colorado St.
Wichita, KS

Los Angeles, CA
March 12

Utah
March 11 — Utah 83-74
Pacific

Utah 70-64

College Park, MD
March 18

UTEP 85-78

College Park, MD
March 19

UTEP 72-65

NATIONAL CHAMPION

Regional Third Place
March 12
at Raleigh, NC
St. Joseph's (Pa.) 92, Davidson 76
at Iowa City, IA
Western Ky. 82, Dayton 62
at Lubbock, TX
Southern Methodist 89, Cincinnati 84
at Los Angeles, CA
Houston 102, Pacific 91

Duke

Duke 79-77

Utah

NATIONAL 3rd PLACE

1966–67

AT A GLANCE

NCAA Champion: UCLA (30-0).

NIT Champion: Southern Illinois (24-2).

NCAA Probation: South Carolina.

NCAA Consensus First-Team All-Americans: Lew Alcindor, C, Soph., UCLA; Clem Haskins, G-F, Sr., Western Kentucky; Elvin Hayes, F-C, Jr., Houston; Bob Lloyd, G, Sr., Rutgers; Wes Unseld, C, Jr., Louisville; Bob Verga, G, Sr., Duke; Jimmy Walker, G, Sr., Providence.

Providence guard Jimmy Walker after winning the 1966 MVP Award at 1966 Holiday Basketball Festival.

UCLA's Lew Alcindor scored 56 points in his varsity debut against Southern California. Alcindor's opening-game outburst was topped just once all season—by his school record 61 against Washington State. He finished his sophomore season ranked among the top seven in the country in field-goal shooting (first at 66.7 percent), scoring (second at 29 points per game), and rebounding (seventh at 15.5 per game). His scoring average is still the highest in Pacific-10 Conference history.

Alcindor was one of seven players to finish within three points of each other for the national scoring lead. Never have so many major collegians finished so close to the top. Providence's Jimmy Walker won the scoring race with a 30.4 average.

Kent's Doug Grayson set an NCAA record for most consecutive successful field goals in a single game with 16 when he went 18 of 19 from the floor against North Carolina.

Rutgers' Bob Lloyd converted 60 consecutive free throws. One of Lloyd's teammates was Jim Valvano, who later made a name for himself as a coach at Iona and North Carolina State. Lloyd went on to serve as coach at his alma mater, where one of his assistants was one low-key Dick Vitale.

Creighton's Bob Portman (51 points against Wisconsin-Milwaukee) and Alabama's Mike Nordholz (50 against Southern Mississippi) established school single-game scoring records.

TCU center James Cash became the first African American to play varsity basketball in the SWC. Cash is now chairman of the Harvard Business School MBA program.

Tennessee led the nation in team defense for the second time in three seasons.

Kentucky suffered its only non-winning record in coach Adolph Rupp's 41 seasons at the helm when the Wildcats went 13-13. They were 8-10 in league competition for their only losing SEC mark in history until UK duplicated that record under Eddie Sutton in 1988–89. Kentucky's defeats included a 92-77 setback against Cornell, the only Ivy League team to beat the Wildcats since 1942.

Louisville's Peck Hickman ended his 23-year coaching career with a 443-183 record. E. C.

Junior forward Don May was instrumental in leading Dayton to the NCAA Final Four.

Houston's mid-sixties teams, coached by Guy Lewis (center), included future NBA stars Elvin Hayes (left) and Don Chaney.

1966–67 FINAL NATIONAL POLLS

AP	UPI	SCHOOL
1	1	UCLA
2	2	Louisville
3	4	Kansas
4	3	North Carolina
5	5	Princeton
6	7	Western Kentucky
7	6	Houston
8	9	Tennessee
9	10	Boston College
10	8	Texas-El Paso
–	11	Toledo
–	12	St. John's
–	13	Tulsa
–	14	Utah St.
–	14	Vanderbilt
–	16	Pacific
–	17	Providence
–	18	New Mexico
–	19	Duke
–	20	Florida

1967 NCAA Tournament

Summary: UCLA won the national championship by a record average of 23.75 points. The

"Doc" Hayes retired as SMU's coach. In 20 seasons with the Mustangs, Hayes won outright or shared eight SWC titles. No other SWC coach has won more than six league championships.

1966–67 INDIVIDUAL LEADERS

SCORING

PLAYER	PTS.	AVG.
Walker, Providence	851	30.4
Alcindor, UCLA	870	29.0
Graham, New York Univ.	688	28.7
Hayes, Houston	881	28.4
Bialosuknia, Connecticut	673	28.0
Lloyd, Rutgers	809	27.9
Gray, Oklahoma City	715	27.5
Anderson, St. Joseph's	690	26.5
Verga, Duke	705	26.1
Tillman, Loyola (Ill.)	553	25.1

Unseld, Louisville	533	19.0
Swagerty, Pacific	518	18.5
May, Dayton	519	16.7
Hayes, Houston	488	15.7
Alcindor, UCLA	466	15.5
Powers, VMI	318	15.1
Lewis, St. Francis (Pa.)	386	14.8
Dove, St. John's	415	14.8

REBOUNDING

PLAYER	REB.	AVG.
Cunningham, Murray St.	479	21.8
Beatty, American	458	19.1

FIELD GOAL PERCENTAGE

PLAYER	FGM	FGA	PCT.
Alcindor, UCLA	346	519	.667
Allen, Bradley	232	373	.622
Lechman, Gonzaga	196	316	.620
Lewis, St. Francis (Pa.)	181	295	.614
Youngblood, Georgia	140	237	.591
Ogden, Santa Clara	186	322	.578
Wagner, Georgia Tech	164	291	.564
Mix, Toledo	227	403	.563
White, Hofstra	161	288	.559
Ware, Virginia Tech	128	230	.557

FREE THROW PERCENTAGE

PLAYER	FTM	FTA	PCT.
Lloyd, Rutgers	255	277	.921
Sandfoss, Morehead St.	106	117	.906
Thompson, Wichita St.	124	137	.905
Sutherland, Clemson	104	116	.897
Cornwall, Syracuse	103	117	.880
Coleman, Missouri	131	150	.873
McPherson, Murray St.	103	118	.873
Chapman, Iowa	114	131	.870
Fritz, Oregon St.	130	150	.867
Heiser, Princeton	93	108	.861

1966–67 TEAM LEADERS

SCORING OFFENSE

SCHOOL	PTS.	AVG.
Oklahoma City	2496	96.0
Northwestern	2009	91.3
UCLA	2687	89.6
Murray St.	2058	89.5
Houston	2765	89.2

SCORING DEFENSE

SCHOOL	PTS.	AVG.
Tennessee	1511	54.0
Memphis St.	1470	56.5
Army	1206	57.4
Princeton	1619	57.8
Kansas	1607	59.5

FIELD GOAL PERCENTAGE

SCHOOL	FGM	FGA	PCT.
UCLA	1082	2081	.520
St. Peter's	773	1498	.516
Bradley	832	1641	.507
Vanderbilt	834	1654	.504
Tulane	843	1679	.502

FREE THROW PERCENTAGE

SCHOOL	FTM	FTA	PCT.
West Texas St.	400	518	.772
Santa Clara	571	742	.770
Kentucky	429	559	.767
Rice	493	648	.761
Georgia	454	598	.759

REBOUNDING

SCHOOL	TOTAL REB.	OWN	PCT.
Florida	2124	1275	.600
Houston	3224	1862	.578
St. Francis (Pa.)	2266	1298	.573
New Mexico	2278	1304	.572
Princeton	2235	1270	.568

Bruins' toughest test was in the West Regional final, where Pacific trailed by fewer than 10 points in the closing minutes until UCLA pulled away to win by 16 (80-64) behind Lew Alcindor's 38 points. The Bruins won 26 of their 30 games by at least 15 points with the only contest in doubt being a 40-35 overtime triumph at Southern Cal in mid-season.

Outcome for Defending Champion: Texas-El Paso compiled a 22-7 with two of the defeats by double-digit margins against New Mexico State.

Biggest Upsets: Dayton wasn't ranked in the UPI top twenty when the Flyers opened the play-offs with a 69-67 overtime triumph against seventh-ranked Western Kentucky as Hilltoppers first-team All-American Clem Haskins, playing with his broken wrist in a cast, was limited to eight points. Dayton also defeated two other top ten teams—Tennessee (ranked ninth by UPI) and North Carolina (third)—before getting clobbered by top-ranked UCLA in the national final.... Charles Beasley was limited to nine points, but fellow SWC first-team selection Denny Holman picked up the slack with 30 points, including a decisive basket with three seconds remaining, to spark SMU (20-6) to an 83-81 victory over second-ranked Louisville (23-5). Wes Unseld and Butch Beard combined for 32 points and 21 rebounds, but it wasn't enough for the Cardinals, who hit just 5 of their 14 free throws.

One and Only: UCLA is the only NCAA champion since World War II not to have a senior on its roster.

Numbers Game: National field-goal accuracy leader UCLA finished among the top 30 teams in that category for the first time in 12 years.

1966–67 NCAA CHAMPION: UCLA

SEASON STATISTICS OF UCLA REGULARS

PLAYER	POS.	CL.	G.	FG%	FT%	PPG	RPG
Lew Alcindor	C	So.	30	.667	.650	29.0	15.5
Lucius Allen	G	So.	30	.479	.713	15.5	5.8
Mike Warren	G	Jr.	30	.465	.758	12.7	4.5
Lynn Shackelford	F	So.	30	.480	.821	11.4	5.9
Ken Heitz	F-G	So.	30	.506	.600	6.1	3.2
Bill Sweek	G	So.	30	.479	.565	4.7	2.8
Jim Nielsen	F-C	So.	27	.519	.455	4.6	3.4
Don Saffer	G	Jr.	27	.451	.542	2.9	0.8
Gene Sutherland	G	Jr.	20	.455	.583	1.9	0.8
Neville Saner	F-C	Jr.	24	.308	.667	1.4	1.9
Joe Chrisman	F	Jr.	19	.320	.364	1.1	1.5
TEAM TOTALS			30	.520	.653	89.6	49.8

1967 FINAL FOUR CHAMPIONSHIP GAME

LOUISVILLE, KY

UCLA (79)	MIN.	FG-A	FT-A	REB.	A	PF	PTS.
Heitz	27	2-7	0-0	6	1	2	4
Shackelford	35	5-10	0-2	3	1	1	10
Alcindor	35	8-12	4-11	18	3	0	20
Allen	36	7-15	5-8	9	2	2	19
Warren	35	8-16	1-1	7	0	1	17
Nielsen	4	0-1	0-1	1	0	3	0
Sweek	8	1-1	0-0	0	0	1	2
Saffer	5	2-5	0-0	0	0	1	4
Saner	5	1-1	0-0	2	0	2	2
Chrisman	4	0-0	1-2	1	0	2	1
Sutherland	4	0-0	0-0	0	0	0	0
Lynn	2	0-1	0-0	0	0	0	0
Team				7			
TOTALS	200	34-69	11-25	54	7	15	79

FG%: .493. FT%: .440.

DAYTON (64)	MIN.	FG-A	FT-A	REB.	A	PF	PTS.
May	40	9-23	3-4	17	3	4	21
Sadlier	26	2-5	1-2	7	0	5	5
Obrovac	5	0-2	0-0	2	1	1	0
Klaus	22	4-7	0-0	0	0	1	8
Hooper	34	2-7	2-4	5	2	2	6
Torain	23	3-14	0-0	4	0	3	6
Waterman	23	4-11	2-3	1	2	3	10
Sharpenter	23	2-5	4-5	5	0	1	8
Samanich	1	0-2	0-0	2	0	0	0
Beckman	1	0-0	0-0	0	0	0	0
Inderrieden	1	0-0	0-0	0	0	0	0
Wannemacher	1	0-0	0-0	0	0	0	0
Team				8			
TOTALS	200	26-76	12-18	51	8	20	64

FG%: .342. FT%: .667.
Halftime: UCLA 38-20.

UCLA's Lew Alcindor shoots over a Dayton defender in the NCAA Tournament final.

ALL-TOURNAMENT TEAM

Lew Alcindor, C, Soph., UCLA*
Lucius Allen, G, Soph., UCLA
Elvin Hayes, F, Jr., Houston
Don May, F, Jr., Dayton
Mike Warren, G, Jr., UCLA
　　*Named Most Outstanding Player

NATIONAL SEMIFINALS

UCLA (73): Heitz 0-0 1-1 1, Shackelford 11-19 0-1 22, Alcindor 6-11 7-13 19, Allen 6-15 5-5 17, Warren 4-10 6-7 14, Nielsen 0-3 0-0 0, Sweek 0-4 0-0 0, Saffer 0-0 0-0 0. Team 27-62 (.435) 19-27 (.704) 73.

HOUSTON (58): Hayes 12-31 1-2 25, Bell 3-11 4-7 10, Kruse 2-5 1-1 5, Grider 2-7 0-0 4, Chaney 3-11 0-2 6, Lentz 1-2 0-3 2, Spain 1-5 0-0 2, Lewis 0-0 0-1 0, Lee 2-3 0-0 4. Team 26-75 (.347) 6-16 (.375) 58.

　　Halftime: UCLA 39-28.

DAYTON (76): May 16-22 2-6 34, Sadlier 4-7 0-1 8, Obrovac 0-0 0-0 0, Klaus 3-6 9-10 15, Hooper 1-7 3-4 5, Torain 4-14 6-8 14, Wannemacher 0-0 0-2 0, Waterman 0-0 0-0 0. Team 28-56 (.500) 20-31 (.645) 76.

NORTH CAROLINA (62): Miller 6-18 1-1 13, Buntin 1-3 1-1 3, Clark 8-14 3-5 19, Lewis 5-18 1-1 11, Grubar 2-7 3-3 7, Gauntlett 1-4 0-0 2, Brown 0-3 0-0 0, Tuttle 3-5 1-1 7. Team 26-72 (.361) 10-12 (.833) 62.

　　Halftime: Dayton 29-23.

1967 CHAMPIONSHIP BRACKET

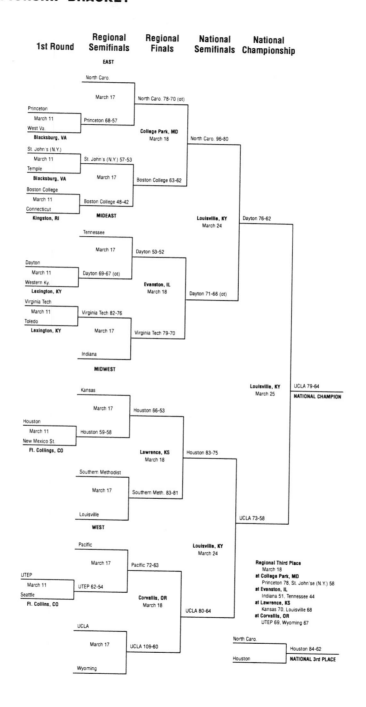

	Regional Semifinals	Regional Finals	National Semifinals	National Championship
1st Round				

EAST

North Caro.

March 17 — North Caro. 78-70 (ot)

Princeton
March 11 — Princeton 68-57
West Va.
Blacksburg, VA

College Park, MD
March 18 — North Caro. 96-80

St. John's (N.Y.)
March 11 — St. John's (N.Y.) 57-53
Temple
Blacksburg, VA

March 17 — Boston College 63-62

Boston College
March 11 — Boston College 48-42
Connecticut
Kingston, RI

Louisville, KY
March 24 — Dayton 76-62

MIDEAST

Tennessee
March 17 — Dayton 53-52

Dayton
March 11 — Dayton 69-67 (ot)
Western Ky.
Lexington, KY

Evanston, IL
March 18 — Dayton 71-66 (ot)

Virginia Tech
March 11 — Virginia Tech 82-76
Toledo
Lexington, KY

March 17 — Virginia Tech 79-70

Indiana

MIDWEST

Louisville, KY
March 25 — UCLA 79-64 **NATIONAL CHAMPION**

Kansas
March 17 — Houston 66-53

Houston
March 11 — Houston 59-58
New Mexico St.
Ft. Collings, CO

Lawrence, KS
March 18 — Houston 83-75

Southern Methodist
March 17 — Southern Meth. 83-81

Louisville

WEST

UCLA 73-58

Pacific
March 17 — Pacific 72-63

Louisville, KY
March 24 — UCLA 80-64

UTEP
March 11 — UTEP 62-54
Seattle
Ft. Collins, CO

Corvallis, OR
March 18

UCLA
March 17 — UCLA 109-60
Wyoming

Regional Third Place
March 18
at College Park, MD
Princeton 78, St. John'se (N.Y.) 58
at Evanston, IL
Indiana 51, Tennessee 44
at Lawrence, KS
Kansas 70, Louisville 68
at Corvallis, OR
UTEP 69, Wyoming 67

North Caro.
Houston 84-62
Houston
NATIONAL 3rd PLACE

1967–68

AT A GLANCE

NCAA Champion: UCLA (29-1).

NIT Champion: Dayton (21-9).

New Rules: The dunk shot is deemed illegal during the game and pregame warmup. NIT field expands from 14 teams to 16.

NCAA Probation: Illinois, Mississippi State, South Carolina.

NCAA Consensus First-Team All-Americans: Lew Alcindor, C, Jr., UCLA; Elvin Hayes, F-C, Sr., Houston; Pete Maravich, G, Soph., Louisiana State; Larry Miller, F, Sr., North Carolina; Wes Unseld, C, Sr., Louisville.

Louisville's Wes Unseld fights off a defender for a rebound.

Houston ended UCLA's 47-game winning streak, 71-69, in the Astrodome in what has been called the "Game of the Century."

Sophomore Pete Maravich scored an amazing 49.3 percent of LSU's points in compiling a 43.8-point average. When Maravich was a prep player, his father, Press, coached at North Carolina State. At the time, the ACC required incoming freshmen to score 800 on their SAT. When Pete apparently had difficulty reaching 800, his father decided that coaching his son was more important than remaining in the ACC. So father and son went to LSU in the SEC. During the 1960s it was widely assumed that the 800 score was the ACC's way of perpetuating segregation. But it wound up costing the league one of the most famous white players in history.

Maravich's 59-point uprising against Alabama was not the season's single-game high. Houston's Elvin Hayes poured in a school-record 62 against Valparaiso.

Florida's Neal Walk became the first Southerner in major-college history to pace the nation in rebounding.

Duke managed just two field goals in a 12-10 defeat against North Carolina State on March 8, 1968. It was the lowest-scoring game involving at least one major team in 26 years, marking the first time a squad won with fewer than 20 points since 1944.

For the only time in ACC history, two members finished the season with at least 20 defeats—Wake Forest (5-21) and Clemson (4-20).

Vanderbilt upset three nationally-ranked teams (North Carolina, Davidson, and Duke) within a week. But the biggest news at Vanderbilt was Perry Wallace breaking the racial barrier and becoming the first African American to play varsity basketball in the SEC. Wallace is now a professor of law at American University.

Establishing school single-game scoring records were Duquesne's Ron Guziak (50 points against St. Francis, Pa.), Southern Illinois' Dick Garrett (46 against Centenary), Louisville's Wes Unseld (45 against Georgetown College), Southern Mississippi's Berlin Ladner (45 against Sam-

1967–68 INDIVIDUAL LEADERS

SCORING

PLAYER	PTS.	AVG.
Maravich, LSU	1138	43.8
Murphy, Niagara	916	38.2
Hayes, Houston	1214	36.8
Travis, Oklahoma City	808	29.9
Portman, Creighton	738	29.5
Mount, Purdue	683	28.5
Hill, W. Texas St.	573	27.3
Halimon, Utah St.	671	26.8
Foster, Miami (Ohio)	617	26.8
Walk, Florida	663	26.5

REBOUNDING

PLAYER	REB.	AVG.
Walk, Florida	494	19.8
Smith, E. Kentucky	472	19.7

Hayes, Houston	624	18.9
Unseld, Louisville	513	18.3
Cunningham, Murray St.	410	17.8
Lewis, St. Francis (Pa.)	443	17.7
Wilson, Idaho St.	420	17.5
Cowens, Florida St.	456	16.9
Alcindor, UCLA	461	16.5
Stephenson, Rhode Island	420	16.2

FIELD GOAL PERCENTAGE

PLAYER	FGM	FGA	PCT.
Allen, Bradley	258	304	.655
Hunt, Army	154	248	.621
Alcindor, UCLA	294	480	.613
Unseld, Louisville	294	480	.613
Sorenson, Ohio St.	196	329	.596
Sidle, Oklahoma	189	321	.589
Webster, St. Peter's	279	477	.585

Lanier, St. Bon.	272	466	.584
Bowen, Bradley	185	317	.584
Lienhard, Georgia	213	366	.582

FREE THROW PERCENTAGE

PLAYER	FTM	FTA	PCT.
Heiser, Princeton	117	130	.900
Ward, Centenary	94	106	.887
Carpenter, Pacific	96	109	.881
Luchini, Marquette	107	124	.863
Williams, Rice	113	131	.863
Garrett, S. Ill.	100	116	.862
Montgomery, W. Forest	134	157	.854
Wininger, Butler	97	114	.851
Moeser, Tulane	125	147	.850
Warren, St. John's	102	120	.850
Washington, Miss. St.	96	113	.850

1967–68 TEAM LEADERS

SCORING OFFENSE

SCHOOL	PTS.	AVG.
Houston	3226	97.8
St. Peter's	2630	93.9
UCLA	2802	93.4
Oklahoma City	2492	92.3
Florida St.	2438	90.3

SCORING DEFENSE

SCHOOL	PTS.	AVG.
Army	1448	57.9
Oklahoma St.	1528	58.8
Tennessee	1548	59.5
Villanova	1696	60.6
Princeton	1579	60.7

SCORING MARGIN

SCHOOL	OFF.	DEF.	MAR.
UCLA	93.4	67.2	26.2

Houston	97.8	72.5	25.3
St. Peter's	93.9	76.1	17.8
Columbia	78.8	61.7	17.1
Boston College	88.8	74.9	13.9

WON-LOST PERCENTAGE

SCHOOL	W-L	PCT.
UCLA	29-1	.967
Houston	31-2	.939
St. Bonaventure	23-2	.920
North Carolina	28-4	.875
St. Peter's	24-4	.857

FIELD GOAL PERCENTAGE

SCHOOL	FGM	FGA	PCT.
Bradley	927	1768	.524
St. Peter's	1019	1953	.522
St. Bonaventure	875	1732	.505
UCLA	1161	2321	.500
Louisville	881	1770	.498

FREE THROW PERCENTAGE

SCHOOL	FTM	FTA	PCT.
Vanderbilt	527	684	.770
Mississippi St.	496	645	.769
Nebraska	504	660	.764
Tulane	528	692	.763
Georgia Tech	404	531	.761

REBOUNDS

SCHOOL	REB.	AVG.
Houston	2074	62.8
Northern Illinois	1383	57.6
St. Francis (Pa.)	1434	57.4
Eastern Kentucky	1348	56.2
American	1459	56.1

ford), and Massachusetts' Billy Tindall (41 against Vermont).

Niagara's Calvin Murphy, a 5-9 sophomore, posted the highest single-season scoring average for a major-college player shorter than 6-0 (38.2 points per game).

Long Island, winner of two of the first four NIT titles (1939 and 1941), participated in the NIT for the first time since 1950.

Oklahoma City coach Abe Lemons, upset when his team trailed Duke, 49-38, at intermission of its NIT opener, kept his team on the Madison Square Garden floor for a 10-minute workout. It didn't help as OCU lost, 97-81.

1967–68 FINAL NATIONAL POLLS

AP	UPI	SCHOOL
1	1	Houston
2	2	UCLA
3	3	St. Bonaventure
4	4	North Carolina
5	5	Kentucky
6	7	New Mexico
7	6	Columbia
8	9	Davidson
9	8	Louisville
10	11	Duke
–	10	Marquette
–	12	New Mexico St.
–	13	Vanderbilt
–	14	Kansas St.
–	15	Princeton
–	16	Army
–	17	Santa Clara
–	18	Utah
–	19	Bradley
–	20	Iowa

UCLA coaching guru John Wooden.

Indiana tied for last place in the Big Ten with a 4-10 league record one season after tying for the title with a 10-4 mark.

1968 NCAA Tournament

Summary: "I've never come out and said it," UCLA coach John Wooden said, "but it would be hard to pick a team over the 1968 team. I will say it would be the most difficult team to prepare for and play against offensively and defensively. It created so many problems. It had such great balance.

"We had the big center (Alcindor) who is the most valuable player of all time. Mike Warren was a three-year starter who may have been the most intelligent floor leader ever, going eight complete games once without a turnover. Lucius Allen was a very physical, talented individual who was extremely quick. Lynn Shackleford was a great shooter out of the corner who didn't allow defenses to sag on Jabbar. Mike Lynn didn't have power, but he had as fine a pair of hands around the boards as I have ever seen."

The roster for UCLA's 1968 national champion included six players with double-digit season scoring averages, but senior forward Edgar Lacey dropped off the team with an 11.9-point average following a dispute with Wooden after a highly-publicized mid-season defeat against

St. Bonaventure's Bob Lanier stetches to block a shot.

Houston's Elvin Hayes (left) and UCLA's Lew Alcindor go head to head in the 1967–68 NCAA Semifinals.

Houston before 52,693 fans at the Astrodome. Lacey, assigned to defend Cougars star Elvin Hayes early in the game, was annoyed with Wooden for singling him out following Hayes' 29-point first-half outburst. Lacey, the leading rebounder for the Bruins' 1965 NCAA titlist when he was an All-Tournament team selection, missed the 1966–67 campaign because of a fractured left kneecap. Houston, entering the tourney undefeated, lost in the national semifinals against UCLA (101-69) when the Cougars' Elvin Hayes, averaging 37.6 points per game entering the Final Four, was restricted to 10 as the Bruins employed a diamond-and-one defense with Lynn Shackelford assigned to cover Hayes. Houston excelled although forward Melvin Bell, the third-leading scorer and second-leading rebounder for the '67 Final Four team, missed the season after undergoing knee surgery.

Star Gazing: St. Bonaventure, undefeated entering the tourney (22-0), lost in the East Regional semifinals against North Carolina (91-72) despite 23 points and nine rebounds by consensus second-team All-American Bob Lanier of the Bonnies.

One and Only: Hayes became the only player to lead the playoffs in scoring and rebounding in back-to-back years. He also became the only player to lead a tournament in scoring by more than 60 points. Alcindor and his UCLA teammates helped hold Hayes to 10 points in the 1968 national semifinals, but the Big E finished with 167 points in five games. Alcindor was runner-up with 103 points in four games. Hayes became the only player in tournament history to collect more than 40 points and 25 rebounds in the same game when he had 49 points and 27 rebounds in a 94-76 decision over Loyola of Chicago in the first round of the Midwest Regional. Hayes holds the records for most rebounds in a playoff series (97 in five games as a senior) and career (222 in

1967–68 NCAA CHAMPION: UCLA

SEASON STATISTICS OF UCLA REGULARS

PLAYER	POS.	CL.	G.	FG%	FT%	PPG	RPG
Lew Alcindor	C	Jr.	28	.613	.616	26.2	16.5
Lucius Allen	G	Jr.	30	.462	.678	15.1	6.0
Mike Warren	G	Sr.	30	.431	.763	12.1	3.7
Lynn Shackelford	F	Jr.	30	.498	.848	10.7	5.0
Mike Lynn	F	Sr.	30	.457	.684	10.3	5.2
Ken Heitz	G	Jr.	27	.500	.743	5.3	2.3
Jim Nielsen	F	Jr.	30	.496	.657	4.6	3.3
Bill Sweek	G	Jr.	27	.471	.654	3.6	1.2
Gene Sutherland	G	Sr.	27	.417	.885	1.6	0.6
Neville Saner	F	Sr.	24	.372	.600	1.5	1.6
TEAM TOTALS			30	.500	.684	93.4	53.4

1968 FINAL FOUR CHAMPIONSHIP GAME

LOS ANGELES, CA

UCLA (78)	MIN.	FG-A	FT-A	REB.	A	PF	PTS.
Shackelford	26	3-5	0-1	2	4	2	6
Lynn	22	1-7	5-7	6	4	2	7
Alcindor	37	15-21	4-4	16	1	4	34
Warren	35	3-7	1-1	3	1	2	7
Allen	35	3-7	5-7	5	5	4	11
Nielsen	10	1-1	0-0	1	0	1	2
Heitz	20	3-6	1-1	2	2	1	7
Sutherland	5	1-2	0-0	2	1	2	2
Sweek	5	0-1	0-0	2	0	0	0
Saner	5	1-3	0-0	2	1	0	2
Team				9			
TOTALS	200	31-60	16-21	48	19	16	78

FG%: .517. FT%: .762. Turnovers: 26.

N. CAROLINA (55)	MIN.	FG-A	FT-A	REB.	A	PF	PTS.
Miller	37	5-13	4-6	6	3	3	14
Bunting	15	1-3	1-2	2	1	5	3
Clark	37	4-12	1-3	8	1	3	9
Scott	35	6-17	0-1	3	2	3	12
Grubar	35	2-5	1-2	0	1	2	5
Fogler	16	1-4	2-2	0	2	0	4
Brown	13	2-5	2-2	5	0	1	6

Tuttle	2	0-0	0-0	0	1	0	0
Frye	3	1-2	0-1	1	0	0	2
Whitehead	1	0-0	0-0	0	0	0	0
Delany	3	0-1	0-0	0	0	0	0
Fletcher	3	0-1	0-0	0	0	0	0
Team				10			
TOTALS	200	22-63	11-19	35	11	17	55

FG%: .349. FT%: .579. Turnovers: 23.
Halftime: UCLA 32-22.

NATIONAL SEMIFINALS

OHIO STATE (66): Howell 6-17 1-2 13, Hosket 4-11 6-9 14, Sorenson 5-17 1-3 11, Schnabel 0-1 0-0 0, Meadors 3-13 2-2 8, Finney 8-13 0-2 16, Smith 2-6 0-0 4, Andreas 0-0 0-0 0, Barclay 0-1 0-0 0, Geddes 0-0 0-0 0. Team 28-79 (.354) 10-18 (.556) 66.

NORTH CAROLINA (80): Miller 10-23 0-1 20, Bunting 4-7 9-10 17, Clark 7-9 1-1 15, Scott 6-16 1-4 13, Grubar 4-9 3-3 11, Fogler 1-2 0-0 2, Brown 0-4 0-0 0, Tuttle 1-1 0-1 2. Team 33-71 (.465) 14-20 (.700) 80.

Halftime: North Carolina 34-27.

HOUSTON (69): Lee 2-15 0-0 4, Hayes 3-10 4-7 10, Spain 4-12 7-10 15, Chaney 5-13 5-7 15, Lewis 2-8 2-2 6, Hamood 3-5 4-6 10, Gribben 0-5 0-1 0, Bell 3-8 3-4 9, Taylor 0-0 0-0 0, Cooper 0-2 0-0 0. Team 22-78 (.282) 25-37 (.676) 69.

UCLA (101): Shackelford 6-10 5-5 17, Lynn 8-10 3-3 19, Alcindor 7-14 5-6 19, Warren 7-18 0-0 14, Allen 9-18 1-2 19, Nielsen 2-3 0-0 4, Heitz 3-6 1-1 7, Sweek 1-1 0-1 2, Sutherland 0-1 0-0 0, Saner 0-2 0-0 0. Team 43-83 (.518) 15-18 (.833) 101.

Halftime: UCLA 53-31.

ALL-TOURNAMENT TEAM

Lew Alcindor, C, Jr., UCLA*
Lucius Allen, G, Jr., UCLA
Larry Miller, F, Sr., North Carolina
Lynn Shackleford, F, Jr., UCLA
Mike Warren, G, Sr., UCLA
   *Named Most Outstanding Player

13 games). He had five games with at least 24 rebounds, including the first three playoff games in 1968, before being held to five in a 101-69 national semifinal loss against UCLA. Hayes also holds the record for most playoff field goals in a career with 152. He averaged almost 24 field goal attempts per game in helping the Cougars win nine of 13 contests.

Numbers Game: UCLA became the only champion to win its two Final Four games by a total of more than 50 points.... This year marked the only time as many as three Final Four teams returned to the national semifinals for a second consecutive season—UCLA (champion both years under Wooden), Houston (third in '67 and fourth in '68 under Guy Lewis), and North Carolina (fourth in '67 and runner-up in '68 under Dean Smith).... Hayes led the tournament in scoring (167 points) and rebounding (97 rebounds) by wide margins for fourth-place Houston, but he wasn't named to the all-tournament team.

1968 CHAMPIONSHIP BRACKET

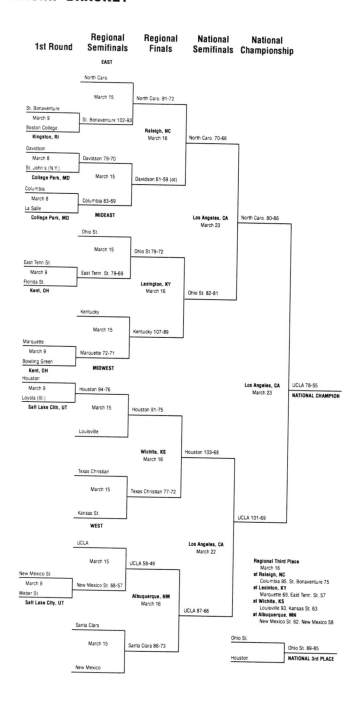

1st Round | Regional Semifinals | Regional Finals | National Semifinals | National Championship

EAST

North Caro.
March 15
North Caro. 91-72
St. Bonaventure
March 9
St. Bonaventure 102-93
Boston College
Kingston, RI
Raleigh, NC
March 16
North Caro. 70-66
Davidson
March 8
Davidson 79-70
St. John's (N.Y.)
College Park, MD
March 15
Davidson 61-59 (ot)
Columbia
March 8
Columbia 83-69
La Salle
College Park, MD

North Caro. 80-66

MIDEAST

Los Angeles, CA
March 23

Ohio St.
March 15
Ohio St 79-72
East Tenn St
March 9
East Tenn. St. 79-69
Florida St.
Kent, OH
Lexington, KY
March 16
Ohio St. 82-81
Kentucky
March 15
Kentucky 107-89
Marquette
March 9
Marquette 72-71
Bowling Green
Kent, OH

MIDWEST

Los Angeles, CA
March 23

UCLA 78-55
NATIONAL CHAMPION

Houston
March 9
Houston 94-76
Loyola (Ill.)
Salt Lake Clth, UT
March 15
Houston 91-75
Louisville
Wichita, KS
March 16
Houston 103-68
Texas Christian
March 15
Texas Christian 77-72
Kansas St.

UCLA 101-69

WEST

UCLA
March 15
UCLA 58-49
New Mexico St.
March 9
New Mexico St. 68-57
Weber St.
Salt Lake City, UT
Los Angeles, CA
March 22
Albuquerque, NM
March 16
UCLA 87-66
Santa Clara
March 15
Santa Clara 86-73
New Mexico

Regional Third Place
March 16
at Raleigh, NC
  Columbia 95. St. Bonaventure 75
at Lexinton, KY
  Marquette 69. East Tenn. St. 57
at Wichita, KS
  Louisville 93. Kansas St. 63
at Albuquerque, MN
  New Mexico St. 62. New Mexico 58

Ohio St.
Ohio St. 89-85
Houston
NATIONAL 3rd PLACE

1968–69

AT A GLANCE

NCAA Champion: UCLA (29-1).

NIT Champion: Temple (22-8).

NCAA Probation: Florida State, Illinois, La Salle, Mississippi State, St. Bonaventure, Texas-Pan American, Utah State.

NCAA Consensus First-Team All-Americans: Lew Alcindor, C, Sr., UCLA; Spencer Haywood, F-C, Jr., Detroit; Pete Maravich, G, Jr., Louisiana State; Rick Mount, G, Jr., Purdue; Calvin Murphy, G, Jr., Niagara.

LSU's Pete Maravich, averaging 44.2 points per game, won the national scoring championship by a larger margin than any player in history (10.9 points higher than Purdue guard Rick Mount). Incredibly, Maravich averaged 46.5 points in 15 road games, compared to 41 at home. Needing 49 in the Tigers' finale at Georgia to set an all-time single-season record, he exploded for 58, including 11 in a second overtime when he climaxed the outburst with a hook shot from midcourt.

A coach who might have wondered about the fuss over Maravich was Tennessee's Ray Mears, whose team employed a helter-skelter defense that was dubbed the "Chinese" defense because it was similar to a Chinese firedrill. In four games over two seasons, the Vols held Pistol Pete to a 19.8 average. No other team held Maravich under 30 points in his first 52 games.

Maravich had three consecutive games with at least 50 points against Division I opponents (66-50-54). His 66 points against Tulane was not the season's single-game high, however. Niagara's Calvin Murphy claimed that distinction by pouring in a school-record 68 against Syracuse.

Michigan's Rudy Tomjanovich, who would go on to coach the 1994 NBA champion Houston Rockets, set a Chicago Stadium college record and school standard with 30 rebounds in a 112-100 overtime defeat to Loyola of Chicago. Earli-er in the season, in another overtime game, he set a Michigan field-goal record with 21 baskets and tied Cazzie Russell's scoring standard with 48 points in an 89-87 victory over Indiana.

Larry Mikan, the son of Hall of Famer George Mikan, led Minnesota in scoring (18.4 ppg) and rebounding (10.5 rpg).

Kentucky became the first school to win 1,000 games.

Wake Forest's Charlie Davis (51 points against American University), St. Bonaventure's Bob Lanier (51 against Seton Hall), and Vanderbilt's Tom Hagan (44 at Mississippi State) set school single-game scoring standards.

Southern Cal ended UCLA's 41-game winning streak, 46-44.

Duke's Vic Bubas retired after a 10-year coaching career with a 213-67 record.

San Diego's Phil Woolpert, who gained national acclaim as coach of San Francisco's back-to-back NCAA champions in the mid-1950s, retired after a 16-year coaching career with a 239-164 record. Woolpert spent much of his later years as a bus driver in the Northwest.

Jerry Tarkanian kicked off his major-college coaching career with a 23-3 record at Long Beach State.

1968–69 FINAL NATIONAL POLLS

AP	UPI	SCHOOL
1	1	UCLA
2	6	La Salle
3	4	Santa Clara
4	2	North Carolina
5	3	Davidson
6	7	Purdue
7	5	Kentucky
8	8	St. John's
9	10	Duquesne
10	15	Villanova
11	11	Drake
12	9	New Mexico St.
13	20	South Carolina
14	14	Marquette
15	13	Louisville
16	15	Boston College
17	–	Notre Dame
18	12	Colorado
19	20	Kansas
20	–	Illinois
–	17	Weber St.
–	17	Wyoming
–	19	Colorado St.

1968–69 INDIVIDUAL LEADERS

SCORING

PLAYER	PTS.	AVG.
Maravich, LSU	1148	44.2
Mount, Purdue	932	33.3
Murphy, Niagara	778	32.4
Haywood, Detroit	699	31.8
B. Tallent, G. Washington	723	28.9
Roberts, Utah St.	718	27.6
Curnutt, Miami (Fla.)	661	27.5
Lanier, St. Bonaventure	654	27.3
Travis, Oklahoma City	729	27.0
Morgan, Jacksonville	613	26.7

REBOUNDING

PLAYER	REB.	AVG.
Haywood, Detroit	472	21.5
Lewis, St. Francis (Pa.)	495	20.6

PLAYER	PTS.	AVG.
Green, Morehead St.	483	17.9
Walk, Florida	481	17.8
Driscoll, Boston College	498	17.8
Cowens, Florida St.	437	17.5
Brown, Middle Tenn. St.	429	16.5
Ladner, S. Mississippi	411	16.4
Grosso, Louisville	432	16.0
Cross, San Francisco	400	16.0

FIELD GOAL PERCENTAGE

PLAYER	FGM	FGA	PCT.
Alcindor, UCLA	303	477	.635
Bunting, N. Carolina	217	363	.598
Wilkes, Virginia	153	256	.598
Awtrey, Santa Clara	240	406	.591
Lanier, St. Bonaventure	270	460	.587
Lienhard, Georgia	235	404	.582
Smith, Syracuse	177	307	.577

Hayes, Boston Univ.	200	351	.570
Dodds, Wyoming	165	290	.569
Gayeska, Massachusetts	142	250	.568

FREE THROW PERCENTAGE

PLAYER	FTM	FTA	PCT.
Justus, Tennessee	133	147	.905
Finney, Ohio St.	99	110	.900
Thomforde, Princeton	123	137	.898
Ward, Centenary	99	112	.884
Davis, Wake Forest	194	220	.882
Mitchell, W. Texas St.	131	149	.879
Powell, Loyola (La.)	106	121	.876
B. Tallent, G. Washington	155	177	.876
Hagan, Vanderbilt	116	133	.872
Mitchell, VMI	99	114	.868

1968–69 TEAM LEADERS

SCORING OFFENSE

SCHOOL	PTS.	AVG.
Purdue	2605	93.0
Hardin-Simmons	2387	91.9
Kentucky	2542	90.8
Michigan	2153	89.7
Louisiana St.	2316	89.1

SCORING DEFENSE

SCHOOL	PTS.	AVG.
Army	1498	53.5
Tennessee	1651	59.0
Oklahoma St.	1482	59.3
Long Island	1372	59.7
Kansas	1625	60.2

SCORING MARGIN

SCHOOL	OFF.	DEF.	MAR.
UCLA	84.7	63.8	20.9
La Salle	89.0	70.9	18.1

Columbia	77.0	61.3	15.7
Santa Clara	77.0	61.3	15.7
Purdue	93.0	79.1	13.9

WON-LOST PERCENTAGE

SCHOOL	W-L	PCT.
UCLA	29-1	.967
La Salle	23-1	.958
Santa Clara	27-2	.931
Weber St.	27-3	.900
Davidson	27-3	.900

FIELD GOAL PERCENTAGE

SCHOOL	FGM	FGA	PCT.
UCLA	1027	1999	.514
Auburn	734	1461	.502
Southern Mississippi	855	1710	.500
Columbia	689	1380	.499
St. Peter's	913	1847	.494

FREE THROW PERCENTAGE

SCHOOL	FTM	FTA	PCT.
Jacksonville	574	733	.783
Purdue	571	730	.782
Tennessee	438	563	.778
Iowa	573	743	.771
Wake Forest	642	833	.771

REBOUNDING

SCHOOL	REB.	AVG.
Middle Tennessee St.	1685	64.8
St. Francis (Pa.)	1411	58.8
Morehead St.	1583	58.6
Indiana	1354	56.4
Maine	1286	55.9

1969 NCAA Tournament

Summary: UCLA's Lew Alcindor, climaxing a streak when he became the only player to earn three consecutive Final Four Most Outstanding Player awards, collected 37 points and 20 rebounds in his final college game, a victory against Purdue (92-72). The 37-point outburst is the fourth-highest point total in championship game history. Teammate Ken Heitz was scoreless in the final but his defense was instrumental in making Boilermakers standout Rick Mount miss 14 consecutive field-goal attempts in one stretch. Fellow guard John Vallely, averaging a modest 10.2 points per game entering the Final Four, erupted for 29 points in the national semifinals and the Bruins needed all of them as they had a nine-point lead with 70 seconds remaining dwindle to one before defeating Drake (85-82).

One and Only: Alcindor, who later changed his name to Kareem Abdul-Jabbar, is the only individual selected the Final Four's Most Outstanding Player three times (1967 through 1969). Alcindor is the only player to couple three unanimous first team All-American seasons with three NCAA titles. He is also the only player to hit better than 70 percent of his field-goal attempts in two different NCAA title games (1968 and 1969).

Numbers Game: The only player to lead a single tournament in scoring with more than 120

1968–69 NCAA CHAMPION: UCLA

SEASON STATISTICS OF UCLA REGULARS

PLAYER	POS.	CL.	G.	FG%	FT%	PPG	RPG
Lew Alcindor	C	Sr.	30	.635	.612	24.0	14.7
Curtis Rowe	F	So.	30	.502	.678	12.9	7.9
John Vallely	G	Jr.	28	.496	.755	11.0	3.3
Sidney Wicks	F	So.	30	.435	.580	7.5	5.1
Lynn Shackelford	F	Sr.	30	.463	.500	7.0	4.0
Ken Heitz	G	Sr.	30	.467	.684	6.5	2.3
Bill Sweek	G	Sr.	30	.506	.625	6.3	2.2
Steve Patterson	C	So.	29	.527	.750	5.0	3.9
Terry Schofield	G	So.	24	.415	.611	2.7	1.6
John Ecker	F	So.	20	.667	.667	1.6	1.2
Bill Seibert	F	So.	15	.261	.714	1.1	0.8
TEAM TOTALS			30	.513	.648	84.7	50.4

1969 FINAL FOUR CHAMPIONSHIP GAME

LOUISVILLE, KY

UCLA (92)	MIN.	FG-A	FT-A	REB.	A	PF	PTS.
Shackelford	35	3-8	5-8	9	0	3	11
Rowe	37	4-4	4-4	12	3	2	12
Alcindor	36	15-20	7-9	20	0	2	37
Heitz	34	0-3	0-1	3	4	4	0
Vallely	31	4-9	7-10	4	0	3	15
Sweek	10	3-3	0-1	1	0	3	6
Wicks	6	0-1	3-6	4	1	1	3
Schofield	3	1-2	0-0	0	0	0	2
Patterson	5	1-1	2-2	2	0	0	4
Seibert	1	0-0	0-0	1	0	0	0
Farmer	1	0-0	0-0	0	0	1	0
Ecker	1	1-1	0-0	0	0	0	2
Team				5			
TOTALS	200	32-58	28-41	61	8	19	92

FG%: .552. FT%: .683. **Turnovers:** 19.

PURDUE (72)	MIN.	FG-A	FT-A	REB.	A	PF	PTS.
Gilliam	32	2-14	3-3	11	3	2	7
Faerber	17	1-2	0-0	3	0	5	2
Johnson	27	4-9	3-4	9	0	2	11
Mount	37	12-36	4-5	1	0	3	28
Keller	32	4-17	3-4	4	3	5	11
Kaufman	13	0-0	2-2	5	0	5	2
Bedford	25	3-8	1-3	8	0	3	7
Weatherford	15	1-5	2-2	1	0	3	4
Reasoner	1	0-1	0-1	1	0	2	0
Taylor	1	0-0	0-0	0	0	0	0
Team				5			
TOTALS	200	27-92	18-24	48	6	30	72

FG%: .293. FT%: .750. **Turnovers:** 4.
Halftime: UCLA 50-41.

NATIONAL SEMIFINALS

NORTH CAROLINA (65): Bunting 7-13 5-7 19, Scott 6-19 4-6 16, Clark 7-9 6-10 20, Fogler 1-4 0-0 2, G. Tuttle 2-4 0-1 4, Delany 0-2 0-0 0, Dedmon 0-1 0-1 0, Brown 1-4 0-0 2, Gipple 0-3 0-0 0, Chadwick 1-2 0-0 2, R. Tuttle 0-1 0-0 0, Eggleston 0-0 0-0 0. Team 25-62 (.403) 15-25 (.600) 65.

PURDUE (92): Gilliam 3-11 0-0 6, Faerber 3-3 2-2 8, Johnson 2-5 1-3 5, Mount 14-28 8-9 36, Keller 9-19 2-3 20, Kaufman 0-1 2-3 2, Weatherford 3-6 1-1 7, Bedford 3-3 0-0 6, Taylor 1-1 0-1 2, Longfellow 0-1 0-0 0, Reasoner 0-0 0-0 0, Young 0-0 0-0 0. Team 38-78 (.487) 16-22 (.727) 92.

Halftime: Purdue 53-30.

DRAKE (82): Pulliam 4-4 4-5 12, Williams 0-1 0-0 0, Wise 5-7 3-4 13, McCarter 10-27 4-4 24, Draper 5-13 2-2 12, Odom 0-2 0-1 0, Wanamaker 4-7 1-1 9, Zeller 4-12 4-6 12, Gwin 0-0 0-1 0. Team 32-83 (.386) 18-24 (.667) 82.

UCLA (85): Shackelford 2-5 2-3 6, Rowe 6-9 2-2 14, Alcindor 8-14 9-16 25, Heitz 3-6 1-3 7, Vallely 9-11 11-14 29, Wicks 0-2 0-0 0, Sweek 0-0 0-0 0, Patterson 0-0 2-2 2, Schofield 0-3 2-4 2. Team 28-50 (.560) 29-44 (.660) 85.

Halftime: UCLA 44-43.

ALL-TOURNAMENT TEAM

Lew Alcindor, C, Sr., UCLA*
Willie McCarter, G, Sr., Drake
Rick Mount, G, Jr., Purdue
Charlie Scott, F-G, Jr., North Carolina
John Vallely, G, Jr., UCLA
    ***Named Most Outstanding Player**

points and not eventually play in the NBA was guard Rick Mount, who scored 122 points in four games for Purdue before playing five seasons in the ABA with four different franchises. Mount (36 points) and Billy Keller (20) accounted for the highest-scoring starting backcourt in a single Final Four game in history when they combined for 56 points in a 92-65 rout of North Carolina in the semifinals.

What If: La Salle, which defeated NCAA Tournament entrants Villanova, St. Joseph's, and Duquesne by a total of 38 points on its way to a No. 2 ranking by AP, was ineligible for the tourney because of NCAA probation.

Putting Things in Perspective: North Carolina starting guard Dick Grubar, averaging 13 points per game, injured a knee in the ACC Tournament and was lost for the NCAA playoffs. A standout defensive player, the senior would have drawn the assignment of facing the explosive Mount, a 36-point scorer in a national semifinal victory over Carolina.

LSU's Pete Maravich (left) was a scoring machine, a three-time All-American—and wore floppy socks!

1960-69 PREMO POWER POLL: BEST TEAMS BY DECADE

RANK	SEASON	SCHOOL
1	1967–68	UCLA* (29-1)
2	1966–67	UCLA* (30-0)
3	1968–69	UCLA* (29-1)
4	1959–60	Ohio St.* (25-3)
5	1963–64	UCLA* (30-0)
6	1960–61	Ohio St. (27-1)
7	1959–60	California (28-2)
8	1961–62	Cincinnati* (29-2)
9	1964–65	UCLA* (28-2)
10	1959–60	Cincinnati (28-2)
11	1962–63	Loyola (Ill.)* (29-2)
12	1967–68	Houston (31-2)
13	1961–62	Ohio St. (26-2)
14	1965–66	Texas Western* (28-1)
15	1960–61	Cincinnati* (27-3)
16	1962–63	Cincinnati (26-2)
17	1968–69	La Salle (23-1)
18	1964–65	Michigan (24-4)
19	1960–61	St. Bonaventure (24-4)
20	1965–66	Kentucky (27-2)
	1963–64	Duke (26-5)

*–NCAA Tournament Champion

1969 CHAMPIONSHIP BRACKET

1st Round	Regional Semifinals	Regional Finals	National Semifinals	National Championship

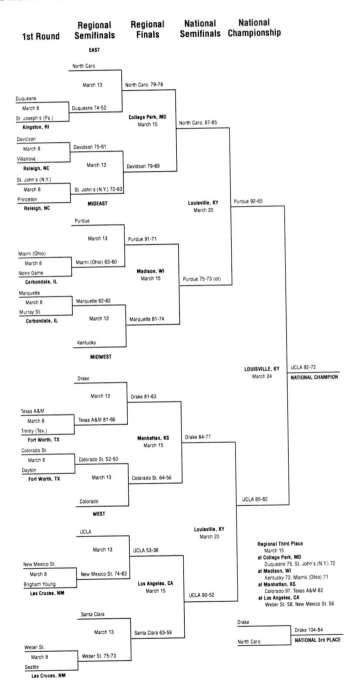

EAST

North Caro.

March 13 — North Caro. 79-78

Duquesne
March 8 — Duquesne 74-52
St. Joseph's (Pa.)
Kingston, RI

College Park, MD
March 15 — North Caro. 87-85

Davidson
March 8 — Davidson 75-61
Villanova
Raleigh, NC
March 13 — Davidson 79-69

St. John's (N.Y.)
March 8 — St. John's (N.Y.) 72-63
Princeton
Raleigh, NC

MIDEAST

Louisville, KY
March 20 — Purdue 92-65

Purdue
March 13 — Purdue 91-71

Miami (Ohio)
March 8 — Miami (Ohio) 63-60
Notre Dame
Carbondale, IL

Madison, WI
March 15 — Purdue 75-73 (ot)

Marquette
March 8 — Marquette 82-62
Murray St.
Carbondale, IL
March 13 — Marquette 81-74

Kentucky

MIDWEST

LOUISVILLE, KY
March 24 — UCLA 92-72
NATIONAL CHAMPION

Drake
March 13 — Drake 81-63

Texas A&M
March 8 — Texas A&M 81-66
Trinity (Tex.)
Fort Worth, TX

Manhattan, KS
March 15 — Drake 84-77

Colorado St.
March 8 — Colorado St. 52-50
Dayton
Fort Worth, TX
March 13 — Colorado St. 64-56

Colorado

WEST

UCLA 85-82

Louisville, KY
March 20 — UCLA 90-52

UCLA
March 13 — UCLA 53-38

New Mexico St.
March 8 — New Mexico St. 74-62
Brigham Young
Las Cruces, NM

Los Angeles, CA
March 15

Santa Clara
March 13 — Santa Clara 63-59

Weber St.
March 8 — Weber St. 75-73
Seattle
Las Cruces, NM

Regional Third Place
March 15
at College Park, MD
Duquesne 75, St. John's (N.Y.) 72
at Madison, WI
Kentucky 72, Miamii (Ohio) 71
at Manhattan, KS
Colorado 97, Texas A&M 82
at Los Angeles, CA
Weber St. 58, New Mexico St. 56

Drake
Drake 104-84
North Caro.
NATIONAL 3rd PLACE

5

EXPLOSION OF NATIONAL POPULARITY: THE 1970s

UCLA's dominance began to erode midway through the 1970s after the NCAA embraced a rule allowing freshman eligibility. More and more regal recruits began to bypass illustrious programs to enroll at schools where they could play immediately. The fresh faces became crucial to the game's popularity because of a growing exodus of standouts leaving college with eligibility remaining to join the pros. By the end of the decade, there was an explosion of interest in the NCAA Tournament, highlighted by a dream duel between All-Americans Larry Bird and Magic Johnson.

1969–70

AT A GLANCE

NCAA Champion: UCLA (28-2).

NIT Champion: Marquette (26-3).

New Conference: PCAA (forerunner of Big West).

NCAA Probation: Centenary, Florida State, La Salle, Yale.

NCAA Consensus First-Team All-Americans: Dan Issel, F-C, Sr., Kentucky; Bob Lanier, C, Sr., St. Bonaventure; Pete Maravich, G, Sr., Louisiana State; Rick Mount, G, Sr., Purdue; Calvin Murphy, G, Sr., Niagara.

Duke, North Carolina, and North Carolina State haven't always dominated the ACC. South Carolina went unbeaten in ACC competition during the 1970 regular season and finished a league-record five games ahead of the Gamecocks' closest rival. The ACC selected its representative to the NCAA playoffs at the time through its own postseason tourney and seven of the eight previous winners reached the Final Four. But the Gamecocks, featuring a starting lineup with current Georgia Tech coach Bobby Cremins as its only senior, lost against North Carolina State in the ACC Tournament final (42-39 in double overtime) when Cremins collected two points, no assists, and no rebounds in 49 minutes. Consensus second-team All-American John Roche, entering the ACC Tournament with a 23.8-point average, sustained a severely sprained ankle in the semifinals and wound up averaging just nine points per contest in three ACC tourney outings.

LSU's Pete Maravich set NCAA single-season records for most points (1,381) and highest average (44.5), finishing his career with NCAA career marks for most points (3,667) and highest average (44.2). He also established an NCAA record for most successful free throws in a game when he converted 30 of 31 foul shots against Oregon State. Maravich is the only player in NCAA Division I history to score more than 1,000 points and average over 40 points per game in each of three seasons. He had 56 games with at least 40 points in his three-year career, including a school-record 69 against Alabama. No other player has had more than 21 games with a minimum of 40. He averaged more than 50 points per game in a 10-game stretch spanning the last three games of 1968–69 and the first seven games of 1969–70. Incredibly, Maravich improved his field-goal accuracy and assists average every year.

Maravich (64) and Kentucky's Dan Issel (51) each scored more than 50 points in the same game when the Wildcats won, 121-105 (see accompanying box score). It was one of eight times in Issel's senior season that he scored at least 40. His high was a school-record 53 against Mississippi.

Purdue's Rick Mount set a Big Ten Conference record with 61 points (13 of his 27 field goals would have been behind the current three-point line), but it wasn't enough to prevent a 108-107 setback against visiting Iowa as the Hawkeyes went unbeaten in league play in coach Ralph Miller's final season at their helm before moving to Oregon State. They had gone 5-9 in the Big Ten the previous season.

Purdue All-American guard Rick Mount scores two of his Big Ten record 61 points against Iowa. The Hawkeyes' Fred Brown (left) and John Johnson can only watch.

Iowa had four players average more than 17 points per game on its way to a league-record 102.9-point average. John Johnson set an Iowa record with 49 points against Northwestern.

Niagara's Calvin Murphy, 5-9, finished his career as the only major-college player in history shorter than 6-0 to score more than 2,500 points.

MORE THAN 50-50 Two of college basketball's most explosive guns met in a classic high-scoring affair on February 21, 1970. Kentucky, led by Dan Issel, travelled to Louisiana State, led by Pistol Pete Maravich. Although the home team lost, 121-105, fans saw Maravich pump in 64 and Issel "settle" for 51 in a winning effort.

KENTUCKY (121)	FG	FT-A	PTS.
Dinwiddie	1	2-2	4
Parker	9	0-0	18
Pratt	11	5-8	27
Key	1	5-7	7
Issel	19	13-17	51
Mills	6	2-3	14
Hollenbeck	0	0-0	0
TOTALS	**47**	**27-37**	**121**

LSU (105)	FG	FT-A	PTS.
Maravich	23	18-22	64
Sanders	5	1-3	11
Tribbett	0	2-3	2
Hester	8	1-2	17
Newton	4	1-1	9
Hickman	1	0-0	2
Lang	0	0-0	0
TOTALS	**41**	**23-31**	**105**

Halftime: Kentucky 56-48. **Fouled Out:** Newton.

1969–70 INDIVIDUAL LEADERS

SCORING

PLAYER	PTS.	AVG.
Maravich, LSU	1381	44.5
Carr, Notre Dame	1106	38.1
Mount, Purdue	708	35.4
Issel, Kentucky	948	33.9
Humes, Idaho St.	733	30.5
Yunkus, Georgia Tech	814	30.1
Tomjanovich, Michigan	722	30.1
Murphy, Niagara	854	29.4
Lanier, St. Bonaventure	757	29.1
Simpson, Michigan St.	667	29.0
Cross, San Francisco	467	18.0
Cowens, Florida St.	447	17.2
Stiles, American	378	17.2
Childress, Colorado St.	392	17.0
Haderlein, Loyola Marymount	442	17.0
Brunson, Furman	401	16.0
Lanier, St. Bonaventure	416	16.0

REBOUNDING

PLAYER	REB.	AVG.
Gilmore, Jacksonville	621	22.2
Erving, Massachusetts	522	20.9

FIELD GOAL PERCENTAGE

PLAYER	FGM	FGA	PCT.
Williams, Florida St.	185	291	.636
Lienhard, Georgia	215	340	.632
Bartolome, Oregon St.	178	286	.622
Chatmon, Baylor	207	345	.600
Cleamons, Ohio St.	211	353	.598
Newton, LSU	143	242	.591
Schoepfer, Boston U.	160	271	.590
Bell, Hofstra	206	353	.584
Cobb, Marquette	158	272	.581
Gilmore, Jacksonville	307	529	.580

FREE THROW PERCENTAGE

PLAYER	FTM	FTA	PCT.
Kaplan, Rutgers	102	110	.927
England, Tennessee	131	146	.897
Finney, Ohio St.	119	134	.888
Murphy, Niagara	222	252	.881
Davis, Wake Forest	196	224	.875
Vidnovic, Iowa	133	152	.875
Newlin, Utah	245	281	.872
Curnutt, Miami (Fla.)	143	166	.861
Foster, Arizona	100	117	.855
Howard, BYU	122	143	.853

1969–70 TEAM LEADERS

SCORING OFFENSE

SCHOOL	PTS.	AVG.
Jacksonville	2809	100.3
Iowa	2467	98.7
Kentucky	2709	96.8
St. Peter's	2247	93.6
Notre Dame	2711	93.5

SCORING DEFENSE

SCHOOL	PTS.	AVG.
Army	1515	54.1
South Carolina	1606	57.4
Fairleigh Dickinson	1409	61.3
Long Island	1532	61.3
Miami (Ohio)	1497	62.4

SCORING MARGIN

SCHOOL	OFF.	DEF.	MAR.
St. Bonaventure	88.4	65.9	22.5

Jacksonville	100.3	78.5	21.8
UCLA	92.0	73.4	18.6
South Carolina	74.0	57.4	16.6
Florida St.	91.7	75.2	16.5

WON-LOST PERCENTAGE

SCHOOL	W-L	PCT.
UCLA	28-2	.933
Jacksonville	27-2	.931
Kentucky	26-2	.929
Pennsylvania	25-2	.926
New Mexico St.	27-3	.900

FIELD GOAL PERCENTAGE

SCHOOL	FGM	FGA	PCT.
Ohio St.	831	1527	.544
Jacksonville	1118	2137	.523
Iowa	959	1834	.523
Georgia Tech	841	1647	.511
Columbia	748	1481	.505

FREE THROW PERCENTAGE

SCHOOL	FTM	FTA	PCT.
Ohio St.	452	559	.809
Iowa	549	704	.780
Rutgers	430	560	.768
Wake Forest	542	706	.768
Boston College	442	581	.761

REBOUNDING

SCHOOL	REB.	AVG.
Florida St.	1451	55.8
Jacksonville	1561	55.8
Western Kentucky	1386	55.4
UNLV	1421	54.7
New Mexico St.	1632	54.4

Auburn's John Mengelt set a school record with 60 points against archrival Alabama.

Georgia Tech center Rich Yunkus, a three-time NCAA Academic All-American, twice scored 47 points in a game (vs. Furman and North Carolina).

Sophomore Julius Erving set a Massachusetts record with 20.9 rebounds per game in powering the 18-7 Minutemen to their most victories in 60 years of basketball.

Jacksonville became the first school to average more than 100 points per game (100.3). The Dolphins also finished runner-up in four categories—field-goal shooting, rebounding scoring margin, and won-lost percentage.

Ohio State led the country in both field-goal shooting (54.4 percent) and free-throw shooting (80.9). The Buckeyes were the first team to hit at least 80 percent of its foul shots in a single season. They were the first team in Big Ten history to have three players average more than 20 points per game—Dave Sorenson (24.2), Jim Cleamons (21.6), and Jody Finney (20.6).

Indiana finished in last place in the Big Ten for the fourth time in five seasons.

Memphis State finished in the Missouri Valley cellar for the third time in three seasons, but ended its MVC losing streak at 27 games with an 85-81 victory over Wichita State.

Davidson of the Southern Conference became the only school since the start of the NCAA Tournament to go undefeated in back-to-back league seasons with different coaches. Terry Holland succeeded Lefty Driesell after Driesell accepted a similar position at Maryland.

Oklahoma State's Hank Iba (767-338 record) and Butler's Tony Hinkle (557-393) retired after 41-year coaching careers. Iba, the only coach with six or more NCAA Tournament appearances to reach the regional finals every time, is hailed as the patriarch of basketball's first family of coaches. He had seven of his former Oklahoma State players eventually coach teams into the NCAA playoffs—John Floyd (Texas A&M), Jack Hartman (Kansas State), Don Haskins (Texas-El Paso), Moe Iba (Nebraska), Bud Mil-

1969-70 FINAL NATIONAL POLLS

AP	UPI	SCHOOL
1	1	Kentucky
2	2	UCLA
3	3	St. Bonaventure
4	5	Jacksonville
5	4	New Mexico St.
6	6	South Carolina
7	7	Iowa
8	10	Marquette
9	8	Notre Dame
10	12	North Carolina St.
11	14	Florida St.
12	11	Houston
13	13	Pennsylvania
14	9	Drake
15	–	Davidson
16	17	Utah St.
17	17	Niagara
18	17	Western Kentucky
19	15	Long Beach St.
20	–	Southern Cal
–	15	Villanova
–	20	Cincinnati
–	20	Texas-El Paso

1969-70 NCAA CHAMPION: UCLA

SEASON STATISTICS OF UCLA REGULARS

PLAYER	POS.	CL.	G.	FG%	FT%	PPG	RPG
Sidney Wicks	F	Jr.	30	.533	.632	18.6	11.9
John Vallely	G	Sr.	30	.486	.721	16.3	3.7
Henry Bibby	G	So.	30	.501	.833	15.6	3.5
Curtis Rowe	F	Jr.	30	.554	.641	15.3	8.7
Steve Patterson	C	Jr.	30	.496	.741	12.5	10.0
John Ecker	F	Jr.	30	.500	.774	3.5	2.5
Kenny Booker	F-G	Jr.	28	.449	.649	3.1	1.5
Terry Schofield	G	Jr.	29	.395	.850	2.7	0.8
Andy Hill	G	So.	24	.289	.714	1.8	0.6
Jon Chapman	C-F	So.	20	.344	.867	1.8	1.7
Rick Betchley	G	So.	23	.462	.625	1.5	0.7
Bill Seibert	F	Jr.	21	.316	.400	1.4	1.6
TEAM TOTALS			30	.496	.696	92.0	50.6

1970 FINAL FOUR CHAMPIONSHIP GAME

COLLEGE PARK, MD

JACKSONVILLE (69)	MIN.	FG-A	FT-A	REB.	A	PF	PTS.
Wedeking	37	6-11	0-0	2	3	2	12
Blevins	19	1-2	1-2	0	1	1	3
Morgan	37	5-11	0-0	4	11	5	10
Burrows	24	6-9	0-0	6	0	1	12
Gilmore	38	9-29	1-1	16	1	5	19
Nelson	16	3-9	2-2	5	0	1	8
Dublin	18	0-5	2-2	1	1	4	2
Baldwin	2	0-0	0-0	0	0	0	0
McIntyre	6	1-3	0-0	3	0	4	2
Hawkins	2	0-1	1-1	1	0	1	1
Selke	1	0-0	0-0	0	0	0	0
Team				2			
TOTALS	200	31-80	7-8	40	17	24	69

FG%: .388. FT%: .875. **Turnovers:** 18 (Morgan 8).

UCLA (80)	MIN.	FG-A	FT-A	REB.	A	PF	PTS.
Rowe	38	7-15	5-5	8	1	4	19
Patterson	38	8-15	1-4	11	2	1	17
Wicks	38	5-9	7-10	18	3	3	17
Vallely	38	5-10	5-7	7	5	2	15
Bibby	38	2-11	4-4	4	2	1	8

Booker	1	0-0	2-3	0	0	0	2
Seibert	2	0-1	0-0	1	0	1	0
Ecker	2	1-1	0-0	0	0	0	2
Betchley	1	0-0	0-1	0	0	0	0
Chapman	2	0-1	0-0	1	0	0	0
Hill	1	0-0	0-1	0	0	0	0
Schofield	1	0-0	0-0	0	0	0	0
Team				3			
TOTALS	200	28-63	24-35	53	13	12	80

FG%: .444. FT%: .686. **Turnovers:** 23 (Vallely 7).
Halftime: UCLA 41-36.

NATIONAL SEMIFINALS

JACKSONVILLE (91): Wedeking 7-15 1-1 15, Morgan 6-15 5-6 17, Burrows 2-4 1-1 5, McIntyre 0-3 0-0 0, Gilmore 9-14 11-15 29, Dublin 1-3 9-9 11, Nelson 1-7 10-12 12, Blevins 1-1 0-0 2, R. Baldwin 0-1 0-1 0. Team 27-63 (.429) 37-45 (.822) 91.

ST. BONAVENTURE (83): Kalbaugh 5-8 2-2 12, Hoffman 4-14 2-4 10, Gary 2-7 5-8 9, T. Baldwin 2-10 1-2 5, Gantt 8-17 0-0 16, Kull 4-7 0-0 8, Thomas 7-17 1-2 15, Grys 1-5 2-2 4, Tepas 0-0 2-2 2, Fahey 1-1 0-0 2. Team 34-86 (.395) 15-22 (.682) 83.

Halftime: Jacksonville 42-34.

UCLA (93): Rowe 4-7 7-11 15, Patterson 5-9 2-2 12, Wicks 10-12 2-5 22, Vallely 7-19 9-10 23, Bibby 8-13 3-3 19, Betchley 0-0 0-0 0, Schofield 0-0 0-0 0, Ecker 0-0 0-0 0, Seibert 0-1 0-0 0, Hill 0-0 0-1 0, Chapman 1-1 0-0 2. Team 35-63 (.556) 23-32 (.719) 93.

NEW MEXICO STATE (77): Criss 6-16 7-9 19, Collins 13-23 2-3 28, Burgess 1-6 0-0 2, Smith 4-11 2-3 10, Lacey 3-9 2-3 8, Reyes 1-6 0-0 2, Neal 2-4 0-0 4, Horne 0-4 2-2 2, Moore 1-1 0-0 2, Lefevre 0-0 0-0 0, Franco 0-0 0-0 0, McCarthy 0-0 0-0 0. Team 31-80 (.388) 15-20 (.750) 77.

Halftime: UCLA 48-41.

ALL-TOURNAMENT TEAM

Jimmy Collins, G, Sr., New Mexico State
Artis Gilmore, C, Jr., Jacksonville
Curtis Rowe, F, Jr., UCLA
John Vallely, G, Sr., UCLA
Sidney Wicks, F, Jr., UCLA*
    ***Named Most Outstanding Player**

likan (Maryland), Doyle Parrack (Oklahoma City), and Eddie Sutton (Creighton, Arkansas, Kentucky, and Oklahoma State).

"Mr. Iba's system was so sound and he inspired such confidence that there was never any question in my mind that his philosophy offered the best opportunity to be successful," Sutton said. "The things he gave us are as valid today as they were 30 years ago."

Five generations of major college coaches emanate from Hank Iba, encompassing those coaches who were either players or assistant coaches for Iba or later generations of coaches with ties to the sage. More than 40 active Division I coaches are branches of Iba's coaching tree.

1970 NCAA Tournament

Summary: Kentucky, after absorbing just one regular-season defeat (at Vanderbilt), was ranked No. 1 in the nation entering the tourney although starting guard Mike Casey missed the entire campaign in the wake of injuries suffered in an auto accident. UK lost to eventual NCAA Tournament runner-up Jacksonville, 106-100, in the Mideast Regional final. Casey was the Wildcats' leading scorer as a sophomore in 1967–68 with 20 points per game and their second-leading scorer as a junior the next year with a 19.1-point average. JU wound up losing to UCLA in the championship game, 80-69, when the Bruins' Sidney Wicks, 6-8, blocked five shots of 7-2 All-American center Artis Gilmore.

Star Gazing: LSU's Pete Maravich became the only three-time first-team All-American to fail to appear in the NCAA playoffs.

One and Only: The best composite winning percentage when four teams arrived at a Final Four occurred as UCLA (26-2), New Mexico State (26-2), Jacksonville (26-1), and St. Bonaventure (25-1) combined for a 103-6 record (.945).

Numbers Game: Notre Dame guard Austin Carr became the only player to score more than 60 points in a single playoff game and the only player to score more than 43 points at least twice. Carr, who tallied 61 points against Ohio University (Southeast Regional first round),

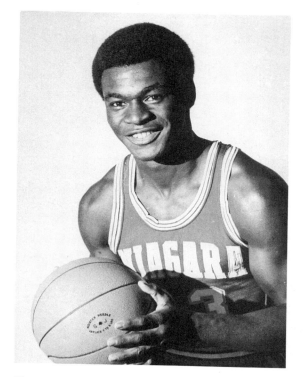

Niagara All-American guard Calvin Murphy helped his team reach the Mideast Regional semifinals.

accounted for half of the eight games in NCAA Tournament history of more than 46 points. He scored 52 points in the next round, but it wasn't enough to prevent a 109-99 defeat against Kentucky as the Wildcats' Dan Issel scored 44 points in the only tourney game in history to have two players score more than 40.

What If: Dave Cowens-led Florida State, which split two games with national runner-up Jacksonville (losing at JU by just four points), was ineligible for the tourney because of NCAA probation.... St. Bonaventure's only regular-season defeat was by two points at Villanova. But the Bonnies' biggest loss against Villanova was in a 23-point victory over the Wildcats in the East Regional final when All-American center Bob Lanier tore a knee ligament in a freak accident. He was clipped accidentally by future Detroit Pistons teammate Chris Ford, who later became coach of the Boston Celtics.

1970 CHAMPIONSHIP BRACKET

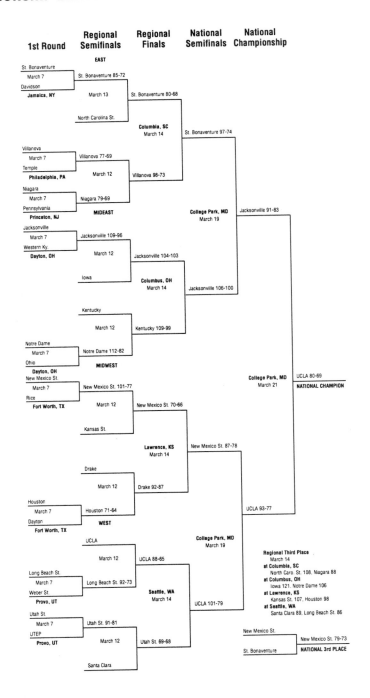

1st Round	Regional Semifinals	Regional Finals	National Semifinals	National Championship

EAST

St. Bonaventure
March 7
Davidson
Jamaica, NY

St. Bonaventure 85-72
March 13

North Carolina St.

Columbia, SC
March 14

St. Bonaventure 80-68

St. Bonaventure 97-74

Villanova
March 7
Temple
Philadelphia, PA

Villanova 77-69
March 12

Villanova 98-73

Niagara
March 7
Pennsylvania
Princeton, NJ

Niagara 79-69

MIDEAST

Jacksonville
March 7
Western Ky.
Dayton, OH

Jacksonville 109-96
March 12

Jacksonville 104-103

College Park, MD
March 19

Jacksonville 91-83

Iowa

Columbus, OH
March 14

Jacksonville 106-100

Kentucky
March 12

Kentucky 109-99

Notre Dame
March 7
Ohio
Dayton, OH

Notre Dame 112-82

MIDWEST

New Mexico St.
March 7
Rice
Fort Worth, TX

New Mexico St. 101-77
March 12

New Mexico St. 70-66

Kansas St.

Lawrence, KS
March 14

New Mexico St. 87-78

College Park, MD
March 21
NATIONAL CHAMPION
UCLA 80-69

New Mexico St. 93-77

Drake
March 12

Drake 92-87

Houston
March 7
Dayton
Fort Worth, TX

Houston 71-64

WEST

UCLA
March 12

UCLA 88-65

College Park, MD
March 19

UCLA 101-79

Long Beach St.
March 7
Weber St.
Provo, UT

Long Beach St. 92-73

Seattle, WA
March 14

Utah St.
March 7
UTEP
Provo, UT

Utah St. 91-81
March 12

Utah St. 69-68

Santa Clara

Regional Third Place
March 14
at Columbia, SC
   North Caro. St. 108, Niagara 88
at Columbus, OH
   Iowa 121, Notre Dame 106
at Lawrence, KS
   Kansas St. 107, Houston 98
at Seattle, WA
   Santa Clara 89, Long Beach St. 86

New Mexico St.

St. Bonaventure

New Mexico St. 79-73
NATIONAL 3rd PLACE

1970–71

NCAA Champion: UCLA (29-1).

NIT Champion: North Carolina (26-6).

New Rules: A nonjumper may not change his position during a jump ball from the time a referee is ready to make the toss until after the ball is tapped. Any school offered an NCAA Tournament bid must accept it or be prohibited from participating in postseason competition.

NCAA Probation: Centenary, Florida State, Yale.

NCAA Consensus First-Team All-Americans: Austin Carr, G, Sr., Notre Dame; Artis Gilmore, C, Sr., Jacksonville; Jim McDaniels, C, Sr., Western Kentucky; Dean Meminger, G, Sr., Marquette; Sidney Wicks, F, Sr., UCLA.

Jacksonville center Artis Gilmore.

UCLA's starting frontcourt of Sidney Wicks, Curtis Rowe, and Steve Patterson combined to average 51.7 points and 32.6 rebounds per game, making it more productive statistically than any of the Bruins' starting frontcourts with all-time great centers Lew Alcindor and Bill Walton.

UCLA's only defeat was an 89-82 setback at Notre Dame when the Bruins' 48-game nonconference winning streak ended. Notre Dame guard Austin Carr scored 46 points, including 15 of the Irish's last 17.

Carr, runner-up to LSU's Pete Maravich in scoring the previous season with a 38-point average, was runner-up again at 38.1 to become the most prolific non-champion ever. Mississippi's Johnny Neumann averaged 40.1 points per game to become the only sophomore in NCAA history other than Maravich (43.8 in 1967–68) to average more than 40. Neumann, bolstered by a school record 63-point outburst against LSU, was threatening Maravich's first-year mark until falling off to a 29.4 average his last five games.

Artis Gilmore, a junior college transfer, finished his two-year career at Jacksonville with an NCAA career rebounding average of 22.7 per game. He is the only player in major-college history to finish his career with averages of more than 22 points and 22 rebounds per game. Gilmore helped Jacksonville win an unprecedented three team statistical titles—offense (99.9-point average), scoring margin (20.9), and field-goal shooting (53.6 percent).

Maryland hit 15 of 18 field-goal attempts (83.3 percent) against South Carolina. North Carolina forward Dennis Wuycik was second from the floor nationally at 60.7 percent and sixth from the foul line at 85.8 percent.

Ohio State ended Marquette's 39-game winning streak, 60-59.

Bill Smith isn't among the top 15 career scorers in Syracuse history, but he tossed in a school-record 47 points against Lafayette. Also establishing school single-game scoring standards were South Carolina's John Roche (56 points against Furman), SMU's Gene Phillips (51 at

1970-71 INDIVIDUAL LEADERS

SCORING

PLAYER	PTS.	AVG.
Neumann, Mississippi	923	40.1
Carr, Notre Dame	1101	38.0
Humes, Idaho St.	777	32.4
McGinnis, Indiana	719	30.0
McDaniels, W. Kentucky	878	29.3
Rinaldi, St. Peter's	687	28.6
Mengelt, Auburn	738	28.4
Phillips, SMU	737	28.3
Meely, Colorado	729	28.0
Brown, Iowa	662	27.6

REBOUNDING

PLAYER	REB.	AVG.
Gilmore, Jacksonville	603	23.2
Washington, American	512	20.5

Erving, Massachusetts	527	19.5
Gianelli, Pacific	509	18.2
Davis, St. John's	479	17.7
Martin, Loyola (Ill.)	387	17.6
Benton, Wichita St.	437	16.8
Kennedy, TCU	416	16.6
Harris, Hardin-Simmons	205	15.8
Frazer, Fairfield	377	15.7

FIELD GOAL PERCENTAGE

PLAYER	FGM	FGA	PCT.
Belcher, Arkansas St.	174	275	.633
Wuycik, North Carolina	182	300	.607
Smith, Syracuse	222	366	.607
Kennedy, TCU	202	340	.594
Szczerbiak, G. Wash.	225	379	.594
Bush, Drake	177	299	.592
Jura, Nebraska	181	306	.592

Sanders, LSU	209	355	.589
Williams, Hardin-Simmons	191	326	.586
Penebacker, Hawaii	165	284	.581

FREE THROW PERCENTAGE

PLAYER	FTM	FTA	PCT.
Starrick, S. Illinois	119	132	.902
Tyler, Brown	128	147	.871
England, Tennessee	143	165	.867
Kaplan, Rutgers	102	118	.864
Davis, Wake Forest	188	218	.862
Wuycik, North Carolina	169	197	.858
Thomason, Pacific	118	138	.855
Bryant, E. Kentucky	122	143	.853
Lowery, Texas Tech	121	143	.846
Phillips, SMU	213	252	.845

1970-71 TEAM LEADERS

SCORING OFFENSE

SCHOOL	PTS.	AVG.
Jacksonville	2598	99.9
Kentucky	2670	95.4
Northern Illinois	2132	92.7
St. Peter's	2221	92.5
Loyola (La.)	2394	92.1

SCORING DEFENSE

SCHOOL	PTS.	AVG.
Fairleigh Dickinson	1236	53.7
Army	1403	58.5
Marquette	1820	62.8
Miami (Ohio)	1591	63.6

SCORING MARGIN

SCHOOL	OFF.	DEF.	MAR.
Jacksonville	99.9	79.0	20.9

Marquette	81.7	62.8	18.9
UCLA	83.5	68.5	15.0
Pennsylvania	81.4	66.8	14.6
Massachusetts	79.7	65.1	14.6

WON-LOST PERCENTAGE

SCHOOL	W-L	PCT.
UCLA	29-1	.967
Marquette	28-1	.966
Pennsylvania	28-1	.966
Southern California	24-2	.923
Kansas	27-3	.900

FIELD GOAL PERCENTAGE

SCHOOL	FGM	FGA	PCT.
Jacksonville	1077	2008	.536
North Carolina	1010	1935	.522
Louisiana St.	897	1725	.520
Loyola (La.)	956	1880	.509
Kentucky	1077	2129	.506

FREE THROW PERCENTAGE

SCHOOL	FTM	FTA	PCT.
Tennessee	538	679	.792
Southern Illinois	460	597	.771
Southern Methodist	552	719	.768
Duke	539	704	.766

REBOUNDING

SCHOOL	REB.	AVG.
Pacific	1643	58.7
West Texas St.	1502	57.8
Hawaii	1596	57.0
Arizona St.	1477	56.8
Los Angeles St.	1458	56.1

Texas), Colorado center Cliff Meely (47 against Oklahoma), and Florida State's Ron King (46 against Georgia Southern).

TCU's Eugene "Goo" Kennedy set an SWC record by grabbing 28 rebounds against Arkansas. He finished the season with a league record rebounding average of 16 per game.

Fairleigh Dickinson shattered Army's streak of three consecutive scoring defense championships. FDU coach Al LoBalbo previously served as an assistant at Army under Bob Knight.

Joe Williams became the only person to be coach of two different universities in back-to-back years when each school made its initial

1970-71 FINAL NATIONAL POLLS

AP	UPI	SCHOOL
1	1	UCLA
2	2	Marquette
3	3	Pennsylvania
4	4	Kansas
5	5	Southern Cal
6	6	South Carolina
7	7	Western Kentucky
8	8	Kentucky
9	9	Fordham
10	10	Ohio St.
11	11	Jacksonville
12	14	Notre Dame
13	13	North Carolina
14	18	Houston
15	18	Duquesne
16	14	Long Beach St.
17	–	Tennessee
18	17	Villanova
19	16	Drake
20	11	Brigham Young
–	20	Weber St.

playoff appearance—Jacksonville in 1970 and Furman in 1971.

Utah's Jack Gardner, who previously coached at Kansas State, ended his 28-year coaching career with a 486-235 record.

1971 NCAA Tournament

Summary: UCLA became the only team to win a national title although its season-leading scorer was held more than 10 points below his average in the championship game. Sidney Wicks, named national player of the year by the U.S. Basketball Writers Association, managed just seven points in a 68-62 victory over Villanova to finish the campaign with a 21.3-point average. The Final Four was tainted when it was disclosed that Villanova star Howard Porter and Western Kentucky standout Jim McDaniels had signed pro contracts before the tourney.

Star Gazing: Julius Erving, leaving Massachusetts with one season of eligibility remaining, didn't participate in the NCAA playoffs despite helping the Minutemen to a composite 41-11 record in 1970 and 1971. He is the only player to score more than 30,000 points in his pro career after never appearing in the NCAA playoffs.... Jacksonville blew a 14-point halftime cushion and lost in the first round of the Mideast Regional against eventual Final Four team Western Kentucky (74-72). Western Kentucky's McDaniels outscored Jacksonville's Artis Gilmore, 23-12, in a battle of seven-foot first-team All-Americans.

UCLA's Sidney Wicks takes careful aim over the outstretched arm of a New Mexico State defender.

Biggest Upsets: Marquette, undefeated entering the tourney (26-0), lost in the Mideast Regional semifinals against Ohio State (60-59) after the Warriors' playmaker, unanimous first-team All-American Dean "The Dream" Meminger, fouled out with five minutes remaining. Teammate Allie McGuire, the coach's son, committed a costly turnover in the closing seconds before Buckeyes guard Allan Hornyak converted a pair of crucial free throws.... Penn, undefeated entering the tourney (26-0), lost in the East

1970–71 NCAA CHAMPION: UCLA

SEASON STATISTICS OF UCLA REGULARS

PLAYER	POS.	CL.	G.	FG%	FT%	PPG	RPG
Sidney Wicks	F	Sr.	30	.524	.661	21.3	12.8
Curtis Rowe	F	Sr.	30	.523	.627	17.5	10.0
Steve Patterson	C	Sr.	30	.420	.620	13.0	9.8
Henry Bibby	G	Jr.	30	.376	.835	11.8	3.5
Terry Schofield	G	Sr.	30	.432	.561	6.2	2.4
Kenny Booker	G	Sr.	30	.441	.480	5.5	2.6
Larry Farmer	F	So.	22	.402	.481	3.6	3.7
John Ecker	F	Sr.	26	.438	.882	2.8	2.0
Rick Betchley	G	Jr.	20	.538	.467	1.8	0.7
Larry Hollyfield	F-G	So.	11	.273	.250	1.7	0.7
Andy Hill	G	Jr.	19	.438	.850	1.6	0.2
Jon Chapman	F-C	Jr.	18	.200	.000	0.4	1.3
TEAM TOTALS			30	.453	.651	83.5	52.5

1971 FINAL FOUR CHAMPIONSHIP GAME

HOUSTON, TX

VILLANOVA (62)	MIN.	FG-A	FT-A	REB.	A	PF	PTS.
Smith	40	4-11	1-1	2	0	4	9
Porter	40	10-21	5-6	8	0	1	25
Siemiontkowski	37	9-16	1-2	6	0	3	19
Inglesby	40	3-9	1-1	4	7	2	7
Ford	40	0-4	2-3	5	10	4	2
McDowell	3	0-1	0-0	2	1	0	0
Team				4			
TOTALS	200	26-62	10-13	31	18	14	62

FG%: .419. FT%: .769. Turnovers: 10 (Ford 7).

UCLA (68)	MIN.	FG-A	FT-A	REB.	A	PF	PTS.
Rowe	40	2-3	4-5	8	2	0	8
Wicks	40	3-7	1-1	9	7	2	7
Patterson	40	13-18	3-5	8	4	1	29
Bibby	40	6-12	5-5	2	3	1	17
Booker	5	0-0	0-0	0	0	0	0
Schofield	26	3-9	0-0	1	4	4	6
Betchley	9	0-0	1-2	1	0	1	1
Team				5			
TOTALS	200	27-49	14-18	34	20	9	68

FG%: .551. FT%: .778. Turnovers: 13.
Halftime: UCLA 45-37.

NATIONAL SEMIFINALS

WESTERN KENTUCKY (89): Glover 5-15 2-4 12, Dunn 11-33 3-6 25, McDaniels 10-24 2-4 22, Rose 8-21 2-3 18, Bailey 5-11 2-3 12, Witt 0-1 0-0 0, Sundmacker 0-0 0-0 0. Team 39-105 (.371) 11-20 (.550) 89.

VILLANOVA (92): Smith 5-14 3-6 13, Porter 10-20 2-3 22, Siemiontkowski 11-20 9-10 31, Inglesby 5-10 4-7 14, Ford 3-6 2-2 8, McDowell 2-3 0-3 4. Team 36-73 (.493) 20-31 (.645) 92.

Halftime: Western Kentucky 38-35. **Regulation:** Tied 74-74. **First Overtime:** Tied 85-85.

KANSAS (60): Robisch 7-19 3-6 17, Russell 5-12 2-2 12, Brown 3-8 1-3 7, Stallworth 5-10 2-4 12, Nash 3-9 1-2 7, Kivisto 1-1 1-4 3, Canfield 0-0 0-0 0, Williams 0-1 2-2 2, Mathews 0-0 0-0 0, Douglas 0-0 0-0 0. Team 24-60 (.400) 12-23 (.522) 60.

UCLA (68): Rowe 7-10 2-4 16, Wicks 5-9 11-13 21, Patterson 3-11 0-0 6, Bibby 6-9 6-6 18, Booker 1-2 1-2 3, Schofield 1-3 0-1 2, Farmer 0-2 0-1 0, Betchley 0-0 0-1 0, Ecker 0-1 2-2 2, Hill 0-0 0-0 0, Chapman 0-0 0-0 0. Team 23-47 (.489) 22-30 (.733) 68.

Halftime: UCLA 32-25.

ALL-TOURNAMENT TEAM

Jim McDaniels, C, Sr., Western Kentucky
Steve Patterson, C, Sr., UCLA
Howard Porter, F, Sr., Villanova*
Hank Siemiontkowski, C, Jr., Villanova
Sidney Wicks, F, Sr., UCLA
     *Named Most Outstanding Player

Regional final against Villanova (90-47) when none of the Quakers players scored more than eight points. Final Four Most Outstanding Player Howard Porter scored 35 points for the Wildcats to more than double the output (16) of three Penn players who wound up in the NBA—Corky Calhoun, Phil Hankinson, and Dave Wohl.

One and Only: UCLA center Steve Patterson became the only player to have a single-digit point total in a national semifinal game (six vs. Kansas) and then increase his output by more than 20 points in the championship game (career- and game-high 29 vs. Villanova).... Western Kentucky became the only Ohio Valley Conference to reach the Final Four.

Numbers Game: The closest result for UCLA during the Bruins' 38-game tourney win-ning streak from 1967 to 1973 came in the West Regional final when they had to erase an 11-point deficit despite 29 percent field-goal shooting to edge Long Beach State (57-55).

What If: Both of Southern Cal's defeats were by a single-digit margin in Pacific-8 Conference competition against national champion-to-be UCLA. The Trojans ranked 5th in both polls.... Houston, minus its third-best scorer and top outside threat Jeff Hickman (declared academically ineligible after the first semester), lost to Final Four-bound Kansas by one point (78-77) in the Midwest Regional semifinals. The Cougars defeated eventual national runner-up Villanova by 15 points on a neutral court early in the season.

1971 CHAMPIONSHIP BRACKET

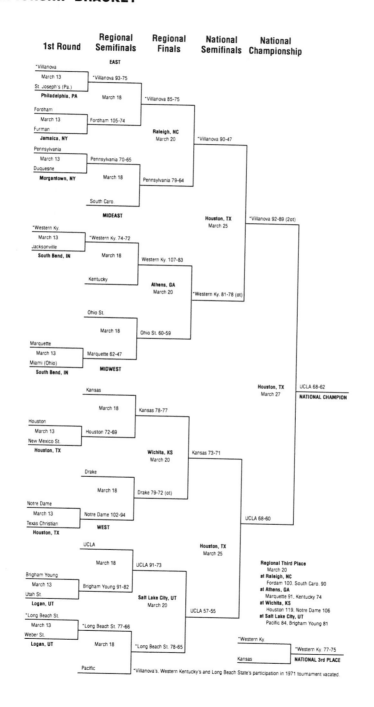

1st Round	Regional Semifinals	Regional Finals	National Semifinals	National Championship

EAST

*Villanova
March 13
St. Joseph's (Pa.)
Philadelphia, PA

*Villanova 93-75
March 18

*Villanova 85-75

Fordham
March 13
Furman
Jamaica, NY

Fordham 105-74

Raleigh, NC
March 20

*Villanova 90-47

Pennsylvania
March 13
Duquesne
Morgantown, NY

Pennsylvania 70-65
March 18

Pennsylvania 79-64

South Caro.

MIDEAST

Houston, TX
March 25

*Villanova 92-89 (2ot)

*Western Ky.
March 13
Jacksonville
South Bend, IN

*Western Ky. 74-72
March 18

Western Ky. 107-83

Kentucky

Athens, GA
March 20

*Western Ky. 81-78 (ot)

Ohio St.
March 18

Ohio St. 60-59

Marquette
March 13
Miami (Ohio)
South Bend, IN

Marquette 62-47

MIDWEST

Houston, TX
March 27

UCLA 68-62
NATIONAL CHAMPION

Kansas
March 18

Kansas 78-77

Houston
March 13
New Mexico St.
Houston, TX

Houston 72-69

Wichita, KS
March 20

Kansas 73-71

Drake
March 18

Drake 79-72 (ot)

Notre Dame
March 13
Texas Christian
Houston, TX

Notre Dame 102-94

WEST

UCLA 68-60

Houston, TX
March 25

UCLA
March 18

UCLA 91-73

Brigham Young
March 13
Utah St.
Logan, UT

Brigham Young 91-82

Salt Lake City, UT
March 20

UCLA 57-55

*Long Beach St.
March 13
Weber St.
Logan, UT

*Long Beach St. 77-66
March 18

*Long Beach St. 78-65

Pacific

Regional Third Place
March 20
at Raleigh, NC
Fordam 100, South Caro. 90
at Athens, GA
Marquette 91, Kentucky 74
at Wichita, KS
Houston 119, Notre Dame 106
at Salt Lake City, UT
Pacific 84, Brigham Young 81

*Western Ky.

*Western Ky. 77-75

Kansas

NATIONAL 3rd PLACE

*Villanova's, Western Kentucky's and Long Beach State's participation in 1971 tournament vacated.

1971-72

AT A GLANCE

NCAA Champion: UCLA (30-0).

NIT Champion: Maryland (27-5).

NCAA Consensus First-Team All-Americans: Henry Bibby, G, Sr., UCLA; Jim Chones, C, Jr., Marquette; Bo Lamar, G, Jr., Southwestern Louisiana; Bob McAdoo, C, Jr., North Carolina; Ed Ratleff, F-G, Jr., Long Beach State; Tom Riker, C, Sr., South Carolina; Bill Walton, C, Soph., UCLA.

Oral Roberts star Richie Fuqua shoots from the outside.

Kentucky's Adolph Rupp, called the "Baron of the Bluegrass," retired after a 41-year coaching career with an 875-190 record.

UCLA's Bill Walton joined Oscar Robertson (Cincinnati '58) as the only players in history to be named national player of the year in their first season of varsity competition. UCLA set an NCAA single-season record for highest average scoring margin (30.3). Incredibly, the Bruins' average halftime margin (17.4) was greater than any other team over an entire game excluding North Carolina's 17.7.

The nation's top three scorers represented teams playing their initial season at the major-college level—Southwestern Louisiana's Bo Lamar (36.3), Oral Roberts' Richie Fuqua (35.9), and Illinois State's Doug Collins (32.6). Fuqua nearly caught Lamar by averaging 41.4 points to Lamar's 38.7 in their last 10 outings. Collins was the star player for Will Robinson, the first black head coach at a predominantly white Division I school.

Southern Illinois' Greg Starrick, who began his college career at Kentucky, finished his career with 90.9 percent free-throw accuracy, an NCAA record.

Kansas' Bud Stallworth set a Big Eight Conference game record with 50 points against Missouri.

Long before premier pivotmen such as Georgetown's Patrick Ewing (Jamaica) and Dikembe Mutombo (Zaire), Houston's Hakeem Olajuwon (Nigeria), Marist's Rik Smits (Nether-

lands), New Mexico's Luc Longley (Australia), and George Washington's Yinka Dare (Nigeria) came from overseas, there was an influential international big man by the name of Kresimir Cosic. The Yugoslavian ranked 42nd in the country by averaging 22.3 points per game as a junior for Brigham Young. His coach, Stan Watts, ended his 23-year coaching career with a 371-254 record.

Jacksonville's Ernie Fleming (59 points against St. Peter's), Florida's Tony Miller (54 against Chicago State), Virginia's Barry Parkhill (51 against Baldwin-Wallace), New Mexico State's John Williamson (48 against California), California's John Coughran (47 against Utah State), and Georgia's Ronnie Hogue (46 against LSU) set school single-game scoring standards.

Detroit ended Marquette's 56-game regular-season winning streak, 70-49, and Temple stopped Penn's 48-game regular-season winning streak, 57-52.

1971–72 INDIVIDUAL LEADERS

SCORING

PLAYER	PTS.	AVG.
Lamar, Southwestern La.	1054	36.3
Fuqua, Oral Roberts	1006	35.9
Collins, Illinois St.	847	32.6
Robinson, West Virginia	706	29.4
Averitt, Pepperdine	693	28.9
Williamson, New Mexico St.	678	27.1
Kohls, Syracuse	748	26.7
Miller, Florida	507	26.7
Taylor, Murray St.	538	25.6
Martiniuk, St. Peter's	611	25.5

REBOUNDING

PLAYER	REB.	AVG.
Washington, American	455	19.8
Gianelli, Pacific	466	17.9

Davidson, West Texas St.	420	17.5
Davis, St. John's	460	17.0
Bradley, Northern Illinois	398	15.9
Jones, Loyola Marymount	395	15.8
Barnes, Providence	424	15.7
Martin, Loyola (Ill.)	329	15.7
Walton, UCLA	466	15.5
Hyland, Iona	350	15.2

FIELD GOAL PERCENTAGE

PLAYER	FGM	FGA	PCT.
Martens, Abilene Christian	136	204	.667
Fullarton, Xavier	149	229	.651
Stewart, Santa Clara	202	312	.647
Walton, UCLA	238	372	.640
Shaeffer, St. John's	186	294	.633
Jackson, Los Angeles St.	222	362	.613
Ebron, Southwestern La.	283	464	.610

Wuycik, North Carolina	189	310	.610
Robinson, Memphis St.	170	279	.609
Traylor, South Carolina	174	292	.596
Sanders, LSU	171	287	.596

FREE THROW PERCENTAGE

PLAYER	FTM	FTA	PCT.
Starrick, Southern Ill.	148	160	.925
Denny, South Alabama	117	128	.914
Garrett, Southern Ill.	130	146	.890
Bullington, Ball St.	142	161	.882
Sherwin, Army	110	125	.880
Roberts, New Mexico	118	135	.874
Bush, Indiana St.	107	123	.870
Rogers, St. Louis	124	143	.867
Edwards, Tennessee	103	119	.866
Kohls, Syracuse	222	257	.864

1971–72 TEAM LEADERS

SCORING OFFENSE

SCHOOL	PTS.	AVG.
Oral Roberts	2943	105.1
Southwestern Louisiana	2840	97.9
Northern Illinois	2380	95.2
UCLA	2838	94.6
Furman	2592	92.6
Houston	2499	92.6

SCORING DEFENSE

SCHOOL	PTS.	AVG.
Minnesota	1451	58.0
Fairleigh Dickinson	1410	58.8
Texas-El Paso	1636	60.6
Marquette	1836	63.3
Pennsylvania	1780	63.6
Temple	1973	63.6

SCORING MARGIN

SCHOOL	OFF.	DEF.	MAR.
UCLA	94.6	64.3	30.3

North Carolina	89.1	71.4	17.7
Marshall	92.4	76.4	16.0
Florida St.	86.9	71.4	15.5
Long Beach St.	84.9	69.8	15.1

WON-LOST PERCENTAGE

SCHOOL	W-L	PCT.
UCLA	30-0	1.000
Oral Roberts	26-2	.929
Pennsylvania	25-3	.893
Hawaii	24-3	.889
Marquette	25-4	.862
Long Beach St.	25-4	.862
Southwestern Louisiana	25-4	.862

FIELD GOAL PERCENTAGE

SCHOOL	FGM	FGA	PCT.
North Carolina	1031	1954	.528
Abilene Christian	792	1566	.506
South Carolina	894	1773	.504
UCLA	1140	2262	.504
Southwestern Louisiana	1153	2295	.502

FREE THROW PERCENTAGE

SCHOOL	FTM	FTA	PCT.
Lafayette	656	844	.777
Brown	560	725	.772
Southern Illinois	522	687	.760
St. Louis	507	669	.758
Tennessee	450	594	.758

REBOUNDING

SCHOOL	REB.	AVG.
Oral Roberts	1686	60.2
West Texas St.	1444	57.8
Pacific	1495	57.5
Hawaii	1462	56.2
Houston	1515	56.1

Notre Dame lost back-to-back road games at Indiana (94-29) and UCLA (114-56) by a total of 123 points in coach Digger Phelps' first season at the Irish helm. Two years later, Notre Dame defeated both teams.

Minnesota center Jim Brewer was anointed as Most Valuable Player in the Big Ten, but he wasn't named to the first or second five for either the AP or UPI All-Big Ten teams. Michigan State's Mike Robinson (27.2 points per game) became the third sophomore in five years to lead the Big Ten in scoring.

Future Hall of Famer Denny Crum embarked on his head coaching career at Louisville with a 26-5 record and a trip to the Final Four.

1972 NCAA Tournament

Summary: UCLA won the national championship by an average of 18 points. Although the Bill Walton-led Bruins trailed Florida State by a season-high seven points in the first half and the final margin of the championship game was just five (81-76), the outcome never seemed in doubt. Excluding a six-point triumph at Oregon State, they won every other game by at least 13 points.

One and Only: Bo Lamar collected 35 points and 11 assists and Roy Ebron contributed 33 points and 20 rebounds in Division I newcomer Southwestern Louisiana's 112-101 victory over Marshall in the first round of the Midwest

Regional when the Ragin' Cajuns scored the most points in the history of the tourney for a school in its first playoff game.

Numbers Game: Kentucky coach Adolph Rupp's final game was a 73-54 defeat against Florida State in the Mideast Regional final. Rupp is the only coach saddled with more than five regional final losses. Rupp sustained eight such setbacks from 1952 through 1972 by an average margin of 10 points. He also incurred a national quarterfinal reversal in 1945 when the first round of the eight-team event was identified as the regional semifinals. Six of Rupp's first seven "field of eight" defeats were against Big Ten teams, including Ohio State four times.

What If: Marquette might have been the team with the best chance to unseat UCLA if Warriors All-American Jim Chones hadn't ended his eligibility after signing a professional contract late in the season during the ABA/NBA bidding war.

1971-72 FINAL NATIONAL POLLS

AP	UPI	SCHOOL
1	1	UCLA
2	2	North Carolina
3	3	Pennsylvania
4	4	Louisville
5	6	Long Beach St.
6	5	South Carolina
7	7	Marquette
8	8	Southwestern La.
9	9	Brigham Young
10	10	Florida St.
11	12	Minnesota
12	18	Marshall
13	13	Memphis St.
14	11	Maryland
15	15	Villanova
16	–	Oral Roberts
17	–	Indiana
18	14	Kentucky
19	–	Ohio St.
20	–	Virginia
–	16	Kansas St.
–	17	Texas-El Paso
–	19	Missouri
–	19	Weber St.

1971-72 NCAA CHAMPION: UCLA

SEASON STATISTICS OF UCLA REGULARS

PLAYER	POS.	CL.	G.	FG%	FT%	PPG	RPG
Bill Walton	C	So.	30	.640	.704	21.1	15.5
Henry Bibby	G	Sr.	30	.450	.806	15.7	3.5
Keith Wilkes	F	So.	30	.531	.696	13.5	8.2
Larry Farmer	F	Jr.	30	.456	.549	10.7	5.5
Greg Lee	G	So.	29	.492	.824	8.7	2.0
Larry Hollyfield	F	Jr.	30	.514	.651	7.3	3.3
Swen Nater	C	Jr.	29	.535	.609	6.7	4.8
Tommy Curtis	G	So.	30	.437	.636	4.1	2.1
Andy Hill	G	Sr.	26	.356	.709	2.7	0.8
Vince Carson	F	So.	28	.400	.667	2.4	2.6
Jon Chapman	F	Sr.	28	.465	.500	1.6	1.6
Gary Franklin	F	So.	26	.412	.438	1.3	1.0
TEAM TOTALS			30	.504	.695	94.6	54.9

1972 FINAL FOUR CHAMPIONSHIP GAME

LOS ANGELES, CA

FLORIDA STATE (76)	MIN.	FG-A	FT-A	REB.	A	PF	PTS.
Garrett	37	1-9	1-1	5	0	1	3
King	31	12-20	3-3	6	1	1	27
Royals	33	5-7	5-6	10	2	5	15
McCray	23	3-6	2-5	6	3	4	8
Samuel	31	3-10	0-0	1	7	1	6
Harris	26	7-13	2-3	6	1	1	16
Petty	9	0-0	1-1	0	2	1	1
Cole	10	0-2	0-0	2	1	1	0
Team				6			
TOTALS	200	31-67	14-19	42	17	15	76

FG%: .463. FT%: .737.

UCLA (81)	MIN.	FG-A	FT-A	REB.	A	PF	PTS.
Wilkes	38	11-16	1-2	10	3	4	23
Farmer	33	2-6	0-0	6	0	2	4
Walton	34	9-17	6-11	20	2	4	24
Lee	16	0-0	0-0	2	4	0	0
Bibby	40	8-17	2-3	3	1	2	18
Curtis	24	4-14	0-1	4	6	1	8
Hollyfield	9	1-6	0-0	2	3	2	2
Nater	6	1-2	0-1	1	0	0	2
Team				2			
TOTALS	200	36-78	9-18	50	19	15	81

FG%: .462. FT%: .500.
Halftime: UCLA 50-39.

NATIONAL SEMIFINALS

NORTH CAROLINA (75): Jones 4-8 1-1 9, Wuycik 7-16 6-6 20, McAdoo 10-19 4-5 24, Previs 1-5 3-6 5, Karl 5-14 1-3 11, Huband 0-1 0-0 0, Chamberlain 2-5 2-3 6, Johnston 0-1 0-0 0, Chambers 0-1 0-1 0-0. Team 29-70 (.414) 17-25 (.680) 75.

FLORIDA STATE (79): Garrett 4-8 3-7 11, King 6-17 10-10 22, Royals 6-8 6-7 18, McCray 3-6 3-6 9, Samuel 2-4 1-4 5, Harris 1-6 2-2 4, Petty 3-5 4-7 10, Gay 0-1 0-0 0. Team 25-55 (.455) 29-43 (.674) 79.

Halftime: Florida State 45-32.

LOUISVILLE (77): Lawhon 0-7 1-2 1, Thomas 2-4 0-0 4, Vilcheck 3-6 0-0 6, Price 11-23 8-9 30, Bacon 5-11 5-7 15, Carter 4-8 0-0 8, Bunton 1-5 1-1 3, Bradley 1-3 0-0 2, Stallings 1-2 0-1 2, Cooper 0-1 2-2 2, Pry 2-3 0-0 4, Meiman 0-1 0-0 0. Team 30-74 (.405) 17-22 (.773) 77.

UCLA (96): Wilkes 5-11 2-2 12, Farmer 6-12 3-5 15, Walton 11-13 11-12 33, Lee 3-6 4-6 10, Bibby 1-5 0-0 2, Curtis 4-5 0-0 8, Hollyfield 3-6 0-0 6, Carson 1-1 0-0 2, Nater 0-0 2-4 2, Hill 1-1 4-4 6, Chapman 0-0 0-1 0, Franklin 0-1 0-0 0. Team 35-61 (.574) 26-34 (.765) 96.

Halftime: UCLA 39-31.

ALL-TOURNAMENT TEAM

Ron King, G, Jr., Florida State
Bob McAdoo, C, Jr., North Carolina
Jim Price, G, Sr., Louisville
Bill Walton, C, Soph., UCLA*
Keith Wilkes, F, Soph., UCLA
     *Named Most Outstanding Player

UCLA star Bill Walton blocks a shot.

1972 CHAMPIONSHIP BRACKET

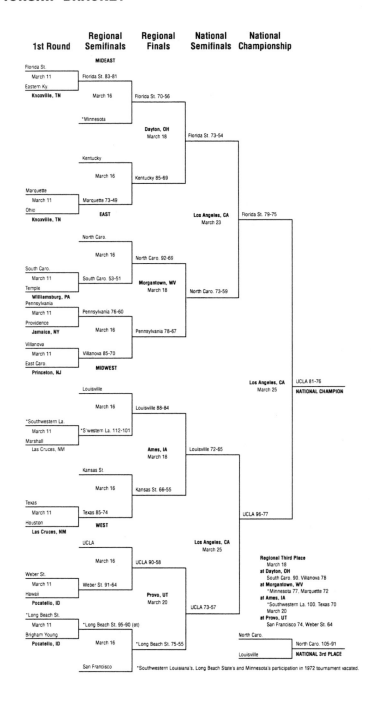

1st Round	Regional Semifinals	Regional Finals	National Semifinals	National Championship

MIDEAST

Florida St.
March 11 — Florida St. 83-81
Eastern Ky.
Knoxville, TN — March 16 — Florida St. 70-56

*Minnesota

Dayton, OH
March 18 — Florida St. 73-54

Kentucky
March 16 — Kentucky 85-69
Marquette
March 11 — Marquette 73-49
Ohio
Knoxville, TN

EAST

Los Angeles, CA
March 23 — Florida St. 79-75

North Caro.
March 16 — North Caro. 92-69
South Caro.
March 11 — South Caro. 53-51
Temple
Williamsburg, PA

Morgantown, WV
March 18 — North Caro. 73-59

Pennsylvania
March 11 — Pennsylvania 76-60
Providence
Jamaica, NY — March 16 — Pennsylvania 78-67
Villanova
March 11 — Villanova 85-70
East Caro.
Princeton, NJ

MIDWEST

Los Angeles, CA
March 25 — UCLA 81-76
NATIONAL CHAMPION

Louisville
March 16 — Louisville 88-84
*Southwestern La.
March 11 — *S'western La. 112-101
Marshall
Las Cruces, NM

Ames, IA
March 18 — Louisville 72-65

Kansas St.
March 16 — Kansas St. 66-55
Texas
March 11 — Texas 85-74
Houston
Las Cruces, NM

WEST

UCLA — UCLA 96-77
March 16 — UCLA 90-58
Weber St.
March 11 — Weber St. 91-64
Hawaii
Pocatello, ID

Los Angeles, CA
March 25 — UCLA 73-57

Provo, UT
March 20

*Long Beach St.
March 11 — *Long Beach St. 95-90 (ot)
Brigham Young
Pocatello, ID — March 16 — *Long Beach St. 75-55

San Francisco

Regional Third Place
March 18
at Dayton, OH
South Caro. 90. Villanova 78
at Morgantown, WV
*Minnesota 77. Marquette 72
at Ames, IA
*Southwestern La. 100. Texas 70
March 20
at Provo, UT
San Francisco 74. Weber St. 64

North Caro.
North Caro. 105-91
Louisville
NATIONAL 3rd PLACE

*Southwestern Louisiana's. Long Beach State's and Minnesota's participation in 1972 tournament vacated.

1972-73

AT A GLANCE

NCAA Champion: UCLA (30-0).

NIT Champion: Virginia Tech (22-5).

New Rules: The free throw on the first six common fouls each half by a team is eliminated. Players cannot attempt to create the false impression that they have been fouled in charging-guarding situations or while setting a screen when the contact was only "incidental." A referee can charge the "actor" with a technical foul for unsportsmanlike conduct if, in the referee's opinion, the acting is making a travesty of the game. NCAA bylaws make freshmen eligible to play varsity ball. NCAA Tournament first-round byes are determined on the basis of an evaluation of the conference's won-lost record over the previous 10 years in playoff competition.

NCAA Probation: Centenary, Duke, Kansas, New Mexico State, North Carolina State, Western Kentucky.

NCAA Consensus First-Team All-Americans: Doug Collins, G, Sr., Illinois State; Ernie DiGregorio, G, Sr., Providence; Bo Lamar, G, Sr., Southwestern Louisiana; Ed Ratleff, F-G, Sr., Long Beach State; David Thompson, F, Soph., North Carolina State; Bill Walton, C, Jr., UCLA; Keith Wilkes, F, Jr., UCLA.

UCLA, spearheaded by center Bill Walton, became the first major college in history to compile back-to-back perfect-record seasons. "Walton might have been a better all-around player (than Lew Alcindor)," Bruins coach John Wooden said. "If you were grading a player for every fundamental skill, Walton would rank the highest of any center who ever played."

Oral Roberts established an NCAA record for most field-goal attempts per game with 98.5. ORU and Southwestern Louisiana finished 1-2 in the team scoring race for the second consecutive season. David Vaughn's 34 rebounds for Oral Roberts against Brandeis is the highest single-game total for a major-college player since freshman eligibility was introduced.

Marquette's 81-game homecourt winning streak, which started in 1967, was snapped by Notre Dame, 81-79, on guard Dwight Clay's right corner jumper with four seconds remaining.

Oklahoma City's Ozzie Edwards (28.4) and Marvin Rich (25.3) became one of only four sets of teammates in NCAA history to each average more than 25 points per game in a single season.

Freshman James "Fly" Williams, the fifth-leading scorer in the country, became a folk hero of sorts by leading Austin Peay State from last place to the Ohio Valley Conference championship. He set a school record with 51 points in two different games (against Tennessee Tech and Georgia Southern).

Los Angeles State's Raymond Lewis (39.9) and Tulsa's Willie Biles (41.6) had staggering scoring averages in their final five games, but they still finished second and third, respectively, in the national scoring race behind Pepperdine's William "Bird" Averitt, who averaged 38.1 points per game in his last 10 contests. Biles set a Tulsa scoring record with 48 points against Wichita State.

American University's Kermit Washington grabbed at least 26 rebounds in each of his last five games to finish the year with a nation-leading 20.4 rebounds per game.

Davidson (Southern), Kentucky (SEC), and Weber State (Big Sky) each captured its sixth consecutive regular-season league championship. Davidson's crown was its ninth undisputed Southern Conference regular-season title in 10 years.

For the first time in ACC Tournament history, the regular-season last-place finisher won a first-round game when Wake Forest (3-9 in the ACC) upset second-place finisher North Carolina State (8-4), 54-52, in overtime.

Arizona's Fred Snowden became the first African-American head coach in the Western Athletic Conference. Arizona freshman Coniel Norman led the WAC in scoring (24 ppg) and Utah freshman Mike Sojourner paced the WAC in rebounding (12.3 rpg).

Temple's Harry Litwack ended his 21-year coaching career with a 373-193 record.

1972-73 INDIVIDUAL LEADERS

SCORING

PLAYER	PTS.	AVG.
Averitt, Pepperdine	848	33.9
Lewis, Los Angeles St.	789	32.9
Biles, Tulsa	788	30.3
Stewart, Richmond	574	30.2
Williams, Austin Peay	854	29.4
Lamar, Southwestern La.	808	28.9
Edwards, Oklahoma City	767	28.4
Terry, Arkansas	735	28.3
Williamson, New Mexico St.	490	27.2
Collins, Illinois St.	650	26.0

REBOUNDING

PLAYER	REB.	AVG.
Washington, American	511	20.4
Barnes, Providence	571	19.0
Parish, Centenary	505	18.7

Padgett, Nevada-Reno	462	17.8
Bradley, N. Illinois	426	17.8
Walton, UCLA	506	16.9
Kenon, Memphis St.	501	16.7
Campion, Manhattan	402	15.5
Cash, Bowling Green	396	15.2
Baker, UNLV	424	15.1
Perry, Pan American	388	14.9

Note: Parish's rebounding totals were discounted by the NCAA because Centenary was on probation.

FIELD GOAL PERCENTAGE

PLAYER	FGM	FGA	PCT.
Hayes, Lamar	146	222	.658
Walton, UCLA	277	426	.650
Stewart, Santa Clara	186	291	.639
Schaeffer, St. John's	265	420	.631

Losch, Tulane	151	240	.629
Armstead, Rutgers	143	232	.616
Starks, Murray St.	162	264	.614
Taylor, Jacksonville	191	313	.610
Jones, North Carolina	206	343	.601
Minniefield, New Mexico	156	260	.600

FREE THROW PERCENTAGE

PLAYER	FTM	FTA	PCT.
Smith, Dayton	111	122	.910
Jellison, Northeastern	122	136	.897
Palubinskas, LSU	137	153	.895
Johnson, Denver	108	121	.893
J. Lee, Syracuse	93	105	.886
Ritter, Indiana	117	134	.873
Bullington, Ball St.	147	170	.865
Edwards, Oklahoma City	103	120	.858
Floyd, Texas A&M	96	112	.857
Kruger, Kansas St.	90	105	.857

1972-73 TEAM LEADERS

SCORING OFFENSE

SCHOOL	PTS.	AVG.
Oral Roberts	2626	97.3
Southwestern Louisiana	2800	96.6
Austin Peay St.	2700	93.1
North Carolina St.	2509	92.9
Houston	2472	91.6

SCORING DEFENSE

SCHOOL	PTS.	AVG.
Texas-El Paso	1460	56.2
Pennsylvania	1606	57.4
Fairleigh Dickinson	1523	58.6
Air Force	1420	59.2
UCLA	1802	60.1

SCORING MARGIN

SCHOOL	OFF.	DEF.	MAR.
North Carolina St.	92.9	71.1	21.8

UCLA	81.3	60.1	21.2
Long Beach St.	90.1	72.3	17.8
St. Joseph's	77.8	63.0	14.8
Houston	91.6	77.1	14.5

WON-LOST PERCENTAGE

SCHOOL	W-L	PCT.
UCLA	30-0	1.000
North Carolina St.	27-0	1.000
Long Beach St.	26-3	.897
Providence	27-4	.871
Marquette	25-4	.862

FIELD GOAL PERCENTAGE

SCHOOL	FGM	FGA	PCT.
North Carolina	1150	2181	.527
Maryland	1089	2094	.520
North Carolina St.	1054	2028	.520
UCLA	1054	2032	.519
St. John's	932	1804	.517

FREE THROW PERCENTAGE

SCHOOL	FTM	FTA	PCT.
Duke	496	632	.785
Jacksonville	426	547	.779
Rhode Island	313	405	.773
William & Mary	483	636	.759
Tennessee	281	371	.757

REBOUND MARGIN

SCHOOL	OWN	OPP.	MAR.
Manhattan	56.5	38.0	18.5
American	56.7	40.3	16.4
Oral Roberts	66.9	50.3	15.6
UCLA	49.0	33.9	15.1
Houston	54.7	40.8	13.9

1972-73 FINAL NATIONAL POLLS

AP	UPI	SCHOOL
1	1	UCLA
2	2	North Carolina St.
3	3	Long Beach St.
4	5	Providence
5	4	Marquette
6	6	Indiana
7	7	Southwestern La.
8	10	Maryland
9	7	Kansas St.
10	9	Minnesota
11	12	North Carolina
12	11	Memphis St.
13	18	Houston
14	14	Syracuse
15	17	Missouri
16	13	Arizona St.
17	15	Kentucky
18	20	Pennsylvania
19	–	Austin Peay St.
20	–	San Francisco
–	16	South Carolina
–	18	Weber St.

1973 NCAA Tournament

Summary: UCLA won the national championship by an average of 16 points. The Bruins' Bill Walton erupted for a championship game-record 44 points in an 87-66 triumph over Memphis State in the final after he was outscored by fellow center Steve Downing, 26-14, in a 70-59 victory against Indiana in the national semifinals. They won 26 of their 30 games by a double-digit margin with the closest results being six-point victories against league rivals Oregon State and Stanford.

Star Gazing: This was the last time a champion had just one representative on the All-NCAA Tournament team (Walton).

1972–73 NCAA CHAMPION: UCLA

SEASON STATISTICS OF UCLA REGULARS

PLAYER	POS.	CL.	G.	FG%	FT%	PPG	RPG
Bill Walton	C	Jr.	30	.650	.569	20.4	16.9
Keith Wilkes	F	Jr.	30	.525	.652	14.8	7.3
Larry Farmer	F	Sr.	30	.511	.701	12.2	5.0
Larry Hollyfield	G	Sr.	30	.466	.492	10.7	2.9
Tommy Curtis	G	Jr.	24	.512	.667	6.4	1.7
Dave Meyers	F	So.	28	.477	.756	4.9	2.9
Greg Lee	G	Jr.	30	.473	.790	4.6	1.3
Swen Nater	C	Sr.	29	.459	.652	3.2	3.3
Pete Trgovich	G-F	So.	25	.382	.400	3.1	1.7
Vince Carson	F	Jr.	26	.514	.471	1.7	2.2
Gary Franklin	F	Jr.	24	.485	.500	1.6	1.3
Bob Webb	G	Jr.	21	.148	.833	0.6	0.2
TEAM TOTALS			30	.519	.632	81.3	49.0

Assists leader: Walton 168.

1973 FINAL FOUR CHAMPIONSHIP GAME

ST. LOUIS, MO

UCLA (87)	MIN.	FG-A	FT-A	REB.	A	PF	PTS.
Wilkes	39	8-14	0-0	7	1	2	16
Farmer	33	1-4	0-0	2	0	2	2
Walton	33	21-22	2-5	13	2	4	44
Lee	34	1-1	3-3	3	14	2	5
Hollyfield	30	4-7	0-0	3	3	2	8
Curtis	11	1-4	2-2	3	9	4	4
Meyers	10	2-7	0-0	3	0	1	4
Nater	7	1-1	0-0	3	0	2	2
Franklin	1	1-2	0-1	1	0	0	2
Carson	1	0-0	0-0	0	0	0	0
Webb	1	0-0	0-0	0	0	0	0
Team				2			
TOTALS	200	40-62	7-11	40	26	18	87

FG%: .645. FT%: .636. Blocks: 5. Turnovers: 17 (Walton 6). Steals: 2.

MEMPHIS ST. (66)	MIN.	FG-A	FT-A	REB.	A	PF	PTS.
Buford	38	3-7	1-2	3	1	1	7
Kenon	34	8-16	4-4	8	3	3	20
Robinson	33	3-6	0-1	7	1	4	6
Laurie	21	0-1	0-0	0	2	0	0
Finch	38	9-21	11-13	1	2	2	29
Westfall	10	0-1	0-0	0	0	5	0
Cook	18	1-4	2-2	0	2	1	4
McKinney	1	0-0	0-0	0	0	0	0
Jones	4	0-0	0-0	0	0	0	0
Tetzlaff	1	0-0	0-2	0	0	1	0
Liss	1	0-1	0-0	0	0	0	0
Andrews	1	0-0	0-0	0	0	0	0
Team				2			
TOTALS	200	24-57	18-24	21	11	17	66

FG%: .421. FT%: .750. Blocks: 1. Turnovers: 8. Steals: 0.
Halftime: Tied 39-39.

NATIONAL SEMIFINALS

MEMPHIS STATE (98): Buford 3-7 0-0 6, Kenon 14-27 0-4 28, Robinson 11-17 2-3 24, Laurie 1-3 2-3 4, Finch 7-16 7-9 21, Cook 3-6 2-3 8, Westfall 2-3 3-4 7, Jones 0-1 0-0 0. Team 41-80 (.513) 16-26 (.615) 98.

PROVIDENCE (85): Crawford 5-12 0-0 10, Costello 5-5 1-1 11, Barnes 5-7 2-3 12, DiGregorio 15-36 2-2 32, Stacom 6-15 3-3 15, King 2-6 0-0 4, Baker 0-0 0-0 0, Dunphy 0-1 1-2 1, Bello 0-0 0-0 0. Team 38-82 (.463) 9-11 (.818) 85.

Halftime: Providence 49-40.

UCLA (70): Wilkes 5-10 3-4 13, Farmer 3-6 1-2 7, Walton 7-12 0-0 14, Lee 0-1 0-0 0, Hollyfield 5-6 0-0 10, Curtis 9-15 4-7 2, Meyers 2-3 0-0 4, Nater 0-0 0-0 0. Team 31-53 (.585) 8-13 (.615) 70.

INDIANA (59): Buckner 3-10 0-1 6, Crews 4-10 0-0 8, Downing 12-20 2-4 26, Green 1-7 0-0 2, Ritter 6-10 1-1 13, Laskowski 1-8 0-0 2, Abernethy 0-1 0-0 0, Smock 0-0 0-0 0, Noort 0-0 0-0 0, Wilson 0-0 0-0 0, Morris 0-0 0-0 0, Ahlfield 0-0 0-0 0, Allen 1-1 0-0 2, Memering 0-0 0-0 0. Team 28-67 (.418) 3-6 (.500) 59.

Halftime: UCLA 40-22.

ALL-TOURNAMENT TEAM

Ernie DiGregorio, G, Sr., Providence
Steve Downing, C, Sr., Indiana
Larry Finch, G, Sr., Memphis State
Larry Kenon, F, Jr., Memphis State
Bill Walton, C, Jr., UCLA*
*Named Most Outstanding Player

Biggest Upset: Coach Jerry Tarkanian's fourth consecutive and last tournament team at Long Beach State (26-3) succumbed against San Francisco, 77-67, when two-time consensus first-team All-American Ed Ratleff hit just 4 of 18 field-goal attempts for the 49ers, who were ranked third by UPI.

One and Only: Walton is the only player to have as many as 20 field goals in an NCAA championship game. He was 21 of 22 from the floor to finish with 44 points in an 87-66 victory against Memphis State.

What If: Undefeated North Carolina State was ineligible for the NCAA Tournament because of NCAA probation.... In the national semifinals, Providence All-American Marvin Barnes suffered a dislocated right kneecap in the first half. The Friars, entering the Final Four with just two defeats, didn't have enough firepower to retain a nine-point halftime lead and wound up losing to Memphis State (98-85).

Putting Things in Perspective: Downing and John Ritter, Indiana's top two scorers, were recruited by coach Bob Knight's predecessor, Lou Watson, who compiled a 17-7 mark in his final season (1970-71) when George McGinnis played his only year in college before turning pro.

Providence guard Ernie DiGregorio was a key reason the Friars made it to the 1973 NCAA Final Four.

1973 CHAMPIONSHIP BRACKET

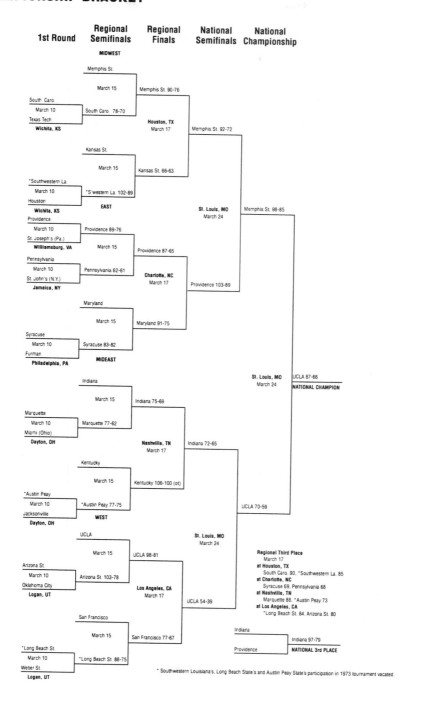

1st Round	Regional Semifinals	Regional Finals	National Semifinals	National Championship

MIDWEST

Memphis St.
March 15
Memphis St. 90-76

South. Caro.
March 10
Texas Tech
Wichita, KS
South Caro. 78-70

Kansas St.
March 15
Kansas St. 66-63

*Southwestern La.
March 10
Houston
Wichita, KS
*S'western La. 102-89

Houston, TX
March 17

Memphis St. 92-72

EAST

Providence
March 10
St. Joseph's (Pa.)
Williamsburg, VA
Providence 89-76

Pennsylvania
March 10
St. John's (N.Y.)
Jamaica, NY
Pennsylvania 62-61

March 15
Providence 87-65

Maryland
March 15
Maryland 91-75

Syracuse
March 10
Furman
Philadelphia, PA
Syracuse 83-82

Charlotte, NC
March 17

Providence 103-89

St. Louis, MO
March 24

Memphis St. 98-85

Providence

MIDEAST

Indiana
March 15
Indiana 75-69

Marquette
March 10
Miami (Ohio)
Dayton, OH
Marquette 77-62

Kentucky
March 15
Kentucky 106-100 (ot)

*Austin Peay
March 10
Jacksonville
Dayton, OH
*Austin Peay 77-75

Nashville, TN
March 17

Indiana 72-65

WEST

UCLA
March 15
UCLA 98-81

Arizona St.
March 10
Oklahoma City
Logan, UT
Arizona St. 103-78

San Francisco
March 15
San Francisco 77-67

*Long Beach St.
March 10
Weber St.
Logan, UT
*Long Beach St. 88-75

Los Angeles, CA
March 17

UCLA 54-39

St. Louis, MO
March 24

Indiana 97-79

UCLA 70-59

St. Louis, MO
March 24

UCLA 87-66
NATIONAL CHAMPION

Regional Third Place
March 17
at Houston, TX
South Caro. 90, *Southwestern La. 85
at Charlotte, NC
Syracuse 69, Pennsylvania 68
at Nashville, TN
Marquette 88, *Austin Peay 73
at Los Angeles, CA
*Long Beach St. 84, Arizona St. 80

Indiana
Indiana 97-79
Providence
NATIONAL 3rd PLACE

* Southwestern Louisiana's, Long Beach State's and Austin Peay State's participation in 1973 tournament vacated.

1973–74

AT A GLANCE

NCAA Champion: North Carolina State (30-1).

NIT Champion: Purdue (21-9).

New Conferences: ECC (after Middle Atlantic disbands), ECAC divided to receive multiple automatic qualification berths in the NCAA Tournament.

New Rules: Referees may penalize players for fouls occurring away from the ball (grabbing, illegal screens, etc.). The NCAA Tournament bracket rotation changes for the first time, eliminating East vs. West bracketing in effect since the event's inception. The first public draw to fill oversubscribed orders for Final Four tickets is administered.

NCAA Probation: Centenary, Long Beach State, Louisiana Tech, McNeese State, New Mexico State, Texas-Pan American, Western Kentucky, Wichita State.

NCAA Consensus First-Team All-Americans: Marvin Barnes, C, Sr., Providence; John Shumate, C-F, Soph., Notre Dame; David Thompson, F, Jr., North Carolina State; Bill Walton, C, Sr., UCLA; Keith Wilkes, F, Sr., UCLA.

Two streaks ended for UCLA. The big one one was the Bruins' NCAA-record 88-game winning streak, which came to a halt when Notre Dame beat them, 71-70 (see accompanying box score). The other was their Pac-8 Conference winning streak of 50 which Oregon State took care of, 61-57. UCLA was 149-2 at Pauley Pavilion under coach John Wooden. Center Bill Walton finished his career with an amazing field-goal percentage of 65.1 although he never won a single-season shooting title. He shot 68.6 percent from the floor in 12 NCAA Tournament games.

Considered in some quarters as the most incredible comeback in major-college history, North Carolina freshman Walter Davis sent the regular-season finale against Duke into overtime with a 30-foot bank shot, climaxing an eight-point rally in the final 17 seconds of regulation. Carolina won in overtime, 96-92, for its first-ever overtime victory against the Blue Devils.

Jerry Tarkanian, the nation's winningest Division I coach by percentage, lost his home debut at UNLV (82-76 to Texas Tech) after Tarkanian-coached teams never lost a home game in five years at Long Beach State or in six years in junior college.

Setting school single-game scoring records were Providence's Marvin Barnes (52 points against Austin Peay State) and Illinois State's Robert "Bubbles" Hawkins (58 against Northern Illinois).

The nation's top three scorers grew up in New York City—Canisius' Larry Fogle, Pan American's Bruce "Sky" King, and Austin Peay State's James "Fly" Williams.

Texas, winner of just one non-conference game, became the only school with a losing overall record to secure an automatic bid by capturing a regular-season league title.

This season marked won-loss records that were the best (27-2 by Maryland-Eastern Shore) and worst (1-25 by Georgia State) for any first-year Division I schools since classification was first introduced in 1948.

In the lowest-scoring game since 1938, Tennessee and Temple combined for a mere 17 points in the Volunteers' 11-6 victory (see accompanying box score).

1973–74 FINAL NATIONAL POLLS

AP	UPI	SCHOOL
1	1	North Carolina St.
2	2	UCLA
3	5	Marquette
4	4	Maryland
5	3	Notre Dame
6	12	Michigan
7	10	Kansas
8	6	Providence
9	9	Indiana
10	11	Long Beach St.
11	–	Purdue
12	8	North Carolina
13	7	Vanderbilt
14	19	Alabama
15	–	Utah
16	14	Pittsburgh
17	13	Southern Cal
18	–	Oral Roberts
19	16	South Carolina
20	19	Dayton
–	15	Louisville
–	17	Creighton
–	18	New Mexico

Maryland, ranking 4th in both polls, lost against eventual NCAA champion North Carolina State in the ACC Tournament final (103-100 in overtime) in what some believe might have been the greatest college game ever played. The Terrapins lost by one point at UCLA in its season opener before dropping both regular-season games against N.C. State by six points and bowing at North Carolina to finish in a tie with the Tar Heels for second place in the ACC standings.

1974 NCAA Tournament

Summary: North Carolina State, unbeaten in 27 games the previous season when it was ineligible to participate in the national tournament because of an NCAA probation, defeated Marquette in the championship game, 76-64, after Warriors coach Al McGuire was assessed two technical fouls late in the first half. The T's helped the Wolfpack score 10 unanswered points in less than a minute and transform a 28-27 deficit into a comfortable 37-28 lead. The

Providence's Marvin Barnes lets it fly.

UCLA'S 88-GAME WINNING STREAK ENDS High drama occurred on January 19, 1974 at Notre Dame's Athletic and Convocation Center when the Irish ended UCLA's NCAA-record 88-game winning streak, 71-70. Guard Dwight Clay's fallaway jump shot from the right baseline climaxed a 12-0 spurt in the last three minutes for the Irish. Clay's teammates Gary Brokaw and John Shumate scored 25 and 24 points respectively.

UCLA (70)	FG-A	FT-A	REB.	PTS.
Tommy Curtis	3-11	3-4	1	9
Pete Trgovich	3-5	1-1	0	7
Bill Walton	12-14	0-0	9	24
Dave Meyers	5-10	0-2	7	10
Keith Wilkes	6-16	6-7	5	18
Greg Lee	0-0	2-2	0	2
Marques Johnson	0-0	0-0	0	0
TOTALS	**29-56**	**12-16**	**27**	**70**

FG%: .518. FT%: .750.

NOTRE DAME (71)	FG-A	FT-A	REB.	PTS.
Gary Brokaw	10-16	5-7	3	25
Dwight Clay	2-5	3-4	6	7
John Shumate	11-22	2-4	11	24
Adrian Dantley	4-12	1-1	8	9
Gary Novak	0-2	0-0	0	0
Bill Paterno	2-4	0-0	1	4
Ray Martin	1-1	0-0	2	2
TOTALS	**30-62**	**11-16**	**31**	**71**

FG%: .484. FT%: .687.
Halftime: UCLA 43-34.

LOWEST-SCORING GAME SINCE 1938

Fans attending the December 15, 1973, match at Tennessee between Temple and the Volunteers probably didn't need to worry about missing any action while standing in line for concessions. The two teams combined for 17 points, the lowest total in a game since 1938. Tennessee's Len Kosmalski was "high scorer" with 5 points.

TEMPLE (6)	FG-A	FT-A	REB.	PTS.
Kevin Washington	0-3	0-0	0	0
Joe Anderson	1-3	2-3	4	4
Joe Newman	1-3	0-0	1	2
Rick Trudeau	0-1	0-0	0	0
John Kneib	0-1	0-0	0	0
Tony Moore	0-0	0-0	0	0
TOTALS	**2-11**	**2-3**	**5**	**6**

FG%: .182. FT%: .667.

TENNESSEE (11)	FG-A	FT-A	REB.	PTS.
Ernie Grunfeld	1-3	0-0	2	2
Wayne Tomlinson	0-0	0-0	2	0
Len Kosmalski	2-3	1-2	3	5
Rodney Woods	0-2	0-0	1	0
John Snow	0-1	4-5	1	4
Austin Clark	0-1	0-0	0	0
Team				3
TOTALS	**3-10**	**5-7**	**12**	**11**

FG%: .300. FT%: .714.
Halftime: Tennessee 7-5.

1973–74 INDIVIDUAL LEADERS

PLAYER	PTS.	AVG.
Fogle, Canisius	835	33.4
King, Pan American	681	31.0
Williams, Austin Peay	687	27.5
Stewart, Richmond	663	26.5
Thompson, North Carolina St.	805	26.0
Bullington, Ball St.	664	25.5
Oleynick, Seattle	653	25.1
Outlaw, North Carolina A&T	647	24.9
Biles, Tulsa	641	24.7
Shumate, Notre Dame	703	24.2

REBOUNDING

PLAYER	REB.	AVG.
Barnes, Providence	597	18.7
McCullough, Pan American	358	16.3
Robinson, Kent St.	423	16.3
Campion, Manhattan	419	15.5

Parish, Centenary*	382	15.3
Padgett, Nevada-Reno	395	15.2
McKinney, Baylor	375	15.0
Meriweather, Southern Ill.	387	14.9
Walton, UCLA	398	14.7
Elmore, Maryland	412	14.7
Warner, Maine	350	14.6

Note: Parish's rebounding totals were discounted by the NCAA because Centenary was on probation.

FIELD GOAL PERCENTAGE

PLAYER	FGM	FGA	PCT.
Fleming, Arizona	136	204	.667
Walton, UCLA	232	349	.665
Cox, Mississippi	152	242	.628
Shumate, Notre Dame	281	448	.627
Skinner, Massachusetts	196	316	.620

Carroll, Howard	205	332	.617
Fry, Mississippi St.	141	233	.605
Morgan, Samford	214	354	.605
Garrett, Purdue	276	465	.594
C. Pondexter, Long Beach St.	167	283	.590

FREE THROW PERCENTAGE

PLAYER	FTM	FTA	PCT.
Medlock, Arkansas	87	95	.916
Snow, Tennessee	81	91	.890
Ferrell, Marshall	128	145	.883
Compton, Vanderbilt	89	102	.873
Kruger, Kansas St.	122	140	.871
Cook, Memphis St.	119	138	.862
Johnson, Denver	120	140	.857
Palubinskas, LSU	121	142	.852
Cosey, West Texas St.	80	94	.851
Bullington, Ball St.	154	183	.842

1973–74 TEAM LEADERS

SCORING OFFENSE

SCHOOL	PTS.	AVG.
Maryland-Eastern Shore	2831	97.6
Oral Roberts	2744	94.6
Virginia Commonwealth	2266	94.4
North Carolina St.	2833	91.4
Utah	2726	90.9

SCORING DEFENSE

SCHOOL	PTS.	AVG.
Texas-El Paso	1413	56.5
Temple	1417	56.7
Princeton	1520	58.5
Marquette	1857	59.9
St. Joseph's	1807	60.2

SCORING MARGIN

SCHOOL	OFF.	DEF.	MAR.
UNC Charlotte	90.2	69.4	20.8
UCLA	82.3	62.7	19.6
Long Beach St.	80.2	61.1	19.1
Notre Dame	89.9	73.0	16.9
Maryland	85.7	69.0	16.7

WON-LOST PERCENTAGE

SCHOOL	W-L	PCT.
North Carolina St.	30-1	.968
Maryland-Eastern Shore	27-2	.931
Long Beach St.	24-2	.923
Notre Dame	26-3	.897
Providence	28-4	.875

FIELD GOAL PERCENTAGE

SCHOOL	FGM	FGA	PCT.
Notre Dame	1056	1992	.530
Long Beach St.	887	1680	.528
North Carolina	1015	1952	.520
Massachusetts	878	1709	.514
UNC Charlotte	996	1948	.511
Stetson	781	1529	.511

FREE THROW PERCENTAGE

SCHOOL	FTM	FTA	PCT.
Vanderbilt	477	595	.802
Princeton	332	423	.785
Davidson	488	623	.783
Seattle	366	479	.764
Denver	311	410	.759

REBOUND MARGIN

SCHOOL	OWN	OPP.	MAR.
Massachusetts	43.7	30.7	13.0
Virginia Commonwealth	55.1	42.1	13.0
Arkansas St.	50.3	39.2	11.1
Iona	51.0	40.0	11.0
Maryland	47.0	36.1	10.9

final in N.C. State's home state at Greensboro was anticlimatic after the Wolfpack avenged an 18-point loss to UCLA earlier in the season on a neutral court by ending the Bruins' 38-game playoff winning streak (80-77 in overtime). N.C. State erased an 11-point deficit midway through the second half and a seven-point deficit in the extra session behind David Thompson's 28 points and 10 rebounds to halt UCLA's string of seven consecutive NCAA championships. The Bruins were ripe to be knocked off. The (Bill) Walton Gang also blew a 17-point advantage in its playoff opener before regrouping to outlast Dayton, 111-100, in triple overtime.

Star Gazing: It's inconceivable to think N.C. State would have won the crown if Thompson hadn't recovered from a nasty fall to the floor after attempting to block a shot by Pitt in the East Regional final. Thompson, cartwheeling over the shoulders of a teammate, landed with a sickening thud on the back of his head and did not move for four minutes. He regained consciousness, was taken to a hospital, and, after getting 15 stitches to mend a head wound, was permitted to return to the arena and watch the end of the game. The mild concussion didn't keep him from being ready for the Final Four, where the junior forward was named Most Outstanding Player.

One and Only: N.C. State starting forward Tim Stoddard is the only individual to play for an NCAA basketball champion and then in a major league baseball World Series (relief pitcher for the Baltimore Orioles in 1979).

Numbers Game: Thompson became the only undergraduate non-center to average more than 23 points per game for a national champion (26 ppg for North Carolina State).

What If: Two-time consensus first-team All-

1973–74 NCAA CHAMPION: NORTH CAROLINA STATE

SEASON STATISTICS OF N.C. STATE REGULARS

PLAYER	POS.	CL.	G.	FG%	FT%	PPG	RPG
David Thompson	F	Jr.	31	.547	.745	26.0	7.9
Tom Burleson	C	Sr.	31	.516	.654	18.1	12.2
Monte Towe	G	Jr.	31	.517	.811	12.8	2.2
Moe Rivers	G	Jr.	30	.484	.654	12.1	2.9
Phil Spence	F	So.	30	.497	.615	6.0	6.3
Tim Stoddard	F	Jr.	31	.416	.697	5.5	4.5
Steve Nuce	F	Sr.	28	.464	.786	4.4	3.2
Greg Hawkins	F	Sr.	25	.469	.735	2.8	1.4
Mark Moeller	G	Jr.	30	.435	.913	2.7	1.2
TEAM TOTALS			**31**	**.499**	**.708**	**91.4**	**46.8**

1974 FINAL FOUR CHAMPIONSHIP GAME

GREENSBORO, NC

MARQUETTE (64)	MIN.	FG-A	FT-A	REB.	A	PF	PTS.
Ellis	39	6-16	0-0	11	1	5	12
Tatum	20	2-7	0-0	3	1	4	4
Lucas	40	7-13	7-9	13	0	4	21
Walton	25	4-10	0-0	2	2	2	8
Washington	35	3-13	5-8	4	0	3	11
Delsman	5	0-0	0-0	0	0	2	0
Daniels	17	1-3	1-2	0	2	3	3
Campbell	12	2-3	0-0	1	0	3	4
Homan	6	0-4	1-2	6	1	2	1
Brennan	1	0-0	0-0	0	0	1	0
Team				3			
TOTALS	**200**	**25-69**	**14-21**	**43**	**7**	**29**	**64**

FG%: .362. **FT%:** .667. **Steals:** 9 (Washington 5). **Blocks:** 3.

N.C. STATE (76)	MIN.	FG-A	FT-A	REB.	A	PF	PTS.
Stoddard	26	3-4	2-2	7	2	5	8
Thompson	40	7-12	7-8	7	2	3	21
Burleson	36	6-9	2-6	11	0	4	14
Rivers	40	4-9	6-9	2	5	2	14
Towe	38	5-10	6-7	3	2	1	16
Spence	18	1-2	1-2	3	3	2	3
Moeller	2	0-0	0-0	0	0	0	0
Team				1			
TOTALS	**200**	**26-46**	**24-34**	**34**	**14**	**17**	**76**

FG%: .565. **FT%:** .706. **Steals:** 12. **Blocks:** 8 (Burleson 7). **Halftime:** North Carolina State 39-30.

NATIONAL SEMIFINALS

UCLA (77): Meyers 6-9 0-1 12, Wilkes 5-17 5-5 15, Walton 13-21 3-3 29, Curtis 4-8 3-4 11, Lee 4-11 0-0 8, Johnson 0-3 0-0 0, McCarter 1-2 0-0 2. Team 33-71 (.465) 11-13 (.846) 77.

NORTH CAROLINA STATE (80): Stoddard 4-11 1-2 9, Thompson 12-25 4-6 28, Burleson 9-20 2-6 20, Rivers 3-8 1-2 7, Towe 4-10 4-4 12, Spence 2-3 0-0 4, Hawkins 0-0 0-0 0. Team 34-77 (.442) 12-20 (.600) 80.

Halftime: Tied 35-35. Regulation: Tied 65-65. First Overtime: Tied 67-67.

KANSAS (51): Cook 1-3 2-4 4, Morningstar 5-13 0-0 10, Knight 0-5 0-0 0, Greenlee 3-7 0-0 6, Kivisto 2-7 2-5 6, Suttle 8-13 3-4 19, Smith 3-4 0-0 6. Team 22-52 (.423) 7-13 (.538) 51.

MARQUETTE (64): Ellis 2-9, 1-2 5, Tatum 5-11 4-6 14, Lucas 7-11 4-4 18, Walton 2-7 3-4 7, Washington 5-12 6-11 16, Daniels 0-2 0-0 0, Campbell 0-1 0-0 0, Homan 1-2 0-0 2, Delsman 0-1 2-2 2, Brennan 0-0 0-0 0, Bryant 0-0 0-0 0, Vollmer 0-0 0-0 0, Johnson 0-0 0-0 0. Team 22-56 (.393) 20-29 (.690) 64.

Halftime: Kansas 24-23.

ALL-TOURNAMENT TEAM

Tom Burleson, C, Sr., North Carolina State
Maurice Lucas, C, Jr., Marquette
David Thompson, F, Jr., North Carolina State*
Monte Towe, G, Jr., North Carolina State
Bill Walton, C, Sr., UCLA
*Named Most Outstanding Player

North Carolina star forward David Thompson.

UCLA's Keith (Jamaal) Wilkes moves down the court.

American forward Keith Wilkes shot better than 50 percent from the floor in his three varsity seasons at UCLA before hitting half of his field-goal attempts in a 12-year NBA career. If only he connected on 41 percent of his field-goal attempts instead of 29.4 percent (5 of 17) in the national semifinals, the Bruins could have defeated North Carolina State rather than lose 80-77.

Putting Things in Perspective: Would North Carolina State have been the kingpin if the Wolfpack didn't play at home (East Regional at Raleigh) and nearby Greensboro, where it ended UCLA's 38-game playoff winning streak with an 80-77 double overtime triumph in the national semifinals?

1974 CHAMPIONSHIP BRACKET

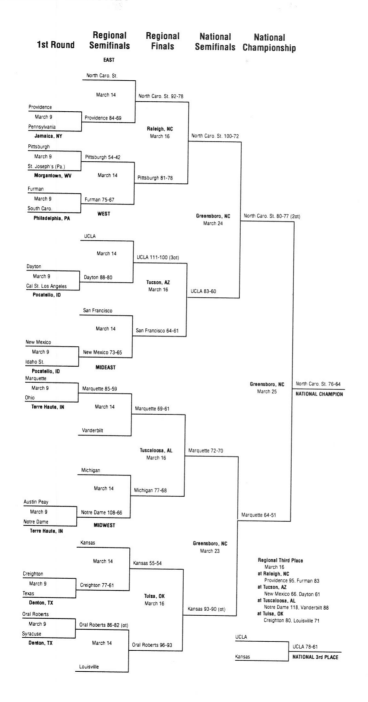

1st Round	Regional Semifinals	Regional Finals	National Semifinals	National Championship

EAST

North Caro. St.
March 14
North Caro. St. 92-78

Providence
March 9
Pennsylvania
Jamaica, NY
Providence 84-69

Raleigh, NC
March 16

North Caro. St. 100-72

Pittsburgh
March 9
St. Joseph's (Pa.)
Morgantown, WV
Pittsburgh 54-42

March 14
Pittsburgh 81-78

Furman
March 9
South Caro.
Philadelphia, PA
Furman 75-67

WEST

North Caro. St. 80-77 (2ot)

UCLA
March 14
UCLA 111-100 (3ot)

Dayton
March 9
Cal St. Los Angeles
Pocatello, ID
Dayton 88-80

Tucson, AZ
March 16

UCLA 83-60

San Francisco
March 14
San Francisco 64-61

New Mexico
March 9
Idaho St.
Pocatello, ID
New Mexico 73-65

MIDEAST

Marquette
March 9
Ohio
Terre Haute, IN
Marquette 85-59

March 14
Marquette 69-61

Vanderbilt

Tuscaloosa, AL
March 16

Marquette 72-70

Michigan
March 14
Michigan 77-68

Austin Peay
March 9
Notre Dame
Terre Haute, IN
Notre Dame 108-66

MIDWEST

Marquette 64-51

Greensboro, NC
March 24

Greensboro, NC
March 25

North Caro. St. 76-64
NATIONAL CHAMPION

Kansas
March 14
Kansas 55-54

Creighton
March 9
Texas
Denton, TX
Creighton 77-61

Tulsa, OK
March 16

Kansas 93-90 (ot)

Oral Roberts
March 9
Syracuse
Denton, TX
Oral Roberts 86-82 (ot)

March 14
Oral Roberts 96-93

Louisville

Greensboro, NC
March 23

Regional Third Place
March 16
at **Raleigh, NC**
Providence 95, Furman 83
at **Tucson, AZ**
New Mexico 66, Dayton 61
at **Tuscaloosa, AL**
Notre Dame 118, Vanderbilt 88
at **Tulsa, OK**
Creighton 80, Louisville 71

UCLA
UCLA 78-61
Kansas
NATIONAL 3rd PLACE

1974–75

AT A GLANCE

NCAA Champion: UCLA (28-3).

NIT Champion: Princeton (22-8).

New Rules: A nonjumper on the restraining circle during a jump ball may move around after the ball leaves the referee's hand. A player assessed a foul is no longer required to raise his hand. A 32-team bracket is adopted for the NCAA Tournament and teams other than the conference champion can be chosen on an at-large basis from the same league for the first time.

NCAA Probation: Centenary, Illinois, Long Beach State, Louisiana Tech, Maryland-Eastern Shore, McNeese State, Southern Methodist, Texas-Pan American, Western Kentucky, Wichita State.

NCAA Consensus First-Team All-Americans: Adrian Dantley, F, Soph., Notre Dame; John Lucas, G, Jr., Maryland; Scott May, F, Jr., Indiana; Dave Meyers, F, Sr., UCLA; David Thompson, F, Sr., North Carolina State.

John Wooden concluded his 29-year coaching career with a 664-162 record. Wooden, the only coach to compile a double-digit total of Final Four victories, notched a 21-3 Final Four record with UCLA in 12 appearances from 1962 to 1975. He won 94 percent of his games in his last 12 seasons (335-22 record). He was replaced by Gene Bartow. Another retiring Pac-8 coach, Howie Dallmar, and his Stanford club, which finished 12-14, upset top-ranked and NCAA champion-to-be UCLA, 64-60.

Richmond's Bob McCurdy won the national scoring title going away with outbursts of 41, 40, 46, and a school-record 53 points in a 17-day stretch at the end of the season. As a freshman for Virginia, McCurdy scored 42 points against Maryland's Len Elmore-Tom McMillen freshmen, but subsequently transferred.

North Carolina State's David Thompson set a school record with 57 points in 34 minutes against Buffalo State. Wake Forest, sparked by guard Skip Brown's 25 points, ended North Carolina State's 37-game winning streak, 83-78.

Purdue's Bruce Parkinson set a Big Ten Conference record with 18 assists against Minnesota.

Texas-El Paso led the nation in team defense for the third consecutive season under coach Don Haskins, a disciple of former Oklahoma State coach Hank Iba.

Penn won its sixth consecutive Ivy League championship.

Seattle's Frank Oleynick made game-winning shots at the buzzer in games against Penn State (62-60), St. Mary's (72-70), and Pepperdine (72-71 in overtime).

An NCAA single-season high of 10 schools were on NCAA probation with sanctions prohibiting them from participating in the NCAA Tournament.

Long Beach State's 75-game homecourt winning streak, which started in 1968, was snapped in its home opener by San Francisco, 94-84.

1974–75 FINAL NATIONAL POLLS

AP	UPI	SCHOOL
1	2	UCLA
2	4	Kentucky
3	1	Indiana
4	3	Louisville
5	5	Maryland
6	–	Syracuse
7	9	North Carolina St.
8	7	Arizona St.
9	10	North Carolina
10	8	Alabama
11	6	Marquette
12	–	Princeton
13	–	Cincinnati
14	14	Notre Dame
15	–	Kansas St.
16	–	Drake
17	14	UNLV
18	–	Oregon St.
19	–	Michigan
20	11	Pennsylvania
–	12	Southern Cal
–	13	Utah St.
–	16	Creighton
–	17	Arizona
–	18	New Mexico St.
–	19	Clemson
–	20	Texas-El Paso

1975 NCAA Tournament

Summary: John Wooden's farewell resulted in another NCAA title. Richard Washington scored 54 points in two Final Four outings as a sophomore for UCLA after averaging a modest

Gene Bartow (left) became coach of the UCLA Bruins after longtime coach John Wooden retired following the 1974–75 season.

4.1 points per game the previous season for the national third-place Bruins. UCLA erased a four-point deficit in the last 50 seconds of regulation to send its national semifinal game against Louisville into overtime. Three Louisville regulars shooting better than 52 percent from the floor for the season (swingman Junior Bridgeman, center Ricky Gallon, and guard Phillip Bond) combined to hit 25 percent (6 of 24) in a 75-74 loss against UCLA. Adding insult to injury for the Cardinals was reserve guard Terry Howard missing the front end of a one-and-one free-throw opportunity in the closing seconds of overtime after he converted all 28 of his previous foul shots that season. The Bruins led a

charmed life throughout the playoffs. They won their opener in overtime after Michigan's C. J. Kupec missed a shot at the end of regulation, and they defeated Montana by three points (67-64) in the West Regional semifinals when future pro standout Micheal Ray Richardson scored just two points for the Grizzlies.

Outcome for Defending Champion: N.C. State (22-6) finished in a three-way tie for second place in the ACC. Despite the presence of national player of the year David Thompson, the ACC Tournament runner-up did not compete in the NCAA playoffs after losing twice against regular-season champion Maryland in league play.

1974-75 INDIVIDUAL LEADERS

SCORING

PLAYER	PTS.	AVG.
McCurdy, Richmond	855	32.9
Dantley, Notre Dame	883	30.4
Thompson, N.C. St.	838	29.9
Burden, Utah	747	28.7
Ivy, Iowa St.	737	28.3
Coleman, Southern Miss.	564	28.2
Oleynick, Seattle	709	27.3
Scaife, Arkansas St.	678	27.1
Rogers, Pan American	588	26.7
Adams, Oklahoma	691	26.6

REBOUNDING

PLAYER	REB.	AVG.
Parish, Centenary	447	15.4
Irving, Hofstra	323	15.4
Warner, Maine	352	14.1

Roane, Md.-Eastern Shore	356	13.7
Mayes, Furman	394	13.6
Robinzine, DePaul	338	13.5
Barnett, Samford	350	13.5
Sorrell, Middle Tenn. St.	373	13.3
King, Pan American	293	13.3
Adams, Oklahoma	346	13.3
Hayes, Idaho St.	346	13.3

Note: Parish's rebounding totals were discounted by the NCAA because Centenary was on probation.

FIELD GOAL PERCENTAGE

PLAYER	FGM	FGA	PCT.
King, Tennessee	273	439	.622
Fleischer, Duke	178	287	.620
Meriweather, S. Ill.	229	370	.619
Roundfield, Central Mich.	216	353	.612
Glenn, Southern Ill.	196	321	.611

Allison, Arkansas	172	282	.610
Andreas, Ohio St.	210	347	.605
Kupchak, North Carolina	239	397	.602
Tampa, East Tenn. St.	117	195	.600
Cutter, Western Michigan	134	224	.598

FREE THROW PERCENTAGE

PLAYER	FTM	FTA	PCT.
Oleynick, Seattle	135	152	.888
Caldwell, Florida	102	115	.887
Brookins, Creighton	98	111	.883
Johnson, Auburn	102	116	.879
Kraft, Air Force	83	95	.874
Lee, Syracuse	98	114	.860
Hays, Montana	91	106	.858
Johnson, Morehead St.	91	106	.858
Krueger, Texas	102	119	.857
Rose, NE Louisiana	83	97	.856

1974-75 TEAM LEADERS

SCORING OFFENSE

SCHOOL	PTS.	AVG.
South Alabama	2412	92.8
North Carolina St.	2596	92.7
Houston	2407	92.6
Kentucky	2858	92.2
Illinois St.	2375	91.3

SCORING DEFENSE

SCHOOL	PTS.	AVG.
Texas-El Paso	1491	57.3
New Mexico St.	1601	59.3
Minnesota	1577	60.7
Princeton	1835	61.2
Marquette	1679	62.2

SCORING MARGIN

SCHOOL	OFF.	DEF.	MAR.
UNC Charlotte	88.9	65.2	23.7

Indiana	88.0	65.9	22.1
Maryland	89.9	74.6	15.3
North Carolina St.	92.7	77.9	14.8
Pan American	87.0	73.2	13.8

WON-LOST PERCENTAGE

SCHOOL	W-L	PCT.
Indiana	31-1	.969
Pan American	22-2	.917
Louisville	28-3	.903
UCLA	28-3	.903
UNC Charlotte	23-3	.885

FIELD GOAL PERCENTAGE

SCHOOL	FGM	FGA	PCT.
Maryland	1049	1918	.547
North Carolina	1037	1933	.536
Arkansas	807	1524	.530
Tennessee	927	1756	.528
Duke	864	1672	.517

FREE THROW PERCENTAGE

SCHOOL	FTM	FTA	PCT.
Vanderbilt	530	692	.766
Florida	456	596	.765
Seattle	303	399	.759
Maryland	509	672	.757
Drake	402	533	.754

REBOUND MARGIN

SCHOOL	OWN	OPP.	MAR.
Stetson	47.1	34.7	12.4
South Alabama	52.6	42.2	10.4
Pan American	45.6	35.7	9.9
Maryland	43.5	34.4	9.1
Minnesota	39.6	30.8	8.8

Star Gazing: Indiana, undefeated entering the tourney (29-0), lost the Mideast Regional final against Kentucky (92-90) despite Kent Benson's 33 points and 23 rebounds. IU coach Bobby Knight said he made a mistake by playing an offensive player (John Laskowski) substanitally more minutes (33 to 3) than defensive standout Tom Abernethy. Kentucky prevailed despite 6 of 19 field-goal shooting by leading scorer Kevin Grevey. UK guards Jimmy Dan Conner and Mike Flynn combined to outscore Indiana counterparts Quinn Buckner and Bobby Wilkerson, 39-22.

One and Only: Louisville is the only school to lead UCLA at halftime in the 20 Final Four games during the Bruins' 10 championship years under coach John Wooden. The Cardinals led UCLA at intermission, 37-33, in the national semifinals before bowing to the Bruins in overtime, 75-74.

Numbers Game: North Carolina started its streak of being the only school to participate in the NCAA Tournament every year since conferences were first permitted to have more than one representative.... Incredibly, Final Four Most Outstanding Players-to-be Jack Givens of Kentucky and Butch Lee of Marquette were blanked in the same game in their freshman season when

1974–75 NCAA CHAMPION: UCLA

SEASON STATISTICS OF UCLA REGULARS

PLAYER	POS.	CL.	G.	FG%	FT%	PPG	RPG
Dave Meyers	F	Sr.	31	.484	.736	18.3	7.9
Richard Washington	C-F	So.	31	.576	.724	15.9	7.8
Marques Johnson	F	So.	29	.543	.686	11.6	7.1
Pete Trgovich	G	Sr.	31	.431	.640	10.2	3.3
Ralph Drollinger	C	Jr.	31	.532	.659	8.8	7.4
Andre McCarter	G	Jr.	31	.359	.729	7.0	2.3
Jim Spillane	G	So.	29	.396	.762	4.5	1.2
Wilbert Olinde	F	So.	22	.474	.560	3.1	2.0
Casey Corliss	F	So.	21	.522	.850	3.1	1.3
Ray Townsend	G	Fr.	20	.410	.667	1.9	0.7
TEAM TOTALS			31	.479	.703	84.7	45.7

Assists leader: McCarter 156.

1975 FINAL FOUR CHAMPIONSHIP GAME

SAN DIEGO, CA

UCLA (92)	MIN.	FG-A	FT-A	REB.	A	PF	PTS.
Meyers	40	9-18	6-7	11	1	4	24
M. Johnson	24	3-9	0-1	7	1	2	6
Washington	40	12-23	4-5	12	3	4	28
Trgovich	40	7-16	2-4	5	4	4	16
McCarter	40	3-6	2-3	2	14	1	8
Drollinger	16	4-6	2-5	13	0	4	10
Team				5			
TOTALS	200	38-78	16-25	55	23	19	92

FG%: .487. FT%: .640. Blocks: 7. Turnovers: 13 (Washington 5). Steals: 3.

KENTUCKY (85)	MIN.	FG-A	FT-A	REB.	A	PF	PTS.
Grevey	36	13-30	8-10	5	1	4	34
Guyette	24	7-11	2-2	7	3	3	16
Robey	14	1-3	0-0	9	1	5	2
Conner	38	4-12	1-2	5	6	1	9
Flynn	25	3-9	4-5	3	2	4	10
Givens	25	3-10	2-3	6	1	3	8
Johnson	17	0-3	0-0	3	1	3	0
Phillips	16	1-7	2-3	6	0	4	4
Lee	3	1-1	0-0	1	0	0	2
Hall	2	0-0	0-0	0	1	1	0
Team				4			
TOTALS	200	33-86	19-25	49	16	28	85

FG%: .384. FT%: .760. Blocks: 1. Turnovers: 13. Steals: 6.
Halftime: UCLA 43-40.

NATIONAL SEMIFINALS

SYRACUSE (79): Hackett 4-6 6-9 14, Sease 7-11 4-4 18, Seibert 2-3 0-2 4, Lee 10-17 3-3 23, Williams 2-9 0-1 4, King 2-8 1-3 5, Kindel 1-3 1-2 3, Shaw 0-0 0-0 0, Parker 2-3 4-7 8, Byrnes 0-0 0-1 0, Kelley 0-1 0-0 0, Meadors 0-0 0-0 0. Team 30-61 (.492) 19-32 (.594) 79.

Halftime: Kentucky 44-32.

KENTUCKY (95): Grevey 5-13 4-5 14, Guyette 2-3 3-4 7, Robey 3-8 3-7 9, Conner 5-9 2-4 12, Flynn 4-9 3-5 11, Givens 10-20 4-8 24, Johnson 2-4 0-0 4, Phillips 5-6 0-2 10, Lee 1-4 0-1 2, Haskins 0-0 2-2 2, Hale 0-1 0-0 0, Hall 0-0 0-0 0, Warford 0-0 0-0 0, Smith 0-1 0-0 0. Team 37-78 (.474) 21-38 (.553) 95.

Halftime: Kentucky 44-32.

LOUISVILLE (74): Murphy 14-28 5-7 33, Cox 5-8 4-11 14, Bunton 3-4 1-2 7, Bridgeman 4-15 4-4 12, Bond 2-6 2-2 6, Whitfield 0-0 0-0 0, Gallon 0-3 0-0 0, Brown 1-1 0-0 2, Wilson 0-0 0-0 0, Howard 0-0 0-1 0. Team 29-65 (.446) 16-27 (.593) 74.

UCLA (75): Meyers 6-16 4-16 16, Johnson 5-10, 0-0 10, Washington 11-19 4-6 26, Trgovich 6-12 0-0 12, McCarter 3-12 0-0 6, Drollinger 1-2 1-2 3, Olinde 0-0 0-0 0, Spillane 1-2 0-0 2. Team 33-73 (.452) 9-14 (.643) 75.

Halftime: Louisville 37-33. **Regulation:** Tied 65-65.

ALL-TOURNAMENT TEAM
Kevin Grevey, F, Sr., Kentucky
Jim Lee, G, Sr., Syracuse
David Meyers, F, Sr., UCLA
Allen Murphy, F, Sr., Louisville
Richard Washington, C-F, Soph., UCLA*
*Named Most Outstanding Player

Kentucky mauled Marquette, 76-54, in the Mideast Regional.

What If: Kentucky had four regulars shoot better than 50 percent from the floor in the 1974–75 campaign—forward Kevin Grevey, guard Jimmy Dan Conner, and centers Rick Robey and Mike Phillips. If only they combined to hit 44.2 percent of their field-goal attempts instead of 36.5 percent (19 of 52) in the champi-onship game, the Wildcats could have defeated UCLA rather than losing 92-85.

Putting Things in Perspective: Consensus first-team All-American forward Scott May's broken arm possibly cost Indiana the national crown. May returned to the lineup against Kentucky, but he was rusty and scored just two points.

1975 CHAMPIONSHIP BRACKET

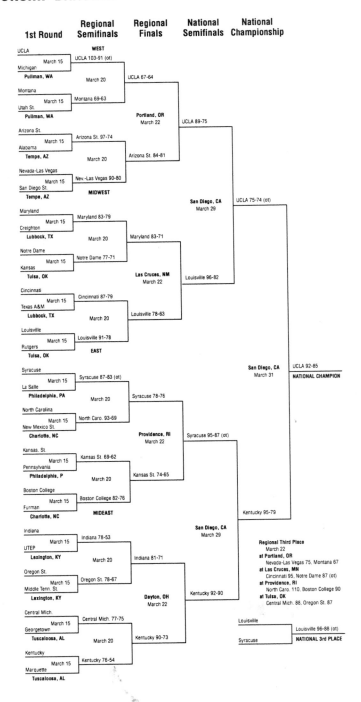

	1st Round	Regional Semifinals	Regional Finals	National Semifinals	National Championship

WEST

UCLA
March 15
Michigan
Pullman, WA
UCLA 103-91 (ot)
March 20
Montana
March 15
Utah St.
Pullman, WA
Montana 69-63
UCLA 67-64
Portland, OR March 22

Arizona St.
March 15
Alabama
Tempe, AZ
Arizona St. 97-74
March 20
Nevada-Las Vegas
March 15
San Diego St.
Tempe, AZ
Nev.-Las Vegas 90-80
Arizona St. 84-81
UCLA 89-75

MIDWEST

Maryland
March 15
Creighton
Lubbock, TX
Maryland 83-79
March 20
Notre Dame
March 15
Kansas
Tulsa, OK
Notre Dame 77-71
Maryland 83-71
Las Cruces, NM March 22

Cincinnati
March 15
Texas A&M
Lubbock, TX
Cincinnati 87-79
March 20
Louisville
March 15
Rutgers
Tulsa, OK
Louisville 91-78
Louisville 78-63
Louisville 96-82

San Diego, CA March 29

UCLA 75-74 (ot)

EAST

Syracuse
March 15
La Salle
Philadelphia, PA
Syracuse 87-83 (ot)
March 20
North Carolina
March 15
New Mexico St.
Charlotte, NC
North Caro. 93-69
Syracuse 78-76
Providence, RI March 22

Kansas. St.
March 15
Pennsylvania
Philadelphia, P
Kansas St. 69-62
March 20
Boston College
March 15
Furman
Charlotte, NC
Boston College 82-76
Kansas St. 74-65
Syracuse 95-87 (ot)

MIDEAST

Indiana
March 15
UTEP
Lexington, KY
Indiana 78-53
March 20
Oregon St.
March 15
Middle Tenn. St.
Lexington, KY
Oregon St. 78-67
Indiana 81-71
Dayton, OH March 22

Central Mich.
March 15
Georgetown
Tuscaloosa, AL
Central Mich. 77-75
March 20
Kentucky
March 15
Marquette
Tuscaloosa, AL
Kentucky 76-54
Kentucky 90-73
Kentucky 92-90

San Diego, CA March 29

Kentucky 95-79

San Diego, CA March 31

UCLA 92-85
NATIONAL CHAMPION

Regional Third Place
March 22
at Portland, OR
Nevada-Las Vegas 75, Montana 67
at Las Cruces, MN
Cincinnati 95, Notre Dame 87 (ot)
at Providence, RI
North Caro. 110, Boston College 90
at Tulsa, OK
Central Mich. 88, Oregon St. 87

Louisville
Syracuse
Louisville 96-88 (ot)
NATIONAL 3rd PLACE

1975-76

AT A GLANCE

NCAA Champion: Indiana (32-0).

NIT Champion: Kentucky (20-10).

New Conferences: Metro, Southland (moved up from Division II).

New Rules: NCAA Tournament regional third-place games are abolished. NIT field reduced from 16 teams to 12 for one year.

NCAA Probation: Canisius, Centenary, Clemson, Long Beach State, Louisiana Tech, Minnesota, Seton Hall, Southwestern Louisiana.

NCAA Consensus First-Team All-Americans: Kent Benson, C, Jr., Indiana; Adrian Dantley, F, Jr., Notre Dame; John Lucas, G, Sr., Maryland; Scott May, F, Sr., Indiana; Richard Washington, C-F, Jr., UCLA.

Tennessee's Ernie Grunfeld.

Indiana tied the 1957 North Carolina team for the all-time record for victories by an undefeated team. The Hoosiers' schedule was one of the most difficult of any NCAA kingpin. In 14 games outside the rigorous Big Ten, their opponents combined to win more than three-fourths of their games excluding the contests with Indiana.

Also in the Big Ten, Purdue (25 of 25) and Wisconsin (22 of 22) combined to sink all 47 of their free-throw attempts in their game on February 7. Minnesota's Mychal Thompson established a Big Ten Conference standard with 12 blocked shots against Ohio State. Michigan State's Terry Furlow set a school record with 50 points against Iowa. And Ohio State's Fred Taylor ended his 18-year coaching career with a 297-158 record.

St. Joseph's had an NCAA-record eight players foul out in a game against Xavier.

Missouri captured its first Big Eight crown since 1930.

UCLA's 98-game homecourt winning streak, which started in 1970, was snapped by Oregon, 65-45. Ducks guard Ron Lee became the only player in Pacific-8 Conference history to be named to the all-league first team four consecutive years.

Tennessee's Ernie Grunfeld (25.3) and Bernard King (25.2) became one of only four sets of teammates in NCAA history to each average more than 25 points per game in a single season. With King idled by a broken right thumb, half of the Bernie-Ernie show was on the sideline and Grunfeld's 36 points weren't enough to prevent an 81-75 defeat against VMI in the first round of the East Regional. The Volunteers defeated national runner-up Michigan early in the season.

North Texas State, which compiled a 6-20 record the previous season, improved by 16 games to 22-4.

Mike Krzyzewski began his distinguished coaching career with an inauspicious 11-14 record at Army.

1975–76 INDIVIDUAL LEADERS

SCORING

PLAYER	PTS.	AVG.
Rogers, Pan American	919	36.8
Williams, Portland St.	834	30.9
Furlow, Michigan St.	793	29.4
Dantley, Notre Dame	829	28.6
Carr, North Carolina St.	798	26.6
Dixon, Hardin-Simmons	707	26.2
Tripucka, Lafayette	679	26.1
Birdsong, Houston	730	26.1
Grunfeld, Tennessee	683	25.3
Smith, Missouri	783	25.3

REBOUNDING

PLAYER	REB.	AVG.
Parish, Centenary	486	18.0
Pellom, Buffalo	420	16.2
Barnett, Samford	354	15.4

Irving, Hofstra	423	14.6
Thomas, Connecticut	402	13.9
Rudd, McNeese St.	328	13.7
Webster, Indiana St.	339	13.6
Terrell, Southern Methodist	374	13.4
Stephens, Drexel	307	13.3
King, Tennessee	325	13.0
Kyle, Cleveland St.	325	13.0

Note: Parish's rebounding totals were discounted by the NCAA because Centenary was on probation.

FIELD GOAL PERCENTAGE

PLAYER	FGM	FGA	PCT.
Moncrief, Arkansas	149	224	.665
Brown, East Tenn. St.	181	274	.661
Thorpe, Virginia Tech	165	251	.657
Shute, Texas-Arlington	136	209	.651
Abrams, S. Illinois	145	224	.647

Cutter, W. Michigan	140	217	.645
Pierson, Georgia St.	187	291	.643
Davis, Florida St.	143	224	.638
Nordhorn, Stetson	146	234	.624
Hillard, Memphis St.	226	366	.617

FREE THROW PERCENTAGE

PLAYER	FTM	FTA	PCT.
Dufelmeier, Loyola (Ill.)	71	80	.888
O'Connell, Stetson	68	77	.883
Drake, Central Mich.	101	115	.878
Furlow, Michigan St.	177	202	.876
Rood, Hofstra	77	88	.875
Brown, Wake Forest	97	111	.874
Carter, Hawaii	117	136	.860
Macy, Purdue	85	99	.859
Rogers, Pan American	197	230	.857
Evans, Kansas St.	70	82	.854

1975–76 TEAM LEADERS

SCORING OFFENSE

SCHOOL	PTS.	AVG.
UNLV	3426	110.5
North Texas St.	2497	96.0
Pan American	2391	95.6
Rutgers	3079	93.3
Notre Dame	2579	88.9

SCORING DEFENSE

SCHOOL	PTS.	AVG.
Princeton	1427	52.9
Texas-El Paso	1480	56.9
Colgate	1390	57.9
Drexel	1364	59.3
Marquette	1742	60.1

SCORING MARGIN

SCHOOL	OFF.	DEF.	MAR.
UNLV	110.5	89.0	21.5
Indiana	82.1	64.8	17.3

Rutgers	93.3	76.9	16.4
UNC Charlotte	84.5	69.0	15.5
Pan American	95.6	80.7	14.9
Florida St.	83.9	69.0	14.9

WON-LOST PERCENTAGE

SCHOOL	W-L	PCT.
Indiana	32-0	1.000
Rutgers	31-2	.939
UNLV	29-2	.935
Marquette	27-2	.931
Western Michigan	25-3	.893

FIELD GOAL PERCENTAGE

SCHOOL	FGM	FGA	PCT.
Maryland	996	1854	.537
Arkansas	910	1715	.531
Oregon St.	839	1594	.526
North Carolina	966	1838	.526
Duke	968	1853	.522

FREE THROW PERCENTAGE

SCHOOL	FGM	FGA	PCT.
Morehead St.	452	577	.783
Bradley	443	572	.774
Central Michigan	328	425	.772
Ohio	412	534	.772
Michigan St.	443	576	.769

REBOUND MARGIN

SCHOOL	OWN	OPP.	MAR.
Notre Dame	46.3	34.1	12.2
Buffalo	51.5	39.7	11.8
Virginia Tech	45.6	35.3	10.3
Connecticut	43.0	32.8	10.2
UNC Charlotte	44.4	34.2	10.2

FINAL NATIONAL POLLS

1975–76

AP	UPI	SCHOOL
1	1	Indiana
2	2	Marquette
3	4	UNLV
4	3	Rutgers
5	5	UCLA
6	7	Alabama
7	8	Notre Dame
8	6	North Carolina
9	9	Michigan
10	19	Western Michigan
11	13	Maryland
12	16	Cincinnati
13	14	Tennessee
14	11	Missouri
15	12	Arizona
16	–	Texas Tech
17	–	DePaul
18	15	Virginia
19	–	Centenary
20	–	Pepperdine
–	10	Washington
–	16	Florida St.
–	18	St. John's
–	19	Princeton

1976 NCAA Tournament

Summary: Indiana's Scott May and Kent Benson combined for 40.8 points and 16.5 rebounds per game for the national champion Hoosiers. IU kept a perfect record intact despite trailing in the second half of three of their five tournament games, including Mideast Regional contests against Alabama and Marquette, accounting for two of the 11 contests they won

Indiana guard Quinn Buckner (left) jumps for the rebound as teammate Scott May looks on.

Rutgers' Phil Sellers hauls down a rebound.

by single-digit margins. The closest result was a two-point triumph at Ohio State in their Big Ten Conference opener. (Knight's alma mater finished in the Big Ten basement that season with a 2-16 league record.) Bob Wilkerson collected 19 rebounds and seven assists in a 65-51 victory over defending champion UCLA in the national semifinals before captain Quinn Buckner contributed 16 points and eight rebounds in the championship game against Michigan. Trailing by six points at intermission in the final and playing without Wilkerson after the guard sustained a concussion early in the game, the Hoosiers shot 60 percent from the floor in the second half to come from behind and win (86-68). May, Benson, and Buckner collaborated for 36 of Indiana's first 38 points in the second half against the Wolverines, an overtime loser at Indiana in Big Ten Conference competition.

Star Gazing: Rutgers, undefeated entering the tourney (28-0), lost in the national semifinals against Michigan (86-70) when the Scarlet Knights' top three scorers for the season—forward Phil Sellers and guards Mike Dabney and Eddie Jordan—combined to shoot 31.4 percent from the floor (16 of 51). John Robinson posted game highs of 20 points and 16 rebounds for the Wolverines.

Biggest Upset: UNLV, ranked third by AP and fourth by UPI entering the tourney, lost to Arizona, 114-109, in overtime in the West Regional semifinals.

One and Only: Buckner was the only one of the Hoosiers' starting quintet to finish his NBA career with a winning playoff record and play for a championship team (Boston Celtics in 1984).

1975-76 NCAA CHAMPION: INDIANA

SEASON STATISTICS OF INDIANA REGULARS

PLAYER	POS.	CL.	G.	FG%	FT%	PPG	RPG
Scott May	F	Sr.	32	.527	.782	23.5	7.7
Kent Benson	C	Jr.	32	.578	.684	17.3	8.8
Tom Abernethy	F	Sr.	32	.561	.743	10.0	5.3
Quinn Buckner	G	Sr.	32	.441	.488	8.9	2.8
Bobby Wilkerson	G-F	Sr.	32	.493	.630	7.8	4.9
Wayne Radford	G	So.	30	.563	.712	4.7	2.1
Jim Crews	G	Sr.	31	.468	.857	3.3	0.7
Jim Wisman	G	So.	26	.367	.724	2.5	0.8
Rich Valavicius	F	Fr.	28	.483	.625	2.4	1.8
TEAM TOTALS			32	.517	.698	82.1	41.4

Assists leader: Wilkerson 171. **Steals leader:** Buckner 65.

1976 FINAL FOUR CHAMPIONSHIP GAME

PHILADELPHIA, PA

MICHIGAN (68)	MIN.	FG-A	FT-A	REB.	A	PF	PTS.
Britt	31	5-6	1-1	3	2	5	11
Robinson	38	4-8	0-1	6	5	2	8
Hubbard	31	4-8	2-2	11	0	5	10
Green	39	7-16	4-5	6	2	3	18
Grote	35	4-9	4-6	1	3	4	12
Bergen	5	0-1	0-0	0	0	1	0
Staton	9	2-5	3-4	2	0	3	7
Baxter	6	0-2	0-0	0	0	2	0
Thompson	2	0-0	0-0	0	0	0	0
Hardy	4	1-2	0-0	2	0	0	2
Team				1			
TOTALS	200	27-57	14-19	32	12	25	68

FG%: .474. FT%: .737. Blocks: 3. Turnovers: 19 (Robinson 6). Steals: 9.

INDIANA (86)	MIN.	FG-A	FT-A	REB.	A	PF	PTS.
Abernethy	35	4-8	3-3	4	1	2	11
May	39	10-17	6-6	8	2	4	26
Benson	39	11-20	3-5	9	2	3	25
Wilkerson	2	0-1	0-0	0	0	1	0
Buckner	39	5-10	6-9	8	4	4	16
Radford	7	0-1	0-0	1	0	0	0
Crews	12	0-1	2-2	1	4	1	2
Wisman	21	0-1	2-3	1	6	4	2
Valavicius	4	1-1	0-0	0	0	0	2
Haymore	1	1-1	0-0	1	0	0	2
Bender	1	0-0	0-0	0	0	0	0
Team				3			
TOTALS	200	32-61	22-28	36	19	19	86

FG%: .525. FT%: .786. Blocks: 2. Turnovers: 13. Steals: 10 (Buckner 5).
Halftime: Michigan 35-29.

NATIONAL SEMIFINALS

MICHIGAN (86): Britt 5-9 1-1 11, Robinson 8-13 4-5 20, Hubbard 8-13 0-3 16, Green 7-16 2-2 16, Grote 4-13 6-6 14, Baxter 2-5 1-2 5, Staton 1-1 0-0 2, Bergen 0-0 0-0 0, Thompson 0-0 0-0 0, Schinnerer 0-0 0-0 0, Hardy 0-0 0-0 0, Jones 0-0 0-0 0, Lillard 0-0 0-0 0. Team 35-70 (.500) 16-21 (.762) 86.

RUTGERS (70): Sellers 5-13 1-3 11, Copeland 7-12 1-1 15, Bailey 1-3 4-6 6, Jordan 6-20 4-4 16, Dabney 5-17 0-1 10, Anderson 3-8 0-1 6, Conlin 2-2 0-0 4, Hefele 1-1 0-0 2. Team 30-76 (.395) 10-16 (.625) 70.

Halftime: Michigan 46-29.

UCLA (51): Washington 6-15 3-4 15, Johnson 6-10 0-1 12, Greenwood 2-5 1-2 5, Townsend 2-10 0-0 4, McCarter 2-9 0-0 4, Drollinger 0-3 2-2 2, Holland 0-2 0-0 0, Spillane 0-2 0-0 0, Smith 3-4 0-0 6, Hamilton 0-1 1-2 1, Vroman 0-0 0-0 0, Lippert 0-0 2-2 2, Olinde 0-0 0-0 0. Team 21-61 (.344) 9-13 (.692) 51.

INDIANA (65): Abernethy 7-8 0-1 14, May 5-16 4-6 14, Benson 6-15 4-6 16, Wilkerson 1-5 3-4 5, Buckner 6-14 0-1 12, Crews 1-1 2-3 4. Team 26-59 (.441) 13-21 (.619) 65.

Halftime: Indiana 34-26.

ALL-TOURNAMENT TEAM

Tom Abernethy, F, Sr., Indiana
Kent Benson, C, Jr., Indiana*
Rickey Green, G, Jr., Michigan
Marques Johnson, F, Jr., UCLA
Scott May, F, Sr., Indiana

   *Named Most Outstanding Player

Numbers Game: This year marked the last time more than half of a set of NCAA first-team All-Americans participated in the Final Four. The five-man All-American squad included Indiana's Benson and May and UCLA's Richard Washington.

What If: Eventual NBA first-round draft choices Leon Douglas and Reggie King combined to score an average of 31.5 points per game for Alabama in the 1975–76 season. If only this frontcourt duo combined for 22 points instead of 16 in the 1976 Mideast Regional semifinals, the Crimson Tide could have defeated unbeaten Indiana rather than lose 74-69. The Hoosiers were also fortunate when eventual NBA players Butch Lee, Lloyd Walton, and Jerome Whitehead struggled from the floor for Marquette in the Mideast Regional final. If only Lee, Walton, and Whitehead had combined to hit 35.1 percent of their field-goal attempts instead of 21.6 percent (8 of 37), the Warriors could have defeated Indiana rather than lose 65-56.

Putting Things in Perspective: North Carolina sophomore playmaker Phil Ford, a second-team consensus All-American, injured a knee in a pickup game after the ACC Tournament and was ineffective (two points, three assists, five turnovers) in the Tar Heels' 79-64 NCAA Tournament first-round defeat against Alabama.

1976 CHAMPIONSHIP BRACKET

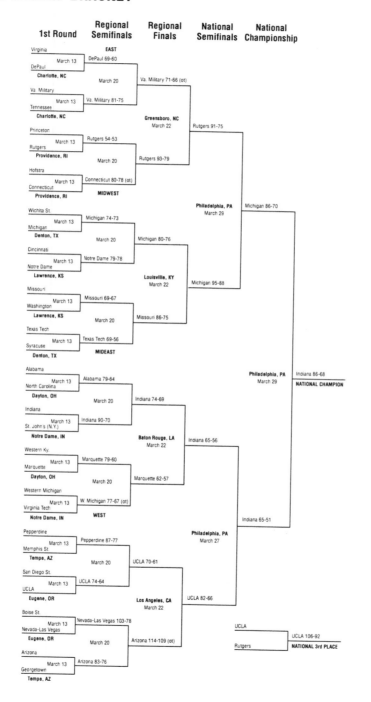

	Regional	Regional	National	National
1st Round	Semifinals	Finals	Semifinals	Championship

EAST

Virginia
DePaul 69-60
March 13
DePaul
Charlotte, NC
March 20
Va. Military 71-66 (ot)
Va. Military
March 13 Va. Military 81-75
Tennessee
Charlotte, NC
Greensboro, NC
March 22
Rutgers 91-75

Princeton
March 13 Rutgers 54-53
Rutgers
Providence, RI
March 20 Rutgers 93-79
Hofstra
March 13 Connecticut 80-78 (ot)
Connecticut
Providence, RI

MIDWEST

Wichita St.
March 13 Michigan 74-73
Michigan
Denton, TX
March 20 Michigan 80-76
Cincinnati
March 13 Notre Dame 79-78
Notre Dame
Lawrence, KS
Louisville, KY
March 22
Michigan 95-88

Missouri
March 13 Missouri 69-67
Washington
Lawrence, KS
March 20 Missouri 86-75
Texas Tech
March 13 Texas Tech 69-56
Syracuse
Denton, TX

Philadelphia, PA
March 29
Michigan 86-70

MIDEAST

Alabama
March 13 Alabama 79-64
North Carolina
Dayton, OH
March 20 Indiana 74-69
Indiana
March 13 Indiana 90-70
St. John's (N.Y.)
Notre Dame, IN
Baton Rouge, LA
March 22
Indiana 65-56

Western Ky.
March 13 Marquette 79-60
Marquette
Dayton, OH
March 20 Marquette 62-57
Western Michigan
March 13 W. Michigan 77-67 (ot)
Virginia Tech
Notre Dame, IN

Philadelphia, PA
March 29
Indiana 86-68
NATIONAL CHAMPION

WEST

Indiana 65-51

Pepperdine
March 13 Pepperdine 87-77
Memphis St.
Tempe, AZ
March 20 UCLA 70-61
San Diego St.
March 13 UCLA 74-64
UCLA
Eugene, OR
Los Angeles, CA
March 22
UCLA 82-66

Philadelphia, PA
March 27

Boise St.
March 13 Nevada-Las Vegas 103-78
Nevada-Las Vegas
Eugene, OR
March 20 Arizona 114-109 (ot)
Arizona
March 13 Arizona 83-76
Georgetown
Tempe, AZ

UCLA
UCLA 106-92
Rutgers
NATIONAL 3rd PLACE

1976-77

AT A GLANCE

NCAA Champion: Marquette (25-7).

NIT Champion: St. Bonaventure (24-6).

New Conference: ECBL (forerunner of Atlantic 10), New Jersey-New York 7 (disbanded three years later), Sun Belt.

New Rules: The dunk shot is allowed again. NIT implements format whereby early-round games are played at locations across the country before the four semifinalists advance to New York.

NCAA Probation: Canisius, Centenary, Clemson, Denver, Minnesota, Montana, Nevada, Southwestern Louisiana, West Texas State.

NCAA Consensus First-Team All-Americans: Kent Benson, C, Sr., Indiana; Otis Birdsong, G, Sr., Houston; Phil Ford, G, Jr., North Carolina; Rickey Green, G, Sr., Michigan; Marques Johnson, F, Sr., UCLA; Bernard King, F, Jr., Tennessee.

Tennessee forward Bernard King.

The first 38 NCAA national champions, from Oregon (29-5 record in 1938–39) through Indiana (the last unbeaten team with a 32-0 mark in 1975–76), averaged barely over two defeats per season. No titlist sustained more than six setbacks until Marquette won the title with a 25-7 worksheet. It was the final game in Al McGuire's coaching career, which included 20-win seasons each of his last 11 years. His average record in his last 10 years was 25-4.

In an amazing turnaround, New Mexico State trailed 28-0 before rallying to defeat Bradley, 117-109. It was the largest deficit before scoring for a team to overcome and still win a game.

Larry Bird, a transfer from Indiana, began to make a name for himself at Indiana State. He averaged 38.3 points per game in his last 15 outings to finish third in the nation in scoring. Oral Roberts' Anthony Roberts finished runner-up in scoring (34 ppg) by averaging 37.3 over the last half of the season, including outbursts of 66 points and 65 (NIT record against Oregon). Portland State's Freeman Williams averaged 40.7 from January 9 through the remainder of the season to lead the country with a 38.8 mark.

Williams poured in 71 points against Southern Oregon—the highest total by a major collegian in 23 years. He averaged 35.3 points on a trip to the South when his team ended New Orleans' 21-game homecourt winning streak, North Texas' 19-game home streak, and Pan American's 20-game home streak in a five-day stretch.

Toledo ended Indiana's 57-game regular-season winning streak, 59-57. Minnesota, compiling a 24-3 record while on NCAA probation, became the only college ever to have three teammates later average more than 20 points per game in any NBA season—Kevin McHale (12 ppg as a freshman), Mychal Thompson (22 ppg as a junior), and Ray Williams (18 ppg as a senior). Wisconsin's Bill Cofield became the first African-American head coach in the Big Ten.

1976–77 INDIVIDUAL LEADERS

SCORING

PLAYER	PTS.	AVG.
Williams, Portland St.	1010	38.8
Roberts, Oral Roberts	951	34.0
Bird, Indiana St.	918	32.8
Birdsong, Houston	1090	30.3
Laurel, Hofstra	908	30.3
Natt, NE Louisiana	782	29.0
McConathy, LSU	716	27.5
Phegley, Bradley	739	27.4
Reynolds, Northwestern (La.)	686	26.4
Hanson, Connecticut	702	26.0

REBOUNDING

PLAYER	REB.	AVG.
Mosley, Seton Hall	473	16.31
Irving, Hofstra	440	16.30
Elmore, Wichita St.	441	15.8

Stephens, Drexel	340	14.8
Landsberger, Arizona St.	359	14.4
King, Tennessee	371	14.3
Bird, Indiana St.	373	13.3
King, Iowa	332	13.3
Jones, Nevada-Reno	355	13.1
Hubbard, Michigan	389	13.0
Hicks, N. Illinois	350	13.0

FIELD GOAL PERCENTAGE

PLAYER	FGM	FGA	PCT.
Senser, W. Chester St.	130	186	.699
Montgomery, VMI	161	247	.652
Moncrief, Arkansas	157	242	.649
Maxwell, UNC Charlotte	244	381	.640
Sowinski, Princeton	163	258	.632
Natt, NE Louisiana	307	493	.623
Cooper, Providence	188	302	.623
Griffin, Wake Forest	198	319	.621

Miller, Cincinnati	180	291	.619
Brewer, Arkansas	199	326	.610
Brown, Iona	150	246	.610

FREE THROW PERCENTAGE

PLAYER	FTM	FTA	PCT.
Smith, UNLV	98	106	.925
Kelly, Vermont	71	77	.922
Thieneman, Va. Tech	98	107	.916
O'Brien, Seattle	89	99	.899
Fagan, Colgate	110	123	.894
DeSantis, Fairfield	116	130	.892
Jonas, Utah	118	133	.887
Mack, Brown	70	79	.886
Hamilton, Iona	68	77	.883
Perry, Holy Cross	156	177	.881
Yoder, Cincinnati	111	126	.881

1976–77 TEAM LEADERS

SCORING OFFENSE

SCHOOL	PTS.	AVG.
UNLV	3426	107.1
Houston	3482	94.1
San Francisco	2904	93.7
North Texas St.	2468	91.4
Detroit	2629	90.7

SCORING DEFENSE

SCHOOL	PTS.	AVG.
Princeton	1343	51.7
Marquette	1900	59.4
Toledo	1604	59.4
Arkansas	1701	60.8
Oregon	1766	60.9

SCORING MARGIN

SCHOOL	OFF.	DEF.	MAR.
UNLV	107.1	87.7	19.4
Clemson	86.6	68.9	17.7
Old Dominion	88.3	70.9	17.4
Detroit	90.7	73.9	16.8
Syracuse	86.9	70.2	16.7

WON-LOST PERCENTAGE

SCHOOL	W-L	PCT.
San Francisco	29-2	.935
Arkansas	26-2	.929
UNLV	29-3	.906
Indiana St.	25-3	.893
Minnesota	24-3	.889

FIELD GOAL PERCENTAGE

SCHOOL	FGM	FGA	PCT.
Arkansas	849	1558	.545
UNC-Wilmington	816	1500	.544
West Texas St.	885	1634	.542
Utah	936	1733	.540
North Carolina	1054	1961	.537

FIELD GOAL PERCENTAGE DEFENSE

SCHOOL	FGM	FGA	PCT.
Minnesota	766	1886	.406
Princeton	548	1336	.410
Oral Roberts	796	1922	.414
Kansas	727	1726	.421
Syracuse	830	1970	.421

FREE THROW PERCENTAGE

SCHOOL	FTM	FTA	PCT.
Utah	499	638	.782
Marquette	446	573	.778
Princeton	391	507	.771
UNLV	610	793	.769
Georgia Tech	434	565	.768

REBOUND MARGIN

SCHOOL	OWN	OPP.	MAR.
Notre Dame	42.4	31.6	10.8
Indiana St.	44.0	33.9	10.1
San Francisco	47.0	37.1	9.9
Arizona	46.7	37.0	9.7
Navy	41.0	32.3	8.7

Houston's Otis Birdsong set an SWC record by averaging 30.3 points per game. Arkansas guards Sidney Moncrief (64.9 percent) and Ron Brewer (61 percent) finished among the top 10 in field-goal shooting to help the Razorbacks lead the country in that category. The Hogs clinched the title by shooting 68 percent against Wake Forest in the NCAA Tournament.

UCLA's 115-game nonconference home-court winning streak was snapped by Notre Dame, 66-63.

San Francisco, undefeated until its final regular-season game at Notre Dame (93-82), was a first-round NCAA loser to UNLV.

Oregon's Greg Ballard set a school record with 43 points against Oral Roberts. It was his third 40-point outing in a month.

Long Beach State won its eighth straight Pacific Coast Athletic Association championship.

Ray Mears, who never had a losing record in his 21-year career at Wittenberg and Tennessee, left coaching with a 399-135 record.

AP	UPI	SCHOOL
1	1	Michigan
2	4	UCLA
3	5	Kentucky
4	6	UNLV
5	3	North Carolina
6	9	Syracuse
7	14	Marquette
8	2	San Francisco
9	–	Wake Forest
10	–	Notre Dame
11	18	Alabama
12	19	Detroit
13	17	Minnesota
14	10	Utah
15	8	Tennessee
16	11	Kansas St.
17	–	UNC Charlotte
18	7	Arkansas
19	13	Louisville
20	–	Va. Military
–	12	Cincinnati
–	15	Providence
–	16	Indiana St.
–	20	Purdue

Marquette's Bo Ellis was named to the 1977 All-Tournament Team.

1977 NCAA Tournament

Summary: Tears of joy flowed for coach Al McGuire when Marquette won the championship in his farewell. Marquette overcame halftime deficits to win its first three playoff games against Cincinnati, Kansas State, and Wake Forest before trailing most of the second half against UNC Charlotte in the national semifinals. Marquette had lost five home games, including its last three, to register the Warriors' worst record in 10 years. They lost those home games in Milwaukee Arena, where during one period McGuire's teams were 145-7, including an 81-game winning streak.

Outcome for Defending Champion: Indiana (14-13) finished fourth in the Big Ten although two defeats to Minnesota were later deemed forfeit victories.

Biggest Upset: Gene Bartow departed after only two seasons as John Wooden's successor following UCLA's 76-75 setback at Idaho State. The Bruins, ranked fourth by UPI entering the tourney, finished with a 24-5 record when guards Roy Hamilton and Brad Holland combined to hit just 8 of 24 field-goal attempts. Idaho State (25-5), prevailing despite shooting just 40.6 percent from the floor, received 27 points and 12 rebounds from Steve Hayes.

One and Only: Cedric "Cornbread" Maxwell is the only player to average more than 20 points and 10 rebounds for an NIT semifinalist one year and an NCAA semifinalist the next season. His coach, Lee Rose, became the only individual to coach teams in the NAIA Tournment, NCAA Division III Tournament, NCAA Division II Tournament, NIT, and NCAA Division I Tournament.... UNLV, which finished in third place, is the only Final Four team to have as many as six players compile a double-digit season scoring average—forwards Eddie Owens (21.8 points per game) and Sam Smith (14.8), guards Glen Gondrezick (14.6), Reggie Theus (14.5), and Robert Smith (12.8), and center Lewis Brown (10.2). The Rebels, averaging 107.1 points as a team on their way to a national third-place finish, also had two other players come close to a double-figure scoring average—guard Tony Smith (9 ppg) and center Larry Moffett (8). Tony Smith

1976–77 NCAA CHAMPION: MARQUETTE

SEASON STATISTICS OF MARQUETTE REGULARS

PLAYER	POS.	CL.	G.	FG%	FT%	PPG	RPG
Butch Lee	G	Jr.	32	.477	.872	19.6	3.8
Bo Ellis	F	Sr.	32	.507	.752	15.6	8.3
Jerome Whitehead	C	Jr.	32	.517	.581	10.5	8.2
Gary Rosenberger	G	Jr.	32	.471	.760	7.3	1.4
Jim Boylan	G	Jr.	32	.456	.922	7.0	2.8
Ulice Payne	F-G	Jr.	21	.488	.933	4.5	2.6
Bernard Toone	F-C	So.	32	.410	.711	4.4	2.2
Bill Neary	F	Sr.	32	.328	.769	1.7	2.8
Jim Dudley	F	So.	17	.417	.600	1.5	1.7
TEAM TOTALS			32	.472	.778	70.5	36.6

Assists leaders: Boylan 114, Lee 104.

1977 FINAL FOUR CHAMPIONSHIP GAME

ATLANTA, GA

N. CAROLINA (59)	MIN.	FG-A	FT-A	REB.	A	PF	PTS.
Davis	33	6-13	8-10	8	3	4	20
O'Koren	31	6-10	2-4	11	1	5	14
Yonakor	25	3-5	0-0	4	1	0	6
Ford	38	3-10	0-0	2	5	3	6
Kuester	31	2-6	1-2	0	6	5	5
Krafcisin	10	1-1	0-0	0	0	0	2
Zaliagiris	10	2-3	0-0	0	0	3	4
Bradley	5	1-1	0-0	0	0	2	2
Buckley	10	0-1	0-0	0	0	1	0
Wolf	3	0-1	0-0	1	0	0	0
Colescott	1	0-0	0-0	0	0	0	0
Coley	1	0-0	0-0	0	0	0	0
Doughton	1	0-0	0-0	0	0	0	0
Virgil	1	0-0	0-0	0	0	1	0
Team				2			
TOTALS	200	24-51	11-16	28	16	24	59

FG%: .471. FT%: .688. Blocks: 1. Turnovers: 14. Steals: 6.

MARQUETTE (67)	MIN.	FG-A	FT-A	REB.	A	PF	PTS.
Ellis	39	5-9	4-5	9	3	4	14
Neary	12	0-2	0-0	0	0	1	0
Whitehead	39	2-8	4-4	11	2	2	8
Lee	40	6-14	7-7	3	2	1	19
Boylan	33	5-7	4-4	4	0	3	14
Rosenberger	8	1-1	4-4	1	1	1	6
Toone	29	3-6	0-1	0	0	1	6
Team				1			
TOTALS	200	22-47	23-25	29	8	13	67

FG%: .468. FT%: .920. Blocks: 3. Turnovers: 11. Steals: 5.
Halftime: Marquette 39-27.

NATIONAL SEMIFINALS

NORTH CAROLINA (84): Davis 7-7 5-6 19, O'Koren 14-19 3-5 31, Yonakor 5-7 1-4 11, Ford 4-10 4-5 12, Kuester 2-5 5-7 9, Zaliagiris 0-1 0-0 0, Krafcisin 0-0 0-1 0, Buckley 1-5 0-0 2, Bradley 0-1 0-0 0, Wolf 0-1 0-0 0, Colescott 0-0 0-0 0. Team 33-56 (.589) 18-28 (.643) 84.

UNLV (83): Owens 7-15 0-0 14, Gondrezick 4-8 0-0 8, Moffett 6-9 1-2 13, R. Smith 4-11 0-1 8, S. Smith 10-18 0-0 20, T. Smith 6-8 0-2 12, Theus 4-11 0-0 8, Brown 0-0 0-0 0. Team 41-80 (.513) 1-5 (.200) 83.

Halftime: UNLV 49-43.

UNC CHARLOTTE (49): Massey 7-13 0-0 14, King 2-7 0-0 4, Maxwell 5-6 7-9 17, Kinch 1-7 2-2 4, Watkins 2-4 2-3 6, Gruber 2-6 0-0 4, Scott 0-0 0-0 0. Team 19-43 (.442) 11-14 (.788) 49.

MARQUETTE (51): Ellis 2-8 0-0 4, Neary 0-1 0-0 0, Whitehead 10-16 1-2 21, Lee 5-18 1-1 11, Boylan 4-9 0-0 8, Toone 2-6 2-2 6, Rosenberger 0-0 1-2 1. Team 23-58 (.397) 5-7 (.714) 51.

Halftime: Marquette 25-22.

ALL-TOURNAMENT TEAM

Walter Davis, F, Sr., North Carolina
Bo Ellis, F, Sr., Marquette
Butch Lee, G, Jr., Marquette*
Cedric Maxwell, C, Sr., UNC Charlotte
Jerome Whitehead, C, Jr., Marquette

*Named Most Outstanding Player

was the only one of the eight players in UNLV's regular rotation to never appear in an NBA game.

Numbers Game: Mike O'Koren became the only freshman to score more than 30 points in a national semifinal or championship game. The North Carolina forward scored 31 in an 84-83 victory over UNLV in the national semifinals.

What If: Guards Phil Ford and John Kuester combined to score 28.4 points per game on 52.7 percent field-goal shooting for North Carolina in the 1976–77 season. If only they combined for 20 points instead of 11 points on 5 of 16 field-goal shooting (31.3 percent) in the championship game, the Tar Heels could have defeated Marquette rather than lose 67-59.… Big Ten runner-up Minnesota, which defeated national champion Marquette on the Warriors' home court, was ineligible for the NCAA Tournament because of an NCAA probation.… Louisville was flying high with a 19-3 record before forward Larry Williams broke his foot against Tulsa in mid-February. The Cardinals went 2-4 to close out the season, erasing memories of an early-season victory at Marquette.

Putting Things in Perspective: North Carolina senior center Tommy LaGarde was averaging 15.1 points and 7.4 rebounds per game when he injured a knee at midseason and was lost for the remainder of the year. Teammate Phil Ford, a first-team consensus All-American and Carolina's leading scorer, hyperextended his shooting elbow in the East Regional semifinals and scored just 20 points in the last three playoff games, including six points against Marquette.

Marquette coach Al McGuire went out a winner as the Warriors won the NCAA Championship in his last game.

1977 CHAMPIONSHIP BRACKET

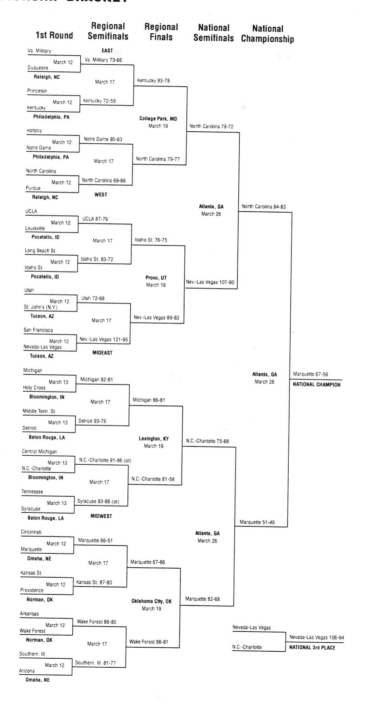

1st Round	Regional Semifinals	Regional Finals	National Semifinals	National Championship

EAST

Va. Military
March 12 — Va. Military 73-66
Duquesne
Raleigh, NC
March 17 — Kentucky 93-78
Princeton
March 12 — Kentucky 72-58
Kentucky
Philadelphia, PA
College Park, MD
March 19
North Carolina 79-72
Hofstra
March 12 — Notre Dame 90-83
Notre Dame
Philadelphia, PA
March 17 — North Carolina 79-77
North Carolina
March 12 — North Carolina 69-66
Purdue
Raleigh, NC

WEST

UCLA
March 12 — UCLA 87-79
Louisville
Pocatello, ID
March 17 — Idaho St. 76-75
Long Beach St.
March 12 — Idaho St. 83-72
Idaho St.
Pocatello, ID
Provo, UT
March 19
Nev.-Las Vegas 107-90
Utah
March 12 — Utah 72-68
St. John's (N.Y.)
Tucson, AZ
March 17 — Nev.-Las Vegas 88-83
San Francisco
March 12 — Nev.-Las Vegas 121-95
Nevada-Las Vegas
Tucson, AZ

Atlanta, GA
March 26
North Carolina 84-83

MIDEAST

Michigan
March 13 — Michigan 92-81
Holy Cross
Bloomington, IN
March 17 — Michigan 86-81
Middle Tenn. St.
March 13 — Detroit 93-76
Detroit
Baton Rouge, LA
Lexington, KY
March 19
N.C.-Charlotte 75-68
Central Michigan
March 13 — N.C.-Charlotte 91-86 (ot)
N.C.-Charlotte
Bloomington, IN
March 17 — N.C.-Charlotte 81-59
Tennessee
March 13 — Syracuse 93-88 (ot)
Syracuse
Baton Rouge, LA

MIDWEST

Cincinnati
March 12 — Marquette 66-51
Marquette
Omaha, NE
March 17 — Marquette 67-66
Kansas St.
March 12 — Kansas St. 87-80
Providence
Norman, OK
Oklahoma City, OK
March 19
Marquette 82-68
Arkansas
March 12 — Wake Forest 86-80
Wake Forest
Norman, OK
March 17 — Wake Forest 86-81
Southern, Ill.
March 12 — Southern. Ill. 81-77
Arizona
Omaha, NE

Atlanta, GA
March 26
Marquette 51-49

Atlanta, GA
March 28
Marquette 67-59
NATIONAL CHAMPION

Nevada-Las Vegas
Nevada-Las Vegas 106-94
N.C.-Charlotte
NATIONAL 3rd PLACE

1977-78

AT A GLANCE

NCAA Champion: Kentucky (30-2).

NIT Champion: Texas (26-5).

New Rule: A seeding process is used in the NCAA Tournament for the first time. A maximum of four automatically-qualifying conference teams are seeded in each of the four regional brackets. These teams are seeded based on their respective conferences' won-lost records in tournament play the previous five years. At-large seeding in each region is based on won-lost records, strength of schedule, and eligibility status of student-athletes for postseason competition.

NCAA Probation: Centenary, Clemson, Hawaii, Idaho, Minnesota, UNLV, Western Carolina.

NCAA Consensus First-Team All-Americans: Larry Bird, F, Jr., Indiana State; Phil Ford, G, Sr., North Carolina; David Greenwood, F, Jr., UCLA; Butch Lee, G, Sr., Marquette; Mychal Thompson, C, Sr., Minnesota.

Evansville's initial year at the Division I level ended in tragedy when coach Bobby Watson and his Purple Aces squad perished in a plane crash just after taking off en route to their fifth game of the season.

North Carolina set an NCAA record for highest field-goal percentage in a half by hitting 16 of 17 shots (94.1 percent) after intermission against Virginia. Duke, after finishing sixth or seventh in the ACC standings the previous four years, improved to second place on its way to the Final Four.

North Carolina A&T, which compiled a 3-24 record the previous season, improved by 16½ games to 20-8.

UNLV's 72-game homecourt winning streak, which started in 1974, was snapped by New Mexico, 89-76.

Portland State guard Freeman Williams became the first major collegian to average more than 30 points per game in his career while playing four seasons in Division I. He scored 81 points as a senior against Rocky Mountain.

West Chester State's Joe Senser, the country's No. 3 pass receiver in Division II football the previous fall, led the nation in field-goal accuracy for the second consecutive year.

Minnesota's Mychal Thompson led the Big Ten Conference in scoring and rebounding, but finished his career as the last NCAA consensus first-team All-American to never participate in the NCAA Tournament.

All five LSU starters fouled out, but the Tigers defeated NCAA champion-to-be Kentucky, 95-94, in overtime.

Purdue's Fred Schaus, who previously coached West Virginia, chose to enter athletic administration, ending his 12-year coaching career with a 251-96 record.

1977-78 FINAL NATIONAL POLLS

AP	UPI	SCHOOL
1	1	Kentucky
2	2	UCLA
3	7	DePaul
4	5	Michigan St.
5	6	Arkansas
6	11	Notre Dame
7	9	Duke
8	3	Marquette
9	14	Louisville
10	8	Kansas
11	13	San Francisco
12	4	New Mexico
13	15	Indiana
14	18	Utah
15	12	Florida St.
16	10	North Carolina
17	19	Texas
18	–	Detroit
19	–	Miami (Ohio)
20	–	Pennsylvania
–	16	Houston
–	17	Utah St.
–	20	Georgetown

1978 NCAA Tournament

Summary: Jack Givens sank 18 of 27 field-goal attempts against Duke's zone defense and scored Kentucky's last 16 points of the first half en route to a 41-point performance in a 94-88 triumph in the final.

Outcome for Defending Champion: Marquette (24-4), making its eighth of 10 consecutive tournament appearances, wasted a five-point, halftime lead and lost in the first round of the

1977–78 INDIVIDUAL LEADERS

SCORING

PLAYER	PTS.	AVG.
Williams, Portland St.	969	35.9
Bird, Indiana St.	959	30.0
Short, Jackson St.	650	29.5
Mack, East Carolina	699	28.0
Phegley, Bradley	663	27.6
Sanders, Southern (La.)	740	27.4
Carter, VMI	736	26.3
Gerdy, Davidson	670	25.8
Brooks, La Salle	696	24.9
Mitchell, Auburn	671	24.9

REBOUNDING

PLAYER	REB.	AVG.
Williams, N. Texas St.	411	14.7
Taylor, Pan American	368	14.2
Uthoff, Iowa St.	378	14.0
King, Alabama	359	13.3
Natt, NE Louisiana	356	13.2
Searcy, Appalachian St.	359	12.8
Brooks, La Salle	358	12.8
Ruland, Iona	332	12.8
Cooper, New Orleans	343	12.7
Knight, Loyola (Ill.)	343	12.7

FIELD GOAL PERCENTAGE

PLAYER	FGM	FGA	PCT.
Senser, W. Chester St.	135	197	.685
O'Koren, N. Carolina	173	269	.643
Cummings, Cincinnati	212	330	.642
Robey, Kentucky	167	263	.635
Daniels, Stetson	180	284	.634
Young, Fairfield	149	237	.629
Fields, UNC-Wilmington	240	382	.628
Haymore, Mass.	162	259	.625
Macklin, LSU	217	349	.622
Ness, Lafayette	227	368	.617

FREE THROW PERCENTAGE

PLAYER	FTM	FTA	PCT.
Gibson, Marshall	84	89	.944
Tucker, Oklahoma St.	114	125	.912
Williams, J'ville	70	77	.909
Appel, Hofstra	67	74	.905
Perry, Holy Cross	181	201	.900
Macy, Kentucky	115	129	.891
Krivacs, Texas	123	138	.891
Miller, Penn St.	73	82	.890
Stamper, Morehead St.	121	136	.890
Hudson, N. Arizona	92	104	.885

1977–78 TEAM LEADERS

SCORING OFFENSE

SCHOOL	PTS.	AVG.
New Mexico	2731	97.5
Pan American	2487	95.7
Southern (La.)	2653	94.8
Detroit	2730	94.1
Houston	3015	91.4

SCORING DEFENSE

SCHOOL	PTS.	AVG.
Fresno St.	1417	52.5
Princeton	1431	55.0
Marquette	1722	61.5
Arkansas	2218	61.6
Middle Tennessee	1623	62.4

SCORING MARGIN

SCHOOL	OFF.	DEF.	MAR.
UCLA	85.3	67.4	17.9
Detroit	94.1	77.2	16.9
Syracuse	87.8	71.6	16.2
Kansas	81.6	66.4	15.2
Pan American	95.7	80.7	15.0

WON-LOST PERCENTAGE

SCHOOL	W-L	PCT.
Kentucky	30-2	.938
DePaul	27-3	.900
UCLA	25-3	.893
Arkansas	32-4	.889
Detroit	25-4	.862

FIELD GOAL PERCENTAGE

SCHOOL	FGM	FGA	PCT.
Arkansas	1060	1943	.546
Southern (La.)	1107	2031	.545
Kentucky	1040	1922	.541
UNC-Wilmington	809	1499	.540
San Francisco	1020	1907	.535

FIELD GOAL PERCENTAGE DEFENSE

SCHOOL	FGM	FGA	PCT.
Delaware St.	733	1802	.407
Kansas	705	1729	.408
Utah St.	803	1915	.419
Air Force	637	1516	.420
Indiana	723	1720	.420

FREE THROW PERCENTAGE

SCHOOL	FTM	FTA	PCT.
Duke	665	841	.791
Furman	557	721	.773
St. Bonaventure	454	590	.769
Bradley	470	615	.764
Morehead St.	363	475	.764

REBOUND MARGIN

SCHOOL	OWN	OPP.	MAR.
Alcorn St.	52.3	36.0	16.3
Southern (La.)	43.1	31.4	11.7
South Carolina St.	49.1	38.4	10.7
South Alabama	40.0	31.1	8.9
Louisiana St.	46.2	37.5	8.7
Pan American	46.0	37.3	8.7

Mideast Regional against Miami of Ohio (84-81 in overtime). Current Ohio State coach Randy Ayers collected 20 points and 10 rebounds for the Redskins to help offset national player of the year Butch Lee's 27 points for Marquette.

Star Gazing: DePaul's Dave Corzine scored a tourney-high 46 points vs. Louisville.

Biggest Upset: Cal State Fullerton (23-9) had four players score from 18 to 23 points and made 62.1 percent of its field-goal attempts to erase a six-point, halftime deficit and upend fourth-ranked New Mexico, 90-85. Future Los Angeles Laker standout Michael Cooper had an off-game for the Lobos (24-4), sinking just six of 15 field-goal attempts. In the second round, Cal State Fullerton overcame a 12-point deficit at intermission to notch a 75-72 triumph over San Francisco (ranked 11th by AP and 13th by UPI). Incredibly, the Titans almost erased a 15-point, halftime deficit in the regional final before losing, 61-58, against Arkansas (ranked 5th by AP and 6th by UPI). Fullerton fell short because of 40.3 percent field-goal shooting compared to 61.7 percent for the Razorbacks.

One and Only: Guard Bob Bender, a member of Indiana's 1976 unbeaten NCAA champion

Marquette All-American guard Butch Lee works his way through the defense.

1977–78 NCAA CHAMPION: KENTUCKY

SEASON STATISTICS OF KENTUCKY REGULARS

PLAYER	POS.	CL.	G.	FG%	FT%	PPG	RPG
Jack Givens	F	Sr.	32	.553	.761	18.1	6.8
Rick Robey	F-C	Sr.	32	.635	.720	14.4	8.2
Kyle Macy	G	So.	32	.536	.891	12.5	2.4
James Lee	F	Sr.	32	.569	.743	10.9	5.2
Mike Phillips	C	Sr.	31	.595	.759	10.2	4.7
Truman Claytor	G	Jr.	32	.466	.774	6.9	0.9
Jay Shidler	G	So.	29	.412	.852	3.7	0.8
Chuck Aleksinas	C	Fr.	27	.569	.694	3.7	2.2
LaVon Williams	F	So.	31	.375	.607	1.9	2.0
Fred Cowan	F	Fr.	19	.500	.667	1.9	0.9
Dwane Casey	G	Jr.	26	.382	.600	1.2	0.7
Tim Stephens	G	So.	19	.333	.857	1.2	0.6
TEAM TOTALS			32	.541	.759	84.2	36.6

Assists leader: Macy 178.

1978 FINAL FOUR CHAMPIONSHIP GAME

ST. LOUIS, MO

DUKE (88)	MIN.	FG-A	FT-A	REB.	A	PF	PTS.
Banks	37	6-12	10-12	8	2	2	22
Dennard	31	5-7	0-0	8	2	5	10
Gminski	37	6-16	8-8	12	2	3	20
Harrell	24	2-2	0-0	0	1	3	4
Spanarkel	40	8-16	5-6	2	3	4	21
Suddath	9	1-3	2-3	2	0	1	4
Bender	16	1-2	5-5	1	4	3	7
Goetsch	6	0-1	0-0	1	0	1	0
Team				1			
TOTALS	200	29-59	30-34	35	14	22	88

FG%: .492. FT%: .882. Blocks: 1. Turnovers: 17. Steals: 6.

KENTUCKY (94)	MIN.	FG-A	FT-A	REB.	A	PF	PTS.
Givens	37	18-27	5-8	8	3	4	41
Robey	32	8-11	4-6	11	0	2	20
Phillips	11	1-4	2-2	2	1	5	4
Macy	38	3-3	3-4	0	8	1	9
Claytor	24	3-5	2-4	0	3	2	8
Lee	20	4-8	0-0	4	2	4	8
Shidler	15	1-5	0-1	1	3	3	2

Aleksinas	1	0-0	0-0	0	0	1	0
Williams	11	1-3	0-0	4	0	2	2
Cowan	8	0-2	0-0	2	0	1	0
Stephens	1	0-0	0-0	0	0	0	0
Courts	1	0-0	0-0	0	0	0	0
Gettelfinger	1	0-0	0-0	0	0	0	0
Casey	0	0-0	0-0	0	0	1	0
TOTALS	200	39-68	16-25	32	20	26	94

FG%: .574. FT%: .573. Blocks: 1. Turnovers: 14. Steals: 9.
Halftime: Kentucky 45-38.

NATIONAL SEMIFINALS

ARKANSAS (59): Counce 2-2 2-3 6, Delph 5-13 5-6 15, Schall 3-5 0-0 6, Brewer 5-12 6-8 16, Moncrief 5-11 3-7 13, Zahn 1-1 1-2 3, Reed 0-0 0-0 0. Team 21-44 (.477) 17-26 (.654) 59.

KENTUCKY (64): Givens 10-16 3-4 23, Robey 3-6 2-2 8, Phillips 1-6 3-4 5, Macy 2-8 3-4 7, Claytor 1-2 0-1 2, Shidler 3-5 0-0 6, Lee 4-8 5-5 13, Casey 0-0 0-0 0, Stephens 0-0 0-0 0, Cowan 0-0 0-0 0, Williams 0-0 0-0 0. Team 24-51 (.471) 16-20 (.800) 64.

Halftime: Kentucky 32-30.

DUKE (90): Banks 8-15 6-7 22, Dennard 2-3 3-5 7, Gminski 13-17 3-4 29, Harrell 0-2 6-6 6, Spanarkel 4-11 12-12 20, Bender 0-1 2-3 2, Goetsch 1-1 0-0 2, Suddath 1-3 0-0 2. Team 29-53 (.547) 32-37 (.865) 90.

NOTRE DAME (86): Tripucka 5-17 2-2 12, Batton 3-6 4-4 10, Flowers 5-8 0-0 10, Branning 4-10 0-0 8, Williams 8-15 0-1 16, Laimbeer 1-5 5-6 7, Hanzlik 3-8 2-2 8, Jackson 5-6 1-2 11, Wilcox 2-2 0-0 4. Team 36-77 (.468) 14-17 (.824) 86.

Halftime: Duke 43-29.

ALL-TOURNAMENT TEAM

Ron Brewer, G, Sr., Arkansas
Jack Givens, F, Sr., Kentucky*
Mike Gminski, C, Soph., Duke
Rick Robey, F-C, Sr., Kentucky
Jim Spanarkel, G, Jr., Duke

*Named Most Outstanding Player

before transferring to Duke, became the only player in NCAA Tournament history to play for two different teams in the championship game.

Numbers Game: None of the five NCAA consensus first-team All-Americans advanced to a regional final, let alone the Final Four.

What If: Arkansas' acclaimed trio—guards Ron Brewer and Sidney Moncrief and forward Marvin Delph—combined to shoot 55.7 percent from the floor in the 1977–78 season. If only they combined to hit half of their field-goal attempts instead of 41.7 percent (15 of 36) in the national semifinals, the Razorbacks could have defeated eventual champion Kentucky rather than lose 64-59. The Wildcats were fortunate to overcome a five-point halftime deficit in their previous game, a 52-49 victory against Michigan State in the Mideast Regional final. Spartans freshman sensation Earvin "Magic" Johnson hit just two of 10 field-goal attempts and committed six turnovers. Johnson shot a lowly 27.8 percent from the floor (10 of 36) in three tourney games.

1978 CHAMPIONSHIP BRACKET

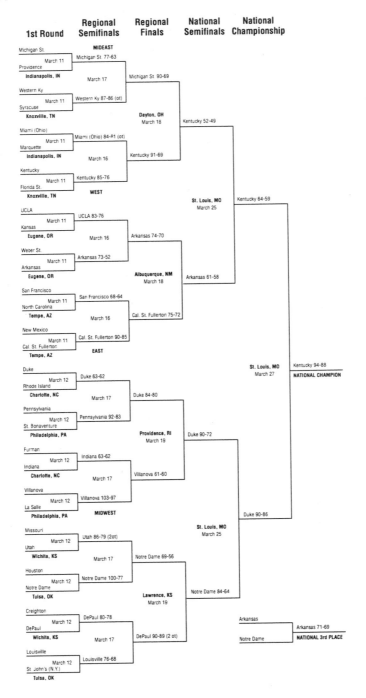

1st Round	Regional Semifinals	Regional Finals	National Semifinals	National Championship

MIDEAST

Michigan St.
March 11
Providence
Indianapolis, IN

Michigan St. 77-63
March 17

Michigan St. 90-69

Western Ky.
March 11
Syracuse
Knoxville, TN

Western Ky 87-86 (ot)

Dayton, OH
March 18

Kentucky 52-49

Miami (Ohio)
March 11
Marquette
Indianapolis, IN

Miami (Ohio) 84-81 (ot)
March 16

Kentucky 91-69

Kentucky
March 11
Florida St.
Knoxville, TN

Kentucky 85-76

WEST

Kentucky 64-59

UCLA
March 11
Kansas
Eugene, OR

UCLA 83-76
March 16

Arkansas 74-70

Weber St.
March 11
Arkansas
Eugene, OR

Arkansas 73-52

Albuquerque, NM
March 18

Arkansas 61-58

San Francisco
March 11
North Carolina
Tempe, AZ

San Francisco 68-64
March 16

Cal. St. Fullerton 75-72

New Mexico
March 11
Cal. St. Fullerton
Tempe, AZ

Cal. St. Fullerton 90-85

EAST

St. Louis, MO
March 25

Kentucky 94-88
NATIONAL CHAMPION

Duke
March 12
Rhode Island
Charlotte, NC

Duke 63-62
March 17

Duke 84-80

Pennsylvania
March 12
St. Bonaventure
Philadelphia, PA

Pennsylvania 92-83

Providence, RI
March 19

Duke 90-72

Furman
March 12
Indiana
Charlotte, NC

Indiana 63-62
March 17

Villanova 61-60

Villanova
March 12
La Salle
Philadelphia, PA

Villanova 103-97

MIDWEST

Duke 90-86

Missouri
March 12
Utah
Wichita, KS

Utah 86-79 (2ot)
March 17

Notre Dame 69-56

Houston
March 12
Notre Dame
Tulsa, OK

Notre Dame 100-77

Lawrence, KS
March 19

Notre Dame 84-64

Creighton
March 12
DePaul
Wichita, KS

DePaul 80-78
March 17

DePaul 90-89 (2 ot)

Louisville
March 12
St. John's (N.Y.)
Tulsa, OK

Louisville 76-68

St. Louis, MO
March 25

St. Louis, MO
March 27

Arkansas

Arkansas 71-69
NATIONAL 3rd PLACE

Notre Dame

1978–79

AT A GLANCE

NCAA Champion: Michigan State (26-6).

NIT Champion: Indiana (22-12).

New Rules: The NCAA Tournament bracket expands from 32 teams to 40 and each entrant is seeded for the first time. Three-man officiating crews are assigned to all tournament games. NIT field expands from 16 teams to 24.

NCAA Probation: Cincinnati, Grambling, Hawaii, UNLV.

NCAA Consensus First-Team All-Americans: Larry Bird, F-C, Sr., Indiana State; Mike Gminski, C, Jr., Duke; David Greenwood, F, Sr., UCLA; Earvin "Magic" Johnson, G, Soph., Michigan State; Sidney Moncrief, G-F, Sr., Arkansas.

Michigan State superstar Earvin "Magic" Johnson.

A ballyhooed matchup between Indiana State's Larry Bird and Michigan State's Magic Johnson aroused fans and generated the largest basketball game rating (24.1) and share (38) in television history. (A share is the percentage of televisions in use at the time.)

Bird was the favorite to lead the nation in scoring until he was limited to four points in a mid-February game against Bradley while Idaho State's Lawrence Butler grabbed the lead with a total of 80 points in two contests. Bird wasn't able to regain the lead despite pouring in a school-record 49 points against Wichita State.

American's Ray Voelkel set an NCAA record for most consecutive successful field goals with 25, covering a nine-game span.

North Texas State's Jon Manning tossed in 41 points against Baylor to become the only player to score 40 or more in a single game for two different schools against Division I opponents. Manning had scored 43 points in January, 1975, as a freshman for Oklahoma City against Tulsa.

UCLA set an NCAA record with its 13th consecutive regular-season conference championship (Pacific-8/Pacific-10). Arizona's Russell Brown set a Pacific-10 Conference record with 19 assists against Grand Canyon.

Denver's Matt Teahan scored the most points in a single game with 61 against Nebraska Wesleyan. Other players who set school single-game scoring records were James Madison's

Steve Stiepler (51 points against Robert Morris), Baylor's Vinnie Johnson (50 against TCU), and Maryland's Ernest Graham (44 against North Carolina State).

South Alabama went undefeated in Sun Belt Conference competition after compiling a 3-7 league mark the previous year.

UNLV led the nation in scoring for the third time in four seasons.

1978–79 FINAL NATIONAL POLLS

AP	UPI	SCHOOL
1	1	Indiana St.
2	2	UCLA
3	4	Michigan St.
4	5	Notre Dame
5	6	Arkansas
6	8	DePaul
7	9	Louisiana St.
8	10	Syracuse
9	3	North Carolina
10	13	Marquette
11	7	Duke
12	17	San Francisco
13	19	Louisville
14	–	Pennsylvania
15	14	Purdue
16	–	Oklahoma
17	–	St. John's
18	–	Rutgers
19	–	Toledo
20	11	Iowa
–	12	Georgetown
–	15	Texas
–	16	Temple
–	18	Tennessee
–	20	Detroit

1979 NCAA Tournament

Summary: Indiana State, undefeated entering the tourney (29-0), lost the national final against Michigan State (75-64) when the Sycamores' Larry Bird, who hit 53.2 percent of his field-goal attempts during the season, made just one-third of his shots from the floor (7 of 21). Magic Johnson scored a game-high 24 points for the Spartans. Michigan State dominated the 1979 NCAA Tournament, handing each one of its five playoff opponents, a quintet averaging 25.6 victories, its worst defeat of the year—Lamar (31-point margin), LSU (16), Notre Dame (12), Penn (34), and Indiana State (11). Consequently, most observers don't remember the glaring defect of

Michigan State forward Greg Kelser scores on a slam.

the Spartans earlier that season when they were defeated by four Big Ten Conference second-division teams. Michigan State required two overtime victories at home to avoid compiling six Big Ten losses in a seven-game span. The Spartans' five Big Ten defeats included an 18-point setback against conference cellar dweller Northwestern, which has 25 consecutive losing league records and finished in the Big Ten basement 12 times in one 16-year stretch.

Outcome for Defending Champion: Kentucky (19-12) incurred its lowest SEC finish (6th) to that point before losing at home in the first round of the NIT.

Star Gazing: Johnson became the only individual to be named Final Four Most Outstanding Player (Michigan State '79) and NBA Finals Most Valuable Player (Los Angeles Lakers '80) in back-to-back seasons.

1978–79 INDIVIDUAL LEADERS

SCORING

PLAYER	PTS.	AVG.
Butler, Idaho St.	812	30.1
Bird, Indiana St.	973	28.6
Galis, Seton Hall	743	27.5
Tillman, E. Kentucky	780	26.9
Dawkins, N. Illinois	695	26.7
Gerdy, Davidson	721	26.7
Hill, Oklahoma City	771	26.6
Stroud, Mississippi	709	26.3
Manning, N. Texas St.	699	25.9
Stielper, James Madison	668	25.7

REBOUNDING

PLAYER	REB.	AVG.
Davis, Tennessee St.	421	16.2
Cartwright, San Francisco	455	15.7
Garrett, Southern (La.)	433	15.5

Bird, Indiana St.	505	14.9
Knight, Loyola (Ill.)	386	14.3
Smith, Alcorn St.	398	13.7
Brooks, La Salle	347	13.3
Stephens, Drexel	360	13.3
Lawrence, McNeese St.	343	12.7

FIELD GOAL PERCENTAGE

PLAYER	FGM	FGA	PCT.
Brown, Florida St.	237	343	.691
Ruland, Iona	233	347	.671
Johnson, Oregon St.	197	298	.661
Green, Tenn. St.	120	183	.656
Peck, Miss. St.	154	239	.644
Mercer, Georgia	146	227	.643
Spain, Pan American	145	227	.639
Lawrence, McNeese St.	226	356	.635
Bouie, Syracuse	176	279	.631

FREE THROW PERCENTAGE

PLAYER	FTM	FTA	PCT.
Mauldin, Campbell	70	76	.921
Kanaskie, La Salle	55	60	.917
Krivacs, Texas	101	111	.910
Orner, Butler	70	77	.909
Perry, Holy Cross	178	196	.908
Goetz, San Diego St.	74	82	.902
Sienkiewicz, Villanova	78	87	.897
White, Marshall	85	95	.895
Huggins, S. Illinois	76	85	.894
Marifke, Northwestern	63	71	.887

1978–79 TEAM LEADERS

SCORING OFFENSE

SCHOOL	PTS.	AVG.
UNLV	2700	93.1
Alcorn St.	2678	92.3
Wichita St.	2485	88.8
Syracuse	2660	88.7
New Mexico	2567	88.5

SCORING DEFENSE

SCHOOL	PTS.	AVG.
Princeton	1452	55.8
Dartmouth	1486	57.2
Fresno St.	1632	58.3
Montana	1628	60.3
Indiana	2080	61.2
Marquette	1775	61.2

SCORING MARGIN

SCHOOL	OFF.	DEF.	MAR.
Syracuse	88.7	71.5	17.2
Notre Dame	79.7	64.1	15.6
Indiana St.	86.8	72.8	14.0
Alcorn St.	92.3	78.9	13.4
Michigan St.	75.7	62.6	13.1

WON-LOST PERCENTAGE

SCHOOL	W-L	PCT.
Indiana St.	33-1	.971
Alcorn St.	28-1	.966
Syracuse	26-4	.867
Temple	25-4	.862
Arkansas	25-5	.833
UCLA	25-5	.833

FIELD GOAL PERCENTAGE

SCHOOL	FGM	FGA	PCT.
UCLA	1053	1897	.555
Fairfield	792	1468	.540
Arkansas	849	1587	.535
The Citadel	864	1616	.535
Syracuse	1052	1970	.534

FIELD GOAL PERCENTAGE DEFENSE

SCHOOL	FGM	FGA	PCT.
Illinois	738	1828	.404
Tennessee St.	717	1707	.420
Wyoming	667	1582	.422
Indiana	847	2008	.422
Princeton	548	1287	.426

FREE THROW PERCENTAGE

SCHOOL	FTM	FTA	PCT.
St. Francis (Pa.)	350	446	.785
Kentucky	666	858	.776
Fairfield	513	666	.770
Villanova	394	514	.767
DePaul	517	676	.765

REBOUND MARGIN

SCHOOL	OWN	OPP.	MAR.
Alcorn St.	50.1	36.3	13.8
Tennessee St.	49.7	37.9	11.8
Pittsburgh	41.3	30.6	10.7
Indiana St.	48.2	38.1	10.1
Syracuse	44.1	34.8	9.3

Biggest Upset: East Regional No. 1 seed North Carolina lost its opener (72-71 against Penn) in the Tar Heels' home state (Raleigh, N.C.).

One and Only: Indiana State is the only school to reach the Final Four in its one and only NCAA Tournament appearance.... Bill Hodges of Indiana State is the only individual to win more than 30 games in earning a trip to the national semifinals in his first season as a head coach. Hodges was named interim coach when Bob King was forced to retire after suffering a stroke in the preseason. The Sycamores, who moved up to Division I status in 1972, haven't compiled a winning season since Hodges guided them to a 16-11 mark in the 1979–80 campaign.

Numbers Game: Penn forward Tony Price is the highest scorer in a tourney for a Final Four team to fail to be named All-Tournament (led playoffs with 142 points for the fourth-place Quakers).

Putting Things in Perspective: Three players who finished their Duke careers with more

1978–79 NCAA CHAMPION: MICHIGAN STATE

SEASON STATISTICS OF MICHIGAN STATE REGULARS

PLAYER	POS.	CL.	G.	FG%	FT%	PPG	RPG
Greg Kelser	F	Sr.	32	.545	.671	18.8	8.7
Earvin Johnson	G	So.	32	.468	.842	17.1	7.3
Jay Vincent	C	So.	31	.496	.581	12.7	5.2
Ron Charles	F	Jr.	32	.665	.622	8.8	5.1
Mike Brkovich	F	So.	32	.509	.803	7.0	1.8
Terry Donnelly	G	Jr.	32	.535	.754	6.6	1.6
Rob Gonzalez	F	Fr.	28	.581	.800	1.7	1.0
TEAM TOTALS			32	.527	.721	75.7	37.1

Assists leader: Johnson 269.

1979 FINAL FOUR CHAMPIONSHIP GAME

SALT LAKE CITY, UT

MICH. STATE (75)	MIN.	FG-A	FT-A	REB.	A	PF	PTS.
M. Brkovich	39	1-2	3-7	4	1	1	5
Kelser	32	7-13	5-6	8	9	4	19
Charles	31	3-3	1-2	7	0	5	7
Donnelly	39	5-5	5-6	4	0	2	15
Johnson	35	8-15	8-10	7	5	3	24
Vincent	19	2-5	1-2	2	0	4	5
Gonzalez	3	0-0	0-0	0	0	0	0
Longaker	2	0-0	0-0	0	0	0	0
Team				2			
TOTALS	200	26-43	23-33	34	15	19	75

FG%: .605. **FT%:** .697. **Blocks:** 2. **Turnovers:** 16. **Steals:** 6.

INDIANA STATE (64)	MIN.	FG-A	FT-A	REB.	A	PF	PTS.
Miley	29	0-0	0-1	3	0	1	0
Gilbert	20	2-3	0-4	4	0	4	4
Bird	40	7-21	5-8	13	2	3	19
Nicks	36	7-14	3-6	2	4	5	17
Reed	36	4-9	0-0	0	9	4	8
Heaton	22	4-14	2-2	6	2	2	10
Staley	17	2-2	0-1	3	0	2	4

Nemcek	2	1-1	0-0	0	1	3	2
Team				3			
TOTALS	200	27-64	10-22	34	18	24	64

FG%: .422. **FT%:** .455. **Blocks:** 2. **Turnovers:** 10 (Bird 6). **Steals:** 6 (Bird 5).

Halftime: Michigan State 37-28.

NATIONAL SEMIFINALS

PENNSYLVANIA (67): Price 7-18 4-4 18, Smith 0-6 0-0 0, White 5-12 3-4 13, Salters 1-5 0-0 2, Willis 4-13 1-3 9, Ross 2-6 0-0 4, Hall 3-8 0-1 6, Reynolds 1-3 0-0 2, Leifsen 0-1 1-2 1, Flick 0-6 6-6 6, Jackson 1-2 4-4 6, Kuhl 0-2 0-0 0, Condon 0-0 0-0 0. Team 24-82 (.293) 19-24 (.792) 67.

MICHIGAN STATE (101): M. Brkovich 6-10 0-0 12, Kelser 12-19 4-6 28, Charles 2-2 0-0 4, Donnelly 3-5 0-0 6, Johnson 9-10 11-12 29, Vincent 0-1 3-4 3, Gonzalez 1-5 0-0 2, Longaker 2-2 0-0 4, Lloyd 0-2 6-7 6, Kaye 2-2 1-3 5, Huffman 0-0 0-1 0, Gilkie 0-1 0-0 0, D. Brkovich 1-1 0-1 2. Team 38-60 (.633) 25-34 (.735) 101.

Halftime: Michigan State 50-17.

DEPAUL (74): Watkins 8-11 0-0 16, Aguirre 9-18 1-2 19, Mitchem 6-11 0-0 12, Bradshaw 4-8 0-0 8, Garland 9-18 1-3 19. Team 36-66 (.545) 2-5 (.400) 74.

INDIANA STATE (76): Miley 2-2 0-0 4, Gilbert 6-7 0-1 12, Bird 16-19 3-4 35, Nicks 4-13 2-2 10, Reed 3-5 0-0 6, Heaton 3-6 0-0 6, Staley 1-4 1-2 3. Team 35-56 (.625) 6-9 (.667) 76.

Halftime: Indiana State 45-42.

ALL-TOURNAMENT TEAM
Mark Aguirre, F, Fr., DePaul
Larry Bird, F-C, Sr., Indiana State
Gary Garland, G, Sr., DePaul
Magic Johnson, G, Soph., Michigan State*
Greg Kelser, F, Sr., Michigan State

*Named Most Outstanding Player

---

than 2,000 points (Gene Banks, Mike Gminski, and Jim Spanarkel) each compiled lower scoring averages than they manufactured the previous year, when Duke was national runner-up. In 1978, Banks, Gminski, and Spanarkel became the only trio to each score at least 20 points in both Final Four games (total of 71 points in a 90-86 victory over Notre Dame in the semifinals and 63 in a 94-88 setback against Kentucky in the championship game). Duke is the only national runner-up to score more than 85 points in an NCAA final. Banks, Gminski, and Spanarkel all scored at least 16 points when they combined to shoot 53.5 percent from the floor against St. John's, but none of their teammates managed more than seven points as the Blue Devils blew a five-point halftime lead.

1970-79 PREMO POWER POLL: BEST TEAMS BY DECADE

RANK	SEASON	SCHOOL
1	1971–72	UCLA* (30-0)
2	1975–76	Indiana* (32-0)
3	1972–73	UCLA* (30-0)
4	1973–74	North Carolina St.* (30-1)
5	1974–75	Indiana (31-1)
6	1969–70	UCLA* (28-2)
7	1973–74	UCLA (26-4)
8	1970–71	UCLA* (29-1)
9	1977–78	Kentucky* (30-2)
10	1972–73	North Carolina St. (27-0)
11	1969–70	St. Bonaventure (25-3)
12	1970–71	Marquette (28-1)
13	1978–79	Indiana St. (33-1)
14	1976–77	UNLV (29-3)
15	1975–76	Marquette (27-2)
16	1970–71	Pennsylvania (28-1)
17	1969–70	Jacksonville (27-2)
18	1973–74	Maryland (23-5)
19	1974–75	UCLA* (28-3)
20	1977–78	Arkansas (32-4)
	1976–77	North Carolina (28-5)
	1971–72	North Carolina (26-5)
	1978–79	Michigan St.* (26-6)

*–NCAA Tournament Champion

1979 CHAMPIONSHIP BRACKET

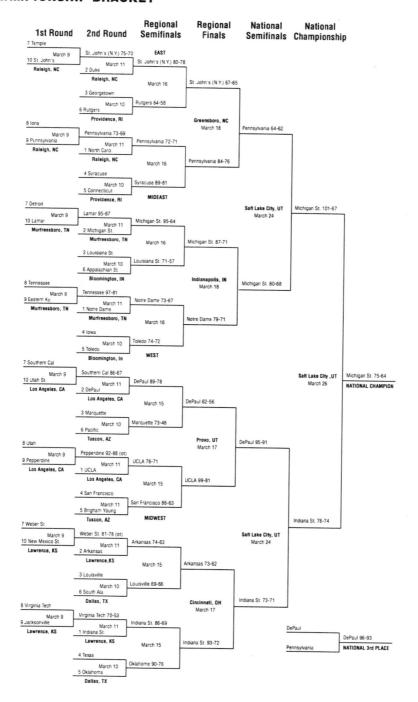

1st Round	2nd Round	Regional Semifinals	Regional Finals	National Semifinals	National Championship

EAST

7. Temple
March 9
10 St. John's
Raleigh, NC

St. John's (N.Y.) 75-70
March 11
2 Duke
Raleigh, NC

St. John's (N.Y.) 80-78

3 Georgetown
March 10
6 Rutgers
Providence, RI

Rutgers 64-58

March 16

St. John's (N.Y.) 67-65

8 Iona
March 9
9 Pennsylvania
Raleigh, NC

Pennsylvania 73-69
March 11
1 North Caro.
Raleigh, NC

Pennsylvania 72-71

Greensboro, NC
March 18

4 Syracuse
March 10
5 Connecticut
Providence, RI

Syracuse 89-81

March 16

Pennsylvania 84-76

Pennsylvania 64-62

MIDEAST

7 Detroit
March 9
10 Lamar
Murfreesboro, TN

Lamar 95-87
March 11
2 Michigan St.
Murfreesboro, TN

Michigan St. 95-64

3 Louisiana St.
March 10
6 Appalachian St.
Bloomington, IN

Louisiana St. 71-57

March 16

Michigan St. 87-71

8 Tennessee
March 9
9 Eastern Ky.
Murfreesboro, TN

Tennessee 97-81
March 11
1 Notre Dame
Murfreesboro, TN

Notre Dame 73-67

Indianapolis, IN
March 18

4 Iowa
March 10
5 Toledo
Bloomington, In

Toledo 74-72

March 16

Notre Dame 79-71

Michigan St. 80-68

Salt Lake City, UT
March 24

Michigan St. 101-67

WEST

7 Southern Cal
March 9
10 Utah St.
Los Angeles, CA

Southern Cal 86-67
March 11
2 DePaul
Los Angeles, CA

DePaul 89-78

3 Marquette
March 10
6 Pacific
Tuscon, AZ

Marquette 73-48

March 15

DePaul 62-56

8 Utah
March 9
9 Pepperdine
Los Angeles, CA

Pepperdine 92-88 (ot)
March 11
1 UCLA
Los Angeles, CA

UCLA 76-71

Provo, UT
March 17

4 San Francisco
March 11
5 Brigham Young
Tuscon, AZ

San Francisco 86-63

March 15

UCLA 99-81

DePaul 95-91

MIDWEST

7 Weber St.
March 9
10 New Mexico St.
Lawrence, KS

Weber St. 81-78 (ot)
March 11
2 Arkansas
Lawrence,KS

Arkansas 74-63

3 Louisville
March 10
6 South Ala.
Dallas, TX

Louisville 69-66

March 15

Arkansas 73-62

8 Virginia Tech
March 9
9 Jacksonville
Lawrence, KS

Virginia Tech 70-53
March 11
1 Indiana St.
Lawrence, KS

Indiana St. 86-69

4 Texas
March 10
5 Oklahoma
Dallas, TX

Oklahoma 90-76

March 15

Indiana St. 93-72

Cincinnati, OH
March 17

Indiana St. 73-71

Salt Lake City, UT
March 24

Indiana St. 76-74

Salt Lake City ,UT
March 26

Michigan St. 75-64

NATIONAL CHAMPION

DePaul

Pennsylvania

DePaul 96-93

NATIONAL 3rd PLACE

6

THE EMERGENCE OF PARITY:

1980s AND 1990s

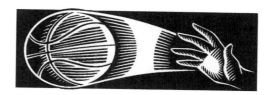

arity became a buzzword for the '80s and '90s as 10 different schools won NCAA championships in a 10-year stretch beginning in 1982. The trite "East is Least" cliche came to an abrupt end with the formation of the Big East Conference. The Big East highlighted a conference reshuffling that saw 10 new Division I leagues in a four-year span from 1980 through 1983. The decade also featured an increased influx of prominent foreign players and the influence of sneaker companies over coaches.

The first half of the 1990s featured the national dominance of two ACC schools—Duke and North Carolina. Developing what many believe is the nation's foremost rivalry, Duke and Carolina or both were represented on the NCAA consensus All-American first- and second-team all but one year (1990) from 1976 through 1994. They combined for more NCAA Tournament victories than the total of over 20 Division I conferences since the playoff field expanded to 64 teams in 1985. The impact of Proposition 48's academic requirements for freshman eligibility escalated, leading to more emphasis on junior college recruits. Debate over

Proposition 48 among other legislative matters fostered an atmosphere whereby the Black Coaches Association (BCA) threatened boycotts for what it thought was discrimination.

1979–80

AT A GLANCE

NCAA Champion: Louisville (33-3).

NIT Champion: Virginia (24-10).

New Conferences: Big East, Midwestern City (forerunner of Midwestern Collegiate), North Atlantic, SWAC (moved up to Division I), Trans America Athletic.

New Rules: The NCAA Tournament bracket expands from 40 teams to 48, including 24 automatic qualifiers and 24 at-large teams. The top 16 seeds receive byes to the second round. The limit of two teams from the same conference allowed in the tournament is lifted. NIT field expands from 24 teams to 32.

NCAA Probation: Auburn, Cincinnati, East Carolina, Memphis State, Oral Roberts, San Francisco.

NCAA Consensus First-Team All-Americans: Mark Aguirre, F, Soph., DePaul; Michael Brooks, F, Sr., La Salle; Joe Barry Carroll, C, Sr., Purdue; Darrell Griffith, G, Sr., Louisville; Kyle Macy, G, Sr., Kentucky.

The NCAA Tournament showed the effect of parity and expansion of the field. This was the only year as many as three Final Four teams finished third or lower in their regular-season league standings—UCLA (fourth in Pacific-10), Purdue (third in Big Ten), and Iowa (fourth in Big Ten).

Missouri established an NCAA single-season record for field-goal percentage (57.2 percent).

Murray State, which compiled a 4-22 record the previous season, improved by 16½ games to 23-8.

Lewis "Magic" Lloyd of Drake finished national runner-up in scoring (30.2) and rebounding (15).

La Salle's Michael Brooks scored a national-high and school record 51 points at Brigham Young.

Maryland guard Greg Manning was sixth nationally in field-goal shooting (64.3 percent) and fourth from the free-throw line (90.8 percent).

Standout freshman forward James Worthy was averaging 12.5 points and 7.4 rebounds per game for North Carolina when he sustained a

1979–80 INDIVIDUAL LEADERS

SCORING

PLAYER	PTS.	AVG.
Murphy, Southern (La.)	932	32.1
Lloyd, Drake	815	30.2
Kelly, Texas Southern	753	29.0
Page, New Mexico	784	28.0
Tillman, E. Kentucky	734	27.2
Belcher, St. Bonaventure	646	26.9
Bowers, American	726	26.9
Nicks, Indiana St.	723	26.8
Aguirre, DePaul	749	26.8
Toney, Southwestern La.	627	26.1

REBOUNDING

PLAYER	REB.	AVG.
Smith, Alcorn St.	392	15.1
Lloyd, Drake	406	15.0

Brown, Mississippi St.	389	14.4
Davis, Tennessee St.	347	13.3
Hooker, Murray St.	356	12.3
Grooms, Kent St.	319	12.3
Schoen, St. Francis (Pa.)	303	12.1
Green, Pan American	337	12.0
Ruland, Iona	407	12.0
Martin, Oral Roberts	334	11.9

FIELD GOAL PERCENTAGE

PLAYER	FGM	FGA	PCT.
Johnson, Oregon St.	211	297	.710
Charles, Mich. St.	169	250	.676
Rhone, Centenary	193	290	.666
Bouie, Syracuse	189	289	.654
Brown, Florida St.	230	356	.646
Manning, Maryland	196	305	.643
Ruland, Iona	256	399	.642

Frazier, Missouri	160	252	.635
McCormick, W. Ky.	165	264	.625
Byrd, Marquette	137	220	.623

FREE THROW PERCENTAGE

PLAYER	FTM	FTA	PCT.
Magid, G. Washington	79	85	.929
Nesbit, The Citadel	74	80	.925
Macy, Kentucky	104	114	.912
Manning, Maryland	79	87	.908
White, Gonzaga	116	130	.892
Matthews, Wisc.	127	143	.888
Salters, Penn	86	97	.887
Nehls, Arizona	108	122	.885
Jones, St. Bon.	84	95	.884
Falconiero, Lafayette	98	111	.883

1979–80 TEAM LEADERS

SCORING OFFENSE

SCHOOL	PTS.	AVG.
Alcorn St.	2729	91.0
Drake	2398	88.8
Oral Roberts	2447	87.4
Utah St.	2329	86.3
Syracuse	2575	85.8

SCORING DEFENSE

SCHOOL	PTS.	AVG.
St. Peter's	1563	50.4
Princeton	1654	55.1
Penn St.	1600	57.1
Wyoming	1644	58.7
Fresno St.	1412	58.8

SCORING MARGIN

SCHOOL	OFF.	DEF.	MAR.
Alcorn St.	91.0	73.6	17.4
Syracuse	85.8	70.4	15.4
South Alabama	76.4	64.5	11.9
Weber St.	75.2	63.3	11.9
Georgetown	80.1	68.8	11.3

WON-LOST PERCENTAGE

SCHOOL	W-L	PCT.
Alcorn St.	28-2	.933
DePaul	26-2	.929
Louisville	33-3	.917
Weber St.	26-3	.897
Oregon St.	26-4	.867
Syracuse	26-4	.867

FIELD GOAL PERCENTAGE

SCHOOL	FGM	FGA	PCT.
Missouri	936	1635	.572
Maryland	985	1789	.551
Oregon St.	943	1732	.544
Syracuse	1025	1902	.539
Toledo	923	1724	.535

FIELD GOAL PERCENTAGE DEFENSE

SCHOOL	FGM	FGA	PCT.
Penn St.	543	1309	.415
St. Peter's	590	1396	.423
UNC-Wilmington	719	1685	.427
Wichita St.	776	1818	.427
Old Dominion	775	1814	.427

FREE THROW PERCENTAGE

SCHOOL	FTM	FTA	PCT.
Oral Roberts	481	610	.789
Southern (La.)	417	537	.777
St. Bonaventure	467	610	.766
Utah St.	605	794	.762
Kentucky	609	802	.759

REBOUND MARGIN

SCHOOL	OWN	OPP.	MAR.
Alcorn St.	49.2	33.8	15.4
Tennessee St.	46.5	34.3	12.2
Wyoming	41.0	30.8	10.2
Northeastern	39.2	31.2	8.0
South Alabama	39.3	31.7	7.6

broken ankle at midseason and was lost for the remainder of the year. The Tar Heels lost their NCAA playoff opener in double overtime against Texas A&M.

Southern (La.) guard Tony Murphy finished his career as the highest scoring two-year player in NCAA history with 1,614 points (28.3 per game).

DePaul won its first 25 games of the season until succumbing at Notre Dame, 76-74, in double overtime. Kelly Tripucka scored 28 points for the Irish.

St. Peter's, coached by ex-Princeton assistant Bob Dukiet, dethroned Princeton as the national leader in scoring defense, yielding only 50.4 points per game—the lowest figure in 19 years.

Princeton and Penn tied for the Ivy League title with 11-3 conference records. It was the first time in 17 years that an Ivy champion lost more than two league games.

Alcorn State led the nation in rebounding margin for the third consecutive season.

South Carolina's Frank McGuire, who previously coached St. John's and North Carolina, retired after a 30-year college coaching career with a 550-235 record.

Louisville All-American guard Darrell Griffith sneaks behind the basket for two.

1979–80 FINAL NATIONAL POLLS

AP	UPI	SCHOOL
1	1	DePaul
2	4	Louisville
3	2	Louisiana St.
4	3	Kentucky
5	5	Oregon St.
6	6	Syracuse
7	7	Indiana
8	8	Maryland
9	11	Notre Dame
10	9	Ohio St.
11	10	Georgetown
12	12	Brigham Young
13	13	St. John's
14	16	Duke
15	15	North Carolina
16	14	Missouri
17	17	Weber St.
18	19	Arizona St.
19	–	Iona
20	–	Purdue
–	18	Texas A&M
–	20	Kansas St.

1980 NCAA Tournament

Summary: All-American Darrell Griffith hit less than 40 percent of his field-goal attempts when Louisville won its first two tourney games in overtime and played only 18 minutes in the Midwest Regional final when the Cardinals overcame an eight-point deficit to defeat LSU. But Griffith was at the top of his game at the Final Four, hitting 23 of 37 shots from the floor against Iowa and UCLA. Louisville excelled with freshman center Rodney McCray, who replaced his injured brother, Scooter.

Outcome for Defending Champion: Michigan State (12-15) became one of only two schools to compile a losing record as defending NCAA champion.

Star Gazing: In a 10-year stretch from 1977 through 1986, Louisville guard Darrell Griffith (22.9 points per game) was the only player to

1979–80 NCAA CHAMPION: LOUISVILLE

SEASON STATISTICS OF LOUISVILLE REGULARS

PLAYER	POS.	CL.	G.	FG%	FT%	PPG	RPG
Darrell Griffith	G	Sr.	36	.553	.713	22.9	4.8
Derek Smith	F	So.	36	.573	.700	14.8	8.3
Wiley Brown	C-F	So.	36	.519	.610	10.4	5.6
Rodney McCray	F-C	Fr.	36	.543	.647	7.8	7.5
Jerry Eaves	G	So.	34	.514	.667	7.7	1.8
Poncho Wright	G-F	So.	36	.450	.729	6.5	2.5
Roger Burkman	G	Jr.	36	.409	.702	3.9	1.7
Tony Branch	G	Sr.	25	.379	.905	1.6	0.1
Greg Deuser	G	So.	22	.360	.682	1.5	0.5
TEAM TOTALS			36	.521	.686	76.9	38.0

Assists leaders: Griffith 138, Burkman 113, Eaves 82.

1980 FINAL FOUR CHAMPIONSHIP GAME

INDIANAPOLIS, IN

UCLA (54)	MIN.	FG-A	FT-A	REB.	A	PF	PTS.
Wilkes	24	1-4	0-0	6	0	3	2
Vandeweghe	37	4-9	6-6	7	0	3	14
Sanders	34	4-10	2-4	6	0	4	10
Foster	38	6-15	4-4	1	5	3	16
Holton	29	1-3	2-2	2	3	2	4
Pruitt	16	2-8	2-2	6	1	2	6
Daye	13	1-3	0-0	1	2	1	2
Allums	4	0-0	0-0	2	0	0	0
Anderson	5	0-0	0-0	0	0	0	0
Team				3			
TOTALS	200	19-52	16-18	34	11	18	54

FG%: .365. FT%: .889. Blocks: 3. Turnovers: 16. Steals: 10 (Foster 6).

LOUISVILLE (59)	MIN.	FG-A	FT-A	REB.	A	PF	PTS.
Brown	34	4-12	0-2	7	3	3	8
Smith	36	3-9	3-4	5	1	2	9
R. McCray	36	2-4	3-4	11	2	4	7
Eaves	30	4-7	0-2	3	3	3	8
Griffith	38	9-16	5-8	2	3	3	23
Burkman	11	0-1	0-0	1	1	4	0
Wright	12	2-4	0-0	4	0	1	4
Branch	3	0-0	0-0	0	0	0	0
Team				3			
TOTALS	200	24-53	11-20	36	13	20	59

FG%: .453. FT%: .550. Blocks: 5. Turnovers: 17. Steals: 8.
Halftime: UCLA 28-26.

NATIONAL SEMIFINALS

IOWA (72): Brookins 6-18 2-2 14, Boyle 0-8 0-0 0, Krafcisin 4-5 4-4 12, Lester 4-4 2-2 10, Arnold 9-17 2-2 20, Waite 4-6 1-1 9, Hansen 2-8 3-4 7, Gannon 0-0 0-0 0, Henry 0-0 0-0 0. Team 29-66 (.439) 14-15 (.933) 72.

LOUISVILLE (80): Brown 1-3 0-2 2, Smith 3-7 7-8 13, R. McCray 5-7 4-4 14, Eaves 2-4 4-5 8, Griffith 14-21 6-8 34, Wright 1-2 0-0 2, Burkman 2-3 3-4 7, Branch 0-0 0-0 0, Deuser 0-0 0-0 0, Cleveland 0-0 0-0 0, Pulliam 0-0-0-0 0. Team 28-47 (.596) 24-31 (.774) 80.

Halftime: Louisville 34-29.

PURDUE (62): Morris 5-14 2-2 12, Hallman 1-7 0-0 2, Carroll 8-14 1-4 17, Edmonson 9-16 5-6 23, B. Walker 1-3 4-5 6, Stallings 0-0 0-0 0, Scearce 0-2 0-0 0, Barnes 1-1 0-0 2, S. Walker 0-1 0-0 0. Team 25-58 (.431) 12-17 (.706) 62.

UCLA (67): Wilkes 2-2 0-0 4, Vandeweghe 9-12 6-6 24, Sanders 3-7 6-6 12, Foster 4-7 1-2 9, Holton 1-3 2-2 4, Allums 0-0 0-2 0, Daye 1-5 4-5 6, Sims 0-3 0-0 0, Pruitt 3-7 2-2 8. Team 23-46 (.500) 21-25 (.840) 67.

Halftime: UCLA 33-25.

ALL-TOURNAMENT TEAM
Joe Barry Carroll, C, Sr., Purdue
Rod Foster, G, Fr., UCLA
Darrell Griffith, G, Sr., Louisville*
Rodney McCray, F-C, Fr., Louisville
Kiki Vandeweghe, F, Sr., UCLA

*Named Most Outstanding Player

average more than 20 the season his school captured a national title.

Biggest Upset: DePaul was the nation's top-ranked team entering the postseason when it lost its West Regional opener to UCLA.

One and Only: Louisville became the only school to win a Division I championship after capturing a small college national tournament. The Cardinals won the 1948 NAIA Tournament by defeating a John Wooden-coached Indiana State in the final.

Numbers Game: Virginia Tech became the only school to erase a halftime deficit of at least 18 points to win a playoff game. The Hokies, Metro Conference runner-up to eventual NCAA champion Louisville, trailed at intermission (48-30) before rallying to edge Western Kentucky

(89-85 in overtime) in the first round of the Mideast Regional.

What If: Forwards Kiki Vandeweghe, Mike Sanders, and James Wilkes, guards Rod Foster, Michael Holton, and Darren Daye, and center Darrell Allums were proficient enough to eventually play in the NBA after they each shot at least 50 percent from the floor for UCLA in the 1979–80 season. If only they combined to hit 45.5 percent of their field-goal attempts instead of 38.6 percent (17 of 44) in the championship game, the Bruins could have defeated Louisville rather than lose 59-54.

Putting Things in Perspective: Louisville lost two of three games in late December, including a 13-point neutral-court defeat to Illinois, which had a losing record in the Big Ten.

1980 CHAMPIONSHIP BRACKET

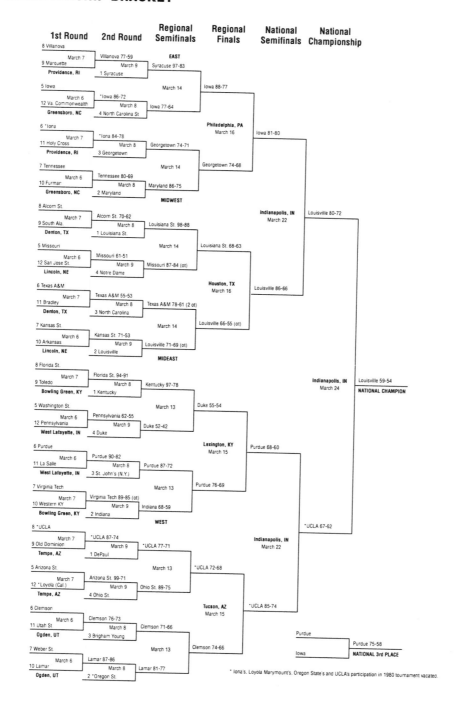

1st Round	2nd Round	Regional Semifinals	Regional Finals	National Semifinals	National Championship

8 Villanova
March 7
9 Marquette
Providence, RI

Villanova 77-59
March 9
1 Syracuse

EAST
Syracuse 97-83

March 14
Iowa 88-77

5 Iowa
March 6
12 Va. Commonwealth
Greensboro, NC

*Iowa 86-72
March 8
4 North Carolina St.

Iowa 77-64

Philadelphia, PA
March 16
Iowa 81-80

6 *Iona
March 7
11 Holy Cross
Providence, RI

*Iona 84-78
March 8
3 Georgetown

Georgetown 74-71

March 14
Georgetown 74-68

7 Tennessee
March 6
10 Furman
Greensboro, NC

Tennessee 80-69
March 8
2 Maryland

Maryland 86-75

MIDWEST

Indianapolis, IN
March 22
Louisville 80-72

8 Alcorn St.
March 7
9 South Ala.
Denton, TX

Alcorn St. 70-62
March 8
1 Louisiana St.

Louisiana St. 98-88

March 14
Louisiana St. 68-63

5 Missouri
March 6
12 San Jose St.
Lincoln, NE

Missouri 61-51
March 9
4 Notre Dame

Missouri 87-84 (ot)

Houston, TX
March 16
Louisville 86-66

6 Texas A&M
March 7
11 Bradley
Denton, TX

Texas A&M 55-53
March 8
3 North Carolina

Texas A&M 78-61 (2 ot)

March 14
Louisville 66-55 (ot)

7 Kansas St.
March 6
10 Arkansas
Lincoln, NE

Kansas St. 71-53
March 9
2 Louisville

Louisville 71-69 (ot)

MIDEAST

Indianapolis, IN
March 24
Louisville 59-54
NATIONAL CHAMPION

8 Florida St.
March 7
9 Toledo
Bowling Green, KY

Florida St. 94-91
March 8
1 Kentucky

Kentucky 97-78

March 13
Duke 55-54

5 Washington St.
March 6
12 Pennsylvania
West Lafayette, IN

Pennsylvania 62-55
March 9
4 Duke

Duke 52-42

Lexington, KY
March 15
Purdue 68-60

6 Purdue
March 6
11 La Salle
West Lafayette, IN

Purdue 90-82
March 8
3 St. John's (N.Y.)

Purdue 87-72

March 13
Purdue 76-69

7 Virginia Tech
March 7
10 Western KY
Bowling Green, KY

Virginia Tech 89-85 (ot)
March 9
2 Indiana

Indiana 68-59

WEST

Indianapolis, IN
March 22
*UCLA 67-62

8 *UCLA
March 7
9 Old Dominion
Tempe, AZ

*UCLA 87-74
March 9
1 DePaul

*UCLA 77-71

March 13
*UCLA 72-68

5 Arizona St.
March 7
12 *Loyola (Cal.)
Tempe, AZ

Arizona St. 99-71
March 9
4 Ohio St.

Ohio St. 89-75

Tucson, AZ
March 15
*UCLA 85-74

6 Clemson
March 6
11 Utah St.
Ogden, UT

Clemson 76-73
March 8
3 Brigham Young

Clemson 71-66

March 13
Clemson 74-66

7 Weber St.
March 6
10 Lamar
Ogden, UT

Lamar 87-86
March 8
2 *Oregon St.

Lamar 81-77

Purdue
Purdue 75-58
NATIONAL 3rd PLACE
Iowa

* Iona's, Loyola Marymount's, Oregon State's and UCLA's participation in 1980 tournament vacated.

1980–81

AT A GLANCE

NCAA Champion: Indiana (26-9).

NIT Champion: Tulsa (26-7).

New Conference: MEAC (moved up from Division II).

New Rule: No more than 50 percent of the NCAA Tournament berths shall be filled by automatic qualifiers.

NCAA Probation: UC Santa Barbara, New Mexico, West Texas State.

NCAA Consensus First-Team All-Americans: Mark Aguirre, F, Jr., DePaul; Danny Ainge, G, Sr., Brigham Young; Steve Johnson, C, Sr., Oregon State; Ralph Sampson, C, Soph., Virginia; Isiah Thomas, G, Soph., Indiana.

Virginia captured its only undisputed ACC regular-season title with a 13-1 league record. Perhaps the national player of the year to struggle the most in a single NCAA Tournament was Virginia sophomore center Ralph Sampson, who had three mediocre playoff games of less than 12 points, including an 11-point outing when the Cavaliers were defeated by North Carolina in the national semifinals.

Oregon State's Steve Johnson, who didn't play basketball until his senior year in high school, set an NCAA single-season record by hitting 74.6 percent of his field-goal attempts (235 of 315). He finished his career at 67.8 percent, an NCAA mark with a minimum of 600 baskets. Johnson is the only player to hit more than 70 percent of his field-goal attempts in two different seasons. His team won its first 26 games before the Beavers were blasted in their regular-season finale by visiting Arizona State, 87-67.

UC Irvine's Kevin Magee, after an unspectacular high school career in Magnolia, Mississippi, and brief stints at three colleges, became the first player ever to finish among the top four nationally in scoring, rebounding, and field-goal shooting.

Tulsa became the only school to win more than 25 games the season after a single-digit victory total. The Golden Hurricanes improved to 26-7 from 8-19 after first-year coach Nolan Richardson brought four of his top players from NJCAA champion Western Texas. Tulsa became the first team to capture the NIT after posting a losing record the previous year.

South Carolina guard Zam Fredrick, entering his senior season with a career scoring average of just 8.1 points per game, ranked in 20th place at 22.5 at mid-season before averaging 36 his last 13 games to finish with a nation-leading mark of 28.9. Colgate's Mike Ferrara, runner-up to Fredrick in scoring (28.6), scored a national-high 50 points against Siena.

Michigan's Mike McGee became the only player to score more than 1,500 points in Big Ten Conference games.

National field-goal shooting improved for the eighth consecutive season to 48 percent.

Five Mid-American teams tied for first place, the most ever for a Division I conference, with 10-6 records.

1980–81 FINAL NATIONAL POLLS

AP	UPI	SCHOOL
1	1	DePaul
2	2	Oregon St.
3	5	Arizona St.
4	4	Louisiana St.
5	3	Virginia
6	6	North Carolina
7	9	Notre Dame
8	8	Kentucky
9	7	Indiana
10	11	UCLA
11	14	Wake Forest
12	13	Louisville
13	12	Iowa
14	10	Utah
15	15	Tennessee
16	17	Brigham Young
17	16	Wyoming
18	20	Maryland
19	18	Illinois
20	–	Arkansas
–	19	Kansas

1981 NCAA Tournament

Summary: North Carolina couldn't cope with two players named Thomas in a 63-50 defeat in the NCAA final. Indiana's Isiah Thomas collected 23 points and five assists and teammate Jim Thomas chipped in with eight assists. Jim Thomas, a defensive standout, became the only player who didn't score a total of more than 10 points in two Final Four games (two points in each game) to be named to an All-NCAA Tournament team.

Star Gazing: Isiah Thomas is the only guard among the eight freshmen and sophomores to lead a national titlist in scoring average.

Biggest Upsets: Defending champion Louis-ville and runner-up UCLA succumbed against Arkansas and Brigham Young, respectively. It was the last time both championship final teams appeared in the tourney again the following season and lost their opening-round games.... Top-ranked DePaul lost its playoff opener (49-48 against St. Joseph's in Mideast Regional). It was the "Year of the Upset" as second-ranked Oregon State succumbed to Kansas State, 50-48, and third-ranked Arizona State was clobbered by Kansas, 88-71, in their playoff openers.

One and Only: DePaul became the only school to be top-ranked entering back-to-back

1980–81 INDIVIDUAL LEADERS

SCORING

PLAYER	PTS.	AVG.
Fredrick, South Carolina	781	28.9
Ferrara, Colgate	772	28.6
Magee, UC Irvine	743	27.5
Lloyd, Drake	762	26.3
Williams, Houston	749	25.0
Jackson, Oklahoma City	719	24.8
Edwards, Cleveland St.	664	24.6
Belcher, St. Bonaventure	637	24.5
Ainge, Brigham Young	782	24.4
McGee, Michigan	732	24.4

REBOUNDING

PLAYER	REB.	AVG.
Watson, Miss. Valley St.	379	14.0
Sappleton, Loyola (Ill.)	374	13.4

Cage, San Diego St.	355	13.1
Magee, UC Irvine	337	12.5
Thompson, Texas	370	12.3
Kellogg, Ohio St.	324	12.0
Atkins, Duquesne	352	11.7
Williams, Maryland	363	11.7
Henry, Oklahoma City	338	11.7
Sampson, Virginia	378	11.5

FIELD GOAL PERCENTAGE

PLAYER	FGM	FGA	PCT.
Johnson, Oregon St.	235	315	.746
Magee, UC Irvine	280	417	.671
Woolridge, Notre Dame	156	240	.650
Williams, Maryland	183	283	.647
Best, Lafayette	164	255	.643
Johnson, UNLV	152	239	.636
Hopson, Idaho	157	247	.636

Payton, Appa. St.	178	281	.633
Palm, Nevada-Reno	204	323	.632
Aleksinas, Conn.	154	244	.631

FREE THROW PERCENTAGE

PLAYER	FTM	FTA	PCT.
Hildahl, Portland St.	76	82	.927
Moore, Nebraska	118	128	.922
Bontrager, O. Roberts	73	81	.901
Stack, N'western	81	90	.900
Leonard, Manhattan	123	138	.891
Simmons, La. Tech	130	146	.890
Greig, Oregon	82	93	.882
Edwards, Cleve. St.	134	152	.882
Wafer, La. Tech	80	91	.879
Ferrara, Colgate	176	201	.876

1980–81 TEAM LEADERS

SCORING OFFENSE

SCHOOL	PTS.	AVG.
UC Irvine	2332	86.4
West Texas St.	2309	85.5
Oklahoma City	2421	83.5
San Francisco	2579	83.2
Long Island	2390	82.4

SCORING DEFENSE

SCHOOL	PTS.	AVG.
Fresno St.	1470	50.7
Princeton	1438	51.4
St. Peter's	1338	51.5
Air Force	1518	56.2
San Jose St.	1699	56.6

SCORING MARGIN

SCHOOL	OFF.	DEF.	MAR.
Wyoming	73.6	57.5	16.1
Oregon St.	76.6	60.9	15.7
Fresno St.	66.1	50.7	15.4
Wichita St.	80.9	66.5	14.4
DePaul	78.9	66.1	12.8
South Alabama	73.8	61.0	12.8

WON-LOST PERCENTAGE

SCHOOL	W-L	PCT.
DePaul	27-2	.931
Oregon St.	26-2	.929
Virginia	29-4	.879
Fresno St.	25-4	.862
Idaho	25-4	.862

FIELD GOAL PERCENTAGE

SCHOOL	FGM	FGA	PCT.
Oregon St.	862	1528	.564
Notre Dame	824	1492	.552
Idaho	816	1484	.550
UC Irvine	934	1703	.548
Pepperdine	918	1709	.537

FIELD GOAL PERCENTAGE DEFENSE

SCHOOL	FGM	FGA	PTS.
Wyoming	637	1589	.401
Penn St.	547	1338	.409
South Florida	701	1682	.417
St. Peter's	521	1248	.417
Air Force	561	1343	.418

FREE THROW PERCENTAGE

SCHOOL	FTM	FTA	PCT.
Connecticut	487	623	.782
Idaho St.	405	522	.776
Davidson	477	626	.762
St. John's	463	612	.757
Tennessee	424	561	.756

REBOUND MARGIN

SCHOOL	OWN	OPP.	MAR.
Northeastern	44.9	32.0	12.9
Wyoming	42.0	30.3	11.7
Wichita St.	44.1	34.0	10.1
Miss. Valley St.	47.1	39.0	8.1
San Francisco	40.1	32.6	7.5

1980–81 NCAA CHAMPION: INDIANA

SEASON STATISTICS OF INDIANA REGULARS

PLAYER	POS.	CL.	G.	FG%	FT%	PPG	RPG
Isiah Thomas	G	So.	34	.554	.742	16.0	3.1
Ray Tolbert	F-C	Sr.	35	.588	.740	12.2	6.4
Randy Wittman	G	Jr.	35	.542	.768	10.4	2.3
Landon Turner	F-C	Jr.	33	.561	.717	9.5	3.7
Ted Kitchel	F	Jr.	34	.465	.854	9.2	3.3
Jim Thomas	G	So.	33	.495	.771	3.7	3.2
Tony Brown	G	So.	28	.458	.536	3.3	1.3
Steve Risley	F	Sr.	31	.452	.651	3.0	2.3
Glen Grunwald	F	Sr.	27	.512	.615	1.9	1.2
Phil Isenbarger	F	Sr.	26	.600	.650	1.7	1.2
Steve Bouchie	F	So.	29	.383	.818	1.6	1.6
Chuck Franz	G	So.	21	.583	.875	1.3	0.3
TEAM TOTALS			35	.530	.744	70.0	32.7

Assists leader: I. Thomas 197. **Blocked shots leader:** Tolbert 35. **Steals leader:** I. Thomas 74.

1981 FINAL FOUR CHAMPIONSHIP GAME

PHILADELPHIA, PA

INDIANA (63)	MIN.	FG-A	FT-A	REB.	A	PF	PTS.
Kitchel	4	0-1	0-0	0	0	3	0
Turner	34	5-8	2-2	6	1	5	12
Tolbert	40	1-4	3-6	11	0	0	5
I. Thomas	40	8-17	7-8	2	5	4	23
Wittman	40	7-13	2-2	4	0	2	16
Risley	13	1-1	3-4	4	0	1	5
J. Thomas	29	1-4	0-0	4	8	2	2
Team				2			
TOTALS	200	23-48	17-22	33	14	17	63

FG%: .479. **FT%:** .773. **Blocks:** 1. **Turnovers:** 14. **Steals:** 8.

NORTH CAROLINA (50)	MIN.	FG-A	FT-A	REB.	A	PF	PTS.
Wood	38	6-13	6-9	6	2	4	18
Worthy	31	3-11	1-2	6	2	5	7
Perkins	39	5-8	1-2	8	1	3	11
Pepper	23	2-5	2-2	1	0	1	6
Black	36	3-4	0-0	2	6	5	6
Budko	1	0-1	0-0	1	0	0	0
Doherty	24	1-2	0-1	4	0	4	2
Braddock	4	0-2	0-0	0	1	1	0
Brust	3	0-0	0-0	0	0	0	0
Kenny	1	0-1	0-0	1	0	0	0
TOTALS	200	20-47	10-16	29	12	23	50

FG%: .426. **FT%:** .625. **Blocks:** 2. **Turnovers:** 19 (Doherty 6). **Steals:** 9. **Halftime:** Indiana 27-26.

NATIONAL SEMIFINALS

INDIANA (67): Kitchel 3-8 4-4 10, Turner 7-19 6-7 20, Tolbert 3-7 1-2 7, I. Thomas 6-8 2-3 14, Wittman 3-10 2-2 8, Risley 0-2 1-2 1, J. Thomas 0-4 2-2 2, Bouchie 0-1 0-0 0, Grunwald 1-2 1-2 3, Brown 0-1 0-1 0, Franz 0-0 2-2 2, LaFave 0-0 0-0 0. Team 23-63 (.365) 21-27 (.778) 67.

LOUISIANA STATE (49): Mitchell 3-10 3-4 9, Macklin 2-12 0-0 4, Cook 3-5 0-0 6, Martin 2-8 3-3 7, Carter 5-10 0-0 10, Sims 2-8 1-2 5, Jones 0-2 0-1 0, Tudor 1-3 4-4 6, Bergeron 0-0 0-0 0, Costello 0-0 0-0 0, Black 1-1 0-0 2. Team 19-59 (.322) 11-14 (.786) 49.

Halftime: Louisiana State 30-27.

NORTH CAROLINA (78): Wood 14-19 11-13 39, Worthy 2-8 4-7 8, Perkins 4-7 3-5 11, Pepper 0-4 0-0 0, Black 4-6 2-3 10, Doherty 0-1 8-9 8, Braddock 0-1 0-0 0, Kenny 1-1 0-0 2. Team 25-47 (.532) 28-37 (.757) 78.

VIRGINIA (65): Lamp 7-18 4-4 18, Sampson 3-10 5-7 11, Wilson 4-7 0-0 8, Jones 5-13 1-1 11, Stokes 0-2 0-0 0, Raker 5-9 3-3 13, Lattimore 1-1 0-0 2. Team 26-61 (.426) 13-15 (.867) 65.

Halftime: Tied 27-27.

ALL-TOURNAMENT TEAM

Jeff Lamp, G, Sr., Virginia
Isiah Thomas, G, Soph., Indiana*
Jim Thomas, G, Soph., Indiana
Landon Turner, F-C, Jr., Indiana
Al Wood, F, Sr., North Carolina

*Named Most Outstanding Player

tournaments but lose both opening playoff games.

Numbers Game: The last player to score the most points in a single game of a tournament and play for a Final Four team was Al Wood. He scored a playoff-high 39 points for North Carolina in the Tar Heels' 78-65 victory against Virginia in the national semifinals before they lost to Indiana in the championship game.

What If: Arizona State, ranked third by AP entering the playoffs with a 24-3 record, had the door open to a possible national title when No. 1 seeds DePaul and Oregon State lost their playoff openers at the buzzer. But the Sun Devils, featuring four upperclassmen who combined for a total of more than 35 seasons in the NBA (guards Fat Lever and Byron Scott, center Alton Lister, and forward Sam Williams), became one of the biggest busts in tourney history. The door to the Final Four was also slammed shut on them in their opener by Kansas (88-71 in Midwest Regional) when they fell behind by 16 points at intermission. ASU had defeated Iowa by eight points early in the season before the Hawkeyes twice upended eventual national champion Indiana in Big Ten Conference competition.

Putting Things in Perspective: Lute Olson's Iowa (21-7) defeated Indiana twice by a total of 16 points before the Hawkeyes lost their NCAA playoff opener in the second round against Wichita State on the Shockers' home court. The Hoosiers got off to a modest 7-5 start, including a defeat on a neutral court against Pan American.

Lute Olson and his Iowa team went to the Final Four in 1980, but they couldn't match that success when the Hawkeyes fell to Wichita State in the opening round of the 1981 tournament.

1981 CHAMPIONSHIP BRACKET

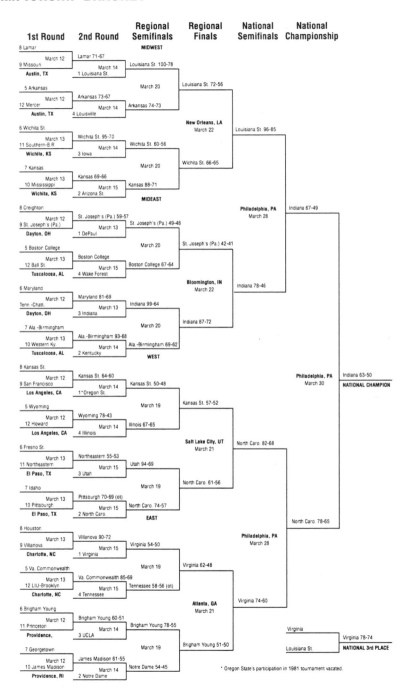

1st Round	2nd Round	Regional Semifinals	Regional Finals	National Semifinals	National Championship

MIDWEST

8 Lamar
March 12
9 Missouri
Austin, TX

Lamar 71-67
March 14
1 Louisiana St.

Louisiana St. 100-78

March 20

Louisiana St. 72-56

5 Arkansas
March 12
12 Mercer
Austin, TX

Arkansas 73-67
March 14
4 Louisville

Arkansas 74-73

New Orleans, LA
March 22

Louisiana St. 96-85

6 Wichita St.
March 13
11 Southern-B.R.
Wichita, KS

Wichita St. 95-70
March 14
3 Iowa

Wichita St. 60-56

March 20

Wichita St. 66-65

7 Kansas
March 13
10 Mississippi
Wichita, KS

Kansas 69-66
March 15
2 Arizona St.

Kansas 88-71

Philadelphia, PA
March 28

Indiana 67-49

MIDEAST

8 Creighton
March 12
9 St. Joseph's (Pa.)
Dayton, OH

St. Joseph's (Pa.) 59-57
March 13
1 DePaul

St. Joseph's (Pa.) 49-48

March 20

St. Joseph's (Pa.) 42-41

5 Boston College
March 13
12 Ball St.
Tuscaloosa, AL

Boston College
March 15
4 Wake Forest

Boston College 67-64

Bloomington, IN
March 22

Indiana 78-46

6 Maryland
March 12
Tenn.-Chatt.
Dayton, OH

Maryland 81-69
March 13
3 Indiana

Indiana 99-64

March 20

Indiana 87-72

7 Ala.-Birmingham
March 13
10 Western Ky.
Tuscaloosa, AL

Ala.-Birmingham 93-68
March 14
2 Kentucky

Ala.-Birmingham 69-62

WEST

8 Kansas St.
March 12
9 San Francisco
Los Angeles, CA

Kansas St. 64-60
March 14
1*Oregon St.

Kansas St. 50-48

March 19

Kansas St. 57-52

5 Wyoming
March 12
12 Howard
Los Angeles, CA

Wyoming 78-43
March 14
4 Illinois

Illinois 67-65

Salt Lake City, UT
March 21

North Caro. 82-68

6 Fresno St.
March 13
11 Northeastern
El Paso, TX

Northeastern 55-53
March 15
3 Utah

Utah 94-69

March 19

North Caro. 61-56

7 Idaho
March 13
10 Pittsburgh
El Paso, TX

Pittsburgh 70-69 (ot)
March 15
2 North Caro.

North Caro. 74-57

EAST

8 Houston
March 13
9 Villanova
Charlotte, NC

Villanova 90-72
March 15
1 Virginia

Virginia 54-50

March 19

Virginia 62-48

5 Va. Commonwealth
March 13
12 LIU-Brooklyn
Charlotte, NC

Va. Commonwealth 85-69
March 15
4 Tennessee

Tennessee 58-56 (ot)

Atlanta, GA
March 21

Virginia 74-60

6 Brigham Young
March 12
11 Princeton
Providence,

Brigham Young 60-51
March 14
3 UCLA

Brigham Young 78-55

March 19

Brigham Young 51-50

7 Georgetown
March 12
10 James Madison
Providence, RI

James Madison 61-55
March 14
2 Notre Dame

Notre Dame 54-45

Philadelphia, PA
March 28

North Caro. 78-65

Philadelphia, PA
March 30

Indiana 63-50

NATIONAL CHAMPION

Virginia

Louisiana St.

Virginia 78-74

NATIONAL 3rd PLACE

* Oregon State's participation in 1981 tournament vacated.

1981-82

AT A GLANCE

NCAA Champion: North Carolina (32-2).

NIT Champion: Bradley (26-10).

New Conferences: Metro Atlantic Athletic, Northeast.

New Rules: The jump ball is employed only at the beginning of the game and the start of each overtime. An alternating arrow indicates possession in jump-ball situations during the game, with the arrow first pointing in the direction of the team that didn't gain possession of the initial jump ball. All fouls assessed to bench personnel are charged to the head coach. National third-place game in the NCAA Tournament is abolished.

NCAA Probation: Arkansas State, UC Santa Barbara, New Mexico, UCLA, Wichita State.

NCAA Consensus First-Team All-Americans: Terry Cummings, F-C, Jr., DePaul; Quintin Dailey, G, Jr., San Francisco; Eric "Sleepy" Floyd, G, Sr., Georgetown; Ralph Sampson, C, Jr., Virginia; James Worthy, F, Jr., North Carolina.

Georgetown's John Thompson took umbrage to depictions of him as the initial African-American coach to direct a team to the Final Four (1982). But the injustices in the past against his race were sufficient reason for placing emphasis on Thompson's achievements with predominantly black rosters.

UC Irvine's Kevin Magee became the only player ever to finish two seasons in the top 10 nationally in scoring, rebounding, and field-goal shooting.

Western Illinois' Joe Dykstra set an NCAA record by converting 64 consecutive free throws (eight-game stretch from December 1 to January 4).

1981-82 FINAL NATIONAL POLLS

AP	UPI	SCHOOL
1	1	North Carolina
2	2	DePaul
3	3	Virginia
4	4	Oregon St.
5	5	Missouri
6	7	Georgetown
7	6	Minnesota
8	8	Idaho
9	9	Memphis St.
10	11	Tulsa
11	10	Fresno St.
12	13	Arkansas
13	12	Alabama
14	17	West Virginia
15	14	Kentucky
16	16	Iowa
17	–	Ala.-Birmingham
18	19	Wake Forest
19	–	UCLA
20	20	Louisville
–	15	Wyoming
–	18	Kansas St.

In the longest game in major-college history, Cincinnati outlasted NIT champion-to-be Bradley, 75-73, in seven overtimes. (see accompanying box score).

LONGEST GAME IN HISTORY Cincinnati and Bradley players anticipating their Christmas break in 1981 had a rude awakening on December 21, 1981. The game between the Braves and the Bearcats went into the seventh overtime before hometeam Bradley lost to Cincinnati, 75-73. Bradley's David Thirdkill and Mitchell Anderson led all scorers with 25 and 20 points, respectively.

CINCINNATI (75)	MIN.	FG-A	FT-A	REB.	PTS.
Gaffney	52	6-16	3-4	8	15
Jones	64	8-14	2-5	15	18
Williams	63	3-11	2-3	15	8
Johnson	63	1-4	0-1	1	2
Austin	73	8-19	2-3	7	18
Schloemer	18	3-3	0-0	3	6
McMillan	13	0-2	0-0	2	0
Robinson	24	2-4	2-3	4	6
Campbell	7	1-1	0-0	1	2
Kecman	1	0-1	0-0	0	0
Team				1	
TOTALS	**375**	**32-75**	**11-19**	**57**	**75**

FG%: .427. **FT%:** .579. **Assists:** 18 (Johnson 7). **Steals:** 7. **Blocked Shots:** 0. **Turnovers:** 19. **Fouled Out:** 2 (Gaffney/6th OT, Jones/6th OT).

BRADLEY (73)	MP	FG-A	FT-A	REB.	PTS.
Anderson	65	8-25	4-6	12	20
Thirdkill	68	10-17	5-8	9	25
Reese	73	4-9	6-8	6	14
Scott	68	0-7	2-3	4	2
Mines	6	0-3	0-0	0	0
Winters	69	6-15	0-2	15	12
Cook	10	0-2	0-0	1	0
Mathews	17	0-1	0-0	1	0
Team				2	
TOTALS	**375**	**28-79**	**17-27**	**50**	**73**

FG%: .354. **FT%:** .630. **Assists:** 20 (Scott 8). **Steals:** 12. **Blocked Shots:** 2. **Turnovers:** 15. **Fouled Out:** 2 (Anderson/5th OT, Winter/2nd half).

Halftime: Bradley 40-35. **Regulation:** Tied 61-61. **First Overtime:** Tied 63-63. **Second Overtime:** Tied 65-65. **Third Overtime:** Tied 65-65. **Fourth Overtime:** Tied 67-67. **Fifth Overtime:** Tied 71-71. **Sixth Overtime:** Tied 73-73.

SCORING

PLAYER	PTS.	AVG.
Kelly, Texas Southern	862	29.7
Pierce, Rice	805	26.8
Callandrillo, Seton Hall	698	25.9
Magee, UC Irvine	732	25.2
Dailey, San Francisco	755	25.2
Jackson, Centenary	693	23.9
Wiggins, Florida St.	523	23.8
Moss, Northeastern	710	23.7
McLaughlin, C. Michigan	581	23.2
Jakubick, Akron	594	22.8

REBOUNDING

PLAYER	REB.	AVG.
Thompson, Texas	365	13.5
Sappleton, Loyola (Ill.)	376	13.0

Tillis, Cleveland St.	346	12.8
McNamara, California	341	12.6
Clarida, Long Island	369	12.3
Norris, Jackson St.	341	12.2
Magee, UC Irvine	353	12.2
Cobb, Pan American	302	12.1
Cummings, DePaul	334	11.9

FIELD GOAL PERCENTAGE

PLAYER	FGM	FGA	PCT.
McNamara, California	231	329	.702
Ellis, Tennessee	257	393	.654
Phillips, Pepperdine	181	280	.646
Culton, Texas-Arl.	200	311	.643
Magee, UC Irvine	272	424	.642
Pinckney, Villanova	169	264	.640
Hopson, Idaho	158	250	.632
Clarida, Long I.	180	285	.632

Jones, Houston Bap.	178	282	.631
Clark, Miss.	251	403	.623

FREE THROW PERCENTAGE

PLAYER	FTA	FTM	PCT.
Foster, UCLA	95	100	.950
Moore, Nebraska	123	131	.939
Dykstra, W. Ill.	147	161	.913
Williams, Idaho St.	70	78	.897
Master, Kentucky	95	106	.896
McGraw, Siena	112	126	.889
Lee, Boise St.	71	80	.888
Carrabino, Harvard	85	97	.876
Gillam, W. Chester St.	85	97	.876
Engelland, Duke	77	88	.875

1981–82 TEAM LEADERS

SCORING OFFENSE

SCHOOL	PTS.	AVG.
Long Island	2605	86.8
Texas Southern	2429	83.8
North Texas St.	2258	83.6
San Francisco	2527	81.5
Houston	2685	81.4

SCORING DEFENSE

SCHOOL	PTS.	AVG.
Fresno St.	1412	47.1
N.C. St.	1570	49.1
Princeton	1277	49.1
Wyoming	1545	51.5
James Madison	1559	52.0

SCORING MARGIN

SCHOOL	OFF.	DEF.	MAR.
Oregon St.	69.6	55.0	14.6
Georgetown	67.6	53.5	14.2
Idaho	71.3	57.5	13.8
Virginia	70.7	57.2	13.5
Tenn.-Chattanooga	72.6	59.9	12.7

WON-LOST PERCENTAGE

SCHOOL	W-L	PCT.
North Carolina	32-2	.941
DePaul	26-2	.929
Fresno St.	27-3	.900
Idaho	27-3	.900
Virginia	30-4	.882

FIELD GOAL PERCENTAGE

SCHOOL	FGM	FGA	PCT.
UC Irvine	920	1639	.561
Mississippi	696	1281	.543
Pepperdine	929	1714	.542
Tennessee	792	1462	.542
Missouri	815	1511	.539

FIELD GOAL PERCENTAGE DEFENSE

SCHOOL	FGM	FGA	PCT.
Wyoming	584	1470	.397
Georgetown	757	1808	.419
Idaho	696	1662	.419
N.C. St.	621	1481	.419
Missouri	742	1766	.420

FREE THROW PERCENTAGE

SCHOOL	FTM	FTA	PCT.
Western Illinois	447	569	.786
Northwestern St. (La.)	489	624	.784
Western Carolina	481	623	.772
Idaho St.	393	522	.753
Ohio St.	415	552	.752

REBOUND MARGIN

SCHOOL	OWN	OPP.	MAR.
Northeastern	41.2	30.8	10.4
Wyoming	36.4	26.7	9.7
Brigham Young	37.3	29.3	8.0
Alabama	37.3	29.5	7.7
Pepperdine	37.7	30.0	7.6

Fresno State posted the best scoring defense of any team since 1952 (47.1 points per game).

Texas got off to a sizzling 14-0 start but finished with a modest 16-11 record after forward Mike Wacker sustained a season-ending knee injury.

Oregon State's 14.6-point margin of victory was the lowest ever by a scoring margin champion.

The national scoring average decreased for the seventh consecutive season, reaching the lowest point since 1952 with 135.1 points per game (both teams combined). Texas Southern's Harry Kelly led the country in scoring with a 29.7-point average, including a national-high 51 points against Texas College.

1982 NCAA Tournament

Summary: Freshman guard Michael Jordan swished a 16-foot jumper from the left side with 16 seconds remaining to provide the title game's final points as North Carolina edged Georgetown, 63-62. Georgetown guard Fred Brown's errant pass directly to Tar Heels forward James

The Louisiana Superdome hosts the 1982 NCAA Final Four.

Worthy prevented the Hoyas from attempting a potential game-winning shot in the closing seconds. Jordan's heroics came after an inauspicious playoff debut when he collected six points, one rebound, no assists, and no steals in 37 minutes of a 52-50 opening-round victory against James Madison in the East Regional.

Outcome for Defending Champion: Indiana (19-10) was eliminated in the second round of the Mideast Regional by Alabama-Birmingham, 80-70.

Star Gazing: Final Four Most Outstanding Player James Worthy hit 20 of 27 field-goal attempts in two Final Four games.

Biggest Upset: DePaul lost its third opener in as many years as a No. 1 seed when the Blue Demons, ranked second nationally, bowed to Boston College, 82-75, in the Midwest Regional.

One and Only: Northeastern's Perry Moss was the only player to crack the 30-point plateau in the tourney. He had 31 against Villanova.

Numbers Game: Guard Rob Williams, Houston's leader in scoring with a 21.1-point average, missed all eight of his field-goal attempts against the Tar Heels in the national semifinals. Nonetheless, he still finished as the tourney's leading scorer because he scored at least 25 points in three previous outings.

1981–82 NCAA CHAMPION: N. CAROLINA

SEASON STATISTICS OF NORTH CAROLINA REGULARS

PLAYER	POS.	CL.	G.	FG%	FT%	PPG	RPG
James Worthy	F	Jr.	34	.573	.674	15.6	6.3
Sam Perkins	C	So.	32	.578	.768	14.3	7.8
Michael Jordan	G	Fr.	34	.534	.722	13.5	4.4
Matt Doherty	F	So.	34	.519	.772	9.3	3.0
Jimmy Black	G	Sr.	34	.513	.738	7.6	1.7
Jim Braddock	G	Jr.	34	.452	.833	1.9	0.5
Chris Brust	F	Sr.	33	.622	.455	1.7	1.7
Buzz Peterson	G	Fr.	30	.390	.429	1.2	0.5
Jeb Barlow	F	Sr.	28	.387	.444	1.0	0.8
TEAM TOTALS			34	.537	.692	66.7	29.4

Assists leader: Black 213. **Blocked shots leader:** Perkins 53. **Steals leader:** Black 58.

1982 FINAL FOUR CHAMPIONSHIP GAME

NEW ORLEANS, LA

GEORGETOWN (62)	MIN.	FG-A	FT-A	REB.	A	PF	PTS.
E. Smith	35	6-8	2-2	3	5	5	14
Hancock	8	0-2	0-0	0	0	1	0
Ewing	37	10-15	3-3	11	1	4	23
F. Brown	29	1-2	2-2	2	5	4	4
Floyd	39	9-17	0-0	3	5	2	18
Spriggs	30	0-2	1-2	1	0	2	1
Jones	10	1-3	0-0	0	0	0	2
B. Martin	5	0-2	0-0	0	0	1	0
G. Smith	7	0-0	0-0	0	0	1	0
Team				2			
TOTALS	200	27-51	8-9	22	16	20	62

FG%: .529. **FT%:** .889. **Blocks:** 2. **Turnovers:** 12. **Steals:** 11.

N. CAROLINA (63)	MIN.	FG-A	FT-A	REB.	A	PF	PTS.
Doherty	39	1-3	2-3	3	1	0	4
Worthy	38	13-17	2-7	4	0	3	28
Perkins	38	3-7	4-6	7	1	2	10
Black	38	1-4	2-2	3	7	2	4
Jordan	34	7-13	2-2	9	2	2	16
Peterson	7	0-3	0-0	1	1	0	0
Braddock	2	0-0	0-0	0	1	1	0
Brust	4	0-0	1-2	1	1	1	1
Team				2			
TOTALS	200	25-47	13-22	30	14	11	63

FG%: .532. **FT%:** .591. **Blocks:** 1. **Turnovers:** 13. **Steals:** 7. **Halftime:** Georgetown 32-31.

NATIONAL SEMIFINALS

HOUSTON (63): Drexler 6-12 5-6 17, Young 1-7 0-1 2, Micheaux 8-14 2-3 18, Rose 10-15 0-2 20, R. Williams 0-8 2-2 2, B. Williams 0-1 0-0 0, Olajuwon 1-3 0-0 2, Davis 1-2 0-0 2, Anders 0-2 0-0 0. Team 27-64 (.422) 9-14 (.643) 63.

NORTH CAROLINA (68): Doherty 2-7 1-2 5, Worthy 7-10 0-0 14, Perkins 9-11 7-7 25, Black 1-2 4-6 6, Jordan 7-14 4-4 18, Peterson 0-0 0-0 0, Brust 0-0-0-0 0, W. Martin 0-0 0-0 0, Braddock 0-0 0-0 0. Team 26-44 (.591) 16-19 (.842) 68.

Halftime: North Carolina 31-29.

LOUISVILLE (46): W. Brown 2-5 0-0 4, D. Smith 4-8 2-4 10, R. McCray 2-5 4-4 8, Gordon 1-6 0-0 2, Eaves 4-9, 0-0 8, Wagner 1-4 0-0 2, Jones 4-7 0-2 8, S. McCray 0-1 0-0 0, Wright 1-3 2-2 4. Team 19-48 (.396) 8-12 (.667) 46.

GEORGETOWN (50): E. Smith 6-10 2-4 14, Hancock 1-3 0-0 2, Ewing 3-8 2-2 8, F. Brown 1-3 2-3 4, Floyd 3-11 7-8 13, Spriggs 2-2 1-3 5, G. Smith 0-0 0-0 0, Jones 2-4 0-0 4, B. Martin 0-0 0-0 0. Team 18-41 (.439) 14-20 (.700) 50.

Halftime: Georgetown 24-22.

ALL-TOURNAMENT TEAM

Patrick Ewing, C, Fr., Georgetown
Sleepy Floyd, G, Sr., Georgetown
Michael Jordan, G, Fr., North Carolina
Sam Perkins, C, Soph., North Carolina
James Worthy, F, Jr., North Carolina*

*Named Most Outstanding Player

What If: Williams, swingman Michael Young, and center Hakeem Olajuwon combined to average 40.3 points per game for Houston. If only they collaborated for 12 points instead of two apiece in the national semifinals, the Cougars could have defeated Carolina rather than lose 68-63.

Putting Things in Perspective: Would North Carolina have captured the crown if the Tar Heels hadn't won three games, two of them by a total of just seven points, in familiar surroundings (second round at Charlotte and East Regional at Raleigh)?

1982 CHAMPIONSHIP BRACKET

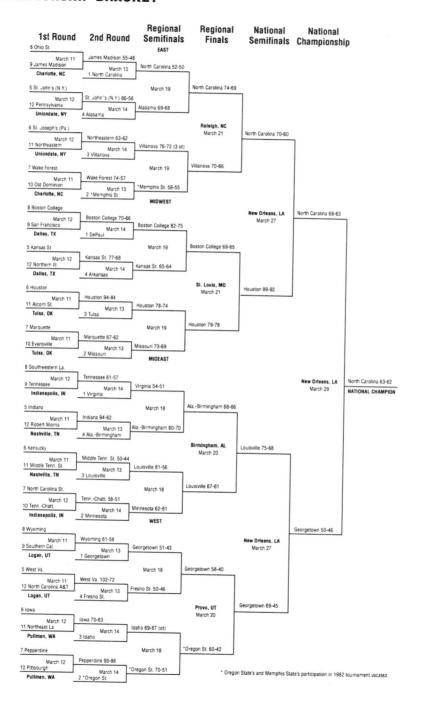

1st Round	2nd Round	Regional Semifinals	Regional Finals	National Semifinals	National Championship

EAST

8 Ohio St.
March 11 — James Madison 55-48
9 James Madison
Charlotte, NC
March 13 — North Carolina 52-50
1 North Carolina
March 19 — North Carolina 74-69

5 St. John's (N.Y.)
March 12 — St. John's (N.Y.) 66-56
12 Pennsylvania
Uniondale, NY
March 14 — Alabama 69-68
4 Alabama

Raleigh, NC
March 21

6 St. Joseph's (Pa.)
March 12 — Northeastern 63-62
11 Northeastern
Uniondale, NY
March 14 — Villanova 76-72 (3 ot)
3 Villanova
March 19 — Villanova 70-66

7 Wake Forest
March 11 — Wake Forest 74-57
10 Old Dominion
Charlotte, NC
March 13 — *Memphis St. 56-55
2 *Memphis St.

North Carolina 70-60

MIDWEST

8 Boston College
March 12 — Boston College 70-66
9 San Francisco
Dallas, TX
March 14 — Boston College 82-75
1 DePaul
March 19 — Boston College 69-65

5 Kansas St
March 12 — Kansas St. 77-68
12 Northern Ill.
Dallas, TX
March 14 — Kansas St. 65-64
4 Arkansas

St. Louis, MO
March 21

6 Houston
March 11 — Houston 94-84
11 Alcorn St.
Tulsa, OK
March 13 — Houston 78-74
3 Tulsa
March 19 — Houston 79-78

7 Marquette
March 11 — Marquette 67-62
10 Evansville
Tulsa, OK
March 13 — Missouri 73-69
2 Missouri

Houston 99-92

New Orleans, LA
March 27

North Carolina 68-63

MIDEAST

8 Southwestern La.
March 12 — Tennessee 61-57
9 Tennessee
Indianapolis, IN
March 14 — Virginia 54-51
1 Virginia
March 18 — Ala.-Birmingham 68-66

5 Indiana
March 11 — Indiana 94-62
12 Robert Morris
Nashville, TN
March 13 — Ala.-Birmingham 80-70
4 Ala.-Birmingham

Birmingham, AL
March 20

6 Kentucky
March 11 — Middle Tenn. St. 50-44
11 Middle Tenn. St.
Nashville, TN
March 13 — Louisville 81-56
3 Louisville
March 18 — Louisville 67-61

7 North Carolina St.
March 12 — Tenn.-Chatt. 58-51
10 Tenn.-Chatt.
Indianapolis, IN
March 14 — Minnesota 62-61
2 Minnesota

Louisville 75-68

New Orleans, LA
March 29

North Carolina 63-62

NATIONAL CHAMPION

WEST

8 Wyoming
March 11 — Wyoming 61-58
9 Southern Cal.
Logan, UT
March 13 — Georgetown 51-43
1 Georgetown
March 18 — Georgetown 58-40

5 West Va.
March 11 — West Va. 102-72
12 North Carolina A&T
Logan, UT
March 13 — Fresno St. 50-46
4 Fresno St.

Provo, UT
March 20

6 Iowa
March 12 — Iowa 70-63
11 Northeast La.
Pullman, WA
March 14 — Idaho 69-67 (ot)
3 Idaho
March 18 — *Oregon St. 60-42

7 Pepperdine
March 12 — Pepperdine 99-88
10 Pittsburgh
Pullman, WA
March 14 — *Oregon St. 70-51
2 *Oregon St.

Georgetown 69-45

New Orleans, LA
March 27

Georgetown 50-46

* Oregon State's and Memphis State's participation in 1982 tournament vacated.

1982–83

AT A GLANCE

NCAA Champion: North Carolina State (26-10).

NIT Champion: Fresno State (25-10).

New Conferences: AMCU (forerunner of Mid-Continent), ECAC South (forerunner of Colonial Athletic).

New Rules: It is no longer a jump-ball situation when the closely guarded five-second count is reached. It is a violation, and the ball is awarded to the defensive team out of bounds. An opening round was added to the NCAA Tournament, requiring the representatives of eight automatic-qualifying conferences to compete for four positions in the 52-team bracket. The current tourney format was established that begins the event the third weekend in March, regional championships on the fourth Saturday and Sunday, and the national semifinals and final the following Saturday and Monday.

NCAA Probation: Oklahoma City, St. Louis, Wichita State.

NCAA Consensus First-Team All-Americans: Dale Ellis, F, Sr., Tennessee; Patrick Ewing, C, Soph., Georgetown; Michael Jordan, G, Soph., North Carolina; Keith Lee, C, Soph., Memphis State; Sam Perkins, C, Jr., North Carolina; Ralph Sampson, C, Sr., Virginia; Wayman Tisdale, C-F, Fr., Oklahoma.

Houston's Clyde Drexler flies past an opponent.

Parity was more than a rhetorical concept this season. In a game hailed as one of the biggest upsets in college basketball history, a Ralph Sampson-led Virginia lost at Chaminade, 77-72, in Hawaii.

Oklahoma's Wayman Tisdale became the first freshman to be named an NCAA consensus first-team All-American. None of the NCAA's seven consensus first-team All-Americans reached the national semifinals.

Texas Southern's Harry Kelly led the nation in scoring with a 28.8-point average, including a national-high 60 points against Jarvis Christian.

Houston's Clyde Drexler set an SWC record with 11 steals against Syracuse.

Wyoming led the nation in field-goal percentage defense for the third consecutive season.

1982–83 FINAL NATIONAL POLLS

AP	UPI	USA/CNN	SCHOOL
1	1	2	Houston
2	2	3	Louisville
3	3	8	St. John's
4	4	5	Virginia
5	5	9	Indiana
6	6	18	UNLV
7	7	16	UCLA
8	8	7	North Carolina
9	9	10	Arkansas
10	12	19	Missouri
11	13	13	Boston College
12	10	6	Kentucky
13	11	11	Villanova
14	–	15	Wichita St.
15	16	–	UT-Chattanooga
16	14	1	North Carolina St.
17	17	12	Memphis St.
18	15	4	Georgia
19	19	–	Oklahoma St.
20	20	20	Georgetown
–	–	14	Iowa
–	–	17	Ohio St.
–	18	–	Illinois St.
–	–	21	Fresno St.
–	–	22	Utah
–	–	23	Syracuse
–	–	24	Washington St.
–	–	25	Tennessee

All-American forward Dale Ellis dunks one for the Tennessee Volunteers.

1982–83 INDIVIDUAL LEADERS

SCORING

PLAYER	PTS.	AVG.
Kelly, Texas Southern	835	28.8
Malone, Miss. St.	777	26.8
Yates, George Mason	723	26.8
Bradley, S. Florida	855	26.7
Jakubick, Akron	774	26.7
Goorjian, Loyola (Cal.)	601	26.1
Hughes, Loyola (Ill.)	744	25.7
Tisdale, Oklahoma	810	24.5
Lyons, N. Texas St.	728	24.3
Jackson, Centenary	697	24.0

REBOUNDING

PLAYER	REB.	AVG.
McDaniel, Wichita St.	403	14.4
Giles, S. Caro. St.	360	12.9

Cage, San Diego St.	354	12.6
Halsel, Northeastern	350	12.5
Cross, Maine	310	11.9
Green, UNLV	368	11.9
Kelly, Texas Southern	340	11.7
Sampson, Virginia	386	11.7
Olajuwon, Houston	388	11.4
Mosley, Nevada-Reno	325	11.2

FIELD GOAL PERCENTAGE

PLAYER	FGM	FGA	PCT.
Mikell, East Tenn. St.	197	292	.675
Phillips, Pepperdine	223	338	.660
McDowell, Florida	203	314	.646
Barkley, Auburn	161	250	.644
Best, St. Peter's	138	215	.642
Thorpe, Providence	204	321	.636
Robinson, Nicholls St.	146	231	.632

Johnson, Grambling	205	325	.631
DeBisschop, Fairfield	203	324	.627
Mosley, Nevada-Reno	184	297	.620

FREE THROW PERCENTAGE

PLAYER	FGM	FGA	PCT.
Gonzalez, Colorado	75	82	.915
Fisher, J. Madison	95	104	.913
Waitkus, Brown	97	108	.898
Cox, Vanderbilt	113	126	.897
Hobdy, Grambling	78	87	.897
Dykstra, W. Ill.	156	176	.886
Allen, Nevada-Reno	117	132	.886
Mullin, St. John's	173	197	.878
Price, Ga. Tech	93	106	.877
Gross, UC S. Barbara	140	160	.875

1982–83 TEAM LEADERS

SCORING OFFENSE

SCHOOL	PTS.	AVG.
Boston College	2697	84.3
Syracuse	2612	84.3
South Carolina St.	2353	84.0
Alabama St.	2352	84.0
Houston	2800	82.4

SCORING DEFENSE

SCHOOL	PTS.	AVG.
Princeton	1507	52.0
Fresno St.	1880	53.7
James Madison	1670	53.9
Notre Dame	1619	55.8
Arkansas St.	1651	56.9

SCORING MARGIN

SCHOOL	OFF.	DEF.	MAR.
Houston	82.4	64.9	17.4
Virginia	81.9	65.0	16.9
Oklahoma	82.3	70.7	11.6
North Carolina	77.0	65.7	11.3
St. John's	75.2	63.9	11.3
Wichita St.	82.3	71.0	11.3

WON-LOST PERCENTAGE

SCHOOL	W-L	PCT.
Houston	31-3	.912
UNLV	28-3	.903
Wichita St.	25-3	.893
Louisville	32-4	.889
Arkansas	26-4	.867

FIELD GOAL PERCENTAGE

SCHOOL	FGM	FGA	PCT.
Kentucky	869	1564	.556
Stanford	752	1373	.548
New Orleans	937	1714	.547
Pepperdine	900	1653	.544
Houston Baptist	712	1319	.540

FIELD GOAL PERCENTAGE DEFENSE

SCHOOL	FGM	FGA	PCT.
Wyoming	599	1441	.416
Virginia	863	2071	.417
Idaho	661	1582	.418
Montana	663	1574	.421
Memphis St.	831	1965	.423

FREE THROW PERCENTAGE

SCHOOL	FTM	FGA	PCT.
Western Illinois	526	679	.775
Dayton	453	586	.773
UC Santa Barbara	413	535	.772
William & Mary	470	609	.772
St. John's	649	843	.770

REBOUND MARGIN

SCHOOL	OWN	OPP.	MAR.
Wichita St.	42.4	33.6	8.8
Virginia	40.6	32.3	8.4
Houston	41.6	33.4	8.1
Wyoming	34.7	27.1	7.6
Alcorn St.	39.8	32.9	6.9

Wichita State's Antoine Carr (47 points against Southern Illinois), Arizona State's Paul Williams (45 against Southern Cal), and South Florida's Charlie Bradley (42 against Florida State) established single-game scoring records for their schools.

The number of independent schools in Division I decreased from 52 to 19. There had been as many as 79 independents in the mid-1970s.

The *USA Today*/CNN poll was introduced, giving fans three top national polls to argue over (along with AP and UPI).

1983 NCAA Tournament

Summary: Sophomore forward Lorenzo Charles scored only four points in the title game, but two of them came when he converted guard Dereck Whittenburg's off-line desperation shot from well beyond the top of the free-throw circle into a decisive dunk as North Carolina State upset Houston, 54-52. N.C. State became the only school to have as many as four playoff games decided by one or two points on its way to a championship.

Outcome for Defending Champion: North Carolina (28-8) was eliminated in the East

Regional final by Georgia, 82-77.

Star Gazing: Hakeem Olajuwon, who collected 41 points and 40 rebounds for national runner-up Houston in two Final Four games, is the only Final Four Most Outstanding Player since 1972 not to play for the championship team.

Biggest Upset: The first meeting between in-state rivals Kentucky and Louisville in more than 24 years was memorable as the Cardinals outscored the Wildcats 18-6 in overtime to reach the Final Four.

One and Only: This was the only year in which all of the Final Four teams won their conference tournaments— North Carolina State (ACC), Houston (SWC), Georgia (SEC), and Louisville (Metro).

Numbers Game: Georgia, seeded No. 4 in the 1983 East Regional in its playoff debut, is the only first-time entrant to be seeded better than fifth since the field expanded to at least 48 teams in 1980.

What If: Houston swingmen Clyde Drexler and Michael Young and forward Larry Micheaux combined to score 47 points per game. If only they combined for 17 points instead of 14 points in the championship game, the Cougars could have defeated North Carolina State rather than lose 54-52.

Putting Things in Perspective: Maryland (20-10) defeated N.C. State twice by a total of 14 points before losing in the second round against eventual national runner-up Houston. Virginia (29-5) defeated the Wolfpack twice by a total of 19 points before losing against N.C. State by one

An explosive Hakeem Olajuwon steals a Louisville pass in the 1983 NCAA Semifinals.

point in the West Regional final. N.C. State lost six of eight games in one span. Five of the Wolfpack's six ACC losses were by at least eight points, including back-to-back defeats by 18 points apiece.

1982-83 NCAA CHAMPION: N.C. STATE

SEASON STATISTICS OF N.C. STATE REGULARS

PLAYER	POS.	CL.	G.	FG%	FT%	PPG	RPG
Dereck Whittenburg	G	Sr.	22	.467	.800	17.5	2.7
Thurl Bailey	F-C	Sr.	36	.501	.717	16.7	7.7
Sidney Lowe	G	Sr.	36	.461	.776	11.3	3.7
Ernie Myers	G	Fr.	35	.446	.607	11.2	2.5
Lorenzo Charles	F	So.	36	.542	.670	8.1	6.0
Terry Gannon	G	So.	36	.521	.903	7.3	0.8
Cozell McQueen	C	So.	36	.431	.576	3.5	5.6
Alvin Battle	F	Jr.	33	.419	.520	2.7	2.0
George McClain	G	Fr.	25	.375	.500	2.7	0.5
Harold Thompson	F	Jr.	26	.353	.500	0.5	0.5
TEAM TOTALS			36	.472	.689	74.2	34.4

Assists leader: Lowe 271. **Blocked shots leader:** Bailey 95. **Steals leader:** Lowe 87.

1983 FINAL FOUR CHAMPIONSHIP GAME

ALBUQUERQUE, NM

N.C. STATE (54)	MIN.	FG-A	FT-A	REB.	A	PF	PTS.
Bailey	39	7-16	1-2	5	0	1	15
Charles	25	2-7	0-0	7	0	2	4
McQueen	34	1-5	2-2	12	1	4	4
Whittenburg	39	6-17	2-2	5	1	3	14
Lowe	40	4-9	0-1	0	8	2	8
Battle	4	0-1	2-2	1	1	1	2
Gannon	18	3-4	1-2	1	2	3	7
Myers	1	0-0	0-0	1	0	0	0
Team				2			
TOTALS	200	23-59	8-11	34	13	16	54

FG%: .390. **FT%:** .727. **Blocks:** 2. **Turnovers:** 6. **Steals:** 7 (Lowe 5).

HOUSTON (52)	MIN.	FG-A	FT-A	REB.	A	PF	PTS.
Drexler	25	1-5	2-2	2	0	4	4
Micheaux	18	2-6	0-0	6	0	1	4
Olajuwon	38	7-15	6-7	18	1	1	20
Franklin	35	2-6	0-1	0	3	0	4
Young	30	3-10	0-4	8	1	0	6
Anders	17	4-9	2-5	2	1	2	10
Gettys	20	2-2	0-0	2	2	3	4
Rose	7	0-1	0-0	1	0	2	0
Williams	10	0-1	0-0	4	1	3	0
Team				1			
TOTALS	200	21-55	10-19	44	9	16	52

FG%: .382. **FT%:** .526. **Blocks:** 8 (Olajuwon 7). **Turnovers:** 13. **Steals:** 0.
Halftime: North Carolina State 33-25.

NATIONAL SEMIFINALS

N.C. STATE (67): Bailey 9-17 2-5 20, Charles 2-2 1-2 5, McQueen 4-5 0-0 8, Whittenburg 8-18, 4-4 20, Lowe 4-6 2-2 10, Battle 0-0 0-0 0, Gannon 1-4 2-2 4. Team 28-52 (.538) 11-15 (.733) 67.

GEORGIA (60): Banks 5-19 3-5 13, Heard 3-5 2-3 8, Fair 2-9 1-2 5, Crosby 5-15 2-2 12, Fleming 7-17 0-0 14, Corhen 3-6 0-1 6, Hartry 1-3 0-0 2, Floyd 0-0 0-0 0. Team 26-74 (.351) 8-13 (.615) 60.

Halftime: North Carolina State 33-32.

LOUISVILLE (81): S. McCray 5-8 0-0 10, R. McCray 3-6 2-8 8, Jones 3-10 6-8 12, Gordon 6-15 5-6 17, Wagner 12-23 0-0 24, Thompson 1-4 4-5 4, Hall 2-4 0-0 4, West 0-0 0-0 0, Valentine 0-0 0-0 0. Team 32-70 (.457) 17-27 (.630) 81.

HOUSTON (94): Drexler 10-15 1-2 21, Micheaux 4-7 0-1 8, Olajuwon 9-14 3-7 21, Franklin 5-8 3-4 13, Young 7-18 2-3 16, Gettys 0-0 0-0 0, Anders 5-9 3-5 13, Rose 0-2 0-0 0, Williams 1-1 0-0 2, Giles 0-0 0-1 0. Team 41-74 (.554) 12-23 (.522) 94.

Halftime: Louisville 41-36.

ALL-TOURNAMENT TEAM
Thurl Bailey, F, Sr., North Carolina State
Sidney Lowe, G, Sr., North Carolina State
Hakeem Olajuwon, C, Soph., Houston*
Milt Wagner, G, Soph., Louisville
Dereck Whittenburg, G, Sr., North Carolina State

***Named Most Outstanding Player**

1983 CHAMPIONSHIP BRACKET

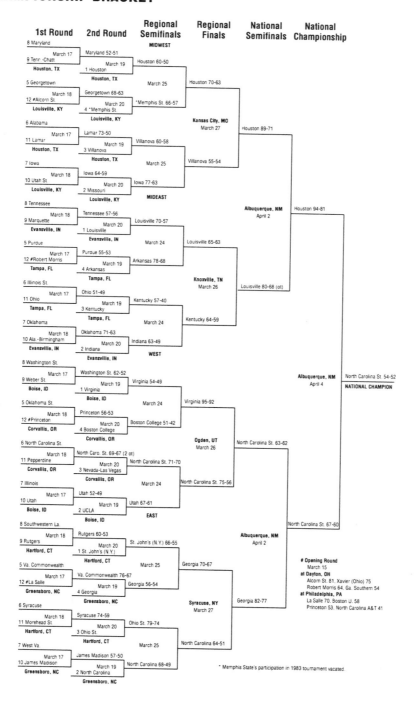

1st Round	2nd Round	Regional Semifinals	Regional Finals	National Semifinals	National Championship

MIDWEST

8 Maryland
March 17
9 Tenn.-Chatt.
Houston, TX
Maryland 52-51
March 19
1 Houston
Houston, TX
Houston 60-50
March 25
Houston 70-63

5 Georgetown
March 18
12 #Alcorn St.
Louisville, KY
Georgetown 68-63
March 20
4 *Memphis St.
Louisville, KY
*Memphis St. 66-57

Kansas City, MO
March 27
Houston 89-71

6 Alabama
March 17
11 Lamar
Houston, TX
Lamar 73-50
March 19
3 Villanova
Houston, TX
Villanova 60-58
March 25
Villanova 55-54

7 Iowa
March 18
10 Utah St
Louisville, KY
Iowa 64-59
March 20
2 Missouri
Louisville, KY
Iowa 77-63

Albuquerque, NM
April 2
Houston 94-81

MIDEAST

8 Tennessee
March 18
9 Marquette
Evansville, IN
Tennessee 57-56
March 20
1 Louisville
Evansville, IN
Louisville 70-57
March 24
Louisville 65-63

5 Purdue
March 17
12 #Robert Morris
Tampa, FL
Purdue 55-53
March 19
4 Arkansas
Tampa, FL
Arkansas 78-68

Knoxville, TN
March 26
Louisville 80-68 (ot)

6 Illinois St.
March 17
11 Ohio
Tampa, FL
Ohio 51-49
March 19
3 Kentucky
Tampa, FL
Kentucky 57-40
March 24
Kentucky 64-59

7 Oklahoma
March 18
10 Ala.-Birmingham
Evansville, IN
Oklahoma 71-63
March 20
2 Indiana
Evansville, IN
Indiana 63-49

WEST

8 Washington St.
March 17
9 Weber St.
Boise, ID
Washington St. 62-52
March 19
1 Virginia
Boise, ID
Virginia 54-49
March 24
Virginia 95-92

5 Oklahoma St.
March 18
12 #Princeton
Corvallis, OR
Princeton 56-53
March 20
4 Boston College
Corvallis, OR
Boston College 51-42

Ogden, UT
March 26
North Carolina St. 63-62

6 North Carolina St.
March 18
11 Pepperdine
Corvallis, OR
North Caro. St. 69-67 (2 ot)
March 20
3 Nevada-Las Vegas
Corvallis, OR
North Carolina St. 71-70
March 24
North Carolina St. 75-56

7 Illinois
March 17
10 Utah
Boise, ID
Utah 52-49
March 19
2 UCLA
Boise, ID
Utah 67-61

Albuquerque, NM
April 4
North Carolina St. 54-52
NATIONAL CHAMPION

North Carolina St. 67-60

EAST

8 Southwestern La.
March 18
9 Rutgers
Hartford, CT
Rutgers 60-53
March 20
1 St. John's (N.Y.)
Hartford, CT
St. John's (N.Y.) 66-55
March 25
Georgia 70-67

5 Va. Commonwealth
March 17
12 #La Salle
Greensboro, NC
Va. Commonwealth 76-67
March 19
4 Georgia
Greensboro, NC
Georgia 56-54

Albuquerque, NM
April 2
Georgia 82-77

6 Syracuse
March 18
11 Morehead St.
Hartford, CT
Syracuse 74-59
March 20
3 Ohio St.
Hartford, CT
Ohio St. 79-74
March 25
North Carolina 64-51

7 West Va.
March 17
10 James Madison
Greensboro, NC
James Madison 57-50
March 19
2 North Carolina
Greensboro, NC
North Carolina 68-49

Syracuse, NY
March 27
Georgia 82-77

Opening Round
March 15
at Dayton, OH
Alcorn St. 81, Xavier (Ohio) 75
Robert Morris 64, Ga. Southern 54
at Philadelphia, PA
La Salle 70, Boston U. 58
Princeton 53, North Carolina A&T 41

* Memphis State's participation in 1983 tournament vacated.

1983-84

AT A GLANCE

NCAA Champion: Georgetown (34-3).

NIT Champion: Michigan (23-10).

New Rules: Two free throws are taken for each common foul committed within the last two minutes of the second half and all of any overtime periods, if the bonus rule is in effect (rule was rescinded one month into the season). One additional NCAA Tournament opening-round game is established, requiring 10 automatic-qualifying conferences to compete for five positions in the 53-team bracket.

NCAA Probation: San Diego State.

NCAA Consensus First-Team All-Americans: Patrick Ewing, C, Jr., Georgetown; Michael Jordan, G, Jr., North Carolina; Hakeem Olajuwon, C, Jr., Houston; Sam Perkins, C, Sr., North Carolina; Wayman Tisdale, C-F, Soph., Oklahoma.

In one of the most ballyhooed regular-season matchups ever, the Ralph Sampson-led Virginia Cavaliers defeated fellow center Patrick Ewing and the Georgetown Hoyas, 68-63. Sampson collected 28 points and 16 rebounds compared to Ewing's 16 points and eight rebounds.

In the first regular-season meeting in 61 years between in-state rivals Kentucky and Louisville, the Wildcats whipped the Cardinals, 65-44.

Houston's Hakeem Olajuwon set an SWC record with 16 blocked shots against Arkansas.

North Carolina was ranked No. 1 with a 19-0 record when the Tar Heels succumbed at Arkansas, 65-64.

Maryland coach Lefty Driesell won his first ACC Tournament in 15 tries.

Oklahoma's Wayman Tisdale poured in a national-high 61 points against Texas-San Antonio.

Akron's Joe Jakubick became the only player in a six-year span to average more than 30 points per game.

Harvard set an NCAA single-season record for free-throw accuracy (82.2 percent).

Lamar's 80-game homecourt winning streak, which started in 1978, was snapped by Louisiana Tech, 68-65, in the Southland Conference Tournament.

1983-84 FINAL NATIONAL POLLS

AP	UPI	USA/CNN	SCHOOL
1	1	4	North Carolina
2	2	1	Georgetown
3	3	3	Kentucky
4	4	6	DePaul
5	5	2	Houston
6	6	5	Illinois
7	8	14	Oklahoma
8	7	13	Arkansas
9	9	20	Texas-El Paso
10	11	17	Purdue
11	10	12	Maryland
12	12	21	Tulsa
13	13	10	UNLV
14	14	22	Duke
15	15	19	Washington
16	16	9	Memphis St.
17	20	–	Oregon St.
18	16	18	Syracuse
19	–	8	Wake Forest
20	–	–	Temple
–	–	7	Virginia
–	18	11	Indiana
–	–	15	Dayton
–	–	16	Louisville
–	19	–	Auburn
–	–	23	Michigan
–	–	24	SMU
–	–	25	Temple

Temple went unbeaten in the Atlantic 10 Conference after posting a losing league record (5-9) the previous year and Northeastern went unbeaten in North Atlantic Conference competition after compiling a 4-6 league mark the previous season.

DePaul's Ray Meyer retired after a 42-year coaching career with a 724-354 record. Meyer, who compiled a 14-16 record in 13 tournament appearances with DePaul, is the only coach to go more than 40 years from his first appearance in the playoffs to his last (1943 to 1984). He averaged 26 victories his last seven seasons after averaging a modest 14 triumphs annually in a 21-year span from 1957 to 1977. He was replaced by his son, Joey, who had been a DePaul assistant coach.

1984 NCAA Tournament

Summary: Georgetown's Patrick Ewing and Houston's Hakeem Olajuwon, the nation's two most celebrated centers, clashed in the champi-

1983–84 INDIVIDUAL LEADERS

SCORING

PLAYER	PTS.	AVG.
Jakubick, Akron	814	30.1
Jackson, Alabama St.	812	29.0
Durrant, Brigham Young	866	27.9
Hughes, Loyola (Ill.)	800	27.6
Tisdale, Oklahoma	919	27.0
Dumars, McNeese St.	817	26.4
Crawford, U.S. Intl.	614	24.6
Cage, San Diego St.	686	24.5
Burtt, Iona	749	24.2
Wood, Cal St. Full.	719	24.0

REBOUNDING

PLAYER	REB.	AVG.
Olajuwon, Houston	500	13.5
Scurry, Long Island	418	13.5
McDaniel, Wichita St.	393	13.1
Newman, Ark.-Little Rock	348	12.9
Cage, San Diego St.	352	12.6
Cross, Maine	339	12.6
Brown, G. Washington	351	12.1

Sanders, Miss. Valley St.	338	12.1
Binion, N. Carolina A&T	335	11.6
Koncak, SMU	378	11.5

ASSISTS

PLAYER	AST.	AVG.
Lathan, Ill.-Chicago	274	9.4
Tarkanian, UNLV	289	8.5
Gettys, Houston	309	8.4
LaFleur, Northeastern	252	7.9
William, Florida St.	215	7.7
Teague, Boston U.	218	7.5
Weingrad, Hofstra	208	7.4
Smith, Massachusetts	212	7.3
Les, Bradley	158	7.2
Stockton, Gonzaga	201	7.2

FIELD GOAL PERCENTAGE

PLAYER	FGM	FGA	PCT.
Olajuwon, Houston	249	369	.675
Hurt, Alabama	168	253	.664
Ewing, Georgetown	242	368	.658
Green, Oregon St.	134	204	.657
Walker, Utica	125	191	.654
Thornton, UC Irvine	151	236	.640
Barkley, Auburn	162	254	.638
Toomer, Florida A&M	149	234	.637
Boldon, C. Mich.	151	238	.634
Burke, Dartmouth	194	306	.634

FREE THROW PERCENTAGE

PLAYER	FTM	FTA	PCT.
Alford, Indiana	137	150	.913
Carrabino, Harvard	153	169	.905
Mullin, St. John's	169	187	.904
Ferry, Harvard	84	93	.903
Cunningham, UTSA	94	107	.879
Golston, Loyola (Ill.)	128	146	.877
Beasley, Arizona St.	112	128	.875
Potter, O. Roberts	82	94	.872
Arnolie, Penn	82	94	.872
White, UT-Chat.	124	143	.867

1983–84 TEAM LEADERS

SCORING OFFENSE

SCHOOL	PTS.	AVG.
Tulsa	2816	90.8
Alabama St.	2485	88.8
Oklahoma	2953	86.9
Marshall	2589	83.5
Oral Roberts	2569	82.9

SCORING DEFENSE

SCHOOL	PTS.	AVG.
Princeton	1403	50.1
Fresno St.	1802	54.6
Tulane	1535	54.8
Oregon St.	1618	55.8
Illinois	1737	56.0

SCORING MARGIN

SCHOOL	OFF.	DEF.	MAR.
Georgetown	74.3	57.9	16.4
North Carolina	80.1	64.8	15.3
Oklahoma	86.9	72.6	14.3
Lamar	78.5	64.8	13.6
UNLV	82.1	68.7	13.4

WON-LOST PERCENTAGE

SCHOOL	W-L	PCT.
Georgetown	34-3	.919
North Carolina	28-3	.903
DePaul	27-3	.900
Texas-El Paso	27-4	.871
Tulsa	27-4	.871

FIELD GOAL PERCENTAGE

SCHOOL	FGM	FGA	PCT.
Houston Baptist	797	1445	.552
North Carolina	966	1779	.543
Southern Methodist	1023	1892	.541
Navy	873	1616	.540
Maryland	941	1745	.539

FIELD GOAL PERCENTAGE DEFENSE

SCHOOL	FGM	FGA	PCT.
Georgetown	799	2025	.395
DePaul	687	1658	.414
Memphis St.	796	1904	.418
Kentucky	796	1894	.420
Southern (La.)	746	1768	.422

FREE THROW PERCENTAGE

SCHOOL	FTM	FTA	PCT.
Harvard	535	651	.822
North Carolina	551	704	.783
Illinois St.	510	659	.774
Fairfield	508	657	.773
St. Louis	400	521	.768

REBOUND MARGIN

SCHOOL	OWN	OPP.	MAR.
Northeastern	40.1	30.3	9.8
Georgetown	40.0	30.5	9.5
St. Joseph's	39.4	30.3	9.1
Auburn	36.9	28.5	8.5
George Washington	38.3	30.8	7.4

onship game but the head-to-head duel didn't live up to its lofty billing. It was little consolation to Olajuwon when he played Ewing to a stand-off on the backboards (each grabbed nine rebounds) and outscored his rival, 15-10. At the end, Olajuwon was on the national runner-up team for the second consecutive season as freshmen Reggie Williams and Michael Graham combined for 33 points to spark the Hoyas to a 84-75 triumph. Ewing, the Hoyas' leading scorer for the season, matched the all-time low scoring total for a Final Four Most Outstanding Player with 18 points in two games (fifth on the team), but he was the key component in Georgetown's suffocating defense. The Hoyas led the nation in field-goal percentage defense (39.5 percent) and exhibited their tenacity in the national semifinals when they harassed Kentucky into shooting a dismal 9.1 percent in the second half (3 of 33) en route to a 53-40 victory. Georgetown's Michael Jackson, a 6-1 guard averaging 1.4 rebounds per game entering the Final Four, retrieved 10

DePaul coach Ray Meyer (left) retired after the 1983–84 season and was replaced by his son, Joey (right) who was an assistant coach.

missed shots against Kentucky's formidable frontline to help the Hoyas overcome a seven-point halftime deficit in the national semifinals.

Outcome for Defending Champion: North Carolina State (19-14) finished in seventh place in the ACC before losing at home to Florida State in the first round of the NIT.

Star Gazing: Ewing, the only individual to fail to score more than 10 points in either the national semifinal or championship game in the year he was named Most Outstanding Player, tallied eight points in a 53-40 triumph over Kentucky in the semifinals and 10 in an 84-75 decision over Houston in the final.

Biggest Upset: Many observers predicted Georgetown would meet top-ranked North Carolina in the national final, but the Tar Heels were upset in the East Regional semifinals by Indiana (72-68) when national player of the year Michael Jordan was limited to 13 points, one rebound, and one assist.

One and Only: Virginia became the only school to reach the Final Four despite compiling a losing record in conference competition (6-8 in ACC) and succumbing in the first round of its league tournament.... Georgetown's John Thompson is the only person to play for an NBA championship team (Boston Celtics '65) before coaching an NCAA titlist.

1983–84 NCAA CHAMPION: GEORGETOWN

SEASON STATISTICS OF GEORGETOWN REGULARS

PLAYER	POS.	CL.	G.	FG%	FT%	PPG	RPG
Patrick Ewing	C	Jr.	37	.658	.656	16.4	10.0
David Wingate	G-F	So.	37	.435	.721	11.2	3.6
Michael Jackson	G	So.	31	.509	.816	10.1	1.7
Reggie Williams	G-F	Fr.	37	.433	.768	9.1	3.5
Bill Martin	F	Jr.	37	.509	.705	8.9	5.9
Michael Graham	F	Fr.	35	.561	.459	4.9	4.0
Horace Broadnax	G	So.	35	.434	.853	4.8	1.4
Gene Smith	G	Sr.	36	.511	.592	3.7	2.1
Fred Brown	G	Sr.	36	.486	.646	3.2	2.6
Ralph Dalton	C-F	Jr.	36	.569	.574	2.8	2.2
TEAM TOTALS			37	.509	.678	74.3	40.0

Assists leader: Jackson 137. **Blocked shots leader:** Ewing 133. **Steals leader:** Smith 67.

1984 FINAL FOUR CHAMPIONSHIP GAME

SEATTLE, WA

HOUSTON (75)	MIN.	FG-A	FT-A	REB.	A	PF	PTS.
Winslow	33	0-1	2-2	6	3	4	2
Young	37	8-21	2-3	5	1	3	18
Olajuwon	32	6-9	3-7	9	0	4	15
Franklin	38	8-15	5-6	2	9	3	21
Gettys	29	3-3	0-0	1	7	2	6
Anders	10	2-2	0-2	0	0	0	4
Clark	1	0-0	0-0	0	0	0	0
Anderson	6	1-1	0-0	2	0	0	2
Dickens	6	2-3	1-2	0	0	5	5
Thomas	2	0-0	0-0	0	0	0	0
Giles	2	0-0	0-0	0	0	0	0
Weaver	1	0-0	0-0	0	0	0	0
Orsak	1	1-1	0-0	0	0	0	2
Alexander	1	0-0	0-0	1	0	0	0
Belcher	1	0-0	0-0	0	0	0	0
Team				3			
TOTALS	200	31-56	13-22	29	20	21	75

FG%: .554. **FT%:** .591. **Blocks:** 4. **Turnovers:** 13. **Steals:** 3.

GEORGETOWN (84)	MIN.	FG-A	FT-A	REB.	A	PF	PTS.
Wingate	32	5-10	6-9	1	3	4	16
Dalton	13	0-0	0-0	2	0	1	0
Ewing	30	4-8	2-2	9	3	4	10
Brown	15	1-2	2-2	4	4	4	4
Jackson	35	3-4	5-5	0	6	4	11
Graham	24	7-9	0-2	5	0	4	14
Williams	26	9-18	1-2	7	3	2	19
Broadnax	8	2-3	0-0	0	0	2	4
Martin	16	3-6	0-0	2	0	0	6
Morris	1	0-0	0-0	0	0	0	0
Team				7			
TOTALS	200	34-60	16-22	37	19	25	84

FG%: .567. **FT%:** .727. **Blocks:** 6 (Ewing 4). **Turnovers:** 9. **Steals:** 0. **Halftime:** Georgetown 40-30.

NATIONAL SEMIFINALS

VIRGINIA (47): Miller 6-15 0-0 12, Edelin 1-2 0-0 2, Polynice 4-7 1-1 9, Wilson 5-12 2-2 12, Carlisle 3-14 2-2 8, Stokes 1-1 0-2 2, Sheehey 1-3 0-0 2. Team 21-54 (.389) 5-7 (.714) 47.

HOUSTON (49): Winslow 4-7 0-0 8, Young 8-16 1-4 17, Olajuwon 4-5 4-6 12, Franklin 2-7 2-2 6, Gettys 3-7 0-0 6, Dickens 0-0 0-0 0, Alexander 0-0 0-0 0. Team 21-42 (.500) 7-12 (.583) 49.

Halftime: Houston 25-23. **Regulation:** Tied 43-43.

GEORGETOWN (53): Wingate 5-8 1-2 11, Dalton 0-1 0-0 0, Ewing 4-6 0-0 8, Brown 0-1 0-1 0, Jackson 4-9 4-6 12, Smith 2-4 1-2 5, Martin 1-4 0-0 2, Graham 4-6 0-2 8, Williams 1-7 0-0 2, Broadnax 2-4 1-2 5. Team 23-50 (.460) 7-15 (.467) 53.

KENTUCKY (40): Bowie 3-10 4-4 10, Walker 1-3 2-2 4, Turpin 2-11 1-2 5, Beal 2-8 2-2 6, Master 2-7 2-2 6, Bennett 1-8 0-0 2, Blackmon 2-5 1-2 5, Bearup 0-0 2-2 2, Harden 0-1 0-0 0. Team 13-53 (.245) 14-16 (.875) 40.

Halftime: Kentucky 29-22.

ALL-TOURNAMENT TEAM

Patrick Ewing, C, Jr., Georgetown*
Alvin Franklin, G, Soph., Houston
Michael Graham, F, Fr., Georgetown
Hakeem Olajuwon, C, Jr., Houston
Michael Young, F, Sr., Houston

*Named Most Outstanding Player

Numbers Game: Dayton forward Roosevelt Chapman became the only non-guard to be the undisputed leading scorer of an NCAA Tournament and not participate in the Final Four (105 points in four games).... Northeastern hit 75 percent from the floor (33 of 44), including 15 of 17 by freshman Reggie Lewis, in the first round, but bowed to Virginia Commonwealth, 70-69.

What If: Eventual top six NBA draft choices Sam Bowie, Melvin Turpin, and Kenny Walker combined to shoot 56.4 percent from the floor to help Kentucky register 51.5 percent field-goal accuracy as a team in the 1983–84 season. If only the Wildcats had managed to hit 30.3 percent of their second-half field-goal attempts instead of 9.1 percent (3 of 33) in the national semifinals, they could have defeated eventual champion Georgetown rather than blow a seven-point halftime lead. Kentucky's starters missed all 21 of their field-goal attempts after intermission. The first-round starting frontcourt of Bowie, Turpin, and Walker combined to shoot 25 percent from the floor (6 of 24) in the entire game.

1984 CHAMPIONSHIP BRACKET

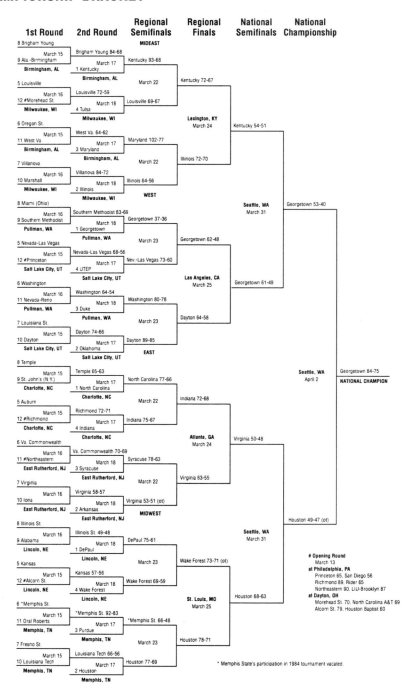

	1st Round	2nd Round	Regional Semifinals	Regional Finals	National Semifinals	National Championship

MIDEAST

8 Brigham Young
March 15
9 Ala.-Birmingham
Birmingham, AL

Brigham Young 84-68
March 17
1 Kentucky
Birmingham, AL

Kentucky 93-68

Kentucky 72-67

5 Louisville
March 16
12 #Morehead St.
Milwaukee, WI

Louisville 72-59
March 18
4 Tulsa
Milwaukee, WI

Louisville 69-67

March 22

Lexington, KY
March 24

Kentucky 54-51

6 Oregon St.
March 15
11 West Va.
Birmingham, AL

West Va. 64-62
March 17
3 Maryland
Birmingham, AL

Maryland 102-77

Illinois 72-70

7 Villanova
March 16
10 Marshall
Milwaukee, WI

Villanova 84-72
March 18
2 Illinois
Milwaukee, WI

Illinois 64-56

March 22

WEST

Georgetown 53-40

8 Miami (Ohio)
March 16
9 Southern Methodist
Pullman, WA

Southern Methodist 83-69
March 18
1 Georgetown
Pullman, WA

Georgetown 37-36

Georgetown 62-48

Seattle, WA
March 31

5 Nevada-Las Vegas
March 15
12 #Princeton
Salt Lake City, UT

Nevada-Las Vegas 68-56
March 17
4 UTEP
Salt Lake City, UT

Nev.-Las Vegas 73-60

March 23

Las Angeles, CA
March 25

Georgetown 61-49

6 Washington
March 16
11 Nevada-Reno
Pullman, WA

Washington 64-54
March 18
3 Duke
Pullman, WA

Washington 80-78

Dayton 64-58

7 Louisiana St.
March 15
10 Dayton
Salt Lake City, UT

Dayton 74-66
March 17
2 Oklahoma
Salt Lake City, UT

Dayton 89-85

March 23

EAST

8 Temple
March 15
9 St. John's (N.Y.)
Charlotte, NC

Temple 65-63
March 17
1 North Carolina
Charlotte, NC

North Carolina 77-66

Indiana 72-68

5 Auburn
March 15
12 #Richmond
Charlotte, NC

Richmond 72-71
March 17
4 Indiana
Charlotte, NC

Indiana 75-67

March 22

Atlanta, GA
March 24

Virginia 50-48

6 Va. Commonwealth
March 16
11 #Northeastern
East Rutherford, NJ

Va. Commonwealth 70-69
March 18
3 Syracuse
East Rutherford, NJ

Syracuse 78-63

Virginia 63-55

Seattle, WA
March 31

7 Virginia
March 16
10 Iona
East Rutherford, NJ

Virginia 58-57
March 18
2 Arkansas
East Rutherford, NJ

Virginia 53-51 (ot)

March 22

MIDWEST

Houston 49-47 (ot)

8 Illinois St.
March 16
9 Alabama
Lincoln, NE

Illinois St. 49-48
March 18
1 DePaul
Lincoln, NE

DePaul 75-61

Wake Forest 73-71 (ot)

5 Kansas
March 15
12 #Alcorn St.
Lincoln, NE

Kansas 57-56
March 17
4 Wake Forest
Lincoln, NE

Wake Forest 69-59

March 23

St. Louis, MO
March 25

Houston 68-63

6 *Memphis St.
March 15
11 Oral Roberts
Memphis, TN

*Memphis St. 92-83
March 17
3 Purdue
Memphis, TN

*Memphis St. 66-48

Houston 78-71

Seattle, WA
April 2

Georgetown 84-75
NATIONAL CHAMPION

7 Fresno St.
March 15
10 Louisiana Tech
Memphis, TN

Louisiana Tech 66-56
March 17
2 Houston
Memphis, TN

Houston 77-69

March 23

 # Opening Round
March 13
at Philadelphia, PA
Princeton 65, San Diego 56
Richmond 89, Rider 65
Northeastern 90, LIU-Brooklyn 87
at Dayton, OH
Morehead St. 70, North Carolina A&T 69
Alcorn St. 79, Houston Baptist 60

* Memphis State's participation in 1984 tournament vacated.

1984–85

NCAA Champion: Villanova (25-10).

NIT Champion: UCLA (21-12).

New Rules: The coaching box is introduced, whereby a coach and all bench personnel must remain in the 28-foot-long box unless seeking information from the scorer's table. The NCAA Tournament bracket is expanded to include 64 teams, eliminating first-round byes.

NCAA Probation: Akron.

NCAA Consensus First-Team All-Americans: Johnny Dawkins, G, Jr., Duke; Patrick Ewing, C, Sr., Georgetown; Keith Lee, C, Sr., Memphis State; Xavier McDaniel, F, Sr., Wichita State; Chris Mullin, G-F, Sr., St. John's; Wayman Tisdale, C-F, Jr., Oklahoma.

Georgia Tech, after finishing in the ACC's second division in its first five seasons in the league, earned a three-way share of the league's regular-season title with a 9-5 conference record. No ACC team had previously finished first with more than three defeats. All eight ACC members participated in the two postseason tourneys—five in the NCAA and three in the NIT—but none reached the national semifinals of either event.

Wichita State's Xavier McDaniel posted the lowest nation-leading scoring average (27.2) since Villanova's Paul Arizin averaged 25.3 in 1950.

Penn State's Craig Collins set an NCAA single-season record for free-throw accuracy by hitting 94 of 98 foul shots (95.9 percent).

Michigan, which was a total of 16 games under .500 in Big Ten competition over the previous six seasons, captured the conference championship with a 16-2 league mark.

Syracuse snapped Kentucky's streak of eight consecutive seasons leading the nation in attendance.

Loyola of Chicago's Alfredrick Hughes (47 points against Detroit) and George Mason's Carlos Yates (42 against Navy) set school single-game scoring records.

LSU was in sixth place in the SEC with a 7-5 record before winning its last six league games to capture the conference crown. The Tigers were believed to be the first team ever to win the SEC title with no seniors on its roster.

Kentucky's Joe B. Hall retired after a 19-year coaching career with a 373-156 record. Washington's Marv Harshman, who previously coached at Pacific Lutheran and Washington State, retired after a 40-year coaching career with a 642-448 record.

1984–85 FINAL NATIONAL POLLS

AP	UPI	USA/CNN	SCHOOL
1	1	2	Georgetown
2	2	9	Michigan
3	3	3	St. John's
4	5	6	Oklahoma
5	4	5	Memphis St.
6	6	4	Georgia Tech
7	7	7	North Carolina
8	8	8	Louisiana Tech
9	9	20	UNLV
10	12	13	Duke
11	11	19	Va. Commonwealth
12	10	11	Illinois
13	13	16	Kansas
14	17	12	Loyola (Ill.)
15	15	17	Syracuse
16	18	10	North Carolina St.
17	16	–	Texas Tech
18	14	–	Tulsa
19	–	–	Georgia
20	19	–	Louisiana St.
1	–	–	Villanova
–	–	14	Auburn
–	–	15	Boston College
–	–	18	Maryland
–	20	–	Michigan St.
–	–	21	Ala.-Birmingham
–	–	22	Alabama
–	–	23	UCLA
–	–	24	Kentucky
–	–	25	Arkansas

1985 NCAA Tournament

Summary: Villanova became the worst seed (#8 in the Southeast Regional) to win a national championship. The Wildcats shot a championship game-record 78.6 percent from the floor in posting a 66-64 victory against defending champion Georgetown, the nation's top-ranked team. They also defeated three other teams with No. 1 or No. 2 seeds (Michigan, North Carolina, and Memphis State). The narrow victory over the Hoyas typified Rollie Massimino's NCAA playoff coaching at Villanova as he won 11 of 12

Oklahoma All-American forward Wayman Tisdale racks up some hang time.

1984–85 INDIVIDUAL LEADERS

SCORING

PLAYER	PTS.	AVG.
McDaniel, Wichita St.	844	27.2
Hughes, Loyola (Ill.)	868	26.3
Palombizio, Ball St.	762	26.3
Dumars, McNeese St.	697	25.8
Catledge, South Alabama	718	25.6
Gervin, Texas-San Ant.	718	25.6
Tisdale, Oklahoma	932	25.2
Smith, Loyola M'mount	678	25.1
Mitchell, Mercer	774	25.0
Harper, Miami (Ohio)	772	24.9

REBOUNDING

PLAYER	REB.	AVG.
McDaniel, Wichita St.	460	14.8
Benjamin, Creighton	451	14.1
Scurry, Long Island	394	14.1
Towns, Monmouth	319	12.3
Sanders, Miss. Valley St.	344	11.9
Stivrins, Colorado	317	11.7
Robinson, Navy	370	11.6

Catledge, S. Alabama	322	11.5
Neal, Cal St. Full.	326	11.2
Williams, Alabama St.	288	11.1

ASSISTS

PLAYER	AST.	AVG.
Weingard, Hofstra	228	9.5
Golston, Loyola (Ill.)	305	9.2
Les, Bradley	263	8.8
Chisholm, Delaware	224	8.0
Carr, Nebraska	237	7.9
James, Brooklyn	211	7.5
Clarington, Tenn. Tech	210	7.5
Moore, SMU	247	7.5
Teague, Boston	217	7.2
McCarthy, Weber St.	209	7.2

FIELD GOAL PERCENTAGE

PLAYER	FGM	FGA	PCT.
Walker, Utica	154	216	.713
Moore, Creighton	265	393	.674

Hoppen, Nebraska	270	418	.646
Robinson, Navy	302	469	.644
Staves, Southern (La.)	164	257	.638
Salley, Ga. Tech	193	308	.627
Ewing, Georgetown	220	352	.625
Daugherty, N. Carolina	238	381	.625
Bantum, Cornell	163	262	.622
Lavodrama, Houst. Bapt.	186	301	.618

FREE THROW PERCENTAGE

PLAYER	FTM	FTA	PCT.
Collins, Penn St.	94	98	.959
Alford, Indiana	116	126	.921
Eggink, Marist	81	88	.920
Nutt, TCU	77	84	.917
Timko, Youngstown St.	78	86	.907
Hagan, Weber St.	86	95	.905
Burden, St. Louis	93	104	.894
Brooks, Tennessee	146	164	.890
Olson, Wisconsin	73	82	.890
Webster, Harvard	96	108	.889

1984–85 TEAM LEADERS

SCORING OFFENSE

SCHOOL	PTS.	AVG.
Oklahoma	3328	89.9
Alcorn St.	2555	85.2
Southern (La.)	2515	83.8
Loyola (Ill.)	2757	83.5
Utah St.	2292	81.9

SCORING DEFENSE

SCHOOL	PTS.	AVG.
Fresno St.	1696	53.0
Princeton	1429	55.0
Colgate	1451	55.8
Temple	1736	56.0
Illinois	2001	57.2

SCORING MARGIN

SCHOOL	OFF.	DEF.	MAR.
Georgetown	74.3	57.3	17.1
Oklahoma	89.9	75.6	14.4
Navy	78.4	65.3	13.0
Louisiana Tech	77.9	65.1	12.8
Illinois	68.9	57.2	11.7

WON-LOST PERCENTAGE

SCHOOL	W-L	PCT.
Georgetown	35-3	.921
Louisiana Tech	29-3	.906
Memphis St.	31-4	.886
St. John's	31-4	.886
UNLV	28-4	.875

FIELD GOAL PERCENTAGE

SCHOOL	FGM	FGA	PCT.
Navy	946	1726	.548
St. John's	978	1806	.542
North Carolina	1039	1925	.540
Iona	898	1669	.538
Michigan St.	837	1559	.537

FIELD GOAL PERCENTAGE DEFENSE

SCHOOL	FGM	FGA	PCT.
Georgetown	833	2064	.404
Illinois	832	1989	.418
West Virginia	693	1652	.419
Iowa	767	1826	.420
Memphis St.	911	2152	.423

FREE THROW PERCENTAGE

SCHOOL	FTM	FTA	PCT.
Harvard	450	555	.811
Davidson	539	692	.779
Weber St.	495	641	.772
The Citadel	529	688	.769
Texas-San Antonio	454	591	.768

REBOUND MARGIN

SCHOOL	OWN	OPP.	MAR.
Georgetown	39.6	30.5	9.1
Michigan	36.7	28.8	7.9
E. Kentucky	40.8	32.9	7.9
Iowa	41.4	33.8	7.7
Washington	34.3	26.9	7.4

NCAA Tournament games decided by fewer than five points.

Star Gazing: Chris Mullin, after averaging 25.5 points in St. John's first four playoff games, became the only national player of the year (UPI, USBWA, and Wooden Award) to score less than 10 points when his school was eliminated in a Final Four contest. The Redmen were routed by Georgetown (77-59) in the national semifinals when Mullin was limited to eight points in 39 minutes.

Biggest Upset: LSU was one of the biggest disappointments in NCAA history. The Tigers, seeded fourth in the Southeast Regional, boasted a roster including eventual NBA first-round draft picks John Williams and Jerry Reynolds and six other players who became NBA draft choices. But they became the only top four seed

1984–85 NCAA CHAMPION: VILLANOVA

SEASON STATISTICS OF VILLANOVA REGULARS

PLAYER	POS.	CL.	G.	FG%	FT%	PPG	RPG
Ed Pinckney	C	Sr.	35	.600	.730	15.6	8.9
Dwayne McClain	F-G	Sr.	35	.574	.774	14.8	4.1
Harold Pressley	F	Jr.	35	.488	.644	12.0	7.9
Gary McLain	G	Sr.	35	.500	.831	8.0	1.2
Dwight Wilbur	G	Jr.	35	.467	.745	7.5	2.0
Harold Jensen	G	So.	32	.434	.813	4.5	1.2
Mark Plansky	F	Fr.	30	.442	.552	3.3	2.0
Chuck Everson	C	Jr.	32	.514	.565	1.5	1.5
TEAM TOTALS			35	.510	.715	68.7	31.8

Assists leader: McLain 150. **Blocked shots leaders:** Pinckney 64, Pressley 38. **Steals leaders:** Pinckney 54, Pressley 53.

1985 FINAL FOUR CHAMPIONSHIP GAME

LEXINGTON, KY

VILLANOVA (66)	MIN.	FG-A	FT-A	REB.	A	PF	PTS.
Pressley	40	4-6	3-4	4	1	1	11
McClain	40	5-7	7-8	1	3	3	17
Pinckney	37	5-7	6-7	6	5	3	16
Wilbur	5	0-0	0-0	0	1	0	0
McLain	40	3-3	2-2	2	2	2	8
Jensen	34	5-5	4-5	1	2	2	14
Plansky	1	0-0	0-1	0	0	1	0
Everson	3	0-0	0-0	0	0	0	0
Team				3			
TOTALS	200	22-28	22-27	17	14	12	66

FG%: .786. **FT%:** .815. **Blocks:** 1. **Turnovers:** 17. **Steals:** 8.

GEORGETOWN (64)	MIN.	FG-A	FT-A	REB.	A	PF	PTS.
Martin	37	4-6	2-2	5	1	2	10
Williams	29	5-9	0-2	4	2	3	10
Ewing	39	7-13	0-0	5	2	4	14
Jackson	37	4-7	0-0	0	9	4	8

Wingate	39	8-14	0-0	2	2	4	16
McDonald	2	0-1	0-0	0	0	0	0
Broadnax	13	1-2	2-2	1	2	4	4
Dalton	4	0-1	2-2	0	0	1	2
TOTALS	200	29-53	6-8	17	18	22	64

FG%: .547. **FT%:** .750. **Blocks:** 1. **Turnovers:** 11. **Steals:** 6.
Halftime: Villanova 29-28.

NATIONAL SEMIFINALS

VILLANOVA (52): Pressley 1-8 1-2 3, McClain 6-9 7-7 19, Pinckney 3-7 6-9 12, Wilbur 0-2 0-0 0, McLain 2-5 5-5 9, Plansky 1-1 1-3 3, Jensen 3-6 0-0 6, Everson 0-0 0-0 0. Team 16-38 (.421) 20-26 (.769) 52.

MEMPHIS STATE (45): Lee 3-9 4-4 10, Holmes 4-8 0-0 8, Bedford 4-9 0-0 8, Turner 5-13 1-2 11, Askew 1-3 0-1 2, Wilfong 0-1 0-0 0, Boyd 0-2 0-0 0, Bailey 1-1 0-0 2, Becton 1-4 2-2 4. Team 19-50 (.380) 7-9 (.778) 45.

Halftime: Tied 23-23.

ST. JOHN'S (59): Berry 4-8 4-5 12, Glass 4-4 5-7 13, Wennington 4-7 4-5 12, Mullin 4-8 0-0 8, Moses 3-7 0-0 6, Bross 0-0 0-0 0, Jackson 3-4 0-2 6, Jones 1-4 0-0 2, Stewart 0-0 0-0 0, Shurina 0-0 0-0 0, Cornegy 0-0 0-0 0. Team 23-42 (.548) 13-19 (.684) 59.

GEORGETOWN (77): Martin 4-8 4-4 12, Williams 8-15 4-4 20, Ewing 7-12 2-4 16, Jackson 2-5 0-0 4, Wingate 3-8 6-8 12, McDonald 0-1 0-0 0, Floyd 0-0 0-0 0, Broadnax 3-4 3-4 9, Lockhart 0-0 0-0 0, Highsmith 0-1 0-0 0, Mateen 0-1 0-0 0, Dalton 2-2 0-0 4. Team 29-57 (.509) 19-24 (.792) 77.

Halftime: Georgetown 32-28.

ALL-TOURNAMENT TEAM

Patrick Ewing, C, Sr., Georgetown
Harold Jensen, G, Soph., Villanova
Dwayne McClain, F-G, Sr., Villanova
Gary McLain, G, Sr., Villanova
Ed Pinckney, C, Sr., Villanova*

*Named Most Outstanding Player

to lose a first-round game by more than 20 points when they were trounced by No. 13 seed Navy, 78-55, when David Robinson collected 18 points and 18 rebounds for the Midshipmen.

One and Only: Massimino became the only individual to be more than 10 games below .500 in his initial campaign as a major-college head coach and subsequently guide a team to a national championship.

Numbers Game: St. John's became the only school to win three times in the regular season over a team that went on to capture the NCAA title. The Redmen won their three games against Villanova by a total of 22 points.... Nike was crowing when all of the Final Four teams wore its "swoosh" sneakers.... Georgetown was the first defending NCAA Tournament champion in 15 years to return to the Final Four the next season.

What If: Center Patrick Ewing, after averaging a modest 13.2 points per game in six Final Four contests with Georgetown, has never averaged fewer than 20 points per game in his eight-year NBA career. If only Ewing averaged 14 points per Final Four game by scoring two more points in the 1982 championship game (63-62 defeat against North Carolina) and three more in the 1985 final (66-64 defeat against Villanova), the Hoyas could have captured three national titles in his college career rather than one.

Putting Things in Perspective: St. John's (31-4) defeated Villanova three times by a total of 22 points before the Redmen lost against Georgetown in the national semifinals. Georgetown (35-3) defeated the Wildcats twice by a total of nine points before losing to Villanova in the national final.

1985 CHAMPIONSHIP BRACKET

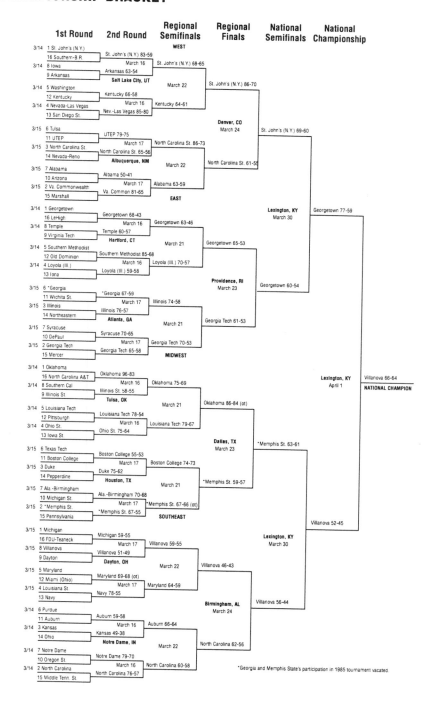

	1st Round	2nd Round	Regional Semifinals	Regional Finals	National Semifinals	National Championship

WEST

3/14 1. St. John's (N.Y.)
16 Southern-B.R.
St. John's (N.Y.) 83-59
March 16
3/14 8 Iowa
9 Arkansas
Arkansas 63-54
Salt Lake City, UT
St. John's (N.Y.) 68-65
March 22
3/14 5 Washington
12 Kentucky
Kentucky 66-58
March 16
3/14 4 Nevada-Las Vegas
13 San Diego St.
Nev.-Las Vegas 85-80
Kentucky 64-61
St. John's (N.Y.) 86-70

Denver, CO
March 24

3/15 6 Tulsa
11 UTEP
UTEP 79-75
March 17
3/15 3 North Carolina St.
14 Nevada-Reno
North Carolina St. 65-56
Albuquerque, NM
North Carolina St. 86-73
March 22
3/15 7 Alabama
10 Arizona
Alabama 50-41
March 17
3/15 2 Va. Commonwealth
15 Marshall
Va. Common 81-65
Alabama 63-59
North Carolina St. 61-55

St. John's (N.Y.) 69-60

Lexington, KY
March 30

EAST

3/14 1 Georgetown
16 LeHigh
Georgetown 68-43
March 16
3/14 8 Temple
9 Virginia Tech
Temple 60-57
Hartford, CT
Georgetown 63-46
March 21
3/14 5 Southern Methodist
12 Old Dominion
Southern Methodist 85-68
March 16
3/14 4 Loyola (Ill.)
13 Iona
Loyola (Ill.) 59-58
Loyola (Ill.) 70-57
Georgetown 65-53

Providence, RI
March 23

3/15 6 *Georgia
11 Wichita St.
*Georgia 67-59
March 17
3/15 3 Illinois
14 Northeastern
Illinois 76-57
Atlanta, GA
Illinois 74-58
March 21
3/15 7 Syracuse
10 DePaul
Syracuse 70-65
March 17
3/15 2 Georgia Tech
15 Mercer
Georgia Tech 65-58
Georgia Tech 70-53
Georgia Tech 61-53

Georgetown 60-54

Georgetown 77-59

MIDWEST

3/14 1 Oklahoma
16 North Carolina A&T
Oklahoma 96-83
March 16
3/14 8 Southern Cal
9 Illinois St.
Illinois St. 58-55
Tulsa, OK
Oklahoma 75-69
March 21
3/14 5 Louisiana Tech
12 Pittsburgh
Louisiana Tech 78-54
March 16
3/14 4 Ohio St.
13 Iowa St.
Ohio St. 75-64
Louisiana Tech 79-67
Oklahoma 86-84 (ot)

Dallas, TX
March 23

3/15 6 Texas Tech
11 Boston College
Boston College 55-53
March 17
3/15 3 Duke
14 Pepperdine
Duke 75-62
Houston, TX
Boston College 74-73
March 21
3/15 7 Ala.-Birmingham
10 Michigan St.
Ala.-Birmingham 70-68
March 17
3/15 2 *Memphis St.
15 Pennsylvania
*Memphis St. 67-55
*Memphis St. 67-66 (ot)
*Memphis St. 59-57

*Memphis St. 63-61

Lexington, KY
April 1

Villanova 66-64
NATIONAL CHAMPION

SOUTHEAST

3/15 1 Michigan
16 FDU-Teaneck
Michigan 59-55
March 17
3/15 8 Villanova
9 Dayton
Villanova 51-49
Dayton, OH
Villanova 59-55
March 22
3/15 5 Maryland
12 Miami (Ohio)
Maryland 69-68 (ot)
March 17
3/15 4 Louisiana St.
13 Navy
Navy 78-55
Maryland 64-59
Villanova 46-43

Birmingham, AL
March 24

3/14 6 Purdue
11 Auburn
Auburn 59-58
March 16
3/14 3 Kansas
14 Ohio
Kansas 49-38
Notre Dame, IN
Auburn 66-64
March 22
3/14 7 Notre Dame
10 Oregon St.
Notre Dame 79-70
March 16
3/14 2 North Carolina
15 Middle Tenn. St.
North Carolina 76-57
North Carolina 60-58
North Carolina 62-56

Villanova 56-44

Villanova 52-45

*Georgia and Memphis State's participation in 1985 tournament vacated.

1985–86

AT A GLANCE

NCAA Champion: Louisville (32-7).

NIT Champion: Ohio State (19-14).

New Conference: Big South.

New Rules: The 45-second clock is introduced with the team in control of the ball having to shoot for a goal within 45 seconds after it attains team control. If a shooter is fouled intentionally and the shot is missed, the penalty will be two shots and possession of the ball out of bounds to the team that was fouled. The head coach may stand throughout the game, while all other bench personnel must remain seated. NCAA Tournament regional games are played at neutral sites. If an institution selected to host this level of competition is a participant in the tourney, it will be bracketed in another regional.

NCAA Probation: Baylor, Idaho State, Southern Illinois.

NCAA Consensus First-Team All-Americans: Steve Alford, G, Jr., Indiana; Walter Berry, F, Jr., St. John's; Len Bias, F, Sr., Maryland; Johnny Dawkins, G, Sr., Duke; Kenny Walker, F, Sr., Kentucky.

Houston's Guy Lewis bid adieu to coaching after 30 years.

It was one of those moments when time seemed to stand still. The fallout stemming from All-American forward Len Bias' cocaine-induced death just four days after the Boston Celtics made him their No. 1 draft pick included the ouster of longtime Maryland coach Lefty Driesell.

Meanwhile, basketball fans in Los Angeles were restless. UCLA's streak of 32 consecutive winning records in conference competition ended when the Bruins finished fourth in the Pac-10 with a 9-9 mark. A few miles away, Southern Cal showed promise with standout freshmen Tom Lewis, Hank Gathers, and Bo Kimble. But all three players wound up transferring to other schools and finished their careers with more than 2,000 points—Lewis at Pepperdine and Gathers and Kimble at Loyola Marymount.

Navy's David Robinson blocked 14 shots in a game against North Carolina-Wilmington en route to finishing the season with an NCAA record 207 rejections.

Chicago State's Darron Brittman became the only player ever to average as many as five steals per game in a single season.

1985–86 FINAL NATIONAL POLLS

AP	UPI	USA/CNN	SCHOOL
1	1	2	Duke
2	2	3	Kansas
3	4	4	Kentucky
4	3	10	St. John's
5	5	14	Michigan
6	6	6	Georgia Tech
7	7	1	Louisville
8	8	7	North Carolina
9	9	16	Syracuse
10	11	21	Notre Dame
11	10	13	UNLV
12	12	15	Memphis St.
13	15	19	Georgetown
14	13	20	Bradley
15	17	24	Oklahoma
16	14	–	Indiana
17	–	8	Navy
18	18	12	Michigan St.
19	20	25	Illinois
20	16	–	Texas-El Paso
–	–	5	Louisiana St.
–	–	9	Auburn
–	–	11	North Carolina St.
–	–	17	Cleveland St.
–	19	18	Alabama
–	–	22	Iowa St.
–	–	23	DePaul

New Mexico hit 35 of 43 field-goal attempts (81.4 percent) against Oregon State. It was the

1985–86 INDIVIDUAL LEADERS

SCORING

PLAYER	PTS.	AVG.
Bailey, Wagner	854	29.4
Skiles, Michigan St.	850	27.4
Yezbak, U.S. Intl.	755	27.0
Miller, UCLA	750	25.9
Harper, Miami (Ohio)	757	24.4
Curry, Virginia Tech	722	24.1
Lewis, Northeastern	714	23.8
Bias, Maryland	743	23.2
Ross, American	645	23.0
Berry, St. John's	828	23.0

REBOUNDING

PLAYER	REB.	AVG.
Robinson, Navy	455	13.0
Anderson, Houston	360	12.9
Sellers, Ohio St.	416	12.6
Harper, Miami (Ohio)	362	11.7
Krystkowiak, Montana	364	11.4
Berry, St. John's	399	11.1
Hill, Bethune-Cookman	317	10.9
Carter, Loyola (Md.)	304	10.9
Boone, Marquette	319	10.6
Grant, Clemson	357	10.9

ASSISTS

PLAYER	AST.	AVG.
Jackson, St. John's	328	9.1
Chisholm, Delaware	230	8.5
Bogues, Wake Forest	245	8.4
Lee, Xavier	251	8.4
Thomas, Monmouth	205	8.2
Smith, Old Dominion	253	8.2
Harmon, McNeese St.	243	8.1
Davis, Marist	248	8.0
Paguaga, St. Francis (N.Y.)	223	8.0
Moody, N'western St. (La.)	198	7.9

BLOCKED SHOTS

PLAYER	BLK.	AVG.
Robinson, Navy	207	5.9
Perry, Temple	123	4.0
Blake, St. Joseph's	121	3.8
Fonville, Jackson St.	93	3.2
Kitchen, South Florida	89	3.2
Seikaly, Syracuse	97	3.0
Tarpley, Michigan	97	2.9
Sellers, Ohio St.	97	2.9
Martin, North Carolina	81	2.8
Smith, Pittsburgh	81	2.8

STEALS

PLAYER	STL.	AVG.
Brittman, Chicago St.	139	5.0
Paguaga, St. Francis (N.Y.)	120	4.3
Allen, Hofstra	100	3.6
Harper, Miami (Ohio)	101	3.3
Starks, Providence	84	3.2
Robinson, Md.-E. Shore	69	3.1
Anderson, Pan American	87	3.1
Bogues, Wake Forest	89	3.1
Anderson, Drexel	92	3.0
Ware, Florida A&M	76	2.8

FIELD GOAL PERCENTAGE

PLAYER	FGM	FGA	PCT.
Daugherty, N. Carolina	284	438	.648
Norman, Illinois	216	337	.641
Gattison, Old Dom.	218	342	.637
McKey, Alabama	178	280	.636
Thomas, Centenary	182	288	.632
Duckworth, E. Ill.	250	396	.631
Jones, N'western St. (La.)	130	207	.628
Turner, Brown	199	317	.628
Smits, Marist	216	347	.622
Williams, SMU	150	242	.620

FREE THROW PERCENTAGE

PLAYER	FTM	FTA	PCT.
Barton, Dartmouth	65	69	.942
Goodwin, Dayton	95	102	.931
Suder, Duquesne	135	147	.918
Coval, Wm. & Mary	111	121	.917
Androlewicz, Lehigh	84	93	.903
Skiles, Mich. St.	188	209	.900
Bajusz, Cornell	89	99	.899
Waddy, W. Carolina	70	78	.897
Newman, Richmond	153	172	.890
Rucker, Davidson	103	116	.888

1985–86 TEAM LEADERS

SCORING OFFENSE

SCHOOL	PTS.	AVG.
U.S. International	2542	90.8
Cleveland St.	2934	88.9
Oklahoma	3077	87.9
North Carolina	2945	86.6
Syracuse	2674	83.6

SCORING DEFENSE

SCHOOL	PTS.	AVG.
Princeton	1429	55.0
St. Peter's	1539	55.0
Fresno St.	1708	56.9
North Carolina A&T	1732	57.7
Tulsa	1854	57.9

SCORING MARGIN

SCHOOL	OFF.	DEF.	MAR.
Cleveland St.	88.9	69.6	19.3
North Carolina	86.6	69.0	17.6
Syracuse	83.6	68.3	15.3
Memphis St.	82.4	67.4	15.0
Notre Dame	78.9	64.8	14.1

WON-LOST PERCENTAGE

SCHOOL	W-L	PCT.
Duke	37-3	.925
Bradley	32-3	.914
Kansas	35-4	.897
Kentucky	32-4	.889
Cleveland St.	29-4	.879

FIELD GOAL PERCENTAGE

SCHOOL	FGM	FGA	PCT.
Michigan St.	1043	1860	.561
North Carolina	1197	2140	.559
Kansas	1260	2266	.556
Georgia Tech	1008	1846	.546
Illinois	990	1828	.542

FIELD GOAL PERCENTAGE DEFENSE

SCHOOL	FGM	FGA	PCT.
St. Peter's	574	1395	.411
South Florida	621	1499	.414
Texas Christian	711	1713	.415
Georgetown	789	1885	.419
Navy	932	2215	.421

REBOUND MARGIN

SCHOOL	OWN	OPP.	MAR.
Notre Dame	36.4	27.8	8.6
Michigan	37.4	29.2	8.1
Syracuse	41.0	32.9	8.1
Ark.-Little Rock	44.6	36.5	8.1
Cleveland St.	38.4	31.0	7.5

second-best team shooting percentage from the floor in a single game in NCAA history.

Michigan State led the country in both field-goal shooting (56.1 percent) and free-throw shooting (79.9).

Princeton became the only school to lead the nation in scoring defense (55 points per game) despite compiling a non-winning record (13-13). Meanwhile, U.S. International became the only school to lead the country in scoring offense (90.8 ppg) while posting a losing record (8-20).

Either Penn or Princeton had won the previous 17 Ivy League championships before Brown won its only Ivy title.

Arkansas' Nolan Richardson became the first African-American head coach in the Southwest Conference.

Houston's Guy Lewis ended his 30-year coaching career with a 592-279 record.

1986 NCAA Tournament

Summary: The only time a group of teams arrived at the Final Four with a total of at least 125 victories was this year as Louisville (30-7), Duke (36-2), Kansas (35-3), and LSU (26-11) combined for a 127-23 record (.847). The two hottest teams of the group—Louisville (16 consecutive victories and Duke (21)—reached the final where freshman Pervis Ellison collected 25 points and 11 rebounds to carry the Cardinals to a 72-69 triumph.

Outcome for Defending Champion: Villanova (23-14) finished fourth in the Big East before being eliminated in the second round of the NCAA Tournament by Georgia Tech, 66-61.

Star Gazing: Duke guard Johnny Dawkins scored 13 of Duke's first 25 points in the final and finished the tourney with 153. No other player scored more than 110.

Biggest Upset: Arkansas-Little Rock, a 17 1/2-underdog, shocked No. 3 seed Notre Dame in the first round of the Midwest Regional (90-83).

One and Only: Cleveland State became the only school seeded in the bottom of a bracket (13 through 16) to reach a Sweet 16. The Vikings, leading the nation in scoring margin, were seeded No. 14 when they won two East Regional games in their only tourney appearance.

On the rebound: Pervis Ellison of Louisville.

Numbers Game: LSU, the No. 11 seed in the Southeast Regional, is the only double-digit seeded team to reach the Final Four. The Tigers reached the national semifinals after finishing in a tie for fifth place in the SEC with a .500 record (9-9).... Maryland earned the best seed (#5) in tourney history for an at-large squad with a losing conference record (6-8 in the ACC).

What If: Forwards Mark Alarie and David Henderson and guard Tommy Amaker combined to make more than 50 percent of their

1985–86 NCAA CHAMPION: LOUISVILLE

SEASON STATISTICS OF LOUISVILLE REGULARS

PLAYER	POS.	CL.	G.	FG%	FT%	PPG	RPG
Billy Thompson	F	Sr.	39	.576	.714	14.9	7.8
Milt Wagner	G	Sr.	39	.495	.862	14.8	3.1
Pervis Ellison	C	Fr.	39	.554	.682	13.1	8.2
Herbert Crook	F	So.	39	.528	.688	11.8	6.5
Jeff Hall	G	Sr.	39	.530	.890	10.3	1.7
Tony Kimbro	F	Fr.	39	.572	.591	5.3	2.5
Mark McSwain	F	Jr.	28	.561	.717	3.6	2.9
Kenny Payne	F	Fr.	34	.437	.773	3.6	1.7
Kevin Walls	G	Fr.	27	.444	.750	2.1	0.4
TEAM TOTALS			39	.531	.733	79.4	37.2

Assists leader: Wagner 165. Blocked shots leader: Ellison 92. Steals leader: Wagner 52.

1986 FINAL FOUR CHAMPIONSHIP GAME

DALLAS, TX

DUKE (69)	MIN.	FG-A	FT-A	REB.	A	PF	PTS.
Henderson	28	5-15	4-4	4	4	5	14
Alarie	33	4-11	4-4	6	0	5	12
Bilas	26	2-3	0-0	3	0	4	4
Amaker	38	3-10	5-6	2	7	3	11
Dawkins	40	10-19	4-4	4	0	1	24
Ferry	20	1-2	2-2	4	0	2	4
Williams	2	0-1	0-0	0	0	0	0
King	13	0-1	0-1	0	1	2	0
Team				4			
TOTALS	200	25-62	19-21	27	12	22	69

FG%: .403. FT%: .905. Blocks: 0. Turnovers: 14. Steals: 13 (Amaker 7).

LOUISVILLE (72)	MIN.	FG-A	FT-A	REB.	A	PF	PTS.
Crook	32	5-9	0-3	12	5	2	10
Thompson	31	6-8	1-3	4	2	4	13
Ellison	35	10-14	5-6	11	1	4	25
Wagner	30	2-6	5-5	3	2	4	9
Hall	33	2-4	0-0	2	2	2	4
McSwain	17	2-4	1-2	3	2	1	5
Walls	8	0-1	0-0	1	0	2	0
Kimbro	14	2-4	2-2	2	2	1	6
Team				1			
TOTALS	200	29-50	14-21	39	16	20	72

FG%: .580. FT%: .667. Blocks: 7. Turnovers: 24 (Crook 9). Steals: 5. Halftime: Duke 37-34.

NATIONAL SEMIFINALS

KANSAS (67): Manning 2-9 0-0 4, Kellogg 11-15 0-0 22, Dreiling 1-7 4-4 6, Hunter 2-5 1-4 5, Thompson 5-12 3-3 13, Turgeon 1-1 0-0 2, Marshall 6-10 1-1 13, Piper 1-1 0-0 2. Team 29-60 (.483) 9-12 (.750) 67.

DUKE (71): Henderson 3-12 7-8 13, Alarie 4-13 4-6 12, Bilas 1-2 5-7 7, Amaker 2-5 3-4 7, Dawkins 11-17 2-4 24, Strickland 0-1 0-0 0, Ferry 4-5 0-1 8, King 0-0 0-0 0. Team 25-55 (.455) 21-30 (.700) 71.

Halftime: Duke 36-33.

LOUISIANA STATE (77): Williams 7-17 0-1 14, Redden 10-20 2-3 22, Blanton 3-5 3-6 9, Taylor 7-17 2-2 16, N. Wilson 7-15 1-1 15, Brown 0-1 1-2 1. Team 34-75 (.453) 9-15 (.600) 77.

LOUISVILLE (88): Crook 8-13 0-1 16, Thompson 10-11 2-5 22, Ellison 5-11 1-2 11, Wagner 8-16 6-6 22, Hall 6-11 2-2 14, McSwain 1-2 1-3 3, Walls 0-2 0-0 0, Kimbro 0-2 0-0 0. Team 38-68 (.559) 12-17 (.708) 88.

Halftime: Louisiana State 44-36.

ALL-TOURNAMENT TEAM

Mark Alarie, F, Sr., Duke
Tommy Amaker, G, Jr., Duke
Johnny Dawkins, G, Sr., Duke
Pervis Ellison, F-C, Fr., Louisville*
Billy Thompson, F, Sr., Louisville

*Named Most Outstanding Player

field-goal attempts for Duke in the 1985–86 season. If only they had combined to hit 39 percent instead of 33.3 percent (12 of 36) in the championship game, the Blue Devils could have defeated Louisville rather than lose 72-69.

Putting Things in Perspective: Kansas (35-4) defeated Louisville twice by a total of seven points before losing to Duke in the national semifinals. The Cardinals lost six of 15 games in one stretch the first half of the season.

1986 CHAMPIONSHIP BRACKET

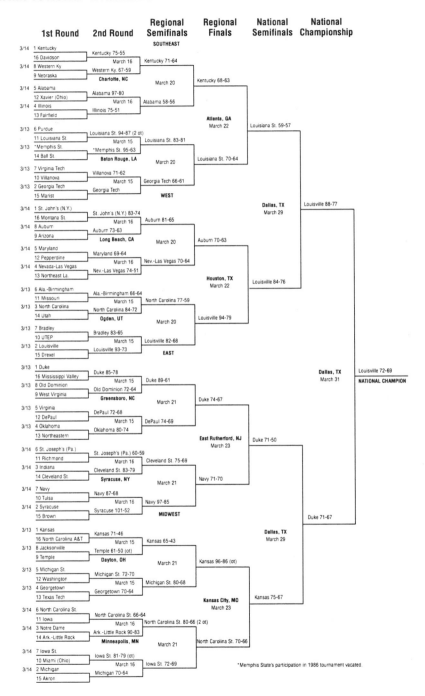

	1st Round	2nd Round	Regional Semifinals	Regional Finals	National Semifinals	National Championship

SOUTHEAST

3/14 1 Kentucky
16 Davidson — Kentucky 75-55
March 16 — Kentucky 71-64
3/14 8 Western Ky.
9 Nebraska — Western Ky. 67-59
Charlotte, NC
March 20 — Kentucky 68-63
3/14 5 Alabama
12 Xavier (Ohio) — Alabama 97-80
March 16 — Alabama 58-56
3/14 4 Illinois
13 Fairfield — Illinois 75-51
Atlanta, GA
March 22 — Louisiana St. 59-57
3/13 6 Purdue
11 Louisiana St. — Louisiana St. 94-87 (2 ot)
March 15 — Louisiana St. 83-81
3/13 *Memphis St.
14 Ball St. — *Memphis St. 95-63
Baton Rouge, LA
March 20 — Louisiana St. 70-64
3/13 7 Virginia Tech
10 Villanova — Villanova 71-62
March 15 — Georgia Tech 66-61
3/13 2 Georgia Tech
15 Marist — Georgia Tech

WEST

3/14 1 St. John's (N.Y.)
16 Montana St. — St. John's (N.Y.) 83-74
March 16 — Auburn 81-65
3/14 8 Auburn
9 Arizona — Auburn 73-63
Long Beach, CA
March 20 — Auburn 70-63
3/14 5 Maryland
12 Pepperdine — Maryland 69-64
March 16 — Nev.-Las Vegas 70-64
3/14 4 Nevada-Las Vegas
13 Northeast La. — Nev.-Las Vegas 74-51
Houston, TX
March 22 — Louisville 84-76
3/13 6 Ala.-Birmingham
11 Missouri — Ala.-Birmingham 66-64
March 15 — North Carolina 77-59
3/13 3 North Carolina
14 Utah — North Carolina 84-72
Ogden, UT
March 20 — Louisville 94-79
3/13 7 Bradley
10 UTEP — Bradley 83-65
March 15 — Louisville 82-68
3/13 2 Louisville
15 Drexel — Louisville 93-73

Louisville 88-77

EAST

3/13 1 Duke
16 Mississippi Valley — Duke 85-78
March 15 — Duke 89-61
3/13 8 Old Dominion
9 West Virginia — Old Dominion 72-64
Greensboro, NC
March 21 — Duke 74-67
3/13 5 Virginia
12 DePaul — DePaul 72-68
March 15 — DePaul 74-69
3/13 4 Oklahoma
13 Northeastern — Oklahoma 80-74
East Rutherford, NJ
March 23 — Duke 71-50
3/14 6 St. Joseph's (Pa.)
11 Richmond — St. Joseph's (Pa.) 60-59
March 16 — Cleveland St. 75-69
3/14 3 Indiana
14 Cleveland St. — Cleveland St. 83-79
Syracuse, NY
March 21 — Navy 71-70
3/14 7 Navy
10 Tulsa — Navy 87-68
March 16 — Navy 97-85
3/14 2 Syracuse
15 Brown — Syracuse 101-52

Duke 71-67

Dallas, TX
March 29

Louisville 72-69
NATIONAL CHAMPION

Dallas, TX
March 31

MIDWEST

3/13 1 Kansas
16 North Carolina A&T. — Kansas 71-46
March 15 — Kansas 65-43
3/13 8 Jacksonville
9 Temple — Temple 61-50 (ot)
Dayton, OH
March 21 — Kansas 96-86 (ot)
3/13 5 Michigan St.
12 Washington — Michigan St. 72-70
March 15 — Michigan St. 80-68
3/13 4 Georgetown
13 Texas Tech — Georgetown 70-64
Kansas City, MO
March 23 — Kansas 75-67
3/14 6 North Carolina St.
11 Iowa — North Carolina St. 66-64
March 16 — North Carolina St. 80-66 (2 ot)
3/14 3 Notre Dame
14 Ark.-Little Rock — Ark.-Little Rock 90-83
Minneapolis, MN
March 21 — North Carolina St. 70-66
3/14 7 Iowa St.
10 Miami (Ohio) — Iowa St. 81-79 (ot)
March 16 — Iowa St. 72-69
3/14 2 Michigan
15 Akron — Michigan 70-64

Dallas, TX
March 29

*Memphis State's participation in 1986 tournament vacated.

1986-87

AT A GLANCE

NCAA Champion: Indiana (30-4).

NIT Champion: Southern Mississippi (23-11).

New Rules: The three-point field goal is introduced nationwide and set at 19 feet 9 inches from the center of the basket. A coach may leave the confines of the bench at any time without penalty to correct a mistake by a scorer or timer. A technical foul is assessed if there is no mistake (rule changed the next year to a timeout). In addition, a television replay may be used to prevent or rectify a scorer's or timer's mistake or a malfunction of the clock. All 64 teams selected for the NCAA Tournament are subjected to drug testing for the first time.

NCAA Probation: Bradley, East Tennessee State, Memphis State.

NCAA Consensus First-Team All-Americans: Steve Alford, G, Sr., Indiana; Danny Manning, F-C, Jr., Kansas; David Robinson, C, Sr., Navy, Kenny Smith, G, Sr., North Carolina; Reggie Williams, F-G, Sr., Georgetown.

Indiana guard Steve Alford tips one in.

The new three-point field-goal shooting rule made an immediate impact. Consider such milestones: NCAA champion Indiana set an NCAA single-season record by hitting more than half of its three-point field-goal attempts (130 of 256 for 50.8 percent). Eastern Kentucky hit 11 consecutive three-point field-goal attempts and was 15 of 18 overall from beyond the arc in a game against North Carolina-Asheville. Butler's Darrin Fitzgerald averaged almost 13 three-point field-goal attempts per game on his way to setting an NCAA single-season record for most treys with 158. Niagara's Gary Bossert set an NCAA record for most consecutive successful three-pointers in a game with 11 vs. Siena.

UNLV's Mark Wade set an NCAA single-season record with 406 assists.

Northeastern's Andre LaFleur finished his career as the tallest player (6-3) with more than 800 assists. He had 894.

Memphis State erased a seven-point deficit in the last 15 seconds to defeat Oral Roberts, 59-58. Memphis State's new head coach was Larry Finch, who was promoted after Dana Kirk encountered extensive legal problems.

Maryland's Bob Wade and Oklahoma State's Leonard Hamilton became the first African-American head coaches in the ACC and Big Eight, respectively.

Lafester Rhodes isn't among Iowa State's top 20 all-time scorers, but he set a school single-game record with 54 points against Iowa. Other players who set school single-game scoring records were Tennessee guard Tony White (51 points against Auburn) and Washington State forward Brian Quinnett (45 against Loyola Marymount).

1986–87 FINAL NATIONAL POLLS

AP	UPI	USA/CNN	SCHOOL
1	1	2	UNLV
2	3	4	North Carolina
3	2	1	Indiana
4	4	7	Georgetown
5	5	9	DePaul
6	7	5	Iowa
7	6	13	Purdue
8	8	17	Temple
9	9	8	Alabama
10	10	3	Syracuse
11	11	20	Illinois
12	12	18	Pittsburgh
13	15	22	Clemson
14	14	23	Missouri
15	13	21	UCLA
16	19	–	New Orleans
17	–	11	Duke
18	18	16	Notre Dame
19	16	–	Texas Christian
20	–	14	Kansas
–	–	6	Providence
–	–	10	Louisiana St.
–	–	15	Florida
–	17	19	Wyoming
–	19	12	Oklahoma
–	19	–	Texas-El Paso
–	–	24	SW Missouri St.
–	–	25	Texas Christian

1987 NCAA Tournament

Summary: Indiana became the only school to win the NCAA championship in four different decades (previous titles were in 1940, 1953, and 1976). Junior college recruit Keith Smart, a guard who was Indiana's fifth-leading scorer, tallied 12 of the Hoosiers' last 15 points, including a 15-foot jumper from the left baseline with five seconds remaining to give them a 74-73 victory over Syracuse in the championship game.

Outcome for Defending Champion: Louisville (18-14) won the Metro Conference regular-season championship.

Star Gazing: Smart, the Final Four Most Outstanding Player, is the only former junior college player to win the award.

Biggest Upsets: Xavier (13th seed) over Missouri (4), 70-69; Southwest Missouri State (13) over Clemson (4), 65-60; and Austin Peay State (14) over Illinois (3), 68-67.

One and Only: Walt Hazzard is the only Final Four Most Outstanding Player (UCLA '64) to later coach his alma mater in the tournament (1-1 playoff record with the Bruins).... UNLV

Syracuse forward Derrick Coleman was named to the 1987 All-Tournament Team.

became the only school to win a regional final game in which it trailed by more than 12 points at halftime. The Rebels were behind Iowa at intermission in the West Regional final by 16 points (58-42) before rallying to win (84-81).

Numbers Game: Georgetown is the only school to defeat two eventual Final Four teams by double-digit margins in the same conference tournament. The Hoyas whipped Providence by 18 points and Syracuse by 10 to win the 1987 Big East Tournament before they were eliminated by Providence in the Southeast Regional final of the NCAA playoffs.... Danny Manning is the only player to score more than 62 percent of his team's points in an NCAA Tournament game. He supplied 62.7 percent of Kansas' offense by scoring 42 points in the Jayhawks' 67-63 victory against Southwest Missouri State in the second round of the Southeast Regional.... UNLV guard

1986–87 INDIVIDUAL LEADERS

SCORING

PLAYER	PTS.	AVG.
Houston, Army	953	32.9
Hopson, Ohio St.	958	29.0
Robinson, Navy	903	28.2
Bailey, Wagner	788	28.1
Hawkins, Bradley	788	27.2
Fitzgerald, Butler	734	26.2
Elmore, VMI	713	25.5
Ross, American	683	25.3
Queenan, Lehigh	720	24.8
Larkin, Xavier	792	24.7

REBOUNDING

PLAYER	REB.	AVG.
Lane, Pittsburgh	444	13.5
Dudley, Yale	320	13.3
Moore, Loyola (Ill.)	360	12.4
Robinson, Navy	378	11.8
Rowsom, UNC-Wilm.	345	11.5
Agbejemisin, Wagner	333	11.5
McCann, Morehead St.	317	11.3
Stewart, Texas S.	316	10.9
Besselink, Conn.	300	10.7
Anderson, Houston	318	10.6

ASSISTS

PLAYER	AST.	AVG.
Johnson, Southern (La.)	333	10.7
Wade, UNLV	406	10.7
Fairley, Baptist	270	9.6
Bogues, Wake Forest	276	9.6
Van Drost, Wagner	260	9.3
Washington, Mid. Tenn. St.	255	8.8
Manuel, Bradley	237	8.8
Smith, Old Dominion	229	8.2
Davis, Marist	227	8.1
Chisholm, Delaware	220	7.9

BLOCKED SHOTS

PLAYER	BLK.	AVG.
Robinson, Navy	144	4.5
Lewis, Maryland	114	4.4
Fonville, Jackson St.	112	3.9
Blake, St. Joseph's	87	3.6
Comegys, DePaul	108	3.5
Perry, Temple	116	3.2
Baugh, Howard	90	3.2
Smith, Pittsburgh	106	3.2
Smith, Ball St.	86	3.2
Brow, Virginia Tech	86	3.1

STEALS

PLAYER	STL.	AVG.
Fairley, Baptist	114	4.1
Usitalo, Boise St.	105	3.5
Jeter, Delaware St.	96	3.4
Ford, Texas-Arl.	96	3.4
Washington, Mid. Tenn. St.	93	3.2
Davis, Marist	88	3.1
Anderson, Drexel	85	3.0
Williams, Baylor	93	3.0
Chisholm, Delaware	84	3.0
Blye, Md.-E. Shore	68	3.0

FIELD GOAL PERCENTAGE

PLAYER	FGM	FGA	PCT.
Williams, Princeton	163	232	.703
Howard, E. Ky.	156	230	.678
Grant, Clemson	256	390	.656
Godbolt, La. Tech	191	295	.647
Williams, N.C. A&T	174	273	.637
Tate, Arkansas St.	216	339	.637
Leckner, Wyoming	246	390	.631
Manning, Kansas	347	562	.617
Rebholz, Hofstra	139	226	.615
Himes, Davidson	196	319	.614

FREE THROW PERCENTAGE

PLAYER	FTM	FTA	PCT.
Houston, Army	268	294	.912
Johnson, Mich. St.	111	122	.910
Haffner, Evansville	80	88	.909
Blackwell, Temple	123	136	.904
Smith, BYU	103	114	.904
White, Tennessee	165	183	.902
McPhee, Gonzaga	105	118	.890
Alford, Indiana	160	180	.889
Adams, Hardin-Simm.	87	98	.888
Farmer, Alabama	118	133	.887

THREE-POINT FIELD GOAL PERCENTAGE

PLAYER	FGM	FGA	PCT.
Jones, Pr. View	64	112	.571
Rhodes, S. F. Austin St.	58	106	.547
Davis, G. Mason	45	84	.536
Dimak, S. F. Austin St.	46	86	.535
Alford, Indiana	107	202	.530

THREE-POINT FIELD GOALS PER GAME

PLAYER	FGM	AVG.
Fitzgerald, Butler	158	5.6
Brooks, UC Irvine	111	4.0
Banks, UNLV	152	3.9
Ivory, Miss. Valley St.	109	3.9
Ross, San Diego St.	104	3.7

1986–87 TEAM LEADERS

SCORING OFFENSE

SCHOOL	PTS.	AVG.
UNLV	3612	92.6
North Carolina	3285	91.2
Oklahoma	3028	89.1
Michigan	2821	88.2
Southern (La.)	2706	87.3

SCORING DEFENSE

SCHOOL	PTS.	AVG.
Southwest Missouri St.	1958	57.6
St. Mary's (Calif.)	1766	58.9
Wis.-Green Bay	1714	59.1
Notre Dame	1902	59.4
San Diego	1810	60.3

SCORING MARGIN

SCHOOL	OFF.	DEF.	MAR.
UNLV	92.6	75.5	17.1
North Carolina	91.2	74.9	16.4
Clemson	86.1	71.5	14.6
DePaul	76.2	62.5	13.7
Georgetown	77.8	64.2	13.5

WON-LOST PERCENTAGE

SCHOOL	W-L	PCT.
UNLV	37-2	.949
DePaul	28-3	.903
North Carolina	32-4	.889
Temple	32-4	.889
Indiana	30-4	.882

FIELD GOAL PERCENTAGE

SCHOOL	FGM	FGA	PCT.
Princeton	601	1111	.541
North Carolina	1238	2304	.537
Marshall	946	1777	.532
Clemson	990	1873	.529
Lafayette	813	1544	.527

FIELD GOAL PERCENTAGE DEFENSE

SCHOOL	FGM	FGA	PCT.
San Diego	660	1645	.401
Houston Baptist	740	1835	.403
Jackson St.	703	1721	.408
Navy	814	1961	.415
DePaul	769	1850	.416

FREE THROW PERCENTAGE

SCHOOL	FTM	FTA	PCT.
Alabama	521	662	.787
Army	491	626	.784
Michigan St.	408	529	.771
Northern Iowa	390	507	.769
UC Irvine	532	693	.768

REBOUND MARGIN

SCHOOL	OWN	OPP.	MAR.
Iowa	43.1	31.5	11.5
Pittsburgh	41.5	31.8	9.7
Western Kentucky	39.6	31.5	8.0
Georgetown	40.4	32.4	8.0
Auburn	39.6	32.0	7.6

THREE-POINT FIELD GOAL PERCENTAGE

SCHOOL	FGM	FGA	PCT.
Indiana	130	256	50.8
Miss. Valley St.	161	322	50.0
Stephen F. Austin St.	120	241	49.8
Niagara	128	275	46.5
Eastern Michigan	144	310	46.5

THREE-POINT FIELD GOALS PER GAME

SCHOOL	FGM	AVG.
Providence	280	8.2
UNLV	309	7.9
Eastern Kentucky	216	7.2
Butler	198	7.1
UC Irvine	187	6.7

1986–87 NCAA CHAMPION: INDIANA

SEASON STATISTICS OF INDIANA REGULARS

PLAYER	POS.	CL.	G.	FG%	FT%	PPG	RPG
Steve Alford	G	Sr.	34	.474	.889	22.0	2.6
Daryl Thomas	F	Sr.	34	.538	.786	15.7	5.7
Rick Calloway	F	So.	29	.531	.742	12.6	4.3
Dean Garrett	C	Jr.	34	.542	.635	11.4	8.5
Keith Smart	G	Jr.	34	.517	.841	11.2	2.9
Steve Eyl	F	Jr.	34	.648	.674	3.0	3.4
Joe Hillman	G	Jr.	32	.483	.742	2.5	1.2
Kreigh Smith	G-F	Jr.	25	.500	.857	1.5	0.8
Todd Meier	F-C	Sr.	29	.450	.591	1.1	1.5
TEAM TOTALS			34	.513	.767	82.5	35.0

Three-point field goals leader: Alford (107 of 202, .530). **Assists leader:** Alford 123. **Blocked shots leader:** Garrett 93. **Steals leader:** Thomas 45.

1987 FINAL FOUR CHAMPIONSHIP GAME

NEW ORLEANS, LA

SYRACUSE (73)	MIN.	FG-A	FT-A	REB.	A	PF	PTS.
Triche	32	3-9	2-4	1	1	4	8
Coleman	37	3-7	2-4	19	1	2	8
Seikaly	34	7-13	4-6	10	1	3	18
Monroe	32	5-11	0-1	2	3	1	12
Douglas	39	8-15	2-2	2	7	3	20
Brower	9	3-3	1-3	1	0	3	7
Thompson	17	0-2	0-0	3	1	0	0
TOTALS	200	29-60	11-20	38	14	16	73

FG%: .483. **FT%:** .550. **Three-point goals:** 4 of 10 (Monroe 2-8, Douglas 2-2). **Blocks:** 7. **Turnovers:** 14. **Steals:** 5.

INDIANA (74)	MIN.	FG-A	FT-A	REB.	A	PF	PTS.
Calloway	14	0-3	0-0	2	1	3	0
Thomas	40	8-18	4-7	7	1	1	20
Garrett	33	5-10	0-0	10	0	4	10
Alford	40	8-15	0-0	3	5	2	23
Smart	35	9-15	3-4	5	6	2	21
Meier	4	0-0	0-1	1	0	0	0
Eyl	13	0-0	0-0	1	1	2	0
Smith	1	0-0	0-0	1	0	1	0
Hillman	20	0-1	0-0	2	6	2	0
Team				4			
TOTALS	200	30-62	7-12	35	20	17	74

FG%: .484. **FT%:** .583. **Three-point goals:** 7 of 11 (Alford 7-10, Smart 0-1). **Blocks:** 3. **Turnovers:** 11. **Steals:** 7.
Halftime: Indiana 34-33.

NATIONAL SEMIFINALS

PROVIDENCE (63): Kipfer 4-10 0-1 8, Lewis 2-12 2-2 7, Duda 2-7 0-1 4, Brooks 4-9 0-0 9, Donovan 3-12 1-1 8, Screen 5-6 7-10 18, Shamsid-Deen 1-2 0-0 2, Conlon 1-1 0-0 2, D. Wright 1-4 0-0 3, S. Wright 1-3 0-0 2, Snedeker 0-0 0-0 0. Team 24-66 (.364) 10-15 (.667) 63.

SYRACUSE (77): Triche 4-10 4-5 12, Coleman 4-6 4-7 12, Seikaly 4-11 8-11 16, Monroe 4-9 6-10 17, Douglas 5-11 2-6 12, Brower 0-1 0-0 0, Thompson 3-5 1-3 7, Harried 0-0 1-2 1. Team 24-53 (.453) 26-44 (.591) 77.

Halftime: Syracuse 36-26. **Three-point field goals:** Providence (5-19). Syracuse (3-8).

UNLV (93): Paddio 2-13 0-0 6, Gilliam 14-26 4-6 32, Basnight 3-4 0-1 6, Wade 1-6 1-2 4, Banks 12-23 4-6 38, Robinson 0-0 0-0 0, Graham 0-5 1-4 1, Hudson 3-4 0-0 6, Willard 0-1 0-0 0. Team 35-82 (.427) 10-19 (.526) 93.

INDIANA (97): Alford 10-19 11-13 33, Smart 5-7 4-5 14, Garrett 7-10 4-5 18, Calloway 6-10 0-0 12, Thomas 3-5 0-0 6, Meier 0-0 0-0 0, Eyl 3-3 1-2 7, Smith 0-2 0-0 0, Hillman 3-4 1-3 7. Team 37-60 (.617) 21-28 (.750) 97.

Halftime: Indiana 53-47. **Three-point field goals:** UNLV (13-35). Indiana (2-4).

ALL-TOURNAMENT TEAM

Steve Alford, G, Sr., Indiana
Derrick Coleman, F, Fr., Syracuse
Sherman Douglas, G, Soph., Syracuse
Armon Gilliam, F-C, Sr., UNLV
Keith Smart, G, Jr., Indiana*

Named Most Outstanding Player

Freddie Banks scored more points than any player in a Final Four game without being selected to the All-Tournament team (38 in a 97-93 defeat in the national semifinals against eventual champion Indiana).... The record for most assists in a playoff game was set by UNLV playmaker Mark Wade with 18 in a 97-93 loss against Indiana (national semifinals). Wade also established the record for most assists in a single playoff series that season with 61 in five games. He had at least nine assists in each of the five contests while scoring a total of just 13 points....

David Robinson furnished 61 percent of Navy's offense by scoring 50 points in the Middies' 97-82 loss against Michigan in the first round of the East Regional.

What If: Forward Derrick Coleman and guards Stephen Thompson and Howard Triche combined to shoot 51.6 percent from the floor for Syracuse in the 1986–87 season. If only they had combined to hit 38.9 percent instead of 33.3 percent (six of 18) in the championship game, the Orangemen could have defeated Indiana rather than lose 74-73.

1987 CHAMPIONSHIP BRACKET

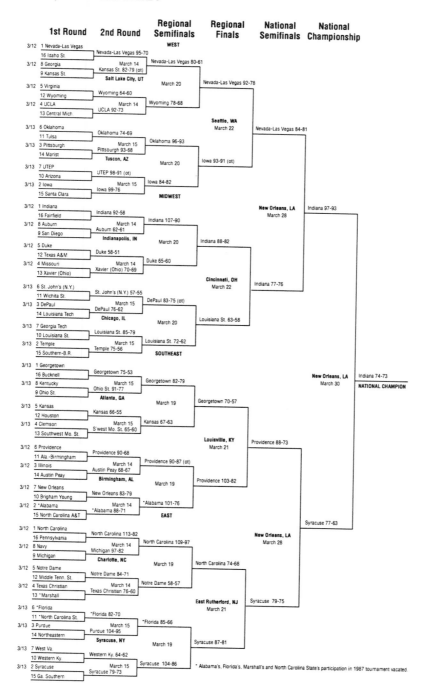

1st Round	2nd Round	Regional Semifinals	Regional Finals	National Semifinals	National Championship

WEST

3/12 1 Nevada-Las Vegas
16 Idaho St.
Nevada-Las Vegas 95-70
3/12 8 Georgia
9 Kansas St.
March 14
Kansas St. 82-79 (ot)
Nevada-Las Vegas 80-61
Salt Lake City, UT
March 20
3/12 5 Virginia
12 Wyoming
Wyoming 64-60
3/12 4 UCLA
13 Central Mich.
March 14
UCLA 92-73
Wyoming 78-68
Nevada-Las Vegas 92-78
Seattle, WA
March 22

3/13 6 Oklahoma
11 Tulsa
Oklahoma 74-69
3/13 3 Pittsburgh
14 Marist
March 15
Pittsburgh 93-68
Oklahoma 96-93
Tuscon, AZ
March 20
3/13 7 UTEP
10 Arizona
UTEP 98-91 (ot)
3/13 2 Iowa
15 Santa Clara
March 15
Iowa 99-76
Iowa 84-82
Iowa 93-91 (ot)

Nevada-Las Vegas 84-81

MIDWEST

3/12 1 Indiana
16 Fairfield
Indiana 92-58
3/12 8 Auburn
9 San Diego
March 14
Auburn 62-61
Indiana 107-90
Indianapolis, IN
March 20
3/12 5 Duke
12 Texas A&M.
Duke 58-51
3/12 4 Missouri
13 Xavier (Ohio)
March 14
Xavier (Ohio) 70-69
Duke 65-60
Indiana 88-82
Cincinnati, OH
March 22

3/13 6 St. John's (N.Y.)
11 Wichita St.
St. John's (N.Y.) 57-55
3/13 3 DePaul
14 Louisiana Tech
March 15
DePaul 76-62
DePaul 83-75 (ot)
Chicago, IL
March 20
3/13 7 Georgia Tech
10 Louisiana St.
Louisiana St. 85-79
3/13 2 Temple
15 Southern-B.R.
March 15
Temple 75-56
Louisiana St. 72-62
Louisiana St. 63-58

Indiana 77-76

Indiana 97-93

SOUTHEAST

3/13 1 Georgetown
16 Bucknell
Georgetown 75-53
3/13 8 Kentucky
9 Ohio St.
March 15
Ohio St. 91-77
Georgetown 82-79
Atlanta, GA
March 19
3/13 5 Kansas
12 Houston
Kansas 66-55
3/13 4 Clemson
13 Southwest Mo. St.
March 15
S'west Mo. St. 65-60
Kansas 67-63
Georgetown 70-57
Louisville, KY
March 21

3/12 6 Providence
11 Ala.-Birmingham
Providence 90-68
3/12 3 Illinois
14 Austin Peay
March 14
Austin Peay 68-67
Providence 90-87 (ot)
Birmingham, AL
March 19
3/12 7 New Orleans
10 Brigham Young
New Orleans 83-79
3/12 2 *Alabama
15 North Carolina A&T
March 14
*Alabama 88-71
*Alabama 101-76
Providence 103-82

Providence 88-73

New Orleans, LA
March 28

Indiana 74-73
NATIONAL CHAMPION

New Orleans, LA
March 30

EAST

3/12 1 North Carolina
16 Pennsylvania
North Carolina 113-82
3/12 8 Navy
9 Michigan
March 14
Michigan 97-82
North Carolina 109-97
Charlotte, NC
March 19
3/12 5 Notre Dame
12 Middle Tenn. St.
Notre Dame 84-71
3/12 4 Texas Christian
13 *Marshall
March 14
Texas Christian 76-60
Notre Dame 58-57
North Carolina 74-68
East Rutherford, NJ
March 21

3/13 6 *Florida
11 *North Carolina St.
*Florida 82-70
3/13 3 Purdue
14 Northeastern
March 15
Purdue 104-95
*Florida 85-66
Syracuse, NY
March 19
3/13 7 West Va.
10 Western Ky.
Western Ky. 64-62
3/13 2 Syracuse
15 Ga. Southern
March 15
Syracuse 79-73
Syracuse 104-86
Syracuse 87-81

Syracuse 79-75

Syracuse 77-63

New Orleans, LA
March 28

* Alabama's, Florida's, Marshall's and North Carolina State's participation in 1987 tournament vacated.

1987-88

AT A GLANCE

NCAA Champion: Kansas (27-11).

NIT Champion: Connecticut (20-14).

New Conference: American South (merged with Sun Belt four years later).

New Rule: Each intentional personal foul carries a two-shot penalty plus possession of the ball.

NCAA Probation: Brooklyn, Eastern Washington, Marist, Minnesota, South Carolina, Virginia Tech.

NCAA Consensus First-Team All-Americans: Sean Elliott, F, Jr., Arizona; Gary Grant, G, Sr., Michigan; Hersey Hawkins, G, Sr., Bradley; Danny Manning, F-C, Sr., Kansas; J. R. Reid, C, Soph., North Carolina.

Bradley's Hersey Hawkins (#33) battles an opponent for a rebound.

Loyola Marymount, which finished in last place in the West Coast Conference the previous season, went unbeaten in league competition. The Lions became the only team to ever have four players average more than 17 points per game in a season—Hank Gathers (22.5 ppg), Bo Kimble (22.2), Mike Yoest (17.6), and Corey Gaines (17.4).

Arizona guard Steve Kerr finished his career with an NCAA-record 38 consecutive games making a three-point field goal.

Holy Cross' Glenn Tropf set an NCAA single-season record for three-point field-goal accuracy by hitting 52 of 82 long-range attempts (63.4 percent).

Southern's Avery Johnson set an NCAA single-season record for assists average with 13.3 scoring feeds per game. Johnson, who began his college career at a junior college, averaged 10.7 assists the previous season to become the only player to twice average double figures in that category. He had 20 or more assists in four games.

Oklahoma's Mookie Blaylock, another J.C. transfer, set an NCAA single-season record with 150 steals, including 13 in one game against Centenary.

Duke's Danny Ferry set an ACC single-game record by pouring in 58 points against

1987–88 INDIVIDUAL LEADERS

SCORING

PLAYER	PTS.	AVG.
Hawkins, Bradley	1125	36.3
Queenan, Lehigh	882	28.5
Mason, Tennessee St.	783	28.0
Hayward, Loyola (Ill.)	756	26.1
Martin, Murray St.	806	26.0
Simmons, Evansville	750	25.9
Middleton, Southern Ill.	711	25.4
Grayer, Iowa St.	811	25.3
Larkin, Xavier	758	25.3
Henderson, Marshall	804	25.1

REBOUNDING

PLAYER	REB.	AVG.
Miller, Loyola (Ill.)	395	13.6
Mack, S. Carolina St.	387	13.3
Lane, Pittsburgh	378	12.2
Sanders, George Mason	339	11.7
White, La. Tech	359	11.6
Canino, Central Conn. St.	321	11.5
Johnson, Baptist	331	11.4
Simmons, La Salle	386	11.4
West, Texas Southern	322	11.1
Coleman, Syracuse	384	11.0

ASSISTS

PLAYER	AST.	AVG.
Johnson, Southern (La.)	399	13.3
Manuel, Bradley	373	12.0
Neal, Georgia Tech	303	9.5
Gaines, L. Marymount	271	8.7
Evans, Temple	294	8.6
Douglas, Syracuse	288	8.2
Smith, Old Dominion	244	8.1
Williams, Holy Cross	234	8.1
Davis, Marist	207	7.7
Brown, Siena	222	7.7

BLOCKED SHOTS

PLAYER	BLK.	AVG.
Blake, St. Joseph's	116	4.0
Smits, Marist	105	3.9
Brown, Canisius	100	3.7
Perry, Temple	118	3.6
Brow, Virginia Tech	100	3.6
Garrett, Indiana	99	3.4
Butts, Bucknell	91	3.4
Campbell, Clemson	88	3.1
Smith, Pittsburgh	96	3.1
Hopkins, Navy	74	3.1

STEALS

PLAYER	STL.	AVG.
Ware, Florida A&M	142	4.9
Johnson, Towson St.	124	4.1
Blaylock, Oklahoma	150	3.8
Workman, Oral Roberts	103	3.6
Johnson, Southern (La.)	106	3.5
Murdock, Providence	90	3.2
Conway, Montana St.	94	3.1
Robertson, Cleveland St.	90	3.0
McDonald, Texas A&M	90	2.9
Strickland, DePaul	75	2.9

FIELD GOAL PERCENTAGE

PLAYER	FGM	FGA	PCT.
Jones, Boise St.	187	283	.661
Brundy, DePaul	194	295	.658
Holifield, Ill. St.	177	273	.648
Basnight, UNLV	184	284	.648
Leckner, Wyoming	181	281	.644
Stuckey, SW Mo. St.	166	259	.641
White, La. Tech	226	354	.638
Perdue, Vanderbilt	234	369	.634
Ambroise, Baptist	171	270	.633
Campbell, Clemson	217	345	.629

FREE THROW PERCENTAGE

PLAYER	FTM	FTA	PCT.
Henson, Kansas St.	111	120	.925
Tullos, Detroit	139	153	.908
Edwards, Indiana	69	76	.908
Barton, Dartmouth	115	127	.906
Smith, Louisville	143	158	.905
Boyd, Memphis St.	111	124	.895
Willingham, S. F. Austin St.	75	84	.893
Harris, Ill. St.	91	102	.892
Nurnberger, S. Ill.	78	88	.886
Lichti, Stanford	174	198	.879

THREE-POINT FIELD GOAL PERCENTAGE

PLAYER	FGM	FGA	PCT.
Tropf, Holy Cross	52	82	.634
Kerr, Arizona	114	199	.573
Joseph, Bucknell	65	116	.560
Jones, Pr. View	85	155	.548
Orlandini, Princeton	60	110	.545

THREE-POINT FIELD GOALS PER GAME

PLAYER	FGM	AVG.
Pollard, Miss. Valley St.	132	4.7
McGill, E. Ky.	104	3.9
Lancaster, Va. Tech	106	3.7
Mooney, Coastal Carolina	102	3.6
Paddio, UNLV	118	3.5

1987–88 TEAM LEADERS

SCORING OFFENSE

SCHOOL	PTS.	AVG.
Loyola Marymount	3528	110.3
Oklahoma	4012	102.9
Southern (La.)	2965	95.6
Xavier	2840	94.7
Iowa	3181	93.6

SCORING DEFENSE

SCHOOL	PTS.	AVG.
Georgia Southern	1725	55.6
Boise St.	1680	56.0
Princeton	1467	56.4
Colorado St.	2007	57.3
St. Mary's (Calif.)	1640	58.6

SCORING MARGIN

SCHOOL	OFF.	DEF.	MAR.
Oklahoma	102.9	81.0	21.9
Arizona	85.1	64.2	20.9
UNLV	84.3	68.2	16.1
Temple	76.8	61.2	15.6
Xavier	94.7	79.5	15.2

WON-LOST PERCENTAGE

SCHOOL	W-L	PCT.
Temple	32-2	.941
Arizona	35-3	.921
Oklahoma	35-4	.897
North Carolina A&T	26-3	.897
Purdue	29-4	.879

FIELD GOAL PERCENTAGE

SCHOOL	FGM	FGA	PCT.
Michigan	1198	2196	.546
Arizona	1147	2106	.545
North Carolina	1013	1892	.535
Purdue	1018	1912	.532
Brigham Young	976	1839	.531

FIELD GOAL PERCENTAGE DEFENSE

SCHOOL	FGM	FGA	PCT.
Temple	777	1981	.392
Marist	617	1537	.401
Kansas	912	2215	.412
UNLV	841	2012	.418
Georgia Southern	640	1529	.419

FREE THROW PERCENTAGE

SCHOOL	FTM	FTA	PCT.
Butler	413	517	.799
Princeton	315	405	.778
Bucknell	477	617	.773
UNC-Asheville	419	543	.772
Auburn	406	527	.770

REBOUND MARGIN

SCHOOL	OFF.	DEF.	MAR.
Notre Dame	36.0	26.2	9.9
South Carolina St.	42.9	33.5	9.4
Ark.-Little Rock	41.3	32.5	8.8
Georgetown	39.2	31.3	7.9
Missouri	41.9	34.3	7.7

THREE-POINT FIELD GOAL PERCENTAGE

SCHOOL	FGM	FGA	PCT.
Princeton	211	429	.492
Prairie View	129	266	.485
Kansas St.	179	370	.484
Arizona	254	526	.483
Bucknell	154	328	.470

THREE-POINT FIELD GOALS PER GAME

SCHOOL	FGM	AVG.
Princeton	211	8.1
Loyola Marymount	251	7.8
Oklahoma	299	7.7
George Mason	219	7.3
Bradley	224	7.2

Miami (Fla.). Bradley's Hersey Hawkins (63 points at Detroit) and San Francisco's Keith Jackson (47 against Loyola Marymount) set school single-game records.

Loyola of Chicago's Kenny Miller became the only freshman ever to lead the nation in rebounding (13.6 per game).

Kansas State's Mitch Richmond poured in 35 points in a 72-61 triumph at Kansas, ending the Jayhawks' 55-game homecourt winning streak.

Pittsburgh, capturing its lone undisputed Big East Conference regular-season championship, became the only school to feature a roster with as many as eight players who would wind up scoring more than 1,000 points before ending their college careers—seniors Charles Smith and Demetreus Gore, junior Jerome Lane, sophomore Rod Brookin, and freshmen Bobby Martin, Jason Matthews, Sean Miller, and Darelle Porter.

North Carolina A&T won its seventh consecutive Mid-Eastern Athletic Conference Tournament.

1987–88 FINAL NATIONAL POLLS

AP	UPI	USA/CNN	SCHOOL
1	1	5	Temple
2	2	3	Arizona
3	3	6	Purdue
4	4	2	Oklahoma
5	5	4	Duke
6	6	9	Kentucky
7	8	7	North Carolina
8	7	13	Pittsburgh
9	9	16	Syracuse
10	10	10	Michigan
11	12	23	Bradley
12	11	22	UNLV
13	14	–	Wyoming
14	13	21	North Carolina St.
15	16	–	Loyola (Ill.)
16	15	20	Illinois
17	18	14	Iowa
18	–	–	Xavier
19	17	–	Brigham Young
20	20	8	Kansas St.
–	–	1	Kansas
–	–	11	Villanova
–	–	12	Rhode Island
–	–	15	Louisville
–	–	17	Vanderbilt
–	–	18	Richmond
–	19	–	Indiana
–	–	19	Loyola Marymount
–	–	24	DePaul
–	–	25	Brigham Young

1988 NCAA Tournament

Summary: The Big Eight went 30 years without winning a Final Four game until Kansas and Oklahoma both won. Kansas won the final after losing three previous title games at Kansas City (1940, 1953, and 1957). Larry Brown became the only coach to leave an NCAA champion before the next season for another coaching job. After winning the NCAA title, Brown quit the Jayhawks before the start of the next NCAA probation-marred campaign to return to the NBA.

Outcome for Defending Champion: Indiana (19-10) finished fifth in the Big Ten before losing its tourney opener to No. 13 seed Richmond, 72-69.

Star Gazing: Danny Manning became the only one of the more than 60 major-college players to score at least 2,500 career points or average a minimum of 28.5 points per game and play for an NCAA championship team. Manning was the only national player of the year from 1981 to 1991 to play for a national titlist. He hit 25 of 45 field-goal attempts and grabbed 28 rebounds at the Final Four.

Biggest Upset: Murray State (14th seed) defeated North Carolina State (3), 78-75.

One and Only: Oklahoma became the only school to compete for the national championship in both football and basketball in the same academic school year (1988). The football Sooners lost to Miami (Fla.) in the Orange Bowl, finishing third in the final wire-service polls.

Numbers Game: Temple, a 63-53 loser against Duke in the East Regional final, is one of only two teams ranked No. 1 by both AP and UPI entering the tourney to lose by a double-digit margin before the Final Four.

What If: Forwards Danny Ferry and Robert Brickey and guard Phil Henderson combined to shoot 50 percent from the floor in their Duke careers. If only they had combined to hit 39.4 percent of their field-goal attempts instead of 27.3 percent (9 of 33) in the national semifinals, the Blue Devils could have defeated eventual

1987–88 NCAA CHAMPION: KANSAS

SEASON STATISTICS OF KANSAS REGULARS

PLAYER	POS.	CL.	G.	FG%	FT%	PPG	RPG
Danny Manning	F-C	Sr.	38	.583	.734	24.8	9.0
Milt Newton	G	Jr.	35	.555	.564	11.6	5.0
Kevin Pritchard	G	So.	37	.486	.739	10.6	2.6
Chris Piper	F	Sr.	34	.537	.705	5.1	3.8
Lincoln Minor	G	Jr.	34	.419	.667	4.8	1.4
Jeff Gueldner	G	So.	34	.422	.681	3.8	2.0
Scooter Barry	G	Jr.	35	.477	.815	3.3	1.3
Keith Harris	F	So.	27	.451	.633	3.1	2.6
Otis Livingston	G	Jr.	27	.650	.613	2.6	1.4
Mike Maddox	F	Fr.	24	.532	.471	2.5	1.5
Mike Masucci	C	Fr.	24	.431	.467	2.1	1.5
TEAM TOTALS			38	.521	.690	75.3	35.6

Three-point field goals leader: Newton (29 of 64, .453). Assists leader: Pritchard 113. Blocked shots leader: Manning 73. Steals leaders: Manning 70, Pritchard 52.

1988 FINAL FOUR CHAMPIONSHIP GAME

KANSAS CITY, MO

KANSAS (83)	MIN.	FG-A	FT-A	REB.	A	PF	PTS.
Piper	37	4-6	0-0	1	2	3	8
Gueldner	15	1-2	0-0	0	1	0	2
Manning	36	13-24	5-7	7	2	3	31
Pritchard	31	6-7	0-0	0	4	1	13
Newton	32	6-6	1-2	0	1	1	15
Barry	9	0-2	1-2	0	2	1	1
Maddox	1	0-0	0-0	0	0	1	0
Harris	12	1-1	0-0	0	0	2	2
Normore	16	3-3	0-1	0	4	3	7
Minor	11	1-4	2-2	0	1	1	4
Team				1			
TOTALS	200	35-55	9-14	8	17	16	83

FG%: .636. FT%: .643. Three-point goals: 4-6 (Pritchard 1-1, Newton 2-2, Normore 1-1, Gueldner 0-1, Manning 0-1). Blocks: 4. Turnovers: 23. Steals: 11 (Manning 5).

OKLAHOMA (79)	MIN.	FG-A	FT-A	REB.	A	PF	PTS.
Grant	40	6-14	2-3	3	1	4	14
Sieger	40	7-15	1-2	3	7	2	22
King	39	7-14	3-3	2	0	3	17
Blaylock	40	6-13	0-1	3	4	4	14
Grace	34	4-14	3-4	3	7	4	12
Mullins	7	0-0	0-0	0	0	1	0
Team				1			
TOTALS	200	30-70	9-13	14	19	18	79

FG%: .429. FT%: .692. Three-point goals: 10-24 (Sieger 7-13, Blaylock 2-4, Grace 1-7). Blocks: 3. Turnovers: 15 (Sieger 6). Steals: 13 (Blaylock 7). Halftime: Tied 50-50.

NATIONAL SEMIFINALS

KANSAS (66): Piper 3-4 4-4 10, Guelder 0-1 0-0 0, Manning 12-21 1-2 25, Pritchard 2-6 2-2 6, Newton 8-14 2-3 20, Barry 1-2 3-4 5, Maddox 0-0 0-0 0, Harris 0-4 0-0 0, Normore 0-0 0-0 0, Minor 0-0 0-0 0, Mattox 0-0 0-0 0. Team 26-52 (.500) 12-15 (.800) 66.

DUKE (59): Ferry 7-22 4-4 19, King 1-4 1-2 3, Brickey 2-9 2-5 6, Snyder 4-10 1-2 9, Strickland 5-13 0-0 10, Koubek 3-5 0-0 8, Abdelnaby 1-2 2-4 4, Smith 0-0 0-0 0, Henderson 0-2 0-0 0, Cook 0-0 0-0 0. Team 23-67 (.343) 10-17 (.588) 59.

Halftime: Kansas 38-27.
Three-point goals: Kansas 2-4 (.500), Duke 3-14 (.214).

ARIZONA (78): Cook 6-13 4-6 16, Elliott 13-23 3-3 31, Tolbert 5-11 1-2 11, McMillan 3-6 0-0 8, Kerr 2-13 0-0 6, Turner 0-0 0-0 0, Mason 0-0 0-0 0, Buechler 2-2 0-0 4, Lofton 1-4 0-0 2. Team 32-72 (.444) 8-11 (.727) 78.

OKLAHOMA (86): Grant 7-14 7-10 21, Sieger 3-8 3-6 10, King 9-16 3-6 21, Blaylock 3-7 1-2 7, Grace 3-10 5-7 13, Mullins 1-1 0-0 3, Wiley 4-8 3-3 11. Team 30-64 (.469) 22-34 (.647) 86.

Halftime: Oklahoma 39-27.
Three-point goals: Arizona 6-23 (.261), Oklahoma 4-14 (.286).

ALL-TOURNAMENT TEAM

Sean Elliott, F, Jr., Arizona
Stacey King, C, Jr., Oklahoma
Danny Manning, F, Sr., Kansas*
Milt Newton, G-F, Jr., Kansas
Dave Sieger, F, Sr., Oklahoma

*Named Most Outstanding Player

champion Kansas rather than lose 66-59.... Oklahoma's Mookie Blaylock set the record for most steals in a playoff series (23 in six games). He had seven steals as a junior guard in an 83-79 championship game loss against Kansas.

Putting Things in Perspective: Kansas State (25-9) defeated Kansas twice by a total of 26 points before losing against KU in the Midwest Regional final. Oklahoma (35-4) defeated the Jayhawks twice by eight points in each Big Eight Conference regular-season game before losing against KU in the national final. Kansas lost five games by double-digit margins. The Jayhawks went almost a month without a victory against a Division I opponent; their only win in a mid-season, six-game stretch was against Hampton (Va.). Nebraska, which was 4-10 in the Big Eight, defeated Kansas, 70-68.

Kansas' Danny Manning (#25) snags a rebound from an opponent.

1988 CHAMPIONSHIP BRACKET

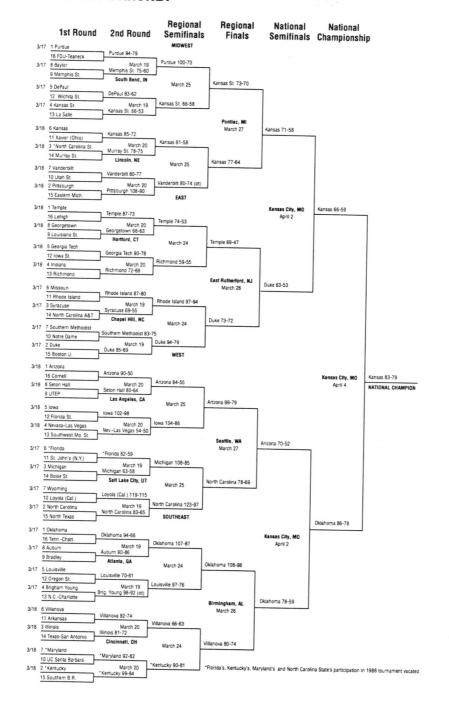

	1st Round	2nd Round	Regional Semifinals	Regional Finals	National Semifinals	National Championship

MIDWEST

3/17 1 Purdue
16 FDU-Teaneck — Purdue 94-79
3/17 8 Baylor
9 Memphis St. — Memphis St. 75-60 — March 19 — Purdue 100-73
South Bend, IN
3/17 5 DePaul
12 Wichita St. — DePaul 83-62 — March 25
3/17 4 Kansas St.
13 La Salle — Kansas St. 66-53 — March 19 — Kansas St. 66-58 — Kansas St. 73-70
3/18 6 Kansas
11 Xavier (Ohio) — Kansas 85-72
3/18 3 *North Carolina St.
14 Murray St. — Murray St. 78-75 — March 20 — Kansas 61-58 — Pontiac, MI March 27
Lincoln, NE
3/18 7 Vanderbilt
10 Utah St. — Vanderbilt 80-77 — March 25 — Kansas 77-64 — Kansas 71-58
3/18 2 Pittsburgh
15 Eastern Mich. — Pittsburgh 108-90 — March 20 — Vanderbilt 80-74 (ot)

EAST

3/18 1 Temple
16 Lehigh — Temple 87-73
3/18 8 Georgetown
9 Louisiana St. — Georgetown 66-63 — March 20 — Temple 74-53
Hartford, CT
3/18 5 Georgia Tech
12 Iowa St. — Georgia Tech 90-78 — March 24 — Kansas City, MO April 2 — Kansas 66-59
3/18 4 Indiana
13 Richmond — Richmond 72-69 — March 20 — Richmond 59-55 — Temple 69-47
3/17 6 Missouri
11 Rhode Island — Rhode Island 87-80
3/17 3 Syracuse
14 North Carolina A&T — Syracuse 69-55 — March 19 — Rhode Island 97-94 — East Rutherford, NJ March 26
Chapel Hill, NC
3/17 7 Southern Methodist
10 Notre Dame — Southern Methodist 83-75 — March 24 — Duke 73-72 — Duke 63-53
3/17 2 Duke
15 Boston U. — Duke 85-69 — March 19 — Duke 94-79

WEST

3/18 1 Arizona
16 Cornell — Arizona 90-50
3/18 8 Seton Hall
9 UTEP — Seton Hall 80-64 — March 20 — Arizona 84-55
Las Angeles, CA
3/18 5 Iowa
12 Florida St. — Iowa 102-98 — March 25
3/18 4 Nevada-Las Vegas
13 Southwest Mo. St. — Nev.-Las Vegas 54-50 — March 20 — Iowa 104-86 — Arizona 99-79
3/17 6 *Florida
11 St. John's (N.Y.) — *Florida 62-59
3/17 3 Michigan
14 Boise St. — Michigan 63-58 — March 19 — Michigan 108-85 — Seattle, WA March 27 — Arizona 70-52
Salt Lake City, UT
3/17 7 Wyoming
10 Loyola (Cal.) — Loyola (Cal.) 119-115 — March 25 — North Carolina 78-69
3/17 2 North Carolina
15 North Texas — North Carolina 83-65 — March 19 — North Carolina 123-97

SOUTHEAST

3/17 1 Oklahoma
16 Tenn.-Chatt. — Oklahoma 94-66
3/17 8 Auburn
9 Bradley — Auburn 90-86 — March 19 — Oklahoma 107-87
Atlanta, GA
3/17 5 Louisville
12 Oregon St. — Louisville 70-61 — March 24
3/17 4 Brigham Young
13 N.C.-Charlotte — Brig. Young 98-92 (ot) — March 19 — Louisville 97-76 — Oklahoma 108-98
3/18 6 Villanova
11 Arkansas — Villanova 82-74
3/18 3 Illinois
14 Texas-San Antonio — Illinois 81-72 — March 20 — Villanova 66-63 — Birmingham, AL March 26
Cincinnati, OH
3/18 7 *Maryland
10 UC Santa Barbara — *Maryland 92-82 — March 24 — Villanova 80-74 — Oklahoma 78-59
3/18 2 *Kentucky
15 Southern B.R. — *Kentucky 99-84 — March 20 — *Kentucky 90-81

Kansas City, MO April 4
Kansas 83-79
NATIONAL CHAMPION

Kansas City, MO April 2
Oklahoma 86-78

*Florida's, Kentucky's, Maryland's and North Carolina State's participation in 1988 tournament vacated.

1988–89

Mr. Clutch: Vanderbilt's Barry Goheen.

AT A GLANCE

NCAA Champion: Michigan (30-7).

NIT Champion: St. John's (20-13).

New Rules: Neutral courts used in all rounds of the NCAA Tournament. Bracket rotation for the tourney is established. Criteria governing automatic qualification for conferences is strengthened.

NCAA Probation: Cincinnati, Cleveland State, Kansas, Marist, Virginia Tech.

NCAA Consensus First-Team All-Americans: Sean Elliott, F, Sr., Arizona; Pervis Ellison, C, Sr., Louisville; Danny Ferry, F-C, Sr., Duke, Chris Jackson, G, Fr., Louisiana State, Stacey King, C, Sr., Oklahoma.

The proliferation of parity and the wisdom of expanding the postseason field was never more evident than in the 1989 playoffs. None of the Final Four teams would have qualified for the NCAA Tournament prior to 1975, the first year more than one league member could be invited. Champion Michigan finished third in the Big Ten Conference, runner-up Seton Hall lost in the Big East Tournament semifinals after finishing runner-up to Georgetown in the regular-season standings, Duke lost in the ACC Tournament final after finishing in a three-way tie for second place behind North Carolina State in the regular-season standings, and Illinois was runner-up in the Big Ten to Indiana.

LSU edged second-ranked Georgetown, 82-

HIGHEST-SCORING GAME IN HISTORY
Loyola Marymount's high scorers met U.S. International on January 31, 1989, in what became the highest-scoring game in history. Marymount defeated U.S. International, 181-150. Marymount's high scorer was Hank Gathers; International's top gun was Steve Smith.

USIU (150)	FG-A	FT-A	REB.	PTS.
Williams	9-12	7-12	5	25
Laffitte	12-18	4-5	7	28
Sterner	5-9	0-0	6	10
Wilson	10-21	1-3	3	21
Smith	11-15	8-8	8	32
Davis	3-4	0-1	3	7
Moore	3-5	0-0	4	6
Judd	3-5	0-0	3	6
Hodges	0-2	0-2	0	0
Howard	6-8	1-4	1	13
Banks	1-2	0-0	0	2
Team			9	
TOTALS	**63-101**	**21-35**	**49**	**150**

FG%: .624. **FT%:** .600. **Three-point shooting:** 3 of 7 (Wilson 0-2, Smith 2-2, Davis 1-2, Hodges 0-1).

LMU (181)	FG-A	FT-A	REB.	PTS.
Stumer	4-11	2-3	5	12
Peabody	2-3	1-2	2	5
Gathers	15-24	11-14	29	41
Fryer	10-24	8-10	2	34
Simmons	10-14	3-4	5	25
Lee	2-2	1-3	1	5
Mister	0-0	1-2	2	1
O'Connell	2-3	1-1	1	5
Lowery	5-9	4-4	4	15
Roscoe	0-0	0-0	0	0
Yoest	3-6	0-0	1	6
Kimble	9-15	0-0	4	20
Knight	1-2	2-2	1	4
Veargason	2-3	0-0	4	4
Morley	0-0	0-0	1	0
Slater	2-3	0-0	0	4
Team			1	
TOTALS	**67-119**	**34-45**	**63**	**181**

FG%: .563. **FT%:** .755. **Three-point shooting:** 13 of 34 (Stumer 2-6, Fryer 6-14, Simmons 2-4, Lowery 1-3, Yoest 0-1, Kimble 2-6).
Halftime: Loyola Marymount 94-76.

Aside from these famous cardboard fans, all spectators were banned from the 1989 North Atlantic Tournament due to a measles outbreak.

80, on Ricky Blanton's last-second rebound basket before 54,321 fans at the Louisiana Superdome (64,144 paid).

LSU guard Chris Jackson became the highest-scoring freshman in major-college history when he averaged 30.2 points per game. His 55 points were in vain in a 113-112 overtime loss at Ole Miss when the Rebels' Gerald Glass offset Jackson's outburst with 53 points. Another Jackson outburst—this time 48 points—also wasn't enough to prevent a 104-95 defeat against visiting Florida when the Gators clinched their lone SEC regular-season title. Helping Florida along the way was an incredible 81-78 overtime victo-

ry at Vanderbilt when the Gators tied the game at the end of regulation after Commodore fans were assessed a two-shot technical for throwing tennis balls at center Dwayne Schintzius, who was involved in a much-publicized incident during which he wielded a tennis racket.

Vanderbilt guard Barry Goheen ended his career as one of the premier clutch players in college history. He made six game-winning shots in the closing seconds and sent an NCAA Tournament game into overtime with two three-point baskets in the final five seconds of regulation.

Duke's Danny Ferry set a school record with 58 points against Miami (Fla.).

1988–89 INDIVIDUAL LEADERS

SCORING

PLAYER	PTS.	AVG.
Gathers, Loyola Marymount	1015	32.7
Jackson, Louisiana St.	965	30.2
Simmons, La Salle	908	28.4
Glass, Mississippi	841	28.0
Edwards, East Carolina	773	26.7
Dudley, Air Force	746	26.6
Coles, Virginia Tech	717	26.6
Smith, Brigham Young	765	26.4
King, Oklahoma	859	26.0
Taft, Marshall	701	26.0

REBOUNDING

PLAYER	REB.	AVG.
Gathers, Loyola Marymount	426	13.7
Hill, Xavier	403	12.2
Draper, American	336	12.0
Battles, Southern (La.)	360	11.6
Simmons, La Salle	365	11.4
Coleman, Syracuse	422	11.4
Burton, Long Island	309	11.0
Mack, South Carolina St.	361	10.9
Sanders, George Mason	326	10.9
Washington, Weber St.	303	10.8

ASSISTS

PLAYER	AST.	AVG.
Williams, Holy Cross	278	9.9
Corchiani, N.C. St.	266	8.6
Douglas, Syracuse	326	8.6
Payton, Oregon St.	244	8.1
Manuel, Bradley	216	8.0
Timberlake, Boston U.	238	7.9
Overton, La Salle	244	7.6
Richardson, UCLA	236	7.6
Sample, Southern (La.)	234	7.5
McGee, New Mexico	243	7.4

BLOCKED SHOTS

PLAYER	BLK.	AVG.
Mourning, Georgetown	169	5.0
Causwell, Temple	124	4.1
Ogg, UAB	129	3.8
Coleman, Syracuse	127	3.4
Butts, Bucknell	100	3.2
Ellison, Louisville	98	3.2
Henderson, Siena	86	3.1
Green, Rhode Island	85	3.0
West, Texas Southern	90	3.0
Campbell, Clemson	87	3.0
Godfread, Evansville	92	3.0

STEALS

PLAYER	STL.	AVG.
Robertson, Cleveland St.	111	4.0
Blaylock, Oklahoma	131	3.7
Applewhite, Tex. S'thern	105	3.5
Screen, Providence	101	3.5
Lee, Towson St.	98	3.4
Tanner, Rice	94	3.4
Murdock, Providence	97	3.3
Workman, Oral Roberts	93	3.3
Blanks, Texas	111	3.3
Newbern, Minnesota	101	3.3

FIELD GOAL PERCENTAGE

PLAYER	FTM	FTA	PCT.
Davis, Florida	179	248	.722
Burns, Miss. St.	167	249	.671
Davis, Clemson	146	218	.670
Mack, S. Carolina St.	204	306	.667
Parker, Cleve. St.	168	253	.664
Ambroise, Baptist	164	247	.664
Vaught, Michigan	201	304	.661
Stewart, Coppin St.	199	302	.659
Smith, Idaho	185	284	.651
Burke, Wagner	215	331	.650

FREE THROW PERCENTAGE

PLAYER	FTM	FTA	PCT.
Smith, BYU	160	173	.925
Henson, Kansas St.	92	100	.920
Simmons, Md.-Balt. C'nty	83	92	.902
Nurnberger, S. Ill.	129	143	.902
Haffner, Evansville	136	151	.901
Matthews, Pitt	142	158	.899
Blevins, Kent	94	105	.895
Lauritzen, Indiana St.	68	76	.895
Peterson, Yale	111	125	.888
Christian, Appa. St.	76	86	.884

THREE-POINT FIELD GOAL PERCENTAGE

PLAYER	FGM	FGA	PCT.
Calloway, Monmouth	48	82	.585
Tribelhorn, Colo. St.	76	135	.563
Joseph, Bucknell	62	115	.539
Bays, Towson St.	71	132	.538
Anglavar, Marquette	53	99	.535

THREE-POINT FIELD GOALS PER GAME

PLAYER	FGM	AVG.
Pollard, Miss. Vly. St.	124	4.4
Grider, SW La.	122	4.2
Fryer, L. Marymount	126	4.1
Barros, Boston College	112	3.9
McCloud, Florida St.	115	3.8

1988–89 TEAM LEADERS

SCORING OFFENSE

SCHOOL	PTS.	AVG.
Loyola Marymount	3486	112.5
Oklahoma	3680	102.2
Southern (La.)	3015	97.3
Texas	3206	94.3
Louisiana St.	2966	92.7

SCORING DEFENSE

SCHOOL	PTS.	AVG.
Princeton	1430	53.0
St. Mary's (Calif.)	1728	57.6
Boise St.	1767	58.9
Colorado St.	2012	61.0
Idaho	1894	61.1

SCORING MARGIN

SCHOOL	OWN	OPP.	MAR.
St. Mary's (Calif.)	76.1	57.6	18.5
Arizona	84.5	66.9	17.6
Michigan	91.7	74.8	16.9
Duke	86.5	69.8	16.8
Siena	85.0	69.8	15.1

WON-LOST PERCENTAGE

SCHOOL	W-L	PCT.
Ball St.	29-3	.906
Arizona	29-4	.879
Illinois	31-5	.861
Georgetown	29-5	.853
West Virginia	26-5	.839

FIELD GOAL PERCENTAGE

SCHOOL	FGM	FGA	PCT.
Michigan	1325	2341	.566
New Mexico	992	1819	.545
Syracuse	1334	2456	.543
Duke	1163	2166	.537
St. Mary's (Calif.)	859	1606	.535

FIELD GOAL PERCENTAGE DEFENSE

SCHOOL	FGM	FGA	PCT.
Georgetown	795	1993	.399
West Virginia	738	1840	.401
St. Mary's (Calif.)	651	1606	.405
Ball St.	688	1687	.408
Seton Hall	934	2265	.412

FREE THROW PERCENTAGE

SCHOOL	FTM	FTA	PCT.
Brigham Young	527	647	.815
Gonzaga	485	614	.790
Bucknell	590	749	.788
Kent	592	755	.784
Louisiana St.	557	723	.770

REBOUND MARGIN

SCHOOL	OWN	OPP.	MAR.
Iowa	41.4	31.8	9.6
Notre Dame	37.7	28.8	9.0
Missouri	42.1	34.2	7.9
Michigan	37.7	30.3	7.4
Stanford	34.8	27.7	7.1

THREE-POINT FIELD GOAL PERCENTAGE

SCHOOL	FGM	FGA	PCT.
Indiana	121	256	.473
Michigan	196	419	.468
The Citadel	153	328	.466
Colorado St.	141	305	.462
Bucknell	160	347	.461

THREE-POINT FIELD GOALS PER GAME

SCHOOL	FGM	AVG.
Loyola Marymount	287	9.3
Valparaiso	257	8.9
Oral Roberts	216	7.7
Mt. St. Mary's (Md.)	202	7.5
Alabama-Birmingham	247	7.3

Memphis State raced to a 24-0 lead at highly-ranked Louisville to upend the Cardinals, 72-67. Louisville and Memphis State combined to capture the previous 10 Metro Conference regular-season championships until Florida State moved atop the league standings.

Loyola Marymount junior Hank Gathers became the only player to lead the nation in scoring (32.7 points per game) in a season he shot better than 60 percent from the floor (60.8). Gathers collected 41 points and a school-record 29 rebounds in 30 minutes in a 181-150 victory over U.S. International that set an NCAA record for most total points in a game (see accompanying box score). The scoring orgy left the following numbers of note: a field goal was attempted an average of every 11 seconds and a basket was scored an average of every 18.5 seconds; the longest span between baskets was 59 seconds; a point was scored an average of every 7.25 seconds; and seven players amassed more points than minutes played.

Evansville's Scott Haffner scored a national-high and school-record 65 points against Dayton.

Kentucky's NCAA-record streak of consecutive non-losing seasons ended at 60 when the Wildcats compiled a 13-19 mark in Eddie Sutton's last year as their coach.

The North Atlantic Tournament was dubbed the MIT (Measles Invitational Tourney) because all spectators were banned due to a measles outbreak.

Oregon State's Ralph Miller, who previously coached at Wichita State and Iowa, retired after a 38-year coaching career with a 657-382 record. C. M. Newton, who coached Transylvania, Alabama, and Vanderbilt, ended his coaching career with a 509-375 record when he became athletic director at his alma mater (Kentucky). Norman Sloan, who previously coached Presbyterian, The Citadel, and North Carolina State, was forced out at Florida, ending his 37-year coaching career with a 624-393 record.

1988-89 FINAL NATIONAL POLLS

AP	UPI	USA/CNN	SCHOOL
1	1	7	Arizona
2	2	5	Georgetown
3	3	3	Illinois
4	5	12	Oklahoma
5	4	8	North Carolina
6	8	11	Missouri
7	9	6	Syracuse
8	6	10	Indiana
9	7	4	Duke
10	10	1	Michigan
11	11	2	Seton Hall
12	13	13	Louisville
13	12	21	Stanford
14	15	16	Iowa
15	14	9	UNLV
16	16	22	Florida St.
17	19	18	West Virginia
18	–	19	Ball St.
19	18	14	North Carolina St.
20	20	–	Alabama
–	–	15	Virginia
–	17	20	Arkansas
–	–	17	Minnesota
–	–	23	Texas-El Paso
–	–	24	South Alabama
–	–	25	UCLA

1989 NCAA Tournament

Summary: Michigan won the championship in bizarre fashion. Just prior to the start of the tournament, Wolverines head coach Bill Frieder announced that he would become head coach at Arizona State the following season. At a press conference a few hours later, Michigan athletic director and former football coaching legend Bo Schembechler announced that assistant coach Steve Fisher would take over for the duration of the tourney. Later, Schembechler said, "I did not want an Arizona State coach coaching Michigan. I wanted a Michigan man." A stunned and saddened Frieder could only lurk in the background, following a team that was no longer his.... U-M became the NCAA titlist to win its two Final Four games by the fewest total of points (three). Sean Higgins' last-second rebound basket gave the Wolverines an 83-81 victory against Illinois in the national semifinals before Rumeal Robinson sank two free throws with three seconds remaining in overtime in an 80-79 triumph against Seton Hall in the final. In the first overtime final since 1963, Seton Hall guard John Morton had the highest scoring output (35 points with 17 in the last eight minutes of regulation) of any player for the losing team in a championship game. Since the introduction of seeding in 1979, this was the only year the championship game did not include at least one No. 1 or No. 2 seed (Michigan and Seton Hall were both No. 3 seeds). The roster Fisher inherited at the start of the playoffs included four future NBA first-round draft choices—Terry Mills, Glen Rice, Robinson, and Loy Vaught.

Outcome for Defending Champion: Kansas (19-12) finished in sixth place in the Big Eight.

Star Gazing: Rice, the Final Four Most Outstanding Player, became the only player to score more than 25 points in two games at a single Final Four from 1975 to 1994. Rice holds the records for most three-point baskets and points in a playoff series (27 treys and 184 points in six games). The senior forward hit 12 of 17 from three-point range on his way to a total of 66 points in Southeast Regional semifinal and final victories over North Carolina (92-87) and Virginia (102-65). Rice's liberal use of the three-pointer enabled him to become the only player from a national champion to average more than 25 points per game in a title season (25.6) since David Thompson finished with a 26-point average for North Carolina State in 1974.

Biggest Upsets: Middle Tennessee State (13th seed) over Florida State (4), 97-83, and Siena (14) over Stanford (3), 80-78.

One and Only: Illinois became the only school to defeat the NCAA champion-to-be twice in one season by at least 12 points when the Illini swept Michigan in Big Ten competition.

Numbers Game: Of the more than 60 different players to score at least 2,500 points and/or rank among the top 25 in career scoring average, Arizona's Sean Elliott finished his career as the only one to have a winning NCAA playoff record in his career as well as post higher scoring, rebounding, and field-goal shooting career playoff averages than he compiled in the regular season.... Xavier became the only school to have the misfortune of opposing eventual national champions in the first round in back-to-back years (Kansas '88 and Michigan '89).... The worst composite conference record in one year of the NCAA playoffs was posted by the SEC, which had all five of its entrants lose their first-round game, with four of them bowing by more than 10 points. Independent South Carolina, a recent addition to the SEC, was also drubbed in its opening-round game, giving the six current SEC members a 13.7-point average margin of defeat.

What If: Forward Nick Anderson (55.3 percent) and center Lowell Hamilton (53.4 percent) rank among the top five Illinois players in career field-goal shooting. If only they had combined for 46.4 percent field-goal shooting instead of 39.3 percent (11 of 28) in the national semifinals, the Illini could have defeated eventual champion Michigan rather than lose 83-81. The Wolverines also dodged a bullet against Seton Hall in the final, when they won 80-79 as Pirates forward Andrew Gaze was restricted to one field goal after contributing at least six baskets in each of the previous four playoff games.

Putting Things in Perspective: Illinois (31-5) defeated Michigan twice by a total of 28 points before losing to the Wolverines by two points in the national semifinals. Indiana (27-8) defeated the Wolverines twice by a total of two points before losing against eventual national runner-up Seton Hall in the West Regional semifinals. Michigan suffered defeats in five of 10 Big Ten games in one span after losing on a neutral court to obscure Alaska-Anchorage.

1988–89 NCAA CHAMPION: MICHIGAN

SEASON STATISTICS OF MICHIGAN REGULARS

PLAYER	POS.	CL.	G.	FG%	FT%	PPG	RPG
Glen Rice	F	Sr.	37	.577	.832	25.6	6.3
Rumeal Robinson	G	Jr.	37	.557	.656	14.9	3.4
Loy Vaught	F	Jr.	37	.661	.778	12.6	8.0
Terry Mills	C	Jr.	37	.564	.769	11.6	5.9
Sean Higgins	F-G	So.	34	.506	.771	12.4	3.1
Mark Hughes	C-F	Sr.	35	.608	.604	6.8	4.1
Kirk Taylor	G	So.	21	.478	.611	4.5	2.2
Mike Griffin	G-F	Jr.	37	.508	.767	2.7	2.4
J. P. Oosterbaan	C	Jr.	22	.564	.692	2.4	1.2
Demetrius Calip	G	So.	30	.440	.824	2.0	0.6
Rob Pelinka	G	Fr.	26	.360	.700	1.1	0.6
TEAM TOTALS			37	.566	.735	91.7	37.7

Three-point field goals leaders: Rice (99 of 192, .516), Higgins (51 of 110 .464), Robinson (30 of 64, .469). **Assists leaders:** Robinson 233, Mills 104, Griffin 103. **Blocked shots leader:** Mills 49. **Steals leader:** Robinson 70.

1989 FINAL FOUR CHAMPIONSHIP GAME

SEATTLE, WA

MICHIGAN (80)	MIN.	FG-A	FT-A	REB.	A	PF	PTS.
Rice	42	12-25	2-2	1	0	2	31
Hughes	25	1-1	0-0	0	0	2	2
Mills	34	4-8	0-0	3	2	2	8
Griffin	17	0-0	0-0	2	3	4	0
Robinson	43	6-13	9-10	1	11	2	21
Vaught	26	4-8	0-0	2	0	2	8
Calip	11	0-2	0-0	0	1	3	0
Higgins	27	3-10	3-4	2	2	3	10
Team				3			
TOTALS	225	30-67	14-16	14	19	20	80

FG%: .448. **FT%:** .875. **Three-point goals:** 6-16 (Rice 5-12, Higgins 1-4). **Blocks:** 4 (Mills 3). **Turnovers:** 14. **Steals:** 3.

SETON HALL (79)	MIN.	FG-A	FT-A	REB.	A	PF	PTS.
Walker	39	5-9	3-4	3	1	2	13
Gaze	39	1-5	2-2	2	3	3	5
Ramos	33	4-9	1-1	0	1	2	9
Morton	37	11-26	9-10	1	3	3	35
Greene	43	5-13	1-3	0	5	3	13

1980–89 PREMO POWER POLL: BEST TEAMS BY DECADE

RANK	SEASON	SCHOOL
1	1983–84	Georgetown* (34-3)
2	1981–82	North Carolina* (32-2)
3	1984–85	Georgetown (35-3)
4	1982–83	Houston (31-3)
5	1985–86	Duke (37-3)
6	1979–80	Louisville* (33-3)
7	1983–84	North Carolina (28-3)
8	1986–87	Indiana* (30-4)
9	1984–85	St. John's (31-4)
10	1980–81	Oregon St. (26-2)
11	1987–88	Oklahoma (35-4)
12	1988–89	Arizona (29-4)
13	1986–87	UNLV (37-2)
14	1979–80	DePaul (26-2)
15	1981–82	Virginia (30-4)
16	1983–84	DePaul (27-3)
17	1987–88	Arizona (35-3)
18	1980–81	DePaul (27-2)
19	1985–86	Kansas (35-4)
20	1982–83	Louisville (32-4)
	1988–89	Georgetown (29-5)

*–NCAA Tournament Champion

Avent	11	1-2	0-0	1	1	0	2
Volcy	7	0-0	0-2	0	0	2	0
Cooper	14	0-0	0-0	0	0	1	0
Wigington	2	1-1	0-0	0	0	1	2
Team				2			
TOTALS	225	28-65	16-22	9	14	17	79

FG%: .431. **FT%:** .727. **Three-point goals:** 7-23 (Morton 4-12, Greene 2-5, Gaze 1-5, Walker 0-1). **Blocks:** 2. **Turnovers:** 11. **Steals:** 4. **Halftime:** Michigan 37-32. **Regulation:** Tied 71-71.

NATIONAL SEMIFINALS

ILLINOIS (81): Anderson 6-14 5-6 17, Battle 10-17 8-10 29, Hamilton 5-14 1-2 11, Gill 5-9 1-1 11, Bardo 1-7 4-4 7, Smith 3-5 0-0 6, Small 0-0 0-0 0, Liberty 0-1 0-0 0. Team 30-67 (.448) 19-23 (.826) 81.

MICHIGAN (83): Rice 12-24 2-2 28, Hughes 4-5 1-1 9, Mills 4-8 0-0 8, Griffin 0-1 0-0 0, Robinson 6-13 2-5 14, Calip 0-1 0-0 0, Higgins 5-12 3-3 14, Vaught 5-13 0-0 10. Team 36-77 (.468) 8-11 (.727) 83.

Three-point goals: Illinois 2-8 (.25), Michigan 3-8 (.375). **Halftime:** Michigan 39-38.

DUKE (78): Brickey 0-3 2-2 2, Ferry 13-29 7-11 34, Laettner 4-5 5-7 13, Henderson 4-16 5-6 13, Snyder 3-10 0-0 8, Koubek 0-3 0-0 0, Davis 1-2 0-2 2, Abdelnaby 0-0 0-0 0, Smith 1-4 3-4 6, Palmer 0-0 0-0 0, Burgin 0-0 0-0 0, Buckley 0-0 0-0 0. Team 26-72 (.361) 22-32 (.688) 78.

SETON HALL (95): Walker 6-9 7-7 19, Gaze 7-14 2-2 20, Ramos 3-8 3-3 9, Morton 4-8 5-6 13, Greene 5-9 6-6 17, Avent 3-4 0-0 6, Volcy 1-2 0-1 2, Cooper 3-4 0-0 6, Wigington 0-0 0-1 0, Monteserin 0-0 0-0 0, Katsikis 1-1 0-1 3, Crowley 0-1 0-0 0, Rebimias 0-1 0-0 0, Long 0-1 0-0 0. Team 33-62 (.532) 23-27 (.852) 95.

Three-point goals: Duke 4-16 (.250), Seton Hall 6-12 (.500). **Halftime:** Duke 38-33.

ALL-TOURNAMENT TEAM

Danny Ferry, F, Sr., Duke
Gerald Greene, G, Sr., Seton Hall
John Morton, G, Sr., Seton Hall
Glen Rice, F, Sr., Michigan*
Rumeal Robinson, G, Jr., Michigan

*Named Most Outstanding Player

1989 CHAMPIONSHIP BRACKET

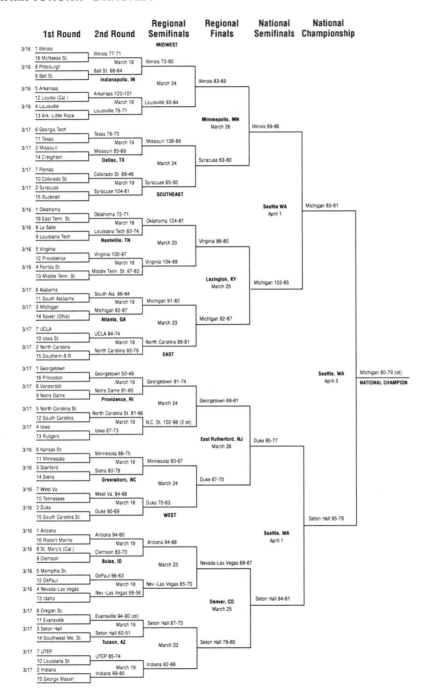

	1st Round	2nd Round	Regional Semifinals	Regional Finals	National Semifinals	National Championship

MIDWEST

3/16 1 Illinois
16 McNeese St.
Illinois 77-71
March 18
3/16 8 Pittsburgh
9 Ball St.
Ball St. 68-64
Illinois 72-60
Indianapolis, IN
March 24
Illinois 83-69
3/16 5 Arkansas
12 Loyola (Cal.)
Arkansas 120-101
March 18
3/16 4 Louisville
13 Ark.-Little Rock
Louisville 76-71
Louisville 93-84
Minneapolis, MN
March 26
Illinois 89-86

3/17 6 Georgia Tech
11 Texas
Texas 76-70
March 19
3/17 3 Missouri
14 Creighton
Missouri 85-69
Missouri 108-89
Dallas, TX
March 24
Syracuse 83-80
3/17 7 Florida
10 Colorado St.
Colorado St. 68-46
March 19
3/17 2 Syracuse
15 Bucknell
Syracuse 104-81
Syracuse 65-50

SOUTHEAST

Seattle WA
April 1
Michigan 83-81

3/16 1 Oklahoma
16 East Tenn. St.
Oklahoma 72-71
March 18
3/16 8 La Salle
9 Louisiana Tech
Louisiana Tech 83-74
Oklahoma 124-81
Nashville, TN
March 23
Virginia 86-80
3/16 5 Virginia
12 Providence
Virginia 100-97
March 18
3/16 4 Florida St.
13 Middle Tenn. St.
Middle Tenn. St. 97-83
Virginia 104-88
Lexington, KY
March 25
Michigan 102-65

3/17 6 Alabama
11 South Alabama
South Ala. 86-84
March 19
3/17 3 Michigan
14 Xavier (Ohio)
Michigan 92-87
Michigan 91-82
Atlanta, GA
March 23
Michigan 92-87
3/17 7 UCLA
10 Iowa St.
UCLA 84-74
March 19
3/17 2 North Carolina
15 Southern-B.R.
North Carolina 93-79
North Carolina 88-81

EAST

Seattle, WA
April 3
Michigan 80-79 (ot)
NATIONAL CHAMPION

3/17 1 Georgetown
16 Princeton
Georgetown 50-49
March 19
3/17 8 Vanderbilt
9 Notre Dame
Notre Dame 81-65
Georgetown 81-74
Providence, RI
March 24
Georgetown 69-61
3/17 5 North Carolina St.
12 South Carolina
North Carolina St. 81-66
March 19
3/17 4 Iowa
13 Rutgers
Iowa 87-73
N.C. St. 102-96 (2 ot)
East Rutherford, NJ
March 26
Duke 85-77

3/16 6 Kansas St.
11 Minnesota
Minnesota 86-75
March 18
3/16 3 Stanford
14 Siena
Siena 80-78
Minnesota 80-67
Greensboro, NC
March 24
Duke 87-70
3/16 7 West Va.
10 Tennessee
West Va. 84-68
March 18
3/16 2 Duke
15 South Carolina St.
Duke 90-69
Duke 70-63

WEST

Seattle, WA
April 1
Seton Hall 95-78

3/16 1 Arizona
16 Robert Morris
Arizona 94-60
March 18
3/16 8 St. Mary's (Cal.)
9 Clemson
Clemson 83-70
Arizona 94-68
Boise, ID
March 23
Nevada-Las Vegas 68-67
3/16 5 Memphis St.
12 DePaul
DePaul 66-63
March 18
3/16 4 Nevada-Las Vegas
13 Idaho
Nev.-Las Vegas 68-56
Nev.-Las Vegas 85-70
Denver, CO
March 25
Seton Hall 84-61

3/17 6 Oregon St.
11 Evansville
Evansville 94-90 (ot)
March 19
3/17 3 Seton Hall
14 Southwest Mo. St.
Seton Hall 60-51
Seton Hall 87-73
Tucson, AZ
March 23
Seton Hall 78-65
3/17 7 UTEP
10 Louisiana St.
UTEP 85-74
March 19
3/17 2 Indiana
15 George Mason
Indiana 99-85
Indiana 92-69

1989–90

AT A GLANCE

NCAA Champion: UNLV (35-5).

NIT Champion: Vanderbilt (21-14).

NCAA Probation: Cleveland State, Kentucky, North Carolina State.

NCAA Consensus First-Team All-Americans: Derrick Coleman, F, Sr., Syracuse; Chris Jackson, G, Soph., Louisiana State; Larry Johnson, F, Jr., UNLV; Gary Payton, G, Sr., Oregon State; Lionel Simmons, F, Sr., La Salle.

Hank Gathers, Loyola Marymount's rising star, collapsed during 1990 tournament play and tragically died soon after.

The most tragic moment in the history of any league tourney occurred in the semifinals of the West Coast Conference Tournament at Loyola Marymount when Hank Gathers, the league's all-time scoring leader and a two-time tourney MVP, collapsed on his home court during the Lions' game with Portland. He died later that evening, the result of a heart ailment, and the tournament was suspended. The Lions still earned an NCAA Tournament bid because of their regular-season crown and advanced to the West Regional final behind the heroics of Bo Kimble, who was Gathers' longtime friend from Philadelphia.

Loyola Marymount, leading the nation in point production for the third consecutive season, set an NCAA record for highest scoring average per game (122.4). The Lions scored at least 99 points in all but two of their 32 games. They also set a mark for largest-ever margin over the national runner-up (21.1 over Oklahoma). Gathers and Kimble became the only set of teammates to surpass the 2,250-point plateau. Kimble (35.3 ppg), Gathers (29), and Jeff Fryer (22.7) combined for 87 points per game to become the highest-scoring trio in a single season in Division I history.

Georgia Tech's perimeter marksmen Dennis Scott (27.7), Brian Oliver (21.3), and Kenny Anderson (20.6) were known in Hoopdom as "Lethal Weapon 3" when they became the first ACC trio to all average more than 20 points per game in the same season. They were also the only threesome to achieve the feat for a Final Four team. Anderson was the sixth Tech player in eight years to be named ACC Rookie of the Year.

Georgia captured its lone SEC regular-season title one year after finishing ninth in the 10-team league.

Ohio University's Dave Jamerson set an NCAA record for most three-point field goals in a game with 14 vs. Charleston. Northwestern's Todd Leslie set an NCAA record for most consecutive successful three-point baskets with 15 in a span covering four games.

La Salle's Lionel Simmons ended his career with an NCAA record 115 consecutive games scoring in double figures.

Oklahoma gave Northeastern Illinois a rude welcome to Division I basketball with a 95-point victory (146-51).

Kentucky had eight different players hit a three-point basket in a 104-73 victory over Furman on December 19, 1989. Four days later, Kentucky (53) and Southwestern Louisiana combined for an NCAA-record 84 three-point field-goal attempts. The Wildcats averaged an NCAA-record 28.9 three-point attempts per game during the season.

Purdue's Steve Scheffler overcame dyslexia to finish with an NCAA career record for field-goal shooting (minimum of 400 baskets). He hit 68.5 percent of his field-goal attempts (408 of 596).

Oregon State's Gary Payton (58 points against Southern Cal) and St. Louis' Anthony Bonner (45 in overtime game against Loyola of Chicago) set school single-game school records.

Clemson captured its only ACC regular-season title.

Seton Hall guard Marko Lokar, a native of Italy making his first college start, scored a Big East Conference-freshman record 41 points against Pittsburgh. In his total of 33 other games with the Pirates this season and a portion of the following year, Lokar scored 99 points with only two double-digit outings (15 and 12). Lokar, a

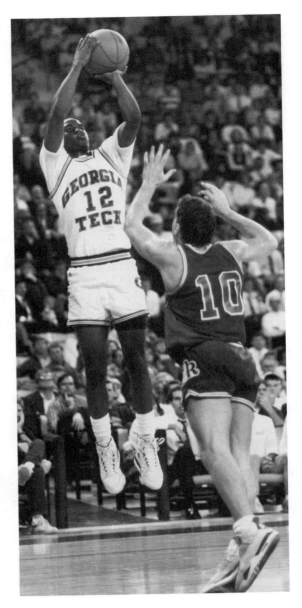

Guard Kenny Anderson—one-third of Georgia Tech's "Lethal Weapon 3"—launches a shot.

pacifist, was opposed to war of any kind and left school because of the reaction he received following his refusal to wear an American flag on his uniform along with the remainder of his teammates during the Gulf War.

North Carolina State coach Jim Valvano was one of college basketball's most colorful characters.

Tennessee's Wade Houston became the first African-American head coach in the SEC.

National personality Jim Valvano was forced out as coach at North Carolina State. He became a popular ESPN and ABC commentator

who died three years later after a courageous fight with cancer.

1989-90 FINAL NATIONAL POLLS

AP	UPI	USA/CNN	SCHOOL
1	1	11	Oklahoma
2	2	1	UNLV
3	3	5	Connecticut
4	4	7	Michigan St.
5	5	14	Kansas
6	6	10	Syracuse
7	8	4	Arkansas
8	9	15	Georgetown
9	7	3	Georgia Tech
10	10	6	Purdue
11	11	20	Missouri
12	13	19	La Salle
13	15	18	Michigan
14	12	21	Arizona
15	14	2	Duke
16	16	24	Louisville
17	17	13	Clemson
18	18	–	Illinois
19	–	–	Louisiana St.
20	–	8	Minnesota
21	–	9	Loyola Marymount
22	–	–	Oregon St.
23	19	16	Alabama
24	20	–	New Mexico St.
25	–	17	Xavier
–	–	12	Texas
–	–	22	Ball St.
–	–	23	UCLA
–	–	25	North Carolina

1990 NCAA Tournament

Summary: UNLV's 103-73 rout of Duke when the Rebels became the only team to score more than 100 points in a championship game established a record for widest margin of victory in a final.

Outcome for Defending Champion: Michigan (23-8), led by interim-less coach Steve Fisher, finished third in the Big Ten.

Star Gazing: UNLV guard Anderson Hunt is the only Final Four Most Outstanding Player since 1954 to never play in the NBA.

Biggest Upset: Northern Iowa (14th seed) over Missouri (3), 74-71.

One and Only: Georgia Tech guard Kenny Anderson became the only freshman on a Final Four team to score more than 20 points in as many as four tournament games.... UNLV became the only school to score more than 100 points in a national championship game and the

1989-90 INDIVIDUAL LEADERS

SCORING

PLAYER	PTS.	AVG.
Kimble, L. Marymount	1131	35.3
Bradshaw, U.S. Intl.	875	31.3
Jamerson, Ohio U.	874	31.2
Ford, Miss. Valley St.	808	29.9
Rogers, Alabama St.	831	29.7
Gathers, L. Marymount	754	29.0
Brooks, Tenn. St.	690	28.8
Jackson, LSU	889	27.8
Scott, Ga. Tech	970	27.7
Stevenson, Duquesne	788	27.2

REBOUNDING

PLAYER	REB.	AVG.
Bonner, St. Louis	456	13.8
McArthur, UC Santa Barb.	377	13.0
Hill, Xavier	402	12.6
Campbell, SW Mo. St.	363	12.5
Ceballos, Cal St. Full.	362	12.5
Shahid, S. Florida	383	12.4
Draper, American	354	12.2
Coleman, Syracuse	398	12.1
O'Neal, LSU	385	12.0
Weatherspoon, S. Miss.	371	11.6

ASSISTS

PLAYER	AST.	AVG.
Lehmann, Drexel	260	9.3
Mitchell, SW La.	264	9.1
Jennings, East Tenn. St.	297	8.7
Livingston, Idaho	262	8.5
Anderson, Ga. Tech	285	8.1
Payton, Oregon St.	235	8.1
Edmond, TCU	234	8.1
Corchiani, N.C. St.	238	7.9
Porter, Pittsburgh	229	7.9
Holt, Prairie View	213	7.9

BLOCKED SHOTS

PLAYER	BLK.	AVG.
Green, Rhode I.	124	4.8
Mutombo, Georgetown	128	4.1
Roberson, Vermont	114	3.8
Williams, Stetson	121	3.8
Roland, Marshall	101	3.6
O'Neal, LSU	115	3.6
Stevenson, Prairie View	97	3.6
Harris, Texas A&M	108	3.5
Longley, New Mexico	117	3.4
Palmer, Dartmouth	85	3.4

STEALS

PLAYER	STL.	AVG.
McMahon, E. Wash.	130	4.5
Dowdell, Coastal Caro.	109	3.8
Henefeld, Conn.	138	3.7
Robinson, Centenary	104	3.5
Payton, Oregon St.	100	3.4
Tanner, Rice	95	3.4
Corchiani, N.C. St.	95	3.2
Rogers, Alabama St.	86	3.1
Giles, Florida A&M	89	3.1
Brown, J'ville	88	3.0

FIELD GOAL PERCENTAGE

PLAYER	FGM	FGA	PCT.
Campbell, SW Mo. St.	192	275	.698
Scheffler, Purdue	173	248	.698
Spencer, Louisville	188	276	.681
Parker, Cleve. St.	155	236	.657
Hill, Evansville	180	278	.647
Stewart, Coppin St.	233	361	.645
Shahid, S. Florida	201	314	.640
French, Hardin-Simm.	212	338	.627
Keefe, Stanford	210	335	.627
Davis, Clemson	205	328	.625

FREE THROW PERCENTAGE

PLAYER	FTM	FTA	PCT.
Robbins, New Mexico	101	108	.935
Joseph, Bucknell	144	155	.929
Jackson, LSU	191	210	.910
Kennedy, UAB	111	123	.902
Henson, Kansas St.	101	112	.902
Matthews, Pittsburgh	141	158	.892
Shreffler, Evansville	84	95	.884
Recasner, Washington	99	112	.884
Venable, Bowling Green	114	129	.884
Franklin, Nevada-Reno	68	77	.883

THREE-POINT FIELD GOAL PERCENTAGE

PLAYER	FGM	FGA	PCT.
Lapin, Princeton	71	133	.534
Iuzzolino, St. Francis (Pa.)	79	153	.516
Oberbrunner, Wisc.-GB	47	93	.505
Mayberry, Arkansas	65	129	.504
Pernell, Holy Cross	81	161	.503

THREE-POINT FIELD GOALS MADE PER GAME

PLAYER	FGM	AVG.
Jamerson, Ohio U.	131	4.7
Grider, SW La.	131	4.5
Alberts, Akron	122	4.4
Fryer, L. Marymount	121	4.3
Brooks, Tenn. St.	95	4.0

1989-90 TEAM LEADERS

SCORING OFFENSE

SCHOOL	PTS.	AVG.
Loyola Marymount	3918	122.4
Oklahoma	3243	101.3
Southern (La.)	3078	99.3
U.S. International	2738	97.8
Centenary	2877	95.9

SCORING DEFENSE

SCHOOL	PTS.	AVG.
Princeton	1378	51.0
Ball St.	1935	58.6
Colorado St.	1778	59.3
Wisc.-Green Bay	1913	59.8
Northern Illinois	1710	61.1

SCORING MARGIN

SCHOOL	OFF.	DEF.	MAR.
Oklahoma	101.3	80.4	21.0
Kansas	92.1	72.3	19.7
Georgetown	81.5	64.8	16.7
Arkansas	95.6	79.8	15.8
Southern (La.)	99.3	84.1	15.2

WON-LOST PERCENTAGE

SCHOOL	W-L	PCT.
La Salle	30-2	.938
UNLV	35-5	.875
Arkansas	30-5	.857
Kansas	30-5	.857
Xavier	28-5	.848

FIELD GOAL PERCENTAGE

SCHOOL	FGM	FGA	PCT.
Kansas	1204	2258	.533
Louisville	1097	2078	.528
Princeton	592	1133	.523
Purdue	778	1491	.522
Loyola Marymount	1456	2808	.519

DEFENSIVE FIELD GOAL PERCENTAGE

SCHOOL	FGM	FGA	PCT.
Georgetown	713	1929	.370
Arizona	780	1990	.392
Ball St.	715	1789	.400
Alabama	784	1952	.402
South Carolina	660	1630	.405

FREE THROW PERCENTAGE

SCHOOL	FTM	FTA	PCT.
Lafayette	461	588	.784
Vanderbilt	742	956	.776
Wisc.-Green Bay	411	532	.773
Murray St.	540	703	.768
Bucknell	502	657	.764

REBOUND MARGIN

SCHOOL	OWN	OPP.	MAR.
Georgetown	44.8	34.0	10.8
Xavier	40.4	30.0	10.4
Ball St.	39.5	30.9	8.6
Michigan St.	38.1	29.8	8.4
Notre Dame	37.9	29.6	8.2

THREE-POINT FIELD GOAL PERCENTAGE

SCHOOL	FGM	FGA	PCT.
Princeton	208	460	45.2
Brigham Young	140	311	45.0
Western Michigan	177	394	44.9
Holy Cross	181	404	44.8
Northwestern	116	260	44.6

THREE-POINT FIELD GOALS MADE

SCHOOL	FGM	AVG.
Kentucky	281	10.0
Loyola Marymount	298	9.3
Southwestern La.	251	8.7
East Tenn. St.	285	8.4
Dayton	261	8.2

UNLV's Anderson Hunt.

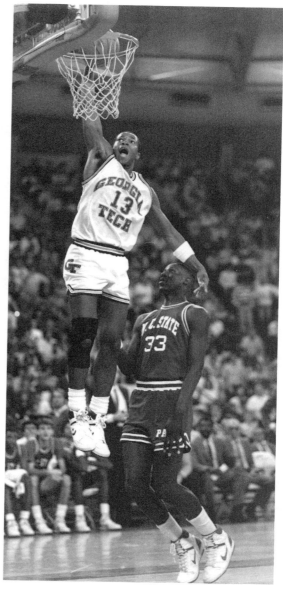

Georgia Tech's Brian Oliver reaches for the hoop.

only school to win an NCAA final by more than 21 points when the Rebels devoured Duke (103-73).

Numbers Game: Georgia Tech is the only Final Four team to have three players each average more than 20 points per game in the same season. The trio, known as "Lethal Weapon 3," included Dennis Scott (27.7), Brian Oliver (21.3), and Anderson (20.6).... Each Final Four participant received more than $1.47 million, a whopping increase of about 2,870 percent in just 20 years. Trying to minimize emphasis on the intrinsic dollar value of "six-figure shots" taken by players, the NCAA implemented a new revenue-sharing formula beginning with the next season.... The record for most three-point field goals in a playoff game was set by Loyola Marymount senior guard Jeff Fryer with 11 against Michigan (West Regional second round). Fryer also has the most playoff three-pointers in a

career with 38. Fryer (41) and Bo Kimble (37) became the only set of teammates to score more than 35 points in the same tourney game when they combined for 78 vs. Michigan.

What If: Anderson averaged 27 points per game in his first four tournament contests as a

1989–90 NCAA CHAMPION: UNLV

SEASON STATISTICS OF UNLV REGULARS

PLAYER	POS.	CL.	G.	FG%	FT%	PPG	RPG
Larry Johnson	F	Jr.	40	.624	.767	20.6	11.4
Anderson Hunt	G	So.	39	.481	.663	15.9	2.2
David Butler	C	Sr.	33	.487	.728	15.8	7.4
Stacey Augmon	F	Jr.	39	.553	.671	14.2	6.9
Greg Anthony	G	Jr.	39	.457	.682	11.2	3.0
Moses Scurry	F-C	Sr.	30	.520	.560	7.7	4.1
Travis Bice	G	So.	33	.480	.818	4.3	0.6
Barry Young	F	Jr.	39	.380	.680	4.2	2.0
James Jones	F	Sr.	31	.527	.550	3.9	2.8
Stacey Cvjanovich	G	Sr.	33	.362	.900	2.6	1.1
TEAM TOTALS			**40**	**.508**	**.699**	**93.5**	**41.7**

Three-point field goals leaders: Hunt (99 of 258, .384), Anthony (45 of 120, .375), Bice (36 of 75, .480), Young (31 of 96, .323). **Assists leaders:** Anthony 289, Hunt 158, Augmon 143. **Blocked shots leaders:** Johnson 56, Augmon 49. **Steals leaders:** Anthony 106, Augmon 69, Johnson 65.

1990 FINAL FOUR CHAMPIONSHIP GAME

DENVER, CO

UNLV (103)	MIN.	FG-A	FT-A	REB.	A	PF	PTS.
Johnson	30	8-12	4-4	2	2	3	22
Augmon	26	6-7	0-1	2	7	5	12
Butler	27	1-4	2-2	0	3	3	4
Hunt	31	12-16	1-2	0	2	0	29
Anthony	30	5-11	3-4	1	6	3	13
Cvjanovich	10	1-2	2-2	1	2	2	5
Bice	9	0-1	0-0	0	0	0	2
Rice	2	0-2	0-0	0	0	0	0
Young	12	2-2	0-0	0	0	1	5
Jones	8	4-5	0-0	0	0	2	8
Scurry	12	2-5	1-2	3	0	2	5
Jeter	3	0-0	0-0	0	2	0	0
Team				2			
TOTALS	**200**	**41-67**	**13-17**	**11**	**24**	**23**	**103**

FG%: .612. **FT%:** .765. **Three-point goals:** 8-14 (Hunt 4-7, Johnson 2-2, Cvjanovich 1-1, Young 1-1, Rice 0-1, Bice 0-1, Anthony 0-1). **Blocks:** 3. **Turnovers:** 17. **Steals:** 16 (Anthony 5).

DUKE (73)	MIN.	FG-A	FT-A	REB.	A	PF	PTS.
Brickey	24	2-4	0-2	1	2	2	4
Laettner	29	5-12	5-6	5	5	4	15
Abdelnaby	24	5-7	4-6	4	0	3	14
Henderson	32	9-20	2-2	1	0	2	21
Hurley	32	0-3	2-2	0	3	3	2
Hill	8	0-2	0-0	1	1	0	0
Davis	21	2-5	2-3	1	0	1	6
McCaffrey	9	1-3	2-2	0	0	1	4
Koubek	14	1-4	0-0	2	0	0	2
Palmer	2	0-0	3-4	0	0	0	3
Buckley	3	0-0	0-0	0	0	0	0
Cook	2	1-1	0-0	0	0	0	2
Team				6			
TOTALS	**200**	**26-61**	**20-27**	**21**	**11**	**16**	**73**

FG%: .426. **FT%:** .741. **Three-point goals:** 1-11 (Henderson 1-8, Hurley 0-2, Koubek 0-1). **Blocks:** 3. **Turnovers:** 23 (Henderson 6, Hurley 5). **Steals:** 5. **Halftime:** UNLV 47-35.

NATIONAL SEMIFINALS

GEORGIA TECH (81): Scott 8-17 6-9 29, Mackey 2-3 0-0 4, McNeil 2-4 0-1 4, Anderson 7-14 1-2 16, Oliver 9-18 6-9 24, Brown 2-3 0-0 4, Barnes 0-0 0-0 0. Team 30-59 (.508) 13-21 (.619) 81.

UNLV (90): Johnson 5-11 4-4 15, Augmon 9-16 3-3 22, Butler 6-10 1-3 13, Hunt 7-15 1-2 20, Anthony 4-9 3-7 14, Cvjanovich 0-0 0-0 0, Bice 0-0 0-0 0, Young 0-0 0-0 0, Jones 0-0 0-0 0, Scurry 3-4 0-0 6. Team 34-65 (.523) 12-19 (.632) 90.

Three-point goals: Georgia Tech 8-21 (.381), UNLV 10-15 (.667). **Halftime:** Georgia Tech 53-46.

DUKE (97): Brickey 8-10 1-3 17, Laettner 5-7 9-12 19, Abdelnaby 8-12 4-5 20, Henderson 10-21 5-5 28, Hurley 0-2 3-6 3, Hill 0-0 0-0 0, Davis 1-4 3-4 5, McCaffrey 0-1 3-4 3, Koubek 1-4 0-0 2, Buckley 0-0 0-0 0, Cook 0-0 0-0 0. Team 33-61 (.541) 28-39 (.718) 97.

ARKANSAS (83): Whitby 0-2 0-0 0, Linn 0-1 0-0 0, Marks 0-0 0-0 0, Day 8-17 7-7 27, Howell 5-9 7-8 18, Credit 2-3 1-4 5, Mayberry 6-18 0-0 12, Bowers 1-6 0-0 2, Murry 2-5 0-0 5, Hawkins 2-4 2-2 6, Miller 1-3 1-2 3, Huery 2-5 1-3 5. Team 29-73 (.397) 19-26 (.731) 83.

Three-point goals: Duke 3-9 (.333), Arkansas 6-21 (.286). **Halftime:** Duke 46-43.

ALL-TOURNAMENT TEAM

Stacey Augmon, F, Jr., UNLV
Phil Henderson, G, Sr., Duke
Anderson Hunt, G, Soph., UNLV*
Larry Johnson, F, Jr., UNLV
Dennis Scott, F, Jr., Georgia Tech

*Named Most Outstanding Player

freshman for Georgia Tech. If only he had reached that figure in his fifth game instead of scoring 16 points in the national semifinals, the Yellow Jackets could have defeated eventual champion UNLV rather than blow a seven-point halftime lead and lose 90-81.

1990 CHAMPIONSHIP BRACKET

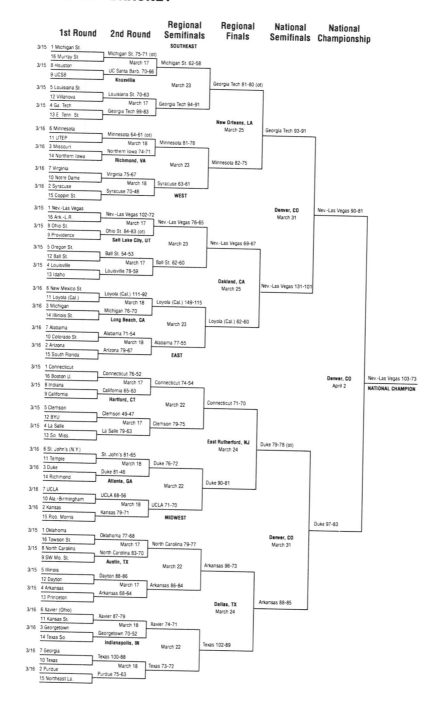

1st Round	2nd Round	Regional Semifinals	Regional Finals	National Semifinals	National Championship

SOUTHEAST

3/15 1 Michigan St.
16 Murray St.
   Michigan St. 75-71 (ot)
3/15 8 Houston   March 17
9 UCSB   UC Santa Barb. 70-66
   Michigan St. 62-58
Knoxville
3/15 5 Louisiana St.
12 Villanova   Louisiana St. 70-63
3/15 4 Ga. Tech   March 17
13 E. Tenn. St.   Georgia Tech 99-83
   March 23
   Georgia Tech 94-91
   Georgia Tech 81-80 (ot)

New Orleans, LA
March 25
Georgia Tech 93-91

3/16 6 Minnesota
11 UTEP   Minnesota 64-61 (ot)
3/16 3 Missouri   March 18
14 Northern Iowa   Northern Iowa 74-71
   Minnesota 81-78
Richmond, VA
3/16 7 Virginia
10 Notre Dame   Virginia 75-67
3/16 2 Syracuse   March 18
15 Coppin St.   Syracuse 70-48
   March 23
   Syracuse 63-61
   Minnesota 82-75

WEST

3/15 1 Nev.-Las Vegas
16 Ark.-L.R.   Nev.-Las Vegas 102-72
3/15 8 Ohio St.   March 17
9 Providence   Ohio St. 84-83 (ot)
   Nev.-Las Vegas 76-65
Salt Lake City, UT
3/15 5 Oregon St.
12 Ball St.   Ball St. 54-53
3/15 4 Louisville   March 17
13 Idaho   Louisville 78-59
   March 23
   Ball St. 62-60
   Nev.-Las Vegas 69-67

Denver, CO
March 31
Nev.-Las Vegas 90-81

3/16 6 New Mexico St.
11 Loyola (Cal.)   Loyola (Cal.) 111-92
3/16 3 Michigan   March 18
14 Illinois St.   Michigan 76-70
   Loyola (Cal.) 149-115
Long Beach, CA
3/16 7 Alabama
10 Colorado St.   Alabama 71-54
3/16 2 Arizona   March 18
15 South Florida   Arizona 79-67
   March 23
   Alabama 77-55
   Loyola (Cal.) 62-60

Oakland, CA
March 25
Nev.-Las Vegas 131-101

EAST

3/15 1 Connecticut
16 Boston U.   Connecticut 76-52
3/15 8 Indiana   March 17
9 California   California 65-63
   Connecticut 74-54
Hartford, CT
3/15 5 Clemson
12 BYU   Clemson 49-47
3/15 4 La Salle   March 17
13 So. Miss.   La Salle 79-63
   March 22
   Clemson 79-75
   Connecticut 71-70

East Rutherford, NJ
March 24
Duke 79-78 (ot)

3/16 6 St. John's (N.Y.)
11 Temple   St. John's 81-65
3/16 3 Duke   March 18
14 Richmond   Duke 81-46
   Duke 76-72
Atlanta, GA
3/16 7 UCLA
10 Ala.-Birmingham   UCLA 68-56
3/16 2 Kansas   March 18
15 Rob. Morris   Kansas 79-71
   March 22
   UCLA 71-70
   Duke 90-81

Denver, CO
April 2
Nev.-Las Vegas 103-73
NATIONAL CHAMPION

Denver, CO
March 31
Duke 97-83

MIDWEST

3/15 1 Oklahoma
16 Towson St.   Oklahoma 77-68
3/15 8 North Carolina   March 17
9 SW Mo. St.   North Carolina 83-70
   North Carolina 79-77
Austin, TX
3/15 5 Illinois
12 Dayton   Dayton 88-86
3/15 4 Arkansas   March 17
13 Princeton   Arkansas 68-64
   March 22
   Arkansas 86-84
   Arkansas 96-73

Dallas, TX
March 24
Arkansas 88-85

3/16 6 Xavier (Ohio)
11 Kansas St.   Xavier 87-79
3/16 3 Georgetown   March 18
14 Texas So.   Georgetown 70-52
   Xavier 74-71
Indianapolis, IN
3/16 7 Georgia
10 Texas   Texas 100-88
3/16 2 Purdue   March 18
15 Northeast La.   Purdue 75-63
   March 22
   Texas 73-72
   Texas 102-89

1990-91

AT A GLANCE

NCAA Champion: Duke (32-7).

NIT Champion: Stanford (20-13).

New Conference: Patriot.

New Rules: Beginning with a team's 10th personal foul in a half, two free throws are awarded for each common foul, except player-control fouls. Three free throws are awarded when a shooter is fouled during an unsuccessful three-point attempt. The definition of "home court" in the NCAA Tournament is amended to include playing no more than three games of a regular-season schedule, excluding league tournaments, in one arena. A preliminary round is used for six of 33 eligible conferences to identify the 30 automatic-qualifying leagues. The conferences with the lowest rankings in the Ratings Percentage Index (RPI) must compete for the available automatic-qualifying positions.

NCAA Probation: Illinois, Kentucky, Marshall, Maryland, Missouri, Northwestern (La.) State, Robert Morris, Southeastern Louisiana.

NCAA Consensus First-Team All-Americans: Kenny Anderson, G, Soph., Georgia Tech; Jim Jackson, G-F, Soph., Ohio State; Larry Johnson, F, Sr., UNLV; Shaquille O'Neal, C, Soph., Louisiana State; Billy Owens, F, Jr., Syracuse.

UNLV's Larry Johnson in motion.

Defending champion UNLV was upset by Duke in the NCAA Tournament. Still, the Rebels will go down as one of the greatest teams in history if only because they're the only squad to have at least four teammates score a minimum of 1,500 points—Stacey Augmon (2,011), Greg Anthony (1,738), Anderson Hunt (1,632), and Larry Johnson (1,617).

U.S. International's Kevin Bradshaw, a Navy veteran who started his college career at Bethune-Cookman, set a single-game record for most points against a major college opponent with 72 vs. Loyola Marymount. Loyola Marymount, a 186-140 winner in the game, established an NCAA record for most points by a team. Bradshaw, who had three other games with at least 53 points, finished his career as the only individual to play for more than one major college and score more than 2,750 points. He had 2,804.

Georgia Tech's Kenny Anderson scored a school-record 50 points against Loyola Marymount.

La Salle guards Randy Woods (46) and Doug Overton (45) became the only set of teammates in history to score more than 40 points in a single game when they combined for 91 in a 133-118 victory at Loyola Marymount.

A national high of 15 different teams averaged more than 90 points per game. Meanwhile, Princeton, limiting its opponents to 48.9 points per game, set a record for highest-ever margin over the runner-up in team defense (8.6 fewer than Northern Illinois).

Connecticut set an NCAA mark for largest lead at the start of a game before an opponent scored, racing to a 32-0 advantage in a victory

1990–91 INDIVIDUAL LEADERS

SCORING

PLAYER	PTS.	AVG.
Bradshaw, U.S. International	1054	37.6
Ford, Miss. Valley St.	915	32.7
McDade, Wisc.-Milw.	830	29.6
Rogers, Alabama St.	852	29.4
Lowery, L. Marymount	884	28.5
Phills, Southern (La.)	795	28.4
O'Neal, LSU	774	27.6
Taft, Marshall	764	27.3
Monroe, N.C. St.	836	27.0
Brandon, Oregon	745	26.6

REBOUNDING

PLAYER	REB.	AVG.
O'Neal, LSU	411	14.7
Jones, Murray St.	469	14.2
Stewart, Coppin St.	403	13.4
Burroughs, J'ville	350	13.0
Kidd, Middle Tenn. St.	370	12.3
Weatherspoon, S'ern Miss.	355	12.2
Johnson, New Orleans	367	12.2
Davis, Delaware St.	366	12.2
Mutombo, Georgetown	389	12.2
Davis, Clemson	340	12.1

ASSISTS

PLAYER	AST.	AVG.
Corchiani, N.C. St.	299	9.6
Tirado, J'ville	259	9.3
Lowery, L. Marymount	283	9.1
Jennings, East Tenn. St.	301	9.1
Anthony, UNLV	310	8.9
Usher, Tenn. Tech	233	8.3
Smart, San Francisco	237	8.2
Johnson, Sam Houston St.	193	8.0

	229	7.9
Cody, Texas-Arl.	229	7.9
Bernard, SW Mo. St.	257	7.6

BLOCKED SHOTS

PLAYER	BLK.	AVG.
Bradley, BYU	177	5.2
Lewis, Maryland	143	5.1
O'Neal, LSU	140	5.0
Mutombo, Georgetown	151	4.7
Roberson, Vermont	104	3.7
Williams, Stetson	113	3.6
Earl, Iowa	106	3.3
McIlvaine, Marquette	92	3.3
Longley, New Mexico	95	3.2
Lopez, Fordham	100	3.0

STEALS

PLAYER	STL.	AVG.
Usher, Tenn. Tech	104	3.7
Burrell, Connecticut	112	3.6
Murdock, Providence	111	3.5
McDade, Wisc.-Milw.	97	3.5
Smith, St. Francis (N.Y.)	100	3.4
Davis, Delaware St.	84	3.4
Ellison, Texas-San Ant.	97	3.3
Jennings, East Tenn. St.	109	3.3
Phills, Southern (La.)	90	3.2
Baldwin, N'western	90	3.2

FIELD GOAL PERCENTAGE

PLAYER	FGM	FGA	PCT.
Miller, Arkansas	254	361	.704
Kidd, Middle Tenn. St.	173	247	.700
Freeman, Akron	175	250	.700
James, St. Francis (N.Y.)	149	215	.693
Kennedy, E. Mich.	240	352	.682

Lightfoot, Montana St.	130	196	.663
Brooks, West Va.	222	335	.663
Johnson, UNLV	308	465	.662
Alexander, Iowa St.	294	446	.659
Longley, New Mex.	229	349	.656

FREE THROW PERCENTAGE

PLAYER	FTM	FTA	PCT.
Archbold, Butler	187	205	.912
Lewis, Monmouth	91	101	.901
Alexander, Okla. St.	96	107	.897
Jennings, East Tenn. St.	136	152	.895
Monroe, N.C. St.	162	183	.885
Iuzzolino, St. Francis (Pa.)	215	243	.885
Bird, Indiana St.	82	94	.872
Marcelic, S. Utah	81	93	.871
Geter, Ohio	137	158	.867
Kennedy, UAB	167	193	.865

THREE-POINT FIELD GOAL PERCENTAGE

PLAYER	FGM	FGA	PCT.
Jennings, East Tenn. St.	84	142	.592
Bennett, Wisc.-GB	80	150	.533
Iuzzolino, St. Francis (Pa.)	103	195	.528
Richardson, L. Marymount	61	116	.526
Mitchell, Samford	41	78	.526

THREE-POINT FIELD GOALS PER GAME

PLAYER	FGM	AVG.
Phills, Southern (La.)	123	4.4
Schmitz, Mo.-KC	116	4.0
Herdman, UC Irvine	112	3.7
Day, Radford	106	3.7
Jackson, Princeton	95	3.5

1990–91 TEAM LEADERS

SCORING OFFENSE

SCHOOL	PTS.	AVG.
Southern (La.)	2924	104.4
Loyola Marymount	3211	103.6
Arkansas	3783	99.6
UNLV	3420	97.7
Oklahoma	3363	96.1

SCORING DEFENSE

SCHOOL	PTS.	AVG.
Princeton	1320	48.9
Northern Illinois	1781	57.5
Yale	1508	58.0
Wisconsin-Green Bay	1893	61.1
Georgetown	1964	61.4

SCORING MARGIN

SCHOOL	OFF.	DEF.	MAR.
UNLV	97.7	71.0	26.7
Arkansas	99.6	80.4	19.2
East Tennessee St.	94.0	76.8	17.3
Ohio St.	84.6	68.5	16.2
North Carolina	87.6	71.6	16.0

WON-LOST PERCENTAGE

SCHOOL	W-L	PCT.
UNLV	34-1	.971
Arkansas	34-4	.895
Princeton	24-3	.889
Utah	30-4	.882
Ohio St.	27-4	.871

FIELD GOAL PERCENTAGE

SCHOOL	FGM	FGA	PCT.
UNLV	1305	2441	.535
Indiana	1043	1955	.534
New Mexico	868	1644	.528
Brooklyn	656	1262	.520
Kansas	1086	2097	.518

DEFENSIVE FIELD GOAL PERCENTAGE

SCHOOL	FGM	FGA	PCT.
Georgetown	680	1847	.368
Northern Illinois	616	1587	.388
Connecticut	682	1753	.389
New Orleans	725	1837	.395
Middle Tennessee St.	793	2007	.395

FREE THROW PERCENTAGE

SCHOOL	FTM	FTA	PCT.
Butler	725	922	.786
Monmouth	422	547	.771
Air Force	483	627	.770
Northwestern	470	612	.768
Wyoming	654	853	.767

REBOUND MARGIN

SCHOOL	OWN	OPP.	MAR.
New Orleans	41.7	32.4	9.3
Murray St.	43.4	34.6	8.7
Stanford	37.9	29.4	8.5
UNLV	42.5	34.8	7.7
Northern Illinois	35.5	28.0	7.5

THREE-POINT FIELD GOAL PERCENTAGE

SCHOOL	FGM	FGA	PCT.
Wisconsin-Green Bay	189	407	.464
Southern Utah St.	158	353	.448
St. Francis (Pa.)	238	534	.446
Eastern Illinois	200	457	.438
Northern Illinois	133	305	.436

THREE-POINT FIELD GOALS PER GAME

SCHOOL	G.	FGM	AVG.
Texas-Arlington	29	265	9.1
East Tennessee St.	33	301	9.1
Dayton	29	256	8.8
UC Irvine	30	263	8.8
Kentucky	28	242	8.6

over New Hampshire. Later, New Hampshire's NCAA-record 32 consecutive homecourt defeats was snapped when the Wildcats defeated Holy Cross, 72-56.

Indiana State set an NCAA record for most consecutive successful free throws by converting 49 in a row in two games in mid-February.

Providence guard Eric Murdock established a Big East Conference record with 48 points against Pittsburgh.

East Tennessee State's Keith "Mister" Jennings (5-7) became the first player under 5-10 to finish his career with more than 900 assists. He had 938.

Georgetown led the nation in field-goal percentage defense for the third consecutive season.

Louisville's NCAA record of consecutive winning seasons was snapped at 46 when the Cardinals went 14-16.

North Carolina's Dean Smith set a national coaching record with his 24th 20-win season.

Tom Young, who previously coached Catholic, American, and Rutgers, was forced out at Old Dominion, ending a 31-year coaching career with a 524-328 record.

UNLV's Stacey Augmon prepares to dish it off to a teammate.

1990–91 FINAL NATIONAL POLLS

AP	UPI	USA/CNN	SCHOOL
1	1	2	UNLV
2	2	5	Arkansas
3	3	9	Indiana
4	4	4	North Carolina
5	5	8	Ohio St.
6	6	1	Duke
7	8	16	Syracuse
8	7	10	Arizona
9	–	17	Kentucky
10	10	12	Utah
11	9	19	Nebraska
12	12	3	Kansas
13	11	6	Seton Hall
14	13	13	Oklahoma St.
15	17	22	New Mexico St.
16	14	25	UCLA
17	15	24	East Tenn. St.
18	20	–	Princeton
19	16	–	Alabama
20	19	7	St. John's
21	18	–	Mississippi St.
22	21	–	Louisiana St.
23	25	–	Texas
24	–	–	DePaul
25	–	–	Southern Mississippi
–	–	15	Connecticut
–	–	18	Eastern Michigan
–	23	20	Georgetown
–	–	21	Pittsburgh
–	22	–	Michigan St.
–	24	23	North Carolina St.

1991 NCAA Tournament

Summary: Duke required nine appearances at the Final Four until the resolute Blue Devils finally won a national title.

Star Gazing: Christian Laettner became the only player with at least 10 championship game free-throw attempts to convert all of them (12 of 12 against Kansas).

Biggest Upsets: Richmond (15th seed) over Syracuse (2), 73-69; Xavier (14) over Nebraska (3), 89-84; and Penn State (13) over UCLA (4), 74-69.

One and Only: North Carolina's Dean Smith became the only coach to direct teams to Final Fours in four different decades, but the Tar Heels lost against Kansas in the national semifinals to give him nine Final Four defeats. No other coach has more than seven Final Four set-

1990–91 NCAA CHAMPION: DUKE

SEASON STATISTICS OF DUKE REGULARS

PLAYER	POS.	CL.	G.	FG%	FT%	PPG	RPG
Christian Laettner	C-F	Jr.	39	.575	.802	19.8	8.7
Billy McCaffrey	G	So.	38	.481	.832	11.6	1.8
Thomas Hill	G-F	So.	39	.552	.743	11.5	3.6
Bobby Hurley	G	So.	39	.423	.728	11.3	2.4
Grant Hill	F-G	Fr.	36	.516	.609	11.2	5.1
Brian Davis	G-F	Jr.	39	.456	.730	7.6	4.1
Greg Koubek	F	Sr.	38	.435	.813	5.9	2.9
Antonio Lang	F-C	Fr.	36	.606	.526	4.3	2.6
Crawford Palmer	C	Jr.	38	.646	.825	3.6	2.0
Marty Clark	G	Fr.	23	.448	.625	2.1	0.7
TEAM TOTALS			39	.511	.726	87.7	36.3

Three-point field goals leaders: Hurley (76 of 188, .404), Koubek (32 of 76, .421). Assists leader: Hurley 289. Blocked shots leader: Laettner 44. Steals leaders: Laettner 75, T. Hill 59.

1991 FINAL FOUR CHAMPIONSHIP GAME

INDIANAPOLIS, IN

KANSAS (65)	MIN.	FG-A	FT-A	REB.	A.	PF.	PTS.
Jamison	29	1-10	0-0	4	5	4	2
Maddox	19	2-4	0-0	3	4	3	4
Randall	33	7-9	3-6	10	2	4	18
Brown	31	6-15	0-0	4	1	1	16
Jordan	34	4-6	1-2	0	3	0	11
Richey	4	0-1	0-0	1	0	0	0
Woodberry	18	1-4	0-0	4	0	4	2
Tunstall	11	1-5	0-0	1	0	3	2
Wagner	3	1-1	0-0	1	0	0	2
Scott	15	3-9	0-0	2	0	1	6
Johanning	3	1-1	0-0	2	1	1	2
TOTALS	200	27-65	4-8	32	16	21	65

FG%: .415. FT%: .500. Three-point goals: 7 of 18 (Jamison 0-2, Randall 1-1, Brown 4-11, Jordan 2-2, Richey 0-1, Tunstall 0-1). Blocks: 2. Turnovers: 14. Steals: 10 (Jamison 4).

DUKE (72)	MIN.	FG-A	FT-A	REB.	A.	PF.	PTS.
Koubek	17	2-4	0-0	4	0	1	5
G. Hill	28	4-6	2-8	8	3	1	10
Laettner	32	3-8	12-12	10	0	3	18
Hurley	40	3-5	4-4	1	9	1	12
T. Hill	23	1-5	0-0	4	1	2	3
McCaffrey	26	6-8	2-2	1	0	1	16
Lang	1	0-0	0-0	0	0	0	0
Davis	24	4-5	0-2	2	1	4	8
Palmer	9	0-0	0-0	0	0	0	0
Team				1			
TOTALS	200	23-41	20-28	31	14	13	72

FG%: .561. FT%: .714. Three-point goals: 6 of 10 (Koubek 1-2, Hurley 2-4, T. Hill 1-1, McCaffrey 2-3). Blocks: 2. Turnovers: 18. Steals: 6. Halftime: Duke 42-34.

NATIONAL SEMIFINALS

DUKE (79): Koubek 1-6 0-0 2, G. Hill 5-8 1-1 11, Laettner 9-14 9-11 28, Hurley 4-7 1-1 12, T. Hill 2-6 2-2 6, McCaffrey 2-3 1-2 5, Lang 0-0 0-0 0, Davis 6-12 3-4 15, Palmer 0-0 0-0 0. Team 29-56 (.518) 17-21 (.810) 79.

UNLV (77): Johnson 5-10 3-4 13, Augmon 3-10 0-1 6, Ackles 3-6 1-2 7, Hunt 11-20 3-5 29, Anthony 8-18 1-1 19, Gray 1-2 0-0 2, Spencer 0-2 1-2 1. Team 31-68 (.456) 9-15 (.600) 77.

Three-point goals: Duke 4-8 (.500), UNLV 6-15 (.400). Halftime: UNLV 43-41.

KANSAS (79): Jamison 4-8 1-3 9, Maddox 4-10 2-2 10, Randall 6-11 4-6 16, Brown 1-10 0-0 3, Jordan 4-11 6-13 16, Richey 1-1 2-2 4, Woodberry 0-0 2-2 2, Tunstall 1-5 2-5 5, Wagner 0-1 0-0 0, Scott 6-9 2-3 14, Johanning 0-0 0-0 0. Team 27-66 (.409) 21-36 (.583) 79.

NORTH CAROLINA (73): Lynch 5-8 3-6 13, Fox 5-22 3-3 13, Chilcutt 2-8 0-0 4, Rice 1-6 3-4 5, Davis 9-16 5-5 25, Montross 3-4 0-1 6, Sullivan 0-0 0-0 0, Harris 0-2 0-0 0, Rodl 0-1 0-0 0, Phelps 0-1 0-2 2, Reese 2-5 0-3 5, Rozier 0-0 0-0 0, Cherry 0-0 0-0 0, Salvadori 0-0 0-0 0, Wenstrom 0-0 0-0 0. Team 28-73 (.384) 14-23 (.609) 73.

Three-point goals: Kansas 4-14 (.286), North Carolina 3-18 (.167). Halftime: Kansas 43-34.

ALL-TOURNAMENT TEAM

Anderson Hunt, G, Jr., UNLV
Bobby Hurley, G, Soph., Duke
Christian Laettner, C, Jr., Duke*
Bill McCaffrey, G, Soph., Duke
Mark Randall, F, Sr., Kansas

*Named Most Outstanding Player

backs.... Eddie Sutton became the only coach to guide four different schools to the NCAA Tournament when his alma mater, Oklahoma State, earned a bid.

Numbers Game: Duke became the only school to reach the NCAA Tournament final in back-to-back seasons after losing by double-digit margins in its conference tournament (defeated by 11 points against Georgia Tech in the 1990 ACC Tournament semifinals before getting trounced in the 1991 ACC Tournament final by 22 points against North Carolina).

What If: Forward Larry Johnson and guard Stacey Augmon combined for 37 points per game on 61 percent field-goal shooting in their two years together as teammates at UNLV. If only they had combined for 22 points instead of 19 points on 40 percent field-goal shooting (8 of 20) in the national semifinals, the seemingly invincible Rebels could have defeated eventual champion Duke rather than lose 79-77.

1991 CHAMPIONSHIP BRACKET

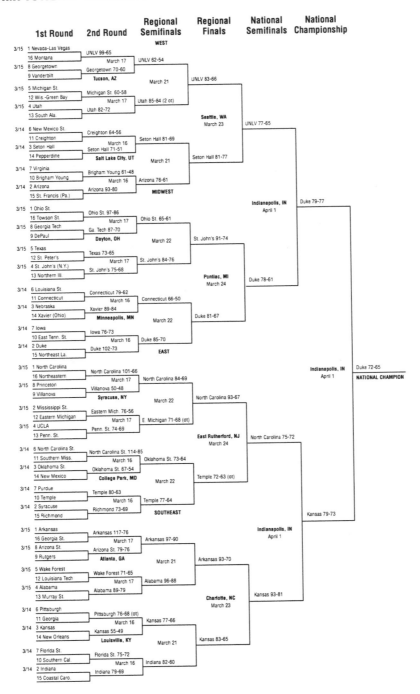

1st Round	2nd Round	Regional Semifinals	Regional Finals	National Semifinals	National Championship

WEST

3/15 1 Nevada-Las Vegas
16 Montana
UNLV 99-65
March 17
UNLV 62-54
3/15 8 Georgetown
9 Vanderbilt
Georgetown 70-60
Tucson, AZ
March 21
UNLV 83-66
3/15 5 Michigan St.
12 Wis.-Green Bay
Michigan St. 60-58
March 17
Utah 85-84 (2 ot)
3/15 4 Utah
13 South Ala.
Utah 82-72
Seattle, WA
March 23
UNLV 77-65
3/14 6 New Mexico St.
11 Creighton
Creighton 64-56
March 16
Seton Hall 81-69
3/14 3 Seton Hall
14 Pepperdine
Seton Hall 71-51
Salt Lake City, UT
March 21
Seton Hall 81-77
3/14 7 Virginia
10 Brigham Young
Brigham Young 61-48
March 16
Arizona 76-61
3/14 2 Arizona
15 St. Francis (Pa.)
Arizona 93-80

Duke 79-77

MIDWEST

Indianapolis, IN
April 1

3/15 1 Ohio St.
16 Towson St.
Ohio St. 97-86
March 17
Ohio St. 65-61
3/15 8 Georgia Tech
9 DePaul
Ga. Tech 87-70
Dayton, OH
March 22
St. John's 91-74
3/15 5 Texas
12 St. Peter's
Texas 73-65
March 17
St. John's 84-76
3/15 4 St. John's (N.Y.)
13 Northern Ill.
St. John's 75-68
Pontiac, MI
March 24
Duke 78-61
3/14 6 Louisiana St.
11 Connecticut
Connecticut 79-62
March 16
Connecticut 66-50
3/14 3 Nebraska
14 Xavier (Ohio)
Xavier 89-84
Minneapolis, MN
March 22
Duke 81-67
3/14 7 Iowa
10 East Tenn. St.
Iowa 76-73
March 16
Duke 85-70
3/14 2 Duke
15 Northeast La.
Duke 102-73

Duke 72-65

NATIONAL CHAMPION

EAST

Indianapolis, IN
April 1

3/15 1 North Carolina
16 Northeastern
North Carolina 101-66
March 17
North Carolina 84-69
3/15 8 Princeton
9 Villanova
Villanova 50-48
Syracuse, NY
March 22
North Carolina 93-67
3/15 2 Mississippi St.
12 Eastern Michigan
Eastern Mich. 76-56
March 17
E. Michigan 71-68 (ot)
3/15 4 UCLA
13 Penn. St.
Penn. St. 74-69
East Rutherford, NJ
March 24
North Carolina 75-72
3/14 6 North Carolina St.
11 Southern Miss.
North Carolina St. 114-85
March 16
Oklahoma St. 73-64
3/14 3 Oklahoma St.
14 New Mexico
Oklahoma St. 67-54
College Park, MD
March 22
Temple 72-63 (ot)
3/14 7 Purdue
10 Temple
Temple 80-63
March 16
Temple 77-64
3/14 2 Syracuse
15 Richmond
Richmond 73-69

SOUTHEAST

Kansas 79-73

Indianapolis, IN
April 1

3/15 1 Arkansas
16 Georgia St.
Arkansas 117-76
March 17
Arkansas 97-90
3/15 8 Arizona St.
9 Rutgers
Arizona St. 79-76
Atlanta, GA
March 21
Arkansas 93-70
3/15 5 Wake Forest
12 Louisiana Tech
Wake Forest 71-65
March 17
Alabama 96-88
3/15 4 Alabama
13 Murray St.
Alabama 89-79
Charlotte, NC
March 23
Kansas 93-81
3/14 6 Pittsburgh
11 Georgia
Pittsburgh 76-68 (ot)
March 16
Kansas 77-66
3/14 3 Kansas
14 New Orleans
Kansas 55-49
Louisville, KY
March 21
Kansas 83-65
3/14 7 Florida St.
10 Southern Cal.
Florida St. 75-72
March 16
Indiana 82-60
3/14 2 Indiana
15 Coastal Caro.
Indiana 79-69

1991–92

AT A GLANCE

NCAA Champion: Duke (35-2).

NIT Champion: Virginia (20-13).

New Conference: Great Midwest.

New Rules: Contact technical fouls count toward the five fouls for player disqualification and toward team fouls in reaching bonus free-throw situations. The shot clock is reset when the ball strikes the basket ring, not when a shot leaves the shooter's hands as it had been since the rule was introduced in 1986.

NCAA Probation: Auburn, Maryland, UNLV, Northwestern (La.) State, Texas A&M.

NCAA Consensus First-Team All-Americans: Jim Jackson, G-F, Jr., Ohio State; Christian Laettner, F-C, Sr., Duke; Harold Miner, G, Jr., Southern California; Alonzo Mourning, C, Sr., Georgetown; Shaquille O'Neal, C, Jr., Louisiana State.

Duke's Christian Laettner hit a dramatic decisive last-second shot against Kentucky in overtime after receiving a long inbounds pass in the East Regional final. The game is acknowledged as one of the most suspenseful in NCAA history.

Embattled coach Jerry Tarkanian was forced out at UNLV, but not before the Rebels captured their 10th consecutive Big West Conference championship. Tarkanian's 307 victories in his last 10 seasons is by far the most successful 10-year stretch in major-college history.

Jackson State guard Lindsey Hunter, who would become a first-round draft choice of the Detroit Pistons the next year, set an NCAA record with 26 three-point field-goal attempts (11 made) in a game at Kansas.

San Francisco's Tomas Thompson set an NCAA record for most three-pointers in a game without a miss when he hit all eight of his attempts from beyond the arc against Loyola Marymount.

Georgetown's Alonzo Mourning finished his career with an NCAA record 453 blocked shots.

LSU's Shaquille O'Neal finished his three-year career with a total of six games with at least 10 blocked shots. He is the only player to twice average at least five rejections per game in a season.

Morehead State's Brett Roberts scored 53 points against Middle Tennessee State to account for the season's game high in scoring.

Height doesn't always determine who excels at blocked shots and field-goal shooting. Vermont's Kevin Roberson finished his career as the shortest player (6-7) to block more than three shots per game (3.65) and Massachusetts' William Herndon finished his career as the shortest player (6-3) to hit more than 63 percent of his field-goal attempts.

Prairie View (0-28) became the first team to go winless in an entire season since The Citadel went 0-17 in 1955.

Cincinnati, coached by Bob Huggins, ranking sixth in winning percentage, had not appeared in the NCAA Tournament for 14 consecutive years until highlighting the Great Midwest Conference's inaugural season by reaching the Final Four. It was the first time for a first-year league member to advance to the national semifinals since UNC Charlotte represented the Sun Belt Conference in 1977, which coincidentally was the last year Cincinnati had participated in the event.

Liberty, after compiling a 5-23 record the previous season, improved by 16 ½ games to 22-7.

Arizona's 71-game homecourt winning streak, which started in 1987, was snapped by UCLA, 89-87.

This season marked the debut of Michigan's Fab Five freshmen—Juwan Howard, Ray Jackson, Jimmy King, Jalen Rose, and Chris Webber—who led the Wolverines to the NCAA championship game in 1992 and 1993, only to lose each time.

Cincinnati coach Bob Huggins argues a call.

St. John's Lou Carnesecca ended his 24-year college coaching career with a 526-200 record.

1991–92 FINAL NATIONAL POLLS

AP	UPI	USA/CNN	SCHOOL
1	1	1	Duke
2	2	7	Kansas
3	4	4	Ohio St.
4	3	8	UCLA
5	6	2	Indiana
6	9	6	Kentucky
7	–	–	UNLV
8	7	11	Southern Cal
9	8	10	Arkansas
10	5	16	Arizona
11	10	9	Oklahoma St.
12	14	5	Cincinnati
13	13	19	Alabama
14	11	20	Michigan St.
15	17	3	Michigan
16	12	18	Missouri
17	21	15	Massachusetts
18	15	12	North Carolina
19	18	13	Seton Hall
20	16	14	Florida St.
21	20	24	Syracuse
22	19	23	Georgetown
23	22	–	Oklahoma
24	23	–	DePaul
25	–	25	LSU
–	–	17	Memphis St.
–	–	21	Georgia Tech
–	–	22	Texas-El Paso
–	24	–	St. John's
–	25	–	Tulane

1992 NCAA Tournament

Summary: Christian Laettner became the NCAA Tournament's all-time leading scorer and teammate Bobby Hurley became the tourney's all-time leader in assists as the Blue Devils became the first school since UCLA (1967–73) to repeat as national champion. Hurley took up the

1991–92 INDIVIDUAL LEADERS

SCORING

PLAYER	PTS.	AVG.
Roberts, Morehead St.	815	28.1
Baker, Hartford	745	27.6
Ford, Miss. Valley St.	714	27.5
Woods, La Salle	847	27.3
Rogers, Alabama St.	764	27.3
Williams, Maryland	776	26.8
Miner, Southern Cal	789	26.3
Lowery, Loyola Marymount	675	26.0
Cunningham, Bethune-Cookman	744	25.7
Casebier, Evansville	634	25.4

REBOUNDING

PLAYER	REB.	AVG.
Jones, Murray St.	431	14.4
O'Neal, Louisiana St.	421	14.0
Burroughs, Jacksonville	370	13.2
Keefe, Stanford	355	12.2
White, Southern (La.)	367	12.2
Sims, Youngstown St.	327	11.7
Ellis, Notre Dame	385	11.7
Stokes, SW La.	370	11.6
Johnson, San Francisco	309	11.4
Henderson, Fairfield	318	11.4
Smith, TCU	386	11.4

ASSISTS

PLAYER	AST.	AVG.
Usher, Tenn. Tech	254	8.8
Crawford, New Mexico St.	282	8.5
Smart, San Francisco	241	8.3
Soares, Nevada	227	7.8
Evans, Miss. St.	219	7.8
Walker, L. Marymount	218	7.8
Dale, S. Miss.	222	7.7
Hurley, Duke	237	7.6

Miller, Marquette	221	7.6
Yelding, S. Alabama	184	7.1

BLOCKED SHOTS

PLAYER	BLK	AVG.
O'Neal, LSU	157	5.2
Mourning, Georgetown	160	5.0
Roberson, Vermont	139	5.0
Earl, Iowa	121	4.0
Baker, Hartford	100	3.7
Van Dyke, UTEP	116	3.5
Horry, Alabama	121	3.5
Jaxon, New Mexico	109	3.3
Chandler, Nebraska	91	3.1
Outlaw, Houston	97	3.1

STEALS

PLAYER	STL.	AVG.
Snipes, NE Illinois	86	3.4
Burcy, Chicago St.	85	3.3
Corbitt, Cent. Conn. St.	88	3.1
Mitchell, Wisc.-Milw.	78	3.1
Soares, Nevada	90	3.1
White, Southern (La.)	93	3.1
Higgins, Maine	95	3.0
Usher, Tenn. Tech	86	3.0
Evans, Miss. St.	83	3.0
Mee, W. Ky.	94	2.9

FIELD GOAL PERCENTAGE

PLAYER	FGM	FGA	PCT.
Outlaw, Houston	156	228	.684
Kidd, Middle Tenn. St.	156	235	.664
Fish, UNC-Wilm.	206	319	.646
McDowell, Texas-Arl.	184	287	.641
Spencer, UNLV	174	273	.637
Robinson, Mo.-KC	199	314	.634

Peplowski, Mich. St.	168	266	.632
Hupmann, Evansville	159	252	.631
Ellis, Notre Dame	227	360	.631
Solis, Brooklyn	150	238	.630

FREE THROW PERCENTAGE

PLAYER	FTM	FTA	PCT.
MacLean, UCLA	197	214	.921
Adkins, UNC-Wilm.	78	85	.918
Shreffler, Evansville	78	85	.918
Hildebrand, Liberty	114	125	.912
Lauritzen, Indiana St.	82	91	.901
Goodman, Utah St.	82	92	.891
Anderson, Old Dom.	96	108	.889
Schmitz, Mo.-KC	76	86	.884
Breslin, Holy Cross	91	103	.883
Marcelic, S. Utah St.	135	153	.882

THREE-POINT FIELD GOAL PERCENTAGE

PLAYER	FGM	FGA	PCT.
Wightman, W. Mich.	48	76	.632
Laettner, Duke	54	97	.557
Barker, Valparaiso	61	117	.521
Batle, Auburn	71	139	.511
Bennett, Wisc.-GB	95	186	.511

THREE-POINT FIELD GOALS PER GAME

PLAYER	FGM	AVG.
Day, Radford	117	4.0
Alberts, Akron	110	3.9
Woods, La Salle	121	3.9
McKelvey, Portland	106	3.8
Hurd, La Salle	113	3.6

1991–92 TEAM LEADERS

SCORING OFFENSE

SCHOOL	PTS.	AVG.
Northwestern St. (La.)	2660	95.0
Oklahoma	2838	94.6
Southern (La.)	2809	93.6
Georgia Southern	2836	91.5
Loyola Marymount	2552	91.1

SCORING DEFENSE

SCHOOL	PTS.	AVG.
Princeton	1349	48.2
Wisc.-Green Bay	1659	55.3
Southwest Missouri St.	1761	56.8
Monmouth	1701	58.7
Ball St.	1959	59.4

SCORING MARGIN

SCHOOL	OFF.	DEF.	MAR.
Indiana	83.4	65.8	17.6
Kansas	84.5	68.1	16.4
Arizona	84.8	68.8	16.0
Cincinnati	79.0	63.1	15.9
Duke	88.0	72.6	15.3

WON-LOST PERCENTAGE

SCHOOL	W-L	PCT.
Duke	34-2	.944

UNLV	26-2	.929
Delaware	27-4	.871
Montana	27-4	.871
Massachusetts	30-5	.857

FIELD GOAL PERCENTAGE

SCHOOL	FGM	FGA	PCT.
Duke	1108	2069	.536
Liberty	790	1519	.520
UNLV	817	1583	.516
Kansas	975	1892	.515
Wisc.-Green Bay	759	1481	.512

FIELD GOAL PERCENTAGE DEFENSE

SCHOOL	FGM	FGA	PCT.
UNLV	628	1723	.364
Princeton	445	1169	.381
Montana	685	1736	.395
Connecticut	734	1843	.398
Charleston Southern	592	1486	.398
Utah	730	1832	.398

FREE THROW PERCENTAGE

SCHOOL	FTM	FTA	PCT.
Northwestern	497	651	.763
Bucknell	550	722	.762
Monmouth	414	544	.761
Washington St.	554	729	.760
Drexel	524	692	.757

REBOUND MARGIN

SCHOOL	OWN	OPP.	MAR.
Delaware	42.1	33.8	8.3
Montana	40.6	32.4	8.2
Wake Forest	36.8	29.1	7.7
Providence	42.8	35.3	7.5
Michigan	40.4	33.0	7.5

THREE-POINT FIELD GOAL PERCENTAGE

SCHOOL	FGM	FGA	PCT.
Wisc.-Green Bay	204	437	.467
Auburn	182	403	.452
Western Michigan	120	267	.449
Louisiana Tech	161	359	.448
Duke	171	394	.434

THREE-POINT FIELD GOALS PER GAME

SCHOOL	FGM	AVG.
La Salle	294	9.5
Northwestern	259	9.3
N.C. St.	265	8.8
Kentucky	317	8.8
Texas-Arlington	255	8.8

slack with 26 points when Laettner was limited to eight points in an 81-78 decision over Indiana in the national semifinals. Laettner closed out his college career with a game-high 19 points in the championship game against Michigan, which became the only school to ever lead an NCAA final at halftime and end up losing the game by at least 20 points. Duke coach Mike Krzyzewski did the unthinkable and temporarily passed UCLA legend John Wooden (47-10, .8246) for the top spot in all-time NCAA playoff winning percentage (minimum of 20 games). Hurley was selected Final Four Most Outstanding Player although dissenters believed that Duke teammate Grant Hill deserved the honor instead. In the two Final Four games, Hill had more field goals than Hurley (14 to 10), outshot him from the floor (61 percent to 41.7), blocked more shots (5 to 0), outrebounded him (16 to 3), and accumulated just as many assists (11 each). Moreover, Hurley's 3 of 12 field-goal shooting in the final against Michigan was the worst marksmanship from the floor

Grant Hill jumps head and shoulders above Michigan's Jalen Rose in the 1992 NCAA final.

for a Final Four Most Outstanding Player in a championship game since Elgin Baylor of runner-up Seattle went 9 of 32 against Kentucky in 1958. It was the second consecutive year for the Final Four Most Outstanding Player to come from Duke and manage just three baskets and shoot less than 50 percent from the floor in the title game. In 1991, Laettner hit 3 of 8 field-goal attempts against Kansas. Duke became the 18th NCAA Tournament champion to win at least two playoff games by fewer than six points

when the Blue Devils edged Kentucky (104-103 in overtime in East Regional final) and Indiana (81-78 in national semifinals).

Star Gazing: Hurley, 6-0, was the shortest player to be selected Final Four Most Outstanding Player since 5-11 Hal Lear led Temple to a national third-place finish in 1956. The only Final Four Most Outstanding Player shorter than Hurley from a championship team was 5-11 Kenny Sailors of the 1943 Wyoming team. Hurley shot a mediocre 41 percent from the floor in his career with the Blue Devils, but his play-making and intangibles helped them win 18 of 20 NCAA playoff games. He holds the career record for most playoff assists (145) although his bid to become the first player to start four consecutive NCAA finals was thwarted when California upset Duke in the second round of the 1993 Midwest Regional despite Hurley's career-high 32 points.

Biggest Upsets: East Tennessee State (14 seed) over Arizona (3), 87-80, and Southwestern Louisiana (13) over Oklahoma (4), 87-83.

One and Only: Guard Jalen Rose is the only freshman to finish with the highest season scoring average for a team reaching the NCAA Tournament championship game. He averaged 17.6 points per game for national runner-up Michigan.

Numbers Game: All three Final Four game winners trailed at halftime.... Duke defied a recent trend by becoming the first top-ranked team in 10 years entering the NCAA Tournament to win the national title. The previous five top-ranked teams failed to reach the championship game.... The final between Duke and Michigan was the most-watched basketball game in television history. An estimated 53 million viewers took in all or part of the title game in the United States' TV homes covered by the Nielsen ratings. CBS estimated that an additional 10 percent of the total audience watched the 1992 final away from home—in taverns, dormitories, and other venues that Nielsen doesn't survey. That's more than 100 times the initial viewing audience estimated at 500,000 in 1946, when the championship game between Oklahoma State and North Carolina was televised locally for the first time in New York by WCBS-TV.... Four of Michigan's Fab Five Freshmen—Rose (107 points), Webber (98), King (83), and Howard (82)—ranked among the top six freshman scorers in a single tournament in the last 13 years.... UNLV's streak of tournament appearances ended at nine when the Rebels were on NCAA probation.... Iowa State compiled the worst league record (5-9 in the Big Eight) of any

Indiana's Calbert Cheaney drives through Michigan's Rob Pelinka (left) and Jimmy King.

team to ever receive an at-large invitation.... Duke won all nine of its NCAA playoff games against Big East and Big Ten teams in a three-year span from 1990 to 1992.

What If: Forwards Calbert Cheaney and Eric Anderson shot better than 50 percent from the floor in their careers for Indiana. If only they had combined to hit 36.8 percent of their field-goal attempts instead of 26.3 percent (5 of 19) in the national semifinals, the Hoosiers could have defeated eventual champion Duke rather than have a five-point halftime lead evaporate and lose 81-78.... Kentucky coach Rick Pitino was criticized in some quarters for leaving Grant Hill unguarded for his approximate 80-foot pass to Laettner with 2.1 seconds remaining in overtime in the East Regional.

1991-92 NCAA CHAMPION: DUKE

SEASON STATISTICS OF DUKE REGULARS

PLAYER	POS.	CL.	G.	FG%	FT%	PPG	RPG
Christian Laettner	C-F	Jr.	39	.575	.802	19.8	8.7
Billy McCaffrey	G	So.	38	.481	.832	11.6	1.8
Thomas Hill	G-F	So.	39	.552	.743	11.5	3.6
Bobby Hurley	G	So.	39	.423	.728	11.3	2.4
Grant Hill	F-G	Fr.	36	.516	.609	11.2	5.1
Brian Davis	G-F	Jr.	39	.456	.730	7.6	4.1
Greg Koubek	F	Sr.	38	.435	.813	5.9	2.9
Antonio Lang	F-C	Fr.	36	.606	.526	4.3	2.6
Crawford Palmer	C	Jr.	38	.646	.825	3.6	2.0
Marty Clark	G	Fr.	23	.448	.625	2.1	0.7
TEAM TOTALS			36	.536	.748	88.0	34.1

Three-point field goals leaders: Hurley (76 of 188, .404), Koubek (32 of 76, .421). Assists leader: Hurley 289. Blocked shots leader: Laettner 44. Steals leaders: Laettner 75, T. Hill 59.

1992 FINAL FOUR CHAMPIONSHIP GAME

MINNEAPOLIS, MN

MICHIGAN (51)	MIN.	FG-A	FT-A	REB.	A.	PF.	PTS.
Webber	30	6-12	2-5	11	1	4	14
Jackson	16	0-1	0-0	1	2	1	0
Howard	29	4-9	1-3	3	0	3	9
Rose	37	5-12	1-2	5	4	4	11
King	40	3-10	0-0	2	1	1	7
Riley	19	2-6	0-0	4	1	2	4
Voskuil	15	1-2	2-2	3	3	2	4
Pelinka	10	1-2	0-0	2	1	0	2
Hunter	2	0-0	0-0	0	0	0	0
Talley	1	0-2	0-0	1	0	0	0
Bossard	1	0-1	0-0	0	0	0	0
Seter	1	0-1	0-0	1	0	0	0
Armer	1	0-0	0-0	0	0	0	0
TOTALS	200	22-58	6-12	35	13	17	51

FG%: .379. FT%: .500. Three-point goals: 1 of 11 (King 1-2, Rose 0-3, Webber 0-1, Howard 0-1, Voskuil 0-1, Talley 0-1, Bossard 0-1). Blocks: 3 (Jackson 2). Turnovers: 20 (Howard 4, Rose 4). Steals: 8 (Webber 2, Rose 2, King 2).

DUKE (71)	MIN.	FG-A	FT-A	REB.	A.	PF.	PTS.
Lang	31	2-3	1-2	4	0	1	5
G. Hill	36	8-14	2-2	10	5	2	18
Laettner	35	6-13	5-6	7	0	1	19
Hurley	36	3-12	2-2	3	7	4	9
T. Hill	34	5-10	5-8	7	0	2	16
Parks	13	1-3	2-2	3	0	3	4
Davis	10	0-2	0-0	0	0	0	0
Ast	1	0-0	0-0	1	0	0	0
Clark	1	0-0	0-0	0	0	0	0
Blakeney	1	0-0	0-0	0	0	0	0
Burt	1	0-0	0-0	0	0	0	0
Meek	1	0-0	0-0	0	0	0	0
TOTALS	200	25-57	17-22	37	12	13	71

FG%: .439. FT%: .773. Three-point goals: 4 of 9 (Laettner 2-4, Hurley 1-3, T. Hill 1-2). Blocks: 4 (G. Hill 2). Turnovers: 14 (Laettner 7). Steals: 9 (G. Hill 3).

Halftime: Michigan 31-30.

NATIONAL SEMIFINALS

DUKE (81): Lang 1-5 2-2 4, Davis 1-3 3-7 5, Laettner 2-8 4-7 8, T. Hill 3-10 4-5 11, Hurley 7-12 6-8 26, G. Hill 6-9 2-4 14, Parks 3-5 2-3 8, Clark 0-0 5-6 5. Team 23-52 (.442) 28-42 (.667) 81.

Halftime: Duke 42-37.

INDIANA (76): Cheaney 4-13 2-4 11, Henderson 6-9 2-2 15, Nover 3-4 2-2 9, Bailey 4-8 0-0 9, Reynolds 1-4 0-0 2, Meeks 1-2 1-2 3, Anderson 1-6 0-1 2, G. Graham 6-9 5-5 18, Leary 3-3 0-0 9. Team 29-58 (.500) 12-16 (.750) 78.

Halftime: Indiana 42-37.

MICHIGAN (76): Webber 8-12 0-2 16, Jackson 1-2 1-2 3, Howard 3-9 6-7 12, Rose 4-13 5-6 13, King 5-9 4-4 17, Talley 1-3 2-3 4, Riley 1-1 0-0 2, Voskuil 2-4 4-5 9. Team 25-53 (.471) 22-29 (.758) 76.

Halftime: Cincinnati 41-38.

CINCINNATI (72): Nelson 2-2 0-0 4, Jones 5-13 2-2 14, Blount 0-3 1-2 1, Buford 6-17 4-4 18, Van Exel 7-15 5-10 21, Martin 4-10 2-3 10, Scott 0-0 0-0 0, Jackson 0-1 0-0 0, Gibson 2-3 0-0 4. Team 26-64 (.406) 14-21 (.667) 72.

Halftime: Cincinnati 41-38.

ALL-TOURNAMENT TEAM

Grant Hill, F, Soph., Duke
Bobby Hurley, G, Jr., Duke*
Christian Laettner, C, Sr., Duke
Jalen Rose, G, Fr., Michigan
Chris Webber, F, Fr., Michigan

*Named Most Outstanding Player

Putting Things in Perspective: Duke (34-2) came close to becoming the eighth NCAA champion to go undefeated. The Blue Devils' two losses were by a total of just six points (ACC road games against North Carolina and Wake Forest to start and end a stretch of five of six contests away from home from February 5 to February 23).

1992 CHAMPIONSHIP BRACKET

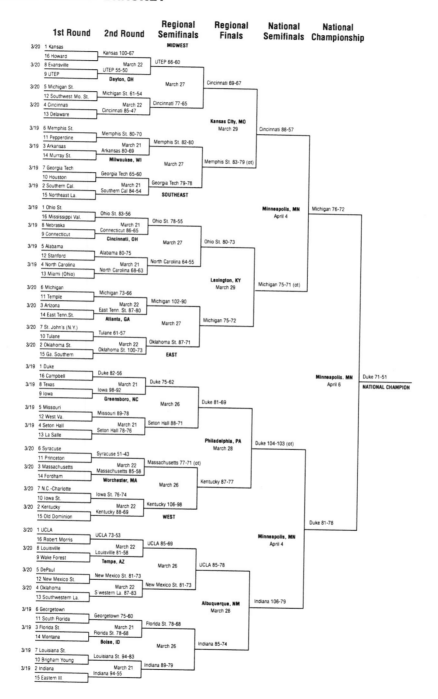

1st Round	2nd Round	Regional Semifinals	Regional Finals	National Semifinals	National Championship

MIDWEST

3/20 1 Kansas
16 Howard — Kansas 100-67
3/20 8 Evansville — March 22 — UTEP 66-60
9 UTEP — UTEP 55-50
Dayton, OH
3/20 5 Michigan St.
12 Southwest Mo. St. — Michigan St. 61-54 — March 27 — Cincinnati 69-67
3/20 4 Cincinnati — March 22 — Cincinnati 77-65
13 Delaware — Cincinnati 85-47

Kansas City, MO — March 29 — Cincinnati 88-57

3/19 6 Memphis St.
11 Pepperdine — Memphis St. 80-70
3/19 3 Arkansas — March 21 — Memphis St. 82-80
14 Murray St. — Arkansas 80-69
Milwaukee, WI
3/19 7 Georgia Tech — March 27 — Memphis St. 83-79 (ot)
10 Houston — Georgia Tech 65-60
3/19 2 Southern Cal. — March 21 — Georgia Tech 79-78
15 Northeast La. — Southern Cal 84-54

SOUTHEAST

Minneapolis, MN — April 4 — Michigan 76-72

3/19 1 Ohio St.
16 Mississippi Val. — Ohio St. 83-56
3/19 8 Nebraska — March 21 — Ohio St. 78-55
9 Connecticut — Connecticut 86-65
Cincinnati, OH
3/19 5 Alabama — March 27 — Ohio St. 80-73
12 Stanford — Alabama 80-75
3/19 4 North Carolina — March 21 — North Carolina 64-55
13 Miami (Ohio) — North Carolina 68-63

Lexington, KY — March 29 — Michigan 75-71 (ot)

3/20 6 Michigan
11 Temple — Michigan 73-66
3/20 3 Arizona — March 22 — Michigan 102-90
14 East Tenn.St. — East Tenn. St. 87-80
Atlanta, GA
3/20 7 St. John's (N.Y.) — March 27 — Michigan 75-72
10 Tulane — Tulane 61-57
3/20 2 Oklahoma St. — March 22 — Oklahoma St. 87-71
15 Ga. Southern — Oklahoma St. 100-73

EAST

Minneapolis, MN — April 6 — Duke 71-51
NATIONAL CHAMPION

3/19 1 Duke
16 Campbell — Duke 82-56
3/19 8 Texas — March 21 — Duke 75-62
9 Iowa — Iowa 98-92
Greensboro, NC
3/19 5 Missouri — March 26 — Duke 81-69
12 West Va. — Missouri 89-78
3/19 4 Seton Hall — March 21 — Seton Hall 88-71
13 La Salle — Seton Hall 78-76

Philadelphia, PA — March 28 — Duke 104-103 (ot)

3/20 6 Syracuse
11 Princeton — Syracuse 51-43
3/20 3 Massachusetts — March 22 — Massachusetts 77-71 (ot)
14 Fordham — Massachusetts 85-58
Worchester, MA
3/20 7 N.C.-Charlotte — March 26 — Kentucky 87-77
10 Iowa St. — Iowa St. 76-74
3/20 2 Kentucky — March 22 — Kentucky 106-98
15 Old Dominion — Kentucky 88-69

WEST

Duke 81-78

3/20 1 UCLA
16 Robert Morris — UCLA 73-53
3/20 8 Louisville — March 22 — UCLA 85-69
9 Wake Forest — Louisville 81-58
Tempe, AZ
3/20 5 DePaul — March 26 — UCLA 85-78
12 New Mexico St. — New Mexico St. 81-73
3/20 4 Oklahoma — March 22 — New Mexico St. 81-73
13 Southwestern La. — S'western La. 87-83

Albuquerque, NM — March 28 — Indiana 106-79

3/19 6 Georgetown
11 South Florida — Georgetown 75-60
3/19 3 Florida St. — March 21 — Florida St. 78-68
14 Montana — Florida St. 78-68
Boise, ID
3/19 7 Louisiana St. — March 26 — Indiana 85-74
10 Brigham Young — Louisiana St. 94-83
3/19 2 Indiana — March 21 — Indiana 89-79
15 Eastern Ill. — Indiana 94-55

1992-93

AT A GLANCE

NCAA Champion: North Carolina (34-4).

NIT Champion: Minnesota (22-10).

New Rule: Unsportsmanlike technical fouls, in addition to contact technical fouls, count toward the five fouls for player disqualification and the team fouls in reaching bonus free-throw situations.

NCAA Probation: Middle Tennessee State, Syracuse, Texas-Pan American, Tulsa.

NCAA Consensus First-Team All-Americans: Calbert Cheaney, F, Sr., Indiana; Anfernee Hardaway, G, Jr., Memphis State; Bobby Hurley, G, Sr., Duke; Jamal Mashburn, F, Jr., Kentucky; Chris Webber, F, Soph., Michigan.

North Carolina coach Dean Smith goes out of his way to emphasize senior leadership and always has his seniors featured on the cover of the Tar Heels' media guide even if they play sparingly. Carolina had several heroes on its way to capturing the national championship, but none loomed larger than senior forward George Lynch, who turned in double doubles (double figures in scoring and rebounding) in his last four games as the Tar Heels won the East Regional at East Rutherford, New Jersey, and the Final Four at New Orleans.

One of Carolina's four defeats was at Wake Forest when Demon Deacons guard Randy Childress erupted for 18 second-half points in less than four minutes.

Duke's Bobby Hurley finished his career with an NCAA-record 1,076 assists.

Iowa had a legitimate shot at a Big Ten title until forward Chris Street, the Hawkeyes' leading rebounder, died in an auto accident.

Mississippi Valley State guard Alphonso Ford finished his Division I career as the only player to score more than 700 points and average more than 25 points per game in each of four seasons. Twice during the season he scored 49 points, game highs for the year.

Connecticut's Scott Burrell finished his career as the tallest player (6-7) to amass more than 300 steals. He had 310.

Marquette's Jim McIlvaine blocked 13 shots in a game against Northeastern Illinois.

J. R. Rider set a UNLV Division I school record with 44 points against Nevada-Reno. UNLV's 59-game homecourt winning streak was ended by Louisville, 90-86.

Florida State became the only school in history to have five active 1,000-point career scorers on their roster at the same time (no transfers from other four-year schools)—Douglas Edwards, Rodney Dobard, Sam Cassell, Chuck Graham, and Bob Sura. Cassell was a junior college transfer.

Tennessee became the first school ever to have nine successive seasons with one or more players scoring at least 600 points. The Volunteers' principal point producers in that stretch were Michael Brooks, Tony White, Dyron Nix, and Allan Houston.

1992-93 FINAL NATIONAL POLLS

AP	UPI	USA/CNN	SCHOOL
1	1	5	Indiana
2	4	3	Kentucky
3	3	2	Michigan
4	2	1	North Carolina
5	5	12	Arizona
6	6	11	Seton Hall
7	7	6	Cincinnati
8	8	8	Vanderbilt
9	9	4	Kansas
10	10	9	Duke
11	11	7	Florida St.
12	12	10	Arkansas
13	13	19	Iowa
14	16	22	Massachusetts
15	14	15	Louisville
16	15	14	Wake Forest
17	18	–	New Orleans
18	19	–	Georgia Tech
19	17	20	Utah
20	24	16	Western Kentucky
21	–	–	New Mexico
22	20	–	Purdue
23	22	–	Oklahoma St.
24	25	–	New Mexico St.
25	21	–	UNLV
–	–	13	Temple
–	–	17	California
–	23	18	Virginia
–	–	19	Iowa
–	–	21	George Washington
–	–	23	Xavier
–	–	24	UCLA
–	–	25	Minnesota

1992–93 INDIVIDUAL LEADERS

SCORING

PLAYER	PTS.	AVG.
Guy, Texas-Pan Am.	556	29.3
Rider, UNLV	814	29.1
Best, Tenn. Tech	799	28.5
Baker, Hartford	792	28.3
Hunter Jackson St.	907	26.7
Ford, Miss. Valley St.	728	26.0
Edwards, Wright St.	757	25.2
Ross, Appa. St.	683	24.4
Robinson, Purdue	676	24.1
Sykes, Grambling St.	644	23.9

REBOUNDING

PLAYER	REB.	AVG.
Kidd, Middle Tenn. St.	386	14.8
Scales, Southern (La.)	393	12.7
Jackson, Nicholls St.	325	12.5
Dunkley, Delaware	367	12.2
Callahan, Northeastern	340	12.1
Johnson, New Orleans	346	11.9
Rogers, Tenn. St.	339	11.7
Rose, Drexel	330	11.4
Smith, Providence	375	11.4
Brown, Colgate	317	11.3

ASSISTS

PLAYER	AST.	AVG.
Crawford, New Mex. St.	310	9.1
Thomas, UNLV	248	8.6
Woods, Wright St.	253	8.4
Hurley, Duke	262	8.2
Evans, Miss. St.	235	8.1
Kidd, California	222	7.7
Miller, Marquette	213	7.6
Haggerty, Baylor	189	7.3
Browne, Lamar	195	7.2
Capers, Arizona St.	200	7.1

BLOCKED SHOTS

PLAYER	BLK.	AVG.
Ratliff, Wyoming	124	4.4
Wright, Clemson	124	4.1
Outlaw, Houston	114	3.8
Rogers, Tenn. St.	93	3.2
Wilson, E. Mich.	96	3.2
Dunkley, Delaware	96	3.2
Dobard, Florida St.	111	3.2
Popa, Miami (Fla.)	85	3.1
Hart, Iona	80	3.1
Thurman, W. III.	83	3.1

STEALS

PLAYER	STL.	AVG.
CALIFORNIA	110	3.8
Goodman, Utah St.	102	3.8
Woods, Wright St.	109	3.6
Bright, Bucknell	94	3.2
Mee, W. Ky.	100	3.1
Myers, St. Francis (N.Y.)	81	3.1
Woods, Charleston	84	3.1
Johnson, Canisius	79	3.0
Peyton, Bucknell	88	3.0
Evans, Oklahoma	97	3.0

FIELD GOAL PERCENTAGE

PLAYER	FGM	FGA	PCT.
Outlaw, Houston	196	298	.658
Grant, Xavier	223	341	.654
Hart, Iona	151	231	.654
Parks, Duke	161	247	.652
Trent, Ohio	194	298	.651
Nahar, Wright St.	190	296	.642
Peplowski, Mich. St.	161	252	.639
Lunsford, Ala. St.	142	223	.637
Kidd, Middle Tenn. St.	167	265	.630
Gay, Winthrop	194	309	.628

FREE THROW PERCENTAGE

PLAYER	FTM	FTA	PCT.
Grant, Utah	104	113	.920
Breslin, Holy Cross	100	111	.901
Lake, Montana	71	79	.899
Schmidt, Valparaiso	70	78	.897
Hartzell, UNC-G'boro	72	81	.889
Holman, Kent	69	78	.885
Ford, Kentucky	104	118	.881
Baldwin, N'western	66	75	.880
Burgess, Radford	109	124	.879
Houston, Tenn.	165	188	.878

THREE-POINT FIELD GOAL PERCENTAGE

PLAYER	FGM	FGA	PCT.
Anderson, Kent	44	82	.537
Moore, S. Houston St.	73	137	.533
Morton, Louisville	51	96	.531
Ford, Kentucky	101	191	.529
Graham, Indiana	57	111	.514

THREE-POINT FIELD GOALS PER GAME

PLAYER	FGM	AVG.
Haslett, S. Miss.	109	4.2
Smith, Arizona St.	113	4.2
Alberts, Akron	107	4.1
Veney, Lamar	106	3.9
Day, Radford	116	3.7

1992–93 TEAM LEADERS

SCORING OFFENSE

SCHOOL	PTS.	AVG.
Southern (La.)	3011	97.1
Northwestern St. (La.)	2357	90.7
UNLV	2592	89.4
Wright St.	2674	89.1
Oklahoma	2850	89.1

SCORING DEFENSE

SCHOOL	PTS.	AVG.
Princeton	1421	54.7
Yale	1444	55.5
Miami (Ohio)	1775	57.3
Cincinnati	1871	58.5
Southwest Missouri St.	1813	58.5

SCORING MARGIN

SCHOOL	OFF.	DEF.	MAR.
North Carolina	86.1	68.3	17.8
Kentucky	87.5	69.8	17.7
Cincinnati	74.5	58.5	16.0
Duke	86.4	71.2	15.2
Indiana	86.5	71.6	14.9

WON-LOST PERCENTAGE

SCHOOL	W-L	PCT.
North Carolina	34-4	.895
Indiana	31-4	.886
Kentucky	30-4	.882
New Orleans	26-4	.867
Michigan	31-5	.861

FIELD GOAL PERCENTAGE

SCHOOL	FGM	FGA	PCT.
Indiana	1076	2062	.522
Northeast Louisiana	1015	1946	.522
James Madison	848	1634	.519
Wright St.	987	1912	.516
Kansas	1109	2154	.515

FIELD GOAL PERCENTAGE DEFENSE

SCHOOL	FGM	FGA	PCT.
Marquette	634	1613	.393
George Washington	708	1794	.395
Arizona	710	1776	.400
Utah	737	1831	.403

FREE THROW PERCENTAGE

SCHOOL	FTM	FTA	PCT.
Utah	476	602	.791
Charleston Southern	408	526	.776
Valparaiso	412	532	.774
Indiana St.	445	580	.767
Brigham Young	697	909	.767

REBOUND MARGIN

SCHOOL	OWN	OPP.	MAR.
Massachusetts	43.9	32.8	11.2
Iowa	42.8	31.7	11.1
Idaho	39.6	29.3	10.3
Arizona	43.1	34.2	9.0
North Carolina	41.1	32.2	8.9

THREE-POINT FIELD GOAL PERCENTAGE

SCHOOL	FGM	FGA	PCT.
Valparaiso	214	500	.428
Princeton	204	479	.426
Indiana	197	464	.425
Kent	162	384	.422
Miami (Ohio)	218	522	.418

THREE-POINT FIELD GOALS PER GAME

SCHOOL	FGM	AVG.
Lamar	271	10.0
Kentucky	340	10.0
Arizona St.	263	9.4
UNC-Asheville	235	8.7
Southern Cal	259	8.6

Forward Tony Dunkin of Coastal Carolina in the Big South Conference became the only player to be named MVP four times in a Division I league. He originally signed with Jacksonville.

Princeton led the nation in team defense for the fifth consecutive season and 11th time in 18 years.

1993 NCAA Tournament

Summary: George Lynch, North Carolina's top rebounder and second-leading scorer, made four big plays in the closing moments of the title game. With Michigan leading, 67-66, he and Eric Montross blocked away a driving layup by Jimmy King. That led to a fastbreak basket by Derrick Phelps and put the Tar Heels ahead to stay with just over three minutes remaining. After a missed Michigan shot, Lynch hit a turn-around jumper from the middle of the lane with 2:28 remaining to increase Carolina's lead to 70-67. On an inbounds play after UNC regained possession, Lynch lofted a perfect pass to Montross for a dunk. The Wolverines rallied to trim the deficit to 73-71 before Lynch and Phelps trapped Chris Webber on the sideline with just 11 seconds remaining and Michigan's consensus first-team All-American called a fateful timeout his team did not have. Donald Williams wrapped the game up with four consecutive free throws.

Outcome for Defending Champion: Duke's streak of five consecutive trips to the Final Four ended when the Blue Devils lost against California in the second round of the Midwest Regional. Duke guard Bobby Hurley was thwarted in his bid to become the first player to start four consecutive NCAA finals, but he is the only player to be credited with more than 125 assists in the tournament. He had 145 in 20 playoff games.

Star Gazing: Final Four Most Outstanding Player Donald Williams scored 25 points in each Final Four game for North Carolina to become the first guard to score at least 25 in both the national semifinals and final since Rick Mount for runner-up Purdue in 1969. The previous guard for a championship team to score at least 25 points in both the national semifinals and final was UCLA's Gail Goodrich in 1965.

Biggest Upsets: In terms of point spreads, Arizona's 64-61 first-round defeat in the West Regional against 20-point underdog Santa Clara was the biggest upset in NCAA playoff history. The Wildcats, ranked fifth by AP entering the tournament, lost against Santa Clara although they scored 25 consecutive points in a 10-minute span bridging the first and second halves. The setback gave Lute Olson five opening-round defeats as coach at Arizona and lowered his record to 2-8 in down-to-the-wire tourney games decided in overtime or in regulation by fewer than six points.... Another first-round shocker was Georgia Tech getting smothered by Southern (93-78), leaving Bobby Cremins of the Yellow Jackets as the only coach to ever lose as many as five playoff games against opponents with double-digit seeds.

One and Only: Williams is the only player to average fewer than four points per game as a freshman and then be named Final Four Most Outstanding Player the next season as a sophomore. After averaging an unsightly 2.2 points per game for North Carolina in 1991–92, he finished with a 14.3-point average in 1992–93.... Dean Smith became the first coach in NCAA Tournament history to reach the 50-win plateau in playoff competition when he raised his record of playoff appearances to 23 and North Carolina won its opening game for the 13th consecutive year.

Quote of Note: Webber's family took his mental lapse in stride and showed that time heals all wounds when his father, Mayce, acquired a vanity license plate that said "Timeout," a reference to his son's excruciating blunder. "It's no big deal," the younger Webber said. "I'm not happy it happened. But I know it's going to help me in some way. It made me a man. It made me grow up a lot faster than if it hadn't happened." Webber left college after his sophomore year and lived up to his words, as he went on to become the NBA's Rookie of the Year in 1993–94.

Numbers Game: Purdue forward Glenn Robinson had the highest-scoring game of the tourney when he tossed in 36 points in a first-round loss against Rhode Island.... Smith and the other three coaches at the Final Four—Michigan's Steve Fisher, Kentucky's Rick Pitino, and Kansas' Roy Williams—had all won more than 70 percent of their NCAA playoff games at that stage in their careers. Fisher, improving his tourney record to 17-3 (.850) by reaching the national final for the third time in five years, moved ahead of Hall of Famer John Wooden (47-10, .825) for the highest winning percentage in tournament history (minimum of 20 games).... The Big East suffered a down year when consecutive tourney appearances for Georgetown (14) and Syracuse (10) came to an end. Syracuse was on NCAA probation.... California freshman guard Jason Kidd's inside baskets on deft moves in the closing seconds helped boost the Bears to victories over two schools making their 10th consecutive NCAA playoff appearance—Duke and LSU.... East Carolina became the eighth school to participate in the NCAA Tournament despite entering the playoffs with a losing record (13-16 after winning the Colonial Athletic Association Tournament). The Pirates' first-round opponent was North Carolina, which handed them their 39th defeat in as many games against the four schools from their state that were charter members of the ACC.... North Carolina's 45-point rout of Rhode Island in the second round represented the sixth-highest margin of victory in any round of the NCAA Tournament.... The ACC and Big Eight tied for the most playoff representatives with six apiece. The ACC notched at least 12 tourney triumphs for the fifth consecutive year.... Temple became the first at-large team in seven years to win fewer than 60 percent of its games but still reach a regional semifinal. The Owls advanced all the way to the West Regional final, where they blew an eight-point, second-half lead and lost against Michigan.... Tennessee's Allan Houston (2,801 points) joined LSU's Pete Maravich (3,667 from 1968 to 1970), Portland State's Freeman Williams (3,249 from 1975 to 1978), Texas Southern's Harry Kelly (3,066 from 1980 to 1983), and Houston's

A distressed Jason Kidd disputes a call.

Otis Birdsong (2,832 from 1974 to 1977) as players to score more than 2,800 points in their major-college careers but never participate in the NCAA Tournament.

What If: Webber absorbed a good deal of grief after his baffling call for a timeout prevented Michigan from having an opportunity to tie the score or take the lead against North Carolina. But why wasn't a Wolverine guard back to bring the ball up after Webber grabbed a rebound off a missed free throw? Webber became the fourth player to secure NCAA All-Tournament team status in back-to-back seasons without winning a national championship either year as Michigan became the third school to lose two consecutive tourney finals.... Indiana was a No. 1 seed entering the tournament, but many experts didn't pick the Hoosiers to reach the Final Four, let alone win the national crown,

1992–93 NCAA CHAMPION: N. CAROLINA

SEASON STATISTICS OF NORTH CAROLINA REGULARS

PLAYER	POS.	CL.	G.	FG%	FT%	PPG	RPG
Eric Montross	C	Jr.	38	.615	.684	15.8	7.6
George Lynch	F	Sr.	38	.501	.667	14.7	9.6
Donald Williams	G	So.	37	.458	.829	14.3	1.9
Brian Reese	F	Jr.	35	.507	.692	11.4	3.6
Derrick Phelps	G	Jr.	36	.457	.675	8.1	4.4
Pat Sullivan	F	Jr.	38	.518	.789	6.4	2.4
Kevin Salvadori	C-F	Jr.	38	.458	.704	4.5	3.6
Henrik Rodl	G	Sr.	38	.496	.658	4.3	1.5
Matt Wenstrom	C	Sr.	33	.557	.593	2.5	1.4
Scott Cherry	G	Sr.	33	.606	.714	2.1	0.7
Dante Calabria	G	Fr.	35	.462	.778	1.8	0.8
TEAM TOTALS			38	**.506**	**.706**	**86.1**	**41.1**

Three-point field goals leader: Williams (83 of 199, .417). **Assists leaders:** Phelps 196, Rodl 136, Reese 83. **Blocked shots leaders:** Montross 47, Salvadori 45. **Steals leaders:** Lynch 89, Phelps 82.

1993 FINAL FOUR CHAMPIONSHIP GAME

NEW ORLEANS, LA

NORTH CAROLINA (77)	MIN.	FG-A	FT-A	REB.	A.	PF.	PTS.
Reese	27	2-7	4-4	5	3	1	8
Lynch	28	6-12	0-0	10	1	3	12
Montross	31	5-11	6-9	5	0	2	16
Phelps	36	4-6	1-2	3	6	0	9
Williams	31	8-12	4-4	1	1	1	25
Sullivan	14	1-2	1-2	1	1	2	3
Salvadori	18	0-0	2-2	4	1	1	2
Rodl	11	1-4	0-0	0	0	0	2
Calabria	1	0-0	0-0	0	0	0	0
Wenstrom	2	0-1	0-0	0	0	0	0
Cherry	1	0-0	0-0	0	0	0	0
TOTALS	200	27-55	18-23	29	13	10	77

FG%: .491. **FT%:** .789. **Three-point goals:** 5 of 11 (Reese 0-1, Phelps 0-1, Williams 5-7, Rodl 0-2). **Blocks:** 4. **Turnovers:** 10 (Phelps 5). **Steals:** 7.

MICHIGAN (71)	MIN.	FG-A	FT-A	REB.	A.	PF.	PTS.
Webber	33	11-18	1-2	11	1	2	23
Jackson	20	2-3	2-2	1	1	5	6
Howard	34	3-8	1-1	7	3	3	7
Rose	40	5-12	0-0	1	4	3	12
King	34	6-13	2-2	6	4	2	15
Riley	14	1-3	0-0	3	1	1	2
Pelinka	17	2-4	0-0	2	1	1	6
Talley	14	0-0	0-0	0	1	1	0
Voskuil	4	0-1	0-0	0	1	0	0
Team				2			
TOTALS	200	30-62	6-7	33	17	18	71

FG%: .484. **FT%:** .857. **Three-point goals:** 5 of 15 (Webber 0-1, Rose 2-6, King 1-5, Pelinka 2-3). **Blocks:** 4. **Turnovers:** 14 (Rose 6). **Steals:** 4. **Halftime:** North Carolina 42-36.

NATIONAL SEMIFINALS

MICHIGAN (81): Webber 10-17 7-9 27, Jackson 4-7 3-5 11, Howard 6-12 5-7 17, Rose 6-16 6-7 18, King 1-3 0-0 2, Riley 2-4 0-0 4, Pelinka 0-1 2-2 2, Voskuil 0-0 0-0 0. Team 29-61 (.475) 23-30 (.767) 81.

KENTUCKY (78): Mashburn 10-18 5-9 26, Prickett 1-6 7-7 9, Dent 2-6 2-2 6, Ford 3-10 4-4 12, Brown 6-10 0-0 16, Rhodes 0-1 1-2 1, Riddick 2-4 0-1 4, Martinez 0-3 0-0 0, Brassow 0-0 0-0 0, Delk 1-3 2-2 4, Braddy 0-0 0-0 0. Team 25-61 (.410) 21-26 (.808) 78.

Three-point goals: Michigan 0-4, Kentucky 7-21 (.333).

Halftime: Michigan 40-35. **Regulation:** Tied 71-71.

KANSAS (68): Hancock 2-5 2-2 6, Scott 3-5 2-2 8, Pauley 2-5 1-1 5, Walters 7-15 0-0 19, Jordan 7-13 0-0 19, Rayford 0-0 0-0 0, Woodberry 2-5 0-0 4, Richey 1-4 0-0 2, Ostertag 0-2 2-2 2, Gurley 1-2 0-0 3, Pearson 0-1 0-0 0. Team 25-57 (.439) 7-7 (1.000) 68.

NORTH CAROLINA (78): Lynch 5-12 4-6 14, Reese 3-5 1-2 7, Montross 9-14 5-8 23, Phelps 1-3 1-2 3, Williams 7-11 6-6 25, Sullivan 0-2 0-0 0, Rodl 0-0 0-0 0, Cherry 0-0 0-0 0, Salvadori 3-5 0-0 6, Wenstrom 0-0 0-0 0, Calabria 0-0 0-0 0, Davis 0-0 0-0 0, Stephenson 0-0 0-0 0, Geth 0-0 0-0 0. Team 28-52 (.538) 17-24 (.708) 78.

Three-point goals: Kansas 11-20 (.550), North Carolina 5-7 (.714). **Halftime:** North Carolina 40-36.

ALL-TOURNAMENT TEAM

George Lynch, F, Sr., North Carolina
Jamal Mashburn, F, Jr., Kentucky
Eric Montross, C, Jr., North Carolina
Chris Webber, F, Soph., Michigan
Donald Williams, G, Soph., North Carolina*

*Named Most Outstanding Player

after star forward Alan Henderson was hampered by a knee injury.

Overcoming Adversity: North Carolina, which finished with a 34-4 record, lost back-to-back ACC road games at Wake Forest (88-62) and Duke (81-67) by a total of 40 points. The Tar Heels' other two defeats were against Michigan (79-78 at the Rainbow Classic in Honolulu) and Georgia Tech (77-75 in the ACC Tournament final when Phelps missed the game because of an injury).

1993 CHAMPIONSHIP BRACKET

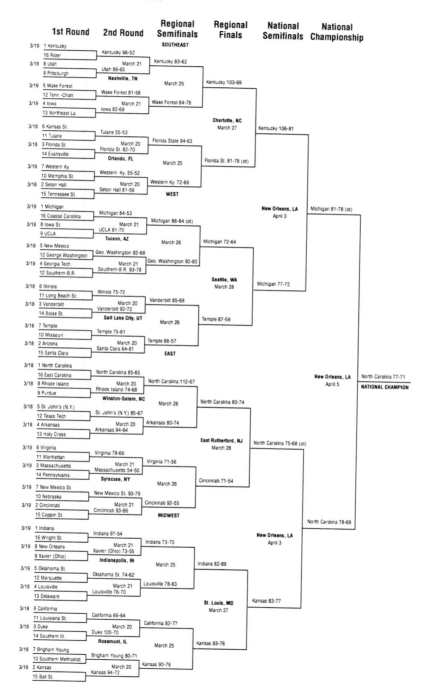

1st Round	2nd Round	Regional Semifinals	Regional Finals	National Semifinals	National Championship

SOUTHEAST

3/19 1 Kentucky
16 Rider
— Kentucky 96-52
3/19 8 Utah — March 21
9 Pittsburgh — Utah 86-65
— Kentucky 83-62
Nashville, TN
3/19 5 Wake Forest
12 Tenn.-Chatt. — Wake Forest 81-58
3/19 4 Iowa — March 21
13 Northeast La. — Iowa 82-69
— Wake Forest 84-78
March 25

Kentucky 103-69

Charlotte, NC
March 27

Kentucky 106-81

3/18 6 Kansas St.
11 Tulane — Tulane 55-53
3/18 3 Florida St. — March 20
14 Evansville — Florida St. 82-70
— Florida State 94-63
Orlando, FL
3/18 7 Western Ky.
10 Memphis St. — Western Ky. 55-52
3/18 2 Seton Hall — March 20
15 Tennessee St. — Seton Hall 81-59
— Western Ky. 72-68
March 25

Florida St. 81-78 (ot)

WEST

3/19 1 Michigan
16 Coastal Carolina — Michigan 84-53
3/19 8 Iowa St. — March 21
9 UCLA — UCLA 81-70
— Michigan 86-84 (ot)
Tucson, AZ
3/19 5 New Mexico
12 George Washington — Geo. Washington 82-68
3/19 4 Georgia Tech. — March 21
12 Southern-B.R. — Southern-B.R. 93-78
— Geo. Washington 90-80
March 26

Michigan 72-64

Seattle, WA
March 28

Michigan 77-72

3/18 6 Illinois
11 Long Beach St. — Illinois 75-72
3/18 3 Vanderbilt — March 20
14 Boise St. — Vanderbilt 92-72
— Vanderbilt 85-68
Salt Lake City, UT
3/18 7 Temple
10 Missouri — Temple 75-61
3/18 2 Arizona — March 20
15 Santa Clara — Santa Clara 64-61
— Temple 68-57
March 26

Temple 67-59

New Orleans, LA
April 3

Michigan 81-78 (ot)

EAST

3/18 1 North Carolina
16 East Carolina — North Carolina 85-65
3/18 8 Rhode Island — March 20
9 Purdue — Rhode Island 74-68
— North Carolina 112-67
Winston-Salem, NC
3/18 5 St. John's (N.Y.)
12 Texas Tech — St. John's (N.Y.) 85-67
3/18 4 Arkansas — March 20
13 Holy Cross — Arkansas 94-64
— Arkansas 80-74
March 26

North Carolina 80-74

East Rutherford, NJ
March 28

North Carolina 75-68 (ot)

3/19 6 Virginia
11 Manhattan — Virginia 78-66
3/19 3 Massachusetts — March 21
14 Pennsylvania — Massachusetts 54-50
— Virginia 71-56
Syracuse, NY
3/19 7 New Mexico St.
10 Nebraska — New Mexico St. 93-79
3/19 2 Cincinnati — March 21
15 Coppin St. — Cincinnati 93-66
— Cincinnati 92-55
March 26

Cincinnati 71-54

MIDWEST

North Carolina 78-68

3/19 1 Indiana
16 Wright St. — Indiana 97-54
3/19 8 New Orleans — March 21
9 Xavier (Ohio) — Xavier (Ohio) 73-55
— Indiana 73-70
Indianapolis, IN
3/19 5 Oklahoma St.
12 Marquette — Oklahoma St. 74-62
3/19 4 Louisville — March 21
13 Delaware — Louisville 76-70
— Louisville 78-63
March 25

Indiana 82-69

St. Louis, MO
March 27

Kansas 83-77

3/18 6 California
11 Louisiana St. — California 66-64
3/18 3 Duke — March 20
14 Southern Ill. — Duke 105-70
— California 82-77
Rosemont, IL
3/18 7 Brigham Young
10 Southern Methodist — Brigham Young 80-71
3/18 2 Kansas — March 20
15 Ball St. — Kansas 94-72
— Kansas 90-76
March 25

Kansas 93-76

New Orleans, LA
April 3

North Carolina 77-71

NATIONAL CHAMPION

New Orleans, LA
April 5

1993–94

AT A GLANCE

NCAA Champion: Arkansas (31-3).

NIT Champion: Villanova (20-12).

New Rules: Shot clock reduced to 35 seconds from 45, five-second defensive pressure call is eliminated, game clock stopped in the last minute after every basket, and trash-talking prohibited.

NCAA Consensus First-Team All-Americans: Grant Hill, F-G, Sr., Duke; Jason Kidd, G, Soph., California; Donyell Marshall, F, Jr., Connecticut; Glenn Robinson, F, Jr., Purdue; Clifford Rozier, C-F, Jr., Louisville.

Purdue's Glenn Robinson became the first Big Ten player since 1966 to lead the country in scoring.

Purdue's Glenn Robinson became the first Big Ten player to lead the country in scoring (30.3 points per game) since Purdue's Dave Schellhase in 1966. Robinson was at his best against the Big Ten's elite, scoring 73 in two games against Michigan and 72 in two outings against Indiana.

Connecticut's Donyell Marshall hit 39 of 40 free throws in averaging 37.7 points per game in three contests against St. John's as the Redmen absorbed their first losing record since 1962–63.

Houston's streak of 34 consecutive non-losing seasons came to a halt.

Kentucky overcame a 31-point, second-half deficit in a 99-95 victory at LSU. The deflating defeat contributed to ending LSU's streak of 17 consecutive non-losing records.

Louisville's Clifford Rozier set an NCAA record by hitting all 15 of his field-goal attempts in a game against Eastern Kentucky.

Cleveland State (39) and Kent (36) established an NCAA standard for most points in overtime periods by both teams, when they combined for 75 in the Vikings' 104-101, four-overtime triumph.

Southern (La.) posted the widest margin of victory in major-college history (97 points) with a 154-57 victory over Patton College.

Dartmouth had nine different players hit a three-pointer, an NCAA record, in a game against Boston College.

Auburn's Wesley Person finished his career with 2,066 points to join his brother, Chuck

Connecticut forward Donyell Marshall concentrates at the free throw line.

AP	UPI	USA/CNN	SCHOOL
1	2	9	North Carolina
2	1	1	Arkansas
3	3	5	Purdue
4	4	7	Connecticut
5	5	6	Missouri
6	6	2	Duke
7	8	13	Kentucky
8	7	15	Massachusetts
9	9	3	Arizona
10	10	10	Louisville
11	11	8	Michigan
12	12	18	Temple
13	13	12	Kansas
14	15	4	Florida
15	14	14	Syracuse
16	16	–	California
17	17	22	UCLA
18	18	16	Indiana
19	19	21	Oklahoma St.
20	21	24	Texas
21	29	17	Marquette
22	24	–	Nebraska
23	23	23	Minnesota
24	22	–	St. Louis
25	–	–	Cincinnati
–	–	11	Boston College
–	–	19	Tulsa
–	–	20	Maryland
–	25	–	Ala.-Birmingham
–	–	25	Pennsylvania

(2,311), as the only brother combination to score more than 2,000 for the same school.

Vermont guard Eddie Benton set a North Atlantic Conference record with 54 points against Drexel.

Askia Jones exploded for a national-high and Big Eight Conference-record 62 points in just 28 minutes and tied an NCAA standard with 14 three-pointers, boosting Kansas State to a 115-77 rout of visiting Fresno State in the quarterfinals of the NIT.

Valparaiso, ending its streak of 16 consecutive losing seasons, compiled a 20-8 record.

Former national coaches of the year Butch van Breda Kolff and Johnny Orr retired at Hofstra and Iowa State, respectively.

1994 NCAA Tournament

Summary: Arkansas ended an SEC dry spell. Despite having an average of three first-round NBA draft choices annually in 15 years since 1979, no current member of the 12-team SEC reached the NCAA Tournament championship game in that span, although every school participated in the playoffs at least once. Arkansas' title vindicated coach Nolan Richardson, who probably would have been dismissed in 1987 after his second season with the Hogs had they not rallied from a 21-point second-half deficit in the NIT to edge Arkansas State, 67-64, in overtime. But that wasn't the most strain he faced that year because his 16-year-old daughter, Yvonne, died of leukemia. Richardson was also a leading figure in a national controversy concerning alleged racial injustices. Pressure was also intense on Scotty Thurman with the shot clock winding down and the score tied with 40 seconds remaining when he lofted a three-point attempt over Duke's Antonio Lang that hit nothing but net.

Outcome for Defending Champion: North Carolina's streak of 13 consecutive trips to a

1993–94 INDIVIDUAL LEADERS

SCORING

PLAYER	PTS.	AVG.
Robinson, Purdue	1030	30.3
Feaster, Holy Cross	785	28.0
Scales, Southern	733	27.1
King, W. Carolina	752	26.9
Neale, Colgate	771	26.6
Benton, Vermont	687	26.4
Bennerman, Siena	858	26.0
Dumas, Mo.-Kansas City	753	26.0
Jones, Air Force	663	25.5
Buchanan, Marist	685	25.4
Trent, Ohio U.	837	25.4
Lightfoot, Idaho	710	25.4

REBOUNDING

PLAYER	REB.	AVG.
Lambert, Baylor	355	14.8
Scales, Southern	384	14.2
Kubel, N'western (La.)	341	13.1
Warren, Va. C'wealth	336	12.4
Rose, Drexel	371	12.4
Vaughn, Memphis	335	12.0
Jackson, Nicholls St.	311	12.0
Simon, New Orleans	355	11.8
Stewart, UNLV	256	11.6
Rogers, Tennessee St.	358	11.5
Smith, Providence	344	11.5

ASSISTS

PLAYER	AST.	AVG.
Kidd, California	272	9.1
Edwards, Texas A&M	265	8.8
Miller, Marquette	274	8.3
O'Bryant, Nevada	232	8.3
Abdullah, Providence	241	8.0
Nathan, Northeast La.	179	7.8
Smart, San Francisco	204	7.6
Pogue, Campbell	207	7.4

Thomas, UNLV	205	7.3
Haggerty, Baylor	161	7.3

BLOCKED SHOTS

PLAYER	BLK.	AVG.
Livingston, Howard	115	4.4
McIlvaine, Marquette	142	4.3
Ratliff, Wyoming	114	4.1
Vaughn, Memphis	107	3.8
Duncan, Wake Forest	124	3.8
Camby, Massachusetts	105	3.6
Cato, South Alabama	85	3.5
Marshall, Connecticut	111	3.3
McDonald, New Orleans	96	3.2
Fleury, UMBC	80	3.2

STEALS

PLAYER	STL.	AVG.
Griggs, S'western La.	120	4.0
Walker, San Francisco	109	3.9
Cradle, Long Island	79	3.8
Kidd, California	94	3.1
Tyler, Texas	87	3.1
Ceasar, LSU	80	3.0
Black, Texas-Pan Am	80	3.0
Thompson, Oklahoma St.	99	2.9
Robertson, Dayton	78	2.9
Golden, Tennessee	78	2.9
Walton, Alcorn St.	63	2.9

FIELD GOAL PERCENTAGE

PLAYER	FGM	FGA	PCT.
Atkinson, Long Beach St.	141	203	.695
Wade, SW Texas St.	232	356	.652
Miller, Mich. St.	162	249	.651
Thomas, Illinois	207	327	.633
Swinson, Auburn	234	371	.631
Ritter, James Madison	230	366	.628

Williamson, Arkansas	237	436	.626
Ardayfio, Army	180	289	.623
Lunsford, Alabama St.	163	263	.620
Rozier, Louisville	247	400	.618

FREE THROW PERCENTAGE

PLAYER	FGM	FGA	PCT.
Basile, Marist	84	89	.944
Evans, Troy St.	72	77	.935
Schmidt, Valparaiso	75	81	.926
Hildebrand, Liberty	149	161	.925
Culuko, James Madison	117	127	.921
Yoder, Colorado St.	107	117	.915
Ford, Kentucky	103	113	.912
Hoover, Notre Dame	76	84	.905
Cline, Morehead St.	73	81	.901
Tucker, N. Illinois	71	79	.899

THREE-POINT FIELD GOAL PERCENTAGE

PLAYER	FGM	FGA	PCT.
Kell, Evansville	62	123	.504
Santiago, Fresno St.	64	128	.500
Born, Tenn.-Chat.	67	135	.496
Young, Canisius	53	109	.486
Eisley, Boston College	91	188	.484

THREE-POINT FIELD GOALS PER GAME

PLAYER	FGM	AVG.
Brown, UC Irvine	122	4.7
Hicks, Coastal Carolina	115	4.4
Durden, Cincinnati	102	4.1
Haslett, Southern Miss.	112	3.7
Townes, La Salle	100	3.7
Ross, George Mason	99	3.7

regional semifinal ended when the Tar Heels lost to Boston College in the second round.

Star Gazing: Final Four Most Outstanding Player Corliss Williamson of Arkansas briefly surpassed Bill Walton's playoff field-goal shooting record (68.6 percent) before missing his first five shots in the final against Duke's Cherokee Parks and finishing the game 10 of 24 from the floor. Williamson's Final Four heroics overshadowed a brilliant performance against him by Michigan's Juwan Howard in a regional final. Howard outscored Williamson, 30-12, and outrebounded him, 13-6, but the Wolverines concentrated so much on "Big Nasty" that Arkansas hit 10 three-pointers.

One and Only: Richardson became the only coach to win national championships in junior college (1980 with Western Texas), the NIT (1981 with Tulsa), and the NCAA.... Duke guard Chris Collins became the first championship game player to be the son of a former NCAA consensus All-American. His father, NBA analyst Doug Collins, became an All-American for Illinois State the year after playing for the 1972 U.S. Olympic team.

Numbers Game: Skip Prosser of Loyola (Md.) became the only active coach to engineer a turnaround that included an NCAA playoff appearance in his first full year at a new job although the school registered a record of more than 20 games below .500 the previous season. The Greyhounds, 2-25 in 1992–93, improved by 13 1/2 games the next year when Prosser assumed control and compiled a 17-13 mark.... Gary Williams, leading Maryland to the Midwest Regional semifinals, became the only individual to win games while coaching schools from the

1993-94 TEAM LEADERS

SCORING OFFENSE

SCHOOL	PTS.	AVG.
Southern (La.)	2727	101.0
Troy St.	2634	97.6
Arkansas	3176	93.4
Texas	3119	91.7
Murray St.	2611	90.0

SCORING DEFENSE

SCHOOL	PTS.	AVG.
Princeton	1361	52.3
Temple	1697	54.7
Wisconsin-Green Bay	1872	55.1
Alabama-Birmingham	1806	60.2
Marquette	2040	61.8

SCORING MARGIN

SCHOOL	OFF.	DEF.	MAR.
Arkansas	93.4	75.6	17.9
Connecticut	84.9	68.6	16.3
Arizona	89.3	74.4	14.9
Southern (La.)	101.0	87.7	13.3
North Carolina	85.6	72.4	13.2

WON-LOST PERCENTAGE

TEAM	W-L	PCT.
Arkansas	31-3	.912
Pennsylvania	25-3	.893
Missouri	28-4	.875
Charleston (S.C.)	24-4	.857
Connecticut	29-5	.853
Purdue	29-5	.853

FIELD GOAL PERCENTAGE

SCHOOL	FGM	FGA	PCT.
Auburn	854	1689	.506
Michigan St.	944	1875	.503
Radford	793	1580	.502
James Madison	890	1783	.499
North Carolina	1091	2188	.499

DEFENSIVE FIELD GOAL PERCENTAGE

SCHOOL	FGM	FGA	PCT.
Marquette	750	2097	.358
Temple	621	1686	.368
Wisconsin-Green Bay	664	1777	.374
Kansas	823	2147	.383
Alabama-Birmingham	661	1718	.385

FREE THROW PERCENTAGE

SCHOOL	FTM	FTA	PCT.
Colgate	511	665	.768
Wisconsin-Green Bay	462	607	.761
Iowa St.	521	687	.758
Davidson	529	704	.751
Vanderbilt	557	742	.751

REBOUND MARGIN

SCHOOL	OWN	OPP.	MAR.
Utah St.	38.4	29.8	8.6
North Carolina	43.7	35.3	8.5
Idaho	41.5	33.1	8.4
UCLA	43.9	36.2	7.7
Baylor	50.3	42.7	7.6

THREE-POINT FIELD GOAL PERCENTAGE

SCHOOL	FGM	FGA	PCT.
Indiana	182	401	.454
Robert Morris	139	323	.430
Evansville	244	570	.428
Oklahoma St.	258	619	.417
Montana	150	369	.407

THREE-POINT FIELD GOALS PER GAME

SCHOOL	FGM	AVG.
Troy St.	262	9.7
New Mexico	300	9.7
Vermont	240	8.9
Arkansas	301	8.9
Kentucky	301	8.9

SCORING DEFENSE

SCHOOL	PTS.	AVG.
Oklahoma A&M	1539	53.1
Duquesne	1551	53.5
Wyoming	1522	54.4
Oregon State	1585	54.7
Oklahoma City	1370	54.8

FIELD GOAL PERCENTAGE

SCHOOL	FGM	FGA	PCT.
George Washington	744	1632	.456
Holy Cross	871	2018	.432
Niagara	778	1817	.428
Maryland	669	1564	.428
Furman	990	2370	.418

three conferences with the best winning percentages in NCAA Tournament history reflecting actual membership—ACC, Big East, and Big Ten. He is also the only coach to win games with as many as three different schools (Boston College, Maryland, and Ohio State) although they were seeded ninth or worse.... Duke's Mike Krzyzewski became the only coach to win his first seven NCAA regional finals.... Boston College's Jim O'Brien defeated two of the three coaches with at least 40 tourney victories (North Carolina's Dean Smith and Indiana's Bob Knight in back-to-back East Regional games).... Arizona guard Khalid Reeves (20th in scoring with 24.2 points per game) was the only player ranking among the nation's top 60 scorers, top 30 in

assists, and top 30 rebounders to participate in the Final Four.... Michigan coach Steve Fisher improved his record to 12-0 in NCAA playoff games decided by five points or less.

Putting Things in Perspective: Arkansas lost two of three SEC road games from January 8 to 19 and nearly lost three of four but capitalized on Thurman's three-pointer in the final 10 seconds to escape with a 65-64 victory at Tennessee, which finished with the worst record in the league (2-14). The Hogs also almost lost at home to a second-division team, but LSU missed two shots in the final 10 seconds to fall short, 84-83, in the only game at Arkansas' brand new Walton Arena that would be less than a double-digit victory.

1994 NCAA CHAMPION: ARKANSAS

SEASON STATISTICS OF ARKANSAS REGULARS

PLAYER	POS.	CL.	G.	FG%	FT%	PPG	RPG
Corliss Williamson	F	So.	34	.626	.700	20.4	7.7
Scotty Thurman	G-F	So.	34	.469	.732	15.9	4.5
Al Dillard	G	Jr.	34	.404	.786	8.9	1.1
Corey Beck	G	Jr.	34	.506	.667	8.8	3.9
Clint McDaniel	G	Jr.	34	.407	.754	8.1	2.8
Dwight Stewart	C	Jr.	34	.453	.647	8.0	5.0
Darnell Robinson	C	Fr.	27	.457	.577	7.6	4.7
Roger Crawford	G	Sr.	30	.556	.679	7.4	1.9
Davor Rimac	G	Jr.	34	.455	.786	4.8	1.9
Lee Wilson	C	Fr.	30	.493	.580	3.4	3.1
Ken Biley	F	Sr.	18	.655	.667	2.8	2.1
Elmer Martin	F	Jr.	27	.308	.692	1.3	1.2
Ray Biggers	F	Jr.	18	.172	.438	1.1	2.2
TEAM TOTALS			34	.488	.680	93.4	41.6

Three-point field goals leaders: Thurman (85 of 198, .429), Dillard (75 of 183, .410), McDaniel (38 of 108, .352), Steward (37 of 95, .389), Rimac (32 of 79, .405). Assists leaders: Beck 169, Thurman 103. Blocked shots leader: Williamson 39. Steals leaders: Beck 68, McDaniel 53, Thurman 47.

1994 FINAL FOUR CHAMPIONSHIP GAME

CHARLOTTE, NC

DUKE (72)	MIN.	FG-A	FT-A	REB.	A.	PF.	PTS.
Lang	34	6-9	3-3	5	3	5	15
Hill	38	4-11	3-5	14	6	3	12
Parks	30	7-10	0-1	7	0	3	14
Capel	35	6-16	0-0	5	4	3	14
Collins	34	4-11	0-0	0	1	1	12
Clark	15	1-6	1-2	1	3	2	3
Meek	14	1-2	0-0	7	0	1	2
Team				5			
TOTALS	200	29-65	7-11	44	17	18	72

FG%: .446. FT%: .636. Three-point goals: 7 of 20 (Hill 1-4, Capel 2-6, Collins 4-8, Clark 0-2). Blocks: 7 (Hill 3). Turnovers: 23 (Hill 9, Capel 6, Lang 5). Steals: 5 (Hill 3).

ARKANSAS (76)	MIN.	FG-A	FT-A	REB.	A.	PF.	PTS.
Biley	3	0-0	0-0	0	0	1	0
Williamson	35	10-24	3-5	8	3	3	23
Stewart	29	3-11	0-0	9	4	3	6
Beck	35	5-11	5-8	10	4	3	15
Thurman	36	6-13	0-0	5	1	2	15
McDaniel	32	2-5	2-4	2	3	2	7
Robinson	12	1-5	0-0	2	0	1	2
Dillard	8	1-5	1-2	1	0	1	4
Rimac	5	0-1	0-0	0	0	0	0
Wilson	5	2-2	0-0	4	0	1	4
Team				3			
TOTALS	200	30-77	11-19	44	15	17	76

FG%: .390. FT%: .579. Three-point goals: 5 of 18 (Stewart 0-5, Beck 0-1, Thurman 3-5, McDaniel 1-3, Dillard 1-4). Blocks: 3. Turnovers: 12 (Williamson 5). Steals: 11 (Stewart 4).
Halftime: Arkansas 34-33.

NATIONAL SEMIFINALS

ARIZONA (82): Owes 7-15 2-2 16, Geary 2-6 0-0 4, Blair 4-7 0-1 8, Reeves 6-19 8-9 20, Stoudamire 5-24 4-4 16, Flanagan 1-1 0-0 2, McLean 1-1 0-0 2, Williams 5-7 0-0 14, Rigdon 0-0 0-0 0, Richey 0-0 0-0 0, Brown 0-0 0-0 0, Kelley 0-0 0-0 0. Team 31-80 (.388) 14-16 (.875) 82.

ARKANSAS (91): Stewart 2-5 1-2 7, Williamson 11-18 7-9 29, Robinson 5-9 2-3 12, Beck 2-5 4-8 9, Thurman 5-13 4-6 14, McDaniel 4-10 2-2 12, Dillard 2-7 0-0 6, Wilson 1-2 0-2 2, Rimac 0-1 0-0 0. Team 32-70 (.457) 20-32 (.625) 91.

Three-point goals: Arizona 6-32, Arkansas 7-24 (.292).
Halftime: Tied 41-41.

FLORIDA (65): Thompson 1-3 2-4 4, DeClercq 7-11 0-2 14, Hill 6-17 4-6 16, Brown 3-9 0-0 8, Cross 3-14 2-4 10, Kuisma 0-2 2-2 2, Anderson 4-6 1-2 9, Dyrkolbotn 0-0 0-0 0, Williams 1-1 0-0 2. Team 25-63 (.397) 11-20 (.550) 65.

DUKE (70): Lang 3-6 6-6 12, Hill 8-13 6-8 25, Parks 4-11 3-4 11, Capel 3-10 1-1 9, Collins 1-4 0-0 2, Clark 3-6 0-0 8, Meek 0-1 3-4 3, Newton 0-0 0-0 0. Team 22-51 (.431) 19-23 (.826) 70.

Three-point goals: Florida 4-9 (.444), Duke 7-14 (.500).
Halftime: Florida 39-32.

ALL-TOURNAMENT TEAM

Corey Beck, G, Jr., Arkansas
Grant Hill, G, Sr., Duke
Antonio Lang, F, Sr., Duke
Scotty Thurman, G-F, Soph., Arkansas
Corliss Williamson, F, Soph., Arkansas*

*Named Most Outstanding Player

1994 CHAMPIONSHIP BRACKET

1st Round	2nd Round	Regional Semifinals	Regional Finals	National Semifinals	National Championship

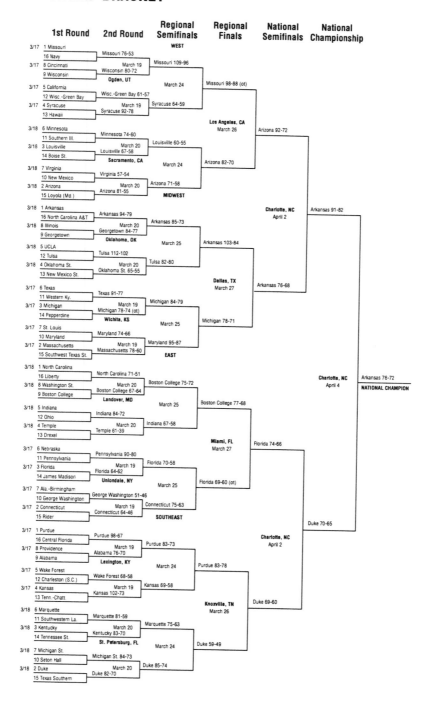

WEST

3/17 1 Missouri
16 Navy — Missouri 76-53
3/17 8 Cincinnati
9 Wisconsin — March 19 Wisconsin 80-72 — Missouri 109-96
Ogden, UT
3/17 5 California
12 Wisc.-Green Bay — Wisc.-Green Bay 61-57 — March 24 — Missouri 98-88 (ot)
3/17 4 Syracuse
13 Hawaii — March 19 Syracuse 92-78 — Syracuse 64-59

3/18 6 Minnesota
11 Southern Ill. — Minnesota 74-60
3/18 3 Louisville
14 Boise St. — March 20 Louisville 67-58 — Louisville 60-55 — **Los Angeles, CA** March 26 — Arizona 92-72
Sacramento, CA
3/18 7 Virginia
10 New Mexico — Virginia 57-54 — March 24 — Arizona 82-70
3/18 2 Arizona
15 Loyola (Md.) — March 20 Arizona 81-55 — Arizona 71-58

MIDWEST

3/18 1 Arkansas
16 North Carolina A&T — Arkansas 94-79
3/18 8 Illinois
9 Georgetown — March 20 Georgetown 84-77 — Arkansas 85-73 — **Charlotte, NC** April 2 — Arkansas 91-82
Oklahoma, OK
3/18 5 UCLA
12 Tulsa — Tulsa 112-102 — March 25 — Arkansas 103-84
3/18 4 Oklahoma St.
13 New Mexico St. — March 20 Oklahoma St. 65-55 — Tulsa 82-80

3/17 6 Texas
11 Western Ky. — Texas 91-77 — **Dallas, TX** March 27 — Arkansas 76-68
3/17 3 Michigan
14 Pepperdine — March 19 Michigan 78-74 (ot) — Michigan 84-79
Wichita, KS
3/17 7 St. Louis
10 Maryland — Maryland 74-66 — March 25 — Michigan 78-71
3/17 2 Massachusetts
15 Southwest Texas St. — March 19 Massachusetts 78-60 — Maryland 95-87

EAST

3/18 1 North Carolina
16 Liberty — North Carolina 71-51
3/18 8 Washington St.
9 Boston College — March 20 Boston College 67-64 — Boston College 75-72 — **Charlotte, NC** April 4 — Arkansas 76-72
Landover, MD
3/18 5 Indiana
12 Ohio — Indiana 84-72 — March 25 — Boston College 77-68 — **NATIONAL CHAMPION**
3/18 4 Temple
13 Drexel — March 20 Temple 61-39 — Indiana 67-58

3/17 6 Nebraska
11 Pennsylvania — Pennsylvania 90-80 — **Miami, FL** March 27 — Florida 74-66
3/17 3 Florida
14 James Madison — March 19 Florida 64-62 — Florida 70-58
Uniondale, NY
3/17 7 Ala.-Birmingham
10 George Washington — George Washington 51-46 — March 25 — Florida 69-60 (ot)
3/17 2 Connecticut
15 Rider — March 19 Connecticut 64-46 — Connecticut 75-63

SOUTHEAST

3/17 1 Purdue
16 Central Florida — Purdue 98-67
3/17 8 Providence
9 Alabama — March 19 Alabama 76-70 — Purdue 83-73 — **Charlotte, NC** April 2 — Duke 70-65
Lexington, KY
3/17 5 Wake Forest
12 Charleston (S.C.) — Wake Forest 68-58 — March 24 — Purdue 83-78
3/17 4 Kansas
13 Tenn.-Chatt. — March 19 Kansas 102-73 — Kansas 69-58

3/18 6 Marquette
11 Southwestern La. — Marquette 81-59 — **Knoxville, TN** March 26 — Duke 69-60
3/18 3 Kentucky
14 Tennessee St. — March 20 Kentucky 83-70 — Marquette 75-63
St. Petersburg, FL
3/18 7 Michigan St.
10 Seton Hall — Michigan St. 84-73 — March 24 — Duke 59-49
3/18 2 Duke
15 Texas Southern — March 20 Duke 82-70 — Duke 85-74

7

NATIONAL INVITATION
TOURNAMENT (NIT)

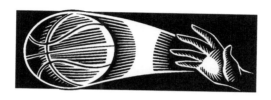

The Final Four hasn't eternally been the final word in national postseason competition, although it appears that's the case. The NCAA Tournament, which previously played second fiddle to the National Invitation Tournament (NIT), seems to haughtily look down upon the NIT as little more than an acronymn contest for derisive entries such as National Insignificant Tournament, Not Influential Tournament, Nominally Important Tournament, No Interest Tournament, Nearly Ignominious Tournament, Naturally Impaired Tournament, Never Impressionable Tournament, and so on.

But the NIT was once superior to the NCAA Tournament during an era when airplanes didn't dominate the transportation industry, television was in its infancy, and New York's Madison Square Garden was the place to be if a team wanted extensive national exposure. If ever there was a concept whose time had arrived, it was the NIT in 1938. If ever there was a location to conduct a national tourney at a time when the sports page was the principal place to get sports news, it was in New York because of Gotham's close to 20 daily newspapers.

Too many were saying for too long such provincial comments as the West was best, the East was least, the North was unable to go forth, and the South was all mouth. Finally, basketball could designate a national champion. Originated by the Metropolitan Basketball Writers Association, responsibility for administering the NIT was transferred two years later to local colleges, and a group first known as the Metropolitan Intercollegiate Basketball Committee, then, in 1948, as the Metropolitan Intercollegiate Basketball Association (MIBA).

And the NIT lived up to its billing. In 1939, the NIT final featured two unbeaten teams when Long Island University defeated Loyola of Chicago, 44-32 (see accompanying box score).

In the early years, the NIT was an extravaganza so hot the NCAA playoffs were actually scheduled after the NIT to prevent the lukewarm reception given the NCAA from turning completely frigid by going head-to-head against what was clearly basketball's showcase event. Such schedule modifications allowed City College of New York to become the only school to win both titles in the same year (1950) and permitted Utah to win the 1944 NCAA crown after the Utes were eliminated in the opening round of the NIT by eventual third-place finisher Kentucky (46-38). The final year teams participated in both national tournaments was 1952, when Dayton, Duquesne, St. John's, and St. Louis doubled up on postseason participation. St. John's was runner-up to Kansas in the NCAA Tournament that year after the Redmen lost their opener in the NIT against La Salle (51-45).

Some observers believe the 1948 NIT, starting the tourney's second decade, was the best from a strength standpoint. If there had been a national poll at the time, it is believed that five of the nation's top seven teams were in the NIT, which was won that year by Ed Macauley-led St. Louis University.

In each of the first two years the Associated Press conducted national rankings (1949 and 1950), five of the top 10 teams participated in the NIT. The four seeded teams in the 1949 NIT all were upset in the quarterfinals after receiving first-round byes—Kentucky, St. Louis, Western Kentucky, and Utah. Four of the 12 teams in the 1953 and 1960 NIT fields were schools ranked in the top 10 of the final AP and/or UPI polls. In 1954, the last four NIT survivors (Holy Cross, Duquesne, Niagara, and Western Kentucky) combined to win 91 percent of their games entering the semifinals, while their NCAA counter-

HOW NIT FIELD HAS INCREASED

A committee of New York writers decided that the inaugural NIT would have two local teams, two from elsewhere in the East, and two from the Midwest or Far West. Three years later, the 1941 NIT included three New York area schools in the first eight-team format.

The final year of the 1940s posed a dilemma when local teams failed to compile sterling records, however. Faced with forgoing any local draws, the NIT made a drastic change and expanded the field to 12 teams, adding an opening round to eliminate four entrants. The 1949 opening-round pair of doubleheaders was a dark day and evening for Big Apple hoops as CCNY, Manhattan, NYU, and St. John's dropped their openers by an average of 18.75 points.

Here is how the NIT field has increased over the years:

1938 (6 entrants), 1941 (8), 1949 (12), 1965 (14), 1968 (16), 1979 (24), and 1980 (32).

parts (La Salle, Bradley, Penn State, and Southern Cal) combined to win barely over 70 percent of their games. Niagara, the third-place finisher in the NIT, defeated 1954 NCAA champion La Salle twice during the regular season by a total of 27 points.

POSTSEASON BATTLE OF UNBEATENS   On March 22, 1939, the NIT final game, held at New York's Madison Square Garden, featured two unbeaten teams—Loyola of Chicago and Long Island University. That game marked the only time in major-college history that two undefeated major colleges met in a national postseason tournament. LIU defeated Loyola, 44-32. LIU finished with a 24-0 record and Loyola 21-1.

LIU (44)	FG	FT	PTS.
Torgoff	5	2	12
King	0	0	0
Kaplowitz	4	1	9
Schwartz	0	2	2
Scharf	0	0	0
Sewitch	0	1	1
Lobelin	0	0	0
Newman	1	1	3
Shelly	1	0	2
Bromberg	2	1	5
Schechtman	4	1	9
Zeitlin	0	1	1
TOTALS	**17**	**10**	**44**

LOYOLA (32)	FG	FT	PTS.
Hogan	2	0	4
Schell	1	0	2
O'Brien	4	1	9
Graham	1	0	2
Novak	0	1	1
Kautz	3	0	6
Driscoll	0	0	0
Wenskus	4	0	8
TOTALS	**15**	**2**	**32**

The NCAA final was also conducted at Madison Square Garden seven times in eight years from 1943 to 1950. NIT crowds averaged more than 18,000 fans per game from 1945 through 1948. But after a point-shaving scandal in 1951 turned New York into a basketball cesspool, the Final Four hasn't come anywhere close to the Big Apple, although the semifinals and final will be held at the Meadowlands in East Rutherford, New Jersey, in 1996.

NCAA Puts on the Pressure

The NCAA, making it mandatory in the mid-1950s for any team winning its conference to participate in the NCAA playoffs, methodically set in motion the forces pressuring the majority of major schools into selecting its national tournament over the NIT. Xavier, right smack in the middle of some bizarre circumstances, is a vivid example of that turbulence. NIT champion-to-be Louisville was ranked 4th in the nation by AP in mid-February when it lost by 40 points at Xavier (99-59). Two years later, Xavier lost 10 of its

St. Louis' Ed Macauley (white uniform, jumping) fights off a defender in a 1949 NIT game.

final 15 regular-season games after a 10-1 start and the NIT asked the Musketeers to give back its NIT bid. But Xavier said no and went on to win the 1958 NIT title.

The issue of "choice" came to a head in 1970 when Marquette, an independent school at the time coached by feisty Al McGuire, won the NIT after rejecting an NCAA at-large invitation because the Warriors were going to be placed in the NCAA Midwest Regional (Fort Worth,

Texas) instead of closer to home in the Mideast Regional (Dayton, Ohio). McGuire's snub led the NCAA to decree that any school offered an NCAA bid must accept it or be prohibited from participating in postseason competition.

The NIT, although imperiled by the NCAA's self-serving maneuvers, more than held its own with the NCAA Tournament because of some scintillating storylines. The final NIT at the old Garden in 1967 belonged to a so-called "small" school, Southern Illinois, sparked by a smooth

Western Kentucky has made 11 NIT appearances, including a second-place finish in 1942. Shown here are members of the 1947–48 team, which took third place in the NIT (from left): Don Ray, John Oldham, Odie Spears, coach E. A. Diddle, Oran McKinney, Dee Gibson, and assistant coach Ted Hornback.

swingman named Walt Frazier. He wasn't Clyde yet, but the future Knick was well on his way.

The competitive NIT, boasting three double overtime games in 1971, was a stark contrast to the "UCLA Invitational." Seemingly invincible UCLA captured seven consecutive NCAA titles from 1967 to 1973 by winning 28 tournament games by an average of almost 18 points per contest. In 1973, the Bruins' four tournament victories were by an average of 16 points, including a 21-point triumph over Memphis State in the championship game. Meanwhile, NIT champion Virginia Tech won four exciting postseason games that year by a total of five points, includ-

ing a game-winning basket at the buzzer in overtime in the final against Notre Dame. The next year, seven of the 12 NIT games in the first round and quarterfinals were decided by four points or less.

Exacerbating the tug of war between the two events was a short-lived, eight-team tournament ostensibly to showcase league runners-up but principally introduced to hamper the NIT field. The new tourney was called the Collegiate Commissioners Association Tournament in 1974, when Indiana won the title at St. Louis, and then changed to the National Commissioners Invitational Tournament in 1975, when Drake won the title at Louisville.

The bottom line: Once network television made its move, it left virtually no choice for schools to choose between the national postseason events. The NCAA inflicted another blow to the NIT in 1978 when NCAA Productions started televising all of the NCAA Tournament games. The occasionally acrimonious battle was over as TV made the NCAA playoffs larger, more affluent, and more visible than it ever fantasized it could become.

While the NCAA pulled strings like a master puppeteer, the NIT's influence eroded. Prominent active coaches such as Lute Olson and Eddie Sutton have never appeared in the NIT. The last consensus first-team All-American to participate in the NIT was forward Larry Bird of Indiana State, a loser at Rutgers in the 1978 quarterfinals. The last wire-service top 10 team to appear in the NIT was North Carolina, a first-round loser against Purdue in 1974.

NIT in Recent Years

For a few years, the NIT served as a springboard to future success for budding powers. In a five-year span from 1980 through 1984 when the NCAA field ranged from 48 to 52 teams, Virginia (1980 NIT champion), DePaul (1983 runner-up), and Michigan (1984 champion) became NCAA regional No. 1 seeds the year after reaching an NIT final. But when the NCAA bracket was increased to 64 in 1985, the move effectively denied the NIT access even to the vast majority of up-and-coming teams. In effect, the NIT champion was reduced to proclaiming "We're No. 65!" although anywhere from nine to 13 teams out of the NIT draw made the NCAA field the following year since the NCAA expanded to 64 entrants.

The NIT has made several strategic alterations over the years, but they've had little impact on how the event is perceived from a national scope. Attendance slipped to an all-time low in 1976 although national power Kentucky

won the title. In 1977, former executive director Pete Carlesimo, the father of former Seton Hall and current Portland Trail Blazers coach P. J. Carlesimo, saved the NIT by implementing a plan whereby early-round games were played at campus sites and locations across the country before the four semifinalists advanced to New York. In 1985, the NIT started a preseason tournament, which evolved into the nation's premier in-season tourney and now probably carries as much clout, if not more, than the postseason NIT.

The memories and tradition of the NIT are marvelous, yet one occasionally wonders how much longer the postseason event can survive when it became so contrived that second- and third-round matchups aren't announced until after the previous games are played. Although the NIT has tinkered with a rule making certain every semifinalist played at least one road game before getting to New York, it is perceived as a tournament awarding home games on the basis of gate-receipt potential or to favor teams bringing the most fans or publicity or both to Madison Square Garden for the tourney's semifinals and final.

Texas-El Paso coach Don Haskins was irked in 1993 when the Miners were consigned to Georgetown's on-campus, 2,200-seat McDonough Gym for a second-round game after UTEP had a near-capacity crowd of 11,800 for a first-round contest against Houston. Haskins, according to AP, called the decision political. "They (NIT officials) want to have Georgetown in New York (for the semifinals and final)," he said. "It's all politics." In 1994, Coppin State, undefeated in the Mid-Eastern Athletic Conference and 22-8 overall with a difficult non-league schedule, rightfully thought the selection process was unjust when it was left out of the NIT. UTEP was also shunned in 1994 despite an 18-12 record.

The NIT's first nine champions lost a total of 25 games, but its seven titlists from 1986 through 1992 combined to go 20 games below .500 in conference competition, including a 4-12 league mark compiled by 1988 Big East cellar dweller

Lenny Wilkens (#14) was a star for the Providence Friars when they were a dominant team in the early 1960s NIT tournaments.

Connecticut. The NIT's "final four" participants combined to average more than 13 defeats per team in the first 10 years after the NCAA field expanded to 64 entrants, including a grim 19-18 mark by 1985 NIT fourth-place finisher Louisville. Louisville was the only school to win two NCAA titles from 1977 to 1986. The 1985 NIT finalists (UCLA and Indiana) have combined for 15 NCAA championships.

"NIT! NIT! NIT!" is chanted at some games by taunting crowds seeking to ridicule opponents who have the potential to participate in the NCAA Tournament but who are on the fence to make it and apparently may have to settle for the NIT. CBS analyst Billy Packer once called the NIT "a gerrymandering tournament with no accountability."

Although NIT-picking observers think the postseason NIT should be taken off life support, the mood in New York is to retain a stiff upper lip. "We think the NIT is still a service to college basketball," said Jack Powers, the NIT's executive director. "Our early-round games frequently play to packed arenas and we still draw reasonably well in the Garden. Because of parity all across the country, there is a place for the teams in our tournament."

NIT Notes

The Big Eight has never won an NIT title although Colorado was champion in 1940 before joining the conference. Colorado had lost the championship game of the inaugural NIT in 1938 when the Buffaloes' roster included future Supreme Court justice Whizzer White.... Georgia Tech was 1971 NIT runner-up to North Carolina before the Yellow Jackets joined the ACC.... The only school from the consensus top conferences to never appear in the NIT is Iowa (Big Ten).... Temple (1938 and 1969) and West Virginia (1942) won NIT championships before the Atlantic 10 was formed.... St. Bonaventure (1977) won an NIT before joining the Atlantic 10.... Current Big East member Villanova was affiliated with the Atlantic 10 when the Wildcats finished in third place in 1977.... St. John's (1943, 1944, 1959, and 1965), Seton Hall (1953), and Providence (1961

Oregon's Ron Lee was Most Valuable Player of the 1975 NIT.

NIT FINAL GAME SUMMARY

YEAR	CHAMPION	RUNNER-UP	MOST VALUABLE PLAYER
1938	Temple	Colorado	Don Shields, Temple
1939	Long Island Univ.	Loyola of Chicago	Bill Lloyd, St. John's
1940	Colorado	Duquesne	Bob Doll, Colorado
1941	Long Island Univ.	Ohio University	Frank Baumholtz, Ohio
1942	West Virginia	Western Kentucky	Rudy Baric, West Virginia
1943	St. John's	Toledo	Harry Boykoff, St. John's
1944	St. John's	DePaul	Bill Kotsores, St. John's
1945	DePaul	Bowling Green St.	George Mikan, DePaul
1946	Kentucky	Rhode Island	Ernie Calverley, Rhode Island
1947	Utah	Kentucky	Vern Gardner, Utah
1948	St. Louis	New York Univ.	Ed Macauley, St. Louis
1949	San Francisco	Loyola of Chicago	Don Lofgan, San Francisco
1950	CCNY	Bradley	Ed Warner, CCNY
1951	Brigham Young	Dayton	Roland Minson, Brigham Young
1952	La Salle	Dayton	Tom Gola and Norm Grekin, La Salle
1953	Seton Hall	St. John's	Walter Dukes, Seton Hall
1954	Holy Cross	Duquesne	Togo Palazzi, Holy Cross
1955	Duquesne	Dayton	Maurice Stokes, St. Francis (Pa.)
1956	Louisville	Dayton	Charlie Tyra, Louisville
1957	Bradley	Memphis St.	Win Wilfong, Memphis St.
1958	Xavier	Dayton	Hank Stein, Xavier
1959	St. John's	Bradley	Tony Jackson, St. John's
1960	Bradley	Providence	Lenny Wilkens, Providence
1961	Providence	St. Louis	Vin Ernst, Providence
1962	Dayton	St. John's	Bill Chmielewski, Dayton
1963	Providence	Canisius	Ray Flynn, Providence
1964	Bradley	New Mexico	Lavern Tart, Bradley
1965	St. John's	Villanova	Ken McIntyre, St. John's
1966	Brigham Young	New York Univ.	Bill Melchionni, Villanova
1967	Southern Illinois	Marquette	Walt Frazier, Southern Illinois
1968	Dayton	Kansas	Don May, Dayton
1969	Temple	Boston College	Terry Driscoll, Boston College
1970	Marquette	St. John's	Dean Meminger, Marquette
1971	North Carolina	Georgia Tech	Bill Chamberlain, N. Carolina
1972	Maryland	Niagara	Tom McMillen, Maryland
1973	Virginia Tech	Notre Dame	John Shumate, Notre Dame
1974	Purdue	Utah	Mike Sojourner, Utah
1975	Princeton	Providence	Ron Lee, Oregon
1976	Kentucky	UNC Charlotte	Cedric Maxwell, UNC Charlotte
1977	St. Bonaventure	Houston	Greg Sanders, St. Bonaventure
1978	Texas	N.C. State	Jim Krivacs and Ron Baxter, Texas
1979	Indiana	Purdue	Butch Carter and Ray Tolbert, Indiana
1980	Virginia	Minnesota	Ralph Sampson, Virginia
1981	Tulsa	Syracuse	Greg Stewart, Tulsa
1982	Bradley	Purdue	Mitchell Anderson, Bradley
1983	Fresno St.	DePaul	Ron Anderson, Fresno St.
1984	Michigan	Notre Dame	Tim McCormick, Michigan
1985	UCLA	Indiana	Reggie Miller, UCLA
1986	Ohio State	Wyoming	Brad Sellers, Ohio State
1987	Southern Miss.	La Salle	Randolph Keys, Southern Miss.
1988	Connecticut	Ohio State	Phil Gamble, Connecticut
1989	St. John's	St. Louis	Jayson Williams, St. John's
1990	Vanderbilt	St. Louis	Scott Draud, Vanderbilt
1991	Stanford	Oklahoma	Adam Keefe, Stanford
1992	Virginia	Notre Dame	Bryant Stith, Virginia
1993	Minnesota	Georgetown	Voshon Lenard, Minnesota
1994	Villanova	Vanderbilt	Doremus Bennerman, Siena

and 1963) won NIT championships before the Big East was formed…. DePaul (1945), St. Louis (1948), Dayton (1962 and 1968), and Marquette (1970) won NIT championships before the Great Midwest was formed.

MOST NIT APPEARANCES (THROUGH 1994)

SCHOOL	APPEARANCES
St. John's*	25
Dayton	17
Bradley*	16
Duquesne	16
Fordham	16
St. Louis	15
Manhattan	15
New Mexico	13
Providence	13
Louisville	12
St. Peter's	12
Temple	12
Villanova	12
DePaul	11
La Salle	11
Memphis State	11
St. Bonaventure	11
Western Kentucky	11
West Virginia	11
Bowling Green State	10
Marquette	10
Seton Hall	10
Utah	10

St. John's (5) and Bradley (4) have the most NIT championships.

8

PLAYER REGISTER

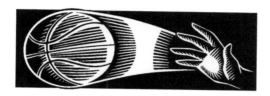

Who were the premier players in major-college history? There's excellence everywhere one turns ... so many greats to choose from ... so many divergent opinions on a seemingly endless list of standout individuals ... so many dilemmas separating pertinent facts from school-submitted fax.

Citing qualifications for determining the cream of the crop is a no-win situation. But in order to whittle the illustrious field of candidates to a manageable number, there must be criteria. Following are the standards used in *Encyclopedia of College Basketball* to determine the greatest college players of all time. There is an emphasis on NBA achievements so as not to forget numerous star players who left college with eligibility remaining.

- NCAA consensus first-team All-American selection or two-time NCAA consensus second-team All-American selection since the NCAA started compiling national statistics in 1948.

- Two-time NCAA consensus first- or second-team All-American selection from the start of the national tournament in 1939 until the NCAA began keeping national statistics.

- Two-time NCAA consensus first-team All-American selection from 1929 until the start of the NCAA Tournament.

- Averaged more than 30 points per game or scored more than 2,750 points in major-college career.

- Collected more than 2,000 points and 1,500 rebounds.

- Led the nation in scoring and rebounding in the same season.

- Two-time national scoring leader.

- Averaged more than 20 points and 20 rebounds per game in college career.

- Two-time All-NCAA Tournament team selection.

- NBA or ABA Most Valuable Player.

- NBA Finals Most Valuable Player.

- Scored more than 15,000 points in NBA and/or ABA career.

- All-NBA first-, second- or third-team selection a minimum of four times.

- Territorial pick or one of the top two choices in an NBA draft since 1955.

The following are abbreviations used throughout this chapter, first in the text, then in the statistical tables.

ABA	American Basketball Association
AP	Associated Press
BAA	Basketball Association of America
NABC	National Association of Basketball Coaches
NBA	National Basketball Association
NBL	National Basketball League
NCAA	National Collegiate Athletic Association
NIT	National Invitation Tournament
ppg	Points per game
UPI	United Press International
USBWA	United States Basketball Writers Association
G	Games played
FGM	Field goals made
FGA	Field goal attempts
FG%	Field goal percentage
FTM	Free throws made
FTA	Free throw attempts
FT%	Free throw percentage
Reb.	Rebounds
Avg.	Average number of rebounds or points per game
Pts.	Points

KAREEM ABDUL-JABBAR
see Lew Alcindor

MAHDI ABDUL-RAHMAD
see Walt Hazzard

MAHMOUD ABDUL-RAUF
see Chris Jackson

MARK AGUIRRE
DePaul
6-6 – F
Chicago, Ill.

Named national player of the year by AP, UPI, and USBWA in 1980.... Naismith Award winner in 1980.... NCAA unanimous first-team All-American in 1980 and 1981.... Leading scorer and second-leading rebounder for 1979 national third-place team (26-6 record).... Member of All-NCAA Tournament team in 1979.... Averaged 20.6 points and 6.1 rebounds in seven NCAA Tournament games from 1979 to 1981 (4-3 record).... Member of 1980 U.S. Olympic team.... Selected as an undergraduate by the Dallas Mavericks in first round of 1981 NBA draft (1st pick overall).

Season	G	FGM	FGA	FG%	FTM	FTA	FT%	Reb.	Avg.	Pts.	Avg.
1978–79	32	302	581	.520	163	213	.765	244	7.6	767	24.0
1979–80	28	281	520	.540	187	244	.766	213	7.6	749	26.8
1980–81	29	280	481	.582	106	137	.774	249	8.6	666	23.0
Totals	89	863	1582	.546	456	594	.768	706	7.9	2182	24.5

DANNY AINGE
Brigham Young
6-5 – G
Eugene, Ore.

Named national player of the year by NABC in 1981.... Wooden Award winner in 1981.... NCAA unanimous first-team All-American in 1981.... Averaged 17.8 points in six NCAA Tournament games from 1979 to 1981 (3-3 record).... Selected by the Boston Celtics in second round of 1981 NBA draft (31st pick overall) after he played three years in the American League as an infielder with the Toronto Blue Jays.

Season	G	FGM	FGA	FG%	FTM	FTA	FT%	Reb.	Avg.	Pts.	Avg.
1977–78	30	243	473	.514	146	169	.864	173	5.8	632	21.1
1978–79	27	206	376	.548	86	112	.768	102	3.8	498	18.4
1979–80	29	229	430	.533	97	124	.782	114	3.9	555	19.1
1980–81	32	309	596	.518	164	199	.824	152	4.8	782	24.4
Totals	118	987	1875	.526	493	604	.816	541	4.6	2467	20.9

LEW ALCINDOR
UCLA
7-2 – C
New York, N.Y.

Named national player of the year by AP, UPI, and the USBWA in 1967 and 1969.... Naismith Award winner in 1969.... NCAA unanimous first-team All-American in 1967, 1968, and 1969.... Led the nation in field-goal shooting in 1967 and 1969.... Named Final Four Most Outstanding Player in 1967, 1968, and 1969.... Leading scorer and rebounder for NCAA champions in 1967 (30-0 record), 1968 (29-1) and 1969 (29-1).... Averaged 25.3 points and 16.8 rebounds in 12 NCAA Tournament games from 1967 to 1969 (12-0 record).... Selected by the Milwaukee Bucks in first round of 1969 NBA draft (1st pick overall).... Changed his name to Kareem Abdul-Jabbar.

Season	G	FGM	FGA	FG%	FTM	FTA	FT%	Reb.	Avg.	Pts.	Avg.
1966–67	30	346	519	.667	178	274	.650	466	15.5	870	29.0
1967–68	28	294	480	.613	146	237	.616	461	16.5	734	26.2
1968–69	30	303	477	.635	115	188	.612	440	14.7	721	24.0
Totals	88	943	1476	.639	439	699	.628	1367	15.5	2325	26.4

STEVE ALFORD
Indiana
6-2 – G
New Castle, Ind.

NCAA unanimous first-team All-American in 1987 and consensus first-team All-American in 1986.... Led the nation in free-throw percentage in 1984.... Leading scorer for 1987 NCAA champion (30-4 record).... Named to All-NCAA Tournament team in 1987.... Averaged 21.3 points in 10 NCAA Tournament games in 1984, 1986 and 1987 (8-2 record).... Averaged 21.6 points in five NIT games for 1985 runner-up.... Member of 1984 U.S. Olympic team.... Selected by the Dallas Mavericks in second round of 1987 NBA draft (26th pick overall).

Season	G	FGM	FGA	FG%	FTM	FTA	FT%	Reb.	Avg.	Pts.	Avg.
1983–84	31	171	289	.592	137	150	.913	82	2.6	479	15.5
1984–85	32	232	431	.538	116	126	.921	101	3.2	580	18.1
1985–86	28	254	457	.556	122	140	.871	75	2.7	630	22.5
1986–87	34	241	508	.474	160	180	.889	87	2.6	749	22.0
Totals	125	898	1685	.533	535	596	.898	345	2.8	2438	19.5

Three-point field goals: 107 of 202 (.530) in 1986–87.

LUCIUS ALLEN
UCLA
6-2 – G
Kansas City, Mo.

NCAA consensus second-team All-American in 1968.... Named to All-NCAA Tournament team in 1967 and 1968.... Second-leading scorer for NCAA champions in 1967 (30-0 record) and 1968 (29-1).... Averaged 15.1 points and 6.8 rebounds in eight NCAA Tournament games in 1967 and 1968 (8-0 record).... Selected by the Seattle SuperSonics in first round of 1969 NBA draft (3rd pick overall).

Season	G	FGM	FGA	FG%	FTM	FTA	FT%	Reb.	Avg.	Pts.	Avg.
1966–67	30	187	390	.479	92	129	.713	175	5.8	466	15.5
1967–68	30	186	403	.462	80	118	.678	181	6.0	452	15.1
1968–69	Did not play because of academic problems.										
Totals	60	373	793	.470	172	247	.696	356	5.9	918	15.3

KENNY ANDERSON
Georgia Tech
6-1 – G
Queens, N.Y.

NCAA unanimous first-team All-American in 1991.... Second-leading scorer and leader in assists for 1990 Final Four team (28-7 record).... Averaged 25.7 points and five assists in seven NCAA Tournament games in 1990 and 1991 (5-2 record).... Selected as an undergraduate by the New Jersey Nets in first round of 1991 NBA draft (2nd pick overall).

Season	G	FGM	FGA	FG%	FTM	FTA	FT%	Reb.	Avg.	Pts.	Avg.
1989–90	35	283	549	.515	107	146	.733	193	5.5	721	20.6
1990–91	30	278	636	.437	155	187	.829	171	5.7	776	25.9
Totals	65	561	1185	.473	262	333	.787	364	5.6	1497	23.0

Three-point field goals: 48 for 117 (.410) in 1989–90 and 65 for 185 (.351) in 1990–91. Totals: 113 for 302 (.374).

NATE ARCHIBALD
Texas-El Paso
6-1 – G
Bronx, N.Y.

Scored 36 points in his only NCAA Tournament game in 1970.... Averaged 29.5 Points in one junior college season at Arizona Western.... Selected by the Cincinnati Royals in second round of 1970 NBA draft (19th pick overall).... Elected to Naismith Memorial Basketball Hall of Fame in 1990.

Season	G	FGM	FGA	FG%	FTM	FTA	FT%	Reb.	Avg.	Pts.	Avg.
1967–68	23	131	281	.466	102	140	.729	81	3.5	364	15.8
1968–69	25	199	374	.532	161	194	.830	69	2.8	559	22.4
1969–70	25	180	351	.513	176	225	.782	66	2.6	536	21.4
Totals	73	510	1006	.507	439	559	.785	216	2.9	1459	20.0

PAUL ARIZIN
Villanova
6-4 – F
Philadelphia, Pa.

Consensus first-team All-American in 1950.... Led the nation in scoring in 1950.... Averaged 26 points in two NCAA Tournament games in 1949 (1-1 record).... Selected by the Philadelphia Warriors in first round of 1950 NBA draft.... Elected to Naismith Memorial Basketball Hall of Fame in 1977.

Season	G	FGM	FGA	FG%	FTM	FTA	FT%	Reb.	Avg.	Pts.	Avg.
1947–48	24	101			65	98	.663			267	11.1
1948–49	27	210			174	233	.747			594	22.0
1949–50	29	260	527	.493	215	278	.773			735	25.3
Totals	80	571			454	609	.745			1596	20.0

WILLIAM (BIRD) AVERITT
Pepperdine
6-1 – G
Hopkinsville, Ky.

Led the nation in scoring in 1973.... Did not play in NCAA Tournament or NIT.... Selected as an undergraduate by the San Diego Conquistadors in second round of 1973 ABA special circumstance draft.

Season	G	FGM	FGA	FG%	FTM	FTA	FT%	Reb.	Avg.	Pts.	Avg.
1971–72	24	263	638	.412	167	225	.742	147	6.1	693	28.9
1972–73	25	352	753	.467	144	211	.682	92	3.7	848	33.9
Totals	49	615	1391	.442	311	436	.713	239	4.9	1541	31.4

CHARLES BARKLEY
Auburn
6-6 – F
Leeds, Ala.

Collected 23 points and 17 rebounds in one NCAA Tournament game in 1984.... Leading scorer (18 points per game) for 1992 U.S. Olympic team.... Selected as an undergraduate by the Philadelphia 76ers in first round of 1984 NBA draft (5th pick overall).

Season	G	FGM	FGA	FG%	FTM	FTA	FT%	Reb.	Avg.	Pts.	Avg.
1981–82	28	144	242	.595	68	107	.636	275	9.8	356	12.7
1982–83	28	161	250	.644	82	130	.631	266	9.5	404	14.4
1983–84	28	162	254	.638	99	145	.683	265	9.5	423	15.1
Totals	84	467	746	.626	249	382	.652	806	9.6	1183	14.1

JIM BARNES
Texas-El Paso
6-8 – F/C
Tuckerman, Ark.

Averaged 17.8 points and 11 rebounds in four NCAA Tournament games in 1963 and 1964 (2-2 record).... Averaged 29.8 points in two junior college seasons at Cameron (Okla.).... Member of 1964 U.S. Olympic team.... Selected by the New York Knicks in first round of 1964 NBA draft (1st pick overall).

Season	G	FGM	FGA	FG%	FTM	FTA	FT%	Reb.	Avg.	Pts.	Avg.
1962–63	26	166	330	.503	160	210	.762	428	16.5	492	18.9
1963–64	28	299	532	.562	218	295	.738	537	19.2	816	29.1
Totals	54	464	862	.540	378	505	.748	965	17.8	1308	24.2

MARVIN BARNES
Providence
6-9 – F/C
Providence, R.I.

NCAA unanimous first-team All-American in 1974.... Led the nation in rebounding in 1974.... Second-leading scorer and leading rebounder for 1973 national fourth-place team (27-4 record).... Averaged 17.1 points and 13.1 rebounds in eight NCAA Tournament games from 1972 to 1974 (5-3 record).... Selected by the Philadelphia 76ers in first round of 1974 NBA draft (2nd pick overall), but he chose to sign a contract with the ABA's Spirits of St. Louis.

Season	G	FGM	FGA	FG%	FTM	FTA	FT%	Reb.	Avg.	Pts.	Avg.
1971–72	27	236	462	.511	112	173	.647	424	15.7	584	21.6
1972–73	30	237	436	.544	237	436	.544	571	19.0	549	18.3
1973–74	32	297	596	.498	112	164	.683	597	18.7	706	22.1
Totals	89	770	1494	.515	461	773	.596	1592	17.9	1839	20.7

RICK BARRY
Miami (Fla.)
6-7 – F
Roselle Park, N.J.

NCAA unanimous first-team All-American in 1965.... Did not play in NCAA Tournament.... Averaged 19.3 points in three NIT games in 1963 and 1964 (1-2 record).... Selected by the San Francisco Warriors in second round of 1965 NBA draft.... Elected to Naismith Memorial Basketball Hall of Fame in 1986.

Season	G	FGM	FGA	FG%	FTM	FTA	FT%	Reb.	Avg.	Pts.	Avg.
1962–63	24	162	341	.475	131	158	.829	351	14.6	455	19.0
1963–64	27	314	572	.549	242	287	.843	448	16.6	870	32.2
1964–65	26	340	651	.522	293	341	.859	475	18.3	973	37.4
Totals	77	816	1564	.522	666	786	.847	1274	16.5	2298	29.8

ELGIN BAYLOR
Seattle
6-6 – F
Washington, D.C.

NCAA unanimous first-team All-American in 1958 and consensus second-team All-American in 1957.... Led the nation in rebounding in 1957.... Named Final Four Most Outstanding Player in 1958.... Leading scorer and rebounder for 1958 national runner-up (24-7 record).... Averaged 27 points in five NCAA Tournament games in 1958 (4-1 record).... Selected as a junior eligible by the Minneapolis Lakers in first round of 1958 NBA draft.... Elected to Naismith Memorial Basketball Hall of Fame in 1976.

Season	G	FGM	FGA	FG%	FTM	FTA	FT%	Reb.	Avg.	Pts.	Avg.
1954–55*	26	332	651	.510	150	232	.647	492	20.5	814	31.3
1955–56			Sat out season after transferring from College of Idaho.								
1956–57	25	271	555	.488	201	251	.801	508	20.3	743	29.7
1957–58	29	353	697	.506	237	308	.769	559	19.3	943	32.5
Totals	80	956	1903	.502	588	791	.743	1559	20.0	2500	31.3

* Rebounds available for 24 of 26 games he played for the College of Idaho his freshman season.

RALPH BEARD
Kentucky
5-11 – G
Louisville, Ky.

NCAA unanimous first-team All-American in 1947 and 1948, and consensus first-team All-American in 1949.... Second-leading scorer for NCAA champions in 1948 (36-3) and 1949 (32-2).... Averaged 9.2 points in six NCAA Tournament games in 1948 and 1949 (6-0 record).... Averaged 12 points in seven NIT games in 1946 (champion), 1947 (runner-up), and 1949 (opening-game loser).... Member of 1948 U.S. Olympic team.... Selected by the Chicago Stags in first round of 1949 BAA draft but a corporation including him and several Kentucky teammates was granted an NBL franchise (the Indianapolis Olympians). When the BAA and NBL merged that summer to form the NBA, the Olympians represented one of the franchises involved in the merger.

Season	G	FGM	FGA	FG%	FTM	FTA	FT%	Reb.	Avg.	Pts.	Avg.
1945–46	30	111			57	110	.518			279	9.3
1946–47	37	157	469	.335	78	115	.678			392	10.6
1947–48	38	194	536	.362	88	149	.591			476	12.5
1948–49	34	144	481	.299	82	115	.713			370	10.9
Totals	139	606			305	489	.624			1517	10.9

ERNIE BECK
Penn
6-4 – F
Philadelphia, Pa.

NCAA consensus first-team All-American in 1953.... Led the nation in rebounding in 1951.... Averaged 23.5 points in two NCAA Tournament games in 1953 (1-1 record).... Selected by the Philadelphia Warriors in 1953 NBA draft.

Season	G	FGM	FGA	FG%	FTM	FTA	FT%	Reb.	Avg.	Pts.	Avg.
1950–51	27	230	532	.432	98	181	.541	556	20.6	558	20.7
1951–52	29	229	561	.408	138	197	.701	551	19.0	596	20.6
1952–53	26	245	625	.392	183	229	.799	450	17.3	673	25.9
Totals	82	704	1718	.410	419	607	.690	1557	19.0	1827	22.3

WALT BELLAMY
Indiana
6-11 – C
New Bern, N.C.

NCAA consensus second-team All-American in 1961.... Did not play in NCAA Tournament.... Member of 1960 U.S. Olympic team.... Selected by the Chicago Packers in first round of 1961 NBA draft (1st pick overall).... Elected to Naismith Memorial Basketball Hall of Fame in 1993.

Season	G	FGM	FGA	FG%	FTM	FTA	FT%	Reb.	Avg.	Pts.	Avg.
1958–59	22	148	289	.512	86	141	.610	335	15.2	382	17.4
1959–60	24	212	396	.535	113	161	.702	324	13.5	537	22.4
1960–61	24	195	389	.501	132	204	.647	428	17.8	522	21.8
Totals	70	555	1074	.517	331	506	.654	1087	15.5	1441	20.6

KENT BENSON
Indiana
6-11 – C
New Castle, Ind.

NCAA unanimous first-team All-American in 1976 and consensus first-team All-American in 1977.... Final Four Most Outstanding Player in 1976.... Leading rebounder and second-leading scorer for undefeated 1976 NCAA champion (32-0 record).... Averaged 19.6 points and 10.9 rebounds in eight NCAA Tournament games in 1975 and 1976 (7-1 record).... Named MVP of 1974 Collegiate Commissioners Association Tournament in powering Indiana to title.... Selected by the Milwaukee Bucks in first round of 1977 NBA draft (1st pick overall).

Season	G	FGM	FGA	FG%	FTM	FTA	FT%	Reb.	Avg.	Pts.	Avg.
1973–74	27	113	224	.504	24	40	.600	222	8.2	250	9.3
1974–75	32	198	366	.541	84	113	.743	286	8.9	480	15.0
1975–76	32	237	410	.578	80	117	.684	282	8.8	554	17.3
1976–77	23	174	346	.503	108	144	.750	241	10.5	456	19.8
Totals	114	722	1346	.536	296	414	.715	1031	9.0	1740	15.3

WALTER BERRY
St. John's
6-8 – F/C
Bronx, N.Y.

Named national player of the year by AP, UPI, USBWA, and NABC in 1986.... Wooden Award winner in 1986.... NCAA unanimous first-team All-American in 1986.... Leading rebounder and second-leading scorer for 1985 Final Four team (31-4 record).... Averaged 20.6 points and 8.6 rebounds in seven NCAA Tournament games in 1985 and 1986 (5-2 record).... Averaged 28.9 points and 14 rebounds in one junior college season at San Jacinto (Tex.).... Selected as an undergraduate by the Portland Trail Blazers in first round of 1986 NBA draft (14th pick overall).

Season	G	FGM	FGA	FG%	FTM	FTA	FT%	Reb.	Avg.	Pts.	Avg.
1982–83			Did not play first year at St. John's due to academic problems.								
1984–85	35	231	414	.558	134	187	.717	304	8.7	596	17.0
1985–86	36	327	547	.598	174	248	.702	399	11.1	828	23.0
Totals	71	558	961	.581	308	435	.708	703	9.9	1424	20.1

LEN BIAS
Maryland
6-8 – F
Landover, Md.

NCAA unanimous first-team All-American in 1986 and consensus second-team All-American in 1985.... Averaged 18.7 points and 7.4 rebounds in nine NCAA Tournament games from 1983 to 1986 (5-4 record).... Selected by the Boston Celtics in first round of 1986 NBA draft (2nd pick overall) but died of a cocaine overdose two days later.

Season	G	FGM	FGA	FG%	FTM	FTA	FT%	Reb.	Avg.	Pts.	Avg.
1982–83	30	86	180	.478	42	66	.636	125	4.2	217	7.2
1983–84	32	211	372	.567	66	86	.767	145	4.5	488	15.3
1984–85	37	274	519	.528	153	197	.777	251	6.8	701	18.9
1985–86	32	267	491	.544	209	242	.864	224	7.0	743	23.2
Totals	131	838	1562	.536	470	591	.795	745	5.7	2149	16.4

Three-point field goals: 3 of 11 (.273) in 1982–83.

HENRY BIBBY
UCLA
6-1 – G
Franklinton, N.C.

NCAA consensus first-team All-American in 1972.... Second-leading scorer for undefeated 1972 NCAA champion (30-0 record), third-leading scorer for 1970 champion (28-2), and fourth-leading scorer for 1971 champion (29-1).... Averaged 15.2 points and 4.4 rebounds in 12 NCAA Tournament games from 1970 to 1972 (12-0 record).... Selected by the New York Knicks in fourth round of 1972 NBA draft (58th pick overall).

Season	G	FGM	FGA	FG%	FTM	FTA	FT%	Reb.	Avg.	Pts.	Avg.
1969–70	30	189	377	.501	90	108	.833	105	3.5	468	15.6
1970–71	30	137	364	.376	81	97	.835	105	3.5	355	11.8
1971–72	30	183	407	.450	104	129	.806	106	3.5	470	15.7
Totals	90	509	1148	.443	275	334	.823	316	3.5	1293	14.4

DAVE BING
Syracuse
6-3 – G
Washington, D.C.

NCAA unanimous first-team All-American in 1966.... Averaged 15 points and 10 rebounds in two NCAA Tournament games in 1966 (1-1 record).... Collected 31 points and nine rebounds in one NIT game in 1964.... Selected by the Detroit Pistons in first round of 1966 NBA draft (2nd pick overall).... Elected to Naismith Memorial Basketball Hall of Fame in 1989.

Season	G	FGM	FGA	FG%	FTM	FTA	FT%	Reb.	Avg.	Pts.	Avg.
1963–64	25	215	460	.467	126	172	.733	206	8.2	556	22.2
1964–65	23	206	444	.464	121	162	.747	277	12.0	533	23.2
1965–66	28	308	569	.541	178	222	.802	303	10.8	794	28.4
Totals	76	729	1473	.495	425	556	.764	786	10.3	1883	24.8

LARRY BIRD
Indiana State
6-9 – F
French Lick, Ind.

Named national player of the year by AP, UPI, USBWA, and NABC in 1979.... Naismith Award and Wooden Award winner in 1979.... NCAA unanimous first-team All-American in 1978 and 1979.... Member of All-NCAA Tournament team in 1979.... Leading scorer and rebounder for 1979 national runner-up (33-1 record).... Averaged 27.2 points and 13.4 rebounds in five NCAA Tournament games in 1979 (4-1 record).... Averaged 31.3 points and 11.7 rebounds in three NIT games in 1977 and 1978 (1-2 record).... Member of 1992 U.S. Olympic team.... Selected as a junior eligible by the Boston Celtics in first round of 1978 NBA draft (6th pick overall).

Season	G	FGM	FGA	FG%	FTM	FTA	FT%	Reb.	Avg.	Pts.	Avg.
1974–75			Left Indiana University before the start of the season.								
1975–76			Sat out the season after transferring to Indiana State.								
1976–77	28	375	689	.544	168	200	.840	373	13.3	918	32.8
1977–78	32	403	769	.524	153	193	.793	369	11.5	959	30.0
1978–79	34	376	707	.532	221	266	.831	505	14.9	973	28.6
Totals	94	1154	2165	.533	542	659	.822	1247	13.3	2850	30.3

OTIS BIRDSONG
Houston
6-4 – G
Winter Haven, Fla.

NCAA consensus first-team All-American in 1977.... Did not play in NCAA Tournament.... Averaged 29 points in four NIT games for 1977 runner-up.... Selected by the Kansas City Kings in first round of 1977 NBA draft (2nd pick overall).

Season	G	FGM	FGA	FG%	FTM	FTA	FT%	Reb.	Avg.	Pts.	Avg.
1973–74	26	154	312	.494	64	92	.696	110	4.2	372	14.3
1974–75	26	268	460	.583	104	143	.727	122	4.7	640	24.6
1975–76	28	302	582	.519	126	191	.660	176	6.3	730	26.1
1976–77	36	452	794	.569	186	249	.747	159	4.4	1090	30.3
Totals	116	1176	2148	.547	480	675	.711	567	4.9	2832	24.4

CHARLES BLACK
Kansas
6-4 – F
Topeka, Kans.

NCAA consensus first-team All-American in 1943 and second-team All-American in 1946.... Averaged 17 points in two NCAA Tournament games in 1942 (1-1 record).

Season	G	FGM	FGA	FG%	FTM	FTA	FT%	Reb.	Avg.	Pts.	Avg.
1941–42	22	101			43	76	.566			245	112.1
1942–43	18	82			42					206	11.4
1943–44	Military Service (Air Force)										
1944–45	Military Service (Air Force)										
1945–46	20	122			82					326	16.3
1946–47	27	107			91	144	.632			305	11.3
Totals	87	412			278					1082	12.4

ROLANDO BLACKMAN
Kansas State
6-6 – G
Brooklyn, N.Y.

Averaged 14.8 points and 4.5 rebounds in six NCAA Tournament games in 1980 and 1981 (4-2 record).... Member of 1980 U.S. Olympic team.... Selected by the Dallas Mavericks in first round of 1981 NBA draft (9th pick overall).

Season	G	FGM	FGA	FG%	FTM	FTA	FT%	Reb.	Avg.	Pts.	Avg.
1977–78	29	127	269	.472	61	93	.656	187	6.4	315	10.9
1978–79	28	200	392	.510	83	113	.735	110	3.9	483	17.3
1979–80	31	226	419	.539	100	145	.690	145	4.7	552	17.8
1980–81	33	202	380	.532	90	115	.783	165	5.0	494	15.0
Totals	121	755	1460	.517	334	466	.717	607	5.0	1844	15.2

RON BONHAM
Cincinnati
6-5 – F
Muncie, Ind.

NCAA consensus first-team All-American in 1963 and consensus second-team All-American in 1964.... Second-leading scorer for 1962 NCAA champion (29-2 record) and leading scorer for 1963 national runner-up (26-2).... Member of All-NCAA Tournament team in 1963.... Averaged 17.8 points in eight NCAA Tournament games in 1962 and 1963 (7-1 record).... Selected by the Boston Celtics in second round of 1964 NBA draft.

Season	G	FGM	FGA	FG%	FTM	FTA	FT%	Reb.	Avg.	Pts.	Avg.
1961–62	31	174	382	.455	95	125	.760	156	5.0	443	14.3
1962–63	28	208	449	.463	173	194	.892	178	6.4	589	21.0
1963–64	26	222	430	.516	190	232	.819	155	6.0	634	24.4
Totals	85	604	1261	.479	458	551	.831	489	5.8	1666	19.6

RON BOONE
Idaho State
6-2 – G
Omaha, Nebr.

Averaged 25.2 points in one junior college season at Iowa Western.... Did not play in NCAA Tournament or NIT.... Selected by the Dallas Chaparrals in eighth round of 1968 ABA draft.

Season	G	FGM	FGA	FG%	FTM	FTA	FT%	Reb.	Avg.	Pts.	Avg.
1965–66	10	46	119	.387	17	26	.654	95	9.5	109	10.9
1966–67	25	199	416	.478	160	215	.744	128	5.1	558	22.3
1967–68	26	223	519	.430	108	159	.679	110	4.2	554	21.3
Totals	61	468	1054	.444	285	400	.713	333	5.5	1221	20.0

BOB BOOZER
Kansas State
6-8 – F
Omaha, Nebr.

NCAA unanimous first-team All-American in 1959 and consensus first-team All-American in 1958.... Leading scorer and rebounder for 1958 national fourth-place team (22-5 record).... Averaged 22 points and 10.7 rebounds in six NCAA Tournament games in 1958 and 1959 (4-2 record).... Member of 1960 U.S. Olympic team.... Selected by the Cincinnati Royals in first round of 1959 NBA draft.

Season	G	FGM	FGA	FG%	FTM	FTA	FT%	Reb.	Avg.	Pts.	Avg.
1956–57	23	136	307	.443	178	231	.771	237	10.3	450	19.6
1957–58	27	195	441	.442	154	215	.716	281	10.4	544	20.1
1958–59	27	247	578	.427	197	258	.764	306	11.3	691	25.6
Totals	77	578	1326	.436	529	704	.751	824	10.7	1685	21.9

VINCE BORYLA
Notre Dame/Denver
6-5 – F
East Chicago, Ind.

NCAA consensus first-team All-American in 1949.... Did not play in NCAA Tournament or NIT.... Member of 1948 U.S. Olympic team.

Season	G	FGM	FGA	FG%	FTM	FTA	FT%	Reb.	Avg.	Pts.	Avg.
1944–45	20	130			62	94	.660			322	16.1
1945–46	21	128	369	.347	65	93	.699			321	15.3
1946–47	Military Service (Army)										
1947–48	Military Service (Army)										
1948–49	33	212			200	253	.791			624	18.9
Totals	74	470			327	440	.743			1267	17.1

Note: Attended Notre Dame his first two seasons before enrolling at Denver for final year in college.

SAM BOWIE
Kentucky
7-1 – C
Lebanon, Pa.

NCAA consensus second-team All-American in 1981.... Leading rebounder and third-leading scorer for 1984 Final Four team (29-5 record).... Averaged

9.7 points and 8.7 rebounds in seven NCAA Tournament games in 1980, 1981 and 1984 (4-3 record).... Member of 1980 U.S. Olympic team.... Selected by the Portland Trail Blazers in first round of 1984 NBA draft (2nd pick overall).

Season	G	FGM	FGA	FG%	FTM	FTA	FT%	Reb.	Avg.	Pts.	Avg.
1979–80	34	165	311	.531	110	144	.764	276	8.1	440	12.9
1980–81	28	185	356	.520	118	164	.720	254	9.1	488	17.4
1981–82	Did not play because of a leg injury.										
1982–83	Did not play because of a leg injury.										
1983–84	34	133	258	.516	91	126	.722	313	9.2	357	10.5
Totals	96	483	925	.522	319	434	.735	843	8.8	1285	13.4

GARY BRADDS
Ohio State
6-8 – C
Jamestown, Ohio

Named national player of the year by AP and UPI in 1964.... NCAA unanimous first-team All-American in 1964 and consensus second-team All-American in 1963.... Sixth-leading scorer for 1962 national runner-up (26-2 record).... Averaged 6.3 points and 3.8 rebounds in four NCAA Tournament games in 1962 (3-1 record).... Selected by the Baltimore Bullets in first round of 1964 NBA draft.

Season	G	FGM	FGA	FG%	FTM	FTA	FT%	Reb.	Avg.	Pts.	Avg.
1961–62	26	50	72	.694	23	40	.575	72	2.8	123	4.7
1962–63	24	237	453	.523	198	248	.798	312	13.0	672	28.0
1963–64	24	276	527	.524	183	231	.792	322	13.4	735	30.6
Totals	74	563	1052	.535	404	519	.778	706	9.5	1530	20.7

BILL BRADLEY
Princeton
6-5 – F
Crystal City, Mo.

Named national player of the year by AP, UPI, and USBWA in 1965.... NCAA unanimous first-team All-American in 1964 and 1965.... Led the nation in free-throw percentage in 1965.... Final Four Most Outstanding Player in 1965.... Leading scorer and rebounder for 1965 national third-place team (23-6 record).... Averaged 33.7 points and 12 rebounds in nine NCAA Tournament games from 1963 to 1965 (5-4 record).... Member of 1964 U.S. Olympic team.... Selected as a territorial pick by the New York Knicks in 1965 NBA draft.... Elected to Naismith Memorial Basketball Hall of Fame in 1982.

Season	G	FGM	FGA	FG%	FTM	FTA	FT%	Reb.	Avg.	Pts.	Avg.
1962–63	25	212	445	.476	258	289	.893	306	12.2	682	27.3
1963–64	29	338	648	.522	260	306	.850	360	12.4	936	32.3
1964–65	29	306	574	.533	273	308	.886	342	11.8	885	30.5
Totals	83	856	1667	.513	791	903	.876	1008	12.1	2503	30.2

SHAWN BRADLEY
Brigham Young
7-6 – C
Castle Dale, Utah

Led NCAA with 5.2 blocked shots per game in 1991.... Averaged nine points, seven rebounds, and six blocked shots in two NCAA Tournament games in 1991 (1-1 record).... Selected as an undergraduate by the Philadelphia 76ers in first round of 1993 NBA draft (2nd pick overall) after spending two years in Australia on a Mormon mission.

Season	G	FGM	FGA	FG%	FTM	FTA	FT%	Reb.	Avg.	Pts.	Avg.
1990–91	34	187	361	.518	128	185	.692	262	7.7	503	14.8

Three-point field goals: 1 of 1 in 1990–91.

JIM BREWER
Minnesota
6-9 – F
Maywood, Ill.

NCAA consensus second-team All-American in 1973.... Averaged 12 points and 18 rebounds in two NCAA Tournament games in 1972 (1-1 record).... Averaged 13.5 points in two NIT games in 1973 (1-1 record).... Member of 1972 U.S. Olympic team.... Selected by the Cleveland Cavaliers in first round of 1973 NBA draft (2nd pick overall).

Season	G	FGM	FGA	FG%	FTM	FTA	FT%	Reb.	Avg.	Pts.	Avg.
1970–71	24	166	413	.402	67	104	.644	331	13.8	399	16.6
1971–72	25	95	260	.365	54	113	.482	275	11.0	244	9.8
1972–73	26	147	317	.464	72	102	.706	301	11.6	366	14.1
Totals	75	408	990	.412	193	319	.605	907	12.1	1009	13.5

GUS BROBERG
Dartmouth
6-1 – G/F
Torrington, Conn.

NCAA consensus first-team All-American in 1940 and 1941.... Averaged 19 points in two NCAA Tournament games in 1941 (1-1 record).

Season	G	FGM	FGA	FG%	FTM	FTA	FT%	Reb.	Avg.	Pts.	Avg.
1938–39	23	127			64	76	.842			318	13.8
1939–40	21	124			57	60	.950			305	14.5
1940–41	23	141			61	76	.803			343	14.9
Totals	67	392			182	212	.858			966	14.4

MICHAEL BROOKS
La Salle
6-7 – F
Philadelphia, Pa.

Named national player of the year by NABC in 1980.... NCAA consensus first-team All-American in 1980.... Averaged 32 points and 13 rebounds in two NCAA Tournament games in 1978 and 1980 (0-2 record).... Leading scorer (13.2 ppg) for 1980 U.S. Olympic team.... Selected by the San Diego Clippers in first round of 1980 NBA draft (9th pick overall).

Season	G	FGM	FGA	FG%	FTM	FTA	FT%	Reb.	Avg.	Pts.	Avg.
1976–77	29	241	490	.492	97	152	.638	311	10.7	579	20.0
1977–78	28	288	490	.588	120	164	.732	358	12.8	696	24.9
1978–79	26	245	443	.553	116	161	.720	347	13.3	606	23.3
1979–80	31	290	553	.524	167	237	.705	356	11.5	747	24.1
Totals	114	1064	1976	.538	500	714	.700	1372	12.0	2628	23.1

BILL BUNTIN
Michigan
6-7 – F/C
Detroit, Mich.

NCAA consensus second-team All-American in 1965.... Leading rebounder and second-leading scorer for 1964 national third-place team (23-5 record) and 1965 national runner-up (24-4).... Named to All-NCAA Tournament team in 1964.... Averaged 22.6 points and 11.4 rebounds in eight NCAA Tournament games in 1964 and 1965 (6-2 record).... Selected as a territorial pick by the Detroit Pistons in 1965 NBA draft.

Season	G	FGM	FGA	FG%	FTM	FTA	FT%	Reb.	Avg.	Pts.	Avg.
1962–63	24	211	491	.430	112	161	.696	376	15.7	534	22.3
1963–64	27	238	481	.495	151	192	.786	338	12.5	627	23.2
1964–65	28	221	454	.487	122	159	.767	323	11.5	564	20.1
Totals	79	670	1426	.470	385	512	.752	1037	13.1	1725	21.8

CARL CAIN
Iowa
6-3 – G
Freeport, Ill.

Member of All-NCAA Tournament team in 1955 and 1956.... Second-leading scorer and rebounder for 1955 national fourth-place team (19-7 record) and 1956 national runner-up (20-6).... Averaged 20.1 points in eight NCAA Tournament games in 1955 and 1956 (5-3 record).... Member of 1956 U.S. Olympic team.... Selected by the Rochester Royals in 1956 NBA draft (did not play in league).

Season	G	FGM	FGA	FG%	FTM	FTA	FT%	Reb.	Avg.	Pts.	Avg.
1953–54	22	106	248	.427	71	119	.597			283	12.9
1954–55	26	133	333	.399	94	140	.671	244	9.4	360	13.8
1955–56	26	165	403	.409	81	112	.723	257	9.9	411	15.8
Totals	74	404	984	.411	246	371	.663			1054	14.2

JOE CALDWELL
Arizona State
6-5 – F
Los Angeles, Calif.

Averaged 22.2 points in five NCAA Tournament games from 1962-64 (2-3 record).... Selected by the Detroit Pistons in first round of 1964 NBA draft (2nd pick overall).

Season	G	FGM	FGA	FG%	FTM	FTA	FT%	Reb.	Avg.	Pts.	Avg.
1961–62	27	141	291	.485	73	115	.635	285	10.6	355	13.1
1962–63	29	239	523	.457	93	152	.612	314	10.8	571	19.7
1963–64	27	231	521	.443	127	193	.658	330	12.2	589	21.8
Totals	83	611	1335	.458	293	460	.637	929	11.2	1515	18.3

AUSTIN CARR
Notre Dame
6-3 – G
Washington, D.C.

Named national player of the year by AP and UPI in 1971.... Naismith Award winner in 1971.... NCAA unanimous first-team All-American in 1971 and consensus second-team All-American in 1970.... Averaged 41.3 points and 7.6 rebounds in seven NCAA Tournament games from 1969 to 1971 (2-5 record).... Selected by the Cleveland Cavaliers in first round of 1971 NBA draft (1st pick overall).

Season	G	FGM	FGA	FG%	FTM	FTA	FT%	Reb.	Avg.	Pts.	Avg.
1968–69	16	143	294	.486	67	85	.788	84	5.3	353	22.1
1969–70	29	444	799	.556	218	264	.826	240	8.3	1106	38.1
1970–71	29	430	832	.517	241	297	.811	214	7.4	1101	38.0
Totals	74	1017	1925	.528	526	646	.814	538	7.3	2560	34.6

JOE BARRY CARROLL
Purdue
7-1 – C
Denver, Colo.

NCAA unanimous first-team All-American in 1980.... Leading scorer and rebounder for 1980 national third-place team (23-10 record).... Member of All-NCAA Tournament team in 1980.... Averaged 23 points and 9.6 rebounds in seven NCAA Tournament games in 1977 and 1980 (5-2 record).... Averaged 25.2 points and 8 rebounds in five NIT games for 1979 runner-up.... Selected by the Golden State Warriors in first round of 1980 NBA draft (1st pick overall).

Season	G	FGM	FGA	FG%	FTM	FTA	FT%	Reb.	Avg.	Pts.	Avg.
1976–77	28	93	187	.497	34	54	.630	206	7.4	220	7.9
1977–78	27	163	312	.522	95	143	.664	288	10.7	421	15.6
1978–79	35	318	545	.583	162	253	.640	352	10.1	798	22.8
1979–80	33	301	558	.539	134	203	.660	302	9.2	736	22.3
Totals	123	875	1602	.546	425	653	.651	1148	9.3	2175	17.7

BILL CARTWRIGHT
San Francisco
6-11 – C
Elk Grove, Calif.

NCAA consensus second-team All-American in 1977 and 1979.... Averaged 24.6 points and nine rebounds in five NCAA Tournament games from 1977 to 1979 (2-3 record).... Scored 5 points in one NIT game in 1976.... Selected by the New York Knicks in first round of 1979 NBA draft (3rd pick overall).

Season	G	FGM	FGA	FG%	FTM	FTA	FT%	Reb.	Avg.	Pts.	Avg.
1975–76	30	151	285	.530	72	98	.735	207	6.9	374	12.5
1976–77	31	241	426	.566	118	161	.733	262	8.5	600	19.4
1977–78	21	168	252	.667	96	131	.733	213	10.1	432	20.6
1978–79	29	268	443	.605	174	237	.734	455	15.7	710	24.5
Totals	111	828	1406	.589	460	627	.734	1137	10.2	2116	19.1

WILT CHAMBERLAIN
Kansas
7-1 – C
Philadelphia, Pa.

NCAA unanimous first-team All-American in 1957 and 1958.... Final Four Most Outstanding Player in 1957.... Leading scorer and rebounder for 1957 national runner-up (24-3 record).... Averaged 30.3 points and 15.5 rebounds in four NCAA Tournament games in 1957 (3-1 record).... Selected as a territorial choice by the Philadelphia Warriors in first round of 1959 NBA draft after he played one season with the Harlem Globetrotters.... Elected to Naismith Memorial Basketball Hall of Fame in 1978.

Season	G	FGM	FGA	FG%	FTM	FTA	FT%	Reb.	Avg.	Pts.	Avg.
1956–57	27	275	588	.468	250	399	.627	510	18.9	800	29.6
1957–58	21	228	482	.473	177	291	.608	367	17.5	633	30.1
Totals	48	503	1070	.470	427	690	.619	877	18.3	1433	29.9

TOM CHAMBERS
Utah
6-10 – F/C
Boulder, Colo.

Averaged 12.8 points and seven rebounds in five NCAA Tournament games from 1978 to 1981 (2-3 record).... Selected by the San Diego Clippers in first round of 1981 NBA draft (8th pick overall).

Season	G	FGM	FGA	FG%	FTM	FTA	FT%	Reb.	Avg.	Pts.	Avg.
1977–78	28	69	139	.496	40	64	.625	104	3.7	178	6.4
1978–79	30	206	379	.544	69	127	.543	266	8.9	481	16.0
1979–80	28	195	359	.543	92	129	.713	244	8.7	482	17.2
1980–81	30	221	372	.594	115	155	.742	262	8.7	557	18.6
Totals	116	691	1249	.553	316	475	.665	876	7.6	1698	14.6

LEN CHAPPELL
Wake Forest
6-8 – F/C
Portage Area, Pa.

NCAA consensus first-team All-American in 1962.... Leading scorer and rebounder for 1962 national third-place team (22-9 record).... Member of All-NCAA Tournament team in 1962.... Averaged 27.6 points and 17.1 rebounds in eight NCAA Tournament games in 1961 and 1962 (6-2 record).... Selected by the Syracuse Nationals in first round of 1962 NBA draft.

Season	G	FGM	FGA	FG%	FTM	FTA	FT%	Reb.	Avg.	Pts.	Avg.
1959–60	28	166	372	.446	156	228	.684	350	12.5	488	17.4
1960–61	28	271	538	.504	203	286	.710	393	14.0	745	26.6
1961–62	31	327	597	.548	278	383	.726	470	15.2	932	30.1
Totals	87	764	1507	.507	637	897	.710	1213	13.9	2165	24.9

CALBERT CHEANEY
Indiana
6-7 – F/G
Evansville, Ind.

Named national player of the year by AP, UPI, NABC, and USBWA in 1993.... Won Naismith Award and Wooden Award in 1993.... NCAA unanimous first-team All-American in 1993.... Leading scorer and third-leading rebounder for 1992 Final Four team (27-7 record).... Averaged 21.5 points and 7.7 rebounds in 13 NCAA Tournament games from 1990-93 (9-4 record).... Selected by the Washington Bullets in first round of 1993 NBA draft (6th pick overall).

Season	G	FGM	FGA	FG%	FTM	FTA	FT%	Reb.	Avg.	Pts.	Avg.
1989–90	29	199	348	.572	72	96	.750	133	4.6	495	17.1
1990–91	34	289	485	.596	113	141	.801	188	5.5	734	21.6
1991–92	34	227	435	.522	112	140	.800	166	4.9	599	17.6
1992–93	35	303	552	.549	132	166	.795	223	6.4	785	22.4
Totals	132	1018	1820	.559	429	543	.790	710	5.4	2613	19.8

Three-point field goals: 25 of 51 (.490) in 1989–90, 43 of 91 (.473) in 1990–91, 33 of 86 (.384) in 1991–92, and 47 of 110 (.427) in 1992–93. **Totals:** 148 of 338 (.438).

JIM CHONES
Marquette
6-11 – C
Racine, Wisc.

NCAA consensus first-team All-American in 1972.... Averaged 22 points and 12 rebounds in three NCAA Tournament games in 1971 (2-1 record).... Signed as an undergraduate by the ABA's New York Nets in 1972.... Drafted by the Los Angeles Lakers in second round of 1973 NBA draft (30th pick overall); rights traded to the Cleveland Cavaliers for a first-round draft choice, May 17, 1974.

Season	G	FGM	FGA	FG%	FTM	FTA	FT%	Reb.	Avg.	Pts.	Avg.
1970–71	29	230	401	.574	60	113	.531	333	11.5	520	17.9
1971–72	21	180	349	.516	72	105	.686	250	11.9	432	20.6
Totals	50	410	750	.547	132	218	.606	583	11.7	952	19.0

JEFF COHEN
William & Mary
6-7 – F/C
Kenosha, Wisc.

Did not play in NCAA Tournament or NIT.... Selected by the Chicago Packers in second round of 1961 NBA draft (did not play in league).

Season	G	FGM	FGA	FG%	FTM	FTA	FT%	Reb.	Avg.	Pts.	Avg.
1957–58	29	146	341	.428	113	164	.689	371	12.8	405	14.0
1958–59	24	150	342	.439	95	142	.669	413	17.2	395	16.5
1959–60	26	230	458	.502	168	232	.724	471	18.1	628	24.2
1960–61	24	193	404	.478	189	246	.768	424	17.7	575	24.0
Totals	103	719	1545	.465	565	784	.721	1679	16.3	2003	19.4

DERRICK COLEMAN
Syracuse
6-9 – F
Detroit, Mich.

NCAA unanimous first-team All-American in 1990.... Leading rebounder and fourth-leading scorer for 1987 national runner-up (31-7 record).... Averaged 12.4 points and 11.1 rebounds in 14 NCAA Tournament games from 1987 to 1990 (10-4 record).... Selected by the New Jersey Nets in first round of 1990 NBA draft (1st pick overall).

Season	G	FGM	FGA	FG%	FTM	FTA	FT%	Reb.	Avg.	Pts.	Avg.
1986–87	38	173	309	.560	107	156	.686	333	8.8	453	11.9
1987–88	35	176	300	.587	121	192	.630	384	11.0	474	13.5
1988–89	37	227	395	.575	171	247	.692	422	11.4	625	16.9
1989–90	33	194	352	.551	188	263	.715	398	12.1	591	17.9
Totals	143	770	1356	.568	587	858	.684	1537	10.7	2143	15.0

Three-point field goals: 1 of 6 (.167) in 1987–88, 0 of 8 in 1988–89, and 15 of 41 (.366) in 1989–90. **Totals:** 16 of 55 (.291).

DOUG COLLINS
Illinois State
6-6 – G
Benton, Ill.

NCAA consensus first-team All-American in 1973.... Did not play in NCAA Tournament or NIT.... Member of 1972 U.S. Olympic team.... Selected by the Philadelphia 76ers in first round of 1973 NBA draft (1st pick overall).

Season	G	FGM	FGA	FG%	FTM	FTA	FT%	Reb.	Avg.	Pts.	Avg.
1970–71	26	273	609	.448	197	235	.838	166	6.4	743	28.6
1971–72	26	352	704	.500	143	177	.808	133	5.1	847	32.6
1972–73	25	269	565	.476	112	137	.818	126	5.0	650	26.0
Totals	77	894	1878	.476	452	549	.823	425	5.5	2240	29.1

BOB COUSY
Holy Cross
6-1 – G
Queens, N.Y.

NCAA unanimous first-team All-American in 1950.... Third-leading scorer for 1947 NCAA champion (27-3 record).... Averaged 10.6 points in eight NCAA Tournament games from 1947 to 1950 (5-3 record).... NBA rights to 1950 first-round draft choice were drawn out of a hat by the Boston Celtics for $8,500 in dispersal of Chicago Stags franchise.... Elected to Naismith Memorial Basketball Hall of Fame in 1970.

Season	G	FGM	FGA	FG%	FTM	FTA	FT%	Reb.	Avg.	Pts.	Avg.
1946–47	30	91			45					227	7.6
1947–48	30	207			72	108	.667			486	16.2
1948–49	27	195			90	134	.672			480	17.8
1949–50	30	216	659	.328	150	199	.754			582	19.4
Totals	117	709			357					1775	15.2

DAVE COWENS
Florida State
6-9 – C
Newport, Ky.

Collected 11 points and four rebounds in one NCAA Tournament game in 1968.... Selected by the Boston Celtics in first round of 1970 NBA draft (4th pick overall).... Elected to Naismith Memorial Basketball Hall of Fame in 1990.

Season	G	FGM	FGA	FG%	FTM	FTA	FT%	Reb.	Avg.	Pts.	Avg.
1967–68	27	206	383	.538	96	131	.733	456	16.9	508	18.8
1968–69	25	202	384	.526	104	164	.634	437	17.5	588	20.3
1969–70	26	174	355	.490	115	169	.680	447	17.2	463	17.8
Totals	78	582	1122	.519	315	464	.679	1340	17.2	1479	19.0

JOHNNY COX
Kentucky
6-4 – F
Hazard, Ky.

NCAA consensus first-team All-American in 1959.... Leading rebounder and second-leading scorer for 1958 NCAA champion (23-6 record).... Member of All-NCAA Tournament team in 1958.... Averaged 18.9 points in eight NCAA Tournament games from 1957 to 1959 (6-2 record).... Selected by the New York Knicks in fourth round of 1959 NBA draft.

Season	G	FGM	FGA	FG%	FTM	FTA	FT%	Reb.	Avg.	Pts.	Avg.
1956–57	28	203	490	.414	138	180	.767	310	11.1	544	19.4
1957–58	29	173	471	.367	86	115	.748	365	12.6	432	14.9
1958–59	27	188	464	.405	109	146	.747	329	12.2	485	18.0
Totals	84	564	1425	.396	333	441	.755	1004	12.0	1461	17.4

CLAIRE CRIBBS
Pittsburgh
6-2 – G
Jeannette, Pa.

NCAA consensus first-team All-American in 1934 and 1935.

STATISTICS NOT AVAILABLE.

TERRY CUMMINGS
DePaul
6-9 – F
Chicago, Ill.

NCAA unanimous first-team All-American in 1982.... Averaged 16.3 points and 9.7 rebounds in three NCAA Tournament games from 1980 to 1982 (0-3 record).... Selected as an undergraduate by the San Diego Clippers in first round of 1982 NBA draft (2nd pick overall).

Season	G	FGM	FGA	FG%	FTM	FTA	FT%	Reb.	Avg.	Pts.	Avg.
1979–80	28	154	303	.508	89	107	.832	263	9.4	397	14.2
1980–81	29	151	303	.498	75	100	.750	260	9.0	377	13.0
1981–82	28	244	430	.567	136	180	.756	334	11.9	624	22.3
Totals	85	549	1036	.530	300	387	.775	857	10.1	1398	16.4

BILLY CUNNINGHAM
North Carolina
6-6 – F
Brooklyn, N.Y.

Did not play in NCAA Tournament or NIT.... Selected by the Philadelphia 76ers in first round of 1965 NBA draft.... Elected to Naismith Memorial Basketball Hall of Fame in 1985.

Season	G	FGM	FGA	FG%	FTM	FTA	FT%	Reb.	Avg.	Pts.	Avg.
1962–63	21	186	380	.489	105	170	.618	339	16.1	477	22.7
1963–64	24	233	526	.443	157	249	.631	379	15.8	623	26.0
1964–65	24	237	481	.493	135	213	.634	344	14.3	609	25.4
Totals	69	656	1387	.473	397	632	.628	1062	15.4	1709	24.8

QUINTIN DAILEY
San Francisco
6-3 – G
Baltimore, Md.

NCAA consensus first-team All-American in 1982.... Averaged 24 points in two NCAA Tournament games in 1981 and 1982 (0-2 record).... Selected as an undergraduate by the Chicago Bulls in first round of 1982 NBA draft (7th pick overall).

Season	G	FGM	FGA	FG%	FTM	FTA	FT%	Reb.	Avg.	Pts.	Avg.
1979–80	29	154	292	.527	85	134	.634	107	3.7	393	13.6
1980–81	31	267	467	.572	159	208	.764	170	5.5	693	22.4
1981–82	30	286	524	.546	183	232	.789	156	5.2	755	25.2
Totals	90	707	1283	.551	427	574	.744	433	4.8	1841	20.5

LOUIE DAMPIER
Kentucky
6-0 – G
Indianapolis, Ind.

NCAA consensus second-team All-American in 1966 and 1967.... Second-leading scorer for 1966 national runner-up (27-2 record).... Averaged 22.8 points and 6.3 rebounds in four NCAA Tournament games in 1966 (3-1 record).... Selected by the Kentucky Colonels in first round of 1967 ABA draft.

Season	G	FGM	FGA	FG%	FTM	FTA	FT%	Reb.	Avg.	Pts.	Avg.
1964–65	25	171	334	.512	84	100	.840	123	4.9	426	17.0
1965–66	29	249	482	.517	114	137	.832	144	5.0	612	21.1
1966–67	26	219	443	.494	99	119	.832	142	5.5	537	20.7
Totals	80	639	1259	.508	297	356	.834	409	5.1	1575	19.7

MEL DANIELS
New Mexico
6-9 – C
Detroit, Mich.

NCAA consensus second-team All-American in 1967.... Averaged 18.3 points in three NIT games in 1965 and 1967 (1-2 record).... Averaged 22.6 points in one junior college season at Burlington (Iowa).... Selected by the Minnesota Muskies in first five rounds of 1967 ABA draft.

Season	G	FGM	FGA	FG%	FTM	FTA	FT%	Reb.	Avg.	Pts.	Avg.
1964–65	27	178	366	.486	111	182	.609	302	11.2	467	17.3
1965–66	23	191	394	.485	107	145	.738	238	10.3	489	21.2
1966–67	27	225	468	.481	131	191	.686	313	11.6	581	21.5
Totals	77	594	1228	.484	349	518	.674	853	11.1	1537	20.0

ADRIAN DANTLEY
Notre Dame
6-5 – F
Washington, D.C.

Named national player of the year by USBWA in 1976.... NCAA unanimous first-team All-American in 1975 and 1976.... Averaged 25.4 points and 8.3 rebounds in eight NCAA Tournament games from 1974 to 1976 (4-4 record).... Member of 1976 U.S. Olympic team who holds U.S. record for highest scoring average in a single Olympiad (19.3 points per game).... Selected as an undergraduate by the Buffalo Braves in first round of 1976 NBA draft (6th pick overall).

Season	G	FGM	FGA	FG%	FTM	FTA	FT%	Reb.	Avg.	Pts.	Avg.
1973–74	28	189	339	.558	133	161	.826	255	9.7	511	18.3
1974–75	29	315	581	.542	253	314	.806	296	10.2	883	30.4
1975–76	29	300	510	.588	229	294	.779	292	10.1	829	28.6
Totals	86	804	1430	.562	615	769	.800	843	9.8	2223	25.8

CHUCK DARLING
Iowa
6-8 – C
Denver, Colo.

NCAA unanimous first-team All-American in 1952.... Did not play in NCAA Tournament or NIT.... Member of 1956 U.S. Olympic team.... Selected by the Rochester Royals in 1952 NBA draft (did not play in league).

Season	G	FGM	FGA	FG%	FTM	FTA	FT%	Reb.	Avg.	Pts.	Avg.
1949–50	19	67	212	.316	41	65	.631			175	9.2
1950–51	22	139	376	.370	80	120	.667	387	17.6	358	16.3
1951–52	22	204	489	.417	153	218	.702			561	25.5
Totals	63	410	1077	.381	274	403	.680			1094	17.4

BRAD DAUGHERTY
North Carolina
7-0 – C
Swannanoa, N.C.

NCAA consensus second-team All-American in 1986.... Led the nation in field-goal shooting in 1986.... Averaged 14.2 points and 8.8 rebounds in 12 NCAA Tournament games from 1983 to 1986 (8-4 record).... Selected by the Cleveland Cavaliers in first round of 1986 NBA draft (1st pick overall).

Season	G	FGM	FGA	FG%	FTM	FTA	FT%	Reb.	Avg.	Pts.	Avg.
1982–83	35	110	197	.558	67	101	.663	181	5.2	287	8.2
1983–84	30	128	210	.610	59	87	.678	167	5.6	315	10.5
1984–85	36	238	381	.625	147	198	.742	349	9.7	623	17.3
1985–86	34	284	438	.648	119	174	.684	306	9.0	687	20.2
Totals	133	760	1226	.620	392	560	.700	1003	7.5	1912	14.2

Three-point field goals: 0 of 1 in 1982–83.

BOB DAVIES
Seton Hall
6-1 – G
Harrisburg, Pa.

NCAA first-team All-American in 1942.... Did not play in NCAA Tournament.... Averaged 11.3 points in three NIT games for 1941 third-place finisher (1-2 record).... Signed as a free agent in 1945 by the NBL's Rochester Royals, which transferred to the BAA for 1948–49 campaign before the NBL and BBA merged to form the NBA for the 1949–50 season.... Coached his alma mater to a 24-3 record in 1946–47, which was the same season he also earned NBL Most Valuable Player honors (averaged 14.3 points in 43 regular-season and playoff games with Rochester).... Elected to Naismith Memorial Basketball Hall of Fame in 1969.

Season	G	FGM	FGA	FG%	FTM	FTA	FT%	Reb.	Avg.	Pts.	Avg.
1939–40	18	78			56					212	11.8
1940–41	22	91			42					224	10.2
1941–42	19	81			63					225	11.8
Totals	59	250			161					661	11.2

WALTER DAVIS
North Carolina
6-6 – G/F
Charlotte, N.C.

Second-leading scorer and rebounder for 1977 national runner-up (28-5 record).... Named to All-NCAA Tournament team in 1977.... Averaged 14.1 points and 5.4 rebounds in eight NCAA Tournament games from 1975 to 1977 (5-3 record; did not play in 1977 opener).... Scored 18 points in one NIT game in 1974.... Member of 1976 U.S. Olympic team.... Selected by the Phoenix Suns in first round of 1977 NBA draft (5th pick overall).

Season	G	FGM	FGA	FG%	FTM	FTA	FT%	Reb.	Avg.	Pts.	Avg.
1973–74	27	161	322	.500	65	82	.793	126	4.7	387	14.3
1974–75	31	200	396	.505	98	130	.754	195	6.3	498	16.1
1975–76	29	190	351	.541	101	130	.777	166	5.7	481	16.6
1976–77	32	203	351	.578	91	117	.778	183	5.7	497	15.5
Totals	119	754	1420	.531	355	459	.773	670	5.6	1863	15.7

JOHNNY DAWKINS
Duke
6-2 – G
Washington, D.C.

Naismith Award winner in 1986.... NCAA unanimous first-team All-American in 1986 and consensus first-team All-American in 1985.... Leading scorer, runner-up in assists and third-leading rebounder for 1986 national runner-up (37-3 record).... Named to All-NCAA Tournament team in 1986.... Averaged 23.8 points and 5.3 rebounds in nine NCAA Tournament games from 1984 to 1986 (6-3 record).... Selected by the San Antonio Spurs in first round of 1986 NBA draft (10th pick overall).

Season	G	FGM	FGA	FG%	FTM	FTA	FT%	Reb.	Avg.	Pts.	Avg.
1982–83	28	207	414	.500	73	107	.682	115	4.1	506	18.1
1983–84	34	263	547	.481	133	160	.831	138	4.1	659	19.4
1984–85	31	225	455	.495	132	166	.795	141	4.5	582	18.8
1985–86	40	331	603	.549	147	181	.812	142	3.6	809	20.2
Totals	133	1026	2019	.508	485	614	.790	536	4.0	2556	19.2

Three-point field goals: 19 of 54 (.352) in 1982–83.

DAVE DEBUSSCHERE
Detroit
6-5 – F
Detroit, Mich.

Scored 38 points and grabbed 19 rebounds in one NCAA Tournament game in 1962.... Averaged 19 points in two NIT games in 1960 and 1961.... Selected as a territorial pick by the Detroit Pistons in first round of 1962 NBA draft.... Elected to Naismith Memorial Basketball Hall of Fame in 1982.

Season	G	FGM	FGA	FG%	FTM	FTA	FT%	Reb.	Avg.	Pts.	Avg.
1959–60	27	288	656	.433	115	196	.587	540	20.0	691	25.6
1960–61	27	256	636	.403	86	155	.555	514	19.0	598	22.1
1961–62	26	267	616	.433	162	242	.669	498	19.2	696	26.8
Totals	80	811	1917	.423	363	593	.612	1552	19.4	1985	24.8

ARCHIE DEES
Indiana
6-8 – C
Mt. Carmel, Ill.

NCAA consensus second-team All-American in 1958.... Averaged 26.5 points and 14.5 rebounds in two NCAA Tournament games in 1958 (1-1 record).... Selected by the Cincinnati Royals in first round of 1958 NBA draft (2nd pick overall).

Season	G	FGM	FGA	FG%	FTM	FTA	FT%	Reb.	Avg.	Pts.	Avg.
1955–56	22	140	332	.422	103	127	.811			383	17.4
1956–57	22	187	440	.425	176	209	.842			550	25.0
1957–58	24	230	480	.479	153	186	.823	345	14.4	613	25.5
Totals	68	557	1252	.445	432	522	.828			1546	22.7

ERNIE DIGREGORIO
Providence
6-0 – G
North Providence, R.I.

NCAA consensus first-team All-American in 1973.... Leading scorer for national fourth-place team in 1973 (27-4 record).... Member of All-NCAA Tournament team in 1973.... Averaged 24.2 points and 6.5 assists in six NCAA Tournament games in 1972 and 1973 (3-3 record).... Averaged 21.5 points in two NIT games in 1971.... Selected by the Buffalo Braves in first round of 1973 NBA draft (3rd pick overall).

Season	G	FGM	FGA	FG%	FTM	FTA	FT%	Reb.	Avg.	Pts.	Avg.
1970–71	28	217	451	.481	88	106	.830	112	4.0	522	18.6
1971–72	27	192	440	.436	93	116	.802	81	3.0	477	17.7
1972–73	31	348	728	.478	65	81	.802	99	3.2	761	24.5
Totals	86	757	1619	.468	246	303	.812	292	3.4	1760	20.5

TERRY DISCHINGER
Purdue
6-7 – F
Terre Haute, Ind.

NCAA unanimous first-team All-American in 1961 and 1962, and consensus second-team All-American in 1960.... Did not play in NCAA Tournament or NIT.... Member of 1960 U.S. Olympic team.... Selected by the Chicago Zephyrs in second round of 1962 NBA draft.

Season	G	FGM	FGA	FG%	FTM	FTA	FT%	Reb.	Avg.	Pts.	Avg.
1959–60	23	201	368	.546	203	260	.781	328	14.3	605	26.3
1960–61	23	215	373	.576	218	261	.835	308	13.4	648	28.2
1961–62	24	217	404	.537	292	350	.834	322	13.4	726	30.3
Totals	70	633	1145	.553	713	871	.819	958	13.7	1979	28.3

CLYDE DREXLER
Houston
6-6 – F/G
Houston, Tex.

NCAA second-team All-American in 1983.... Second-leading scorer and leading rebounder for 1982 Final Four team (25-8 record) and second-leading scorer and second-leading rebounder for 1983 national runner-up (31-3).... Averaged 13.4 points and 6.9 rebounds in 11 NCAA Tournament games from 1981 to 1983 (8-3 record).... Member of 1992 U.S. Olympic team.... Selected as an undergraduate by the Portland Trail Blazers in first round of 1983 NBA draft (14th pick overall).

Season	G	FGM	FGA	FG%	FTM	FTA	FT%	Reb.	Avg.	Pts.	Avg.
1980–81	30	153	303	.505	50	85	.588	314	10.5	356	11.9
1981–82	32	206	362	.569	73	120	.608	336	10.5	485	15.2
1982–83	34	236	440	.536	70	95	.737	298	8.8	542	15.9
Totals	96	595	1105	.538	193	300	.643	948	9.9	1383	14.4

WALTER DUKES
Seton Hall
6-10 – C
Rochester, N.Y.

NCAA unanimous first-team All-American in 1953.... One of six players to average more than 20 points and 20 rebounds per game in his career.... Did not play in NCAA Tournament.... NIT Most Valuable Player in 1953.... Averaged 22.5 points in four NIT games in 1952 (first-round loser) and 1953 (champion).... Played two full seasons with the Harlem Globetrotters before signing with the New York Knicks, who picked him in the 1953 NBA draft.

Season	G	FGM	FGA	FG%	FTM	FTA	FT%	Reb.	Avg.	Pts.	Avg.
1951–52	26	169	402	.420	186	280	.664	513	19.7	524	20.2
1952–53	33	272	574	.474	317	426	.744	734	22.2	861	26.1
Totals	59	441	976	.452	503	706	.712	1247	21.1	1385	23.5

JOE DUMARS
McNeese State
6-3 – G
Natchitoches, La.

Did not play in NCAA Tournament or NIT.... Selected by the Detroit Pistons in first round of 1985 NBA draft (18th pick overall).

Season	G	FGM	FGA	FG%	FTM	FTA	FT%	Reb.	Avg.	Pts.	Avg.
1981–82	29	206	464	.444	115	160	.719	64	2.1	527	18.2
1982–83	29	212	487	.435	140	197	.711	128	4.4	569	19.6
1983–84	31	275	586	.469	267	324	.824	164	5.3	817	26.4
1984–85	27	248	501	.495	201	236	.852	132	4.9	697	25.8
Totals	116	941	2038	.462	723	917	.788	488	4.2	2610	22.5

Three-point field goals: 5 of 8 (.625) in 1982–83.

SEAN ELLIOTT
Arizona
6-8 – F
Tucson, Ariz.

Named national player of the year by AP and NABC in 1989.... Wooden Award winner in 1989.... NCAA unanimous first-team All-American in 1988 and 1989.... Member of All-NCAA Tournament team in 1988.... Leading scorer and rebounder for 1988 Final Four team (35-3 record).... Averaged 23.6 points and 6.8 rebounds in 10 NCAA Tournament games from 1986 to 1989 (6-4 record).... Selected by the San Antonio Spurs in first round of 1989 NBA draft (3rd pick overall).

Season	G	FGM	FGA	FG%	FTM	FTA	FT%	Reb.	Avg.	Pts.	Avg.
1985–86	32	187	385	.486	125	167	.749	171	5.3	499	15.6
1986–87	30	209	410	.510	127	165	.770	181	6.0	578	19.3
1987–88	38	263	461	.570	176	222	.793	219	5.8	743	19.6
1988–89	33	237	494	.480	195	232	.841	237	7.2	735	22.3
Totals	133	896	1750	.512	623	786	.793	808	6.1	2555	19.2

Three-point field goals: 33 of 89 (.371) in 1986–87, 41 of 87 (.471) in 1987–88 and 66 of 151 (.437) in 1988–89. **Totals:** 140 of 327 (.428).

DALE ELLIS
Tennessee
6-7 – F
Marietta, Ga.

NCAA consensus first-team All-American in 1983 and consensus second-team All-American in 1982.... Averaged 14.5 points and 5.5 rebounds in eight NCAA Tournament games from 1980 to 1983 (4-4 record).... Selected by the Dallas Mavericks in first round of 1983 NBA draft (9th pick overall).

Season	G	FGM	FGA	FG%	FTM	FTA	FT%	Reb.	Avg.	Pts.	Avg.
1979–80	27	81	182	.445	31	40	.775	96	3.6	193	7.1
1980–81	29	215	360	.597	83	111	.748	185	6.4	513	17.7
1981–82	30	257	393	.654	121	152	.796	189	6.3	635	21.2
1982–83	32	279	464	.601	166	221	.751	209	6.5	724	22.6
Totals	118	832	1399	.595	401	524	.765	679	5.8	2065	17.5

PERVIS ELLISON
Louisville
6-9 – F/C
Savannah, Ga.

NCAA consensus first-team All-American in 1989.... Final Four Most Outstanding Player in 1986.... Member of All-NCAA Tournament team in 1986.... Third-leading scorer and leading rebounder for 1986 NCAA champion (32-7 record).... Averaged 17 points and 10.1 rebounds in 12 NCAA Tournament games in 1986, 1988, and 1989 (10-2 record).... Selected by the Sacramento Kings in first round of 1989 NBA draft (1st pick overall).

Season	G	FGM	FGA	FG%	FTM	FTA	FT%	Reb.	Avg.	Pts.	Avg.
1985–86	39	210	379	.554	90	132	.682	318	8.2	510	13.1
1986–87	31	185	347	.533	100	139	.719	270	8.7	470	15.2
1987–88	35	235	391	.601	146	211	.692	291	8.3	617	17.6
1988–89	31	227	369	.615	92	141	.652	270	8.7	546	17.6
Totals	136	857	1486	.577	428	623	.687	1149	8.4	2143	15.8

Three-point field goals: 1 of 2 (.500) in 1987–88 and 0 of 1 in 1988–89. Totals: 1 of 3 (.333).

ALEX ENGLISH
South Carolina
6-7 – F
Columbia, S.C.

Averaged 16.8 points and 11 rebounds in four NCAA Tournament games in 1973 and 1974 (2-2 record).... Averaged 15.5 points in two NIT games in 1975.... Selected by the Milwaukee Bucks in second round of 1976 NBA draft (23rd pick overall).

Season	G	FGM	FGA	FG%	FTM	FTA	FT%	Reb.	Avg.	Pts.	Avg.
1972–73	29	189	368	.514	44	70	.629	306	10.6	422	14.6
1973–74	27	209	395	.529	75	112	.670	237	8.8	493	18.3
1974–75	28	199	359	.554	49	77	.636	244	8.7	447	16.0
1975–76	27	258	468	.551	94	134	.701	277	10.3	610	22.6
Totals	111	855	1590	.538	262	393	.667	1064	9.6	1972	17.8

JULIUS ERVING
Massachusetts
6-6 – F
Roosevelt, N.Y.

One of six players to average more than 20 points and 20 rebounds per game in his career.... Did not play in NCAA Tournament.... Averaged 15.5 points in two NIT games in 1970 and 1971 (0-2 record).... Selected by the Milwaukee Bucks in first round of 1972 NBA draft (12th pick overall) although he was already playing in the ABA after signing as an undergraduate free agent with the Virginia Squires.... Elected to Naismith Memorial Basketball Hall of Fame in 1993.

Season	G	FGM	FGA	FG%	FTM	FTA	FT%	Reb.	Avg.	Pts.	Avg.
1969–70	25	238	468	.509	167	230	.726	522	20.9	643	25.7
1970–71	27	286	609	.470	155	206	.752	527	19.5	727	26.9
Totals	52	524	1077	.487	322	436	.739	1049	20.2	1370	26.3

PATRICK EWING
Georgetown
7-0 – C
Cambridge, Mass.

Named national player of the year by AP and NABC in 1985.... Naismith Award winner in 1985.... NCAA unanimous first-team All-American in 1984 and 1985, and consensus first-team All-American in 1983.... Final Four Most Outstanding Player in 1984.... Member of All-NCAA Tournament team in 1982, 1984, and 1985.... Leading scorer and rebounder for 1984 NCAA champion (34-3 record) and 1985 national runner-up (35-3).... Second-leading scorer and leading rebounder for 1982 national runner-up (30-7).... Averaged 14.2 points and eight rebounds in 18 NCAA Tournament games from 1982 to 1985 (15-3 record).... Member of 1984 and 1992 U.S. Olympic teams .... Selected by the New York Knicks in first round of 1985 NBA draft (1st pick overall).

Season	G	FGM	FGA	FG%	FTM	FTA	FT%	Reb.	Avg.	Pts.	Avg.
1981–82	37	183	290	.631	103	167	.617	279	7.5	469	12.7
1982–83	32	212	372	.570	141	224	.629	325	10.2	565	17.7
1983–84	37	242	368	.658	124	189	.656	371	10.0	608	16.4
1984–85	37	220	352	.625	102	160	.638	341	9.2	542	14.6
Totals	143	857	1382	.620	470	740	.635	1316	9.2	2184	15.3

ARNIE FERRIN
Utah
6-4 – F
Ogden, Utah

NCAA consensus first-team All-American in 1945 and second-team All-American in 1947 and 1948.... Final Four Most Outstanding Player in 1944.... Leading scorer with 13.3 points per game during 1944 tournament for NCAA champion (22-4 record).... Did not play in the 1945 playoffs after entering the service the day after the regular season ended.... Averaged 13.5 points in four NIT games in 1944 (first-round loser) and 1947 (champion).

Season	G	FGM	FGA	FG%	FTM	FTA	FT%	Reb.	Avg.	Pts.	Avg.
1943–44	24	127			47					301	12.5
1944–45	18									315	17.4
1945–46		Military Service (Army)									
1946–47	20	82			63					227	11.4
1947-48	20	96			90					282	14.1
Totals	82									1125	13.7

DANNY FERRY
Duke
6-10 – F/C
Bowie, Md.

Named national player of the year by UPI and NABC in 1989.... Naismith
Award winner in 1989.... NCAA unanimous first-team All-American in 1989
and consensus second-team All-American in 1988.... Member of All-NCAA
Tournament team in 1989.... Leading scorer and rebounder for Final Four
teams in 1988 (28-7 record) and 1989 (28-8).... Sixth-leading scorer and
second-leading rebounder for 1986 national runner-up (37-3).... Averaged
14.2 points and 6.9 rebounds in 19 NCAA Tournament games from 1986-89
(15-4 record).... Selected by the Los Angeles Clippers in first round of 1989
NBA draft (2nd pick overall); the Clippers subsequently traded his draft
rights to the Cleveland Cavaliers.

Season	G	FGM	FGA	FG%	FTM	FTA	FT%	Reb.	Avg.	Pts.	Avg.
1985–86	40	91	198	.460	54	86	.628	221	5.5	236	5.9
1986–87	33	172	383	.449	92	109	.844	256	7.8	461	14.0
1987–88	35	247	519	.476	135	163	.828	266	7.6	667	19.1
1988–89	35	300	575	.522	146	193	.756	260	7.4	791	22.6
Totals	143	810	1675	.484	427	551	.775	1003	7.0	2155	15.1

Three-point field goals: 25 of 63 (.397) in 1986–87, 38 of 109 (.349) in
1987–88, and 45 of 106 (.425) in 1988–89. Totals: 108 of 278 (.388).

ROD FLETCHER
Illinois
6-4 – G
Champaign, Ill.

NCAA consensus first-team All-American in 1952.... Second-leading scorer
for 1952 national third-place finisher (22-4 record) and third-leading scorer
for 1951 national third-place finisher (22-5).... Averaged 14 points in eight
NCAA Tournament games in 1951 and 1952 (6-2 record).... Selected by the
Minneapolis Lakers in 1952 NBA draft (did not play in league).

Season	G	FGM	FGA	FG%	FTM	FTA	FT%	Reb.	Avg.	Pts.	Avg.
1949–50	22	39	176	.222	24	48	.500			102	4.6
1950–51	27	115	338	.340	60	111	.541			290	10.7
1951–52	22	90	311	.289	65	116	.560			245	11.1
Totals	71	244	825	.296	149	275	.542			637	9.0

DARRELL FLOYD
Furman
6-1 – G/F
Morehead, Ky.

NCAA consensus second-team All-American in 1955 and 1956.... Led the
nation in scoring in 1955 and 1956.... Did not play in NCAA Tournament or
NIT.... Selected by the St. Louis Hawks in third round of 1956 NBA draft
(did not play in league).

Season	G	FGM	FGA	FG%	FTM	FTA	FT%	Reb.	Avg.	Pts.	Avg.
1953–54	18	185	417	.444	68	81	.840	141	7.8	438	24.3
1954–55	25	344	796	.432	209	267	.783	208	8.3	897	35.9
1955–56	28	339	850	.399	268	350	.766	262	9.4	946	33.8
Totals	71	868	2063	.421	545	698	.781	611	8.6	2281	32.1

ERIC (SLEEPY) FLOYD
Georgetown
6-3 – G
Gastonia, N.C.

NCAA unanimous first-team All-American in 1982.... Member of All-NCAA
Tournament team in 1982.... Leading scorer and third-leading rebounder for
1982 national runner-up (30-7 record).... Averaged 18 points in 10 NCAA
Tournament games from 1979 to 1982 (6-4 record).... Selected by the New
Jersey Nets in first round of 1982 NBA draft (13th pick overall).

Season	G	FGM	FGA	FG%	FTM	FTA	FT%	Reb.	Avg.	Pts.	Avg.
1978–79	29	177	388	.456	126	155	.813	119	4.1	480	16.6
1979–80	32	246	444	.554	106	140	.757	98	3.1	598	18.7
1980–81	32	237	508	.467	133	165	.806	133	4.2	607	19.0
1981–82	37	249	494	.504	121	168	.720	127	3.4	619	16.7
Totals	130	909	1834	.496	486	628	.774	477	3.7	2304	17.7

ALPHONSO FORD
Mississippi Valley State
6-1 – G
Greenwood, Miss.

Scored 16 points in one NCAA Tournament game in 1992.... Selected by
the Philadelphia 76ers in second round of 1993 NBA draft (did not play in
league).

Season	G	FGM	FGA	FG%	FTM	FTA	FT%	Reb.	Avg.	Pts.	Avg.
1989–90	27	289	656	.441	126	171	.737	133	4.9	808	29.9
1990–91	28	325	668	.487	179	234	.765	167	6.0	915	32.7
1991–92	26	255	567	.450	137	181	.757	145	5.6	714	27.5
1992–93	28	252	578	.436	148	187	.791	147	5.3	728	26.0
Totals	109	1121	2469	.454	590	773	.763	592	5.4	3165	29.0

Three-point field goals: 104 of 288 (.361) in 1989–90, 86 of 260 (.331) in
1990–91, 67 of 221 (.303) in 1991–92, and 76 of 216 (.352) in 1992–93.
Totals: 333 of 985 (.338).

PHIL FORD
North Carolina
6-2 – G
Rocky Mount, N.C.

Named national player of the year by NABC and USBWA in 1978.... Wooden
Award winner in 1978.... NCAA unanimous first-team All-American in 1978,
consensus first-team All-American in 1977 and consensus second-team All-
American in 1977.... Leading scorer for 1977 national runner-up (28-5
record).... Averaged 14.7 points and 4.9 assists in 10 NCAA Tournament
games from 1975 to 1978 (6-4 record).... Member of 1976 U.S. Olympic
team.... Selected by the Kansas City Kings in first round of 1978 NBA draft
(2nd pick overall).

Season	G	FGM	FGA	FG%	FTM	FTA	FT%	Reb.	Avg.	Pts.	Avg.
1974–75	31	191	370	.516	126	161	.783	85	2.7	508	16.4
1975–76	29	206	387	.532	128	164	.780	51	1.8	540	18.6
1976–77	33	230	431	.534	157	184	.853	63	1.9	617	18.7
1977–78	30	238	452	.527	149	184	.810	62	2.1	625	20.8
Totals	123	865	1640	.527	560	693	.808	261	2.1	2290	18.6

CHET FORTE
Columbia
5-9 – G
Hackensack, N.J.

Named national player of the year by UPI in 1957.... NCAA consensus first-
team All-American in 1957.... Did not play in NCAA Tournament or NIT....
Selected by the Cincinnati Royals in seventh round of 1957 NBA draft (did
not play in league).

Season	G	FGM	FGA	FG%	FTM	FTA	FT%	Reb.	Avg.	Pts.	Avg.
1954–55	25	186	465	.400	187	222	.842	100	4.0	559	22.4
1955–56	16	122	288	.424	114	139	.820	82	5.1	358	22.4
1956–57	24	235	583	.403	224	263	.852	108	4.5	694	28.9
Totals	65	543	1336	.406	525	624	.841	290	4.5	1611	24.8

ROBIN FREEMAN
Ohio State
5-11 – G
Cincinnati, Ohio

NCAA unanimous first-team All-American in 1956 and consensus second-team All-American in 1955.... Did not play in NCAA Tournament or NIT.... Selected by the St. Louis Hawks in fourth round of 1956 NBA draft (did not play in league).

Season	G	FGM	FGA	FG%	FTM	FTA	FT%	Reb.	Avg.	Pts.	Avg.
1953–54	22	185	461	.401	95	122	.779			465	21.1
1954–55	13	149	341	.437	111	137	.810			409	31.5
1955–56	22	259	562	.461	205	253	.810			723	32.9
Totals	57	593	1364	.435	411	512	.803			1597	28.0

RICHIE FUQUA
Oral Roberts
6-4 – G
Chattanooga, Tenn.

NCAA consensus second-team All-American in 1972.... Did not play in NCAA Tournament.... Averaged 30.7 points in three NIT games in 1972 and 1973 (1-2 record).... Selected by the Boston Celtics in fourth round of 1973 NBA draft (did not play in league).

Season	G	FGM	FGA	FG%	FTM	FTA	FT%	Reb.	Avg.	Pts.	Avg.
1969–70	31	228	483	.472	105	147	.714	154	5.0	561	18.1
1970–71	26	353	701	.504	120	171	.702	116	4.5	826	31.8
1971–72	28	423	941	.450	160	210	.762	140	5.0	1006	35.9
1972–73	26	269	713	.377	73	130	.562	113	4.3	611	23.5
Totals	111	1273	2838	.449	458	658	.696	523	4.7	3004	27.1

Note: Oral Roberts was a Division II school in his first two seasons.

DICK GARMAKER
Minnesota
6-3 – F
Hibbing, Mich.

NCAA consensus first-team All-American in 1955.... Did not play in NCAA Tournament or NIT.... Played 1950–51 and 1951–52 seasons at Hibbing (Minn.) Junior College.... Selected by the Minneapolis Lakers in both the 1954 and 1955 NBA drafts (territorial pick in 1955).

Season	G	FGM	FGA	FG%	FTM	FTA	FT%	Reb.	Avg.	Pts.	Avg.
1952–53				Sat out season under Big Ten rules for junior college transfers.							
1953–54	22	147	327	.450	181	251	.721	155	7.0	475	21.6
1954–55	22	186	507	.367	161	209	.770	185	8.4	533	24.2
Totals	44	333	834	.399	342	460	.743	340	7.7	1008	22.9

ERIC (HANK) GATHERS
Loyola Marymount
6-7 – F/C
Philadelphia, Pa.

NCAA consensus second-team All-American in 1990.... Led the nation in scoring and rebounding in 1989.... Averaged 21.3 points and 13.7 rebounds in three NCAA Tournament games in 1988 and 1989 (1-2 record; died of heart ailment before the 1990 tournament in which the Lions were 3-1).

Season	G	FGM	FGA	FG%	FTM	FTA	FT%	Reb.	Avg.	Pts.	Avg.
1985–86	28	90	170	.529	53	92	.576	143	5.1	233	8.3
1986–87			Sat out entire year after transferring from Southern Cal.								
1987–88	32	304	541	.562	113	208	.543	278	8.7	721	22.5
1988–89	31	419	689	.608	177	315	.562	426	13.7	1015	32.7
1989–90	26	314	528	.595	126	222	.568	281	10.8	754	29.0
Totals	117	1127	1928	.585	469	837	.560	1128	9.6	2723	23.3

Three-point field goals: 0 of 1 in 1987–88 and 0 of 1 in 1989–90. Totals: 0 of 2.

ARMON GILLIAM
UNLV
6-9 – F
Bethel Park, Pa.

NCAA consensus second-team All-American in 1987.... Leading scorer and rebounder for 1987 Final Four team (37-2 record).... Averaged 21.5 points and 9.3 rebounds in 10 NCAA Tournament games from 1985 to 1987 (7-3 record).... Averaged 16.9 points and 8.3 rebounds in one junior college season at Independence (Kans.).... Selected by the Phoenix Suns in first round of 1987 NBA draft (2nd pick overall).

Season	G	FGM	FGA	FG%	FTM	FTA	FT%	Reb.	Avg.	Pts.	Avg.
1983–84			Sat out the entire season as a redshirt.								
1984–85	31	136	219	.621	98	150	.653	212	6.8	370	11.9
1985–86	37	221	418	.529	140	190	.737	315	8.5	582	15.7
1986–87	39	359	598	.600	185	254	.728	363	9.3	903	23.2
Totals	107	716	1235	.580	423	594	.712	890	8.3	1855	17.3

ARTIS GILMORE
Jacksonville
7-2 – C
Chipley, Fla.

NCAA unanimous first-team All-American in 1971.... Led the nation in rebounding in 1970 and 1971.... Only player to average more than 22 points and 22 rebounds per game in his career.... Leading scorer and rebounder for 1970 national runner-up (27-2 record).... Named to All-NCAA Tournament team in 1970.... Averaged 24 points and 19.2 rebounds in six NCAA Tournament games in 1970 and 1971 (4-2 record).... Averaged 22.5 points in two junior college seasons at Gardner-Webb (N.C.).... Selected by the Chicago Bulls in seventh round of 1971 NBA draft (117th pick overall) and by the Kentucky Colonels in first round of 1971 ABA draft.

Season	G	FGM	FGA	FG%	FTM	FTA	FT%	Reb.	Avg.	Pts.	Avg.
1969–70	28	307	529	.580	128	202	.634	621	22.2	742	26.5
1970–71	26	229	405	.565	112	188	.596	603	23.2	570	21.9
Totals	54	536	934	.574	240	390	.615	1224	22.7	1312	24.3

GEORGE GLAMACK
North Carolina
6-6 – C
Allentown, Pa.

NCAA consensus first-team All-American in 1940 and 1941.... Averaged 20 points in two NCAA Tournament games in 1941 (0-2 record).

Season	G	FGM	FGA	FG%	FTM	FTA	FT%	Reb.	Avg.	Pts.	Avg.
1938–39					Statistics not available.						
1939–40					Statistics not available.						
1940–41	28									578	20.6
Totals					Totals not available.						

MIKE GMINSKI
Duke
6-11 – C
Monroe, Conn.

NCAA consensus first-team All-American in 1979 and consensus second-team All-American in 1980.... Named to All-NCAA Tournament team in 1978.... Leading rebounder and second-leading scorer for 1978 national runner-up (27-7 record).... Averaged 19.8 points and 8.3 rebounds in nine NCAA Tournament games from 1978 to 1980 (6-3 record).... Selected by the New Jersey Nets in first round of 1980 NBA draft (7th pick overall).

Season	G	FGM	FGA	FG%	FTM	FTA	FT%	Reb.	Avg.	Pts.	Avg.
1976–77	27	175	340	.515	64	91	.703	289	10.7	414	15.3
1977–78	32	246	450	.547	148	176	.841	319	10.0	640	20.0
1978–79	30	218	420	.519	129	177	.729	275	9.2	565	18.8
1979–80	33	262	487	.538	180	214	.841	359	10.9	704	21.3
Totals	122	901	1697	.531	521	658	.792	1242	10.2	2323	19.0

TOM GOLA
La Salle
6-6 – F
Philadelphia, Pa.

Named national player of the year by UPI in 1955.... NCAA unanimous first-team All-American in 1954 and 1955, and consensus first-team All-American in 1953.... Final Four Most Outstanding Player in 1954.... Named to All-NCAA Tournament teams in 1954 and 1955.... Leading scorer and rebounder for 1954 NCAA champion (26-4 record) and 1955 national runner-up (26-5).... Averaged 22.9 points in 10 NCAA Tournament games in 1954 and 1955 (9-1 record).... Co-Most Valuable Player of 1952 NIT with teammate Norm Grekin.... Averaged 14 points in five NIT games in 1952 (champion) and 1953 (opening-game loser).... Selected as a territorial choice by the Philadelphia Warriors in 1955 NBA draft.... Elected to Naismith Memorial Basketball Hall of Fame in 1975.

Season	G	FGM	FGA	FG%	FTM	FTA	FT%	Reb.	Avg.	Pts.	Avg.
1951–52	29	192	528	.364	121	170	.712	497	17.1	505	17.4
1952–53	28	186	451	.412	145	186	.780	434	15.5	517	18.5
1953–54	30	252	619	.407	186	254	.732	652	21.7	690	23.0
1954–55	31	274	624	.439	202	267	.757	618	19.9	750	24.2
Totals	118	904	2222	.407	654	877	.746	2201	18.7	2462	20.9

GAIL GOODRICH
UCLA
6-1 – G
Pasadena, Calif.

NCAA unanimous first-team All-American in 1965.... Named to All-NCAA Tournament team in 1964 and 1965.... Leading scorer and fourth-leading rebounder for NCAA champions in 1964 (30-0 record) and 1965 (28-2).... Averaged 23.5 points and four rebounds in 10 NCAA Tournament games from 1963 to 1965 (8-2 record).... Selected as a territorial pick by the Los Angeles Lakers in 1965 NBA draft.

Season	G	FGM	FGA	FG%	FTM	FTA	FT%	Reb.	Avg.	Pts.	Avg.
1962–63	29	117	280	.418	66	103	.641	101	3.5	300	10.3
1963–64	30	243	530	.458	160	225	.711	156	5.2	646	21.5
1964–65	30	277	528	.525	190	265	.717	158	5.3	744	24.8
Totals	89	637	1338	.476	416	593	.702	415	4.7	1690	19.0

OTTO GRAHAM
Northwestern/Colgate
6-0 – F
Waukegan, Ill.

NCAA consensus first-team All-American in 1944 and second-team All-American in 1943.... Did not play in NCAA Tournament or NIT.

Season	G	FGM	FGA	FG%	FTM	FTA	FT%	Reb.	Avg.	Pts.	Avg.
1941–42	21	103			86					292	13.9
1942–43	16	86			51					223	13.9
1943–44	17	75			37					187	11.0
Totals	54	264			174					702	13.0

Note: 1943–44 statistics include four games with Colgate in which he had a total of 28 field goals and eight free throws.

GARY GRANT
Michigan
6-3 – G
Canton, Ohio

NCAA unanimous first-team All-American in 1988.... Averaged 11.2 points and 6.1 assists in nine NCAA Tournament games from 1985-88 (5-4 record).... Selected by the Seattle SuperSonics in first round of 1988 NBA draft (15th pick overall); they promptly traded his draft rights to the Los Angeles Clippers.

Season	G	FGM	FGA	FG%	FTM	FTA	FT%	Reb.	Avg.	Pts.	Avg.
1984–85	30	169	307	.550	49	60	.817	76	2.5	387	12.9
1985–86	33	172	348	.494	58	78	.744	104	3.2	402	12.2
1986–87	32	286	533	.537	111	142	.782	159	5.0	716	22.4
1987–88	34	269	508	.530	135	167	.808	116	3.4	717	21.1
Totals	129	896	1696	.528	353	447	.790	455	3.5	2222	17.2

Three-point field goals: 33 of 68 (.485) in 1986–87 and 44 of 99 (.444) in 1987–88. Totals: 77 of 167 (.461).

DON GRATE
Ohio State
6-2 – F
Greenfield, Ohio

NCAA consensus second-team All-American in 1944 and 1945.... Leading scorer for 1944 national semifinalist (14-7 record) and second-leading scorer for 1945 national semifinalist (15-5).... Averaged 11.3 points in four NCAA Tournament games in 1944 and 1945 (2-2 record).... Signed pro baseball contract with the Philadelphia Phillies as a pitcher prior to his senior season.

Season	G	FGM	FGA	FG%	FTM	FTA	FT%	Reb.	Avg.	Pts.	Avg.
1943–44	21									272	13.0
1944–45	20	95			46					236	11.8
Totals	41									508	12.4

RICKEY GREEN
Michigan
6-0 – G
Chicago, Ill.

NCAA unanimous first-team All-American in 1977.... Named to All-NCAA Tournament team in 1976.... Leading scorer for 1976 national runner-up (25-7 record).... Averaged 18.6 points, 4.5 rebounds and 5 assists in eight NCAA Tournament games in 1976 and 1977 (6-2 record).... Averaged 19 points in two junior college seasons at Vincennes (Ind.).... Selected by the Golden State Warriors in first round of 1977 NBA draft (16th pick overall).

Season	G	FGM	FGA	FG%	FTM	FTA	FT%	Reb.	Avg.	Pts.	Avg.
1975–76	32	266	542	.491	106	135	.785	117	3.7	638	19.9
1976–77	28	224	464	.483	98	128	.766	81	2.9	546	19.5
Totals	60	490	1006	.487	204	263	.776	198	3.3	1184	19.7

SI GREEN
Duquesne
6-3 – G
Brooklyn, N.Y.

NCAA unanimous first-team All-American in 1956 and consensus first-team All-American in 1955.... Did not play in NCAA Tournament.... Averaged 21.3 points in eight NIT games in 1954 (runner-up), 1955 (champion), and 1956 (lost in quarterfinals).... Selected by the Rochester Royals in 1956 NBA draft.

Season	G	FGM	FGA	FG%	FTM	FTA	FT%	Reb.	Avg.	Pts.	Avg.
1953–54	29	151	377	.401	88	146	.603	239	8.2	390	13.4
1954–55	25	206	470	.438	139	235	.591	341	13.6	551	22.0
1955–56	27	241	570	.423	180	258	.698	356	13.2	662	24.5
Totals	81	598	1417	.422	407	639	.637	936	11.6	1603	19.8

DAVID GREENWOOD
UCLA
6-9 – F
Los Angeles, Calif.

NCAA unanimous first-team All-American in 1978 and consensus first-team All-American in 1979.... Seventh-leading scorer and fourth-leading rebounder for 1976 national third-place team (27-5 record).... Averaged 13.9 points and 7.7 rebounds in 12 NCAA Tournament games from 1976 to 1979 (8-4 record).... Selected by the Chicago Bulls in first round of 1979 NBA draft (2nd pick overall).

Season	G	FGM	FGA	FG%	FTM	FTA	FT%	Reb.	Avg.	Pts.	Avg.
1975–76	31	62	122	.508	28	35	.800	114	3.7	152	4.9
1976–77	29	202	395	.511	80	112	.714	280	9.7	484	16.7
1977–78	28	196	364	.538	97	133	.729	319	11.4	489	17.5
1978–79	30	247	421	.587	102	126	.810	309	10.3	596	19.9
Totals	118	707	1302	.543	307	406	.756	1022	8.7	1721	14.6

HAL GREER
Marshall
6-2 – G
Huntington, W.V.

Scored 12 points in his only NCAA Tournament game in 1956.... Selected by the Syracuse Nationals in second round of 1958 NBA draft (14th pick overall).... Elected to Naismith Memorial Basketball Hall of Fame in 1981.

Season	G	FGM	FGA	FG%	FTM	FTA	FT%	Reb.	Avg.	Pts.	Avg.
1955–56	23	128	213	.601	101	145	.697	153	6.6	357	15.5
1956–57	24	167	329	.508	119	156	.763	332	13.8	453	18.9
1957–58	24	236	432	.546	95	114	.833	280	11.7	567	23.6
Totals	71	531	974	.545	315	415	.759	765	10.8	1377	19.4

ROD GRIFFIN
Wake Forest
6-6 – F
Fairmont, N.C.

NCAA consensus second-team All-American in 1977 and 1978.... Averaged 21.3 points and 6.3 rebounds in three NCAA Tournament games in 1977 (2-1 record).... Selected by the Denver Nuggets in first round of 1978 NBA draft (17th pick overall).

Season	G	FGM	FGA	FG%	FTM	FTA	FT%	Reb.	Avg.	Pts.	Avg.
1974–75	25	142	290	.490	64	97	.660	190	7.6	348	13.9
1975–76	27	190	367	.518	102	135	.756	242	9.0	482	17.9
1976–77	26	198	319	.621	136	174	.782	224	8.6	532	20.5
1977–78	29	243	424	.573	137	191	.717	291	10.0	623	21.5
Totals	107	773	1400	.552	439	597	.735	947	8.9	1985	18.6

DARRELL GRIFFITH
Louisville
6-4 – G
Louisville, Ky.

Wooden Award winner in 1980.... NCAA unanimous first-team All-American in 1980.... Final Four Most Outstanding Player in 1980.... Leading scorer and fourth-leading rebounder for 1980 NCAA champion (33-3 record).... Averaged 20.3 points and 4.7 rebounds in 10 NCAA Tournament games from 1977-80 (7-3 record).... Selected by the Utah Jazz in first round of 1980 NBA draft (2nd pick overall).

Season	G	FGM	FGA	FG%	FTM	FTA	FT%	Reb.	Avg.	Pts.	Avg.
1976–77	28	150	299	.502	59	93	.634	109	3.8	359	12.8
1977–78	30	240	460	.522	78	110	.709	162	5.4	558	18.6
1978–79	32	242	487	.497	107	151	.709	140	4.4	591	18.5
1979–80	36	349	631	.553	127	178	.713	174	4.8	825	22.9
Totals	126	981	1877	.523	371	532	.697	585	4.6	2333	18.5

DICK GROAT
Duke
6-0 – G
Swissvale, Pa.

NCAA unanimous first-team All-American in 1952 and consensus second-team All-American in 1951.... Finished second in the nation in assists with 7.6 per game in 1952.... Did not play in NCAA Tournament or NIT.... Appeared in College World Series in 1952.... Selected by the Fort Wayne Pistons in 1952 NBA draft.

Season	G	FGM	FGA	FG%	FTM	FTA	FT%	Reb.	Avg.	Pts.	Avg.
1949–50	19	109	256	.426	57	98	.582			275	14.5
1950–51	33	285	713	.400	261	331	.789			831	25.2
1951–52	30	288	700	.411	204	281	.726			780	26.0
Totals	82	682	1669	.409	522	710	.735			1886	23.0

ALEX GROZA
Kentucky
6-7 – C
Martins Ferry, Ohio

NCAA consensus first-team All-American in 1947 and 1949, and consensus second-team All-American in 1948.... Final Four Most Outstanding Player in 1948 and 1949.... Leading scorer for NCAA champions in 1948 (36-3 record) and 1949 (32-2).... Averaged 22.7 points in six NCAA Tournament games in 1948 and 1949 (6-0 record).... Averaged 13.3 points in four NIT games in 1947 (runner-up) and 1949 (opening-game loser).... Leading scorer (11.1 points per game) for 1948 U.S. Olympic team.... Selected by the Indianapolis Olympians in 1949 NBA draft.

Season	G	FGM	FGA	FG%	FTM	FTA	FT%	Reb.	Avg.	Pts.	Avg.
1944–45	10	62			41					165	16.5
1945–46	Military Service (Army)										
1946–47	37	146	372	.392	101	160	.631			393	10.6
1947–48	39	200	530	.377	88	140	.629			488	12.5
1948–49	34	259	612	.423	180	248	.726			698	20.5
Totals	120	667			410					1744	14.5

CLIFF HAGAN
Kentucky
6-4 – F/C
Owensboro, Ky.

NCAA consensus first-team All-American in 1952 and 1954.... Leading scorer for 1954 undefeated team that chose not to participate in national postseason competition (25-0 record).... Fifth-leading scorer for 1951 NCAA champion (32-2).... Averaged 12 points in six NCAA Tournament games in 1951 and 1952 (5-1 record).... Selected by the Boston Celtics in third round of 1953 NBA draft; draft rights traded to St. Louis Hawks after he served two years in the military.... Elected to Naismith Memorial Basketball Hall of Fame in 1977.

Season	G	FGM	FGA	FG%	FTM	FTA	FT%	Reb.	Avg.	Pts.	Avg.
1950–51	20	69	188	.367	45	61	.738	169	8.5	183	9.2
1951–52	32	264	633	.417	164	235	.698	528	16.5	692	21.6
1952–53	Kentucky prohibited from playing because of NCAA probation.										
1953–54	25	234	514	.455	132	191	.691	338	13.5	600	24.0
Totals	77	567	1335	.425	341	487	.700	1035	13.4	1475	19.2

DALE HALL
Army
5-10 – F
Parsons, Kans.

NCAA consensus second-team All-American in 1944 and 1945.... Did not play in NCAA Tournament or NIT.

Season	G	FGM	FGA	FG%	FTM	FTA	FT%	Reb.	Avg.	Pts.	Avg.
1942–43	12	41			11					93	7.8
1943–44	15	122			29					273	18.2
1944–45	15	91			31					213	14.2
Totals	42	254			71					579	13.8

ANFERNEE HARDAWAY
Memphis State
6-7 – G
Memphis, Tenn.

NCAA unanimous first-team All-American in 1993.... Averaged 17.6 points, 5.4 rebounds, and five assists in five NCAA Tournament games in 1992 and 1993 (3-2 record).... Selected as an undergraduate by the Golden State Warriors in first round of 1993 NBA draft (3rd pick overall); draft rights promptly traded to the Orlando Magic.

Season	G	FGM	FGA	FG%	FTM	FTA	FT%	Reb.	Avg.	Pts.	Avg.
1990–91	Did not play–failed to meet requirements of Proposition 48.										
1991–92	34	209	483	.433	103	158	.652	237	7.0	590	17.4
1992–93	32	249	522	.477	158	206	.767	273	8.5	729	22.8
Totals	66	458	1005	.456	261	364	.717	510	7.7	1319	20.0

Three-point field goals: 69 of 190 (.363) in 1991–92 and 73 of 220 (.332) in 1992–93. **Totals:** 142 of 410 (.346).

JERRY HARKNESS
Loyola of Chicago
6-2 – F
New York, N.Y.

NCAA consensus first-team All-American in 1963.... Leading scorer and third-leading rebounder for 1963 NCAA champion (29-2 record).... Averaged 21.2 points and nine rebounds in five NCAA Tournament games in 1963 (5-0 record).... Averaged 15.7 points in three games for 1962 NIT third-place team.... Selected by the New York Knicks in second round of 1963 NBA draft (10th pick overall).

Season	G	FGM	FGA	FG%	FTM	FTA	FT%	Reb.	Avg.	Pts.	Avg.
1960–61	23	185	372	.497	150	198	.758	198	8.6	520	22.6
1961–62	27	202	438	.461	163	229	.712	234	8.7	567	21.0
1962–63	31	244	484	.504	174	240	.725	236	7.6	662	21.4
Totals	81	631	1294	.488	487	667	.730	668	8.2	1749	21.6

CLEM HASKINS
Western Kentucky
6-3 – G/F
Campbellsville, Ky.

NCAA consensus first-team All-American in 1967.... Averaged 17 points and 11.3 rebounds in four NCAA Tournament games in 1966 and 1967 (2-2 record).... Averaged 17 points in two NIT games in 1965.... Selected by the Chicago Bulls in first round of 1967 NBA draft (3rd pick overall).

Season	G	FGM	FGA	FG%	FTM	FTA	FT%	Reb.	Avg.	Pts.	Avg.
1964–65	27	252	561	.449	129	190	.679	293	10.9	633	23.4
1965–66	28	213	461	.462	146	189	.772	280	10.0	572	20.4
1966–67	21	170	377	.451	135	167	.808	236	11.2	475	22.6
Totals	76	635	1399	.454	410	546	.751	809	10.6	1680	22.1

JOHN HAVLICEK
Ohio State
6-5 – G/F
Bridgeport, Ohio

NCAA consensus second-team All-American in 1962.... Fourth-leading scorer and second-leading rebounder on 1960 NCAA champion (25-3 record), third-leading scorer and second-leading rebounder on 1961 national runner-up (27-1), and second-leading scorer and rebounder on 1962 national runner-up (26-2).... Named to All-NCAA Tournament team in 1962.... Averaged 13 points and 8.8 rebounds in 12 NCAA Tournament games from 1960 to 1962 (10-2 record).... Selected by the Boston Celtics in first round of 1962 NBA draft.... Elected to Naismith Memorial Basketball Hall of Fame in 1983.

Season	G	FGM	FGA	FG%	FTM	FTA	FT%	Reb.	Avg.	Pts.	Avg.
1959–60	28	144	312	.462	53	74	.716	205	7.3	341	12.2
1960–61	28	173	321	.539	61	87	.701	244	8.7	407	14.5
1961–62	28	196	377	.520	83	109	.761	271	9.7	475	17.0
Totals	84	513	1010	.508	197	270	.730	720	8.6	1223	14.6

HERSEY HAWKINS
Bradley
6-3 – G
Chicago, Ill.

Named national player of the year by AP, UPI and NABC in 1988.... NCAA unanimous first-team All-American in 1988.... Led the nation in scoring in 1988.... Averaged 29 points and 7.3 rebounds in three NCAA Tournament games in 1986 and 1988 (1-2 record).... Collected 13 points and 10 rebounds in one NIT game in 1985.... Member of 1988 U.S. Olympic team.... Selected by the Los Angeles Clippers in first round of 1988 NBA draft (6th pick overall); draft rights promptly traded to the Philadelphia 76ers.

Season	G	FGM	FGA	FG%	FTM	FTA	FT%	Reb.	Avg.	Pts.	Avg.
1984–85	30	179	308	.581	81	105	.771	182	6.1	439	14.6
1985–86	35	250	461	.542	156	203	.768	200	5.7	656	18.7
1986–87	29	294	552	.533	169	213	.793	195	6.7	788	27.2
1987–88	31	377	720	.524	284	335	.848	241	7.8	1125	36.3
Totals	125	1100	2041	.539	690	856	.806	818	6.5	3008	24.1

Three-point field goals: 31 of 108 (.287) in 1986–87 and 87 of 221 (.394) in 1987–88. Totals: 118 of 329 (.359).

ELVIN HAYES
Houston
6-9 – F
Rayville, La.

Named national player of the year by AP, UPI, and USBWA in 1968.... NCAA unanimous first-team All-American in 1967 and 1968.... Member of All-NCAA Tournament team in 1967.... Leading scorer and rebounder for 1967 national third-place team (27-4 record) and 1968 fourth-place team (31-2).... Averaged 27.5 points and 17.4 rebounds in 13 NCAA Tournament games from 1966 to 1968 (9-4 record).... Selected by the San Diego Rockets in first round of 1968 NBA draft (1st pick overall).... Elected to Naismith Memorial Basketball Hall of Fame in 1989.

Season	G	FGM	FGA	FG%	FTM	FTA	FT%	Reb.	Avg.	Pts.	Avg.
1965–66	29	323	570	.567	143	257	.556	490	16.9	789	27.2
1966–67	31	373	750	.497	135	227	.595	488	15.7	881	28.4
1967–68	33	519	945	.549	176	285	.618	624	18.9	1214	36.8
Totals	93	1215	2265	.536	454	769	.590	1602	17.2	2884	31.0

SPENCER HAYWOOD
Detroit
6-8 – F/C
Detroit, Mich.

NCAA unanimous first-team All-American in 1969.... Led the nation in rebounding in 1969.... Did not play in NCAA Tournament or NIT.... Averaged 28.2 points and 22.1 rebounds in one junior college season at Trinidad State (Colo.).... Leading scorer (16.1 points per game) for 1968 U.S. Olympic team.... Signed as an undergraduate free agent by the ABA's Denver Rockets in 1969.

Season	G	FGM	FGA	FG%	FTM	FTA	FT%	Reb.	Avg.	Pts.	Avg.
1968–69	24	288	508	.567	195	254	.768	530	22.1	771	32.1

WALT HAZZARD
UCLA
6-2 – G
Philadelphia, Pa.

Named national player of the year by USBWA in 1964.... NCAA unanimous first-team All-American in 1964.... Second-leading scorer for undefeated 1964 NCAA champion (30-0 record) and third-leading scorer for 1962 fourth-place finisher (18-11).... Final Four Most Outstanding Player and member of All-NCAA Tournament team in 1964.... Averaged 16.2 points and 5.7 rebounds in 10 NCAA Tournament games from 1962 to 1964 (6-4 record).... Member of 1964 U.S. Olympic team.... Selected as a territorial pick by the Los Angeles Lakers in first round of 1964 NBA draft.... Changed his name to Mahdi Abdul-Rahmad.

Season	G	FGM	FGA	FG%	FTM	FTA	FT%	Reb.	Avg.	Pts.	Avg.
1961–62	28	134	338	.396	102	143	.713	163	5.8	370	13.2
1962–63	29	170	380	.447	133	193	.689	170	5.9	473	16.3
1963–64	30	204	458	.445	150	209	.718	142	4.7	558	18.6
Totals	87	508	1176	.432	385	545	.706	475	5.5	1401	16.1

TOM HEINSOHN
Holy Cross
6-7 – F
Union City, N.J.

NCAA consensus first-team All-American in 1956.... Collected 26 points and 20 rebounds in one NCAA Tournament game in 1956.... Averaged 18.3 points in four NIT games in 1954 (champion) and 1955 (first-round loser).... Selected as a territorial pick by the Boston Celtics in 1956 NBA draft.... Elected to Naismith Memorial Basketball Hall of Fame in 1985.

Season	G	FGM	FGA	FG%	FTM	FTA	FT%	Reb.	Avg.	Pts.	Avg.
1953–54	28	175	364	.481	94	142	.662	300	10.7	444	15.9
1954–55	26	232	499	.465	141	215	.656	385	14.8	605	23.3
1955–56	27	254	630	.403	232	304	.763	569	21.1	740	27.4
Totals	81	661	1493	.443	467	661	.707	1254	15.4	1789	22.1

NED (DICKIE) HEMRIC
Wake Forest
6-6 – F/C
Jonesville, N.C.

NCAA consensus second-team All-American in 1955.... Averaged 29 points and 17.5 rebounds in two NCAA Tournament games in 1953 (1-1 record).... Selected by the Boston Celtics in 1955 NBA draft.

Season	G	FGM	FGA	FG%	FTM	FTA	FT%	Reb.	Avg.	Pts.	Avg.
1951–52	24	182	413	.441	174	310	.561	447	18.6	538	22.4
1952–53	25	212	452	.469	199	336	.592	416	16.6	623	24.9
1953–54	28	225	446	.504	230	310	.742	424	15.1	680	24.3
1954–55	27	222	429	.517	302	403	.749	515	19.1	746	27.6
Totals	104	841	1740	.483	905	1359	.666	1802	17.3	2587	24.9

DON HENNON
Pittsburgh
5-9 – G
Wampum, Pa.

NCAA consensus first-team All-American in 1958 and consensus second-team All-American in 1959.... Averaged 25.8 points in four NCAA Tournament games in 1957 and 1958 (1-3 record).... Selected by the Cincinnati Royals in sixth round of 1959 NBA draft.

Season	G	FGM	FGA	FG%	FTM	FTA	FT%	Reb.	Avg.	Pts.	Avg.
1956–57	27	225	541	.416	123	149	.826	95	3.5	573	21.2
1957–58	25	267	654	.408	117	140	.836	118	4.7	651	26.0
1958–59	24	231	632	.366	155	191	.812	105	4.4	617	25.7
Totals	76	723	1827	.396	395	480	.823	318	4.2	1841	24.2

FRED HETZEL
Davidson
6-8 – F/C
Washington, D.C.

NCAA unanimous first-team All-American in 1965 and consensus second-team All-American in 1964.... Did not play in NCAA Tournament.... Selected by the San Francisco Warriors in first round of 1965 NBA draft.

Season	G	FGM	FGA	FG%	FTM	FTA	FT%	Reb.	Avg.	Pts.	Avg.
1962–63	27	245	460	.533	144	181	.796	359	13.3	634	23.5
1963–64	26	273	498	.548	163	211	.773	351	13.5	709	27.3
1964–65	26	273	471	.580	143	178	.803	384	14.8	689	26.5
Totals	79	791	1429	.554	450	570	.789	1094	13.8	2032	25.7

Season	G	FGM	FGA	FG%	FTM	FTA	FT%	Reb.	Avg.	Pts.	Avg.
1959–60	30	152	264	.576	63	130	.485	331	11.0	367	12.2
1960–61	30	208	391	.532	87	168	.518	374	12.5	503	16.8
1961–62	31	211	424	.498	99	175	.566	383	12.4	521	16.8
Totals	91	571	1079	.529	249	473	.526	1088	12.0	1391	15.3

ART HEYMAN
Duke
6-5 – F
Rockville Center, N.Y.

Named national player of the year by AP, UPI, and USBWA in 1963.... NCAA unanimous first-team All-American in 1963 and consensus second-team All-American in 1962.... Leading scorer and rebounder for 1963 national third-place team (27-3 record).... Averaged 22.3 points and 10.5 rebounds in four NCAA Tournament games in 1963 (3-1 record).... Selected by the New York Knicks in first round of 1963 NBA draft.

Season	G	FGM	FGA	FG%	FTM	FTA	FT%	Reb.	Avg.	Pts.	Avg.
1960–61	25	229	488	.469	171	263	.650	272	10.9	629	25.2
1961–62	24	219	506	.433	170	276	.616	269	11.2	608	25.3
1962–63	30	265	586	.452	217	314	.691	324	10.8	747	24.9
Totals	79	713	1580	.451	558	853	.654	865	10.9	1984	25.1

GRANT HILL
Duke
6-8 – G/F
Reston, Va.

NCAA unanimous first-team All-American in 1994 and consensus second-team All-American in 1993.... Fifth-leading scorer and second-leading rebounder for 1991 NCAA championship team (32-7 record), second-leading rebounder and third-leading scorer for 1992 NCAA championship team (34-2), and leading scorer and second-leading rebounder for 1994 NCAA runner-up (28-6).... Named to All-NCAA Tournament team in 1992 and 1994.... Averaged 13.5 points, 6.7 rebounds, and 4.3 assists in 20 NCAA Tournament games from 1991 to 1994 (18-2 record).... Selected by the Detroit Pistons in first round of 1994 NBA draft (3rd pick overall).

Season	G	FGM	FGA	FG%	FTM	FTA	FT%	Reb.	Avg.	Pts.	Avg.
1990–91	36	160	310	.516	81	133	.609	183	5.1	402	11.2
1991–92	33	182	298	.611	99	135	.733	187	5.7	463	14.0
1992–93	26	185	320	.578	94	126	.746	166	6.4	468	18.0
1993–94	34	218	472	.462	116	165	.703	233	6.9	591	17.4
Totals	129	745	1400	.532	390	559	.698	769	6.0	1924	14.9

Three-point field goals: 1 of 2 (.500) in 1990–91, 0 of 1 in 1991–92, 4 of 14 (.286) in 1992–93, and 39 of 100 in 1993–94. **Totals:** 44 of 117 (.376).

PAUL HOGUE
Cincinnati
6-9 – C
Knoxville, Tenn.

Leading scorer and rebounder for 1962 NCAA champion (29-2 record), leading rebounder and second-leading scorer for 1961 NCAA champion (27-3), and third-leading scorer and second-leading rebounder for 1960 national third-place team (28-2).... Averaged 18.4 points and 13.3 rebounds in 12 NCAA Tournament games from 1960 to 1962 (11-1 record).... Named to All-NCAA Tournament team in 1962.... Selected by the New York Knicks in first round of 1962 NBA draft (2nd pick overall).

JOE HOLUP
George Washington
6-6 – C
Swoyersville, Pa.

Led the nation in field-goal shooting in 1954 and 1956.... Led the nation in rebounding in 1956.... Scored 13 points in one NCAA Tournament game in 1954.... Selected by the Syracuse Nationals in first round of 1956 NBA draft.

Season	G	FGM	FGA	FG%	FTM	FTA	FT%	Reb.	Avg.	Pts.	Avg.
1952–53	22	154	301	.512	119	167	.713	396	18.0	427	19.4
1953–54	26	179	313	.572	189	255	.741	484	18.6	547	21.0
1954–55	30	223	373	.598	155	208	.745	546	18.2	601	20.0
1955–56	26	200	309	.647	251	331	.758	604	23.2	651	25.0
Totals	104	756	1296	.583	714	961	.743	2030	19.5	2226	21.4

BOB HOUBREGS
Washington
6-7 – F/C
Seattle, Wash.

NCAA unanimous first-team All-American in 1953 and consensus second-team All-American in 1952.... Leading scorer and rebounder for 1953 national third-place team (30-3 record).... Member of All-NCAA Tournament team in 1953.... Averaged 27.4 points in seven NCAA Tournament games in 1951 and 1953 (5-2 record).... Selected by the Milwaukee Hawks in 1953 NBA draft.... Elected to Naismith Memorial Basketball Hall of Fame in 1986.

Season	G	FGM	FGA	FG%	FTM	FTA	FT%	Reb.	Avg.	Pts.	Avg.
1950–51	30							292	9.7	408	13.6
1951–52	28	189	440	.430	142	195	.728	298	10.6	520	18.6
1952–53	33	325	604	.538	196	264	.742	381	11.5	846	25.6
Totals	91							971	10.7	1774	19.5

ALLAN HOUSTON
Tennessee
6-6 – G
Louisville, Ky.

Did not play in NCAA Tournament.... Averaged 25.8 points and 6.5 rebounds in four NIT games in 1990 and 1992 (2-2 record).... Selected by the Detroit Pistons in first round of 1993 NBA draft (11th pick overall).

Season	G	FGM	FGA	FG%	FTM	FTA	FT%	Reb.	Avg.	Pts.	Avg.
1989–90	30	203	465	.437	120	149	.805	88	2.9	609	20.3
1990–91	34	265	550	.482	177	205	.863	104	3.1	806	23.7
1991–92	34	223	492	.453	189	225	.840	180	5.3	717	21.1
1992–93	30	211	454	.465	165	188	.878	145	4.8	669	22.3
Totals	128	902	1961	.460	651	767	.849	517	4.0	2801	21.9

Three-point field goals: 83 of 192 (.432) in 1989–90, 99 of 231 (.429) in 1990–91, 82 of 196 (.418) in 1991–92, and 82 of 198 (.414) in 1992–93. **Totals:** 346 of 817 (.424).

BAILEY HOWELL
Mississippi State
6-7 – F
Middleton, Tenn.

NCAA unanimous first-team All-American in 1959 and consensus second-team All-American in 1958.... Led the nation in field-goal percentage in 1957.... Did not play in NCAA Tournament or NIT.... Selected by the Detroit Pistons in first round of 1959 NBA draft.

Season	G	FGM	FGA	FG%	FTM	FTA	FT%	Reb.	Avg.	Pts.	Avg.
1956–57	25	217	382	.568	213	285	.747	492	19.7	647	25.9
1957–58	25	226	439	.515	243	315	.771	406	16.2	695	27.8
1958–59	25	231	464	.498	226	292	.774	379	15.2	688	27.5
Totals	**75**	**674**	**1285**	**.525**	**682**	**892**	**.765**	**1277**	**17.0**	**2030**	**27.1**

LOU HUDSON
Minnesota
6-5 – G/F
Greensboro, N.C.

Did not play in NCAA Tournament or NIT.... Selected by the St. Louis Hawks in first round of 1966 NBA draft (4th pick overall).

Season	G	FGM	FGA	FG%	FTM	FTA	FT%	Reb.	Avg.	Pts.	Avg.
1963–64	24	191	435	.439	53	85	.624	191	8.0	435	18.1
1964–65	24	231	463	.499	96	123	.780	247	10.3	558	23.3
1965–66	17	143	303	.472	50	77	.649	138	8.1	336	19.8
Totals	**65**	**565**	**1201**	**.470**	**199**	**285**	**.698**	**576**	**8.1**	**1329**	**20.4**

ALFREDRICK HUGHES
Loyola of Chicago
6-5 – F
Chicago, Ill.

Averaged 15.3 points and 7.3 rebounds in three NCAA Tournament games in 1985 (2-1 record).... Selected by the San Antonio Spurs in first round of 1985 NBA draft (14th pick overall).

Season	G	FGM	FGA	FG%	FTM	FTA	FT%	Reb.	Avg.	Pts.	Avg.
1981–82	29	216	538	.401	70	109	.642	177	6.1	502	17.3
1982–83	29	318	711	.447	108	188	.574	254	8.8	744	25.7
1983–84	29	326	655	.498	148	209	.708	237	8.2	800	27.6
1984–85	33	366	756	.484	136	195	.697	314	9.5	868	26.3
Totals	**120**	**1226**	**2660**	**.461**	**462**	**701**	**.659**	**982**	**8.2**	**2914**	**24.3**

WILLIE HUMES
Idaho State
6-1 – F
Madison, Ind.

Did not play in NCAA Tournament or NIT.... Averaged 22.6 points and 6.5 rebounds in two junior college seasons at Vincennes (Ind.).... Selected by the Atlanta Hawks in sixth round of 1971 NBA draft (did not play in league).

Season	G	FGM	FGA	FG%	FTM	FTA	FT%	Reb.	Avg.	Pts.	Avg.
1969–70	24	278	620	.448	177	237	.747	151	6.3	733	30.5
1970–71	24	287	723	.397	203	272	.746	187	7.8	777	32.4
Totals	**48**	**565**	**1343**	**.421**	**380**	**509**	**.747**	**338**	**7.0**	**1510**	**31.5**

ROD HUNDLEY
West Virginia
6-4 – G/F
Charleston, W.V.

NCAA consensus first-team All-American in 1957 and consensus second-team All-American in 1956.... Averaged 17.3 points in three NCAA Tournament games from 1955 to 1957 (0-3 record).... Selected by the Cincinnati Royals in 1957 NBA draft (1st pick overall).

Season	G	FGM	FGA	FG%	FTM	FTA	FT%	Reb.	Avg.	Pts.	Avg.
1954–55	30	260	756	.344	191	255	.749	244	8.1	711	23.7
1955–56	30	290	814	.356	218	326	.669	392	13.1	798	26.6
1956–57	29	235	648	.363	201	254	.791	305	10.5	671	23.1
Totals	**89**	**785**	**2218**	**.354**	**610**	**835**	**.731**	**941**	**10.6**	**2180**	**24.5**

ANDERSON HUNT
UNLV
6-2 – G
Detroit, Mich.

Second-leading scorer and leader in assists for 1990 NCAA champion (35-5 record) and second-leading scorer for 1991 national runner-up (34-1).... Member of All-NCAA Tournament team in 1990 and 1991.... Averaged 14.4 points and 3.2 assists in 15 NCAA Tournament games from 1989 to 1991 (13-2 record).... Left school with one season of eligibility remaining, but he wasn't drafted by an NBA team.

Season	G	FGM	FGA	FG%	FTM	FTA	FT%	Reb.	Avg.	Pts.	Avg.
1987–88	Sat out the season as a Proposition 48 casualty.										
1988–89	37	158	396	.399	48	70	.686	64	1.7	443	12.0
1989–90	39	230	478	.481	61	92	.663	87	2.2	620	15.9
1990–91	33	218	455	.479	28	42	.667	53	1.6	569	17.2
Totals	**109**	**606**	**1329**	**.456**	**137**	**204**	**.672**	**204**	**1.9**	**1632**	**15.0**

Three-point field goals: 79 of 218 (.362) in 1988–89, 99 of 258 (.384) in 1989–90, and 105 of 263 (.399) in 1990–91. **Totals:** 283 of 739 (.383).

BOBBY HURLEY
Duke
6-0 – G
Jersey City, N.J.

NCAA unanimous first-team All-American in 1993.... Holds NCAA career record for most assists.... Final Four Most Outstanding Player in 1992.... Third-leading scorer and leader in assists for 1992 NCAA champion (34-2 record), fourth-leading scorer and leader in assists for 1991 NCAA champion (32-7), and fifth-leading scorer and leader in assists for 1990 Final Four team (29-9).... Averaged 12 points and 8.1 assists in 20 NCAA Tournament games from 1990 to 1993 (18-2 record).... Selected by the Sacramento Kings in first round of 1993 NBA draft (7th pick overall).

Season	G	FGM	FGA	FG%	FTM	FTA	FT%	Reb.	Avg.	Pts.	Avg.
1989–90	38	92	262	.351	110	143	.769	68	1.8	335	8.8
1990–91	39	141	333	.423	83	114	.728	93	2.4	441	11.3
1991–92	31	123	284	.433	105	133	.789	61	2.0	410	13.2
1992–93	32	157	373	.421	143	178	.803	84	2.6	545	17.0
Totals	**140**	**513**	**1252**	**.410**	**441**	**568**	**.776**	**306**	**2.2**	**1731**	**12.4**

Three-point field goals: 41 of 115 (.357) in 1989–90, 76 of 188 (.404) in 1990–91, 59 of 140 (.421) in 1991–92, and 88 of 209 (.421) in 1992–93. **Totals:** 264 of 652 (.405).

CHUCK HYATT
Pittsburgh
6-0 – F
Uniontown, Pa.

NCAA consensus first-team All-American in 1929 and 1930.... Elected to Naismith Memorial Basketball Hall of Fame in 1959.

Season	G	FGM	FGA	FG%	FTM	FTA	FT%	Reb.	Avg.	Pts.	Avg.
1927–28	110		46							266	
1928–29	118		64							300	
1929–30	138		38							314	
Totals	366		148							880	

DARRALL IMHOFF
California
6-10 – C
Alhambra, Calif.

NCAA unanimous first-team All-American in 1960.... Second-leading scorer and leading rebounder for 1959 NCAA champion (25-4 record).... Leading scorer and rebounder for 1960 national runner-up (28-2).... Member of All-NCAA Tournament team in 1959 and 1960.... Averaged 14 points in 10 NCAA Tournament games from 1958 to 1960 (9-1 record; did not play in 1958 West Regional final defeat).... Member of 1960 U.S. Olympic team.... Selected by the New York Knicks in first round of 1960 NBA draft (3rd pick overall).

Season	G	FGM	FGA	FG%	FTM	FTA	FT%	Reb.	Avg.	Pts.	Avg.
1957–58	16	6	17	.353	2	5	.400	23	1.4	14	0.9
1958–59	29	134	316	.424	61	114	.535	318	11.0	329	11.3
1959–60	30	154	346	.445	102	162	.630	371	12.4	410	13.7
Totals	75	294	679	.433	165	281	.587	712	9.5	753	10.0

DAN ISSEL
Kentucky
6-9 – F/C
Batavia, Ill.

NCAA unanimous first-team All-American in 1970 and consensus second-team All-American in 1969.... Averaged 29.3 points and 11.3 rebounds in six NCAA Tournament games from 1968 to 1970 (3-3 record).... Selected by the Kentucky Colonels in first round of 1970 ABA draft.... Elected to Naismith Memorial Basketball Hall of Fame in 1993.

Season	G	FGM	FGA	FG%	FTM	FTA	FT%	Reb.	Avg.	Pts.	Avg.
1967–68	27	171	390	.438	102	154	.662	328	12.1	444	16.4
1968–69	28	285	534	.534	176	232	.759	381	13.6	746	26.6
1969–70	28	369	667	.553	210	275	.764	369	13.2	948	33.9
Totals	83	825	1591	.519	488	661	.738	1078	13.0	2138	25.8

CHRIS JACKSON
Louisiana State
6-1 – G
Gulfport, Miss.

NCAA consensus first-team All-American in 1989 and 1990.... Compiled highest scoring average for a freshman in NCAA history.... Averaged 20.7 points in three NCAA Tournament games in 1989 and 1990 (1-2 record).... Selected as an undergraduate by the Denver Nuggets in first round of 1990 NBA draft (3rd pick overall).... Changed his name to Mahmoud Abdul-Rauf.

Season	G	FGM	FGA	FG%	FTM	FTA	FT%	Reb.	Avg.	Pts.	Avg.
1988–89	32	359	739	.486	163	200	.815	108	3.4	965	30.2
1989–90	32	305	662	.461	191	210	.910	81	2.5	889	27.8
Totals	64	664	1401	.474	354	410	.863	189	3.0	1854	29.0

Three-point field goals: 84 of 216 (.389) in 1988–89 and 88 of 246 (.358) in 1989–90. **Totals:** 172 of 462 (.372).

JIM JACKSON
Ohio State
6-6 – G
Toledo, Ohio

NCAA unanimous first-team All-American in 1992 and consensus first-team All-American in 1991.... Averaged 17.7 points, 6.4 rebounds, and 4.4 assists in nine NCAA Tournament games from 1990 to 1992 (6-3 record).... Selected as an undergraduate by the Dallas Mavericks in first round of 1992 NBA draft (4th pick overall).

Season	G	FGM	FGA	FG%	FTM	FTA	FT%	Reb.	Avg.	Pts.	Avg.
1989–90	30	194	389	.499	73	93	.785	166	5.5	482	16.1
1990–91	31	228	441	.517	112	149	.752	169	5.5	585	18.9
1991–92	32	264	535	.493	146	180	.811	217	6.8	718	22.4
Totals	93	686	1365	.503	331	422	.784	552	5.9	1785	19.2

Three-point field goals: 21 of 59 (.356) in 1989–90, 17 of 51 (.333) in 1990–91, and 44 of 108 (.407) in 1991–92. **Totals:** 82 of 218 (.376).

TONY JACKSON
St. John's
6-4 – F
Brooklyn, N.Y.

NCAA consensus second-team All-American in 1960 and 1961.... Collected 26 points and six rebounds in one NCAA Tournament game in 1961.... NIT Most Valuable Player in 1959.... Averaged 19.8 points in five NIT games in 1959 (champion) and 1960 (opening-game loser).... Selected by the New York Knicks in third round of 1961 NBA draft (24th pick overall).

Season	G	FGM	FGA	FG%	FTM	FTA	FT%	Reb.	Avg.	Pts.	Avg.
1958–59	26	215	470	.457	91	130	.700	401	15.4	521	20.0
1959–60	25	187	456	.410	157	196	.801	286	11.4	531	21.2
1960–61	25	203	400	.508	145	180	.806	310	12.4	551	22.0
Totals	76	605	1326	.456	393	506	.777	997	13.1	1603	21.1

CHESTER (CHET) JAWORSKI
Rhode Island
5-11 – G
Worcester, Mass.

NCAA consensus first-team All-American in 1939.... Led the nation in scoring in 1938 and 1939.... Did not play in NCAA Tournament or NIT.

Season	G	FGM	FGA	FG%	FTM	FTA	FT%	Reb.	Avg.	Pts.	Avg.
1936–37										301	
1937–38	21	177			87					441	21.0
1938–39	21	201			73					475	22.6
Totals										1217	

DENNIS JOHNSON
Pepperdine
6-4 – G
Compton, Calif.

Averaged 13 points and six rebounds in two NCAA Tournament games in 1976 (1-1 record).... Played two junior college seasons at Los Angeles Harbor (Calif.).... Selected as an undergraduate by the Seattle SuperSonics in second round of 1976 NBA draft (29th pick overall).

Season	G	FGM	FGA	FG%	FTM	FTA	FT%	Reb.	Avg.	Pts.	Avg.
1975–76	27	181	378	.479	63	112	.563	156	5.8	425	15.7

EARVIN (MAGIC) JOHNSON
Michigan State
6-9 – G
Lansing, Mich.

NCAA unanimous first-team All-American in 1979.... Final Four Most Outstanding Player and member of All-NCAA Tournament team in 1979.... Second-leading scorer and rebounder for 1979 national champion (26-6 record).... Averaged 17.8 points, eight rebounds, and 9.5 assists in eight NCAA Tournament games in 1978 and 1979 (7-1 record).... Member of 1992 U.S. Olympic team.... Selected as an undergraduate by the Los Angeles Lakers in first round of 1979 NBA draft (1st pick overall).

Season	G	FGM	FGA	FG%	FTM	FTA	FT%	Reb.	Avg.	Pts.	Avg.
1977–78	30	175	382	.458	161	205	.785	237	7.9	511	17.0
1978–79	32	173	370	.468	202	240	.842	234	7.3	548	17.1
Totals	62	348	752	.463	363	445	.816	471	7.6	1059	17.1

EDDIE JOHNSON
Illinois
6-7 – F
Chicago, Ill.

Averaged 17 points and eight rebounds in two NCAA Tournament games in 1981 (1-1 record).... Averaged 18.6 points and 8.4 rebounds in five NIT games for 1980 third-place team.... Selected by the Kansas City Kings in second round of 1981 NBA draft (29th pick overall).

Season	G	FGM	FGA	FG%	FTM	FTA	FT%	Reb.	Avg.	Pts.	Avg.
1977–78	27	100	234	.427	20	27	.741	84	3.1	220	8.1
1978–79	30	168	405	.415	26	49	.531	170	5.7	362	12.1
1979–80	35	266	576	.462	78	119	.655	310	8.9	610	17.4
1980–81	29	219	443	.494	62	82	.756	267	9.2	500	17.2
Totals	121	753	1658	.454	186	277	.671	831	6.9	1692	14.0

GUS JOHNSON
Idaho
6-6 – F
Akron, Ohio

Did not play in NCAA Tournament or NIT.... Played two junior college seasons at Boise (Idaho) JC.... Selected by the Baltimore Bullets in second round of 1963 NBA draft (11th pick overall).

Season	G	FGM	FGA	FG%	FTM	FTA	FT%	Reb.	Avg.	Pts.	Avg.
1959–60	Left the University of Akron before the start of the season.										
1962–63	23	188	438	.429	62	105	.590	466	20.3	438	19.0

KEVIN JOHNSON
California
6-1 – G
Sacramento, Cal.

Did not play in NCAA Tournament.... Averaged 25.8 points and 4.8 assists in four NIT games in 1986 and 1987 (2-2 record).... Selected by the Cleveland Cavaliers in first round of 1987 NBA draft (7th pick overall).

Season	G	FGM	FGA	FG%	FTM	FTA	FT%	Reb.	Avg.	Pts.	Avg.
1983–84	28	98	192	.510	75	104	.721	83	3.0	271	9.7
1984–85	27	127	282	.450	94	142	.662	104	3.9	348	12.9
1985–86	29	164	335	.490	123	151	.815	104	3.6	451	15.6
1986–87	34	212	450	.471	113	138	.819	132	3.9	585	17.2
Totals	115	601	1259	.477	405	535	.757	423	3.7	1655	14.0

Three-point field goals: 48 of 124 (.387) in 1986–87.

LARRY JOHNSON
UNLV
6-7 – F
Dallas, Tex.

Named national player of the year by NABC and USBWA in 1991.... Naismith Award and Wooden Award winner in 1991.... NCAA unanimous first-team All-American in 1991 and consensus first-team All-American in 1990.... Named to All-NCAA Tournament team in 1990.... Leading scorer and rebounder for 1990 NCAA champion (35-5 record) and 1991 Final Four team (34-1).... Averaged 20.2 points and 11.5 rebounds in 11 NCAA Tournament games in 1990 and 1991 (10-1 record).... Averaged 26 points and 11.6 rebounds in two junior college seasons at Odessa (Tex.).... Selected by the Charlotte Hornets in first round of 1991 NBA draft (1st pick overall).

Season	G	FGM	FGA	FG%	FTM	FTA	FT%	Reb.	Avg.	Pts.	Avg.
1989–90	40	304	487	.624	201	262	.767	457	11.4	822	20.6
1990–91	35	308	465	.662	162	198	.818	380	10.9	795	22.7
Totals	75	612	952	.643	363	460	.789	837	11.2	1617	21.6

Three-point field goals: 13 of 38 (.342) in 1989–90 and 17 of 48 (.354) in 1990–91. **Totals:** 30 of 86 (.349).

MARQUES JOHNSON
UCLA
6-7 – F
Los Angeles, Calif.

Named national player of the year by AP, UPI, USBWA, and NABC in 1977.... Naismith Award and Wooden Award winner in 1977.... NCAA unanimous first-team All-American in 1977.... Member of All-NCAA Tournament team in 1976.... Third-leading scorer and rebounder for 1975 national champion (28-3 record).... Second-leading scorer and rebounder for 1976 national third-place team (27-5).... Averaged 14.6 points and 8.6 rebounds in 16 NCAA Tournament games from 1974 to 1977 (13-3 record).... Selected by the Milwaukee Bucks in first round of 1977 NBA draft (3rd pick overall).

Season	G	FGM	FGA	FG%	FTM	FTA	FT%	Reb.	Avg.	Pts.	Avg.
1973–74	27	83	131	.634	28	38	.737	90	3.3	194	7.2
1974–75	29	138	254	.543	59	86	.686	205	7.1	335	11.6
1975–76	32	223	413	.540	106	140	.757	301	9.4	552	17.3
1976–77	27	244	413	.591	90	145	.621	301	11.1	578	21.4
Totals	115	688	1211	.568	283	409	.692	897	7.8	1659	14.4

STEVE JOHNSON
Oregon State
6-10 – C
San Bernardino, Calif.

NCAA consensus first-team All-American in 1981.... Led the nation in field-goal percentage in 1980 and 1981.... Averaged 20 points and 12 rebounds in two NCAA Tournament games in 1980 and 1981 (0-2 record).... Collected 22 points and eight rebounds in one NIT game in 1979.... Selected by the Kansas City Kings in first round of 1981 NBA draft (7th pick overall).

Season	G	FGM	FGA	FG%	FTM	FTA	FT%	Reb.	Avg.	Pts.	Avg.
1976–77	28	159	267	.596	61	91	.670	156	5.6	379	13.5
1977–78	3	26	45	.578	8	13	.615	29	9.7	60	20.0
1978–79	27	197	298	.661	104	169	.615	178	6.6	498	18.4
1979–80	30	211	297	.710	87	145	.600	207	6.9	509	17.0
1980–81	28	235	315	.746	119	174	.684	215	7.7	589	21.0
Totals	116	828	1222	.678	379	592	.640	785	6.8	2035	17.5

Note: Missed most of 1977–78 season after suffering a broken left foot.

K. C. JONES

San Francisco
6-1 – G
San Francisco, Calif.

NCAA consensus second-team All-American in 1956.... Third-leading scorer for 1955 champion (28-1 record) and second-leading scorer for undefeated 1956 champion (29-0).... Member of All-NCAA Tournament team in 1955.... Averaged 13.6 points in five NCAA Tournament games in 1955.... Ineligible to play in 1956 NCAA Tournament because he was playing his fifth season of college basketball.... Member of 1956 U.S. Olympic team.... Selected by the Boston Celtics in second round of 1956 NBA draft.... Elected to Naismith Memorial Basketball Hall of Fame in 1988.

Season	G	FGM	FGA	FG%	FTM	FTA	FT%	Reb.	Avg.	Pts.	Avg.
1951–52	24	44	128	.344	46	64	.719	94	3.9	134	5.6
1952–53	23	63	159	.396	79	149	.544			205	8.9
1953–54	1	3	12	.250	2	2	1.000	3	3.0	8	8.0
1954–55	29	105	293	.358	97	144	.674	148	5.1	307	10.6
1955–56	25	76	208	.365	93	142	.655	130	5.2	245	9.8
Totals	102	291	800	.364	319	501	.637			901	8.8

Note: Missed majority of 1953–54 season after undergoing an appendectomy.

MICHAEL JORDAN

North Carolina
6-6 – G/F
Wilmington, N.C.

NCAA unanimous first-team All-American in 1983 and 1984.... Named national player of the year by AP, UPI, USBWA, and NABC in 1984.... Naismith Award and Wooden Award winner in 1984.... Member of All-NCAA Tournament team in 1982.... Third-leading scorer and rebounder for 1982 national champion (32-2 record).... Member of 1984 and 1992 U.S. Olympic teams.... Averaged 16.5 points and 4.2 rebounds in 10 NCAA Tournament games from 1982 to 1984 (8-2 record).... Selected as an undergraduate by the Chicago Bulls in first round of 1984 NBA draft (3rd pick overall).

Season	G	FGM	FGA	FG%	FTM	FTA	FT%	Reb.	Avg.	Pts.	Avg.
1981–82	34	191	358	.534	78	108	.722	149	4.4	460	13.5
1982–83	36	282	527	.535	123	167	.737	197	5.5	721	20.0
1983–84	31	247	448	.551	113	145	.779	163	5.3	607	19.6
Totals	101	720	1333	.540	314	420	.748	509	5.0	1788	17.7

Three-point field goals: 34 of 76 (.447) in 1982–83.

GEORGE KAFTAN

Holy Cross
6-3 – F
New York, N.Y.

NCAA consensus second-team All-American in 1947 and 1948.... Final Four Most Outstanding Player in 1947.... Leading scorer for 1947 NCAA champion (27-3 record) and second-leading scorer for 1948 national third-place team (26-4).... Averaged 17.3 points in six NCAA Tournament games in 1947 and 1948 (5-1 record).

Season	G	FGM	FGA	FG%	FTM	FTA	FT%	Reb.	Avg.	Pts.	Avg.
1945–46	15	90			57					237	15.8
1946–47	28	119			72					310	11.1
1947–48	30	187			94					468	15.6
1948–49	14	68			26					162	11.6
Totals	87	464			249					1177	13.5

ROGER KAISER

Georgia Tech
6-1 – G
Dale, Ind.

NCAA consensus first-team All-American in 1961 and consensus second-team All-American in 1960.... Averaged 26 points and 5.5 rebounds in two NCAA Tournament games in 1960 (1-1 record).... Selected by the Chicago Packers in first round of 1961 NBA draft (did not play in league).

Season	G	FGM	FGA	FG%	FTM	FTA	FT%	Reb.	Avg.	Pts.	Avg.
1958–59	26	138	342	.404	106	127	.835	182	7.0	382	14.7
1959–60	28	237	503	.471	164	190	.863	154	5.5	638	22.8
1960–61	26	216	517	.418	176	203	.867	106	4.1	608	23.4
Totals	80	591	1362	.434	446	520	.858	442	5.5	1628	20.4

DEAN KELLEY

Kansas
6-0 – G
McCune, Kans.

Named to All-NCAA Tournament team in 1952 and 1953.... Fourth-leading scorer for 1952 NCAA champion (28-3 record) and third-leading scorer for 1953 national runner-up (19-6).... Averaged 9.8 points in eight NCAA Tournament games in 1952 and 1953 (7-1 record).... Member of 1952 U.S. Olympic team.... Selected by the Fort Wayne Pistons in 1953 NBA draft (did not play in the league).

Season	G	FGM	FGA	FG%	FTM	FTA	FT%	Reb.	Avg.	Pts.	Avg.
1950–51	18	7			0	4	.000			14	0.8
1951–52	31	77	194	.397	49	81	.605	101	3.3	203	6.5
1952–53	25	81	236	.343	80	115	.696	76	3.0	242	9.7
Totals	74	165			129	200	.645			459	6.2

HARRY KELLY

Texas Southern
6-7 – F
Jackson, Miss.

Led the nation in scoring in 1982 and 1983.... Did not play in NCAA Tournament or NIT.... Selected by the Atlanta Hawks in fourth round of 1983 NBA draft (did not play in league).

Season	G	FGM	FGA	FG%	FTM	FTA	FT%	Reb.	Avg.	Pts.	Avg.
1979–80	26	313	612	.511	127	163	.779	205	7.8	753	29.0
1980–81	26	252	538	.468	112	149	.751	205	7.9	616	23.7
1981–82	29	336	658	.511	190	260	.730	335	11.6	862	29.7
1982–83	29	333	736	.452	169	222	.761	340	11.7	835	28.8
Totals	110	1234	2544	.485	598	794	.753	1085	9.9	3066	27.9

JASON KIDD

California
6-4 – G
Oakland, Calif.

NCAA unanimous first-team All-American in 1994.... Led the nation in steals with 3.8 per game in 1993.... Averaged 13 points, 7.8 rebounds, 9.5 assists, and four steals in four NCAA Tournament games in 1993 and 1994 (2-2 record).... Selected as an undergraduate by the Dallas Mavericks in first round of 1994 NBA draft (2nd pick overall).

Season	G	FGM	FGA	FG%	FTM	FTA	FT%	Reb.	Avg.	Pts.	Avg.
1992–93	29	133	287	.463	88	134	.657	142	4.9	378	13.0
1993–94	30	166	352	.472	117	169	.692	207	6.9	500	16.7
Totals	59	299	639	.468	205	303	.677	349	5.9	878	14.9

Three-point field goals: 24 of 84 (.286) in 1992–93 and 51 of 141 (.362) in 1993–94. **Totals:** 75 of 225 (.333).

BERNARD KING
Tennessee
6-7 – F
Brooklyn, N.Y.

NCAA consensus first-team All-American in 1977 and consensus second-team All-American in 1976.... Led the nation in field-goal percentage in 1975.... Collected 23 points and 12 rebounds in one NCAA Tournament game in 1977.... Selected as an undergraduate by the New Jersey Nets in first round of 1977 NBA draft (7th pick overall).

Season	G	FGM	FGA	FG%	FTM	FTA	FT%	Reb.	Avg.	Pts.	Avg.
1974–75	25	273	439	.622	115	147	.782	308	12.3	661	26.4
1975–76	25	260	454	.573	109	163	.669	325	13.0	629	25.2
1976–77	26	278	481	.578	116	163	.712	371	14.3	672	25.8
Totals	76	811	1374	.590	340	473	.719	1004	13.2	1962	25.8

STACEY KING
Oklahoma
6-10 – C
Lawton, Okla.

NCAA unanimous first-team All-American in 1989.... Member of All-NCAA Tournament team in 1988.... Leading scorer and rebounder for 1988 national runner-up (35-4 record).... Averaged 20.5 points and 7.8 rebounds in 12 NCAA Tournament games from 1987 to 1989 (9-3 record).... Selected by the Chicago Bulls in first round of 1989 NBA draft (6th pick overall).

Season	G	FGM	FGA	FG%	FTM	FTA	FT%	Reb.	Avg.	Pts.	Avg.
1985–86	14	26	67	.388	32	43	.744	53	3.8	84	6.0
1986–87	28	71	162	.438	54	87	.621	108	3.8	196	7.0
1987–88	39	337	621	.543	195	289	.675	332	8.5	869	22.3
1988–89	33	324	618	.524	211	294	.718	332	10.1	859	26.0
Totals	114	758	1468	.516	492	713	.690	825	7.2	2008	17.6

Three-point field goals: 0 of 1 in 1986–87 and 0 of 1 in 1987–88. **Totals:** 0 of 2.

Note: Missed 1986 NCAA Tournament because of academic problems.

BOB KINNEY
Rice
6-6 – C
San Antonio, Tex.

NCAA consensus first-team All-American in 1942 and consensus second-team All-American in 1941.... Averaged 10 points in four NCAA Tournament games in 1940 and 1942 (1-3 record).

Season	G	FGM	FGA	FG%	FTM	FTA	FT%	Reb.	Avg.	Pts.	Avg.
1939–40	27	145			48					338	12.5
1940–41	24	128			96	144	.667			352	14.7
1941–42	27	147			75	136	.551			369	13.7
Totals	78	420			219					1059	13.6

LEO KLIER
Notre Dame
6-1 – F
Washington, Ind.

NCAA consensus first-team All-American in 1944 and 1946.

Season	G	FGM	FGA	FG%	FTM	FTA	FT%	Reb.	Avg.	Pts.	Avg.
1942–43	3	4			0	0				8	2.7
1943–44	19	117			59	98	.602			293	15.4
1944–45		Military Service (Navy)									
1945–46	21	147	513	.287	61	115	.530			355	16.9
Totals	43	268			120	213	.563			656	15.3

JOHN KOTZ
Wisconsin
6-3 – F
Rhinelander, Wisc.

NCAA consensus first-team All-American in 1942 and second-team All-American in 1943.... Second-leading scorer for 1941 NCAA champion (20-3 record).... Final Four Most Outstanding Player in 1941.... Averaged 12.3 points in three NCAA Tournament games in 1941.

Season	G	FGM	FGA	FG%	FTM	FTA	FT%	Reb.	Avg.	Pts.	Avg.
1940–41	23	79			47					205	8.9
1941–42	21	125			75					325	15.5
1942–43	21	114			79					307	14.6
Totals	65	318			201					837	12.9

BARRY KRAMER
New York University
6-4 – F
Schenectady, N.Y.

NCAA consensus first-team All-American in 1963.... Averaged 25.2 points and 9.3 rebounds in six NCAA Tournament games in 1962 and 1963 (3-3 record).... Averaged 21.3 points in four NIT games for 1964 fourth-place team.... Selected by the San Francisco Warriors in first round of 1964 NBA draft.

Season	G	FGM	FGA	FG%	FTM	FTA	FT%	Reb.	Avg.	Pts.	Avg.
1961–62	24	152	349	.436	120	161	.745	219	9.1	424	17.7
1962–63	23	220	463	.475	235	283	.830	276	12.0	675	29.3
1963–64	27	209	488	.428	150	198	.758	195	7.2	568	21.0
Totals	74	581	1300	.447	505	642	.787	690	9.3	1667	22.5

ED (MOOSE) KRAUSE
Notre Dame
6-3 – C
Chicago, Ill.

NCAA consensus first-team All-American in 1932, 1933, and 1934.

Season	G	FGM	FGA	FG%	FTM	FTA	FT%	Reb.	Avg.	Pts.	Avg.
1931–32	18	48			42					138	7.7
1932–33	21	77			59					213	10.1
1933–34	23	76			44					196	8.5
Totals	62	201			145					547	8.8

JIM KREBS
SMU
6-8 – C
Webster Groves, Mo.

NCAA consensus first-team All-American in 1957.... Leading scorer and rebounder for 1965 national fourth-place team (26-4 record).... Averaged 21.6 points in nine NCAA Tournament games from 1955-57 (4-5 record).... Selected by the Minneapolis Lakers in first round of 1957 NBA draft (3rd pick overall).

Season	G	FGM	FGA	FG%	FTM	FTA	FT%	Reb.	Avg.	Pts.	Avg.
1954–55	26	209	478	.437	137	189	.725	228	8.8	555	21.3
1955–56	30	228	532	.429	118	156	.756	299	10.0	574	19.1
1956–57	26	233	486	.479	158	200	.790	313	12.0	624	24.0
Totals	82	670	1496	.448	413	545	.758	840	10.2	1753	21.4

BOB KURLAND
Oklahoma A&M
7-0 – C
St. Louis, Mo.

NCAA consensus first-team All-American in 1944, 1945, and 1946.... Final Four Most Outstanding Player in 1945 and 1946.... Leading scorer for NCAA champions in 1945 (27-4 record) and 1946 (31-2).... Averaged 22.8 points in six NCAA Tournament games in 1945 and 1946 (6-0 record).... Averaged 13.7 points in three NIT games for 1944 fourth-place finisher (1-2 record).... Member of 1948 and 1952 U.S. Olympic teams.... Elected to Naismith Memorial Basketball Hall of Fame in 1961.

Season	G	FGM	FGA	FG%	FTM	FTA	FT%	Reb.	Avg.	Pts.	Avg.
1942–43	21	22			9					53	2.5
1943–44	33	182			80					444	13.5
1944–45	31	214			101					529	17.1
1945–46	33	257			129					643	19.5
Totals	118	675			319					1669	14.1

CHRISTIAN LAETTNER
Duke
6-11 – C/F
Angola, N.Y.

Named national player of the year by AP, UPI, USBWA, and NABC in 1992.... Naismith Award and Wooden Award winner in 1992.... NCAA unanimous first-team All-American in 1992 and consensus second-team All-American in 1991.... Final Four Most Outstanding Player in 1991.... Member of All-NCAA Tournament team in 1991 and 1992.... Leading scorer and rebounder for 1992 national champion (34-2 record), what about 1991 (32-7) and 1990 (29-9).... Averaged 17.7 points and 7.3 rebounds in 23 NCAA Tournament games from 1989 to 1992 (21-2 record).... Member of 1992 U.S. Olympic team.... Selected by the Minnesota Timberwolves in first round of 1992 NBA draft (3rd pick overall).

Season	G	FGM	FGA	FG%	FTM	FTA	FT%	Reb.	Avg.	Pts.	Avg.
1988–89	36	115	159	.723	88	121	.727	170	4.7	319	8.9
1989–90	38	194	380	.511	225	269	.836	364	9.6	619	16.3
1990–91	39	271	471	.575	211	263	.802	340	8.7	771	19.8
1991–92	35	254	442	.575	189	232	.815	275	7.9	751	21.5
Totals	148	834	1452	.574	713	885	.806	1149	7.8	2460	16.6

Three-point field goals: 1 of 1 in 1988–89, 6 of 12 (.500) in 1989–90, 18 of 53 (.340) in 1990–91, and 54 of 97 (.557) in 1991–92. **Totals:** 79 of 163 (.485).

DWIGHT (BO) LAMAR
Southwestern Louisiana
6-1 – G
Columbus, Ohio

NCAA unanimous first-team All-American in 1972 and consensus first-team All-American in 1973.... Led the nation in scoring in 1972.... Averaged 29.2 points in six NCAA Division I Tournament games in 1972 and 1973 (3-3 record).... Averaged 33.2 points in five NCAA Division II Tournament games for 1971 national third-place team.... Selected by the San Diego Conquistadors in first round of 1973 ABA draft (1st pick overall).

Season	G	FGM	FGA	FG%	FTM	FTA	FT%	Reb.	Avg.	Pts.	Avg.
1969–70	26	253	608	.416	81	107	.757	132	5.1	587	22.6
1970–71	29	424	910	.466	196	261	.751	102	3.5	1044	36.0
1971–72	29	429	949	.452	196	268	.731	78	2.7	1054	36.3
1972–73	28	339	741	.457	130	166	.783	94	3.4	808	28.9
Totals	112	1445	3208	.450	603	802	.752	406	3.6	3493	31.2

BOB LANIER
St. Bonaventure
6-11 – C
Buffalo, N.Y.

NCAA unanimous first-team All-American in 1970 and consensus second-team All-American in 1968.... Leading scorer and rebounder for 1970 national fourth-place team (25-3 record).... Averaged 25.2 points and 14.2 rebounds in six NCAA Tournament games in 1968 and 1970 (4-2 record).... Selected by the Detroit Pistons in first round of 1970 NBA draft (1st pick overall).

Season	G	FGM	FGA	FG%	FTM	FTA	FT%	Reb.	Avg.	Pts.	Avg.
1967–68	25	272	466	.584	112	175	.640	390	15.6	656	26.2
1968–69	24	270	460	.587	114	181	.630	374	15.5	654	27.3
1969–70	26	308	549	.561	141	194	.727	416	16.0	757	29.1
Totals	75	850	1475	.576	367	550	.667	1180	15.7	2067	27.6

TONY LAVELLI
Yale
6-3 – G
Somerville, Mass.

NCAA consensus first-team All-American in 1949 and consensus second-team All-American in 1946 and 1948.... Led the nation in scoring in 1949.... Averaged 17.5 points in two NCAA Tournament games in 1949 (0-2 record).... Selected by the Boston Celtics in 1949 NBA draft.

Season	G	FGM	FGA	FG%	FTM	FTA	FT%	Reb.	Avg.	Pts.	Avg.
1945–46	15	124			72	90	.800			320	21.3
1946–47	25	152			115	159	.723			419	16.8
1947–48	27	196			162	212	.764			554	20.5
1948–49	30	228	652	.350	215	261	.824			671	22.4
Totals	97	700			564	722	.781			1964	20.2

ALFRED (BUTCH) LEE
Marquette
6-2 – G
Bronx, N.Y.

Named national player of the year by AP and UPI in 1978.... Naismith Award winner in 1978.... NCAA unanimous first-team All-American in 1978 and consensus second-team All-American in 1977.... Final Four Most Outstanding Player and member of All-NCAA Tournament team in 1977.... Leading scorer and third-leading rebounder for 1977 NCAA champion (25-7 record).... Averaged 16 points in 10 NCAA Tournament games from 1975 to 1978 (7-3 record).... Selected by the Atlanta Hawks in first round of 1978 NBA draft (10th pick overall).

Season	G	FGM	FGA	FG%	FTM	FTA	FT%	Reb.	Avg.	Pts.	Avg.
1974–75	26	85	188	.452	45	56	.804	63	2.4	215	8.3
1975–76	29	160	354	.452	77	98	.786	104	3.6	397	13.7
1976–77	32	239	501	.477	150	172	.872	121	3.8	628	19.6
1977–78	28	182	360	.506	131	149	.879	87	3.1	495	17.7
Totals	115	666	1403	.475	403	475	.848	375	3.3	1735	15.1

CLYDE LEE
Vanderbilt
6-9 – C
Nashville, Tenn.

NCAA unanimous first-team All-American in 1966 and consensus second-team All-American in 1965.... Averaged 26 points and 17.5 rebounds in two NCAA Tournament games in 1965 (1-1 record).... Selected by the San Francisco Warriors in first round of 1966 NBA draft (3rd pick overall).

Season	G	FGM	FGA	FG%	FTM	FTA	FT%	Reb.	Avg.	Pts.	Avg.
1963–64	25	176	410	.429	119	176	.676	391	15.6	471	18.8
1964–65	28	239	516	.463	153	228	.671	420	15.0	631	22.5
1965–66	26	218	457	.477	153	206	.743	412	15.8	589	22.7
Totals	79	633	1383	.458	425	610	.697	1223	15.5	1691	21.4

KEITH LEE
Memphis State
6-10 – C/F
West Memphis, Ark.

NCAA unanimous first-team All-American in 1985 and consensus first-team All-American in 1983.... Consensus second-team All-American in 1984.... Leading scorer and rebounder for 1985 Final Four team (31-4 record).... Averaged 18.3 points and 8.9 rebounds in 12 NCAA Tournament games from 1982 to 1985 (8-4 record).... Selected by the Chicago Bulls in first round of 1985 NBA draft (11th pick overall); draft rights promptly traded to the Cleveland Cavaliers.

Season	G	FGM	FGA	FG%	FTM	FTA	FT%	Reb.	Avg.	Pts.	Avg.
1981–82	29	199	370	.538	134	178	.753	320	11.0	532	18.3
1982–83	31	220	438	.502	141	172	.820	336	10.8	581	18.7
1983–84	33	245	453	.541	117	151	.775	357	10.8	607	18.4
1984–85	35	266	536	.496	156	200	.780	323	9.2	688	19.7
Totals	128	930	1797	.518	548	701	.782	1336	10.4	2408	18.8

BOB LLOYD
Rutgers
6-1 – G
Upper Darby, Pa.

NCAA consensus first-team All-American in 1967.... Led the nation in free-throw percentage in 1967.... Did not play in NCAA Tournament.... Averaged 32.3 points in four NIT games for 1967 third-place team.... Selected by the Minnesota Muskies in first five rounds of 1967 ABA draft.

Season	G	FGM	FGA	FG%	FTM	FTA	FT%	Reb.	Avg.	Pts.	Avg.
1964–65	24	237	543	.436	127	145	.876	72	3.0	601	25.0
1965–66	24	237	517	.458	161	183	.880	70	2.9	635	26.5
1966–67	29	277	579	.478	255	277	.921	96	3.3	809	27.9
Totals	77	751	1639	.458	543	605	.898	238	3.1	2045	26.6

CLYDE LOVELLETTE
Kansas
6-9 – C
Terre Haute, Ind.

NCAA consensus first-team All-American in 1951 and 1952.... Led the nation in scoring in 1952.... Leading scorer and rebounder for 1952 NCAA champion (28-3 record).... Final Four Most Outstanding Player in 1952.... Averaged 35.3 points in four NCAA Tournament games in 1952.... Leading scorer (14.1 points per game) for 1952 U.S. Olympic team.... Selected by the Minneapolis Lakers in 1952 NBA draft.... Elected to Naismith Memorial Basketball Hall of Fame in 1987.

Season	G	FGM	FGA	FG%	FTM	FTA	FT%	Reb.	Avg.	Pts.	Avg.
1949–50	25	214	499	.429	117	181	.646	192	7.7	545	21.8
1950–51	24	245	554	.442	58	89	.652	237	9.9	548	22.8
1951–52	28	315	660	.477	165	224	.737	357	12.8	795	28.4
Totals	77	774	1713	.452	340	494	.688	786	10.2	1888	24.5

JERRY LUCAS
Ohio State
6-8 – C
Middletown, Ohio

Named national player of the year by AP, UPI, and USBWA in 1961 and 1962.... NCAA unanimous first-team All-American in 1960, 1961, and 1962.... Led the nation in field-goal percentage in 1960, 1961, and 1962.... Led nation in rebounding in 1961 and 1962 ... Final Four Most Outstanding Player in 1960 and 1961.... Member of All-NCAA Tournament team in 1960, 1961, and 1962.... Leading scorer and rebounder for 1960 NCAA champion (25-3 record) and national runners-up in 1961 (27-1) and 1962 (26-2).... Averaged 22.2 points and 16.4 rebounds in 12 NCAA Tournament games from 1960 to 1962 (10-2 record).... Tied with Oscar Robertson for scoring leadership (17 points per game) on 1960 U.S. Olympic team.... Selected as a territorial pick by the Cincinnati Royals in first round of 1962 NBA draft (did not play professionally in 1962-63 after signing with the Cleveland Pipers before they dropped out of the American Basketball League prior to the start of the season).... Elected to Naismith Memorial Basketball Hall of Fame in 1979.

Season	G	FGM	FGA	FG%	FTM	FTA	FT%	Reb.	Avg.	Pts.	Avg.
1959–60	27	283	444	.637	144	187	.770	442	16.4	710	26.3
1960–61	27	256	411	.623	159	208	.764	470	17.4	671	24.9
1961–62	28	237	388	.611	135	169	.799	499	17.8	609	21.8
Totals	82	776	1243	.624	438	564	.777	1411	17.2	1990	24.3

JOHN LUCAS
Maryland
6-3 – G
Durham, N.C.

NCAA consensus first-team All-American in 1975 and 1976.... Averaged 22.2 points in five NCAA Tournament games in 1973 and 1975 (3-2 record).... Selected by the Houston Rockets in first round of 1976 NBA draft (1st pick overall).

Season	G	FGM	FGA	FG%	FTM	FTA	FT%	Reb.	Avg.	Pts.	Avg.
1972–73	30	190	353	.538	45	64	.703	83	2.8	425	14.2
1973–74	28	253	495	.511	58	77	.753	82	2.9	564	20.1
1974–75	24	186	339	.549	97	116	.836	100	4.2	469	19.5
1975–76	28	233	456	.511	91	117	.778	109	3.9	557	19.9
Totals	110	862	1643	.525	291	374	.778	374	3.4	2015	18.3

ANGELO (HANK) LUISETTI
Stanford
6-2 – F
San Francisco, Calif.

NCAA consensus All-American in 1936, 1937, and 1938.... Led the nation in scoring in 1936 and 1937.... Did not play in NCAA Tournament or NIT.... Elected to Naismith Memorial Basketball Hall of Fame in 1959.

Season	G	FGM	FGA	FG%	FTM	FTA	FT%	Reb.	Avg.	Pts.	Avg.
1935–36	29									416	20.3
1936–37	24									410	17.1
1937–38	27									465	17.2
Totals	80									1291	16.1

BOB MCADOO
North Carolina
6-9 – F/C
Greensboro, N.C.

NCAA consensus first-team All-American in 1972.... Named to All-NCAA Tournament team in 1972.... Leading scorer and rebounder for 1972 national third-place team (29-5 record).... Averaged 20.5 points and 14 rebounds in four NCAA Tournament games in 1972 (3-1 record).... Averaged 21.9 points and 10.5 rebounds in two junior college seasons at Vincennes (Ind.).... Selected as an undergraduate by the Buffalo Braves in first round of 1972 NBA draft (2nd pick overall).

Season	G	FGM	FGA	FG%	FTM	FTA	FT%	Reb.	Avg.	Pts.	Avg.
1971–72	31	243	471	.516	118	167	.707	312	10.1	604	19.5

ED MACAULEY
St. Louis
6-8 – C/F
St. Louis, Mo.

NCAA unanimous first-team All-American in 1949 and consensus first-team All-American in 1948.... Led the nation in field-goal percentage in 1949.... Did not play in NCAA Tournament.... NIT Most Valuable Player in 1948.... Averaged 16.5 points in four NIT games in 1948 (champion) and 1949 (first-round loser).... Selected as a territorial pick by the St. Louis Bombers of the Basketball Association of America in 1949.... Elected to Naismith Memorial Basketball Hall of Fame in 1960.

Season	G	FGM	FGA	FG%	FTM	FTA	FT%	Reb.	Avg.	Pts.	Avg.
1945–46	23	94			71					259	11.3
1946–47	28	141			104					386	13.8
1947–48	27	132	324	.407	104	159	.654			368	13.6
1948–49	26	144	275	.524	116	153	.758			404	15.5
Totals	104	511			395					1417	13.6

XAVIER MCDANIEL
Wichita State
6-7 – F
Columbia, S.C.

NCAA consensus first-team All-American in 1985... One of only two players in NCAA history to lead the nation in scoring and rebounding in the same season (1985); also led the nation in rebounding in 1983.... Collected 22 points and 11 rebounds in one NCAA Tournament game in 1985.... Collected 16 points and 10 rebounds in one NIT game in 1984.... Selected by the Seattle SuperSonics in first round of 1985 NBA draft (4th pick overall).

Season	G	FGM	FGA	FG%	FTM	FTA	FT%	Reb.	Avg.	Pts.	Avg.
1981–82	28	68	135	.504	27	43	.628	103	3.7	163	5.8
1982–83	28	223	376	.593	80	148	.541	403	14.4	526	18.8
1983–84	30	251	445	.564	117	172	.680	393	13.1	619	20.6
1984–85	31	351	628	.559	142	224	.634	460	14.8	844	27.2
Totals	117	893	1584	.564	366	587	.624	1359	11.6	2152	18.4

JIM MCDANIELS
Western Kentucky
7-0 – C
Scottsdale, Ky.

NCAA consensus first-team All-American in 1971.... Leading scorer and rebounder for 1971 national third-place team (24-6 record).... Member of All-NCAA Tournament team in 1971.... Averaged 29.3 points and 12.2 rebounds in six NCAA Tournament games in 1970 and 1971 (4-2 record).... Selected by the Utah Stars in first round of a "secret" ABA draft in January 1971 before signing a contract with the ABA (no specific team) sometime before the end of the season.

Season	G	FGM	FGA	FG%	FTM	FTA	FT%	Reb.	Avg.	Pts.	Avg.
1968–69	26	273	544	.502	98	152	.645	324	12.5	644	24.8
1969–70	25	305	535	.570	106	141	.752	340	13.6	716	28.6
1970–71	30	357	684	.522	164	221	.742	454	15.1	878	29.3
Totals	81	935	1763	.530	368	514	.716	1118	13.8	2238	27.6

BILLY MCGILL
Utah
6-9 – C
Los Angeles, Calif.

NCAA unanimous first-team All-American in 1962 and consensus first-team All-American in 1961.... Led the nation in scoring in 1962.... Leading scorer and rebounder for 1961 national fourth-place team (23-8 record).... Averaged 23.7 points and 10.7 rebounds in seven NCAA Tournament games in 1960 and 1961 (4-3 record).... Selected by the Chicago Zephyrs in first round of 1962 NBA draft.

Season	G	FGM	FGA	FG%	FTM	FTA	FT%	Reb.	Avg.	Pts.	Avg.
1959–60	29	179	374	.479	92	138	.667	285	9.8	450	15.5
1960–61	31	343	650	.528	176	249	.707	430	13.9	862	27.8
1961–62	26	394	705	.559	221	302	.732	391	15.0	1009	38.8
Totals	86	916	1729	.530	489	689	.710	1106	12.9	2321	27.0

GEORGE MCGINNIS
Indiana
6-8 – F
Indianapolis, Ind.

Did not play in NCAA Tournament or NIT.... Signed as an undergraduate free agent by the ABA's Indiana Pacers in 1971 in lieu of 1972 first-round draft choice.

Season	G	FGM	FGA	FG%	FTM	FTA	FT%	Reb.	Avg.	Pts.	Avg.
1970–71	24	283	615	.460	153	249	.614	352	14.7	719	30.0

KEVIN MCHALE
Minnesota
6-10 – F/C
Hibbing, Minn.

Did not play in NCAA Tournament.... Averaged 12 points in five NIT games for 1980 runner-up.... Selected by the Boston Celtics in first round of 1980 NBA draft (3rd pick overall).

Season	G	FGM	FGA	FG%	FTM	FTA	FT%	Reb.	Avg.	Pts.	Avg.
1976–77	27	133	241	.552	58	77	.753	218	8.1	324	12.0
1977–78	26	143	242	.591	54	77	.701	192	7.4	340	13.1
1978–79	27	202	391	.517	79	96	.823	259	9.6	483	17.9
1979–80	32	236	416	.567	85	107	.794	281	8.8	557	17.4
Totals	112	714	1290	.553	276	357	.773	950	8.5	1704	15.2

JIM MCINTYRE
Minnesota
6-10 – C
Minneapolis, Minn.

NCAA consensus first-team All-American in 1948.... Did not play in NCAA Tournament or NIT.... Did not play in NBA although several teams held his rights (Rochester Royals, Tri-Cities Blackhawks, and Milwaukee Hawks). He chose instead to get involved in the Youth for Christ Movement although he did play two seasons (1952–53 and 1953–54) with the Akron Goodyears in the National Industrial Basketball League.

Season	G	FGM	FGA	FG%	FTM	FTA	FT%	Reb.	Avg.	Pts.	Avg.
1945–46	20	74			47					195	9.8
1946–47	21	107			100					314	15.0
1947–48	19	125			110					360	18.9
1948–49	21	126			102	146	.699			354	16.9
Totals	81	432			359					1223	15.1

KYLE MACY
Kentucky
6-3 – G
Peru, Ind.

NCAA unanimous first-team All-American in 1980.... Third-leading scorer for 1978 NCAA champion (30-2 record).... Averaged 10.3 points in seven NCAA Tournament games in 1978 and 1980 (6-1 record).... Scored 20 points in one NIT game in 1979.... Selected as a junior eligible by the Phoenix Suns in first round of 1979 NBA draft (22nd pick overall).

Season	G	FGM	FGA	FG%	FTM	FTA	FT%	Reb.	Avg.	Pts.	Avg.
1975–76	27	144	293	.491	85	99	.859	75	2.8	373	13.8
1976–77				Sat out the season after transferring from Purdue.							
1977–78	32	143	267	.536	115	129	.891	76	2.4	401	12.5
1978–79	31	179	355	.504	112	129	.868	82	2.6	470	15.2
1979–80	35	218	415	.525	104	114	.912	85	2.4	540	15.4
Totals	125	684	1330	.514	416	471	.883	318	2.5	1784	14.3

JEFF MALONE
Mississippi State
6-4 – G
Macon, Ga.

Did not play in NCAA Tournament or NIT.... Selected by the Washington Bullets in first round of 1983 NBA draft (10th pick overall).

Season	G	FGM	FGA	FG%	FTM	FTA	FT%	Reb.	Avg.	Pts.	Avg.
1979–80	27	139	303	.459	42	51	.824	90	3.3	320	11.9
1980–81	27	219	447	.490	105	128	.820	113	4.2	543	20.1
1981–82	27	225	410	.549	52	70	.743	111	4.1	502	18.6
1982–83	29	323	608	.531	131	159	.824	106	3.7	777	26.8
Totals	110	906	1768	.512	330	408	.809	420	3.8	2142	19.5

KARL MALONE
Louisiana Tech
6-9 – F
Summerfield, La.

Averaged 19.6 points and 12 rebounds in five NCAA Tournament games in 1984 and 1985 (3-2 record).... Member of 1992 U.S. Olympic team.... Selected as an undergraduate by the Utah Jazz in 1985 NBA draft (13th pick overall).

Season	G	FGM	FGA	FG%	FTM	FTA	FT%	Reb.	Avg.	Pts.	Avg.
1981–82				Did not play because he was academically ineligible.							
1982–83	28	217	373	.582	152	244	.623	289	10.3	586	20.9
1983–84	32	220	382	.576	161	236	.682	282	8.8	601	18.8
1984–85	32	216	399	.541	97	170	.571	288	9.0	529	16.5
Totals	92	653	1154	.566	410	650	.631	859	9.3	1716	18.7

DANNY MANNING
Kansas
6-10 – F/C
Greensboro, N.C.

NCAA unanimous first-team All-American in 1987 and 1988, and consensus second-team All-American in 1986.... Named national player of the year by NABC in 1988.... Naismith Award and Wooden Award winner in 1988.... Member of All-NCAA Tournament team in 1988 when he was Final Four Most Outstanding Player.... Leading scorer and rebounder for 1988 NCAA champion (27-11 record), and leading scorer and second-leading rebounder for 1986 Final Four team (35-4).... Member of 1988 U.S. Olympic team.... Averaged 20.5 points and 7.3 rebounds in 16 NCAA Tournament games from 1985-88 (13-3 record).... Selected by the Los Angeles Clippers in first round of 1988 NBA draft (1st pick overall).

Season	G	FGM	FGA	FG%	FTM	FTA	FT%	Reb.	Avg.	Pts.	Avg.
1984–85	34	209	369	.566	78	102	.765	258	7.6	496	14.6
1985–86	39	279	465	.600	95	127	.748	245	6.3	653	16.7
1986–87	36	347	562	.617	165	226	.730	342	9.5	860	23.9
1987–88	38	381	653	.583	171	233	.734	342	9.0	942	24.8
Totals	147	1216	2049	.593	509	688	.740	1187	8.1	2951	20.1

Three-point field goals: 1 of 3 (.333) in 1986–87 and 9 of 26 (.346) in 1987–88. **Totals:** 10 of 29 (.345).

PETE MARAVICH
Louisiana State
6-5 – G
Raleigh, N.C.

NCAA unanimous first-team All-American in 1968, 1969, and 1970.... Named national player of the year by AP, UPI, and USBWA in 1970.... Naismith Award winner in 1970.... Led the nation in scoring in 1968, 1969, and 1970.... Did not play in NCAA Tournament.... Averaged 25.7 points, five rebounds, and 7.7 assists in three NIT games for 1970 fourth-place team (did not play in one game).... Selected by the Atlanta Hawks in first round of 1970 NBA draft (3rd pick overall).... Elected to Naismith Memorial Basketball Hall of Fame in 1986.

Season	G	FGM	FGA	FG%	FTM	FTA	FT%	Reb.	Avg.	Pts.	Avg.
1967–68	26	432	1022	.423	274	338	.811	195	7.5	1138	43.8
1968–69	26	433	976	.444	282	378	.746	169	6.5	1148	44.2
1969–70	31	522	1168	.447	337	436	.773	164	5.3	1381	44.5
Totals	83	1387	3166	.438	893	1152	.775	528	6.4	3667	44.2

DONYELL MARSHALL
Connecticut
6-9 – F
Reading, Pa.

NCAA unanimous first-team All-American in 1994.... Averaged 17.2 points and 10.4 rebounds in five NCAA Tournament games in 1992 and 1994 (3-2 record).... Collected 22 points and 12 rebounds in one NIT game in 1993.... Selected as an undergraduate by the Minnesota Timberwolves in first round of 1994 NBA draft (4th pick overall).

Season	G	FGM	FGA	FG%	FTM	FTA	FT%	Reb.	Avg.	Pts.	Avg.
1991–92	30	125	295	.424	69	93	.742	183	6.1	334	11.1
1992–93	27	166	332	.500	107	129	.829	210	7.8	459	17.0
1993–94	34	306	599	.511	200	266	.752	302	8.9	853	25.1
Totals	91	597	1226	.487	376	488	.770	695	7.6	1646	18.1

Three-point field goals: 15 of 62 (.242) in 1991–92, 20 of 54 (.370) in 1992–93, and 41 of 132 (.311) in 1993–94. **Totals:** 76 of 248 (.306).

LARUE MARTIN

Loyola of Chicago
6-11 – C
Chicago, Ill.

Did not play in NCAA Tournament or NIT.... Selected by the Portland Trail Blazers in first round of 1972 NBA draft (1st pick overall).

Season	G	FGM	FGA	FG%	FTM	FTA	FT%	Reb.	Avg.	Pts.	Avg.
1969–70	24	168	332	.506	63	100	.630	346	14.4	399	16.6
1970–71	22	166	406	.409	80	127	.630	387	17.6	412	18.7
1971–72	21	159	359	.443	93	114	.816	329	15.7	411	19.6
Totals	67	493	1097	.449	236	341	.692	1062	15.9	1222	18.2

JAMAL MASHBURN

Kentucky
6-8 – F
Bronx, N.Y.

NCAA unanimous first-team All-American in 1993.... Leading scorer and rebounder for 1993 Final Four team (30-4 record).... Averaged 21.4 points and eight rebounds in nine NCAA Tournament games in 1992 and 1993 (7-2 record).... Selected as an undergraduate by the Dallas Mavericks in first round of 1993 NBA draft (4th pick overall).

Season	G	FGM	FGA	FG%	FTM	FTA	FT%	Reb.	Avg.	Pts.	Avg.
1990–91	28	137	289	.474	64	88	.727	195	7.0	362	12.9
1991–92	36	279	492	.567	151	213	.709	281	7.8	767	21.3
1992–93	34	259	526	.492	130	194	.670	284	8.4	714	21.0
Totals	98	675	1307	.516	345	495	.697	760	7.8	1843	18.8

Three-point field goals: 23 of 82 (.280) in 1990–91, 58 of 132 (.439) in 1991–92, and 66 of 180 (.367) in 1992–93. Totals: 147 of 394 (.373).

DON MAY

Dayton
6-4 – F
Dayton, Ohio

NCAA consensus second-team All-American in 1967 and 1968.... Leading scorer and rebounder for 1967 national runner-up (25-6 record).... Named to All-NCAA Tournament team in 1967.... Averaged 20.1 points and 12.9 rebounds in eight NCAA Tournament games in 1966 and 1967 (5-3 record).... Most Valuable Player of 1968 NIT.... Averaged 26.5 points in four NIT games for 1968 champion.... Selected by the New York Knicks in third round of 1968 NBA draft (30th pick overall).

Season	G	FGM	FGA	FG%	FTM	FTA	FT%	Reb.	Avg.	Pts.	Avg.
1965–66	29	238	505	.471	114	166	.687	331	11.4	590	20.3
1966–67	31	258	543	.475	173	213	.812	519	16.7	689	22.2
1967–68	30	239	509	.470	223	284	.785	451	15.0	701	23.4
Totals	90	735	1557	.472	510	663	.769	1301	14.5	1980	22.0

SCOTT MAY

Indiana
6-7 – F
Sandusky, Ohio

Named national player of the year by AP, UPI, and NABC in 1976.... Naismith Award winner in 1976.... NCAA unanimous first-team All-American in 1976 and consensus first-team All-American in 1975.... Leading scorer and second-leading rebounder for undefeated 1976 NCAA champion (32-0 record).... Named to All-NCAA Tournament team in 1976.... Averaged 14.4 points and 4.9 rebounds in eight NCAA Tournament games in 1975 and 1976 (7-1 record).... Leading rebounder (6.2 rpg) and second-leading scorer (16.7 ppg) for 1976 U.S. Olympic team.... Selected by the Chicago Bulls in first round of 1976 NBA draft (2nd pick overall).

Season	G	FGM	FGA	FG%	FTM	FTA	FT%	Reb.	Avg.	Pts.	Avg.
1972–73		Did not play because he was academically ineligible.									
1973–74	28	154	313	.492	43	56	.768	150	5.4	351	12.5
1974–75	30	204	400	.510	82	107	.766	199	6.6	490	16.3
1975–76	32	308	584	.527	136	174	.782	245	7.7	752	23.5
Totals	90	666	1297	.513	261	337	.774	594	6.6	1593	17.7

CEDRIC (CORNBREAD) MAXWELL

UNC Charlotte
6-8 – F/C
Kinston, N.C.

Leading scorer and rebounder for 1977 NCAA fourth-place finisher (30-5 record).... Named to All-NCAA Tournament team in 1977.... Averaged 24.6 points and 12.8 rebounds in five NCAA Tournament games in 1977 (3-2 record).... NIT Most Valuable Player in 1976 when he averaged 27.3 points and 11.5 rebounds in four games for second-place finisher.... Selected by the Boston Celtics in first round of 1977 NBA draft (12th pick overall).

Season	G	FGM	FGA	FG%	FTM	FTA	FT%	Reb.	Avg.	Pts.	Avg.
1973–74	26	98	154	.636	41	77	.532	161	6.2	237	9.1
1974–75	34	142	237	.535	64	88	.727	230	8.8	318	12.2
1975–76	29	201	371	.541	177	215	.823	350	12.1	579	20.0
1976–77	31	244	381	.640	202	263	.768	376	12.1	690	22.3
Totals	112	670	1143	.586	484	643	.753	1117	10.0	1824	16.3

GENE MELCHIORRE

Bradley
5-8 – G
Highland Park, Ill.

NCAA consensus first-team All-American in 1951.... Second-leading scorer for 1950 NCAA runner-up (32-5 record).... Averaged 15.3 points in three NCAA Tournament games for 1950 national runner-up.... Averaged 16.7 points in six NIT games for 1949 fourth-place team and 1950 runner-up.... Selected by the Baltimore Bullets in 1951 NBA draft (did not play in league).

Season	G	FGM	FGA	FG%	FTM	FTA	FT%	Reb.	Avg.	Pts.	Avg.
1947–48	31	111	279	.398	82	137	.599			304	9.8
1948–49	34	142	328	.433	116	177	.655			400	11.8
1949–50	37	153	384	.398	134	202	.663			440	11.9
1950–51	35	138			161					437	12.5
Totals	137	544			493					1581	11.5

DEAN MEMINGER

Marquette
6-1 – G
New York, N.Y.

NCAA unanimous first-team All-American in 1971.... Averaged 18.2 points and 5.7 rebounds in six NCAA Tournament games in 1969 and 1971 (4-2 record).... Averaged 17.8 points in four NIT games for 1970 champion.... NIT Most Valuable Player in 1970.... Selected by the New York Knicks in first round of 1971 NBA draft (16th pick overall).

Season	G	FGM	FGA	FG%	FTM	FTA	FT%	Reb.	Avg.	Pts.	Avg.
1968–69	29	172	409	.421	131	233	.562	187	6.4	475	16.4
1969–70	29	184	400	.460	178	279	.638	142	4.9	546	18.8
1970–71	29	216	425	.508	184	250	.736	117	4.0	616	21.2
Totals	87	572	1234	.464	493	762	.647	446	5.1	1637	18.8

DAVE MEYERS
UCLA
6-8 – F
La Habra, Calif.

NCAA unanimous first-team All-American in 1975.... Leading scorer and rebounder for 1975 NCAA champion (28-3 record), third-leading scorer and rebounder for 1974 national third-place team (26-4), and sixth-leading scorer for undefeated 1973 NCAA champion (30-0).... Member of All-NCAA Tournament team in 1975.... Averaged 12.7 points and 6.8 rebounds in 13 NCAA Tournament games from 1973 to 1975 (12-1 record).... Selected by the Los Angeles Lakers in first round of 1975 NBA draft (2nd pick overall). Rights promptly traded to the Milwaukee Bucks.

Season	G	FGM	FGA	FG%	FTM	FTA	FT%	Reb.	Avg.	Pts.	Avg.
1972–73	28	52	109	.477	34	45	.756	82	2.9	138	4.9
1973–74	30	144	295	.488	54	77	.701	171	5.7	342	11.4
1974–75	31	230	475	.484	106	144	.736	244	7.9	566	18.3
Totals	89	426	879	.485	194	266	.729	497	5.6	1046	11.8

GEORGE MIKAN
DePaul
6-10 – C
Joliet, Ill.

NCAA consensus first-team All-American in 1944, 1945 and 1946.... Led the nation in scoring in 1945 and 1946.... Final Four Most Outstanding Player in 1955.... Leading scorer for 1943 Final Four team (19-5 record).... Averaged 15.5 points in two NCAA Tournament games in 1943 (1-1 record).... NIT Most Valuable Player in 1945.... Leading scorer in NIT in 1944 and 1945 when he averaged 28.2 points in six games.... Signed by the NBA's Chicago Stags in 1946.... Elected to Naismith Memorial Basketball Hall of Fame in 1959.

Season	G	FGM	FGA	FG%	FTM	FTA	FT%	Reb.	Avg.	Pts.	Avg.
1942–43	24	97			77	111	.694			271	11.3
1943–44	26	188			110	169	.651			486	18.7
1944–45	24	218			122	199	.613			558	23.3
1945–46	24	206			143	186	.769			555	23.1
Totals	98	709			452	665	.680			1870	19.1

LARRY MILLER
North Carolina
6-4 – F
Catasauqua, Pa.

NCAA consensus first-team All-American in 1968 and consensus second-team All-American in 1967.... Leading scorer and second-leading rebounder for 1968 national runner-up (28-4 record) and 1967 national fourth-place team (26-6).... Member of All-NCAA Tournament team in 1968.... Averaged 17.5 points and 9.1 rebounds in eight NCAA Tournament games in 1967 and 1968 (5-3 record).... Selected by the Los Angeles Stars in first five rounds of 1968 ABA draft.

Season	G	FGM	FGA	FG%	FTM	FTA	FT%	Reb.	Avg.	Pts.	Avg.
1965–66	27	219	400	.548	127	187	.679	277	10.3	565	20.9
1966–67	32	278	553	.503	144	218	.661	299	9.3	700	21.9
1967–68	32	268	545	.492	181	256	.707	258	8.1	717	22.4
Totals	91	765	1498	.511	452	661	.684	834	9.2	1982	21.8

HAROLD MINER
Southern California
6-5 – G
Inglewood, Calif.

NCAA unanimous first-team All-American in 1992.... Averaged 19 points and five rebounds in three NCAA Tournament games in 1991 and 1992 (1-2 record).... Selected as an undergraduate by the Miami Heat in first round of 1992 NBA draft (12th pick overall).

Season	G	FGM	FGA	FG%	FTM	FTA	FT%	Reb.	Avg.	Pts.	Avg.
1989–90	28	206	436	.472	106	126	.841	101	3.6	578	20.6
1990–91	29	235	519	.453	152	190	.800	159	5.5	681	23.5
1991–92	30	250	571	.438	232	286	.811	211	7.0	789	26.3
Totals	87	691	1526	.453	490	602	.814	471	5.4	2048	23.5

Three-point field goals: 60 of 142 (.423) in 1989–90, 59 of 175 (.337) in 1990–91, and 57 of 162 (.352) in 1991–92. **Totals:** 176 of 479 (.367).

MIKE MITCHELL
Auburn
6-7 – F
Atlanta, Ga.

Did not play in NCAA Tournament or NIT.... Selected by the Cleveland Cavaliers in first round of 1978 NBA draft (15th pick overall).

Season	G	FGM	FGA	FG%	FTM	FTA	FT%	Reb.	Avg.	Pts.	Avg.
1974–75	26	204	426	.479	53	98	.541	286	11.4	461	18.4
1975–76	26	210	431	.487	66	96	.688	249	9.6	486	18.7
1976–77	26	229	429	.534	47	69	.681	220	8.5	505	19.4
1977–78	27	283	544	.520	105	135	.778	241	8.9	671	24.9
Totals	104	926	1830	.506	271	398	.681	996	9.6	2123	20.4

BILL MLKVY
Temple
6-4 – F
Palmerton, Pa.

NCAA unanimous first-team All-American in 1951.... Led the nation in scoring in 1951.... Second in the nation in rebounding and assists in 1951.... Did not play in NCAA Tournament or NIT.... Selected by the Philadelphia Warriors in 1952 NBA draft.

Season	G	FGM	FGA	FG%	FTM	FTA	FT%	Reb.	Avg.	Pts.	Avg.
1949–50	24	152			86	110	.782			390	16.3
1950–51	25	303	964	.314	125	181	.691	472	18.9	731	29.2
1951–52	24	169			80	103	.777	379	15.8	418	17.4
Totals	73	624			291	394	.739			1539	21.1

STAN MODZELEWSKI
Rhode Island
5-11 – G
Worcester, Mass.

NCAA consensus second-team All-American in 1941 and 1942.... Led the nation in scoring in 1940, 1941, and 1942.... Did not play in NCAA Tournament.... Averaged 14 points in two NIT first-round defeats in 1941 and 1942.... . Changed his name to Stan Stutz.

Season	G	FGM	FGA	FG%	FTM	FTA	FT%	Reb.	Avg.	Pts.	Avg.
1939–40	22	210			89					509	23.1
1940–41	25	178			107					463	18.5
1941–42	22	182			106	131	.809			470	21.4
Totals	69	570			302					1442	20.9

JOHN MOIR
Notre Dame
6-2 – F
Niagara Falls, N.Y.

NCAA consensus first-team All-American in 1937 and 1938.

Season	G	FGM	FGA	FG%	FTM	FTA	FT%	Reb.	Avg.	Pts.	Avg.
1935–36	23	112			36					260	11.3
1936–37	22	113			64					290	13.2
1937–38	22	92			46					230	10.5
Totals	67	317			146					780	11.6

SIDNEY MONCRIEF
Arkansas
6-3 – G
Little Rock, Ark.

NCAA consensus first-team All-American in 1979.... Led the nation in field-goal percentage in 1976.... Leading rebounder and second-leading scorer for 1978 national third-place team (32-4 record).... Averaged 17 points and 7.1 rebounds in nine NCAA Tournament games from 1977 to 1979 (6-3 record).... Selected by the Milwaukee Bucks in first round of 1979 NBA draft (5th pick overall).

Season	G	FGM	FGA	FG%	FTM	FTA	FT%	Reb.	Avg.	Pts.	Avg.
1975–76	28	149	224	.665	56	77	.727	213	7.6	354	12.6
1976–77	28	157	242	.649	117	171	.684	235	8.4	431	15.4
1977–78	36	209	354	.590	203	256	.793	278	7.7	621	17.3
1978–79	30	224	400	.560	212	248	.855	289	9.6	660	22.0
Totals	122	739	1220	.606	588	752	.782	1015	8.3	2066	16.9

ERIC MONTROSS
North Carolina
7-0 – C
Indianapolis, Ind.

NCAA consensus second-team All-American in 1993 and 1994.... Leading scorer and second-leading rebounder for 1993 NCAA champion (34-4 record).... Fourth-leading rebounder and sixth-leading scorer for 1991 Final Four team (29-6).... Named to All-NCAA Tournament team in 1993.... Averaged 13.9 points and 6.9 rebounds in 16 NCAA Tournament games from 1991 to 1994 (13-3 record).... Selected by the Boston Celtics in first round of 1994 NBA draft (9th pick overall).

Season	G	FGM	FGA	FG%	FTM	FTA	FT%	Reb.	Avg.	Pts.	Avg.
1990–91	35	81	138	.587	41	67	.612	148	4.2	203	5.8
1991–92	31	140	244	.574	68	109	.624	218	7.0	348	11.2
1992–93	38	222	361	.615	156	228	.684	290	7.6	600	15.8
1993–94	35	183	327	.560	110	197	.558	285	8.1	476	13.6
Totals	139	626	1070	.585	375	601	.624	941	6.8	1629	11.7

MAX MORRIS
Northwestern
6-1 – C-F
West Frankfort, Ill.

NCAA consensus first-team All-American in 1946 and second-team All-American in 1945.... Did not play in NCAA Tournament or NIT.

Season	G	FGM	FGA	FG%	FTM	FTA	FT%	Reb.	Avg.	Pts.	Avg.
1943–44		Earned letter in football at the University of Illinois.									
1944–45	19									292	15.4
1945–46	20	133			78					344	17.2
Totals	39									636	16.3

RICK MOUNT
Purdue
6-4 – G
Lebanon, Ind.

NCAA unanimous first-team All-American in 1969 and 1970.... Leading scorer with 30.5-point average in four NCAA Tournament games for 1969 national runner-up (23-5 record).... Member of All-NCAA Tournament team in 1969.... Selected by the Indiana Pacers in 1970 ABA draft.

Season	G	FGM	FGA	FG%	FTM	FTA	FT%	Reb.	Avg.	Pts.	Avg.
1967–68	24	259	593	.437	165	195	.846	67	2.8	683	28.5
1968–69	28	366	710	.515	200	236	.847	90	3.2	932	33.3
1969–70	20	285	582	.490	138	166	.831	54	2.7	708	35.4
Totals	72	910	1885	.483	503	597	.843	211	2.9	2323	32.3

ALONZO MOURNING
Georgetown
6-10 – C
Chesapeake, Va.

NCAA consensus first-team All-American in 1992 and consensus second-team All-American in 1990.... Led the nation in blocked shots (five per game) in 1989.... Averaged 15.3 points, 8.5 rebounds, and 3.7 blocked shots in 10 NCAA Tournament games from 1989 to 1992 (6-4 record).... Selected by the Charlotte Hornets in first round of 1992 NBA draft (2nd pick overall).

Season	G	FGM	FGA	FG%	FTM	FTA	FT%	Reb.	Avg.	Pts.	Avg.
1988–89	34	158	262	.603	130	195	.667	248	7.3	447	13.1
1989–90	31	145	276	.525	220	281	.783	265	8.5	510	16.5
1990–91	23	105	201	.522	149	188	.793	176	7.7	363	15.8
1991–92	32	204	343	.595	272	359	.758	343	10.7	681	21.3
Totals	120	612	1082	.566	771	1023	.754	1032	8.6	2001	16.7

Three-point field goals: 1 of 4 (.250) in 1988–89, 0 of 2 in 1989–90, 4 of 13 (.308) in 1990–91, and 6 of 23 (.261) in 1991–92. Totals: 11 of 42 (.262).

CHRIS MULLIN
St. John's
6-6 – G/F
Brooklyn, N.Y.

Named national player of the year by UPI and USBWA in 1985.... Wooden Award winner in 1985.... NCAA unanimous first-team All-American in 1985 and consensus second-team All-American in 1984.... Leading scorer and third-leading rebounder for 1985 Final Four team (31-4 record).... Averaged 20.7 points, 4.3 rebounds, and 3.9 assists in 10 NCAA Tournament games from 1982 to 1985 (6-4 record).... Member of 1984 and 1992 U.S. Olympic teams.... Selected by the Golden State Warriors in first round of 1985 NBA draft (7th pick overall).

Season	G	FGM	FGA	FG%	FTM	FTA	FT%	Reb.	Avg.	Pts.	Avg.
1981–82	30	175	328	.534	148	187	.791	97	3.2	498	16.6
1982–83	33	228	395	.577	173	197	.878	123	3.7	629	19.1
1983–84	27	225	394	.571	169	187	.904	120	4.4	619	22.9
1984–85	35	251	482	.521	192	233	.824	169	4.8	694	19.8
Totals	125	879	1599	.550	682	804	.848	509	4.1	2440	19.5

CALVIN MURPHY
Niagara
5-9 – G
Norwalk, Conn.

NCAA consensus first-team All-American in 1969 and 1970, and consensus second-team All-American in 1968.... Averaged 29.3 points and 6.3 rebounds in three NCAA Tournament games in 1970 (1-2 record).... Selected by the San Diego Rockets in second round of 1970 NBA draft (18th pick overall).

Season	G	FGM	FGA	FG%	FTM	FTA	FT%	Reb.	Avg.	Pts.	Avg.
1967–68	24	337	772	.437	242	288	.840	118	4.9	916	38.2
1968–69	24	294	700	.420	190	230	.826	87	3.6	778	32.4
1969–70	29	316	692	.457	222	252	.881	103	3.6	854	29.4
Totals	77	947	2164	.438	654	770	.849	308	4.0	2548	33.1

CHARLES (STRETCH) MURPHY
Purdue
6-6 – C
Marion, Ind.

NCAA consensus first-team All-American in 1929 and 1930.... Elected to Naismith Memorial Basketball Hall of Fame in 1960.

Season	G	FGM	FGA	FG%	FTM	FTA	FT%	Reb.	Avg.	Pts.	Avg.
1927–28	17	70			37					177	10.4
1928–29	17	76			54					206	12.1
1929–30	15	73			44					190	12.7
Totals	49	219			135					573	11.7

LARRY NANCE
Clemson
6-10 – F/C
Anderson, S.C.

Averaged 14.5 points and 9.3 rebounds in four NCAA Tournament games in 1980 (3-1 record).... Averaged 15.3 points and 6 rebounds in three NIT games in 1979 and 1981 (1-2 record).... Selected by the Phoenix Suns in first round of 1981 NBA draft (20th pick overall).

Season	G	FGM	FGA	FG%	FTM	FTA	FT%	Reb.	Avg.	Pts.	Avg.
1977–78	25	35	75	.467	8	17	.471	78	3.1	78	3.1
1978–79	29	137	264	.519	49	77	.636	210	7.2	323	11.1
1979–80	32	174	338	.515	98	164	.598	259	8.1	446	13.9
1980–81	31	207	360	.575	80	116	.690	237	7.6	494	15.9
Totals	117	553	1037	.533	235	374	.628	784	6.7	1341	11.5

CHARLES (COTTON) NASH
Kentucky
6-5 – F
Lake Charles, La.

NCAA unanimous first-team All-American in 1964 and consensus second-team All-American in 1962 and 1963.... Averaged 17.5 points and 9.8 rebounds in four NCAA Tournament games in 1962 and 1964 (1-3 record).... Selected by the Los Angeles Lakers in second round of 1964 NBA draft (14th pick overall).

Season	G	FGM	FGA	FG%	FTM	FTA	FT%	Reb.	Avg.	Pts.	Avg.
1961–62	26	221	489	.452	166	218	.761	345	13.3	608	23.4
1962–63	25	176	471	.374	162	236	.686	300	12.0	514	20.6
1963–64	27	248	588	.422	152	198	.768	317	11.7	648	24.0
Totals	78	645	1548	.417	480	652	.736	962	12.3	1770	22.7

CALVIN NATT
Northeast Louisiana
6-6 – F
Bastrop, La.

NCAA consensus second-team All-American in 1979.... Did not play in NCAA Tournament.... Collected 38 points and 8 rebounds in one NIT game in 1979.... Selected by the New Jersey Nets in first round of 1979 NBA draft (8th pick overall).

Season	G	FGM	FGA	FG%	FTM	FTA	FT%	Reb.	Avg.	Pts.	Avg.
1975–76	25	207	371	.558	102	129	.791	274	11.0	516	20.6
1976–77	27	307	493	.623	168	226	.743	340	12.6	782	29.0
1977–78	27	220	401	.549	136	186	.731	356	13.2	576	21.3
1978–79	29	283	506	.559	141	178	.792	315	10.9	707	24.4
Totals	108	1017	1771	.574	547	719	.761	1285	11.9	2581	23.9

JOHNNY NEUMANN
Mississippi
6-6 – F/G
Memphis, Tenn.

NCAA consensus second-team All-American in 1971.... Led the nation in scoring in 1971.... Did not play in NCAA Tournament or NIT.... Signed as an undergraduate free agent by the Memphis Pros of the ABA in 1971.

Season	G	FGM	FGA	FG%	FTM	FTA	FT%	Reb.	Avg.	Pts.	Avg.
1970–71	23	366	792	.462	191	250	.764	152	6.6	923	40.1

PAUL NOWAK
Notre Dame
6-6 – C
South Bend, Ind.

NCAA consensus first-team All-American in 1936, 1937, and 1938.

Season	G	FGM	FGA	FG%	FTM	FTA	FT%	Reb.	Avg.	Pts.	Avg.
1935–36	23	65			31					161	7.0
1936–37	21	56			40					152	7.2
1937–38	23	68			37					173	7.5
Totals	67	189			108					486	7.3

JOHNNY O'BRIEN
Seattle
5-8 – G
South Amboy, N.J.

NCAA unanimous first-team All-American in 1953 and consensus second-team All-American in 1952.... Averaged 32 points in three NCAA Tournament games in 1953 (2-1 record).... Selected by the Milwaukee Hawks in 1953 NBA draft.

Season	G	FGM	FGA	FG%	FTM	FTA	FT%	Reb.	Avg.	Pts.	Avg.
1950–51	37	275	484	.568	216	290	.745			766	20.7
1951–52	37	345	646	.534	361	475	.760			1051	28.4
1952–53	32	284	535	.531	348	430	.809	173	5.4	916	28.6
Totals	106	904	1665	.543	925	1195	.774			2733	25.8

Note: Seattle was classified a Division II school in 1951 and 1952.

MIKE O'KOREN
North Carolina
6-8 – F
Jersey City, N.J.

NCAA consensus second-team All-American in 1979 and 1980.... Leading rebounder and third-leading scorer for 1977 national runner-up (28-5 record).... Member of All-NCAA Tournament team in 1977.... Averaged 15.8 points and 8.6 rebounds in eight NCAA Tournament games from 1977 to 1980 (4-4 record).... Selected by the New Jersey Nets in first round of 1980 NBA draft (6th pick overall).

Season	G	FGM	FGA	FG%	FTM	FTA	FT%	Reb.	Avg.	Pts.	Avg.
1976–77	33	172	298	.577	114	157	.726	217	6.6	458	13.9
1977–78	27	173	269	.643	122	163	.748	180	6.7	468	17.3
1978–79	28	135	259	.521	144	188	.766	202	7.2	414	14.8
1979–80	29	163	298	.547	99	152	.651	216	7.4	425	14.7
Totals	**117**	**643**	**1124**	**.572**	**479**	**660**	**.726**	**815**	**7.0**	**1765**	**15.1**

HAKEEM OLAJUWON
Houston
7-0 – C
Lagos, Nigeria

NCAA consensus first-team All-American in 1984.... Led the nation in rebounding, field-goal percentage, and blocked shots (5.6 per game) in 1984.... Final Four Most Outstanding Player in 1983.... Second-leading scorer and leading rebounder for 1984 national runner-up (32-5 record), third-leading scorer and leading rebounder for 1983 national runner-up (31-3), and sixth-leading scorer and third-leading rebounder for 1982 Final Four team (25-8).... Member of All-NCAA Tournament team in 1983 and 1984.... Averaged 15.1 points and 10.2 rebounds in 15 NCAA Tournament games from 1982-84 (12-3 record).... Selected as an undergraduate by the Houston Rockets in first round of 1984 NBA draft (1st pick overall).

Season	G	FGM	FGA	FG%	FTM	FTA	FT%	Reb.	Avg.	Pts.	Avg.
1980–81			Did not play first year after coming to the U.S. from Nigeria.								
1981–82	29	91	150	.607	58	103	.563	179	6.2	240	8.3
1982–83	34	192	314	.611	88	148	.595	388	11.4	472	13.9
1983–84	37	249	369	.675	122	232	.526	500	13.5	620	16.8
Totals	**100**	**532**	**833**	**.639**	**268**	**483**	**.555**	**1067**	**10.7**	**1332**	**13.3**

SHAQUILLE O'NEAL
Louisiana State
7-1 – C
San Antonio, Tex.

Named national player of the year by AP and UPI in 1991.... NCAA unanimous first-team All-American in 1991 and 1992.... Led the nation in rebounding in 1991 and in blocked shots (5.2 per game) in 1992.... Averaged 24 points, 13.2 rebounds, and 5.8 blocked shots in five NCAA Tournament games from 1990-92 (2-3 record).... Selected as an undergraduate by the Orlando Magic in first round of 1992 NBA draft (1st pick overall).

Season	G	FGM	FGA	FG%	FTM	FTA	FT%	Reb.	Avg.	Pts.	Avg.
1989–90	32	180	314	.573	85	153	.556	385	12.0	445	13.9
1990–91	28	312	497	.628	150	235	.638	411	14.7	774	27.6
1991–92	30	294	478	.615	134	254	.528	421	14.0	722	24.1
Totals	**90**	**786**	**1289**	**.610**	**369**	**642**	**.575**	**1217**	**13.5**	**1941**	**21.6**

KEVIN O'SHEA
Notre Dame
6-1 – G
San Francisco, Calif.

NCAA unanimous first-team All-American in 1948 and consensus second-team All-American in 1950.... Did not play in NCAA Tournament or NIT.... Selected by the Minneapolis Lakers in 1950 NBA draft.

Season	G	FGM	FGA	FG%	FTM	FTA	FT%	Reb.	Avg.	Pts.	Avg.
1946–47	22	91	261	.349	28	57	.491			210	9.5
1947–48	23	100	316	.316	65	106	.613			265	11.5
1948–49	22	85	268	.317	62	92	.674			232	10.5
1949–50	24	133	390	.341	92	141	.652			358	14.9
Totals	**91**	**409**	**1235**	**.331**	**247**	**396**	**.624**			**1065**	**11.7**

BILLY OWENS
Syracuse
6-9 – F
Carlisle, Pa.

NCAA unanimous first-team All-American in 1991.... Averaged 18.9 points and 8.6 rebounds in eight NCAA Tournament games from 1989 to 1991 (5-3 record).... Selected as an undergraduate by the Sacramento Kings in first round of 1991 NBA draft (3rd pick overall); traded to the Golden State Warriors before the start of his rookie season.

Season	G	FGM	FGA	FG%	FTM	FTA	FT%	Reb.	Avg.	Pts.	Avg.
1988–89	38	196	376	.521	94	145	.648	263	6.9	494	13.0
1989–90	33	228	469	.486	127	176	.722	276	8.4	602	18.2
1990–91	32	282	554	.509	157	233	.674	371	11.6	744	23.3
Totals	**103**	**706**	**1399**	**.505**	**378**	**554**	**.682**	**910**	**8.8**	**1840**	**17.9**

Three-point field goals: 8 of 36 (.222) in 1988–89, 19 of 60 (.317) in 1989–90, and 23 of 58 (.397) in 1990–91. **Totals:** 50 of 154 (.325).

ROBERT PARISH
Centenary
7-0 – C
Shreveport, La.

Led the nation in rebounding in 1975 and 1976.... Did not play in NCAA Tournament or NIT.... Selected by the Golden State Warriors in first round of 1976 NBA draft (8th pick overall).

Season	G	FGM	FGA	FG%	FTM	FTA	FT%	Reb.	Avg.	Pts.	Avg.
1972–73	27	285	492	.579	50	82	.610	505	18.7	620	23.0
1973–74	25	224	428	.523	49	78	.628	382	15.3	497	19.9
1974–75	29	237	423	.560	74	112	.661	447	15.4	548	18.9
1975–76	27	288	489	.589	93	134	.694	486	18.0	669	24.8
Totals	**108**	**1034**	**1832**	**.564**	**266**	**406**	**.655**	**1820**	**16.9**	**2334**	**21.6**

JOHN PAXSON
Notre Dame
6-2 – G
Kettering, Ohio

NCAA consensus second-team All-American in 1982 and 1983.... Averaged five points in three NCAA Tournament games in 1980 and 1981 (1-2 record).... Scored 17 points in one NIT game in 1983.... Selected by the San Antonio Spurs in first round of 1983 NBA draft (19th pick overall).

Season	G	FGM	FGA	FG%	FTM	FTA	FT%	Reb.	Avg.	Pts.	Avg.
1979–80	27	42	87	.483	41	55	.745	34	1.3	125	4.6
1980–81	29	113	218	.518	61	89	.685	53	1.8	287	9.9
1981–82	27	185	346	.535	72	93	.774	55	2.0	442	16.4
1982–83	29	219	411	.533	74	100	.740	63	2.2	512	17.7
Totals	**112**	**559**	**1062**	**.526**	**248**	**337**	**.736**	**205**	**1.8**	**1366**	**12.2**

GARY PAYTON
Oregon State
6-3 – G
Oakland, Calif.

NCAA unanimous first-team All-American in 1990.... Averaged 18 points, four rebounds, and seven assists in three NCAA Tournament games from 1988 to 1990 (0-3 record).... Averaged 15.5 points and six assists in two NIT games in 1987 (1-1 record).... Selected by the Seattle SuperSonics in first round of 1990 NBA draft (2nd pick overall).

Season	G	FGM	FGA	FG%	FTM	FTA	FT%	Reb.	Avg.	Pts.	Avg.
1986–87	30	153	333	.459	55	82	.671	120	4.0	374	12.5
1987–88	31	180	368	.489	58	83	.699	103	3.3	449	14.5
1988–89	30	208	438	.475	105	155	.677	122	4.1	603	20.1
1989–90	29	288	571	.504	118	171	.690	135	4.7	746	25.7
Totals	120	829	1710	.485	336	491	.684	480	4.0	2172	18.1

Three-point field goals: 13 of 35 (.371) in 1986–87, 31 of 78 (.397) in 1987–88, 82 of 213 (.385) in 1988–89, and 52 of 156 (.333) in 1989–90. **Totals:** 178 of 482 (.369).

SAM PERKINS

North Carolina
6-10 – F/C
Latham, N.Y.

NCAA consensus first-team All-American in 1983 and 1984, and consensus second-team All-American in 1982.... Second-leading scorer and leading rebounder for 1982 NCAA champion (32-2 record).... Second-leading scorer and rebounder for 1981 national runner-up (29-8).... Named to All-NCAA Tournament team in 1982.... Averaged 15.8 points and 8.6 rebounds in 15 NCAA Tournament games from 1981 to 1984 (12-3 record).... Member of U.S. Olympic team in 1984.... Selected by the Dallas Mavericks in first round of 1984 NBA draft (4th pick overall).

Season	G	FGM	FGA	FG%	FTM	FTA	FT%	Reb.	Avg.	Pts.	Avg.
1980–81	37	199	318	.626	152	205	.741	289	7.8	550	14.9
1981–82	32	174	301	.578	109	142	.768	250	7.8	457	14.3
1982–83	35	218	414	.527	145	177	.819	330	9.4	593	16.9
1983–84	31	195	331	.589	155	181	.856	298	9.6	545	17.6
Totals	135	786	1364	.576	561	705	.796	1167	8.6	2145	15.9

Three-point field goals: 12 of 28 (.429) in 1982–83.

BOB PETTIT

Louisiana State
6-9 – F/C
Baton Rouge, La.

NCAA consensus first-team All-American in 1954 and consensus second-team All-American in 1953.... Leading scorer and rebounder for 1953 national fourth-place team (22-3 record).... Averaged 30.5 points in six NCAA Tournament games in 1953 and 1954 (3-3 record).... Selected by the Milwaukee Hawks in first round of 1954 NBA draft.... Elected to Naismith Memorial Basketball Hall of Fame in 1970.

Season	G	FGM	FGA	FG%	FTM	FTA	FT%	Reb.	Avg.	Pts.	Avg.
1951–52	23	237	549	.432	115	192	.599	315	13.1	589	25.6
1952–53	21	193	394	.490	133	215	.619	263	16.3	519	24.7
1953–54	25	281	573	.490	223	308	.724	432	17.3	785	31.4
Totals	69	711	1516	.469	471	715	.659	1010	14.6	1893	27.4

ANDY PHILLIP

Illinois
6-2 – F
Granite City, Ill.

NCAA consensus first-team All-American in 1942 and 1943, and consensus second-team All-American in 1947.... Averaged 5.5 points in two NCAA Tournament games in 1942 (0-2 record).... Elected to Naismith Memorial Basketball Hall of Fame in 1961.

Season	G	FGM	FGA	FG%	FTM	FTA	FT%	Reb.	Avg.	Pts.	Avg.
1941–42	23	87			58					232	10.1
1942–43	18	131			43	57	.754			305	16.9
1943–44		Military Service (Marine Corps)									
1944–45		Military Service (Marine Corps)									
1945–46		Military Service (Marine Corps)									
1946–47	20	81			30	61	.492			192	9.6
Totals	61	299			131					729	12.0

MARK PRICE

Georgia Tech
6-0 – G
Enid, Okla.

NCAA consensus second-team All-American in 1985.... Averaged 17.9 points in seven NCAA Tournament games in 1985 and 1986 (5-2 record).... Collected 13 points and five assists in one NIT game in 1984.... Selected by the Dallas Mavericks in second round of 1986 NBA draft (25th pick overall); rights promptly traded to the Cleveland Cavaliers for a 1989 second-round draft choice and cash.

Season	G	FGM	FGA	FG%	FTM	FTA	FT%	Reb.	Avg.	Pts.	Avg.
1982–83	28	201	462	.435	93	106	.877	105	3.8	568	20.3
1983–84	29	191	375	.509	70	85	.824	61	2.1	452	15.6
1984–85	35	223	462	.483	137	163	.840	71	2.0	583	16.7
1985–86	34	233	441	.528	124	145	.855	94	2.8	590	17.4
Totals	126	848	1740	.487	424	499	.850	331	2.6	2193	17.4

Three-point field goals: 73 of 166 (.440) in 1982–83.

FRANK RAMSEY

Kentucky
6-3 – F
Madisonville, Ky.

NCAA consensus second-team All-American in 1954.... Second-leading scorer for undefeated 1954 team that chose not to participate in national postseason competition (25-0 record).... Second-leading rebounder and fourth-leading scorer for 1951 national champion (32-2).... Averaged 11.2 points in six NCAA Tournament games in 1951 and 1952 (5-1 record).... Selected by the Boston Celtics in first round of 1953 NBA draft.... Elected to Naismith Memorial Basketball Hall of Fame in 1981.

Season	G	FGM	FGA	FG%	FTM	FTA	FT%	Reb.	Avg.	Pts.	Avg.
1950–51	34	135	413	.327	75	123	.610	434	12.8	345	10.1
1951–52	32	185	470	.394	139	214	.650	383	12.0	509	15.9
1952–53		Kentucky prohibited from playing because of NCAA probation.									
1953–54	25	179	430	.416	132	181	.729	221	8.8	490	19.6
Totals	91	499	1313	.380	346	518	.668	1038	11.4	1344	14.8

SAM RANZINO

North Carolina State
6-1 – G/F
Gary, Ind.

NCAA consensus first-team All-American in 1951.... Leading scorer for 1950 national third-place team (27-6 record).... Averaged 25.7 points in three NCAA Tournament games in 1950 (2-1 record; he and star teammates Paul Horvath and Vic Bubas were ineligible for the 1951 NCAA Tournament because they were in their fourth season of varsity competition).... Averaged 13 points in two NIT opening-game defeats (1948 and 1951).... Selected by the Rochester Royals in 1951 NBA draft.

Season	G	FGM	FGA	FG%	FTM	FTA	FT%	Reb.	Avg.	Pts.	Avg.
1947–48	32	105			46	71	.648			256	8.0
1948–49	33	157			67	97	.691			381	11.5
1949–50	33	241	721	.334	142	197	.721			624	18.9
1950–51	34	241	760	.317	224	305	.734	220	6.5	706	20.8
Totals	132	744			479	670	.715			1967	14.9

ED RATLEFF

Long Beach State
6-6 – F/G
Columbus, Ohio

NCAA unanimous first-team All-American in 1972 and 1973.... Averaged 18.8 points and 7.3 rebounds in nine NCAA Tournament games from 1971 to 1973 (6-3 record).... Member of 1972 U.S. Olympic team.... Selected by the Houston Rockets in first round of 1973 NBA draft (6th pick overall).

Season	G	FGM	FGA	FG%	FTM	FTA	FT%	Reb.	Avg.	Pts.	Avg.
1970–71	27	218	485	.449	103	132	.780	239	8.9	539	20.0
1971–72	29	250	517	.484	121	157	.771	220	7.6	621	21.4
1972–73	29	275	549	.501	110	138	.797	251	8.7	660	22.8
Totals	85	743	1551	.479	334	427	.782	710	8.4	1820	21.4

J. R. REID
North Carolina
6-9 – F/C
Virginia Beach, Va.

NCAA unanimous first-team All-American in 1988.... Averaged 20.4 points and 8.5 rebounds in 10 NCAA Tournament games from 1987 to 1989 (7-3 record).... Member of 1988 U.S. Olympic team.... Selected as an undergraduate by the Charlotte Hornets in 1989 NBA draft (5th pick overall).

Season	G	FGM	FGA	FG%	FTM	FTA	FT%	Reb.	Avg.	Pts.	Avg.
1986–87	36	198	339	.584	132	202	.653	268	7.4	528	14.7
1987–88	33	222	366	.607	151	222	.680	293	8.9	595	18.0
1988–89	27	164	267	.614	101	151	.669	170	6.3	429	15.9
Totals	96	584	972	.601	384	575	.668	731	7.6	1552	16.2

JOE REIFF
Northwestern
6-2 – F
Chicago, Ill.

NCAA consensus first-team All-American in 1931 and 1933.

Season	G	FGM	FGA	FG%	FTM	FTA	FT%	Reb.	Avg.	Pts.	Avg.
1930–31	12	43			37					123	10.3
1931–32	12	36			32					104	8.7
1932–33	12	53			61					167	13.9
Totals	36	132			130					394	10.9

Note: Statistics are for Big Ten Conference games only.

GLEN RICE
Michigan
6-7 – F/G
Flint, Mich.

NCAA consensus second-team All-American in 1989.... Leading scorer and second-leading rebounder for 1989 NCAA champion (30-7 record).... Final Four Most Outstanding Player in 1989.... Named to All-NCAA Tournament team in 1989.... Averaged 23.7 points and 6.3 rebounds in 13 NCAA Tournament games from 1986 to 1989 (10-3 record).... Selected by the Miami Heat in first round of 1989 NBA draft (4th pick overall).

Season	G	FGM	FGA	FG%	FTM	FTA	FT%	Reb.	Avg.	Pts.	Avg.
1985–86	32	105	191	.550	15	25	.600	97	3.0	225	7.0
1986–87	32	226	402	.562	85	108	.787	294	9.2	540	16.9
1987–88	33	308	539	.571	79	98	.806	236	7.2	728	22.1
1988–89	37	363	629	.577	124	149	.832	232	6.3	949	25.6
Totals	134	1002	1761	.569	303	380	.797	859	6.4	2442	18.2

Three-point field goals: 3 of 12 (.250) in 1986–87, 33 of 77 (.429) in 1987–88, and 99 of 192 (.516) in 1988–89. **Totals:** 135 of 281 (.480).

DICK RICKETTS
Duquesne
6-8 – F/C
Pottstown, Pa.

NCAA consensus first-team All-American in 1955 and consensus second-team All-American in 1954.... Averaged 18 points in two NCAA Tournament games in 1952 (1-1 record).... Averaged 17.8 points in 13 NIT games in 1952 (fourth place), 1953 (third place), 1954 (runner-up), and 1955 (champion).... Selected by the St. Louis Hawks in 1955 NBA draft.

Season	G	FGM	FGA	FG%	FTM	FTA	FT%	Reb.	Avg.	Pts.	Avg.
1951–52	27	130	331	.393	76	105	.724	290	10.7	336	12.4
1952–53	29	229	637	.359	148	226	.655	318	11.0	606	20.9
1953–54	29	205	488	.420	88	121	.727	301	10.4	498	17.2
1954–55	26	174	435	.400	175	225	.778	450	17.3	523	20.1
Totals	111	738	1891	.390	487	677	.719	1359	12.2	1963	17.7

TOM RIKER
South Carolina
6-10 – C
Oyster Bay, N.Y.

NCAA consensus first-team All-American in 1972.... Averaged 23.6 points and 10.2 rebounds in five NCAA Tournament games in 1971 and 1972 (2-3 record).... Selected by the New York Knicks in first round of 1972 NBA draft (8th pick overall).

Season	G	FGM	FGA	FG%	FTM	FTA	FT%	Reb.	Avg.	Pts.	Avg.
1969–70	28	143	277	.516	101	151	.669	251	9.0	387	13.8
1970–71	29	148	313	.473	110	173	.636	231	8.0	406	14.0
1971–72	28	208	375	.555	134	187	.717	292	10.4	550	19.6
Totals	85	499	965	.517	345	511	.675	774	9.1	1343	15.8

OSCAR ROBERTSON
Cincinnati
6-5 – G/F
Indianapolis, Ind.

Named national player of the year by UPI and USBWA in 1958, 1959, and 1960.... NCAA unanimous first-team All-American in 1958, 1959, and 1960.... Led the nation in scoring in 1958, 1959, and 1960.... Leading scorer and rebounder for national third-place teams in 1959 (26-4 record) and 1960 (28-2).... Member of All-NCAA Tournament team in 1959 and 1960.... Averaged 32.4 points and 13.1 rebounds in 10 NCAA Tournament games from 1958 to 1960 (7-3 record).... Tied with Jerry Lucas for scoring leadership (17 points per game) on 1960 U.S. Olympic team.... Selected as a territorial pick by the Cincinnati Royals in 1960 NBA draft.... Elected to Naismith Memorial Basketball Hall of Fame in 1979.

Season	G	FGM	FGA	FG%	FTM	FTA	FT%	Reb.	Avg.	Pts.	Avg.
1957–58	28	352	617	.571	280	355	.789	425	15.2	984	35.1
1958–59	30	331	650	.509	316	398	.794	489	16.3	978	32.6
1959–60	30	369	701	.526	273	361	.756	424	14.1	1011	33.7
Totals	88	1052	1968	.535	869	1114	.780	1338	15.2	2973	33.8

DAVID ROBINSON
Navy
7-0 – C
Woodbridge, Va.

Named national player of the year by AP, UPI, USBWA, and NABC in 1987.... Wooden Award and Naismith Award winner in 1987.... NCAA unanimous first-team All-American in 1987 and consensus second-team All-American in 1986.... Led the nation in rebounding in 1986.... Led the nation in blocked shots in 1986 (5.9 per game) and 1987 (4.5 per game).... Averaged 28.6 points and 12.3 rebounds in seven NCAA Tournament games from 1985 to 1987 (4-3 record).... Member of 1988 and 1992 U.S. Olympic teams.... Selected by the San Antonio Spurs in first round of 1987 NBA draft (1st pick overall).

Season	G	FGM	FGA	FG%	FTM	FTA	FT%	Reb.	Avg.	Pts.	Avg.
1983–84	28	86	138	.623	42	73	.575	111	4.0	214	7.6
1984–85	32	302	469	.644	152	243	.626	370	11.6	756	23.6
1985–86	35	294	484	.607	208	331	.628	455	13.0	796	22.7
1986–87	32	350	592	.591	202	317	.637	378	11.8	903	28.2
Totals	127	1032	1683	.613	604	964	.627	1314	10.3	2669	21.0

Three-point field goals: 1 for 1 in 1986–87.

GLENN ROBINSON
Purdue
6-8 – F
Gary, Ind.

Named national player of the year by AP, UPI, USBWA, and NABC in 1994.... Wooden Award and Naismith Award winner in 1994.... NCAA unanimous first-team All-American in 1994.... Led the nation in scoring in 1994.... Averaged 31.4 points and 9.8 rebounds in five NCAA Tournament games in 1993 and 1994 (3-2 record).... Selected by the Milwaukee Bucks in first round of 1994 NBA draft (1st pick overall).

Season	G	FGM	FGA	FG%	FTM	FTA	FT%	Reb.	Avg.	Pts.	Avg.
1991–92				Sat out the entire season as a Proposition 48 casualty.							
1992–93	28	246	519	.474	152	205	.741	258	9.2	676	24.1
1993–94	34	368	762	.483	215	270	.796	344	10.1	1030	30.3
Totals	62	614	1281	.479	367	475	.773	602	9.7	1706	27.5

Three-point field goals: 32 of 80 (.400) in 1992–93 and 79 of 208 (.380) in 1993–94. Totals: 111 of 288 (.385).

JOHN ROCHE
South Carolina
6-3 – G
New York, N.Y.

NCAA consensus second-team All-American in 1970 and 1971.... Averaged 11 points in two NCAA Tournament defeats in 1971.... Averaged 21 points in two NIT games in 1969 (1-1 record).... Selected by the Phoenix Suns in first round of 1971 NBA draft (14th pick overall).

Season	G	FGM	FGA	FG%	FTM	FTA	FT%	Reb.	Avg.	Pts.	Avg.
1968–69	28	239	507	.471	184	226	.814	73	2.6	662	23.6
1969–70	28	222	469	.473	179	216	.829	70	2.5	623	22.3
1970–71	29	205	493	.416	215	262	.821	67	2.3	625	21.6
Totals	85	666	1469	.453	578	704	.821	210	2.5	1910	22.5

GUY RODGERS
Temple
6-0 – G
Philadelphia, Pa.

NCAA unanimous first-team All-American in 1958 and consensus second-team All-American in 1957.... Leading scorer for 1958 national third-place team (27-3 record).... Member of All-NCAA Tournament team in 1958.... Averaged 17.9 points in nine NCAA Tournament games in 1956 and 1958 (7-2 record).... Averaged 23.3 points in three NIT games for 1957 third-place team.... Selected as a territorial pick by the Philadelphia Warriors in 1958 NBA draft.

Season	G	FGM	FGA	FG%	FTM	FTA	FT%	Reb.	Avg.	Pts.	Avg.
1955–56	31	243	552	.440	87	155	.561	186	6.0	573	18.5
1956–57	29	216	565	.382	159	224	.710	202	7.0	591	20.4
1957–58	30	249	564	.441	105	171	.614	199	6.6	603	20.1
Totals	90	708	1681	.421	351	550	.638	587	6.5	1767	19.6

LENNIE ROSENBLUTH
North Carolina
6-5 – F
New York, N.Y.

NCAA consensus first-team All-American in 1957.... Leading scorer and second-leading rebounder for undefeated 1957 NCAA champion (32-0 record).... Member of All-NCAA Tournament team in 1957.... Averaged 28 points and 9.2 rebounds in five NCAA Tournament games in 1957 (5-0 record).... Selected by the Philadelphia Warriors in first round of 1957 NBA draft (6th pick overall).

Season	G	FGM	FGA	FG%	FTM	FTA	FT%	Reb.	Avg.	Pts.	Avg.
1954–55	21	189	444	.426	158	222	.712	246	11.7	536	25.5
1955–56	23	227	496	.458	160	217	.737	264	11.5	614	26.7
1956–57	32	305	631	.483	285	376	.758	280	8.8	895	28.0
Totals	76	721	1571	.459	603	815	.740	790	10.4	2045	26.9

CLIFFORD ROZIER
Louisville
6-9 – F/C
Bradenton, Fla.

NCAA consensus first-team All-American in 1994.... Averaged 8.3 points and 5.5 rebounds in 11 NCAA Tournament games in 1991 (five games with North Carolina), 1993, and 1994 (8-3 record).... Fifth-leading rebounder and seventh-leading scorer for North Carolina's 1991 Final Four team (29-6 record).... Selected as an undergraduate by the Golden State Warriors in first round of 1994 NBA draft (16th pick overall).

Season	G	FGM	FGA	FG%	FTM	FTA	FT%	Reb.	Avg.	Pts.	Avg.
1990–91	34	64	136	.471	39	69	.565	101	3.0	167	4.9
1991–92				Sat out the season after transferring from North Carolina.							
1992–93	31	192	342	.561	104	183	.568	338	10.9	488	15.7
1993–94	34	247	400	.618	122	224	.545	377	11.1	616	18.1
Totals	99	503	898	.560	265	476	.557	816	8.2	1271	12.8

Three-point field goals: 0 of 2 in 1992–93 and 0 of 1 in 1993–94. Totals: 0 of 3.

BILL RUSSELL
San Francisco
6-9 – C
Oakland, Calif.

Named national player of the year by UPI in 1956.... NCAA unanimous first-team All-American in 1956 and consensus first-team All-American in 1955.... One of six players to average more than 20 points and 20 rebounds per game in his career.... Final Four Most Outstanding Player in 1955.... Leading scorer and rebounder for NCAA championship teams in 1955 (28-1 record) and 1956 (29-0).... Member of All-NCAA Tournament team in 1955 and 1956.... Averaged 23.2 points in nine NCAA Tournament games in 1955 and 1956 (9-0 record).... Leading scorer (14.1 points per game) for 1956 U.S. Olympic team.... Selected by the Boston Celtics in first round of 1956 NBA draft (3rd pick overall).... Elected to Naismith Memorial Basketball Hall of Fame in 1974.

Season	G	FGM	FGA	FG%	FTM	FTA	FT%	Reb.	Avg.	Pts.	Avg.
1953–54	21	150	309	.485	117	212	.552	403	19.2	417	19.9
1954–55	29	229	423	.541	164	278	.590	594	20.5	622	21.4
1955–56	29	246	480	.513	105	212	.495	609	21.0	597	20.6
Totals	79	625	1212	.516	386	702	.550	1606	20.3	1636	20.7

CAZZIE RUSSELL
Michigan
6-5 – G
Chicago, Ill.

Named national player of the year by AP, UPI, and USBWA in 1966.... NCAA unanimous first-team All-American in 1965 and 1966, and consensus second-team All-American in 1964.... Leading scorer and third-leading rebounder for 1964 national third-place team (23-5 record) and 1965 runner-up (24-4).... Member of All-NCAA Tournament team in 1965.... Averaged 24.6 points and 7.4 rebounds in eight NCAA Tournament games from 1964 to 1966 (5-3 record; didn't play in 1964 national third-place game because of a swollen ankle).... Selected by the New York Knicks in first round of 1966 NBA draft (1st pick overall).

Season	G	FGM	FGA	FG%	FTM	FTA	FT%	Reb.	Avg.	Pts.	Avg.
1963–64	27	260	507	.513	150	178	.843	244	9.0	670	24.8
1964–65	27	271	558	.486	152	186	.817	213	7.9	694	25.7
1965–66	26	308	595	.518	184	223	.825	219	8.4	800	30.8
Totals	80	839	1660	.505	486	587	.828	676	8.5	2164	27.1

FOREST (AGGIE) SALE
Kentucky
6-4 – F/C
Lawrenceburg, Ky.

NCAA consensus first-team All-American in 1932 and 1933.

Season	G	FGM	FGA	FG%	FTM	FTA	FT%	Reb.	Avg.	Pts.	Avg.
1930–31										62	
1931–32	17									235	13.8
1932–33	23									324	14.0
Totals										621	

RALPH SAMPSON
Virginia
7-4 – C
Harrisonburg, Va.

Named national player of the year by AP, UPI, and USBWA in 1981, 1982, and 1983, and by NABC in 1982 and 1983.... Wooden Award winner in 1982 and 1983.... Naismith Award winner in 1981, 1982, and 1983.... NCAA unanimous first-team All-American in 1981, 1982, and 1983.... Leading rebounder and second-leading scorer for 1981 national third-place team (29-4 record).... Averaged 16.4 points and 11.3 rebounds in 10 NCAA Tournament games from 1981 to 1983 (7-3 record).... NIT Most Valuable Player in 1980.... Averaged 19.2 points and 13.8 rebounds in five NIT games for 1980 champion.... Selected by the Houston Rockets in first round of 1983 NBA draft (1st pick overall).

Season	G	FGM	FGA	FG%	FTM	FTA	FT%	Reb.	Avg.	Pts.	Avg.
1979–80	34	221	404	.547	66	94	.702	381	11.2	508	14.9
1980–81	33	230	413	.557	125	198	.631	378	11.5	585	17.7
1981–82	32	198	353	.561	110	179	.615	366	11.4	506	15.8
1982–83	33	250	414	.604	126	179	.704	386	11.7	629	19.1
Totals	132	899	1584	.568	427	650	.657	1511	11.4	2228	16.9

Three-point field goals: 3 of 5 (.600) in 1982–83.

DOLPH SCHAYES
New York University
6-8 – F/C
Bronx, N.Y.

Third-leading scorer for 1945 national runner-up (16-8 record).... Averaged 8.8 points in five NCAA Tournament games in 1945 and 1946 (3-2 record).... Averaged 10 points in three NIT games for 1948 runner-up.... Selected by the Tri-Cities Hawks in 1948 National Basketball League draft before his rights were acquired by the Syracuse Nationals of the NBA.... Elected to Naismith Memorial Basketball Hall of Fame in 1972.

Season	G	FGM	FGA	FG%	FTM	FTA	FT%	Reb.	Avg.	Pts.	Avg.
1944–45	11	46			23					115	10.5
1945–46	22	54			41					149	6.8
1946–47	21	66			63					195	9.3
1947–48	26	124			108					356	13.7
Totals	80	290			235					815	10.2

DAVE SCHELLHASE
Purdue
6-4 – F
Evansville, Ind.

NCAA unanimous first-team All-American in 1966 and consensus second-team All-American in 1965.... Led the nation in scoring in 1966.... Did not play in NCAA Tournament or NIT.... Selected by the Chicago Bulls in first round of 1966 NBA draft (10th pick overall).

Season	G	FGM	FGA	FG%	FTM	FTA	FT%	Reb.	Avg.	Pts.	Avg.
1963–64	24	213	441	.483	163	211	.773	271	11.3	589	24.5
1964–65	24	249	559	.445	206	262	.786	195	8.1	704	29.3
1965–66	24	284	611	.465	213	276	.772	255	10.6	781	32.5
Totals	72	746	1611	.463	582	749	.777	721	10.0	2074	28.8

DON SCHLUNDT
Indiana
6-10 – C
South Bend, Ind.

NCAA consensus first-team All-American in 1954 and consensus second-team All-American in 1953.... Leading scorer and rebounder for 1953 NCAA champion (23-3 record).... Member of All-NCAA Tournament team in 1953.... Averaged 27 points in six NCAA Tournament games in 1953 and 1954 (5-1 record).... Selected by the Syracuse Nationals in 1955 NBA draft (never played in league).

Season	G	FGM	FGA	FG%	FTM	FTA	FT%	Reb.	Avg.	Pts.	Avg.
1951–52	22	131	289	.453	114	171	.667	158	7.2	376	17.1
1952–53	26	206	477	.432	249	310	.803	220	8.5	661	25.4
1953–54	24	177	354	.500	229	296	.774	267	11.1	583	24.3
1954–55	22	169	377	.448	234	299	.783	215	9.8	572	26.0
Totals	94	683	1497	.456	826	1076	.768	860	9.1	2192	23.3

DICK SCHNITTKER
Ohio State
6-5 – F
Sandusky, Ohio

NCAA unanimous first-team All-American in 1950.... Averaged 21.5 points in two NCAA Tournament games in 1950 (1-1 record).... Selected by the Washington Capitols in 1950 NBA draft.

Season	G	FGM	FGA	FG%	FTM	FTA	FT%	Reb.	Avg.	Pts.	Avg.
1946–47	2	1	1	1.000	0	0				2	1.0
1947–48	20	116	281	.413	90	120	.750			322	16.1
1948–49	19	125	275	.455	86	125	.688			336	17.7
1949–50	22	158	390	.405	153	204	.750			469	21.3
Totals	63	400	947	.422	329	449	.733			1129	17.9

CHARLIE SCOTT
North Carolina
6-5 – G/F
New York, N.Y.

NCAA consensus second-team All-American in 1969 and 1970.... Leading scorer and third-leading rebounder for 1969 national fourth-place team (27-5 record).... Second-leading scorer and fourth-leading rebounder for 1968 national runner-up (28-4).... Member of All-NCAA Tournament team in 1969.... Averaged 21.2 points and 5.3 rebounds in eight NCAA Tournament games in 1968 and 1969.... Scored 26 points in one NIT game in 1970.... Selected by the Washington Capitols in first round of "secret" ABA draft in January 1970; NBA rights traded by the Boston Celtics to the Phoenix Suns for future considerations, March 14, 1972.

Season	G	FGM	FGA	FG%	FTM	FTA	FT%	Reb.	Avg.	Pts.	Avg.
1967–68	32	234	490	.478	94	141	.667	191	6.0	562	17.6
1968–69	32	290	577	.503	134	191	.702	226	7.1	714	22.3
1969–70	27	281	611	.460	169	215	.786	232	8.6	731	27.1
Totals	91	805	1678	.480	397	547	.726	649	7.1	2007	22.1

FRANK SELVY
Furman
6-3 – F
Corbin, Ky.

NCAA consensus first-team All-American in 1954 and consensus second-team All-American in 1953.... Holds NCAA record for most points in a single game with 100 against Newberry on February 13, 1954.... Led the nation in scoring in 1953 and 1954.... Did not play in NCAA Tournament or NIT.... Selected by the Baltimore Bullets in 1954 NBA draft.

Season	G	FGM	FGA	FG%	FTM	FTA	FT%	Reb.	Avg.	Pts.	Avg.
1951–52	24	223	556	.401	145	199	.729			591	24.6
1952–53	25	272	646	.421	194	263	.738			738	29.5
1953–54	29	427	941	.454	355	444	.800	400	13.8	1209	41.7
Totals	78	922	2143	.430	694	906	.766			2538	32.5

BILL SHARMAN
Southern California
6-1 – G
Porterville, Calif.

NCAA consensus first-team All-American in 1950.... Did not play in NCAA Tournament or NIT.... Selected by the Washington Capitols in second round of 1950 NBA draft.... Elected to Naismith Memorial Basketball Hall of Fame in 1975.

Season	G	FGM	FGA	FG%	FTM	FTA	FT%	Reb.	Avg.	Pts.	Avg.
1946–47	10	16			9	12	.750			41	4.1
1947–48	24	100			38	44	.864			238	9.9
1948–49	24	142			98	125	.784			382	15.9
1949–50	24	171	421	.406	104	129	.806			446	18.6
Totals	82	429			249	310	.803			1107	13.5

RON SHAVLIK
North Carolina State
6-9 – C
Denver, Colo.

NCAA consensus first-team All-American in 1956 and consensus second-team All-American in 1955.... Averaged 19.3 points in four NCAA Tournament games in 1954 and 1956 (2-2 record).... Selected by the New York Knicks in 1956 NBA draft.

Season	G	FGM	FGA	FG%	FTM	FTA	FT%	Reb.	Avg.	Pts.	Avg.
1953–54	33	204	536	.381	115	203	.567	441	13.4	523	15.8
1954–55	32	260	646	.402	187	267	.700	581	18.2	707	22.1
1955–56	28	177	429	.413	156	227	.687	545	19.5	510	18.2
Totals	93	641	1611	.398	458	697	.657	1567	16.8	1740	18.7

JOHN SHUMATE
Notre Dame
6-9 – F/C
Elizabeth, N.J.

NCAA unanimous first-team All-American in 1974.... Averaged 28.7 points and eight rebounds in three NCAA Tournament games in 1974 (2-1 record).... Averaged 23.8 points and 8.8 rebounds in four NIT games for 1973 runner-up.... Selected with eligibility remaining by the Phoenix Suns in first round of 1974 NBA draft (4th pick overall).

Season	G	FGM	FGA	FG%	FTM	FTA	FT%	Reb.	Avg.	Pts.	Avg.
1971–72	Sat out the entire season because of a blood clot in a lung.										
1972–73	30	257	434	.592	117	179	.654	365	12.2	631	21.0
1973–74	29	281	448	.627	141	196	.719	319	11.0	703	24.2
Totals	59	538	882	.610	258	375	.688	684	11.6	1334	22.6

PAUL SILAS
Creighton
6-7 – F/C
Oakland, Calif.

Holds NCAA record for most rebounds in a three-year career.... Led the nation in rebounding in 1963.... One of six players to average more than 20 points and 20 rebounds in his career.... Averaged 17.5 points in six NCAA Tournament games in 1962 and 1964 (3-3 record).... Selected by the St. Louis Hawks in second round of 1964 NBA draft (12th pick overall).

Season	G	FGM	FGA	FG%	FTM	FTA	FT%	Reb.	Avg.	Pts.	Avg.
1961–62	25	213	524	.406	125	215	.581	563	22.5	551	22.0
1962–63	27	220	531	.414	133	228	.583	557	20.6	573	21.2
1963–64	29	210	529	.397	117	194	.603	631	21.8	537	18.5
Totals	81	643	1584	.406	375	637	.589	1751	21.6	1661	20.5

LIONEL SIMMONS
La Salle
6-7 – F
Philadelphia, Pa.

Named national player of the year by AP, UPI, NABC, and USBWA in 1990.... Naismith Award and Wooden Award winner in 1990.... NCAA unanimous first-team All-American in 1990 and consensus second-team All-American in 1989.... Averaged 26.5 points and 12 rebounds in four NCAA Tournament games from 1988 to 1990 (1-3 record).... Averaged 23.4 points and 10.4 rebounds in five NIT games for 1987 runner-up.... Selected by the Sacramento Kings in first round of 1990 NBA draft (7th pick overall).

Season	G	FGM	FGA	FG%	FTM	FTA	FT%	Reb.	Avg.	Pts.	Avg.
1986–87	33	263	500	.526	142	186	.763	322	9.8	670	20.3
1987–88	34	297	613	.485	196	259	.757	386	11.4	792	23.3
1988–89	32	349	716	.487	189	266	.711	365	11.4	908	28.4
1989–90	32	335	653	.513	146	221	.661	356	11.1	847	26.5
Totals	131	1244	2482	.501	673	932	.722	1429	10.9	3217	24.6

Three-point field goals: 2 of 6 (.333) in 1986–87, 2 of 8 (.250) in 1987–88, 21 of 56 (.375) in 1988–89, and 31 of 65 (.477) in 1989–90. **Totals:** 56 of 135 (.415).

KENNY SMITH
North Carolina
6-3 – G
Queens, N.Y.

NCAA unanimous first-team All-American in 1987.... Averaged 13.4 points and 6.6 assists in 13 NCAA Tournament games from 1984 to 1987 (9-4 record).... Selected by the Sacramento Kings in first round of 1987 NBA draft (6th pick overall).

Season	G	FGM	FGA	FG%	FTM	FTA	FT%	Reb.	Avg.	Pts.	Avg.
1983–84	23	83	160	.519	44	55	.800	40	1.7	210	9.1
1984–85	36	173	334	.518	98	114	.860	92	2.6	444	12.3
1985–86	34	164	318	.516	80	99	.808	75	2.2	408	12.0
1986–87	34	208	414	.502	71	88	.807	76	2.2	574	16.9
Totals	127	628	1226	.512	293	356	.823	283	2.2	1636	12.9

Three-point field goals: 87 of 213 (.408) in 1986–87.

RIK SMITS
Marist
7-4 – C
Eindhoven, Holland

Averaged 19 points and three rebounds in two NCAA Tournament games in 1986 and 1987 (0-2 record).... Selected by the Indiana Pacers in first round of 1988 NBA draft (2nd pick overall).

Season	G	FGM	FGA	FG%	FTM	FTA	FT%	Reb.	Avg.	Pts.	Avg.
1984–85	29	132	233	.567	60	104	.577	162	5.6	324	11.2
1985–86	30	216	347	.622	98	144	.681	242	8.1	530	17.7
1986–87	21	157	258	.609	109	151	.722	171	8.1	423	20.1
1987–88	27	251	403	.623	166	226	.735	236	8.7	668	24.7
Totals	107	756	1241	.609	433	625	.693	811	7.6	1945	18.2

BILL SPIVEY
Kentucky
7-0 – C
Warner Robins, Ga.

NCAA unanimous first-team All-American in 1951.... Leading scorer and rebounder for 1951 NCAA champion (32-2 record).... Averaged 18 points and 13.8 rebounds in four NCAA Tournament games in 1951 (4-0 record).... Scored 15 points in one NIT game in 1950.... Allegedly wasn't drafted by any NBA team because of possible repercussions stemming from a game-fixing scandal involving Kentucky.

Season	G	FGM	FGA	FG%	FTM	FTA	FT%	Reb.	Avg.	Pts.	Avg.
1949–50	30	225	619	.363	128	176	.727			578	19.3
1950–51	33	252	632	.399	131	211	.621	567	17.2	635	19.2
Totals	63	477	1251	.381	259	387	.669			1213	19.3

Note: Didn't play in 1951–52 because of a knee injury at the start of the season and then later was dropped from Kentucky's team because of possible involvement in the game-fixing scandals.

DAVE STALLWORTH
Wichita State
6-7 – F
Dallas, Tex.

NCAA unanimous first-team All-American in 1964 and consensus second-team All-American in 1965.... Averaged 29.5 points and 19.5 rebounds in two NCAA Tournament games in 1964 (1-1 record).... Averaged 17 points in two NIT games in 1962 and 1963 (0-2 record).... Selected by the New York Knicks in second round of 1965 NBA draft.

Season	G	FGM	FGA	FG%	FTM	FTA	FT%	Reb.	Avg.	Pts.	Avg.
1961–62	7	56	127	.441	28	35	.800	64	9.1	140	20.0
1962–63	27	222	421	.527	165	199	.829	275	10.2	609	22.6
1963–64	29	283	518	.546	203	279	.728	294	10.1	769	26.5
1964–65	16	153	275	.556	94	139	.676	194	12.1	400	25.0
Totals	79	714	1341	.532	490	652	.752	827	10.5	1918	24.3

Note: Did not play for national fourth-place team in 1965 NCAA playoffs because his eligibility expired after the first semester.

STEVE STIPANOVICH
Missouri
6-10 – C
St. Louis, Mo.

NCAA consensus second-team All-American in 1983.... Averaged 11.9 points and 6.6 rebounds from seven NCAA Tournament games from 1980-83 (3-4 record).... Selected by the Indiana Pacers in first round of 1983 NBA draft (2nd pick overall).

Season	G	FGM	FGA	FG%	FTM	FTA	FT%	Reb.	Avg.	Pts.	Avg.
1979–80	31	180	331	.598	85	127	.669	199	6.4	445	14.4
1980–81	32	143	286	.500	120	162	.741	237	7.4	406	12.7
1981–82	31	140	278	.504	79	104	.760	248	8.0	359	11.6
1982–83	34	246	454	.542	134	187	.717	300	8.8	626	18.4
Totals	128	709	1319	.538	418	580	.721	984	7.7	1836	14.3

TOM STITH
St. Bonaventure
6-5 – F
Brooklyn, N.Y.

NCAA unanimous first-team All-American in 1961 and consensus first-team All-American in 1960.... Averaged 29 points in three NCAA Tournament games in 1961 (2-1 record).... Averaged 24.8 points in five NIT games in 1959 (opening-game loser) and 1960 (fourth place).... Selected by the New York Knicks in first round of 1961 NBA draft (2nd pick overall).

Season	G	FGM	FGA	FG%	FTM	FTA	FT%	Reb.	Avg.	Pts.	Avg.
1958–59	22	162	295	.549	79	129	.612	224	10.2	403	18.3
1959–60	26	318	614	.518	183	261	.701	296	11.4	819	31.5
1960–61	28	327	622	.526	176	265	.664	191	6.8	830	29.6
Totals	76	807	1531	.527	438	655	.669	711	9.4	2052	27.0

JOHN STOCKTON
Gonzaga
6-1 – G
Spokane, Wash.

Did not play in NCAA Tournament or NIT.... Member of 1992 U.S. Olympic team.... Selected by the Utah Jazz in first round of 1984 NBA draft (16th pick overall).

Season	G	FGM	FGA	FG%	FTM	FTA	FT%	Reb.	Avg.	Pts.	Avg.
1980–81	25	26	45	.578	26	35	.743	11	0.4	78	3.1
1981–82	27	117	203	.576	69	102	.676	67	2.5	303	11.2
1982–83	27	142	274	.518	91	115	.791	87	3.2	375	13.9
1983–84	28	229	397	.577	126	182	.692	66	2.4	584	20.9
Totals	107	514	919	.559	312	434	.719	231	2.2	1340	12.5

MAURICE STOKES

St. Francis (Pa.)
6-6 – C
Pittsburgh, Pa.

Did not play in NCAA Tournament.... NIT Most Valuable Player in 1955....
Averaged 31 points in six NIT games in 1954 (quarterfinals loser) and 1956
(fourth-place team).... Selected by the Rochester Royals in first round of
1955 NBA draft (2nd pick overall).

Season	G	FGM	FGA	FG%	FTM	FTA	FT%	Reb.	Avg.	Pts.	Avg.
1951–52	30	206	450	.458	93	166	.560			505	16.8
1952–53	18	170	331	.514	77	125	.616	397	22.1	417	23.2
1953–54	26	234	549	.426	132	190	.695	689	26.5	600	23.1
1954–55	28	302	707	.427	156	218	.716	733	26.2	760	27.1
Totals	102	912	2037	.448	458	699	.655	1617		2282	22.4

STAN STUTZ

see Stan Modzelewski

SID TANNENBAUM

New York University
6-0 – G
Brooklyn, N.Y.

NCAA consensus first-team All-American in 1946 and 1947.... Second-
leading scorer for 1945 national runner-up (16-8 record).... Averaged 9.8
points in five NCAA Tournament games in 1945 and 1946 (3-2 record).

Season	G	FGM	FGA	FG%	FTM	FTA	FT%	Reb.	Avg.	Pts.	Avg.
1943–44	16	88			34					210	13.1
1944–45	24	121			60					302	12.6
1945–46	22	113			58					284	12.9
1946–47	21	117			44					278	13.2
Totals	83	439			196					1074	12.9

TOM THACKER

Cincinnati
6-2 – F/G
Covington, Ky.

NCAA consensus first-team All-American in 1963.... Third-leading scorer
and rebounder for 1961 NCAA champion (27-3 record), third-leading scorer
and second-leading rebounder for 1962 NCAA champion (29-2), and
second-leading scorer and rebounder for 1963 national runner-up (26-2)....
Member of All-NCAA Tournament team in 1962 and 1963.... Averaged 12
points and 9.3 rebounds in 12 NCAA Tournament games from 1961 to 1963
(11-1 record).... Selected as a territorial pick by the Cincinnati Royals in
1963 NBA draft.

Season	G	FGM	FGA	FG%	FTM	FTA	FT%	Reb.	Avg.	Pts.	Avg.
1960–61	30	139	531	.396	91	133	.684	284	9.5	369	12.3
1961–62	31	134	331	.405	74	121	.612	266	8.6	342	11.0
1962–63	28	169	357	.473	103	155	.665	281	10.0	441	15.8
Totals	89	442	1219	.363	268	409	.655	831	9.3	1152	12.9

REGGIE THEUS

UNLV
6-7 – G
Inglewood, Calif.

Fourth-leading scorer and fifth-leading rebounder for 1977 national third-
place team (29-3 record).... Averaged 13.9 points and 4.1 rebounds in
seven NCAA Tournament games in 1976 and 1977 (5-2 record).... Selected
as an undergraduate by the Chicago Bulls in first round of 1978 NBA draft
(9th pick overall).

Season	G	FGM	FGA	FG%	FTM	FTA	FT%	Reb.	Avg.	Pts.	Avg.
1975–76	31	68	163	.417	48	60	.800	53	1.7	184	5.9
1976–77	32	178	358	.497	108	132	.818	145	4.5	464	14.5
1977–78	28	181	389	.465	167	207	.807	191	6.8	529	18.9
Totals	91	427	910	.469	323	399	.810	389	4.3	1177	12.9

ISIAH THOMAS

Indiana
6-1 – G
Chicago, Ill.

NCAA unanimous first-team All-American in 1981.... Final Four Most
Outstanding Player in 1981.... Led 1981 NCAA champion in scoring and
assists (26-9 record).... Averaged 19.7 points and 7.9 assists in seven
NCAA Tournament games in 1980 and 1981 (6-1 record).... Member of
1980 U.S. Olympic team.... Selected as an undergraduate by the Detroit
Pistons in first round of 1981 NBA draft (2nd pick overall).

Season	G	FGM	FGA	FG%	FTM	FTA	FT%	Reb.	Avg.	Pts.	Avg.
1979–80	29	154	302	.510	115	149	.772	116	4.0	423	14.6
1980–81	34	212	383	.554	121	163	.742	105	3.1	545	16.0
Totals	63	366	685	.534	236	312	.756	221	3.5	968	15.4

DAVID THOMPSON

North Carolina State
6-4 – F
Shelby, N.C.

Named national player of the year by
UPI, USBWA, and NABC in 1975, and
by AP in 1974 and 1975.... Naismith
Award winner in 1975.... NCAA
unanimous first-team All-American in
1973, 1974, and 1975.... Final Four
Most Outstanding Player and
member of All-NCAA Tournament
team in 1974.... Leading scorer and
second-leading rebounder for 1974
NCAA champion (30-1 record)....
Averaged 24.3 points and 7.3
rebounds in four NCAA Tournament
games in 1974 (4-0 record).... Selected as an undergraduate by the Virginia
Squires in first round of 1975 ABA draft; rights traded to the Denver
Nuggets, July 14, 1975.

Season	G	FGM	FGA	FG%	FTM	FTA	FT%	Reb.	Avg.	Pts.	Avg.
1972–73	27	267	469	.569	132	160	.825	220	8.1	666	24.7
1973–74	31	325	594	.547	155	208	.745	245	7.9	805	26.0
1974–75	28	347	635	.546	144	197	.731	229	8.2	838	29.9
Totals	86	939	1698	.553	431	565	.763	694	8.1	2309	26.8

JOHN (CAT) THOMPSON

Montana State
5-10 – F
St. George, Utah

NCAA consensus first-team All-American in 1929 and 1930.... Elected to
Naismith Memorial Basketball Hall of Fame in 1962.

Season	G	FGM	FGA	FG%	FTM	FTA	FT%	Reb.	Avg.	Pts.	Avg.
1926–27	12	69			29					167	13.9
1927–28	38	274			81					629	16.6
1928–29	36	262			73					597	16.6
1929–30	12	45			18					108	9.0
Totals											

Note: Statistics in 1926–27 and 1929–30 are for conference games
only.

MYCHAL THOMPSON
Minnesota
6-10 – F/C
Nassau, Bahamas

NCAA unanimous first-team All-American in 1978 and consensus second-team All-American in 1977.... Did not play in NCAA Tournament or NIT.... Selected by the Portland Trail Blazers in first round of 1978 NBA draft (1st pick overall).

Season	G	FGM	FGA	FG%	FTM	FTA	FT%	Reb.	Avg.	Pts.	Avg.
1974–75	23	114	215	.530	59	78	.756	176	7.7	287	12.5
1975–76	25	264	461	.573	119	171	.696	312	12.5	647	25.9
1976–77	27	251	414	.606	93	132	.705	240	8.9	595	22.0
1977–78	21	194	362	.536	75	119	.630	228	10.9	463	22.0
Totals	96	823	1452	.567	346	500	.692	956	10.0	1992	20.8

ROD THORN
West Virginia
6-4 – F/G
Princeton, W.V.

NCAA consensus second-team All-American in 1962 and 1963.... Averaged 29.3 points and 8.8 rebounds in four NCAA Tournament games in 1962 and 1963 (2-2 record).... Selected by the Baltimore Bullets in first round of 1963 NBA draft.

Season	G	FGM	FGA	FG%	FTM	FTA	FT%	Reb.	Avg.	Pts.	Avg.
1960–61	24	192	416	.462	61	106	.575	299	12.5	445	18.5
1961–62	29	259	586	.442	170	241	.705	351	12.1	688	23.7
1962–63	29	241	557	.433	170	221	.769	262	9.0	652	22.5
Totals	82	692	1559	.444	401	568	.706	912	11.1	1785	21.8

NATE THURMOND
Bowling Green State
6-11 – C
Akron, Ohio

NCAA consensus second-team All-American in 1963.... Averaged 17.5 points and 21 rebounds in four NCAA Tournament games in 1962 and 1963 (1-3 record).... Selected by the San Francisco Warriors in first round of 1963 NBA draft.... Elected to Naismith Memorial Basketball Hall of Fame in 1984.

Season	G	FGM	FGA	FG%	FTM	FTA	FT%	Reb.	Avg.	Pts.	Avg.
1960–61	24	170	427	.398	87	129	.674	449	18.7	427	17.8
1961–62	25	163	358	.455	67	113	.593	394	15.8	393	15.7
1962–63	27	206	466	.442	124	197	.629	452	16.7	536	19.9
Totals	76	539	1251	.431	278	439	.633	1295	17.0	1356	17.8

WAYMAN TISDALE
Oklahoma
6-8 – F
Tulsa, Okla.

NCAA unanimous first-team All-American in 1984 and 1985, and consensus first-team All-American in 1983.... Averaged 22.6 points and 9.6 rebounds in seven NCAA Tournament games from 1983 to 1985 (4-3 record).... Leading rebounder (6.4 rpg) for 1984 U.S. Olympic team.... Selected as an undergraduate by the Indiana Pacers in first round of 1985 NBA draft (2nd pick overall).

Season	G	FGM	FGA	FG%	FTM	FTA	FT%	Reb.	Avg.	Pts.	Avg.
1982–83	33	338	583	.580	134	211	.635	341	10.3	810	24.5
1983–84	34	369	639	.577	181	283	.640	329	9.7	919	27.0
1984–85	37	370	640	.578	192	273	.703	378	10.2	932	25.2
Totals	104	1077	1862	.578	507	767	.661	1048	10.1	2661	25.6

RUDY TOMJANOVICH
Michigan
6-8 – F
Hamtramck, Mich.

Did not play in NCAA Tournament or NIT.... Selected by the San Diego Rockets in first round of 1970 NBA draft (2nd pick overall).

Season	G	FGM	FGA	FG%	FTM	FTA	FT%	Reb.	Avg.	Pts.	Avg.
1967–68	24	210	446	.471	49	78	.628	323	13.5	469	19.5
1968–69	24	269	541	.497	79	131	.603	340	14.2	617	25.7
1969–70	24	286	604	.474	150	200	.750	376	15.7	722	30.1
Totals	72	765	1591	.481	278	409	.680	1039	14.4	1808	25.1

KELLY TRIPUCKA
Notre Dame
6-6 – F/G
Bloomfield, N.J.

NCAA consensus second-team All-American in 1979 and 1981.... Third-leading scorer and rebounder for 1978 national fourth-place team (23-8 record).... Averaged 16 points and 4.8 rebounds in 11 NCAA Tournament games from 1978 to 1981 (6-5 record).... Selected by the Detroit Pistons in first round of 1981 NBA draft (12th pick overall).

Season	G	FGM	FGA	FG%	FTM	FTA	FT%	Reb.	Avg.	Pts.	Avg.
1977–78	31	141	247	.571	80	108	.741	161	5.2	362	11.7
1978–79	29	143	277	.516	129	151	.854	125	4.3	415	14.3
1979–80	23	150	270	.556	115	151	.762	151	6.6	415	18.0
1980–81	29	195	354	.551	137	168	.815	169	5.8	527	18.2
Totals	112	629	1148	.548	461	578	.798	606	5.4	1719	15.3

GERRY TUCKER
Oklahoma
6-4 – C
Winfield, Kans.

NCAA consensus first-team All-American in 1947 and consensus second-team All-American in 1943.... Leading scorer for 1947 national runner-up (24-7 record).... Averaged 16.6 points in five NCAA Tournament games in 1943 and 1947 (3-2 record).

Season	G	FGM	FGA	FG%	FTM	FTA	FT%	Reb.	Avg.	Pts.	Avg.
1941–42	12	71			44					186	15.5
1942–43	26	144			85					373	14.3
1943–44		Military Service (Army)									
1944–45		Military Service (Army)									
1945–46		Military Service (Army)									
1946–47	31	111			103	136	.757			325	10.5
Totals	69	326			232					884	12.8

JACK TWYMAN
Cincinnati
6-6 – F
Pittsburgh, Pa.

Did not play in NCAA Tournament.... Averaged 19.7 points in three NIT games for 1955 third-place finisher (2-1 record).... Selected by the Rochester Royals in second round of 1955 NBA draft (10th pick overall).... Elected to Naismith Memorial Basketball Hall of Fame in 1982.

Season	G	FGM	FGA	FG%	FTM	FTA	FT%	Reb.	Avg.	Pts.	Avg.
1951–52	16	27	83	.325	13	27	.481	55	3.4	67	4.2
1952–53	24	136	323	.421	89	143	.622	362	15.1	361	15.0
1953–54	21	174	443	.393	110	145	.759	347	16.5	458	21.8
1954–55	29	285	628	.454	142	192	.740	478	16.5	712	24.6
Totals	90	622	1477	.421	354	507	.698	1242	13.8	1598	17.8

CHARLIE TYRA
Louisville
6-8 – C
Louisville, Ky.

NCAA consensus first-team All-American in 1957.... Did not play in NCAA Tournament.... NIT Most Valuable Player in 1956.... Averaged 20.2 points in six NIT games in 1954 (first-round loser), 1955 (second-round loser), and 1956 (champion).... Selected by the Detroit Pistons in first round of 1957 NBA draft (2nd pick overall).

Season	G	FGM	FGA	FG%	FTM	FTA	FT%	Reb.	Avg.	Pts.	Avg.
1953–54	13	36	82	.439	13	38	.342	84	6.5	85	6.5
1954–55	27	149	379	.393	100	158	.633	368	13.6	398	14.7
1955–56	29	262	592	.443	166	256	.648	645	22.2	690	23.8
1956–57	26	193	452	.427	169	234	.722	520	20.0	555	21.3
Totals	95	640	1505	.425	448	686	.653	1617	17.0	1728	18.2

PAUL UNRUH
Bradley
6-4 – F
Toulon, Ill.

NCAA unanimous first-team All-American in 1950.... Leading scorer for 1950 national runner-up (32-5 record).... Averaged 9.3 points in three NCAA Tournament games in 1950.... Averaged 16.1 points in eight NIT games in 1947 (first-round loser), 1949 (fourth place), and 1950 (runner-up).... Selected by the Indianapolis Olympians in second round of 1950 NBA draft (did not play in league).

Season	G	FGM	FGA	FG%	FTM	FTA	FT%	Reb.	Avg.	Pts.	Avg.
1946–47	32	156	465	.335	71	115	.617			383	12.0
1947–48	29	176	461	.382	103	157	.656			455	15.7
1948–49	35	202	522	.387	105	156	.673			509	14.5
1949–50	37	189	480	.394	97	149	.651			475	12.8
Totals	133	723	1928	.375	376	577	.652			1822	13.7

WES UNSELD
Louisville
6-7 – C
Louisville, Ky.

NCAA unanimous first-team All-American in 1967 and 1968.... Averaged 20.5 points and 17.5 rebounds in four NCAA Tournament games in 1967 and 1968 (1-3 record).... Collected 35 points and 26 rebounds in one NIT game in 1966.... Selected by the Baltimore Bullets in first round of 1968 NBA draft (2nd pick overall).... Elected to the Naismith Memorial Basketball Hall of Fame in 1987.

Season	G	FGM	FGA	FG%	FTM	FTA	FT%	Reb.	Avg.	Pts.	Avg.
1965–66	26	195	374	.521	128	202	.634	505	19.4	518	19.9
1966–67	28	201	374	.537	121	177	.684	533	19.0	523	18.7
1967–68	28	234	382	.613	177	275	.644	513	18.3	645	23.0
Totals	82	630	1130	.558	426	654	.651	1551	18.9	1686	20.6

JOHN VALLELY
UCLA
6-2 – G
Corona Del Mar, Calif.

Named to All-NCAA Tournament team in 1969 and 1970.... Second-leading scorer for NCAA champion in 1970 (28-2 record) and third-leading scorer for NCAA champion in 1969 (29-1).... Averaged 16.4 points in eight NCAA Tournament games in 1969 and 1970 (8-0 record).... Averaged 23.3 points and 9.7 rebounds in two junior college seasons at Orange Coast (Calif.).... Selected by the Atlanta Hawks in first round of 1970 NBA draft (14th pick overall).

Season	G	FGM	FGA	FG%	FTM	FTA	FT%	Reb.	Avg.	Pts.	Avg.
1968–69	28	116	234	.496	77	102	.755	91	3.3	309	11.0
1969–70	30	192	395	.486	106	147	.721	111	3.7	490	16.3
Totals	58	308	629	.490	183	249	.735	202	3.5	799	13.8

DICK VAN ARSDALE
Indiana
6-5 – F
Indianapolis, Ind.

Did not play in NCAA Tournament or NIT.... Selected by the New York Knicks in third round of 1965 NBA draft (18th pick overall).

Season	G	FGM	FGA	FG%	FTM	FTA	FT%	Reb.	Avg.	Pts.	Avg.
1962–63	24	95	225	.422	102	142	.718	213	8.9	292	12.2
1963–64	24	178	396	.449	179	223	.803	298	12.4	535	22.3
1964–65	24	146	327	.446	121	142	.852	208	8.7	413	17.2
Totals	72	419	948	.442	402	507	.793	719	10.0	1240	17.2

BOB VERGA
Duke
6-0 – G
Sea Girt, N.J.

NCAA consensus first-team All-American in 1967 and consensus second-team All-American in 1966.... Second-leading scorer for national third-place team in 1966.... Averaged 15.5 points in four NCAA Tournament games in 1966 (3-1 record).... Scored 24 points in one NIT game in 1967.... Selected by the Kentucky Colonels in first five rounds of 1967 ABA draft.

Season	G	FGM	FGA	FG%	FTM	FTA	FT%	Reb.	Avg.	Pts.	Avg.
1964–65	25	229	431	.531	76	116	.655	84	3.4	534	21.4
1965–66	28	216	441	.490	87	119	.731	113	4.0	519	18.5
1966–67	27	283	614	.461	139	179	.777	102	3.8	705	26.1
Totals	80	728	1486	.490	302	414	.729	299	3.7	1758	22.0

NEAL WALK
Florida
6-9 – C
Miami Beach, Fla.

Led the nation in rebounding in 1968.... Did not play in NCAA Tournament.... Scored 26 points in one NIT game in 1969.... Selected by the Phoenix Suns in first round of 1969 NBA draft (2nd pick overall).

Season	G	FGM	FGA	FG%	FTM	FTA	FT%	Reb.	Avg.	Pts.	Avg.
1966–67	25	109	210	.519	70	97	.722	206	8.2	288	11.5
1967–68	25	239	507	.471	185	244	.758	494	19.8	663	26.5
1968–69	27	224	449	.499	201	278	.723	464	17.2	649	24.0
Totals	77	572	1166	.491	456	619	.737	1164	15.1	1600	20.8

CHET WALKER
Bradley
6-6 – F
Benton Harbor, Mich.

NCAA unanimous first-team All-American in 1962 and consensus first-team All-American in 1961.... Did not play in NCAA Tournament.... Averaged 23.5 points in four NIT games in 1960 (champion) and 1962 (first-round loser).... Selected by the Syracuse Nationals in second round of 1962 NBA draft (14th pick overall).

Season	G	FGM	FGA	FG%	FTM	FTA	FT%	Reb.	Avg.	Pts.	Avg.
1959–60	29	244	436	.560	144	234	.615	388	13.4	632	21.8
1960–61	26	238	423	.563	180	250	.720	327	12.6	656	25.2
1961–62	26	268	500	.536	151	236	.640	321	12.3	687	26.4
Totals	81	750	1359	.552	475	720	.660	1036	12.8	1975	24.4

JIMMY WALKER
Providence
6-3 – G
Boston, Mass.

NCAA unanimous first-team All-American in 1967 and consensus first-team All-American in 1966.... Led the nation in scoring in 1967.... Averaged 20 points in four NCAA Tournament games in 1965 and 1966 (2-2 record).... Averaged 36.5 points in two NIT games in 1967 (1-1 record).... Selected by the Detroit Pistons in first round of 1967 NBA draft (1st pick overall).

Season	G	FGM	FGA	FG%	FTM	FTA	FT%	Reb.	Avg.	Pts.	Avg.
1964–65	26	211	444	.475	110	143	.769	158	6.1	532	20.5
1965–66	27	248	488	.508	166	215	.772	182	6.7	662	24.5
1966–67	28	323	659	.490	205	256	.801	169	6.0	851	30.4
Totals	81	782	1591	.492	481	614	.783	509	6.3	2045	25.2

KENNY WALKER
Kentucky
6-8 – F
Roberta, Ga.

NCAA unanimous first-team All-American in 1986 and consensus second-team All-American in 1985.... Second-leading scorer and third-leading rebounder for 1984 Final Four team (29-5 record).... Averaged 16.1 points and 5.8 rebounds in 14 NCAA Tournament games from 1983 to 1986 (10-4 record).... Selected by the New York Knicks in first round of 1986 NBA draft (5th pick overall).

Season	G	FGM	FGA	FG%	FTM	FTA	FT%	Reb.	Avg.	Pts.	Avg.
1982–83	31	88	144	.611	51	77	.662	151	4.9	227	7.3
1983–84	34	171	308	.555	80	109	.734	200	5.9	422	12.4
1984–85	31	246	440	.559	218	284	.768	315	10.2	710	22.9
1985–86	36	260	447	.582	201	263	.764	276	7.7	721	20.0
Totals	132	765	1339	.571	550	733	.750	942	7.1	2080	15.8

BILL WALTON
UCLA
6-11 – C
La Mesa, Calif.

NCAA unanimous first-team All-American in 1972, 1973, and 1974.... Named national player of the year by UPI and USBWA in 1972, 1973, and 1974, and by AP in 1972 and 1973.... Naismith Award winner in 1972, 1973, and 1974.... Final Four Most Outstanding Player in 1972 and 1973.... Leading scorer and rebounder for undefeated NCAA champions in 1972 (30-0 record) and

1973 (30-0) and national third-place team in 1974 (26-4).... Member of All-NCAA Tournament team in 1972, 1973, and 1974.... Averaged 21.2 points and 14.7 rebounds in 12 NCAA Tournament games from 1972 to 1974 (11-1 record).... Selected by the Portland Trail Blazers in first round of 1974 NBA draft (1st pick overall).... Elected to Naismith Memorial Basketball Hall of Fame in 1993.

Season	G	FGM	FGA	FG%	FTM	FTA	FT%	Reb.	Avg.	Pts.	Avg.
1971–72	30	238	372	.640	157	223	.704	466	15.5	633	21.1
1972–73	30	277	426	.650	58	102	.569	506	16.9	612	20.4
1973–74	27	232	349	.665	58	100	.580	398	14.7	522	19.3
Totals	87	747	1147	.651	273	425	.642	1370	15.7	1767	20.3

MIKE WARREN
UCLA
5-11 – G
South Bend, Ind.

Named to All-NCAA Tournament team in 1967 and 1968.... Third-leading scorer for NCAA champions in 1967 (30-0 record) and 1968 (29-1).... Averaged 13.6 points and 4.9 rebounds in eight NCAA Tournament games in 1967 and 1968 (8-0 record).... Selected by the Seattle SuperSonics in 14th round of 1968 NBA draft (did not play in league).

Season	G	FGM	FGA	FG%	FTM	FTA	FT%	Reb.	Avg.	Pts.	Avg.
1965–66	26	162	368	.440	108	146	.740	96	3.7	432	16.6
1966–67	30	144	310	.465	94	124	.758	134	4.5	382	12.7
1967–68	30	152	353	.431	58	76	.763	111	3.7	362	12.1
Totals	86	458	1031	.444	260	346	.751	341	4.0	1176	13.7

KERMIT WASHINGTON
American
6-8 – C/F
Washington, D.C.

NCAA consensus second-team All-American in 1973.... Led the nation in rebounding in 1972 and 1973.... One of six players to average more than 20 points and 20 rebounds per game in his career.... Did not play in NCAA Tournament.... Collected 29 points and 15 rebounds in one NIT game in 1973.... Selected by the Los Angeles Lakers in first round of 1973 NBA draft (5th pick overall).

Season	G	FGM	FGA	FG%	FTM	FTA	FT%	Reb.	Avg.	Pts.	Avg.
1970–71	25	173	370	.468	119	183	.650	512	20.5	465	18.6
1971–72	23	193	355	.544	96	144	.667	455	19.8	482	21.0
1972–73	25	211	426	.495	98	132	.742	511	20.4	520	20.8
Totals	73	577	1151	.501	313	459	.682	1478	20.2	1467	20.1

RICHARD WASHINGTON
UCLA
6-10 – F/C
Portland, Ore.

NCAA consensus first-team All-American in 1976.... Leading scorer and second-leading rebounder for national third-place team in 1976 (27-5 record), second-leading scorer and rebounder for 1975 NCAA champion (28-3), and eighth-leading scorer and fifth-leading rebounder for 1974 national third-place team (26-4).... Final Four Most Outstanding Player in 1975.... Member of All-NCAA Tournament team in 1975.... Averaged 16.1 points and 7.6 rebounds in 13 NCAA Tournament games from 1974 to 1976 (12-1 record; did not play in 1974 national semifinal defeat).... Selected as an undergraduate by the Kansas City Kings in first round of 1976 NBA draft (3rd pick overall).

Season	G	FGM	FGA	FG%	FTM	FTA	FT%	Reb.	Avg.	Pts.	Avg.
1973–74	24	41	80	.513	17	34	.500	66	2.8	99	4.1
1974–75	31	204	354	.576	84	116	.724	242	7.8	492	15.9
1975–76	32	276	538	.513	92	125	.736	274	8.6	644	20.1
Totals	87	521	972	.536	193	275	.702	582	6.7	1235	14.2

MAYCE (CHRIS) WEBBER
Michigan
6-9 – F
Detroit, Mich.

NCAA unanimous first-team All-American in 1993.... Leading scorer and rebounder for 1993 NCAA runner-up (31-5 record), and leading rebounder and second-leading scorer for 1992 NCAA runner-up (25-9).... Named to All-NCAA Tournament team in 1992 and 1993.... Averaged 17.9 points, 10.5 rebounds, and 2.7 blocked shots in 12 NCAA Tournament games in 1992 and 1993 (10-2 record).... Selected as an undergraduate by the Orlando Magic in first round of 1993 NBA draft (1st pick overall); draft rights promptly traded to the Golden State Warriors.

Season	G	FGM	FGA	FG%	FTM	FTA	FT%	Reb.	Avg.	Pts.	Avg.
1991–92	34	229	412	.556	56	113	.496	340	10.0	528	15.5
1992–93	36	281	454	.619	101	183	.552	362	10.1	690	19.2
Totals	70	510	866	.589	157	296	.530	702	10.0	1218	17.4

Three-point field goals: 14 of 54 (.259) in 1991–92 and 27 of 80 (.338) in 1992–93. Totals: 41 of 134 (.306).

NICK WERKMAN
Seton Hall
6-3 – F
Trenton, N.J.

Led the nation in scoring in 1963.... Did not play in NCAA Tournament or NIT.... Selected by the Boston Celtics in fifth round of 1964 NBA draft (did not play in league).

Season	G	FGM	FGA	FG%	FTM	FTA	FT%	Reb.	Avg.	Pts.	Avg.
1961–62	24	271	563	.481	251	347	.723	413	17.2	793	33.0
1962–63	22	221	502	.440	208	325	.640	278	12.6	650	29.5
1963–64	25	320	734	.436	190	308	.617	345	13.8	830	33.2
Totals	71	812	1799	.451	649	980	.662	1036	14.6	2273	32.0

JERRY WEST
West Virginia
6-3 – G/F
Cabin Creek, W.V.

NCAA unanimous first-team All-American in 1959 and 1960.... Final Four Most Outstanding Player in 1959.... Leading scorer and rebounder for 1959 national runner-up (29-5 record).... Member of All-NCAA Tournament team in 1959.... Averaged 30.6 points and 13.8 rebounds in nine NCAA Tournament games from 1958 to 1960 (6-3 record).... Member of 1960 U.S. Olympic team.... Selected by the Los Angeles Lakers in first round of 1960 NBA draft (2nd pick overall).... Elected to Naismith Memorial Basketball Hall of Fame in 1979.

Season	G	FGM	FGA	FG%	FTM	FTA	FT%	Reb.	Avg.	Pts.	Avg.
1957–58	28	178	359	.496	142	194	.732	311	11.1	498	17.8
1958–59	34	340	656	.518	223	320	.697	419	12.3	903	26.6
1959–60	31	325	645	.504	258	337	.766	510	16.5	908	29.3
Totals	93	843	1660	.508	623	851	.732	1240	13.3	2309	24.8

PAUL WESTPHAL
Southern California
6-4 – G
Redondo Beach, Calif.

Did not play in NCAA Tournament or NIT.... Selected by the Boston Celtics in first round of 1972 NBA draft (10th pick overall).

Season	G	FGM	FGA	FG%	FTM	FTA	FT%	Reb.	Avg.	Pts.	Avg.
1969–70	26	147	277	.531	84	110	.764	68	2.6	378	14.5
1970–71	26	157	328	.479	109	150	.727	84	3.2	423	16.3
1971–72	14	106	219	.484	72	95	.758	74	5.3	284	20.3
Totals	66	410	824	.498	265	355	.746	226	3.4	1085	16.4

JO JO WHITE
Kansas
6-3 – G
St. Louis, Mo.

NCAA consensus second-team All-American in 1968 and 1969.... Averaged 17.3 points and 6.5 rebounds in four NCAA Tournament games in 1966 and 1967 (2-2 record).... Averaged 13.8 points and 3.5 rebounds in four NIT games for 1968 runner-up.... Member of 1968 U.S. Olympic team.... Selected by the Boston Celtics in first round of 1969 NBA draft (9th pick overall).

Season	G	FGM	FGA	FG%	FTM	FTA	FT%	Reb.	Avg.	Pts.	Avg.
1965–66	9	44	112	.393	14	26	.538	68	7.6	102	11.3
1966–67	27	170	416	.409	59	72	.819	150	5.6	399	14.8
1967–68	30	188	462	.407	83	115	.722	107	3.6	459	15.3
1968–69	18	134	286	.469	58	79	.734	84	4.7	326	18.1
Totals	84	536	1276	.420	214	292	.733	409	4.9	1286	15.3

SIDNEY WICKS
UCLA
6-8 – F/C
Los Angeles, Calif.

Named national player of the year by USBWA in 1971.... NCAA unanimous first-team All-American in 1971 and consensus second-team All-American in 1970.... Leading scorer and rebounder for NCAA champions in 1970 (28-2 record) and 1971 (29-1).... Fourth-leading scorer and third-leading rebounder for 1969 NCAA champion (29-1).... Final Four Most Outstanding Player in 1970.... Member of All-NCAA Tournament team in 1970 and 1971.... Averaged 13.3 points and 9.3 rebounds in 12 NCAA Tournament games from 1969 to 1971 (12-0 record).... Averaged 26 points and 19.5 rebounds in one season of junior college basketball at Santa Monica Community College.... Selected by the Portland Trail Blazers in first round of 1971 NBA draft (2nd pick overall).

Season	G	FGM	FGA	FG%	FTM	FTA	FT%	Reb.	Avg.	Pts.	Avg.
1968–69	30	84	193	.435	58	100	.580	153	5.1	226	7.5
1969–70	30	221	415	.533	117	185	.632	357	11.9	559	18.6
1970–71	30	244	466	.524	150	227	.661	384	12.8	638	21.3
Totals	90	549	1074	.511	325	512	.635	894	9.9	1423	15.8

MURRAY WIER
Iowa
5-9 – G
Muscatine, Iowa

NCAA consensus first-team All-American in 1948.... Led the nation in scoring in 1948.... Did not play in NCAA Tournament.... Selected by the Tri-Cities Blackhawks in 1948 NBL draft.

Season	G	FGM	FGA	FG%	FTM	FTA	FT%	Reb.	Avg.	Pts.	Avg.
1944–45	17	58			18	33	.545			134	7.9
1945–46	18	57			39	62	.629			153	8.5
1946–47	18	105	348	.302	62	93	.667			272	15.1
1947–48	19	152	429	.354	95	136	.699			399	21.0
Totals	72	372			214	324	.660			958	13.3

LENNY WILKENS
Providence
6-1 – G
Brooklyn, N.Y.

NCAA consensus second-team All-American in 1960.... Did not play in NCAA Tournament.... NIT Most Valuable Player in 1960.... Averaged 20.3 points in eight NIT games in 1959 (fourth place) and 1960 (runner-up).... Selected by the St. Louis Hawks in first round of 1960 NBA draft.... Elected to Naismith Memorial Basketball Hall of Fame in 1988.

Season	G	FGM	FGA	FG%	FTM	FTA	FT%	Reb.	Avg.	Pts.	Avg.
1957–58	24	137	316	.434	84	130	.646	190	7.9	358	14.9
1958–59	27	167	390	.428	89	144	.618	188	7.0	423	15.7
1959–60	29	157	362	.434	98	140	.700	205	7.1	412	14.2
Totals	80	461	1068	.432	271	414	.655	583	7.3	1193	14.9

JAMAAL WILKES
see Keith Wilkes

KEITH WILKES
UCLA
6-7 – F
Santa Barbara, Calif.

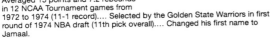

NCAA unanimous first-team All-American in 1974 and consensus first-team All-American in 1973.... Second-leading scorer and rebounder for undefeated 1973 NCAA champion (30-0 record) and 1974 third-place team (26-4).... Third-leading scorer and second-leading rebounder for undefeated 1972 NCAA champion (30-0).... Member of All-NCAA Tournament team in 1972.... Averaged 15 points and 7.2 rebounds in 12 NCAA Tournament games from 1972 to 1974 (11-1 record).... Selected by the Golden State Warriors in first round of 1974 NBA draft (11th pick overall).... Changed his first name to Jamaal.

Season	G	FGM	FGA	FG%	FTM	FTA	FT%	Reb.	Avg.	Pts.	Avg.
1971–72	30	171	322	.531	64	92	.696	245	8.2	406	13.5
1972–73	30	200	381	.525	43	66	.652	220	7.3	443	14.8
1973–74	30	209	426	.491	82	94	.872	198	6.6	500	16.7
Totals	90	580	1129	.514	189	252	.750	663	7.4	1349	15.0

DOMINIQUE WILKINS
Georgia
6-8 – F
Washington, N.C.

Did not play in NCAA Tournament.... Averaged 21.5 points and 9 rebounds in six NIT games in 1981 (second-round loser) and 1982 (semifinals loser).... Selected as an undergraduate by the Utah Jazz in first round of 1982 NBA draft (3rd pick overall).

Season	G	FGM	FGA	FG%	FTM	FTA	FT%	Reb.	Avg.	Pts.	Avg.
1979–80	16	135	257	.525	27	37	.730	104	6.5	297	18.6
1980–81	31	310	582	.533	112	149	.752	234	7.5	732	23.6
1981–82	31	278	526	.529	103	160	.644	250	8.1	659	21.3
Totals	78	723	1365	.530	242	346	.699	588	7.5	1688	21.6

CHARLES (BUCK) WILLIAMS
Maryland
6-8 – F
Rocky Mount, N.C.

Averaged 16.5 points and 12.5 rebounds in four NCAA Tournament games in 1980 and 1981 (2-2 record).... Averaged 10.5 points and 14 rebounds in two NIT games in 1979.... Selected as an undergraduate by the New Jersey Nets in first round of 1981 NBA draft (3rd pick overall).

Season	G	FGM	FGA	FG%	FTM	FTA	FT%	Reb.	Avg.	Pts.	Avg.
1978–79	30	120	206	.583	60	109	.550	323	10.8	300	10.0
1979–80	24	143	236	.606	85	128	.664	242	10.1	371	15.5
1980–81	31	183	283	.647	116	182	.637	363	11.7	482	15.5
Totals	85	446	725	.615	261	419	.623	928	10.9	1153	13.6

FREEMAN WILLIAMS
Portland State
6-4 – G
Los Angeles, Calif.

NCAA consensus second-team All-American in 1978.... Led the nation in scoring in 1977 and 1978.... Did not play in NCAA Tournament or NIT.... Selected by the Boston Celtics in first round of 1978 NBA draft (8th pick overall).

Season	G	FGM	FGA	FG%	FTM	FTA	FT%	Reb.	Avg.	Pts.	Avg.
1974–75	26	186	435	.428	64	81	.790	89	3.4	436	16.8
1975–76	27	356	781	.456	122	155	.787	111	4.1	834	30.9
1976–77	26	417	838	.498	176	221	.796	126	4.8	1010	38.8
1977–78	27	410	872	.470	149	191	.780	132	4.9	969	35.9
Totals	106	1369	2926	.468	511	648	.789	458	4.3	3249	30.7

REGGIE WILLIAMS
Georgetown
6-7 – F/G
Baltimore, Md.

NCAA unanimous first-team All-American in 1987.... Fourth-leading scorer for 1984 NCAA champion (34-3 record) and 1985 national runner-up (35-3).... Averaged 15.3 points and 5.5 rebounds in 17 NCAA Tournament games from 1984 to 1987 (14-3 record).... Selected by the Los Angeles Clippers in first round of 1987 NBA draft (4th pick overall).

Season	G	FGM	FGA	FG%	FTM	FTA	FT%	Reb.	Avg.	Pts.	Avg.
1983–84	37	130	300	.433	76	99	.768	131	3.5	336	9.1
1984–85	35	168	332	.506	80	106	.755	200	5.7	416	11.9
1985–86	32	227	430	.528	109	149	.732	261	8.2	563	17.6
1986–87	34	284	589	.482	156	194	.804	294	8.6	802	23.6
Totals	138	809	1651	.490	421	548	.768	886	6.4	2117	15.3

Three-point field goals: 78 of 202 (.386) in 1986–87.

GEORGE WILSON
Cincinnati
6-8 – C/F
Chicago, Ill.

Named to All-NCAA Tournament team in 1963.... Fourth-leading scorer and third-leading rebounder for 1962 NCAA champion (29-2 record) and third-leading scorer and leading rebounder for 1963 national runner-up (26-2).... Averaged 13.1 points and 8.9 rebounds in eight NCAA Tournament games in 1962 and 1963 (7-1 record).... Member of 1964 U.S. Olympic team.... Selected as a territorial choice by the Cincinnati Royals in 1964 NBA draft.

Season	G	FGM	FGA	FG%	FTM	FTA	FT%	Reb.	Avg.	Pts.	Avg.
1961–62	31	109	216	.505	67	101	.663	248	8.0	285	9.2
1962–63	28	160	299	.535	101	170	.594	314	11.2	421	15.0
1963–64	26	164	343	.478	90	173	.520	326	12.5	418	16.1
Totals	85	433	858	.505	258	444	.581	888	10.4	1124	13.2

LES WITTE
Wyoming
6-0 – F
Lincoln, Nebr.

NCAA consensus first-team All-American in 1932 and 1934.

Season	G	FGM	FGA	FG%	FTM	FTA	FT%	Reb.	Avg.	Pts.	Avg.
1930–31	23									274	11.9
1931–32	20									238	11.9
1932–33	23									234	10.2
1933–34	27									323	12.0
Totals	93									1069	11.5

JOHN WOODEN
Purdue
5-10 – G
Martinsville, Ind.

NCAA consensus first-team All-American in 1930, 1931, and 1932.... Elected to Naismith Memorial Basketball Hall of Fame as a player in 1960.

Season	G	FGM	FGA	FG%	FTM	FTA	FT%	Reb.	Avg.	Pts.	Avg.
1929–30	13	45			26					116	8.9
1930–31	17	53			34	49	.694			140	8.2
1931–32	18	79			61	86	.709			219	12.2
Totals	48	177			121					475	9.9

JAMES WORTHY
North Carolina
6-9 – F
Gastonia, N.C.

NCAA consensus first-team All-American in 1982.... Final Four Most Outstanding Player in 1982.... Leading scorer and second-leading rebounder for 1982 NCAA champion (32-2 record).... Third-leading scorer and leading rebounder for 1981 national runner-up (29-8).... Averaged 15.3 points and 5.5 rebounds in 10 NCAA Tournament games in 1981 and 1982 (9-1 record).... Selected as an undergraduate by the Los Angeles Lakers in first round of 1982 NBA draft (1st pick overall).

Season	G	FGM	FGA	FG%	FTM	FTA	FT%	Reb.	Avg.	Pts.	Avg.
1979–80	14	74	126	.587	27	45	.600	104	7.4	175	12.5
1980–81	36	208	416	.500	96	150	.640	301	8.4	512	14.2
1981–82	34	203	354	.573	126	187	.674	215	6.3	532	15.6
Totals	84	485	896	.541	249	382	.652	620	7.4	1219	14.5

JEWELL YOUNG
Purdue
6-0 – F
Lafayette, Ind.

NCAA consensus first-team All-American in 1937 and 1938.

Season	G	FGM	FGA	FG%	FTM	FTA	FT%	Reb.	Avg.	Pts.	Avg.
1935–36	20	74			29	43	.674			177	8.9
1936–37	20	97			49	65	.754			243	12.2
1937–38	20	117			55	73	.753			289	14.5
Totals	60	288			133	181	.735			709	11.8

Reggie Lewis (center) holds up his new jersey after the Boston Celtics selected him as their first pick in the 1987 NBA draft; Celtics president Red Auerbach (left) looks on. Lewis was a college star in the Celtics' backyard, scoring over 2700 points for Northeastern University. Tragedy struck in July 1993 when Lewis died of a heart attack after tests revealed he had a heart condition.

ADDITIONAL COLLEGE STARS

FOUR-YEAR PLAYERS WITH 2000+ POINTS

Player	School	Final Year	G	Pts.	Avg.
Reggie Lewis	Northeastern	1987	122	2708	22.2
Daren Queenan	Lehigh	1988	118	2703	22.9
Byron Larkin	Xavier	1988	121	2696	22.3
Mark Macon	Temple	1991	126	2609	20.7
Don MacLean	UCLA	1992	127	2608	20.5
Terrance Bailey	Wagner	1987	110	2591	23.6
Dickie Hemric	Wake Forest	1955	104	2587	24.9
Derrick Chievous	Missouri	1988	130	2580	19.8
Skip Henderson	Marshall	1988	125	2574	20.6
Rodney Monroe	N.C. State	1991	124	2551	20.6
Willie Jackson	Centenary	1984	114	2535	22.2
Steve Burtt	Iona	1984	121	2534	20.9
Steve Rogers	MTSU/Alabama St.	1992	113	2534	22.4
Joe Jakubick	Akron	1984	108	2530	23.4
Andrew Toney	Southwestern La.	1980	107	2526	23.6
Ron Perry	Holy Cross	1980	109	2524	23.2
Mike Olliver	Lamar	1981	122	2518	20.6
Bryant Stith	Virginia	1992	131	2516	19.2
Jeff Grayer	Iowa State	1899	125	2502	20.0
Terry Dehere	Seton Hall	1993	128	2494	19.5
Bimbo Coles	Virginia Tech	1990	115	2485	21.6
Jeff Martin	Murray State	1989	117	2484	21.2
John Gerdy	Davidson	1979	106	2483	23.4
Tony Dumas	Mo.-Kansas City	1994	112	2459	22.0
Vernon Maxwell	Florida	1988	130	2450	18.8
Mike McGee	Michigan	1981	114	2439	21.4
Gay Elmore	Va. Military	1987	113	2422	21.4
Carlos Yates	George Mason	1985	109	2420	22.2
Phil Sellers	Rutgers	1976	114	2399	21.0
Malik Sealy	St. John's	1992	127	2394	18.9
Todd Day	Arkansas	1992	127	2394	18.9
Lindsey Hunter	Alcorn/Jackson St.	1993	120	2393	19.9
Dell Curry	Virginia Tech	1986	126	2385	18.9
John Newman	Richmond	1986	122	2383	19.5
Henry Williams	UNC Charlotte	1992	118	2383	20.2
Byron Houston	Oklahoma State	1992	127	2379	18.7
Ron Harper	Miami of Ohio	1986	120	2377	19.8
Jim McCoy	Massachusetts	1992	126	2374	18.8
John S. Williams	Indiana State	1986	113	2370	21.0
George Dalton	John Carroll	1955	101	2357	23.3
Bo Kimble	USC/Loyola (Cal.)	1990	104	2350	22.6
Dana Barros	Boston College	1989	119	2342	19.7
Mitchell Anderson	Bradley	1982	122	2341	19.2
Anthony Roberts	Oral Roberts	1977	108	2341	21.7
Todd Lichti	Stanford	1989	124	2336	18.8
Dave Jamerson	Ohio Univ.	1990	115	2336	20.3
John Taft	Marshall	1991	107	2332	21.8
John Stroud	Mississippi	1980	110	2328	21.2
Kevin Houston	Army	1987	113	2325	20.6
Chad Tucker	Butler	1988	117	2321	19.8
Adam Keefe	Stanford	1992	125	2319	18.6
Michael Smith	Brigham Young	1989	122	2319	19.0
Jeff Lamp	Virginia	1981	123	2317	18.8
Lucious Harris	Long Beach State	1993	122	2312	19.0
Fennis Dembo	Wyoming	1988	129	2311	17.9
Chuck Person	Auburn	1986	126	2311	18.3
Dom Flora	Washington & Lee	1958	105	2310	22.0
Bill Edwards	Wright State	1993	114	2303	20.2
Joe Anderson	St. Francis (Pa.)	1991	116	2301	19.8
Jonathan Moore	Furman	1980	117	2299	19.6
Gary Winton	Army	1978	105	2296	21.9
Ben Hinson	Baptist	1987	116	2295	19.8
Kevin Brooks	SW Louisiana	1991	116	2294	19.8
Kenneth Lyons	North Texas State	1983	111	2291	20.6
Tony Bennett	Wisc.-Green Bay	1992	118	2285	19.4
Devin Durrant	Brigham Young	1984	117	2285	19.5
Marc Brown	Siena	1991	123	2284	18.6
Travis Mays	Texas	1990	124	2279	18.4
Ernie Hill	Oklahoma City	1980	110	2276	20.7
Tim McAlister	Oklahoma	1987	136	2275	16.7
Tom Davis	Delaware State	1991	95	2274	23.9
Charlie Bradley	South Florida	1985	118	2273	19.3
Eric Brown	Miami (Fla.)	1989	120	2270	18.9
Jeff Webster	Oklahoma	1994	125	2264	18.1
Steve Smith	Michigan State	1991	122	2263	18.5
Mouse McFadden	Cleveland State	1989	117	2256	19.3
Ernie Grunfeld	Tennessee	1977	101	2249	22.3
Steve Harris	Tulsa	1985	122	2248	18.4
Joe Dykstra	Western Illinois	1983	117	2248	19.2
Vin Baker	Hartford	1993	112	2238	20.0
Greg Sanders	St. Bonaventure	1978	112	2238	20.0
Franklin Edwards	Cleveland State	1981	102	2235	21.9
Roosevelt Chapman	Dayton	1984	118	2233	18.9
Ron Carter	Va. Military	1978	116	2228	19.2
Ray Hall	Canisius	1985	115	2226	19.4
Jeff Hodge	South Alabama	1989	119	2221	18.7
Eddie Owens	UNLV	1977	118	2221	18.8
Tony White	Tennessee	1987	127	2219	17.5
Darrick Suber	Rider	1993	116	2219	19.1
Elliot Perry	Memphis State	1991	126	2209	17.5
Michael Anderson	Drexel	1988	115	2208	19.2
Rufus Harris	Maine	1980	103	2206	21.4
Greg Dennis	East Tennessee St.	1992	127	2204	17.4
Ronnie Valentine	Old Dominion	1980	101	2204	21.8
Terrell Lowery	Loyola Marymount	1992	118	2201	18.7
Bailey Alston	Rutgers/Liberty	1990	108	2195	20.3
Earl Wise	Tennessee Tech	1990	112	2194	19.6
Barry Stevens	Iowa State	1985	117	2190	18.7
Terry Teagle	Baylor	1982	110	2189	19.9
Doug Smith	Missouri	1991	128	2184	17.1
Kenny Battle	No. Ill./Illinois	1989	123	2184	17.8
Ray Dudley	Air Force	1990	109	2178	20.0
Kenny Sanders	George Mason	1989	109	2177	20.0
Ron Simpson	Adelphi/Rider	1988	107	2172	20.3
Keith Herron	Villanova	1978	117	2170	18.5
Paul Graham	Ohio Univ.	1989	110	2170	19.7
Reggie King	Alabama	1979	118	2168	18.4
Dave Hoppen	Nebraska	1986	111	2167	19.5
John Long	Detroit	1978	110	2167	19.7
Pete Harris	Northeastern	1981	109	2167	19.9
Cleo Littleton	Wichita State	1955	113	2164	19.2
Jim Barton	Dartmouth	1989	104	2158	20.8
James Lacy	Loyola (Md.)	1949	119	2154	18.1
Kevin Green	Loyola (Md.)	1992	112	2154	19.2
Tony Dunkin	Coastal Carolina	1993	104	2151	20.7
Lew Massey	UNC Charlotte	1978	111	2149	19.4
Chris Smith	Connecticut	1992	128	2145	16.8
Mike Perry	Richmond	1981	108	2145	19.9
Joe Binion	No. Carolina A&T	1984	116	2143	18.5
Jesse Arnelle	Penn State	1955	102	2138	21.0
Mark Alarie	Duke	1986	133	2136	16.1
Dale Solomon	Virginia Tech	1982	116	2136	18.4
Bob Elliott	Arizona	1977	114	2131	18.7
Clarence Weatherspoon	Southern Miss.	1992	117	2130	18.2
Jesse Ratliff	North Texas	1994	114	2130	18.7
Deon Thomas	Illinois	1994	118	2129	18.0
Jon Manning	OCU/North Texas	1979	108	2129	19.7
Steve Steilper	James Madison	1980	104	2126	20.4
Greg Grant	Utah State	1986	115	2124	18.5
Scott Skiles	Michigan State	1986	118	2120	18.0
Charles Price	Grambling/Tex. So.	1990	116	2119	18.3
Rick Bullock	Texas Tech	1976	107	2118	19.8
Roy Marble	Iowa	1989	134	2116	15.8
Mike Evans	Kansas State	1978	117	2115	18.1
Carlton Owens	Rhode Island	1988	120	2111	17.6
Litterial Green	Georgia	1992	116	2111	18.2
John Rankin	Drexel	1989	110	2111	19.1
Bob Harstad	Creighton	1991	128	2110	16.5
Doremus Bennerman	Siena	1994	125	2109	16.9
Ray McCallum	Ball State	1983	115	2108	18.3
Stan Kimbrough	Central Fla./Xavier	1989	123	2103	17.1
Reggie Johnson	Tennessee	1980	115	2103	18.3
Bill Curley	Boston College	1994	126	2102	16.7
Rich Laurel	Hofstra	1977	95	2102	22.1
Dwight Stewart	Fla. International	1993	118	2101	17.8
Darryl Kennedy	Oklahoma	1987	137	2097	15.3
Dennis Hopson	Ohio State	1987	125	2096	16.8
Reggie Miller	UCLA	1987	122	2095	17.2
Butch Graves	Yale	1984	103	2091	20.3
Ronnie Williams	Florida	1984	110	2086	19.0
Ron Lee	Oregon	1976	112	2085	18.6
B. B. Davis	Lamar	1981	119	2084	17.5

ADDITIONAL COLLEGE STARS (CONTD.)

FOUR-YEAR PLAYERS WITH 2000+ POINTS

Player	School	Final Year	G	Pts.	Avg.
Tom Hammonds	Georgia Tech	1989	123	2081	16.9
Gene Banks	Duke	1981	124	2080	16.8
Chris Mills	Kentucky/Arizona	1993	126	2078	16.5
Rudy Macklin	Louisiana State	1981	123	2078	16.9
Joe Harvell	Mississippi	1993	114	2078	18.2
Steve Smith	Marist	1983	107	2077	19.4
Earl Belcher	St. Bonaventure	1981	104	2077	20.0
Ralph Crosthwaite	Western Kentucky	1959	103	2076	20.2
Anthony Mason	Tennessee State	1988	111	2075	18.7
Christian Welp	Washington	1987	129	2073	16.1
Herb Stamper	Morehead State	1979	99	2072	20.9
Sidney Green	UNLV	1983	119	2069	17.4
Mel McLaughlin	Central Michigan	1983	102	2068	20.3
Sherman Douglas	Syracuse	1989	138	2067	15.0
Fred West	Texas Southern	1990	118	2066	17.5
Wesley Person	Auburn	1994	108	2066	19.1
Ron Cornelius	Pacific	1981	115	2065	18.0
Roger Phegley	Bradley	1978	103	2064	20.0
Mike Woodson	Indiana	1980	104	2061	19.8
Greg Tynes	Seton Hall	1978	110	2059	18.7
Forrest McKenzie	Loyola Marymount	1986	110	2059	18.7
David Rivers	Notre Dame	1988	118	2058	17.4
Albert King	Maryland	1981	118	2058	17.4
Popeye Jones	Murray State	1992	123	2057	16.7
Boo Bowers	American	1981	93	2056	22.1
Bill McCaffrey	Duke/Vanderbilt	1994	142	2050	14.4
Tom Lewis	USC/Pepperdine	1990	114	2050	18.0
Charles Smith	Pittsburgh	1988	122	2045	16.8
Dan Majerle	Central Michigan	1988	94	2045	21.8
Michael Young	Houston	1984	134	2043	15.2
Terry Brooks	Alabama State	1989	112	2042	18.2
Troy Lewis	Purdue	1988	124	2038	16.4
Jack Givens	Kentucky	1978	123	2038	16.6
Mark Acres	Oral Roberts	1985	110	2038	18.5
Doug West	Villanova	1989	138	2037	14.8
James Bailey	Rutgers	1979	122	2034	16.7
Skip Brown	Wake Forest	1977	108	2034	18.8
Larry Chanay	Montana State	1960	101	2034	20.1
Jason Reese	Northern Iowa	1990	114	2033	17.8
Mike McConathy	Louisiana Tech	1977	98	2033	20.7
Doug Day	Radford	1993	117	2027	17.3
Kenny Williams	Illinois-Chicago	1994	121	2025	16.7
John Pinone	Villanova	1983	126	2024	16.1
Eric Murdock	Providence	1991	117	2021	17.3
Chad Kinch	UNC Charlotte	1980	112	2020	18.0
Bruce Collins	Weber State	1980	120	2019	16.8
Darrin Fitzgerald	Butler	1987	113	2019	17.9
Howie Crittenden	Murray State	1956	104	2019	19.4
Larry Krystkowiak	Montana	1986	120	2017	16.8
Ken Epperson	Toledo	1985	112	2016	18.0
Al Wood	North Carolina	1981	126	2015	16.0
Jim McPhee	Gonzaga	1990	118	2015	17.1
Greg Kelser	Michigan State	1979	115	2014	17.5
Brian Gilgeous	American	1993	115	2013	17.5
Jim Spanarkel	Duke	1979	114	2012	17.6
Bob Schafer	Villanova	1955	106	2012	19.0
Steve Black	La Salle	1985	102	2012	19.7
Stacey Augmon	UNLV	1991	145	2011	13.9
Clyde Vaughan	Pittsburgh	1984	122	2011	16.5
Herb Williams	Ohio State	1981	114	2011	17.6
Tony George	Fairfield	1986	115	2006	17.4
Tyrone Hill	Xavier	1990	126	2003	15.9
Jay Handlan	Washington & Lee	1952	94	2002	21.3
Josh Grant	Utah	1993	131	2000	15.3
Devin Boyd	Towson State	1993	116	2000	17.2

THREE-YEAR PLAYERS WITH 1550+ POINTS

Player	School	Final Year	G	Pts.	Avg.
Gerald Glass*	Delta State/Miss.	1990	93	2425	26.1
Buzz Wilkinson	Virginia	1955	78	2233	28.6
Rich Yunkus	Georgia Tech	1971	84	2232	26.6
Frank Burgess	Gonzaga	1961	78	2196	28.2
Jack Foley	Holy Cross	1965	79	2185	27.7
Dennis Scott	Georgia Tech	1990	99	2115	21.4

THREE-YEAR PLAYERS WITH 1550+ POINTS

Player	School	Final Year	G	Pts.	Avg.
Orlando Lightfoot	Idaho	1994	91	2102	23.1
Rich Travis	Oklahoma City	1969	80	2086	26.1
Flynn Robinson	Wyoming	1965	78	2049	26.3
Howard Porter	Villanova	1971	89	2026	22.8
Keith Gailes	Loyola (Ill.)	1991	82	2026	24.7
Don Curnutt	Miami (Fla.)	1970	77	2005	26.0
Wayne Estes	Utah State	1965	75	2001	26.7
Mel Counts	Oregon State	1964	89	1973	22.2
Tracy Tripucka	Lafayette	1972	79	1973	25.0
Charlie Davis	Wake Forest	1971	79	1970	24.9
Henry Finkel	Dayton	1966	83	1968	23.7
Cliff Meely	Colorado	1971	80	1940	24.3
Reggie Isaac	Coppin State	1991	92	1938	21.1
Lewis Jackson*	Alabama State	1984	82	1936	23.6
Gene Phillips	SMU	1971	74	1931	26.1
John Mengelt	Auburn	1971	77	1920	24.9
Tom Kerwin	Centenary	1966	74	1910	25.8
Desi Wilson	Fair. Dickinson	1991	88	1902	21.6
Cornell Green	Utah State	1962	84	1890	22.5
Hub Reed	Oklahoma City	1958	81	1887	23.3
Jeff Mullins	Duke	1964	86	1884	21.9
Ron Warner	Gettysburg	1962	77	1880	24.4
Harry Hollines	Denver	1968	75	1879	25.1
Shawn Vandiver	Colorado	1991	91	1876	20.6
Bob Portman	Creighton	1969	76	1876	24.7
Larry Finch	Memphis State	1973	84	1869	22.3
Don Meineke	Dayton	1952	97	1866	19.2
Terry Catledge	South Alabama	1985	86	1866	21.7
Jeff Ruland	Iona	1980	89	1855	20.8
Jerry Smith	Furman	1963	80	1855	23.2
Will Robinson	West Virginia	1972	75	1850	24.7
Mike Newlin	Utah	1971	80	1849	23.1
Ricky Pierce	Rice	1982	82	1847	22.5
Eddie Miles	Seattle	1963	80	1846	23.1
Marvin Roberts	Utah State	1982	78	1844	23.6
Rob Williams	Houston	1982	88	1838	20.9
Bob Lewis	North Carolina	1967	83	1836	22.1
John Austin	Boston College	1966	68	1835	27.0
Butch Komives	Bowling Green	1964	71	1834	25.8
Larry Stewart	Coppin State	1991	91	1824	20.0
Tom Hawkins	Notre Dame	1959	79	1820	23.0
Randy Woods	La Salle	1992	88	1817	20.6
Bob Zawoluk	St. John's	1952	80	1817	22.7
Don Boldebuck*	Neb. Wslyn/Houston	1956	79	1817	23.0
Russell Lee	Marshall	1972	76	1815	23.9
James Robinson	Alabama	1993	96	1813	18.9
Chris Gatling	Old Dominion	1991	85	1811	21.3
Tom McMillen	Maryland	1974	88	1807	20.5
Allan Bristow	Virginia Tech	1973	78	1804	23.1
Kevin Grevey	Kentucky	1975	84	1801	21.4
Tom Chilton	East Tennessee St.	1961	69	1801	26.1
Jervaughn Scales	Southern (La.)	1994	88	1797	20.4
Tracy Murray	UCLA	1992	98	1792	18.3
Rubin Jackson	Oklahoma City	1982	83	1791	21.6
Luther Burden	Utah	1975	80	1790	22.4
Jalen Rose	Michigan	1994	102	1788	17.5
Manny Newsome	Western Michigan	1964	68	1786	26.3
Leonard Coulter	Morehead State	1974	77	1781	23.1
Sly Williams	Rhode Island	1979	84	1777	21.2
Bruce King	Cor. Chr./Pan Am.	1974	73	1776	24.3
George Thompson	Marquette	1971	87	1773	20.4
Kenny Carr	N.C. State	1977	86	1772	20.6
Louis Dunbar	Houston	1975	79	1765	22.3
Joe Allen	Bradley	1968	79	1763	22.3
Butch Zatezalo	Clemson	1970	75	1761	23.5
Jim McMillian	Columbia	1970	77	1758	22.8
Dave Robisch	Kansas	1971	83	1754	21.1
Bud Koper	Oklahoma City	1964	80	1752	21.9
Steve Chubin	Rhode Island	1966	80	1751	21.9
Alex Blackwell	Monmouth	1992	86	1749	20.3
Jerry Harkness	Loyola (Ill.)	1963	81	1749	21.6
Larry Bullington	Ball State	1974	74	1747	23.6
Jim McCaffrey*	St. Mich./H. Cross	1986	79	1745	22.1
Jim Cunningham	Fordham	1958	76	1744	22.9
Dwight Davis	Houston	1972	84	1741	20.7

ADDITIONAL COLLEGE STARS (CONTD.)

THREE-YEAR PLAYERS WITH 1550+ POINTS

Player	School	Final Year	G	Pts.	Avg.
Jim Darrow	Kentucky	1960	72	1740	24.2
Fred Crawford	St. Bonaventure	1963	77	1738	22.6
Jimmy Collins	New Mexico State	1970	89	1734	19.5
Bill Shepherd	Butler	1972	72	1733	24.1
Billy Knight	Pittsburgh	1974	78	1731	22.2
Cliff Anderson	St. Joseph's	1967	84	1728	20.6
Willie Somerset	Duquesne	1965	84	1725	20.5
Pat Tallent	George Washington	1976	83	1725	20.8
Bill Buntin	Michigan	1965	79	1725	21.8
Larry Fogle	SW La./Canisius	1975	72	1724	23.9
George Stone	Marshall	1968	77	1723	22.4
Dick O'Neal	TCU	1957	72	1723	23.9
Steve Thomas	Xavier	1966	73	1722	23.6
Fred Taylor	Pan American	1970	76	1721	22.6
Rodney Rogers	Wake Forest	1993	89	1720	19.3
Mike Robinson	Michigan State	1974	71	1717	24.2
Mal Graham	NYU	1967	78	1716	22.0
Ira Terrell	SMU	1976	80	1715	21.4
Kevin Porter	St. Francis (Pa.)	1972	71	1712	24.1
Gary Gray	Oklahoma City	1967	85	1710	20.1
Darrell McGhee	Kent State	1979	79	1710	21.6
Alvan Adams	Oklahoma	1975	73	1707	23.4
Jim Haderlein	Loyola Marymount	1971	78	1706	21.9
Winfred Boynes	San Francisco	1978	90	1702	18.9
Howard Wright	Austin Peay	1970	73	1700	23.3
Ken Charles	Fordham	1973	84	1697	20.2
Frank Oleynick	Seattle	1975	75	1696	22.6
Leo Byrd	Marshall	1959	72	1695	23.5
Dick Snyder	Davidson	1966	80	1693	21.2
Derrick Gervin	Tex.-San Antonio	1985	80	1691	21.1
Lamond Murray	California	1994	88	1688	19.2
Ron Williams	West Virginia	1968	84	1687	20.1
Mike Bantom	St. Joseph's	1973	84	1684	20.0
Roy Ebron	SW Louisiana	1973	87	1683	19.3
Larry Hennessey	Villanova	1953	73	1683	23.1
Bill Green	Colorado State	1963	76	1682	22.1
Ken Durrett	La Salle	1971	71	1679	23.6
Jim Hayes	Boston Univ.	1970	69	1679	24.3
Steve Mix	Toledo	1969	73	1676	23.0
Dennis Awtrey	Santa Clara	1970	84	1675	19.9
Bob Florence	UNLV	1974	77	1674	21.7
Michael Allen	Southwestern La.	1994	91	1673	18.4
Wes Bialosuknia	Connecticut	1967	71	1673	23.6
Don Smith	Iowa State	1968	75	1672	22.3
Bobby Rascoe	Western Kentucky	1967	80	1670	20.9
Ken House	Seton Hall	1972	77	1670	21.7
Ollie Johnson	San Francisco	1965	84	1669	19.9
Arnie Berman	Brown	1972	77	1668	21.7
Bob Arnzen	Notre Dame	1969	82	1665	20.3
Mike Maloy	Davidson	1970	86	1661	19.3
George Knighton	New Mexico State	1962	75	1660	22.1
John Gianelli	Pacific	1972	81	1659	20.5
Bob Leinhard	Georgia	1970	75	1659	22.1
Randy Denton	Duke	1971	84	1658	19.7
Red Murrell	Drake	1958	73	1657	22.7
Alex Ellis	Niagara	1958	81	1656	20.4
Don Smith	Dayton	1974	81	1655	20.4
Don Scaife	Arkansas State	1975	74	1652	22.3
Henry Wilmore	Michigan	1973	70	1652	23.6
Aaron McKie	Temple	1994	92	1650	17.9
Keith Swagerty	Pacific	1967	82	1650	20.1
Marshall Rogers	Kansas/Pan Amer.	1976	65	1645	25.3
Keven McDonald	Penn	1978	79	1644	20.8
Stan Love	Oregon	1971	78	1644	21.1
Tom Lipsey	Los Angeles State	1976	78	1641	21.0
Bob Leonard	Wake Forest	1966	80	1637	20.5
Granville Williams	Morehead State	1962	76	1637	21.5
Bob Quick	Xavier	1968	78	1636	21.0
Sam Drummer	APSU/Ga. Tech	1979	80	1635	20.4
Brian Shorter	Pittsburgh	1991	92	1633	17.8
Togo Palazzi	Holy Cross	1954	80	1633	20.4
Bill O'Connor	Canisius	1963	70	1630	23.3
John Bagley	Boston College	1982	91	1629	17.9
Bill Uhl	Dayton	1956	88	1627	18.5
Ty Marioneaux	Loyola (La.)	1971	76	1627	21.4
Willie McCarter	Drake	1969	77	1626	21.1

THREE-YEAR PLAYERS WITH 1550+ POINTS

Player	School	Final Year	G	Pts.	Avg.
Bob McCarty	Virginia	1956	83	1625	19.6
Walter Luckett	Ohio Univ.	1975	79	1625	20.6
Dave Sorenson	Ohio State	1970	77	1622	21.1
John Garrett	Purdue	1975	82	1620	19.8
Tom Ingelsby	Villanova	1973	87	1616	18.6
Bill Melchionni	Villanova	1966	84	1612	19.2
Ed Siudet	Holy Cross	1969	72	1611	22.4
Hubie White	Villanova	1962	78	1608	20.6
Paul Erland	Dartmouth	1975	75	1606	21.4
Doug Edwards	Florida State	1993	93	1604	17.2
Joe Gibbon	Mississippi	1957	86	1601	18.6
Tom Burleson	N.C. State	1974	84	1598	19.0
Carl Ashley	Wyoming	1970	80	1598	20.0
Paul Long	Va. Tech/Wake Forest	1967	76	1598	21.0
Robin Freeman	Ohio State	1956	57	1597	28.0
Al Butler	Niagara	1961	70	1596	22.8
Dick Stricklin	Seattle	1957	85	1595	18.8
Harry Hall	Wyoming	1969	83	1595	19.2
John Beasley	Texas A&M	1966	73	1594	21.8
Jerry Wells	Oklahoma City	1966	78	1591	20.4
Bob Duffy	Colgate	1962	70	1591	22.7
Bob Fazio	St. Peter's	1977	83	1590	19.2
Clyde Mayes	Furman	1975	89	1589	17.9
Eddie Bodkin	Eastern Kentucky	1966	75	1587	21.2
Phil Hicks	Tulane	1976	75	1586	21.1
Hank Washington	Southeastern La.	1993	83	1585	19.1
Lloyd Batts	Cincinnati	1974	79	1585	20.1
Butch Beard	Louisville	1969	83	1580	19.0
Bob Whitmore	Notre Dame	1969	83	1580	19.0
Glenn Price	St. Bonaventure	1974	76	1579	20.8
Bill Ebben	Detroit	1957	77	1578	20.5
Dennis McDermott	St. Francis, N.Y.	1974	74	1578	21.3
Walt Piatkowski	Bowling Green	1968	73	1577	21.6
Sonny Dove	St. John's	1967	83	1576	19.0
Hubie Marshall	La Salle	1967	74	1576	21.3
Benoit Benjamin	Creighton	1985	89	1575	17.7
Mel Thompson	N.C. State	1954	97	1574	16.2
Byron Scott	Arizona State	1983	90	1572	17.5
Alan Hornyak	Ohio State	1973	69	1572	22.8
Rich Rinaldi	St. Peter's	1971	74	1571	21.2
Johnny Jones	Villanova	1969	80	1568	19.6
Voshon Lenard	Minnesota	1994	96	1567	16.3
John Fultz	Rhode Island	1970	77	1566	20.3
Claude Terry	Stanford	1972	76	1566	20.6
Sherman Dillard*	James Madison	1978	74	1566	21.2
Walter Devlin	George Washington	1955	78	1564	20.1
Willie Sojourner	Weber State	1971	81	1563	19.3
Johnny Davis	Dayton	1976	81	1562	19.3
Lee Marshall	Washington & Lee	1957	76	1561	20.5
Wendell Ladner	Southern Miss.	1970	76	1561	20.5
Tom Kozelko	Toledo	1973	75	1561	20.8
John Clune	Navy	1954	70	1561	22.3
Art Crump	Idaho State	1964	74	1557	21.0
Bill Taylor	La Salle	1975	82	1554	19.0
Bill Yarborough	Clemson	1956	85	1553	18.3
Mark Workman	West Virginia	1952	76	1553	20.4
Don Kessinger	Mississippi	1964	70	1553	22.2

* Began his career with a school that was classified as a small college at the time.

TWO-YEAR PLAYERS WITH 1170+ POINTS

Player	School	Final Year	G	Pts.	Avg.
Tony Murphy	Southern (La.)	1980	57	1614	28.3
Lewis Lloyd	Drake	1981	56	1577	28.2
Fly Williams	Austin Peay	1974	54	1541	28.5
Kevin Magee	UC Irvine	1982	56	1475	26.3
Grady Wallace	South Carolina	1957	52	1456	28.0
Lawrence Butler	Idaho State	1979	53	1430	27.0
Sidney Grider	Southwestern La.	1990	58	1419	24.5
Ozzie Edwards	Oklahoma City	1973	55	1414	25.7
Jerry Chambers	Utah	1966	57	1400	24.6
Willie Smith	Missouri	1976	58	1387	23.9
Joe Yezbak	U.S. International	1987	56	1374	24.5

ADDITIONAL COLLEGE STARS (CONTD.)

TWO-YEAR PLAYERS WITH 1170+ POINTS

Player	School	Final Year	G	Pts.	Avg.
Elnardo Webster	St. Peter's	1969	56	1374	24.5
J. R. Rider	UNLV	1993	55	1372	24.9
Martin Terry	Arkansas	1973	52	1368	26.3
Ledell Eackles	New Orleans	1988	59	1358	23.0
Bob McCurdy	Richmond	1975	54	1347	24.9
Mookie Blaylock	Oklahoma	1989	74	1338	18.1
Mitch Richmond	Kansas State	1988	64	1327	20.7
Leonard White	Southern	1993	60	1292	21.5
Shaler Halimon	Utah State	1968	51	1284	25.2
Cedric Ceballos	Cal St. Fullerton	1990	58	1284	22.1
Chris Cheeks	Va. Commonwealth	1989	63	1273	20.2
Terrell Brandon	Oregon	1991	57	1263	22.2
Winston Garland	SW Missouri State	1987	66	1248	18.9
Larry Robinson	Centenary	1990	60	1247	20.8
Darnell Sneed	Charleston South.	1993	57	1240	21.8
Brian Taylor	Princeton	1972	51	1239	24.3
Ryan Stuart	NE Louisiana	1993	58	1238	21.3
Aron Stewart	Richmond	1974	44	1237	28.1
Ron Peaks	Canisius	1979	54	1237	22.9
Mark Brisker	Stetson	1992	59	1236	20.9
Marvin Johnson	New Mexico	1978	57	1235	21.7
Jacky Dorsey	Georgia	1976	52	1234	23.7
Vinnie Johnson	Baylor	1979	51	1231	24.1
Ollie Taylor	Houston	1970	56	1231	22.0
Paul Long	Wake Forest	1967	53	1225	23.1
Sam Cassell	Florida State	1993	66	1211	18.3
Kenny Cunningham	Western Michigan	1980	56	1207	21.6
Riley Smith	Idaho	1990	62	1195	19.3
Coniel Norman	Arizona	1974	50	1194	23.9
Ollie Mack	East Carolina	1979	52	1194	23.0
Rico Washington	Weber State	1989	57	1194	20.9
Alton Lee Gipson	Florida State	1985	61	1194	19.6
Marvin Rich	Oklahoma City	1973	51	1192	23.4
Simmie Hill	West Texas State	1969	47	1189	25.3
Terry Boyd	Western Carolina	1992	51	1189	23.3
Dave Wagnon	Idaho State	1966	49	1183	24.1
Blue Edwards	East Carolina	1989	57	1177	20.6
Sam Williams	Iowa	1968	49	1176	24.0
Ken Green	Nevada-Reno	1983	57	1176	20.6

9

COACH DIRECTORY

Determining the greatest coaches in college basketball history is an inexact science. Actually, many of the most efficient coaches toiled in anonymity at obscure schools with inferior talent. Nonetheless, here is a look at the achievements of major-college coaches, both active and retired. The following criteria were used to determine the greatest college coaches of all time.

• Coached at least one NCAA championship team.

• Directed two or more teams to the Final Four.

• Had a total of 600 victories (minimum of 20 seasons in Division I).

• Won more than two-thirds of games in career with at least 20 years in Division I.

• Made at least 10 NCAA Tournament appearances.

Active College Coaching Greats

GENE BARTOW
Northeast Missouri State
'53
Browning, Mo.

NABC national coach of the year in 1973.... Reached NCAA Final Four two times—1973 (runner-up with Memphis State) and 1976 (third with UCLA).... Coach of NIT third-place teams in 1989 and 1993.... Coach of four Sun Belt Conference Tournament champions—1982, 1983, 1984, and 1987.

Year	School	Overall	League	Finish	Postseason
61–62	Central Mo. St.	16-6	7-3	3d (MIAA)	DNP
62–63	Central Mo. St.	17-6	7-3	T2d (MIAA)	DNP
63–64	Central Mo. St.	14-9	6-4	T2d (MIAA)	DNP
64–65	Valparaiso	13-12	5-7	T3d (ICC)	DNP
65–66	Valparaiso	19-9	7-5	4th (ICC)	NCAA DII (1-1)
66–67	Valparaiso	21-8	7-5	2d (ICC)	NCAA DII (2-1)
67–68	Valparaiso	11-15	3-9	6th (ICC)	DNP
68–69	Valparaiso	16-12	4-4	T2d (ICC)	NCAA DII (1-1)
69–70	Valparaiso	13-13	2-6	5th (ICC)	DNP
70–71	Memphis St.	18-8	8-6	T4th (Mo. Valley)	DNP
71–72	Memphis St.*	21-7	12-2	T1st (Mo. Valley)	NIT (0-1)
72–73	Memphis St.	24-6	12-2	1st (Mo. Valley)	NCAA (3-1)
73–74	Memphis St.	19-11			NIT (1-1)
74–75	Illinois	8-18	4-14	T9th (Big Ten)	Probation
75–76	UCLA	27-5	12-2	1st (Pac-10)	NCAA (4-1)
76–77	UCLA	24-5	11-3	1st (Pac-10)	NCAA (1-1)
78–79	Ala.-Birm.	15-11			DNP
79–80	Ala.-Birm.	18-12	10-4	T2d (Sun Belt)	NIT (0-1)
80–81	Ala.-Birm.	23-9	9-3	T1st (Sun Belt)	NCAA (2-1)
81–82	Ala.-Birm.	25-6	9-1	1st (Sun Belt)	NCAA (2-1)

82–83	Ala.-Birm.	19-14	9-5	3d (Sun Belt)	NCAA (0-1)
83–84	Ala.-Birm.	23-11	8-6	5th (Sun Belt)	NCAA (0-1)
84–85	Ala.-Birm.	25-9	11-3	2d (Sun Belt)	NCAA (1-1)
85–86	Ala.-Birm.	25-11	9-5	T3d (Sun Belt)	NCAA (1-1)
86–87	Ala.-Birm.	21-11	10-4	3d (Sun Belt)	NCAA (0-1)
87–88	Ala.-Birm.	16-15	7-7	5th (Sun Belt)	DNP
88–89	Ala.-Birm.	22-12	8-6	4th (Sun Belt)	NIT (4-1)
89–90	Ala.-Birm.	22-9	12-2	1st (Sun Belt)	NCAA (0-1)
90–91	Ala.-Birm.	18-13	9-5	2d (Sun Belt)	NIT (0-1)
91–92	Ala.-Birm.	20-9	4-6	5th (G. M'west)	NIT (0-1)
92–93	Ala.-Birm.	21-14	5-5	4th (G. M'west)	NIT (4-1)
93–94	Ala.-Birm.	22-8	8-4	T2d (G. M'west)	NCAA (0-1)

* Lost Missouri Valley Conference playoff game against regular-season co-champion Louisville (83-72) for automatic berth in NCAA Tournament.

32-Year Coaching Record: 616-324 (.655) overall, not including forfeit victory over Oregon State in 1975–76; 47-21 (.691) in three years at Central Missouri State; 93-69 (.574) in six years at Valparaiso; 82-32 (.719) in four years at Memphis State; 8-18 (.308) in one year at Illinois; 51-10 (.836) in two years at UCLA; 335-174 (.658) in first 16 years at Alabama-Birmingham; 20-10 (.667) in Missouri Intercollegiate Athletic Association; 28-36 (.438) in Indiana Collegiate Conference; 32-10 (.762) in Missouri Valley; 4-14 (.222) in Big Ten; 23-5 (.821) in Pacific-10; 111-51 (.685) in Sun Belt; 17-15 (.531) in Great Midwest; 19-8 (.704) in Sun Belt Tournament; 0-3 in Great Midwest Tournament; 4-3 (.571) in NCAA Division II Tournament with Valparaiso; 14-12 (.538) in NCAA Division I Tournament; 9-7 (.563) in NIT.

JIM BOEHEIM
Syracuse '66
Lyons, N.Y.

Coach of 1987 NCAA Tournament runner-up.... Coach of 1981 NIT runner-up.... Coach of three Big East Tournament champions—1981, 1988 and 1992.... Assistant coach at Syracuse under Roy Danforth for seven seasons from 1970 to 1976.

Year	School	Overall	League	Finish	Postseason
76–77	Syracuse	26-4			NCAA (1-1)
77–78	Syracuse	22-6			NCAA (1-1)
78–79	Syracuse	26-4			NCAA (1-1)
79–80	Syracuse	26-4	5-1	T1st (Big East)	NCAA (1-1)
80–81	Syracuse	22-12	6-8	6th (Big East)	NIT (4-1)
81–82	Syracuse	16-13	7-7	T5th (Big East)	NIT (1-1)
82–83	Syracuse	21-10	9-7	5th (Big East)	NCAA (1-1)
83–84	Syracuse	23-9	12-4	T2d (Big East)	NCAA (1-1)
84–85	Syracuse	22-9	9-7	T3d (Big East)	NCAA (1-1)
85–86	Syracuse	26-6	14-2	T1st (Big East)	NCAA (1-1)
86–87	Syracuse	31-7	12-4	T1st (Big East)	NCAA (5-1)
87–88	Syracuse	26-9	11-5	2d (Big East)	NCAA (1-1)
88–89	Syracuse	30-8	10-6	3d (Big East)	NCAA (3-1)
89–90	Syracuse	26-7	12-4	T1st (Big East)	NCAA (2-1)
90–91	Syracuse	26-6	12-4	1st (Big East)	NCAA (0-1)
91–92	Syracuse	22-10	10-8	T5th (Big East)	NCAA (0-1)
92–93	Syracuse	20-9	10-8	3d (Big East)	Probation
93–94	Syracuse	23-7	13-5	2d (Big East)	NCAA (2-1)

18-Year Coaching Record: 434-140 (.756) overall; 152-80 (.655) in Big East; 24-12 (.667) in Big East Tournament; 21-15 (.583) in NCAA Tournament; 5-2 (.714) in NIT.

DALE BROWN
Minot St. '57
Minot, N.D.

Guided LSU to Final Four appearances in 1981 (4th) and 1986 (T-3d).... Second-winningest coach in SEC history (behind Adolph Rupp) in both overall and SEC games.... Led Tigers to 15 consecutive postseason tournaments (1979–93).... Coach of 1980 SEC Tournament champion.... Assistant coach on Ladell Andersen's staff at Utah State (1966–71) before a one-year stint under Marv Harshman at Washington State (1971–72).

Year	School	Overall	League	Finish	Postseason
72–73	LSU	14-10	9-9	5th (SEC)	DNP
73–74	LSU	12-14	6-12	8th (SEC)	DNP
74–75	LSU	10-16	6-12	7th (SEC)	DNP
75–76	LSU	12-14	5-13	9th (SEC)	DNP
76–77	LSU	15-12	8-10	5th (SEC)	DNP

77–78	LSU	18-9	12-6	2d (SEC)	DNP
78–79	LSU	23-6	14-4	1st (SEC)	NCAA (1-1)
79–80	LSU	26-6	14-4	2d (SEC)	NCAA (2-1)
80–81	LSU	31-5	17-1	1st (SEC)	NCAA (3-2)
81–82	LSU	14-14	11-7	T4th (SEC)	NIT (0-1)
82–83	LSU	19-13	10-8	T2d (SEC)	NIT (0-1)
83–84	LSU	18-11	11-7	T3d (SEC)	NCAA (0-1)
84–85	LSU	19-10	13-5	1st (SEC)	NCAA (0-1)
85–86	LSU	26-12	9-9	T5th (SEC)	NCAA (4-1)
86–87	LSU	24-15	8-10	T6th (SEC)	NCAA (3-1)
87–88	LSU	16-14	10-8	T4th (SEC)	NCAA (0-1)
88–89	LSU	20-12	11-7	T4th (SEC)	NCAA (0-1)
89–90	LSU	23-9	12-6	T2d (SEC)	NCAA (1-1)
90–91	LSU	20-10	13-5	T1st (SEC)	NCAA (0-1)
91–92	LSU	21-10	12-4	2d-W (SEC)	NCAA (1-1)
92–93	LSU	22-10	9-7	2d-W (SEC)	NCAA (0-1)
93–94	LSU	11-16	5-11	5th-W (SEC)	DNP

22-Year Coaching Record: 414-249 (.651) in 22 years at LSU; 225-165 (.577) in Southeastern Conference; 12-15 (.444) in SEC Tournament; 15-14 (.517) in NCAA Tournament; 0-2 in NIT.

PETE CARRIL
Lafayette '52
Bethlehem, Pa.

Captured the Ivy League's only NIT championship in 1975.... Has only one losing record in 27 seasons at Princeton.

Year	School	Overall	League	Finish	Postseason
66–67	Lehigh	11-12		Middle Atlantic	DNP
67–68	Princeton	20-6	12-2	T1st (Ivy)	DNP
68–69	Princeton	19-7	14-0	1st (Ivy)	NCAA (0-1)
69–70	Princeton	16-9	9-5	3d (Ivy)	DNP
70–71	Princeton	14-11	9-5	T3d (Ivy)	DNP
71–72	Princeton	20-7	12-2	2d (Ivy)	NIT (1-1)
72–73	Princeton	16-9	11-3	2d (Ivy)	DNP
73–74	Princeton	16-10	11-3	T2d (Ivy)	DNP
74–75	Princeton	22-8	12-2	2d (Ivy)	NIT (4-0)
75–76	Princeton	22-5	14-0	1st (Ivy)	NCAA (0-1)
76–77	Princeton	21-5	13-1	1st (Ivy)	NCAA (0-1)
77–78	Princeton	17-9	11-3	T2d (Ivy)	DNP
78–79	Princeton	14-12	7-7	3d (Ivy)	DNP
79–80	Princeton	15-15	11-3	T1st (Ivy)	DNP
80–81	Princeton	18-10	13-1	T1st (Ivy)	NCAA (0-1)
81–82	Princeton	13-13	9-5	T2d (Ivy)	DNP
82–83	Princeton	20-9	12-2	1st (Ivy)	NCAA (2-1)
83–84	Princeton	18-10	10-4	1st (Ivy)	NCAA (1-1)
84–85	Princeton	11-15	7-7	T4th (Ivy)	DNP
85–86	Princeton	13-13	7-7	T4th (Ivy)	DNP
86–87	Princeton	16-9	9-5	T2d (Ivy)	DNP
87–88	Princeton	17-9	9-5	3d (Ivy)	DNP
88–89	Princeton	19-8	11-3	1st (Ivy)	NCAA (0-1)
89–90	Princeton	20-7	11-3	1st (Ivy)	NCAA (0-1)
90–91	Princeton	24-3	14-0	1st (Ivy)	NCAA (0-1)
91–92	Princeton	22-6	12-2	1st (Ivy)	NCAA (0-1)
92–93	Princeton	15-11	7-7	4th (Ivy)	DNP
93–94	Princeton	18-8	11-3	2d (Ivy)	DNP

28-Year College Coaching Record: 487-256 (.655) overall; 11-12 (.478) in one year at Lehigh; 476-244 (.661) in 27 years at Princeton; 292-90 (.764) in Ivy League; 3-10 (.231) in NCAA Tournament; 5-1 (.833) in NIT.

GALE CATLETT
West Virginia '63
Hedgesville, W.V.

Never compiled a losing record.... Winningest coach in West Virginia and Atlantic 10 Conference history.... Directed West Virginia to NIT semifinals (4th) in 1981.... Coached Cincinnati to Metro Tournament titles in 1976 and 1977.... Directed West Virginia to back-to-back Atlantic 10 Tournament championships in 1983 and 1984.... Assistant coach under Richmond's Lew Mills, Davidson's Lefty Driesell, Kansas' Ted Owens, and Kentucky's Adolph Rupp.

Year	School	Overall	League	Finish	Postseason
72–73	Cincinnati	17-9			DNP
73–74	Cincinnati	19-8			NIT (0-1)

Year	School	Overall	League	Finish	Postseason
74–75	Cincinnati	23-6			NCAA (2-1)
75–76	Cincinnati	25-6	2-1	(Metro 6)	NCAA (0-1)
76–77	Cincinnati	25-5	4-2	2d (Metro 7)	NCAA (0-1)
77–78	Cincinnati	17-10	6-6	T4th (Metro 7)	DNP
78–79	West Va.	16-12	7-3	T2d (East. 8)	DNP
79–80	West Va.	15-14	4-6	7th (East. 8)	DNP
80–81	West Va.	23-10	9-4	3d (East. 8)	NIT (3-2)
81–82	West Va.	27-4	13-1	1st (East. 8)	NCAA (1-1)
82–83	West Va.	23-8	10-4	T1st-W (Atl. 10)	NCAA (0-1)
83–84	West Va.	20-12	9-9	T4th (Atl. 10)	NCAA (1-1)
84–85	West Va.	20-9	16-2	1st (Atl. 10)	NIT (0-1)
85–86	West Va.	22-11	15-3	T2d (Atl. 10)	NCAA (0-1)
86–87	West Va.	23-8	15-3	2d (Atl. 10)	NCAA (0-1)
87–88	West Va.	18-14	12-6	3d (Atl. 10)	NIT (0-1)
88–89	West Va.	26-5	17-1	1st (Atl. 10)	NCAA (1-1)
89–90	West Va.	16-12	11-7	T3d (Atl. 10)	DNP
90–91	West Va.	17-14	10-8	T3d (Atl. 10)	NIT (1-1)
91–92	West Va.	20-12	10-6	3d (Atl. 10)	NCAA (0-1)
92–93	West Va.	17-12	7-7	6th (Atl. 10)	NIT (1-1)
93–94	West Va.	17-12	8-8	T3d (Atl. 10)	NIT (1-1)

22-Year Coaching Record: 446-213 (.677) overall; 126-44 (.741) in six years at Cincinnati; 320-169 (.654) in first 16 years at West Virginia; 12-9 (.571) in Metro Conference; 173-78 (.689) in Atlantic 10 Conference; 5-1 (.833) in Metro Tournament; 21-14 (.600) in Atlantic 10 Tournament; 5-10 (.333) in NCAA Tournament; 6-8 (.429) in NIT.

JOHN CHANEY
Bethune-Cookman '55
Philadelphia, Pa.

Named national coach of the year by the USBWA in 1987 and by AP, UPI, NABC, and USBWA in 1988.... Coach of NCAA Division II champion in 1978 and third-place finisher in 1979.... Won four Atlantic 10 Conference Tournament titles (1985, 1987, 1988, and 1990).

Year	School	Overall	League	Finish	Postseason
72–73	Cheyney St.	23-5	12-2	1st-E (Pa. Conf.)	NCAA-II (1-1)
73–74	Cheyney St.	19-7	11-1	T1st-E (Pa. Conf.)	DNP
74–75	Cheyney St.	16-9	9-5	2d-E (Pa. Conf.)	DNP
75–76	Cheyney St.	24-5	11-1	1st-E (Pa. Conf.)	NCAA-II (2-1)
76–77	Cheyney St.	20-8	10-2	1st-E (Pa. Conf.)	NCAA-II (2-1)
77–78	Cheyney St.	27-2	12-0	1st-E (Pa. Conf.)	NCAA-II (5-0)
78–79	Cheyney St.	24-7	10-2	1st-E (Pa. Conf.)	NCAA-II (4-1)
79–80	Cheyney St.	23-5	12-0	1st-E (Pa. Conf.)	NCAA-II (1-1)
80–81	Cheyney St.	21-8	9-3	T1st-E (Pa. Conf.)	NCAA-II (1-1)
81–82	Cheyney St.	28-3	11-1	1st-E (Pa. Conf.)	NCAA-II (2-1)
82–83	Temple	14-15	5-9	3d-E (Atl. 10)	DNP
83–84	Temple	26-5	18-0	1st (Atl. 10)	NCAA (1-1)
84–85	Temple	25-6	15-3	2d (Atl. 10)	NCAA (1-1)
85–86	Temple	25-6	15-3	T2d (Atl. 10)	NCAA (1-1)
86–87	Temple	32-4	17-1	1st (Atl. 10)	NCAA (1-1)
87–88	Temple	32-2	18-0	1st (Atl. 10)	NCAA (3-1)
88–89	Temple	18-12	15-3	2d (Atl. 10)	NIT (0-1)
89–90	Temple	20-11	15-3	1st (Atl. 10)	NCAA (0-1)
90–91	Temple	24-10	13-5	2d (Atl. 10)	NCAA (3-1)
91–92	Temple	17-13	11-5	2d (Atl. 10)	NCAA (0-1)
92–93	Temple	20-13	8-6	T2d (Atl. 10)	NCAA (3-1)
93–94	Temple	23-8	12-4	2d (Atl. 10)	NCAA (1-1)

22-Year Coaching Record: 501-164 (.753) overall; 225-59 (.792) in 10 years at Cheyney State; 276-105 (.724) in first 12 years at Temple; 107-17 (.863) in Pennsylvania Conference; 162-42 (.794) in Atlantic 10 Conference; 23-8 (.742) in Atlantic 10 Tournament; 14-10 (.583) in NCAA Division I Tournament; 0-1 in NIT; 18-7 (.720) in NCAA Division II Tournament.

BOBBY CREMINS
South Carolina '70
Bronx, N.Y.

Led Georgia Tech to Final Four appearance in 1990.... Naismith national coach of the year in 1990.... His three ACC Tournament championships (1985, 1990, and 1993) are second only to Dean Smith's among active coaches.... Led Appalachian State to 1979 Southern Conference Tournament title.... Served as an assistant coach at Point Park (Pa.) and under Frank McGuire at South Carolina.

Year	School	Overall	League	Finish	Postseason
75–76	Appala. St.	13-14	6-6	5th (Southern)	DNP
76–77	Appala. St.	17-12	8-4	3d (Southern)	DNP
77–78	Appala. St.	15-13	9-3	1st (Southern)	DNP
78–79	Appala. St.	23-6	11-3	1st (Southern)	NCAA (0-1)
79–80	Appala. St.	12-16	6-10	T6th (Southern)	DNP
80–81	Appala. St.	20-9	11-5	T1st (Southern)	DNP
81–82	Ga. Tech	10-16	3-11	8th (ACC)	DNP
82–83	Ga. Tech	13-15	4-10	6th (ACC)	DNP
83–84	Ga. Tech	18-11	6-8	T5th (ACC)	NIT (0-1)
84–85	Ga. Tech	27-8	9-5	T1st (ACC)	NCAA (3-1)
85–86	Ga. Tech	27-7	11-3	2d (ACC)	NCAA (2-1)
86–87	Ga. Tech	16-13	7-7	5th (ACC)	NCAA (0-1)
87–88	Ga. Tech	22-10	8-6	4th (ACC)	NCAA (1-1)
88–89	Ga. Tech	20-12	8-6	5th (ACC)	NCAA (0-1)
89–90	Ga. Tech	28-7	8-6	T3d (ACC)	NCAA (4-1)
90–91	Ga. Tech	17-13	6-8	T5th (ACC)	NCAA (1-1)
91–92	Ga. Tech	23-12	8-8	T4th (ACC)	NCAA (0-1)
92–93	Ga. Tech	19-11	8-8	6th (ACC)	NCAA (0-1)
93–94	Ga. Tech	16-13	7-9	6th (ACC)	NIT (0-1)

19-Year Coaching Record: 356-218 (.620) overall; 100-70 (.588) in six years at Appalachian State; 256-148 (.634) in first 13 years at Georgia Tech; 51-31 (.622) in Southern Conference; 93-95 (.495) in Atlantic Coast Conference; 10-5 (.667) in Southern Conference Tournament; 13-10 (.565) in ACC Tournament; 13-10 (.565) in NCAA Tournament; 0-2 in NIT.

DENNY CRUM
UCLA '58
San Fernando, Calif.

Reached NCAA Final Four six times—1972 (fourth), 1975 (third), 1980 (champion), 1982 (tied for third), 1983 (tied for third), and 1986 (champion).... Coach of 1985 NIT fourth-place team.... Coach of 10 Metro Conference Tournament champions—1978, 1980, 1981, 1983, 1986, 1988, 1989, 1990, 1993, and 1994.... Assistant coach at UCLA for six seasons under John Wooden from 1959 to 1971 sandwiched around six-year stint at Pierce (Calif.) Community College.... Elected to Naismith Memorial Basketball Hall of Fame in 1994.

Year	School	Overall	League	Finish	Postseason
71–72	Louisville*	26-5	12-2	T1st (Mo. Valley)	NCAA (2-2)
72–73	Louisville	23-7	11-3	2d (Mo. Valley)	NIT (1-1)
73–74	Louisville	21-7	11-1	1st (Mo. Valley)	NCAA (0-2)
74–75	Louisville	28-3	12-2	1st (Mo. Valley)	NCAA (4-1)
75–76	Louisville	20-8	2-1	(Metro)	NIT (0-1)
76–77	Louisville	21-7	6-1	1st (Metro)	NCAA (0-1)
77–78	Louisville	23-7	9-3	2d (Metro)	NCAA (1-1)
78–79	Louisville	24-8	9-1	1st (Metro)	NCAA (1-1)
79–80	Louisville	33-3	12-0	1st (Metro)	NCAA (5-0)
80–81	Louisville	21-9	11-1	1st (Metro)	NCAA (0-1)
81–82	Louisville	23-10	8-4	T2d (Metro)	NCAA (3-1)
82–83	Louisville	32-4	12-0	1st (Metro)	NCAA (3-1)
83–84	Louisville	24-11	11-3	T1st (Metro)	NCAA (2-1)
84–85	Louisville	19-18	6-8	T4th (Metro)	NIT (3-2)
85–86	Louisville	32-7	10-2	1st (Metro)	NCAA (6-0)
86–87	Louisville	18-14	9-3	1st (Metro)	DNP
87–88	Louisville	24-11	9-3	1st (Metro)	NCAA (2-1)
88–89	Louisville	24-9	8-4	T2d (Metro)	NCAA (2-1)
89–90	Louisville	27-8	12-2	1st (Metro)	NCAA (1-1)
90–91	Louisville	14-16	4-10	8th (Metro)	DNP
91–92	Louisville	19-11	7-5	T2d (Metro)	NCAA (1-1)
92–93	Louisville	22-9	11-1	1st (Metro)	NCAA (2-1)
93–94	Louisville	26-6	10-2	1st (Metro)	NCAA (2-1)

* Won Missouri Valley Conference playoff game against regular-season co-champion Memphis St. (83-72) to earn invitation to NCAA Tournament.

23-Year Coaching Record: 544-198 (.733) at Louisville; 46-8 (.852) in four years in Missouri Valley; 166-54 (.755) in first 19 years in Metro Conference; 30-9 (.769) in Metro Tournament; 37-18 (.673) in NCAA Tournament; 4-4 (.500) in NIT.

CHARLES (LEFTY) DRIESELL
Duke '54
Norfolk, Va.

Coach of 1972 NIT champion.... Coach of five conference tournament champions—three in Southern Conference (1966, 1968, and 1969), one in ACC (1984), and one in Colonial Athletic Association (1994).

Year	School	Overall	League	Finish	Postseason
60–61	Davidson	9-14	2-10	9th (Southern)	DNP
61–62	Davidson	14-11	5-6	5th (Southern)	DNP
62–63	Davidson	20-7	8-3	2d (Southern)	DNP
63–64	Davidson	22-4	9-2	1st (Southern)	DNP
64–65	Davidson	24-2	12-0	1st (Southern)	DNP
65–66	Davidson	21-7	11-1	1st (Southern)	NCAA (1-2)
66–67	Davidson	15-12	8-4	2d (Southern)	DNP
67–68	Davidson	24-5	9-1	1st (Southern)	NCAA (2-1)
68–69	Davidson	27-3	9-0	1st (Southern)	NCAA (2-1)
69–70	Maryland	13-13	5-9	6th (ACC)	DNP
70–71	Maryland	14-12	5-9	T6th (ACC)	DNP
71–72	Maryland	27-5	8-4	T2d (ACC)	NIT (4-0)
72–73	Maryland	23-7	7-5	3d (ACC)	NCAA (1-1)
73–74	Maryland	23-5	9-3	T2d (ACC)	DNP
74–75	Maryland	24-5	10-2	1st (ACC)	NCAA (2-1)
75–76	Maryland	22-6	7-5	T2d (ACC)	DNP
76–77	Maryland	19-8	7-5	4th (ACC)	DNP
77–78	Maryland	15-13	3-9	T6th (ACC)	DNP
78–79	Maryland	19-11	6-6	4th (ACC)	NIT (1-1)
79–80	Maryland	24-7	11-3	1st (ACC)	NCAA (1-1)
80–81	Maryland	21-10	8-6	4th (ACC)	NCAA (1-1)
81–82	Maryland	16-13	5-9	5th (ACC)	NIT (1-1)
82–83	Maryland	20-10	8-6	T3d (ACC)	DNP
83–84	Maryland	24-8	9-5	2nd (ACC)	NCAA (1-1)
84–85	Maryland	25-12	8-6	T4th (ACC)	NCAA (2-1)
85–86	Maryland	19-14	6-8	6th (ACC)	NCAA (1-1)
88–89	J. Madison	16-14	6-8	T5th (CAA)	DNP
89–90	J. Madison	20-11	11-3	1st (CAA)	NIT (0-1)
90–91	J. Madison	19-10	12-2	1st (CAA)	NIT (0-1)
91–92	J. Madison	21-11	12-2	T1st (CAA)	NIT (0-1)
92–93	J. Madison	21-9	11-3	T1st (CAA)	NIT (0-1)
93–94	J. Madison	20-10	10-4	T1st (CAA)	NCAA (0-1)

32-Year Coaching Record: 641-289 (.689) overall; 176-65 (.730) in nine years at Davidson; 348-159 (.686) in 17 years at Maryland; 117-65 (.643) in first six years at James Madison; 73-27 (.730) in Southern Conference; 122-100 (.550) in ACC; 62-22 (.738) in Colonial Athletic Association; 15-5 (.750) in Southern Conference Tournament; 17-16 (.515) in ACC Tournament; 9-5 (.643) in CAA Tournament; 15-13 (.536) in NCAA Tournament; 6-6 (.500) in NIT.

HUGH DURHAM
Florida St. '59
Louisville, Ky.

One of only three coaches in NCAA history to win at least 200 games at two Division I schools.... His Florida State squad was runner-up to UCLA in the 1972 NCAA Tournament finals, and his 1983 Georgia team reached the national semifinals.... Guided Georgia to 1982 NIT semifinals (T3rd).... Led Georgia to 1983 SEC Tournament title.... Assistant coach at his alma mater under Bud Kennedy.

Year	School	Overall	League	Finish	Postseason
66–67	Florida St.	11-15			DNP
67–68	Florida St.	19-8			NCAA (0-1)
68–69	Florida St.	18-8			Probation
69–70	Florida St.	23-3			Probation
70–71	Florida St.	17-9			Probation
71–72	Florida St.	27-6			NCAA (4-1)
72–73	Florida St.	18-8			DNP
73–74	Florida St.	18-8			DNP
74–75	Florida St.	18-8			DNP
75–76	Florida St.	22-5			DNP
76–77	Florida St.	16-11	2-4	5th (Metro)	DNP
77–78	Florida St.	23-6	11-1	1st (Metro)	NCAA (0-1)
78–79	Georgia	14-14	7-11	7th (SEC)	DNP
79–80	Georgia	14-13	7-11	T6th (SEC)	DNP
80–81	Georgia	19-12	9-9	5th (SEC)	NIT (1-1)
81–82	Georgia	19-12	10-8	6th (SEC)	NIT (3-1)
82–83	Georgia	24-10	9-9	T4th (SEC)	NCAA (3-1)
83–84	Georgia	17-13	8-10	T7th (SEC)	NIT (0-1)
84–85*	Georgia	22-9	12-6	2d (SEC)	NCAA (1-1)
85–86	Georgia	17-13	9-9	T5th (SEC)	NIT (1-1)
86–87	Georgia	18-12	10-8	T3d (SEC)	NCAA (0-1)
87–88	Georgia	20-16	8-10	7th (SEC)	NIT (1-1)
88–89	Georgia	15-16	6-12	9th (SEC)	DNP
89–90	Georgia	20-9	13-5	1st (SEC)	NCAA (0-1)
90–91	Georgia	17-13	9-9	5th (SEC)	NCAA (0-1)
91–92	Georgia	15-14	7-9	4th-E (SEC)	DNP
92–93	Georgia	15-14	8-8	4th-E (SEC)	NIT (0-1)
93–94	Georgia	14-16	7-9	4th-E (SEC)	DNP

* NCAA Tournament games later vacated by action of the NCAA

28-Year Coaching Record: 510-301 (.629); 230-95 (.708) in 12 years at Florida State; 280-206 (.576) in first 16 years at Georgia; 13-5 (.722) in Metro Conference; 139-143 (.493) in Southeastern Conference; 1-2 (.333) in Metro Tournament; 17-15 (.531) in SEC Tournament; 8-8 (.500) in NCAA Tournament; 6-6 (.500) in NIT.

STEVE FISHER
Illinois St. '67
Herrin, Ill.

Reached NCAA Final Four three times—1989 (champion), 1992 (runner-up), and 1993 (runner-up).... Assistant coach at Western Michigan under Les Wothke for three seasons from 1980 to 1982 and at Michigan under Bill Frieder for seven seasons from 1983 to 1989.

Year	School	Overall	League	Finish	Postseason
88–89	Michigan	6-0*			NCAA (6-0)
89–90	Michigan	23-8	12-6	3d (Big Ten)	NCAA (1-1)
90–91	Michigan	14-15	7-11	8th (Big Ten)	NIT (0-1)
91–92	Michigan	25-9	11-7	3d (Big Ten)	NCAA (5-1)
92–93	Michigan	31-5	13-5	2d (Big Ten)	NCAA (5-1)
93–94	Michigan	24-8	13-5	2d (Big Ten)	NCAA (3-1)

*Promoted from assistant to head coach just before the start of the 1989 tournament after head coach Bill Frieder announced he had accepted the head coaching position at Arizona State.

Six-Year Coaching Record: 123-45 (.732) overall; 58-32 (.644) in Big Ten; 20-4 (.833) in NCAA Tournament; 0-1 in NIT.

JIM HARRICK
Charleston '60
Charleston, W.V.

Assistant under Dutch Belnap for four years at Utah State and under Gary Cunningham for two years at UCLA.

Year	School	Overall	League	Finish	Postseason
79–80	Pepperdine	17-11	9-7	T5th (WCAC)	NIT (0-1)
80–81	Pepperdine	16-12	11-3	T1st (WCAC)	DNP
81–82	Pepperdine	22-7	14-0	1st (WCAC)	NCAA (1-1)
82–83	Pepperdine	20-9	10-2	1st (WCAC)	NCAA (0-1)
83–84	Pepperdine	15-13	6-6	T4th (WCAC)	DNP
84–85	Pepperdine	23-9	11-1	1st (WCAC)	NCAA (0-1)
85–86	Pepperdine	25-5	13-1	1st (WCAC)	NCAA (0-1)
86–87	Pepperdine	12-18	5-9	7th (WCAC)	DNP
87–88	Pepperdine	17-13	8-6	4th (WCAC)	NIT (0-1)
88–89	UCLA	21-10	13-5	T3d (Pac-10)	NCAA (1-1)
89–90	UCLA	22-11	11-7	4th (Pac-10)	NCAA (2-1)
90–91	UCLA	23-9	11-7	2d (Pac-10)	NCAA (1-1)
91–92	UCLA	28-5	16-2	1st (Pac-10)	NCAA (3-1)
92–93	UCLA	22-11	11-7	T3d (Pac-10)	NCAA (1-1)
93–94	UCLA	21-7	13-5	T2nd (Pac-10)	NCAA (0-1)

15-Year Coaching Record: 304-150 (.670) overall; 167-97 (.633) in nine years at Pepperdine; 137-53 (.721) in first six years at UCLA; 87-35 (.713) in West Coast Athletic Conference; 75-33 (.694) in Pacific-10 Conference; 3-2 (.600) in WCAC Tournament; 3-2 (.600) in Pac-10 Tournament; 8-10 (.444) in NCAA Tournament; 0-2 in NIT.

DON HASKINS
Oklahoma State '53
Enid, Okla.

Coach of 1966 NCAA champion.... Coach of four Western Athletic Conference Tournament champions— 1984, 1986, 1989, and 1990.... U.S. Olympic team assistant coach in 1972.

Year	School	Overall	League	Finish	Postseason
61–62	Texas West.*	18-6			DNP
62–63	Texas West.*	19-7			NCAA (0-1)
63–64	Texas West.*	25-3			NCAA (2-1)
64–65	Texas West.*	16-9			NIT (0-1)
65–66	Texas West.*	28-1			NCAA (5-0)
66–67	Texas West.*	22-6			NCAA (2-1)
67–68	Texas-El Paso	14-9			DNP
68–69	Texas-El Paso	16-9			DNP
69–70	Texas-El Paso	17-8	10-4	1st (WAC)	NCAA (0-1)
70–71	Texas-El Paso	15-10	9-5	T2d (WAC)	NIT (4-0)
71–72	Texas-El Paso	20-7	9-5	T2d (WAC)	NIT (0-1)
72–73	Texas-El Paso	16-10	6-8	5th (WAC)	DNP
73–74	Texas-El Paso	18-7	8-6	5th (WAC)	DNP
74–75	Texas-El Paso	20-6	10-4	2d (WAC)	NCAA (0-1)
75–76	Texas-El Paso	19-7	9-5	T2d (WAC)	DNP
76–77	Texas-El Paso	11-15	3-11	8th (WAC)	DNP
77–78	Texas-El Paso	10-16	2-12	8th (WAC)	DNP
78–79	Texas-El Paso	11-15	3-9	T6th (WAC)	DNP
79–80	Texas-El Paso	20-8	10-4	T2d (WAC)	NIT (1-1)
80–81	Texas-El Paso	18-12	9-7	4th (WAC)	NIT (1-1)
81–82	Texas-El Paso	20-8	11-5	T2d (WAC)	DNP
82–83	Texas-El Paso	19-10	11-5	T1st (WAC)	NIT (0-1)
83–84	Texas-El Paso	27-4	13-3	1st (WAC)	NCAA (0-1)
84–85	Texas-El Paso	22-10	12-4	1st (WAC)	NCAA (1-1)
85–86	Texas-El Paso	27-6	12-4	T1st (WAC)	NCAA (0-1)
86–87	Texas-El Paso	25-7	13-3	1st (WAC)	NCAA (1-1)
87–88	Texas-El Paso	23-10	10-6	4th (WAC)	NCAA (0-1)
88–89	Texas-El Paso	26-7	11-5	T2d (WAC)	NCAA (1-1)
89–90	Texas-El Paso	21-11	10-6	T3d (WAC)	NCAA (0-1)
90–91	Texas-El Paso	16-13	7-9	T5th (WAC)	DNP
91–92	Texas-El Paso	27-7	12-4	T1st (WAC)	NCAA (2-1)
92–93	Texas-El Paso	21-13	10-8	4th (WAC)	NIT (1-1)
93–94	Texas-El Paso	18-12	8-10	T5th (WAC)	DNP

*School's official name changed to Texas-El Paso in 1967.

33-Year Coaching Record: 645-288 (.691) at Texas-El Paso; 228-154 (.597) in Western Athletic Conference; 20-7 (.741) in WAC Tournament; 14-13 (.519) in NCAA Tournament; 3-6 (.333) in NIT.

GEORGE (JUD) HEATHCOTE
Washington State '50
Port Orchard, Wash.

Named national coach of the year by NABC in 1990.... Coach of 1979 NCAA champion.... Coach of 1989 NIT fourth-place team.... Served as an assistant coach at Washington State under Marv Harshman from 1965 to 1971.

Year	School	Overall	League	Finish	Postseason
71–72	Montana	14-12	7-7	T5th (Big Sky)	DNP
72–73	Montana	13-13	7-7	4th (Big Sky)	DNP
73–74	Montana*	19-8	11-3	T1st (Big Sky)	DNP
74–75	Montana	21-8	13-1	1st (Big Sky)	NCAA (1-2)
75–76	Montana	13-12	7-7	5th (Big Sky)	DNP
76–77	Mich. St.	12-15	9-9	5th (Big Ten)	DNP
77–78	Mich. St.	25-5	15-3	1st (Big Ten)	NCAA (2-1)
78–79	Mich. St.	26-6	13-5	1st (Big Ten)	NCAA (5-0)
79–80	Mich. St.	12-15	6-12	9th (Big Ten)	DNP
80–81	Mich. St.	13-14	7-11	8th (Big Ten)	DNP
81–82	Mich. St.	12-16	7-11	T7th (Big Ten)	DNP
82–83	Mich. St.	17-13	9-9	T6th (Big Ten)	NIT (1-1)
83–84	Mich. St.	16-12	9-9	5th (Big Ten)	DNP
84–85	Mich. St.	19-10	10-8	T5th (Big Ten)	NCAA (0-1)
85–86	Mich. St.	23-8	12-6	3d (Big Ten)	NCAA (2-1)
86–87	Mich. St.	11-17	6-12	7th (Big Ten)	DNP
87–88	Mich. St.	10-18	5-13	8th (Big Ten)	DNP
88–89	Mich. St.	18-15	6-12	T8th (Big Ten)	NIT (3-2)
89–90	Mich. St.	28-6	15-3	1st (Big Ten)	NCAA (2-1)
90–91	Mich. St.	19-11	11-7	T3d (Big Ten)	NCAA (1-1)
91–92	Mich. St.	22-8	11-7	T3d (Big Ten)	NCAA (1-1)
92–93	Mich. St.	15-13	7-11	T8th (Big Ten)	NIT (0-1)
93–94	Mich. St.	20-12	10-8	T4th (Big Ten)	NCAA (1-1)

* Lost Big Sky Conference playoff game against regular-season co-champion Idaho St. (60-57) for automatic berth in NCAA Tournament.

23-Year Coaching Record: 398-267 (.598) overall; 80-53 (.602) in five years at Montana; 318-214 (.598) in first 18 years at Michigan State; 45-25 (.643) in Big Sky Conference; 168-156 (.519) in Big Ten Conference; 15-9 (.625) in NCAA Tournament; 4-4 (.500) in NIT.

LOU HENSON
New Mexico State '55
Okay, Okla.

Coach of two NCAA Final Four teams—1970 (third with New Mexico St.) and 1989 (tied for third with Illinois).... Coach of 1980 NIT third-place team.

Year	School	Overall	League	Finish	Postseason
62–63	Hardin-Simm.	10-16			DNP
63–64	Hardin-Simm.	20-6			DNP
64–65	Hardin-Simm.	17-8			DNP
65–66	Hardin-Simm.	20-6			DNP
66–67	New Mex. St.	15-11			NCAA (0-1)
67–68	New Mex. St.	23-6			NCAA (0-1)
68–69	New Mex. St.	24-5			NCAA (1-2)
69–70	New Mex. St.	27-3			NCAA (4-1)
70–71	New Mex. St.	19-8			NCAA (0-1)
71–72	New Mex. St.	19-6			DNP
72–73	New Mex. St.	12-14	6-8	T5th (Mo. Valley)	Probation
73–74	New Mex. St.	14-11	7-6	T3d (Mo. Valley)	Probation
74–75	New Mex. St.	20-7	11-3	2d (Mo. Valley)	NCAA (0-1)
75–76	Illinois	14-13	7-11	T7th (Big Ten)	DNP
76–77	Illinois*	14-16	6-12	7th (Big Ten)	DNP
77–78	Illinois	13-14	7-11	7th (Big Ten)	DNP
78–79	Illinois	19-11	7-11	7th (Big Ten)	DNP
79–80	Illinois	22-13	8-10	T6th (Big Ten)	NIT (4-1)
80–81	Illinois	21-8	12-6	3d (Big Ten)	NCAA (1-1)
81–82	Illinois	18-11	10-8	6th (Big Ten)	NIT (1-1)
82–83	Illinois	21-11	11-7	T2d (Big Ten)	NCAA (0-1)
83–84	Illinois	26-5	15-3	T1st (Big Ten)	NCAA (2-1)
84–85	Illinois	26-9	12-6	2d (Big Ten)	NCAA (2-1)
85–86	Illinois	22-10	11-7	T4th (Big Ten)	NCAA (1-1)
86–87	Illinois	23-8	13-5	4th (Big Ten)	NCAA (0-1)
87–88	Illinois	23-10	12-6	T3d (Big Ten)	NCAA (1-1)
88–89	Illinois	31-5	14-4	2d (Big Ten)	NCAA (4-1)
89–90	Illinois	21-8	11-7	T4th (Big Ten)	NCAA (1-1)
90–91	Illinois	21-10	11-7	T3d (Big Ten)	Probation
91–92	Illinois	13-15	7-11	8th (Big Ten)	DNP
92–93	Illinois	19-13	11-7	T3d (Big Ten)	NCAA (1-1)
93–94	Illinois	17-11	10-8	T4th (Big Ten)	NCAA (0-1)

* Overall record is 16-14 and Big Ten mark is 8-10, including two forfeit victories awarded from Minnesota after the season.

32-Year Coaching Record: 626-306 (.672) overall; 67-36 (.650) in four years at Hardin-Simmons; 173-71 (.709) in nine years at New Mexico State; 386-199 (.660) in first 19 years at Illinois; 24-17 (.585) in Missouri Valley Conference; 197-145 (.576) in Big Ten Conference; 19-18 (.514) in NCAA Tournament; 5-2 (.714) in NIT.

GENE KEADY
Kansas State '58
Larned, Kans.

Named national coach of the year by USBWA in 1984 and co-coach of the year (with Nolan Richardson) by the NABC in 1994.... Member of National Junior College Basketball Hall of Fame (as player and coach). Compiled 187-48 record (.796) in eight seasons at Hutchinson (Kan.) Community

College.... Guided three Purdue teams to NIT semifinal round—1981 (3rd), 1982 (2nd), and 1993 (4th).... Assistant coach at Arkansas under Eddie Sutton for four seasons from 1975 to 1978.

Year	School	Overall	League	Finish	Postseason
78–79	Western Ky.	17-11	7-5	T2d (OVC)	DNP
79–80	Western Ky.	21-8	10-2	T1st (OVC)	NCAA (0-1)
80–81	Purdue	21-11	10-8	4th (Big Ten)	NIT (4-1)
81–82	Purdue	18-14	11-7	5th (Big Ten)	NIT (4-1)
82–83	Purdue	21-9	11-7	T2d (Big Ten)	NCAA (1-1)
83–84	Purdue	22-7	15-3	T1st (Big Ten)	NCAA (0-1)
84–85	Purdue	20-9	11-7	T3d (Big Ten)	NCAA (0-1)
85–86	Purdue	25-10	11-7	T4th (Big Ten)	NCAA (0-1)
86–87	Purdue	25-5	15-3	T1st (Big Ten)	NCAA (1-1)
87–88	Purdue	29-4	16-2	1st (Big Ten)	NCAA (2-1)
88–89	Purdue	15-16	8-10	T6th (Big Ten)	DNP
89–90	Purdue	22-8	13-5	2d (Big Ten)	NCAA (1-1)
90–91	Purdue	17-12	9-9	T5th (Big Ten)	NCAA (0-1)
91–92	Purdue	18-15	8-10	T6th (Big Ten)	NIT (2-1)
92–93	Purdue	18-10	9-9	T5th (Big Ten)	NCAA (0-1)
93–94	Purdue	29-5	14-4	1st (Big Ten)	NCAA (3-1)

16-Year Coaching Record: 335-154 (.685) overall; 38-19 (.667) in two years at Western Kentucky; 297-135 (.688) in first 14 years at Purdue; 17-7 (.708) in Ohio Valley Conference; 161-91 (.639) in Big Ten Conference; 8-11 (.421) In NCAA Tournament; 10-3 (.769) in NIT.

BOB KNIGHT
Ohio St. '62
Orrville, Ohio

Named national coach of the year by NABC in 1975; by AP and USBWA in 1976, 1976, and 1989; by UPI in 1976 and 1989; and by Naismith in 1987.... Reached NCAA Final Four five times—1973 (third), 1976 (champion), 1981 (champion), 1987 (champion), and 1992 (tied for third).... Coach of five NIT semifinalists—1966 (fourth), 1969 (fourth), 1970 (third), 1979 (champion), and 1985 (runner-up).... Coach of 1974 Collegiate Commissioners Association Tournament champion.... Winningest coach in Big Ten Conference history.... U.S. Olympic team coach in 1984.... Assistant coach at Army under Tates Locke for two seasons (1963–64 and 1964–65).... Elected to Naismith Memorial Basketball Hall of Fame in 1990.

Year	School	Overall	League	Finish	Postseason
65–66	Army	18-8			NIT (2-2)
66–67	Army	13-8			DNP
67–68	Army	20-5			NIT (0-1)
68–69	Army	18-10			NIT (2-2)
69–70	Army	22-6			NIT (3-1)
70–71	Army	11-13			DNP
71–72	Indiana	17-8	9-5	T3d (Big Ten)	NIT (0-1)
72–73	Indiana	22-6	11-3	1st (Big Ten)	NCAA (3-1)
73–74	Indiana	23-5	12-2	T1st (Big Ten)	CCA (3-0)
74–75	Indiana	31-1	18-0	1st (Big Ten)	NCAA (2-1)
75–76	Indiana	32-0	18-0	1st (Big Ten)	NCAA (5-0)
76–77	Indiana*	14-13	9-9	5th (Big Ten)	DNP
77–78	Indiana	21-8	12-6	T2d (Big Ten)	NCAA (1-1)
78–79	Indiana	22-12	10-8	5th (Big Ten)	NIT (4-0)
79–80	Indiana	21-8	13-5	1st (Big Ten)	NCAA (1-1)
80–81	Indiana	26-9	14-4	1st (Big Ten)	NCAA (5-0)
81–82	Indiana	19-10	12-6	T2d (Big Ten)	NCAA (1-1)
82–83	Indiana	24-6	13-5	1st (Big Ten)	NCAA (1-1)
83–84	Indiana	22-9	13-5	3d (Big Ten)	NCAA (2-1)
84–85	Indiana	19-14	7-11	7th (Big Ten)	NIT (4-1)
85–86	Indiana	21-8	13-5	2d (Big Ten)	NCAA (0-1)
86–87	Indiana	30-4	15-3	T1st (Big Ten)	NCAA (6-0)
87–88	Indiana	19-10	11-7	5th (Big Ten)	NCAA (0-1)
88–89	Indiana	27-8	15-3	1st (Big Ten)	NCAA (2-1)
89–90	Indiana	18-11	8-10	T7th (Big Ten)	NCAA (0-1)
90–91	Indiana	29-5	15-3	T1st (Big Ten)	NCAA (2-1)
91–92	Indiana	27-7	14-4	2d (Big Ten)	NCAA (4-1)
92–93	Indiana	31-4	17-1	1st (Big Ten)	NCAA (3-1)
93–94	Indiana	21-9	12-6	3d (Big Ten)	NCAA (2-1)

* Overall record is 16-11 and Big Ten mark is 11-7, including two forfeit victories awarded from Minnesota after the season.

29-Year Coaching Record: 638-225 (.739) overall; 102-50 (.671) in six years at Army; 536-175 (.754) in first 23 years at Indiana; 291-111 (.724) in Big Ten; 40-15 (.727) in NCAA Tournament; 15-8 (.652) in NIT.

Future coaching success stories: Mike Krzyzewski (left), here a player for Army, then the head coach at Army, and now the head coach at Duke; and Bob Knight, here the head coach at Army, and now the head coach at Indiana.

MIKE KRZYZEWSKI
Army '69
Chicago, Ill.

UPI national coach of the year in 1986.... Naismith national coach of the year in 1989 and NABC national coach of the year in 1991.... Coach of 1991 and 1992 NCAA champions.... Reached NCAA Final Four seven times in nine years from 1986 to 1994.... Coach of three ACC Tournament champions–1986, 1988 and 1992.... U.S. Olympic team assistant coach in 1992.... Assistant coach at Indiana under Bob Knight for one season in 1974–75.

Year	School	Overall	League	Finish	Postseason
75–76	Army	11-14			DNP
76–77	Army	20-8			DNP
77–78	Army	19-9			NIT (0-1)
78–79	Army	14-11			DNP
79–80	Army	9-17			DNP
80–81	Duke	17-13	6-8	6th (ACC)	NIT (2-1)
81–82	Duke	10-17	4-10	T6th (ACC)	DNP
82–83	Duke	11-17	3-11	7th (ACC)	DNP
83–84	Duke	24-10	7-7	3d (ACC)	NCAA (0-1)
84–85	Duke	23-8	8-6	4th (ACC)	NCAA (1-1)
85–86	Duke	37-3	12-2	1st (ACC)	NCAA (5-1)
86–87	Duke	24-9	9-5	3d (ACC)	NCAA (2-1)
87–88	Duke	28-7	9-5	3d (ACC)	NCAA (4-1)
88–89	Duke	28-8	9-5	T2d (ACC)	NCAA (4-1)
89–90	Duke	29-9	9-5	2d (ACC)	NCAA (5-1)
90–91	Duke	32-7	11-3	1st (ACC)	NCAA (6-0)
91–92	Duke	34-2	14-2	1st (ACC)	NCAA (6-0)
92–93	Duke	24-8	10-6	T3d (ACC)	NCAA (1-1)
93–94	Duke	28-5	12-4	1st (ACC)	NCAA (5-1)

19-Year Coaching Record: 422-182 (.699) overall; 73-59 (.553) in five years at Army; 349-123 (.739) in first 14 years at Duke; 123-79 (.609) in ACC; 17-11 (.607) in ACC Tournament; 39-9 (.813) in NCAA Tournament; 2-2 (.500) in NIT.

ROLLIE MASSIMINO
Vermont '56
Hillside, N.J.

Coach of NCAA national champion in 1985.... Coach of 1977 NIT third-place team.... Coach of two Eastern Athletic Association Tournament champions—1978 and 1980.... Assistant coach at Penn under Chuck Daly for three seasons from 1972 to 1974.

Year	School	Overall	League	Finish	Postseason
69–70	Stony Brook	19-6	9-0	1st (K'bocker)	NCAA-III (0-1)
70–71	Stony Brook	15-10	7-2	T2d (K'bocker)	DNP
73–74	Villanova	7-19			DNP
74–75	Villanova	9-18			DNP
75–76	Villanova	16-11			DNP
76–77	Villanova	23-10	6-1	2d (ECBL East)	NIT (3-1)
77–78	Villanova	23-9	7-3	T1st (East. 8)	NCAA (2-1)
78–79	Villanova	15-13	9-1	1st (East. 8)	DNP
79–80	Villanova	23-8	7-3	T1st (East. 8)	NCAA (1-1)
80–81	Villanova	20-11	8-6	T3d (Big East)	NCAA (1-1)
81–82	Villanova	24-8	11-3	1st (Big East)	NCAA (2-1)
82–83	Villanova	24-8	12-4	T1st (Big East)	NCAA (2-1)
83–84	Villanova	19-12	12-4	T2d (Big East)	NCAA (1-1)
84–85	Villanova	25-10	9-7	T3d (Big East)	NCAA (6-0)
85–86	Villanova	23-14	10-6	4th (Big East)	NCAA (1-1)
86–87	Villanova	15-16	6-10	6th (Big East)	NIT (0-1)
87–88	Villanova	24-13	9-7	T3d (Big East)	NCAA (3-1)
88–89	Villanova	18-16	7-9	T5th (Big East)	NIT (2-1)
89–90	Villanova	18-15	8-8	T5th (Big East)	NCAA (0-1)
90–91	Villanova	17-15	7-9	T7th (Big East)	NCAA (1-1)
91–92	Villanova	14-15	11-7	4th (Big East)	NIT (0-1)
92–93	UNLV	21-8	15-3	2d (Big West)	NIT (0-1)
93–94	UNLV	15-12	10-8	T5th (Big West)	DNP

23-Year Coaching Record: 425-276 (.606) overall; 34-16 (.680) in two years at SUNY-Stony Brook; 357-241 (.597) in 19 years at Villanova; 36-20 (.643) in first two years at UNLV; 16-2 (.889) in two years in Knickerbocker Conference; 29-8 (.784) in four years in Eastern 8 Conference; 110-80 (.579) in 12 years in Big East Conference; 23-13 (.639) in Big West Conference; 9-2 (.818) in Eastern 8 Tournament; 13-12 (.520) in Big East Tournament; 2-2 (.500) in Big West Tournament; 0-1 in NCAA Division III Tournament; 20-10 (.667) in NCAA Division I Tournament; 5-5 (.500) in NIT.

ROBERT (LUTE) OLSON
Augsburg (Minn.) '57
Mayville, N.D.

Named national coach of the year by NABC in 1980.... Reached NCAA Final Four three times—1980 (fourth with Iowa), 1988 (tied for third with Arizona) and 1994 (tied for third with Arizona).... Coach of three Pacific-10 Conference Tournament champions—1988, 1989, and 1990.... Coached at Long Beach City College, including the 1971 California community college champion.

Year	School	Overall	League	Finish	Postseason
73–74	L. Beach St.	24-2	12-0	1st (PCAA)	Probation
74–75	Iowa	10-16	7-11	7th (Big Ten)	DNP
75–76	Iowa	19-10	9-9	5th (Big Ten)	DNP
76–77	Iowa	20-7	12-6	4th (Big Ten)	DNP
77–78	Iowa	12-15	5-13	8th (Big Ten)	DNP
78–79	Iowa	20-8	13-5	T1st (Big Ten)	NCAA (0-1)
79–80	Iowa	23-10	10-8	4th (Big Ten)	NCAA (4-2)
80–81	Iowa	21-7	13-5	2d (Big Ten)	NCAA (0-1)
81–82	Iowa	21-8	12-6	T2d (Big Ten)	NCAA (1-1)
82–83	Iowa	21-10	10-8	5th (Big Ten)	NCAA (2-1)
83–84	Arizona	11-17	8-10	T5th (Pac-10)	DNP
84–85	Arizona	21-10	12-6	T3d (Pac-10)	NCAA (0-1)
85–86	Arizona	23-9	14-4	1st (Pac-10)	NCAA (0-1)
86–87	Arizona	18-12	13-5	2d (Pac-10)	NCAA (0-1)
87–88	Arizona	35-3	17-1	1st (Pac-10)	NCAA (4-1)
88–89	Arizona	29-4	17-1	1st (Pac-10)	NCAA (2-1)
89–90	Arizona	25-7	15-3	T1st (Pac-10)	NCAA (1-1)
90–91	Arizona	28-7	14-4	1st (Pac-10)	NCAA (2-1)
91–92	Arizona	24-7	13-5	3d (Pac-10)	NCAA (0-1)
92–93	Arizona	24-4	17-1	1st (Pac-10)	NCAA (0-1)
93–94	Arizona	29-6	14-4	1st (Pac-10)	NCAA (4-1)

21-Year Coaching Record: 458-179 (.719) overall; 24-2 (.943) in one year at Long Beach State; 167-91 (.647) in nine years at Iowa; 267-86 (.756) in first 11 years at Arizona; 12-0 (1.000) in Pacific Coast Athletic Association; 91-71 (.562) in Big Ten; 154-42 (.786) in Pacific-10; 9-1 (.900) in Pacific-10 Tournament; 20-16 (.556) in NCAA Tournament.

RICK PITINO
Massachusetts '74
New York, N.Y.

Reached NCAA Final Four on two occasions—once with Providence (1987) and once with Kentucky (1993).... Coach of North Atlantic Conference Tournament champion in 1983 and SEC Tournament champions from 1992 through 1994.... Compiled 90-74 regular-season record and 6-7 playoff mark in two seasons as coach of the NBA's New York Knicks (1987–88 and 1988–89).... Assistant coach at Hawaii under Bruce O'Neil for two seasons (1974–75 and 1975–76), at Syracuse under Jim Boeheim for two seasons (1976–77 and 1977–78), and with the Knicks under Hubie Brown for two seasons (1983–84 and 1984–85).

Year	School	Overall	League	Finish	Postseason
78–79	Boston U.	17-9			DNP
79–80	Boston U.	21-9			NIT (0-1)
80–81	Boston U.	13-14			DNP
81–82	Boston U.	19-9	6-2	4th (N. Atl.)	DNP
82–83	Boston U.	21-10	8-2	T1st (N. Atl.)	NCAA (0-1)
85–86	Prov.	17-14	7-9	5th (Big East)	DNP
86–87	Prov.	25-9	10-6	T4th (Big East)	NIT (2-1)
89–90	Kentucky	14-14	10-8	T4th (SEC)	Probation
90–91	Kentucky	22-6	14-4	1st (SEC)	Probation
91–92	Kentucky	29-7	12-4	1st (SEC East)	NCAA (3-1)
92–93	Kentucky	30-4	13-3	2d (SEC East)	NCAA (4-1)
93–94	Kentucky	25-7	12-4	T1st (SEC East)	NCAA (1-1)

12-Year College Coaching Record: 253-112 (.693) overall; 91-51 (.641) in five years at Boston University; 42-23 (.646) in two years at Providence; 120-38 (.759) in first five years at Kentucky; 14-4 (.778) in North Atlantic Conference; 17-15 (.531) in Big East; 61-23 (.726) in SEC; 16-5 (.762) in postseason conference tournaments; 8-4 (.667) in NCAA Tournament; 2-2 (.500) in NIT.

NOLAN RICHARDSON
Texas-El Paso '65
El Paso, Tex.

Received Naismith Award as national coach of the year and shared similar NABC award in 1994.... Coach of two Final Four teams—1990 (tied for third place) and 1994 (champion).... Coach of 1981 NIT champion.... Coach of five conference tournament champions—Missouri Valley (1982 and 1984) and Southwest Conference (1989, 1990, and 1991).... Coach at Western Texas Junior College for three seasons, including the 1980 NJCAA championship team that compiled a 37-0 record.

Year	School	Overall	League	Finish	Postseason
80–81	Tulsa	26-7	11-5	T2d (Mo. Valley)	NIT (5-0)
81–82	Tulsa	24-6	12-4	2d (Mo. Valley)	NCAA (0-1)
82–83	Tulsa	19-12	11-7	T3d (Mo. Valley)	NIT (0-1)
83–84	Tulsa	27-4	13-3	T1st (Mo. Valley)	NCAA (0-1)
84–85	Tulsa	23-8	12-4	1st (Mo. Valley)	NCAA (0-1)
85–86	Arkansas	12-16	4-12	7th (SWC)	DNP
86–87	Arkansas	19-14	8-8	5th (SWC)	NIT (1-1)
87–88	Arkansas	21-9	11-5	T2d (SWC)	NCAA (0-1)
88–89	Arkansas	25-7	13-3	1st (SWC)	NCAA (1-1)
89–90	Arkansas	30-5	14-2	1st (SWC)	NCAA (4-1)
90–91	Arkansas	34-4	15-1	1st (SWC)	NCAA (3-1)
91–92	Arkansas	26-8	13-3	1st (SEC West)	NCAA (1-1)
92–93	Arkansas	22-9	10-6	1st (SEC West)	NCAA (2-1)
93–94	Arkansas	31-3	14-2	1st (SEC West)	NCAA (6-0)

14-Year Coaching Record: 339-112 (.752) overall; 119-37 (.763) in five years at Tulsa; 220-75 (.746) in first nine years at Arkansas; 59-23 (.720) in Missouri Valley; 65-31 (.677) in SWC; 37-11 (.771) in SEC; 11-3 (.786) in MVC Tournament; 10-3 (.769) in SWC Tournament; 3-3 (.500) in SEC Tournament; 17-9 (.654) in NCAA Tournament; 6-2 (.750) in NIT.

WINFREY (WIMP) SANDERSON
North Alabama '59
Florence, Ala.

Only second coach in SEC history (Kentucky's Adolph Rupp was the first) to win three consecutive SEC Tournament titles (1989–91). Also, led 'Bama to SEC postseason tournament titles in 1982 and 1987 for a total of five.... New Arkansas-Little Rock head coach was an assistant at Alabama for 20 years under Hayden Riley and C. M. Newton.

Year	School	Overall	League	Finish	Postseason
80–81	Alabama	18-11	10-8	4th (SEC)	NIT (1-1)
81–82	Alabama	24-7	12-6	3d (SEC)	NCAA (1-1)
82–83	Alabama	20-12	8-10	T8th (SEC)	NCAA (0-1)
83–84	Alabama	18-12	10-8	5th (SEC)	NCAA (0-1)
84–85	Alabama	23-10	11-7	T3d (SEC)	NCAA (2-1)
85–86	Alabama	24-9	13-5	T2d (SEC)	NCAA (2-1)
86–87*	Alabama	28-5	16-2	1st (SEC)	NCAA (2-1)
87–88	Alabama	14-17	6-12	T8th (SEC)	DNP
88–89	Alabama	23-8	12-6	T2d (SEC)	NCAA (0-1)
89–90	Alabama	26-9	12-6	T2d (SEC)	NCAA (2-1)
90–91	Alabama	23-10	12-6	3d (SEC)	NCAA (2-1)
91–92	Alabama	26-9	10-6	3d (SEC)	NCAA (1-1)

* NCAA Tournament games later vacated by action of the NCAA.

12-Year Coaching Record: 267-119 (.692) in 12 years at Alabama; 132-82 (.617) in Southeastern Conference; 25-7 (.781) in SEC Tournament; 12-10 (.545) in NCAA Tournament; 1-1 (.500) in NIT.

DEAN SMITH
Kansas '53
Topeka, Kans.

NABC national coach of the year in 1977 and USBWA national coach of the year in 1979.... All-time winningest coach in NCAA Tournament competition.... Reached NCAA Final Four nine times—1967 (fourth), 1968 (runner-up), 1969 (fourth), 1972 (runner-up), 1977 (runner-up), 1981 (runner-up), 1982 (champion), 1991 (tied for third), and 1993 (champion).... Coach of 1971 NIT champion and 1973 third-place team.... Coach of 12 ACC Tournament champions—1967, 1968, 1969, 1972, 1975, 1977, 1979, 1981, 1982, 1989, 1991, and 1994.... U.S. Olympic team coach in 1976.... Assistant coach under Kansas' Dick Harp, Air Force's Bob Spear, and North Carolina's Frank McGuire.... Elected to Naismith Memorial Basketball Hall of Fame in 1982.

Year	School	Overall	League	Finish	Postseason
61–62	N. Caro.	8-9	7-7	T4th (ACC)	DNP
62–63	N. Caro.	15-6	10-4	3d (ACC)	DNP
63–64	N. Caro.	12-12	6-8	5th (ACC)	DNP
64–65	N. Caro.	15-9	10-4	T2d (ACC)	DNP
65–66	N. Caro.	16-11	8-6	T3d (ACC)	DNP
66–67	N. Caro.	26-6	12-2	1st (ACC)	NCAA (2-2)
67–68	N. Caro.	28-4	12-2	1st (ACC)	NCAA (3-1)
68–69	N. Caro.	27-5	12-2	1st (ACC)	NCAA (2-2)
69–70	N. Caro.	18-9	9-5	T2d (ACC)	NIT (0-1)
70–71	N. Caro.	26-6	11-3	1st (ACC)	NIT (4-0)
71–72	N. Caro.	26-5	9-3	1st (ACC)	NCAA (3-1)
72–73	N. Caro.	25-8	8-4	2d (ACC)	NIT (3-1)
73–74	N. Caro.	22-6	9-3	T2d (ACC)	NIT (0-1)
74–75	N. Caro.	23-8	8-4	T2d (ACC)	NCAA (2-1)
75–76	N. Caro.	25-4	11-1	1st (ACC)	NCAA (0-1)
76–77	N. Caro.	28-5	9-3	1st (ACC)	NCAA (4-1)
77–78	N. Caro.	23-8	9-3	1st (ACC)	NCAA (0-1)
78–79	N. Caro.	23-6	9-3	T1st (ACC)	NCAA (0-1)
79–80	N. Caro.	21-8	9-5	T2d (ACC)	NCAA (4-1)
80–81	N. Caro.	29-8	10-4	2d (ACC)	NCAA (5-0)
81–82	N. Caro.	32-2	12-2	T1st (ACC)	NCAA (2-1)
82–83	N. Caro.	28-8	12-2	T1st (ACC)	NCAA (1-1)
83–84	N. Caro.	28-3	14-0	1st (ACC)	NCAA (1-1)
84–85	N. Caro.	27-9	9-5	T1st (ACC)	NCAA (3-1)
85–86	N. Caro.	28-6	10-4	3d (ACC)	NCAA (2-1)
86–87	N. Caro.	32-4	14-0	1st (ACC)	NCAA (3-1)
87–88	N. Caro.	27-7	11-3	1st (ACC)	NCAA (2-1)
88–89	N. Caro.	29-8	9-5	T2d (ACC)	NCAA (2-1)
89–90	N. Caro.	21-13	8-6	T3d (ACC)	NCAA (4-1)
90–91	N. Caro.	29-6	10-4	2nd (ACC)	NCAA (4-1)
91–92	N. Caro.	23-10	9-7	3d (ACC)	NCAA (2-1)
92–93	N. Caro.	34-4	14-2	1st (ACC)	NCAA (6-0)
93–94	N. Caro.	26-7	11-5	2d (ACC)	NCAA (1-1)

33-Year Coaching Record: 800-230 (.777) at North Carolina; 331-121 (.732) in ACC; 53-21 (.716) in ACC Tournament; 56-24 (.700) in NCAA Tournament; 7-3 (.700) in NIT.

NORM STEWART
Missouri '56
Shelbyville, Mo.

UPI national coach of the year in 1982 and 1994. Also named by AP in 1994.... Coach of six Big Eight Tournament champions—1978, 1982, 1987, 1989, 1991, and 1993.... Winningest coach in Big Eight Conference history.... Coach of NCAA Division II fourth-place team in 1964.... Assistant coach at Missouri under Sparky Stalcup for four seasons from 1958 to 1961.

Year	School	Overall	League	Finish	Postseason
61–62	N. Iowa	19-5	8-4	T1st (N. Cent.)	DNP
62–63	N. Iowa	15-8	8-4	2d (N. Cent.)	DNP
63–64	N. Iowa	23-4	11-1	1st (N. Cent.)	NCAA-II (3-2)
64–65	N. Iowa	16-7	8-4	2d (N. Cent.)	DNP
65–66	N. Iowa	13-7	9-3	2d (N. Cent.)	DNP
66–67	N. Iowa	11-11	6-6	T2d (N. Cent.)	DNP
67–68	Missouri	10-16	5-9	6th (Big Eight)	DNP
68–69	Missouri	14-11	7-7	5th (Big Eight)	DNP
69–70	Missouri	15-11	7-7	T3d (Big Eight)	DNP
70–71	Missouri	17-9	9-5	T2d (Big Eight)	DNP
71–72	Missouri	21-6	10-4	2d (Big Eight)	NIT (0-1)
72–73	Missouri	21-6	9-5	T2d (Big Eight)	NIT (0-1)
73–74	Missouri	12-14	3-11	T7th (Big Eight)	DNP
74–75	Missouri	18-9	9-5	3d (Big Eight)	DNP
75–76	Missouri	26-5	12-2	1st (Big Eight)	NCAA (2-1)
76–77	Missouri	21-8	9-5	T2d (Big Eight)	DNP
77–78	Missouri	14-16	4-10	T6th (Big Eight)	NCAA (0-1)
78–79	Missouri	13-15	8-6	T2d (Big Eight)	DNP
79–80	Missouri	25-6	11-3	1st (Big Eight)	NCAA (2-1)
80–81	Missouri	22-10	10-4	1st (Big Eight)	NCAA (0-1)
81–82	Missouri	27-4	12-2	1st (Big Eight)	NCAA (1-1)
82–83	Missouri	26-8	12-2	1st (Big Eight)	NCAA (0-1)
83–84	Missouri	16-14	5-9	T6th (Big Eight)	DNP
84–85	Missouri	18-14	7-7	T3d (Big Eight)	NIT (0-1)
85–86	Missouri	21-14	8-6	T3d (Big Eight)	NCAA (0-1)
86–87	Missouri	24-10	11-3	1st (Big Eight)	NCAA (0-1)
87–88	Missouri	19-11	7-7	4th (Big Eight)	NCAA (0-1)
88–89	Missouri	29-8	10-4	2d (Big Eight)	NCAA (2-1)
89–90	Missouri	26-6	12-2	1st (Big Eight)	Probation
90–91	Missouri	20-10	8-6	4th (Big Eight)	Probation
91–92	Missouri	21-9	8-6	T2d (Big Eight)	NCAA (1-1)
92–93	Missouri	19-14	5-9	7th (Big Eight)	NCAA (0-1)
93–94	Missouri	28-4	14-0	1st (Big Eight)	NCAA (3-1)

33-Year Coaching Record: 640-310 (.674) overall; 97-42 (.698) in six years at Northern Iowa; 543-268 (.670) in first 27 years at Missouri; 50-22 (.694) in North Central Conference; 232-146 (.614) in Big Eight; 28-12 (.700) in Big Eight Tournament; 11-14 (.440) in NCAA Division I Tournament; 0-3 in NIT; 3-2 (.600) in NCAA Division II Tournament.

EDDIE SUTTON
Oklahoma St. '58
Bucklin, Kans.

Named national coach of the year by USBWA in 1977, by AP and UPI in 1978, and by AP and NABC in 1986.... Coach of NCAA Final Four team in 1978 with Arkansas.... Only coach to guide four different colleges to the NCAA playoffs.... Coach of five conference tournament champions—SWC (1977, 1979, and 1982 with Arkansas) and SEC (1986 and 1988 with Kentucky).... Assistant coach at Oklahoma State under Henry Iba for one season (1958–59).... Coach at Southern Idaho Junior College for three seasons from 1967 to 1969.

Year	School	Overall	League	Finish	Postseason
69–70	Creighton	15-10			DNP
70–71	Creighton	14-11			DNP
71–72	Creighton	15-11			DNP
72–73	Creighton	15-12			DNP
73–74	Creighton	23-6			NCAA (2-1)
74–75	Arkansas	17-9	11-3	T2d (SWC)	DNP
75–76	Arkansas	19-9	9-7	4th (SWC)	DNP

Year	School	Overall	League	Finish	Postseason
76–77	Arkansas	26-2	16-0	1st (SWC)	NCAA (0-1)
77–78	Arkansas	32-4	14-2	T1st (SWC)	NCAA (4-1)
78–79	Arkansas	25-5	13-3	T1st (SWC)	NCAA (2-1)
79–80	Arkansas	21-8	13-3	2d (SWC)	NCAA (0-1)
80–81	Arkansas	24-8	13-3	1st (SWC)	NCAA (2-1)
81–82	Arkansas	23-6	12-4	1st (SWC)	NCAA (0-1)
82–83	Arkansas	26-4	14-2	2d (SWC)	NCAA (1-1)
83–84	Arkansas	25-7	14-2	2d (SWC)	NCAA (0-1)
84–85	Arkansas	22-13	10-6	T2d (SWC)	NCAA (1-1)
85–86	Kentucky	32-4	17-1	1st (SEC)	NCAA (3-1)
86–87	Kentucky	18-11	10-8	T3d (SEC)	NCAA (2-1)
87–88	Kentucky	27-6	13-5	1st (SEC)	NCAA (2-1)
88–89	Kentucky	13-19	8-10	T6th (SEC)	DNP
90–91	Okla. St.	24-8	10-4	T1st (Big Eight)	NCAA (2-1)
91–92	Okla. St.	28-8	8-6	T2d (Big Eight)	NCAA (2-1)
92–93	Okla. St.	20-9	8-6	T2d (Big Eight)	NCAA (1-1)
93–94	Okla. St.	24-10	10-4	2d (Big Eight)	NCAA (1-1)

24-Year Coaching Record: 528-200 (.725) overall; 82-50 (.621) in five years at Creighton; 260-75 (.776) in 11 years at Arkansas; 96-35 (.733) in four years at Kentucky; 90-40 (.692) in first four years at Oklahoma State; 139-35 (.799) in Southwest Conference; 48-24 (.667) in Southeastern Conference; 36-20 (.643) in Big Eight Conference; 13-7 (.650) in SWC Tournament; 6-2 (.750) in SEC Tournament; 5-4 (.556) in Big Eight Tournament; 23-17 (.575) in NCAA Tournament.

JOHN THOMPSON
Providence '64
Washington, D.C.

Named national coach of year by USBWA in 1982, by the NABC in 1985, and by UPI in 1987.... Reached NCAA Final Four three times—1982 (runner-up), 1984 (champion), and 1985 (runner-up).... Coach of two NIT semifinalists—1978 (fourth) and 1993 (runner-up).... Coach of six Big East Conference champions—1980, 1982, 1984, 1985, 1987, and 1989.... U.S. Olympic head coach in 1988 and assistant coach in 1976.

Year	School	Overall	League	Finish	Postseason
72–73	Georgetown	12-15			DNP
73–74	Georgetown	13-13			DNP
74–75	Georgetown	18-10			NCAA (0-1)
75–76	Georgetown	21-7			NCAA (0-1)
76–77	Georgetown	19-9			NIT (0-1)
77–78	Georgetown	23-8			NIT (2-2)
78–79	Georgetown	24-5			NCAA (0-1)
79–80	Georgetown	26-6	5-1	T1st (Big East)	NCAA (2-1)
80–81	Georgetown	20-12	9-5	2d (Big East)	NCAA (0-1)
81–82	Georgetown	30-7	10-4	2d (Big East)	NCAA (4-1)
82–83	Georgetown	22-10	11-5	4th (Big East)	NCAA (1-1)
83–84	Georgetown	34-3	14-2	1st (Big East)	NCAA (5-0)
84–85	Georgetown	35-3	14-2	2d (Big East)	NCAA (5-1)
85–86	Georgetown	24-8	11-5	3d (Big East)	NCAA (1-1)
86–87	Georgetown	29-5	12-4	T1st (Big East)	NCAA (3-1)
87–88	Georgetown	20-10	9-7	T3d (Big East)	NCAA (1-1)
88–89	Georgetown	29-5	13-3	1st (Big East)	NCAA (3-1)
89–90	Georgetown	24-7	11-5	3d (Big East)	NCAA (1-1)
90–91	Georgetown	19-13	8-8	6th (Big East)	NCAA (1-1)
91–92	Georgetown	22-10	12-6	T1st (Big East)	NCAA (1-1)
92–93	Georgetown	20-13	8-10	8th (Big East)	NIT (4-1)
93–94	Georgetown	19-12	10-8	T4th (Big East)	NCAA (1-1)

22-Year Coaching Record: 503-190 (.726) at Georgetown; 157-75 (.677) in Big East Conference; 28-9 (.757) in Big East Tournament; 29-16 (.644) in NCAA Tournament; 6-4 (.600) in NIT.

BILLY TUBBS
Lamar '58
Tulsa, Okla.

Directed Oklahoma to 12 consecutive 20-win seasons (1982–93), a Big Eight best.... Took the Sooners to postseason play his last 13 years with them (9 NCAA/4 NIT) before moving to TCU for the 1994-95 season.... His '88 OU squad advanced to the national championship game against Kansas.... OU teams advanced to NIT semifinals in 1982 (T3rd) and 1991 (2nd).... Led Oklahoma to three Big Eight Tournament championships—1985, 1988 and 1990.

Year	School	Overall	League	Finish	Postseason
71–72	S'western	12-14	7-5	T2d (Big St.)	DNP
72–73	S'western	19-8	9-3	2d (Big St.)	DNP
76–77	Lamar	12-17	6-4	3d (Southland)	DNP
77–78	Lamar	18-9	8-2	T1st (Southland)	DNP
78–79	Lamar	23-9	8-1	1st (Southland)	NCAA (1-1)
79–80	Lamar	22-11	8-2	1st (Southland)	NCAA (2-1)
80–81	Oklahoma	9-18	4-10	7th (Big Eight)	DNP
81–82	Oklahoma	22-11	8-6	3d (Big Eight)	NIT (3-1)
82–83	Oklahoma	24-9	10-4	2d (Big Eight)	NCAA (1-1)
83–84	Oklahoma	29-5	13-1	1st (Big Eight)	NCAA (0-1)
84–85	Oklahoma	31-6	13-1	1st (Big Eight)	NCAA (3-1)
85–86	Oklahoma	26-9	8-6	T3d (Big Eight)	NCAA (1-1)
86–87	Oklahoma	24-10	9-5	T2d (Big Eight)	NCAA (2-1)
87–88	Oklahoma	35-4	12-2	1st (Big Eight)	NCAA (5-1)
88–89	Oklahoma	30-6	12-2	1st (Big Eight)	NCAA (2-1)
89–90	Oklahoma	27-5	11-3	2d (Big Eight)	NCAA (1-1)
90–91	Oklahoma	20-15	5-9	T6th (Big Eight)	NIT (4-1)
91–92	Oklahoma	21-9	8-6	T2d (Big Eight)	NCAA (0-1)
92–93	Oklahoma	20-12	7-7	T5th (Big Eight)	NIT (1-1)
93–94	Oklahoma	15-13	6-8	5th (Big Eight)	NIT (0-1)

20-Year Coaching Record: 439-200 (.687) overall; 31-22 (.585) in two years at Southwestern; 75-46 (.620) in four years at Lamar; 333-132 (.716) in 14 years at Oklahoma; 16-8 (.667) in Big State; 30-9 (.769) in Southland Conference; 126-70 (.643) in Big Eight Conference; 18-11 (.621) in Big Eight Tournament; 18-11 (.621) in NCAA Tournament; 8-4 (.667) in NIT.

ROY WILLIAMS
North Carolina '72
Skyland, N.C.

USBWA national coach of the year in 1990.... Reached NCAA Final Four two times—1991 (runner-up) and 1993 (tied for third).... Coach of 1992 Big Eight Tournament champion.... Assistant coach at North Carolina under Dean Smith for 10 seasons from 1979 to 1988.

Year	School	Overall	League	Finish	Postseason
88–89	Kansas	19-12	6-8	6th (Big Eight)	Probation
89–90	Kansas	30-5	11-3	T2d (Big Eight)	NCAA (1-1)
90–91	Kansas	27-8	10-4	T1st (Big Eight)	NCAA (5-1)
91–92	Kansas	27-5	11-3	1st (Big Eight)	NCAA (1-1)
92–93	Kansas	29-7	11-3	1st (Big Eight)	NCAA (4-1)
93–94	Kansas	27-8	9-5	3d (Big Eight)	NCAA (2-1)

Six-Year Coaching Record: 159-45 (.779) at Kansas; 58-26 (.690) in Big Eight Conference; 7-5 (.583) in Big Eight Tournament; 13-5 (.722) in NCAA Tournament.

Former College Coaching Greats

FORREST (PHOG) ALLEN
Kansas '06
Independence, Mo.

Elected to Naismith Memorial Basketball Hall of Fame in 1959.... U.S. Olympic team assistant coach in 1952.... Reached NCAA Final Four three times—1940 (2nd), 1952 (1st), and 1953 (2nd).... His 1922 and 1923 Kansas teams were selected as national champions by the Helms Foundation.... Holds the NCAA career record for most years coached.

Year	School	Overall	League	Finish	Postseason
05–6	Baker	18-3			
06–7	Baker	14-0			
07–8	Baker	13-6			
07–8	Kansas	18-6	6-0	1st (MVC)	

08–9	Kansas	25-3	8-2	1st (MVC)	
08–9	Haskell	27-5			
12–13	Central Mo. St.	11-7			
13–14	Central Mo. St.	15-4			
14–15	Central Mo. St.	13-4			
15–16	Central Mo. St	9-4			
16–17	Central Mo. St.	13-2			
17–18	Central Mo. St.	9-4			
18–19	Central Mo. St.	14-6			
19–20	Kansas	10-7	9-7	3d (MVC)	
20–21	Kansas	10-8	10-8	4th (MVC)	
21–22	Kansas	16-2	15-1	T1st (MVC)	
22–23	Kansas	17-1	16-0	1st (MVC)	
23–24	Kansas	16-3	15-1	1st (MVC)	
24–25	Kansas	17-1	15-1	1st (MVC)	
25–26	Kansas	16-2	16-2	1st (MVC)	
26–27	Kansas	15-2	10-2	1st (MVC)	
27–28	Kansas	9-9	9-9	4th (MVC)	
28–29	Kansas	3-15	2-8	T5th (Big Six)	
29–30	Kansas	14-4	7-3	2d (Big Six)	
30–31	Kansas	15-3	7-3	1st (Big Six)	
31–32	Kansas	13-5	7-3	1st (Big Six)	
32–33	Kansas	13-4	8-2	1st (Big Six)	
33–34	Kansas	16-1	9-1	1st (Big Six)	
34–35	Kansas	15-5	12-4	2d (Big Six)	
35–36	Kansas	21-2	10-0	1st (Big Six) Olympic Playoffs (3-2)	
36–37	Kansas	15-4	8-2	T1st (Big Six)	
37–38	Kansas	18-2	9-1	1st (Big Six)	DNP
38–39	Kansas	13-7	6-4	3d (Big Six)	DNP
39–40	Kansas	19-6	8-2	T1st (Big Six)	NCAA (2-1)
40–41	Kansas	12-6	7-3	T1st (Big Six)	DNP
41–42	Kansas	17-5	8-2	T1st (Big Six)	NCAA (1-1)
42–43	Kansas	22-6	10-0	1st (Big Six)	DNP
43–44	Kansas	17-9	5-5	3d (Big Six)	DNP
44–45	Kansas	12-5	7-3	2d (Big Six)	DNP
45–46	Kansas	19-2	10-0	1st (Big Six)	DNP
46–47	Kansas	8-5	5-5	T3d (Big Six)	DNP
47–48	Kansas	9-15	4-8	T6th (Big Seven)	DNP
48–49	Kansas	12-12	3-9	T6th (Big Seven)	DNP
49–50	Kansas	14-11	8-4	T1st (Big Seven)	DNP
50–51	Kansas	16-8	8-4	T2d (Big Seven)	DNP
51–52	Kansas	26-2	11-1	1st (Big Seven)	NCAA (4-0)
52–53	Kansas	19-6	10-2	1st (Big Seven)	NCAA (3-1)
53–54	Kansas	16-5	10-2	T1st (Big Seven)	DNP
54–55	Kansas	11-10	5-7	5th (Big Seven)	DNP
55–56	Kansas	14-9	6-6	5th (Big Seven)	DNP

48-Year Coaching Record: 746-264 (.739) overall; 45-9 (.833) in three years at Baker; 27-5 (.844) in one year at Haskell; 84-31 (.730) in seven years at Central Missouri State; 588-218 (.730) in 39 years at Kansas; 115-31 (.788) in Missouri Valley Conference; 210-94 (.691) in Big Eight Conference; 10-3 (.769) in NCAA Tournament.

Note: Coached two teams during the 1907-8 and 1908-9 seasons.

FORDDY ANDERSON
Stanford '42
Gary, Ind.

One of only 10 coaches to take two different teams to the Final Four.... Reached NCAA Final Four three times—1950 (2nd with Bradley), 1954 (2nd with Bradley), and 1957 (4th with Michigan State).... Led Bradley to fourth-place finish in 1949 NIT and second-place finish in 1950 NIT.... Assistant coach under Everett Dean at Stanford while completing work for college degree following World War II.

Year	School	Overall	League	Finish	Postseason
46–47	Drake	18-11	8-4	T2d (MVC)	DNP
47–48	Drake	14-12	5-5	3d (MVC)	DNP
48–49	Bradley	27-8	6-4	3d (MVC)	NIT (2-2)
49–50	Bradley	32-5	11-1	1st (MVC)	NCAA (2-1); NIT (2-1)
50–51	Bradley	32-6	11-3	T2d (MVC)	DNP
51–52	Bradley	17-12			DNP
52–53	Bradley	15-12			Probation
53–54	Bradley	19-13			NCAA (4-1)
54–55	Mich. St.	13-9	8-6	4th (Big Ten)	DNP
55–56	Mich. St.	13-9	7-7	5th (Big Ten)	DNP
56–57	Mich. St.	16-10	10-4	T1st (Big Ten)	NCAA (2-2)
57–58	Mich. St.	16-6	9-5	3d (Big Ten)	DNP
58–59	Mich. St.	19-4	12-2	1st (Big Ten)	NCAA (1-1)
59–60	Mich. St.	10-11	5-9	8th (Big Ten)	DNP
60–61	Mich. St.	7-17	3-11	9th (Big Ten)	DNP
61–62	Mich. St.	8-14	3-11	T9th (Big Ten)	DNP
62–63	Mich. St.	4-16	3-11	9th (Big Ten)	DNP
63–64	Mich. St.	14-10	8-6	T4th (Big Ten)	DNP
64–65	Mich. St.	5-18	1-13	10th (Big Ten)	DNP
65–66	Hiram Scott	12-3			
66–67	Hiram Scott	19-4			
67–68	Hiram Scott	15-5			
68–69	Hiram Scott	13-8			
69–70	Hiram Scott	10-11			

24-Year Coaching Record: 368-234 (.611) overall; 32-23 (.582) in two years at Drake; 142-56 (.717) in six years at Bradley; 125-124 (.502) in 11 years at Michigan State; 69-31 (.690) in five years at Hiram Scott; 41-17 (.707) in Missouri Valley Conference; 69-85 (.448) in Big Ten Conference; 9-5 (.643) in NCAA Tournament; 4-3 (.571) in NIT.

LEW ANDREAS
Syracuse '21
Sterling, Ill.

His 1926 team was selected as national champion by the Helms Foundation.

Year	School	Overall	League	Finish	Postseason
24–25	Syracuse	14-2			
25–26	Syracuse	19-1			
26–27	Syracuse	15-4			
27–28	Syracuse	10-6			
28–29	Syracuse	11-4			
29–30	Syracuse	18-2			
30–31	Syracuse	16-4			
31–32	Syracuse	13-7			
32–33	Syracuse	14-2			
33–34	Syracuse	15-2			
34–35	Syracuse	15-2			
35–36	Syracuse	12-5			
36–37	Syracuse	13-4			
37–38	Syracuse	13-5			DNP
38–39	Syracuse	14-4			DNP
39–40	Syracuse	10-8			DNP
40–41	Syracuse	14-5			DNP
41–42	Syracuse	15-6			DNP
42–43	Syracuse	8-10			DNP
44–45	Syracuse	7-12			DNP
45–46	Syracuse	23-4			NIT (0-1)
46–47	Syracuse	19-6			DNP
47–48	Syracuse	11-13			DNP
48–49	Syracuse	18-7			DNP
49–50	Syracuse	18-9			NIT (1-1)

25-Year Coaching Record: 355-134 (.726) overall; 1-2 (.333) in NIT.

CLAIR BEE
Waynesburg '25
Grafton, W.V.

Elected to Naismith Memorial Basketball Hall of Fame in 1967.... Coached LIU-Brooklyn to NIT titles in 1939 and 1941.... Second on the all-time coaches list for career winning percentage.... Compiled a 34-116 record with the NBA's Baltimore Bullets from 1952–53 through 1954–55.

Year	School	Overall	League	Finish	Postseason
28–29	Rider	19-3			
29–30	Rider	17-2			
30–31	Rider	17-2			
31–32	LIU-Bk'lyn	16-4			
32–33	LIU-Bk'lyn	6-11			
33–34	LIU-Bk'lyn	26-1			
34–35	LIU-Bk'lyn	24-2			
35–36	LIU-Bk'lyn	25-0			
36–37	LIU-Bk'lyn	28-3			
37–38	LIU-Bk'lyn	23-5			NIT (0-1)
38–39	LIU-Bk'lyn	23-0			NIT (3-0)
39–40	LIU-Bk'lyn	19-4			NIT (0-1)
40–41	LIU-Bk'lyn	25-2			NIT (3-0)
41–42	LIU-Bk'lyn	25-3			NIT (0-1)
42–43	LIU-Bk'lyn	13-6			DNP

45–46	LIU-Bk'lyn	14-9	DNP
46–47	LIU-Bk'lyn	17-5	NIT (0-1)
47–48	LIU-Bk'lyn	17-4	DNP
48–49	LIU-Bk'lyn	18-12	DNP
49–50	LIU-Bk'lyn	20-5	NIT (0-1)
50–51	LIU-Bk'lyn	20-4	DNP

21-Year Coaching Record: 412-87 (.826) overall; 53-7 (.883) in three years at Rider; 359-80 (.818) in 18 years at LIU-Brooklyn; 6-5 (.545) in NIT.

LARRY BROWN
North Carolina '63
Long Beach, N.Y.

Naismith coach of the year in 1988.... Coach of 1988 NCAA champion, 1980 runner-up, and 1986 Final Four team.... Coach of two Big Eight Conference Tournament champions— 1984 and 1986.... U.S. Olympic team assistant coach in 1980.... Compiled a 229-107 (.682) regular-season record and 20-22 (.476) playoff mark in four seasons as coach in the ABA from 1972–73 through 1975–76 before compiling a 481-377 (.561) regular-season record and 29-32 (.475) playoff mark in his first 11 years as coach of five different NBA franchises from 1976–77 through 1993–94.... Assistant coach at North Carolina under Dean Smith for two seasons (1965–66 and 1966–67).

Year	School	Overall	League	Finish	Postseason
79–80	UCLA	22-10	12-6	4th (Pac-10)	NCAA (5-1)
80–81	UCLA	20-7	13-5	3d (Pac-10)	NCAA (0-1)
83–84	Kansas	22-10	9-5	2d (Big Eight)	NCAA (1-1)
84–85	Kansas	26-8	11-3	2d (Big Eight)	NCAA (1-1)
85–86	Kansas	35-4	13-1	1st (Big Eight)	NCAA (4-1)
86–87	Kansas	25-11	9-5	T2d (Big Eight)	NCAA (2-1)
87–88	Kansas	27-11	9-5	3d (Big Eight)	NCAA (6-0)

Seven-Year College Coaching Record: 177-61 (.744) overall; 42-17 (.712) in two years at UCLA; 135-44 (754) in five years at Kansas; 25-11 (.694) in Pacific-10 Conference; 51-19 (.729) in Big Eight; 10-3 (.769) in Big Eight Tournament; 19-6 (.760) in NCAA Tournament.

VIC BUBAS
N.C. St. '51
Gary, Ind.

Reached NCAA Final Four three times—1963 (3rd), 1964 (2nd), and 1966 (3rd).... Coach of four Atlantic Coast Conference Tournament champions— 1960, 1963, 1964, and 1966.... Assistant coach under Everett Case at his alma mater from 1951–52 through 1958–59.

Year	School	Overall	League	Finish	Postseason
59–60	Duke	17-11	7-7	4th (ACC)	NCAA (2-1)
60–61	Duke	22-6	10-4	3d (ACC)	DNP
61–62	Duke	20-5	11-3	2d (ACC)	DNP
62–63	Duke	27-3	14-0	1st (ACC)	NCAA (3-1)
63–64	Duke	26-5	13-1	1st (ACC)	NCAA (3-1)
64–65	Duke	20-5	11-3	1st (ACC)	DNP
65–66	Duke	26-4	12-2	1st (ACC)	NCAA (3-1)
66–67	Duke	18-9	9-3	2d (ACC)	NIT (0-1)
67–68	Duke	22-6	11-3	2d (ACC)	NIT (1-1)
68–69	Duke	15-13	8-6	T3d (ACC)	DNP

10-Year Coaching Record: 213-67 (.761) overall; 106-32 (.768) in Atlantic Coast Conference; 22-6 (.786) in ACC Tournament; 11-4 (.733) in NCAA Tournament; 1-2 (.333) in NIT.

LOU CARNESECCA
St. John's '46
Manhattan, N.Y.

Named national coach of the year by NABC and USBWA in 1983, and by UPI and USBWA in 1985.... Coach of 1985 NCAA Final Four team.... Coach of three NIT semifinalists—1970 (runner-up), 1975 (fourth place), and 1989 (champion).... Compiled 114-138 record in three seasons with ABA's New York Nets from 1970–71 through 1972–73.... Assistant coach at St. John's for nine seasons under Joe Lapchick from 1957 to 1965.... Elected to Naismith Memorial Basketball Hall of Fame in 1991.

Year	School	Overall	League	Finish	Postseason
65–66	St. John's	18-8			NIT (0-1)
66–67	St. John's	23-5			NCAA (1-1)
67–68	St. John's	19-8			NCAA (0-1)
68–69	St. John's	23-6			NCAA (1-1)
69–70	St. John's	21-8			NIT (3-1)
73–74	St. John's	20-7			NIT (0-1)
74–75	St. John's	21-10			NIT (2-2)
75–76	St. John's	23-6			NCAA (0-1)
76–77	St. John's	22-9			NCAA (0-1)
77–78	St. John's	21-7			NCAA (0-1)
78–79	St. John's	21-11			NCAA (0-1)
79–80	St. John's	24-5	5-1	T1st (Big East)	NCAA (0-1)
80–81	St. John's	17-11	8-6	T3d (Big East)	NIT (0-1)
81–82	St. John's	21-9	9-5	3d (Big East)	NCAA (1-1)
82–83	St. John's	28-5	12-4	T1st (Big East)	NCAA (1-1)
83–84	St. John's	18-12	8-8	T4th (Big East)	NCAA (0-1)
84–85	St. John's	31-4	15-1	1st (Big East)	NCAA (4-1)
85–86	St. John's	31-5	14-2	1st (Big East)	NCAA (1-1)
86–87	St. John's	21-9	10-6	T4th (Big East)	NCAA (1-1)
87–88	St. John's	17-12	8-8	T5th (Big East)	NCAA (0-1)
88–89	St. John's	20-13	6-10	T7th (Big East)	NIT (5-0)
89–90	St. John's	24-10	10-6	4th (Big East)	NCAA (1-1)
90–91	St. John's	23-9	10-6	2d (Big East)	NCAA (3-1)
91–92	St. John's	19-11	12-6	T1st (Big East)	NCAA (1-1)

24-Year College Coaching Record: 526-200 (.725) overall; 127-69 (.648) in Big East; 12-11 (.522) in Big East Tournament; 17-20 (.459) in NCAA Tournament; 10-6 (.625) in NIT.

EVERETT CASE
Wisconsin '23
Anderson, Ind.

Elected to Naismith Memorial Basketball Hall of Fame in 1981.... Reached Final Four in 1950 (3rd).... Coach of six Southern Conference Tournament champions—1947, 1948, 1949, 1950, 1951, and 1953.... Coach of four Atlantic Coast Conference Tournament champions—1954, 1955, 1956, and 1959.

Year	School	Overall	League	Finish	Postseason
46–47	N.C. St.	26-5	11-2	1st (Southern)	NIT (2-1)
47–48	N.C. St.	29-3	12-0	1st (Southern)	NIT (0-1)
48–49	N.C. St.	25-8	14-1	1st (Southern)	DNP
49–50	N.C. St.	27-6	12-2	1st (Southern)	NCAA (2-1)
50–51	N.C. St.	30-7	13-1	1st (Southern)	NCAA (1-2): NIT (0-1)
51–52	N.C. St.	24-10	12-2	2d (Southern)	NCAA (1-1)
52–53	N.C. St.	26-6	13-3	1st (Southern)	DNP
53–54	N.C. St.	26-7	5-3	4th (ACC)	NCAA (2-1)
54–55	N.C. St.	28-4	12-2	1st (ACC)	DNP
55–56	N.C. St.	24-4	11-3	T1st (ACC)	NCAA (0-1)
56–57	N.C. St.	15-11	7-7	T4th (ACC)	DNP
57–58	N.C. St.	18-6	10-4	T2d (ACC)	DNP
58–59	N.C. St.	22-4	12-2	T1st (ACC)	DNP
59–60	N.C. St.	11-15	5-9	6th (ACC)	DNP
60–61	N.C. St.	16-9	8-6	4th (ACC)	DNP
61–62	N.C. St.	11-6	10-4	3d (ACC)	DNP
62–63	N.C. St.	10-11	5-9	T4th (ACC)	DNP
63–64	N.C. St.	8-11	4-10	T7th (ACC)	DNP
64–65	N.C. St.	1-1	0-1		DNP

19-Year Coaching Record: 377-134 (.738) overall; 87-11 (.888) in Southern Conference; 89-60 (.597) in Atlantic Coast Conference; 20-1 (.952) in Southern Conference Tournament; 15-7 (.682) in ACC Tournament; 6-6 (.500) in NCAA Tournament; 2-3 (.400) in NIT.

HARRY COMBES

Illinois '37
Monticello, Ill.

Reached NCAA Final Four three times—1949 (3rd), 1951 (3rd), and 1952 (3rd).

Year	School	Overall	League	Finish	Postseason
47–48	Illinois	15-5	7-5	T3d (Big Ten)	DNP
48–49	Illinois	21-4	10-2	1st (Big Ten)	NCAA (2-1)
49–50	Illinois	14-8	7-5	T3d (Big Ten)	DNP
50–51	Illinois	22-5	13-1	1st (Big Ten)	NCAA (3-1)
51–52	Illinois	22-4	12-2	1st (Big Ten)	NCAA (3-1)
52–53	Illinois	18-4	14-4	2d (Big Ten)	DNP
53–54	Illinois	17-5	10-4	T3d (Big Ten)	DNP
54–55	Illinois	17-5	10-4	T2d (Big Ten)	DNP
55–56	Illinois	18-4	11-3	2d (Big Ten)	DNP
56–57	Illinois	14-8	7-7	7th (Big Ten)	DNP
57–58	Illinois	11-11	5-9	T8th (Big Ten)	DNP
58–59	Illinois	12-10	7-7	T5th (Big Ten)	DNP
59–60	Illinois	16-7	8-6	T3d (Big Ten)	DNP
60–61	Illinois	9-15	5-9	7th (Big Ten)	DNP
61–62	Illinois	15-8	7-7	T4th (Big Ten)	DNP
62–63	Illinois	20-6	11-3	T1st (Big Ten)	NCAA (1-1)
63–64	Illinois	13-11	6-8	T6th (Big Ten)	DNP
64–65	Illinois	18-6	10-4	3d (Big Ten)	DNP
65–66	Illinois	12-12	8-6	T3d (Big Ten)	DNP
66–67	Illinois	12-12	6-8	7th (Big Ten)	DNP

20-Year Coaching Record: 316-150 (.678) overall; 174-104 (.626) in Big Ten Conference; 9-4 (.692) in NCAA Tournament.

CHARLES (CHICK) DAVIES

Duquesne '34
New Castle, Pa.

Reached NCAA Final Four in 1940 (tied for third place).... Coach of second-place finisher in 1940 NIT.

Year	School	Overall	League	Finish	Postseason
24–25	Duquesne	12-6			
25–26	Duquesne	15-4			
26–27	Duquesne	16-4			
27–28	Duquesne	15-7			
28–29	Duquesne	12-8			
29–30	Duquesne	18-10			
30–31	Duquesne	12-6			
31–32	Duquesne	14-6			
32–33	Duquesne	15-1			
33–34	Duquesne	19-2			
34–35	Duquesne	18-1			
35–36	Duquesne	14-3			
36–37	Duquesne	13-6			
37–38	Duquesne	6-11			DNP
38–39	Duquesne	14-4			DNP
39–40	Duquesne	20-3			NCAA (1-1); NIT (2-1)
40–41	Duquesne	17-3			NIT (0-1)
41–42	Duquesne	15-6			DNP
42–43	Duquesne	12-7			DNP
46–47	Duquesne	20-2			NIT (0-1)
47–48	Duquesne	17-6			DNP

21-Year Coaching Record: 314-106 (.748) overall; 1-1 (.500) in NCAA Tournament; 2-3 (.400) in NIT.

EVERETT DEAN

Indiana '21
Salem, Ind.

Elected to Naismith Memorial Basketball Hall of Fame in 1966.... Coached Stanford to the 1942 NCAA championship.

Year	School	Overall	League	Finish	Postseason
21–22	Carleton	14-2		1st (Midwest)	
22–23	Carleton	17-2		1st (Midwest)	
23–24	Carleton	14-0		1st (Midwest)	
24–25	Indiana	12-5	8-4	T2d (Western)	
25–26	Indiana	12-5	8-4	T1st (Western)	
26–27	Indiana	13-4	9-3	2d (Western)	
27–28	Indiana	15-2	10-2	1st (Western)	
28–29	Indiana	7-10	4-8	8th (Western)	
29–30	Indiana	8-9	7-5	T4th (Western)	
30–31	Indiana	9-8	5-7	6th (Western)	
31–32	Indiana	8-10	4-8	7th (Western)	
32–33	Indiana	10-8	6-6	T6th (Western)	
33–34	Indiana	13-7	6-6	T5th (Western)	
34–35	Indiana	14-6	8-4	T4th (Western)	
35–36	Indiana	18-2	11-1	T1st (Western)	
36–37	Indiana	13-7	6-6	T6th (Western)	
37–38	Indiana	10-10	4-8	8th (Western)	DNP
38–39	Stanford	16-9	6-6	3d (PCC-S)	DNP
39–40	Stanford	14-9	6-6	2d (PCC-S)	DNP
40–41	Stanford	21-5	10-2	1st (PCC-S)	DNP
41–42	Stanford	27-4	11-1	1st (PCC-S)	NCAA (3-0)
42–43	Stanford	10-10	4-4	T2d (PCC-S)	DNP
45–46	Stanford	6-18	0-12	4th (PCC-S)	DNP
46–47	Stanford	15-16	5-7	3d (PCC-S)	DNP
47–48	Stanford	15-11	3-9	T3d (PCC-S)	DNP
48–49	Stanford	19-9	5-7	3d (PCC-S)	DNP
49–50	Stanford	11-14	3-9	4th (PCC-S)	DNP
50–51	Stanford	12-14	5-7	3d (PCC-S)	DNP

28-Year Coaching Record: 374-217 (.633) overall; 45-4 (.918) in three years at Carleton; 162-93 (.635) in 14 years at Indiana; 167-120 (.582) in 11 years at Stanford; 96-72 (.571) in Western Conference (forerunner of Big Ten); 53-70 (.431) in Pacific Coast Conference-South Division; 3-0 in NCAA Tournament.

ED DIDDLE

Centre '21
Columbia, Ky.

Elected to Naismith Memorial Basketball Hall of Fame in 1971.... Coach of four Ohio Valley Conference Tournament champions—1949, 1952, 1953, and 1954.... Coach of second-place finisher in 1942 NIT, third-place finisher in 1948, and fourth-place finisher in 1954.... Tied with DePaul's Ray Meyer for the NCAA career record for most years coached at one school with 42 seasons.

Year	School	Overall	League	Finish	Postseason
22–23	Western Ky.	12-2			
23–24	Western Ky.	9-9			
24–25	Western Ky.	8-6			
25–26	Western Ky.	10-4		KIAC	
26–27	Western Ky.	12-7		KIAC	
27–28	Western Ky.	10-7		KIAC	
28–29	Western Ky.	8-10		KIAC	
29–30	Western Ky.	4-12		KIAC	
30–31	Western Ky.	11-3		KIAC	
31–32	Western Ky.	15-8		KIAC	
32–33	Western Ky.	16-6		KIAC	
33–34	Western Ky.	28-8		KIAC	
34–35	Western Ky.	24-3		KIAC	
35–36	Western Ky.	26-4		KIAC	
36–37	Western Ky.	21-2		KIAC	
37–38	Western Ky.	30-3		KIAC	DNP
38–39	Western Ky.	22-3		KIAC	DNP
39–40	Western Ky.	24-6		KIAC	NCAA (0-1)
40–41	Western Ky.	22-4		KIAC	DNP
41–42	Western Ky.	29-5		KIAC	NIT (2-1)
42–43	Western Ky.	24-3	3-1	T2d (KIAC)	NIT (0-1)
43–44	Western Ky.	13-9		KIAC	DNP
44–45	Western Ky.	17-10		KIAC	DNP
45–46	Western Ky.	15-19	2-6	8th (KIAC)	DNP
46–47	Western Ky.	25-4	6-2	2d (KIAC)	NIT (2-1)
47–48	Western Ky.	28-2	10-0	1st (KIAC)	NIT (0-1)
48–49	Western Ky.	25-4	8-2	1st (OVC)	NIT (1-1)
49–50	Western Ky.	25-6	8-0	1st (OVC)	DNP
50–51	Western Ky.	19-10	4-4	4th (OVC)	DNP
51–52	Western Ky.	26-5	9-1	1st (OVC)	NIT (1-1)
52–53	Western Ky.	25-6	8-2	2d (OVC)	NIT (1-1)
53–54	Western Ky.	29-3	9-1	1st (OVC)	NIT (1-2)
54–55	Western Ky.	18-10	8-2	1st (OVC)	DNP
55–56	Western Ky.	16-12	7-3	T1st (OVC)	DNP
56–57	Western Ky.	17-9	9-1	T1st (OVC)	DNP
57–58	Western Ky.	14-11	5-5	3d (OVC)	DNP
58–59	Western Ky.	16-10	8-4	2d (OVC)	DNP

Year	School	Overall	League	Finish	Postseason
59–60	Western Ky.	21-7	10-2	1st (OVC)	NCAA (2-1)
60–61	Western Ky.	18-8	9-3	T1st (OVC)	DNP
61–62	Western Ky.	17-10	11-1	1st (OVC)	NCAA (1-2)
62–63	Western Ky.	5-16	3-9	7th (OVC)	DNP
63–64	Western Ky.	5-16	3-11	8th (OVC)	DNP

42-Year Coaching Record: 759-302 (.715) overall; 21-9 (.700) in Kentucky Intercollegiate Athletic Conference; 119-51 (.700) in Ohio Valley Conference; 54-7 (.885) in KIAC Tournament; 35-7 (.833) in Southern Intercollegiate Athletic Association Tournament; 3-4 (.429) in NCAA Tournament; 7-9 (.438) in NIT.

Note: No regular-season standings, only postseason conference tournaments, for the Kentucky Intercollegiate Athletic Conference except for one season through 1944–45. The SIAA Tournament included champions and at-large teams from various southern conferences.

BRUCE DRAKE
Oklahoma '29
Oklahoma City, Okla.

Elected to Naismith Memorial Basketball Hall of Fame in 1972.... U.S. Olympic Team coach in 1956.... Reached NCAA Final Four two times—1939 (tied for third) and 1947 (2nd).... Assistant coach under Hugh McDermott at Oklahoma.

Year	School	Overall	League	Finish	Postseason
38–39	Oklahoma	12-9	7-3	T1st (Big Six)	NCAA (1-1)
39–40	Oklahoma	12-7	8-2	T1st (Big Six)	DNP
40–41	Oklahoma	6-12	5-5	4th (Big Six)	DNP
41–42	Oklahoma	11-7	8-2	T1st (Big Six)	DNP
42–43	Oklahoma	18-9	7-3	2d (Big Six)	NCAA (1-1)
43–44	Oklahoma	15-8	9-1	T1st (Big Six)	DNP
44–45	Oklahoma	12-13	5-5	T3d (Big Six)	DNP
45–46	Oklahoma	11-10	7-3	2d (Big Six)	DNP
46–47	Oklahoma	24-7	8-2	1st (Big Six)	NCAA (2-1)
47–48	Oklahoma	13-9	7-5	T2d (Big Seven)	DNP
48–49	Oklahoma	14-9	9-3	T1st (Big Seven)	DNP
49–50	Oklahoma	12-10	6-6	T3d (Big Seven)	DNP
50–51	Oklahoma	14-10	6-6	4th (Big Seven)	DNP
51–52	Oklahoma	7-17	4-8	T4th (Big Seven)	DNP
52–53	Oklahoma	8-13	5-7	T4th (Big Seven)	DNP
53–54	Oklahoma	8-13	4-8	6th (Big Seven)	DNP
54–55	Oklahoma	3-18	1-11	7th (Big Seven)	DNP

17-Year Coaching Record: 200-181 (.525) overall; 106-80 (.570) in Big Eight Conference (previously known as Big Six and Big Seven); 4-3 (.571) in NCAA Tournament.

CLARENCE (HEC) EDMUNDSON
Idaho '10
Moscow, Idaho

Year	School	Overall	League	Finish	Postseason
16–17	Idaho	8-8			
17–18	Idaho	12-1			
20–21	Washington	18-4	10-4	3d (PCC)	
21–22	Washington	13-5	11-5	4th (PCC)	
22–23	Washington	12-4	5-3	T1st (PCC-N)	
23–24	Washington	12-4	7-2	1st (PCC-N)	
24–25	Washington	14-7	5-5	T3d (PCC-N)	
25–26	Washington	10-6	5-5	4th (PCC-N)	
26–27	Washington	15-4	7-3	T2d (PCC-N)	
27–28	Washington	22-6	9-1	1st (PCC-N)	
28–29	Washington	18-2	10-0	1st (PCC-N)	
29–30	Washington	21-7	12-4	1st (PCC-N)	
30–31	Washington	25-3	14-2	1st (PCC-N)	
31–32	Washington	19-6	12-4	1st (PCC-N)	
32–33	Washington	22-6	10-6	2d (PCC-N)	
33–34	Washington	20-5	14-2	1st (PCC-N)	
34–35	Washington	16-8	11-5	2d (PCC-N)	
35–36	Washington	25-7	13-3	1st (PCC-N)	
36–37	Washington	15-11	11-5	T1st (PCC-N)	
37–38	Washington	29-7	13-7	2d (PCC-N)	DNP
38–39	Washington	20-5	11-5	2d (PCC-N)	DNP
39–40	Washington	10-15	6-10	4th (PCC-N)	DNP
40–41	Washington	12-13	7-9	T3d (PCC-N)	DNP
41–42	Washington	18-7	10-6	2d (PCC-N)	DNP

Year	School	Overall	League	Finish	Postseason
42–43	Washington	24-7	12-4	1st (PCC-N)	NCAA (0-2)
43–44	Washington	26-6	15-1	1st (PCC-N)	DNP
44–45	Washington	22-18	5-11	4th (PCC-N)	DNP
45–46	Washington	14-14	6-10	4th (PCC-N)	DNP
46–47	Washington	16-8	8-8	3d (PCC-N)	DNP

29-Year Coaching Record: 508-204 (.713) overall; 20-9 (.690) in two years at Idaho; 488-195 (.714) in 27 years at Washington; 259-130 (.666) in Pacific-10 (Pacific Coast Conference); 0-2 in NCAA Tournament.

HAROLD "BUD" FOSTER
Wisconsin '30
Mason City, Iowa

Elected to Naismith Memorial Basketball Hall of Fame in 1964.... Coach of 1941 NCAA championship team.

Year	School	Overall	League	Finish	Postseason
34–35	Wisconsin	15-5	9-3	T1st (Big Ten)	DNP
35–36	Wisconsin	11-9	4-8	8th (Big Ten)	DNP
36–37	Wisconsin	8-12	3-9	T8th (Big Ten)	DNP
37–38	Wisconsin	10-10	5-7	7th (Big Ten)	DNP
38–39	Wisconsin	10-10	4-8	7th (Big Ten)	DNP
39–40	Wisconsin	5-15	3-9	9th (Big Ten)	DNP
40–41	Wisconsin	20-3	11-1	1st (Big Ten)	NCAA (3-0)
41–42	Wisconsin	14-7	10-5	T2d (Big Ten)	DNP
42–43	Wisconsin	12-9	6-6	T4th (Big Ten)	DNP
43–44	Wisconsin	12-9	9-3	T2d (Big Ten)	DNP
44–45	Wisconsin	10-11	4-8	T6th (Big Ten)	DNP
45–46	Wisconsin	4-17	1-11	9th (Big Ten)	DNP
46–47	Wisconsin	16-6	9-3	1st (Big Ten)	NCAA (1-1)
47–48	Wisconsin	12-8	7-5	T3d (Big Ten)	DNP
48–49	Wisconsin	12-10	5-7	7th (Big Ten)	DNP
49–50	Wisconsin	17-5	9-3	2d (Big Ten)	DNP
50–51	Wisconsin	10-12	7-7	T4th (Big Ten)	DNP
51–52	Wisconsin	10-12	5-9	7th (Big Ten)	DNP
52–53	Wisconsin	13-9	10-8	5th (Big Ten)	DNP
53–54	Wisconsin	12-10	6-8	T5th (Big Ten)	DNP
54–55	Wisconsin	10-12	5-9	T6th (Big Ten)	DNP
55–56	Wisconsin	6-16	4-10	T8th (Big Ten)	DNP
56–57	Wisconsin	5-17	3-11	9th (Big Ten)	DNP
57–58	Wisconsin	8-14	3-11	10th (Big Ten)	DNP
58–59	Wisconsin	3-19	1-13	10th (Big Ten)	DNP

25-Year Coaching Record: 265-267 (.498) overall; 143-182 (.440) in Big Ten Conference; 4-1 (.800) in NCAA Tournament.

JACK GARDNER
Southern Cal '32
Redlands, Calif.

Elected to Naismith Memorial Basketball Hall of Fame in 1983.... Reached NCAA Final Four four times—1948 (4th with Kansas St.), 1951 (2nd with Kansas St.), 1961 (4th with Utah), and 1966 (4th with Utah).

Year	School	Overall	League	Finish	Postseason
39–40	Kansas St.	6-12	2-8	T4th (Big Six)	DNP
40–41	Kansas St.	6-12	3-7	5th (Big Six)	DNP
41–42	Kansas St.	8-10	3-7	5th (Big Six)	DNP
46–47	Kansas St.	14-10	3-7	T5th (Big Six)	DNP
47–48	Kansas St.	22-6	9-3	1st (Big Seven)	NCAA (1-2)
48–49	Kansas St.	13-11	8-4	3d (Big Seven)	DNP
49–50	Kansas St.	17-7	8-4	T1st (Big Seven)	DNP
50–51	Kansas St.	25-4	11-1	1st (Big Seven)	NCAA (3-1)
51–52	Kansas St.	19-5	10-2	2d (Big Seven)	DNP
52–53	Kansas St.	17-4	9-3	2d (Big Seven)	DNP
53–54	Utah	12-14	7-7	T4th (Sky. Eight)	DNP
54–55	Utah	24-4	13-1	1st (Sky. Eight)	NCAA (1-1)
55–56	Utah	22-6	12-2	1st (Sky. Eight)	NCAA (1-1)
56–57	Utah	19-8	10-4	2d (Sky. Eight)	NIT (0-1)
57–58	Utah	20-7	9-5	T2d (Sky. Eight)	NIT (0-1)
58–59	Utah	21-7	13-1	1st (Sky. Eight)	NCAA (0-2)
59–60	Utah	26-3	13-1	1st (Sky. Eight)	NCAA (2-1)
60–61	Utah	23-8	12-2	T1st (Sky. Eight)	NCAA (2-2)
61–62	Utah	23-3	13-1	1st (Sky. Eight)	Probation
62–63	Utah	12-14	5-5	3d (WAC)	DNP
63–64	Utah	19-9	4-6	T4th (WAC)	DNP
64–65	Utah	17-9	3-7	6th (WAC)	DNP

Year	School	Overall	League	Finish	Postseason
65–66	Utah	23-8	7-3	1st (WAC)	NCAA (2-2)
66–67	Utah	15-11	5-5	T3d (WAC)	DNP
67–68	Utah	17-9	5-5	T2d (WAC)	DNP
68–69	Utah	13-13	5-5	T3d (WAC)	DNP
69–70	Utah	18-11	9-5	T2d (WAC)	NIT (1-1)
70–71	Utah	15-11	9-5	T2d (WAC)	DNP

28-Year Coaching Record: 486-235 (.674) overall; 147-81 (.645) in 10 years at Kansas State; 339-154 (.688) in 18 years at Utah; 66-46 (.589) in Big Eight Conference (Big Six, Big Seven); 102-24 (.810) in Skyline Eight Conference; 52-46 (.531) in Western Athletic Conference; 12-12 (.500) in NCAA Tournament; 1-3 (.250) in NIT.

AMORY "SLATS" GILL
Oregon St. '24
Salem, Oreg.

Elected to Naismith Memorial Basketball Hall of Fame in 1967.... Reached NCAA Final Four two times—1949 (4th) and 1963 (4th).

Year	School	Overall	League	Finish	Postseason
28–29	Oregon St.	12-8	4-6	4th (PCC-N)	
29–30	Oregon St.	14-13	7-9	4th (PCC-N)	
30–31	Oregon St.	19-9	9-7	3d (PCC-N)	
31–32	Oregon St.	12-12	8-8	3d (PCC-N)	
32–33	Oregon St.	21-6	12-4	1st (PCC-N)	
33–34	Oregon St.	14-10	7-9	3d (PCC-N)	
34–35	Oregon St.	19-9	12-4	1st (PCC-N)	
35–36	Oregon St.	16-9	10-6	2d (PCC-N)	
36–37	Oregon St.	11-14	5-11	4th (PCC-N)	
37–38	Oregon St.	17-16	6-14	5th (PCC-N)	DNP
38–39	Oregon St.	13-11	6-10	4th (PCC-N)	DNP
39–40	Oregon St.	27-11	12-4	1st (PCC-N)	DNP
40–41	Oregon St.	19-9	9-7	2d (PCC-N)	DNP
41–42	Oregon St.	18-9	11-5	1st (PCC-N)	DNP
42–43	Oregon St.	19-9	8-8	4th (PCC-N)	DNP
43–44	Oregon St.	8-16	5-11	T3d (PCC-N)	DNP
44–45	Oregon St.	20-8	10-6	3d (PCC-N)	DNP
45–46	Oregon St.	13-11	10-6	2d (PCC-N)	DNP
46–47	Oregon St.	28-5	13-3	1st (PCC-N)	NCAA (1-1)
47–48	Oregon St.	21-13	10-6	T1st (PCC-N)	DNP
48–49	Oregon St.	24-12	12-4	1st (PCC-N)	NCAA (1-2)
49–50	Oregon St.	13-14	8-8	T2d (PCC-N)	DNP
50–51	Oregon St.	14-18	6-10	4th (PCC-N)	DNP
51–52	Oregon St.	9-19	3-13	5th (PCC-N)	DNP
52–53	Oregon St.	11-18	6-10	4th (PCC-N)	DNP
53–54	Oregon St.	19-10	11-5	1st (PCC-N)	NCAA (1-1)
54–55	Oregon St.	22-8	15-1	1st (PCC-N)	DNP
55–56	Oregon St.	8-18	5-11	T7th (PCC)	DNP
56–57	Oregon St.	11-15	6-10	6th (PCC)	DNP
57–58	Oregon St.	20-6	12-4	T1st (PCC)	DNP
58–59	Oregon St.	13-13	7-9	6th (PCC)	DNP
59–60	Oregon St.*	9-3			DNP
60–61	Oregon St.	14-12			DNP
61–62	Oregon St.	24-5			NCAA (2-1)
62–63	Oregon St.	22-9			NCAA (3-2)
63–64	Oregon St.	25-4			NCAA (0-1)

* Missed 14 games (6-8 record) in 1959–60 because of illness. Replaced by Paul Valenti, who later succeeded him.

36-Year Coaching Record: 599-392 (.604) overall; 265-229 (.536) in Pacific-10 Conference (Pacific Coast); 8-8 (.500) in NCAA Tournament.

HUGH GREER
Connecticut '26
Suffield, Conn.

Finished lower than second place in Yankee Conference just once in 17 seasons.

Year	School	Overall	League	Finish	Postseason
46–47*	Conn.	12-0	5-0	2d (Yankee)	DNP
47–48	Conn.	17-6	6-1	1st (Yankee)	DNP
48–49	Conn.	19-6	7-1	1st (Yankee)	DNP
49–50	Conn.	17-8	5-2	2d (Yankee)	DNP
50–51	Conn.	22-4	6-1	1st (Yankee)	NCAA (0-1)
51–52	Conn.	20-7	6-1	1st (Yankee)	DNP
52–53	Conn.	17-4	5-1	1st (Yankee)	DNP
53–54	Conn.	23-3	7-0	1st (Yankee)	NCAA (0-1)
54–55	Conn.	20-5	7-0	1st (Yankee)	NIT (0-1)
55–56	Conn.	17-11	6-1	1st (Yankee)	NCAA (1-2)
56–57	Conn.	17-8	8-0	1st (Yankee)	NCAA (0-1)
57–58	Conn.	17-10	10-2	1st (Yankee)	NCAA (0-1)
58–59	Conn.	17-7	8-2	1st (Yankee)	NCAA (0-1)
59–60	Conn.	17-9	8-2	1st (Yankee)	NCAA (0-1)
60–61	Conn.	11-13	6-4	3d (Yankee)	DNP
61–62	Conn.	16-8	7-3	T2d (Yankee)	DNP
62–63	Conn.	7-3	9-1	1st (Yankee)	DNP

* Greer coached only last 12 games of 16-2 season and 6-1 conference record.

17-Year Coaching Record: 286-112 (.719) overall; 116-22 (.841) in Yankee Conference; 1-8 (.111) in NCAA Tournament; 0-1 in NIT.

JOE B. HALL
Sewanee '51
Cynthiana, Ky.

Reached NCAA Final Four three times—1975 (2nd), 1978 (1st), and 1984 (tied for third).... Led Kentucky to 1976 NIT title.... Coach of 1984 Southeastern Conference Tournament champion.

Year	School	Overall	League	Finish	Postseason
59–60	Regis (Colo.)	10-11			DNP
60–61	Regis (Colo.)	10-10			DNP
61–62	Regis (Colo.)	10-11			DNP
62–63	Regis (Colo.)	15-9			DNP
63–64	Regis (Colo.)	12-9			DNP
64–65	Central Mo. St.	19-6	9-1	1st (MIAA)	NCAA-II (1-1)
72–73	Kentucky	20-8	14-4	1st (SEC)	NCAA (1-1)
73–74	Kentucky	13-13	9-9	T4th (SEC)	DNP
74–75	Kentucky	26-5	15-3	T4th (SEC)	NCAA (4-1)
75–76	Kentucky	20-10	11-7	T4th (SEC)	NIT (4-0)
76–77	Kentucky	26-4	16-2	T1st (SEC)	NCAA (5-0)
77–78	Kentucky	30-2	16-2	1st (SEC)	NCAA (5-0)
78–79	Kentucky	19-12	10-8	6th (SEC)	NIT (0-1)
79–80	Kentucky	29-6	15-3	1st (SEC)	NCAA (1-1)
80–81	Kentucky	22-6	15-3	2d (SEC)	NCAA (0-1)
81–82	Kentucky	22-8	13-5	T1st (SEC)	NCAA (1-1)
82–83	Kentucky	23-8	13-5	1st (SEC)	NCAA (2-1)
83–84	Kentucky	29-5	14-4	1st (SEC)	NCAA (3-1)
84–85	Kentucky	18-13	11-7	T3d (SEC)	NCAA (2-1)

19-Year Coaching Record: 373-156 (.705) overall; 57-50 (.533) in five years at Regis (Colorado); 19-6 (.760) in one year at Central Missouri State; 297-100 (.748) in 13 years at Kentucky; 9-1 (.900) in Missouri Intercollegiate Athletic Association; 172-62 (.735) in Southeastern Conference; 10-6 (.625) in SEC Tournament; 20-9 (.690) in NCAA Tournament; 4-1 (.800) in NIT; 1-1 (.500) in NCAA Division II Tournament.

MARV HARSHMAN
Pacific Lutheran '42
Lake Stevens, Wash.

Named national coach of the year by the NABC in 1984.... Elected to Naismith Memorial Basketball Hall of Fame in 1984.

Year	School	Overall	League	Finish	Postseason
45–46	Pac. Luth.	10-18	3-13	4th (WIAC)	DNP
46–47	Pac. Luth.	15-14	6-6	3d (WIAC)	DNP

Year	School	Overall	League	Finish	Postseason
47–48	Pac. Luth.	17-15	12-3	1st (WIAC)	DNP
48–49	Pac. Luth.	25-7	11-3	T2d (Evergreen)	DNP
49–50	Pac. Luth.	19-8	8-6	4th (Evergreen)	DNP
50–51	Pac. Luth.	20-11	10-4	T2d (Evergreen)	DNP
51–52	Pac. Luth.	22-10	7-5	3d (Evergreen)	DNP
52–53	Pac. Luth.	16-10	8-4	T2d (Evergreen)	DNP
53–54	Pac. Luth.	18-10	8-4	2d (Evergreen)	DNP
54–55	Pac. Luth.	17-6	10-2	T1st (Evergreen)	DNP
55–56	Pac. Luth.	25-6	15-3	1st (Evergreen)	DNP
56–57	Pac. Luth.	28-1	12-0	1st (Evergreen)	DNP
57–58	Pac. Luth.	21-6	12-0	1st (Evergreen)	DNP
58–59	Wash. St.	10-16	3-13	8th (PCC-N)	DNP
59–60	Wash. St.	13-13			DNP
60–61	Wash. St.	10-16			DNP
61–62	Wash. St.	8-18			DNP
62–63	Wash. St.	5-20			DNP
63–64	Wash. St.	5-21	2-13	6th (Pac-8)	DNP
64–65	Wash. St.	9-17	6-8	5th (Pac-8)	DNP
65–66	Wash. St.	15-11	6-8	4th (Pac-8)	DNP
66–67	Wash. St.	15-11	8-6	2d (Pac-8)	DNP
67–68	Wash. St.	16-9	8-6	3d (Pac-8)	DNP
68–69	Wash. St.	18-8	11-3	2d (Pac-8)	DNP
69–70	Wash. St.	19-7	9-5	2d (Pac-8)	DNP
70–71	Wash. St.	12-14	2-12	7th (Pac-8)	DNP
71–72	Washington	20-6	10-4	2d (Pac-8)	DNP
72–73	Washington	16-11	6-8	T5th (Pac-8)	DNP
73–74	Washington	16-10	7-7	4th (Pac-8)	DNP
74–75	Washington	16-10	6-8	T5th (Pac-8)	DNP
75–76	Washington	23-5	10-4	3d (Pac-8)	NCAA (0-1)
76–77	Washington	17-10	8-6	T3d (Pac-8)	DNP
77–78	Washington	14-13	6-8	T5th (Pac-8)	DNP
78–79	Washington	11-16	6-12	T8th (Pac-10)	DNP
79–80	Washington	18-10	9-9	5th (Pac-10)	NIT (0-1)
80–81	Washington	14-13	8-10	T5th (Pac-10)	DNP
81–82	Washington	19-10	11-7	4th (Pac-10)	NIT (1-1)
82–83	Washington	16-15	7-11	T6th (Pac-10)	DNP
83–84	Washington	24-7	15-3	T1st (Pac-10)	NCAA (2-1)
84–85	Washington	22-10	13-5	T1st (Pac-10)	NCAA (0-1)

40-Year Coaching Record: 654-449 (.589) overall; 253-122 (.675) in 13 years at Pacific Lutheran; 155-181 (.461) in 13 years at Washington State; 246-146 (.628) in 14 years at Washington; 21-22 (.488) in Washington Intercollegiate Athletic Conference; 101-31 (.765) in Evergreen Intercollegiate Conference; 176-177 (.499) in Pacific-10 Conference (Pacific Coast-Northern, Pacific-8); 2-3 (.400) in NCAA Tournament; 1-2 (.333) in NIT.

BILL HENDERSON
Howard Payne
Ballinger, Tex. '25

Reached Final Four two times—1948 (2d) and 1950 (4th).... Assistant coach under Ralph Wolf at Baylor.

Year	School	Overall	League	Finish	Postseason
41–42	Baylor	11-9	6-6	T3d (SWC)	DNP
42–43	Baylor	6-14	3-9	7th (SWC)	DNP
45–46	Baylor	25-5	11-1	1st (SWC)	NCAA (0-2)
46–47	Baylor	11-11	6-6	4th (SWC)	DNP
47–48	Baylor	24-8	11-1	1st (SWC)	NCAA (2-1)
48–49	Baylor	14-10	9-3	T1st (SWC)	DNP
49–50	Baylor	14-13	8-4	T1st (SWC)	NCAA (1-2)
50–51	Baylor	8-16	3-9	6th (SWC)	DNP
51–52	Baylor	6-18	5-7	T3d (SWC)	DNP
52–53	Baylor	10-11	6-6	4th (SWC)	DNP
53–54	Baylor	12-11	6-6	3d (SWC)	DNP
54–55	Baylor	13-11	7-5	4th (SWC)	DNP
55–56	Baylor	6-17	3-9	5th (SWC)	DNP
56–57	Baylor	9-15	6-6	3d (SWC)	DNP
57–58	Baylor	5-19	3-11	8th (SWC)	DNP
58–59	Baylor	11-13	7-7	4th (SWC)	DNP
59–60	Baylor	12-12	6-8	6th (SWC)	DNP
60–61	Baylor	4-20	2-12	8th (SWC)	DNP

19-Year Coaching Record: 201-233 (.463) overall; 108-116 (.482) in Southwest Conference; 3-5 (.375) in NCAA Tournament.

CAM HENDERSON
Salem '17
Joe Town, W.V.

Coach of 1947 NAIA Tournament champion.

Year	School	Overall	League	Finish	Postseason
19–20	Muskingum	10-8			
20–21	Muskingum	20-4			
21–22	Muskingum	8-10			
22–23	Muskingum	6-11			
23–24	Davis & Elkins	10-7			
24–25	Davis & Elkins	22-0			
25–26	Davis & Elkins	15-4			
26–27	Davis & Elkins	23-3			
27–28	Davis & Elkins	24-4			
28–29	Davis & Elkins	20-5			
29–30	Davis & Elkins	22-3			
30–31	Davis & Elkins	17-4			
31–32	Davis & Elkins	19-2			
32–33	Davis & Elkins	15-8			
33–34	Davis & Elkins	11-6			
34–35	Davis & Elkins	27-4			
35–36	Marshall	6-10	1-9	T5th (Buckeye)	
36–37	Marshall	23-8	9-1	T1st (Buckeye)	
37–38	Marshall	28-4			NAIA (1-1)
38–39	Marshall	22-5			DNP
39–40	Marshall	25-4			DNP
40–41	Marshall	14-9			DNP
41–42	Marshall	15-9			DNP
42–43	Marshall	10-7			DNP
43–44	Marshall	15-7			DNP
44–45	Marshall	17-9			DNP
45–46	Marshall	24-10			DNP
46–47	Marshall	32-5			NAIA (5-0)
47–48	Marshall	22-11			NAIA (1-1)
48–49	Marshall	16-12	2-2	4th (OVC)	DNP
49–50	Marshall	15-9	5-4	3d (OVC)	DNP
50–51	Marshall	13-13	2-6	6th (OVC)	DNP
51–52	Marshall	15-11	5-7	4th (OVC)	DNP
52–53	Marshall	20-4			DNP
53–54	Marshall	12-9	6-7	4th (MAC)	DNP
54–55	Marshall	17-4	10-4	2d (MAC)	DNP

35-Year Coaching Record: 630-243 (.722) overall; 44-33 (.571) in four years at Muskingum; 225-50 (.818) in 12 years at Davis & Elkins; 361-160 (.693) in 20 years at Marshall; 10-10 (.500) in Buckeye Conference; 14-19 (.424) in Ohio Valley Conference; 16-11 (.593) in Mid-American Conference; 7-2 (.778) in NAIA Tournament.

BERNARD (PECK) HICKMAN
Western Kentucky '35
Central City, Ky.

Coached team to the NIT title in 1956.... Led Louisville to five NCAA Tournament appearances, including a fourth-place finish in 1959.... Coach of 1948 NAIA Tournament champion.

Year	School	Overall	League	Finish	Postseason
44–45	Louisville	16-3		KIAC	DNP
45–46	Louisville	22-6	10-2	2d (KIAC)	DNP
46–47	Louisville	17-6	5-3	5th (KIAC)	DNP
47–48	Louisville	29-6	7-3	2d (KIAC)	NAIB (5-0)
48–49	Louisville	23-10	6-3	3d (OVC)	DNP
49–50	Louisville	21-11			DNP
50–51	Louisville	19-7			NCAA (0-1)
51–52	Louisville	20-6			NIT (0-1)
52–53	Louisville	22-6			NIT (1-1)
53–54	Louisville	22-7			NIT (0-1)
54–55	Louisville	19-8			NIT (1-1)
55–56	Louisville	26-3			NIT (3-0)
56–57	Louisville	21-5			Probation
57–58	Louisville	13-12			DNP
58–59	Louisville	19-12			NCAA (3-2)
59–60	Louisville	15-11			DNP
60–61	Louisville	21-8			NCAA (2-1)
61–62	Louisville	15-10			DNP
62–63	Louisville	14-11			DNP
63–64	Louisville	15-10			NCAA (0-1)
64–65	Louisville	15-10			DNP

| 65–66 | Louisville | 16-10 | | | NIT (0-1) |
| 66–67 | Louisville | 23-5 | | | NCAA (0-2) |

23-Year Coaching Record: 443-183 (.708) overall; 22-8 (.733) in Kentucky Intercollegiate Athletic Conference; 6-3 (.667) in Ohio Valley Conference; 5-3 (.625) in Kentucky Intercollegiate Athletic Conference Tournament; 2-1 (.667) in Ohio Valley Conference Tournament; 5-7 (.417) in NCAA Tournament; 5-5 (.500) in NIT; 5-0 in NAIB.

Note: No regular-season standings, only postseason conference tournament, for the Kentucky Intercollegiate Athletic Conference in 1944–45.

HOWARD HOBSON
Oregon '26
Portland, Oreg.

Elected to Naismith Memorial Basketball Hall of Fame in 1965.... U.S. Olympic team manager in 1952.... Coach of 1939 NCAA champion.

Year	School	Overall	League	Finish	Postseason
32–33	S. Oreg.	19-5			
33–34	S. Oreg	23-5			
34–35	S. Oreg	26-5			
35–36	Oregon	20-11	7-9	4th (PCC-N)	DNP
36–37	Oregon	20-9	11-5	T1st(PCC-N)	DNP
37–38	Oregon	25-8	14-6	1st (PCC-N)	DNP
38–39	Oregon	29-5	14-2	1st (PCC-N)	NCAA (3-0)
39–40	Oregon	19-12	10-6	2d (PCC-N)	DNP
40–41	Oregon	18-18	7-9	T3d (PCC-N)	DNP
41–42	Oregon	12-15	7-9	4th (PCC-N)	DNP
42–43	Oregon	19-10	10-6	2d (PCC-N)	DNP
43–44	Oregon	16-10	11-5	2d (PCC-N)	DNP
45–46	Oregon	16-17	8-8	3d (PCC-N)	DNP
46–47	Oregon	18-9	7-9	4th (PCC-N)	DNP
47–48	Yale	14-13	4-8	6th (EIBL)	DNP
48–49	Yale	22-8	9-3	1st (EIBL)	NCAA (0-2)
49–50	Yale	17-9	7-5	T3d (EIBL)	DNP
50–51	Yale	14-13	4-8	5th (EIBL)	DNP
51–52	Yale	14-14	4-8	T5th (EIBL)	DNP
52–53	Yale	10-15	6-6	T3d (EIBL)	DNP
53–54	Yale	12-14	7-7	4th (EIBL)	DNP
54–55	Yale	3-21	3-11	T6th (Ivy)	DNP
55–56	Yale	15-11	7-7	T5th (Ivy)	DNP

23-Year Coaching Record: 401-257 (.609) overall; 68-15 (.819) in three years at Southern Oregon; 212-124 (.631) in 11 years at Oregon; 121-118 (.506) in nine years at Yale; 106-74 (.589) in Pacific Coast Conference; 51-63 (.447) in Ivy League (Eastern Intercollegiate Basketball League); 3-2 (.600) in NCAA Tournament.

TERRY HOLLAND
Davidson '64
Clinton, N.C.

Reached NCAA Final Four with Virginia in 1981 (3d) and 1984 (tied for 3d).... Coach of 1980 NIT champion.... Coach of 1970 Southern Conference Tournament champion with Davidson and 1976 Atlantic Coast Conference Tournament champion with Virginia.... Assistant coach under Lefty Driesell at Davidson from 1969–70 through 1973–74.

Year	School	Overall	League	Finish	Postseason
69–70	Davidson	22-5	10-0	1st (Southern)	NCAA (0-1)
70–71	Davidson	15-11	9-1	1st (Southern)	DNP
71–72	Davidson	19-9	8-2	1st (Southern)	NIT (0-1)
72–73	Davidson	18-9	9-1	1st (Southern)	DNP
73–74	Davidson	18-9	7-3	3d (Southern)	DNP
74–75	Virginia	12-13	4-8	5th (ACC)	DNP
75–76	Virginia	18-12	4-8	6th (ACC)	NCAA (0-1)
76–77	Virginia	12-17	2-10	6th (ACC)	DNP
77–78	Virginia	20-8	6-6	4th (ACC)	NIT (0-1)
78–79	Virginia	19-10	7-5	3d (ACC)	NIT (1-1)
79–80	Virginia	24-10	7-7	5th (ACC)	NIT (5-0)
80–81	Virginia	29-4	13-1	1st (ACC)	NCAA (4-1)
81–82	Virginia	30-4	12-2	1st (ACC)	NCAA (1-1)
82–83	Virginia	29-5	12-2	1st (ACC)	NCAA (2-1)
83–84	Virginia	21-12	6-8	5th (ACC)	NCAA (4-1)
84–85	Virginia	17-16	3-11	8th (ACC)	NIT (2-1)
85–86	Virginia	19-11	7-7	4th (ACC)	NCAA (0-1)

86–87	Virginia	21-10	8-6	4th (ACC)	NCAA (0-1)
87–88	Virginia	13-18	5-9	6th (ACC)	DNP
88–89	Virginia	22-11	9-5	T2d (ACC)	NCAA (3-1)
89–90	Virginia	20-12	6-8	T4th (ACC)	NCAA (1-1)

21-Year Coaching Record: 418-216 (.659) overall; 92-43 (.681) in five years at Davidson; 326-173 (.653) in 16 years at Virginia; 43-7 (.860) in Southern Conference; 111-103 (.519) in Atlantic Coast Conference; 15-15 (.500) in ACC Tournament; 7-4 (.636) in Southern Conference Tournament; 15-10 (.600) in NCAA Tournament; 8-4 (.667) in NIT.

NAT HOLMAN
Savage School of Phys.
  Ed. '17
New York, N.Y.

Elected to Naismith Memorial Basketball Hall of Fame in 1964.... Coach of NCAA and NIT titlists in 1950, the only time a team won both crowns in the same year. Also finished fourth in 1947 NCAA Tournament.... Coach of 1941 NIT third-place finisher.

Year	School	Overall	League	Finish	Postseason
19–20	CCNY	13-3			
20–21	CCNY	11-4			
21–22	CCNY	10-2			
22–23	CCNY	12-1			
23–24	CCNY	12-1			
24–25	CCNY	12-2			
25–26	CCNY	9-5			
26–27	CCNY	9-3			
27–28	CCNY	11-4			
28–29	CCNY	9-5			
29–30	CCNY	11-3			
30–31	CCNY	12-4			
31–32	CCNY	16-1			
32–33	CCNY	13-1			
33–34	CCNY	14-1			
34–35	CCNY	10-6			
35–36	CCNY	10-4			
36–37	CCNY	10-6			
37–38	CCNY	13-3			DNP
38–39	CCNY	11-6			DNP
39–40	CCNY	8-8			DNP
40–41	CCNY	17-5			NIT (2-1)
41–42	CCNY	16-3			NIT (0-1)
42–43	CCNY	8-10			DNP
43–44	CCNY	6-11			DNP
44–45	CCNY	12-4			DNP
45–46	CCNY	14-4			DNP
46–47	CCNY	17-6			NCAA (1-2)
47–48	CCNY	18-3			DNP
48–49	CCNY	17-8			NIT (0-1)
49–50	CCNY	24-5			NCAA (3-0); NIT (4-0)
50–51	CCNY	12-7			DNP
51–52	CCNY	8-11			DNP
54–55	CCNY	8-10			DNP
55–56	CCNY	4-14			DNP
58–59	CCNY	6-12			DNP
59–60	CCNY	0-4			DNP

37-Year Coaching Record: 423-190 (.690) overall; 4-2 (.667) in NCAA Tournament; 6-3 (.667) in NIT.

HENRY (HANK) IBA
Westminster, Mo. '28
Easton, Mo.

Elected to Naismith Memorial Basketball Hall of Fame in 1968.... U.S. Olympic Team coach in 1964, 1968, and 1972.... Reached Final Four on four occasions—1945 (1st), 1946 (1st), 1949 (2d), and 1951 (4th).... Coach of three teams that reached NIT semifinals—1938 (3d), 1940 (3d), and 1944 (4th).... Holds the NCAA career record for most games coached at 1,105.

Year	School	Overall	League	Finish	Postseason
29–30	NW Mo. St.	31-0	16-0	1st (MIAA)	
30–31	NW Mo. St.	32-6	3-5	T3d (MIAA)	
31–32	NW Mo. St.	26-2	7-1	1st (MIAA)	
32–33	NW Mo. St.	12-6	6-2	1st (MIAA)	
33–34	Colorado	11-8	7-5	2d (RMC)	
34–35	Okla. St.	9-9	5-7	T5th (MVC)	
35–36	Okla. St.	16-8	8-4	T1st (MVC)	
36–37	Okla. St.	20-3	11-1	1st (MVC)	
37–38	Okla. St.	25-3	13-1	1st (MVC)	NIT (1-1)
38–39	Okla. St.	19-8	11-3	T1st (MVC)	DNP
39–40	Okla. St.	26-3	12-0	1st (MVC)	NIT (1-1)
40–41	Okla. St.	18-7	8-4	2d (MVC)	DNP
41–42	Okla. St.	20-6	9-1	T1st (MVC)	DNP
42–43	Okla. St.	14-10	7-3	T2d (MVC)	DNP
43–44	Okla. St.	27-6		Mo. Valley	NIT (1-2)
44–45	Okla. St.	27-4		Mo. Valley	NCAA (3-0)
45–46	Okla. St.	31-2	12-0	1st (MVC)	NCAA (3-0)
46–47	Okla. St.	24-8	8-4	T2d (MVC)	DNP
47–48	Okla. St.	27-4	10-0	1st (MVC)	DNP
48–49	Okla. St.	23-5	9-1	1st (MVC)	NCAA (2-1)
49–50	Okla. St.	18-9	7-5	T3d (MVC)	DNP
50–51	Okla. St.	29-6	12-2	1st (MVC)	NCAA (2-2)
51–52	Okla. St.	19-8	7-3	2d (MVC)	DNP
52–53	Okla. St.	23-7	8-2	1st (MVC)	NCAA (1-1)
53–54	Okla. St.	24-5	9-1	1st (MVC)	NCAA (1-1)
54–55	Okla. St.	12-13	5-5	3d (MVC)	DNP
55–56	Okla. St.	18-9	8-4	T2d (MVC)	NIT (0-1)
56–57	Okla. St.	17-9	8-6	T3d (MVC)	DNP
57–58	Okla. St.	21-8			NCAA (2-1)
58–59	Okla. St.	11-14	5-9	T5th (Big Eight)	DNP
59–60	Okla. St.	10-15	4-10	T7th (Big Eight)	DNP
60–61	Okla. St.	15-10	9-5	3d (Big Eight)	DNP
61–62	Okla. St.	14-11	7-7	4th (Big Eight)	DNP
62–63	Okla. St.	16-9	7-7	5th (Big Eight)	DNP
63–64	Okla. St.	15-10	7-7	T4th (Big Eight)	DNP
64–65	Okla. St.	20-7	12-2	1st (Big Eight)	NCAA (1-1)
65–66	Okla. St.	4-21	2-12	7th (Big Eight)	DNP
66–67	Okla. St.	7-18	2-12	7th (Big Eight)	DNP
67–68	Okla. St.	10-16	3-11	T7th (Big Eight)	DNP
68–69	Okla. St.	12-13	5-9	T6th (Big Eight)	DNP
69–70	Okla. St.	14-12	5-9	T7th (Big Eight)	DNP

41-Year Coaching Record: 767-338 (.694) overall; 101-14 (.878) in four years at Northwest Missouri St.; 11-8 (.579) in one year at Colorado; 655-316 (.675) in 36 years at Oklahoma St.; 32-8 (.800) in Missouri Intercollegiate Athletic Association; 7-5 (.583) in Rocky Mountain Conference; 187-57 (.766) in Missouri Valley Conference; 68-100 (.405) in Big Eight Conference; 15-7 (.682) in NCAA Tournament; 3-5 (.375) in NIT.

GEORGE IRELAND
Notre Dame '36
Prairie du Chien, Wisc.

Coach of 1963 NCAA champion and 1962 NIT third-place finisher.

Year	School	Overall	League	Finish	Postseason
51–52	Loyola (Ill.)	17-8			DNP
52–53	Loyola (Ill.)	8-15			DNP
53–54	Loyola (Ill.)	7-15			DNP
54–55	Loyola (Ill.)	13-11			DNP
55–56	Loyola (Ill.)	10-14			DNP
56–57	Loyola (Ill.)	14-10			DNP
57–58	Loyola (Ill.)	16-8			DNP
58–59	Loyola (Ill.)	11-13			DNP
59–60	Loyola (Ill.)	10-12			DNP
60–61	Loyola (Ill.)	15-8			DNP
61–62	Loyola (Ill.)	23-4			NIT (2-1)
62–63	Loyola (Ill.)	29-2			NCAA (5-0)
63–64	Loyola (Ill.)	22-6			NCAA (2-1)
64–65	Loyola (Ill.)	11-14			DNP
65–66	Loyola (Ill.)	22-3			NCAA (0-1)
66–67	Loyola (Ill.)	13-9			DNP
67–68	Loyola (Ill.)	15-9			NCAA (0-1)
68–69	Loyola (Ill.)	9-14			DNP
69–70	Loyola (Ill.)	13-11			DNP
70–71	Loyola (Ill.)	4-20			DNP
71–72	Loyola (Ill.)	8-14			DNP
72–73	Loyola (Ill.)	8-15			DNP
73–74	Loyola (Ill.)	12-14			DNP
74–75	Loyola (Ill.)	8-6			DNP

24-Year Coaching Record: 318-255 (.555) overall; 7-3 (.700) in NCAA Tournament; 2-1 (.667) in NIT.

ED JUCKER
Cincinnati '40
Cincinnati, Ohio

Named national coach of the year by UPI and the USBWA in 1963.... Led Cincinnati to three consecutive Final Four appearances—1961 (1st), 1962 (1st), and 1963 (2d).... Holds the NCAA Tournament all-time record (minimum of 10 games) for highest winning percentage at 91.7% (11-1).

Year	School	Overall	League	Finish	Postseason
45–46	King's Pt.	14-0			DNP
46–47	King's Pt.	12-4			DNP
48–49	Rensselaer	13-3			DNP
49–50	Rensselaer	12-3			DNP
50–51	Rensselaer	9-9			DNP
51–52	Rensselaer	4-11			DNP
52–53	Rensselaer	8-9			DNP
60–61	Cincinnati	27-3	10-2	1st (MVC)	NCAA (4-0)
61–62	Cincinnati	29-2	10-2	T1st (MVC)	NCAA (4-0)
62–63	Cincinnati	26-2	11-1	1st (MVC)	NCAA (3-1)
63–64	Cincinnati	17-9	6-6	T4th (MVC)	DNP
64–65	Cincinnati	14-12	5-9	7th (MVC)	DNP
72–73	Rollins	13-11			DNP
73–74	Rollins	18-9			NCAA II (1-2)
74–75	Rollins	15-7			DNP
75–76	Rollins	19-6	8-2	2d (Sunshine)	NCAA II(1-1)
76–77	Rollins	16-9	6-4	T2d (Sunshine)	

17-Year Coaching Record: 266-109 (.709) overall; 26-4 (.867) in two years at King's Point; 46-35 (.568) in five years at Rensselaer; 113-28 (.801) in five years at Cincinnati; 81-42 (.659) in five years at Rollins; 42-20 (.667) in Missouri Valley Conference; 14-6 (.700) in Sunshine St. Conference; 11-1 (.917) in NCAA Tournament; 2-3 (.400) in NCAA Division II Tournament.

ALVIN (DOGGIE) JULIAN
Bucknell '23
Reading, Pa.

Elected to Naismith Memorial Basketball Hall of Fame in 1967.... Led Holy Cross to two NCAA Final Four appearances—1947 (1st) and 1948 (3d).... Compiled a 47-81 record as coach of the NBA's Boston Celtics in 1948–49 and 1949–50.

Year	School	Overall	League	Finish	Postseason
27–28	Albright	6-13			
28–29	Albright	3-13			
36–37	Muhlenberg	9-9			
37–38	Muhlenberg	9-11			
38–39	Muhlenberg	13-8			
39–40	Muhlenberg	11-9			
40–41	Muhlenberg	13-10			
41–42	Muhlenberg	17-7	9-3	2d (Eastern Pa.)	
42–43	Muhlenberg	13-8	7-3	2d (Eastern Pa.)	
43–44	Muhlenberg	20-5			NIT (0-1)
44–45	Muhlenberg	24-4			DNP
45–46	Holy Cross	12-3			DNP
46–47	Holy Cross	27-3			NCAA (3-0)
47–48	Holy Cross	26-4			NCAA (2-1)
50–51	Dartmouth	3-23	1-11	7th (EIBL)	DNP
51–52	Dartmouth	11-19	4-8	T5th (EIBL)	DNP
52–53	Dartmouth	12-14	5-7	T5th (EIBL)	DNP
53–54	Dartmouth	13-13	5-9	6th (EIBL)	DNP
54–55	Dartmouth	18-7	9-5	4th (Ivy)	DNP
55–56	Dartmouth	18-11	10-4	1st (Ivy)	NCAA (2-1)
56–57	Dartmouth	18-7	10-4	2d (Ivy)	DNP
57–58	Dartmouth	22-5	11-3	1st (Ivy)	NCAA (2-1)
58–59	Dartmouth	22-6	14-1	1st (Ivy)	NCAA (0-1)
59–60	Dartmouth	14-9	10-4	2d (Ivy)	DNP
60–61	Dartmouth	5-19	4-10	T6th (Ivy)	DNP

61–62	Dartmouth	6-18	3-11	T6th (Ivy)	DNP
62–63	Dartmouth	7-18	2-12	8th (Ivy)	DNP
63–64	Dartmouth	2-23	0-14	8th (Ivy)	DNP
64–65	Dartmouth	4-21	1-13	8th (Ivy)	DNP
65–66	Dartmouth	3-21	0-14	8th (Ivy)	DNP
66–67	Dartmouth	7-17	1-13	8th (Ivy)	DNP

32-Year College Coaching Record: 388-358 (.520) overall; 9-26 (.257) in two years at Albright; 129-71 (.645) in nine years at Muhlenberg; 65-10 (.867) in three years at Holy Cross; 185-251 (.424) in 17 years at Dartmouth; 16-6 (.727) in Eastern Pennsylvania Collegiate League; 90-143 (.386) in Ivy League (Eastern Intercollegiate Basketball League); 9-4 (.692) in NCAA Tournament; 0-1 in NIT Tournament.

FRANK KEANEY
Bates '11
Boston, Mass.

Led Rhode Island to a fourth-place finish in 1945 NIT and a second-place finish in 1946 NIT.... Elected to Naismith Memorial Basketball Hall of Fame in 1960.

Year	School	Overall	League	Finish	Postseason
21–22	Rhode I.	3-7			
22–23	Rhode I.	9-4			
23–24	Rhode I.	9-6			
24–25	Rhode I.	11-5			
25–26	Rhode I.	8-8			
26–27	Rhode I.	13-4			
27–28	Rhode I.	15-5			
28–29	Rhode I.	15-1			
29–30	Rhode I.	10-5			
30–31	Rhode I.	13-4			
31–32	Rhode I.	13-3			
32–33	Rhode I.	14-4			
33–34	Rhode I.	13-3			
34–35	Rhode I.	12-6			
35–36	Rhode I.	13-5			
36–37	Rhode I.	18-3	8-0	1st (New England)	
37–38	Rhode I.	19-2	8-0	1st (New England)	DNP
38–39	Rhode I.	17-4	7-1	1st (New England)	DNP
39–40	Rhode I.	19-3	8-0	1st (New England)	DNP
40–41	Rhode I.	21-4	7-1	T1st (New England)	NIT (0-1)
41–42	Rhode I.	18-4	8-0	1st (New England)	NIT (0-1)
42–43	Rhode I.	16-3	7-1	1st (New England)	DNP
43–44	Rhode I.	14-6		New England	DNP
44–45	Rhode I.	20-5		New England	NIT (1-2)
45–46	Rhode I.	21-3	4-0	1st (New England)	NIT (2-1)
46–47	Rhode I.	17-3	4-1	3d (Yankee)	DNP
47–48	Rhode I.	16-7	5-1	2d (Yankee)	DNP

27-Year Coaching Record: 387-117 (.768) overall; 57-3 (.950) in New England Conference; 9-2 (.818) in Yankee Conference; 3-5 (.375) in NIT.

GEORGE KEOGAN
Minnesota
Detroit Lakes, Minn.

Coach of Notre Dame teams in 1927 and 1936 that were selected as national champions by the Helms Foundation.... Elected to Naismith Memorial Basketball Hall of Fame in 1961.

Year	School	Overall	League	Finish	Postseason
15–16	St. Louis	13-6			
18–19	Allegheny	14-1			
19–20	Valparaiso	12-8			
20–21	Valparaiso	19-5			
23–24	Notre Dame	15-8			
24–25	Notre Dame	11-11			
25–26	Notre Dame	19-1			
26–27	Notre Dame	19-1			
27–28	Notre Dame	18-4			
28–29	Notre Dame	15-5			
29–30	Notre Dame	14-6			
30–31	Notre Dame	12-8			
31–32	Notre Dame	18-2			
32–33	Notre Dame	16-6			
33–34	Notre Dame	20-4			
34–35	Notre Dame	13-9			
35–36	Notre Dame	22-2-1			
36–37	Notre Dame	20-3			
37–38	Notre Dame	20-3			DNP
38–39	Notre Dame	15-6			DNP
39–40	Notre Dame	15-6			DNP
40–41	Notre Dame	17-5			DNP
41–42	Notre Dame	16-6			DNP
42–43	Notre Dame	12-1			DNP

24-Year Coaching Record: 385-117 (.767) overall; 13-6 (.684) in one year at St. Louis; 14-1 (.933) in one year at Allegheny; 31-13 (.705) in two years at Valparaiso; 327-97 (.771) in 20 years at Notre Dame.

WARD (PIGGY) LAMBERT
Wabash '11
Crawfordsville, Ind.

Coach of 1932 team that was selected as national champion by the Helms Foundation.... Elected to Naismith Memorial Basketball Hall of Fame in 1960.

Year	School	Overall	League	Finish	Postseason
16–17	Purdue	11-3	7-2	3d (Big Ten)	
18–19	Purdue	6-8	4-7	7th (Big Ten)	
19–20	Purdue	16-4	8-2	2d (Big Ten)	
20–21	Purdue	13-7	8-4	T1st (Big Ten)	
21–22	Purdue	15-3	8-1	1st (Big Ten)	
22–23	Purdue	9-6	7-5	T4th (Big Ten)	
23–24	Purdue	12-5	7-5	T4th (Big Ten)	
24–25	Purdue	9-5	7-4	4th (Big Ten)	
25–26	Purdue	13-4	8-4	T1st (Big Ten)	
26–27	Purdue	12-5	9-3	T2d (Big Ten)	
27–28	Purdue	15-2	10-2	T1st (Big Ten)	
28–29	Purdue	13-4	9-3	3d (Big Ten)	
29–30	Purdue	13-2	10-0	1st (Big Ten)	
30–31	Purdue	12-5	8-4	2d (Big Ten)	
31–32	Purdue	17-1	11-1	1st (Big Ten)	
32–33	Purdue	11-7	6-6	T5th (Big Ten)	
33–34	Purdue	17-3	10-2	1st (Big Ten)	
34–35	Purdue	17-3	9-3	T1st (Big Ten)	
35–36	Purdue	16-4	11-1	T1st (Big Ten)	
36–37	Purdue	15-5	8-4	4th (Big Ten)	
37–38	Purdue	18-2	10-2	1st (Big Ten)	DNP
38–39	Purdue	12-7	6-6	5th (Big Ten)	DNP
39–40	Purdue	16-4	10-2	1st (Big Ten)	DNP
40–41	Purdue	13-7	6-6	6th (Big Ten)	DNP
41–42	Purdue	14-7	9-6	T5th (Big Ten)	DNP
42–43	Purdue	9-11	6-6	T4th (Big Ten)	DNP
43–44	Purdue	11-10	8-4	T4th (Big Ten)	DNP
44–45	Purdue	9-11	6-6	4th (Big Ten)	DNP
45–46	Purdue	7-7	2-4	8th (Big Ten)	DNP

29-Year Coaching Record: 371-152 (.709) overall; 228-105 (.685) in Big Ten Conference.

JOE LAPCHICK
Did not attend college
New York, N.Y.

Led St. John's to NIT titles in 1943, 1944, 1959, and 1965.... Elected to Naismith Memorial Basketball Hall of Fame in 1966.... Compiled a 326-247 record (.569) as coach of the New York Knicks for nine seasons (1947–48 through 1955–56), reaching the NBA Finals in 1951 and 1952.

Year	School	Overall	League	Finish	Postseason
36–37	St. John's	13-7			
37–38	St. John's	15-4			DNP
38–39	St. John's	18-4			NIT (1-2)
39–40	St. John's	15-4			NIT (0-1)
40–41	St. John's	11-6			DNP
41–42	St. John's	16-5			DNP
42–43	St. John's	21-3			NIT (3-0)
43–44	St. John's	18-5			NIT (3-0)
44–45	St. John's	21-3			NIT (2-1)
45–46	St. John's	17-6			NIT (0-1)
46–47	St. John's	16-7			NIT (0-1)
56–57	St. John's	14-9			DNP

Year	School	Overall			Postseason
57–58	St. John's	18-8			NIT (2-2)
58–59	St. John's	20-6			NIT (4-0)
59–60	St. John's	17-8			NIT (0-1)
60–61	St. John's	20-5			NCAA (0-1)
61–62	St. John's	21-5			NIT (2-1)
62–63	St. John's	9-15			DNP
63–64	St. John's	14-11			DNP
64–65	St. John's	21-8			NIT (4-0)

20-Year Coaching Record: 335-129 (.722) overall; 0-1 in NCAA Tournament; 21-10 (.677) in NIT.

GUY LEWIS
Houston '47
Arp, Tex.

Named national coach of the year by AP, UPI, and the USBWA in 1968, and again by AP in 1983.... Reached NCAA Final Four five times—1967 (3d), 1968 (4th), 1982 (tied for 3d), 1983 (2d), and 1984 (2d).... Coach of four Southwest Conference Tournament champions—1978, 1981, 1983, and 1984.... Assistant under Alden Pasche at Houston for three seasons from 1953–54 through 1955–56.

Year	School	Overall	League	Finish	Postseason
56–57	Houston	10-16	5-9	5th (MVC)	NCAA (0-2)
57–58	Houston	9-16	4-10	6th (MVC)	DNP
58–59	Houston	12-14	6-8	5th (MVC)	DNP
59–60	Houston	13-12	6-8	4th (MVC)	DNP
60–61	Houston	17-11			NCAA (1-2)
61–62	Houston	21-6			NIT (0-1)
62–63	Houston	15-11			DNP
63–64	Houston	16-10			DNP
64–65	Houston	19-10			NCAA (1-2)
65–66	Houston	23-6			NCAA (2-1)
66–67	Houston	27-4			NCAA (4-1)
67–68	Houston	31-2			NCAA (3-2)
68–69	Houston	16-10			DNP
69–70	Houston	25-5			NCAA (1-2)
70–71	Houston	22-7			NCAA (2-1)
71–72	Houston	20-7			NCAA (0-1)
72–73	Houston	23-4			NCAA (0-1)
73–74	Houston	17-9			DNP
74–75	Houston	16-10			DNP
75–76	Houston	17-11	7-9	6th (SWC)	DNP
76–77	Houston	29-8	13-3	2d (SWC)	NIT (3-1)
77–78	Houston	25-8	11-5	3d (SWC)	NCAA (0-1)
78–79	Houston	16-15	6-10	T6th (SWC)	DNP
79–80	Houston	14-14	8-8	T4th (SWC)	DNP
80–81	Houston	21-9	10-6	T2d (SWC)	NCAA (0-1)
81–82	Houston	25-8	11-5	2d (SWC)	NCAA (4-1)
82–83	Houston	31-3	16-0	1st (SWC)	NCAA (4-1)
83–84	Houston	32-5	15-1	1st (SWC)	NCAA (4-1)
84–85	Houston	16-14	8-8	T5th (SWC)	NIT (0-1)
85–86	Houston	14-14	8-8	6th (SWC)	DNP

30-Year Coaching Record: 592-279 (.680) overall; 21-35 (.375) in Missouri Valley Conference; 113-63 (.642) in Southwest Conference; 18-7 (.720) in SWC Tournament; 26-18 (.591) in NCAA Tournament; 3-3 (.500) in NIT.

HARRY LITWACK
Temple '30
Philadelphia, Pa.

Elected to Naismith Memorial Basketball Hall of Fame in 1975.... Led team to 1969 NIT title and third-place finish in 1957 NIT.... Reached NCAA Final Four two times—1956 (3d) and 1958 (3d).... Assistant coach at Temple under Jimmy Usilton, Ernie Messikomer, and Josh Cody.... Assistant under Ed Gottlieb of the NBA's Philadelphia Warriors in 1950–51.

Year	School	Overall	League	Finish	Postseason
52–53	Temple	16-10			DNP
53–54	Temple	15-12			DNP
54–55	Temple	11-10			DNP
55–56	Temple	27-4			NCAA (4-1)
56–57	Temple	20-9			NIT (2-1)
57–58	Temple	27-3			NCAA (3-1)
58–59	Temple	6-19	4-7	9th (Mid. Atl.)	DNP
59–60	Temple	17-9	9-2	3d (Mid. Atl.)	NIT (0-1)
60–61	Temple	20-8	9-1	2d (Mid. Atl.)	NIT (1-1)
61–62	Temple	18-9	8-2	2d (Mid. Atl.)	NIT (1-1)
62–63	Temple	15-7	6-3	4th (Mid. Atl.)	DNP
63–64	Temple	17-8	6-1	1st (Mid. Atl.)	NCAA (0-1)
64–65	Temple	14-10		4th (Mid. Atl.)	DNP
65–66	Temple	21-7		2d (Mid. Atl.)	NIT (1-1)
66–67	Temple	20-8		1st (Mid. Atl.)	NCAA (0-1)
67–68	Temple	19-9		3d (Mid. Atl.)	NIT (0-1)
68–69	Temple	22-8		1st (Mid. Atl.)	NIT (4-0)
69–70	Temple	15-13	2-3	T2d (Mid. Atl.-E)	NCAA (0-1)
70–71	Temple	13-12	3-3	4th (Mid. Atl.-E)	DNP
71–72	Temple	23-8	6-0	1st (Mid. Atl.-E)	NCAA (0-1)
72–73	Temple	17-10	5-1	2d (Mid. Atl.-E)	DNP

21-Year Coaching Record: 373-193 (.659) overall; 58-23 (.716) in Middle Atlantic Conference; 7-6 (.538) in NCAA Tournament; 9-6 (.600) in NIT.

KEN LOEFFLER
Penn St. '24
Beaver Falls, Pa.

Led La Salle to 1952 NIT championship and 1954 NCAA title. Also directed team to second-place finish in 1955 NCAA Tournament.... Elected to the Naismith Memorial Basketball Hall of Fame in 1964.... Coach of the NBA's St. Louis Bombers in 1946–47 and 1947–48 and Providence Steamrollers in 1948–49, guiding Bombers to the league's best regular-season record in 1947–48.

Year	School	Overall	League	Finish	Postseason
28–29	Geneva	14-5			
29–30	Geneva	10-9			
30–31	Geneva	13-10			
31–32	Geneva	13-7		(Eastern Pa.)	
32–33	Geneva	13-6	10-2	1st (Eastern Pa.)	
33–34	Geneva	13-9	11-1	1st (Eastern Pa.)	
34–35	Geneva	16-7			
35–36	Yale	8-16	6-6	3d (Ivy)	
36–37	Yale	12-8	7-5	3d (Ivy)	
37–38	Yale	7-12	3-9	7th (Ivy)	DNP
38–39	Yale	4-16	3-9	6th (Ivy)	DNP
39–40	Yale	13-6	7-5	3d (Ivy)	DNP
40–41	Yale	10-12	4-8	4th (Ivy)	DNP
41–42	Yale	7-12	3-9	6th (Ivy)	DNP
49–50	La Salle	21-4			NIT (1-1)
50–51	La Salle	22-7			NIT (0-1)
51–52	La Salle	24-5			NIT (4-0)
52–53	La Salle	25-3			NIT (0-1)
53–54	La Salle	26-4			NCAA (5-0)
54–55	La Salle	26-5			NCAA (4-1)
55–56	Texas A&M	6-18	3-9	T5th (SWC)	DNP
56–57	Texas A&M	7-17	3-9	T6th (SWC)	Probation

22-Year College Coaching Record: 310-198 (.610) overall; 92-53 (.634) in seven years at Geneva; 61-82 (.427) in seven years at Yale; 144-28 (.837) in six years at La Salle; 13-35 (.271) in two years at Texas A&M; 33-51 (.393) in Eastern Intercollegiate Basketball League (forerunner of Ivy League); 6-18 (.250) in Southwest Conference; 9-1 (.900) in NCAA Tournament; 5-3 (.625) in NIT.

BRANCH McCRACKEN

Indiana '30
Monrovia, Ind.

Led Indiana to two NCAA Tournament championships—1940 and 1953.... Only coach to participate in at least two Final Fours and win all of his games there.... Elected to Naismith Memorial Basketball Hall of Fame as a player in 1960.

Year	School	Overall	League	Finish	Postseason
30–31	Ball St.	9-5	8-5	6th (Ind. Col.)	
31–32	Ball St.	9-7		(Indiana Col.)	
32–33	Ball St.	7-9		(Indiana Col.)	
33–34	Ball St.	9-10		(Indiana Col.)	
34–35	Ball St.	9-9		(Indiana Col.)	
35–36	Ball St.	13-7		3d (Indiana Col.)	
36–37	Ball St.	13-6		(Indiana Col.)	
37–38	Ball St.	17-4		(Indiana Col.)	DNP
38–39	Indiana	17-3	9-3	2d (Western)	DNP
39–40	Indiana	20-3	9-3	2d (Western)	NCAA (3-0)
40–41	Indiana	17-3	10-2	2d (Western)	DNP
41–42	Indiana	15-6	10-5	2d (Western)	DNP
42–43	Indiana	18-2	11-2	2d (Western)	DNP
46–47	Indiana	12-8	8-4	T2d (Western)	DNP
47–48	Indiana	8-12	3-9	T8th (Western)	DNP
48–49	Indiana	14-8	6-6	T4th (Big Ten)	DNP
49–50	Indiana	17-5	7-5	T3d (Big Ten)	DNP
50–51	Indiana	19-3	12-2	2d (Big Ten)	DNP
51–52	Indiana	16-6	9-5	4th (Big Ten)	DNP
52–53	Indiana	23-3	17-1	1st (Big Ten)	NCAA (4-0)
53–54	Indiana	20-4	12-2	1st (Big Ten)	NCAA (1-1)
54–55	Indiana	8-14	5-9	T6th (Big Ten)	DNP
55–56	Indiana	13-9	6-8	T6th (Big Ten)	DNP
56–57	Indiana	14-8	10-4	T1st (Big Ten)	DNP
57–58	Indiana	13-11	10-4	1st (Big Ten)	NCAA (1-1)
58–59	Indiana	11-11	7-7	T5th (Big Ten)	DNP
59–60	Indiana	20-4	11-3	2d (Big Ten)	DNP
60–61	Indiana	15-9	8-6	T4th (Big Ten)	Probation
61–62	Indiana	13-11	7-7	T4th (Big Ten)	Probation
62–63	Indiana	13-11	9-5	3d (Big Ten)	Probation
63–64	Indiana	9-15	5-9	8th (Big Ten)	Probation
64–65	Indiana	19-5	9-5	4th (Big Ten)	DNP

32-Year Coaching Record: 450-231 (.661) overall; 86-57 (.601) in eight years at Ball State; 364-174 (.677) in 24 years at Indiana; 210-116 (.644) in Big Ten Conference; 9-2 (.818) in NCAA Tournament.

AL McGUIRE

St. John's '51
Brooklyn, N.Y.

Named national coach of the year by AP, UPI, and the USBWA in 1971, and by the NABC in 1974.... Coached Marquette to the NIT title in 1970 and the NCAA championship in 1977. His 1974 Marquette squad finished runner-up to North Carolina State in the NCAA Tournament and his 1967 team lost to Southern Illinois in the NIT final.... Elected to Naismith Memorial Basketball Hall of Fame in 1991.... Assistant coach at Dartmouth under Doggie Julian.

Year	School	Overall	League	Finish	Postseason
57–58	Belmont Abbey	24-3			
58–59	Belmont Abbey	21-2			
59–60	Belmont Abbey	19-6			
60–61	Belmont Abbey	17-7			
61–62	Belmont Abbey	16-9			NAIA (0-1)
62–63	Belmont Abbey	6-19			
63–64	Belmont Abbey	6-18			
64–65	Marquette	8-18			DNP
65–66	Marquette	14-12			DNP
66–67	Marquette	21-9			NIT (3-1)
67–68	Marquette	23-6			NCAA (2-1)
68–69	Marquette	24-5			NCAA (2-1)
69–70	Marquette	26-3			NIT (4-0)
70–71	Marquette	28-1			NCAA (2-1)
71–72	Marquette	25-4			NCAA (1-2)
72–73	Marquette	25-4			NCAA (2-1)
73–74	Marquette	26-5			NCAA (4-1)
74–75	Marquette	23-4			NCAA (0-1)
75–76	Marquette	27-2			NCAA (2-1)
76–77	Marquette	26-6			NCAA (5-0)

20-Year Coaching Record: 405-143 (.739) overall; 110-63 (.636) in seven years at Belmont Abbey; 295-80 (.787) in 13 years at Marquette; 20-9 (.690) in NCAA Tournament; 7-1 (.875) in NIT; 0-1 in NAIA Tournament.

FRANK McGUIRE

St. John's '36
New York, N.Y.

Coached 11 years at St. Xavier H.S. (126-39).... Only coach to win more than 100 games for three colleges—St. John's (103), North Carolina (164), and South Carolina (283).... Directed North Carolina to an undefeated record (32-0) en route to the 1957 NCAA Tournament title.... Led St. John's to back-to-back NIT third-place finishes in 1950 and 1951.... Named national coach of the year by UPI in 1957.... Also served as head baseball coach at St. John's, where he took the Redmen to the 1949 College World Series.... Elected to Naismith Memorial Basketball Hall of Fame in 1976.... Guided North Carolina to 1957 ACC Tournament title and South Carolina to the 1971 ACC Tournament championship.... Compiled 49-31 regular-season record for the NBA's Philadelphia Warriors in 1961–62.

Year	School	Overall	League	Finish	Postseason
47–48	St. John's	12-11			DNP
48–49	St. John's	16-9			NIT (0-1)
49–50	St. John's	24-5			NIT (2-1)
50–51	St. John's	26-5			NCAA (2-1); NIT (2-1)
51–52	St. John's	25-5			NCAA (3-1); NIT (0-1)
52–53	N. Carolina	17-10	15-6	8th (Southern)	DNP
53–54	N. Carolina	11-10	5-6	5th (ACC)	DNP
54–55	N. Carolina	10-11	8-6	T4th (ACC)	DNP
55–56	N. Carolina	18-5	11-3	T1st (ACC)	DNP
56–57	N. Carolina	32-0	14-0	1st (ACC)	NCAA (5-0)
57–58	N. Carolina	19-7	10-4	T2d (ACC)	DNP
58–59	N. Carolina	20-5	12-2	T1st (ACC)	NCAA (0-1)
59–60	N. Carolina	18-6	12-2	T1st (ACC)	DNP
60–61	N. Carolina	19-4	12-2	1st (ACC)	Probation
64–65	S. Carolina	6-17	2-12	8th (ACC)	DNP
65–66	S. Carolina	11-13	4-10	T6th (ACC)	DNP
66–67	S. Carolina	16-7	8-4	3d (ACC)	Probation
67–68	S. Carolina	15-7	9-5	4th (ACC)	Probation
68–69	S. Carolina	21-7	11-3	2d (ACC)	NIT (1-1)
69–70	S. Carolina	25-3	14-0	1st (ACC)	DNP
70–71	S. Carolina	23-6	10-4	2d (ACC)	NCAA (0-2)
71–72	S. Carolina	24-5			NCAA (2-1)
72–73	S. Carolina	22-7			NCAA (2-1)
73–74	S. Carolina	22-5			NCAA (0-1)
74–75	S. Carolina	19-9			NIT (1-1)
75–76	S. Carolina	18-9			DNP
76–77	S. Carolina	14-12			DNP
77–78	S. Carolina	16-12			DNP
78–79	S. Carolina	15-12			DNP
79–80	S. Carolina	16-11			DNP

30-Year College Coaching Record: 550-235 (.701) overall; 102-36 (.739) in five years at St. John's; 164-58 (.739) in nine years at North Carolina; 283-142 (.666) in 16 years at South Carolina; 15-6 (.714) in Southern Conference; 142-63 (.693) in Atlantic Coast Conference (84-25, .771, at UNC; 58-38, .604, at USC); 0-1 (.000) in Southern Conference Tournament; 17-12 (.586) in ACC Tournament (8-6, .571, at UNC; 9-6, .600, at USC); 14-8 (.636) in NCAA Tournament; 6-6 (.500) in NIT.

DR. WALTER MEANWELL

Maryland '09
Leeds, England

Led teams to nine conference titles in the first 12 seasons of his 22-year career.... Coach of Wisconsin teams in 1912, 1914, and 1916 that were selected as national champions by the Helms Foundation.... Elected to Naismith Memorial Basketball Hall of Fame in 1959.... Charter member of the National Association of Basketball Coaches.

Year	School	Overall	League	Finish	Postseason
11–12	Wisconsin	15-0	12-0	1st (Big Ten)	
12–13	Wisconsin	14-1	11-1	1st (Big Ten)	
13–14	Wisconsin	15-0	12-0	1st (Big Ten)	
14–15	Wisconsin	13-4	8-4	3d (Big Ten)	
15–16	Wisconsin	20-1	11-1	1st (Big Ten)	
16–17	Wisconsin	15-3	9-3	4th (Big Ten)	
17–18	Missouri	17-1	15-1	1st (MVC)	
19–20	Missouri	17-1	17-1	1st (MVC)	
20–21	Wisconsin	13-4	8-4	T1st (Big Ten)	
21–22	Wisconsin	14-5	8-4	T2d (Big Ten)	
22–23	Wisconsin	12-3	11-1	T1st (Big Ten)	
23–24	Wisconsin	11-5	8-4	T1st (Big Ten)	
24–25	Wisconsin	6-11	3-9	9th (Big Ten)	
25–26	Wisconsin	8-9	4-8	T8th (Big Ten)	
26–27	Wisconsin	10-7	7-5	T4th (Big Ten)	
27–28	Wisconsin	13-4	9-3	T3d (Big Ten)	
28–29	Wisconsin	15-2	10-2	T1st (Big Ten)	
29–30	Wisconsin	15-2	8-2	2d (Big Ten)	
30–31	Wisconsin	8-9	4-8	T7th (Big Ten)	
31–32	Wisconsin	8-10	3-9	T8th (Big Ten)	
32–33	Wisconsin	7-13	4-8	8th (Big Ten)	
33–34	Wisconsin	14-6	8-4	T2d (Big Ten)	

22-Year Coaching Record: 280-101 (.735) overall; 246-99 (.713) in 20 years at Wisconsin; 34-2 (.944) in two years at Missouri; 158-80 (.660) in Big Ten Conference; 32-2 (.941) in Missouri Valley Conference.

RAY MEARS
Miami (Ohio) '49
Dover, Ohio

Coached Wittenberg to 1961 NCAA College Division championship.... His 1969 Tennessee squad finished third in the NIT.

Year	School	Overall	League	Finish	Postseason
56–57	Wittenberg	15-6	11-3	3d (Ohio)	DNP
57–58	Wittenberg	19-3	14-1	2d (Ohio)	DNP
58–59	Wittenberg	19-3	13-1	1st (Ohio)	NCAA DII (1-1)
59–60	Wittenberg	22-2	12-0	1st (Ohio)	DNP
60–61	Wittenberg	25-4	10-0	1st (Ohio)	NCAA DII (5-0)
61–62	Wittenberg	21-5	10-2	2d (Ohio)	NCAA DII (2-1)
62–63	Tennessee	13-11	6-8	7th (SEC)	DNP
63–64	Tennessee	16-8	9-5	T2d (SEC)	DNP
64–65	Tennessee	20-5	12-4	2d (SEC)	DNP
65–66	Tennessee	18-8	10-6	T3d (SEC)	DNP
66–67	Tennessee	21-7	15-3	1st (SEC)	NCAA (0-2)
67–68	Tennessee	20-6	13-5	2d (SEC)	DNP
68–69	Tennessee	21-7	13-5	2d (SEC)	NIT (3-1)
69–70	Tennessee	16-9	10-8	5th (SEC)	DNP
70–71	Tennessee	21-7	13-5	2d (SEC)	NIT (1-1)
71–72	Tennessee	19-6	14-4	T1st (SEC)	DNP
72–73	Tennessee	15-9	13-5	T2d (SEC)	DNP
73–74	Tennessee	17-9	12-6	3d (SEC)	DNP
74–75	Tennessee	18-8	12-6	T3d (SEC)	DNP
75–76	Tennessee	21-6	14-4	2d (SEC)	NCAA (0-1)
76–77	Tennessee	22-6	16-2	T1st (SEC)	NCAA (0-1)

21-Year Coaching Record: 399-135 (.747) overall; 121-23 (.840) in six years at Wittenberg; 278-112 (.713) in 15 years at Tennessee; 70-7 (.909) in Ohio Conference; 182-76 (.705) in Southeastern Conference; 0-4 in NCAA Tournament; 4-2 (.667) in NIT; 8-2 (.800) in NCAA College Division Tournament.

RAY MEYER
Notre Dame '38
Chicago, Ill.

Elected to Naismith Memorial Basketball Hall of Fame in 1978.... Coached three teams to the NIT championship game (1944, 1945, and 1983), winning the title in 1945. His 1948 squad finished fourth at the NIT.... Twice took teams to NCAA Final Four—1943 (T3d) and 1979 (3d).... Shares the longest coaching tenure (42 years) at one school with Western Kentucky's Ed Diddle.... Named coach of the year by UPI and AP in 1980 and 1984, by the USBWA in 1978 and 1980, and by the NABC in 1979.... Assistant coach at Notre Dame under George Keogan for two years in 1940–41 and 1941–42.

Year	School	Overall	League	Finish	Postseason
42–43	DePaul	19-5			NCAA (1-1)
43–44	DePaul	22-4			NIT (2-1)
44–45	DePaul	21-3			NIT (3-0)
45–46	DePaul	19-5			DNP
46–47	DePaul	16-9			DNP
47–48	DePaul	22-8			NIT (1-2)
48–49	DePaul	16-9			DNP
49–50	DePaul	12-13			DNP
50–51	DePaul	13-12			DNP
51–52	DePaul	19-8			DNP
52–53	DePaul	19-9			NCAA (1-2)
53–54	DePaul	11-10			DNP
54–55	DePaul	16-6			DNP
55–56	DePaul	16-8			NCAA (0-1)
56–57	DePaul	8-14			DNP
57–58	DePaul	8-12			DNP
58–59	DePaul	13-11			NCAA (1-2)
59–60	DePaul	17-7			NCAA (2-1)
60–61	DePaul	17-8			NIT (0-1)
61–62	DePaul	13-10			DNP
62–63	DePaul	15-8			NIT (0-1)
63–64	DePaul	21-4			NIT (0-1)
64–65	DePaul	17-10			NCAA (1-2)
65–66	DePaul	18-8			NIT (0-1)
66–67	DePaul	17-8			DNP
67–68	DePaul	13-12			DNP
68–69	DePaul	14-11			DNP
69–70	DePaul	12-13			DNP
70–71	DePaul	8-17			DNP
71–72	DePaul	12-11			DNP
72–73	DePaul	14-11			DNP
73–74	DePaul	16-9			DNP
74–75	DePaul	15-10			DNP
75–76	DePaul	20-9			NCAA (1-1)
76–77	DePaul	15-12			DNP
77–78	DePaul	27-3			NCAA (2-1)
78–79	DePaul	26-6			NCAA (4-1)
79–80	DePaul	26-2			NCAA (0-1)
80–81	DePaul	27-2			NCAA (0-1)
81–82	DePaul	26-2			NCAA (0-1)
82–83	DePaul	21-12			NIT (4-1)
83–84	DePaul	27-3			NCAA (1-1)

42-Year Coaching Record: 724-354 (.672); 14-16 (.467) in NCAA Tournament; 10-8 (.556) in NIT.

RALPH MILLER
Kansas '42
Chanute, Kans.

Elected to Naismith Memorial Basketball Hall of Fame in 1987.... Recorded 33 winning records in 38 seasons at three schools.... Compiled eight 20-win seasons during the 1980s.... Named national coach of the year by UPI, USBWA, and NABC in 1981. Voted coach of the year by AP in 1981 and 1982.... Played college basketball for Phog Allen at Kansas.

Year	School	Overall	League	Finish	Postseason
51–52	Wichita	11-19	2-8	6th (MVC)	DNP
52–53	Wichita	16-11	3-7	6th (MVC)	DNP
53–54	Wichita	27-4	8-2	2d (MVC)	NIT (0-1)
54–55	Wichita	17-9	4-6	4th (MVC)	DNP
55–56	Wichita	14-12	7-5	4th (MVC)	DNP
56–57	Wichita	15-11	8-6	T4th (MVC)	DNP
57–58	Wichita	14-12	6-8	4th (MVC)	DNP
58–59	Wichita	14-12	7-7	4th (MVC)	DNP
59–60	Wichita	14-12	6-8	T4th (MVC)	DNP
60–61	Wichita	18-8	6-6	4th (MVC)	DNP
61–62	Wichita	18-9	7-5	3d (MVC)	NIT (0-1)
62–63	Wichita	19-8	7-5	2d (MVC)	NIT (0-1)
63–64	Wichita	23-6	10-2	T1st (MVC)	NCAA (1-1)
64–65	Iowa	14-10	8-6	5th (Big Ten)	DNP
65–66	Iowa	17-7	8-6	3d (Big Ten)	DNP
66–67	Iowa	16-8	9-5	3d (Big Ten)	DNP
67–68	Iowa	16-9	10-4	T1st (Big Ten)	DNP
68–69	Iowa	12-12	5-9	T8th (Big Ten)	DNP
69–70	Iowa	20-5	14-0	1st (Big Ten)	NCAA (1-1)
70–71	Oregon St.	12-14	4-10	6th (Pac-8)	DNP
71–72	Oregon St.	18-10	9-5	T3d (Pac-8)	DNP
72–73	Oregon St.	15-11	6-8	T5th (Pac-8)	DNP
73–74	Oregon St.	13-13	6-8	5th (Pac-8)	DNP

74–75	Oregon St.	19-12	10-4	2d (Pac-8)	NCAA (1-2)
75–76#	Oregon St.	18-9	10-4	T2d (Pac-8)	DNP
76–77	Oregon St.	16-13	8-6	T3d (Pac-8)	DNP
77–78	Oregon St.	16-11	9-5	2d (Pac-8)	DNP
78–79	Oregon St.	18-10	11-7	3d (Pac-10)	NIT (0-1)
79–80*	Oregon St.	26-4	16-2	1st (Pac-10)	NCAA (0-1)
80–81*	Oregon St.	26-2	17-1	1st (Pac-10)	NCAA (0-1)
81–82*	Oregon St.	25-5	16-2	1st (Pac-10)	NCAA (2-1)
82–83	Oregon St.	20-11	12-6	T3d (Pac-10)	NIT (2-1)
83–84	Oregon St.	22-7	15-3	T1st (Pac-10)	NCAA (0-1)
84–85	Oregon St.	22-9	12-6	T3d (Pac-10)	NCAA (0-1)
85–86	Oregon St.	12-15	8-10	T5th (Pac-10)	DNP
86–87	Oregon St.	19-11	10-8	T3d (Pac-10)	NIT (1-1)
87–88	Oregon St.	20-11	12-6	T2d (Pac-10)	NCAA (0-1)
88–89	Oregon St.	22-8	13-5	T3d (Pac-10)	NCAA (0-1)

#–15 wins later forfeited by action of NCAA Council.

*–NCAA Tournament games later vacated by action of the NCAA.

38-Year Coaching Record: 674-370 (.646) overall; 220-133 (.623) in 13 years at Wichita State (Wichita); 95-51 (.651) in six years at Iowa; 359-186 (.659) in 19 years at Oregon State; 81-75 (.519) in Missouri Valley Conference; 54-30 (.643) in Big Ten Conference; 204-114 (.642) in Pacific-10 Conference; 3-3 (.500) in Pac-10 Tournament; 5-11 (.313) in NCAA Tournament; 3-6 (.333) in NIT.

DONALD (DUDEY) MOORE
Duquesne '34
Pittsburgh, Pa.

Led Duquesne to the semifinal round of the NIT on five occasions—1950 (4th), 1952 (4th), 1953 (3d), 1954 (2d), and 1955 (1st).

Year	School	Overall	League	Finish	Postseason
48–49	Duquesne	17-5			DNP
49–50	Duquesne	23-6			NIT (1-2)
50–51	Duquesne	16-11			DNP
51–52	Duquesne	23-4			NIT (1-2); NCAA (1-1)
52–53	Duquesne	21-8			NIT (3-1)
53–54	Duquesne	26-3			NIT (2-1)
54–55	Duquesne	22-4			NIT (3-0)
55–56	Duquesne	17-10			NIT (1-1)
56–57	Duquesne	16-7			DNP
57–58	Duquesne	10-12			DNP
58–59	La Salle	16-7			DNP
59–60	La Salle	16-6			DNP
60–61	La Salle	15-7			DNP
61–62	La Salle	16-9			DNP
62–63	La Salle	16-8			NIT (0-1)

15-Year Coaching Record: 270-107 (.716) overall; 191-70 (.732) in 10 years at Duquesne; 79-37 (.681) in five years at La Salle; 1-1 (.500) in NCAA Tournament; 11-8 (.579) in NIT.

PETE NEWELL
Loyola (Calif.) '40
Vancouver, B.C.

Guided California to back-to-back NCAA Final Four appearances in 1959 (1st) and 1960 (2d).... Named national coach of the year by UPI and the USBWA in 1960.... Elected to Naismith Memorial Basketball Hall of Fame in 1978.... Coach of gold medal-winning 1960 U.S. Olympic Team.... Led San Francisco to 1949 NIT title.

Year	School	Overall	League	Finish	Postseason
46–47	San Fran.	13-14			DNP
47–48	San Fran.	13-11			DNP
48–49	San Fran.	25-5			NIT (4-0)
49–50	San Fran.	19-7			DNP
50–51	Mich. St.	10-11	5-9	7th (Big Ten)	DNP
51–52	Mich. St.	13-9	6-8	T5th (Big Ten)	DNP
52–53	Mich. St.	13-9	11-7	T3d (Big Ten)	DNP
53–54	Mich. St.	9-13	4-10	8th (Big Ten)	DNP
54–55	California	9-16	1-11	4th (PCC-S)	DNP
55–56	California	17-8	10-6	T3d (PCC)	DNP
56–57	California	21-5	14-2	1st (PCC)	NCAA (1-1)
57–58	California	19-9	12-4	T1st (PCC)	NCAA (1-1)
58–59	California	25-4	14-2	1st (PCC)	NCAA (4-0)
59–60	California	28-2	11-1	1st (AAWU)	NCAA (4-1)

14-Year Coaching Record: 234-123 (.655) overall; 70-37 (.654) in four years at San Francisco; 45-42 (.517) in four years at Michigan State; 119-44 (.730) in six years at California; 26-34 (.433) in Big Ten Conference; 62-26 (.705) in Pacific-10 Conference (Pacific Coast Conference/AAWU); 10-3 (.769) in NCAA Tournament; 4-0 in NIT.

FRANK (BUCKY) O'CONNER
Drake '38
Newton, Iowa

Took Iowa to back-to-back NCAA Final Four appearances in 1955 (4th) and 1956 (2d).... Assistant coach at Iowa under Pops Harrison and Rollie Williams.

Year	School	Overall	League	Finish	Postseason
49–50	Iowa	6-5	5-5	5th (Big Ten)	DNP
51–52	Iowa	19-3	11-3	2d (Big Ten)	DNP
52–53	Iowa	12-10	9-9	6th (Big Ten)	DNP
53–54	Iowa	17-5	11-3	2d (Big Ten)	DNP
54–55	Iowa	19-7	11-3	1st (Big Ten)	NCAA (2-2)
55–56	Iowa	20-6	13-1	1st (Big Ten)	NCAA (3-1)
56–57	Iowa	8-14	4-10	8th (Big Ten)	DNP
57–58	Iowa	13-9	7-7	6th (Big Ten)	DNP

Eight-Year Coaching Record: 114-59 (.659) in eight years at Iowa; 71-41 (.634) in Big Ten Conference; 5-3 (.625) in NCAA Tournament.

HAROLD OLSEN
Wisconsin '17
Rice Lake, Wisc.

Directed Ohio State to title game (runner-up to Oregon) in first NCAA Tournament in 1939.... Finished in third place in 1946 NCAA Tournament.... Elected to Naismith Memorial Basketball Hall of Fame in 1959.... Compiled a 95-63 record (.601) as coach of the NBA's Chicago Stags for three seasons (1946–47 through 1948–49).

Year	School	Overall	League	Finish	Postseason
18–19	Bradley	5-7			
19–20	Ripon	10-2			
20–21	Ripon	9-3			
21–22	Ripon	7-5			
22–23	Ohio St.	4-11	1-11	T9th (Western)	
23–24	Ohio St.	12-5	7-5	T4th (Western)	
24–25	Ohio St.	14-2	11-1	1st (Western)	
25–26	Ohio St.	10-7	6-6	5th (Western)	
26–27	Ohio St.	11-6	6-6	7th (Western)	
27–28	Ohio St.	5-12	3-9	T7th (Western)	
28–29	Ohio St.	9-8	6-6	T5th (Western)	
29–30	Ohio St.	4-11	1-9	9th (Western)	
30–31	Ohio St.	4-13	3-9	9th (Western)	
31–32	Ohio St.	9-9	5-7	6th (Western)	
32–33	Ohio St.	17-3	10-2	T1st (Western)	
33–34	Ohio St.	8-12	4-8	T8th (Western)	
34–35	Ohio St.	13-6	8-4	T4th (Western)	
35–36	Ohio St.	12-8	5-7	T6th (Western)	
36–37	Ohio St.	13-7	7-5	5th (Western)	
37–38	Ohio St.	12-8	7-5	T3d (Western)	DNP
38–39	Ohio St.	16-7	10-2	1st (Western)	NCAA (2-1)
39–40	Ohio St.	13-7	8-4	3d (Western)	DNP
40–41	Ohio St.	10-10	7-5	T3d (Western)	DNP
41–42	Ohio St.	6-14	4-11	9th (Western)	DNP
42–43	Ohio St.	8-9	5-7	T6th (Western)	DNP
43–44	Ohio St.	14-7	10-2	1st (Western)	NCAA (1-1)
44–45	Ohio St.	15-5	10-2	2d (Western)	NCAA (1-1)
45–46	Ohio St.	16-5	10-2	1st (Western)	NCAA (2-1)
50–51	N'western	12-10	7-7	T4th (Big Ten)	DNP
51–52	N'western	7-15	4-10	T8th (Big Ten)	DNP

30-Year College Coaching Record: 305-234 (.566); 5-7 (.416) in one year at Bradley; 26-11 (.703) in three years at Ripon; 255-192 (.570) in 24 years at Ohio State; 19-25 (.432) in two years at Northwestern; 165-152 (.521) in Big Ten Conference (154-135, .533, at OSU; 11-17, .393, at NU); 6-4 (.600) in NCAA Tournament.

JOHNNY ORR
Beloit, Wis. '49
Taylorville, Ill.

All-time winningest coach at Michigan (209) and Iowa State (218), joining Ralph Miller (Wichita State and Oregon State) as the only individuals to be the winningest coaches at two different schools.... First Big Ten coach to lead his team to four consecutive NCAA berths.... Named national coach of the year by the NABC in 1976.... Led Michigan to the 1976 NCAA Tournament title game versus Indiana.... His 1977 Michigan team was ranked No. 1 in the final wire service polls.... Assistant at Wisconsin under John Erickson and under Dave Strack at Michigan.

Year	School	Overall	League	Finish	Postseason
63–64	Mass.	15-9	5-5	3d (Yankee)	DNP
64–65	Mass.	13-11	8-2	2d (Yankee)	DNP
65–66	Mass.	11-13	5-5	3d (Yankee)	DNP
68–69	Michigan	13-11	7-7	4th (Big Ten)	DNP
69–70	Michigan	10-14	5-9	6th (Big Ten)	DNP
70–71	Michigan	19-7	12-2	2d (Big Ten)	NIT (1-1)
71–72	Michigan	14-10	9-5	T3d (Big Ten)	DNP
72–73	Michigan	13-11	6-8	T5th (Big Ten)	DNP
73–74	Michigan	22-5	12-2	T1st (Big Ten)	NCAA (1-1)
74–75	Michigan	19-8	12-6	2d (Big Ten)	NCAA (0-1)
75–76	Michigan	25-7	14-4	2d (Big Ten)	NCAA (4-1)
76–77	Michigan	26-4	16-2	1st (Big Ten)	NCAA (2-1)
77–78	Michigan	16-11	11-7	T4th (Big Ten)	DNP
78–79	Michigan	15-12	8-10	6th (Big Ten)	DNP
79–80	Michigan	17-13	8-10	T6th (Big Ten)	NIT (2-1)
80–81	Iowa St.	9-18	2-12	8th (Big Eight)	DNP
81–82	Iowa St.	10-17	5-9	6th (Big Eight)	DNP
82–83	Iowa St.	13-15	5-9	5th (Big Eight)	DNP
83–84	Iowa St.	16-13	6-8	T4th (Big Eight)	NIT (0-1)
84–85	Iowa St.	21-13	7-7	3d (Big Eight)	NCAA (0-1)
85–86	Iowa St.	22-11	9-5	2d (Big Eight)	NCAA (2-1)
86–87	Iowa St.	13-15	5-9	6th (Big Eight)	DNP
87–88	Iowa St.	20-12	6-8	T5th (Big Eight)	NCAA (0-1)
88–89	Iowa St.	17-12	7-7	T4th (Big Eight)	NCAA (0-1)
89–90	Iowa St.	10-18	4-10	6th (Big Eight)	DNP
90–91	Iowa St.	12-19	6-8	5th (Big Eight)	DNP
91–92	Iowa St.	21-13	5-9	T6th (Big Eight)	NCAA (1-1)
92–93	Iowa St.	20-11	8-6	T2d (Big Eight)	NCAA (0-1)
93–94	Iowa St.	14-13	4-10	T6th (Big Eight)	DNP

29-Year Coaching Record: 466-346 (.574) overall; 39-33 (.542) in three years at Massachusetts; 209-113 (.649) in 12 years at Michigan; 218-200 (.522) in 14 years at Iowa State; 18-12 (.600) in Yankee Conference; 120-72 (.625) in Big Ten Conference; 81-117 (.409) in Big Eight Conference; 7-14 (.333) in Big Eight Tournament; 10-10 (.500) in NCAA Tournament; 3-3 (.500) in NIT.

TED OWENS
Oklahoma '51
Hollis, Okla.

Reached NCAA Final Four two times—1971 (4th) and 1974 (4th).... Finished runner-up in the 1968 NIT.... Led Kansas to 1981 Big Eight Tournament title.... Assistant at Oklahoma under Bruce Drake in 1951–52 and at Kansas under Dick Harp from 1960–61 through 1963–64.

Year	School	Overall	League	Finish	Postseason
64–65	Kansas	17-8	9-5	2d (Big Eight)	DNP
65–66	Kansas	23-4	13-1	1st (Big Eight)	NCAA (1-1)
66–67	Kansas	23-4	13-1	1st (Big Eight)	NCAA (1-1)
67–68	Kansas	22-8	10-4	2d (Big Eight)	NIT (3-1)
68–69	Kansas	20-7	9-5	T2d (Big Eight)	NIT (0-1)
69–70	Kansas	17-9	8-6	2d (Big Eight)	DNP
70–71	Kansas	27-3	14-0	1st (Big Eight)	NCAA (2-2)
71–72	Kansas	11-15	7-7	T4th (Big Eight)	DNP
72–73	Kansas	8-18	4-10	T6th (Big Eight)	Probation
73–74	Kansas	23-7	13-1	1st (Big Eight)	NCAA (2-2)
74–75	Kansas	19-8	11-3	1st (Big Eight)	NCAA (2-2)
75–76	Kansas	13-13	6-8	T4th (Big Eight)	DNP
76–77	Kansas	18-10	8-6	4th (Big Eight)	DNP
77–78	Kansas	24-5	13-1	1st (Big Eight)	NCAA (0-1)
78–79	Kansas	18-11	8-6	T2d (Big Eight)	DNP
79–80	Kansas	15-14	7-7	T3d (Big Eight)	DNP
80–81	Kansas	24-8	9-5	1st (Big Eight)	NCAA (2-1)
81–82	Kansas	13-14	4-10	7th (Big Eight)	DNP
82–83	Kansas	13-16	4-10	T7th (Big Eight)	DNP

VADAL PETERSON
Utah '20
Huntsville, Utah

After losing to Kentucky in NIT, led the Utes to NCAA title in 1944.... Coached Utah to NIT title in 1947.

Year	School	Overall	League	Finish	Postseason
27–28	Utah	6-11	5-7	T2d-W (RMC)	
28–29	Utah	8-9	3-9	4th-W (RMC)	
29–30	Utah	13-11	4-8	4th-W (RMC)	
30–31	Utah	20-5	8-4	1st-W (RMC)	
31–32	Utah	12-8	8-4	T1st-W (RMC)	
32–33	Utah	13-9	9-3	T1st-W (RMC)	
33–34	Utah	14-9	7-5	T2d-W (RMC)	
34–35	Utah	8-8	5-7	3d-W (RMC)	
35–36	Utah	9-13	4-8	4th-W (RMC)	
36–37	Utah	17-7	7-5	T1st-W (RMC)	
37–38	Utah	17-4	10-2	T1st (RMC)	DNP
38–39	Utah	12-7	7-5	T3d (MSC)	DNP
39–40	Utah	18-4	8-4	2d (MSC)	DNP
40–41	Utah	14-7	9-3	2d (MSC)	DNP
41–42	Utah	13-7	7-5	4th (MSC)	DNP
42–43	Utah	10-12	1-7	3d-W (MSC)	DNP
43–44	Utah	21-4			NIT (0-1); NCAA (3-0)
44–45	Utah	17-4			NCAA (0-2)
45–46	Utah	12-8	8-4	3d (MSC)	DNP
46–47	Utah	19-5	10-2	2d (MSC)	NIT (3-0)
47–48	Utah	11-9	6-4	T2d (MSC)	DNP
48–49	Utah	24-8	14-6	2d (MSC)	NIT (0-1)
49–50	Utah	26-18	8-12	5th (MSC)	DNP
50–51	Utah	23-13	12-8	3d (MSC)	DNP
51–52	Utah	19-9	8-6	4th (MSC)	DNP
52–53	Utah	10-14	5-9	T5th (MSC)	DNP

26-Year Coaching Record: 386-223 (.634) in 26 years at Utah; 70-62 (.530) in Rocky Mountain Conference; 103-75 (.579) in Mountain States Conference; 3-2 (.600) in NCAA Tournament; 3-2 (.600) in NIT.

Year	School	Overall	League	Finish	Postseason
85–86	Oral Roberts	10-18	5-7	5th (MW Coll.)	DNP
86–87	Oral Roberts	11-17	5-7	T5th (MW Coll.)	DNP

21-Year College Coaching Record: 369-217 (.594) overall; 348-182 (.657) in 19 years at Kansas; 21-35 (.375) in two years at Oral Roberts; 170-96 (.639) in Big Eight Conference; 10-14 (.417) in Midwestern Collegiate Conference; 10-6 (.625) in Big Eight Tournament; 0-2 in MCC Tournament; 10-10 (.500) in NCAA Tournament; 3-2 (.600) in NIT.

LEE ROSE
Transylvania '58
Lexington, Ky.

In second year at UNC Charlotte, guided the 49ers to the Final Four.... Coached Purdue to third-place finish in 1980 NCAA Tournament.... His 1976 UNC Charlotte squad advanced to the NIT championship game, as did his 1979 Purdue team.... Guided UNCC to the Sun Belt Tournament championship in 1977.... Assistant coach at Transylvania from 1961–62 through 1963–64 and at Cincinnati under Tay Baker from 1965–66 through 1967–68.... Assistant coach in the NBA with the San Antonio Spurs (1986–87 and 1987–88), New Jersey Nets (1988–89), and Milwaukee Bucks (1991–92).

Year	School	Overall	League	Finish	Postseason
64–65*	Transylvania	21-10			NAIA (0-1)
68–69	Transylvania	20-7			NCAA DII (1-1)
69–70	Transylvania	21-7			NCAA DII (0-2)
70–71	Transylvania	21-3			DNP
71–72	Transylvania	21-6			NCAA DII (0-2)
72–73	Transylvania	20-7			NCAA DII (1-2)
73–74	Transylvania	16-10			DNP
74–75	Transylvania	20-7			NCAA DIII (1-1)
75–76	UNC Charl.	24-6			NIT (3-1)
76–77	UNC Charl.	28-5	5-1	1st (Sun Belt)	NCAA (3-2)
77–78	UNC Charl.	20-7	9-1	1st (Sun Belt)	DNP
78–79	Purdue	27-8	13-5	T1st (Big Ten)	NIT (4-1)
79–80	Purdue	23-10	11-7	3d (Big Ten)	NCAA (5-1)
80–81	S. Fla.	18-11	7-5	4th (Sun Belt)	NIT (0-1)

81–82	S. Fla.	17-11	4-6	4th (Sun Belt)	DNP
82–83	S. Fla.	22-10	8-6	4th (Sun Belt)	NIT (1-1)
83–84	S. Fla.	17-11	9-5	T2d (Sun Belt)	DNP
84–85	S. Fla.	18-12	6-8	T4th (Sun Belt)	NIT (1-1)
85–86	S. Fla.	14-14	5-9	T6th (Sun Belt)	DNP

    * Interim head coach.

19-Year Coaching Record: 388-162 (.705) overall; 160-57 (.737) in eight years at Transylvania; 72-18 (.800) in three years at UNC Charlotte; 50-18 in two years at Purdue; 106-69 (.606) in six years at South Florida; 24-12 (.667) in Big Ten Conference; 53-41 (.564) in Sun Belt Conference (14-2, .875, at UNCC; 39-39, .500, at USF); 6-7 (.462) in Sun Belt Tournament (2-1, .667, at UNCC; 4-6, .400, at USF); 8-3 (.727) in NCAA Division I Tournament; 9-5 (.643) in NIT; 0-1 in NAIA Tournament; 2-7 (.222) in NCAA Division II Tournament; 1-1 (.500) in NCAA Division III Tournament.

ADOLPH RUPP
Kansas '23
Halstead, Kans.

Coached teams to four NCAA titles (1948, 1949, 1951, and 1958).... His 1942 squad finished tied for third in the 1942 NCAA Tournament and his 1966 team was runner-up to Texas Western.... Elected to Naismith Memorial Basketball Hall of Fame in 1968.... Named national coach of the year by UPI in 1959 and 1966, and by the USBWA in 1966.... Directed Kentucky to 1946 NIT title. Coached UK to NIT championship game again in 1947. His 1944 UK team finished fourth at NIT.... Coach of 1933 Kentucky team that was selected as national champion by the Helms Foundation.... Holds NCAA career record for most victories.... Coached Kentucky to an SEC-record 24 conference and 13 tournament titles.... Played college ball for Phog Allen at Kansas.

Year	School	Overall	League	Finish	Postseason
30–31	Kentucky	15-3			
31–32	Kentucky	15-2			
32–33	Kentucky	20-3	8-0	1st (SEC)	
33–34	Kentucky	16-1	11-0		
34–35	Kentucky	19-2	11-0	T1st (SEC)	
35–36	Kentucky	15-6	6-2		
36–37	Kentucky	17-5	5-3	1st (SEC)	
37–38	Kentucky	13-5	6-0		DNP
38–39	Kentucky	16-4	5-2	1st (SEC)	DNP
39–40	Kentucky	15-6	4-4	1st (SEC)	DNP
40–41	Kentucky	17-8	8-1		DNP
41–42	Kentucky	19-6	6-2	1st (SEC)	NCAA (1-1)
42–43	Kentucky	17-6	8-1		DNP
43–44	Kentucky	19-2	0-0	1st (SEC)	NIT (2-1)
44–45	Kentucky	22-4	4-1	1st (SEC)	NCAA (1-1)
45–46	Kentucky	28-2	6-0	1st (SEC)	NIT (3-0)
46–47	Kentucky	34-3	11-0	1st (SEC)	NIT (2-1)
47–48	Kentucky	36-3	9-0	1st (SEC)	NCAA (3-0)
48–49	Kentucky	32-2	13-0	1st (SEC)	NIT (0-1), NCAA (3-0)
49–50	Kentucky	25-5	11-2	1st (SEC)	NIT (0-1)
50–51	Kentucky	32-2	14-0	1st (SEC)	NCAA (4-0)
51–52	Kentucky	29-3	14-0	1st (SEC)	NCAA (1-1)
53–54	Kentucky	25-0	14-0	T1st (SEC)	DNP
54–55	Kentucky	23-3	12-2	1st (SEC)	NCAA (1-1)
55–56	Kentucky	20-6	12-2	2d (SEC)	NCAA (1-1)
56–57	Kentucky	23-5	12-2	1st (SEC)	NCAA (1-1)
57–58	Kentucky	23-6	12-2	1st (SEC)	NCAA (4-0)
58–59	Kentucky	24-3	12-2	T2d (SEC)	NCAA (1-1)
59–60	Kentucky	18-7	10-4	3d (SEC)	DNP
60–61	Kentucky	19-9	10-4	T2d (SEC)	NCAA (1-1)
61–62	Kentucky	23-3	13-1	T1st (SEC)	NCAA (1-1)
62–63	Kentucky	16-9	8-6	5th (SEC)	DNP
63–64	Kentucky	21-6	11-3	1st (SEC)	NCAA (0-2)
64–65	Kentucky	15-10	10-6	5th (SEC)	DNP
65–66	Kentucky	27-2	15-1	1st (SEC)	NCAA (3-1)
66–67	Kentucky	13-13	8-10	T5th (SEC)	DNP
67–68	Kentucky	22-5	15-3	1st (SEC)	NCAA (1-1)
68–69	Kentucky	23-5	16-2	1st (SEC)	NCAA (1-1)
69–70	Kentucky	26-2	17-1	1st (SEC)	NCAA (1-1)
70–71	Kentucky	22-6	16-2	1st (SEC)	NCAA (0-2)
71–72	Kentucky	21-7	14-4	T1st (SEC)	NCAA (1-1)

    Note: Kentucky did not field a team in 1952–53. From 1933 to 1950 the SEC champion was determined by a tournament, except for 1935.

41-Year Coaching Record: 875-190 (.822) at Kentucky; 397-75 (.845) in Southeastern Conference; 57-6 (.905) in SEC Tournament; 30-18 (.625) in NCAA Tournament; 7-4 (.636) in NIT.

EVERETT SHELTON
Phillips '23
Cunningham, Kans.

Elected to Naismith Memorial Basketball Hall of Fame in 1979.... Directed Wyoming to 1943 NCAA title.... Won 850 games in a 46-year coaching career that included eight years at the high school level and eight years at AAU.

Year	School	Overall	League	Finish	Postseason
23–24	Phillips	11-16			
24–25	Phillips	15-5			
25–26	Phillips	22-8			
39–40	Wyoming	7-10	3-9	T5th (MSC)	DNP
40–41	Wyoming	13-6	10-2	1st (MSC)	NCAA (0-2)
41–42	Wyoming	15-5	9-3	T2d (MSC)	DNP
42–43	Wyoming	31-2	4-0	1st-E (MSC)	NCAA (3-0)
44–45	Wyoming	10-17			DNP
45–46	Wyoming	22-4	10-2	1st (MSC)	DNP
46–47	Wyoming	22-6	11-1	1st (MSC)	NCAA (0-2)
47–48	Wyoming	18-9	6-4	T2d (MSC)	NCAA (0-2)
48–49	Wyoming	25-10	15-5	1st (MSC)	NCAA (0-2)
49–50	Wyoming	25-11	13-7	T2d (MSC)	DNP
50–51	Wyoming	26-11	13-7	2d (MSC)	DNP
51–52	Wyoming	28-7	13-1	1st (MSC)	NCAA (1-1)
52–53	Wyoming	20-10	12-2	1st (MSC)	NCAA (0-2)
53–54	Wyoming	19-9	10-4	2d (MSC)	DNP
54–55	Wyoming	17-9	9-5	T3d (MSC)	DNP
55–56	Wyoming	7-19	5-9	T6th (MSC)	DNP
56–57	Wyoming	6-19	4-10	7th (MSC)	DNP
57–58	Wyoming	13-14	10-4	1st (MSC)	NCAA (0-1)
58–59	Wyoming	4-22	1-13	T7th (MSC)	DNP
59–60	Sacra. St.	10-13	6-4	3d (Far West.)	DNP
60–61	Sacra. St.	18-8	8-2	2d (Far West.)	DNP
61–62	Sacra. St.	21-10	10-2	1st (Far West.)	NCAA Div. II (4-1)
62–63	Sacra. St.	10-16	4-8	6th (Far West.)	DNP
63–64	Sacra. St.	8-18	6-6	T4th (Far West.)	DNP
64–65	Sacra. St.	10-16	4-8	6th (Far West.)	DNP
65–66	Sacra. St.	10-16	6-6	T4th (Far West.)	DNP
66–67	Sacra. St.	15-11	10-4	T2d (Far West.)	DNP
67–68	Sacra. St.	16-10	9-5	3d (Far West.)	DNP

31-Year Coaching Record: 494-347 (.587) overall; 328-201 (.620) in 19 seasons at Wyoming; 221-133 (.624) in Mountain States Conference; 63-45 (.583) in Far Western Conference; 4-12 (.250) in NCAA Tournament; 4-1 (.800) in NCAA College Division Tournament.

NORMAN SLOAN
North Carolina St. '51
Anderson, Ind.

Led alma mater North Carolina State to the national championship in 1974.... Named national coach of the year in 1974 by AP and the USBWA.... Selected as head coach of 1980 British Olympic team.... Guided N.C. State to third place (1976) and second place (1978) showings at the NIT. His 1986 Florida team advanced to NIT semifinals (4th).... Coached N.C. State to 1970, 1973, and 1974 ACC Tournament titles.... Assistant coach at Memphis State under Eugene Lambert for one year in 1955–56.

Year	School	Overall	League	Finish	Postseason
51–52	P'byterian	21-7			
52–53	P'byterian	11-15	4-2	2d (S.C. Little 4)	
53–54	P'byterian	17-8	4-2	2d (S.C. Little 4)	
54–55	P'byterian	20-6	6-0	1st (S.C. Little 4)	
56–57	The Citadel	11-14	5-9	7th (Southern)	DNP
57–58	The Citadel	16-11	9-6	4th (Southern)	DNP
58–59	The Citadel	15-5	7-4	3d (Southern)	DNP
59–60	The Citadel	15-8	4-4	4th (Southern)	DNP
60–61	Florida	15-11	9-5	4th (SEC)	DNP
61–62	Florida	12-11	8-6	4th (SEC)	DNP
62–63	Florida	12-14	5-9	T8th (SEC)	DNP

		Overall	League	Finish	Postseason
63–64	Florida	12-10	6-8	T9th (SEC)	DNP
64–65	Florida	18-7	11-5	T3d (SEC)	DNP
65–66	Florida	16-10	9-7	T5th (SEC)	DNP
66–67	N.C. St.	7-19	2-12	8th (ACC)	DNP
67–68	N.C. St.	16-10	9-5	T3d (ACC)	DNP
68–69	N.C. St.	15-10	8-6	T3d (ACC)	DNP
69–70	N.C. St.	23-7	9-5	T2d (ACC)	NCAA (1-1)
70–71	N.C. St.	13-14	5-9	T6th (ACC)	DNP
71–72	N.C. St.	16-10	6-6	T4th (ACC)	DNP
72–73	N.C. St.	27-0	12-0	1st (ACC)	Probation
73–74	N.C. St.	30-1	12-0	1st (ACC)	NCAA (4-0)
74–75	N.C. St.	22-6	8-4	T2d (ACC)	DNP
75–76	N.C. St.	21-9	7-5	T2d (ACC)	NIT (3-1)
76–77	N.C. St.	17-11	6-6	5th (ACC)	DNP
77–78	N.C. St.	21-10	7-5	3d (ACC)	NIT (3-1)
78–79	N.C. St.	18-12	3-9	6th (ACC)	DNP
79–80	N.C. St.	20-8	9-5	T2d (ACC)	NCAA (0-1)
80–81	Florida	12-16	5-13	8th (SEC)	DNP
81–82	Florida	5-22	2-16	10th (SEC)	DNP
82–83	Florida	13-18	5-13	10th (SEC)	DNP
83–84	Florida	16-13	11-7	T3d (SEC)	NIT (0-1)
84–85	Florida	18-12	9-9	T5th (SEC)	NIT (0-1)
85–86	Florida	19-14	10-8	4th (SEC)	NIT (3-2)
86–87*	Florida	23-11	12-6	2d (SEC)	NCAA (2-1)
87–88*	Florida	23-12	11-7	T2d (SEC)	NCAA (1-1)
88–89	Florida	21-13	13-5	1st (SEC)	NCAA (0-1)

* NCAA Tournament games later vacated by action of the NCAA.

37-Year Coaching Record: 627-395 (.614) overall; 69-36 (.657) in four years at Presbyterian; 57-38 (.600) in four years at The Citadel; 266-127 (.677) in 14 years at North Carolina State; 235-194 (.548) in 15 years at Florida; 29-23 (.558) in Southern Conference; 103-77 (.573) in Atlantic Coast Conference; 126-124 (.504) in Southeastern Conference; 2-4 (.333) in Southern Conference Tournament; 14-11 (.560) in ACC Tournament; 5-9 (.357) in SEC Tournament; 8-5 (.615) in NCAA Tournament; 9-6 (.600) in NIT.

GEORGE SMITH
Cincinnati '35
Mount Vernon, Ohio

Reached NCAA Final Four two times—1959 (3d) and 1960 (3d).... His 1955 Cincinnati squad finished third in the NIT.... Voted national coach of the year by the Rockne Club in 1960.... Assistant at Cincinnati under John Wiethe for four seasons from 1948–49 through 1951–52.

Year	School	Overall	League	Finish	Postseason
52–53	Cincinnati	11-13	9-3	2d (MAC)	DNP
53–54	Cincinnati	11-10			DNP
54–55	Cincinnati	21-8			NIT (2-1)
55–56	Cincinnati	17-7			Probation
56–57	Cincinnati	15-9			DNP
57–58	Cincinnati	25-3	13-1	1st (MVC)	NCAA (1-1)
58–59	Cincinnati	26-4	13-1	1st (MVC)	NCAA (3-1)
59–60	Cincinnati	28-2	13-1	1st (MVC)	NCAA (3-1)

Eight-Year Coaching Record: 154-56 (.733) in eight years; 9-3 (.750) in Mid-American Conference; 39-3 (.929) in Missouri Valley Conference; 7-3 (.700) in NCAA Tournament; 2-1 (.667) in NIT.

DAVE STRACK
Michigan '45
Indianapolis, Ind.

Guided Michigan to back-to-back Final Four appearances in 1964 (3d) and 1965 (2d).... Voted UPI national coach of the year in 1965.... Assistant at Michigan under Bill Perigo for 10 years from 1949–50 through 1958–59.

Year	School	Overall	League	Finish	Postseason
59–60	Idaho	11-15			DNP
60–61	Michigan	6-18	2-12	10th (Big Ten)	DNP
61–62	Michigan	7-17	5-9	8th (Big Ten)	DNP
62–63	Michigan	16-8	8-6	4th (Big Ten)	DNP
63–64	Michigan	23-5	11-3	T1st (Big Ten)	NCAA (3-1)
64–65	Michigan	24-4	13-1	1st (Big Ten)	NCAA (3-1)
65–66	Michigan	18-8	11-3	1st (Big Ten)	NCAA (1-1)
66–67	Michigan	8-16	2-12	10th (Big Ten)	DNP
67–68	Michigan	11-13	6-8	6th (Big Ten)	DNP

Nine-Year Coaching Record: 124-104 (.544) overall; 11-15 (.423) in one year at Idaho; 113-89 (.559) in eight years at Michigan; 58-54 (.518) in Big Ten Conference; 7-3 (.700) in NCAA Tournament.

JERRY TARKANIAN
Fresno State '55
Pasadena, Calif.

UPI national coach of the year in 1983.... Coach of 1990 NCAA champion.... Reached NCAA Final Four four times in 15 years from 1977 to 1991.... Compiled highest career winning percentage in Division I history.... Coach of seven Big West Tournament champions—1983, 1985, 1986, 1987, 1989, 1990, and 1991.... Compiled 9-11 record in brief stint with NBA's San Antonio Spurs at the start of 1992–93 season.... Compiled 212-26 (.891) record in seven seasons as coach at two community colleges in California.

Year	School	Overall	League	Finish	Postseason
68–69	Long Beach St.	23-3	?-?	1st (CCAA)	DNP
69–70	Long Beach St.	24-5	10-0	1st (PCAA)	NCAA (1-2)
70–71	Long Beach St.	24-5	10-0	1st (PCAA)	NCAA (2-1)
71–72	Long Beach St.	25-4	10-2	1st (PCAA)	NCAA (2-1)
72–73	Long Beach St.	26-3	10-2	1st (PCAA)	NCAA (2-1)
73–74	UNLV	20-6	10-4	3d (WCAC)	DNP
74–75	UNLV	24-5	13-1	1st (WCAC)	NCAA (2-1)
75–76	UNLV	29-2			NCAA (1-1)
76–77	UNLV	29-3			NCAA (4-1)
77–78	UNLV	20-8			Probation
78–79	UNLV	21-8			Probation
79–80	UNLV	23-9			NIT (3-2)
80–81	UNLV	16-12			DNP
81–82	UNLV	20-10			NIT (1-1)
82–83	UNLV	28-3	15-1	1st (PCAA)	NCAA (0-1)
83–84	UNLV	29-6	16-2	1st (PCAA)	NCAA (2-1)
84–85	UNLV	28-4	17-1	1st (PCAA)	NCAA (1-1)
85–86	UNLV	33-5	16-2	1st (PCAA)	NCAA (2-1)
86–87	UNLV	37-2	18-0	1st (PCAA)	NCAA (4-1)
87–88	UNLV	28-6	15-3	1st (PCAA)	NCAA (1-1)
88–89	UNLV	29-8	16-2	1st (Big West)	NCAA (3-1)
89–90	UNLV	35-5	16-2	T1st (Big West)	NCAA (6-0)
90–91	UNLV	34-1	18-0	1st (Big West)	NCAA (4-1)
91–92	UNLV	26-2	18-0	1st (Big West)	Probation

24-Year College Coaching Record: 631-125 (.837) overall; 122-20 (.859) in five years at Long Beach State; 509-105 (.829) in 19 years at UNLV; 23-5 (.821) in West Coast Athletic Conference; 205-17 (.923) in Pacific Coast Athletic Association and Big West Conference; 24-2 (.923) in Big West Tournament; 37-16 (.698) in NCAA Tournament; 4-3 (.571) in NIT.

FRED TAYLOR
Ohio St. '50
Zanesville, Ohio

Coached Ohio State to NCAA title in 1960. Finished runner-up to Cincinnati in 1961 and 1962. Finished third in fourth Final Four appearance in 1968.... Elected to Naismith Memorial Basketball Hall of Fame in 1985.... Named coach of the year by UPI and USBWA in 1961 and 1962.... Assistant coach under Floyd Stahl until succeeding him.

Year	School	Overall	League	Finish	Postseason
58–59	Ohio St.	11-11	7-7	T5th (Big Ten)	DNP
59–60	Ohio St.	25-3	13-1	1st (Big Ten)	NCAA (4-0)
60–61	Ohio St.	27-1	14-0	1st (Big Ten)	NCAA (3-1)
61–62	Ohio St.	26-2	13-1	1st (Big Ten)	NCAA (3-1)
62–63	Ohio St.	20-4	11-3	T1st (Big Ten)	DNP
63–64	Ohio St.	16-8	11-3	T1st (Big Ten)	DNP
64–65	Ohio St.	12-12	6-8	6th (Big Ten)	DNP
65–66	Ohio St.	11-13	5-9	8th (Big Ten)	DNP
66–67	Ohio St.	13-11	6-8	T7th (Big Ten)	DNP
67–68	Ohio St.	21-8	10-4	T1st (Big Ten)	NCAA (3-1)
68–69	Ohio St.	17-7	9-5	T2d (Big Ten)	DNP
69–70	Ohio St.	17-7	8-6	T3d (Big Ten)	DNP
70–71	Ohio St.	20-6	13-1	1st (Big Ten)	NCAA (1-1)
71–72	Ohio St.	18-6	10-4	2d (Big Ten)	DNP
72–73	Ohio St.	14-10	8-6	T3d (Big Ten)	DNP
73–74	Ohio St.	9-15	4-10	8th (Big Ten)	DNP
74–75	Ohio St.	14-14	8-10	6th (Big Ten)	DNP
75–76	Ohio St.	6-20	2-16	10th (Big Ten)	DNP

18-Year Coaching Record: 297-158 (.653) at Ohio State; 158-102 (.608) in Big Ten Conference; 14-4 (.778) in NCAA Tournament.

JIM VALVANO
Rutgers '67
Seaford, N.Y.

Directed North Carolina State to a stunning 54-52 win over top-ranked Houston to capture the 1983 NCAA championship.... Coached N.C. State to 1983 and 1987 ACC Tournament titles.... Assistant under Bill Foster at Rutgers for two seasons (1967–68 and 1968–69) and under Dee Rowe at Connecticut for two seasons (1970–71 and 1971–72).

Year	School	Overall	League	Finish	Postseason
68–69	Johns Hopkins	3-14	3-9	10th-S (Mid. Atl.)	DNP
72–73	Bucknell	11-14	6-4	T2d-W (Mid. Atl.)	DNP
73–74	Bucknell	8-16	2-8	T5th-W (Mid. Atl.)	DNP
74–75	Bucknell	14-12	4-4	T3d-W (ECC)	DNP
75–76	Iona	11-15			DNP
76–77	Iona	15-10			DNP
77–78	Iona	17-10			DNP
78–79	Iona	23-6			NCAA (0-1)
79–80*	Iona	29-5			NCAA (1-1)
80–81	N.C. St.	14-13	4-10	7th (ACC)	DNP
81–82	N.C. St.	22-10	7-7	4th (ACC)	NCAA (0-1)
82–83	N.C. St.	26-10	8-6	T3d (ACC)	NCAA (6-0)
83–84	N.C. St.	19-14	4-10	7th (ACC)	NIT (0-1)
84–85	N.C. St.	23-10	9-5	T1st (ACC)	NCAA (3-1)
85–86	N.C. St.	21-13	7-7	4th (ACC)	NCAA (3-1)
86–87*	N.C. St.	20-15	6-8	6th (ACC)	NCAA (0-1)
87–88*	N.C. St.	24-8	10-4	2d (ACC)	NCAA (0-1)
88–89	N.C. St.	22-9	10-4	1st (ACC)	NCAA (2-1)
89–90	N.C. St.	18-12	6-8	T4th (ACC)	Probation

* NCAA Tournament games later vacated by action of the NCAA

19-Year Coaching Record: 338-214 (.612) overall; 3-14 (.176) in one year at Johns Hopkins; 33-42 (.440) in three years at Bucknell; 95-46 (.674) in five years at Iona; 209-114 (.647) in 10 years at North Carolina State; 11-21 (344) in Middle Atlantic Conference; 4-4 (.500) in East Coast Conference; 71-69 (.507) in Atlantic Coast Conference; 9-8 (.529) in ACC Tournament; 15-8 (.652) in NCAA Tournament; 0-1 in NIT.

FRED (TEX) WINTER
Southern California '47
Wellington, Tex.

Owns best winning percentage in Kansas State history (.691).... Guided K-State to two Final Fours—1958 (4th) and 1964 (4th).... Named national coach of the year by UPI in 1958.... His 1959 K-State squad finished No. 1 in both the final AP and UPI polls.... Assistant under Jack Gardner at Kansas St. for four seasons (1947–48 through 1950–51).... Longtime Chicago Bulls assistant compiled a 51-78 record as head coach of the Houston Rockets in 1971–72 and 1972–73.

Year	School	Overall	League	Finish	Postseason
51–52	Marquette	12-14			DNP
52–53	Marquette	13-11			DNP
53–54	Kansas St.	11-10	5-7	T4th (Big Seven)	DNP
54–55	Kansas St.	11-10	6-6	T3d (Big Seven)	DNP
55–56	Kansas St.	17-8	9-3	1st (Big Seven)	NCAA (1-1)
56–57	Kansas St.	15-8	8-4	2d (Big Seven)	DNP
57–58	Kansas St.	22-5	10-2	1st (Big Seven)	NCAA (3-2)
58–59	Kansas St.	25-2	14-0	1st (Big Eight)	NCAA (1-1)
59–60	Kansas St.	16-10	10-4	T1st (Big Eight)	DNP
60–61	Kansas St.	23-4	13-1	1st (Big Eight)	NCAA (1-1)
61–62	Kansas St.	22-3	12-2	2d (Big Eight)	DNP
62–63	Kansas St.	16-9	11-3	T1st (Big Eight)	DNP
63–64	Kansas St.	22-7	12-2	1st (Big Eight)	NCAA (2-2)
64–65	Kansas St.	12-13	5-9	T6th (Big Eight)	DNP
65–66	Kansas St.	14-11	9-5	3d (Big Eight)	DNP
66–67	Kansas St.	17-8	9-5	4th (Big Eight)	DNP
67–68	Kansas St.	19-9	11-3	1st (Big Eight)	NCAA (0-2)
68–69	Washington	13-13	6-8	4th (Pac-8)	DNP
69–70	Washington	17-9	7-7	5th (Pac-8)	DNP
70–71	Washington	15-13	6-8	5th (Pac-8)	DNP
73–74	N'western	9-15	3-11	9th (Big Ten)	DNP
74–75	N'western	6-20	4-14	T9th (Big Ten)	DNP
75–76	N'western	12-14	7-11	T7th (Big Ten)	DNP
76–77	N'western	9-18	7-11	T7th (Big Ten)	DNP
77–78	N'western	8-19	4-14	T9th (Big Ten)	DNP
78–79	Long Beach St.	16-12	7-7	T4th (PCAA)	DNP
79–80	Long Beach St.	21-9	11-3	2d (PCAA)	NIT (1-1)
80–81	Long Beach St.	15-13	9-5	T3d (PCAA)	DNP
81–82	Long Beach St.	12-16	7-7	T4th (PCAA)	DNP
82–83	Long Beach St.	13-16	6-10	7th (PCAA)	DNP

30-Year College Coaching Record: 454-333 (.577) overall; 25-25 (.500) in two years at Marquette; 262-117 (.691) in 15 years at Kansas State; 45-35 (.563) in three years at Washington; 44-87 (.336) in five years at Northwestern; 78-69 (.531) in five years at Long Beach State; 106-36 (.746) in Big Eight Conference; 19-23 (.452) in Pacific-10 Conference (Pacific-8); 24-61 (.282) in Big Ten Conference; 40-32 (.556) in Big West Conference (PCAA); 6-5 (.545) in Big West Tournament (PCAA); 8-9 (.471) in NCAA Tournament; 1-1 (.500) in NIT.

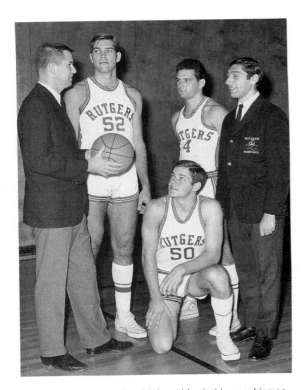

A young Jim Valvano (far right) got his start in coaching as an assistant under Rutgers' Bill Foster (far left) in the late 1960s.

JOHN WOODEN
Purdue '32
Martinsville, Ind.

From 1964 to 1975, UCLA won an NCAA-record 10 national titles, including seven straight from 1967 though 1973.... Elected to Naismith Memorial Basketball Hall of Fame as a coach in 1972.... Named national coach of the year by AP in 1967, 1969, 1970, 1972, and 1973; by UPI in 1964, 1967, 1969, 1970, 1972, and 1973; by the USBWA in 1964, 1967, 1970, 1972, and 1973; and by the NABC in 1969, 1970, and 1972.... His 1962 team finished fourth in the NCAA Tournament and his 1974 squad finished third.... Won 13 conference titles in his last 14 years.

Year	School	Overall	League	Finish	Postseason
46–47	Indiana St.	17-8			DNP
47–48	Indiana St.	27-7			NAIA (4-1)
48–49	UCLA	22-7	10-2	1st-S (PCC)	DNP
49–50	UCLA	24-7	10-2	1st-S (PCC)	NCAA (0-2)
50–51	UCLA	19-10	9-4	T1st-S (PCC)	DNP
51–52	UCLA	19-12	8-4	1st-S (PCC)	NCAA (0-2)
52–53	UCLA	16-8	6-6	3d-S (PCC)	DNP
53–54	UCLA	18-7	7-5	2d-S (PCC)	DNP
54–55	UCLA	21-5	11-1	1st-S (PCC)	DNP
55–56	UCLA	22-6	16-0	1st (PCC)	NCAA (1-1)
56–57	UCLA	22-4	13-3	T2d (PCC)	Probation
57–58	UCLA	16-10	10-6	3d (PCC)	DNP
58–59	UCLA	16-9	10-6	T3d (PCC)	DNP
59–60	UCLA	14-12	7-5	2d (AAWU)	DNP
60–61	UCLA	18-8	7-5	2d (AAWU)	DNP
61–62	UCLA	18-11	10-2	1st (AAWU)	NCAA (2-2)
62–63	UCLA	20-9	8-5	T1st (AAWU)	NCAA (0-2)
63–64	UCLA	30-0	15-0	1st (AAWU)	NCAA (4-0)
64–65	UCLA	28-2	14-0	1st (AAWU)	NCAA (4-0)
65–66	UCLA	18-8	10-4	2d (AAWU)	DNP
66–67	UCLA	30-0	14-0	1st (AAWU)	NCAA (4-0)
67–68	UCLA	29-1	14-0	1st (AAWU)	NCAA (4-0)
68–69	UCLA	29-1	13-1	1st (Pac-8)	NCAA (4-0)
69–70	UCLA	28-2	12-2	1st (Pac-8)	NCAA (4-0)
70–71	UCLA	29-1	14-0	1st (Pac-8)	NCAA (4-0)
71–72	UCLA	30-0	14-0	1st (Pac-8)	NCAA (4-0)
72–73	UCLA	30-0	14-0	1st (Pac-8)	NCAA (4-0)
73–74	UCLA	26-4	12-2	1st (Pac-8)	NCAA (3-1)
74–75	UCLA	28-3	12-2	1st (Pac-8)	NCAA (5-0)

29-Year Coaching Record: 664-162 (.804) overall; 44-15 (.746) in two years at Indiana State; 620-147 (.808) in 27 years at UCLA; 304-74 (.810) In Pacific-10 Conference; 47-10 (.825) in NCAA Tournament; 4-1 (.800) in NAIA Tournament.

PHIL WOOLPERT
Loyola (La.) '40
Los Angeles, Calif.

Coached San Francisco to back-to-back NCAA titles in 1955 and 1956 before finishing third in 1957.... Named national coach of the year by UPI in 1955 and 1956.... Elected to Naismith Memorial Basketball Hall of Fame in 1991.... Freshman coach at San Francisco under Pete Newell in 1948–49 and 1949–50 while coaching St. Ignatius High School.... Coached the San Francisco Saints for one season in the old American Basketball League.

Year	School	Overall	League	Finish	Postseason
50–51	San Fran.	9-17			DNP
51–52	San Fran.	11-13			DNP
52–53	San Fran.	10-11	6-2	T1st (CBA)	DNP
53–54	San Fran.	14-7	8-4	2d (CBA)	DNP
54–55	San Fran.	28-1	12-0	1st (CBA)	NCAA (5-0)
55–56	San Fran.	29-0	14-0	1st (WCAC)	NCAA (4-0)
56–57	San Fran.	21-7	12-2	1st (WCAC)	NCAA (3-1)
57–58	San Fran.	25-2	12-0	1st (WCAC)	NCAA (1-1)
58–59	San Fran.	6-20	3-9	6th (WCAC)	DNP
62–63	San Diego	4-15			DNP
63–64	San Diego	13-13			DNP
64–65	San Diego	14-11			DNP
65–66	San Diego	17-11			DNP
66–67	San Diego	13-11			DNP
67–68	San Diego	15-10			DNP
68–69	San Diego	10-15			DNP

16-Year College Coaching Record: 239-164 (.593) overall; 153-78 (.662) in nine years at San Francisco; 86-86 (.500) in seven years at San Diego; 67-17 (.798) in West Coast Conference (CBA/WCAC); 13-2 (.867) in NCAA Tournament.

10

THEY PLAYED THE GAME, TOO

There is a theory in some quarters that basketball players are the most versatile team sport athletes in the world. What other sport demands such an abundance of speed, strength, stamina, coordination, quickness, jumping ability, teamwork, timing, guile, and creativity?

Long before Michael Jordan abandoned hoops for baseball, or before Charlie Ward mulled over a choice between basketball and football, or before the widespread jacks-of-all-trades fascination with football/baseball standouts Bo Jackson and Deion Sanders, there was a host of college basketball players who also excelled in other fields of endeavor. Some of the names will surprise you. Here is a summary of former college hoopsters who made a bigger name for themselves off the hardwood—in other sports, as prominent businessmen, and as entertainers.

MAJOR LEAGUE BASEBALL PLAYERS

MARK ACRE, New Mexico State

Pitcher for the Oakland A's.... The 6-8, 220-pound forward-center averaged 1.9 points and 1.2 rebounds per game while playing sparingly for the Aggies in 1988–89 and 1989–90 after averaging 25.1 points and 9.6 rebounds per game in his final junior college season at the College of the Siskiyous in Weed, Calif.

JERRY ADAIR, Oklahoma State

Hit .254 in 1,165 games in 13 seasons (1958–70) with the Baltimore Orioles, Chicago White Sox, Boston Red Sox, and Kansas City Athletics. Set a major league record for highest fielding average (.994) and fewest errors (five) by a second baseman in a season in 1964 and set a major league record for consecutive errorless games by a second baseman (89) in 1964 and 1965.... Before signing a pro baseball contract, he played two varsity seasons of basketball at Oklahoma State (third-leading scorer with a 9.7-points-per-game average in 1956–57 and second-leading scorer with an 11.9 average in 1957–58). Ranked among the nation's top 11 free-throw shooters both seasons.

JOE ADCOCK, Louisiana State

First baseman hit .277 with 336 home runs and 1,122 RBIs in 17 seasons (1950–66) with the

Cincinnati Reds, Milwaukee Braves, Cleveland Indians, and the Los Angeles/California Angels. Hit four homers and a double for the Braves against the Brooklyn Dodgers on July 31, 1954, setting a major league record for most total bases in a game (18). Braves' regular first baseman for 1957 and 1958 National League champions.... He played three seasons (1944–45 through 1946–47) at LSU as a 6-4, 190-pound center. Leading scorer with an 18.6-points-per-game average on the 1945–46 Tigers team that compiled an 18-3 record and lost against Kentucky in the Southeastern Conference Tournament final. Set SEC Tournament record with 15 field goals in a game against Tulane in 1946.

BILL ALMON, Brown

Signed $90,000 bonus contract with the San Diego Padres after becoming the first player selected in the 1974 baseball draft. Shortstop hit .254 in 15 seasons (1974–88) with the Padres, Montreal Expos, New York Mets, Chicago White Sox, Oakland A's, Pittsburgh Pirates, and Philadelphia Phillies.... The 6-3, 175-pound guard averaged 6.4 points per game for the 1971–72 Brown freshman team and 2.5 ppg for the 1972–73 varsity.

WALTER ALSTON, Miami of Ohio

Baseball Hall of Famer managed the Brooklyn and Los Angeles Dodgers for 23 seasons (1954–76), winning seven National League pennants and three World Series.... The 6-2, 195-pound Alston lettered in basketball at Miami in 1932–33, 1933–34, and 1934–35. Scored 10 of Miami's 15 points in a 32-15 defeat against Indiana in his senior season. Charter member of alma mater's Athletic Hall of Fame.

GEORGE ALTMAN, Tennessee State

First baseman hit .269 with 102 home runs in nine seasons (1959–67) with the Chicago Cubs, St. Louis Cardinals, and New York Mets.... The 6-4_ forward earned four letters on Tennessee A&I teams that compiled an 88-17 from 1951–52 through 1954–55. The school appeared in the NAIA Tournament in 1953 and 1954.

ELDON AUKER, Kansas State

Pitcher who compiled a 130-101 record in 10 seasons (1933–42) with the Detroit Tigers, Boston Red Sox, and St. Louis Browns. Led American League in winning percentage in 1935 with .720 mark (18-7 record). Appeared in 1934 and 1935 World Series with the Tigers, hurling a complete game, 10-4 victory over the St. Louis Cardinals in Game Four of the '34 Series.... Three-year basketball letterman was named to the first five on the All-Big Six team in his final college season (1931–32).... The *Spalding Official Basketball Guide* called the 6-2 guard an "outstanding performer, with height, endurance and skill beyond the ordinary."

STEVE BARBER, Riverside City College

Pitcher compiled a 1-0 record in 22 games with the Minnesota Twins in 1970 and 1971.... Starting guard for Jerry Tarkanian-coached community college powers that combined for a 64-6 record in 1964–65 and 1965–66.

FRANKIE BAUMHOLTZ, Ohio University

Outfielder hit .290 in 1,019 games in 10 seasons (1947–49, 1951–57) with the Chicago Cubs, Cincinnati Reds, and Philadelphia Phillies. Led National League in pinch hits in 1955 and 1956.... First player in Ohio U. history to score 1,000 points in a career. Led the school to three-year record of 49-18. Capped college career by earning MVP honors in 1941 NIT as he led the tourney in scoring with 53 points in three games for the second-place Bobcats. Named to first five on Converse 1940–41 All-America team.... Earned second-team all-league honors with the Youngstown Bears in the National Basketball League in 1945–46 and the Cleveland Rebels in the Basketball Association of America in 1946–47.

LOUIS (BOZEY) BERGER, Maryland

Infielder hit .236 in six seasons (1932, 1935 through 1939) with the Cleveland Indians, Chicago White Sox, and Boston Braves.... The 6-2 forward led Maryland to the 1931 Southern Conference championship with a league-high

19.1-point scoring average in conference competition. Maryland's first basketball All-American was an NCAA consensus first-team selection the next year as a senior.

LOU BOUDREAU, Illinois

Baseball Hall of Famer was an infielder for 15 seasons (1938–52) with the Cleveland Indians and Boston Red Sox. Managed Indians, Red Sox, Kansas City Athletics, and Chicago Cubs, starting his managerial career at the age of 24 in 1942. As player-manager in 1948, the shortstop led Cleveland to the American League title and earned MVP honors by hitting .355 with 116 RBIs.... Played two varsity basketball seasons at Illinois (1936–37 and 1937–38). As a sophomore, he led the Illini in scoring with an 8.7-point average as the team shared the Big Ten Conference title. Compiled 8.8 average the next year. After helping the Illini upset St. John's in a game at Madison Square Garden, the *New York Daily News* described him as "positively brilliant" and said he "set up countless plays in breathtaking fashion." ... Averaged 8.2 points per game for the Hammond (Ind.) Ciesar All-Americans in the National Basketball League in 1938–39.

CARL BOULDIN, Cincinnati

Compiled 3-8 pitching record in four seasons (1961–64) with the Washington Senators.... Starting guard and co-captain as a senior on 1961 NCAA champion. Averaged 2.8 points per game as a sophomore, 5.8 as a junior, and 11.7 as

a senior. The Bearcats reached the Final Four all three of his varsity seasons (third-place finishes in 1959 and 1960), compiling an 81-9 record in that span.... Sketch in school guide: "Poised, unruffled backcourt leader. Exceptionally fine ball handler and playmaker possesses clever offensive moves. Especially dependable in clutch situations."

RALPH BRANCA, New York University

Compiled an 88-68 pitching record in 12 seasons (1944–54, 1956) with the Brooklyn Dodgers, Detroit Tigers, and New York Yankees. Appeared in 1947 and 1949 World Series with the Dodgers. Best remembered for throwing the pitch that Bobby Thomson of the New York Giants hit for a homer in the decisive game of the 1951 playoff for the National League title.... A 6-2, 190-pound center, he was the sixth-leading scorer for NYU in 1943–44 with an average of 3.8 points per game.

BOB CERV, Nebraska

Outfielder played 12 seasons (1951–62) with the New York Yankees, Kansas City Athletics, Los Angeles Angels, and Houston Colt .45s. Played in the 1955, 1956, and 1960 World Series with the Yankees. In 1958, he batted .305 with 38 home runs and 104 RBIs for Kansas City.... He averaged 6.2 points per game for the Cornhuskers in four varsity seasons (1946–47 through 1949–50), ranking fourth on the school's career scoring list when he finished his career.... Excerpt from school guide: "One of the finest defensive guards to perform on the Nebraska maples. Combines unusual speed with a sixth sense of timing to steal the ball or tie up the ball handler."

MARTY CLARY, Northwestern

Pitcher compiled a 5-14 record in 58 games with the Atlanta Braves in 1987, 1989, and 1990.... The 6-4 guard was a letterman with the Wildcats in 1982 and 1983. He hit 82.8 percent of his free throws (24 of 29).

GENE CONLEY, Washington State

Compiled a 91-96 pitching record in 11 seasons (1952, 1954–63) with the Boston/Milwaukee Braves, Philadelphia Phillies, and Boston Red Sox. Three-time All-Star Game performer finished second in the National League rookie of the year voting in 1954 when he had a 14-9 record and 2.97 ERA for the Braves.... Led the Cougars and Pacific Coast Conference Northern Division in scoring in 1949–50 as a sophomore (13.3 points per game) in his only season of varsity basketball before signing a pro contract. Played six seasons in the NBA with the Boston Celtics and New York Knicks, averaging 5.9 points and 6.3 rebounds per game. Member of Celtic championship teams in 1959, 1960, and 1961.... Excerpt in school guide: "Unusually fast and active for a boy his size (6-7, 215 pounds)."

ROGER CRAIG, North Carolina State

Former National League pitcher and manager. Compiled a 74-98 record and 3.83 ERA in 12 seasons (1955–66) with the Brooklyn/Los Angeles Dodgers, New York Mets, St. Louis Cardinals, Cincinnati Reds, and Philadelphia Phillies. Led N.L. in losses with the Mets in 1962 (10-24) and 1963 (5-22). Pitched in seven World Series games with the Dodgers and Cardinals. Managed 10 seasons with the San Diego Padres and San Francisco Giants, winning the 1989 N.L. title with the Giants.... The 6-4, 180-pound forward scored 33 points as a member of the 1949–50 N.C. State freshman basketball team before signing a pro baseball contract.

GUY CURTRIGHT, Northeast Missouri State

Outfielder hit .276 with Chicago White Sox from 1943 to 1946. Set major league rookie record (subsequently broken) with a 26-game hitting streak.... Two-time all-conference selection as a 5-11, 200-pound forward in the Missouri Intercollegiate Athletic Association. Led Bulldog basketball team in scoring each of his four seasons.

WALT DROPO, Connecticut

First baseman hit .270 with 152 home runs and 704 RBIs in 13 seasons from 1949 to 1961

with the Boston Red Sox, Detroit Tigers, Chicago White Sox, Cincinnati Reds, and Baltimore Orioles. Named American League Rookie of the Year in 1950 after hitting .322 with 34 homers and a league-leading 144 RBIs for the Red Sox. Tied major league record with 12 consecutive hits in 1952.... The 6-5 Dropo averaged 21.7 points per game in 1942–43, 21 in 1945–46, and 19.7 in 1946–47 in a Huskies career interrupted by World War II. The first player in UConn history to average 20 points for a season, he has the second-highest scoring average in school annals (20.7).

SAMMY ESPOSITO, Indiana

Utility infielder hit .207 in 560 games during 10-year career (1952, 1955–63) with the Chicago White Sox and Kansas City Athletics. Saw action in two World Series games in 1959 with the White Sox. Baseball coach at North Carolina State from 1967 through 1987, leading the Wolfpack to third-place finish in 1968 College World Series.... Played one season (1951–52) of varsity basketball at Indiana before signing pro baseball contract, averaging seven points per game as a starting guard for the Hoosiers. Assistant basketball coach at N.C. State for 14 years, including the 1974 NCAA champion.... Sketch in school guide: "Only 5-9, he is fast, a peerless playmaker and one of the best defensive men on the squad."

DARRELL EVANS, Pasadena City College

Infielder-outfielder hit .248 with 414 homers and 1,254 RBIs in 21 seasons (1969–89) with the Atlanta Braves, San Francisco Giants, and Detroit Tigers. Led the American League with 40 homers for the Tigers in 1985, becoming the oldest player to win a home run title in the majors (38).... As a sophomore for Pasadena (Calif.) City College in 1966–67, he was a member of a Jerry Tarkanian-coached club that won the state junior college crown.

DAN FIFE, Michigan

Pitcher compiled a 3-2 record in 14 games with the Minnesota Twins in 1973 and 1974.... The father of Michigan guard Dugan Fife averaged 12.6 points per game as the Wolverines' third-leading scorer each year in three varsity seasons (1968–69 through 1970–71).... Excerpt from school guide: "One of the most intense players in country. Greatest hustler in the whole Big Ten."

JOHNNY GEE, Michigan

One of the tallest players ever to play major league baseball. Compiled 7-12 record in 44 games during six seasons (1939, 1941, 1943–46) with the Pittsburgh Pirates and New York Giants.... Senior captain of Wolverines team in 1936–37 that compiled a 16-4 record and third-place finish in the Big Ten. The 6-9, 225-pounder was sixth in the Big Ten in scoring that season with an average of 8.8 points per game.... In his history of Michigan basketball, Jeff Mortimer wrote: "Gee looked upon a rebound as something that was his property unless it could be taken away by force."

JOE GIBBON, Mississippi

Compiled a 61-65 record and 3.52 ERA in 419 games during 13 seasons (1960–72) with the Pittsburgh Pirates, San Francisco Giants, Cincinnati Reds, and Houston Astros. Pitched in two games in 1960 World Series for the Pirates.... Finished four-year career as the Rebels' leader in career scoring (1,601 points for 18.9 average) and rebounds (827 for 9.6 average). Nation's second-leading scorer as a senior in 1956–57 with an average of 30 points per game, finishing ahead of Seattle's Elgin Baylor (29.7) and Kansas' Wilt Chamberlain (29.7). Named to first team on Helms Foundation All-America squad and second team on United Press All-America team.... School guide described him as "Ole Miss' big weapon, a portsided, long-range bomber who is accurate from the corner, from the front and through crowded defenses for drive-in baskets."

BOB GIBSON, Creighton

Baseball Hall of Famer compiled a 251-174 pitching record with 3,117 strikeouts and 2.91 ERA in 17 seasons (1959–75) with the St. Louis Cardinals. Notched a 7-3 mark and 1.89 ERA in nine games in the 1964, 1967, and 1968 World Series. Set a World Series record with 17 strikeouts against the Detroit Tigers on October 2, 1968.... First Creighton player to average 20 points per game for his career (20.2). Led school in scoring in 1955-56 (40th in the country with 22 ppg) and 1956–57 and was second-leading scorer in 1954–55 before playing one season (1957–58) with the Harlem Globetrotters.... Sketch from school brochure: "Possesses outstanding jump shot and for height (6-1) is a terrific rebounder."

DALLAS GREEN, Delaware

New York Mets manager compiled 20-22 pitching record in eight seasons (1960–67) with the Philadelphia Phillies, Washington Senators, and Mets. Managed the Phillies to victory over the Kansas City Royals in 1980 World Series.... The 6-5 Green played two seasons of varsity basketball for the Blue Hens, averaging 6.5 points per game in 22 games as a sophomore in 1953–54 and 12.1 points in 21 games as a junior in 1954–55, when he was the school's second-leading scorer and rebounder (10.6 per game).

DICK GROAT, Duke

Shortstop hit .286 in 1,929 games in 14 seasons (1952, 1955–67) with the Pittsburgh Pirates, St. Louis Cardinals, Philadelphia Phillies, and San Francisco Giants. Eight-time All-Star Game performer started on World Championship teams with the Pirates in 1960 and Cardinals in 1964.... Named College Basketball Player of the Year by the Helms Foundation in 1950–51. Nation's fourth-leading scorer as a junior (25.2 points per game) and runner-up as a senior (26 ppg). Averaged 14.5 as a sophomore in 1949–50. Scored 48 points against North Carolina on February 29, 1952. Played 26 games in the NBA, averaging 11.9 points per game for the Fort

Wayne Pistons in 1952–53.... In 1951, Virginia coach Gus Tebell said Groat is "the finest player I've seen in the South in my 27 years of coaching. An All-American on anybody's team. I recall the brilliance of Hank Luisetti and I must put Groat in the same category with him. Excellent shot and remarkable ballhandler."

TONY GWYNN, San Diego State

San Diego Padres outfielder hit .329 in first 12 seasons (1982–93), winning National League batting titles in 1984, 1987, 1988, and 1989. Played in nine All-Star games.... Averaged 8.6 points and 5.5 assists per game in 107 games with the Aztecs in four seasons (1977–78 through 1980–81). The 5-11, 170-pound guard was named second-team All-Western Athletic Conference as both a junior and senior. Led WAC in assists as both a sophomore and junior and was third as a senior. Led San Diego State in steals each of his last three seasons. Selected in the 10th round of 1981 NBA draft by the San Diego Clippers.

ED HALICKI, Monmouth (N.J.)

Pitcher compiled a 55-66 record in seven seasons (1974–80) with the San Francisco Giants and California Angels. His best season was 1977 when he posted a 16-12 record for the Giants. Hurled a no-hitter for them vs. the New York Mets on August 24, 1975.... The 6-7, 220-pound forward-center collected 1,777 points and 1,266 rebounds in four seasons (1968–69 through 1971–72). Holds Monmouth single-game rebounding record with 40 in his junior year. Named to NAIA All-American third team as a senior when he led the Hawks in scoring with 21 points per game.

STEVE HAMILTON, Morehead State

Lefthanded pitcher compiled a 40-31 record, 3.05 ERA, and 42 saves in 421 games during 12 seasons (1961–72) with the Cleveland Indians, Washington Senators, New York Yankees, Chicago White Sox, San Francisco Giants, and Chicago Cubs. Appeared in 1963 and 1964 World Series with the Yankees.... Averaged 17.9 points and 16.4 rebounds per game in four-year college

basketball career (1954–55 through 1957–58), leading the Eagles in scoring and rebounding as a junior and senior. He ranked 15th in the country in scoring as a junior (24.2 ppg) and among the nation's top 10 rebounders as a senior (19.1 rpg). The 6-7, 195-pound forward-center averaged 18.5 points in four NCAA Tournament games in 1956 and 1957. He had a 51-point game against Ohio University as a junior. He also lettered as a pole vaulter in track. Currently the athletic director at his alma mater, he averaged 4.5 points and 3.4 rebounds per game in two seasons with the NBA's Minneapolis Lakers. He is the only athlete to play in the World Series and the NBA Finals (rookie in 1959 when the Lakers were swept by the Boston Celtics).

ATLEE HAMMAKER, East Tennessee State

Pitcher for more than ten years (1981–85, 1987–91, and 1994) with the Kansas City Royals, San Francisco Giants, San Diego Padres, and Chicago White Sox.... The 6-2, 185-pound guard averaged 5.3 points per game as a freshman in 1976–77 and 4.9 as a sophomore in 1977–78.... Excerpt from school guide: "Probably most exciting player on club. Has ability to come off the bench and provide much needed spark at times."

CHUCK HARMON, Toledo

Utilityman for four seasons (1954–57) with the Cincinnati Reds, St. Louis Cardinals, and Philadelphia Phillies.... Second-leading scorer for the Rockets as a sophomore in 1946–47 (13.6 points per game) and as a junior in 1947–48 (8.8). As a freshman starter in 1942–43, the swingman was Toledo's second-leading scorer in the NIT on a 22-4 team that finished runner-up to St. John's.... Sketch in school guide: "Master of tricky play and a whirlwind on the backboards."

BILLY HARRELL, Siena

Infielder hit .231 in 173 games with the Cleveland Indians (1955, 1957, 1958) and Boston Red Sox (1961).... The 6-1, 180-pounder averaged 10.3 points per game in three seasons of varsity basketball for Siena. When he finished his college career, he held school records for most points in a season (396 in 1951–52), career and game (28 against Arizona State in 1951) and most rebounds in a season (387 in 1949–50)…. Excerpt from school guide: "Seems to have steel springs for legs and extension hooks for hands. Can reach the top of the backboard if necessary. Shifty and speedy. Has variety of shots. He'll often pass up scoring chance to give ball to teammate."

RICK HERRSCHER, Southern Methodist

Played 35 games as an infielder-outfielder for the 1962 New York Mets team that finished with a 40-120 record…. Averaged 11.5 points per game in three seasons (1955–56 through 1957–58) of varsity basketball as a 6-3, 185-pound swingman. Led team with 17.5 average as a senior. Helped Mustangs win two Southwest Conference titles. Member of SMU squad that reached the 1956 Final Four…. Excerpt from school guide: "Captain is most versatile cager ever to play for the Mustangs. He possesses great finesse and can fake and evade the man who is guarding him. He knows all the tricks of a postman. His outside shot demands the respect of all opponents. He is an excellent feeder."

ORAL HILDEBRAND, Butler

Compiled 83-78 record in 10 seasons (1931–40) with the Cleveland Indians, St. Louis Browns, and New York Yankees. Named to 1933 American League All-Star Game team. Pitched four shutout innings as fourth-game starter for Yankees in 1939 World Series after posting 10-4 record during the season…. Three-year letterman (1927–28 through 1929–30) on Butler teams that combined for a 48-11 record. Senior captain scored 32 points in 24 minutes in a game against Evansville. Named to second five on 1928–29 *College Humor Magazine* All-American team and third five on 1929–30 *College Humor* All-American squad.

JAY HOOK, Northwestern

Compiled a 39-62 pitching record in eight seasons (1957 through 1964) with the Cincinnati Reds and New York Mets…. The 6-2, 185-pound

swingman was the Wildcats' third-leading scorer as a sophomore with 10.7 points per game. He had a 5.3-point average the next season (1956–57).

FRANK HOWARD, Ohio State

New York Mets coach was outfielder/first baseman for 16 seasons from 1958 to 1973 with the Los Angeles Dodgers, Washington Senators, Texas Rangers, and Detroit Tigers. In 1,902 major league games, he hit .273 with 382 home runs and 1,119 RBIs. Howard led the American League in homers with 44 in 1968 and 1970…. Played three seasons (1955–56 through 1957–58) of varsity basketball with the Buckeyes, leading them in both scoring and rebounding as a junior (20.1 points and 15.3 rebounds) and senior (16.9 and 13.6). He was 54th in the country in scoring as a junior. Finished college career as OSU's third-leading career scorer and leading rebounder. The 6-6, 220-pound Howard was a first-team All-American selection by the U.S. Basketball Writers/*Look Magazine,* Converse, and NEA as a junior when he ranked eighth in the nation in rebounding…. Excerpt from school guide: "One of the strongest players in college basketball and one of the top rebounders. Shoots very well from the outside."

RON JACKSON, Western Michigan

First baseman for seven seasons with the Chicago White Sox and Boston Red Sox (1954–60)…. Second-team All-Mid-American Conference choice in 1952, 1953, and 1954. The 6-6, 225-pound center led WMU in scoring in 1952–53 (15.7 points per game) and 1953–54 (19.7)…. Excerpt from sketch in *Dell Basketball Magazine:* "Scores with one-hand flip inside, has a good one-hand push near the foul circle, a two-hand set from the side well out. Good pass, good speed, good rebound, and his team's strongest defensive player to boot."

DAVE JOHNSON, Texas A&M

Cincinnati Reds manager guided New York Mets to victory over Boston Red Sox in 1986 World Series. Hit .261 as an infielder in 13-year career (1965–75, 1977–78) with the Baltimore Orioles, Atlanta Braves, Philadelphia Phillies, and Chicago Cubs. Hit 43 homers for the Braves in 1973.... Averaged 1.7 points per game as a sophomore in his only varsity season (1961–62) with the Aggies before signing a pro baseball contract in 1962.

DUANE JOSEPHSON, Northern Iowa

Catcher hit .258 in eight seasons with the Chicago White Sox (1965–70) and Boston Red Sox (1971–72) ... Averaged 13.4 points per game as a 6-0, 190-pound guard in three varsity seasons (1961-62 through 1963–64) at what was then call the State College of Iowa. Led the team in scoring as a junior and senior and was named to the All-North Central Conference team both of those seasons. Averaged 17.4 points in five NCAA College Division Tournament games in 1964 when SCI finished fourth.

HOWIE JUDSON, Illinois

Compiled 17-37 pitching record in seven seasons with the Chicago White Sox (1948–52) and Cincinnati Reds (1953 and 1954).... Lettered in basketball with the Illini as a freshman in 1943–44 and as a sophomore in 1944–45 (third-leading scorer with average of 8.5 points per game).

CHARLIE KELLER, Maryland

Outfielder hit .286 with 189 home runs and 760 RBIs in 13 seasons (1939–43 and 1945–52) with the New York Yankees and Detroit Tigers. Hit .306 for the Yanks in 19 World Series games (1939, 1941–43).... Three-year basketball letterman with the Terrapins from 1934–35 through 1936–37.

DON KESSINGER, Mississippi

Infielder played 16 seasons (1964–79) with the Chicago Cubs, St. Louis Cardinals, and Chicago White Sox. Managed White Sox in 1979. Led National League shortstops in putouts three times, assists four times, and double plays four times. Played in six All-Star Games.... Selected to the 10-man All-Southeastern Conference team all three of his varsity seasons (1961–62 through

1963–64) as he ranked among the nation's top 45 scorers each year. In scoring for all games, he ranked third in the SEC as a sophomore (21.4 points per game), second as a junior (21.8), and second as a senior (23.5). He scored 49 points against Tulane on February 2, 1963, and 48 against Tennessee 10 nights later.... Excerpt from school guide: "One of the nation's most gifted athletes, he features every shot in the book but the specifics are one-handed push shots, usually a jumper, and driving layups."

JERRY KINDALL, Minnesota

Infielder hit .213 in nine seasons (1956–58, 1960–65) with the Chicago Cubs, Cleveland Indians, and Minnesota Twins. Baseball coach at Arizona for more than 20 years, leading the Wildcats to three College World Series titles (1976, 1980, and 1986).... Played two seasons of varsity basketball for Minnesota, averaging 1.4 points per game as a sophomore in 1954–55 and 6.9 as a junior in 1955–56.... Excerpt from school guide: "Exceptionally quick reflexes and a good eye are his main attributes although he also has tremendous spring making him a good rebounder."

JIM KONSTANTY, Syracuse

National League MVP in 1950 when he pitched in a major league record 74 games, all in relief, and compiled a 16-7 record and 2.66 ERA for the N.L. champion Philadelphia Phillies. Lost 1950 World Series opener to the New York Yankees as a starter, 1-0, before relieving in two other Series games. Compiled career record of 66-48 in 11 seasons (1944, 1946, 1948–56) with the Cincinnati Reds, Boston Braves, Phillies, Yankees, and St. Louis Cardinals.... Member of 1937–38 and 1938–39 Syracuse basketball teams.

CAL KOONCE, Campbell

Compiled a 47-49 record in 10 seasons with the Chicago Cubs, New York Mets, and Boston

Mississippi basketball star Don Kessinger became a six-time All-Star shortstop in the major leagues.

Speedy Arizona guard Kenny Lofton turned into a speedy Cleveland Indian rookie of the year.

Red Sox (1962–71). He was a reliever for the 1969 Amazin' Mets World Series champions.... Standout basketball player for Campbell in 1960 and 1961 when the North Carolina-based school was a junior college.

SANDY KOUFAX, Cincinnati

Baseball Hall of Famer compiled a 165-87 record and 2.76 ERA in 12 seasons as a lefthanded pitcher with the Brooklyn (1955–57) and Los Angeles (1958–66) Dodgers. Led the National League in ERA in each of his last five seasons. Was 25-5 in 1963, 26-8 in 1965, and 27-9 in 1966 when he won the Cy Young Award. Named N.L. MVP in 1963. Pitched four no-hit games. Compiled a 4-3 record and 0.95 ERA in eight World Series games in 1959, 1963, 1965, and 1966.... Attended Cincinnati one year on a combination basketball/baseball scholarship before signing a pro baseball contract. Third-leading scorer with

9.7-point average as a 6-1, 190-pound forward for the Bearcats' freshman team in 1953–54.... Ed Jucker, coach of Cincinnati's NCAA titlists in 1961 and 1962, coached the Bearcats' 1953–54 freshman team. Jucker said of Koufax's basketball ability: "He could jump extremely well, was a strong kid and a good driver. He would have made a fine varsity player. We certainly could have used him."

KENNY LOFTON, Arizona

Led Cleveland Indians with a .325 batting mark (fourth in the American League) and paced majors with 70 stolen bases in 1993. After his brief major league debut with the Houston Astros in 1991, he was traded to Cleveland where he hit .285 in 1992 and led the A.L. in stolen bases with 66, a record for an A.L. rookie.... Averaged 4.8 points and 2.6 assists per game in four seasons (1985–86 through 1988–89) with the Wildcats. Set school records for steals in a season (67 in 1988–89) and career (200). Member of team that compiled a 35-3 record and reached the 1988 Final Four.

JERRY LUMPE, Southwest Missouri State

Infielder hit .268 in 12-year career (1956–67) with the New York Yankees, Kansas City Athletics, and Detroit Tigers. Played in 1957 and 1958 World Series with the Yankees.... Member of Southwest Missouri squads that won 1952 and 1953 NAIA Tournament titles.

DON LUND, Michigan

Outfielder hit .240 in seven-year career (1945, 1947–49, 1952–54) with the Brooklyn Dodgers, St. Louis Browns, and Detroit Tigers.... First-round selection as a fullback/linebacker by the Chicago Bears in the 1945 NFL draft. Rejected $100 a game offer from the Bears and never played pro football.... He was a starting guard as a junior for the Wolverines' basketball team and starting center as a senior.... In his history of Michigan basketball, Jeff Mortimer wrote of the school's World War II squads: "Lund, rejected for military service because of a trick knee, was the mainstay of these teams." ... Following his playing career, he served as baseball coach at Michigan (won 1962 College World Series), farm system director for the Tigers, and associate athletic director at his alma mater.

TONY LUPIEN, Harvard

First baseman hit .268 in six seasons (1940, 1942–45, and 1948) with the Boston Red Sox, Philadelphia Phillies, and Chicago White Sox. The former baseball coach at Dartmouth was co-author of the book *The Imperfect Diamond: The Story of Baseball's Reserve Clause and the Men Who Fought to Change It*.... The 5-10, 185-pound guard was captain of the 1938–39 Harvard basketball squad. The previous season, he was the school's second-leading scorer in conference competition with 5.4 points per game.

TED LYONS, Baylor

Baseball Hall of Famer spent entire career with the Chicago White Sox (1923–42, 1946) after never playing in the minors. Managed White Sox from 1946 through 1948. Three-time 20-game winner compiled a 260-230 record and 3.67 ERA in 594 games. Pitched no-hitter against

Boston Red Sox in 1926.... Earned four basketball letters at Baylor from 1919–20 through 1922–23. Consensus first-team selection on All-Southwest Conference squad as a sophomore and senior.

BILL McCAHAN, Duke

Pitcher for four seasons (1946–49) with the Philadelphia Athletics. Hurled seven-inning shutout in his first major league game and no-hitter vs. Washington on September 3, 1947.... Three-year letterman for Duke basketball teams that finished second in the Southern Conference Tournament in 1940 and won title in 1941 and 1942. Named to United Press all-tourney team in 1942 when the 5-11, 200-pound guard finished second on the Blue Devils in scoring. Played briefly for the Syracuse Nationals in the National Basketball League in the 1946-47 season.

BEN McDONALD, Louisiana State

Baltimore Orioles pitcher since 1989 won at least 12 games in 1992, 1993, and 1994, including a team record first seven decisions in 1994.... Played in 32 games, starting six, as a 6-6 freshman forward for LSU in 1986–87. Averaged 2.8 points per game with a high of 13 against Auburn. Played in six basketball games the next season before concentrating on his baseball career.

MEL McGAHA, Arkansas

Former manager of the Cleveland Indians (1962) and Kansas City Athletics (June 11, 1964–May 14, 1965).... The first player in Arkansas history to earn four letters in basketball (1943–44 through 1946–47). Played for the New York Knickerbockers of the Basketball Association of America in 1948–49.

SAM MELE, New York University

Major league outfielder (1947–56) and manager of Minnesota Twins (1961–67). Hit .267 in 1,046 games with the Boston Red Sox, Washington Senators, Chicago White Sox, Baltimore Orioles, Cincinnati Reds, and Cleveland Indians. Led American League with 36 doubles for the

Senators in 1951 and drove in six runs in one inning in a 1952 game for the White Sox. Managed Twins in 1965 when they won A.L. title.... The 6-0, 180-pound guard played two seasons of varsity basketball before entering the military. Named to the first five on the All-Metropolitan New York team as a sophomore in 1942–43 when he was the Violets' leading scorer in the NCAA Tournament (losses against Georgetown and Dartmouth).

EDDIE O'BRIEN, Seattle

Infielder-outfielder played five seasons (1953, 1955–58) with the Pittsburgh Pirates, hitting .236 in 231 games. Twin brother of former major leaguer Johnny O'Brien, a teammate at Seattle.... Averaged 12.1 points per game in 1950–51, 10.6 in 1951–52, and 16.5 in 1952–53. Third-team All-American selection on Converse and United Press All-American squads as a senior. Averaged 15.3 points per game in three NCAA Tournament games in 1953. Finished college career as Seattle's second-leading career scorer (behind Johnny) with 1,237 points.

JOHNNY O'BRIEN, Seattle

Infielder/pitcher played six seasons (1953, 1955–59) with the Pittsburgh Pirates, St. Louis Cardinals, and Milwaukee Braves. Hit .250 and compiled 1-3 pitching record in 339 games. Twin brother of former major leaguer Eddie O'Brien, a teammate at Seattle.... The 5-9, 160-pound guard scored 2,733 points in three varsity seasons (1950–51 through 1952–53), averaging 20.7 points per game as a sophomore, 28.4 as a junior, and 28.6 as a senior. Scored 51 points against Gonzaga on February 15, 1953. NCAA consensus All-American second-team choice as a junior and consensus first-team selection as a senior. Averaged 32 points per game in three games in the 1953 NCAA Tournament. Became first college player to score 1,000 points in a season when he scored 1,051 in 37 games in 1951–52.

LOU PINIELLA, Tampa

Seattle Mariners manager hit .291 as an outfielder during 18 seasons (1964, 1968–84) with the Baltimore Orioles, Cleveland Indians, Kansas City Royals, and New York Yankees. Named American League Rookie of the Year in 1969 after hitting .282 for the Royals. Hit .319 in 22 World Series games with the Yankees in 1976, 1977, 1978, and 1981. Also managed the Yankees (1986–88) and Cincinnati Reds (1990–92). Led the Reds to a four-game sweep of the Oakland A's in the 1990 World Series.... Accepted a college basketball scholarship in 1961 after establishing a Tampa city single-season high school scoring record that stood until 1984. Less than a year after enrolling at UT, he signed a baseball contract with the Cleveland Indians.

PAUL POPOVICH, West Virginia

Infielder hit .233 in 11 seasons (1964, 1966–75) with the Chicago Cubs, Los Angeles Dodgers, and Pittsburgh Pirates. Went three-for-three in pinch-hitting appearances for the Pirates in 1974 National League Championship series.... Averaged 3.3 points per game in a reserve role in his one season (1959–60) of varsity basketball with the Mountaineers before signing pro baseball contract. Led freshman team in scoring with 18.8 average. Teammate of Jerry West on squad that compiled a 26-5 record and played in the 1960 NCAA Tournament.... Excerpt from school guide: "Brings poise and confidence, born of extensive baseball training."

CURTIS PRIDE, William & Mary

Outfielder made major league debut with Montreal Expos in 1993 and hit .444 in 10 games. Born with 95 percent hearing disability, he is one of few deaf athletes to ever play major league baseball.... Averaged 5.6 points and 3.1 assists in four seasons (1986–87 through 1989–90) with the Tribe. The 6-0, 185-pound guard led team in steals three times and in assists twice. Named to the Colonial Athletic Association All-Rookie team as a freshman and to the CAA All-Defensive team as a sophomore and junior.... Excerpt from school guide: "Strong player for his size. Exceptionally quick player has moves to penetrate. Frustrates other ball handlers with his ability to make the big steal."

DENNIS RASMUSSEN, Creighton

Compiled 91-76 record in his first 10 seasons (1984–93) with the San Diego Padres, New York Yankees, Cincinnati Reds, Chicago Cubs, and Kansas City Royals.... The 6-7, 215-pound forward averaged 5.1 points per game in three seasons (1977–78 through 1979–80) for Creighton before signing a pro baseball contract.... Excerpt from school guide: "Super sub proved a valuable contributor. Anchoring an important sixthman role, Rasmussen sparks the Bluejay offense with deadeye shooting."

RON REED, Notre Dame

Compiled 146-140 pitching record and 3.46 ERA in 19 seasons (1966–84) with the Atlanta Braves, St. Louis Cardinals, Philadelphia Phillies, and Chicago White Sox. Pitched for Phillies in 1980 and 1983 World Series.... The 6-5, 205-pound forward averaged 18.9 points and 14.3 rebounds in three varsity seasons (1962–63 through 1964–65). Averaged 20 points and 17.7 rebounds as a junior and 21 points and 13.2 rebounds as a senior. Named to Helms Foundation 36-man All-American team as a senior.... Third-round selection of the Detroit Pistons in the 1965 NBA draft, he played two seasons with the franchise, averaging eight points and 6.4 rebounds per game.

STEVE RENKO, Kansas

Compiled 134-146 pitching record in 15 seasons (1969–83) with the Montreal Expos, Chicago Cubs, Chicago White Sox, Oakland Athletics, Boston Red Sox, California Angels, and Kansas City Royals.... Averaged 9.9 points and 5.8 rebounds per game as a sophomore before concentrating on his career as a football quarterback and baseball pitcher.... Excerpt from school guide: "Versatile shooter, tough rebounder and promising playmaker."

DAVE RICKETTS, Duquesne

Catcher hit .249 in six seasons (1962, 1965, 1967–70) with the St. Louis Cardinals and Pittsburgh Pirates. Played with Cardinals in 1967,

and 1968 World Series. Coach, instructor and minor league manager in the Cardinals' organization since 1976.... The 6-2, 190-pound guard was a three-year starter who led the Dukes in scoring in his senior season with a 17.9 average in 1956–57, finishing fourth in the nation in free-throw percentage with an 86.2 mark. Sophomore member of team that compiled a 22-4 record and finished sixth in the final AP poll after winning the NIT.

DICK RICKETTS, Duquesne

Compiled a 1-6 pitching record in his only season with the St. Louis Cardinals in 1959.... The 6-8, 215-pound forward/center was a second-team consensus All-American choice as a junior in 1953-54 and first five consensus All-American selection as a senior in 1954-55. Averaged 17.7 points and 12.2 rebounds per game in starting all 111 games in his four-year Duquense career. First-round pick of the Milwaukee Hawks in the 1955 NBA draft. Played three seasons in the NBA with the St. Louis Hawks and Rochester/Cincinnati Royals, averaging 9.6 points and 6.3 rebounds per game.... Following pro sports career, he was an executive with Eastman Kodak. Died of leukemia on March 6, 1988.

ROBIN ROBERTS, Michigan State

Baseball Hall of Famer compiled a 286-245 record in 19 seasons (1948–66) with the Philadelphia Phillies, Baltimore Orioles, Houston Astros, and Chicago Cubs. Twenty-game winner for six consecutive seasons with the Phillies (1950–55).... Played three seasons of basketball with the Spartans. Averaged 10.6 points per game as a freshman (team's third-leading scorer as he was eligible because of WWII), 9.8 as a sophomore (second-leading scorer), and 9.0 as a junior (second-leading scorer). Forward led team in field-goal percentage as a junior.... Sketch from school basketball guide: "Regarded by newsmen as one of the greatest players today in college basketball. A poll by the *Detroit Free Press* named him the 'most valuable' collegiate player in Michigan. He is not especially fast, but he's extremely well-coordinated, passes exceptionally well, and is a beautiful one-hand shot artist."

JACKIE ROBINSON, UCLA

Member of Baseball Hall of Fame was an infielder who hit .311 and was a regular on six National League pennant winners with the Brooklyn Dodgers in 10 seasons (1947–56).... Football, basketball and track standout at Pasadena City College in 1937–38 and 1938–39. Named to All-Southern California Junior College Conference Western Division all-star basketball team both years, a span in which UCLA was winless in league competition. First athlete in UCLA history to letter in football, basketball, baseball, and track. Forward compiled highest scoring average in the Pacific Coast Conference both seasons at UCLA (12.3 points per league game in 1939–40 and 11.1 in 1940–41). In his last UCLA athletic contest, he accounted for more than half of the Bruins' output with 20 points in a 52-37 loss to Southern Cal.

GARRY ROGGENBURK, Dayton

Lefthanded pitcher compiled a 6-9 record during five seasons (1963, 1965, 1966, 1968, 1969) with the Minnesota Twins, Boston Red Sox, and Seattle Pilots.... The 6-6, 190-pound forward led the Flyers in scoring all three of his varsity seasons (16.1 points per game as a sophomore and junior and 16 ppg as a senior) and led the team in rebounding as a sophomore (13.8 per game) and junior (12.5). Named to third team on Helms All-American squad as a senior in 1962 when Dayton won the NIT.

MARIUS RUSSO, Long Island University

Compiled a 45-34 record and 3.13 ERA in six seasons (1939–43, 1946) with the New York Yankees. Registered a pair of 2-1 World Series victories (over the Brooklyn Dodgers in 1941 and St. Louis Cardinals in 1943).... Played on two of the premier teams in college basketball history when LIU went 24-2 in 1934–35 and 26-0 in 1935–36. Named to the first five on the 1935–36 Metropolitan New York Basketball Writers Association All-Star Team.

TED SAVAGE, Lincoln (Mo.)

Director of target marketing for the St. Louis Cardinals. Outfielder hit .233 in nine seasons (1962–63, 1965–75) with the Philadelphia Phillies, Pittsburgh Pirates, St. Louis Cardinals, Chicago Cubs, Los Angeles Dodgers, Cincinnati Reds, Milwaukee Brewers, and Kansas City Royals.... The 6-0, 175-pounder led Jefferson City, Missouri-based Lincoln in scoring with an average of 13.5 points per game in 1955–56.

DON SCHWALL, Oklahoma

Compiled a 49-48 pitching record in seven seasons (1961–67) with the Boston Red Sox, Pittsburgh Pirates, and Atlanta Braves. Named American League Rookie of the Year in 1961 when he posted a 15-7 mark and 3.22 ERA for the Red Sox.... As a 6-5, 190-pound sophomore forward in 1956–57, he led the Sooners in rebounding with 8.7 per game and finished as the team's second-leading scorer with a 15.9-point average. Scored 23, 20, and 30 points in three defeats against Wilt Chamberlain-led Kansas. Dropped off OU squad in December of junior year after signing a bonus contract with the Red Sox for a reported $50,000.... Excerpt from school guide: "Became highest scoring sophomore in Sooner history. Tremendous rebounder and has exceptional speed for a man his size. Can work inside or outside."

JEFF SHAW, Rio Grande

Pitcher for the Montreal Expos after previously playing for the Cleveland Indians.... He averaged 1.3 points per game as a 6-2, 170-pound freshman guard on the 1984–85 Rio Grande squad that compiled a 31-5 record and reached the second round of the NAIA Tournament.

ROLLIE SHELDON, Connecticut

Compiled a 38-36 pitching record in five seasons (1961, 1962, and 1964–1966) with the

New York Yankees, Kansas City Athletics, and Boston Red Sox. He was 11-5 as a rookie with the American League champion Yankees.... The 6-4 sophomore forward was the third-leading scorer with 13.5 points per game for the Huskies' NCAA Tournament basketball team in 1959–60. He also averaged 7.1 rebounds per game.

NORM SIEBERN, Southwest Missouri State

First baseman-outfielder hit .272 with 132 home runs in 12 seasons (1956, 1958–68) with the New York Yankees, Kansas City Athletics, Baltimore Orioles, California Angels, San Francisco Giants, and Boston Red Sox. Played in 1956 and 1958 World Series with the Yankees and 1967 World Series with the Red Sox.... Member of Southwest Missouri squads that won back-to-back NAIA Tournament titles in 1952 and 1953.

SONNY SIEBERT, Missouri

Compiled a 140-114 pitching record in 12 seasons (1964–75) with the Cleveland Indians, Boston Red Sox, Texas Rangers, St. Louis Cardinals, San Diego Padres, and Oakland A's. Pitched a no-hitter for the Indians against the Washington Senators on June 10, 1966. Selected for All-Star Game in 1966 and 1971.... A 6-3 guard, he played two seasons of varsity basketball for the Tigers (1956–57 and 1957–58) before signing a pro baseball contract. Averaged 13.4 points per game as a sophomore (school record at the time for scoring by a first-year player) and 16.7 as a junior. Led Mizzou in scoring in his junior season, including a 31-point outburst against Oklahoma on February 15, 1958.... Sketch in school guide: "Feathery jump shooter who owns a wide repertoire of shots. Handles the ball well to clear many of his shot tries. Good driver can play either outside or in."

JOHN SIMMONS, New York University

Outfielder with the Washington Senators in 1949.... Starting guard averaged 8.7 points per game for NYU's 17-6 NCAA Tournament team in 1943.

LEE SMITH, Northwestern (La.) State

All-time major league career saves leader, notching more than 400 in his first 15 seasons (1980–94) with the Chicago Cubs, Boston Red Sox, St. Louis Cardinals, New York Yankees, and Baltimore Orioles. Set a record in 1991 (subsequently broken) for most saves in a season by a National League pitcher with 47 for the Cardinals. Six-time All-Star finished 1993 season with a 2.91 ERA in 850 games.... The 6-5, 215-pound forward averaged 3.4 points and 1.9 rebounds per game with the Demons in his only season of college basketball.

TIM STODDARD, North Carolina State

Pitched in 485 games, all as a reliever, in 13 seasons (1975, 1978–89) with the Chicago White Sox, Baltimore Orioles, Chicago Cubs, San Diego Padres, New York Yankees, and Cleveland Indians. Compiled a 41-35 record with 3.95 ERA and 76 saves. Recorded 26 saves for the Orioles in 1980 the year after being the winning pitcher for them in Game Four of the 1979 World Series against the Pittsburgh Pirates.... Played three seasons (1972–73 through 1974–75) of varsity basketball at N.C. State as a 6-7, 230-pound forward. Averaged 7.9 points and 5.3 rebounds as a sophomore, 5.5 and 4.5 as a junior, and 5.6 and 4.8 as a senior as the Wolfpack won 69 of 76 games in that span. Starting forward opposite David Thompson on 1974 NCAA champion.... Sketch in school guide: "Filled a vital role as a starter with his rebounding and defensive play. Has proven himself a clutch performer on numerous occasions."

TED TAPPE, Washington State

Outfielder with Cincinnati Reds (1950 and 1951) and Chicago Cubs (1955).... The 6-3, 185-pound guard was the leading scorer in the 1949 NJCAA national tournament with 81 points in four games in helping Olympic Junior College (Bremerton, Wash.) to a fourth-place finish. He was the third-leading scorer (6.8 points per game) in his only season with the Cougars before signing a pro baseball contract.

JIM UMBRICHT, Georgia

Compiled a 9-5 record and 3.00 ERA in 88 games in five seasons (1959–63) with the Pittsburgh Pirates and Houston Colt .45s before dying of cancer on April 9, 1964.... Three-year basketball letterman captained the Georgia team as a senior in 1951–52.

CECIL UPSHAW, Centenary

Reliever compiled a 34-36 record with 3.13 ERA and 86 saves in nine seasons (1966–69, 1971–75) with the Atlanta Braves, Houston Astros, Cleveland Indians, New York Yankees, and Chicago White Sox. Posted 2.84 ERA in three relief appearances for the Braves in 1969 National League Championship Series. Led Braves in saves five times, including career-high 27 for 1969 N.L. Western Division champions.... The 6-6, 185-pound forward averaged 13.7 points and six rebounds per game from 1961–62 through 1963–64. Led team in scoring as a junior (15.4) and finished as Centenary's third-leading career scorer.... Excerpt from school guide: "Deadly shooter from the corner but lacks strength to battle the boards with the bigger boys."

INMAN (COOT) VEAL, Auburn

Infielder for six seasons (1958–63) with the Detroit Tigers, Washington Senators, and Pittsburgh Pirates. Named to *The Sporting News* Rookie All-Star Team in 1958 after hitting .256 for the Tigers.... Led Auburn in scoring as a sophomore in his only season of varsity basketball (10.9 points per game in 1951–52) before signing a pro baseball contract.

BOB VEALE, Benedictine College (Kan.)

Compiled a 120-95 pitching record and 3.08 ERA in 13 seasons (1962–74) with the Pittsburgh Pirates and Boston Red Sox. Lefthander led National League in strikeouts with 250 in 1964, the first of four consecutive years he won at least 16 games. Two-time N.L. All-Star twice struck out 16 batters in a game.... Scored 1,160 points in three seasons (1955–56 through 1957–58) as a 6-5, 205-pound center for the Atchison (Kan.)-based school that was then called St. Benedict's.

PRESTON WARD, Southwest Missouri State

First baseman-outfielder hit .253 in nine seasons (1948, 1950, 1953–59) with the Brooklyn Dodgers, Chicago Cubs, Pittsburgh Pirates, Cleveland Indians, and Kansas City Athletics.... The 6-4, 190-pound Ward was the second-leading scorer on Southwest Missouri's Teams in 1946–47 (8.1 points per game) and 1948–49 (12.2). Named to the first five on the All-Missouri Intercollegiate Athletic Association team both of those seasons.

BILLY WERBER, Duke

Infielder hit .271 in 11 seasons (1930, 1933–42) with the New York Yankees, Boston Red Sox, Philadelphia Athletics, Cincinnati Reds, and New York Giants. Led American League in stolen bases in 1934, 1935, and 1937. Regular third baseman on the Reds' National League pennant winners in 1939 and 1940. First player to bat in a televised major league game (Reds vs. Brooklyn on August 26, 1939).... First Duke player to earn All-American honors in basketball. He was named to the 10-man Christy Walsh Syndicate All-American team following his senior season in 1929–30 when the Blue Devils were 18-2. Second-leading scorer on Southern Conference Tournament runner-up as both a junior and senior.

SAMMY WHITE, Washington

Catcher hit .262 in 11 seasons with the Boston Red Sox (1951–59), Milwaukee Braves (1961), and Philadelphia Phillies (1962).... Averaged 10.1 points per game as a 6-3, 195-pound forward with the Huskies in three varsity seasons (1946–47 through 1948–49). Named to first five on All-Pacific Coast Conference Northern Division team as a junior and senior.... Sketch in school guide: "White's variations on traditional tosses not only make him a treacherous offensive weapon, but one of the greatest crowd pleasers to perform under the Husky banner in many a moon. Perhaps the fastest man on club, and although his forte is offensive punch, he is far from impotent on defense."

DAVE WINFIELD, Minnesota

Outfielder has hit .285 in 21 seasons so far (1973–88, 1990–94) with the San Diego Padres, New York Yankees, California Angels, Toronto Blue Jays, and Minnesota Twins. Played in 12 All-Star Games. Reached 3,000-hit mark during 1993 season.... Played two seasons of varsity basketball as a 6-6, 220-pound forward with the Gophers, averaging 6.9 points and 5.4 rebounds per game as a junior in 1971–72 and 10.5 points and 6.1 rebounds as a senior in 1972–73.... Selected by the Atlanta Hawks in the fifth round of the 1973 NBA draft and the Utah Stars in the sixth round of the 1973 ABA draft. Didn't play college football, but chosen in 17th round of the 1973 NFL draft by the Minnesota Vikings.... Excerpt from school guide: "Recruited out of intramural ranks to lend depth, became a starter and was a giant in the stretch drive. Amazing athlete leaps like a man catapulted. Soft touch from medium range."

BOBBY WINKLES, Illinois Wesleyan

Coached Arizona State to College World Series titles in 1965, 1967, and 1969 before managing the California Angels in 1973 and through the first 74 games of 1974. Reggie Jackson, Rick Monday, and Sal Bando were among the more than 20 future major leaguers he coached at ASU.... Led Illinois Wesleyan in scoring as a senior in 1950–51 (12 points per game). The 5-9, 170-pound guard was a first-team selection in the College Conference of Illinois.

CHUCK WORKMAN, Central Missouri State

Outfielder-third baseman hit .242 in six seasons (1938, 1941, 1943–46) with the Cleveland Indians, Boston Braves, and Pittsburgh Pirates. Finished second in the National League in home runs in 1945 with 25 for the Braves.... Led team in scoring as sophomore (8.9 points per game in 1934–35) and junior (10.5) and was second-leading scorer as a senior (9.5). Leading scorer in tourney with 38 points in three games when Central Missouri won the first National Intercollegiate Tournament (now NAIA Tournament) at

Kansas City in 1937.... First five selection on the Missouri Intercollegiate Athletic Association all-star team as a sophomore and junior.

FOOTBALL STANDOUTS

WARREN AMLING, Ohio State

College Football Hall of Famer is one of few athletes to earn consensus All-American honors at two positions (guard in 1945 and tackle in 1946). Member of 1944 Ohio State football team that finished with a 9-0 record, won the Big Ten title, and finished second behind Army in the final Associated Press poll.... Three-year letterman for the Buckeyes' basketball team from 1944–45 through 1946–47. Starting guard on Final Four squads in 1945 and 1946. Second-team All-Big Ten selection in basketball in 1945–46.

KEN ANDERSON, Augustana (Ill.)

Quarterback passed for 32,838 yards and 197 touchdowns in 16 seasons (1975–85) with the Cincinnati Bengals. Played in three NFL Pro Bowl games and one Super Bowl.... Swingman finished Augustana career as the fifth-leading scorer in school history with 1,044 points. Led team in field goal and free throw shooting as a freshman and sophomore. High school teammate of college and pro star Dan Issel.... Quote from Augustana coach Jim Borcherding in school guide: "His outstanding ability and leadership qualities make him an inspiration both to his teammates and to the fans."

DOUG ATKINS, Tennessee

Member of College Football Hall of Fame and Pro Football Hall of Fame. Eight-time Pro Bowl game participant played 17 seasons (1953–69) as a defensive end in the NFL with the Cleveland Browns, Chicago Bears, and New Orleans Saints....

Originally enrolled on a basketball scholarship at Tennessee, where he played one season of varsity basketball before concentrating on football. The 6-5, 210-pound center averaged 9.9 points per game for the 1950–51 Volunteers, ranking third on the team in scoring.

MORRIS (RED) BADGRO, Southern Cal

Pro Football Hall of Famer was an offensive and defensive end with the New York Yankees (1927), New York Giants (1930–35), and Brooklyn Dodgers (1936) in an NFL career that was interrupted by a stint in major league baseball. Hit .257 in two seasons (1929 and 1930) as an outfielder with the St. Louis Browns.... Earned varsity basketball letters for the Trojans in 1924–25 and 1926–27. Named to the first five on the All-Pacific Coast Conference team as a forward in 1926–27 when he was USC's MVP.

AL (BUBBA) BAKER, Colorado State

Played in three Pro Bowl games during 13-year NFL career from 1978–90 as a defensive end with the Detroit Lions, St. Louis Cardinals, Cleveland Browns, and Minnesota Vikings. Named NFC rookie of the year by *The Sporting News* in 1978.... Averaged 4.1 points and 3.5 points per game as a 6-6, 255-pound forward-center for the CSU Rams from 1974–75 through 1977–78.

TERRY BAKER, Oregon State

College Football Hall of Famer won the 1962 Heisman Trophy as a senior quarterback after rushing 115 times for 538 yards (4.7 per carry), completing 112 of 203 passes for a nation-leading 1,738 yards and 15 touchdowns. He also led the country in total offense (2,276 yards) and touchdowns responsible (24). His 99-yard run from scrimmage for a TD accounted for the only points in a 6-0 victory against Villanova in the Liberty Bowl. Played in the NFL with the Los Angeles Rams (1963–65) and in the Canadian Football League with Edmonton (1967).... The 6-3 guard averaged 7.4 points per game in 1960–61, 10.7 in 1961–62, and 13.4 in 1962–63. Second-leading scorer for Beavers squad that reached the 1963 Final Four.... Excerpt from school guide: "Referred to by *Sports Illustrated* as 'Best Athlete in College.' Leader of fastbreak offense."

ERICH BARNES, Purdue

Defensive back intercepted 45 passes in 14 seasons with the Chicago Bears, New York Giants, and Cleveland Browns. Played in six Pro Bowls and six NFL championship games.... He was a 6-3, 190-pound forward-center who played briefly for the Boilermakers' varsity basketball team as a sophomore in 1955–56.

ROOSEVELT BARNES, Purdue

Linebacker with the Detroit Lions in the NFL (1982–85).... Member of 1980 Final Four team. Played briefly for Fort Wayne in the CBA.... Excerpt from school's NIT guide: "Known around the Big Ten as a defensive specialist. Probably Purdue's most emotional cager. Quickness, strength and jumping ability are his strongest assets."

CLIFF BATTLES, West Va. Wesleyan College

Halfback became member of College Football and Pro Football Halls of Fame. Led the NFL in rushing as a rookie in 1932 and in his final season in 1937. First NFL player to rush for 200 yards in a game (215 yards in 16 carries for the Boston Redskins against the New York Giants in 1933).... Played four seasons of varsity basketball in college.

SAMMY BAUGH, Texas Christian

College Football and Pro Football Hall of Famer is considered by many as the finest quarterback in history. Consensus All-American in 1936. Passed for 21,886 yards and 186 touchdowns in 16 years (1937–52) with the Washington Redskins. Led the NFL in passing five times, in punting five times, and in pass interceptions once. Held almost all NFL passing records when he retired.... Three-year letterman in basketball at TCU was an honorable mention selection on the All-Southwest Conference team as a senior in 1936–37.

DICK BEETSCH, Northern Iowa

Set NCAA Small College Division (now Division II) record for most pass receptions in a season in 1953 when he caught 54 passes for 837 yards and nine touchdowns as a sophomore.... He averaged 12 points per game in four seasons of basketball, leading the team in scoring as a sophomore (13.3 ppg) and senior (13.8).

JIM BENTON, Arkansas

Standout end with the Cleveland Rams, Chicago Bears, and Los Angeles Rams (1938–40, 1942–47) after leading the nation's major-college players in pass receptions in 1937. Starter on two NFL champions (Bears '43 and Rams '45). Caught 288 passes for 4,801 yards and 45 touchdowns, finishing NFL career ranked second behind all-time great Don Hutson in pass receptions, receiving yardage, and receiving touchdowns. Led league in pass receptions in 1946 and in pass reception yardage in 1945 and 1946. Caught 10 passes for 303 yards in a 1945 game.... The 6-3, 185-pound forward was the Razorbacks' third-leading scorer in SWC play (7.2 points per game) as a senior in 1937–38 when they won the league title with an 11-1 mark and compiled a 19-3 overall record.

MATT BLUNDIN, Virginia

Quarterback was a second-round pick by the Kansas City Chiefs in the NFL draft after passing for 2,696 yards and 25 touchdowns in his college career. Named ACC offensive football player of the year as a senior.... Started most of his sophomore basketball season, when he averaged six points and 5.8 rebounds per game. The 6-7, 230-pound forward finished his four-year basketball career with averages of 3.6 points and 4.5 rebounds. He averaged 4.7 points and 5.6 rebounds in seven NCAA Tournament games from 1989–91.

ALBIE BOOTH, Yale

College Football Hall of Famer was an All-American single wing tailback in 1929, 1930, and 1931. Gained nationwide attention when he scored all of Yale's points in a 21-13 victory over Army.... The 5-6, 145-pound forward was named to the All-Eastern Intercollegiate League second five as a senior in 1930–31.

GEORGE BORK, Northern Illinois

First college football player to pass for more than 3,000 yards in a season (completed 244 of 374 passes for 3,077 yards and 32 touchdowns in nine games in 1963). Led NCAA college division in passing and total offense in 1962 and 1963.... Led the Interstate Intercollegiate Athletic Conference in scoring and was named to the first team on the IIAC all-star squad as a junior in 1961–62 (21.7 points per game) and as a senior in 1962–63 (23.2). Had a 44-point game against Winona State on February 20, 1962.

ORDELL BRAASE, South Dakota

Defensive end with the Baltimore Colts in 12 NFL seasons (1957–68). Played in two Pro Bowl games and four NFL championship games. Member of 1958, 1959, and 1968 NFL championship teams.... The 6-4, 215-pound center in basketball was a first-team selection in the All-North Central Conference when he averaged 7.8 points per game in 1952–53 and 11 points in 1953–54.

DARRELL (PETE) BREWSTER, Purdue

Receiver caught 210 passes for 3,758 yards and 21 touchdowns in nine seasons (1952–60) with the Cleveland Browns and Pittsburgh Steelers. Played in two Pro Bowl games and started for Cleveland in five NFL championship games. Member of the Browns' 1954 an 1955 NFL champions.... The 6-3, 200-pound forward-center was the Boilermakers' fourth-leading scorer as a junior (6.8 points per game) and senior (5.9 ppg).

JOHNNY BRIGHT, Drake

Canadian Football League Hall of Famer ranked second on the CFL all-time rushing list at the end of his 13-year career. He led the nation's major college players in total offense yardage in 1949 (1,950) and 1950 (2,400) and finished fifth in the 1951 Heisman Trophy voting. Concluded career as major college leader in all-time total offense yardage (5,903).... Scored 35 points in 17 games for the 1949–50 Bulldogs basketball team.

JIM BROWN, Syracuse

Movie actor is member of College Football Hall of Fame and Pro Football Hall of Fame. Earned All-American honors in football and lacrosse. Averaged 6.2 yards per carry as a senior in 1956 and scored 43 points in a game against Colgate. Established NFL career records for yards rushing (12,312), rushing attempts (2,359), rushing average (5.2 per carry), touchdowns (126), and years leading league in rushing (eight) in his nine seasons (1957–65) with the Cleveland Browns.... Averaged 14.9 points per game for the Orangemen basketball team as a sophomore and 11.3 as a junior. He is reluctant to specifically say why he quit the team before his senior season when Syracuse participated in the NCAA Tournament for the first time, but indicated it was because of a racial quota. "They basically didn't want to start more than two blacks although nobody could outrun, outjump, or outshoot me," Brown said.... Excerpt from school guide: "Brownie is a powerfully built youth, who helps under the boards, and is an excellent shot as well."

FRANK BROYLES, Georgia Tech

Arkansas athletic director compiled 149-62-6 record in 20 seasons as head football coach at Missouri (1957) and Arkansas (1958–76). Guided 10 teams to bowl games, winning the AP and UPI national title in 1964.... Four-year starting guard in basketball for Tech. Named to second five on the SEC All-Tournament team in 1944, 1945, and

1947. Second-leading scorer for Tech with a 10.4-point average as a senior in 1946–47.

BOB CAREY, Michigan State

Consensus All-American was captain and leading pass receiver on undefeated and untied 1951 MSU football team. First-round choice of the Los Angeles Rams in 1952 finished his NFL career with the Chicago Bears in 1958.... A forward-center in basketball, he averaged 8.8 points per game in three varsity seasons.... Excerpt from school guide: "Extremely fast for his size (6-5, 220). Ranks as finest all-around athlete in school history."

HAROLD CARMICHAEL, Southern (La.)

Wide receiver caught 590 passes for 8,985 yards and 79 touchdowns in 14-year career with the Philadelphia Eagles (1971–83) and Dallas Cowboys (1984). Four-time Pro Bowl Game participant established an NFL record for most consecutive games with a pass reception (127).... Former Southern basketball coach Dick Mack said Carmichael was a starter his last two seasons with the Jaguars and their top rebounder.

CHUCK CARNEY, Illinois

College Football Hall of Famer was a consensus All-American choice as an end in 1920. Only Illini athlete to earn All-American honors in both football and basketball.... The Helms Foundation named him to its 10-man All-American basketball teams for the 1919–20 and 1921–22 seasons and named him player of the year for the 1921–22 season. Led the Big Ten in scoring with 15.7 points per game in 1919-20 and 14.3 in 1921-22.... Sketch in *Spalding Official Basketball Guide*: "Possessed of reach, height, speed and a good eye for the basket, he had all the requisites of a star. No guard was able to hold him in check."

RICK CASARES, Florida

Fullback for 12 NFL seasons (1955–66) with the Chicago Bears, Washington Redskins, and Miami Dolphins. Led league in rushing (1,136 yards) and touchdowns (14) in 1957. Ranks second on Bears career rushing list behind Walter Payton with 5,675 yards.... The 6-2, 205-pound forward led the Gators in scoring and rebounding in both of his varsity seasons—14.9 points and 11.3 rebounds as a sophomore in 1951–52 and 15.5 points and 11.5 rebounds as a junior in 1952–53.

SAM CLANCY, Pittsburgh

Defensive end had 49 sacks in his first 11 seasons in pro football with the Seattle Seahawks, Cleveland Browns, and Indianapolis Colts in the NFL and Pittsburgh and Memphis in the USFL. Played in two AFC championship games with the Browns.... The 6-7, 235-pound basketball center was a member of the gold-medal winning U.S. team in the 1979 Pan American Games. Averaged 14.4 points and 11.6 rebounds per game for Pitt from 1977–78 through 1980–81. Chosen in the third round of 1981 NBA draft by the Phoenix Suns after finishing his college career as the Panthers' all-time leading rebounder. Played 1981–82 season with Billings in the CBA, averaging 11.5 points and 8.3 rebounds per game.... Quote in school guide from West Virginia coach Gale Catlett: "Clancy is Superman in shorts. He's one of the best players I've seen and that includes some great ones."

EARL (DUTCH) CLARK, Colorado College

Member of College Football and Pro Football Halls of Fame. Halfback and quarterback was named to All-NFL team in six of his seven seasons with Portsmouth (1931–32) and Detroit (1934–38). Led NFL in scoring in 1932, 1935, and 1936. Player-coach of Detroit (1937–38) and head coach of Cleveland Rams (1939–42). First-team QB on the 1928 AP All-America team. Scored at least one touchdown in 21 consecutive college football games.... The 6-0, 180-pounder was an All-Rocky Mountain Conference choice in basketball all four seasons (first team as a freshman and senior, second team as a junior, and third team as a sophomore).... Sketch in *Spalding Official Guide*: "There isn't a man who could match Clark as a floor guard. The best dribbler ever to bounce a ball in the conference."

GEORGE CONNOR, Notre Dame

College Football and Pro Football Hall of Famer was Outland Trophy winner (outstanding interior lineman) as a tackle on Notre Dame's 1946 national championship team. Consensus All-American football choice in 1946 and 1947. Earned All-American honors as a tackle at Holy Cross in 1943 before transferring to Notre Dame. Played offensive and defensive tackle and linebacker with the Chicago Bears from 1948 through 1955, earning All-NFL first-team honors from 1949 through 1953.... Averaged 2.5 points per game as a 6-3, 225-pound center on the Irish's 1946–47 basketball team.

CHARLIE COWAN, New Mexico Highlands

Three-time Pro Bowl game participant was an offensive tackle for 15 seasons with the Los Angeles Rams (1961–75).... The 6-4, 260-pound basketball center averaging 15 points and 15.6 rebounds per game in his college career (20.7 points and 18.3 rebounds as a junior and 19.5 points and 18.3 rebounds as a senior).... Excerpt from school guide: "Rugged under the basket but moves with the grace of a cat playing at the post. He will drive the basket from either side and also has a good hook shot."

HERBERT (FRITZ) CRISLER, Chicago

College Football Hall of Famer compiled 116-32-9 record in 18 seasons as football coach at Minnesota (1930-31), Princeton (1932-37), and Michigan (1938-47). The only team he coached with a losing record was in his first year. His last seven Michigan teams finished in the top 10 in the final Associated Press Poll. The 1947 Wolverines had a 10-0 record, defeated Southern Cal in the Rose Bowl (49-0), and finished second in the final AP poll behind Notre Dame.... Named to third five on All-Big Ten basketball team in 1919–20 when the University of Chicago was a member of the league.

ERNIE DAVIS, Syracuse

Heisman Trophy winner in 1961. Halfback was consensus All-American choice in 1960 and

1961 after Syracuse won the 1959 national championship. College Football Hall of Famer averaged 6.6 yards per carry and scored 35 touchdowns. Selected by the Washington Redskins as the first player picked in the 1962 NFL draft. His rights were acquired for the great Bobby Mitchell by the Cleveland Browns, who signed Davis that summer before he was diagnosed with leukemia. He never played in the NFL and died on May 18, 1963.... A 6-2, 205-pound forward on the 1960–61 Syracuse varsity basketball team, his rebound average (9.6) was highest on the team and his scoring average (10.2) ranked second.

GLENN DAVIS, Army

College Football Hall of Famer was a consensus All-American in 1944, 1945, and 1946. The 5-9, 170-pound halfback averaged 8.3 yards per carry and scored 59 touchdowns for Army teams that compiled a 34-2-2 record in his four seasons. Won Heisman Trophy in 1946 and was runner-up in 1944 and 1945. Played with the Los Angeles Rams in the NFL in 1950 and 1951.... Member of Army basketball teams as a junior in 1944–45 and as a senior in 1945–46.

LEN DAWSON, Purdue

Pro Football Hall of Famer completed 2,136 for 28,731 yards and 239 touchdowns in 19 seasons (1957–75) with the Cleveland Browns, Dallas Texans, and Kansas City Chiefs. Quarterbacked the Chiefs to victory over the Minnesota Vikings in Super Bowl following 1969 season.... Played in two games as a 6-0, 180-pound guard for Purdue's basketball team in the 1956–57 season.

VERN DEN HERDER, Central College

Defensive lineman played in four Super Bowls with the Miami Dolphins during his 12-year NFL career (1971–82). Starting defensive left end on undefeated 1972 Miami team (17-0).... The 6-6, 220-pound basketball center finished his four-season career at Central College as the Pella, Iowa-based school's all-time leading scorer (15.5 ppg) and rebounder (12.4 rpg). He grabbed a

school-record 29 rebounds in a game his senior season (1970–71).

MIKE DITKA, Pittsburgh

College Football and Pro Football Hall of Famer is a CBS analyst and former coach of the Chicago Bears. The tight end caught 427 passes for 5,812 yards and 43 touchdowns in 12 NFL seasons (1961–72) with the Chicago Bears, Philadelphia Eagles, and Dallas Cowboys. Coached Super Bowl winner in 1985 season when Bears compiled an 18-1 overall record. Registered 112-68 mark in 11 years (1982–92) as coach of the Bears.... Played two seasons as a 6-2, 205-pound forward for the Panthers, averaging 2.8 points and 2.6 rebounds per game.... Sketch in school basketball guide: "A natural athlete who never quits. If Pitt wins a few games, there is a good chance he will be in the thick of things."

VINCE DOOLEY, Auburn

Won national championship in 1980 and six SEC titles as coach at Georgia. Compiled a 201-66-10 record as 20 teams played in bowl games in his 25 seasons (1964–88).... Averaged 6.3 points per game as a starting guard in 1951–52 in his only season of varsity basketball at Auburn before he concentrated on football.

JACK DUGGER, Ohio State

Consensus All-American end on the 1944 OSU football team that finished second behind Army in the final AP poll. Played pro football with three different franchises from 1946 to 1949.... Three-year letterman in basketball was a 6-4, 205-pound starting forward for the Buckeyes' Final Four teams in 1944 and 1945. Played briefly for the Syracuse Nationals in the National Basketball League in 1946–47.

PETE ELLIOTT, Michigan

Pro Football Hall of Fame executive director earned All-American honors as a quarterback on the Wolverines' 1948 national champion. Former head coach at Nebraska (1956), California (1957–59) and Illinois (1960–66) led Cal, and the

Illini to Rose Bowl berths.... A four-year starter as a 6-0, 190-pound guard on Michigan teams from 1945–46 through 1948–49. Captain of squad as a sophomore and member of Big Ten championship team in 1947–48. First-team all-conference choice as a junior and second-team selection as a senior. Second-team pick on Helms All-American team in 1947–48.... Excerpt from school guide: "At times his defensive work was almost uncanny as he held high-scoring opposition practically scoreless in several games. Outstanding at recovering rebounds."

RAY EVANS, Kansas

College Football Hall of Famer earned All-American honors as a back in 1942 and 1947 in a career interrupted by World War II. Led nation's major-college players in passes attempted (200) and completed (101) and interceptions (10) in 1942 for a rare triple crown. Played in NFL with the Pittsburgh Steelers in 1948 before becoming a prominent Kansas City bank official.... Four-year basketball letterman was the second-leading scorer in 1942 NCAA Tournament for the Jayhawks. Earned Helms Foundation All-American honors in 1941–42 and 1942–43.

WEEB EWBANK, Miami of Ohio

Pro Football Hall of Famer is only head coach to win championships in both the NFL (Baltimore Colts in 1958 and 1959) and AFL (New York Jets in 1968).... Two-year basketball letterman at Miami (1926–27 and 1927–28) was head basketball coach at Brown University in 1946–47.

BEATTIE FEATHERS, Tennessee

Became first NFL player to rush for 1,000 yards or more in season when he had 1,004 yards (9.9 per carry) as a rookie with the Chicago Bears in 1934. College Football Hall of Famer was a consensus All-American halfback in 1933. Played seven seasons in the NFL with the Bears (1934–37), Brooklyn Dodgers (1938–39) and Green Bay Packers (1940).... Regular on the 1931–32 Volunteers' basketball squad.

WES FESLER, Ohio State

College Football Hall of Famer was consensus All-American end in 1928, 1929, and 1930. Named to Grantland Rice's all-time All-American team in 1939. Coach at Pittsburgh (1946), Ohio State (1947–50), and Minnesota (1951–53).... The 6-0, 185-pounder was a second-team All-Big Ten basketball selection as a sophomore and a first-team choice as a senior.

JIM FINKS, Tulsa

Recently deceased NFL executive was a defensive back and quarterback with the Pittsburgh Steelers (1949–55). Selected to the Pro Bowl following 1952 season after leading NFL in touchdown passes with 20. Led NFL in passes attempted (344), passes completed (165), and passing yardage (2,270) in 1955. Played with Calgary in the Canadian Football League in 1957.... The 6-0, 170-pound Finks was a four-year varsity basketball player at Tulsa, leading the team in scoring average as a sophomore with 8.9 points per game in 1946–47. Held school single-game scoring record at the time with 28 points against Drake.

ARNOLD GALIFFA, Army

College Football Hall of Famer was a consensus All-American selection in 1949 and finished fourth in voting for Heisman Trophy. Quarterback of Cadet teams that compiled a 31-2-3 record from 1946 through 1949. Played in the NFL and CFL.... Army's third-leading scorer in basketball as a freshman (6.2 points per game) and as a junior (9.1) before becoming second-leading scorer as a senior (9.2).... Served as an aide to Gen. Matthew Ridgeway and Gen. Mark Clark during the Korean War before becoming an executive with U.S. Steel.

PETE GENT, Michigan State

Flanker and tight end caught 68 passes for 989 yards and four touchdowns with the Dallas

Cowboys from 1964–68…. Author of several novels, including *North Dallas Forty* and *The Franchise*. His most recent title is *The Conquering Heroes,* a cynical look at a fictional renegade college basketball program…. Averaged 17.4 points and 8.3 rebounds per game in leading the Spartans in scoring each of his three varsity seasons (1961–62 through 1963–64). The 6-4, 200-pound forward scored 34 points against Bowling Green State in his senior year when he ranked 62nd in the country in scoring with 21.1 ppg…. Excerpt from school guide: "Fine playmaker with excellent ability in shooting, driving, dribbling and passing. Hardnosed competitor."

GEORGE GIPP, Notre Dame

College Football Hall of Famer earned All-American football honors in 1919 and 1920. Legendary halfback scored 12 points in four games for the 1918–19 Irish basketball team.

OTTO GRAHAM, Northwestern

Member of College Football and Pro Football Halls of Fame. Quarterback earned All-American honors and finished third in Heisman Trophy voting as a senior in 1943. Played 10 seasons (1946–55) with the Cleveland Browns and led team to championship game each year (All-American Football Conference from 1946 to 1949 and NFL from 1950 to 1955). Compiled a 105-17-4 record in regular-season pro competition, completing 1,464 of 2,626 passes for 23,584 yards and 174 touchdowns…. Played three seasons of varsity basketball, finishing second in the Big Ten in scoring as a sophomore (13.1 points per game) and as a junior (15.8). The 6-0 forward earned second-team All-Big Ten honors in 1941–42 and first five honors in 1942–43. Also played for Colgate as a senior. NCAA consensus first-team All-American in 1944 and second-team All-American in 1943. Left Northwestern with the highest scoring total in school history with more than 600 points. Played one season with the Rochester Royals in the National Basketball League, averaging 5.2 points per game for the 1945–46 squad that won the NBL title.

HARRY (BUD) GRANT, Minnesota

Former NFL and CFL end and coach. Played with Philadelphia in the NFL from 1951 to 1952 and Winnipeg of the CFL from 1953 to 1956. Caught 88 passes for 4,197 yards and 20 touchdowns in six pro seasons, leading the CFL in pass receptions in 1953, 1954, and 1956. Coached Winnipeg in the CFL (1957–66) and Minnesota in the NFL (1967–85). Coach of four CFL champions and four NFL Super Bowl teams…. Third-leading scorer for the Gophers' basketball squad in 1948–49 (8.5 points per game) after being named team MVP the previous season over first-team All-American Jim McIntyre. Finished 13th in the Big Ten in scoring in 1946–47 with a 9.3 average. Played two seasons in the NBA, including a rookie year when he was a member of the Minneapolis Lakers' 1950 championship team.

CORNELL GREEN, Utah State

Intercepted 34 passes in 13 years as a defensive back with the Dallas Cowboys (1962–74). Played in five Pro Bowl games and two Super Bowls…. Finished his three-year varsity career as Utah State's all-time leading scorer with 1,890 points. The 6-4 forward led the Aggies in scoring with 21.2 points per game in 1959–60 (34th in the nation), 20.3 in 1960–61 (57th) and 25.6 in 1961–62 (13th). Held under 10 points only once in college career and scored 46 against New Mexico on March 3, 1962. The school's all-time leading rebounder set a single-season record with 403 boards in 1959–60. Helms Foundation second-team All-American as a senior, when he averaged 24.3 points per game in three NCAA Tournament contests…. Review of his career in school guide: "He had an array of moves and shots that ranged from quick reverse pivots under the hoop to overpowering physical strength as a rebounder and tap shot artist."

BOB GRIESE, Purdue

TV analyst and member of College Football and Pro Football Halls of Fame. Quarterback played 14 seasons (1967–80) with the Miami Dolphins, completing 1,926 of 3,429 passes for 25,093 yards and 192 touchdowns. Played in six Pro Bowl games and three Super Bowls.... As a 6-1, 185-pound sophomore guard in 1964–65, he scored 22 points in 16 games in his only varsity basketball season with the Boilermakers.

GEORGE HALAS, Illinois

Pro Football Hall of Famer compiled a 324-151-31 record as an NFL coach, guiding the Chicago Bears to seven NFL titles. His 40-year NFL coaching career also included stints with the Decatur/Chicago Staleys.... The 6-0, 175-pound Halas was a starting guard for the Illini team that won the Big Ten basketball title in 1916–17 with a 10-2 record. He was captain of the squad the next season before entering the armed forces.

DALE HALL, Army

Successor to legendary Red Blaik as football coach at Army. Compiled w4-4-1, 6-3-1 and 6-4 records from 1959 to 1961.... Named college basketball player of the year by *The Sporting News* in 1943–44 when he was the leading scorer (18.2 points per game) for a Cadet team that compiled a 15-0 record and was ranked No. 1 in the nation by the Dick Dunkel rankings. The next season as a senior, he was the team scoring leader (14.2 ppg) for a 14-1 squad. NCAA consensus second-team All-American in 1944 and 1945. Recipient of the Army Athletic Association trophy presented annually to the man who renders "the most valuable service to athletics during his cadet career."

VIC HANSON, Syracuse

Consensus All-American end in 1926 served as head football coach at his alma mater from 1930 through 1936, compiling a 33-21-5 record, including a 7-1-1 mark in 1931.... Forward was named to Helms Athletic Foundation 10-man All-American basketball teams selected in 1943 for the 1924–25, 1925–26, and 1926–27 seasons. Naismith Memorial Hall of Famer was designated college basketball player of the year by Helms in his senior season.

WAYNE HARDIN, Pacific

Head football coach at U.S. Naval Academy (1959–64) and Temple (1970–82). Coached Heisman Trophy winner Roger Staubach in 1963 when Navy finished second in the nation in the final AP poll with a 9-2 record.... Letterman on four Pacific basketball teams in the late 1940s.

KEVIN HARDY, Notre Dame

Defensive end and tackle for four seasons in the NFL with three different teams. Two-time All-American with the Irish, including 1966 as a junior on the school's national championship football team.... The 6-5, 260-pound forward-center averaged 2.1 points and 2.3 rebounds per game in his one season of basketball (1964–65).

TOM HARMON, Michigan

Two-time consensus All-American halfback won Heisman Trophy in 1940. Played two seasons (1946 and 1947) with the Los Angeles Rams following World War II military service.... Averaged 7.6 points per game as a sophomore in 1938–39 and led the Wolverines in scoring in five contests. Posted 2.5-point average the next year as a junior.... Michigan coach Bennie Oosterbaan said Harmon "had a great fake and cut, a great shot, and aggressiveness."

HOWARD (RED) HICKEY, Arkansas

Coach of San Francisco 49ers (1959–63) after playing end for the Cleveland and Los Angeles Rams (1941–42, 1945–48). Finished sixth in the NFL in pass receptions in 1941. Member of the Rams' 1945 NFL title team.... The 6-2, 195-pound guard was a second-team All-Southwest Conference choice as a sophomore and junior and a first-team selection as a senior. He was a member of the 1941 team that won the SWC title with a 12-0 record, finished 20-3 overall, and reached the Final Four in its NCAA Tournament debut.

ELROY (CRAZY LEGS) HIRSCH, Wisconsin/Michigan

Member of College Football and Pro Football Halls of Fame. Played halfback, defensive back, and offensive end as a pro with the Chicago Rockets of the All-American Football Conference and Los Angeles Rams of the NFL. Caught 387 passes and scored 66 touchdowns as a pro. Played in four NFL championship games.... Starting center for the Wolverines' basketball team while undergoing military training there.... Sketch in Michigan guide: "Naval transfer from Wisconsin was a big aid, chiefly through his flaming competitive spirit."

PAUL HORNUNG, Notre Dame

College Football and Pro Football Hall of Famer earned All-American honors as a quarterback in 1955 and 1956. Won Heisman Trophy as a senior after finishing fifth as a junior. Played nine seasons as a halfback with the Green Bay Packers, leading the NFL in scoring in 1959, 1960, and 1961. Played in five NFL championship games.... Played varsity basketball for the Irish as a sophomore, averaging 6.1 points per game in 10 contests.

PERCY HOWARD, Austin Peay State

Wide receiver failed to catch a pass in eight regular-season games for the Dallas Cowboys in 1975, but caught a 34-yard touchdown pass from Roger Staubach for their final TD in a 21-17 loss to the Pittsburgh Steelers in Super Bowl X.... Averaged 12.4 points and 7.3 rebounds per game in three varsity seasons (1972–73 through 1974–75) for the Governors as a 6-4, 215-pound forward. He averaged seven points and seven rebounds per game in four NCAA Tournament contests in 1973 and 1974 as a teammate of the celebrated James "Fly" Williams.

JIM LEE HOWELL, Arkansas

New York Giants end (1937–42, 1946–48) and head coach (1954–60). Started for them in four NFL championship games, including 1938 titlist. Coach of Giants team that routed the Chicago Bears, 47-7, in 1956 NFL title game. Also guided New York to 1958 and 1959 NFL championship games.... A 6-5, 200-pounder, he was named to the first five on the All-Southwest Conference team in his senior season (1935–36) as a member of an Arkansas squad that won the league title, compiled a 24-3 record and participated in the U.S. Olympic basketball trials.

JOHNNY JOHNSON, San Jose State

Rushed for 3,147 yards in his first four seasons in the NFL. Played first three pro years with the Phoenix Cardinals before he was traded to the New York Jets and led the Jets in rushing in 1993. Appeared in Pro Bowl following rookie season. As a junior at San Jose State in 1988, he was the first player in NCAA history to rush for more than 1,200 yards (1,219) and catch at least 60 passes (61) in a single season.... Averaged 11.2 points and 6.5 rebounds per game as a 6-3, 210-pound junior forward in 1988–89. Led the Spartans in scoring (23 points) and rebounding (12) in a 95-66 loss to UNLV.

ED (TOO TALL) JONES, Tennessee State

Defensive lineman with the Dallas Cowboys for 15 seasons (1974–78, 1980–89). Appeared in three Super Bowls and three Pro Bowl games.... He was a 6-8, 230-pound backup post player when he averaged 1.7 points and 2.6 rebounds for the Tigers in his freshman and sophomore seasons (1969–70 and 1970–71).

RALPH (SHUG) JORDAN, Auburn

Compiled a 176-83-6 record as head football coach at his alma mater from 1951 to 1975. Led Auburn to berths in 12 bowl games and an AP national title in 1957 with a 10-0 record.... Three-year basketball letterman was captain of the team in his junior season (1930–31).

JOE KAPP, California

Quarterback with Calgary (1959–60) and Vancouver (1961–66) in the Canadian Football League and Minnesota (1967–69) and Boston (1970) in the NFL. Member of CFL Hall of Fame. Passed for 28,836 yards and 194 touchdowns in his pro career. Finished fifth in Heisman Trophy voting in 1958 when he led Cal to a Rose Bowl berth.... The Bears won Pacific Coast Conference titles both years (1956–57 and 1957–58) when he was a 6-3, 195-pound backup forward.... Sketch in school guide: "Powerfully built player has an excellent long jump shot."

LARRY KELLEY, Yale

Heisman Trophy winner in 1936. End earned All-American football honors in 1934, 1935, and 1936.... The 6-1, 190-pound swingman finished 12th in the Eastern Intercollegiate League in scoring in 1935–36 and was seventh in the league in scoring the next season. Honorable mention on all-league team as a junior.

GLENN KILLINGER, Penn State

College Football Hall of Famer was a 1921 consensus All-American as a quarterback-halfback. He played in the NFL with the Canton Bulldogs (1921) and New York Giants (1926).... Three-year basketball letterman on teams that compiled an overall record of 37-5. Captain of team as a senior in 1920–21.

BILLY KILMER, UCLA

Quarterback with the San Francisco 49ers, New Orleans Saints, and Washington Redskins (1961–62, 1964, 1966, 1967–78).... Scored eight points in six games for coach John Wooden's 1959–60 UCLA basketball team.... Excerpt from school guide: "Tried basketball, but his football ankle failed to allow him to perform at his best."

NILE KINNICK, Iowa

Heisman Trophy winner as a quarterback-halfback in 1939 when he rushed and passed for 1,012 yards, intercepted eight passes, punted for a 39.9-yard average, and averaged 11.9 yards on punt returns and 25.1 yards on kickoff returns. Phi Beta Kappa graduate was selected by the Philadelphia Eagles in the first round of 1940 NFL draft.... Bypassed pro football to attend law school. He was killed in a plane crash in 1943 while serving in the Navy during World War II.... The 5-8, 165-pounder played basketball for Iowa during his sophomore year, averaging 6.1 points per game as the team's second-leading scorer.

TERRY KIRBY, Virginia

Miami Dolphins running back started as a rookie and was their leading pass receiver and second-leading rusher after being a third-round pick in the 1993 NFL draft. Set Virginia career rushing record with 3,348 yards on 567 carries.... Averaged 3.4 points per game as a freshman in 1989–90 and 2.1 as a sophomore in 1990–91. Scored 18 points in seven minutes of playing time (hitting 8 of 10 field-goal attempts) against North Carolina State on January 31, 1990.

RON KRAMER, Michigan

Offensive end for 10 seasons (1957 and 1959–67) with Green Bay Packers and Detroit Lions. Caught 229 passes for 3,272 yards and 16 touchdowns in the NFL.... The 6-3, 220-pound forward-center led the Wolverines in scoring as a sophomore (16 points per game) and as a junior (20.4) before finishing second on the team as a senior (14.5). Second-team All-American selection by Converse and third-team pick by National Association of Basketball Coaches as a senior.... Excerpt from school guide: "Can leap and battle as well as shoot, and he's an inspirational type of player who picks up his teammates when he's in there."

JOHN LATTNER, Notre Dame

Consensus All-American halfback won Heisman Trophy in 1953 after finishing fifth in the Heisman voting the previous year. College Football Hall of Famer helped the Irish compile a 23-4-2 record in his three varsity football seasons (1951–53). Played with the Pittsburgh Steelers in the NFL in 1954 before suffering a career-ending knee injury while in military service.... Scored 12 points in four games for the 1951–52 Notre Dame basketball team as a 6-2 forward.

ELMER LAYDEN, Notre Dame

College Football Hall of Famer was a full-back in the famed Four Horseman backfield of the 1920s. Consensus All-American selection in 1924. Head football coach of the Irish from 1934 through 1940, compiling a 47-12-2 record. His 1938 Notre Dame team was named national champion by the Dickinson System.... NFL commissioner from 1941–46.... Scored seven points in 10 games for the 1922–23 Notre Dame basketball squad.

DAVE LOGAN, Colorado

Wide receiver caught 263 passes for 4,250 yards and 24 touchdowns in nine seasons (1976–84) with the Cleveland Browns and Denver Broncos.... Averaged 14.1 points and 6.3 rebounds per game in 58 varsity basketball games for the Buffaloes from 1972–73 through 1975–76 (missed 1974–75 because of a knee injury). Team's second-leading scorer as both a sophomore and senior.

JOHN LUJACK, Notre Dame

Heisman Trophy winner in 1947 after finishing third in voting the previous year. In his three years as quarterback, the College Football Hall of Famer helped the Irish win a national championship each season and a 26-1-1 record overall. Was quarterback, defensive back, and kicker for the Chicago Bears from 1948 through 1951, leading them in scoring all four years. He intercepted a team-high eight passes as a rookie and holds the franchise record for most passing

yards in a game with 468 in a 1949 contest.... Averaged 3.4 points per game as a starting guard for Notre Dame's basketball team in 1943–44.

LAMAR LUNDY, Purdue

Member of the "Fear-some Foursome" for the Los Angeles Rams in his 13–year NFL career (1957-69).... He averaged 10.5 points and 8.5 rebounds per game in three varsity seasons, leading the Boilermakers in rebounding as a junior and senior. He finished 30th in the country in field-goal shooting (48.1 percent) in 1957.... Sketch in school guide: "The most improved player in the Big Ten. The 6-6, 225-pound Lundy was more often than not the equal of or better than opposing centers reaching 6-8 or 6-9. His unusual speed and defensive ability make him a valuable asset."

BOB MacLEOD, Dartmouth

College Football Hall of Famer was consensus All-American halfback in 1938 when he finished fourth in Heisman Trophy voting. Three-year letterman on Dartmouth football teams that compiled a 21-3-3 record under the legendary Red Blaik. Selected by Brooklyn in the first round of the 1939 NFL draft.... Ranked among the Eastern Intercollegiate League's top 20 scorers all three years in college for Dartmouth teams that won the league his last two seasons. Named to first five on all-league team as a senior and second team as a junior.

JACK (CY) McCLAIREN, Bethune-Cookman

Split end with the Pittsburgh Steelers from 1955 through 1960. Finished third in the NFL in pass receptions with 46 in 1957.... A 6-4, 210-pound forward-center in basketball, he was a two-time All-Southern Intercollegiate Athletic Conference selection. In the championship game of the 1953 SIAC tourney, he scored 36 points to lead his team to victory over Xavier of New

Orleans. Served as head basketball coach at his alma mater for 31 seasons before retiring following the 1992–93 campaign.

BANKS McFADDEN, Clemson

College Football Hall of Famer became Clemson's first football All-American in 1939. The halfback finished eighth in the Heisman Trophy voting that year. Selected by the Brooklyn Dodgers in the first round (third player overall) of the 1940 NFL draft. Finished fourth in rushing in the NFL in 1940, averaging 6.3 yards per carry, before entering military service.... Led Clemson in scoring in each of his three seasons on his way to becoming the school's first All-American basketball player. The 6-3, 175-pound center was named to the first five on the Southern Conference all-tournament team three times.

KEITH McKELLER, Jacksonville (Ala.) State

Buffalo Bills tight end has played in four Super Bowl games.... Starting center on Jacksonville State's 1985 NCAA Division II championship team. Led Gulf South Conference in rebounding each of his first three seasons and finished second as a senior. Four-time all-league pick averaged 12.5 points and 10.1 rebounds per game in his career (1982–83 through 1985–86).

GEORGE MARTIN, Oregon

Defensive end who played 14 seasons (1975–88) with the New York Giants. Started for the 1986 Giants team that defeated the Denver Broncos, 39-20, in the Super Bowl. Scored six touchdowns in his NFL career (84-yard run with blocked field goal, three pass interception returns, and two runs with fumble recoveries).... The 6-5, 225-pound forward-center averaged just over 10 points and 10 rebounds per game for the Ducks' freshman squad in 1971–72. He played briefly for the varsity the next season.

PETE METZELAARS, Wabash (Ind.)

Tight end played in five AFC championship games and four Super Bowls in his 13-year career (1982–94) with the Seattle Seahawks and Buffalo Bills. He led the Bills with 68 receptions in 1993.... As a 6-8, 235-pound center at Wabash, he averaged 19.2 points and 11.4 rebounds per game in four varsity seasons. Set NCAA Division III field-goal shooting records for a single season (75.3 percent in 1981–82 as a senior) and career (72.4). Led Wabash to the 1982 Division III Tournament title, scoring a tourney record 129 points in five games and earning tourney outstanding player honors. Collected 45 points and 13 rebounds in the championship game.

DON MILLER, Notre Dame

Halfback in Irish's famous "Four Horsemen" backfield. College Football Hall of Famer earned All-American honors in 1923 and 1924. Former president of the U.S. Attorney's Association was a longtime judge and attorney in Ohio.... Played for Notre Dame's basketball team in 1922–23 and 1923–24.

GEORGE MUSSO, Millikin (Ill.)

Pro Football Hall of Famer played for seven divisional winners and four NFL title teams. The 6-2, 270-pound guard and tackle played for 12 seasons (1933–44) with the Chicago Bears. As a collegian, he played against future president Ronald Reagan, who attended Eureka. As a member of the Bears in 1935, Musso played against future president Gerald Ford in the Bears-College All-Star Game in Chicago.... Three-year basketball letterman in college.

ERNIE NEVERS, Stanford

Member of College Football and Pro Football Halls of Fame. He was a consensus All-American selection as a senior fullback in 1925 before playing in the NFL with the Duluth Eskimos (1926–27) and Chicago Cardinals (1929–31). Set NFL record with a 40-point game against the Chicago Bears in 1929.... Compiled a 6-12 pitching record in three seasons (1926–28) with the St. Louis

Browns.... Lettered in basketball at Stanford as a sophomore and junior. Named to the All-Pacific Coast Conference second five as a junior.... Historians say he was a fine shooter, an excellent dribbler, tough on defense, and generally a terrifying figure for the opposition. The *Spalding Basketball Guide* said: "He is almost as good a basketball player as he is a football star. With his speed, weight and general all-around ability, he was a stellar performer."

GIFFORD NIELSEN, Brigham Young

Quarterback finished sixth in Heisman Trophy voting in 1976. In three seasons at BYU (1975–77), he completed 415 of 708 passes for 5,833 yards and 55 touchdowns. Played six seasons in the NFL with the Houston Oilers (1978–83).... The 6-5, 190-pound forward-guard averaged 6.5 points and 2.7 rebounds per game in 44 varsity contests during the 1973–74 and 1974–75 seasons. Fourth-leading scorer on 1974–75 squad with an 8.7 average.

ELMER OLIPHANT, Purdue/Army

One of the legendary athletes in the history of college sports. Earned nine letters (three in football and two each in basketball, baseball, and track) at Purdue before graduating in 1914. Won 12 letters at Army (U.S. Military Academy) in football, basketball, baseball, track, boxing, and hockey before graduating in 1918. Consensus All-American halfback in 1916 and 1917.... The 5-7, 175-pound Oliphant was named to the 10-man All-American basketball teams selected in 1957 by the Helms Foundation for the 1913–14 and 1914–15 seasons.... *Spalding's Official Basketball Guide* called him "the fastest and most aggressive floor worker in the conference."

BENNIE OOSTERBAAN, Michigan

College Football Hall of Famer coached Michigan's football team to a 63-33-4 record in 11 seasons (1948-58). His first team finished with a 9-0 record and was voted national champion in the AP poll. Won Big Ten titles in 1948, 1949, and 1950.... In 1943, the Helms Athletic Foundation named him to its 10-man All-American basket-

ball teams it selected for the 1926–27 and 1927–28 seasons. Finished third in Big Ten scoring in 1926–27 (9.3 points per game) and led conference as a senior the next year (10.8 ppg).

R. C. OWENS, College of Idaho

Split end caught 206 passes for 3,285 yards and 22 touchdowns in his eight seasons (1957–64) with the San Francisco 49ers, Baltimore Colts, and New York Giants. Gained fame as the receiver on "Alley-Oop" pass play in which he made receptions by leaping high above pass defenders. Became the first 49er to gain 1,000 yards on pass receptions in a season when he caught 55 passes for 1,032 yards in 1961.... The 6-3, 195-pound center had three standout basketball seasons. He averaged 23.5 points and 27.1 rebounds per game in 1952–53 and finished third in the nation among NCAA small college rebounders. Led in rebounding the next season with 27.1 per game while also averaging 23.5 points. In 1954–55, on a team that also included all-time great Elgin Baylor (31.3 ppg and 20.5 rpg), Owens averaged 18.1 ppg and 21.3 rpg. Owens was named to AAU All–American team in 1956-57 as a member of the Seattle Buchan Bakers.

ARA PARSEGHIAN, Miami of Ohio

College Football Hall of Famer compiled a 170-58-6 record as coach at Miami of Ohio (1951–55), Northwestern (1956–63), and Notre Dame (1964–74). Guided Notre Dame to three national football titles (1964, 1966, and 1973). Halfback on Cleveland Browns team that won All-American Football Conference title in 1948.... Played for Miami basketball squads in 1946–47 and 1947–48.

JOE PATERNO, Brown

Penn State's head coach since 1966 guided the Nittany Lions to national championships in 1983 and 1986. Entering 1994, he had compiled a 257-69-3 record, including a 15-8-1 record in bowl games.... He earned varsity basketball letters at Brown in 1947–48 and 1948–49. His 7.3-points-per-game scoring average in 1947–48 was second highest on the team.

HAL PATTERSON, Kansas

Canadian Football League Hall of Famer averaged 20.6 yards per pass reception in his 14-year career with 460 catches for 9,473 yards and 64 touchdowns. He also played defensive back for Montreal and Hamilton.... Named to NJCAA All-Tournament team in 1952 when he averaged 20 points per game for Garden City (Kan.) before enrolling at Kansas. The 6-1, 185-pound forward averaged 9.5 ppg in 1952–53 for the Jayhawks' NCAA runner-up and averaged 11.2 ppg the next season. Excerpt from school guide: "Fierce battler. Exceptionally high jumper under the backboards. Good close range shooter."

PRESTON PEARSON, Illinois

Did not play college football, but rushed for 3,609 yards in 941 carries, caught 254 passes for 3,095 yards, and returned 114 kickoffs for 2,801 yards in 14 NFL seasons (1967–80) with the Baltimore Colts, Pittsburgh Steelers, and Dallas Cowboys. Played in five Super Bowl games.... Guard-forward averaged 8.7 points and six rebounds per game as a senior in 1966–67 to finish his three-year varsity career with 5.2 ppg and 3.6 rpg.... Excerpt from school guide: "Aggressive, scrappy play made him a crowd favorite. Although he's not big (6-1, 190) by present basketball standards, Preston is one of the strongest men in any game."

DICK PLASMAN, Vanderbilt

Member of two NFL championship teams with the Chicago Bears (1940 and 1941) and one with the Chicago Cardinals (1947). Led Bears in pass receptions in 1939 and 1941.... Starter as 6-5 center on basketball team in 1934–35 and 1935–36. Named to the second five on the 1936 SEC All-Tournament team.

ART POWELL, San Jose State

Offensive end caught 512 passes for 8,699 yards and 85 touchdowns in 11 seasons (1957, 1959–68) in the Canadian Football League, AFL, and NFL. Led AFL in pass reception yards in 1962 and 1963 and in touchdowns on pass receptions in 1960 (14) and 1963 (16). Played in four AFL All-Star Games. Led the nation's major-college players in pass receptions as a sophomore in 1956 with 40 before signing CFL contract the next year.... The 6-2, 190-pound forward averaged 10.5 points and 8.2 rebounds per game in nine contests for the Spartans varsity basketball team in 1956–57.

GREG PRUITT, Oklahoma

Consensus All-American running back was third in the Heisman Trophy voting in 1971 and second in 1972. Rushed for 5,672 yards in 12 seasons (1973–84) with the Cleveland Browns and Los Angeles Raiders.... A 5-10, 180-pound guard in basketball, he averaged 13.3 points per game in three contests for the 1969–70 Sooners freshman team before concentrating on football.

RAY RAMSEY, Bradley

Offensive and defensive halfback in the All-America Football Conference from 1947 through 1949 with three different franchises (Chicago Rockets, Brooklyn Dodgers, and Chicago Hornets) before playing in the NFL for four seasons from 1950 through 1953 with the Chicago Cardinals. Led the Rockets in pass receptions, punt returns, kickoff returns, and scoring and finished second in rushing as a rookie in 1947. Tied for second in the NFL in pass interceptions with 10 in his final season.... Led Bradley's basketball team in scoring in 1941–42 (12.3 ppg) and 1942–43 (13.3 ppg) before having his career interrupted by World War II. He was captain of the Braves' 1946–47 squad that compiled a 25-7 record.

WAYNE RASMUSSEN, South Dakota State

Defensive back intercepted 16 passes for 189 yards in nine seasons (1964–72) with the Detroit Lions.... A guard in basketball, he averaged 11.6 points per game in three varsity seasons. He was named MVP in the eight-team 1963 NCAA College Division Tournament after scoring a tourney high 56 points in three games to lead the Jackrabbits to the national title.... Excerpt from school guide: "An intense competitor, he's at his best when the chips are down and the going is toughest. Ability to start quickly and shift immediately into full speed are assets that make him a strong driver. He plays tall for his height (6-1)."

GEORGE RATTERMAN, Notre Dame

Quarterback with Buffalo in the All-American Football Conference, New York Yankees and Cleveland Browns in the NFL, and Montreal Alouettes in the CFL. Played in AAFC championship game in 1948 and NFL championship games in 1953, 1954, and 1955. Second-team QB on Notre Dame's 1946 national championship football team…. Third-leading scorer with 11.7 points per game as 6-0 forward on 1944–45 Irish basketball team that compiled a 15-5 record and 8.6 ppg on 1945–46 squad that went 17-4. Scored 4.9 ppg as a senior reserve. In 1945–46, he scored Notre Dame's last 11 points in a 56-47 upset of Kentucky club that finished with a 28-2 mark…. Sketch in school guide: "Considered one of the 'slickest' players in college ball."

PAT RICHTER, Wisconsin

Tight end with Washington Redskins for nine seasons after being their first-round pick in the 1962 NFL draft. Caught 99 passes for 1,315 yards and 14 touchdowns and averaged 41.9 yards per punt on 338 punts for the Redskins. Consensus football All-American in 1962 at Wisconsin, where he is now the athletic director. Led school's baseball team in hits, home runs, and RBIs for three consecutive seasons…. Three-year letterman in basketball collected 103 points and 145 rebounds in 38 games as a 6-5, 230-pound center.

ANDRE RISON, Michigan State

Wide receiver averaged almost 80 receptions per year in his first five seasons in the NFL with the Indianapolis Colts (1989) and Atlanta

Football was—and continues to be—Andre Rison's forte, but he did spend some time as a backup guard for the Michigan State Spartans in the mid-1980s.

Falcons (1990–93). Played in four Pro Bowl games in that span, leading the Falcons in pass receptions (fourth in NFL with 86) and touchdowns (15) in 1993…. The 6-1, 185-pound guard in basketball, was a backup for the Spartans in two seasons (1985–86 and 1987–88).

GENE RONZANI, Marquette

Halfback-quarterback with the Chicago Bears for eight seasons and coach of the Green Bay Packers from 1950–53. Played in three NFL championship games (1933, 1934, and 1937). Led Bears in passing in 1934 and in rushing in 1935…. A 5-10 guard in basketball, he was the Warriors' fourth-leading scorer in 1931–32 (3.8 points per game) and third-leading scorer in 1932–33 (3.5 ppg).

OTTO SCHNELLBACHER, Kansas

Defensive back intercepted 34 passes in four pro seasons. Led AAFC with 11 interceptions for the New York Yankees in 1948 and led NFL with 11 in 1951 for the New York Giants. Named to All-NFL team in 1951 by AP and UPI.... Averaged 11 points per game in four-year basketball career at Kansas, earning All-Big Six/Seven Conference honors each season. The 6-3, 180-pound forward ranked second on the school's career scoring list when his career ended at the conclusion of the 1947–48 campaign. Averaged 6.4 ppg in 43 games for the Providence Steamrollers and St. Louis Bombers as a rookie in the Basketball Association of America the next season.

WEAR SCHOONOVER, Arkansas

End was Arkansas' initial football first-team All-American (Grantland Rice in 1929).... All-SWC basketball selection in 1928, 1929, and 1930 when the Razorbacks extended their streak of league titles to five in a row. Selected as a senior to the second five on *College Humor Magazine*'s All-American team.

JOE SENSER, West Chester (Pa.) State

Tight end caught 165 passes for 1,822 yards and touchdowns in four-year career (1980–82, 1984) with the Minnesota Vikings. Selected for the Pro Bowl following the 1981 season in which he caught 79 passes for 1,004 yards and eight touchdowns.... Averaged 11.4 points and 7.4 rebounds per game and shot 66.2 percent from the floor in his four-year college basketball career as a 6-5, 230-pound center. Led NCAA Division I in field-goal shooting in 1976–77 (69.9 percent) and 1977–78 (68.5).

ART SHELL, Maryland-Eastern Shore

Pro Football Hall of Famer has been head coach of the Los Angeles Raiders since 1989. Offensive tackle for the Raiders from 1968 to 1982 played in eight Pro Bowl games.... Two-year basketball letterman as a 6-5, 265-pound center at school that was then known as Maryland State College.... Sketch from school guide:

"Pure muscle. Amazing agility. Uncompromising under the boards, nobody pushes big Art without a battle."

VERNON (CATFISH) SMITH, Georgia

College Football Hall of Famer was a consensus All-American end as a senior in 1931. Scored all of Georgia's points and was a standout on defense in a shocking 15-0 upset of Yale in his sophomore season.... Three-year basketball letterman was senior captain and starting center on Bulldogs team that defeated Duke in the semifinals and North Carolina in the final to win the 1932 Southern Conference Tournament. Named to second five on the all-tourney team.

J. NEIL (SKIP) STAHLEY, Penn State

Head football coach for Delaware (1934), Brown (1941–43), George Washington (1946–47), Toledo (1948–49) and Idaho (1954–60). Backfield coach of the NFL's Chicago Cardinals in 1953.... Leading scorer for Penn State's basketball team in 1928–29 and captain of the squad the next season.

ROGER STAUBACH, Navy

College Football and Pro Football Hall of Famer won Heisman Trophy in 1963. Passed for 3,571 yards and rushed for 682 in his career at Navy (1961–64). Quarterback in four Super Bowls during his 11 seasons with the Dallas Cowboys. Five-time Pro Bowl player passed for 22,700 yards and 153 touchdowns.... Averaged 9.3 points per game for the 1961–62 Navy plebe (freshman) basketball team. The 6-2, 190-pound forward scored five points in four games for Midshipmen varsity squad the next season.

JOE STYDAHAR, West Virginia

Member of College Football and Pro Football Halls of Fame. Earned All-American honors as a 6-4, 230-pound tackle in 1935. Played nine seasons (1936–42, 1945–46) with the Chicago Bears after being their first-round pick in the first NFL draft in 1936. Named to All-NFL team four times from 1937 through 1940. Coached Los Angeles Rams (1950–51) and Chicago Cardinals

(1953–54), leading Rams to 1951 NFL title.... Four-year basketball letterman was captain of the Mountaineers' 1934–35 team that compiled a 16-6 record. Selected to the first five on West Virginia's Pre-World War II team that was named as part of the university's all-time basketball squad.

HUGH (BONES) TAYLOR, Tulane/Okla. City

Offensive end caught 272 passes for 5,233 yards and 58 touchdowns in eight seasons (1947–54) with the Washington Redskins. Led NFL in average per reception in 1950 (21.4 yards) and 1952 (23.4) and in touchdown receptions (nine) in 1949. Led Redskins in pass receptions from 1949 through 1954. Coach of Houston Oilers in the AFL in 1965.... Lettered in basketball for Tulane and Oklahoma City, leading OCU in scoring as a senior with 11.4 points per game.

LIONEL TAYLOR, New Mexico Highlands

First player in pro football history to catch 100 passes in a season holds the all-time AFL record for most pass receptions in a career with 587 as a wide receiver for the Denver Broncos (1960–66) and Houston Oilers (1967–68). Led AFL in pass receptions in 1960 (92), 1961 (100), 1962 (77), 1963 (78), and 1965 (85). Caught 13 passes in a single game in 1964.... The 6-2, 205-pounder averaged 16 points per game during his basketball career, leading the team in scoring average with 13.6 ppg in 1955–56 and 20.3 in 1956–57.

OTIS TAYLOR, Prairie View

Wide receiver caught 410 passes for 7,306 yards and 57 touchdowns in 11 seasons (1965–75) with the Kansas City Chiefs. He also rushed 30 times for a 5.4-yard average and three touchdowns. Taylor led the AFL in average per reception in 1966 (22.4 yards) and led the NFL in pass reception yardage in 1971 (1,110). Played in two Super Bowl games and caught 10 passes for 128 yards and a touchdown.... He was a backup small forward in the Prairie View era after the school's glory years with Zelmo Beaty. Former Prairie View coach Leroy Moore remembers Taylor for his "all-around great athletic ability."

ARNOLD TUCKER, Army

Quarterback on the great Army football teams that compiled a 27-0-1 record from 1944 through 1946, winning national titles the first two years. Earned All-American honors as a junior and senior. Won the Sullivan Award in 1946 as the nation's outstanding amateur athlete. Tied for the national lead in pass interceptions with eight in 1946 and finished fifth in the Heisman Trophy voting.... Played basketball as a Navy V-12 trainee at Miami (Fla.) and Florida prior to entering West Point. Played three seasons of basketball for Army and was captain of the team as a senior.

EMLEN TUNNELL, Toledo

Pro Football Hall of Famer played in nine Pro Bowl games. Defensive back established career records for interceptions (79), yards gained on interceptions (1,282) and yards gained on punt returns (2,209) in 14 seasons (1948–61) with the New York Giants and Green Bay Packers.... The 6-1, 180-pound forward was a top reserve for the 1942–43 Toledo basketball team that compiled a 22-4 record and finished second in the NIT.

BOB VOIGTS, Northwestern

All-American football tackle in 1938 and head football coach for his alma mater from 1946 to 1954. Starter on 1936 Northwestern team that won the only Big Ten football title in the school's history (6-0 in league play and 7-1 overall). Coach of the only Northwestern team ever to play in the Rose Bowl. The Wildcats, ranked seventh in the final AP poll in 1946, finished second in the Big Ten behind national champion Michigan, compiled an 8-2 overall record, and defeated California, 20-14, in the Rose Bowl.... The 5-11, 205-pound Voigts was a three-year letterman in basketball and captain of the team his senior season.

VIRGIL WAGNER, Millikin (Ill.)

Canadian Football League Hall of Famer played halfback for the Montreal Alouettes from 1946 through 1954. Led CFL in scoring in 1947,

1948, and 1949 and tied for scoring title in 1946. Scored two touchdowns for the Alouettes in their 28-15 victory over Calgary in the 1949 Grey Cup game (CFL championship).... Second-leading scorer for Millikin's basketball team in 1941–42 and 1942–43.

CHARLIE WARD, Florida State

Heisman Trophy winner and consensus All-American quarterback captured the 1993 Sullivan Award winner as the nation's top amateur athlete. Led the Seminoles to 1993 national title by passing for 3,032 yards and 27 touchdowns and rushing for 339 yards and four touchdowns. Passed and rushed for 6,636 yards in his college football career.... Averaged 8.1 points and 4.4 assists per game in his four-year basketball career (1990–91 through 1993–94). The 6-2 guard set a school career record with 238 steals.... Excerpt from school guide: "Lightning quick defender excels in every facet of the game. Great decision maker and poised leader."

JAMES WHATLEY, Alabama

Tackle and end for the NFL's Brooklyn Dodgers from 1936 to 1938. Starting tackle for 1934 Alabama football team that compiled a 10-0 record and defeated Stanford, 29-13, in the Rose Bowl. All-SEC first-team selection and All-American second-team pick in football in 1935.... The 6-4½ center in basketball was a sophomore starter and fourth-leading scorer in the league for the 1933–34 squad that won the school's first SEC title and compiled a 16-2 record. He was a first-team selection on the All-SEC Tournament team in 1934 and 1936. Whatley served as head basketball coach at Western Carolina, Mississippi (1946–47 through 1948–49), and Georgia (1949–50 and 1950–51).

RON WIDBY, Tennessee

Averaged 42 yards per punt in six seasons (1968–73) with the Dallas Cowboys and Green Bay Packers. Played in the Pro Bowl following the 1971 season and appeared in 1970 and 1971 NFL title games with the Cowboys.... He averaged 14.5 points and 8.3 rebounds as a sopho-

more, 17.3 points and eight rebounds as a junior, and 22.1 points and 8.7 rebounds as a senior. The 6-4, 210-pound forward scored 50 points vs. LSU as a senior on his way to becoming SEC player of the year in 1967. Named to second five on AP All-American team and third five on UPI All-American team in 1966–67. He played briefly with the New Orleans Buccaneers in the ABA in 1967–68.

BOB ZUPPKE, Wisconsin

College Football Hall of Famer compiled a 131-81-13 record as head football coach at Illinois from 1913 through 1941. Directed the Illini to four national titles (1914, 1919, 1923, and 1927) and seven Big Ten championships.... Two-year letterman on Wisconsin's basketball team. The seven-man 1904–5 squad was called the "Western intercollegiate champions" by *Spalding's Official Basketball Guide*.

BOXING, GOLF, TENNIS, AND TRACK STARS

JIM BAUSCH, Kansas

Olympic decathlon champion in 1932 won the Sullivan Award that year as the nation's outstanding amateur athlete. Member of College Football Hall of Fame and Track and Field Hall of Fame played in the NFL in 1933.... Starter for 1929–30 Jayhawks basketball team that compiled a 13-game winning streak on its way to a 14-4 record and second-place finish in the Big Six Conference.... The *Spalding Official Basketball Guide* said that he "solved the center problem which had bothered Kansas for several seasons."

JOE CAMPBELL, Purdue

Professional Golfers Association Rookie of the Year in 1959. Won Texas Open (1961), Baton

Rouge Open (1962), and Tucson Open (1966) before a back injury ended his PGA Tour career. NCAA golf champion in 1955 has been coach of eight Purdue golf teams that won Big Ten titles.... Averaged 7.7 points per game in three seasons of varsity basketball. The 5-7, 165-pound guard was the team's third-leading scorer (11.9 ppg) and leading free-throw shooter (73.6 percent) as a senior in 1956–57.

OTIS DAVIS, Oregon

Double gold medal winner in track and field in the 1960 Olympic Games. Won the 400 meters with a world record time of 44.9 seconds and anchored the 1600-meter relay team as it set a world record of 3.02.2.... Played briefly for the Ducks' basketball team in 1957–58 after transferring from Los Angeles City College.

WALTER (BUDDY) DAVIS, Texas A&M

Winner of gold medal in 1952 Olympic Games high jump with a leap of 6 feet, 8_ inches. Won AAU high jump titles in 1952 and 1953. Set then-world high jump record of 6 feet, 11_ inches in 1953.... Played three seasons of varsity basketball with the Aggies, averaging 9.9 points per game as a sophomore, 12.1 as a junior (NCAA Tournament team), and 15.1 as a senior. First five selection on All-Southwest Conference team as both a junior and senior. Held school season (362 points) and career (952 points) scoring records when he graduated in 1952. Named to Helms Foundation All-American third team as a junior. The 6-8, 210-pound center-forward averaged 4.8 points and 4.3 rebounds in five seasons (1953–54 through 1957–58) in the NBA with the Philadelphia Warriors and St. Louis Hawks. Member of two NBA championship teams—Warriors in 1956 and Hawks in 1958.

JAMES (BUSTER) DOUGLAS, Coffeyville (Kan.) Community College

Won world heavyweight boxing title with a 10th-round knockout of Mike Tyson in Tokyo on February 10, 1990. Lost title to Evander Holyfield on a third-round KO in Las Vegas on October 23, 1990.... A 6-4, 210-pound forward, he averaged nine points and eight rebounds per game for the 1978–79 Coffeyville team that compiled a 25-8 record. He scored 20 points and grabbed 18 rebounds in an 89-65 rout of Tunxis County CC (Conn.) in the NJCAA national tournament.

DWIGHT (DIKE) EDDLEMAN, Illinois

Member of 1948 U.S. Olympic track and field team finished fourth in the high jump with a mark of 6 feet, 4¾ inches. Won 1948 NCAA high jump title (6 feet, 7 inches), placed fourth in 1946, and tied for second in 1947. Holds Illini football records for highest punting average in a season (43 yards per kick in 1948), longest punt (88 yards vs. Iowa in 1948), punt return average in a season (32.8 in 1948), and longest punt return (92 yards vs. Western Michigan in 1947).... Led Illinois basketball squad in scoring in 1947–48 (13.9 points per game) and 1948–49 (13.1). The 6-3, 180-pound guard-forward was named to the second five on Associated Press All-American team in 1947–48 and 1948–49 and first team on Converse All-American team in 1948–49. Played four seasons in the NBA (1949–50 through 19522-53) with the Tri-Cities Blackhawks, Milwaukee Hawks, and Fort Wayne Pistons.

RAFER JOHNSON, UCLA

Former world record holder in the decathlon. Won gold medal in the decathlon in the 1955 Pan American Games and the 1960 Olympic Games and was runner-up in the 1956 Olympics. Won Sullivan Award in 1960 as the nation's No. 1 amateur athlete.... Lettered in basketball with the Bruins two seasons as a 6-3 forward-guard. Averaged 2.5 points per game in 1957–58 and 8.2 points in 1958–59. Third-leading scorer and rebounder on 1958–59 team that he led in field-goal percentage (50.7).... Sketch in school guide: "Had to miss practice sessions because of his duties as the Associated Students (student body) president, and, as a result, hasn't come along as fast as hoped for. But this great athlete figures to be mighty valuable."

RANDY MATSON, Texas A&M

Former world record holder in the shot put became first shot putter to exceed 70 feet with a toss of 70 feet, 7¼ inches in 1965. Won gold medal in shot put in 1968 Olympic Games and silver medal in 1964. Won both shot put and discus in the 1966 and 1967 NCAA and AAU meets. Sullivan Award winner in 1967 as the nation's outstanding amateur athlete.... In his only season of varsity basketball (1965–66), the 6-6½, 250-pound forward-center averaged 8.2 points and 10.1 rebounds per game. In Southwest Conference competition, he finished third in field-goal shooting (54.9 percent) and fifth in rebounding (10 rpg).

JESSE MORTENSEN, Southern Cal

Track and Field Hall of Famer coached his alma mater to seven NCAA titles (1951, 1952, 1953, 1954, 1955, 1958, and 1961) and a 79-0 mark in dual meets. He won the AAU and NCAA javelin title in 1929 and was AAU decathlon champion in 1931.... Three-year basketball letterman was named to the first five on the Pacific Coast Conference all-league team in 1927–28 and 1929–30. The forward-center was the third-leading scorer in the PCC Southern Division as a sophomore (10.8 points per game) and fourth-leading scorer as a junior (6.4). Third-team All-American selection on 1928–29 *College Humor Magazine* team and first-team choice on 1929–30 Christy Walsh Syndicate squad.

PETER MULLINS, Washington State

Sixth-place finisher in the 1948 Olympic Games decathlon as a member of the Australian team.... Captain as a senior in 1952–53 when he led the Cougars' basketball squad with 13.3 points per game. He was the school's second-leading scorer as a sophomore (8 ppg) and third-leading scorer as a junior (8.7 ppg).

STEVE PAULY, Oregon State

AAU decathlon champion in 1963 after finishing third in 1962.... Played three seasons (1960–61 through 1962–63) of varsity basketball with the Beavers as a 6-4, 200-pound guard-forward. Third-leading scorer on team as both a junior (11.5 points per game) and senior (9.2). Scoring average was 6.2 as a sophomore. Helped Oregon State reach 1963 Final Four by scoring 21 points against Arizona State in West Regional final.... Sketch in school guide: "Big, fairly quick and can shoot. Can also play defense with the best of 'em."

JOHN RAMBO, Long Beach State

Bronze medal winner in the high jump in the 1964 Olympic Games with a jump of 7 feet, 1 inch, which was two inches under his career best mark. NCAA high jump champion in 1964 before winning the AAU indoor high jump championships in 1967 and 1969.... The 6-7, 195-pound forward averaged 19.8 points and 11 rebounds per game in two years (California Collegiate Athletic Association first-team all-star choice in 1963–64 and 1964–65). He led the 49ers in scoring (20.3 points per game) and rebounding (12.7) in his second season. Had a 42-point, 31-rebound outing against San Diego.

MARTY RIESSEN, Northwestern

Nine times ranked among the top 10 men's singles tennis players in the United States. Member of five U.S. Davis Cup teams (1963, 1965, 1967, 1973, 1981).... A 6-1, 170-pound guard, he averaged 6.5 points per game for Northwestern from 1961–62 through 1963–64.... Sketch in school guide: "Reputation as a rugged, poised performer. Cool head makes him a logical floor leader."

HARLOW ROTHERT, Stanford

Member of two U.S. Olympic track and field teams placed seventh in the shot put in 1928 and won silver medal in the event in 1932. NCAA shot put champion in 1928, 1929, and 1930. Second in discus in 1930 AAU meet and fourth in

1930 AAU decathlon.... A 6-2, 225-pounder, he was named to the 10-man Helms Foundation 1928–29 All-American team selected in 1943.... Excerpt from *Spalding Basketball Guide*: "The opinion seemed to be nearly unanimous that Rothert is the best guard in the (Pacific Coast) conference. Rangy and aggressive, he is clever at getting the ball off the backboard and putting it back in play, and is a dangerous scorer when in shooting distance."

VIC SEIXAS, North Carolina

Tennis Hall of Famer was Wimbledon champion in 1953. Ranked No. 1 in the U.S. in 1951, 1954, and 1957. Member of U.S. Davis Cup team from 1951 through 1957, he shared French and Australian doubles titles with Tony Trabert in 1953.... Scored six points in one basketball game for the Tar Heels in 1946–47.

FRED SHEFFIELD, Utah

First athlete to place in NCAA high jump for four consecutive years. Finished first with a best jump of 6-8 in 1943, second in 1944, tied for first in 1945, and tied for second in 1946.... The 6-2, 165-pounder was the starting center as a junior for the 1943–44 Utah team that won the NCAA Tournament and compiled a 22-4 record. Played for the Philadelphia Warriors in the Basketball Association of America in 1946–47 and Sunbury in the Eastern Basketball League in 1948–49.

JACK TORRANCE, Louisiana State

Broke world shot put record five times in the 1930s. Mark of 57 feet, 1 inch set in 1934 stood as the world record until 1948. Helped LSU win NCAA track title in 1933 with a first-place finish in the shot put and third-place finish in the discus throw. All-SEC lineman in 1933 when he captained the Tigers' undefeated football team (7-0-3). Played tackle with the Chicago

Bears in 1939 and 1940.... A 6-3, 240-pound center in basketball, he finished third in the SEC in scoring in 1931–32 and 10th in 1933–34.

TONY TRABERT, Cincinnati

International Tennis Hall of Famer won NCAA singles title in 1951 before winning singles titles in French (1954 and 1955), United States (1955), and Wimbledon (1955) tournaments. Ranked the No. 1 men's player in the world by the *London Daily Telegraph* in 1953 and 1955.... Played two seasons of varsity basketball for the Bearcats in a college career interrupted by military service. Averaged 6.9 points in 22 games in 1950–51 and scored 11 points in four games in 1953–54. Starting guard as a 6-0 sophomore for the '51 team that played in the NIT and had an 18-4 record.... Sketch in school guide: "Great surprise in early basketball drills. His improvement has been rapid and he should be a great help to the club."

SAMMY URZETTA, St. Bonaventure

United States Amateur golf champion in 1950 when he defeated all-time great Frank Stranahan on the 39th hole in the title match in one of the biggest surprises in the tourney's history. *Sport* magazine called him a "pre-tourney 100-1 shot." ... Averaged 6.2 points per game in four-year varsity career with the Bonnies from 1946–47 through 1949–50. Led nation in free-throw percentage as a sophomore (92.2 percent) and senior (88.5).... Sketch in school guide: "One of the finest floor men in college. Equally adept at scoring from underneath or out front. One of the best defensive men in the business."

RICK WANAMAKER, Drake

Winner of the decathlon title in 1971 Pan American Games, 1971 National AAU meet, and 1970 NCAA meet.... Averaged 4.8 points per game in three-year varsity career with the Bulldogs (1967–68 through 1969–70). Drake won the national third-place game in 1969 after his nine points and seven rebounds weren't enough to prevent an 85-82 loss against UCLA in the NCAA Tournament semifinals.... Sketch in school guide: "Without batting an eye, he batted away a Lew Alcindor shot. When Alcindor hesitated to come out to the top of the key to cover him, the lanky lad popped in a couple of quick jumpers. Wanamaker forced Dick Fosbury to make his first seven-foot jump of the season in the Drake Relays. Rick cleared 6-11."

CELEBRATED ACTORS, BUSINESSMEN, AND POLITICIANS

ROBERT B. ADAMS, Canisius

Served in the U.S. Army for 31 years, retiring with the rank of major general, before he was appointed commissioner of the New York State Office of General Services by Governor Mario Cuomo. Listed in *Who's Who in America* and *Who's Who of American Business Leaders*.... Third-leading scorer (9.2 points per game) as a senior for Canisius' first NCAA Tournament team in 1955.

DAVID ADKINS, Denver

Comedian known as "Sinbad" has a show by that name on the Fox Network. He vaulted to TV prominence as a co-star on the hit series *A Different World*.... Adkins averaged 4.2 points and 4.4 rebounds for the Pioneers in his varsity career (1974–75 through 1977–78) when they were classified as a major college independent. He never shot less than 50 percent from the floor in any of his four seasons.

BOB AMES, La Salle

Director of the Central Intelligence Agency's Office of Analysis of the Near East and South Asia in 1983 when he was killed in Beirut. A truck loaded with TNT on a suicide mission rammed into the facility where Ames was staying while serving as a liaison trying to allay contacts among the Lebanese, Syrians, and Israelis in hopes of calming the escalating discord.... Backup forward for La Salle's 1954 NCAA titlist and 1955 national runner-up in his sophomore and junior seasons.

Known as David Adkins when he played for the University of Denver, comedian Sinbad now has his own TV show.

NOLAN ARCHIBALD, Weber State

President and chief executive officer of Black & Decker.... Named to National Junior College Athletic Association All-America second team in 1966 when he averaged 25.3 points per game for Dixie College (Utah). The 6-5, 195-pound forward averaged 15.2 points and 9 rebounds per game as a junior at Weber State and 11.9 points and 7.1 rebounds as a senior. Named to second five on All-Big Sky Conference all-star team in 1967–68.

JESSE ARNELLE, Penn State

Founding partner of San Francisco-based Arnelle & Hastie, one of the first minority-owned national corporate law firms in America. The four-year football letterman and one of the finest ends ever to play for the Nittany Lions is vice president of his alma mater's board of trustees.... The 6-5, 220-pound Arnelle averaged 20.2 points per game in 10 NCAA Tournament games in 1952, 1954, and 1955. He remains the school's all-time leader in scoring (2,138 points) and rebounding (1,238) after pacing the Nittany Lions in those two categories all four varsity seasons. He had 15 games of 30 or more points. Arnelle averaged 4.7 points per game in one season in the NBA (1955–56) with the Fort Wayne Pistons.

SCOTTY BAESLER, Kentucky

Mayor of Lexington, Ky., from 1982 to 1992 represented Kentucky's Sixth District in the U.S. House of Representatives before running for governor.... The 5-11, 180-pound guard averaged 8.4 points per game in three varsity seasons (1960–61 through 1962–63). Scored 26 points as a junior against Southern California. Senior captain hit 16 of 17 free throws in a game against Vanderbilt.... Sketch in school guide: "Typifies the 'we ain't scared of nothing' attitude of 'Fearless Five.' The self-made man type that sportswriters like to laud in success stories."

RICHARD T. (DICK) BAKER, Ohio State

Managing partner and CEO of major accounting firm Ernst and Ernst for 13 years, starting in 1964. Accounting Hall of Famer served on the boards of directors of such firms as General Electric, Anheuser-Busch, and Hershey Foods.... Three-year letterman was Ohio State's second-leading scorer as a starting senior forward for a team that finished runner-up to Oregon in the first NCAA Tournament in 1939. He scored a game-high 25 points for the Buckeyes in their tourney opener, a 64-52 victory over Wake Forest.

BILL BRADLEY, Princeton

United States senator (D-N.J.).... Elected to Naismith Memorial Basketball Hall of Fame in 1982. Averaged 30.2 points and 12.1 rebounds per game in three varsity seasons as a 6-5 forward. Scored 58 points against Wichita State in the national third-place game in 1965 when he was named Most Outstanding Player in the

NCAA Tournament. Averaged 33.7 points in nine playoff games from 1963 through 1965. Named college player of the year as a senior in 1964–65 season by Associated Press, United Press International, and the United States Basketball Writers Association.... Member of gold-medal winning U.S. basketball team in the 1964 Olympic Games. Played 10 seasons in the NBA with the New York Knicks, averaging 12.4 points, 3.4 assists, and 3.2 rebounds per game. Member of 1970 and 1973 NBA championship teams.

LLOYD VERNET (BEAU) BRIDGES, UCLA

Actor with the hit movie *The Fabulous Baker Boys* among his credits.... Averaged 0.6 points and 1.4 rebounds per game for the Bruins' 1960–61 freshman team that compiled a 20-2 record. He was a frosh teammate of Fred Slaughter, the starting center for UCLA's first NCAA championship team in 1964.

AVERY BRUNDAGE, Illinois

AAU president in the 1930s before becoming president of the International Olympic Committee from 1952 to 1972. Competed in the decathlon and pentathlon in the 1912 Olympic Games.... Basketball letterman with the Illini in 1907–8.

DR. CALVIN W. BURNETT, St. Louis

President of Coppin State in Baltimore since 1970. Listed in *Who's Who in America*.... Three-year letterman averaged 5.2 points and 8.2 rebounds per game with the Billikens (1956–57 through 1958–59). The 6-5, 190-pound forward led team in rebounding with 14.9 per game as a sophomore.... Excerpt from sketch in school guide: "Strong, fast and a fine competitor, Cal favors a leaping one-hander from medium range. He is 'sure death' on follows."

JAMES B. BURNS, Northwestern

U.S. attorney for the Northern Illinois District.... Career average of 19.5 points per game in leading the Wildcats in scoring each of his three varsity seasons (1964–65 through 1966–67). The 6-4 guard was Northwestern's all-time leading scorer when he finished his career. Named to third five on AP and NABC All-American teams as a senior.... Sketch in school guide: "Converted forward is especially effective driving the baseline for acrobatic layups." ... Played briefly for the Chicago Bulls in the NBA and Dallas Chaparrals in the ABA in the 1967–68 season.

WAYNE CALLOWAY, Wake Forest

Chairman of the Board and CEO of Pepsi-Co.... The business administration major scored 29 points in 15 games for the Demon Deacons in 1957–58 as a 6-1, 180-pound guard. "One of the unique aspects of being on a team is that you clearly learn to share responsibility and share the credit," Calloway says. "You find out that there is definitely a reason for working together. In today's business world, you discover this in a hurry. You only get so far by yourself."

JAMES CASH, Texas Christian

Became the first black tenured professor at Harvard in 1976. He was named chairman of the Harvard Business School MBA program in 1992.... The first African-American to play in the Southwest Conference averaged 13.9 points and 11.6 rebounds per game in three seasons from 1966–67 through 1968–69. The 6-6, 220-pound center had a 37-point game and 26-, 25-, and 23-rebound games for TCU. He was the SWC's leading rebounder as a senior with 12.9 per game.

TED CASSIDY, Stetson

Actor played the role of Lurch in the TV comedy *The Addams Family* in the 1960s.... He died prematurely during a heart bypass operation in 1975.... The 6-9, 245-pounder played four seasons for Stetson in the first half of the 1950s after a mysterious brief stint at West Liberty State College. When his college career was interrupted one year because of academic problems, he served as a disc jockey for two different radio stations. Cassidy, a sophomore member of the Stetson squad that participated in the 1953 NAIA Tournament, was the team's leading scorer (17.7 ppg) and rebounder (10.7 rpg) as a senior in 1954–55.

DALE COMEY, Connecticut

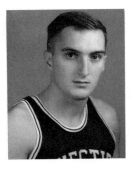

Executive Vice President of ITT, a global enterprise with sales in excess of $23 billion specializing in diversified products and services in three areas—financial and business, manufactured products, and Sheraton Hotels. He earns more than $1 million per year.... Comey averaged nine points per game in three varsity seasons after leading the school's freshman team in scoring (16 ppg). The 5-9, 150-pound guard was an All-Yankee Conference second-team selection as a senior when he scored 17 points in a 77-71 defeat to West Virginia in the first round of the 1963 NCAA Tournament.

KEVIN (CHUCK) CONNORS, Seton Hall

Longtime star of the television series *The Rifleman*.... Played major league baseball with the Brooklyn Dodgers (1949) and Chicago Cubs (1951).... Scored 32 points in 15 varsity games for Seton Hall in 1941–42 before leaving school for military service. The 6-5, 190-pound forward-center played for the Rochester Royals in the National Basketball League in 1945–46 and Boston of the Basketball Association of America in 1946-47 and 1947–48.

MIKE CONNORS, UCLA

Real name of actor, who had a hit TV series (*Mannix*), is Jay Kerkon O'Hanian.... The 6-1, 180-pounder averaged 4.6 points per game for the Bruins' 1946–47 freshman team that compiled a 15-3 record.

DR. DENTON COOLEY, Texas

World famous heart surgeon has performed about 20,000 open-heart operations.... Three-year letterman (1938–39 through 1940–41) on Texas teams that combined for a 51-21 record. He saw action in both of the Longhorns' games in the inaugural NCAA Tournament in 1939 after they captured the Southwest Conference championship.

KRESIMIR COSIC, Brigham Young

Deputy ambassador to the United States for Croatia.... A 6-11, 195-pound center, he averaged 19.1 points and 11.6 rebounds per game in three-year varsity career (1970–71 through 1972–73). Led the Cougars in rebounding all three seasons and led in scoring as a junior and senior. Earned All-American honors in 1971–72 (Coaches fourth team and UPI third team) and 1972–73 (Coaches fourth team and Helms Foundation 36-man team). Member of Yugoslavian Olympic teams.

MICHAEL CRICHTON, Harvard

Nationally-acclaimed fiction writer has authored numerous best-selling novels, including *Andromeda Strain* (1969), *The Terminal Man* (1972), *The Great Train Robbery* (1975), *Jurassic Park* (1991) and *Disclosure* (1994).... The tallest player (6-8) on Harvard's squad as a sophomore in 1961–62 scored three points (all free throws) in nine games. He averaged 6.3 points per game in 12 outings for Harvard's freshman team the previous year when his best performance was a 16-point, 14-rebound effort against Andover.

R. HAL DEAN, Grinnell (Ia.)

Former chairman of Ralston Purina Company.... Played basketball for Grinnell when it was a member of the Missouri Valley Conference. In 1936–37, he was named to the second five on the All-MVC team and finished fifth in league scoring with an average of 7.5 points per game. The next season, he was again named to the All-

MVC second five and finished 16th in conference scoring with an average of 6.5 per game.... The *Spalding Official Guide* described him as a "sparkplug" and "one of the Midland's best guards."

JOHN DICK, Oregon

Retired with the rank of admiral after 32 years of service in the U.S. Navy. Commanded the aircraft carrier *Saratoga* for two years and served as chief of staff for all carrier forces in the Western Pacific.... Starting junior forward for first NCAA Tournament champion in 1939 when he led the Ducks in scoring in three playoff games, including a game-high 15 points in the final against Ohio State. NCAA consensus first-team All-American the next season when he paced the Pacific Coast Conference Northern Division in scoring with 183 points in 16 games.

JAY DICKEY, Arkansas

Republican member of the U.S. House of Representatives from the Fourth District of Arkansas that includes President Clinton's birthplace (Hope, Ark.).... Dickey scored eight points in six games for the Razorbacks' basketball team in 1959–60 before he was stricken with polio.

ROBERT J. DOLE, Kansas

U.S. senator from Kansas since 1969. Senate minority leader since 1987 after being Senate majority leader from 1985 to 1987. Republican nominee for vice president of the U.S. in 1976.... Member of Kansas freshman basketball team in 1942–43 before enlisting in the Army during World War II.

DR. EDDIE DURNO, Oregon

U.S. congressman in 1961 and 1962 lost primary for U.S. Senate before serving as Oregon chairman for Barry Goldwater's presidential campaign in 1964. Durno was a physician in Medford, Oregon, for more than 30 years after graduating cum laude from Harvard Medical School.... Scored half of Oregon's entire point total as a sophomore forward in 1918–19 when he led the league in scoring for the Pacific Coast

Conference titlist. Named to Helms Foundation 10-man All-American team for the 1920–21 season (selected in 1943).... Excerpt from *Spalding Basketball Guide*: "He is small, but makes up for the handicap with his speed and clever dodging and dribbling. He makes long shots as well as short ones from any angle on the floor."

DR. PAUL ALLEN EBERT, Ohio State

Director of the American College of Surgeons since 1986. Nationally-recognized authority on children's thoracic and cardiovascular surgery is listed in *Who's Who in America*.... Earned All-American recognition by averaging more than 20 points per game each of his three varsity seasons (1951–52 through 1953–54). All-Big Ten choice each year finished his career as the school's career scoring leader. Had a 40-point game against Michigan as a sophomore. He was second in the Big Ten in scoring as a sophomore (20.1 ppg) and junior (21.7) and third as a senior (23.5).

DR. HARRY F. EDWARDS, San Jose State

Nationally-known liberal sociologist and special consultant for the San Francisco 49ers.... The 6-8, 240-pound center averaged 10 points and 5.9 rebounds per game in three seasons of varsity basketball (1961–62 through 1963–64). He was the Spartans' second-leading scorer (10.2) and rebounder (5.8) as a senior.

CLIFF EHRLICH, Brown

Senior vice-president of the Marriott Corporation is listed in *Who's Who in America*.... The 6-4, 200-pound forward was a three-year letterman (1957–58 through 1959–60). He led Brown in scoring as a junior with 13.9 points per game and was named to the second five on the All-Ivy League team.

RAYMOND L. FLYNN, Providence

U.S. ambassador to the Vatican is former mayor of Boston.... Averaged 12.5 points per game as a 6-0 guard in his three varsity seasons with the Friars (1960–61 through 1962–63). As a senior captain, he tied with John Thompson for team scoring honors with an average of 18.9

points per game. Member of NIT championship teams in 1961 and 1963, winning NIT Most Valuable Player award in 1963 after leading tourney in scoring with 83 points in three games.... Sketch in school guide: "One of the fiercest competitors and greatest outside shooters in Providence history. Admired by his teammates for his intense devotion to basketball, manifested by his constant effort to improve."

GILBERT (GIB) FORD, Texas

President of Converse.... The 6-4, 190-pound guard-forward averaged 7.6 points and 5.9 rebounds per game in three varsity seasons (1951–52 through 1953–54). Leading rebounder (7.8 per game) and third-leading scorer (9.8 ppg) as a junior. Earned a spot on the 1956 U.S. Olympic team as a member of the Armed Forces All-Stars while serving in the Air Force.

CHET FORTE, Columbia

Former director of *Monday Night Football* on ABC Television. Nine-time Emmy Award winner also produced or directed Olympic Games, World Series, and Indianapolis 500 before a gambling addiction cost him almost $4 million and led to a guilty plea to fraud and tax evasion charges. Forte, who last bet in April 1988, has been host of a San Diego radio show and was slated to return to the NFL in 1994 to direct several games on NBC.... The 5-9, 145-pound guard averaged 24.8 points per game in three varsity seasons (1954–55 through 1956–57). Named college player of the year by UPI as a senior when he was the nation's fifth-leading scorer (28.9 ppg) and ranked sixth in free-throw shooting (85.2 percent).

AL GORE, Harvard

Vice President in Bill Clinton's administration was a Democratic senator from Tennessee.... Gore averaged 2.8 points per game for Harvard's 12-4 freshman team in 1965–66.

STEDMAN GRAHAM, Hardin-Simmons

Public relations executive and longtime beau of TV personality Oprah Winfrey.... The

In his college days, Ray Flynn (left) was a star Providence guard; he "grew up" to become mayor of Boston and U.S. ambassador to the Vatican.

6-6, 200-pound forward averaged 10.7 points and 7.4 rebounds per game in his three-year varsity career, averaging 12.3 ppg and 10 rpg as a junior in 1972–73 and 15.2 ppg and 8.5 rpg as a senior in 1973–74.

LEE H. HAMILTON, DePauw (Ind.)

Chairman of the House Foreign Affairs Committee represents Indiana's Ninth District in the U.S. House of Representatives.... Ranked fourth on DePauw's career scoring list when he graduated in 1952. Led team in scoring as a junior (11.4 points per game) and was the second-leading scorer as a sophomore (9.8 ppg) and senior (10.9 ppg).

HARRY HOPKINS, Grinnell (Ia.)

Advisor to President Franklin D. Roosevelt (1933–45), including stint as secretary of commerce (1938–40). Headed the Federal Emergency Relief Administration and the Works Progress Administration during the Depression.... Played varsity basketball for Grinnell in 1910–11 and 1911–12. *Scarlet and Black,* the school newspaper, said Hopkins was the game's "bright and shining light" when Grinnell upset Missouri Valley Conference champion Kansas, 17-16, on February 22, 1911.

DR. FREDERICK L. HOVDE, Minnesota

President of Purdue University (1946–70)....

Fourth-leading scorer for Gophers in Big Ten basketball competition in 1928–29.... Described by *Spalding's Official Basketball Guide* as "a small, hard driving floor man."

MANNIE JACKSON, Illinois

Senior vice president, Honeywell, Inc., head of International and Home Building Control unit. The owner of the Harlem Globetrotters, a team he played for after graduating from Illinois, is the ultimate rags to riches story. Jackson was born in a boxcar in East St. Louis.... Three-year starter averaged 11.1 points per game in 1957–58, 13.6 in 1958–59, and 16.4 in 1959–60. Named to second five on UPI All-Big Ten team as a senior after finishing 10th in the league in scoring. Had 32-point game against Iowa as a senior captain. Finished Illini career as fourth-leading scorer in school history with 922 points.... Excerpt from school guide: "A spring-legged jump shooter played forward his first year before being shifted to guard. Quick hands and an excellent eye for the basket."

E. HENRY (HANK) KNOCHE,
Colorado/Washington & Jefferson

Deputy director of the Central Intelligence Agency in 1976 under President-to-be George Bush.... Led the Mountain States (Big Seven) Conference in scoring in 1945–46 with a 16.4-points-per-game average before transferring from Colorado to Washington & Jefferson to play on a 16-4 team with two of his brothers. The father of American University coach Chris Knoche, he was reputedly the first player selected in the NBA's first college draft in 1947 by the Pittsburgh Ironmen although the league doesn't have any official draft records prior to 1949.

ART LINKLETTER, San Diego State

Longtime radio and television personality was master of ceremonies of such popular shows as *People Are Funny* and *Art Linkletter's House Party*.... Three-year letterman led the Aztecs in scoring in 1932–33 (7 points per game) and 1933–34 (8.8 ppg). Named to Southern California Intercollegiate Athletic Conference all-star team as a sophomore and senior. Captain of team as a senior when he finished second in conference competition in scoring.

JIM LUISI, St. Francis (N.Y.)

Actor played part of Lt. Chapman on television series *The Rockford Files*... Led the Terriers in scoring in 1949–50 (14.7 points per game) and 1950–51 (14.6). Finished his career in third place on the school's career scoring list. Played briefly for the Baltimore Bullets in the NBA in 1953–54.... Excerpt from school guide: "Shooting ability and deceptive dribbling, together with his indomitable courage in the face of the toughest opposition, make him an invaluable asset."

TOM McMILLEN, Maryland

Co-chairman of President's Council on Physical Fitness under Bill Clinton. Former member of the U.S. House of Representatives from Maryland.... The 6-11 center averaged 20.5 points and 9.8 rebounds per game in three seasons for Maryland from 1971–72 through 1973–74. Member of 1972 U.S. Olympic team.... Averaged 8.1 points and four rebounds in 11 NBA seasons (1975–76 through 1985–86) with the Buffalo Braves, New York Knicks, Atlanta Hawks, and Washington Bullets.

REV. EDWARD A. MALLOY, C.S.C., Notre Dame

President of the University of Notre Dame.... The 6-4, 190-pound guard-forward scored two points in three games as a sophomore in 1960–61, 19 in 11 games as a junior in 1961–62, and six in seven games as a senior in 1962–63. He was a high school teammate of John Thompson, a star center for Providence who played briefly in the NBA before becoming coach at Georgetown.

Maryland center Tom McMillen became a politician after his successful 11-year career in the NBA.

JAMES E. MARTIN, Auburn

The 14th president of Auburn (1984–1992) was a scholarship basketball player at the same school. A three-year letterman, he started as a 6-6 sophomore center in 1951–52, when he was runner-up in scoring (9.1 points per game) and led in rebounding (eight per game). Averaged 7.1 points and 6.8 rebounds in his three-year varsity career.

TONY MASIELLO, Canisius

Mayor of Buffalo.... Averaged 15.1 points and 8.9 rebounds per game in three varsity seasons (1966–67 through 1968–69). The 6-4, 190-pound forward led Canisius in scoring and rebounding as a junior (18.2 ppg, 10.5 rpg) and senior (19.9 ppg, 9.3 rpg). He culminated his college career with 35 points in an 83-79 victory over Calvin Murphy-led Niagara.... Excerpt from school guide: "Became captain of the Golden Griffins through concentrated team play and aggressive individual performance. Backbone of the team."

HENRY (HANK) NOWAK, Canisius

Never received less than 75 percent of the general electorate vote while representing Buffalo area for nine terms (1975–93) in the U.S. House of Representatives.... Leading rebounder for the only three Canisius teams to participate in the NCAA Tournament. He averaged 19.4 points per game in nine NCAA playoff contests. Led the Golden Griffins in scoring as a senior (51st in the country with 20.1 ppg). The school's all-time leading rebounder (880) is third in career scoring (1,449 points).... Excerpt from school guide: "Quiet and unassuming lad when off the court, but when going up for a tap or rebound, he becomes transformed into a whirling mass of arms and legs."

JAY KERKON O'HANION

see MIKE CONNORS

DR. HUNTER RAWLINGS III, Haverford (Pa.)

President of the University of Iowa.... The 6-7 center was a four-year starter in college. As a senior in 1965–66, he averaged 16.2 points and 16.4 rebounds per game and was named MVP in the Southern College Division of the Middle Atlantic Conference after leading his team to a 13-3 league record.

PAUL ROBESON, Rutgers

World renowned singer and actor.... He was a 6-3, 215-pound center for the Scarlet Knights' basketball team.... Earned Phi Beta Kappa honors from Rutgers when he graduated in 1919. Earned law degree from Columbia, financing way through school by playing pro football with the Akron Pros and Milwaukee Badgers.

TOM SELLECK, Southern Cal

Television and movie star who won an Emmy in 1984 for his work on *Magnum, P.I.* Was a 6-4, 200-pound forward with the Trojans. After serving as captain of the basketball team at Los Angeles Valley Community College, he scored four points in seven games for USC in 1965–66 and was scoreless in three games in 1966–67.... Excerpt from school guide: "Agile and quick performer who adds depth on front line. Business administration major is good jumper with fine mobility. Rapidly improving shooter has impressed coaches with his hustle in practice. Needs to work on defense."

DR. KENNETH A. SHAW, Illinois State

Chancellor of Syracuse University represented the Big East Conference on the NCAA Presidents Commission.... Known as "Buzz" in college, he was a 6-2, 185-pound guard who averaged 12.9 points per game in his varsity career. He led the Redbirds in scoring as a junior with a 15-point average. Set school records (subsequently broken) for most games played (108) and highest career free-throw percentage (.831).

C. J. (PETE) SILAS, Georgia Tech

Chairman and chief executive officer of Phillips Petroleum Company.... The 6-6, 180-pound forward led the Yellow Jackets in scoring in each of his three varsity seasons (11.6 points per game in 1950–51, 17.8 ppg in 1951–52, and 17 ppg in 1952–53). He set school records at the time for points in a game (39) and in a season (393 as a junior). Member of gold-medal winning U.S. Pan American Games team in 1955 while serving in the Armed Forces.

SINBAD

see DAVID ADKINS

GEORGE SMATHERS, Florida

Prominent Washington lobbyist after serving as U.S. senator from Florida for 19 years until retiring in 1969.... Lettered on Gator teams from 1933–34 through 1935–36. Captain of squad his senior season.

PAUL TAGLIABUE, Georgetown

NFL commissioner since October 26, 1989.... Averaged 11.4 points and nine rebounds per game in three varsity seasons as a 6-5 forward. Led the Hoyas in rebounding as a sophomore and junior and was second-leading rebounder as a senior captain.... Sketch in school guide: "One of the toughest competitors ever to wear the Blue and Gray. At his best when the going gets toughest. Fierce rebounder, an excellent shooter and a tireless performer. President of his class."

JOSEPH P. (JOE) TEASDALE, Benedictine College

Former governor of Missouri (1977–81) gained national attention by walking across the state while campaigning.... Member of 1953–54 team from Kansas (then called St. Benedict's) that compiled a 24-5 record en route to winning the NAIA Tournament. Converted 19 of 20 free throws the next season in a game against William Jewell College on his way to finishing as the team's second-leading scorer with an 11.9-point average.

MONROE TROUT, Harvard

Considered among the trading elite on Chicago's volatile commodity markets. According to the New York Times, his Trout Trading Company earned profits in 69 of 79 consecutive months, an outstanding ratio.... He set a school record for season field-goal shooting (65.9 percent) as a sophomore in 1981–82. The 6-9 center averaged 10 and 10.6 points per game in his sophomore and junior seasons before slipping to 3.4 ppg as a senior.

MORRIS (MO) UDALL, Arizona

Former member of the U.S. House of Representatives and former candidate for the Democratic Party's presidential nomination.... He was the Wildcats' second-leading scorer with an average of 10 points per game on the 1946–47 team that won the Border Conference title and finished with a 21-3 record. The next year, he was the leading scorer (13.3 average) on a squad that successfully defending its league crown. The 6-5, 200-pound forward-center was named to the first five on the 1947–48 Border Conference all-star team and finished second in the league in scoring. He played with the Denver Nuggets in the National Basketball League in 1948–49.

REV. MAURICE E. VAN ACKEREN, S.J., Creighton

Former chancellor of Rockhurst College in Kansas City.... First-team All-Missouri Valley Conference selection as a sophomore (second-leading scorer in league) and junior (leading scorer) and second-team choice as a senior (third-leading scorer). Creighton tied for the MVC title his first two years and won the conference crown with an 8-0 record and finished with 17-4 overall mark his senior year in 1932 when he captained the team.

RICHARD VINROOT, North Carolina

Mayor of Charlotte.... The 6-7, 210-pound center played briefly for the Tar Heels in coach Dean Smith's first two seasons (1961–62 and 1962–63).... Excerpt from school guide: "Diligent worker. President of junior and senior classes."

ROBERT JAMES WALLER, Northern Iowa

Best-selling author of *The Bridges of Madison County* and *Slow Waltz in Cedar Bend*.... Averaged 11.8 points per game as a 6-0 guard in three varsity seasons (1959–60 through 1961–62). Earned All-North Central Conference honors as a senior when he finished 10th in the league in scoring (14.2 ppg) and fourth in free-throw shooting (78.4 percent). Helped the Panthers

UCLA star guard Mike Warren went on to become the likable Officer Bobby Hill on TV's Hill Street Blues.

earn their first NCAA Tournament appearance in the college division.

MIKE WARREN, UCLA

Television star who portrayed Officer Bobby Hill on *Hill Street Blues*.... The 5-11, 160-pound guard averaged 16.6 points per game in 1965–66 as a sophomore, 12.7 in 1966–67 as a junior, and 12.1 in 1967–68 as a senior. He was an All-NCAA Tournament selection in 1967 and 1968 when the Bruins won national titles by combining for a 59-1 record. Warren was named to Converse and Helms All-American squads as a junior. In his senior season, he was named to the 10-man United States Basketball Writers Association All-American team and was a third five selection on the Associated Press and United Press International All-American squads.... Excerpt from school guide: "Named on the Academic All-American first team. One of UCLA's all-time great ball handlers as well as being an outstanding driver and jump shooter."

BYRON (WHIZZER) WHITE, Colorado

Former U.S. Supreme Court Justice.... Finished second in 1937 Heisman Trophy voting after rushing for national-leading 1,121 yards, passing for 475, returning punts and kickoffs for 746, punting for a 42.5-yard average, intercepting four passes, and scoring a nation-leading 122 points. Played three seasons in the NFL with the Pittsburgh Steelers (1938) and Detroit Lions (1940–41). Led the NFL in rushing in 1938 and 1940 and in punt returns in 1941.... In a low-scoring era of basketball, he averaged 6.8 points per game for the Buffaloes in conference play in three varsity seasons (1935–36 through 1937–38). Third-team all-league as a sophomore (Rocky Mountain) and first team as a junior (RMC) and senior (Mountain States).... After Colorado's 48-47 victory over NYU in the 1938 NIT, the *New York Times* wrote that "White was the guiding genius of the team and its steadying influence. The Rhodes Scholar, with a build as solid as an oak tree, was all-powerful on defense and an excellent shot when he chose."

DR. JOHN EDGAR WIDEMAN, Penn

Award-winning writer/novelist is an English literature professor at the University of Massachusetts. Books authored include *Hurry Home* (1969), *The Lynchers* (1973), *Sent for You Yesterday* (1983), *Brothers and Keepers* (1984), and *Philadelphia Fire* (1990). Rhodes Scholar has been listed in Who's Who in America.... The 6-1, 180-pound forward led Penn in scoring as a junior (13.2 points per game in 1961–62) and as a senior (13.8 ppg in 1962–63). Also led the Quakers in rebounding as a junior (7.6 per game).

KENNY WOLFE, Harvard

Producer for ABC's Monday Night Football.... The 6-2, 165-pound guard was an honorable mention All-Ivy League pick as a senior in 1973–74 when he was the team's third-leading scorer with 9.8 points per game. Wolfe averaged seven points per game in his three-year varsity career.

11

WOMEN'S HOOPS

Just months after Dr. James Naismith put up his first peach basket in Springfield, Mass., a physical education teacher at a nearby women's college asked him to explain the new game of "basket ball" in hopes of introducing it to her students. In early 1892, Lithuanian-born Senda Berenson adopted the same general concept of the game as Naismith, but rewrote a substantial portion of his original rule book to suit prevailing Victorian assumptions of femininity and the kind of physical stress that females could endure. Not surprisingly, the first contests that Berenson organized at Smith College limited players to one of three sections of the court and prohibited them from snatching the ball from an opponent.

Other women teachers flocked to write their own rules. Games sprung up at Mount Holyoke College and at Sophie Newcomb College (now part of Tulane University), where women played 11 to a side, and all were restricted to a small portion of the floor. Players could guard opponents only vertically, and the no-snatch rule, which would dominate most women's rules for years, continued to apply. In some places dribbling was not allowed and defenders could not try to steal or bat away an opponent's pass. Bounce passes also were taboo for many years. All these rules were part of an effort to eliminate the roughness that Berenson and her peers found appalling in the basketball games they saw men play.

The controls on women's rules, which fit like the typical corset of the day, began a pattern of events that steered women's basketball for more than 70 years, until women began playing the five-player version that exists today. Women physical educators steadfastly believed that the purpose of basketball and any other sport was for the fitness and well-being of the athlete, and not for competition's sake. Basketball simply was too rough for societal acceptance and their own ideals of physical activity, so future rules revisions that opened up the game came slowly and in some instances, with great reluctance.

As a result, the experience of women in basketball has been drastically different from that of men, although they've been playing just as long. It also explains women's delayed entry into more competitive brands of basketball, and why the women's college game today, despite dramatic progress in the last 20 years, lacks the overt commercialization of men's basketball. The perspective and approach of women leaders, both in the physical education realm through the 1960s and by feminist-minded coaches and athletic administrators since then, in some ways resonate with the values and aspirations of the founders of the women's game.

In addition to the restrictive rules, Berenson and colleagues emphasized the importance of only women teaching and coaching female athletes. This issue has become a highly volatile aspect of the contentious gender equity debate currently roaring through college athletic departments, in which male coaching candidates occasionally are bypassed in favor of women.

One other turn-of-the-century issue still has delicate ramifications and is a hot-button topic that surfaces in larger question of women's rights in sports. Arguments raged for years about whether females would be made more masculine if they undertook athletic pursuits. Then and now, women coaches and teachers pleaded that such activity ideally fosters the well-being, health, vitality, self-image, and confidence of young women. Discussions of women, sports, and sexuality often are laced with connotations of what constitutes feminine nature. Ardent women's sports leaders now contend that health benefits from sports are necessary for all girls and women, and charge their critics routinely engage in homophobic scare tactics to stunt women's advances in athletics.

In April 1896, four years after Berenson published the first Spalding rules for women, the first known women's intercollegiate varsity basketball game was played. Stanford defeated California 2-1 after playing two 20-minute halves, precisely the same time rules that govern the current women's college game. Each team played with nine players and although 700 people cheered with interest, they all were women. At California's request, men were strictly forbidden from watching women compete. Women

teachers across the country feared a co-ed audience would prevent them from fulfilling their educational ideals, which did not include spectators who may be interested in something besides their athletic abilities. This philosophy, rooted in the creed of universal participation, rather than elite competition by a talented few, did not pass easily from the scene.

But there was more than a sporadic staging of women's basketball in colleges and high schools between 1900 and 1920. This reflected a new-found sense of independence by some women and a desire by others to strive for more competition than what was offered in intramural programs. While they are the forerunners of the pro-competition feminists in the 1970s and 1980s, and descended from the earliest American women's rights leaders, neither were they terribly interested in upsetting the societal equilibrium of the time. Ironically, as many American women were expressing some limited social freedoms by adopting a Jazz Age flapper lifestyle, women physical education teachers took steps to force female athletic participation into a very narrow domain. They worried that women would not be allowed to take part in sports activities at all if they veered too far away from traditional cultural prescriptions that still dominated educational institutions. Throughout the first half of the 20th century, women's athletic experiences in the educational realm consisted mostly of "play days," large intramural events that emphasized the values their teachers held dear.

Women's collegiate competition whittled away quickly in the 1920s and did not return on a significant national scale until the late 1960s. High school teams were more commonplace and were most popular in the South and some parts of the Midwest. But the Amateur Athletic Union, which was virtually all male, eyed women's basketball and other women's sports to increase its membership and offerings for athletes. Naturally, the women teachers resisted, and in the early 1920s, tenaciously fought the AAU's efforts. They feared a pro-competition avenue opening for women that they regarded as exploitive and exclusive. Some leaders quickly met to form organizations that worked to oppose women's participation in the Olympic games and denied attempts by the AAU to be affiliated with them.

The AAU fanned the flames by proposing to nationalize women's basketball rules and speed up the game to augment high-level competition. It wasn't until the 1930s that the AAU was allowed membership in women's sports groups. By then, pockets of basketball hotbeds were creating unprecedented opportunities for girls and women. The earliest national-caliber players hailed not from college campuses but from factory and mill towns and thousands of high school communities that placed their female basketball teams on a rare pedestal of respect and admiration.

Women's Basketball Tournaments Increase

That tradition was especially passionate in Iowa, where the famous girls high school basketball tournament got its start in the mid-1920s. The Iowa Girls High School Athletic Union (IGHSAU) was set up expressly to offer interscholastic basketball competition at the same time other states were moving in the opposite direction. Eventually, the girls tournament would come to outdraw the boys and offer a fervent rallying point for fans in Des Moines all the way down to the smallest farming villages. It was as if all the controversies about how females should play basketball missed Iowa completely; the men who set up the IGHSAU firmly believed that girls would benefit from the experience regardless of their life's ambitions. In 1985, however, the six-player tournament got some competition when a five-player option was offered for the first time. By 1993, six-player basketball had been phased out altogether. All across the South, industrial leagues sprang up between the world wars, providing substantial competition for working women and others who wanted to continue playing after high school. Between 1927 and 1932, a Dallas insurance firm, Employers Casualty Company, built a powerful team called the Golden

Cyclones that won an AAU national tournament and featured future Olympic champion and golfing legend Babe Didrikson. Two other Dallas teams, the Sunoco Oil Company Oilers and the Schepps Aces, also won national titles, fueling rivalries that were widely reported in the local papers. The Depression forced numerous companies to disband their teams, and the Golden Cyclones were an early victim.

Southern industrial teams continued to dominate the AAUs in the post-war period, producing most of the players on the first American women's national teams. However, a number of college teams cropped up into the fray, signalling the very earliest calls for a pro-varsity existence that was still at least a generation away.

Another Texas school, Wayland Baptist in the Panhandle region, was one of the first institutions to offer basketball scholarships to women. Claude Hutcherson, who sponsored the team, known as the Flying Queens, also arranged for first class travel. They flew to major competition in such places as Mexico and Madison Square Garden in a fleet of Beechcraft Bonanzas he owned. During the 1950s, the Flying Queens locked horns for national supremacy with Nashville Business College (NBC), which boasted Nera White, who later would be inducted into the Naismith Memorial Basketball Hall of Fame. The United States won the first two women's World Championship tournaments in 1953 and 1957, primarily with players from NBC and Hutcherson's Flying Queens.

Away from the playing courts, women's sports leaders actively debated the possibility of strengthening interscholastic competition. Some more traditionally-minded women balked, arguing that women would adopt male patterns of athletic behavior they believed were corrupting and contrary to the best interests of student-athletes. A host of rules changes opened the doors even further. By 1961, the six-player game allowed two players on each side to rove fullcourt, and an unlimited dribble was permitted five years later. And in 1969, as the first organization devoted to women's varsity collegiate competition was formed, another dramatic new set of rules, ironically introduced on an experimental basis, permanently changed the look of women's basketball. The five-player, full-court game also was played with a 30-second shot clock to speed up the tempo. Not only was this a reward for elite players, but it symbolized the advent of modern college basketball for women.

AIAW and Title IX

As the women's liberation movement gathered steam in the late 1960s, the first major intercollegiate women's basketball tournament set off a wave of activity that permanently changed the game. Although disputes continued for the rest of the decade over how scholarships, recruiting, professional coaches, and competition would be implemented, women had decided firmly that intercollegiate play was a positive and necessary development in increasing women's opportunities in sports.

The National Collegiate Athletic Association had refused repeatedly to sponsor championships for women. In 1966, however, a group of women's sports leaders created the Commission on Intercollegiate Athletics for Women (CIAW) to look into that possibility, piquing the interest of the NCAA. The two groups would clash for 15 years until the NCAA usurped women's separate administration of varsity sports in 1981.

In 1969, a physical education teacher at West Chester (Pa.) State College quietly planted the seeds for championship-oriented competition. Carol Eckman organized the first women's invitational tournament, attracting top college teams from around the nation and showcasing the college game for the first time. Her West Chester team won the title and the event continued for two more years. The CIAW evolved into the Association of Intercollegiate Athletics for Women (AIAW), which first offered a national basketball championship tournament for the 1971–72 season.

But the biggest instrument toward full competition for women came in 1972 when Congress passed a package of laws to order sex equity in education. Title IX of those Education Amendments strictly prohibited federal funds to schools, colleges, and universities that practiced sex discrimination, whether it was in the biology lab or on the basketball court. The most celebrated Title IX cases, however, involved women's athletics, and many of those controversies rage today. It was not until the late 1970s, as the NCAA's interest in sponsoring women's sports soared, that nominal enforcement of Title IX began.

Reflecting the education-oriented philosophies of the AIAW, small colleges coached by prominent women physical education teachers dominated the early years. Immaculata College, a tiny, all-women's institution outside Philadelphia, won the first three titles behind the play of center Theresa Shank; now Theresa Grentz, she is the respected coach at Rutgers and of the 1992 U.S. Olympic team. Two of her teammates also would become leading coaches: Rene Portland of Penn State, and Marianne Stanley, who led Old Dominion to three national titles. Immaculata's coach was Cathy Rush, who like her peers received little or no stipend for coaching. However, after leaving coaching in the late 1970s, she opened up a girls sports camp business and has been a color analyst on women's television games.

Delta State University in Cleveland, Miss., won the next three titles, from 1975 to 1977. Alumna Margaret Wade was brought in to start the program from scratch in 1973, and she relied on a supremely talented local player, 6-3 Lusia Harris, the first true athletic center in the women's college game, to help lead the way. Both are in the Naismith Memorial Basketball Hall of Fame.

The early AIAW years weren't lost on a sports media intrigued by chronicling what was then a novelty. When Queens College played host to the 1973 AIAW national tournament, reporters from all the New York papers, including the *New York Times*, profiled players and coaches and ran box scores. Players congregated in a hospitality room to enjoy juice, cookies, and fellowship after games.

Two years later, New York again was the center of attention as Madison Square Garden officials invited Queens and Immaculata to face off in what became at the time the largest crowd in the United States to watch a women's game. Nearly 12,000 spectators saw Immaculata win in a preliminary to a men's game, a normal practice in women's basketball until the 1980s. Players warmed up to Helen Reddy's popular song that began: "I Am Woman, Hear Me Roar." The Garden was the site for in-season tournaments sponsored by Manufacturers Hanover that featured top college teams throughout the 1970s. The first Kodak All-American team, started by Rush, was unveiled in 1975, and is considered the most prestigious women's All-American honor today.

Although women played with a shot clock to speed up the game, it generally remained mechanical and lacked widespread athleticism for a number of years. The AIAW's first guidelines prohibited females who received athletic scholarships from competing in its sanctioned events. This ban eventually was struck down after a female college tennis player went to court. Scholarships were awarded in limited quantities beginning in 1974, a practice that eventually would benefit large, public universities. The smaller schools, with limited resources, would be pushed out of the national scope by the end of the decade.

Other AIAW policies reflected the leaders' beliefs that the interests of athletes should come first. Student-athletes had to maintain academic averages required of all students at their schools. Women players also could transfer and play immediately at their new college, since other students who transferred could participate in other extracurricular activities once they became academically eligible. No women's basketball team took greater advantage of this rule than Tennessee, which emerged nationally in large part because of transfers. Coach Pat Head persuaded 1976 Olympic teammates Pat Roberts

and Cindy Brogdon to transfer to her program. They closed out their careers with the Lady Volunteers and helped Tennessee reach the upper echelon of the AIAW tournament for the first time.

The Olympic team, which won a silver medal, was perhaps the most telling indicator of how women's basketball in the United States had progressed. After being throttled by the Soviets, who boasted a starting lineup with a 7-2 center and a 6-8 forward, American coaches began searching for taller, more athletically-inclined players. They found one in Anne Donovan, a thin 6-8 player from a strong high school program in New Jersey. She joined Old Dominion in time to help win a national championship and later became a national player of the year and a three-time Olympian.

By 1978, big schools were becoming fixtures on the national scene and at the first AIAW Final Four played at UCLA. The home team, led by All-American Ann Meyers, won the title by defeating Maryland in the finals. This ushered in a new period of women's basketball as the recruiting of female players and the professionalization of coaches began in earnest. Many of the women physical education teachers who pioneered the college game were going back to the classroom. Their protégés, in many cases former players barely out of college, filled full-time positions and took the initial steps toward emulating their men's counterparts. They attended camps and tournaments that showcased top high school players, went on publicity tours, and informally organized for their professional common good.

Media attention stepped up that same season, when *Philadelphia Inquirer* reporter Mel Greenberg began the first Associated Press women's basketball poll. Those rankings framed the sport for reporters and gave schools fodder for press releases and brochures. *Parade Magazine* also began choosing girls' high school All-American basketball teams that served as a useful recruiting resource.

UCLA All-American Ann Meyers celebrates her team's 1978 AIAW national championship.

The 1978 Final Four also marked the end of the remarkable career of Carol Blazejowski, who set a women's record by averaging 38.6 points per game that season for Montclair (N.J.) State College. She is widely considered the finest jump shooter ever to play women's basketball and once scored 52 points in a game at Madison Square Garden. As she bowed out, the most decorated women's player ever jumped into prominence. Lynette Woodard of Kansas was the first true all-around athlete to play women's college basketball, starting at all five positions during her career. She scored 3,649 points, only 18 behind Pete Maravich's all-time college mark and became an All-American, Olympian, and the first woman to suit up for the Harlem Globetrotters.

Old Dominion's 1979 and 1980 national title teams exemplified more than basketball supremacy; they were an entertaining band of players who captured the attention of basketball fans in general. Flashy guard Nancy Lieberman was a street-tough New Yorker who learned the game playing against men in the playgrounds of Harlem. Center Inge Nissen, a native of Denmark, was a worldly traveler who occasionally smoked cigarettes and drank coffee during halftime. Their coach, Marianne Stanley, came on the scene after her predecessor, the fiery Pam Parsons, was the subject of complaints from players.

By the time Old Dominion rose to the top, televised women's games were not unprecedented. The first TV game was carried by NBC in 1975 between Immaculata and Maryland. NBC also carried the national title game beginning in 1978 through the early 1980s, although regular season games virtually were non-existent on the tube.

And it was over television that the final rifts between the AIAW and the NCAA erupted, resulting in an ugly, visible dispute marked by the lawsuits, intense rhetoric, and power struggles that highlight recent battles over gender equity. Title IX had forced initial compliance with its provisions in regard to use of facilities, travel and recruiting budgets, and more playing opportunities for athletes, but they hardly amounted to a drop in the basket of what women's sports leaders expected and later would demand.

AIAW leaders were optimistic as the 1970s drew to a close that a lucrative TV contract and other corporate sponsorships could lead to greater self-sufficiency. In 1980, the AIAW signed a four-year contract with NBC that amounted to $200,000 per year in television rights alone and worked other deals to help pay for partial travel expenses for national tournament teams, something it declined to do previously. But the very progress of the AIAW, and of Title IX, led to the ultimate demise of the women-dominated group. Greater demand for scholarship aid, calls from outspoken feminists for equity to match the exact level of support for men's programs, and takeover caveats from the NCAA forced their hand.

The NCAA offered a women's basketball tournament for the 1981–82 season that included promises for more television exposure and program expansion and full reimbursement for travel and expenses to the championships. That last pledge prompted most athletic directors to go with the NCAA, since their costs would be minimized and they were under Title IX threats to broaden women's offerings. Even many women basketball coaches, especially from bigger schools, thought the change would enhance the sport.

The AIAW staged its final basketball tournament the same year, but lost nearly $10,000 in the process. Rutgers defeated Texas in the Palestra in Philadelphia, but only a handful of the nation's top teams remained with the AIAW. Louisiana Tech won the first NCAA women's title on live TV and before a sold-out crowd of more than 10,000 in Norfolk, Va.

Trying to stay alive, the AIAW filed an antitrust lawsuit soon after, but later its members voted to disband. The novel experiment of a student-centered model of college sports was in place for only 11 seasons, but it opened the doors to high-level competition and produced many of the elite coaches who have controlled women's basketball since the 1980s. How they handled their new association with the NCAA proved to be an exciting experience although somewhat contentious.

The NCAA Digs In: Coming of Age in a Time of Transition

With the bitter breakup of the AIAW still fresh in their minds, women's sports leaders looked ahead to a future under the NCAA umbrella with some trepidation. Title IX was nowhere closer to being enforced, and large numbers of women coaches were leaving their positions. Men began filling many of those jobs, especially in basketball, and women feared they were losing their grip on the control of women's athletics.

But on the court, women's basketball experienced a virtual explosion of growth and interest in the 1980s. Players with superb athletic as well as basketball skills were starring in all parts of the country. Many would become Olympic stars later in the decade, as the United States replaced the Soviet Union as the dominant force in international women's basketball.

Just months after Louisiana Tech won the first NCAA title in 1982, elite coaches awaited the recruiting decision of a California teenager who came to personify the sport in an unprecedented fashion. Cheryl Miller finally cast her lot with USC, noting its major media market and academic program in public relations. Not only was Miller one of the most gifted women ever to play basketball, but her personal flair and theatrics attracted national attention and gave the sport an unmistakable identity.

She would become the first four-time Kodak All-American, and in her first two seasons guided USC to national championships. USC fans loved her emotional fury, as she pumped her fists in the air after a spectacular play. Opposing coaches and fans were infuriated when she blew kisses to the crowd or slammed down a ball after a call didn't go her way. However she was perceived by individual supporters or foes, Miller meant one thing to women's basketball. She injected personality, pizazz, and a sense of the dramatic. For once, the game was the viable entertainment option its leaders hoped it would be.

USC reached the title game in Miller's senior season, but lost to Texas in 1986. She was the leading scorer for the 1984 Olympic team that won the gold medal in Los Angeles, and continued a sports career in broadcasting after graduation. In late 1993, she took over the coaching reins at her alma mater.

There was no lack of exciting players and teams to challenge USC. In the Deep South, the Southeastern Conference asserted itself as the best league in the nation. Tennessee had been strong since the 1970s, but with the NCAA era came an increase in funding and commitment at schools like Auburn and Georgia. LSU, Vanderbilt, and Mississippi also were regular contenders for postseason play.

Georgia turned heads by recruiting some of the top high school players in the country. In 1981, Janet Harris, a 6-3 center from Chicago, headed to Georgia to begin a migration that continues today. In the next two years, homegrown talent in guard Teresa Edwards and center Katrina McClain would join forces on one of the most talented teams ever to play. Georgia reached the Final Four in 1983 and in 1985 was favored to win the national title, but was tripped up by Old Dominion in the championship game.

What Georgia and other SEC schools embodied was the full acceptance of recruiting as a tool to advance the game. As gifted athletes who played nearly year-round on national teams and in summer leagues, these players represented the kind of student-athlete that AIAW leaders abhorred. These young women were tied down to their athletic obligations like male athletes had been for years, and there were no signs of turning back. Even more women coaches with physical education backgrounds left the profession, leaving the door open to men and women who fit the new prototype.

A win-at-all-costs recruiting mentality began to materialize at the highest levels of women's basketball, since there aren't nearly the numbers of blue chip players as come out of boys high school ranks. Toward the end of the AIAW era, a scandal rocked women's basketball badly enough to illustrate that women could fall victim to the corrupting influences the game's pioneers dreaded would happen.

When coach Pam Parsons left Old Dominion in 1977 because of protests from her players,

TRACK STAR JOYNER-KERSEE WAS CAGER, TOO

There's an argument in some sexist quarters that women's basketball is inferior because of an absence of female players with all-around athletic skills. It's easy to refute that stance, however, when one recalls Jackie Joyner-Kersee, acknowledged as the greatest female athlete in history.

Joyner, a four-year starter, averaged 9.6 points and 6.2 rebounds per game in her UCLA basketball career from 1980–81 through 1982–83 and 1984–85.

Later, she earned national acclaim with an extraordinary track and field career. Her achievements include:

- Won five medals in Olympic track and field competition, including the gold medal in the heptathlon in 1988 and 1992 and the long jump in 1988.

- Established women's world heptathlon record (7,290 points) and women's American long jump record (24 feet, 5 1/2 inches).

- Earned Sullivan Award as the nation's premier amateur athlete in 1986.

- Named Female Athlete of the Year by the Associated Press in 1987.

she latched on at South Carolina, turning that school into an instant power. She embarked on a national recruiting effort—landing Evelyn Johnson, the talented younger sister of Magic Johnson, among others—to build her program. South Carolina reached the AIAW Final Four in 1980 and was a favorite to get back. But allegations of illegal recruiting, financial and academic activities, and sexual improprieties jolted the school and the sport and led to Parsons' resignation early in the 1980–81 season. A *Sports Illustrated* article detailing the situation included accusations that she was personally involved with one of her players, a charge she vehemently denied. Parsons sued the magazine for libel, but later was convicted of perjury.

The AIAW believed in self-policing of rules violations, but the South Carolina imbroglio clearly demonstrated that approach could not control flagrant abuses. The only major recruiting scandal during the NCAA era was widely reported around the country. Northeast Louisiana made the national rankings in the mid-1980s because of aggressive, nationwide recruiting. When a Mississippi high school star, 6-4 Chana Perry, caught college coaches' attention in 1983, Northeast Louisiana boosters allegedly offered her use of automobiles and other gifts and promised her jobs after graduation. An assistant provided illegal transportation and lodging during a recruiting trip and Perry was given an illegal tryout while still in high school.

Perry signed with Northeast Louisiana and in 1985 helped her team to the Final Four. But soon after, the NCAA placed the school on probation, giving it the maximum penalty for a women's program: it was not eligible for postseason play. Perry also was not allowed to play there any longer and finished her career at San Diego State.

A host of new schools reached prominent levels during the 1980s, especially from the major conferences. In the Atlantic Coast Conference, Maryland and North Carolina State received a new rival in Virginia, which dominated into the early 1990s behind the guard play of Dawn Staley. The Big Ten featured annual clashes between Ohio State and Iowa, and Purdue entered the fray toward the end of the decade. Colorado and Kansas were the most solid programs in the Big Eight. USC owned the Pacific-10 during the Miller years, but budding programs at Washington and Stanford would shift the balance northward in years to come.

Texas had the Southwest Conference all to itself, winning 188 consecutive league games and leading the nation in attendance for most of the 1980s. In 1986, the Lady Longhorns became the only NCAA champion to go undefeated, posting a 34-0 record and featuring the play of freshman forward Clarissa Davis, who earned Final Four MVP honors. She was one of four players on that team later to become an All-American, and one of three from Texas to make an Olympic team. Injuries cut short Davis' career, but not before she scored 45 points at Tennessee before a world record crowd of nearly 25,000 fans in early 1987.

And Tennessee, after several tries without success, finally won a national title in 1987, the first of three in five seasons for coach Pat Head Summitt, who had learned the recruiting game

very well. She developed a pipeline to Michigan to sign the best of that state's deep talent base, and went to Florida to get Bridgette Gordon, a smooth forward who keyed her first title and a repeat performance in 1989. The Lady Volunteers won the crown again in 1991, making Summitt the only women's coach to earn three NCAA championships.

The advent of tougher academic requirements, such as Proposition 48, also changed the national picture. Tara VanDerveer left Ohio State to revive the Stanford program in 1985. She also recruited nationwide for top prep athletes, but many of them were class valedictorians and honor students. Five years later, Stanford won the national title and duplicated the feat in 1992. The 1990 Final Four, played in the spacious 25,000-seat arena on the Tennessee campus, marked another women's watershed. Although Tennessee had been ousted in the regionals, Summitt and other school officials persuaded partisan fans to come. More than 20,000 spectators watched Stanford, led by Knoxville-area native Jennifer Azzi, take the crown.

The Final Four's first advance sellout in 1993 was a fitting finale for Texas Tech senior Sheryl Swoopes, who electrified the crowd of more than 15,000 in Atlanta with a 47-point performance against Ohio State in the title game. That broke Bill Walton's Final Four record of 44 points in 1973 and made her a household name in basketball circles.

Off-the-court issues dominated news stories and NCAA policies in the early 1990s. Women sports activists stepped up efforts to push women coaches for plum jobs, and men coaches complained of reverse discrimination. And the concept of gender equity became a major source of controversy. The NCAA Task Force on Gender Equity mapped out a plan to make athletic programs comply with Title IX toward the end of the decade. But feminist demands for resources proportionate to female student enrollment placed women at severe odds with some athletic directors and football coaches, who saw their revenue-producing programs threatened.

Several basketball programs faced extinction as the 1990s opened. Oklahoma suddenly dropped its women's team during the 1990 Final Four, but threats of a lawsuit forced a change in plans. Similar pressure was put on athletic administrators at William & Mary, which proposed cutting women's basketball for financial reasons. That decision also was reversed after extensive reports appeared in major newspapers and magazines.

In 1984, Title IX was imperiled when the U.S. Supreme Court ruled that the law did not apply if specific departments of an educational institution received no federal funds. The ruling threatened to remove athletics from the realm of Title IX, but Congress overrode the court's action in 1988 by passing the Civil Rights Restoration Act, which mandated universal Title IX compliance.

Women's basketball coaches began to enter the high rent district in terms of salary and benefits in the early 1990s. No less than a half dozen coaches received six-figure contracts following the 1992–93 season, with the equal pay component of gender equity a major factor. Summitt, VanDerveer, Virginia's Debbie Ryan, and several others received the same base pay as the men's coaches at their schools. Others came close to the male standard. After coaching Texas Tech to the 1993 title, Marsha Sharp received a Lexus automobile from the school as a bonus. It was featured on the cover of the school's media guide the next season.

But an equal pay dispute at USC erupted into a full-scale controversy in late 1993. Marianne Stanley, who had retooled the program into a winner, demanded the same salary as men's coach George Raveling during contract negotiations. The school offered her slightly less, near the $100,000 mark, a figure she rejected. Her contract expired and Cheryl Miller was hired, but Stanley filed an $8 million sex discrimination lawsuit. She sought reinstatement for the 1993–94 season, but her petition was rejected by the U.S. Supreme Court.

Women's coaches rushed to Stanley's side, publicly blasting USC and suggesting boycotts

Southeastern Louisiana's Robin Roberts (right) is now a successful ESPN reporter.

against the Miller-coached team. But the school contended that since Raveling's team produces revenue and the women lose money, the pressures on them to produce are different and therefore their job descriptions were not the same.

Despite the internal squabbles, women's college basketball continued to attract more fans and media interest. Attendance records have been set every season during the NCAA period, to more than four million for the 1992–93 season. The NCAA tournament was expanded three times and now matches the men's 64-team field. Television exposure also increased, as various schools and conferences signed their own deals and the NCAA demanded several women's games as part of its men's tournament package awarded to CBS.

Marketing, promotions, and business deals will dictate the viability of women's basketball in the sports marketplace. Coaches sign endorsement contracts, speak before civic and business groups, and are positioning themselves to administer the sport when their coaching days are concluded. Recruiting and evaluation camps and tournaments have helped prepare high school players for the rigors of the college game. Developmental programs have been started by USA Basketball to foster intense competition at a younger age and instill a wider range of basketball skills. International events such as the Olympics and professional leagues for women in Europe have continued the playing careers of elite players, some of whom are competing into their 30s.

The chaste beginnings of women's basketball 100 years ago have given way completely to a modern sport that reflects the emancipation of women in society. For instance, Robin Roberts, who still ranks among the top five scorers and rebounders in Southeastern Louisiana women's history, became one of ESPN's top announcers. In their struggles to achieve full equality, however, women in basketball still cling to some of the educational precepts that have formed the game's heritage. Finding a balance between those ideals will continue to be their biggest challenge as women's basketball moves into its second century.

WOMEN'S CHAMPIONSHIPS, ATTENDANCE, AND TV

With judicious placement of host schools in the bracket, the NCAA women's championship almost doubled in attendance in a 10-year span from 2,455 per session in 1983 to 4,800 in 1992. There has also been an increase in the size of the field. In an era of gender equality, the bracket expanded from 32 to 40 teams in 1988, from 40 to 48 the next year, and from 48 to the same size as the men's tournament (64) in 1994. Another possible change is moving the dates of the women's tourney so it isn't overshadowed as much by the men's event.

Prior to the NCAA's first women's tournament in 1982, several alterations occurred under the auspices of the former governing body, the Association of Intercollegiate Athletics for Women (AIAW). In 1978, the 16-team, one-site event (games were played morning, noon, and night) was transformed into sectional play (four at each regional). A year later, the AIAW field was increased to 24. It decreased to 16 in its 11th and final competition in 1982, when the majority of noteworthy Division I schools chose to compete in the first NCAA championship.

Women's basketball, with few national personalities, is a difficult sell for the television networks. But NCAA executives, terrified of strident cries from Title IX muckrakers, mandated that a women's package be part of CBS' billion dollar deal to carry the men's Final Four. One of the trade-offs, however, was forcing the women's semifinals and final to be played on back-to-back days. The format is rigorous for any athlete to endure and can be a deterrent to the women putting their best foot forward on national TV in the championship game. The lack of time to physically recuperate didn't stop Texas Tech's Sheryl Swoopes from scoring more points, 47, than any player, male or female, ever managed in an NCAA final in 1993 when she helped the Red Raiders outlast Ohio State (84-82). Swoopes was acknowledged as the best women's player since Southern Cal's Cheryl Miller in the mid-1980s.

The women's championship game has been telecast on CBS since 1987 although it hasn't generated the audience a network needs to keep it going and growing. The ratings for the first six finals were abysmal, starting with a somewhat promising 6.1 (18 share) in 1987 but falling to as low as a 3.7 (11 share) in 1990. But Swoopes' performance in a close game in 1993 helped the women notch a 5.5 rating, a 34 percent increase from the previous year and the highest since 1987. The highest-rated women's basketball game came in 1982, when Louisiana Tech defeated Cheyney on CBS in the NCAA's first female championship game. It drew a 7.3 rating.

In addition to Swoopes' pristine performance, here are other factors demonstrating why women's basketball might be on the horizon of becoming a legitimate form of sports entertainment:

• The four teams at Atlanta in 1993 were Final Four first-timers, showing perhaps the women's game could be on the verge of extensive parity similar to the men.

• In 1993, there was the first advance sellout since the women embraced a Final Four format in 1978.

• The ladies generated enough attention to make the Las Vegas bookmakers' lines.

AIAW CHAMPIONS

YEAR	CHAMPION	COACH	RUNNER-UP	SITE
1972	Immaculata	Cathy Rush	West Chester	West Chester, Pa.
1973	Immaculata	Cathy Rush	Queens (N.Y.)	Flushing, N.Y.
1974	Immaculata	Cathy Rush	Miss. College	Manhattan, Kans.
1975	Delta St.	Margaret Wade	Immaculata	Harrisonburg, Va.
1976	Delta St.	Margaret Wade	Immaculata	University Park, Pa.
1977	Delta St.	Margaret Wade	LSU	Minneapolis
1978	UCLA	Billie Moore	Maryland	Los Angeles
1979	Old Dominion	Marianne Stanley	La. Tech	Greensboro, N.C.
1980	Old Dominion	Marianne Stanley	Tenn.	Mt. Pleasant, Mich.
1981	Louisiana Tech	Sonja Hogg	Tenn.	Eugene, Ore.
1982	Rutgers	Theresa Grentz	Texas	Philadelphia

NCAA WOMEN'S CHAMPIONS

YEAR	CHAMPION	COACH	RUNNER-UP	SITE
1982	La. Tech	Sonja Hogg	Cheyney (Pa.)	Norfolk, Va.
1983	Southern Cal	Linda Sharp	La. Tech	Norfolk, Va.
1984	Southern Cal	Linda Sharp	Tennessee	Los Angeles
1985	Old Dominion	Marianne Stanley	Georgia	Austin, Tex.
1986	Texas	Jody Conradt	Southern Cal	Lexington, Ky.
1987	Tennessee	Pat Summitt	La. Tech	Austin, Tex.
1988	La. Tech	Leon Barmore	Auburn	Tacoma, Wash.
1989	Tennessee	Pat Summitt	Auburn	Tacoma, Wash.
1990	Stanford	Tara VanDerveer	Auburn	Knoxville, Tenn.
1991	Tennessee	Pat Summitt	Virginia	New Orleans
1992	Stanford	Tara VanDerveer	W. Kentucky	Los Angeles
1993	Texas Tech	Marsha Sharp	Ohio State	Atlanta
1994	N. Carolina	Sylvia Hatchell	La. Tech	Richmond, Va.

NCAA OUTSTANDING PLAYER AWARD WINNERS

1982: Janice Lawrence, Louisiana Tech
1983: Cheryl Miller, Southern Cal
1984: Cheryl Miller, Southern Cal
1985: Tracy Claxton, Old Dominion
1986: Clarissa Davis, Texas
1987: Tonya Edwards, Tennessee
1988: Erica Westbrooks, Louisiana Tech
1989: Bridgette Gordon, Tennessee
1990: Jennifer Azzi, Stanford
1991: Dawn Staley, Virginia
1992: Molly Goodenbour, Stanford
1993: Sheryl Swoopes, Texas Tech
1994: Charlotte Smith, North Carolina

WOMEN'S TOURNAMENT FACTS

THROUGH 1993–94 SEASON

Most NCAA titles by school: Tennessee (3), Louisiana Tech (2), Southern Cal (2), Stanford (2).

Most NCAA victories by school: Louisiana Tech (39), Tennessee (38), Southern Cal (26), Auburn (20), Texas (20).

Coach Sylvia Hatchell and her North Carolina team won the 1994 NCAA Championship.

All-Time Great Women's Players

LORRI BAUMAN
Drake
6-3 – C
Des Moines, Iowa

The first woman to score 3,000 points while playing a majority of her games under NCAA auspices.... Still holds seven NCAA tournament marks, including 50 points in a game in the 1982 West Regional final in a loss to Maryland.... Only one of nine women to score more than 3,000 points and collect more than 1,000 rebounds.... Drake qualified for three NCAA Tournament trips during her career.... In 120 games, she missed double figures in scoring only four times.... Played six-on-six basketball in high school in Iowa, averaging 48 points per game as a senior.

Year	G	FGM	FGA	FG%	FTM	FTA	FT%	Reb.	Avg.	Pts.	Avg.
80–81	28	263	465	.566	212	264	.803	248	8.9	738	26.4
81–82	35	273	513	.532	275	325	.846	372	9.2	821	23.5
82–83	28	264	445	.593	209	251	.833	264	9.4	737	26.3
83–84	29	304	508	.598	211	250	.844	216	7.4	819	28.2
Totals	120	1104	1931	.572	907	1090	.832	1050	8.8	3115	26.0

CAROL BLAZEJOWSKI
Montclair State
5-11 – F
Cranford, N.J.

Still holds women's career scoring average (31.7 points) and season average (38.6) and is third on the all-time women's scoring charts (3,199 points).... Was inducted in the Naismith Hall of Fame in 1993.... Owns the women's single-season scoring mark with 1,235 points as a senior.... A three-time Kodak All-American and the first Wade Trophy winner.... Helped Montclair State reach the first AIAW Final Four in 1978.... Montclair also played in two other AIAW national tournaments.... Continues to play on barnstorming teams in the Northeast.... Currently is director of licensing for the National Basketball Association.

Year	G	FGM	FGA	FG%	FTM	FTA	FT%	Reb.	Avg.	Pts.	Avg.
74–75	17	138	320	.430	57	80	.711	171	10.0	333	19.6
75–76	25	298	540	.551	116	150	.773	255	10.2	712	28.5
76–77	27	393	695	.565	133	167	.796	272	10.1	919	34.0
77–78	32	515	905	.569	205	245	.837	317	9.9	1235	38.6
Totals	101	1344	2460	.550	511	642	.795	1015	10.4	3199	31.7

CATHY BOSWELL
Illinois State
5-11 – F
Joliet, Ill.

Illinois State's all-time leading women's scorer (2,005 points) holds six school records and is the only woman athlete at the school to have her number retired.... Twice a finalist for the Wade Trophy.

Year	G	FGM	FGA	FG%	FTM	FTA	FT%	Reb.	Avg.	Pts.	Avg.
79–80	33	242	490	.494	51	84	.607	301	9.1	535	16.2
80–81	36	274	537	.510	101	119	.849	343	9.5	649	18.0
81–82	22	165	347	.476	28	44	.636	159	7.2	358	16.3
82–83	30	208	444	.468	47	62	.758	257	8.6	463	15.4
Totals	121	889	1818	.489	227	309	.735	1060	8.8	2005	16.6

DEBBIE BROCK
Delta State
4-11 – G
Forest City, Miss.

The tiny guard played for three AIAW national championship teams from 1975 to 1977.... Averaged only 7 points a game during her career, but was known for her excellent passing to future Hall of Fame teammate Lusia Harris.... An All-American her final two seasons.... Scored 22 points in the 1977 national title game against LSU from what now is the 3-point range.

Year	G	FGM	FGA	FG%	FTM	FTA	FT%	Reb.	Avg.	Pts.	Avg.
74–75	25	63	119	.529	65	77	.844	60	2.4	191	7.6
75–76	34	65	128	.507	62	78	.794	111	3.2	192	5.6
76–77	35	100	221	.452	65	77	.844	78	2.2	95	7.6
77–78	32	85	200	.425	85	103	.825	94	2.9	255	7.9
Totals	126	313	668	.469	277	335	.827	343	2.7	903	7.1

CINDY BROGDON
Mercer/Tennessee
5-10 – F
Buford, Ga.

The second all-time leading women's scorer with 3,240 points.... Tennessee made its first trip to the Final Four in her senior year in 1979.... Played her first two seasons for Mercer before transferring.... Was a two-time Kodak All-American, once at each school.

Year	G	FGM	FGA	FG%	FTM	FTA	FT%	Reb.	Avg.	Pts.	Avg.
75–76	30	348	706	.490	206	247	.830	319	10.6	902	30.1
76–77	28	335	690	.490	174	216	.810	286	10.2	844	30.1
77–78	31	286	593	.482	102	118	.864	238	7.6	674	21.7
78–79	39	344	639	.538	96	118	.813	185	4.7	784	20.1
Totals	128	1313	2628	.500	578	699	.827	1028	8.3	3240	25.0

ANUCHA BROWNE
Northwestern
6-1 – F
Brooklyn, N.Y.

Holds 24 school records and is Northwestern's first Kodak All-American (1985).... As a senior, she led the country in scoring with 30.5 points a game.... Set an NCAA record by scoring 30 points or more in six consecutive games.... The second all-time leading scorer in Big Ten history with 2,307 points, she was a three-time all-league pick and twice was its Player of the Year.... A finalist for the Wade Trophy and the Naismith Award.

Year	G	FGM	FGA	FG%	FTM	FTA	FT%	Reb.	Avg.	Pts.	Avg.
81–82	29	136	266	.511	74	116	.638	174	6.0	346	11.9
82–83	27	221	396	.558	110	170	.647	249	9.2	552	20.4
83–84	26	221	481	.459	112	179	.651	271	10.4	554	21.3
84–85	28	341	666	.512	173	254	.681	257	9.2	855	30.5
Totals	110	919	1809	.508	469	719	.652	951	8.6	2307	21.0

VICKY BULLETT
Maryland
6-2 – F/C
Martinsburg, W.V.

A two-time Kodak All-American.... The leading scorer and rebounder in school history.... Leading scorer and rebounder on Maryland's 1989 Final Four team.... Helped team to two Atlantic Coast Conference titles.... A three-time All-ACC pick.

Year	G	FGM	FGA	FG%	FTM	FTA	FT%	Reb.	Avg.	Pts.	Avg.
85–86	21	87	175	.470	44	61	.721	135	6.4	218	10.4
86–87	29	197	357	.552	49	77	.636	243	8.4	443	15.3
87–88	32	243	404	.602	95	134	.709	303	9.6	581	18.2
88–89	32	289	503	.675	108	136	.794	287	9.0	688	21.4
Totals	114	816	1439	.567	296	408	.725	888	7.8	1928	16.9

DENISE CURRY
UCLA
6-1 – F
Davis, Calif.

UCLA's all-time leading scorer (3,198 points) and rebounder (1,310 boards) who played on 1978 AIAW national championship team as a freshman.... Set a collegiate record by scoring in double figures in all 130 games of her career.... A three-time Kodak All-American who helped the Bruins to two West Coast Athletic Association titles and two AIAW national appearances.... Holds 14 UCLA career records.... Currently an assistant coach at the University of California.

Year	G	FGM	FGA	FG%	FTM	FTA	FT%	Reb.	Avg.	Pts.	Avg.
77–78	30	280	451	.621	50	65	.769	273	9.1	610	20.3
78–79	34	355	586	.606	93	115	.809	340	10.0	803	23.6
79–80	30	361	599	.604	133	149	.893	337	11.2	855	28.5
80–81	36	390	647	.603	150	192	.781	360	10.0	930	25.8
Totals	130	1386	2283	.607	426	521	.818	1310	10.1	3198	24.6

CLARISSA DAVIS-WRIGHTSIL
Texas
6-1 – F
San Antonio, Tex.

The all-time Southwest Conference career scoring and third-best scorer in school history despite being cut down by injuries during her career (knee injury as junior).... Was MVP of the 1986 Final Four as a freshman as Texas won the NCAA title.... A two-time Kodak All-American and Wade Trophy winner.... Also named National Player of the Year as a senior by Naismith, Champion Products, and the USBWA/Mercedes.... Scored 45 points in 97-78 Texas win at Tennessee in which a world attendance record (24,563) was set.... Established a Texas record by scoring 843 points during senior year.... Currently playing professional basketball in Turkey, where her husband also is a pro player.

Year	G	FGM	FGA	FG%	FTM	FTA	FT%	Reb.	Avg.	Pts.	Avg.
85–86	34	180	309	.583	99	150	.660	262	7.7	459.	13.5
86–87	26	196	340	.576	91	146	.632	217	8.3	483	18.6
87–88	9	93	145	.641	37	50	.740	87	9.7	223	24.8
88–89	32	324	585	.559	188	262	.718	316	9.9	843	26.3
Totals	101	793	1379	.580	415	608	.680	882	8.7	2008	19.8

ANNE DONOVAN
Old Dominion
6-8 – C
Ridgewood, N.J.

Old Dominion's all-time leading scorer and rebounder played for two national championship squads and two gold medal Olympic squads.... The first exceptionally tall impact player in women's college basketball.... A four-year starter, she was leading scorer and rebounder as a freshman, playing alongside All-Americans Nancy Lieberman and Inge Nissen on national title team.... A three-time Kodak All-American and the 1983 National Player of the Year.

Year	G	FGM	FGA	FG%	FTM	FTA	FT%	Reb.	Avg.	Pts.	Avg.
79–80	38	290	460	.630	68	126	.539	491	12.9	648	17.0
80–81	35	377	591	.638	125	175	.714	569	16.2	879	25.1
81–82	28	240	375	.640	99	142	.697	412	14.7	579	14.7
82–83	35	263	428	.614	87	130	.669	504	14.4	613	17.5
Totals	136	1170	1854	.631	379	573	.661	1976	14.5	2719	19.9

TERESA EDWARDS
Georgia
5-11 – G
Cairo, Ga.

A two-time Kodak All-American and three-time Olympian.... Played on Georgia's Final Four teams in 1983 and 1985.... Jersey number was the first to be retired for a Georgia basketball player, male or female.... Named all-SEC three times.... Had extensive professional career in Japan and Europe between Olympic stints.... Her international play spanned from 1981 to the 1992 Olympics and she participated in 13 major competitions.

Year	G	FGM	FGA	FG%	FTM	FTA	FT%	Reb.	Avg.	Pts.	Avg.
82–83	33	189	412	.459	52	82	.634	73	2.2	430	13.0
83–84	33	207	397	.521	51	65	.785	81	2.5	465	14.1
84–85	30	203	385	.527	58	79	.734	84	2.8	464	15.5
85–86	32	274	491	.558	82	104	.788	146	4.6	630	19.7
Totals	128	873	1685	.518	243	330	.736	384	3.0	1989	15.5

PEGGIE GILLOM
Mississippi
6-0 – F
Abbeville, Miss.

The leading scorer and rebounder in school history.... Led Ole Miss to two AIAW regional tournament trips.... Was a finalist for the Wade Trophy in 1980... Drafted by the Dallas Diamonds of the Women's Professional Basketball League in 1980 and played one season before returning to Ole Miss, where she has been an assistant coach since 1981.... Her younger sister, Jennifer, also scored more than 2,000 points for the Lady Rebels, earned a gold medal with the 1988 U.S. Olympic team, and is the school's only Kodak All-American.

Year	G	FGM	FGA	FG%	FTM	FTA	FT%	Reb.	Avg.	Pts.	Avg.
76–77	28	159	314	.506	41	67	.612	240	8.6	359	12.8
77–78	40	312	583	.535	97	132	.735	329	8.2	721	8.0
78–79	39	288	571	.504	116	152	.763	341	8.7	692	17.7
79–80	37	293	652	.449	128	181	.707	361	9.8	714	19.3
Totals	144	1052	2120	.496	382	532	.718	1271	8.8	2486	17.3

BRIDGETTE GORDON
Tennessee
6-0 – F
DeLand, Fla.

The all-time leading scorer and most decorated player in school history.... Led Tennessee to its first two national championships in 1987 and 1989, and is one of three Lady Volunteers to reach the Final Four in all four of her college seasons. No other women's program holds that distinction.... A two-time Kodak All-American and MVP of the 1989 Final Four.... The all-time leading scorer in NCAA women's tournament history with 388 points and a 21.6 average.... Tennessee was 115-21 during her career, winning two SEC titles, and she was the league's Player of the Year twice.... Led her professional team to the Italian League championship in 1991.

Year	G	FGM	FGA	FG%	FTM	FTA	FT%	Reb.	Avg.	Pts.	Avg.
85–86	34	206	429	.480	69	109	.633	209	6.2	418	14.2
86–87	34	222	459	.484	115	160	.719	232	6.8	559	16.4
87–88	33	286	529	.541	106	151	.702	225	6.8	687	20.8
88–89	36	298	557	.535	131	188	.697	251	7.0	733	20.4
Totals	137	1012	1974	.513	421	608	.692	917	6.1	2460	18.0

JERILYNN HARPER
Tennessee/Tennessee Tech
6-1 – F
Jefferson City, Tenn.

The second all-time career scorer for one of the early powers from the Southeast.... Helped Tech to appearances in the National Women's Invitational Tournament and the first NCAA tournament in 1982.... Owns 10 of the top 11 individual single-game scoring records at Tech.... Scored 40 or more points six different times in her career and in 32 games scored 30 points or more.... Played her freshman year at Tennessee, where she was a reserve on the 1979 Final Four team, before transferring to Tennessee Tech.

Year	G	FGM	FGA	FG%	FTM	FTA	FT%	Reb.	Avg.	Pts.	Avg.
78–79	37	152	271	.561	61	84	.726	170	4.6	365	9.9
79–80	27	159	293	.543	78	100	.780			396	14.7
80–81	34	410	653	.628	191	242	.789			1011	29.7
81–82	31	343	601	.571	191	242	.784			831	26.8
Totals	129	1064	1818	.585	521	668	.780	961	7.4	2603	20.2

JANET HARRIS
Georgia
6-3 – F/C
Chicago, Ill.

Georgia's all-time leading scorer and rebounder, a three-time Kodak All-American, and a member of two U.S. National Sports teams.... Took Georgia to the NCAA Final Four in 1983 and 1985.... Is one of three Georgia women's players to have a jersey number retired.... While at Georgia, the team earned four straight NCAA Tournament trips.... A three-time All-SEC selection, she led Georgia to consecutive league crowns in 1983 and 1984.

Year	G	FGM	FGA	FG%	FTM	FTA	FT%	Reb.	Avg.	Pts.	Avg.
81–82	30	281	517	.533	101	160	.631	371	12.4	663	22.4
82–83	34	299	537	.557	94	155	.606	397	11.7	692	20.4
83–84	33	249	472	.528	88	126	.698	279	8.5	586	17.8
84–85	34	298	503	.592	104	147	.707	351	10.3	700	20.6
Totals	131	1127	2029	.555	387	588	.658	1398	10.7	2641	20.2

LUSIA HARRIS STEWART
Delta State
6-3 – C
Minter City, Miss.

The first female college player to be inducted into the Naismith Basketball Hall of Fame in 1992.... The first prototypical modern center in the women's college game.... Led the Lady Statesmen to three consecutive AIAW national titles from 1975 to 1977. She was MVP of all three national tournaments.... A member of the 1976 silver medal U.S. Olympic team, she scored the first points ever by a female player in the Olympics.... The Olympians' top scorer (15.0) and rebounder (7.0).... A three-time All-American and two-time national Player of the Year.... The nation's top scorer as a junior, averaging 31.2 points.... Delta State's first women's basketball recruit after a 40-year layoff.... Currently a high school teacher and coach in Ruleville, Miss.

Year	G	FGM	FGA	FG%	FTM	FTA	FT%	Reb.	Avg.	Pts.	Avg.
73–74	18	147	226	.650	58	103	.563	252	14.0	352	19.6
74–75	28	300	458	.655	107	145	.738	400	14.3	707	25.3
75–76	34	457	738	.619	146	217	.672	514	15.1	1060	31.2
76–77	35	363	579	.627	136	200	.680	496	14.2	862	24.6
Totals	115	1266	2001	.633	447	665	.672	1662	14.5	2979	25.9

Year	G	FGM	FGA	FG%	FTM	FTA	FT%	Reb.	Avg.	Pts.	Avg.
80–81	34	192	326	.589	123	189	.651	283	8.3	507	14.9
81–82	36	202	363	.556	124	174	.713	253	7.0	528	14.7
82–83	33	272	455	.598	141	222	.635	301	9.1	685	20.7
83–84	32	268	433	.619	147	207	.710	301	8.1	683	21.3
Totals	135	934	1577	.592	535	792	.676	1097	8.1	2403	17.8

PAM KELLY
Louisiana Tech
6-0 – F
Columbia, La.

Captained Louisiana Tech to national titles in 1981 and 1982 as the Lady Techsters rolled up a dominating record of 69-1 over those seasons, prompting one coach to proclaim they had the two best teams in America.... The school's career leader in points (2,979) and rebounds (1,511) as well as in 19 other categories.... A three-time Kodak All-American and the 1982 Wade Trophy winner.... A member of the Louisiana Tech Hall of Fame and the Louisiana College Athlete of the Year in 1981.... Scored in double figures in 140 of her 153 college games, and notched rebounding double-figure games 80 times.... Had a career-high of 41 points against UCLA as a senior.... The Lady Techsters were 143-10 during her career.

Year	G	FGM	FGA	FG%	FTM	FTA	FT%	Reb.	Avg.	Pts.	Avg.
78–79	38	273	564	.484	62	92	.674	372		721	19.0
79–80	45	369	710	.520	79	114	.693	491	10.9	932	20.7
80–81	34	204	449	.454	53	70	.757	322	9.5	595	17.5
81–82	36	280	435	.644	171	247	.692	326	9.1	732	20.3
Totals	153	1126	2158	.522	365	531	.687	1511	9.8	2979	19.4

NANCY LIEBERMAN CLINE
Old Dominion
5-10 – G
Far Rockaway, N.Y.

One of the first flash-and-dash players of the modern women's era.... She was captain of two national championship teams and a three-time Kodak All-American.... The 1980 national Player of the Year.... Named to the 1976 U.S. Olympic team as an 18-year-old high school graduate.... A first-round draft choice of the Dallas Diamonds in 1980, leading them to a league title.... Was a physical trainer and confidante of tennis champion Martina Navratilova.... Has played in the U.S. Basketball League and currently has several basketball and sports marketing businesses in operation.... Wrote an autobiography entitled *Lady Magic* for the nickname she earned because of her fancy passing abilities.

Year	G	FGM	FGA	FG%	FTM	FTA	FT%	Reb.	Avg.	Pts.	Avg.
76–77	27	240	507	.473	88	117	.709	272	10.1	563	20.9
77–78	34	281	651	.432	119	163	.730	325	9.6	681	20.2
78–79	36	243	500	.478	139	176	.790	276	7.7	625	17.4
79–80	37	203	390	.533	145	186	.779	294	7.9	561	15.2
Totals	134	973	2056	.472	486	642	.757	1167	8.7	2430	18.1

BARBARA KENNEDY
Clemson
6-1 – F/C
Rome, Ga.

A Kodak All-American selection in 1981–82, when she averaged 29 points a game, currently the 10th best seasonal average in NCAA history.... Still holds the Atlantic Coast Conference record for career scoring average and is the league's career rebounding leader... Clemson was 84-42 during her career, qualifying for three AIAW tournaments and the first NCAA women's tournament.... She scored the first points in NCAA women's tournament history against Penn State on March 12, 1982.... A member of the Clemson Athletic Hall of Fame, she also was a Clemson assistant coach and is now an athletic academic counselor at the school.

Year	G	FGM	FGA	FG%	FTM	FTA	FT%	Reb.	Avg.	Pts.	Avg.
78–79	29	227	477	.476	87	130	.669	248	8.6	541	18.7
79–80	36	382	729	.524	89	137	.650	298	8.3	853	23.7
80–81	31	348	722	.482	115	175	.657	306	9.9	811	26.2
81–82	31	392	760	.516	124	172	.721	400	12.9	908	29.3
Totals	127	1349	2688	.502	415	614	.676	1252	9.9	3113	24.5

KATRINA MCCLAIN
Georgia
6-2 – C
Charleston, S.C.

The 1987 Player of the Year by Champion Products, the Women's Basketball News Service, the American Women's Sports Foundation, and the *Shreveport Journal*.... A two-time All-American and two-time Olympian.... Was named to two All-SEC teams.... Starting center on Georgia team that reached the 1985 national title game.

Year	G	FGM	FGA	FG%	FTM	FTA	FT%	Reb.	Avg.	Pts.	Avg.
83–84	33	137	197	.695	66	95	.695	254	7.7	340	10.3
84–85	29	164	262	.626	70	105	.667	234	8.1	398	13.7
85–86	31	262	396	.662	137	176	.778	314	10.1	661	21.3
86–87	32	310	552	.562	176	240	.733	391	12.2	796	24.9
Totals	125	873	1407	.620	449	616	.729	1193	9.5	2195	17.6

JANICE LAWRENCE
Louisiana Tech
6-3 – C
Lucedale, Miss.

A three-time Kodak All-American and a national Player of the Year who guided the Lady Techsters to two national titles in 1980–81 and 1981–82. Those title teams were among the most dominating in women's college annals, going a collective 69-1.... The MVP of the first NCAA Women's Final Four in 1982.... The national player of the year in 1984 as well as the Wade Trophy winner.

SUZIE MCCONNELL SERIO
Penn State
5-5 – G
Pittsburgh, Pa.

A 1988 Kodak All-American and a two-time Olympian.... The NCAA's all-time women's assists leader, totaling 1,307 for an average of 10.2 a game.... Guided the Nittany Lions to four NCAA Tournament berths.... Named the Frances Pomeroy Naismith winner in 1988 as the top small player in the country .... Had 71 double-figure assist games.... Currently a high school and AAU coach in Pittsburgh.

Year	G	FGM	FGA	FG%	FTM	FTA	FT%	Reb.	Avg.	Pts.	Avg.
84–85	33	157	343	.458	101	136	.743	93	2.8	415	12.6
85–86	32	148	335	.442	86	109	.789	94	2.9	382	11.9
86–87	30	169	337	.502	68	94	.723	141	4.7	418	13.9
87–88	33	255	511	.499	116	143	.811	165	5.0	682	20.6
Totals	128	729	1526	.478	371	482	.770	493	3.9	1897	14.8

PAM MCGEE
Southern Cal
6-3 – F/C
Flint, Mich.

A Kodak All-American in 1984 as a senior.... Member of national title teams in 1983 and 1984.... The identical twin of USC forward Paula McGee.... Was a finalist for the Wade Trophy in 1983 and the Naismith Award in 1984.... USC's all-time leader in career field-goal shooting.

Year	G	FGM	FGA	FG%	FTM	FTA	FT%	Reb.	Avg.	Pts.	Avg.
80–81	34	217	398	.545	75	148	.506	294	8.6	509	14.8
81–82	27	219	381	.575	91	143	.636	312	11.6	529	19.6
82–83	33	249	408	.610	110	174	.632	329	10.0	608	18.4
83–84	33	250	420	.595	68	131	.519	320	8.7	568	17.2
Totals	127	935	1607	.582	365	596	.613	1255	9.9	2214	17.4

PAULA MCGEE
Southern Cal
6-3 – F/C
Flint, Mich.

Was a Kodak All-American in 1981 and 1983.... Helped the Trojans to national titles in 1983 and 1984.... The identical twin of USC forward Pam McGee.... No other USC freshman, including Cheryl Miller, scored as many points (683).

Year	G	FGM	FGA	FG%	FTM	FTA	FT%	Reb.	Avg.	Pts.	Avg.
80–81	34	289	567	.510	105	165	.636	318	9.4	683	20.1
81–82	27	226	461	.490	94	130	.723	278	10.3	546	20.2
82–83	33	282	493	.572	68	91	.747	305	9.2	632	19.2
83–84	33	207	393	.527	71	110	.645	259	7.8	485	14.7
Totals	127	993	1941	.524	338	496	.681	1160	9.1	2346	17.5

CAROL MENKEN SCHAUDT
Oregon State
6-5 – C
Jefferson, Ore.

A 1981 Kodak All-American and 1984 U.S. Olympian.... Owns a majority of Oregon State's individual women's records, despite playing only three seasons for the Beavers after one year of junior college ball.... As a senior, led the nation in field-goal percentage, hitting 75 percent of her shots and helping OSU to a 22-6 record, one of its best ever.... Once scored 51 points in a game.... A three-time all-conference selection of the Northwest College Women's Sports Association.

Year	G	FGM	FGA	FG%	FTM	FTA	FT%	Reb.	Avg.	Pts.	Avg.
78–79	22	239	379	.630	106	173	.612	274	12.5	584	26.5
79–80	31	353	518	.681	125	217	.576	325	10.5	831	26.8
80–81	28	363	484	.750	102	161	.634	302	10.9	828	29.6
Totals	81	955	1381	.692	333	551	.604	901	11.1	2243	27.7

ANN MEYERS
UCLA
5-8 – G
LaHabra, Calif.

Inducted into the Naismith Basketball Hall of Fame in 1993.... With late husband, baseball great Don Drysdale, made history by becoming part of first married couple to both be elected into the halls of fame of their respective sports.... Team captain of 1978 AIAW national championship as a senior.... First woman awarded an athletic scholarship at UCLA.... Older brother Dave Meyers played on national title teams at UCLA in early 1970s.... Drafted by the Indiana Pacers in 1978, the first woman ever selected by an NBA team... Played two seasons for the New Jersey Gems of the Women's Professional Basketball League.

Year	G	FGM	FGA	FG%	FTM	FTA	FT%	Reb.	Avg.	Pts.	Avg.
74–75	23	183	346	.529	56	73	.767	191	8.3	422	18.3
75–76	23	129	303	.426	65	89	.730	189	8.2	323	14.0
76–77	22	160	317	.505	82	99	.828	161	7.3	402	18.3
77–78	29	221	420	.526	96	120	.800	278	9.6	538	18.6
Totals	97	693	1386	.500	299	381	.785	819	8.4	1685	17.4

CHERYL MILLER
Southern Cal
6-3 – F
Riverside, Calif.

A four-time All-American and three-time Naismith Award winner.... Led USC to national titles in 1983 and 1984 and the championship game in 1986.... Named 1980s Player of the Decade by the WBCA and the U.S. Basketball Writers Association.... USC career leader in points, rebounds, field goals, free throws, and steals.... Scored a state-record 105 points in a high school game.... The first four-time *Parade* high school All-American, male or female.... The only USC basketball player, male or female, to have her number retired.... Was a sports commentator for ABC-TV and ESPN before being named USC's head coach in September 1993.... Grew up in an athletic family, with an older brother formerly a major league baseball prospect and younger brother, Reggie, currently starring for the NBA's Indiana Pacers.

Year	G	FGM	FGA	FG%	FTM	FTA	FT%	Reb.	Avg.	Pts.	Avg.
82–83	33	268	486	.551	137	186	.737	320	9.7	673	20.4
83–84	33	281	493	.570	164	218	.752	350	10.6	726	22.0
84–85	30	302	572	.528	201	289	.753	474	15.8	805	26.8
85–86	32	308	506	.609	198	263	.753	390	12.2	814	25.4
Totals	128	1159	2057	.563	702	956	.734	1534	12.0	3018	23.6

KIM MULKEY ROBERTSON
Louisiana Tech
5-4 – G
Hammond, La.

Piloted Lady Techsters to national titles in 1981 and 1982.... A two-time Kodak All-American, she won 1984 Francis Pomeroy Naismith Award as the best women's player under 5-6.... Also selected as an Academic All-American twice.... Currently an assistant coach at Louisiana Tech.

Year	G	FGM	FGA	FG%	FTM	FTA	FT%	Reb.	Avg.	Pts.	Avg.
80–81	34	88	172	.512	76	118	.644	46	1.4	252	7.4
81–82	36	77	158	.487	46	76	.605	56	1.6	200	5.6
82–83	31	78	159	.491	53	85	.624	55	1.8	209	6.7
83–84	32	101	205	.493	81	120	.675	72	2.3	283	8.8
Totals	133	344	694	.496	256	399	.642	229	1.7	944	7.1

INGE NISSEN
Old Dominion
6-5 – C
Randers, Denmark

Member of dominating Old Dominion national title teams in 1979 and 1980.... Second-leading scorer and rebounder in school history.... A two-time Kodak All-American.... Currently an assistant coach at Florida International.... Lady Monarch MVP three times.... Established a school single-game record with 28 rebounds.... One of the first foreign female players to excel in the college game, she recruits many European players as a coach.... Played on professional title teams in Denmark, Norway, and France .... Holds the National Women's Invitational Tournament mark with 20 field goals in a game.... Played briefly in the now-defunct U.S. women's pro leagues.

Year	G	FGM	FGA	FG%	FTM	FTA	FT%	Reb.	Avg.	Pts.	Avg.
76–77	32	255	408	.523	82	152	.539	410	12.8	592	18.5
77–78	32	257	544	.472	148	209	.708	378	11.8	662	20.7
78–79	34	300	576	.521	148	198	.747	339	9.9	749	22.0
79–80	37	252	576	.437	140	199	.703	382	10.3	644	17.4
Totals	135	1064	2184	.487	518	758	.683	1509	11.2	2647	19.6

JUNE OLKOWSKI
Rutgers
6-0 – F
Philadelphia, Pa.

The only Rutgers player to have her jersey number retired.... Was captain and second-leading scorer of 1982 team that won the final AIAW national championship... A two-time Kodak All-American.... Has been an assistant coach at Auburn and Maryland and a head coach at Arizona and Butler, where she has been since the 1993–94 season.

Year	G	FGM	FGA	FG%	FTM	FTA	FT%	Reb.	Avg.	Pts.	Avg.
78–79	32	197	426	.462	102	152	.671	304	9.5	496	15.5
79–80	30	186	379	.491	91	138	.659	225	7.5	463	15.4
80–81	17	101	190	.532	54	78	.692	95	5.6	256	15.1
81–82	24	116	261	.444	53	73	.726	156	6.5	285	11.9
Totals	103	600	1256	.480	300	441	.680	780	7.7	1500	14.8

VICKIE ORR
Auburn
6-3 – C
Decatur, Ala.

A three-time Kodak All-American.... Was a finalist for the Champion/WBCA and Naismith Player of the Year Awards.... Led Auburn to national championship games in 1988 and 1989 ... Was SEC Player of the Year in 1988 ... Was named an assistant coach at Auburn in 1992.

Year	G	FGM	FGA	FG%	FTM	FTA	FT%	Reb.	Avg.	Pts.	Avg.
85–86	30	165	297	.555	65	98	.663	233	7.8	395	13.2
86–87	33	239	396	.604	72	110	.656	252	7.6	550	16.7
87–88	35	248	461	.538	69	90	.767	237	6.8	565	16.1
88–89	33	212	374	.567	101	135	.748	284	8.6	525	15.9
Totals	131	864	1528	.565	307	433	.709	1006	7.7	2035	15.5

SHELLY PENNEFATHER
Villanova
6-1 – F
Utica, N.Y.

The all-time leading career scorer (2,408 points) in school history and for the Philadelphia Big Five .... A two-time All-American and the 1987 Wade Trophy winner.... Named to the All-Big East team three times, and was the league's MVP three times as well.... Is the Big East's women's career scoring and rebounding leader.... Villanova won two Big East regular-season crowns and averaged 23 wins a season during her career.... The first Big East player, male or female, to earn the conference's player of the week award three consecutive times.... Was inducted into the Big Five Hall of Fame in 1993.... She played professionally in Japan for four seasons.... Currently is a member of the Order of St. Claire, a cloistered nunnery in Virginia.

Year	G	FGM	FGA	FG%	FTM	FTA	FT%	Reb.	Avg.	Pts.	Avg.
83–84	29	220	411	.535	64	82	.780	253	9.7	504	19.4
84–85	29	245	459	.534	54	73	.740	317	10.9	544	18.8
85–86	31	302	527	.573	81	99	.818	293	9.5	685	22.1
86–87	31	306	523	.585	68	82	.768	308	9.9	675	21.8
Totals	120	1073	1920	.558	262	336	.779	1171	9.7	2408	20.0

Villanova's Shelly Pennefather maneuvers around the opposition's defense.

LATAUNYA POLLARD
Long Beach State
5-10 – G/F
East Chicago, Ind.

One of just 13 women players with 3,000 career points or more.... Instrumental in turning Long Beach State into a national power in the early 1980s.... The 1983 Wade Trophy winner and a three-time All-American.... Twice named the player of the year by the West Coast Athletic Association.... Holds four major career and three single season school records, including scoring, scoring average, and field goals made.... Guided the 49ers to four postseason bids (three AIAW and one NCAA).... A prototype full-court athlete who helped speed up the transition game in women's basketball.... Was such a popular figure during her college days that she once rode on the City of Long Beach float at the Tournament of Roses parade.

Year	G	FGM	FGA	FG%	FTM	FTA	FT%	Reb.	Avg.	Pts.	Avg.
79–80	34	295	570	.518	70	94	.745	176	5.1	660	19.4
80–81	34	325	602	.540	83	121	.686	193	5.8	733	21.6
81–82	29	292	540	.541	117	154	.760	177	6.1	701	24.2
82–83	31	376	721	.521	155	201	.771	275	8.9	907	29.2
Totals	128	1288	2433	.530	425	570	.745	821	6.4	3001	23.5

JILL RANKIN
Wayland Baptist/Tennessee
6-3 – C
Phillips, Tex.

A Kodak All-American in her only season at Tennessee, which went 35-5 and finished second in the AIAW national tournament.... The last national caliber player at Wayland Baptist, a tiny Texas Panhandle school that was one of the first institutions to give women basketball scholarships as early as the 1950s.... Helped Wayland reach three AIAW national tournaments during its college-era heyday in the late 1970s and was a Kodak choice as a junior.... Scored 81 points in a high school game.

Year	G	FGM	FGA	FG%	FTM	FTA	FT%	Reb.	Avg.	Pts.	Avg.
76–77	36	218	368	.592	91	131	.695	257	7.0	527	14.6
77–78	38	259	426	.607	76	121	.628	264	6.9	594	15.6
78–79	34	410	698	.587	180	234	.769	305	9.0	1000	29.4
79–80	38	296	536	.552	138	172	.802	277	7.3	730	19.2
Totals	146	1183	2028	.583	485	658	.737	1101	7.6	2851	19.2

THERESA SHANK GRENTZ
Immaculata
5-10 – C
Springfield, Pa.

The first dominating center in women's college basketball.... A two-time All-American who paced Immaculata to the first three AIAW national championships from 1972 to 1974.... Bypassed an opportunity to try out for the 1976 Olympic team to get married and begin a family.... One of the first women's coaches to earn a professional salary that did not include teaching duties.... Taught elementary school after graduation before being named head coach at St. Joseph's.... Went to Rutgers in 1977 and coached the last AIAW national championship team in 1982.

Year	G	FGM	FGA	FG%	FTM	FTA	FT%	Reb.	Avg.	Pts.	Avg.
70–71	3	58	101	.574	8	11	.727	44	14.6	66	22.0
71–72	20	188	321	.585	120	170	.705	389	19.4	496	24.8
72–73	16	124	247	.500	59	90	.655	269	16.8	307	19.1
73–74	20	123	257	.478	76	114	.660	263	13.1	322	16.1
Totals	59	493	926	.532	263	385	.683	965	16.3	1191	20.2

BEV SMITH
Oregon
5-11 – F
Salmon Arm, B.C.

The only Oregon player to be named a Kodak All-American (1981 and 1982).... Is the school's career rebounding leader and second leading all-time scorer.... Owns or shares 12 school records... A four-year starter, she led the Ducks to a 103-20 record, two AIAW national tournament appearances, and one trip to the NCAA tourney.... Was nominated for the Wade Trophy twice.... MVP of the National Women's Invitational Tournament as a freshman.... Played for the 1984 Canadian Olympic team and in the 1979 World Championships.

Year	G	FGM	FGA	FG%	FTM	FTA	FT%	Reb.	Avg.	Pts.	Avg.
78–79	25	166	356	.466	47	86	.547	323	12.9	379	15.2
79–80	27	240	441	.544	99	129	.767	367	13.6	579	21.4
80–81	32	259	485	.534	114	157	.726	376	11.8	632	19.8
81–82	26	192	400	.480	89	119	.748	296	11.4	473	18.2
Totals	110	857	1682	.510	349	491	.711	1362	12.4	2063	18.8

DAWN STALEY
Virginia
5-6 – G
Philadelphia, Pa.

Named national player of the year as a junior and senior by a variety of organizations.... Was a three-time Kodak All-American.... Led Virginia to

three Final Four appearances.... Named the 1991 Honda-Broderick Cup Award winner, signifying the top collegiate woman athlete.... Was MVP of the 1991 Final Four, sharing a single-game record of 28 points in a losing effort against Tennessee in the national title game.... The NCAA career steals leader with 454.... The only player in ACC history, male or female, to register at least 2,000 points, 700 rebounds, 700 assists and 400 steals.... The first woman in school history to score 2,000 points.... Led Virginia to an ACC tournament title and was a two-time league Player of the Year.... Learned the game on the same playgrounds as former Loyola Marymount All-Americans Hank Gathers and Bo Kimble.

Year	G	FGM	FGA	FG%	FTM	FTA	FT%	Reb.	Avg.	Pts.	Avg.
88–89	31	197	431	.457	147	177	.831	158	5.1	574	18.5
89–90	32	203	449	.452	132	169	.781	214	6.7	574	17.9
90–91	34	176	391	.450	108	131	.824	209	6.1	495	14.6
91–92	34	177	366	.484	118	146	.808	191	5.6	492	14.5
Totals	131	753	1637	.460	505	623	.811	772	5.9	2135	16.3

MARIANNE CRAWFORD STANLEY
Immaculata
5-6 – G
Upper Darby, Pa.

A two-time All-American who played on two AIAW national championship teams.... Considered one of the first guards to speed up the game with a full-court transition game and heady point guard play.... Played on the same Immaculata teams with Theresa Grentz, head coach at Rutgers, and Rene Portland of Penn State.... Averaged nearly six assists a game during her career.... Was an assistant coach at Immaculata for one season before beginning her head coaching career at Old Dominion, where she coached three national championship teams.... Moved to USC in 1989 before suing the school on equal pay grounds.

Year	G	FGM	FGA	FG%	FTM	FTA	FT%	Reb.	Avg.	Pts.	Avg.
72–73	16	74	158	.468	56	81	.691	83	5.1	204	12.7
73–74	20	65	168	.386	41	65	.630	62	3.1	171	8.5
74–75	26	86	219	.392	45	70	.642	80	3.0	217	8.3
75–76	27	60	147	.408	34	51	.666	63	2.3	154	5.7
Totals	89	692	285	.418	176	267	.659	288	3.2	746	8.3

VALERIE STILL
Kentucky
6-1 – F/C
Cherry Hill, N.J.

The all-time leading scorer, male or female, in Kentucky basketball history with 2,763 points.... A two-time All-American and finalist for the Wade Trophy.... Led the Lady Kats to their best season ever as a senior, reaching the NCAA Tournament and achieving a No. 4 national ranking.... Guided Kentucky to its only SEC tournament championship in 1982 by averaging 30 points and 11 rebounds in three games and earning MVP honors.... She holds nearly a dozen school career records.... The only woman at Kentucky to have her jersey retired.... Began her playing career in Europe shortly after graduation and is currently playing there, perhaps with the most longevity of any American female.... The younger sister of former Kansas City Chiefs All-Pro lineman Art Still.

Year	G	FGM	FGA	FG%	FTM	FTA	FT%	Reb.	Avg.	Pts.	Avg.
79–80	29	256	463	.553	129	183	.700	403	13.9	641	22.1
80–81	30	260	447	.581	108	154	.701	329	10.9	628	20.9
81–82	32	329	565	.582	136	199	.683	457	14.3	794	24.8
82–83	28	273	456	.599	154	212	.726	336	12.0	700	25.0
Totals	119	1118	1931	.580	527	748	.700	1525	12.8	2763	23.2

SHERYL SWOOPES
Texas Tech
6-0 – F
Brownfield, Tex.

Played just two years of major college basketball, but as a senior guided Texas Tech to the NCAA championship in 1993.... She shattered Bill Walton's Final Four single-game scoring record of 44 points by tallying 47 against Ohio State in the title contest.... Was a unanimous national Player of the Year and twice earned Kodak All-American honors.... Scored in double figures in all but two of her 66 games at Texas Tech and finished as the school's second all-time scoring leader with 1,645 points.... Was the national Junior College Player of the Year at South Plains Junior College in Texas, where she holds 28 school records.

Year	G	FGM	FGA	FG%	FTM	FTA	FT%	Reb.	Avg.	Pts.	Avg.
91–92	32	275	527	.503	135	167	.808	285	8.9	690	21.6
92–93	34	356	652	.546	211	243	.868	312	9.2	955	28.0
Totals	66	631	1179	.535	346	410	.843	597	9.0	1645	24.9

JOYCE WALKER
LSU
5-8 – G
Seattle, Wash.

A two-time Kodak All-American and the school's career scoring leader with 2,906 points.... The only player in LSU history to rank in the Top 10 in scoring, rebounding, assists, steals, and blocked shots.... Second-leading SEC career scoring leader at 24.9 points, she also leads the league in career field goals made and attempted.... Helped LSU to an AIAW national tournament appearance as a freshman and to the NCAA regionals in her senior season.

Year	G	FGM	FGA	FG%	FTM	FTA	FT%	Reb.	Avg.	Pts.	Avg.
80–81	30	277	489	.566	67	107	.626	157	5.2	621	20.7
81–82	30	340	500	.576	67	99	.677	136	4.5	747	24.9
82–83	27	312	540	.578	120	161	.745	186	6.9	744	27.6
83–84	30	330	619	.533	134	165	.812	119	4.0	794	26.5
Totals	117	1259	2238	.562	388	532	.729	598	5.1	2906	24.8

ROSIE WALKER
Stephen F. Austin
6-1 – F
Dallas, Tex.

Despite playing only two years, is one of the most decorated players in school history.... A two-time All-American at Stephen F. Austin after being named a junior college All-American.... Holds seven school records in all.... The Ladyjacks recorded a 57-11 during her two seasons and one national AIAW tournament trip.... Scored 30 or more points in 18 different games.

Year	G	FGM	FGA	FG%	FTM	FTA	FT%	Reb.	Avg.	Pts.	Avg.
78–79	35	395	607	.650	122	174	.701	448	12.8	912	26.0
79–80	31	263	390	.674	123	170	.724	354	11.4	649	20.9
Totals	66	658	997	.660	245	344	.712	802	12.2	1561	23.7

TERESA WEATHERSPOON
Louisiana Tech
5-8 – G
Pineland, Tex.

The all-time assists leader in Louisiana Tech history who guided the Lady Techsters to their third national title in 1988.... A two-time Kodak All-American and the 1988 Wade Trophy Winner.... Also the 1988 recipient of the Honda/Broderick Cup, awarded to the top collegiate female athlete in all sports.... Named to the all-Women's Final Four team twice.... In 1993 became one of the first two Americans to play professional basketball in

Russia as a member of the Moscow Red Army team.

Year	G	FGM	FGA	FG%	FTM	FTA	FT%	Reb.	Avg.	Pts.	Avg.
84–85	33	72	140	.514	51	100	.510	127	3.8	195	5.9
85–86	32	110	226	.487	61	112	.545	125	3.9	281	8.7
86–87	33	122	234	.521	67	95	.705	137	4.2	311	9.4
87–88	33	119	249	.478	57	86	.663	144	4.4	300	9.1
Totals	131	423	849	.498	236	393	.601	533	4.1	1087	8.3

LYNETTE WOODARD
Kansas
6-0 – F
Wichita, Kans.

The all-time women's scoring leader, with 3,649 points, only 18 points shy of Pete Maravich's career college record... A four-time All-American and two-time Olympian, captaining the 1984 U.S. gold medal squad.... The 1981 Wade Trophy Winner, awarded to the top female collegian.... Selected the Big Eight's Player of the Decade for the 1980s.... A member of the Kansas and National High School Athletic Halls of Fame.... Paced Kansas to a 108-32 record and three AIAW national tournament appearances.... Holds eight career, eight single-season, and five single-game school records.... Was the first woman to play for the Harlem Globetrotters.... Played professionally in Italy and Japan and briefly was a Kansas assistant coach.... Currently is athletic director for Kansas City public schools.... The first female inducted into the GTE Academic All-American Hall of Fame in 1992.

Year	G	FGM	FGA	FG%	FTM	FTA	FT%	Reb.	Avg.	Pts.	Avg.
77–78	33	366	736	.497	101	152	.664	490	14.8	833	25.2
78–79	38	519	924	.562	139	212	.656	545	14.3	1177	31.0
79–80	37	372	738	.504	137	192	.714	389	10.5	881	23.8
80–81	31	315	594	.533	128	186	.688	310	10.0	758	24.5
Totals	139	1572	2992	.525	505	742	.681	1734	12.4	3649	26.3

All-Time Great Women's Coaches

LEON BARMORE
Louisiana Tech '67

The winningest coach by percentage in women's college basketball history.... Served as an assistant and associate head coach and was co-head coach with Sonja Hogg for three seasons before getting the job to himself in 1985.... Tech won two national titles while he was an assistant and again in 1988.... Named co-Coach of the Decade for the 1980s by the U.S. Basketball Writers Association.... Named Naismith National Coach of the Year in 1988.... Until 1990–91, Tech had never finished lower than fifth in the final regular-season AP poll.... Lady Techsters upset No. 1 Tennessee and Southern Cal to reach the 1994 Final Four, losing only on a last-second shot by North Carolina in the finals.

Year	School	Overall	League	Postseason
82–83	La. Tech	26-6		NCAA Runnerup
83–84	La. Tech	30-3		NCAA Final Four
84–85	La. Tech	29-4		NCAA Regional
85–86	La. Tech	27-5		NCAA Regional
86–87	La. Tech	30-3		NCAA Runnerup
87–88	La. Tech	32-2	8-0 (ASC)	NCAA Champion
88–89	La. Tech	32-4	12-0 (ASC)	NCAA Final Four
89–90	La. Tech	32-1	14-0 (ASC)	NCAA Final Four
90–91	La. Tech	18-12	10-4 (ASC)	NCAA 1st Round
91–92	La. Tech	20-10	11-3 (SBC)	NCAA 1st Round
92–93	La. Tech	26-6	13-1 (SBC)	NCAA Regional
93–94	La. Tech	32-3	14-0 (SBC)	NCAA Runnerup
93–94	La. Tech	31-4	14-0 (SBC)	NCAA Runnerup

12-Year Coaching Record: 338-56 (.857) overall; 31-11 (.738) in the NCAA Tournament.

JODY CONRADT
Baylor '63

The all-time winningest coach in women's college basketball history and the only coach with more than 600 career victories.... Her 1986 Texas team went 34-0 and finished as the only undefeated women's NCAA title team ever.... Earned Southwest Conference Coach of the Year honors four times and was the National Coach of the Year in 1980 and 1986.... Texas won a record 188 consecutive SWC victories until Arkansas snapped the string during the 1989–90 season.... Texas also was the national attendance leader during the 1980s.... Coached the U.S. to a gold medal in the 1987 Pan American Games.... Women's athletic director at Texas since 1992.... A young 1993–94 Lady Longhorn team upset defending NCAA champion Texas Tech with a last-second shot to win the Southwest Conference Tournament.

Year	School	Overall	League	Postseason
69–70	Sam Houston St.	15-4		
70–71	Sam Houston St.	20-6		
71–72	Sam Houston St.	19-6		
72–73	Sam Houston St.	20-7		
73–74	UT-Arlington	9-14		
74–75	UT-Arlington	11-14		
75–76	UT-Arlington	23-11		
76–77	Texas	36-10		AIAW Regional
77–78	Texas	29-10		AIAW Regional
78–79	Texas	37-4		AIAW Regional
79–80	Texas	33-4		5th AIAW
80–81	Texas	28-8		AIAW Nationals
81–82	Texas	35-4		2nd AIAW
82–83	Texas	30-3	8-0 (SWC)	NCAA Regional
83–84	Texas	32-3	16-0 (SWC)	NCAA Regional
84–85	Texas	28-3	16-0 (SWC)	NCAA Regional
85–86	Texas	34-0	16-0 (SWC)	NCAA Champion
86–87	Texas	31-2	16-0 (SWC)	NCAA Final Four
87–88	Texas	32-3	16-0 (SWC)	NCAA Regional
88–89	Texas	27-5	16-0 (SWC)	NCAA Regional
89–90	Texas	27-5	15-1 (SWC)	NCAA Regional
90–91	Texas	21-9	14-2 (SWC)	NCAA 1st Round
91–92	Texas	21-10	13-4 (SWC)	NCAA 2nd Round
92–93	Texas	22-8	13-3 (SWC)	NCAA 2nd Round
93–94	Texas	22-9	10-4 (SWC)	NCAA 2nd Round

25-Year Coaching Record: 642-162 (.798) overall; 525-100 (.840) at Texas; 169-11 (.948) in Southwest Conference; 69-24 (.740) in the postseason.

SUE GUNTER
Peabody '62

She is the only women's coach with as many as 30 years of heading coaching experience.... Was an All-American AAU player in 1960 for Nashville Business College.... The first women's coach to earn 200 career victories at two different schools.... Coached LSU to the SEC Tournament championship in 1991.... Her LSU team won the National Women's Invitational Tournament in 1985.

Year	School	Overall	League	Postseason
62–63	Middle Tenn. St.	N/A		
63–64	Middle Tenn. St.	N/A		
64–65	Stephen F. Austin	N/A		
65–66	Stephen F. Austin	N/A		
66–67	Stephen F. Austin	N/A		
67–68	Stephen F. Austin	N/A		
69–70	Stephen F. Austin	6-4		
70–71	Stephen F. Austin	12-2		
71–72	Stephen F. Austin	19-9		
72–73	Stephen F. Austin	21-6		
73–74	Stephen F. Austin	27-7		AIAW Tr.
74–75	Stephen F. Austin	32-8		AIAW Tr.
75–76	Stephen F. Austin	30-4		
76–77	Stephen F. Austin	28-6		AIAW Regional
77–78	Stephen F. Austin	25-13		AIAW Tr.
78–79	Stephen F. Austin	30-5		AIAW Regional
79–80	Stephen F. Austin	27-6		AIAW Regional
82–83	LSU	20-7	6-2 (SEC)	
83–84	LSU	23-7	5-3 (SEC)	NCAA Regional
84–85	LSU	20-9	4-4 (SEC)	NWIT Champion
85–86	LSU	27-6	6-3 (SEC)	NCAA Regionals
86–87	LSU	20-8	6-3 (SEC)	NCAA 2nd Round
87–88	LSU	18-11	6-3 (SEC)	NCAA 1st Round
88–89	LSU	19-11	5-4 (SEC)	NCAA Regional
89–90	LSU	21-9	4-5 (SEC)	NCAA 1st Round
90–91	LSU	24-7	5-4 (SEC)	NCAA 2nd Round
91–92	LSU	16-13	4-7 (SEC)	
92–93	LSU	9-18	0-11 (SEC)	
93–94	LSU	11-16	2-9 (SEC)	

30-Year Coaching Record: 494-209 (.702) overall; 266-87 (.754) at Stephen F. Austin; 228-122 (.651) at LSU; 53-58 (.477) in the Southeastern Conference; 31-30 (.508) in the postseason.

SONJA HOGG
Louisiana Tech '70

Began the famed Louisiana Tech program and coached it to national titles in 1981 and 1982.... Set a women's single-season record of 40 victories in 1979–90.... The 1980–81 team that went 34-0 is only one of two women's teams to go undefeated in a season.... In her later years at Tech, became a marketing and public relations ambassador for the team, leaving Leon Barmore to handle on-court responsibilities.... Left Tech in 1985 and became a high school coach in Texas briefly in the late 1980s.... Was director of marketing for the women's athletic department at Texas and also was the chief fundraiser for a women's basketball hall of fame to be built near Jackson, Tenn.... Named head coach at Baylor in April 1994.

Year	School	Overall	League	Postseason
74–75	La. Tech	13-9		
75–76	La. Tech	19-10		
76–77	La. Tech	22-9		AIAW Regional
77–78	La. Tech	20-8		AIAW Regional
78–79	La. Tech	34-4		AIAW Tr.
79–80	La. Tech	40-5		AIAW Final Four
80–81	La. Tech	34-0		AIAW Champions
81–82	La. Tech	35-1		NCAA Champions
82–83	La. Tech	31-2		NCAA Final Four
83–84	La. Tech	30-3		NCAA Final Four
84–85	La. Tech	29-4		NCAA Regional

11-Year Coaching Record: 307-55 (.848) at Louisiana Tech; 37-11 (.771) in postseason.

LUCILLE KYVALLOS
Springfield College

One of the pioneering college coaches of the early 1970s.... Queens participated in the earliest National Invitation Tournament and later became an AIAW runnerup under her tutelage.... The college coach of former Immaculata mentor Cathy Rush.... Helped organize the first women's college game at Madison Square Garden in 1975 in which her team was defeated by Immaculata before a crowd of more than 12,000 spectators.... Was named the first recipient of the U.S. Basketball Writers Association's Pioneer Award in 1990 .... Still a member of the physical education faculty at Queens.

Year	School	Overall	League	Postseason
62–66	W. Chester St.	54-2		
68–69	Queens	N/A		
69–70	Queens	N/A		W. Carolina Inv.
70–71	Queens	N/A		
71–72	Queens	27-2		AIAW Tournament
72–73	Queens	22-5		2nd AIAW Tr.
73–74	Queens	22-4		
74–75	Queens	19-8		
75–76	Queens	20-5		
76–77	Queens	18-13		
77–78	Queens	24-3		
78–79	Queens	N/A		
79–80	Queens	23-6		

Incomplete 16-Year Coaching Record: 229-48 (.826) overall; 54-2 (.964) at West Chester State; 175-46 (.791) at Queens.

DARLENE MAY
Cal State Fullerton '67

The winningest coach in Division II history, topping the 500-victory mark early in the 1993–94 season and is third among all active women's coaches.... Coached three national championship teams and eight AIAW and NCAA Final Four teams.... Cal Poly-Pomona has never finished below first place in conference play.... Has won the Converse national Division II Coach of the Year award two times.... Also has had a distinguished officiating career, becoming the first woman to referee a women's Olympic contest during the 1984 games in Los Angeles, including the bronze medal game.... Retired after 1993–94 season.

Year	School	Overall	League	Postseason
74–75	Cal Poly-Pomona	16-6		5th AIAW
75–76	Cal Poly-Pomona	20-6		8th AIAW
76–77	Cal Poly-Pomona	28-6	10-0 (SCAA)	5th AIAW
77–78	Cal Poly-Pomona	31-4	10-0 (SCAA)	
78–79	Cal Poly-Pomona	24-7	10-0 (SCAA)	
79–80	Cal Poly-Pomona	27-13	9-1 (SCAA)	6th AIAW
80–81	Cal Poly-Pomona	30-9	12-0 (CCAA)	AIAW Final Four
81–82	Cal Poly-Pomona	29-7	12-0 (CCAA)	NCAA Final Four
82–83	Cal Poly-Pomona	29-3	11-0 (CCAA)	NCAA Final Four
83–84	Cal Poly-Pomona	22-7	11-1 (CCAA)	
84–85	Cal Poly-Pomona	26-7	11-1 (CCAA)	NCAA Champion
85–86	Cal Poly-Pomona	30-3	12-0 (CCAA)	NCAA Champion
86–87	Cal Poly-Pomona	29-3	11-1 (CCAA)	NCAA Final Four
87–88	Cal Poly-Pomona	28-4	12-0 (CCAA)	NCAA Regional
88–89	Cal Poly-Pomona	28-6	11-1 (CCAA)	NCAA Final Four
89–90	Cal Poly-Pomona	29-4	12-0 (CCAA)	NCAA Final Four
90–91	Cal Poly-Pomona	22-9	11-1 (CCAA)	NCAA Regional
91–92	Cal Poly-Pomona	23-6	12-0 (CCAA)	
92–93	Cal Poly-Pomona	27-3	11-1 (CCAA)	NCAA Regional
93–94	Cal Poly-Pomona	21-6	9-1 (CCAA)	NCAA 1st Round

19-Year Coaching Record: 519-119 (.813) overall; 195-8 (.961) in the Southern California Athletic Association and California Collegiate Athletic Association.

BILLIE JEAN MOORE
Washburn '66

Coached Cal State Fullerton and UCLA to national championships during a 24-year career that culminated with her retirement in April 1993.... Won the first AIAW Final Four in 1978 in her first year at UCLA.... Her Fullerton team won a national crown in her first year on the job there, predating the official beginning of the AIAW tournament.... Also coached the first U.S. women's Olympic team to a silver medal in 1976.... Teams went to postseason play 16 out of 24 seasons, winning nine conference titles and eight national Top 10 finishes.

Year	School	Overall	League	Postseason
69–70	CS Fullerton	17-1		NIT Champion
70–71	CS Fullerton	20-1		
71–72	CS Fullerton	19-1		3rd AIAW
72–73	CS Fullerton	13-1		
73–74	CS Fullerton	19-2		
74–75	CS Fullerton	19-2		3rd AIAW
75–76	CS Fullerton	14-5		
76–77	CS Fullerton	19-2		
77–78	UCLA	27-3	8-0 (WCAA)	AIAW Champion
78–79	UCLA	24-10	7-1 (WCAA)	4th AIAW
79–80	UCLA	18-12	9-3 (WCAA)	AIAW Regional
80–81	UCLA	29-7	9-3 (WCAA)	5th AIAW
81–82	UCLA	16-14	7-5 (WCAA)	
82–83	UCLA	18-11	9-5 (WCAA)	NCAA Regional
83–84	UCLA	17-12	6-8 (WCAA)	
84–85	UCLA	20-10	10-4 (WCAA)	NCAA Regional
85–86	UCLA	12-16	3-5 (Pac West)	
86–87	UCLA	18-10	11-7 (Pac-10)	
87–88	UCLA	19-11	12-6 (Pac-10)	
88–89	UCLA	12-16	8-10 (Pac-10)	
89–90	UCLA	17-12	12-6 (Pac-10)	NCAA 1st Round
90–91	UCLA	15-13	10-8 (Pac-10)	
91–92	UCLA	21-10	12-6 (Pac-10)	NCAA Regional
92–93	UCLA	13-14	8-10 (Pac-10)	

24-Year Coaching Record: 436-196 (.689) overall; 140-15 (.903) at Cal State Fullerton; 296-181 (.620) at UCLA; 73-35 (.579) in Pacific-10 games; 59-18 (.766) in postseason games.

CATHY RUSH
West Chester State

A women's coaching pioneer who led Immaculata to the first three AIAW national titles... Three of her former players are distinguished college

coaches—Theresa Grentz (Rutgers), Rene Portland (Penn State), and Marianne Stanley (formerly of Old Dominion, Pennsylvania, and USC).... Made history in 1975 when Immaculata played Queens in Madison Square Garden, drawing nearly 12,000 spectators.... After retiring in 1977, got into sports camp business for girls, her current occupation.... She runs the camps with her husband, NBA referee Ed Rush.... Is a commentator on women's TV games.... Named the 1994 recipient of the U.S. Basketball Writers Association's Pioneer Award.

Year	School	Overall	League	Postseason
70–71	Immaculata	12-2		
71–72	Immaculata	20-1		AIAW champion
72–73	Immaculata	20-0		AIAW champion
73–74	Immaculata	20-1		AIAW champion
74–75	Immaculata	23-3		AIAW runnerup
75–76	Immaculata	25-3		AIAW nationals
76–77	Immaculata	29-6		AIAW nationals

7-Year Coaching Record: 149-16 (.903) overall.

BOB SPENCER
Parsons College '57

Retired following 1992–93 season with 578 wins, the second most of any women's coach ever, trailing only Jody Conradt of Texas.... A native of Iowa, a girls high school hotbed where he coached some of the first women's intercollegiate teams in the mid-1960s.... Started programs at John F. Kennedy College and William Penn College, two of the earliest Midwestern college powers.... William Penn won seven Iowa AIAW titles, six regional crowns, and a national ranking in each of his eight seasons.... The 1973 team finished fourth in the AIAW national tournament.

Year	School	Overall	League	Postseason
66–70	JFK	73-42		
71–73	Parsons	67-39		
73–81	William Penn	40-43		
81–82	Fresno St.	8-17		
82–83	Fresno St.	15-12		
83–84	Fresno St.	18-11		
84–85	Fresno St.	20-9		
85–86	Fresno St.	21-9		
86–87	Fresno St.	22-8	12-6	(Big W.)
87–88	Fresno St.	16-12	11-7	(Big W.)
88–89	Fresno St.	18-12	9-9	(Big W.)
89–90	Fresno St.	21-12	11-7	(Big W.)
90–91	Fresno St.	16-13	9-9	(Big W.)
91–92	Fresno St.	13-15	7-11	(Big W.)
92–93	Fresno St.	10-17	4-10	(WAC)

27-Year Coaching Record: 578-274 (.678) overall; 198-137 (.591) at Fresno State.

MARIANNE STANLEY
Immaculata '76

A three-time national championship coach who left USC in an equal pay dispute in September 1993 and sued the institution.... Won two AIAW and one NCAA title at Old Dominion, becoming the only women's coach to win crowns in both associations.... Revived the USC program in her final two seasons, as the Trojans reached the regional finals and regionals.... Two-time national Coach of the Year (1979, 1985).... Old Dominion won titles in 1979 and 1980 and the NCAA crown in 1985.... In her first season of college coaching, Old Dominion won the National Women's Invitational Tournament.... An All-American player at Immaculata (Pa.) College, which won two national titles while she was there.... Hired to market women's basketball at Stanford while her lawsuit is pending.

Year	School	Overall	League	Postseason
77–78	Old Dominion	30-4		NWIT Champion
78–79	Old Dominion	35-1		AIAW Champion
79–80	Old Dominion	37-1		AIAW Champion
80–81	Old Dominion	28-7		AIAW Final Four
81–82	Old Dominion	22-6		AIAW Regional
82–83	Old Dominion	29-6		NCAA Final Four
83–84	Old Dominion	24-5		NCAA Regional
84–85	Old Dominion	31-3		NCAA Champion
85–86	Old Dominion	15-13		
86–87	Old Dominion	18-13		NCAA Regional

UCLA coach Billie Moore hoists the 1978 AIAW trophy, cheered on by her team.

87–88	Pennsylvania	6-20		
88–89	Pennsylvania	5-21		
89–90	USC	8-19	6-12 (Pac-10)	
90–91	USC	18-12	11-7 (Pac-10)	NCAA 2nd Round
91–92	USC	23-8	14-4 (Pac-10)	NCAA Regional
92–93	USC	22-7	14-4 (Pac 10)	NCAA Regional

16-Year Coaching Record: 351-146 (.706) overall; 269-59 (.820) at Old Dominion; 11-41 (.212) at Pennsylvania; 71-46 (.606) at USC; 56-27 (.674) in the Pacific-10 Conference; 17-7 (.708) in the NCAA Tournament.

C. VIVIAN STRINGER
Slippery Rock '70

The 1993 Converse National Coach of the Year after guiding Iowa to its first Final Four appearance and overcoming the death of her husband early in the season.... Coached Cheyney State (Pa.) College to the first women's NCAA title game in 1982.... Also Converse Coach of the Year in 1988.... Iowa has won outright or shared six Big Ten championships since she arrived in 1983.

Year	School	Overall	League	Postseason
71–83	Cheyney St.	251-51		
83–84	Iowa	17-10	11-7 (Big 10)	
84–85	Iowa	20-8	14-4 (Big 10)	
85–86	Iowa	22-7	15-3 (Big 10)	NCAA 2nd Round
86–87	Iowa	26-5	17-1 (Big 10)	NCAA Regional
87–88	Iowa	29-2	17-1 (Big 10)	NCAA Regional
88–89	Iowa	27-5	16-2 (Big 10)	NCAA Regional
89–90	Iowa	23-6	15-3 (Big 10)	NCAA 2nd Round
90–91	Iowa	21-9	13-5 (Big 10)	NCAA 2nd Round
91–92	Iowa	25-4	16-2 (Big 10)	NCAA 2nd Round
92–93	Iowa	27-4	16-2 (Big 10)	NCAA Final Four
93–94	Iowa	21-7	13-5 (Big 10)	NCAA 2nd Round

23-Year Coaching Record: 509-118 (.811) overall; 258-67 (.819) at Iowa; 163-35 (.823) in Big Ten; 11-9 (.550) in NCAA Tournament.

PAT HEAD SUMMITT
Tennessee-Martin '74

Only women's coach to win three NCAA titles (1987, 1989, 1991).... Earned her 500th career win in the first game of the 1993–94 season, becoming the second winningest active Division I coach behind Jody Conradt of Texas.... Coached the U.S. women to the 1984 Olympic gold medal, and played on the first Olympic team in 1976 that won a silver medal.... Her teams have qualified for 11 Final Fours and have won 20 or more games 17 consecutive seasons.... The Naismith National Coach of the Year in 1987, 1989, and 1994.... Named co-coach of the decade for the 1980s by the U.S. Basketball Writers Association.... The first woman to receive the John Bunn Award given by the Naismith Basketball Hall of Fame in 1990.... An inductee of the Women's Sports Foundation Hall of Fame in 1990.

Year	School	Overall	League	Postseason
74–75	Tennessee	16-8		
75–76	Tennessee	16-11		
76–77	Tennessee	28-5		3rd AIAW
77–78	Tennessee	27-4		1st AIAW Poll
78–79	Tennessee	30-9		AIAW Final Four
79–80	Tennessee	33-5		2nd AIAW
80–81	Tennessee	25-6		2nd AIAW
81–82	Tennessee	22-10		NCAA Final Four
82–83	Tennessee	25-8	7-1 (SEC)	NCAA Regional
83–84	Tennessee	23-10	7-1 (SEC)	2nd Final Four
84–85	Tennessee	22-10	4-4 (SEC)	NCAA Regional
85–86	Tennessee	24-10	5-4 (SEC)	NCAA Final Four
86–87	Tennessee	28-6	6-3 (SEC)	NCAA Champion
87–88	Tennessee	31-3	8-1 (SEC)	NCAA Final Four
88–89	Tennessee	35-2	8-1 (SEC)	NCAA Champion
89–90	Tennessee	27-6	8-1 (SEC)	NCAA Regional
90–91	Tennessee	30-5	6-3 (SEC)	NCAA Champion
91–92	Tennessee	28-3	10-1 (SEC)	NCAA Regional
92–93	Tennessee	29-3	11-0 (SEC)	NCAA Regional
93–94	Tennessee	31-2	11-0 (SEC)	NCAA Regionals

20-Year Coaching Record: 430-126 (.807) overall; 91-20 (.819) in Southeastern Conference; 107-30 (.781) in postseason play.

MARGARET WADE
Delta State

Became the first woman college coach inducted into the Naismith Basketball Hall of Fame in 1984.... Coached Delta State to three AIAW national titles from 1975 to 1977, and collected a career record of 157-23 in six seasons.... Revived a dormant Delta State program and retired from coaching in 1979. Her star player, Lusia Harris Stewart, also is a member of the Hall of Fame.... Came to Delta State to teach physical education in 1959 and began a women's varsity program there 14 years later.... Her Delta State team, nicknamed the "Cadillac Kids," once posed for a *Sports Illustrated* photograph along with Wade seated on the hood of a Cadillac.... The Wade Trophy, given to the top woman player each season, is named after her.

Year	School	Overall	League	Postseason
73–74	Delta State	16-2		
74–75	Delta State	28-0		AIAW Champion
75–76	Delta State	33-1		AIAW Champion
76–77	Delta State	32-3		AIAW Champion
77–78	Delta State	27-5		AIAW Tournament
78–79	Delta State	21-12		AIAW Tournament

6-Year Coaching Record: 157-23 (.872) overall.

DEAN WEESE
Wayland Baptist College

Ushered tiny Wayland Baptist College from an AAU powerhouse into a national contender on the women's college scene during the mid-1980s. Wayland won two AAU championships and finished fifth or higher in the AIAW nationals five times in his six seasons.... Wayland was one of the first colleges to offer basketball scholarships to women and his teams were instantly dominant in Texas when the AIAW era began.... Was honored with the 1991 Pioneer Award by the U.S. Basketball Writers Association.... Since leaving Wayland, has been a successful high school coach in west Texas, currently coaching at Levelland High School.

Year	School	Overall	League	Postseason
73–74	Wayland Baptist	37-5		AAU Champion; 5th AIAW
74–75	Wayland Baptist	34-1		AAU Champion; 5th AIAW
75–76	Wayland Baptist	34-5		2nd AAU; 3rd AIAW
76–77	Wayland Baptist	31-5		
77–78	Wayland Baptist	33-5		4th AIAW
78–79	Wayland Baptist	24-10		AIAW Quarterfinals

6-Year College Coaching Record: 193-91 (.862) overall.

CHRIS WELLER
Maryland '66

Has spent most of her adult life at Maryland as a student, coach, and administrator.... The Naismith and U.S. Basketball Writers Association national Coach of the Year in 1992.... A two-time ACC Coach of the Year whose teams have won a record eight ACC titles.... Has missed coaching in a national tournament only twice.... Played basketball and lacrosse and swam during college career.... Coach of the U.S. Jones Cup team in 1992 and the 1994 U.S. Select Team.

Year	School	Overall	League	Postseason
75–76	Maryland	20-4		
76–77	Maryland	17-6		
77–78	Maryland	27-4	5-1 (ACC)	2nd AIAW
78–79	Maryland	22-7	6-1 (ACC)	AIAW Regional
79–80	Maryland	21-9	5-2 (ACC)	AIAW Regional
80–81	Maryland	19-9	5-2 (ACC)	AIAW Regional
81–82	Maryland	25-7	6-1 (ACC)	NCAA Final Four
82–83	Maryland	26-5	10-3 (ACC)	NCAA Regional
83–84	Maryland	19-10	10-4 (ACC)	NCAA Regional
84–85	Maryland	9-18	4-10 (ACC)	
85–86	Maryland	17-13	6-8 (ACC)	NCAA Regional
86–87	Maryland	15-14	6-8 (ACC)	
87–88	Maryland	26-6	12-2 (ACC)	NCAA Regional
88–89	Maryland	29-3	13-1 (ACC)	NCAA Final Four

89–90	Maryland	19-11	7-7 (ACC)	NCAA Regional
90–91	Maryland	17-13	9-5 (ACC)	NCAA Regional
91–92	Maryland	25-6	13-3 (ACC)	NCAA Regional
92–93	Maryland	22-8	11-5 (ACC)	NCAA 2nd Round
93–94	Maryland	15-13	8-8 (ACC)	

19-Year Coaching Record: 390-166 (.701) overall; 136-71 (.657) in Atlantic Coast Conference.

12

SMALL COLLEGES:

J.C., DIVISIONS II & III, AND NAIA

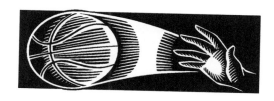

Junior College Action

Junior college (J.C.) players were perceived in some quarters for an extended period as the rogues of recruiting. But now they are in vogue throughout the vast majority of major four-year universities because of an improved image amid the advent of stiffer academic requirements for Division I freshman eligibility.

Although many tunnel-vision Division I coaches were once standoffish, it seems as if virtually everyone except Ivy League schools are flocking toward J.C. recruits these days, especially after "juco" signees frequented the rosters of recent Final Four teams—Arkansas (1990 and 1994), Cincinnati (1992), Indiana (1987), Kansas (1988, 1991, and 1993), Kentucky (1993), Oklahoma (1988), and UNLV (1987, 1990, and 1991).

It wasn't too long ago when only a splinter group of maverick coaches were bold enough to liberally dot their rosters with J.C. players stereotyped as discipline problems, academic risks, or simply unsuitable to go directly from high school to major college programs. "Jucoland" was labeled by misguided observers as little more than where free-lance players

enjoyed the free reins to make Great Plains arenas their own personal H-O-R-S-E stables.

But now major colleges aren't nearly so reluctant to bring "quick fix" junior college players aboard for two seasons. It is no longer demeaning to recruit at the juco level because the entire recruiting process is based on the law of supply and demand and harsher academic requirements at the NCAA level increase the amount of talent at the J.C. level.

The talent pool in the National Junior College Athletic Association (NJCAA) Tournament might have never been greater than in 1968, when eight of the 10 members of the All-Tournament Team either eventually played or were at least drafted by the NBA and/or ABA, and a ninth All-Tournament Team member played several years with the Harlem Globetrotters.

The misconceptions regarding junior college basketball aren't helped when network TV pulls a snafu such as when it was mistakenly inferred that recent Kentucky guard Dale Brown was the first instance of the Wildcats recruiting a junior college player. Actually, Hall of Fame coach Adolph Rupp, a Kansas native, regularly attended the NJCAA Tournament at Hutchinson, Kansas, in the 1950s and recruited four tournament MVPs or leading scorers. Two of the four didn't play much for Kentucky or transferred, but the other two—Bob Burrow (Lon Morris) and Sid Cohen (Kilgore)—proved to be pivotal players for the Wildcats and were selected in the NBA draft. Burrow was an NCAA consensus second-team All-American in 1956.

Two decades earlier, Alabama, after finishing 12th in the 13-team SEC in 1937–38 with a 4-12 record, topped the league's regular-season standings the next year with a 13-4 mark. 'Bama's squad included three junior college graduates, led by center George Prather, who was named to the SEC All-Tournament first five.

Junior college products made a difference for national titlists, too. Keith Erickson, Jack Hirsch, and Sidney Wicks were instrumental in helping UCLA win five of its NCAA championships (1964, 1965, 1969, 1970, 1971) and former J.C. player Bobby Joe Hill was the sparkplug for Texas Western when the Miners captured the 1966 title.

Success has not been limited to just basketball ability. The most notable student-athlete to come out of junior college might be Nolan Archibald, an Academic All-American selection as a senior and player for Weber State's first NCAA Tournament team in 1968. An All-American selection at Dixie Junior College in his native state of Utah, Archibald graduated cum laude from Weber State before earning an M.S. degree in business administration from the Harvard Business School in 1970. As Black & Decker's chairman of the board, president, and chief executive officer since 1986, he heads a $5 billion corporation. Archibald is one of the youngest CEOs of a publicly held Fortune 100 company and has been recognized by *Fortune* and *Business Week* as one of the nation's outstanding managers.

A glance at NBA rosters and the backgrounds of many of the nation's prominent Division I coaches suggests there probably never should have been a stigma attached to the J.C. ranks. One

Southeastern Oklahoma's Dennis Rodman slams one home, though he went on to become an NBA rebounding machine.

seldom hears NBA commentators credit a J.C. beginning, but about 40 NBA players annually played for a two-year school at some point in their college careers, including recent regulars

Ron Anderson, Mookie Blaylock, Anthony Bowie, Sam Cassell, Cedric Ceballos, Mark Eaton, Blue Edwards, Kevin Edwards, Craig Ehlo, Kevin Gamble, Winston Garland, Armon Gilliam, Harvey Grant, Avery Johnson, Larry Johnson, Nate McMillan, Ken Norman, Ricky Pierce, Mitch Richmond, J. R. Rider, Alvin Robertson, Dennis Rodman, Latrell Sprewell, John Starks, Tom Tolbert, Darrell Walker, Spud Webb, Gerald Wilkins, Kenny Williams, and Kevin Willis. Embellishing junior college credentials even more are all-time pro greats with a J.C. connection such as Tiny Archibald, Ron Boone, Fred Brown, Mack Calvin, Michael Cooper, Artis Gilmore, Spencer Haywood, Lionel Hollins, Dennis Johnson, Gus Johnson, Vinnie Johnson, Bob McAdoo, and Paul Pressey.

Furthermore, about 40 current Division I head coaches previously served in a similar capacity at a junior college. The list includes the following high profile coaches: Louisville's Denny Crum (Pierce, Calif.), Purdue's Gene Keady (Hutchinson, Kans.), Arizona's Lute Olson (Long Beach City, Calif.), Arkansas' Nolan Richardson (Western Texas), St. Louis' Charlie Spoonhour (Moberly, Mo., and Southwestern, Iowa), and Oklahoma State's Eddie Sutton (Southern Idaho). Former long-time UNLV coach Jerry Tarkanian also had stints at Riverside (Calif.) City and Pasadena (Calif.) City. Tarkanian, Crum, and Olson, however, never coached in the NJCAA Tournament. California community college administrators conduct an in-state tournament because they don't want their athletes participating in national competition.

The NJCAA Tournament is a five-day, 16-team, 26-game double-elimination affair. It has been played in Hutchinson, Kansas, since 1949.

NJCAA CHAMPIONS

YEAR	CHAMPION		
1949	Tyler (Tex.)	1971	Ellsworth (Iowa)
1950	Los Angeles (Calif.)	1972	Vincennes (Ind.)
1951	Tyler (Tex.)	1973	Mercer County (N.J.)
1952	Wharton (Tex.)	1974	Mercer County (N.J.)
1953	El Dorado (Kans.)	1975	Western Texas
1954	Moberly (Mo.)	1976	Southern Idaho
1955	Moberly (Mo.)	1977	Independence (Kans.)
1956	Kilgore (Tex.)	1978	Independence (Kans.)
1957	San Angelo (Tex.)	1979	Three Rivers (MO)
1958	Kilgore (Tex.)	1980	Western Texas
1959	Weber (Utah)	1981	Westark (Ark.)
1960	Parsons (Kans.)	1983	San Jacinto (Tex.)
1961	Pueblo (Colo.)	1984	San Jacinto (Tex.)
1962	Coffeyville (Kans.)	1985	Dixie (Utah)
1963	Independence (Kans.)	1986	San Jacinto (Tex.)
1964	Dodge City (Kans.)	1987	Southern Idaho
1965	Vincennes (Ind.)	1988	Hutchinson (Kans.)
1966	Moberly (Mo.)	1989	NE Oklahoma A&M
1967	Moberly (Mo.)	1990	Connors State (Okla.)
1968	San Jacinto (Tex.)	1991	Aquinas (Tenn.)
1969	Paducah (Ky.)	1992	Three Rivers (Mo.)
1970	Vincennes (Ind.)	1993	Pensacola (Fla.)
		1994	Hutchinson (Kans.)

Multiple NJCAA titles by school: Moberly (4), San Jacinto (4), Independence (3), Vincennes (3), Hutchinson (2), Kilgore (2), Mercer County (2), Southern Idaho (2), Three Rivers (2), Tyler (2), Western Texas (2).

Most NJCAA titles by state: Texas (13; seven different schools), Kansas (9; six different schools), Missouri (6; two different schools).

1950s Odds and Trends: Longtime NBA coach Lowell (Cotton) Fitzsimmons is believed to hold the record for the longest shot made in NJCAA Tournament history. Fitzsimmons, playing for Hannibal-LaGrange (Mo.), hit a basket estimated at 70 feet just before the end of the first half of the 1952 national third-place game. The next year, Fitzsimmons averaged 25.4 points per game. Incidentally, Fitzsimmons was coach of Moberly (Mo.) when the school won back-to-back national titles in 1966 and 1967.... John Keller, a swingman on 1950 national third-place finisher Garden City (Kan.), became a member of the Clyde Lovellette-led Kansas team that won the 1952 NCAA Tournament. Keller was among the Jayhawks' seven players on the 1952 U.S. Olympic team as he became the first former NJCAA Tournament player to earn a gold medal in the Olympics.... Another Garden City product, forward Hal Patterson, was an All-Tournament team selection in 1952 before playing for Kansas' NCAA runner-up in 1953. He also was an end who was named to the Canadian Football League Hall of Fame after a 14-year career

(1954–67) during which he averaged 20.6 yards per pass reception with 460 catches for 9,473 yards and 64 touchdowns.... Network television announcer Gary Bender is the son of Herb Bender, who coached Dodge City (Kan.) to five consecutive national junior college tournament appearances from 1948 to 1952.... Jim Carey, a member of the back-to-back champions for Moberly (Mo.) in 1954 and 1955, is the only tourney participant to have played and coached on an NJCAA champion. He guided Ellsworth (Iowa) to the 1971 title.... "Jungle Jim" Loscutoff of Grant Tech (Calif.) was the first NJCAA Tournament alumnus to reach the NBA. After graduating from Oregon, he enjoyed a successful career with the Boston Celtics from 1956 through 1964, a period in which they won seven NBA championships.

1960s and 1970s Odds and Trends: The 1962 Jack Hartman-coached Coffeyville (Kan.) became the first undefeated team (32-0) to win the NJCAA Tournament.... The leading rebounder for 1963 runner-up Moberly (Mo.) was 6-3 Larry "Butch" Mantle, a younger brother of New York Yankees Hall of Famer Mickey Mantle.... Allegany Community College of Cumberland, Md., defeated Baltimore Institute, 210-23, on February 8, 1964. Allegany led 90-8 at halftime and hit 92 of 127 field-goal attempts in the debacle.... Longtime pro standout Artis Gilmore, the NJCAA Tournament's first seven-footer, had a disappointing juco tourney experience. His Gardner-Webb (N.C.) teams lost their openers in 1968 and 1969.... Essex County of Newark, N.J., set a NJCAA scoring record in a 210-67 rout of Englewood Cliffs during the 1973–74 season. Essex led at halftime, 110-29. Essex's Lou Grimsley scored 44 points on 22 of 26 field-goal shooting.

1980s and 1990s Odds and Trends: An NJCAA Tournament standard is listed in The Guinness Book of World Records. In a 1982 first-round game against Mercer County, Dixie College's Chris McMullin (later a player for Utah State) hit 29 free throws without a miss.... The NJCAA employs a ticket purchasing plan similar to those used by pro teams and high profile colleges. Season-ticket holders have the right to repurchase their seats for the next year in the 6,800-seat Hutchinson (Kan.) Sports Arena as long as they renew before a May 31 deadline. Consequently, except for standing-room-only tickets, the tournament has sold out nine months in advance every year since 1979.... No individual has played on both an NJCAA and an NCAA Division I championship team. The two players to come closest were guards Jerry Tetzlaff of Ellsworth (1971) and Terry Brown of Northeastern Oklahoma A&M (1989). Tetzlaff played sparingly for 1973 NCAA runner-up Memphis State, and Brown was a starter and three-point specialist for 1991 NCAA runner-up Kansas. Elmore Spencer of Connors (1990) was a center on UNLV's team that was undefeated until getting upset by eventual champion Duke in the 1991 NCAA semifinals.... No college team ever blew a game more incredibly than Shasta (Calif.) in its 1990 contest against Butte (Calif.). Shasta squandered an 18-point lead in the final 77 seconds of regulation. Then, the Knights assembled an 11-point advantage only to see that margin evaporate, too. They finally lost in double overtime, 116-115.

Divisions II and III: Bevo and Friends

The spotlight on Division I leaves the vast majority of Division II and III players toiling in virtual obscurity. But perhaps the greatest folk hero in college basketball history was a small-college player named Clarence "Bevo" Francis, who set an all-time collegiate scoring record with 113 points for Rio Grande (Ohio) College in a 134-95 victory over Hillsdale on February 2, 1954 (see accompanying box for box score). Francis' revolutionary jump shot helped him average 46.5 points per game that season.

Francis proved he could score against major-college teams by pouring in 39 points vs. Villanova, 41 vs. Providence, 48 vs. Miami (Fla.), 34 vs. North Carolina State, 32 vs. Wake Forest, 48 vs. Butler, and 49 and 41 vs. Creighton. Rio Grande won the Providence, Miami, Wake Forest, and Butler games and the first Creighton contest.

"I really don't remember much about the 113-point game," said Francis, a factory worker who was selected by the Philadelphia Warriors in the 1956 draft but couldn't reach a contract agreement with them and never played in the NBA. "It was just another time when I was double- and triple-teamed. Their coach told me after the game that if he could have dressed out, he would have guarded me, too."

No stat sheet exists to detail how many shots the 6-9 Francis attempted en route to his 37 field goals against Hillsdale. "Most of them were outside," he said. "With the three-pointer, I know I would have come close to 150 points."

The scoring outburst might not have had much of an impact on him because he scored even more points—116—as a freshman the previous season against Ashland (Ky.) Junior College. Francis averaged 50.1 points that year for a 39-0 team that reportedly generated sufficient gate receipts to save the school from bankruptcy. However, his single-game total against Ashland and his season average were later expunged from the NCAA record book because 27 of the opponents for Rio Grande (pronounced RYE-o Grand) were junior colleges, military teams, and vocational schools.

Bevo got his nickname because his father was fond of Beve Beer, a root beer-type soft drink. Francis rejected offers from larger universities to follow his Wellsville, Ohio, high school coach, Newt Oliver, to a college with an enrollment of 92 full-time students. Francis, who had a wife and an infant when he arrived at Rio Grande, left school after his sophomore season and signed a three-year contract worth $13,000 annually to play on a national barnstorming tour for a team that opposed the Harlem Globetrotters.

Francis' scoring exploits completely overshadowed the rebounding records established by Tom Hart, a 6-4 center for Middlebury. Hart finished his career in 1955–56 with an average of 27.6 rebounds per game, including an average of 29.5 in each of the previous two years. His career average and his season standards are still NCAA marks.

The most recognizable small-college coach in history probably is Clarence "Bighouse" Gaines, who compiled 828 victories in 47 seasons at Winston-Salem State. Gaines' prize pupil was future Hall of Famer Earl "The Pearl" Monroe, a 6-3 guard who averaged 41.5 points per game for the Rams' 1967 College Division titlist. Winston-Salem was the first historically black college to win an NCAA basketball championship. Monroe's presence at Winston-Salem overshadowed one of the most remarkable achievements in hoop history. The next season, 6-6 William English outscored the opposition by

BEVO BREAKS LOOSE! On February 2, 1954, Hillsdale visited Rio Grande in a game that featured the amazing scoring of Clarence "Bevo" Francis. In an era where there was no three-point zone, Francis wowed the crowd with an all-time scoring total of 113 points (see accompanying text for more details).

HILLSDALE (91)	FG	FT	PTS.
Lowry	4	1	9
Helsted	6	7	19
Kincannon	0	3	3
Wagner	1	0	2
Davis	7	11	25
Sewell	0	3	3
Fake	0	2	2
Neff	4	4	12
Check	1	1	3
Allinder	1	2	4
Thiendeck	1	0	2
Vushan	2	0	4
Tallmen	1	1	3
TOTALS	**28**	**35**	**91**

RIO GRANDE (134)	FG	FT	PTS.
Wiseman	1	2	4
Barr	1	0	2
Ripperger	2	5	9
Francis	38	37	113
McKenzie	0	0	0
Vyhnalek	0	0	0
Moses	1	0	2
Gossett	0	1	1
Weiher	1	0	2
Myers	0	1	1
TOTALS	**44**	**46**	**134**

Pan American's Luke Jackson (far right) comes down hard with a rebound, accidentally kicking Rockhurst College's Dick Hennier in an NAIA tournament game in the mid-1960s.

himself with 77 points for the Rams in a 146–74 victory over Fayetteville.

Joining Monroe among the most memorable players in the small-college ranks were George Gervin (Eastern Michigan), Walt Frazier (Southern Illinois), Jerry Buse (Evansville), and Jerry Sloan (Evansville), but many were lost in the shuffle as schools shed small-college status to be classifed as major colleges or had a dual affiliation with the NAIA. After several unsuccessful attempts to restructure its membership in the early 1970s, the NCAA conducted its first-ever special convention at Chicago in August 1973, to realign schools for legislative and competitive purposes. The outcome was to divide the membership by creating Divisions I, II, and III. Division III schools were grouped together because they don't award athletic scholarships. Division II has in the neighborhood of 220 members while Division III usually has between 310 and 325.

The 32-team Division II Tournament introduced an "Elite Eight" finals format in 1989, with quarterfinal pairings at one site featuring teams from eight regions (East, Great Lakes, New England, North Central, South, South Atlantic, South Central, and West). Springfield, Massachusetts, was the site of the finals for 14 consecutive seasons; the event will be held in Louisville in 1995.

Division III has a 40-team bracket. Wittenberg, the only school to win national titles at both Division II (1961) and Division III (1977), was host of four Division III Tournament semifinals and finals from 1989 through 1992. Buffalo State was designated as host of the event from 1993 through 1995.

NCAA DIVISION II CHAMPIONS

YEAR	CHAMPION	(RECORD)
1957	Wheaton (Ill.)	(28-1)
1958	South Dakota	(22-5)
1959	Evansville (Ind.)	(21-6)
1960	Evansville (Ind.)	(25-4)
1961	Wittenberg (Ohio)	(25-4)
1962	Mt. St. Mary's (Md.)	(24-6)
1963	South Dakota State	(22-5)
1964	Evansville (Ind.)	(26-3)
1965	Evansville (Ind.)	(29-0)
1966	Kentucky Wesleyan	(24-6)
1967	Winston-Salem State (N.C.)	(30-2)
1968	Kentucky Wesleyan	(28-3)
1969	Kentucky Wesleyan	(25-5)
1970	Philadelphia Textile (Pa.)	(29-2)
1971	Evansville (Ind.)	(22-8)
1972	Roanoke (Va.)	(28-4)
1973	Kentucky Wesleyan	(24-6)
1974	Morgan State (Md.)	(28-5)
1975	Old Dominion (Va.)	(25-6)
1976	Puget Sound (Wash.)	(27-7)
1977	Tennessee-Chattanooga	(27-5)
1978	Cheyney State (Pa.)	(27-2)
1979	North Alabama	(22-9)
1980	Virginia Union	(26-4)
1981	Florida Southern	(24-8)
1982	District of Columbia	(25-5)
1983	Wright State (Ohio)	(28-4)
1984	Central Missouri State	(29-3)
1985	Jacksonville State (Ala.)	(30-1)
1986	Sacred Heart (Conn.)	(30-4)
1987	Kentucky Wesleyan	(28-5)
1988	Lowell (Mass.)	(27-7)
1989	North Carolina Central	(28-4)
1990	Kentucky Wesleyan	(31-2)
1991	North Alabama	(29-4)
1992	Virginia Union	(30-3)
1993	Cal State-Bakersfield	(33-0)
1994	Cal State-Bakersfield	(27-6)

Most Division II titles by school: Kentucky Wesleyan (6), Evansville (5).

NCAA DIVISION III CHAMPIONS

YEAR	CHAMPION	(RECORD)
1975	Lemoyne-Owen (Tenn.)	(27-5)
1976	Scranton (Pa.)	(27-5)
1977	Wittenberg (Ohio)	(23-5)
1978	North Park (Ill.)	(29-2)
1979	North Park (Ill.)	(26-5)
1980	North Park (Ill.)	(28-3)
1981	Potsdam State (N.Y.)	(30-2)
1982	Wabash (Ind.)	(24-4)
1983	Scranton (Pa.)	(19-7)
1984	Wisconsin-Whitewater	(27-4)
1985	North Park (Ill.)	(26-4)
1986	Potsdam State (N.Y.)	(32-0)
1987	North Park (Ill.)	(28-3)
1988	Ohio Wesleyan	(27-5)
1989	Wisconsin-Whitewater	(29-2)
1990	Rochester (N.Y.)	(27-5)
1991	Wisconsin-Platteville	(28-3)
1992	Calvin (Mich.)	(31-1)
1993	Ohio Northern	(28-2)
1994	Lebanon Valley (Pa.)	(28-4)

Most Division III titles by school: North Park (5), Potsdam State (2), Scranton (2), Wisconsin-Whitewater (2).

NAIA Tournament

Perhaps no postseason competition factors in endurance in such a brief span as much as the National Association of Intercollegiate Athletics Tournament. When 32 of the finest small colleges in the country collide, a champion emerges after winning five games in one week. The NAIA Tournament is also a grueling test for spectators. Fans sit through more than 12 hours of basketball each of three consecutive days covering the first two rounds of the 32-team event.

There have been numerous NAIA players to warrant such attention, however. These former NAIA Tournament standouts went on to play at least three seasons in the NBA and/or ABA: Dick Barnett (Tennessee State), John Barnhill (Tennessee State), Billy Ray Bates (Kentucky State), Zelmo Beaty (Prairie View A&M), M. L. Carr

(Guilford), World B. Free (Guilford), Joe Fulks (Murray State), Travis Grant (Kentucky State), Luke Jackson (Pan American), Kevin Loder (Alabama State), Vern Mikkelsen (Hamline), Earl Monroe (Winston-Salem State), Terry Porter (Wisconsin-Stevens Point), Willis Reed (Grambling), Dennis Rodman (Southeastern Oklahoma), Jack Sikma (Illinois Wesleyan), Elmore Smith (Kentucky State), Al Tucker (Oklahoma Baptist), and Foots Walker (West Georgia).

"We're Goin' to Kansas City" served as the theme song for countless small schools across the country for the final time in 1993. After being a fixture for more than 40 years as the Kansas City masterpiece, the week-long marathon shifted along with the NAIA headquarters to Tulsa, beginning in 1994. Attendance had waned in Kansas City for more than a decade, but the principal reason for the move was to escape what had overshadowed the NAIA for years: the nearby headquarters of the NCAA, the Big Eight Conference Tournament, the NFL (Chiefs), and major league baseball (Royals).

The NAIA split into two divisions in 1992. NAIA Division II schools, which conduct a 24-team national tournament, are those that distribute no more than five scholarships.

Divisions II & III and NAIA Roundup

1940s Odds and Trends: York (Neb.) College, with an enrollment of 50, upset Akron, 52-49, in the first round of the NAIA Tournament before losing to North Texas, 51-49, in the second round. Brothers Jim and Wayne Kaeding scored 78 of York's 101 points.... North Carolina College's Rocky Roberson scored 58 points in a game against Shaw in the 1942–43 season for what was believed to be a college record at the

NAIA CHAMPIONS

YEAR	CHAMPION	RECORD
1937	Central Missouri St.	(17-3)
1938	Central Missouri St.	(24-3)
1939	Southwestern (Kans.)	(21-2)
1940	Tarkio (Mo.)	(20-4)
1941	San Diego St. (Calif.)	(24-7)
1942	Hamline (Minn.)	(20-2)
1943	Southeast Missouri St.	(19-6)
1944	No tournament due to World War II	
1945	Loyola (La.)	(19-5)
1946	Southern Illinois	(20-6)
1947	Marshall (W.V.)	(32-5)
1948	Louisville (Ky.)	(29-6)
1949	Hamline (Minn.)	(29-1)
1950	Indiana St.	(27-8)
1951	Hamline (Minn.)	(27-2)
1952	Southwest Missouri St.	(27-5)
1953	Southwest Missouri St.	(24-4)
1954	St. Benedict's (Kans.)	(24-5)
1955	East Texas St.	(29-5)
1956	McNeese St. (La.)	(33-3)
1957	Tennessee St.	(31-4)
1958	Tennessee St.	(31-3)
1959	Tennessee St.	(32-1)
1960	Southwest Texas St.	(28-3)
1961	Grambling (La.)	(30-4)
1962	Prairie View A&M (Tex.)	(27-3)
1963	Pan American (Tex.)	(26-6)
1964	Rockhurst (Mo.)	(27-6)
1965	Central St. (Ohio)	(30-0)
1966	Oklahoma Baptist	(26-7)
1967	St. Benedict's (Kans.)	(27-2)
1968	Central St. (Ohio)	(29-4)
1969	Eastern New Mexico	(24-7)
1970	Kentucky St.	(29-3)
1971	Kentucky St.	(31-2)
1972	Kentucky St.	(28-5)
1973	Guilford (N.C.)	(29-5)
1974	West Georgia	(29-4)
1975	Grand Canyon (Ariz.)	(30-3)
1976	Coppin State (Md.)	(39-2)
1977	Texas Southern	(31-5)
1978	Grand Canyon (Ariz.)	(30-3)
1979	Drury (Mo.)	(33-2)
1980	Cameron (Okla.)	(36-3)
1981	Bethany Nazarene (Okla.)	(36-6)
1982	Spartanburg (S.C.)	(27-5)
1983	Charleston (S.C.)	(33-5)
1984	Fort Hays St. (Kans.)	(35-2)
1985	Fort Hays St. (Kans.)	(35-3)
1986	David Lipscomb (Tenn.)	(35-4)
1987	Washburn (Kans.)	(35-4)
1988	Grand Canyon (Ariz.)	(37-6)
1989	St. Mary's (Tex.)	(28-5)
1990	Birmingham Southern (Ala.)	(31-3)
1991	Oklahoma City	(34-3)
1992	Oklahoma City	(38-0)
1993	Hawaii Pacific	(30-4)
1994	Oklahoma City	(28-7)

Most NAIA titles by school: Grand Canyon (3), Hamline (3), Kentucky State (3), Oklahoma City (3), Tennessee State (3).

Most NAIA Tournament appearances: Central Washington (24), Wisconsin-Eau Claire (20).

time.... Howie Schultz, a star for Hamline (Minn.) in the early 1940s, replaced Jackie Robinson at first base in Robinson's first regular-season game for the Brooklyn Dodgers in 1947.... More than 100 current NCAA Division I schools previously competed in the NAIA Tournament. Thirteen of the 17 different colleges to win NAIA titles from 1941 through 1963 are currently classified as NCAA Division I institutions. One of the 13 universities is Southeast Missouri State, which captured the 1943 crown after losing its first four games of the season.... Former NFL commissioner Pete Rozelle was athletic publicity director at Compton (Calif.) College in 1946–47 when the school played 26 consecutive games without calling a timeout en route to their 36-4 record.... CIAA champion West Virginia State was the nation's only undefeated college team in 1947–48, finishing with a 23-0 record. The squad, coached by Mark Cardwell, included future NBA players Bob Wilson and Earl Lloyd.... UCLA legend John Wooden was in his final season as coach of Indiana State when the Sycamores lost to Louisville in the 1948 final. The all-tourney first five included Beloit's Johnny Orr, who went on to become a longtime major-college coach. Two years later, Indiana State won the NAIA title.... Tennessee State, coached by Henry A. Kean, was the nation's only undefeated team in 1948–49 with a 24-0 record. The Tigers' leading scorers, Clarence Wilson and Joshua Grider, were both eventually longtime standouts with the Harlem Globetrotters.... Hamline (Minn.), the 1949 NAIA champion, had two players—center Vern Mikkelsen and forward Hal Haskins—on Converse's first three five-man All-American teams.

1950s Odds and Trends: Morris Harvey's George King became the first college player to average 30 or more points per game in a seson when he led the nation's small-college players with a 31.2-point average in 1949–50.... The first black college to take the floor in an integrated national collegiate tournament was Tennessee State (then Tennessee A&I) in 1953. Hall of Famer John McLendon coached Tennessee State to three consecutive national titles (1957–59). Oddly, the '53 Tennessee State team defeated McLendon-coached North Carolina College for the opportunity to go to Kansas City.... Southwest Missouri, winning the 1953 crown to become the first school to capture back-to-back titles with a 32-team format, played the last 3½ minutes of its semifinal game with only four players on the court after encountering foul problems. The principal reason Southwest Missouri was shorthanded stemmed from two squad members being in spring training on their way to playing 12 seasons of major league baseball—infielder Jerry Lumpe and first baseman/outfielder Norm Siebern.... West Virginia Tech averaged more than 100 points per game four consecutive seasons from 1954–55 through 1957–58.... McNeese State's Bill Reigel, playing for his third college in six seasons, led the nation's small-college players with a 33.9-point average when he paced McNeese to the 1956 NAIA Tournament title. Reigel had averaged 18 points per game for the Duquesne freshman team in 1950–51 and 16.3 points per game for the Duke varsity in 1952–53 before entering military service. He later coached

John Barnhill (left) and Dick Barnett—each of whom went on to NBA careers—were members of Tennessee State, the first historically black institution to participate in post-season competition.

McNeese for three seasons from 1971–72 through 1973–74.... Western Illinois missed an opportunity to become the nation's only undefeated college team in 1957–58 when it lost to Tennessee State, 85-73, in the NAIA Tournament championship game. Western had defeated Tennessee State, 79-76, earlier in the season. It was one of three consecutive NAIA titles won by Tennessee State, which boasted future pros Dick Barnett, John Barnhill, and Ben Warley.... Davis & Elkins' Paul Wilcox, 6-6, became the only player to lead the NAIA in scoring (22.6 ppg) and rebounding (22.3 rpg) in the same season (1958–59).

1960s Odds and Trends: The NAIA All-Stars upset NCAA champion Ohio State, 76-69, in a first-round games in the 1960 Olympic Trials. The NAIA zone defense limited Buckeye All-American Jerry Lucas to 14 points.... Midwestern (Tex.) defeated Austin College, 14-11, in overtime in 1964. Midwestern held a 4-1 halftime lead and the teams were tied at 8-8 at the end of regulation. Midwestern had won an earlier game that season with Austin by 40 points, 92-52.... Sam Alford, father of former Indiana All-American guard Steve Alford, led the NAIA in free-throw shooting in 1963–64. The elder Alford hit 91.2 percent of his foul shots for Franklin (Ind.) that season.... Youngstown State's John McElroy became the shortest player (6-0) ever to score 70 or more points in a game involving NCAA colleges when he scored 72 against Wayne State (Mich.) on February 26, 1969.

1970s and 1980s Odds and Trends: Doug Williams, a 32-year-old Air Force veteran, earned NAIA first-team All-American honors for St. Mary's (Tex.) in 1969–70 when he averaged 18.9 points per game. He scored 24 in a 76-66 upset of Houston.... Elmore Smith, a 7-0 center for 1970 NAIA champion Kentucky State, was called for goaltending 12 times in a 116-98 defeat to Eastern Michigan.... Tennessee State edged Oglethorpe, 7-4, on February 16, 1971, in what is believed to be the lowest-scoring college game since the center jump was eliminated prior to the 1937–38 season. Tennessee State had overwhelmed Oglethorpe, 82-43, earlier in the season.... Birmingham-Southern's Russell Thompson scored 25 points without making a field-goal attempt in a 55-46 victory over Florence State in the 1970–71 season. He converted 25 of 28 free throws.... Kentucky State's Travis "Machine Gun" Grant

Despite being called for goaltending 12 times in a late 1960s game, Kentucky State's Elmore Smith (right) holds the collegiate record for most rebounds in a season.

set the single-game NAIA Tournament scoring record with 60 points against Minot State in 1972. Grant finished his four-year college career with 4,045 points and a 33.4-point average.... Guilford (N.C.) and Tennessee State are the only two small colleges to have two players score more than 20 points per game in an NBA season—World B. Free and Bob Kaufmann attended Guilford, and Dick Barnett and Truck Robinson attended Tennessee State.... Guilford won the 1973 NAIA Tournament with a lineup that included three future NBA players—Free, M. L. Carr, and Greg Jackson. Guilford's top reserve was Steve Hankins, a 6-6, 220-pound, 28-year-old Marine Corps veteran who had served 44 months in Vietnam and was one of the military pallbearers at President John F. Kennedy's funeral.... Leon Gobczynski, a 6-10 center, averaged 36.1 points per game for Millikin (Ill.) in the 1973–74 season despite being blanked by Augustana (Ill.) in an 88-61 defeat. Gobczynski, who had scored 43 points in an earlier game that year between the two teams, missed all nine of his field-goal attempts in 36 minutes of playing time.... Albany (Ga.) State's Major Jones led NCAA Division II rebounders with an average of 22.5 per game. Jones, 6-9, is the last Division I or Division II player to average at least 20 per game.... Amherst's Jim Rehnquist, son of Supreme Court Justice William Rehnquist, finished fifth in NCAA Division III scoring with an average of 27.8 points per game.... Salem College's (W. Va.) Archie Talley set an NAIA record for most points in a season (1,347) in 1975–76 when he averaged 40.8 per game.... Phoenix Suns coach Paul Westphal guided Grand Canyon to the 1988 NAIA title.

1990s Odds and Trends: Central Arkansas ranks among the top three schools for most NAIA Tournament appearances with 14 through 1994 but none of those were when 1992 U.S. basketball Olympian Scottie Pippen of the Chicago Bulls played for the Bears.... Missouri and Texas are the states with the most different colleges to win the tournament with six apiece.... The 1992 NAIA championship game going into overtime wasn't a rarity. Four of the eight finals from 1981 through 1988 required extra sessions. Nine of the last 11 championship games were decided in overtime or by fewer than six points in regulation.... Bob Hoffman was deprived of becoming the first coach in NAIA history to guide men's and women's champions when No. 1 seed Oklahoma Baptist bowed to Hawaii Pacific, 88-83, in the 1993 championship game. Hoffman had directed Southern Nazarene (Okla.) to the 1989 NAIA women's title.... John Pierce of Lipscomb

(Tenn.) became college basketball's all-time leading scorer after totaling 33 points in his 1993–94 regular-season finale, a 119-102 triumph over Cumberland Pierce; his 4,110 total career points broke former roommate Phil Hutcheson's mark of 4,106 set in the 1990 NAIA Tournament.

Humble Backgrounds

Small colleges have supplied many of the biggest names in coaching. Highly regarded Alabama-Birmingham coach Gene Bartow, for instance, began his coaching career at Central Missouri State, a Division II power that lists Division I championship coaches Phog Allen of Kansas and Joe B. Hall of Kentucky among its former head coaches. Allen posted an 84-31 record in seven seasons at Central Missouri from 1913 to 1919, Bartow was 47-21 in three seasons from 1962 to 1964, and Hall was 19-6 in one season (1964–65).

Central Missouri, winner of the first two NAIA Tournaments in 1937 and 1938, captured the NCAA Division II crown in 1984 under Lynn Nance, the coach at St. Mary's (Calif.) in 1989 when the Gaels made their first NCAA Tournament appearance in 30 years. Another former CMSU coach, Louisiana Tech's Jim Wooldridge, directed Southwest Texas State to its first-ever NCAA playoff appearance in 1994.

Here is an alphabetical list including Bartow and a striking number of other prominent active major-college coaches who worked their way up the ladder after graduating from a small school:

DIVISION I COACH	ALMA MATER
Dana Altman	Eastern New Mexico '80
Ronnie Arrow	Southwest Texas State '69
Rick Barnes	Lenoir-Rhyne (N.C.) '76
J. D. Barnett	Winona (Minn.) State '66
Gene Bartow	Northeast Missouri State '53
Dick Bennett	Ripon (Wisc.) '65
Dale Brown	Minot (N.D.) State '57
Jim Calhoun	American International (Mass.) '67
John Calipari	Clarion (Pa.) State '82
John Chaney	Bethune-Cookman (Fla.) '55
Perry Clark	Gettysburg (Pa.) '74
Gary Colson	David Lipscomb (Tenn.) '56
Tom Davis	Wisconsin-Platteville '60
Mike Deane	Potsdam (N.Y.) State '74
James Dickey	Central Arkansas '76
Bob Donewald	Hanover (Ind.) '64
Steve Fisher	Illinois State '67
Bill Foster	Carson-Newman (Tenn.) '58
Ned Fowler	East Texas State '66

Leonard Hamilton	Tennessee-Martin '71
Jim Harrick	Morris Harvey (W. Va.) '60
Rich Herrin	McKendree (Ill.) '56
Ben Jobe	Fisk (Tenn.) '56
Pat Kennedy	King's (Pa.) '75
Steve Lappas	City College of New York '77
Nick Macarchuk	Fairfield (Conn.) '63
John MacLeod	Bellarmine (Ky.) '59
Neil McCarthy	Sacramento (Calif.) State '65
Eldon Miller	Wittenberg (Ohio) '61
Jim Molinari	Illinois Wesleyan '77
Danny Nee	St. Mary of the Plains (Kan.) '71
Dave Odom	Guilford (N.C.) '65
Lute Olson	Augsburg (Minn.) '56
Kevin O'Neill	McGill (Que., Canada) '79
Bruce Parkhill	Lock Haven (Pa.) '71
Bobby Paschal	Stetson (Fla.) '64
Oliver Purnell	Old Dominion (Va.) '75
Kelvin Sampson	Pembroke (N.C.) State '78
Wimp Sanderson	Florence (Ala.) State '59
Sonny Smith	Milligan (Tenn.) '58
Tubby Smith	High Point (N.C.) '73
Charlie Spoonhour	Ozarks (Ark.) '61
Billy Tubbs	Lamar (Tex.) '58
M. K. Turk	Livingston (Ala.) '64
Rudy Washington	Redlands (Calif.) '73

Notes: Bethune-Cookman, Fairfield, Illinois State, Lamar, Old Dominion, Southwest Texas State, Stephen F. Austin State, and Stetson are now classified as NCAA Division I colleges.... Several of these coaches who graduated from small colleges started their careers at major universities before transferring—Barnett (Missouri), Calipari (North Carolina-Wilmington), Harrick (Marshall), Molinari (Kansas State), and Nee (Marquette).... Morris Harvey College is now the University of Charleston and Florence State is now the University of North Alabama.

Current Iowa coach Tom Davis graduated from small college Wisconsin-Platteville in 1960.

SMALL-SCHOOL STANDOUTS

Here is an alphabetical list of the career statistics for a smattering of recognizable small-college stars.

PLAYER	SCHOOL	LAST YEAR	G.	FG%	FT%	RPG	PPG
Al Attles	North Carolina A&T	1960	53	.561	.636		13.1
Dick Barnett	Tennessee St.	1959	136				23.6
John Barnhill	Tennessee St.	1959	103				13.8
Zelmo Beaty	Prairie View (Tex.)	1962	108	.655	.775	19.0	24.7
Don Buse	Evansville	1972	84	.497	.784	6.3	17.0
M. L. Carr	Guilford (N.C.)	1973	111	.573	.618	11.4	18.0
Bob Dandridge	Norfolk (Va.) St.	1969	77	.578	.745	13.0	22.6
John Drew	Gardner-Webb (N.C.)	1974	51	.518	.692	11.0	25.2
Walt Frazier	Southern Illinois	1967	50	.471	.751	10.6	17.7
Lloyd Free	Guilford (N.C.)	1975	85	.485	.731	6.5	23.6
Joe Fulks	Murray St.	1943	47		.665		13.2
Harry Gallatin	Northeast Missouri	1948	62				13.2
George Gervin	Eastern Michigan	1972	39	.582	.776	14.4	26.8
Travis "Machine Gun" Grant	Kentucky St.	1972	121	.638	.774	9.4	33.4
Mike Green	Louisiana Tech	1973	102	.580	.723	15.4	22.9
Luke Jackson	Pan American (Tex.)	1964	77	.544	.730	18.5	24.1
Phil Jackson	North Dakota	1967	86	.510	.738	12.9	19.9
George Johnson	Dillard (La.)	1970	90	.472	.590	15.0	12.3
Mickey Johnson	Aurora (Ill.)	1974	94	.561	.660	20.9	26.1
Caldwell Jones	Albany (Ga.) St.	1973	109	.506	.674	20.3	20.5
Sam Jones	North Carolina Central	1957	100	.463	.697	9.0	17.7
Bob Kauffman	Guilford (N.C.)	1968	113			15.9	22.8
Bob Love	Southern (La.)	1965	104	.561	.749	11.2	23.1
Rick Mahorn	Hampton (Va.) Institute	1980	119	.534	.682	12.3	20.3
Vern Mikkelsen	Hamline (Minn.)	1949	104				13.6
Earl Monroe	Winston-Salem (N.C.) St.	1967	110				26.7
Scottie Pippen	Central Arkansas	1987	93	.563	.695	8.1	17.2
Terry Porter	Wisconsin-Stevens Point	1985	117	.589	.796	3.8	13.5
Willis Reed	Grambling (La.)	1964	122	.597	.740	15.2	18.7
Len "Truck" Robinson	Tennessee St.	1974	111	.521	.645	13.5	20.3
Dennis Rodman	Southeastern Oklahoma	1986	96	.637	.625	15.7	25.7
Dan Roundfield	Central Michigan	1975	79	.542	.631	13.1	16.7
Woody Sauldsberry	Texas Southern	1955	29				18.5
Bruce Seals	Xavier (La.)	1973	53	.520	.617	13.0	22.2
Purvis Short	Jackson (Miss.) St.	1978	104	.534	.733	9.3	23.4
Jack Sikma	Illinois Wesleyan	1977	107	.592	.765	13.1	21.2
James Silas	Stephen F. Austin (Tex.)	1972	99	.572	.803	4.7	18.7
Jerry Sloan	Evansville	1965	85	.403	.721	12.4	15.5
Elmore Smith	Kentucky St.	1971	85	.584	.566	22.6	21.3
Randy Smith	Buffalo St.	1971	74	.497	.657	13.2	23.1
Sedale Threatt	West Virginia Tech	1983	120	.498	.724	3.7	20.7
Dave Twardzik	Old Dominion	1972	82	.506	.799	5.5	20.2
Charles "Chico" Vaughn	Southern Ill.	1962	85	.439	.737	7.8	24.5
Clarence "Foots" Walker	West Georgia	1974	61	.492	.760	7.4	20.9
Ben Warley	Tennessee St.	1960	74	.424	.843	10.3	13.8
Don "Slick" Watts	Xavier (La.)	1973	80	.490	.620	4.2	17.6
Marvin Webster	Morgan St. (Md.)	1975	114	.524	.658	19.9	17.5

Notes: Attles' statistics are available for only the last two of four seasons.... Barnhill's freshman statistics are unavailable.... L. Jackson also played for Texas Southern but those statistics are unavailable.... Sauldsberry's freshman statistics are unavailable.... E. Smith also played for Wiley (Tex.) College but those statistics are unavailable.... Warley's complete statistics are unavailable and the figures listed are based on available figures....

Central Michigan, Eastern Michigan, Evansville, Grambling, Jackson State, Louisiana Tech, Morgan State, Murray State, North Carolina A&T, Old Dominion, Pan American, Prairie View,m Southern (La.), Southern Illinois, Stephen F. Austin State, Tennessee State, and Texas Southern subsequently moved up to NCAA Division I status.

Purvis Short was a standout for Jackson State University.

13

THE OLYMPIC GAMES

D r. James Naismith is credited for inventing the game of basketball in 1891, but it wasn't until June 1932, in Geneva, Switzerland, that an international federation was formed to focus solely on men's basketball. In the Olympics of 1904, 1924, and 1928, basketball was classified as only a demonstration sport; but in 1935, the International Basketball Federation (FIBB) was officially recognized by the International Olympic Committee (IOC), helping pave the path for men's basketball to be implemented at the 1936 Berlin Summer Olympic Games. The FIBB is the forerunner of the International Basketball Federation (FIBA).

The 1936 U.S. team was split into two groups: one from Universal movie studio and another known as the McPherson Globe Oilers. The McPherson group wound up playing for the gold: they defeated Canada, 19-8, in an outdoors game that featured a torrential rainstorm that flooded the court, making dribbling impossible.

The Amateur Athletic Union (AAU) was recognized as the organization that would be responsible for United States teams in international competitions when the United States

joined the FIBA as a member in 1934. Various committees controlled the selection of the U.S. Olympic teams and coaching staffs. For instance, the Games Committee selected from eight teams at the 1960 Olympics Trials—three AAU squads, the NCAA Tournament champion, an NCAA university all-star team, an NCAA college all-star team, an Armed Forces all-star team, and a National Association of Intercollegiate Athletics (NAIA) all-star team.

Just prior to the 1972 Olympics, FIBA revoked its recognition of the AAU and instructed the United States to form a new organization containing representation from the numerous basketball outlets in the country. In 1974, the Amateur Basketball Federation of the United States of America (ABAUSA) was formed. ABAUSA changed its name to USA Basketball in October 1989, shortly after the FIBA modified its rules to allow professional basketball players to participate in international competitions. The result of that, of course, was 1992's "Dream Team," which consisted of such active NBA stars as Larry Bird, Charles Barkley, and Michael Jordan, the recently retired Magic Johnson, and the lone college player, Duke's Christian Laettner.

Women's basketball was added as a medal sport in 1976. The U.S. team has won gold at two of the five Olympics (the U.S. boycotted the 1980 Olympics), while the Soviet Union and the Unified teams have won the other three (the Soviets boycotted the 1984 games).

Men's Basketball

1936   BERLIN, GERMANY

MEDAL WINNERS: 1. U.S. (5-0); 2. Canada (5-1); 3. Mexico (5-2).

U.S. COACH: James Needles, Universal Pictures (Calif.).

FAST FACT: Each basketball team was limited to seven players per game, which was played on outdoor facilities. A rule banning players taller than 6-2 was rescinded only after the U.S. complained.

U.S. MEN'S RESULTS

U.S. 2, Spain 0*
U.S. 52, Estonia 28
U.S. 56, Philippines 23
U.S. 25, Mexico 10
U.S. 19, Canada 8

* The U.S. was awarded a forfeit victory when its first opponent (Spain) failed to appear because of the Spanish civil war.

U.S. MEN'S ROSTER AND STATISTICS

PLAYER	POS.	AFFILIATION/SCHOOL	PPG.
Sam Balter	G	Universal Pictures (UCLA)	8.5
Ralph Bishop	F	Washington	2.0
Joe Fortenberry	C	Globe Oilers (Wichita State)	14.5
John Gibbons	G	Globe Oilers (Southwestern)	6.0
Francis Johnson	G	Globe Oilers (Wichita State)	10.0
Carl Knowles	F	Universal Pictures (UCLA)	3.0
Frank Lubin	F	Universal Pictures (UCLA)	11.0
Art Mollner	G	Universal Pictures (L.A.J.C.)	2.0
Don Piper	G	Universal Pictures (UCLA)	2.0
Jack Ragland	G	Globe Oilers (Wichita State)	3.5
Willard Schmidt	C	Globe Oilers (Creighton)	8.0
Carl Shy	G	Universal Pictures (UCLA)	5.0
Dwayne Swanson	F	Universal Pictures (USC)	2.0
William Wheatley	F	Globe Oilers (Kansas Wesleyan)	4.5

Note: The team was divided into two seven-man units, each of whom played one game and then sat out the next contest.

1948   LONDON, ENGLAND

MEDAL WINNERS: 1. U.S. (8-0); 2. France (5-2); 3. Brazil (7-1).

U.S. COACH: Omar Browning, Phillips Oilers (Okla.).

FAST FACT: The Phillips Oilers, winners of the national AAU title, defeated Kentucky, the 1948 NCAA champion, in the final game of the U.S. Olympic Trials (53-49). Each of the finalists wound up with five representatives on the U.S. squad. NIT champion St. Louis rejected an invitation to the eight-team Olympic Trials because the school's administration believed the players would miss too much class time.

U.S. MEN'S RESULTS

U.S. 86, Switzerland 21
U.S. 53, Czechoslovakia 28
U.S. 59, Argentina 57
U.S. 66, Egypt 28
U.S. 61, Peru 33
U.S. 63, Uruguay 28
U.S. 71, Mexico 40
U.S. 65, France 21

U.S. MEN'S ROSTER AND STATISTICS

PLAYER	POS.	AFFILIATION/SCHOOL	PPG.
Cliff Barker	F	Kentucky	3.8
Don Barksdale	C	Oakland Bittners (UCLA)	9.0
Ralph Beard	G	Kentucky	3.7
Lewis Beck	G	Phillips Oilers (Oregon State)	4.7
Vince Boryla*	G	Denver Nuggets (Notre Dame)	5.6
Gordon Carpenter	C-F	Phillips Oilers (Kansas)	7.0
Alex Groza	C	Kentucky	11.1
Wallace Jones	C-F	Kentucky	7.2
Bob Kurland	C	Phillips Oilers (Oklahoma State)	9.3
Ray Lumpp	G	NYU	7.2
R. C. Pitts	F	Phillips Oilers (Arkansas)	7.8
Jesse Renick	G	Phillips Oilers (Oklahoma State)	5.6
Jack Robinson	G	Baylor	2.6
Ken Rollins	G	Kentucky	4.0

* Boryla played two seasons at Notre Dame (1944–45 and 1945–46) and then served in the military for two years before finishing his college career at the University of Denver (1948–49).

1952   HELSINKI, FINLAND

MEDAL WINNERS: 1. U.S. (8-0); 2. Soviet Union (6-2); 3. Uruguay (5-3).

U.S. COACH: Warren Womble, Peoria Caterpillars (Ill.).

FAST FACT: U.S. Olympic team captain Ron Bontemps was a high school (Taylorville, Ill.) and college (Illinois and Beloit, Wisc.) teammate of former Massachusetts, Michigan, and Iowa State coach Johnny Orr. Their 1944 state high school championship team compiled a 45-0 record. Bontemps averaged a team-high 22 points per game for a Beloit squad that earned a bid to the 1951 NIT after defeating larger schools such as Washington State, Marshall, San Jose State, and Loyola (Ill.). Beloit had an enrollment of 1,060 students.

U.S. MEN'S RESULTS

U.S. 66, Hungary 48
U.S. 72, Czechoslovakia 47
U.S. 57, Uruguay 44
U.S. 86, USSR 58
U.S. 103, Chile 55
U.S. 57, Brazil 53
U.S. 85, Argentina 76
U.S. 36, USSR 25

U.S. MEN'S ROSTER AND STATISTICS

PLAYER	POS.	AFFILIATION/SCHOOL	PPG.
Ron Bontemps	G	Peoria Caterpillars (Ill./Beloit)	7.1
Marcus Freiberger	C	Peoria Caterpillars (Oklahoma)	6.3
Wayne Glasgow	G-F	Phillips 66ers	4.5
Charlie Hoag	G-F	Kansas	2.9
Bill Hougland	G	Kansas	6.0
John Keller	G-F	Kansas	1.5
Dean Kelley	G	Kansas	0.7
Bob Kenney	F	Kansas	10.9
Bob Kurland	C	Phillips 66ers (Oklahoma State)	9.6
Bill Lienhard	F	Kansas	4.0
Clyde Lovellette	C-F	Kansas	14.1
Frank McCabe	F	Peoria Caterpillars (Marquette)	3.0
Dan Pippin	G	Peoria Caterpillars (Missouri)	7.0
Howie Williams	G	Peoria Caterpillars (Purdue)	3.4

1956   MELBOURNE, AUSTRALIA

MEDAL WINNERS: 1. U.S. (8-0); 2. Soviet Union (5-3); 3. Uruguay (6-2).

U.S. COACH: Gerald Tucker, Phillips 66ers (OK).

FAST FACT: The XVIth Olympiad was held during the United States' late autumn season (Nov. 22–Dec. 1) because the seasons are reversed in Australia; this delayed Bill Russell's NBA debut. Swingman Gib Ford became president of Converse after serving in the Air Force.

U.S. MEN'S RESULTS

U.S. 98, Japan 40
U.S. 101, Thailand 29
U.S. 121, Philippines 53
U.S. 85, Bulgaria 44
U.S. 113, Brazil 51
U.S. 85, USSR 55
U.S. 101, Uruguay 38
U.S. 89, USSR 55

U.S. MEN'S ROSTER AND STATISTICS

PLAYER	POS.	AFFILIATION/SCHOOL	PPG.
Dick Boushka	F	Wichita Vickers (St. Louis Univ.)	8.0
Carl Cain	F	Iowa	1.5
Chuck Darling	C	Phillips 66ers (Iowa)	9.3
Bill Evans	G	U.S. Armed Forces (Kentucky)	6.8
Gib Ford	G-F	U.S. Armed Forces (Texas)	4.9
Burdette Haldorson	F	Phillips 66ers (Colorado)	8.6
Bill Hougland	F	Phillips 66ers (Kansas)	5.8
Bob Jeangerard	F	Phillips 66ers (Colorado)	12.5
K. C. Jones	G	San Francisco	10.9
Bill Russell	C	San Francisco	14.1
Ron Tomsic	G	U.S. Armed Forces (Stanford)	11.1
Jim Walsh	G	Phillips 66ers (Stanford)	9.1

U.S. MEN'S RESULTS

U.S. 78, Australia 45
U.S. 77, Finland 51
U.S. 60, Peru 45
U.S. 83, Uruguay 28
U.S. 69, Yugoslavia 61
U.S. 86, Brazil 53
U.S. 116, South Korea 50
U.S. 62, Puerto Rico 42
U.S. 73, USSR 59

U.S. MEN'S ROSTER AND STATISTICS

PLAYER	POS.	AFFILIATION/SCHOOL	PPG.
Jim Barnes	C	Texas Western	8.5
Bill Bradley	G-F	Princeton	10.1
Larry Brown	G	Goodyear Wingfoots (N. Carolina)	4.1
Joe Caldwell	G-F	Arizona State	9.0
Mel Counts	C	Oregon State	6.6
Dick Davies	G	Goodyear Wingfoots (LSU)	3.4
Walt Hazzard	G-F	UCLA	3.8
Luke Jackson	F	Pan American	10.0
Pete McCaffrey	F	Goodyear Wingfoots (St. Louis Univ.)	5.1
Jeff Mullins	G-F	Duke	2.3
Jerry Shipp	G	Phillips 66ers (SE Oklahoma State)	12.4
George Wilson	F-C	Chicago Jamaco Saints (Cincinnati)	5.4

1960   ROME, ITALY

MEDAL WINNERS: 1. U.S. (8-0); 2. Soviet Union (6-2); 3. Brazil (6-2).

U.S. COACH: Pete Newell, California.

FAST FACT: Eight members of the 12-man U.S. roster in 1960 went on to play at least nine seasons in the NBA.

U.S. MEN'S RESULTS

U.S. 88, Italy 54
U.S. 125, Japan 66
U.S. 107, Hungary 63
U.S. 104, Yugoslavia 42
U.S. 108, Uruguay 50
U.S. 81, USSR 57
U.S. 112, Italy 81
U.S. 90, Brazil 63

U.S. MEN'S ROSTER AND STATISTICS

PLAYER	POS.	AFFILIATION/SCHOOL	PPG.
Jay Arnette	F	Texas	2.9
Walter Bellamy	C	Indiana	7.9
Bob Boozer	F	Peoria Caterpillars (Kansas State)	6.8
Terry Dischinger	F	Purdue	11.8
Burdette Haldorson	F	Phillips 66ers (Colorado)	2.9
Darrall Imhoff	C	California	4.8
Allen Kelley	G	Peoria Caterpillars (Kansas)	0.8
Lester Lane	G	Wichita Vickers (Oklahoma)	5.9
Jerry Lucas	F-C	Ohio State	17.0
Oscar Robertson	F	Cincinnati	17.0
Adrian Smith	G	U.S. Armed Forces (Kentucky)	10.9
Jerry West	G	West Virginia	13.8

1964   TOKYO, JAPAN

MEDAL WINNERS: 1. U.S. (9-0); 2. Soviet Union (8-1); 3. Brazil (6-3).

U.S. COACH: Hank Iba, Oklahoma State.

FAST FACT: Current UNC Charlotte coach Jeff Mullins compiled the lowest scoring average on the 12-man U.S. roster despite averaging 24.2 points per game for NCAA runner-up Duke. Mullins scored 14 of his 18 points against Puerto Rico in the semifinals.

Houston's Ken Spain was part of the 1968 Olympic basketball team.

1968   MEXICO CITY, MEXICO

MEDAL WINNERS: 1. U.S. (9-0); 2. Yugoslavia (7-2); 3. Soviet Union (8-1).

U.S. COACH: Hank Iba, Oklahoma State.

FAST FACT: Spencer Haywood, the leading scorer for the U.S. squad, was at that time the youngest player (19) to ever earn a spot on the U.S. Olympic basketball team.

U.S. MEN'S RESULTS

U.S. 81, Spain 46
U.S. 93, Senegal 36
U.S. 96, Philippines 75
U.S. 73, Yugoslavia 58
U.S. 95, Panama 60
U.S. 100, Italy 61
U.S. 61, Puerto Rico 56
U.S. 75, Brazil 63
U.S. 65, Yugoslavia 50

U.S. MEN'S ROSTER AND STATISTICS

PLAYER	POS.	AFFILIATION/SCHOOL	PPG.
Mike Barrett	G	U.S. Armed Forces (West Va. Tech)	6.2
John Clawson	G	U.S. Armed Forces (Michigan)	3.6
Don Dee	F	St. Mary of the Plains (Kans.)	4.7
Calvin Fowler	G	Goodyear Wingfoots (St. Francis, Pa.)	6.4
Spencer Haywood	C	Trinidad State J.C. (Colo.)	16.1
Bill Hosket	F	Ohio State	8.6
Jim King	F	Goodyear Wingfoots (Oklahoma State)	1.8
Glynn Saulters	G	Northeast Louisiana	5.3
Charlie Scott	F-G	North Carolina	8.0
Mike Silliman	F	U.S. Armed Forces (Army)	9.0
Ken Spain	C	Houston	4.4
Jo Jo White	G	Kansas	11.7

1972   MUNICH, WEST GERMANY

MEDAL WINNERS: 1. Soviet Union (9-0); 2. U.S. (8-1); 3. Cuba (7-2).

U.S. COACH: Hank Iba, Oklahoma State.

FAST FACT: The United States' 62-game Olympic winning streak ended in the most controversial game in international basketball history. In the final game, three seconds were put back on the clock on two separate occasions before the USSR's Aleksander Belov received a length-of-the-court pass between two U.S. players and converted a game-winning layup. UCLA's Bill Walton became a postdefeat whipping boy in some quarters for not playing on the team.

U.S. MEN'S RESULTS

U.S. 66, Czechoslovakia 35
U.S. 81, Australia 55
U.S. 67, Cuba 48
U.S. 61, Brazil 54
U.S. 96, Egypt 31
U.S. 72, Spain 56
U.S. 99, Japan 33
U.S. 68, Italy 38
USSR 51, U.S. 50

U.S. MEN'S ROSTER AND STATISTICS

PLAYER	POS.	AFFILIATION/SCHOOL	PPG.
Mike Bantom	F	St. Joseph's	7.7
Jim Brewer	F-C	Minnesota	7.6
Tom Burleson	C	North Carolina State	3.4
Doug Collins	G	Illinois State	7.3
Kenny Davis	G	Marathon Oil (Georgetown College)	1.8
Jim Forbes	F	Texas-El Paso	5.1
Tom Henderson	G	St. Jacinto J.C. (Tex.)	9.2
Bobby Jones	F	North Carolina	4.1
Dwight Jones	C	Houston	9.2
Kevin Joyce	G	South Carolina	5.3
Tom McMillen	F	Maryland	6.8
Ed Ratleff	F-G	Long Beach State	6.4

St. Joseph's Mike Bantom, shown here in a regular season game, averaged nearly 8 points per game for the 1972 Olympic basketball team.

1976   MONTREAL, QUEBEC, CANADA

MEDAL WINNERS: 1. U.S. (7-0); 2. Yugoslavia (5-2); 3. Soviet Union (5-2).

U.S. MEN'S COACH: Dean Smith, North Carolina.

FAST FACT: Seven members of the 12-man U.S. roster were from coach Dean Smith's conference although the ACC didn't notch a victory in the 1976 NCAA Tournament. One of the non-ACC players was Notre Dame forward Adrian Dantley, who managed the highest-ever scoring average for a U.S. player in a single Olympiad (19.3 points per game).

U.S. MEN'S RESULTS

U.S. 106, Italy 86
U.S. 95, Puerto Rico 94
U.S. 112, Yugoslavia 93
U.S. 2, Egypt 0*
U.S. 81, Czechoslovakia 76
U.S. 95, Canada 77
U.S. 95, Yugoslavia 74

* The U.S. was awarded a forfeit victory when Egypt withdrew for political reasons.

U.S. MEN'S ROSTER AND STATISTICS

PLAYER	POS.	AFFILIATION/SCHOOL	PPG.	RPG.
Tate Armstrong	G	Duke	2.7	0.4
Quinn Buckner	G	Indiana	7.3	3.0
Kenny Carr	F	North Carolina State	6.8	3.2
Adrian Dantley	F	Notre Dame	19.3	5.7
Walter Davis	F-G	North Carolina	4.3	1.7
Phil Ford	G	North Carolina	11.3	2.2
Ernie Grunfeld	F	Tennessee	3.5	0.7
Phil Hubbard	F	Michigan	4.7	3.8
Mitch Kupchak	C	North Carolina	12.5	5.7
Tom LaGarde	C	North Carolina	6.7	1.8
Scott May	F	Indiana	16.7	6.2
Steve Sheppard	F-G	Maryland	1.5	1.0

1980   MOSCOW, SOVIET UNION

MEDAL WINNERS: 1. Yugoslavia (8-0); 2. Italy (5-3); 3. Soviet Union (6-2).

U.S. MEN'S COACH: Dave Gavitt, Providence.

FAST FACT: Argentina, Canada, China, Mexico, Puerto Rico, and the U.S. all qualified for the Olympics, but they boycotted the Moscow Games in protest of the Soviet Union's invasion of Afghanistan.

U.S. MEN'S ROSTER AND STATISTICS

PLAYER	POS.	SCHOOL	PPG.	RPG.
Mark Aguirre	F	DePaul	11.3	5.0
Rolando Blackman	G-F	Kansas State	8.0	4.7
Sam Bowie	C	Kentucky	11.8	6.9
Michael Brooks	F	La Salle	13.2	6.0
Bill Hanzlik	G	Notre Dame	1.8	1.0
Alton Lister	C	Arizona State	1.7	1.0
Rodney McCray	F	Louisville	0.6	0.8
Isiah Thomas	G	Indiana	9.5	2.0
Darnell Valentine	G	Kansas	5.7	2.0
Danny Vranes	F	Utah	6.8	2.8
Buck Williams	F	Maryland	4.9	4.0
Al Wood	F-G	North Carolina	10.0	2.9

Note: Statistics are for six games (5-1 record) in the "Gold Medal Series" in various U.S. cities against NBA All-Star teams.

1984   LOS ANGELES, CALIFORNIA, USA

MEDAL WINNERS: 1. U.S. (8-0); 2. Spain (6-2); 3. Yugoslavia (7-1).

U.S. MEN'S COACH: Bob Knight, Indiana.

FAST FACT: Political repercussions persisted as the Soviet bloc countries boycotted the Olympic Games in Los Angeles.

U.S. MEN'S RESULTS

U.S. 97, China 49
U.S. 89, Canada 68
U.S. 104, Uruguay 68
U.S. 120, France 62
U.S. 101, Spain 68
U.S. 78, West Germany 67
U.S. 78, Canada 59
U.S. 96, Spain 65

U.S. MEN'S ROSTER AND STATISTICS

PLAYER	POS.	SCHOOL	PPG.	RPG.
Steve Alford	G	Indiana	10.3	3.3
Patrick Ewing	C	Georgetown	11.0	5.6
Vern Fleming	G	Georgia	7.7	2.7
Michael Jordan	G-F	North Carolina	17.1	3.0
Joe Kleine	C	Arkansas	3.4	2.0
Jon Koncak	C	SMU	3.3	2.4
Chris Mullin	G-F	St. John's	11.6	2.5
Sam Perkins	F-C	North Carolina	8.1	5.4
Alvin Robertson	G	Arkansas	7.8	2.8
Wayman Tisdale	F	Oklahoma	8.6	6.4
Jeff Turner	F	Vanderbilt	1.6	2.1
Leon Wood	G	Cal State Fullerton	5.9	2.0

1988   SEOUL, SOUTH KOREA

MEDAL WINNERS: 1. Soviet Union (7-1); 2. Yugoslavia (6-2); 3. U.S. (7-1).

U.S. MEN'S COACH: John Thompson, Georgetown.

FAST FACT: Hersey Hawkins, the team's top outside threat, was sidelined because of an injury when the U.S. sustained a semifinal loss to the USSR in the first Olympic matchup between the superpowers since the controversial 1972 final in Munich.

U.S. MEN'S RESULTS

U.S. 97, Spain 53
U.S. 76, Canada 70
U.S. 102, Brazil 87
U.S. 108, China 57
U.S. 102, Egypt 35
U.S. 94, Puerto Rico 57
USSR 82, U.S. 76
U.S. 78, Australia 49

U.S. MEN'S ROSTER AND STATISTICS

PLAYER	POS.	SCHOOL	PPG.	RPG.
Willie Anderson	G	Georgia	5.0	1.9
Stacey Augmon	F	UNLV	1.2	1.8
Bimbo Coles	G	Virginia Tech	7.1	1.8
Jeff Grayer	F-G	Iowa State	6.9	3.4
Hersey Hawkins	G	Bradley	8.8	1.0
Dan Majerle	F-G	Central Michigan	14.1	4.8
Danny Manning	F	Kansas	11.4	6.0
J. R. Reid	F-C	North Carolina	6.0	3.3
Mitch Richmond	G-F	Kansas State	8.9	3.4
David Robinson	C	Navy	12.8	6.8
Charles D. Smith	F	Pittsburgh	7.8	4.1
Charles E. Smith	G	Georgetown	8.6	1.3

1992   BARCELONA, SPAIN

MEDAL WINNERS: 1. U.S. (8-0); 2. Croatia (6-2); 3. Lithuania (6-2).

U.S. MEN'S COACH: Chuck Daly, New Jersey Nets.

FAST FACT: The "Dream Team," which won its eight games by an average of 43.8 points, was assembled after international rules, which previously prevented only NBA players from being eligible for Olympic basketball, were changed by the FIBA membership on April 7, 1989, by virtue of a 56-13 vote in favor of "open competition."

U.S. MEN'S RESULTS

U.S. 116, Angola 48
U.S. 103, Croatia 70
U.S. 111, Germany 68
U.S. 127, Brazil 83
U.S. 122, Spain 81
U.S. 115, Puerto Rico 77
U.S. 127, Lithuania 76
U.S. 117, Croatia 85

Louisiana Tech's Karl Malone went on to stardom in the NBA as the Utah Jazz's "Mailman" and as a member of the 1992 Olympic "Dream Team."

U.S. MEN'S ROSTER AND STATISTICS

PLAYER	POS.	NBA TEAM/SCHOOL	PPG.	RPG.
Charles Barkley	F	Phoenix Suns (Auburn)	18.0	4.1
Larry Bird	F	Boston Celtics (Indiana State)	8.4	3.8
Clyde Drexler	G	Portland Trail Blazers (Houston)	10.5	3.0
Patrick Ewing	C	New York Knicks (Georgetown)	9.5	5.3
Earvin "Magic" Johnson	G	Los Angeles Lakers (Michigan St.	8.0	2.3
Michael Jordan	G	Chicago Bulls (North Carolina)	14.9	2.4
Christian Laettner*	F	Duke	4.8	2.5
Karl Malone	F	Utah Jazz (Louisiana Tech)	13.0	5.3
Chris Mullin	F-G	Golden State Warriors (St. John's)	12.9	1.6
Scottie Pippen	F	Chicago Bulls (Central Arkansas)	9.0	2.1
David Robinson	C	San Antonio Spurs (Navy)	9.0	4.1
John Stockton	G	Utah Jazz (Gonzaga)	2.8	0.3

* Drafted by the Minnesota Timberwolves.

Women's Basketball

1976 MONTREAL, QUEBEC, CANADA

MEDAL WINNERS: 1. Soviet Union (5-0); 2. U.S. (3-2); 3. Bulgaria (3-2).

U.S. WOMEN'S COACH: Billie Jean Moore, Cal State Fullerton.

U.S. WOMEN'S RESULTS

Japan 84, U.S. 71
U.S. 95, Bulgaria 79
U.S. 89, Canada 75
USSR 112, U.S. 77
U.S. 83, Czechoslovakia 67

U.S. WOMEN'S LEADING SCORERS

PLAYER	POS.	SCHOOL	PPG.
Lusia Harris	F	Delta State (Miss.)	15.2
Nancy Dunkle	C	Cal State Fullerton	13.0
Patricia Roberts	F	Tennessee	12.0
Ann Meyers	G	UCLA	9.6

1980 MOSCOW, SOVIET UNION

MEDAL WINNERS: 1. Soviet Union (6-0); 2. Bulgaria (4-2); 3. Yugoslavia (4-2).

U.S. WOMEN'S COACH: Sue Gunter, Stephen F. Austin State (Tex.).

U.S. WOMEN'S LEADING SCORERS

PLAYER	POS.	SCHOOL	PPG.
Denise Curry	F	UCLA	17.8
Cindy Noble	C	Tennessee	13.8
Rosie Walker	F	Stephen F. Austin State	12.7
LaTaunya Pollard	F	Long Beach State	12.0
Carol Blazejowski	G	Montclair State (N.J.)	10.7
Tara Heiss	G	Maryland	5.7
Anne Donovan	C	Old Dominion	5.2

Note: Statistics are for six of seven games (6-1 record) in the FIBA Pre-Olympic Qualifying Tournament in Bulgaria.

1984 LOS ANGELES, CALIFORNIA, USA

MEDAL WINNERS: 1. U.S. (6-0); 2. South Korea (4-2); 3. Canada (3-3).

U.S. WOMEN'S COACH: Pat Head Summitt, Tennessee.

U.S. WOMEN'S RESULTS

U.S. 83, Yugoslavia 55
U.S. 81, Australia 47
U.S. 84, South Korea 47
U.S. 91, China 55
U.S. 92, Canada 61
U.S. 85, South Korea 55

U.S. WOMEN'S LEADING SCORERS

PLAYER	POS.	SCHOOL	PPG.
Cheryl Miller	F	Southern Cal	16.5
Lynette Woodard	G	Kansas	10.5
Janice Lawrence	C	Louisiana Tech	9.5
Cindy Noble	C	Tennessee	8.7
Anne Donovan	C	Old Dominion	7.5
Denise Curry	F	UCLA	7.0
Pam McGee	C	Southern Cal	6.2

1988 SEOUL, SOUTH KOREA

MEDAL WINNERS: 1. U.S. (5-0); 2. Yugoslavia (3-2); 3. Soviet Union (3-2).

U.S. WOMEN'S COACH: Kay Yow, North Carolina State.

U.S. WOMEN'S RESULTS

U.S. 87, Czechoslovakia 81
U.S. 101, Yugoslavia 74
U.S. 94, China 79
U.S. 102, USSR 88
U.S. 77, Yugoslavia 70

U.S. WOMEN'S LEADING SCORERS

PLAYER	POS.	SCHOOL	PPG.
Katrina McClain	F	Georgia	17.6
Teresa Edwards	G	Georgia	16.6
Cynthia Cooper	G	Southern Cal	14.2
Bridgette Gordon	F	Tennessee	8.8
Suzie McConnell	G	Penn State	8.4
Cindy Brown	F	Long Beach State	8.0
Andrea Lloyd	F	Texas	6.6

North Carolina State's Kay Yow coached the 1988 women's Olympic basketball team to a gold medal.

BARCELONA, SPAIN

MEDAL WINNERS: 1. Unified Team (5-0); 2. China (4-1); 3. U.S. (4-1).
U.S. WOMEN'S COACH: Theresa Grentz, Rutgers.

U.S. WOMEN'S RESULTS

U.S. 111, Czechoslovakia 55
U.S. 114, Spain 59
U.S. 93, China 67
Unified 79, U.S. 73
U.S. 88, Cuba 74

U.S. WOMEN'S LEADING SCORERS

PLAYER	POS.	SCHOOL	PPG.
Medina Dixon	F	Old Dominion	15.8
Clarissa Davis	F	Texas	13.0
Teresa Edwards	F	Georgia	12.6
Katrina McClain	F	Georgia	11.4
Cynthia Cooper	G	Southern Cal	7.6
Vickie Orr	F	Auburn	7.6
Tammy Jackson	C	Florida	7.2
Suzie McConnell	G	Penn State	6.8
Daedra Charles	C	Tennessee	6.2

14

CONFERENCE DIRECTORY

The nation's NCAA Division I schools have been in a frenetic restructuring of conferences although the quest for megaleagues might be a delusion because they're vying for television revenue that simply doesn't exist anymore as network sports divisions operate at ample deficits.

Only three Division I conferences have remained intact since the late 1980s—the Ivy League, Pacific-10, and West Coast. Although the TV well is dry and no amount of realigning will alter the marketplace, almost one-fourth of the nearly 300 Division I schools changed conferences or shed independent status in the first half of the 1990s. Many of the recent moves failed to cause a ripple on the national landscape, but conference conflicts have existed for an extended period. For instance, the Big Eight and Missouri Valley are still debating which league can legitimately be credited with being the oldest conference west of the Mississippi. They both stake a claim to the 21 seasons of the old Missouri Valley Intercollegiate Athletic Association from 1908 to 1928.

A time-honored argument also rages each season on the court: Which conference plays the best basketball? The debate attained new heights in 1980, the Big East's initial campaign and the year the NCAA Tournament expanded its field to 48 teams. Naturally, the NCAA playoffs are an accurate barometer to determine the longstanding or recent strength of a league. Consider the following postseason achievements:

- The Atlantic Coast Conference (ACC) is the only league to have each of its members play at least 10 games in the NCAA playoffs. Incredibly, all nine ACC members have winning NCAA Tournament records and have advanced to the Sweet 16 since the field expanded to 64 teams. Perhaps the greatest testimony to the ACC's consistent brilliance is the league's average of 11 tournament victories annually since the field expanded to at least 52 teams in 1983. No other league through 1994 had ever enjoyed back-to-back tourneys with more than 10 triumphs.

- The Big East is the only league to have three representatives at a single Final Four— Georgetown, St. John's, and Villanova in 1985 after they all defeated ACC members in 1985 regional finals.

- Following the 1993–94 season, the Big Ten had the most Final Four teams (33) and the most different members win the NCAA title (five).

- The Big Eight sent more teams (six) to the 1992 NCAA Tournament than any league and tied the ACC for the most playoff delegates in 1993 with six. In 1988, Kansas and Oklahoma enabled the Big Eight to become the only league to have two members meet in the NCAA final from 1986 to 1994.

- The Great Midwest entered the 1994–95 season as the only league with all of its members (seven) having reached the national semifinals of the NCAA Tournament or NIT.

- The Pacific-10, with nine of its 10 schools advancing to the national semifinals at least once, boasts the highest percentage of present league members to reach the Final Four.

- In 1994, the SEC compiled the best winning percentage in a single tourney for a league with at least three entrants (12-3 record, .800).

Putting provincialism aside, here are vital facts on Division I conferences. Each season is denoted by a single year. For example, the ACC's first season in 1953–54 is listed as 1954. The numbers in parentheses after schools with regular-season champions denote undisputed titles first and then ties.

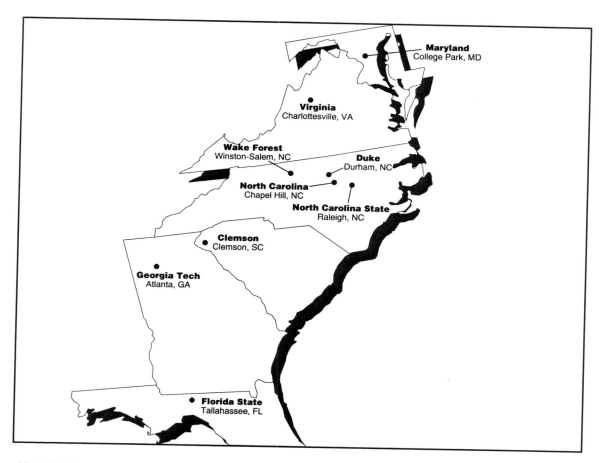

Maryland
College Park, MD

Virginia
Charlottesville, VA

Wake Forest
Winston-Salem, NC

Duke
Durham, NC

North Carolina
Chapel Hill, NC

North Carolina State
Raleigh, NC

Clemson
Clemson, SC

Georgia Tech
Atlanta, GA

Florida State
Tallahassee, FL

ATLANTIC COAST

ADDRESS: 6011 Landmark Center Boulevard, P.O. Drawer ACC, Greensboro, NC 27419-6999.

TELEPHONE/FAX: (910) 854-8787/8797.

CURRENT MEMBERS: Clemson (1954–), Duke (1954–), Florida State (1992–), Georgia Tech (1980–), Maryland (1954–), North Carolina (1954–), North Carolina State (1954–), Virginia (1954–), Wake Forest (1954–).

FORMER MEMBER: South Carolina (1954–71).

NCAA TITLES (7): Duke (1991 and 1992), North Carolina (1957-82-93), North Carolina State (1974 and 1983).

NIT TITLES (4): Maryland (1972), North Carolina (1971), Virginia (1980 and 1992).

ALL-TIME LEADING SCORER: Johnny Dawkins, Duke (2,556 points, 1983–86). Dickie Hemric of Wake Forest (1952–55) scored 2,587 points but the first two seasons of his career preceded the formation of the ACC.

REGULAR-SEASON CHAMPIONS: Clemson (1 outright-0 ties), Duke (11-0), Georgia Tech (0-1), Maryland (2-0), North Carolina (14-7), North Carolina State (4-3), South Carolina (1-0), Virginia (1-2), Wake Forest (1-1).

ACC TOURNAMENT TITLES: North Carolina (13), N.C. State (10), Duke (9), Georgia Tech (3), Maryland (2), Wake Forest (2), South Carolina (1), Virginia (1).

YEAR-BY-YEAR CHAMPIONS (incl. conference records): 1954—Duke (9-1); **1955**—N.C. State (12-2); **1956**—North Carolina (11-3), N.C. State (11-3); **1957**—North Carolina (14-0); **1958**—Duke (11-3); **1959**—North Carolina (12-2), N.C. State (12-2); **1960**—North Carolina (12-2), Wake Forest (12-2); **1961**—North Carolina (12-2); **1962**—Wake Forest (12-2); **1963**—Duke (14-0); **1964**—Duke (13-1); **1965**—Duke (11-3); **1966**—Duke (12-2); **1967**—North Carolina (12-2); **1968**—North Carolina (12-2); **1969**—North Carolina (12-2); **1970**—South Carolina (14-0); **1971**—North Carolina (11-3); **1972**—North Carolina (9-3); **1973**—N.C. State (12-0); **1974**—N.C. State (12-0); **1975**—Maryland (10-2); **1976**—North Carolina (11-1); **1977**—North Carolina (9-3); **1978**—North Carolina (9-3); **1979**—Duke (9-3), North Carolina (9-3); **1980**—Maryland (11-3); **1981**—Virginia (13-1); **1982**—North Carolina (12-2), Virginia (12-2); **1983**—North Carolina (12-2), Virginia (12-2); **1984**—North Carolina (14-0); **1985**—Georgia Tech (9-3), North Carolina (9-3), N.C. State (9-3); **1986**—Duke (12-2); **1987**—North Carolina (14-0); **1988**—North Carolina (11-3); **1989**—N.C. State (10-4); **1990**—Clemson (10-4); **1991**—Duke (11-3); **1992**—Duke (14-2); **1993**—North Carolina (14-2); **1994**—Duke (12-4).

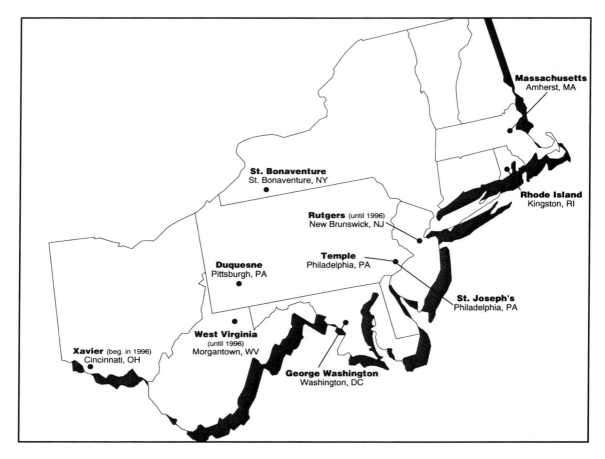

ATLANTIC 10

ADDRESS: 101 Interchange Plaza, Suite 202, Cranbury, NJ 08512.

TELEPHONE/FAX: (609) 860-9100/0142.

PREVIOUS NAMES: Eastern Collegiate Basketball League (1977), Eastern Athletic Association or Eastern 8 (1978–1982).

CURRENT MEMBERS: Duquesne (1977– , except for 1993), George Washington (1977–), Massachusetts (1977–), Rhode Island (1981–), Rutgers (1977– ; slated to join Big East in 1996), St. Bonaventure (1980–), St. Joseph's (1983–), Temple (1983–), West Virginia (1977– ; slated to join Big East in 1996. Xavier will join Atlantic 10 in 1996.

FORMER MEMBERS: Penn State (1977–79 and 1983–91), Pittsburgh (1977–82), Villanova (1977–80).

NIT TITLES (5): Duquesne (1955), St. Bonaventure (1977), Temple (1938 and 1969) and West Virginia (1942) won before joining Atlantic 10.

ALL-TIME LEADING SCORER: Mark Macon, Temple (2,609 points, 1988–91).

REGULAR-SEASON CHAMPIONS: Duquesne (0 outright-2 ties), Massachusetts (3-0), Penn State (0-1), Rhode Island (0-1), Rutgers (3-2), St. Bonaventure (0-1), St. Joseph's (1-0), Temple (4-0), Villanova (1-2), West Virginia (3-2).

ATLANTIC 10 TOURNAMENT TITLES: Temple (4), Massachusetts (3), Pittsburgh (2), Rutgers (2), Villanova (2), West Virginia (2), Duquesne (1), St. Joseph's (1).

YEAR-BY-YEAR CHAMPIONS (incl. conference records): **1977**—Rutgers (7-1/E), Penn State (5-5/W), West Virginia (5-5/W); **1978**—Rutgers (7-3), Villanova (7-3); **1979**—Villanova (9-1); **1980**—Duquesne (7-3), Rutgers (7-3), Villanova (7-3); **1981**—Duquesne (10-3), Rhode Island (10-3); **1982**—West Virginia (13-1); **1983**—Rutgers (11-3/E), St. Bonaventure (10-4/W), West Virginia (10-4/W); **1984**—Temple (18-0); **1985**—West Virginia (16-2); **1986**—St. Joseph's (16-2); **1987**—Temple (17-1); **1988**—Temple (18-0); **1989**—West Virginia (17-1); **1990**—Temple (15-3); **1991**—Rutgers (14-4); **1992**—Massachusetts (13-3); **1993**—Massachusetts (11-3); **1994**—Massachusetts (14-2).

Note: The Atlantic 10 had Eastern and Western Divisions for one season in 1982–83.

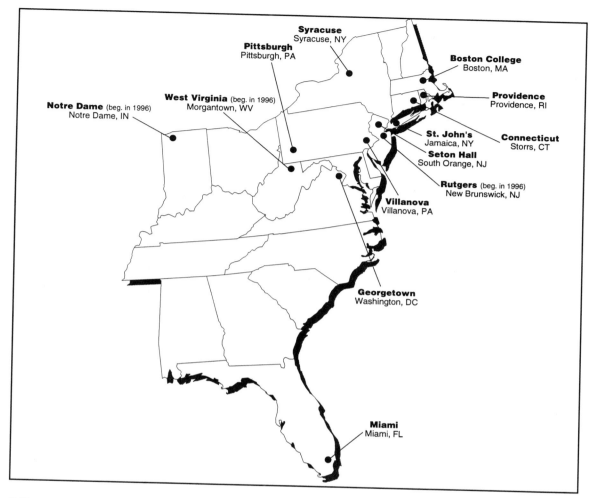

BIG EAST

ADDRESS: 56 Exchange Terrace, Providence, RI 02903.

TELEPHONE/FAX: (401) 272-9108/751-8540.

CURRENT MEMBERS: Boston College (1980–), Connecticut (1980–), Georgetown (1980–), Miami, Fla. (1992–), Pittsburgh (1983–), Providence (1980–), St. John's (1980–), Seton Hall (1980–), Syracuse (1980–), Villanova (1981–). Notre Dame, Rutgers, and West Virginia are slated to join in 1996.

NCAA TITLES (2): Georgetown (1984) and Villanova (1985).

NIT TITLES (10): Connecticut (1988), Providence (1961 and 1963), St. John's (1943-44-59-65-89), Seton Hall (1953), Villanova (1994). Three of the titles were earned since the formation of the league.

ALL-TIME LEADING SCORER: Terry Dehere, Seton Hall (2,494 points, 1990–93).

REGULAR-SEASON CHAMPIONS: Boston College (1 outright-1 tie), Connecticut (1-1), Georgetown (2-3), Pittsburgh (1-1), St. John's (1-3), Seton Hall (1-1), Syracuse (1-4), Villanova (1-1).

BIG EAST TOURNAMENT TITLES: Georgetown (6), Syracuse (3), St. John's (2), Seton Hall (2), Connecticut (1), Providence (1).

YEAR-BY-YEAR CHAMPIONS (incl. conference records): 1980—Georgetown (5-1), St. John's (5-1), Syracuse (5-1); **1981**—Boston College (10-4); **1982**—Villanova (11-3); **1983**—Boston College (12-4), St. John's (12-4), Villanova (12-4); **1984**—Georgetown (14-2); **1985**—St. John's (15-1); **1986**—St. John's (14-2), Syracuse (14-2); **1987**—Georgetown (12-4), Pittsburgh (12- 4), Syracuse (12-4); **1988**—Pittsburgh (12-4); **1989**—Georgetown (13-3); **1990**—Connecticut (12-4), Syracuse (12-4); **1991**—Syracuse (12-4); **1992**—Georgetown (12-6), St. John's (12-6), Seton Hall (12-6); **1993**—Seton Hall (14-4); **1994**—Connecticut (16-2).

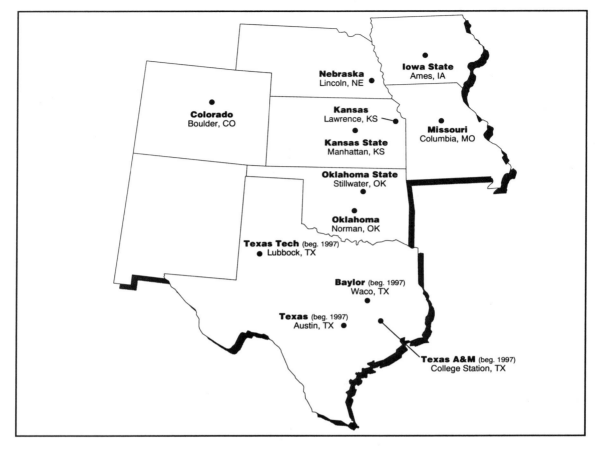

BIG EIGHT

ADDRESS: 104 West 9th Street, Suite 408, Kansas City, MO 64105-1755.

TELEPHONE/FAX: (816) 471-5088/4601.

PREVIOUS NAMES: Big Six (1929–47), Big Seven (1948–58).

FUTURE NAME: Big 12 (starting in 1997 when Baylor, Texas, Texas A&M, and Texas Tech are slated to join).

CURRENT MEMBERS: Colorado (1948–), Iowa State (1929–), Kansas (1929–), Kansas State (1929–), Missouri (1929–), Nebraska (1929–), Oklahoma (1929–), Oklahoma State (1959–).

NCAA TITLES (4): Oklahoma State (1945 and 1946), Kansas (1952 and 1988). Oklahoma State's titles came before the school joined the Big Eight.

NIT TITLES (1): Colorado (1940 before joining league).

ALL-TIME LEADING SCORER: Danny Manning, Kansas (2,951 points, 1985–88).

REGULAR-SEASON CHAMPIONS (SINCE 1929): Colorado (3 outright-2 ties), Iowa State (2-2), Kansas (20-8), Kansas State (12-3), Missouri (9-2), Nebraska (0-3), Oklahoma (7-5), Oklahoma State (1-1).

BIG EIGHT TOURNAMENT TITLES: Missouri (6), Kansas (4), Oklahoma (4), Kansas State (2), Nebraska (1), Oklahoma State (1).

YEAR-BY-YEAR CHAMPIONS (incl. conference records): 1929—Oklahoma (10-0); 1930—Missouri (8-2); 1931—Kansas (7-3); 1932—Kansas (7-3); 1933—Kansas (8-2); 1934—Kansas (9-1); 1935—Iowa State (8-2);

1936—Kansas (10-0); 1937—Kansas (8-2), Nebraska (8-2); 1938—Kansas (9-1); 1939—Missouri (7-3), Oklahoma (7-3); 1940—Kansas (8-2)*, Missouri (8-2), Oklahoma (8-2); 1941—Iowa State (7-3), Kansas (7-3); 1942—Kansas (8-2), Oklahoma (8-2); 1943—Kansas (10-0); 1944—Iowa State (9-1), Oklahoma (9-1); 1945—Iowa State (8-2); 1946—Kansas (10-0); 1947—Oklahoma (8-2); 1948—Kansas State (9-3); 1949—Nebraska (9-3), Oklahoma (9-3); 1950—Kansas (8-4), Kansas State (8-4), Nebraska (8-4); 1951—Kansas State (11-1); 1952—Kansas (11-1); 1953—Kansas (10-2); 1954—Colorado (10-2), Kansas (10-2); 1955—Colorado (11-1); 1956—Kansas State (9-3); 1957—Kansas (11-1); 1958—Kansas State (10-2); 1959—Kansas State (14-0); 1960—Kansas (10-4)*, Kansas State (10-4); 1961—Kansas State (13-1); 1962—Colorado (13-1); 1963—Colorado (11-3), Kansas State (11-3); 1964—Kansas State (12-2); 1965—Oklahoma State (12-2); 1966—Kansas (13-1); 1967—Kansas (13-1); 1968—Kansas State (11-3); 1969—Colorado (10-4); 1970—Kansas State (10-4); 1971—Kansas (14-0); 1972—Kansas State (12-2); 1973—Kansas State (12-2); 1974—Kansas (13-1); 1975—Kansas (11-3); 1976—Missouri (12-2); 1977—Kansas State (11-3); 1978—Kansas (13-1); 1979—Oklahoma (10-4); 1980—Missouri (11-3); 1981—Missouri (10-4); 1982—Missouri (12-2); 1983—Missouri (12-2); 1984—Oklahoma (13-1); 1985—Oklahoma (13-1); 1986—Kansas (13-1); 1987—Missouri (11-3); 1988—Oklahoma (12-2); 1989—Oklahoma (12-2); 1990—Missouri (12-2); 1991—Kansas (10-4), Oklahoma State (10-4); 1992—Kansas (11-3); 1993—Kansas (11-3); 1994—Missouri (14-0).

* Won playoff period.

Note: Kansas won 13 of the 21 Missouri Valley Intercollegiate Athletic Association titles from 1908 to 1928.

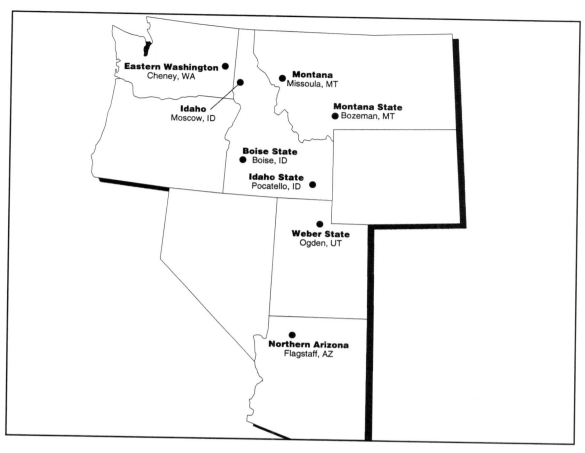

BIG SKY

ADDRESS: 106 North Sixth Street, Suite 202, Boise, ID 83702.

TELEPHONE/FAX: (208) 345-0281/343-6804.

CURRENT MEMBERS: Boise State (1971–), Eastern Washington (1988–), Idaho (1964–), Idaho State (1964–), Montana (1964–), Montana State (1964–), Northern Arizona (1971–), Weber State (1964–).

FORMER MEMBERS: Gonzaga (1964–79), Nevada–Reno (1980-92).

ALL-TIME LEADING SCORER: Orlando Lightfoot, Idaho (2,102 points, 1992–94).

REGULAR-SEASON CHAMPIONS: Boise State (1 outright-2 ties), Gonzaga (0-2), Idaho (4-1), Idaho State (1-3), Montana (4-2), Montana State (2-1), Nevada-Reno (1-1), Northern Arizona (0-1), Weber State (10-4).

BIG SKY TOURNAMENT TITLES: Boise State (4), Idaho (4), Weber State (4), Idaho State (2), Montana (2), Nevada (2), Montana State (1).

YEAR-BY-YEAR CHAMPIONS (incl. conference records): 1964—Montana State (8-2); **1965**—Weber State (8-2); **1966**—Gonzaga (8-2), Weber State (8-2); **1967**—Gonzaga (7-3), Montana State (7-3); **1968**—Weber State (12-3); **1969**—Weber State (15-0); **1970**—Weber State (12-3); **1971**—Weber State (12-2); **1972**—Weber State (10-4); **1973**—Weber State (13-1); **1974**—Idaho State (11-3)*, Montana (11-3); **1975**—Montana (13-1); **1976**—Boise State (9-5), Idaho (9-5), Weber State (9-5); **1977**—Idaho State (13-1); **1978**—Montana (12-2); **1979**—Weber State (10-4); **1980**—Weber State (13-1); **1981**—Idaho (12-2); **1982**—Idaho (13-1); **1983**—Nevada (10-4), Weber State (10-4); **1984**—Weber State (12-2); **1985**—Nevada (11-3); **1986**—Montana (9-5), Northern Arizona (9-5); **1987**—Montana State (12-2); **1988**—Boise State (13-3); **1989**—Boise State (13-3), Idaho (13-3); **1990**—Idaho (13-3); **1991**—Montana (13-3); **1992**—Montana (14-2); **1993**—Idaho (11-3); **1994**—Idaho State (10-4), Weber State (10-4).

   * Won playoff.

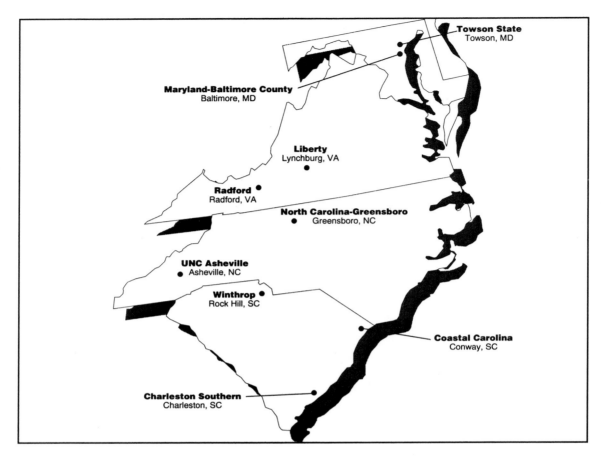

Towson State
Towson, MD

Maryland-Baltimore County
Baltimore, MD

Liberty
Lynchburg, VA

Radford
Radford, VA

North Carolina-Greensboro
Greensboro, NC

UNC Asheville
Asheville, NC

Winthrop
Rock Hill, SC

Coastal Carolina
Conway, SC

Charleston Southern
Charleston, SC

BIG SOUTH

ADDRESS: 1551 21st Avenue North, Suite 11, Myrtle Beach, SC 29577.

TELEPHONE/FAX: (803) 448-9998/626-7167.

CURRENT MEMBERS: Charleston Southern (1986–), Coastal Carolina (1986–), Liberty (1992–), Maryland-Baltimore County (1993–), UNC Asheville (1986–), North Carolina-Greensboro (1993–), Radford (1986–), Towson State (1993–), Winthrop (1986–).

FORMER MEMBERS: Armstrong State (1986 and 1987), Augusta (1986–91), Campbell (1986–94), Davidson (1991 and 1992).

ALL-TIME LEADING SCORER: Tony Dunkin, Coastal Carolina (2,151 points, 1990–93).

REGULAR-SEASON CHAMPIONS: Charleston Southern (2 outright-0 ties), Coastal Carolina (4-0), Radford (1-0), Towson State (2-0).

BIG SOUTH TOURNAMENT TITLES: Coastal Carolina (3), Charleston Southern (2), Liberty (1), Campbell (1), UNC Asheville (1), Winthrop (1).

YEAR-BY-YEAR CHAMPIONS (incl. conference records): 1986—Charleston Southern (5-1); **1987**—Charleston Southern (12-2); **1988**—Coastal Carolina (9-3); **1989**—Coastal Carolina (9-3); **1990**—Coastal Carolina (11-1); **1991**—Coastal Carolina (13-1); **1992**—Radford (12-2); **1993**—Towson State (14-2); **1994**—Towson State (16-2).

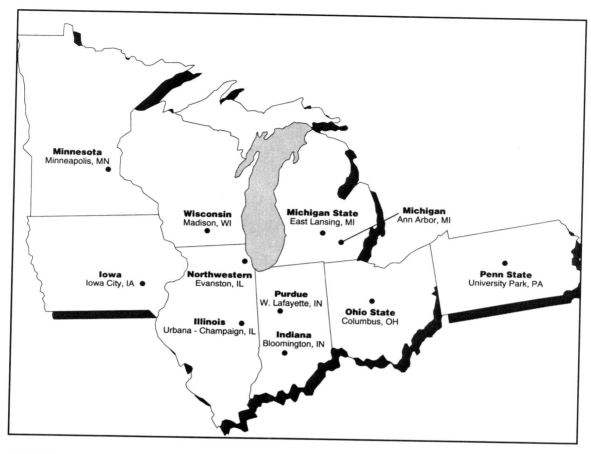

BIG TEN

ADDRESS: 1500 West Higgins Road, Park Ridge, IL 60068-6300.

TELEPHONE/FAX: (708) 696-1010/1110.

PREVIOUS NAME: Intercollegiate Conference of Faculty Representatives or Western Conference.

CURRENT MEMBERS: Illinois (1906–), Indiana (1906–), Iowa (1909–), Michigan (1918–), Michigan State (1951–), Minnesota (1906–), Northwestern (1909–), Ohio State (1913–), Penn State (1993–), Purdue (1906–), Wisconsin (1906–).

FORMER MEMBER: University of Chicago (1906–46).

NCAA TITLES (9): Indiana (1940-53-76-81-87), Michigan (1989), Michigan State (1979), Ohio State (1960), Wisconsin (1941).

NIT TITLES (5): Indiana (1979), Michigan (1984), Minnesota (1993), Ohio State (1986), Purdue (1974).

ALL-TIME LEADING SCORER: Calbert Cheaney, Indiana (2,613 points, 1990–93).

REGULAR-SEASON CHAMPIONS: Chicago (3 outright-3 ties), Illinois (6-6), Indiana (11-8), Iowa (4-4), Michigan (7-5), Michigan State (3-3), Minnesota (4-4), Northwestern (1-1), Ohio State (10-5), Purdue (9-9), Wisconsin (7-7).

YEAR-BY-YEAR CHAMPIONS (incl. conference records): 1906—Minnesota (6-1); **1907**—Chicago (6-2), Minnesota (6-2); **1908**—Chicago (7-1), Wisconsin (7-1); **1909**—Chicago (12-0); **1910**—Chicago (9-3); **1911**—Minnesota (8-4), Purdue (8-4); **1912**—Wisconsin (12-0); **1913**—Wisconsin (11-1); **1914**—Wisconsin (12-0); **1915**—Illinois (12-0);

1916—Wisconsin (11-1); **1917**—Illinois (10-2), Minnesota (10-2); **1918**—Wisconsin (9-3); **1919**—Minnesota (10-0); **1920**—Chicago (10-2); **1921**—Michigan (8-4), Purdue (8-4), Wisconsin (8-4); **1922**—Purdue (8-1); **1923**—Iowa (11-1), Wisconsin (11-1); **1924**—Chicago (8-4), Illinois (8-4), Wisconsin (8-4); **1925**—Ohio State (11-1); **1926**—Indiana (8-4), Iowa (8-4), Michigan (8-4), Purdue (8-4); **1927**—Michigan (10-2); **1928**—Indiana (10-2), Purdue (10-2); **1929**—Michigan (10-2), Wisconsin (10-2); **1930**—Purdue (10-0); **1931**—Northwestern (11-1); **1932**—Purdue (11-1); **1933**—Northwestern (10-2), Ohio State (10-2); **1934**—Purdue (10-2); **1935**—Illinois (9-3), Purdue (9-3), Wisconsin (9-3); **1936**—Indiana (11-1), Purdue (11-1); **1937**—Illinois (10-2), Minnesota (10-2); **1938**—Purdue (10-2); **1939**—Ohio State (10-2); **1940**—Purdue (10-2); **1941**—Wisconsin (11-1); **1942**—Illinois (13-2); **1943**—Illinois (12-0); **1944**—Ohio State (10-2); **1945**—Iowa (11-1); **1946**—Ohio State (10-2); **1947**—Wisconsin (9-3); **1948**—Michigan (10-2); **1949**—Illinois (10-2); **1950**—Ohio State (11-1); **1951**—Illinois (13-1); **1952**—Illinois (12-2); **1953**—Indiana (17-1); **1954**—Indiana (12-2); **1955**—Iowa (11-3); **1956**—Iowa (13-1); **1957**—Indiana (10-4), Michigan State (10-4); **1958**—Indiana (10-4); **1959**—Michigan State (12-2); **1960**—Ohio State (13-1); **1961**—Ohio State (14-0); **1962**—Ohio State (13-1); **1963**—Illinois (11-3), Ohio State (11-3); **1964**—Michigan (11-3), Ohio State (11-3); **1965**—Michigan (13-1); **1966**—Michigan (11-3); **1967**—Indiana (10-4), Michigan State (10-4); **1968**—Iowa (10-4), Ohio State (10-4); **1969**—Purdue (13-1); **1970**—Iowa (14-0); **1971**—Ohio State (13-1); **1972**—Minnesota (11-3); **1973**—Indiana (11-3); **1974**—Indiana (12-2); **1975**—Indiana (18-0); **1976**—Indiana (18-0); **1977**—Michigan (16-2); **1978**—Michigan State (15-3), Purdue (13-5); **1979**—Iowa (13-5), Michigan State (13-5); **1980**—Indiana (13-5); **1981**—Indiana (14-4); **1982**—Minnesota (14-4); **1983**—Indiana (13-5); **1984**—Illinois (15-3), Purdue (15-3); **1985**—Michigan (16-2); **1986**—Michigan (14-4); **1987**—Indiana (15-3), Purdue (15-3); **1988**—Purdue (16-2); **1989**—Indiana (15-3); **1990**—Michigan State (15-3); **1991**—Indiana (15-3), Ohio State (15-3); **1992**—Ohio State (15-3); **1993**—Indiana (17-1); **1994**—Purdue (14-4).

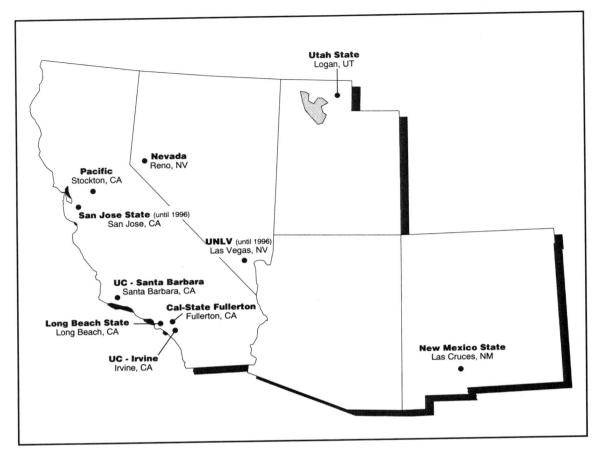

BIG WEST

ADDRESS: 2 Corporate Park, Suite 206, Irvine, CA 92714.

TELEPHONE/FAX: (714) 261-2525/2528.

PREVIOUS NAME: Pacific Coast Athletic Association.

CURRENT MEMBERS: UC Irvine (1978–), UC Santa Barbara (1970–74 and 1977–), Cal State Fullerton (1975–), Long Beach State (1970–), Nevada (1993–), New Mexico State (1984–), Pacific (1972–), San Jose State (1970–95; will join Western Athletic in 1996), UNLV (1983–95; will join Western Athletic in 1996), Utah State (1979–).

FORMER MEMBERS: Cal State Los Angeles (1970–74), Fresno State (1970–92), San Diego State (1970–78).

NCAA TITLES (1): UNLV (1990).

ALL-TIME LEADING SCORER: Lucious Harris, Long Beach State (2,312 points, 1990–93).

REGULAR-SEASON CHAMPIONS: Cal State Fullerton (0 outright–1 tie), Fresno State (2-1), Long Beach State (6-2), New Mexico State (2-1), Pacific (1-0), San Diego State (0-2), UNLV (9-1), Utah State (1-0).

BIG WEST TOURNAMENT TITLES: UNLV (7), Fresno State (3), Long Beach State (2), New Mexico State (2), Cal State Fullerton (1), Pacific (1), San Diego State (1), San Jose State (1), Utah State (1).

YEAR-BY-YEAR CHAMPIONS (incl. conference records): 1970—Long Beach State (10-0); **1971**—Long Beach State (10-0); **1972**—Long Beach State (10-2); **1973**—Long Beach State (10-2); **1974**—Long Beach State (12-0); **1975**—Long Beach State (8-2); **1976**—Cal State Fullerton (6-4), Long Beach State (6-4); **1977**—Long Beach State (9-3), San Diego State (9-3); **1978**—Fresno State (11-3), San Diego State (11-3); **1979**—Pacific (11-3); **1980**—Utah State (11-2); **1981**—Fresno State (12-2); **1982**—Fresno State (13-1); **1983**—UNLV (15-1); **1984**—UNLV (16-2); **1985**—UNLV (17-1); **1986**—UNLV (16-2); **1987**—UNLV (18-0); **1988**—UNLV (15-3); **1989**—UNLV (16-2); **1990**—New Mexico State (16-2), UNLV (16-2); **1991**—UNLV (18-0); **1992**—UNLV (18-0); **1993**—New Mexico State (15-3); **1994**—New Mexico State (12-6).

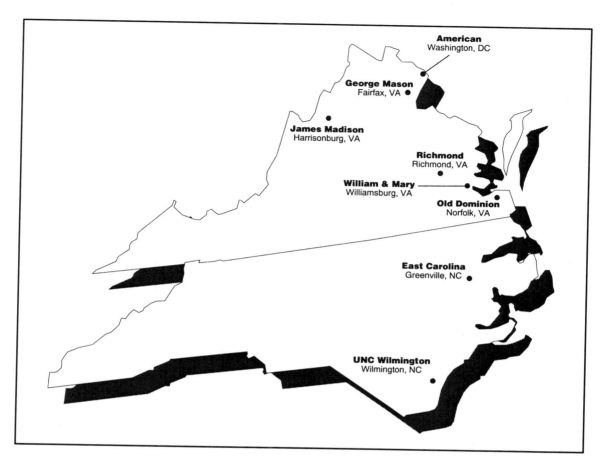

COLONIAL ATHLETIC ASSOCIATION

ADDRESS: 8625 Patterson Avenue, Richmond, VA 23229-6349.

TELEPHONE/FAX: (804) 754-1616/1830.

PREVIOUS NAME: ECAC South (1983-86).

CURRENT MEMBERS: American (1985–), East Carolina (1983–), George Mason (1983–), James Madison (1983–), UNC Wilmington (1985–), Old Dominion (1992–), Richmond (1983–), William & Mary (1983–).

FORMER MEMBER: Navy (1983–91).

ALL-TIME LEADING SCORER: David Robinson, Navy (2,669 points, 1984–87).

REGULAR-SEASON CHAMPIONS: James Madison (2 outright-3 ties), Navy (2-1), Old Dominion (0-2), Richmond (3-2), William & Mary (1-0).

CAA TOURNAMENT TITLES: Richmond (4), Navy (3), James Madison (2), East Carolina (1), George Mason (1), Old Dominion (1).

YEAR-BY-YEAR CHAMPIONS (incl. conference records): 1983—William & Mary (9-0); **1984**—Richmond (7-3); **1985**—Navy (11-3), Richmond (11-3); **1986**—Navy (13-1); **1987**—Navy (13-1); **1988**—Richmond (11-3); **1989**—Richmond (13-1); **1990**—James Madison (11-3); **1991**—James Madison (12-2), Richmond (12-2); **1992**—James Madison (12-2); **1993**—James Madison (11-3), Old Dominion (11-3); **1994**—James Madison (10-4), Old Dominion (10-4).

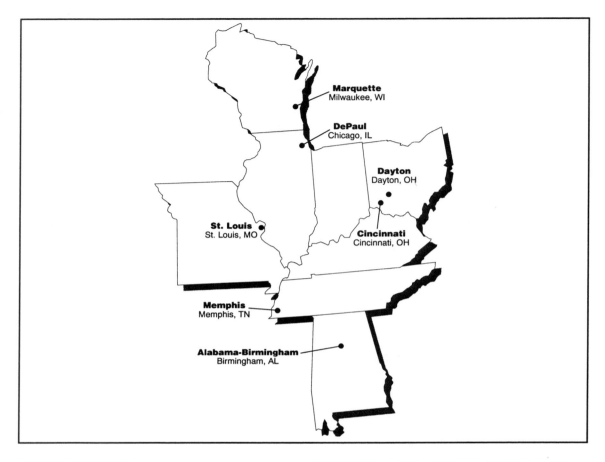

GREAT MIDWEST

ADDRESS: 35 East Wacker Drive, Suite 650, Chicago, IL 60601.

TELEPHONE/FAX: (312) 553-0483/0495.

CURRENT MEMBERS: Alabama-Birmingham (1992–), Cincinnati (1992–), Dayton (1994–), DePaul (1992–), Marquette (1992–), Memphis (1992–), St. Louis (1992–).

NCAA TITLES (3): Cincinnati (1961 and 1962), Marquette (1977). Titles were before formation of league.

NIT TITLES (4): Dayton (1962 and 1968), DePaul (1945), St. Louis (1948). Titles were before formation of league.

REGULAR-SEASON CHAMPIONS: Cincinnati (1 outright-1 tie), DePaul (0-1), Marquette (1-0).

GMC TOURNAMENT TITLES: Cincinnati (3).

YEAR-BY-YEAR CHAMPIONS (incl. conference records): 1992—Cincinnati (8-2), DePaul (8-2); **1993—**Cincinnati (8-2); **1994—**Marquette (10-2).

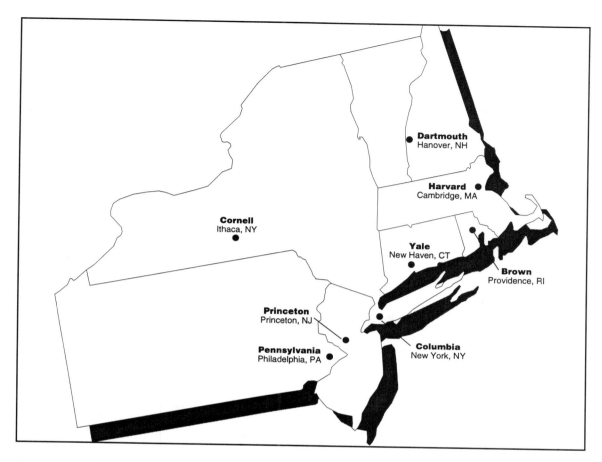

IVY LEAGUE

ADDRESS: 120 Alexander Street, Princeton, NJ 08544.

TELEPHONE/FAX: (609) 258-6426/1690.

PREVIOUS NAME: Eastern Intercollegiate Basketball League (1902–54).

CURRENT MEMBERS: Brown (1954–), Columbia (1902–), Cornell (1902–), Dartmouth (1912–), Harvard (1902–09 and 1934–), Pennsylvania (1904–), Princeton (1902–), Yale (1902–).

NIT TITLES (1): Princeton (1975).

ALL-TIME LEADING SCORER: Bill Bradley, Princeton (2,503 points, 1963–65).

REGULAR-SEASON CHAMPIONS: Brown (1 outright-0 ties), Columbia (11-5), Cornell (3-2), Dartmouth (9-3), Penn (24-6), Princeton (18-12), Yale (10-1).

YEAR-BY-YEAR CHAMPIONS (incl. conference records): 1902—Yale (6-2); **1903**—Yale (7-1); **1904**—Columbia (10-0); **1905**—Columbia (8-0); **1906**—Pennsylvania (9-1); **1907**—Yale (9-1); **1908**—Pennsylvania (8-0); **1909**—Columbia (7-1)*; **1910**—Columbia (6-0)*; **1911**—Columbia (7-1); **1912**—Columbia (8-2); **1913**—Cornell (7-1); **1914**—Columbia (8-2), Cornell (8-2); **1915**—Yale (8-2); **1916**—Pennsylvania (8-2), Princeton (8-2); **1917**—Yale (9-1); **1918**—Pennsylvania (9-1); **1919**—Pennsylvania (7-1); **1920**—Pennsylvania (10-0); **1921**—Pennsylvania (9-1); **1922**—Princeton (9-2); **1923**—Yale (7-3); **1924**—Cornell (8-2); **1925**—Princeton (9-1); **1926**—Columbia (9-1); **1927**—Dartmouth (7-3), Princeton (7-3); **1928**—Pennsylvania (7-3), Princeton (7-3); **1929**—Pennsylvania (8-2); **1930**—Columbia (9-1); **1931**—Columbia (10-0); **1932**—Columbia (8-2), Princeton (8-2); **1933**—Yale (8-2); **1934**—Pennsylvania (10-2); **1935**—Columbia (10-2), Pennsylvania (10-2); **1936**—Columbia (12-0); **1937**—Pennsylvania (12-0); **1938**—Dartmouth (8-4); **1939**—Dartmouth (10-2); **1940**—Dartmouth (11-1); **1941**—Dartmouth (10-2); **1942**—Dartmouth (10-2), Princeton (10-2); **1943**—Dartmouth (11-1); **1944**—Dartmouth (8-0); **1945**—Pennsylvania (5-1); **1946**—Dartmouth (7-1); **1947**—Columbia (11-1); **1948**—Columbia (11-1); **1949**—Yale (9-3); **1950**—Princeton (11-1); **1951**—Columbia (12-0); **1952**—Princeton (10-2); **1953**—Pennsylvania (10-2); **1954**—Cornell (12-3); **1955**—Princeton (11-4); **1956**—Dartmouth (10-4); **1957**—Yale (12-2); **1958**—Dartmouth (11-3); **1959**—Dartmouth (14-1); **1960**—Princeton (11-3); **1961**—Princeton (11-3); **1962**—Yale (13-1); **1963**—Princeton (12-3); **1964**—Princeton (12-2); **1965**—Princeton (13-1); **1966**—Pennsylvania (12-2); **1967**—Princeton (13-1); **1968**—Columbia (13-2); **1969**—Princeton (14-0); **1970**—Pennsylvania (14-0); **1971**—Pennsylvania (14-0); **1972**—Pennsylvania (13-1); **1973**—Pennsylvania (12-2); **1974**—Pennsylvania (13-1); **1975**—Pennsylvania (13-1); **1976**—Princeton (14-0); **1977**—Princeton (13-1); **1978**—Pennsylvania (12-2); **1979**—Pennsylvania (13-1); **1980**—Pennsylvania (11-3), Princeton (11-3); **1981**—Pennsylvania (13-1), Princeton (13-1); **1982**—Pennsylvania (12-2); **1983**—Princeton (12-2); **1984**—Princeton (10-4); **1985**—Pennsylvania (10-4); **1986**—Brown (10-4); **1987**—Pennsylvania (10-4); **1988**—Cornell (11-3); **1989**—Princeton (11-3); **1990**—Princeton (11-3); **1991**—Princeton (14-0); **1992**—Princeton (12-2); **1993**—Pennsylvania (14-0); **1994**—Pennsylvania (14-0).

* Informal competition.

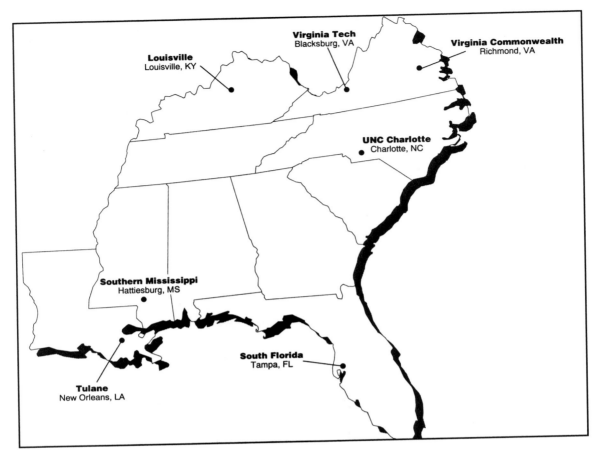

METRO

ADDRESS: Two Ravinia Drive, Suite 210, Atlanta, GA 30346.

TELEPHONE/FAX: (404) 395-6444/6423.

CURRENT MEMBERS: Louisville (1976–), UNC Charlotte (1992–), Southern Mississippi (1983–), South Florida (1992–), Tulane (1976–85 and 1990–), Virginia Commonwealth (1992–), Virginia Tech (1979–).

FORMER MEMBERS: Cincinnati (1976–91), Florida State (1977–91), Georgia Tech (1976–78), Memphis (1976–91), St. Louis (1976–82), South Carolina (1984–91).

NCAA TITLES (2): Louisville (1980 and 1986).

NIT TITLES (1): Southern Mississippi (1987).

ALL-TIME LEADING SCORER: Bimbo Coles, Virginia Tech (2,484 points, 1987–90).

REGULAR-SEASON CHAMPIONS: Florida State (2 outright-0 ties), Louisville (11-1), Memphis (2-1), Southern Mississippi (1-0), Tulane (1-0).

METRO TOURNAMENT TITLES: Louisville (10), Memphis (4), Cincinnati (2), Florida State (1), UNC Charlotte (1), Virginia Tech (1).

YEAR-BY-YEAR CHAMPIONS (incl. conference records): 1976—Tulane (1-0); **1977**—Louisville (6-1); **1978**—Florida State (11-1); **1979**—Louisville (9-1); **1980**—Louisville (12-0); **1981**—Louisville (11-1); **1982**—Memphis (10-2); **1983**—Louisville (12-0); **1984**—Louisville (11-3); Memphis (11-3); **1985**—Memphis (13-1); **1986**—Louisville (10-2); **1987**—Louisville (9-3); **1988**—Louisville (9-3); **1989**—Florida State (9-3); **1990**—Louisville (12-2); **1991**—Southern Miss. (10-4); **1992**—Tulane (8-4); **1993**—Louisville (11-1); **1994**—Louisville (10-2).

Note: Tulane's 1976 "title" is not recognized because the most league games any member played in that inaugural season was three.

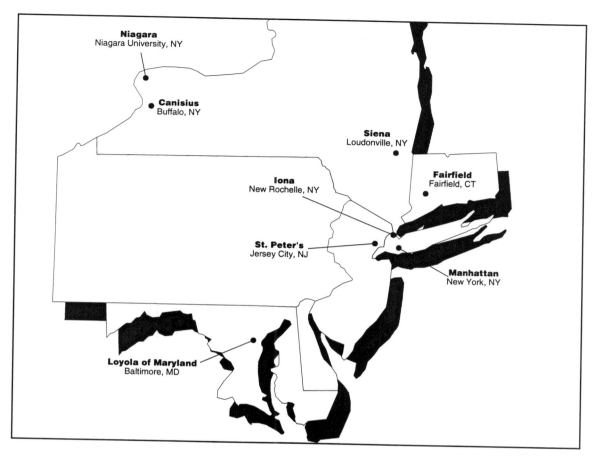

METRO ATLANTIC ATHLETIC

ADDRESS: 1090 Amboy Avenue, Edison, NJ 08837-2847.

TELEPHONE/FAX: (908) 225-0202/5440.

CURRENT MEMBERS: Canisius (1990–), Fairfield (1982–), Iona (1982–), Loyola, Md. (1990–), Manhattan (1982–), Niagara (1990–), St. Peter's (1982–), Siena (1990–).

FORMER MEMBERS: Army (1982–90), Fordham (1982–90), Holy Cross (1984–90), La Salle (1984–92).

ALL-TIME LEADING SCORER: Lionel Simmons, La Salle (3,217 points, 1987–90).

REGULAR-SEASON CHAMPIONS: Canisius (1 outright-0 ties), Fairfield (1-0), Holy Cross (1-0), Iona (2-1), La Salle (3-1), Manhattan (2-0), St. Peter's (2-1), Siena (1-0).

MAAC TOURNAMENT TITLES: La Salle (4), Iona (3), Fairfield (2), Fordham (1), Loyola, Md. (1), Manhattan (1), St. Peter's (1).

YEAR-BY-YEAR CHAMPIONS (incl. conference records): **1982**—St. Peter's (9-1); **1983**—Iona (8-2); **1984**—Iona (11-3), La Salle (11-3), St. Peter's (11-3); **1985**—Iona (11-3); **1986**—Fairfield (13-1); **1987**—St. Peter's (11-3); **1988**—La Salle (14-0); **1989**—La Salle (13-1); **1990**—Holy Cross (14-2/N), La Salle (16-0/S); **1991**—Siena (12-4); **1992**—Manhattan (13-3); **1993**—Manhattan (12-2); **1994**—Canisius (12-2).

Note: The MAAC had North and South Divisions for one season in 1989–90.

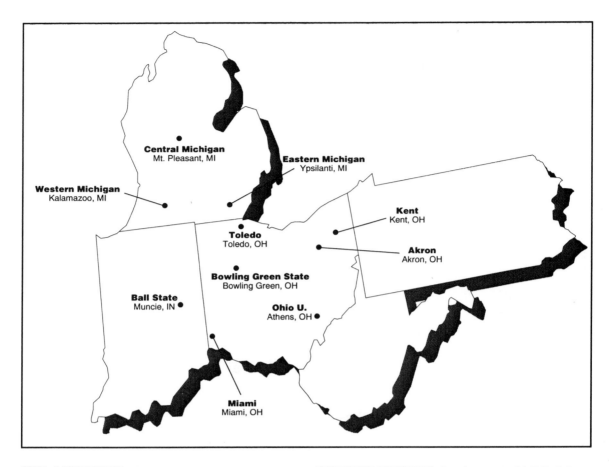

MID-AMERICAN

ADDRESS: Four SeaGate, Suite 102, Toledo, OH 43604.

TELEPHONE/FAX: (419) 249-7177/7199.

CURRENT MEMBERS: Akron (1993–), Ball State (1976–), Bowling Green State (1954–), Central Michigan (1973–), Eastern Michigan (1975–), Kent (1952–), Miami of Ohio (1948–), Ohio University (1947–), Toledo (1952–), Western Michigan (1948–).

FORMER MEMBERS: Butler (1947–50), Cincinnati (1947–53), Marshall (1954–69), Northern Illinois (1976–86), Wayne State (1947), Western Reserve (1947–55).

ALL-TIME LEADING SCORER: Ron Harper, Miami of Ohio (2,377 points, 1983–86).

REGULAR-SEASON CHAMPIONS: Ball State (3 outright-2 ties), Bowling Green State (4-2), Butler (0-1), Central Michigan (2-2), Cincinnati (4-1), Eastern Michigan (2-0), Marshall (1-0), Miami of Ohio (12-5), Northern Illinois (0-1), Ohio U. (7-2), Toledo (3-3), Western Michigan (1-2).

MAC TOURNAMENT TITLES: Ball State (5), Ohio U. (3), Eastern Michigan (2), Miami of Ohio (2), Central Michigan (1), Northern Illinois (1), Toledo (1).

YEAR-BY-YEAR CHAMPIONS (incl. conference records): 1947—Butler (6-2), Cincinnati (6-2); **1948**—Cincinnati (7-2); **1949**—Cincinnati (9-1); **1950**—Cincinnati (10-0); **1951**—Cincinnati (7-1); **1952**—Miami of Ohio (9-3), Western Michigan (9-3); **1953**—Miami of Ohio (10-2); **1954**—Toledo (10-2); **1955**—Miami of Ohio (11-3); **1956**—Marshall (10-2); **1957**—Miami of Ohio (11-1); **1958**—Miami of Ohio (12-0); **1959**—Bowling Green (9-3), Miami of Ohio (9-3); **1960**—Ohio U. (10-2); **1961**—Ohio U. (10-2); **1962**—Bowling Green (11-1); **1963**—Bowling Green (9-3); **1964**—Ohio U. (10-2); **1965**—Miami of Ohio (11-1), Ohio U. (11-1); **1966**—Miami of Ohio (11-1); **1967**—Toledo (11-1); **1968**—Bowling Green (10-2); **1969**—Miami of Ohio (10-2); **1970**—Ohio U. (9-1); **1971**—Miami of Ohio (9-1); **1972**—Ohio U. (7-3), Toledo (7-3); **1973**—Miami of Ohio (9-2); **1974**—Ohio U. (9-3); **1975**—Central Michigan (10-4); **1976**—Western Michigan (15-1); **1977**—Central Michigan (13-3), Miami of Ohio (13-3); **1978**—Miami of Ohio (12-4); **1979**—Central Michigan (13-3), Toledo (13-3)*; **1980**—Toledo (14-2); **1981**—Ball State (10-6), Bowling Green (10-6), Northern Illinois (10-6), Toledo (10-6), Western Michigan (10-6); **1982**—Ball State (12-4); **1983**—Bowling Green (15-3); **1984**—Miami of Ohio (16-2); **1985**—Ohio U. (14-4); **1986**—Miami of Ohio (16-2); **1987**—Central Michigan (14-2); **1988**—Eastern Michigan (14-2); **1989**—Ball State (14-2); **1990**—Ball State (13-3); **1991**—Eastern Michigan (13-3); **1992**—Miami of Ohio (13-3); **1993**—Ball State (14-4, Miami of Ohio (14-4); **1994**—Ohio U. (14-4).

* Won playoff.

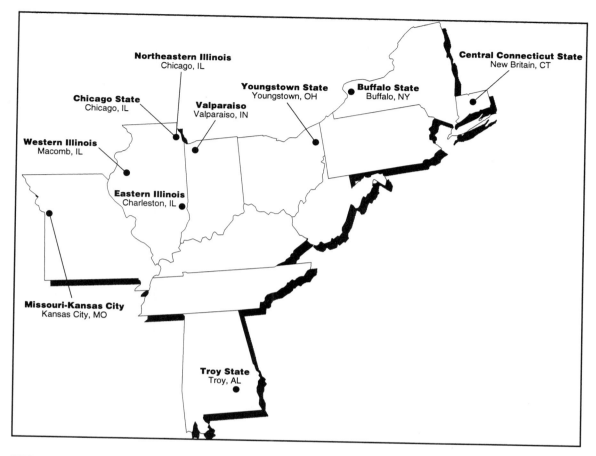

Northeastern Illinois
Chicago, IL

Chicago State
Chicago, IL

Valparaiso
Valparaiso, IN

Youngstown State
Youngstown, OH

Buffalo State
Buffalo, NY

Central Connecticut State
New Britain, CT

Western Illinois
Macomb, IL

Eastern Illinois
Charleston, IL

Missouri-Kansas City
Kansas City, MO

Troy State
Troy, AL

MID-CONTINENT

ADDRESS: 40 Shuman Boulevard, Suite 118, Naperville, IL 60563.

TELEPHONE/FAX: (708) 416-7560/7564.

PREVIOUS NAME: Association of Mid–Continent Universities (1983-89).

CURRENT MEMBERS: Buffalo State (1995–), Central Connecticut State (1995–), Chicago State (1995–), Eastern Illinois (1983–), Missouri-Kansas City (1995–), Northeastern Illinois (1995–), Troy State (1995–), Valparaiso (1983–), Western Illinois (1983–), Youngstown State (1992–).

FORMER MEMBERS: Akron (1991 and 1992), Cleveland State (1983–94), Illinois-Chicago (1983–94), Northern Illinois (1991–94), Northern Iowa (1983–91), Southwest Missouri State (1983–90), Wisconsin-Green Bay (1983–94), Wisconsin-Milwaukee (1993 and 1994), Wright State (1992–94).

ALL-TIME LEADING SCORER: Tony Bennett, Wisconsin-Green Bay (2,285 points, 1989–92).

REGULAR-SEASON CHAMPIONS: Cleveland State (3 outright-0 ties), Illinois-Chicago (1-0), Northern Illinois (1-0), Southwest Missouri State (4-0), Western Illinois (1-0), Wisconsin-Green Bay (2-0).

MID-CONTINENT TOURNAMENT TITLES: Eastern Illinois (2), Southwest Missouri State (2), Wisconsin-Green Bay (2), Cleveland State (1), Northern Iowa (1), Wright State (1).

YEAR-BY-YEAR CHAMPIONS (incl. conference records): 1983—Western Illinois (9-3); **1984**—Illinois-Chicago (12-2); **1985**—Cleveland State (11-3); **1986**—Cleveland State (13-1); **1987**—Southwest Missouri State (13-1); **1988**—Southwest Missouri State (12-2); **1989**—Southwest Missouri State (10-2); **1990**—Southwest Missouri State (11-1); **1991**—Northern Illinois (14-2); **1992**—Wisconsin-Green Bay (14-2); **1993**—Cleveland State (15-1); **1994**—Wisconsin-Green Bay (15-3).

Note: Cleveland State would have won the 1989 regular-season championship instead of Southwest Missouri State had the Vikings' league games counted. But Cleveland State was on NCAA probation and was declared ineligible by the league so that the Mid-Continent Conference wouldn't risk losing its automatic bid to the NCAA Tournament.

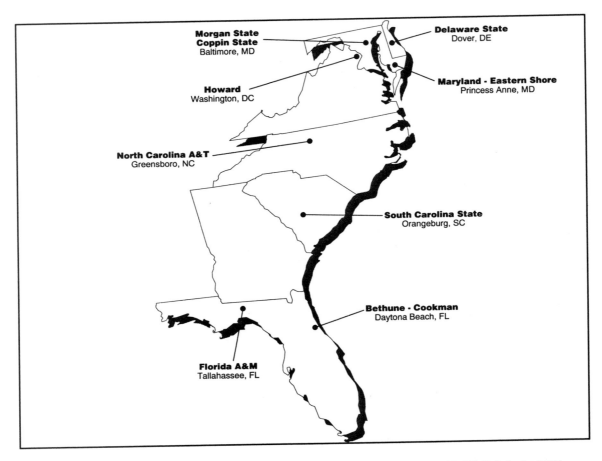

Morgan State
Coppin State
Baltimore, MD

Delaware State
Dover, DE

Howard
Washington, DC

Maryland - Eastern Shore
Princess Anne, MD

North Carolina A&T
Greensboro, NC

South Carolina State
Orangeburg, SC

Bethune - Cookman
Daytona Beach, FL

Florida A&M
Tallahassee, FL

MID-EASTERN ATHLETIC

ADDRESS: 102 North Elm Street, Suite 401, P.O. Box 21205, Greensboro, NC 27401.

TELEPHONE/FAX: (910) 275-9961/9964.

CURRENT MEMBERS: Bethune-Cookman (1981–), Coppin State (1986–), Delaware State (1972–), Florida A&M (1980–), Howard (1972–), Maryland-Eastern Shore (1972–79 and 1983–), Morgan State (1972–80 and 1985–), North Carolina A&T (1972–), South Carolina State (1972–).

FORMER MEMBER: North Carolina Central (1972–80).

ALL-TIME LEADING SCORER: Tom Davis, Delaware State (2,274 points, 1988–91).

DIVISION I REGULAR-SEASON CHAMPIONS (SINCE 1972): Coppin State (4 outright-0 ties), Howard (3-1), Maryland-Eastern Shore (1-1), Morgan State (0-2), North Carolina A&T (10-2), South Carolina State (2-0).

MEAC TOURNAMENT TITLES (SINCE 1981): North Carolina A&T (8), Coppin State (2), Howard (2), Florida A&M (1), South Carolina State (1).

YEAR-BY-YEAR CHAMPIONS (incl. conference records): 1972—North Carolina A&T (9-3); **1973**—Maryland-Eastern Shore (10-2); **1974**—Maryland-Eastern Shore (11-1), Morgan State (11-1); **1975**—North Carolina A&T (10-2); **1976**—Morgan State (11-1), North Carolina A&T (11-1); **1977**—South Carolina State (10-2); **1978**—North Carolina A&T (11-1); **1979**—North Carolina A&T (11-1); **1980**—No standings; **1981**—North Carolina A&T (7-3); **1982**—North Carolina A&T (10-2); **1983**—Howard (11-1); **1984**—North Carolina A&T (9-1); **1985**—North Carolina A&T (10-2); **1986**—North Carolina A&T (12-2); **1987**—Howard (13-1); **1988**—North Carolina A&T (16-0); **1989**—South Carolina State (14-2); **1990**—Coppin State (15-1); **1991**—Coppin State (14-2); **1992**—Howard (12-4), North Carolina A&T (12-4); **1993**—Coppin State (16-0); **1994**—Coppin State (16-0).

Note: The MEAC moved up to Division I status in 1981.

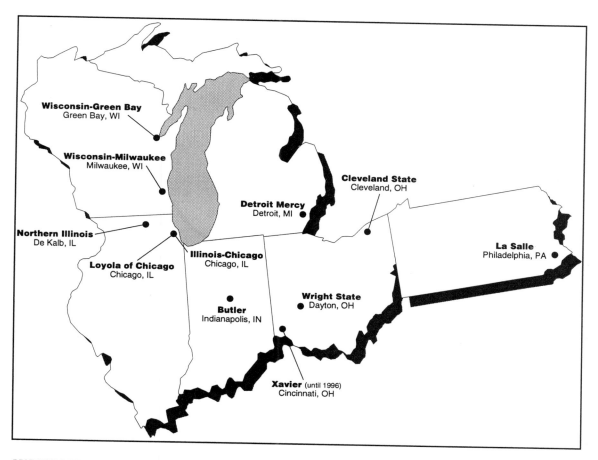

MIDWESTERN COLLEGIATE

ADDRESS: Pan American Plaza, 201 South Capitol Avenue, Suite 500, Indianapolis, IN 46225.

TELEPHONE/FAX: (317) 237-5622/5620.

PREVIOUS NAME: Midwestern City (1980–85).

CURRENT MEMBERS: Butler (1980–), Cleveland State (1995–), Detroit Mercy (1981–), Illinois-Chicago (1995–), La Salle (1993–), Loyola of Chicago (1980–), Northern Illinois (1995–), Wisconsin-Green Bay (1995–), Wisconsin-Milwaukee (1995–), Wright State (1995–), Xavier (1980–95; plans to join Atlantic 10 in 1996).

FORMER MEMBERS: Dayton (1989–93), Duquesne (1993), Evansville (1980–94), Marquette (1990 and 1991), Oklahoma City (1980–85), Oral Roberts (1980–87), St. Louis (1983–91).

NCAA TITLES (2): La Salle (1954), Loyola of Chicago (1963). Both NCAA titles occurred before the conference was formed.

NIT TITLES (2): La Salle (1952), Xavier (1958). Both NIT titles occurred before the conference was formed.

ALL-TIME LEADING SCORER: Alfredrick Hughes, Loyola of Chicago (2,906 points, 1982–85).

REGULAR-SEASON CHAMPIONS: Evansville (3 outright-2 ties), Loyola of Chicago (3-1), Oral Roberts (1-0), Xavier (6-1).

MCC TOURNAMENT TITLES: Xavier (5), Evansville (3), Oral Roberts (2), Dayton (1), Detroit Mercy (1), Loyola of Chicago (1), Oklahoma City (1).

YEAR-BY-YEAR CHAMPIONS (incl. conference records): 1980—Loyola of Chicago (5-0); **1981**—Xavier (8-3); **1982**—Evansville (10-2); **1983**—Loyola of Chicago (12-2); **1984**—Oral Roberts (11-3); **1985**—Loyola of Chicago (13-1); **1986**—Xavier (10-2); **1987**—Evansville (8-4), Loyola of Chicago (8-4); **1988**—Xavier (9-1); **1989**—Evansville (10-2); **1990**—Xavier (12-2); **1991**—Xavier (11-3); **1992**—Evansville (8-2); **1993**—Evansville (12-2), Xavier (12-2); **1994**—Xavier (8-2).

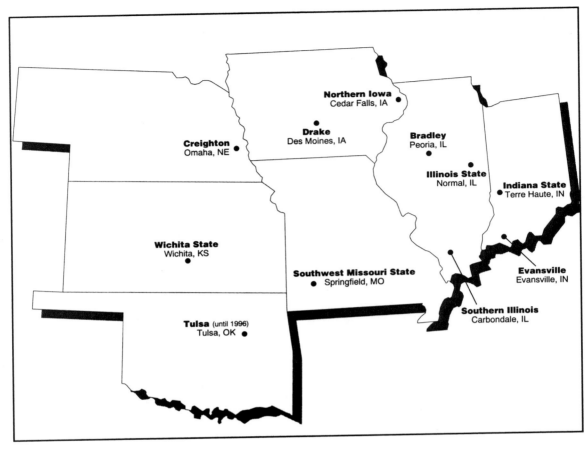

MISSOURI VALLEY

ADDRESS: 100 North Broadway, Suite 1135, St. Louis, MO 63102.

TELEPHONE/FAX: (314) 421-0339/3505.

PREVIOUS NAME: Missouri Valley Intercollegiate Athletic Association.

CURRENT MEMBERS: Bradley (1949–51 and 1956–), Creighton (1929–48 and 1977–), Drake (1908–51 and 1957–), Evansville (1995–), Illinois State (1981–), Indiana State (1977–), Northern Iowa (1992–), Southern Illinois (1975–), Southwest Missouri State (1991–), Tulsa (1935–95; will join Western Athletic in 1996), Wichita State (1946–).

FORMER MEMBERS: Butler (1933 and 1934), Cincinnati (1958–70), Detroit (1950–57), Grinnell, Ia. (1919–39), Houston (1951–60), Iowa State (1908–28), Kansas (1908–28), Kansas State (1914–28), Louisville (1965–75), Memphis (1968–73), Missouri (1908–28), Nebraska (1908–28), New Mexico State (1971–83), North Texas (1958–75), Oklahoma (1920–28), Oklahoma A&M (1926–57), St. Louis (1938–74), Washburn, Kan. (1935–41), Washington, Mo. (1908–47), West Texas State (1971–86).

NIT TITLES (5): Bradley (1957-60-64-82), Southern Illinois (1967).

ALL-TIME LEADING SCORER: Hersey Hawkins, Bradley (3,008 points, 1985–88).

REGULAR-SEASON CHAMPIONS (SINCE 1929): Bradley (5 outright-1 tie), Butler (2-0), Cincinnati (6-1), Creighton (6-5), Drake (1-6), Houston (1-0), Illinois State (1-2), Indiana State (1-0), Louisville (4-3), Memphis (1-1), New Mexico State (0-1), Oklahoma A&M (9-4), St. Louis (3-2), Southern Illinois (1-2), Tulsa (3-2), Washington, Mo. (1-2), Wichita State (4-1).

MVC TOURNAMENT TITLES: Creighton (4), Southern Illinois (3), Tulsa (3), Bradley (2), Illinois State (2), Wichita State (2), Indiana State (1), Southwest Missouri State (1).

YEAR-BY-YEAR CHAMPIONS (incl. conference records): 1929—Washington, Mo. (7-0); **1930**—Creighton (6-2), Washington, Mo. (6-2); **1931**—Creighton (5-3), Oklahoma A&M (5-3), Washington, Mo. (5-3); **1932**—Creighton (8-0); **1933**—Butler (9-1); **1934**—Butler (9-1); **1935**—Creighton (8-4), Drake (8-4); **1936**—Creighton (8-4), Drake (8-4), Oklahoma A&M (8-4); **1937**—Oklahoma A&M (11-1); **1938**—Oklahoma A&M (13-1); **1939**—Drake (11-3), Oklahoma A&M (11-3); **1940**—Oklahoma A&M (12-0); **1941**—Creighton (9-3); **1942**—Creighton (9-1), Oklahoma A&M (9-1); **1943**—Creighton (10-0); **1944**—No competition due to WWII; **1945**—No competition due to WWII; **1946**—Oklahoma A&M (12-0); **1947**—St. Louis (11-1); **1948**—Oklahoma A&M (10-0); **1949**—Oklahoma A&M (9-1); **1950**—Bradley (11-1); **1951**—Oklahoma A&M (12-2); **1952**—St. Louis (9-1); **1953**—Oklahoma A&M (8-2); **1954**—Oklahoma A&M (9-1); **1955**—St. Louis (8-2), Tulsa (8-2); **1956**—Houston (9-3); **1957**—St. Louis (12-2); **1958**—Cincinnati (13-1); **1959**—Cincinnati (13-1); **1960**—Cincinnati (13-1); **1961**—Cincinnati (10-2); **1962**—Bradley (10-2), Cincinnati (10-2)*; **1963**—Cincinnati (11-1); **1964**—Drake (10-2), Wichita State (10-2)*; **1965**—Wichita State (11-3); **1966**—Cincinnati (10-4); **1967**—Louisville (12-2); **1968**—Louisville (14-2); **1969**—Drake (13-3), Louisville (13-3)*; **1970**—Drake (14-2); **1971**—Drake (9-5)*, Louisville (9-5), St. Louis (9-5); **1972**—Louisville (12-2)*, Memphis (12-2); **1973**—Memphis (12-2); **1974**—Louisville (11-1); **1975**—Louisville (12-2); **1976**—Wichita State (10-2); **1977**—New Mexico State (8-4), Southern Illinois (8-4); **1978**—Creighton (12-4); **1979**—Indiana State (16-0); **1980**—Bradley (13-3); **1981**—Wichita State (12-4); **1982**—Bradley (13-3); **1983**—Wichita State (17-1); **1984**—Illinois State (13-3), Tulsa (13-3); **1985**—Tulsa (12-4); **1986**—Bradley (16-0); **1987**—Tulsa (11-3); **1988**—Bradley (12-2); **1989**—Creighton (11-3); **1990**—Southern Illinois (10-4); **1991**—Creighton (12-4); **1992**—Illinois State (14-4), Southern Illinois (14-4); **1993**—Illinois State (13-5); **1994**—Tulsa (15-3).

* **Won playoff. Note:** The MVIAA had North and South Divisions from 1908 to 1910 and from 1912 to 1914. There was no conference competition in 1944 and 1945 because of World War II. The nucleus of what is now the Big Eight Conference split from the other MVIAA's members prior to the start of the 1928–29 season.

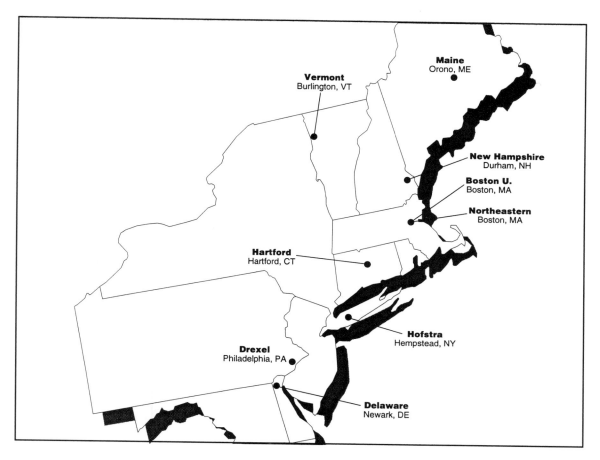

NORTH ATLANTIC

ADDRESS: 28 Main Street, P.O. Box 69, Orono, ME 04473.

TELEPHONE/FAX: (207) 866-2383/7524.

PREVIOUS NAME: ECAC North.

CURRENT MEMBERS: Boston University (1980–), Delaware (1992–), Drexel (1992–), Hartford (1986–), Hofstra (1995–), Maine (1980–), New Hampshire (1980–), Northeastern (1980–), Vermont (1980–).

FORMER MEMBERS: Canisius (1980–89), Colgate (1980–90), Holy Cross (1980–83), Niagara (1980–89), Rhode Island (1980), Siena (1985–89).

ALL-TIME LEADING SCORER: Reggie Lewis, Northeastern (2,709 points, 1984–87).

REGULAR-SEASON CHAMPIONS: Boston U. (0 outright-2 ties), Canisius (0-1), Delaware (1-0), Drexel (1-1), New Hampshire (0-1), Northeastern (5-3), Siena (2-0).

NAC TOURNAMENT TITLES: Northeastern (7), Boston U. (3), Delaware (2), Drexel (1), Holy Cross (1), Siena (1).

YEAR-BY-YEAR CHAMPIONS (incl. conference records): 1982—Northeastern (8-1); **1983**—Boston U. (8-2), New Hampshire (8-2); **1984**—Northeastern (14-0); **1985**—Canisius (13-3), Northeastern (13-3); **1986**—Northeastern (16-2); **1987**—Northeastern (16-2); **1988**—Siena (16-2); **1989**—Siena (16-1); **1990**—Boston U. (9-3), Northeastern (9-3); **1991**—Northeastern (8-2); **1992**—Delaware (14-0); **1993**—Drexel (12-2), Northeastern (12-2); **1994**—Drexel (12-2).

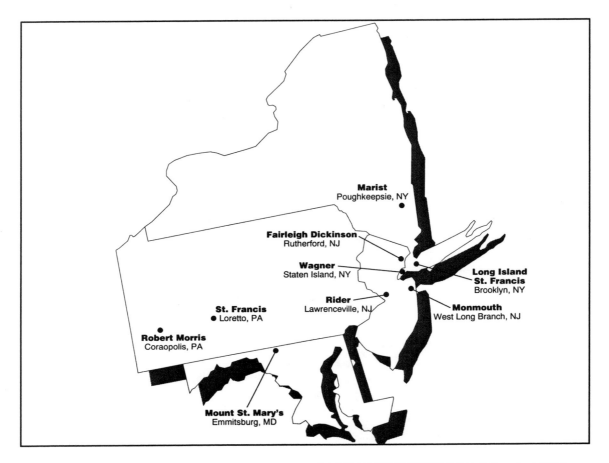

Marist
Poughkeepsie, NY

Fairleigh Dickinson
Rutherford, NJ

Wagner
Staten Island, NY

Long Island
St. Francis
Brooklyn, NY

Rider
Lawrenceville, NJ

Monmouth
West Long Branch, NJ

St. Francis
● Loretto, PA

Robert Morris
Coraopolis, PA

Mount St. Mary's
Emmitsburg, MD

NORTHEAST

ADDRESS: 900 Route 9, Woodbridge, NJ 07095.

TELEPHONE/FAX: (908) 636-9119/6496.

CURRENT MEMBERS: Fairleigh Dickinson (1982–), Long Island (1982–), Marist (1982–), Monmouth (1986–), Mount St. Mary's (1990–), Rider (1993–), Robert Morris (1982–), St. Francis, N.Y. (1982–), St. Francis, Pa. (1982–), Wagner (1982–).

FORMER MEMBERS: Baltimore (1982 and 1983), Loyola, Md. (1982–89), Siena (1982–84), Towson State (1982).

NIT TITLES (2): Long Island (1939 and 1941). Both titles occurred before the league was formed.

ALL-TIME LEADING SCORER: Terrance Bailey, Wagner (2,591 points, 1984–87).

REGULAR-SEASON CHAMPIONS: Fairleigh Dickinson (2 outright-2 ties), Long Island (1-1), Marist (2-1), Rider (2-0), Robert Morris (5-1), St. Francis, Pa. (0-1).

NORTHEAST TOURNAMENT TITLES: Robert Morris (5), Fairleigh Dickinson (2), Marist (2), Rider (2), Long Island (1), St. Francis, Pa. (1).

YEAR-BY-YEAR CHAMPIONS (incl. conference records): 1982—Fairleigh Dickinson (12-3/North), Robert Morris (9-5/South); **1983**—Long Island (11-3/N), Robert Morris (12-2/S); **1984**—Long Island (11-5), Robert Morris (11-5); **1985**—Marist (11-3); **1986**—Fairleigh Dickinson (13-3); **1987**—Marist (15-1); **1988**—Fairleigh Dickinson (13-3), Marist (13-3); **1989**—Robert Morris (12-4); **1990**—Robert Morris (12-4); **1991**—Fairleigh Dickinson (13-3), St. Francis, Pa. (13-3); **1992**—Robert Morris (12-4); **1993**—Rider (14-4); **1994**—Rider (14-4).

Note: The NEC had North and South Divisions in its first two seasons in 1982 and 1983.

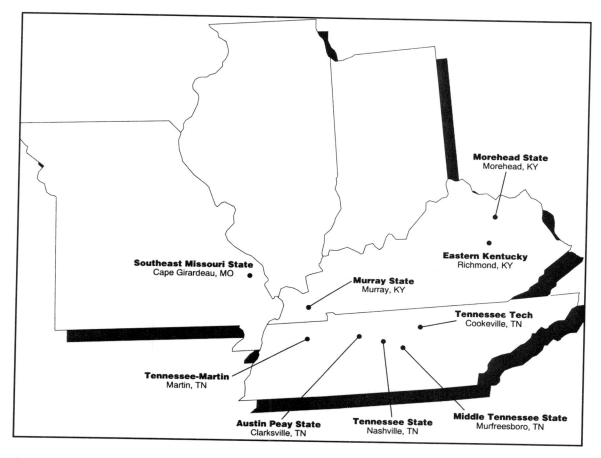

Morehead State
Morehead, KY

Eastern Kentucky
Richmond, KY

Southeast Missouri State
Cape Girardeau, MO

Murray State
Murray, KY

Tennessee Tech
Cookeville, TN

Tennessee-Martin
Martin, TN

Austin Peay State
Clarksville, TN

Tennessee State
Nashville, TN

Middle Tennessee State
Murfreesboro, TN

OHIO VALLEY

ADDRESS: 278 Franklin Road, Suite 103, Brentwood, TN 37027.

TELEPHONE/FAX: (615) 371-1698/1788.

CURRENT MEMBERS: Austin Peay State (1964–), Eastern Kentucky (1949–), Middle Tennessee State (1953–), Morehead State (1949–), Murray State (1949–61 and 1963–), Southeast Missouri State (1992–), Tennessee-Martin (1993–), Tennessee State (1988–), Tennessee Tech (1949–).

FORMER MEMBERS: Akron (1981–87), East Tennessee State (1959–78), Evansville (1949–52), Marshall (1949–52), Western Kentucky (1949–82), Youngstown State (1982–88).

ALL-TIME LEADING SCORER: Joe Jakubick, Akron (2,583 points, 1981–84).

REGULAR-SEASON CHAMPIONS: Akron (0 outright-1 tie), Austin Peay State (2-1), Eastern Kentucky (4-2), East Tennessee State (0-2), Middle Tennessee State (2-3), Morehead State (1-7), Murray State (8-5), Tennessee State (1-0), Tennessee Tech (2-2), Western Kentucky (13-6).

OVC TOURNAMENT TITLES: Western Kentucky (10), Murray State (6), Middle Tennessee State (5), Eastern Kentucky (3), Morehead State (2), Tennessee State (2), Akron (1), Austin Peay State (1), Tennessee Tech (1).

YEAR-BY-YEAR CHAMPIONS (incl. conference records): 1949—Western Kentucky (8-2); **1950**—Western Kentucky (8-0); **1951**—Murray State (9-3); **1952**—Western Kentucky (9-1); **1953**—Eastern Kentucky (9-1); **1954**—Western Kentucky (9-1); **1955**—Western Kentucky (8-2); **1956**—Morehead State (7-3), Tennessee Tech (7-3), Western Kentucky (7-3); **1957**—Morehead State (9-1), Western Kentucky (9-1); **1958**—Tennessee Tech (8-2); **1959**—Eastern Kentucky (10-2); **1960**—Western Kentucky (10-2); **1961**—Eastern Kentucky (9-3), Morehead State (9-3), Western Kentucky (9-3); **1962**—Western Kentucky (11-1); **1963**—Morehead State (8-4), Tennessee Tech (8-4); **1964**—Murray State (11-3); **1965**—Eastern Kentucky (13-1); **1966**—Western Kentucky (14-0); **1967**—Western Kentucky (13-1); **1968**—East Tennessee State (10-4), Murray State (10-4); **1969**—Morehead State (11-3), Murray State (11-3); **1970**—Western Kentucky (14-0); **1971**—Western Kentucky (12-2); **1972**—Eastern Kentucky (9-5), Morehead State (9-5); —Western Kentucky (9-5); **1973**—Austin Peay (11-3); **1974**—Austin Peay (10-4), Morehead State (10-4); **1975**—Middle Tennessee State (12-2); **1976**—Western Kentucky (11-3); **1977**—Austin Peay (13-1); **1978**—East Tennessee State (10-4), Middle Tennessee State (10-4); **1979**—Eastern Kentucky (9-3); **1980**—Murray State (10-2), Western Kentucky (10-2); **1981**—Western Kentucky (12-2); **1982**—Murray State (13-3), Western Kentucky (13-3); **1983**—Murray State (11-3); **1984**—Morehead State (12-2); **1985**—Tennessee Tech (11-3); **1986**—Akron (10-4), Middle Tennessee State (10-4); **1987**—Middle Tennessee State (11-3); **1988**—Murray State (13-1); **1989**—Middle Tennessee State (10-2), Murray State (10-2); **1990**—Murray State (10-2); **1991**—Murray State (10-2); **1992**—Murray State (11-3); **1993**—Tennessee State (13-3); **1994**—Murray State (15-1).

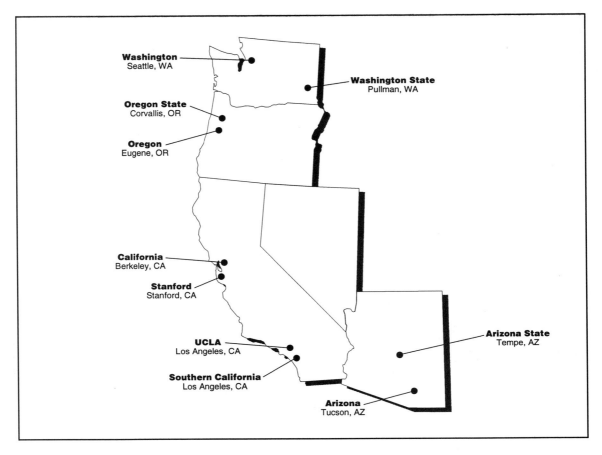

PACIFIC-10

ADDRESS: 800 South Broadway, Suite 400, Walnut Creek, CA 94596.

TELEPHONE/FAX: (510) 932-4411/4601.

PREVIOUS NAMES: Pacific Coast Conference (1916–59), Athletic Association of Western Universities (1960–68), Pacific-8 (1969–78).

CURRENT MEMBERS: Arizona (1979–), Arizona State (1979–), California (1916–), Oregon (1916–59 and 1965–), Oregon State (1916–59 and 1965–), Southern California (1922–), Stanford (1917–), UCLA (1928–), Washington (1916–), Washington State (1917–59 and 1964–).

FORMER MEMBERS: Idaho (1922–59), Montana (1924–29).

NCAA TITLES (13): California (1959), Oregon (1939), UCLA (1964-65-67-68-69-70-71-72-73-75), Stanford (1942).

NIT TITLES (2): Stanford (1991), UCLA (1985).

ALL-TIME LEADING SCORER: Don MacLean, UCLA (2,608 points, 1989–92).

REGULAR-SEASON CHAMPIONS (SINCE 1916): Arizona (6 outright-1 tie), California (10-4), Idaho (2-0), Oregon (2-1), Oregon State (8-4), Southern California (6-1), Stanford (5-2), UCLA (22-2), Washington (6-3), Washington State (2-0).

PACIFIC-10 TOURNAMENT TITLES (1987–90): Arizona (3), UCLA (1).

YEAR-BY-YEAR CHAMPIONS (incl. conference records): 1916—California (5-3), Oregon State (5-3); **1917**—Washington State (8-1); **1918**—No league competition; **1919**—Oregon (11-3); **1920**—Stanford (9-1); **1921**—California (8-3), Stanford (8-3); **1922**—Idaho (7-0); **1923**—Idaho (5-3/North)*; **1924**—California (5-3/South)*; **1925**—California (3-1/S)*; **1926**—California (5-0/S)*; **1927**—California (5-0/S)*; **1928**—Southern Cal (6-3/S)*; **1929**—California (9-0/S)*; **1930**—Southern Cal (7-2/S)*; **1931**—Washington (14-2/N)*; **1932**—California (8-3/S)*; **1933**—Oregon State (12-4/N)*; **1934**—Washington (14-2/N)*; **1935**—Southern Cal (11-1/S)*; **1936**—Stanford (8-4/S)*; **1937**—Stanford (10-2/S)*; **1938**—Stanford (10-2/S)*; **1939**—Oregon (14-2/N)*; **1940**—Southern Cal (10-2/S)*; **1941**—Washington (13-3/N)*; **1942**—Stanford (11-1/S)*; **1943**—Washington (12-4/N)*; **1944**—Washington (15-1/N), California (4-0/S); **1945**—Oregon (11-5/N), UCLA (3-1/S); **1946**—California (11-1/S)*; **1947**—Oregon State (13-3/N)*; **1948**—Washington (10-6/N)*; **1949**—Oregon State (12-4/N)*; **1950**—UCLA (10-2/S)*; **1951**—Washington (11-5/N)*; **1952**—UCLA (8-4/S)*; **1953**—Washington (15-1/N)*; **1954**—Southern Cal (8-4/S)*; **1955**—Oregon State (15-1/N)*; **1956**—UCLA (16-0); **1957**—California (14-2); **1958**—California (12-4), Oregon State (12-4); **1959**—California (14-2); **1960**—California (11-1); **1961**—Southern Cal (9-3); **1962**—UCLA (10-2); **1963**—Stanford (7-5), UCLA (7-5); **1964**—UCLA (15-0); **1965**—UCLA (14-0); **1966**—Oregon State (12-2); **1967**—UCLA (14-0); **1968**—UCLA (14-0); **1969**—UCLA (13-1); **1970**—UCLA (12-2); **1971**—UCLA (14-0); **1972**—UCLA (14-0); **1973**—UCLA (14-0); **1974**—UCLA (12-2); **1975**—UCLA (12-2); **1976**—UCLA (12-2); **1977**—UCLA (11-3); **1978**—UCLA (14-0); **1979**—UCLA (15-3); **1980**—Oregon State (16-2); **1981**—Oregon State (17-1); **1982**—Oregon State (16-2); **1983**—UCLA (15-3); **1984**—Oregon State (15-3), Washington (15-3); **1985**—Southern Cal (13-5), Washington (13-5); **1986**—Arizona (14-4); **1987**—UCLA (14-4); **1988**—Arizona (17-1); **1989**—Arizona (17-1); **1990**—Arizona (15-3), Oregon State (15-3); **1991**—Arizona (14-4); **1992**—UCLA (16-2); **1993**—Arizona (17-1); **1994**—Arizona (14-4).

* Won divisional playoff.

Note: The PCC had North and South Divisions from 1923 to 1955. No official league competition in 1917–18.

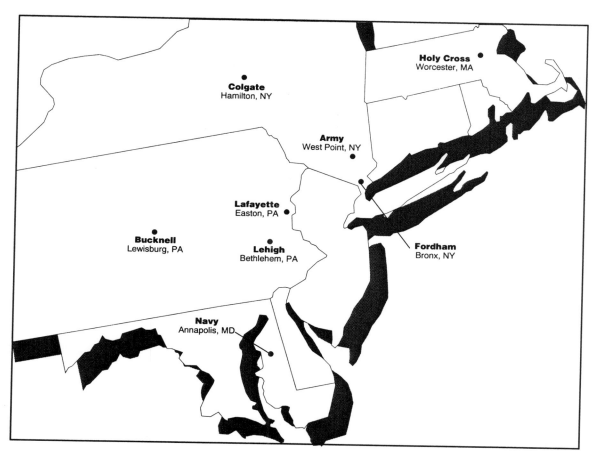

PATRIOT

ADDRESS: 3897 Adler Place, Building C, Suite 310, Bethlehem, PA 18017.

TELEPHONE/FAX: (215) 691-2414/8414.

CURRENT MEMBERS: Army (1991–), Bucknell (1991–), Colgate (1991–), Fordham (1991–), Holy Cross (1991–), Lafayette (1991–), Lehigh (1991–), Navy (1992–).

REGULAR-SEASON CHAMPIONS: Bucknell (1 outright-1 tie), Colgate (0-1), Fordham (2-2), Holy Cross (0-1), Navy (0-1).

PATRIOT TOURNAMENT TITLES: Fordham (2), Holy Cross (1), Navy (1).

YEAR-BY-YEAR CHAMPIONS (incl. conference records): 1991—Fordham (11-1); **1992**—Bucknell (11-3), Fordham (11-3); **1993**—Bucknell (13-1); **1994**—Colgate (9-5), Fordham (9-5), Holy Cross (9-5), Navy (9-5).

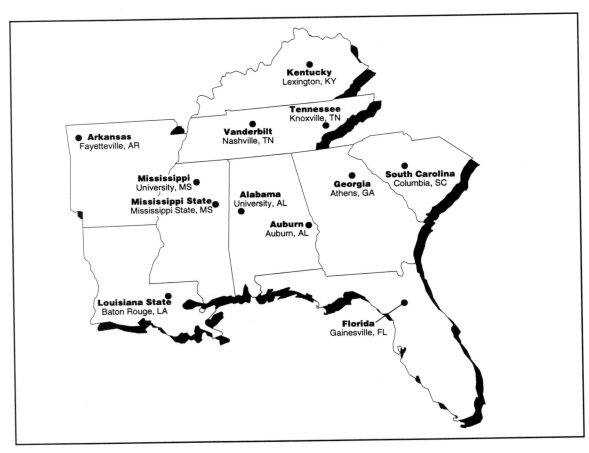

SOUTHEASTERN

ADDRESS: 2201 Civic Center Boulevard, Birmingham, AL 35203-1103.

TELEPHONE/FAX: (205) 458-3010/3030.

CURRENT MEMBERS: Alabama (1933–), Arkansas (1992–), Auburn (1933–), Florida (1933–), Georgia (1933–), Kentucky (1933–), Louisiana State (1933–), Mississippi (1933–), Mississippi State (1933–), South Carolina (1992–), Tennessee (1933–), Vanderbilt (1933–).

FORMER MEMBERS: Georgia Tech (1933–64), Sewanee (1933–40), Tulane (1933–66).

NCAA TITLES (6): Arkansas (1994), Kentucky (1948-49-51-58-78).

NIT TITLES (3): Kentucky (1946 and 1976), Vanderbilt (1990).

ALL-TIME LEADING SCORER: Pete Maravich, LSU (3,667 points, 1968–70).

REGULAR-SEASON CHAMPIONS: Alabama (5 outright-2 ties), Arkansas (3-0), Auburn (1-0), Florida (1-1), Georgia (1-0), Georgia Tech (1-0), Kentucky (29-10), Louisiana State (4-4), Mississippi State (3-2), Tennessee (2-4), Tulane (1-0), Vanderbilt (2-1).

SEC TOURNAMENT TITLES: Kentucky (18), Alabama (6), Tennessee (4), Auburn (1), Georgia (1), Georgia Tech (1), LSU (1), Mississippi (1), Vanderbilt (1).

YEAR-BY-YEAR CHAMPIONS (incl. conference records): 1933—Kentucky (8-0); **1934**—Kentucky (11-0); **1935**—Kentucky (11-0), Louisiana State (12-0); **1936**—Kentucky (6-2); **1937**—Georgia Tech (10-0); **1938**—Kentucky (6-0); **1939**—Alabama (13-4); **1940**—Alabama (14-4); **1941**—Kentucky (8-1); **1942**—Tennessee (7-1); **1943**—Kentucky (8-1); **1944**—Tulane (4-0); **1945**—Kentucky (4-1), Tennessee (8-2); **1946**—Kentucky (6-0), Louisiana State (8-0); **1947**—Kentucky (11-0); **1948**—Kentucky (9-0); **1949**—Kentucky (13-0); **1950**—Kentucky (11-2); **1951**—Kentucky (14-0); **1952**—Kentucky (14-0); **1953**—Louisiana State (13-0); **1954**—Kentucky (14-0), Louisiana State (14-0); **1955**—Kentucky (12-2); **1956**—Alabama (14-0); **1957**—Kentucky (12-2); **1958**—Kentucky (12-2); **1959**—Mississippi State (13-1); **1960**—Auburn (12-2); **1961**—Mississippi State (11-3); **1962**—Kentucky (13-1), Mississippi State (13-1); **1963**—Mississippi State (12-2); **1964**—Kentucky (11-3); **1965**—Vanderbilt (15-1); **1966**—Kentucky (15-1); **1967**—Tennessee (15-3); **1968**—Kentucky (15-3); **1969**—Kentucky (16-2); **1970**—Kentucky (17-1); **1971**—Kentucky (16-2); **1972**—Kentucky (14-4), Tennessee (14-4); **1973**—Kentucky (14-4); **1974**—Alabama (15-3), Vanderbilt (15-3); **1975**—Alabama (15-3), Kentucky (15-3); **1976**—Alabama (15-3), Tennessee (15-3); **1977**—Kentucky (16-2), Tennessee (16-2); **1978**—Kentucky (16-2); **1979**—Louisiana State (14-4); **1980**—Kentucky (15-3); **1981**—Louisiana State (17-1); **1982**—Kentucky (13-5), Tennessee (13-5); **1983**—Kentucky (13-5); **1984**—Kentucky (14-4); **1985**—Louisiana State (13-5); **1986**—Kentucky (17-1); **1987**—Alabama (16-2); **1988**—Kentucky (13-5); **1989**—Florida (13-5); **1990**—Georgia (13-5); **1991**—Louisiana State (13-5), Mississippi State (13-5); **1992**—Kentucky (12-4/E), Arkansas (13-3/W); **1993**—Vanderbilt (14-2/E), Arkansas (10-6/W); **1994**—Florida (12-4/E), Kentucky (12-4/E), Arkansas (14-2/W).

Note: The SEC introduced Eastern and Western Divisions for the first time in the 1991–92 season.

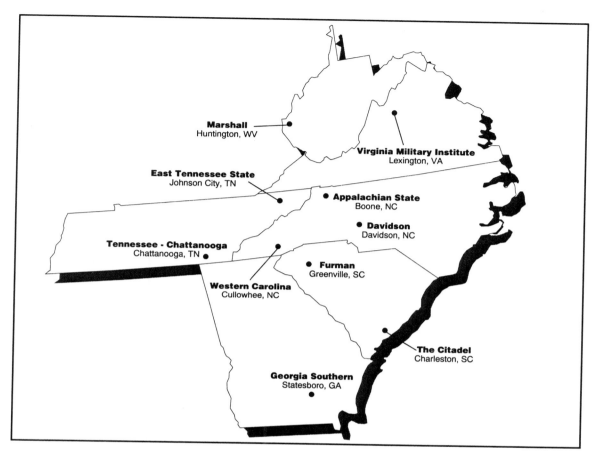

Marshall
Huntington, WV

Virginia Military Institute
Lexington, VA

East Tennessee State
Johnson City, TN

Appalachian State
Boone, NC

Davidson
Davidson, NC

Tennessee - Chattanooga
Chattanooga, TN

Furman
Greenville, SC

Western Carolina
Cullowhee, NC

The Citadel
Charleston, SC

Georgia Southern
Statesboro, GA

SOUTHERN

ADDRESS: One West Pack Square, Suite 1508, Asheville, NC 28801.

TELEPHONE/FAX: (704) 255-7872/251-5006.

PREVIOUS NAME: Southern Intercollegiate.

CURRENT MEMBERS: Appa. St. (1973–), The Citadel (1937–), Davidson (1937–88 and 1993–), E. Tenn. St. (1980–), Furman (1937–), Georgia Southern (1993–), Marshall (1978–), Tenn.-Chat. (1978–), Virginia Military (1926–), Western Carolina (1978–).

FORMER MEMBERS: Alabama (1922–32), Auburn (1922–32), Clemson (1922–53), Duke (1929–53), E. Carolina (1966–77), George Washington (1942 and 1943 and 1946–70), Georgia (1922–32), Georgia Tech (1922–32), Kentucky (1922–32), Louisiana St. (1923–32), Maryland (1924–53), Mississippi (1923–32), Mississippi St. (1922–32), N.C. (1922–53), Richmond (1937–76), University of the S. (1924–32), S. Carolina (1923–53), Tenn. (1922–32), Tulane (1923–32), Vanderbilt (1923–32), Virginia (1922–37), Virginia Tech (1922–65), Wake Forest (1937–53), Washington & Lee (1922–58), W. Virginia (1951–68), William & Mary (1937–77).

ALL-TIME LEADING SCORER: Skip Henderson, Marshall (2,574 points, 1985–88).

REGULAR-SEASON CHAMPIONS: Alabama (1 outright-0 ties), Appa. St. (2-1), Auburn (1-0), Davidson (9-1), E. Tenn. St. (1-2), Furman (3-2), George Washington (1-1), Georgia (1-0), Marshall (3-0), Maryland (0-1), N.C. (7-0), N.C. St. (6-0), S. Carolina (4-0), Tenn.-Chat. (7-3), Tulane (1-0), Virginia (1-0), Virginia Military (1-1), Virginia Tech (1-0), Wake Forest (1-0), Washington & Lee (3-0), W. Virginia (9-1).

SC TOURNAMENT TITLES: W. Virginia (10), N.C. (8), N.C. St. (7), Furman (6), UT-Chat. (6), Davidson (5), Duke (5), E. Tenn. St. (4), George Washington (3), Marshall (3), VMI (3), Washington & Lee (2), Alabama (1), Appa. St. (1), Clemson (1), E. Carolina (1), Georgia (1), Kentucky (1), Maryland (1), Mississippi (1), Mississippi St. (1), S. Carolina (1), Vanderbilt (1), Wake Forest (1).

YEAR-BY-YEAR CHAMPIONS (incl. conference records): **1922**—Virginia (5-0); **1923**—N.C. (5-0); **1924**—Tulane (10-0); **1925**—N.C. (8-0); **1926**—Kentucky (8-0); **1927**—S. Carolina (9-1); **1928**—Auburn (12-1); **1929**—Washington & Lee (7-1); **1930**—Alabama (10-0); **1931**—Georgia (15-1); **1932**—Kentucky (9-1), Maryland (9-1); **1933**—S. Carolina (3-0); **1934**—S. Carolina (6-0); **1935**—N.C. (12-1); **1936**—Washington & Lee (10-1); **1937**—Washington & Lee (11-1); **1938**—N.C. (13-3); **1939**—Wake Forest (15-3); **1940**—Duke (13-2); **1941**—N.C. (14-1); **1942**—Duke (15-1); **1943**—Duke (12-1); **1944**—N.C. (9-1); **1945**—S. Carolina (9-0); **1946**—N.C. (13-1); **1947**—N.C. St. (11-2); **1948**—N.C. St. (12-0); **1949**—N.C. St. (14-1); **1950**—N.C. St. (12-2); **1951**—N.C. St. (13-1); **1952**—W. Virginia (15-1); **1953**—N.C. St. (13-3); **1954**—George Washington (10-0); **1955**—W. Virginia (9-1); **1956**—George Washington (10-2), W. Virginia (10-2); **1957**—W. Virginia (12-0); **1958**—W. Virginia (12-0); **1959**—W. Virginia (9-1); **1960**—Virginia Tech (12-1); **1961**—W. Virginia (11-1); **1962**—W. Virginia (12-1); **1963**—W. Virginia (11-2); **1964**—Davidson (9-2); **1965**—Davidson (12-0); **1966**—Davidson (11-1); **1967**—W. Virginia (9-1); **1968**—Davidson (9-1); **1969**—Davidson (9-0); **1970**—Davidson (10-0); **1971**—Davidson (9-1); **1972**—Davidson (8-2); **1973**—Davidson (9-1); **1974**—Furman (11-1); **1975**—Furman (12-0); **1976**—Virginia Military (9-3); **1977**—Furman (8-2), Virginia Military (8-2); **1978**—Appa. St. (9-3); **1979**—Appa. St. (11-3); **1980**—Furman (14-1); **1981**—Appa. St. (11-5), Davidson (11-5), Tenn.-Chat. (11-5); **1982**—Tenn.-Chat. (15-1); **1983**—Tenn.-Chat. (15-1); **1984**—Marshall (13-3); **1985**—Tenn.-Chat. (14-2); **1986**—Tenn.-Chat. (12-4); **1987**—Marshall (15-1); **1988**—Marshall (14-2); **1989**—Tenn.-Chat. (10-4); **1990**—E. Tenn. St. (12-2); **1991**—E. Tenn. St. (11-3), Furman (11-3), Tenn.-Chat. (11-3); **1992**—E. Tenn. St. (12-2), Tenn.-Chat. (12-2); **1993**—Tenn.-Chat. (16-2); **1994**—Tenn.-Chat. (14-4).

Note: League split into two divisions—Northern and Southern—in 1995.

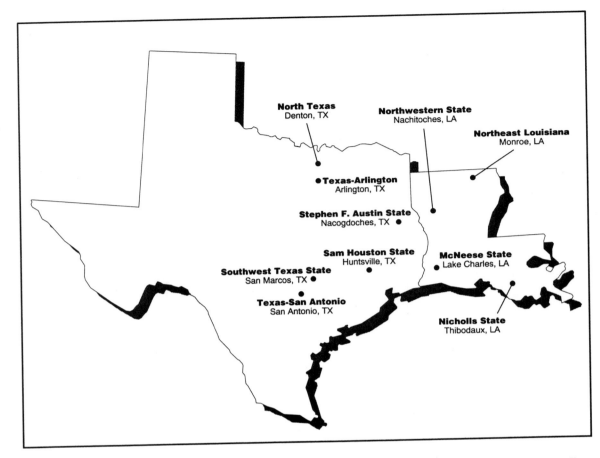

North Texas
Denton, TX

Northwestern State
Nachitoches, LA

Northeast Louisiana
Monroe, LA

●Texas-Arlington
Arlington, TX

Stephen F. Austin State
Nacogdoches, TX ●

Sam Houston State
Huntsville, TX ●

McNeese State
● Lake Charles, LA

Southwest Texas State
San Marcos, TX ●

Texas-San Antonio
San Antonio, TX ●

Nicholls State
Thibodaux, LA

SOUTHLAND

ADDRESS: 1309 West 15th, Suite 303, Plano, TX 75075.

TELEPHONE/FAX: (214) 424-4833/4099.

CURRENT MEMBERS: McNeese State (1973–), Nicholls State (1992–), North Texas (1983–), Northeast Louisiana (1983–), Northwestern State, La. (1988–), Sam Houston State (1988–), Stephen F. Austin State (1988–), Southwest Texas State (1988–), Texas-Arlington (1969–86 and 1988–), Texas-San Antonio (1992–).

FORMER MEMBERS: Abilene Christian (1969–73), Arkansas State (1969–87), Lamar (1969–87), Louisiana Tech (1972–87), Southwestern Louisiana (1972–82), Trinity, Tex. (1969–72).

ALL-TIME LEADING SCORER: Dwight "Bo" Lamar, Southwestern Louisiana (3,493 points, 1970–73).

REGULAR-SEASON CHAMPIONS (SINCE 1964): Abilene Christian (2 outright-1 tie), Arkansas State (3-1), Lamar (7-1), Louisiana Tech (5-0), McNeese State (1-1), Northeast Louisiana (5-0), North Texas (2-0), Southwestern Louisiana (2-0), Texas-San Antonio (1-0), Trinity (1-0).

SLC TOURNAMENT TITLES: Northeast Louisiana (5), Louisiana Tech (3), Lamar (2), McNeese State (1), North Texas (1), Southwestern Louisiana (1), Southwest Texas State (1).

YEAR-BY-YEAR CHAMPIONS (incl. conference records): 1964—Lamar (7-1); **1965**—Abilene Christian (6-2), Arkansas State (6-2); **1966**—Abilene Christian (8-0); **1967**—Arkansas State (8-0); **1968**—Abilene Christian (6-2); **1969**—Trinity, Tex. (7-1); **1970**—Lamar (7-1); **1971**—Arkansas State (6-2); **1972**—Southwestern Louisiana (8-0); **1973**—Southwestern Louisiana (12-0); **1974**—Arkansas State (4-0); **1975**—McNeese State (6-2); **1976**—Louisiana Tech (9-1); **1977**—Southwestern Louisiana (8-2); **1978**—Lamar (8-2), McNeese State (8-2); **1979**—Lamar (9-1); **1980**—Lamar (8-2); **1981**—Lamar (8-2); **1982**—Southwestern Louisiana (8-2); **1983**—Lamar (9-3); **1984**—Lamar (11-1); **1985**—Louisiana Tech (11-1); **1986**—Northeast Louisiana (9-3); **1987**—Louisiana Tech (9-1); **1988**—North Texas (12-2); **1989**—North Texas (10-4); **1990**—Northeast Louisiana (13-1); **1991**—Northeast Louisiana (13-1); **1992**—Texas-San Antonio (15-3); **1993**—Northeast Louisiana (17-1); **1994**—Northeast Louisiana (15-3).

Note: The SLC moved up to Division I status in 1975–76.

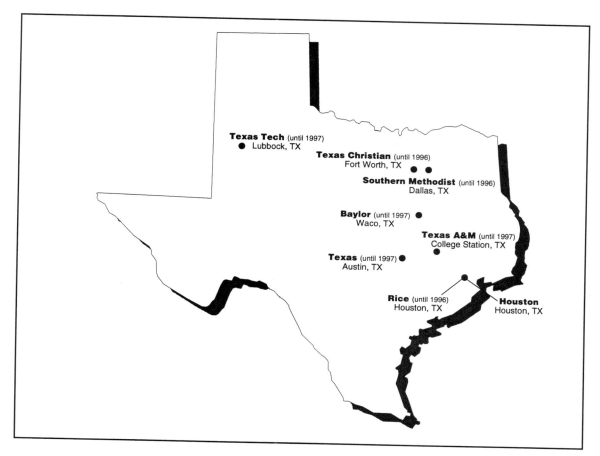

SOUTHWEST

ADDRESS: 1300 West Mockingbird Lane, Suite 444, Dallas, TX 75247-0427.

TELEPHONE/FAX: (214) 634-7353/920-1758.

PREVIOUS NAME: Southwest Intercollegiate Athletic.

CURRENT MEMBERS: Baylor (1915–96; will join Big Eight in 1997), Houston (1976–), Rice (1915–95; will join Western Athletic in 1996), Southern Methodist (1919–95; will join Western Athletic in 1996), Texas (1915–96; will join Big Eight in 1997), Texas A&M (1915–96; will join Big Eight in 1997), Texas Christian (1924–95; will join Western Athletic in 1996), Texas Tech (1958–96; will join Big Eight in 1997).

FORMER MEMBERS: Arkansas (1924–91), Oklahoma A&M (1918 and 1922–25), Phillips, Okla. (1920), Southwestern, Tex. (1915 and 1916).

NIT TITLES (1): Texas (1978).

ALL-TIME LEADING SCORER: Travis Mays, Texas (2,279 points, 1987–90).

REGULAR-SEASON CHAMPIONS: Arkansas (14 outright-8 ties), Baylor (3-2), Houston (2-1), Oklahoma A&M (1-0), Rice (4-6), Southern Methodist (8-5), Texas (12-9), Texas A&M (9-2), Texas Christian (8-2), Texas Tech (3-1).

SWC TOURNAMENT TITLES: Arkansas (6), Houston (5), Texas Tech (4), Texas A&M (2), SMU (1), Texas (1).

YEAR-BY-YEAR CHAMPIONS (incl. conference records): 1915—Texas (5-0); **1916**—Texas (6-0); **1917**—Texas (7-1); **1918**—Rice (7-3); **1919**—Texas (11-2); **1920**—Texas A&M (16-0); **1921**—Texas A&M (10-2); **1922**—Texas A&M (13-3); **1923**—Texas A&M (15-3); **1924**—Texas (20-0); **1925**—Oklahoma A&M (12-2); **1926**—Arkansas (11-1); **1927**—Arkansas (8-2); **1928**—Arkansas (12-0); **1929**—Arkansas (11-1); **1930**—Arkansas (10-2); **1931**—Texas Christian (9-3); **1932**—Baylor (10-2); **1933**—Texas (11-1); **1934**—Texas Christian (10-2); **1935**—Arkansas (9-3), Rice (9-3), Southern Methodist (9-3); **1936**—Arkansas (11-1); **1937**—Southern Methodist (10-2); **1938**—Arkansas (11-1); **1939**—Texas (10-2); **1940**—Rice (10-2); **1941**—Arkansas (12-0); **1942**—Arkansas (10-2), Rice (10-2); **1943**—Rice (9-3), Texas (9-3); **1944**—Arkansas (11-1), Rice (11-1); **1945**—Rice (12-0); **1946**—Baylor (11-1); **1947**—Texas (12-0); **1948**—Baylor (11-1); **1949**—Arkansas (9-3)*, Baylor (9-3); Rice (9-3); **1950**—Arkansas (8-4), Baylor (8-4); **1951**—Texas (8-4), Texas A&M (8-4), Texas Christian (8-4); **1952**—Texas Christian (11-1); **1953**—Texas Christian (9-3); **1954**—Rice (9-3)*, Texas (9-3); **1955**—Southern Methodist (9-3); **1956**—Southern Methodist (12-0); **1957**—Southern Methodist (11-1); **1958**—Arkansas (9-5)*, Southern Methodist (9-5); **1959**—Texas Christian (12-2); **1960**—Texas (11-3); **1961**—Texas Tech (11-3); **1962**—Southern Methodist (11-3), Texas Tech (11-3)*; **1963**—Texas (13-1); **1964**—Texas A&M (13-1); **1965**—Southern Methodist (10-4)*, Texas (10-4); **1966**—Southern Methodist (11-3); **1967**—Southern Methodist (12-2); **1968**—Texas Christian (9-5); **1969**—Texas A&M (12-2); **1970**—Rice (10-4); **1971**—Texas Christian (11-3); **1972**—Southern Methodist (10-4), Texas (10-4)*; **1973**—Texas Tech (11-3); **1975**—Texas A&M (12-2); **1976**—Texas A&M (14-2); **1977**—Arkansas (16-0); **1978**—Arkansas (14-2), Texas (14-2); **1979**—Arkansas (13-3), Texas (13-3); **1980**—Texas A&M (14-2); **1981**—Arkansas (13-3); **1982**—Texas (12-4); **1983**—Houston (16-0); **1984**—Houston (15-1); **1985**—Texas Tech (12-4); **1986**—Texas (12-4), Texas A&M (12-4); **1987**—Texas Christian (14-2); **1988**—Southern Methodist (12-4); **1989**—Arkansas (13-3); **1990**—Arkansas (14-2); **1991**—Arkansas (15-1); **1992**—Houston (11-3), Texas (11-3); **1993**—Southern Methodist (12-2); **1994**—Texas (12-2).

* Won playoff.

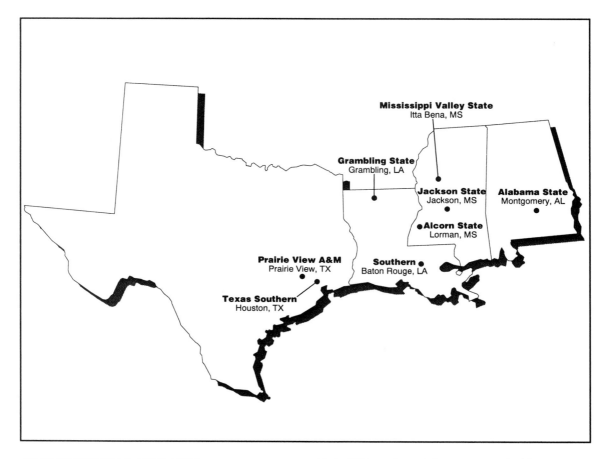

Mississippi Valley State
Itta Bena, MS

Grambling State
Grambling, LA

Jackson State
Jackson, MS

Alabama State
Montgomery, AL

Alcorn State
Lorman, MS

Prairie View A&M
Prairie View, TX

Southern
Baton Rouge, LA

Texas Southern
Houston, TX

SOUTHWESTERN ATHLETIC

ADDRESS: 1500 Sugar Bowl Drive, Louisiana Superdome, New Orleans, LA 70112.

TELEPHONE/FAX: (504) 523-7574/7513.

CURRENT MEMBERS: Alabama State (1983–), Alcorn State (1963–), Grambling State (1959–), Jackson State (1959–), Mississippi Valley State (1969–), Prairie View A&M (1921– , except for 1990–91), Southern (1935–), Texas Southern (1955–).

FORMER MEMBERS: Arkansas AM&N (1937–70), Bishop (1921–56), Langston (1932–57), Paul Quinn (1921–29), Sam Houston (1921–59), Texas College (1921–61), Wiley (1921–68).

ALL-TIME LEADING SCORER: Harry Kelly, Texas Southern (3,066 points, 1980–83).

REGULAR-SEASON CHAMPIONS (SINCE JOINING NCAA IN 1957): Alcorn State (7 outright-5 ties), Arkansas AM&N (0-1), Grambling (6-3), Jackson State (5-4), Mississippi Valley State (0-1), Prairie View (2-0), Southern (3-4), Texas Southern (5-2).

SWAC TOURNAMENT TITLES: Southern (6), Alcorn State (5), Jackson State (2), Mississippi Valley State (2), Texas Southern (2).

YEAR-BY-YEAR CHAMPIONS (incl. conference records): 1957—Texas Southern; 1958—Texas Southern; 1959—Grambling; 1960—Grambling; 1961—Prairie View; 1962—Prairie View; 1963—Grambling; 1964—Grambling, Jackson State; 1965—Southern; 1966—Alcorn State, Grambling; 1967—Alcorn State, Arkansas AM&N, Grambling; 1968—Alcorn State, Jackson State; 1969—Alcorn State; 1970—Jackson State; 1971—Grambling; 1972—Grambling; 1973—Alcorn State; 1974—Jackson State; 1975—Jackson State; 1976—Alcorn State; 1977—Texas Southern; 1978—Jackson State, Southern; 1979—Alcorn State; 1980—Alcorn State; 1981—Alcorn State, Southern; 1982—Alcorn State, Jackson State; 1983—Texas Southern; 1984—Alcorn State; 1985—Alcorn State; 1986—Alcorn State; 1987—Grambling; 1988—Southern; 1989—Grambling, Southern, Texas Southern; 1990—Southern; 1991—Jackson State; 1992—Mississippi Valley State, Texas Southern; 1993—Jackson State; 1994—Texas Southern.

Note: The SWAC, which started in 1921, moved up to Division I status in 1980.

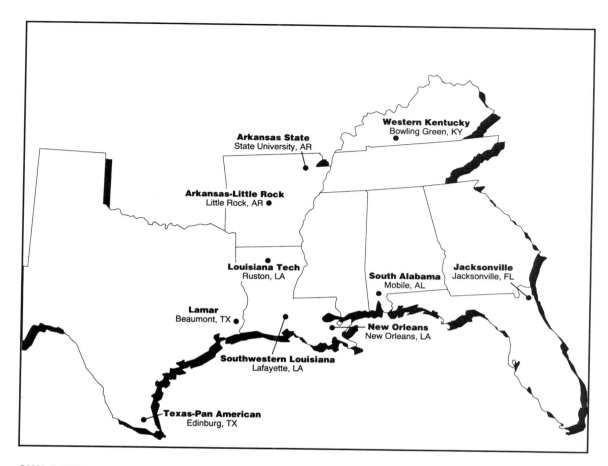

Arkansas State
State University, AR

Western Kentucky
Bowling Green, KY

Arkansas-Little Rock
Little Rock, AR

Louisiana Tech
Ruston, LA

South Alabama
Mobile, AL

Jacksonville
Jacksonville, FL

Lamar
Beaumont, TX

New Orleans
New Orleans, LA

Southwestern Louisiana
Lafayette, LA

Texas-Pan American
Edinburg, TX

SUN BELT

ADDRESS: One Galleria Boulevard, Suite 2115, Metairie, LA 70001.

TELEPHONE/FAX: (504) 834-6600/6806.

CURRENT MEMBERS: Arkansas-Little Rock (1992–), Arkansas State (1992–), Jacksonville (1977–), Lamar (1992–), Louisiana Tech (1992–), New Orleans (1977–80 and 1992–), South Alabama (1977–), Southwestern Louisiana (1992–), Texas-Pan American (1992–), Western Kentucky (1983–).

FORMER MEMBERS: Alabama-Birmingham (1980–91), Central Florida (1992), Georgia State (1977–81), UNC Charlotte (1977–91), Old Dominion (1983–91), South Florida (1977–91), Virginia Commonwealth (1980–91).

ALL-TIME LEADING SCORER: Charles Bradley, South Florida (2,273 points, 1982–85).

REGULAR-SEASON CHAMPIONS: Alabama-Birmingham (2 outright-1 tie), Louisiana Tech (0-1), New Orleans (1-0), UNC Charlotte (3-0), Old Dominion (1-1), South Alabama (4-1), Southwestern Louisiana (0-1), Virginia Commonwealth (2-2), Western Kentucky (2-0).

SUN BELT TOURNAMENT TITLES: Alabama-Birmingham (4), Virginia Commonwealth (3), Jacksonville (2), UNC Charlotte (2), South Alabama (2), Southwestern Louisiana (2), New Orleans (1), South Florida (1), Western Kentucky (1).

YEAR-BY-YEAR CHAMPIONS (incl. conference records): 1977—UNC Charlotte (5-1); **1978**—UNC Charlotte (9-1); **1979**—South Alabama (10-0); **1980**—South Alabama (12-2); **1981**—Alabama-Birmingham (9-3), South Alabama (9-3), Virginia Commonwealth (9-3); **1982**—Alabama-Birmingham (9-1); **1983**—Old Dominion (12-2), Virginia Commonwealth (12-2); **1984**—Virginia Commonwealth (11-3); **1985**—Virginia Commonwealth (12-2); **1986**—Old Dominion (11-3); **1987**—Western Kentucky (12-2); **1988**—UNC Charlotte (11-3); **1989**—South Alabama (11-3); **1990**—Alabama-Birmingham (12-2); **1991**—South Alabama (11-3); **1992**—Louisiana Tech (13-3); **1993**—New Orleans (18-0); **1994**—Western Kentucky (14-4).

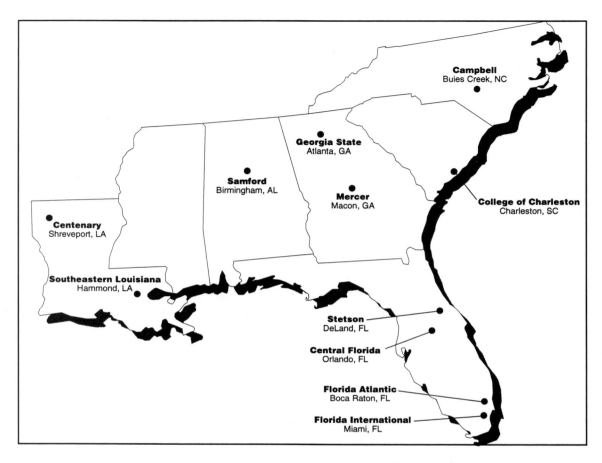

TRANS AMERICA ATHLETIC

ADDRESS: The Commons, Suite 108-B, 3370 Vineville Avenue, Macon, GA 31204.

TELEPHONE/FAX: (912) 474-3394/4272.

CURRENT MEMBERS: Campbell (1995–), Centenary (1980–), Central Florida (1994–), College of Charleston, S.C. (1994–), Florida Atlantic (1996–), Florida International (1992–), Georgia State (1985–), Mercer (1980–), Samford (1980–), Southeastern Louisiana (1992–), Stetson (1987–).

FORMER MEMBERS: Arkansas-Little Rock (1981–91), Georgia Southern (1981–92), Hardin-Simmons (1980–90), Houston Baptist (1980–89), Northeast Louisiana (1980–82), Northwestern State, La. (1981–84), Texas-Pan American (1980), Texas-San Antonio (1987–91).

ALL-TIME LEADING SCORER: Willie Jackson, Centenary (2,535 points, 1981–84).

REGULAR-SEASON CHAMPIONS: Arkansas-Little Rock (4 outright-1 tie), Centenary (1-0), College of Charleston (1-0), Florida International (1-0), Georgia Southern (3-1), Houston Baptist (2-0), Northeast Louisiana (2-0), Texas-San Antonio (1-0).

TAAC TOURNAMENT TITLES: Arkansas-Little Rock (3), Georgia Southern (3), Mercer (2), Northeast Louisiana (2), Centenary (1), Central Florida (1), Georgia State (1), Houston Baptist (1), Texas-San Antonio (1).

YEAR-BY-YEAR CHAMPIONS (incl. conference records): 1980—Northeast Louisiana (6-0); **1981**—Houston Baptist (9-3); **1982**—Arkansas-Little Rock (12-4); **1983**—Arkansas-Little Rock (12-2); **1984**—Houston Baptist (11-3); **1985**—Georgia Southern (11-3); **1986**—Arkansas-Little Rock (12-2); **1987**—Arkansas-Little Rock (16-2); **1988**—Arkansas-Little Rock (15-3), Georgia Southern (15-3); **1989**—Georgia Southern (16-2); **1990**—Centenary (14-2); **1991**—Texas-San Antonio (12-2); **1992**—Georgia Southern (13-1); **1993**—Florida International (9-3); **1994**—College of Charleston (14-2).

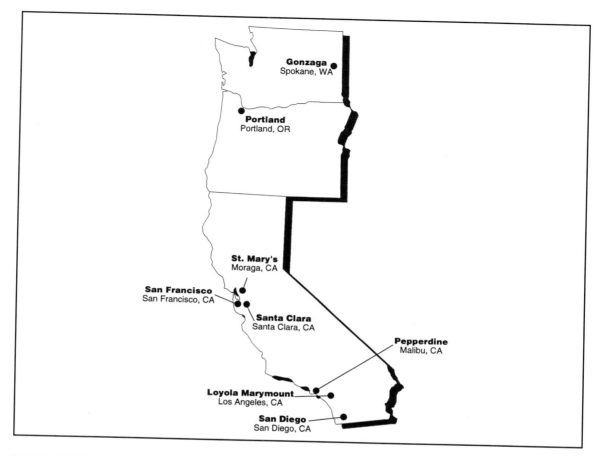

WEST COAST

ADDRESS: 400 Oyster Point Boulevard, Suite 221, South San Francisco, CA 94080.

TELEPHONE/FAX: (415) 873-8622/7846.

PREVIOUS NAMES: California Basketball Association and West Coast Athletic.

CURRENT MEMBERS: Gonzaga (1980–), Loyola Marymount (1956–), Pepperdine (1956–), Portland (1977–), St. Mary's (1953–), San Diego (1980–), San Francisco (1953–), Santa Clara (1953–).

FORMER MEMBERS: UC Santa Barbara (1965–69), Fresno State (1956 and 1957), Nevada-Reno (1970–79), Pacific (1953–71), San Jose State (1953–69), Seattle (1972–80), UNLV (1970–75).

NCAA TITLES (2): San Francisco (1955 and 1956).

ALL-TIME LEADING SCORER: Hank Gathers, Loyola Marymount (2,490 points, 1988–90).

REGULAR-SEASON CHAMPIONS: Gonzaga (1 outright-0 ties), Loyola Marymount (3-0), Pacific (3-0), Pepperdine (9-1), St. Mary's (2-1), San Diego (2-0), San Francisco (13-2), Santa Clara (6-0), UNLV (1-0).

WCC TOURNAMENT TITLES: Pepperdine (3), Loyola Marymount (2), Santa Clara (2).

YEAR-BY-YEAR CHAMPIONS (incl. conference records): 1953—San Francisco (6-2), Santa Clara (6-2)*; **1954**—Santa Clara (9-3); **1955**—San Francisco (12-0); **1956**—San Francisco (14-0); **1957**—San Francisco (12-2); **1958**—San Francisco (12-0); **1959**—St. Mary's (11-1); **1960**—Loyola Marymount (9-3), Santa Clara (9-3)*; **1961**—Loyola Marymount (10-2); **1962**—Pepperdine (11-1); **1963**—San Francisco (10-2); **1964**—San Francisco (12-0); **1965**—San Francisco (13-1); **1966**—Pacific (13-1); **1967**—Pacific (14-0); **1968**—Santa Clara (13-1); **1969**—Santa Clara (13-1); **1970**—Pacific (11-3), Santa Clara (11-3)*; **1971**—Pacific (12-2); **1972**—San Francisco (13-1); **1973**—San Francisco (12-2); **1974**—San Francisco (12-2); **1975**—UNLV (13-1); **1976**—Pepperdine (10-2); **1977**—San Francisco (14-0); **1978**—San Francisco (12-2); **1979**—San Francisco (12-2); **1980**—San Francisco (11-5), St. Mary's (11-5); **1981**—Pepperdine (11-3), San Francisco (11-3); **1982**—Pepperdine (14-0); **1983**—Pepperdine (10-2); **1984**—San Diego (9-3); **1985**—Pepperdine (11-1); **1986**—Pepperdine (13-1); **1987**—San Diego (13-1); **1988**—Loyola Marymount (14-0); **1989**—St. Mary's (12-2); **1990**—Loyola Marymount (13-1); **1991**—Pepperdine (13-1); **1992**—Pepperdine (14-0); **1993**—Pepperdine (11-3); **1994**—Gonzaga (12-2).

* Won playoff.

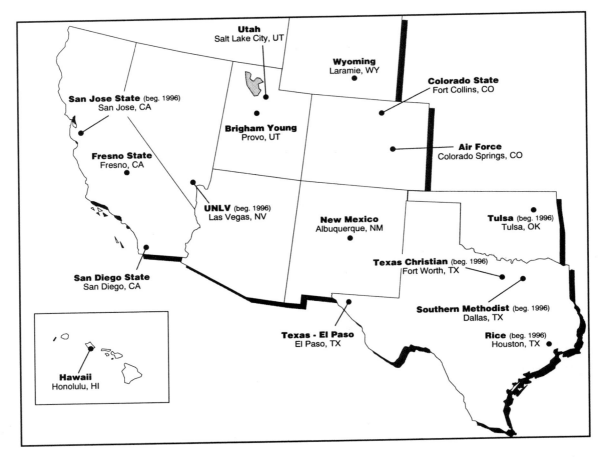

WESTERN ATHLETIC

ADDRESS: 14 West Dry Creek Circle, Littleton, CO 80120-4478.

TELEPHONE/FAX: (303) 795-1962/1960.

CURRENT MEMBERS: Air Force (1981–), Brigham Young (1963–), Colorado State (1970–), Fresno State (1993–), Hawaii (1980–), New Mexico (1963–), San Diego State (1979–), Texas-El Paso (1970–), Utah (1963–), Wyoming (1963–). Rice, San Jose State, Southern Methodist, Texas Christian, Tulsa, and UNLV are slated to join the league in 1996.

FORMER MEMBERS: Arizona (1963–78), Arizona State (1963–78).

NCAA TITLES (1): Texas-El Paso (1966). UTEP won the title before joining the WAC.

NIT TITLES (4): Brigham Young (1951 and 1966), Fresno State (1983), Utah (1947). The only one of the four NIT titles won as a member of the WAC was BYU in 1966.

ALL-TIME LEADING SCORER: Danny Ainge, Brigham Young (2,467 points, 1978–81).

REGULAR-SEASON CHAMPIONS: Arizona (1 outright-0 ties), Arizona State (3-1), Brigham Young (6-5), Colorado State (1-1), New Mexico (4-1), Texas-El Paso (4-3), Utah (3-4), Wyoming (1-4).

WAC TOURNAMENT TITLES: Texas-El Paso (4), Brigham Young (2), Wyoming (2), Hawaii (1), New Mexico (1), San Diego State (1).

YEAR-BY-YEAR CHAMPIONS (incl. conference records): 1963—Arizona State (9-1); **1964**—Arizona State (7-3), New Mexico (7-3); **1965**—Brigham Young (8-2); **1966**—Utah (7-3); **1967**—Brigham Young (8-2), Wyoming (8-2); **1968**—New Mexico (8-2); **1969**—Brigham Young (6-4), Wyoming (6-4); **1970**—Texas-El Paso (10-4); **1971**—Brigham Young (10-4); **1972**—Brigham Young (12-2); **1973**—Arizona State (10-4); **1974**—New Mexico (10-4); **1975**—Arizona State (12-2); **1976**—Arizona (11-3); **1977**—Utah (11-3); **1978**—New Mexico (13-1); **1979**—Brigham Young (10-2); **1980**—Brigham Young (13-1); **1981**—Utah (13-3), Wyoming (13-3); **1982**—Wyoming (14-2); **1983**—Brigham Young (11-5), Texas-El Paso (11-5), Utah (11-5); **1984**—Texas-El Paso (13-3); **1985**—Texas-El Paso (12-4); **1986**—Texas-El Paso (12-4), Utah (12-4), Wyoming (12-4); **1987**—Texas-El Paso (13-3); **1988**—Brigham Young (13-3); **1989**—Colorado State (12-4); **1990**—Brigham Young (11-5), Colorado State (11-5); **1991**—Utah (15-1); **1992**—Brigham Young (12-4), Texas-El Paso (12-4); **1993**—Brigham Young (15-3), Utah (15-3); **1994**—New Mexico (14-4).

FORMER MAJOR COLLEGE CONFERENCES

AMERICAN SOUTH (1988–91):

Merged with the Sun Belt.

YEAR-BY-YEAR CHAMPIONS (incl. conference records): 1988—Louisiana Tech (7-3), New Orleans (7-3); 1989—New Orleans (7-3); 1990—Louisiana Tech (8-2), New Orleans (8-2); 1991—Arkansas State (9-3), New Orleans (9-3).

BORDER (1932–62):

Disbanded when the WAC was formed.

YEAR-BY-YEAR CHAMPIONS (incl. conference records): 1932—Arizona; 1933—Texas Tech; 1934—Texas Tech; 1935—Texas Tech; 1936—Arizona; 1937—New Mexico State; 1938—New Mexico State; 1939—New Mexico State; 1940—New Mexico State; 1941—DNP; 1942—West Texas A&M; 1943—West Texas A&M; 1944—Northern Arizona; 1945—New Mexico; 1946—Arizona; 1947—Arizona; 1948—Arizona; 1949—Arizona; 1950—Arizona; 1951—Arizona; 1952—New Mexico State, West Texas A&M; 1953—Arizona, Hardin-Simmons; 1954—Texas Tech; 1955—Texas Tech, West Texas A&M; 1956—Texas Tech; 1957—Texas Western; 1958—Arizona State; 1959—Arizona State, New Mexico State, Texas Western; 1960—New Mexico State; 1961—Arizona State, New Mexico State; 1962—Arizona State.

EAST COAST (1975–94):

Merged with Mid-Continent prior to start of 1994–95 season. Featured divisional format first nine years.

YEAR-BY-YEAR CHAMPIONS (incl. conference records): 1975—American (East), La Salle (East), Lafayette (West); 1976—St. Joseph's (East), Lafayette (West); 1977—Temple (East), Hofstra (East), Lafayette (West); 1978—La Salle (East), Lafayette (West); 1979—Temple (East), Bucknell (West); 1980—St. Joseph's (East), Lafayette (West); 1981—American (East), Lafayette (West), Rider (West); 1982—Temple (East), West Chester (West); 1983—American (East), La Salle (East), Hofstra (East), Rider (West); 1984—Bucknell; 1985—Bucknell; 1986—Drexel; 1987—Bucknell; 1988—Lafayette; 1989—Bucknell; 1990—Towson State, Hofstra, Lehigh; 1991—Towson State; 1992—Hofstra; 1993—DNP.

GULF STAR (1985–87):

Members joined Southland or became independents before joining Trans America Athletic.

YEAR-BY-YEAR CHAMPIONS (incl. conference records): 1985—Southeastern Louisiana; 1986—Sam Houston State; 1987—Stephen F. Austin.

METROPOLITAN COLLEGIATE (1966–69):

Disbanded with eight members, including Fairleigh Dickinson, Hofstra, Iona, Long Island, Manhattan, St. Peter's, Seton Hall, and Wagner.

METROPOLITAN NEW YORK (1943–63):

Brooklyn, CCNY, Fordham, Manhattan, New York University, St. Francis (N.Y.), and St. John's made up this conference as of its last season in 1962–63.

YEAR-BY-YEAR CHAMPIONS (incl. conference records): 1943—St. John's; 1944—DNP; 1945—DNP; 1946—New York U., St. John's; 1947—St. John's; 1948—New York U.; 1949—Manhattan, St. John's; 1950—CCNY; 1951—St. John's; 1952—St. John's; 1953—Manhattan; 1954—St. Francis (N.Y.); 1955—Manhattan; 1956—St. Francis (N.Y.); 1957—New York U.; 1958—St. John's; 1959—Manhattan; 1960—New York U.; 1961—St. John's; 1962—St. John's; 1963—Fordham.

MIDDLE ATLANTIC (1959–74):

Split into Eastern and Western sections the last five years of its existence before the majority of members wound up forming the East Coast Conference.

MOUNTAIN STATES (1938–62):

The Mountain States Conference was also known informally as the Big Seven before embracing the Skyline Six and Skyline Eight label.

YEAR-BY-YEAR CHAMPIONS (incl. conference records): 1938—Colorado, Utah; 1939—Colorado; 1940—Colorado; 1941—Wyoming; 1942—Colorado; 1943—Wyoming; 1944—Utah; 1945—Utah; 1946—Wyoming; 1947—Wyoming; 1948—Brigham Young; 1949—Wyoming; 1950—Brigham Young; 1951—Brigham Young; 1952—Wyoming; 1953—Wyoming; 1954—Colorado; 1955—Utah; 1956—Utah; 1957—Brigham Young; 1958—Wyoming; 1959—Utah; 1960—Utah; 1961—Colorado State, Utah; 1962—Utah.

NEW ENGLAND (1938–46), YANKEE (1947–75):

This league disbanded with members Boston University, Connecticut, Maine, Massachusetts, New Hampshire, Rhode Island, and Vermont.

YEAR-BY-YEAR CHAMPIONS (incl. conference records): 1938—Rhode Island; 1939—Rhode Island; 1940—Rhode Island; 1941—Rhode Island; 1942—Rhode Island; 1943—Rhode Island; 1944—Rhode Island; 1945—DNP; 1946—Rhode Island. 1947—Vermont; 1948—Connecticut; 1949—Connecticut; 1950—Rhode Island; 1951—Connecticut; 1952—Connecticut; 1953—Connecticut; 1954—Connecticut; 1955—Connecticut; 1956—Connecticut; 1957—Connecticut; 1958—Connecticut; 1959—Connecticut; 1960—Connecticut; 1961—Rhode Island; 1962—Massachusetts; 1963—Connecticut; 1964—Connecticut, Rhode Island; 1965—Connecticut; 1966—Connecticut, Rhode Island; 1967—Connecticut; 1968—Massachusetts, Rhode Island; 1969—Massachusetts; 1970—Connecticut, Massachusetts; 1971—Massachusetts; 1972—Rhode Island; 1973—Massachusetts; 1974—Massachusetts; 1975—Massachusetts.

ROCKY MOUNTAIN (1922–60):

Divisional format from 1925 to 1937. Seven members dropped out of the Rocky Mountain and formed the Mountain States Intercollegiate Athletic Conference after the 1936–37 season.

YEAR-BY-YEAR CHAMPIONS (incl. conference records): 1922—Colorado Col.; 1923—Colorado Col.; 1924—Colorado Col.; 1925—Colorado Col. (East), Brigham Young (West); 1926—Colorado State (East), Utah (West); 1927—Colorado Col. (East), Montana State (West); 1928—Wyoming (East), Montana State (West); 1929—Colorado (East), Montana State (West); 1930—Colorado (East), Montana State, Utah State (West); 1931—Wyoming (East), Utah (West); 1932—Wyoming (East), Brigham Young, Utah (West); 1933—Wyoming (East), Colorado State (East), Brigham Young (West), Utah (West); 1934—Wyoming (East), Brigham Young, Utah State (West); 1935—Northern Colorado (East), Utah State (West); 1936—Wyoming (East), Utah (West); 1937—Denver (East), Colorado (East), Montana State (West), Utah (West); 1938—Montana State; 1939—Northern Colorado; 1940—Northern Colorado; 1941—Northern Colorado; 1942—Northern Colorado; 1943—Northern Colorado; 1944—Colorado College; 1945—Colorado College; 1946—Colorado State; 1947—Montana State; 1948—Colorado State; 1949—Colorado State; 1950—Montana State; 1951—Montana State; 1952—Colorado State, Montana State; 1953—Idaho State; 1954—Idaho State; 1955—Idaho State; 1956—Idaho State; 1957—Idaho State; 1958—Idaho State; 1959—Idaho State; 1960—Idaho State.

BASKETBALL ORGANIZATIONS

College Sports Information Directors of America

c/o Fred Nuesch
Texas A&M-Kingsville
Campus Box 114A
Kingsville, TX 78363
Phone: (512) 595-3908

Community College League of California

2017 "O" Street
Sacramento, CA 95814
Phone: (916) 444-8641

Naismith Memorial Hall of Fame

1150 West Columbus Avenue
Springfield, MA 01101-0179
Phone: (413) 781-6500

National Association of Basketball Coaches

9300 West 110th Street, Suite 640
Overland Park, KS 66210-1486
Phone: (913) 469-1001

National Association of Intercollegiate Athletics

6120 South Yale, Suite 1450
Tulsa, OK 74136
Phone: (918) 494-8828

National Collegiate Athletic Association

6201 College Boulevard
Overland Park, KS 66211-2422
Phone: (913) 339-1906

National Invitation Tournament

Downtown Athletic Club
19 West Street, Suite 2010
New York, NY 10004
Phone: (212) 425-6510

National Junior College Athletic Association

P.O. Box 7305
Colorado Springs, CO 80933
Phone: (719) 590-9788

United States Basketball Writers Association

100 North Broadway, Suite 1135
St. Louis, MO 63102
Phone: (314) 421-0339

USA Basketball

1750 East Boulder Street
Colorado Springs, CO 80909
Phone: (719) 632-7687

15

SCHOOL DIRECTORY

I n 1950, 145 schools were classified as major colleges. Forty years later, the number of NCAA Division I institutions had more than doubled to over 300. The following are vital facts for over 200 schools classified as major colleges for more than 40 years, who have had at least one player earn a spot as an NCAA consensus first-team All-American, have won at least one NCAA Tournament game, have reached the NIT semifinals, or are a current member of a conference that has had an NCAA champion.

AIR FORCE

NICKNAME: Falcons.

ADDRESS: Building 2169, Room 1050, Colorado Springs, CO 80840-5461.

PHONE/FAX: (719) 472-2313/3798.

ENROLLMENT: 4,400.

ARENA: Cadet Fieldhouse (6,000).

SCHOOL COLORS: Blue and silver.

CONFERENCE:: Western Athletic.

NCAA TOURNAMENT APPEARANCES (2): 1960 and 1962; 0-2 record.

NIT APPEARANCES: None.

CAREER LEADING SCORER: Raymond Dudley (2,178 points, 1987–90).

CAREER LEADING REBOUNDER: Reggie Jones (776, 1978–81).

ALABAMA

NICKNAME: Crimson Tide.

ADDRESS: P.O. Box 870391, Tuscaloosa, AL 35487-0391.

PHONE/FAX: (205) 348-6084/8841.

ENROLLMENT: 20,000.

ARENA: Coleman Coliseum (15,043).

SCHOOL COLORS: Crimson and white.

CONFERENCE:: Southeastern.

FINAL AP TOP 10 RANKINGS (4): 1956-75-76-87.

NCAA TOURNAMENT APPEARANCES (13): 1975-76-82-83-84-85-86-87-89-90-91-92-94; 14-13 record (.519); never reached regional final.

NIT APPEARANCES (6): 1973-77-79-80-81-93; 10-8 record (.556); finished 4th in 1973, 4th in 1977, and 3d in 1979.

CAREER LEADING SCORER: Reggie King (2,168 points, 1976–79).

CAREER LEADING REBOUNDER: Jerry Harper (1,688, 1953–56).

ALABAMA-BIRMINGHAM

NICKNAME: Blazers.

ADDRESS: 115 UAB Arena, Birmingham, AL 35294-1160.

PHONE/FAX: (205) 934-0722/7505.

ENROLLMENT: 16,660.

ARENA: UAB Arena (8,500).

SCHOOL COLORS: Green, gold, and white.

CONFERENCE: Great Midwest.

NCAA TOURNAMENT APPEARANCES (9): 1981-82-83-84-85-86-87-90-94; 6-9 record (.400); reached regional final in 1982.

NIT APPEARANCES (5): 1980-89-91-92-93; 8-5 record (.615); finished 3d in 1989 and 1993.

CAREER LEADING SCORER: Steve Mitchell (1,867 points, 1983–86).

CAREER LEADING REBOUNDER: Jerome Mincy (933, 1983–86).

ALCORN STATE

NICKNAME: Braves.

ADDRESS: P.O. Box 510, Lorman, MS 39096.

PHONE/FAX: (601) 877-6466/3821.

ENROLLMENT: 3,300.

ARENA: Davey L. Whitney Complex (7,000).

SCHOOL COLORS: Purple and old gold.

CONFERENCE: Southwestern Athletic.

NCAA TOURNAMENT APPEARANCES (4): 1980-82-83-84; 3-4 record (.429).

NIT APPEARANCES (2): 1979 and 1985; 1-2 record (.333).

CAREER LEADING SCORER: Richard Smith (2,527 points, 1953–56).

CAREER LEADING REBOUNDER: Alfred Milton (1,432, 1972–75).

ARIZONA

NICKNAME: Wildcats.

ADDRESS: McKale Center, Tucson, AZ 85721.

PHONE/FAX: (602) 621-4163/2681.

ENROLLMENT: 34,000.

ARENA: McKale Center (13,814).

SCHOOL COLORS: Cardinal and navy.

CONFERENCE: Pacific-10.

FINAL AP TOP 10 RANKINGS (6): 1988-89-91-92-93-94.

NCAA TOURNAMENT APPEARANCES (13): 1951-76-77-85-86-87-88-89-90-91-92-93-94; 15-13 record (.536); reached Final Four in 1988 (T3d) and 1994 (T3d).

NIT APPEARANCES (3): 1946-50-51; 0-3 record.

CAREER LEADING SCORER: Sean Elliott (2,535 points, 1986–89).

CAREER LEADING REBOUNDER: Al Fleming (1,190, 1973–76).

NCAA CONSENSUS FIRST-TEAM ALL-AMERICANS (2): Sean Elliott (1988 and 1989).

ARIZONA STATE

NICKNAME: Sun Devils.

ADDRESS: IAC Building, Room 105, Tempe, AZ 85287-2505.

PHONE/FAX: (602) 965-3482/5408.

ENROLLMENT: 42,625.

ARENA: University Activity Center (14,287).

SCHOOL COLORS: Maroon and gold.

CONFERENCE: Pacific-10.

FINAL AP TOP 10 RANKINGS (3): 1963-75-81.

NCAA TOURNAMENT APPEARANCES (10): 1958-61-62-63-64-73-75-80-81-91; 9-11 record (.450); regional runner-up in 1961, 1963, and 1975.

NIT APPEARANCES (5): 1983-90-92-93-94; 2-5 record (.286).

CAREER LEADING SCORER: Stevin Smith (1,673 points, 1991–94).

CAREER LEADING REBOUNDER: Tony Cerkvenik (1,022, 1960–63).

ARKANSAS

NICKNAME: Razorbacks.

ADDRESS: P.O. Box 7777, Fayetteville, AR 72702.

PHONE/FAX: (501) 575-2751/7481.

ENROLLMENT: 14,200.

ARENA: Bud Walton Arena (18,600).

SCHOOL COLORS: Cardinal and white.

CONFERENCE: Southeastern.

FINAL AP TOP 10 RANKINGS (8): 1978-79-83-84-90-91-92-94.

NCAA TOURNAMENT APPEARANCES (20): 1941-45-49-58-77-78-79-80-81-82-83-84-85-88-89-90-91-92-93-94; 30-20 record (.600); reached Final Four in 1941 (T3d), 1945 (T3d), 1978 (3d), 1990 (T3d), and 1994 (1st).

NIT APPEARANCES (1): 1987; 1-1 record (.500).

CAREER LEADING SCORER: Todd Day (2,395 points, 1989–92).

CAREER LEADING REBOUNDER: Sidney Moncrief (1,015, 1976–79).

NCAA CONSENSUS FIRST-TEAM ALL-AMERICANS (3): Ike Poole (1936), John Adams (1941), and Sidney Moncrief (1979).

ARKANSAS-LITTLE ROCK

NICKNAME: Trojans.

ADDRESS: 2801 South University Avenue, Little Rock, AR 72204.

PHONE/FAX: (501) 569-3449/3030.

ENROLLMENT: 12,420.

ARENA: Barton Coliseum (8,303).

SCHOOL COLORS: Maroon and gold.

CONFERENCE: Sun Belt.

NCAA TOURNAMENT APPEARANCES (3): 1986-89-90; 1-3 record (.250).

NIT APPEARANCES (2): 1987 and 1988; 3-3 record (.500); finished 4th in 1987.

CAREER LEADING SCORER: James Scott (1,731 points, 1988–91).

CAREER LEADING REBOUNDER: Larry Johnson (1,315, 1975–78).

ARMY

NICKNAMES: Black Knights, Cadets.

ADDRESS: 639 Howard Road, West Point, NY 10996-9906.

PHONE/FAX: (914) 938-3512/446-2556.

ENROLLMENT: 4,200.

ARENA: Christl Arena (5,043).

SCHOOL COLORS: Black, gold, and gray.

CONFERENCE: Patriot.

NCAA TOURNAMENT APPEARANCES: None.

NIT APPEARANCES (8): 1961-64-65-66-68-69-70-78; 13-10 record (.565); finished 3d in 1964, 3d in 1965, 4th in 1966, 4th in 1969, and 3d in 1970.

CAREER LEADING SCORER: Kevin Houston (2,325 points, 1984–87).

CAREER LEADING REBOUNDER: Gary Winton (1,168, 1975–78).

AUBURN

NICKNAME: Tigers.

ADDRESS: P.O. Box 351, Auburn, AL 36831-0351.

PHONE/FAX: (205) 844-9701/9708.

ENROLLMENT: 21,800.

ARENA: Beard-Eaves-Memorial Coliseum (12,500).

SCHOOL COLORS: Burnt orange and navy blue.

CONFERENCE: Southeastern.

FINAL AP TOP 10 RANKINGS (1): 1959.

NCAA TOURNAMENT APPEARANCES (5): 1984-85-86-87-88; 7-5 record (.583); regional runner-up in 1986.

NIT APPEARANCES (1): 1993; 0-1 record.

CAREER LEADING SCORER: Chuck Person (2,311 points, 1983–86).

CAREER LEADING REBOUNDER: Mike Mitchell (996, 1975–78).

AUSTIN PEAY STATE

NICKNAME: Governors.

ADDRESS: Box 4515, Clarksville, TN 37044.

PHONE/FAX: (615) 648-7561/7562.

ENROLLMENT: 8,200.

ARENA: Dunn Center (9,000).

SCHOOL COLORS: Red and white.

CONFERENCE: Ohio Valley.

NCAA TOURNAMENT APPEARANCES (3): 1973-74-87; 2-4 record (.333).

NIT APPEARANCES: None.

CAREER LEADING SCORER: Tom Morgan (1,850 points in 1953 and 1956–58).

CAREER LEADING REBOUNDER: Tom Morgan (1,431 in 1953 and 1956–58).

BALL STATE

NICKNAME: Cardinals.

ADDRESS: HP 120, Muncie, IN 47306-0929.

PHONE/FAX: (317) 285-8242/8929.

ENROLLMENT: 20,717.

ARENA: University Arena (11,500).

SCHOOL COLORS: Cardinal and white.

CONFERENCE: Mid-American.

NCAA TOURNAMENT APPEARANCES (5): 1981-86-89-90-93; 3-5 record (.375).

NIT APPEARANCES (2): 1991 and 1992; 0-2 record.

CAREER LEADING SCORER: Ray McCallum (2,109 points, 1980–83).

CAREER LEADING REBOUNDER: Ed Butler (1,231, 1962–64).

BAYLOR

NICKNAME: Bears.

ADDRESS: 3031 Dutton, Waco, TX 76711.

PHONE/FAX: (817) 755-3042/1369.

ENROLLMENT: 12,500.

ARENA: Ferrell Center (10,084).

SCHOOL COLORS: Green and gold.

CONFERENCE: Southwest (will join Big 12, now Big Eight, in 1997).

NCAA TOURNAMENT APPEARANCES (4): 1946-48-50-88; 3-6 record (.333); reached Final Four in 1948 (2d) and 1950 (4th).

NIT APPEARANCES (2): 1987 and 1990; 0-2 record.

CAREER LEADING SCORER: Terry Teagle (2,189 points, 1979–82).

CAREER LEADING REBOUNDER: Jerry Mallett (877, 1955–57).

BOSTON COLLEGE

NICKNAME: Eagles.

ADDRESS: Conte Forum 321, Chestnut Hill, MA 02167.

PHONE/FAX: (617) 552-3004/4903.

ENROLLMENT: 9,165.

ARENA: Silvio O. Conte Forum (8,606).

SCHOOL COLORS: Maroon and gold.

CONFERENCE: Big East.

FINAL AP TOP 10 RANKINGS (1): 1967.

NCAA TOURNAMENT APPEARANCES (9): 1958-67-68-75-81-82-83-85-94; 14-10 record (.583); regional runner-up in 1967, 1982, and 1994.

NIT APPEARANCES (9): 1965-66-69-74-80-84-88-92-93; 15-10 record (.600); finished 2d in 1969, 3d in 1974, and 4th in 1988.

CAREER LEADING SCORER: Dana Barros (2,342 points, 1986–89).

CAREER LEADING REBOUNDER: Terry Driscoll (1,071, 1967–69).

BOSTON UNIVERSITY

NICKNAME: Terriers.

ADDRESS: 285 Babcock Street, Boston, MA 02215.

PHONE/FAX: (617) 353-2872/4286.

ENROLLMENT: 13,665.

ARENA: Case Gym (2,500).

SCHOOL COLORS: Scarlet and white.

CONFERENCE: North Atlantic.

NCAA TOURNAMENT APPEARANCES (4): 1959-83-88-90; 2-4 record (.333); regional runner-up in 1959.

NIT APPEARANCES (2): 1980 and 1986; 0-2 record.

CAREER LEADING SCORER: Drederick Irving (1,931 points, 1985–88).

CAREER LEADING REBOUNDER: James Garvin (935, 1971–73).

BOWLING GREEN STATE

NICKNAME: Falcons.

ADDRESS: BGSU Athletic Department, Bowling Green, OH 43403-0030.

PHONE/FAX: (419) 372-7076/6015.

ENROLLMENT: 17,300.

ARENA: Anderson Arena (5,000).

SCHOOL COLORS: Seal brown and burnt orange.

CONFERENCE: Mid-American.

FINAL AP TOP 10 RANKINGS (2): 1949 and 1962.

NCAA TOURNAMENT APPEARANCES (4): 1959-62-63-68; 1-5 record (.167).

NIT APPEARANCES (10): 1944-45-46-48-49-54-80-83-90-91; 6-10 record (.375); finished 2d in 1945 and 3d in 1949.

CAREER LEADING SCORER: Howard Komives (1,834 points, 1962–64).

CAREER LEADING REBOUNDER: Nate Thurmond (1,295, 1961–63).

NCAA CONSENSUS FIRST-TEAM ALL-AMERICANS (1): Wyndol Gray (1945, before playing for Harvard the next season).

BRADLEY

NICKNAME: Braves.

ADDRESS: 1501 West Bradley Avenue, Peoria, IL 61625.

PHONE/FAX: (309) 677-2624/2626.

ENROLLMENT: 6,000.

ARENA: Carver Arena (10,474).

SCHOOL COLORS: Red and white.

CONFERENCE: Missouri Valley.

FINAL AP TOP 10 RANKINGS (8): 1949-50-51-54-59-60-61-62.

NCAA TOURNAMENT APPEARANCES (6): 1950-54-55-80-86-88; 9-6 record (.600); reached Final Four in 1950 (2d) and 1954 (2d).

NIT APPEARANCES (16): 1938-39-47-49-50-57-58-59-60-62-64-65-68-82-85-94; 23-13 record (.639); finished 3d in 1939, 4th in 1949, 2d in 1950, 1st in 1957, 2d in 1959, 1st in 1960, 1st in 1964, and 1st in 1982.

CAREER LEADING SCORER: Hersey Hawkins (3,008 points, 1985–88).

CAREER LEADING REBOUNDER: Dick Estergard (1,414, 1952–54).

NCAA CONSENSUS FIRST-TEAM ALL-AMERICANS (5): Paul Unruh (1950), Gene Melchiorre (1951), Chet Walker (1961 and 1962), and Hersey Hawkins (1988).

BRIGHAM YOUNG

NICKNAME: Cougars.

ADDRESS: 106 Smith Fieldhouse, Provo, UT 84602.

PHONE/FAX: (801) 378-4911/3520.

ENROLLMENT: 26,000.

ARENA: Marriott Center (22,700).

SCHOOL COLORS: Blue and white.

CONFERENCE: Western Athletic.

FINAL AP TOP 10 RANKINGS (2): 1965 and 1972.

NCAA TOURNAMENT APPEARANCES (17): 1950-51-57-65-69-71-72-79-80-81-84-87-88-90-91-92-93; 11-20 record (.355); regional runner-up in 1950, 1951, and 1981.

NIT APPEARANCES (7): 1951-53-54-66-82-86-94; 9-5 record (.643); finished 1st in 1951 and 1966.

CAREER LEADING SCORER: Danny Ainge (2,467 points, 1978–81).

CAREER LEADING REBOUNDER: Michael Smith (922, 1984–89; missed 1984–85 and 1985–86 seasons while on a Latter Day Saints mission).

NCAA CONSENSUS FIRST-TEAM ALL-AMERICANS (2): Elwood Romney (1931) and Danny Ainge (1981).

BROWN

NICKNAME: Bears.

ADDRESS: Box 1932, Providence, RI 02912.

PHONE/FAX: (401) 863-2219, 2259/1436.

ENROLLMENT: 5,500.

ARENA: Pizzitola Sports Center (2,800).

SCHOOL COLORS: Seal brown, cardinal red, and white.

CONFERENCE: Ivy League.

NCAA TOURNAMENT APPEARANCES (2): 1939 and 1986; 0-2 record.

NIT APPEARANCES: None.

CAREER LEADING SCORER: Arnie Berman (1,668 points, 1970–72).

CAREER LEADING REBOUNDER: Phil Brown (931, 1973–75).

BUCKNELL

NICKNAME: Bison.

ADDRESS: Lewisburg, PA 17837-2005.

PHONE/FAX: (717) 524-1227/1660.

ENROLLMENT: 3,400.

ARENA: David Gymnasium (2,300).

SCHOOL COLORS: Orange and blue.

CONFERENCE: Patriot.

NCAA TOURNAMENT APPEARANCES (2): 1987 and 1989; 0-2 record.

NIT APPEARANCES: None.

CAREER LEADING SCORER: Al Leslie (1,973 points, 1978–81).

CAREER LEADING REBOUNDER: Hal Danzig (1,134, 1957–59).

BUTLER

NICKNAME: Bulldogs.

ADDRESS: 4600 Sunset Avenue, Indianapolis, IN 46208.

PHONE/FAX: (317) 283-9375/9808.

ENROLLMENT: 4,200.

ARENA: Hinkle Fieldhouse (11,043).

SCHOOL COLORS: Blue and white.

CONFERENCE: Midwestern Collegiate.

NCAA TOURNAMENT APPEARANCES (1): 1962; 2-1 record (.333).

NIT APPEARANCES (5): 1958-59-85-91-92; 1-5 record (.167).

CAREER LEADING SCORER: Chad Tucker (2,321 points, 1984–88; sat out most of 1986–87 season because of shoulder injury).

CAREER LEADING REBOUNDER: Daryl Mason (961, 1972–74).

CALIFORNIA

NICKNAME: Golden Bears.

ADDRESS: Memorial Stadium, Berkeley, CA 94720.

PHONE/FAX: (510) 642-5363/643-7778.

ENROLLMENT: 31,000.

ARENAS: Harmon Arena (6,578) and Oakland/Alameda County Coliseum (15,025).

SCHOOL COLORS: Blue and gold.

CONFERENCE: Pacific-10.

FINAL AP TOP 10 RANKINGS (1): 1960.

NCAA TOURNAMENT APPEARANCES (8): 1946-57-58-59-60-90-93-94; 14-8 record (.636); reached Final Four in 1946 (4th), 1959 (1st), and 1960 (2d).

NIT APPEARANCES (3): 1986-87-89; 3-3 record (.500).

CAREER LEADING SCORER: Lamond Murray (1,688 points, 1992–94).

CAREER LEADING REBOUNDER: Bob McKeen (1,019, 1952–55).

NCAA CONSENSUS FIRST-TEAM ALL-AMERICANS (3): Vern Corbin (1929), Darrall Imhoff (1960), and Jason Kidd (1994).

UC IRVINE

NICKNAME: Anteaters.

ADDRESS: Campus and University Drive, Irvine, CA 92717.

PHONE/FAX: (714) 856-5814/5260.

ENROLLMENT: 16,700.

ARENA: Bren Events Center (5,000).

SCHOOL COLORS: Blue and gold.

CONFERENCE: Big West.

NCAA TOURNAMENT APPEARANCES: None.

NIT APPEARANCES (2): 1982 and 1986; 2-2 record (.500).

CAREER LEADING SCORER: Tod Murphy (1,778 points, 1983–86).

CAREER LEADING REBOUNDER: Dave Baker (926, 1972–75).

UC SANTA BARBARA

NICKNAME: Gauchos.

ADDRESS: Ward Memorial Freeway, Santa Barbara, CA 93106.

PHONE/FAX: (805) 893-3428/4537.

ENROLLMENT: 18,200.

ARENA: The Thunderdome (6,000).

SCHOOL COLORS: Blue and gold.

CONFERENCE: Big West.

NCAA TOURNAMENT APPEARANCES (2): 1988 and 1990; 1-2 record (.333).

NIT APPEARANCES (3): 1989-92-93; 0-3 record.

CAREER LEADING SCORER: Carrick DeHart (1,687 points, 1987–90).

CAREER LEADING REBOUNDER: Eric McArthur (904, 1987–90).

CAL STATE FULLERTON

NICKNAME: Titans.

ADDRESS: 800 North State College Boulevard, Fullerton, CA 92634-9480.

PHONE/FAX: (714) 773-3970/3141.

ENROLLMENT: 22,500.

ARENA: Titan Gym (4,000).

SCHOOL COLORS: Blue, orange, and white.

CONFERENCE: Big West.

NCAA TOURNAMENT APPEARANCES (1): 1978; reached regional final with a 2-1 record.

NIT APPEARANCES (2): 1983 and 1987; 0-2 record.

CAREER LEADING SCORER: Leon Wood (1,876 points, 1981–84).

CAREER LEADING REBOUNDER: Tony Neal (1,115, 1982–85).

CANISIUS

NICKNAME: Golden Griffins.

ADDRESS: 2001 Main Street, Buffalo, NY 14208.

PHONE/FAX: (716) 888-2970/2980.

ENROLLMENT: 4,525.

ARENAS: Koessler Athletic Center (1,800) and Memorial Auditorium (16,476).

SCHOOL COLORS: Blue and gold.

CONFERENCE: Metro Atlantic Athletic.

NCAA TOURNAMENT APPEARANCES (3): 1955-56-57; 6-3 record (.667); regional runner-up in 1955 and 1956.

NIT APPEARANCES (4): 1944-63-85-94; 2-3 record (.400); finished 2d in 1963.

CAREER LEADING SCORER: Ray Hall (2,226 points, 1982–85).

CAREER LEADING REBOUNDER: Henry Nowak (880, 1955–57).

CENTRAL MICHIGAN

NICKNAME: Chippewas.

ADDRESS: 101 West Hall, Mount Pleasant, MI 48859.

PHONE/FAX: (517) 774-3277/7324.

ENROLLMENT: 16,250.

ARENA: Dan Rose Arena (6,000).

SCHOOL COLORS: Maroon and gold.

CONFERENCE: Mid-American.

NCAA TOURNAMENT APPEARANCES (3): 1975-77-87; 2-3 record (.400).

NIT APPEARANCES (1): 1979; 0-1 record.

CAREER LEADING SCORER: Melvin McLaughlin (2,071 points, 1980–83).

CAREER LEADING REBOUNDER: Dan Roundfield (1,031, 1973–75).

CINCINNATI

NICKNAME: Bearcats.

ADDRESS: 340 Shoemaker Center, Cincinnati, OH 45221-0021.

PHONE/FAX: (513) 556-5191/0619.

ENROLLMENT: 36,000.

ARENA: Myrl Shoemaker Center (13,176).

SCHOOL COLORS: Red and black.

CONFERENCE: Great Midwest.

FINAL AP TOP 10 RANKINGS (8): 1958-59-60-61-62-63-66-93.

NCAA TOURNAMENT APPEARANCES (13): 1958-59-60-61-62-63-66-75-76-77-92-93-94; 27-12 record (.692); reached Final Four in 1959 (3d), 1960 (3d), 1961 (1st), 1962 (1st), 1963 (2d), and 1992 (3d).

NIT APPEARANCES (8): 1951-55-57-70-74-85-90-91; 5-8 record (.385); finished 3d in 1955.

CAREER LEADING SCORER: Oscar Robertson (2,973 points, 1958–60).

CAREER LEADING REBOUNDER: Oscar Robertson (1,338, 1958–60).

NCAA CONSENSUS FIRST-TEAM ALL-AMERICANS (5): Oscar Robertson (1958, 1959, and 1960), Ron Bonham (1963), and Tom Thacker (1963).

THE CITADEL

NICKNAME: Bulldogs.

ADDRESS: Charleston, SC 29409.

PHONE/FAX: (803) 953-5120/4058.

ENROLLMENT: 2,000.

ARENA: McAlister Field House (6,200).

SCHOOL COLORS: Citadel blue and white.

CONFERENCE: Southern.

NCAA TOURNAMENT APPEARANCES: None.

NIT APPEARANCES: None.

CAREER LEADING SCORER: Regan Truesdale (1,661 points, 1982–85).

CAREER LEADING REBOUNDER: Ray Graves (924, 1958–60).

CLEMSON

NICKNAME: Tigers.

ADDRESS: 100 Perimeter Road, P.O. Box 632, Clemson, SC 29633.

PHONE/FAX: (803) 365-2114/656-0299.

ENROLLMENT: 17,665.

ARENA: Littlejohn Coliseum (11,020).

SCHOOL COLORS: Purple and orange.

CONFERENCE: Atlantic Coast.

NCAA TOURNAMENT APPEARANCES (4): 1980-1987-89-90; 6-4 record (.600); regional runner-up in 1980.

NIT APPEARANCES (9): 1975-79-81-82-85-86-88-93-94; 6-9 record (.400).

CAREER LEADING SCORER: Elden Campbell (1,880 points, 1987–90).

CAREER LEADING REBOUNDER: Tree Rollins (1,311, 1974–77).

CLEVELAND STATE

NICKNAME: Vikings.

ADDRESS: Convocation Center, 2000 Prospect Avenue, Cleveland, OH 44115.

PHONE/FAX: (216) 687-4818/523-7257.

ENROLLMENT: 19,090.

ARENA: CSU Convocation Center (13,610).

SCHOOL COLORS: Forest green and white.

CONFERENCE: Midwestern Collegiate.

NCAA TOURNAMENT APPEARANCES (1): 1986; 2-1 record (.667).

NIT APPEARANCES (2): 1987 and 1988; 2-2 record (.500).

CAREER LEADING SCORER: Ken "Mouse" McFadden (2,256 points, 1986–89).

CAREER LEADING REBOUNDER: Weldon Kytle (1,241, 1962–65).

COLGATE

NICKNAME: Red Raiders.

ADDRESS: 13 Oak Drive, Hamilton, NY 13346-1398.

PHONE/FAX: (315) 824-7566/0042.

ENROLLMENT: 2,700.

ARENA: Cotterell Court (3,000).

SCHOOL COLORS: Maroon, gray, and white.

CONFERENCE: Patriot.

NCAA TOURNAMENT APPEARANCES: None.

NIT APPEARANCES: None.

CAREER LEADING SCORER: Mike Ferrara (1,763 points, 1978–81); Tucker Neale expected to break record in 1994–95.

CAREER LEADING REBOUNDER: Jack Nichols (1,082, 1955–57).

NCAA CONSENSUS FIRST-TEAM ALL-AMERICANS (1): Otto Graham (1944; also played with Northwestern).

COLORADO

NICKNAME: Buffaloes.

ADDRESS: CU Fieldhouse Annex, Box 357, Boulder, CO 80309.

PHONE/FAX: (303) 492-5626/3811.

ENROLLMENT: 25,090.

ARENA: Coors Event Center (11,199).

SCHOOL COLORS: Silver, gold, and black.

CONFERENCE: Big Eight (will be renamed Big 12 in 1997).

FINAL AP TOP 10 RANKINGS (2): 1962 and 1963.

NCAA TOURNAMENT APPEARANCES (8): 1940-42-46-54-55-62-63-69; 8-10 record (.444); reached Final Four in 1942 (T3d) and 1955 (3d).

NIT APPEARANCES (3): 1938-40-91; 7-2 record (.778); finished 2d in 1938, 1st in 1940, and 3d in 1991.

CAREER LEADING SCORER: Cliff Meely (1,940 points, 1969–71; Donnie Boyce is on a pace to become all-time leader in 1995).

CAREER LEADING REBOUNDER: Cliff Meely (971, 1969–71).

COLORADO STATE

NICKNAME: Rams.

ADDRESS: 202 B Moby Arena, Fort Collins, CO 80523.

PHONE/FAX: (303) 491-5067/1348.

ENROLLMENT: 20,600.

ARENA: Moby Arena (9,000).

SCHOOL COLORS: Green and gold.

CONFERENCE: Western Athletic.

NCAA TOURNAMENT APPEARANCES (7): 1954-63-65-66-69-89-90; 3-8 record (.273); regional runner-up in 1969.

NIT APPEARANCES (3): 1961-62-88; 4-3 record (.571); finished 3d in 1988.

CAREER LEADING SCORER: Pat Durham (1,980 points, 1986–89).

CAREER LEADING REBOUNDER: Pat Durham (851, 1986–89).

COLUMBIA

NICKNAME: Lions.

ADDRESS: 406 Dodge Physical Fitness Center, New York, NY 10027.

PHONE/FAX: (212) 854-2534/8168.

ENROLLMENT: 5,200.

ARENA: Levien Gymnasium (3,408).

SCHOOL COLORS: Columbia blue and white.

CONFERENCE: Ivy League.

FINAL AP TOP 10 RANKINGS (2): 1951 and 1968.

NCAA TOURNAMENT APPEARANCES (3): 1948-51-68; 2-4 record (.333).

NIT APPEARANCES: None.

CAREER LEADING SCORER: Buck Jenkins (1,766 points, 1990–93).

CAREER LEADING REBOUNDER: Frank Thomas (1,022, 1954–56).

NCAA CONSENSUS FIRST-TEAM ALL-AMERICANS (2): George Gregory (1931) and Chet Forte (1957).

CONNECTICUT

NICKNAMES: Huskies, UConn.

ADDRESS: 2095 Hillside Road, U-78, Storrs, CT 06269-3078.

PHONE/FAX: (203) 486-3531/5085.

ENROLLMENT: 25,885.

ARENAS: Gampel Pavilion (8,241) and Hartford Civic Center (16,294).

SCHOOL COLORS: National flag blue and white.

CONFERENCE: Big East.

FINAL AP TOP 10 RANKINGS (2): 1990 and 1994.

NCAA TOURNAMENT APPEARANCES (17): 1951-54-56-57-58-59-60-63-64-65-67-76-79-90-91-92-94; 12-18 record (.400); regional runner-up in 1964 and 1990.

NIT APPEARANCES (9): 1955-74-75-80-81-82-88-89-93; 9-8 record (.529); finished 1st in 1988.

CAREER LEADING SCORER: Chris Smith (2,145 points, 1989–92).

CAREER LEADING REBOUNDER: Art Quimby (1,716, 1952–55).

NCAA CONSENSUS FIRST-TEAM ALL-AMERICANS (1): Donyell Marshall (1994).

CORNELL

NICKNAME: Big Red.

ADDRESS: Box 729, Ithaca, NY 14851.

PHONE/FAX: (607) 255-3752/9791.

ENROLLMENT: 12,900.

ARENA: Alberding Field House (4,750).

SCHOOL COLORS: Carnellian red and white.

CONFERENCE: Ivy League.

NCAA TOURNAMENT APPEARANCES (2): 1954 and 1988; 0-3 record.

NIT APPEARANCES: None.

CAREER LEADING SCORER: John Bajusz (1,663 points, 1984–87).

CAREER LEADING REBOUNDER: George Farley (1,089, 1958–60).

CREIGHTON

NICKNAME: Bluejays.

ADDRESS: Vinardi Athletic Center, 2500 California Plaza, Omaha, NE 68178-0810.

PHONE/FAX: (402) 280-2488/2495.

ENROLLMENT: 6,340.

ARENA: Omaha Civic Auditorium (9,481).

SCHOOL COLORS: Blue and white.

CONFERENCE: Missouri Valley.

NCAA TOURNAMENT APPEARANCES (9): 1941-62-64-74-75-78-81-89-91; 7-10 record (.412); regional runner-up in 1941.

NIT APPEARANCES (5): 1942-43-77-84-90; 2-5 record (.286); finished 3d in 1942.

CAREER LEADING SCORER: Bob Harstad (2,110 points, 1988–91).

CAREER LEADING REBOUNDER: Paul Silas (1,751, 1962–64).

NCAA CONSENSUS FIRST-TEAM ALL-AMERICANS (1): Ed Beisser (1943).

DARTMOUTH

NICKNAME: Big Green.

ADDRESS: Box G, 6083 Alumni Gym, Hanover, NH 03755-3512.

PHONE/FAX: (603) 646-2468/1286.

ENROLLMENT: 4,000.

ARENA: Leede Arena (2,100).

SCHOOL COLORS: Dartmouth green and white.

CONFERENCE: Ivy League.

NCAA TOURNAMENT APPEARANCES (7): 1941-42-43-44-56-58-59; 10-7 record (.588); reached Final Four in 1942 (2d) and 1944 (2d).

NIT APPEARANCES: None.

CAREER LEADING SCORER: Jim Barton (2,158 points, 1986–89).

CAREER LEADING REBOUNDER: Rudy LaRusso (1,239, 1957–59).

NCAA CONSENSUS FIRST-TEAM ALL-AMERICANS (3): Gus Broberg (1940 and 1941) and Audley Brindley (1944).

DAVIDSON

NICKNAME: Wildcats.

ADDRESS: Davidson, NC 28036.

PHONE/FAX: (704) 892-2374/2636.

ENROLLMENT: 1,550.

ARENA: Belk Arena (6,000).

SCHOOL COLORS: Red and black.

CONFERENCE: Southern.

FINAL AP TOP 10 RANKINGS (4): 1964-65-68-69.

NCAA TOURNAMENT APPEARANCES (5): 1966-68-69-70-86; 5-6 record (.455); regional runner-up in 1968 and 1969.

NIT APPEARANCES (2): 1972 and 1994; 0-2 record.

CAREER LEADING SCORER: John Gerdy (2,487 points, 1976–79).

CAREER LEADING REBOUNDER: Mike Maloy (1,111, 1968–70).

NCAA CONSENSUS FIRST-TEAM ALL-AMERICANS (1): Fred Hetzel (1965).

DAYTON

NICKNAME: Flyers.

ADDRESS: 300 College Park, Dayton, OH 45469-1238.

PHONE/FAX: (513) 229-4460/4461.

ENROLLMENT: 6,300.

ARENA: Dayton Arena (13,455).

SCHOOL COLORS: Red and blue.

CONFERENCE: Great Midwest.

FINAL AP TOP 10 RANKINGS (2): 1955 and 1956.

NCAA TOURNAMENT APPEARANCES (10): 1952-65-66-67-69-70-74-84-85-90; 13-12 record (.520); reached Final Four in 1967 (2d).

NIT APPEARANCES (17): 1951-52-54-55-56-57-58-60-61-62-68-71-78-79-81-82-86; 29-16 record (.644); finished 2d in 1951, 2d in 1952, 2d in 1955, 2d in 1956, 2d in 1958, 4th in 1961, 1st in 1962, and 1st in 1968.

CAREER LEADING SCORER: Roosevelt Chapman (2,233 points, 1981–84).

CAREER LEADING REBOUNDER: John Horan (1,341, 1952–55).

DEPAUL

NICKNAME: Blue Demons.

ADDRESS: 1011 West Belden Avenue, Chicago, IL 60614.

PHONE/FAX: (312) 362-8551/8076.

ENROLLMENT: 16,415.

ARENA: Rosemont Horizon (17,500).

SCHOOL COLORS: Royal blue and scarlet.

CONFERENCE: Great Midwest.

FINAL AP TOP 10 RANKINGS (8): 1964-78-79-80-81-82-84-87.

NCAA TOURNAMENT APPEARANCES (20): 1943-53-56-59-60-65-76-78-79-80-81-82-84-85-86-87-88-89-91-92; 20-23 record (.465); reached Final Four in 1943 (T3d) and 1979 (3d).

NIT APPEARANCES (11): 1940-44-45-48-61-63-64-66-83-90-94; 13-12 record (.520); finished 4th in 1940, 2d in 1944, 1st in 1945, 4th in 1948, and 2d in 1983.

CAREER LEADING SCORER: Mark Aguirre (2,182 points, 1979–81).

CAREER LEADING REBOUNDER: Dave Corzine (1,151, 1975–78).

NCAA CONSENSUS FIRST-TEAM ALL-AMERICANS (6): George Mikan (1944, 1945, and 1946), Mark Aguirre (1980 and 1981), and Terry Cummings (1982).

DETROIT MERCY

NICKNAME: Titans.

ADDRESS: 4001 West McNichols Road, P.O. Box 19900, Detroit, MI 48219-0900.

PHONE/FAX: (313) 993-1745/1765.

ENROLLMENT: 7,800.

ARENA: Cobo Arena (11,143).

SCHOOL COLORS: Red, white, and blue.

CONFERENCE: Midwestern Collegiate.

NCAA TOURNAMENT APPEARANCES (3): 1962-77-79; 1-3 record (.250).

NIT APPEARANCES (4): 1960-61-65-78; 2-4 record (.333).

CAREER LEADING SCORER: John Long (2,167 points, 1975–78).

CAREER LEADING REBOUNDER: Dave DeBusschere (1,552, 1960–62).

NCAA CONSENSUS FIRST-TEAM ALL-AMERICANS (1): Spencer Haywood (1969).

DRAKE

NICKNAME: Bulldogs.

ADDRESS: Drake Fieldhouse, Des Moines, IA 50311.

PHONE/FAX: (515) 271-3012/3015.

ENROLLMENT: 4,000.

ARENA: Knapp Center (7,002).

SCHOOL COLORS: Blue and white.

CONFERENCE: Missouri Valley.

NCAA TOURNAMENT APPEARANCES (3): 1969-70-71; 5-3 record (.625); reached Final Four in 1969 (3d).

NIT APPEARANCES (3): 1964-81-86; 1-3 record (.250).

CAREER LEADING SCORER: Red Murrell (1,657 points, 1956–58).

CAREER LEADING REBOUNDER: Melvin Mathis (854, 1983–86).

DUKE

NICKNAME: Blue Devils.

ADDRESS: P.O. Box 90557, 115 Cameron Indoor Stadium, Durham, NC 27708-0557.

PHONE/FAX: (919) 684-2633/2489.

ENROLLMENT: 6,130.

ARENA: Cameron Indoor (9,314).

SCHOOL COLORS: Royal blue and white.

CONFERENCE: Atlantic Coast.

FINAL AP TOP 10 RANKINGS (17): 1958-61-62-63-64-65-66-68-78-85-86-88-89-91-92-93-94.

NCAA TOURNAMENT APPEARANCES (19): 1955-60-63-64-66-78-79-80-84-85-86-87-88-89-90-91-92-93-94; 56-17 record (.767); reached Final Four in 1963 (3d), 1964 (2d), 1966 (3d), 1978 (2d), 1986 (2d), 1988 (T3d), 1989 (T3d), 1990 (2d), 1991 (1st), 1992 (1st), and 1994 (2d).

NIT APPEARANCES (5): 1967-68-70-71-81; 5-6 record (.455); finished 4th in 1971.

CAREER LEADING SCORER: Johnny Dawkins (2,556 points, 1983–86).

CAREER LEADING REBOUNDER: Mike Gminski (1,242, 1977–80).

NCAA CONSENSUS FIRST-TEAM ALL-AMERICANS (10): Dick Groat (1952), Art Heyman (1963), Mike Gminski (1979), Johnny Dawkins (1985 and 1986), Danny Ferry (1989), Christian Laettner (1992), Bobby Hurley (1993), and Grant Hill (1994).

DUQUESNE

NICKNAME: Dukes.

ADDRESS: A. J. Palumbo Center, 600 Forbes Avenue, Pittsburgh, PA 15282.

PHONE/FAX: (412) 396-6560/6210.

ENROLLMENT: 8,600.

ARENA: A. J. Palumbo Center (6,200).

SCHOOL COLORS: Red and blue.

CONFERENCE: Atlantic 10.

FINAL AP TOP 10 RANKINGS (6): 1950-52-53-54-55-69.

NCAA TOURNAMENT APPEARANCES (5): 1940-52-69-71-77; 4-5 record (.444); reached Final Four in 1940 (T3d).

NIT APPEARANCES (16): 1940-41-47-50-52-53-54-55-56-62-64-68-70-80-81-94; 17-18 record (.486); finished 2d in 1940, 4th in 1950, 4th in 1952, 3d in 1953, 2d in 1954, 1st in 1955, and 4th in 1962.

CAREER LEADING SCORER: Dick Ricketts (1,963 points, 1952–55).

CAREER LEADING REBOUNDER: Dick Ricketts (1,496, 1952–55).

NCAA CONSENSUS FIRST-TEAM ALL-AMERICANS (3): Dick Ricketts (1955) and Si Green (1955 and 1956).

EAST TENNESSEE STATE

NICKNAME: Buccaneers.

ADDRESS: Johnson City, TN 37614.

PHONE/FAX: (615) 929-4220/6138.

ENROLLMENT: 12,105.

ARENA: Memorial Center (12,000).

SCHOOL COLORS: Blue and gold.

CONFERENCE: Southern.

NCAA TOURNAMENT APPEARANCES (5): 1968-89-90-91-92; 2-6 record (.250).

NIT APPEARANCES (1): 1983; 0-1 record.

CAREER LEADING SCORER: Greg Dennis (2,204 points, 1989–92).

EASTERN KENTUCKY

NICKNAMES: Colonels, Maroons.

ADDRESS: 205 Begley Building, Richmond, KY 40475-3105.

PHONE/FAX: (606) 622-1253/1230.

ENROLLMENT: 16,500.

ARENA: McBrayer Arena (6,500).

SCHOOL COLORS: Maroon and white.

CONFERENCE: Ohio Valley.

NCAA TOURNAMENT APPEARANCES (5): 1953-59-65-72-79; 0-5 record.

NIT APPEARANCES: None.

CAREER LEADING SCORER: Antonio Parris (1,723 points, 1984–87).

CAREER LEADING REBOUNDER: Mike Smith (977, 1989–92).

EASTERN MICHIGAN

NICKNAME: Eagles.

ADDRESS: 200 Bowen Field House, Ypsilanti, MI 48197.

PHONE/FAX: (313) 487-0317/485-3840.

ENROLLMENT: 25,835.

ARENA: Bowen Field House (5,600).

SCHOOL COLORS: Dark green and white.

CONFERENCE: Mid-American.

NCAA TOURNAMENT APPEARANCES (2): 1988 and 1991; 2-2 record (.500).

NIT APPEARANCES: None.

CAREER LEADING SCORER: Kennedy McIntosh (2,219 points, 1968–71).

CAREER LEADING REBOUNDER: Kennedy McIntosh (1,426, 1968–71).

EVANSVILLE

NICKNAME: Aces.

ADDRESS: 1800 Lincoln Avenue, Evansville, IN 47722.

PHONE/FAX: (812) 479-2350/2199.

ENROLLMENT: 2,300.

ARENA: Roberts Stadium (12,300).

SCHOOL COLORS: Purple and white.

CONFERENCE: Missouri Valley.

NCAA TOURNAMENT APPEARANCES (4): 1982-89-92-93; 1-4 record (.200).

NIT APPEARANCES (2): 1988 and 1994; 1-2 record (.333).

CAREER LEADING SCORER: Larry Humes (2,236 points, 1964–66).

CAREER LEADING REBOUNDER: Dale Wise (1,197, 1959–61).

FLORIDA

NICKNAME: Gators.

ADDRESS: P.O. Box 14485, Gainesville, FL 32604.

PHONE/FAX: (904) 375-4683/4809.

ENROLLMENT: 35,000.

ARENA: Stephen C. O'Connell Center (12,000).

SCHOOL COLORS: Orange and blue.

CONFERENCE: Southeastern.

NCAA TOURNAMENT APPEARANCES (4): 1987-88-89-94; 7-4 record (.636); reached Final Four in 1994 (T3d).

NIT APPEARANCES (6): 1969-84-85-86-92-93; 6-8 record (.429); finished 4th in 1986 and 1992.

CAREER LEADING SCORER: Ronnie Williams (2,090 points, 1980–84).

CAREER LEADING REBOUNDER: Neal Walk (1,181, 1967–69).

FLORIDA STATE

NICKNAME: Seminoles.

ADDRESS: Moore Athletic Center, P.O. Drawer 2195, Tallahassee, FL 32316.

PHONE/FAX: (904) 644-1403/3820.

ENROLLMENT: 29,000.

ARENA: Tallahassee Civic Center (12,500).

SCHOOL COLORS: Garnet and gold.

CONFERENCE: Atlantic Coast.

FINAL AP TOP 10 RANKINGS (1): 1972.

NCAA TOURNAMENT APPEARANCES (9): 1968-72-78-80-88-89-91-92-93; 11-9 record (.550); reached Final Four in 1972 (2d).

NIT APPEARANCES (2): 1984 and 1987; 2-2 record (.500).

CAREER LEADING SCORER: Jim Oler (1,820 points, 1953–56); Bob Sura is expected to break the record in 1994–95.

CAREER LEADING REBOUNDER: Dave Cowens (1,340, 1968–70).

FORDHAM

NICKNAME: Rams.

ADDRESS: Rose Hill Gym, Bronx, NY 10458-9993.

PHONE/FAX: (718) 817-4240/4244.

ENROLLMENT: 14,500.

ARENA: Rose Hill Gym (3,470).

SCHOOL COLORS: Maroon and white.

CONFERENCE: Patriot.

FINAL AP TOP 10 RANKINGS (1): 1971.

NCAA TOURNAMENT APPEARANCES (4): 1953-54-71-92; 2-4 record (.333).

NIT APPEARANCES (16): 1943-58-59-63-65-68-69-72-81-82-83-84-85-88-90-91; 5-17 record (.227); finished 4th in 1943.

CAREER LEADING SCORER: Ed Conlin (1,886 points, 1952–55).

CAREER LEADING REBOUNDER: Ed Conlin (1,930, 1952–55).

FRESNO STATE

NICKNAME: Bulldogs.

ADDRESS: 5305 North Campus Drive, Fresno, CA 93740-0027.

PHONE/FAX: (209) 278-2509/4689.

ENROLLMENT: 19,600.

ARENA: Selland Arena (10,132).

SCHOOL COLORS: Cardinal and blue.

CONFERENCE: Western Athletic.

NCAA TOURNAMENT APPEARANCES (3): 1981-82-84; 1-3 record (.250).

NIT APPEARANCES (3): 1983-85-94; 9-2 record (.818); finished 1st in 1983.

CAREER LEADING SCORER: Wil Hooker (1,739 points, 1989–92).

CAREER LEADING REBOUNDER: Gary Alcorn (1,080, 1957–59).

FURMAN

NICKNAME: Paladins.

ADDRESS: 3300 Poinsett Highway, Greenville, SC 29613.

PHONE/FAX: (803) 294-2061/3061.

ENROLLMENT: 2,500.

ARENA: Greenville Memorial Auditorium (5,344).

SCHOOL COLORS: Purple and white.

CONFERENCE: Southern.

NCAA TOURNAMENT APPEARANCES (6): 1971-73-74-75-78-80; 1-7 record (.125).

NIT APPEARANCES (1): 1991; 0-1 record.

CAREER LEADING SCORER: Frank Selvy (2,538 points, 1952–54).

CAREER LEADING REBOUNDER: Jonathan Moore (1,242, 1977–80).

NCAA CONSENSUS FIRST-TEAM ALL-AMERICANS (1): Frank Selvy (1954).

GEORGE WASHINGTON

NICKNAME: Colonials.

ADDRESS: Smith Center, Room 107, 600 22d Street NW, Washington, DC 20052.

PHONE/FAX: (202) 994-8604/2713.

ENROLLMENT: 17,000.

ARENA: Charles E. Smith Center (5,000).

SCHOOL COLORS: Buff and blue.

CONFERENCE: Atlantic 10.

NCAA TOURNAMENT APPEARANCES (4): 1954-61-93-94; 3-4 record (.429).

NIT APPEARANCES (1): 1991; 0-1 record.

CAREER LEADING SCORER: Joe Holup (2,226 points, 1953–56).

CAREER LEADING REBOUNDER: Joe Holup (2,030, 1953–56).

GEORGETOWN

NICKNAME: Hoyas.

ADDRESS: Washington, DC 20057.

PHONE/FAX: (202) 687-2492/2491.

ENROLLMENT: 6,085.

ARENA: USAir Arena (19,035).

SCHOOL COLORS: Blue and gray.

CONFERENCE: Big East.

FINAL AP TOP 10 RANKINGS (6): 1982-84-85-87-89-90.

NCAA TOURNAMENT APPEARANCES (18): 1943-75-76-79-80-81-82-83-84-85-86-87-88-89-90-91-92-94; 31-17 record (.646); reached Final Four in 1943 (2d), 1982 (2d), 1984 (1st), and 1985 (2d).

NIT APPEARANCES (5): 1953-70-77-78-93; 6-6 record (.500); finished 4th in 1978 and 2d in 1993.

CAREER LEADING SCORER: Eric Floyd (2,304 points, 1979–82).

CAREER LEADING REBOUNDER: Patrick Ewing (1,316, 1982–85).

NCAA CONSENSUS FIRST-TEAM ALL-AMERICANS (6): Eric Floyd (1982), Patrick Ewing (1983, 1984, and 1985), Reggie Williams (1987), and Alonzo Mourning (1992).

GEORGIA

NICKNAME: Bulldogs.

ADDRESS: P.O. Box 1472, Athens, GA 30613.

PHONE/FAX: (706) 542-1621/1140.

ENROLLMENT: 28,690.

ARENA: Georgia Coliseum (10,512).

SCHOOL COLORS: Red and black.

CONFERENCE: Southeastern.

NCAA TOURNAMENT APPEARANCES (5): 1983-85-87-90-91; 4-5 record (.444); reached Final Four in 1983 (T3d).

NIT APPEARANCES (6): 1981-82-84-86-88-93; 6-6 record (.500); reached semifinals in 1982.

CAREER LEADING SCORER: Litterial Green (2,111 points, 1989–92).

CAREER LEADING REBOUNDER: Bob Lienhard (1,116, 1968–70).

GEORGIA TECH

NICKNAMES: Yellow Jackets, Rambling Wreck.

ADDRESS: 150 Bobby Dodd Way, NW, Atlanta, GA 30332-0455.

PHONE/FAX: (404) 894-5445/853-2674.

ENROLLMENT: 12,900.

ARENA: Alexander Memorial Coliseum (10,026).

SCHOOL COLORS: Old gold and white.

CONFERENCE: Atlantic Coast.

FINAL AP TOP 10 RANKINGS (3): 1985-86-90.

NCAA TOURNAMENT APPEARANCES (10): 1960-85-86-87-88-89-90-91-92-93; 14-10 record (.583); reached Final Four in 1990 (T3d).

NIT APPEARANCES (4): 1970-71-84-94; 4-4 record (.500); finished 2d in 1971.

CAREER LEADING SCORER: Rich Yunkus (2,232 points, 1969–71).

CAREER LEADING REBOUNDER: Malcolm Mackey (1,205, 1990–93).

NCAA CONSENSUS FIRST-TEAM ALL-AMERICANS (2): Roger Kaiser (1961), Kenny Anderson (1991).

GONZAGA

NICKNAME: Zags.

ADDRESS: East 502 Boone Avenue, Spokane, WA 99258.

PHONE/FAX: (509) 328-4220/484-2830.

ENROLLMENT: 5,000.

ARENA: Charlotte Martin Centre (4,000).

SCHOOL COLORS: Blue, red and white.

CONFERENCE: West Coast.

NCAA TOURNAMENT APPEARANCES: None.

NIT APPEARANCES (1): 1994; 1-1 record (.500).

CAREER LEADING SCORER: Frank Burgess (2,196 points, 1959–61).

CAREER LEADING REBOUNDER: Jerry Vermillion (1,670, 1952–55).

HARVARD

NICKNAME: Crimson.

ADDRESS: 60 John F. Kennedy Street, Cambridge, MA 02138.

PHONE/FAX: (617) 495-2206/2130.

ENROLLMENT: 6,675.

ARENA: Briggs Athletic Center (3,000).

SCHOOL COLORS: Crimson, black, and white.

CONFERENCE: Ivy League.

NCAA TOURNAMENT APPEARANCES (1): 1946; 0-2 record.

NIT APPEARANCES: None.

CAREER LEADING SCORER: Joe Carrabino (1,880 points, 1982–85).

CAREER LEADING REBOUNDER: Ron Mitchell (803, 1989–92).

HAWAII

NICKNAME: Rainbows.

ADDRESS: 1337 Lower Campus Road, Honolulu, HI 96822.

PHONE/FAX: (808) 956-7523/4470.

ENROLLMENT: 19,810.

ARENA: Blaisdell Arena (7,575).

SCHOOL COLORS: Green and white.

CONFERENCE: Western Athletic.

NCAA TOURNAMENT APPEARANCES (2): 1972 and 1994; 0-2 record.

NIT APPEARANCES (4): 1971-74-89-90; 4-4 record (.500).

CAREER LEADING SCORER: Chris Gaines (1,734 points, 1987–90).

CAREER LEADING REBOUNDER: Melton Werts (1,098, 1973–76).

HOLY CROSS

NICKNAME: Crusaders.

ADDRESS: 1 College Street, Worcester, MA 01610-2395.

PHONE/FAX: (508) 793-2583/2309.

ENROLLMENT: 2,600.

ARENA: Hart Recreation Center (3,600).

SCHOOL COLORS: Royal purple, and white.

CONFERENCE: Patriot.

FINAL AP TOP 10 RANKINGS (2): 1950 and 1954.

NCAA TOURNAMENT APPEARANCES (8): 1947-48-50-53-56-77-80-93; 7-8 record (.467); reached Final Four in 1947 (1st) and 1948 (3d).

NIT APPEARANCES (11): 1952-54-55-60-61-62-75-76-79-81-90; 10-10 record (.500); finished 1st in 1954 and 3d in 1961.

CAREER LEADING SCORER: Ronnie Perry (2,524 points, 1977–80).

CAREER LEADING REBOUNDER: Tom Heinsohn (1,254, 1954–56).

NCAA CONSENSUS FIRST-TEAM ALL-AMERICANS (2): Bob Cousy (1950) and Tom Heinsohn (1956).

HOUSTON

NICKNAME: Cougars.

ADDRESS: Department of Athletics, Houston, TX 77204-5121.

PHONE/FAX: (713) 743-9404/9411.

ENROLLMENT: 33,000.

ARENA: Hofheinz Pavilion (10,145).

SCHOOL COLORS: Scarlet and white.

CONFERENCE: Southwest.

FINAL AP TOP 10 RANKINGS (4): 1967-63-83-84.

NCAA TOURNAMENT APPEARANCES (18): 1956-61-65-66-67-68-70-71-72-73-78-81-82-83-84-87-90-92; 26-23 record (.531); reached Final Four in 1967 (3d), 1968 (4th), 1982 (T3d), 1983 (2d), and 1984 (2d).

NIT APPEARANCES (6): NIT Appearances (6): 1962-77-85-88-91-93; 4-6 record (.400); finished 2d in 1977.

CAREER LEADING SCORER: Elvin Hayes (2,884 points, 1966–68).

CAREER LEADING REBOUNDER: Elvin Hayes (1,602, 1966–68).

NCAA CONSENSUS FIRST-TEAM ALL-AMERICANS (4): Elvin Hayes (1967 and 1968), Otis Birdsong (1977), and Hakeem Olajuwon (1984).

IDAHO

NICKNAME: Vandals.

ADDRESS: East End Kibbie Dome, Moscow, ID 83843.

PHONE/FAX: (208) 885-0211/0255.

ENROLLMENT: 14,395.

ARENA: Kibbie ASUI Dome (10,000).

SCHOOL COLORS: Silver and gold.

CONFERENCE: Big Sky.

FINAL AP TOP 10 RANKINGS (1): 1982.

NCAA TOURNAMENT APPEARANCES (4): 1981-82-89-90; 1-4 record (.200).

NIT APPEARANCES (1): 1983; 0-1 record.

CAREER LEADING SCORER: Orlando Lightfoot (2,102 points, 1992–94).

CAREER LEADING REBOUNDER: Deon Watson (877, 1991–94).

IDAHO STATE

NICKNAME: Bengals.

ADDRESS: P.O. Box 8124, Pocatello, ID 83209.

PHONE/FAX: (208) 236-3651/3659.

ENROLLMENT: 11,155.

ARENA: Holt Arena (7,938).

SCHOOL COLORS: Orange and black.

CONFERENCE: Big Sky.

NCAA TOURNAMENT APPEARANCES (11): 1953-54-55-56-57-58-59-60-74-77-87; 8-13 record (.381); regional runner-up in 1977.

NIT APPEARANCES: None.

CAREER LEADING SCORER: Steve Hayes (1,933 points, 1974–77).

CAREER LEADING REBOUNDER: Steve Hayes (1,147, 1974–77).

ILLINOIS

NICKNAME: Fighting Illini.

ADDRESS: 1817 South Neil, Suite 201, Champaign, IL 61820.

PHONE/FAX: (217) 333-1390/5540.

ENROLLMENT: 35,000.

ARENA: Assembly Hall (16,321).

SCHOOL COLORS: Orange and blue.

CONFERENCE: Big Ten.

FINAL AP TOP 10 RANKINGS (7): 1949-51-52-56-63-84-89.

NCAA TOURNAMENT APPEARANCES (16): 1942-49-51-52-63-81-83-84-85-86-87-88-89-90-93-94; 21-17 record (.553); reached Final Four in 1949 (3d), 1951 (3d), 1952 (3d), and 1989 (T3d).

NIT APPEARANCES (2): 1980 and 1982; 5-2 record (.714); finished 3d in 1980.

CAREER LEADING SCORER: Deon Thomas (2,129 points, 1991–94).

CAREER LEADING REBOUNDER: Efrem Winters (853, 1983–86).

NCAA CONSENSUS FIRST-TEAM ALL-AMERICANS (5): Bill Hapac (1940), Andy Phillip (1942 and 1943), Walt Kirk (1945), and Rod Fletcher (1952).

ILLINOIS STATE

NICKNAME: Redbirds.

ADDRESS: Horton Field House 133, College at Delaine, Normal, IL 61790-7130.

PHONE/FAX: (309) 438-3825/5634.

ENROLLMENT: 21,000.

ARENA: Redbird Arena (10,600).

SCHOOL COLORS: Red and white.

CONFERENCE: Missouri Valley.

NCAA TOURNAMENT APPEARANCES (4): 1983-84-85-90; 2-4 record (.333).

NIT APPEARANCES (5): 1977-78-80-87-88; 4-5 record (.444).

CAREER LEADING SCORER: Doug Collins (2,240 points, 1971–73).

CAREER LEADING REBOUNDER: Ron deVries (1,033, 1972–74).

NCAA CONSENSUS FIRST-TEAM ALL-AMERICANS (1): Doug Collins (1973).

INDIANA

NICKNAME: Hoosiers.

ADDRESS: Assembly Hall, Bloomington, IN 47405.

PHONE/FAX: (812) 855-2421/9401.

ENROLLMENT: 35,000.

ARENA: Assembly Hall (17,357).

SCHOOL COLORS: Cream and crimson.

CONFERENCE: Big Ten.

FINAL AP TOP 10 RANKINGS (16): 1951-53-54-60-73-74-75-76-80-81-83-87-89-91-92-93.

NCAA TOURNAMENT APPEARANCES (23): 1940-53-54-58-67-73-75-76-78-80-81-82-83-84-86-87-88-89-90-91-92- 93-94; 50-18 record (.735); reached Final Four in 1940 (1st), 1953 (1st), 1973 (3d), 1976 (1st), 1981 (1st), 1987 (1st), and 1992 (T3d).

NIT APPEARANCES (3): 1972-79-85; 8-2 record (.800); finished 1st in 1979 and 2d in 1985.

CAREER LEADING SCORER: Calbert Cheaney (2,613 points, 1990–93).

CAREER LEADING REBOUNDER: Walt Bellamy (1,088, 1959–61).

NCAA CONSENSUS FIRST-TEAM ALL-AMERICANS (13): Branch McCracken (1930), Vern Huffman (1936), Ernie Andres (1939), Ralph Hamilton (1947), Don Schlundt (1954), Scott May (1975 and 1976), Kent Benson (1976 and 1977), Isiah Thomas (1981), Steve Alford (1986 and 1987), and Calbert Cheaney (1993).

INDIANA STATE

NICKNAME: Sycamores.

ADDRESS: ISU Arena, 4th & Chestnut, Terre Haute, IN 47809.

PHONE/FAX: (812) 237-4160/4157.

ENROLLMENT: 12,270.

ARENA: Hulman Center (10,200).

SCHOOL COLORS: Blue and white.

CONFERENCE: Missouri Valley.

FINAL AP TOP 10 RANKINGS (1): 1979.

NCAA TOURNAMENT APPEARANCES (1): 1979; finished 2d with a 4-1 record.

NIT APPEARANCES (2): 1977 and 1978; 1-2 record (.333).

CAREER LEADING SCORER: Larry Bird (2,850 points, 1977–79).

CAREER LEADING REBOUNDER: Larry Bird (1,247, 1977–79).

NCAA CONSENSUS FIRST-TEAM ALL-AMERICANS (2): Larry Bird (1978 and 1979).

IONA

NICKNAME: Gaels.

ADDRESS: 715 North Avenue, New Rochelle, NY 10801-1890.

PHONE/FAX: (914) 633-2334/2072.

ENROLLMENT: 7,500.

ARENA: Mulcahy Center (3,200).

SCHOOL COLORS: Maroon and gold.

CONFERENCE: Metro Atlantic Athletic.

NCAA TOURNAMENT APPEARANCES (4): 1979-80-84-85; 1-4 record (.200).

NIT APPEARANCES (2): 1982 and 1983; 1-2 record (.333).

CAREER LEADING SCORER: Steve Burtt (2,534 points, 1981–84).

CAREER LEADING REBOUNDER: Warren Isaac (1,124, 1963–65).

IOWA

NICKNAME: Hawkeyes.

ADDRESS: 205 Carver-Hawkeye Arena, Iowa City, IA 52242.

PHONE/FAX: (319) 335-9411/9417.

ENROLLMENT: 28,000.

ARENA: Carver-Hawkeye Arena (15,500).

SCHOOL COLORS: Old gold and black.

CONFERENCE: Big Ten.

FINAL AP TOP 10 RANKINGS (6): 1952-55-56-61-70-87.

NCAA TOURNAMENT APPEARANCES (16): 1955-56-70-79-80-81-82-83-85-86-87-88-89-91-92-93; 22-18 record (.550); reached Final Four in 1955 (4th), 1956 (2d), and 1980 (4th).

NIT APPEARANCES: None.

CAREER LEADING SCORER: Roy Marble (2,116 points, 1986–89).

CAREER LEADING REBOUNDER: Kevin Kunnert (914, 1971–73).

NCAA CONSENSUS FIRST-TEAM ALL-AMERICANS (2): Murray Wier (1948), Chuck Darling (1952).

IOWA STATE

NICKNAME: Cyclones.

ADDRESS: Olsen Building Annex, Ames, IA 50011.

PHONE/FAX: (515) 294-3372/0558.

ENROLLMENT: 25,260.

ARENA: James H. Hilton Coliseum (14,020).

SCHOOL COLORS: Cardinal and gold.

CONFERENCE: Big Eight (will be renamed Big 12 in 1997).

NCAA TOURNAMENT APPEARANCES (7): 1944-85-86-88-89-92-93; 4-7 record (.364); reached Final Four in 1944 (T3d).

NIT APPEARANCES (1): 1984; 0-1 record.

CAREER LEADING SCORER: Jeff Grayer (2,502 points, 1985–88).

CAREER LEADING REBOUNDER: Dean Uthoff (1,233, 1977–80).

JACKSONVILLE

NICKNAME: Dolphins.

ADDRESS: 2800 University Boulevard North, Jacksonville, FL 32211.

PHONE/FAX: (904) 744-7402/743-0067.

ENROLLMENT: 2,400.

ARENA: Jacksonville Coliseum (10,000).

SCHOOL COLORS: Green and gold.

CONFERENCE: Sun Belt.

FINAL AP TOP 10 RANKINGS (1): 1970.

NCAA TOURNAMENT APPEARANCES (5): 1970-71-73-79-86; 4-5 record (.444); reached Final Four in 1970 (2d).

NIT APPEARANCES (4): 1972-74-80-87; 5-5 record (.500); finished 3d in 1972 and 4th in 1974.

CAREER LEADING SCORER: Ralph Tiner (2,184 points, 1962–65).

CAREER LEADING REBOUNDER: Artis Gilmore (1,224 in 1970 and 1971).

NCAA CONSENSUS FIRST-TEAM ALL-AMERICANS (1): Artis Gilmore (1971).

JAMES MADISON

NICKNAME: Dukes.

ADDRESS: Harrisonburg, VA 22807.

PHONE/FAX: (703) 568-6154/3703.

ENROLLMENT: 11,500.

ARENA: JMU Convocation Center (7,612).

SCHOOL COLORS: Purple and gold.

CONFERENCE: Colonial Athletic Association.

NCAA TOURNAMENT APPEARANCES (4): 1981-82-83-94; 3-4 record (.429).

NIT APPEARANCES (5): 1987-90-91-92-93; 0-5 record.

CAREER LEADING SCORER: Steve Stiepler (2,126 points, 1977–80).

CAREER LEADING REBOUNDER: Steve Stiepler (917, 1977–80).

KANSAS

NICKNAME: Jayhawks.

ADDRESS: 202 Allen Fieldhouse, Lawrence, KS 66045.

PHONE/FAX: (913) 864-3417/7944.

ENROLLMENT: 29,150.

ARENA: Allen Fieldhouse (15,800).

SCHOOL COLORS: Crimson and blue.

CONFERENCE: Big Eight (will be renamed Big 12 in 1997).

FINAL AP TOP 10 RANKINGS (13): 1952-53-57-58-66-67-71-74-78-86-90-92-93.

NCAA TOURNAMENT APPEARANCES (23): 1940-42-52-53-57-60-66-67-71-74-75-78-81-84-85-86-87-88-90-91-92- 93-94; 49-23 record (.681); reached Final Four in 1940 (2d), 1952 (1st), 1953 (2d), 1957 (2d), 1971 (4th), 1974 (4th), 1986 (T3d), 1988 (1st), 1991 (2d), and 1993 (T3d).

NIT APPEARANCES (2): 1968 and 1969; 3-2 record (.600); finished 2d in 1968.

CAREER LEADING SCORER: Danny Manning (2,951 points, 1985–88).

CAREER LEADING REBOUNDER: Danny Manning (1,187, 1985–88).

NCAA CONSENSUS FIRST-TEAM ALL-AMERICANS (9): Fred Pralle (1938), Howard Engleman (1941), Charles Black (1943), Clyde Lovellette (1951 and 1952), Wilt Chamberlain (1957 and 1958), and Danny Manning (1987 and 1988).

KANSAS STATE

NICKNAME: Wildcats.

ADDRESS: 144 Bramlage Coliseum, 1800 College Avenue, Manhattan, KS 66502.

PHONE/FAX: (913) 532-6531/6093.

ENROLLMENT: 21,220.

ARENA: Fred Bramlage Coliseum (13,500).

SCHOOL COLORS: Purple and white.

CONFERENCE: Big Eight (will be renamed Big 12 in 1997).

FINAL AP TOP 10 RANKINGS (7): 1951-52-58-59-61-62-73.

NCAA TOURNAMENT APPEARANCES (21): 1948-51-56-58-59-61-64-68-70-72-73-75-77-80-81-82-87-88-89-90-93; 27-25 record (.519); reached Final Four in 1948 (4th), 1951 (2d), 1958 (4th), and 1964 (4th).

NIT APPEARANCES (3): 1976-92-94; 4-4 record (.500); finished 4th in 1994.

CAREER LEADING SCORER: Mike Evans (2,115 points, 1975–78).

CAREER LEADING REBOUNDER: Ed Nealy (1,071, 1979–82).

NCAA CONSENSUS FIRST-TEAM ALL-AMERICANS (2): Bob Boozer (1958 and 1959).

KENT

NICKNAME: Golden Flashes.

ADDRESS: MAC Center, Kent, OH 44242-0001.

PHONE/FAX: (216) 672-2110/2112.

ENROLLMENT: 30,965.

ARENA: Memorial Athletic and Convocation Center (6,327).

SCHOOL COLORS: Blue and gold.

CONFERENCE: Mid-American.

NCAA TOURNAMENT APPEARANCES: None.

NIT APPEARANCES (3): 1985-89-90; 0-3 record.

CAREER LEADING SCORER: Burrell McGhee (1,710 points, 1977–79).

CAREER LEADING REBOUNDER: Trent Grooms (1,012, 1977–80).

KENTUCKY

NICKNAME: Wildcats.

ADDRESS: Memorial Coliseum, Avenue of Champions, Lexington, KY 40506-0019.

PHONE/FAX: (606) 257-8000/323-4310.

ENROLLMENT: 24,200.

ARENA: Rupp Arena (23,000).

SCHOOL COLORS: Blue and white.

CONFERENCE: Southeastern.

FINAL AP TOP 10 RANKINGS (29): 1949-50-51-52-54-55-56-57-58-59-62-64-66-68-69-70-71-75-77-78-80- 81-84-86-88-91-92-93-94.

NCAA TOURNAMENT APPEARANCES (36): 1942-45-48-49-51-52-55-56-57-58-59-61-62-64-66-68-69-70-71-72-73- 75-77-78-80-81-82-83-84-85-86-87-88-92-93-94; 63-33 record (.656); reached Final Four in 1942 (T3d), 1948 (1st), 1949 (1st), 1951 (1st), 1958 (1st), 1966 (2d), 1975 (2d), 1978 (1st), 1984 (T3d), and 1993 (T3d).

NIT APPEARANCES (7): 1944-46-47-49-50-76-79; 11-5 record (.688); finished 3d in 1944, 1st in 1946, 2d in 1947, and 1st in 1976.

CAREER LEADING SCORER: Dan Issel (2,138 points, 1968–70).

CAREER LEADING REBOUNDER: Dan Issel (1,078, 1968–70).

NCAA CONSENSUS FIRST-TEAM ALL-AMERICANS (18): Forest Sale (1932 and 1933), Leroy Edwards (1935), Bob Brannum (1944), Ralph Beard (1947, 1948, and 1949), Alex Groza (1947 and 1949), Bill Spivey (1951), Cliff Hagan (1952 and 1954), Johnny Cox (1959), Cotton Nash (1964), Dan Issel (1970), Kyle Macy (1980), Kenny Walker (1986), and Jamal Mashburn (1993).

LA SALLE

NICKNAME: Explorers.

ADDRESS: 1900 West Olney Avenue, Box 805, Philadelphia, PA 19141-1199.

PHONE/FAX: (215) 951-1513/1694.

ENROLLMENT: 6,500.

ARENA: Philadelphia Civic Center (10,000).

SCHOOL COLORS: Blue and gold.

CONFERENCE: Midwestern Collegiate.

FINAL AP TOP 10 RANKINGS (5): 1950-53-54-55-69.

NCAA TOURNAMENT APPEARANCES (11): 1954-55-68-75-78-80-83-88-89-90-92; 11-10 record (.524); reached Final Four in 1954 (1st) and 1955 (2d).

NIT APPEARANCES (11): 1948-50-51-52-53-63-65-71-84-87-91; 9-10 record (.474); finished 1st in 1952 and 2d in 1987.

CAREER LEADING SCORER: Lionel Simmons (3,217 points, 1987–90).

CAREER LEADING REBOUNDER: Tom Gola (2,201, 1952–55).

NCAA CONSENSUS FIRST-TEAM ALL-AMERICANS (5): Tom Gola (1953, 1954, and 1955), Michael Brooks (1980), and Lionel Simmons (1990).

LAFAYETTE

NICKNAME: Leopards.

ADDRESS: 17 Watson Hall, Easton, PA 18042-1768.

PHONE/FAX: (610) 250-5122/5127.

ENROLLMENT: 2,000.

ARENA: Allan P. Kirby Field House (3,500).

SCHOOL COLORS: Maroon and white.

CONFERENCE: Patriot.

NCAA TOURNAMENT APPEARANCES (1): 1957; 0-2 record.

NIT APPEARANCES (5): 1955-56-72-75-80; 1-5 record (.167).

CAREER LEADING SCORER: Tracy Tripucka (1,973 points, 1970–72).

CAREER LEADING REBOUNDER: Jim Radcliff (1,148, 1955–57).

LAMAR

NICKNAME: Cardinals.

ADDRESS: P.O. Box 10066, Beaumont, TX 77710.

PHONE/FAX: (409) 880-2323/2338.

ENROLLMENT: 9,110.

ARENA: Montagne Center (10,080).

SCHOOL COLORS: Red and white.

CONFERENCE: Sun Belt.

NCAA TOURNAMENT APPEARANCES (4): 1979-80-81-83; 5-4 record (.556).

NIT APPEARANCES (4): 1982-84-85-86; 2-4 record (.333).

CAREER LEADING SCORER: Mike Olliver (2,518 points, 1978–81).

CAREER LEADING REBOUNDER: Clarence Kea (1,143, 1977–80).

LEHIGH

NICKNAME: Engineers.

ADDRESS: 641 Taylor Street, Bethlehem, PA 18015-3187.

PHONE/FAX: (610) 758-3174/4407.

ENROLLMENT: 4,400.

ARENA: Stabler Arena (5,600).

SCHOOL COLORS: Brown and white.

CONFERENCE: Patriot.

NCAA TOURNAMENT APPEARANCES (2): 1985 and 1988; 0-2 record.

NIT APPEARANCES: None.

CAREER LEADING SCORER: Daren Queenan (2,703 points, 1985–88).

CAREER LEADING REBOUNDER: Daren Queenan (1,013, 1985–88).

LONG BEACH STATE

NICKNAME: 49ers.

ADDRESS: 1250 Bellflower Boulevard, Long Beach, CA 90840.

PHONE/FAX: (310) 985-7978/8197.

ENROLLMENT: 27,445.

ARENA: The Gold Mine (1,900).

SCHOOL COLORS: Black and gold.

CONFERENCE: Big West.

FINAL AP TOP 10 RANKINGS (3): 1972-73-74.

NCAA TOURNAMENT APPEARANCES (6): 1970-71-72-1973-77-93; 7-7 record (.500); regional runner-up in 1971 and 1972.

NIT APPEARANCES (3): 1980-88-90; 2-3 record (.400).

CAREER LEADING SCORER: Lucious Harris (2,312 points, 1990–93).

CAREER LEADING REBOUNDER: Francois Wise (896, 1977–80).

NCAA CONSENSUS FIRST-TEAM ALL-AMERICANS (2): Ed Ratleff (1972 and 1973).

LONG ISLAND

NICKNAME: Blackbirds.

ADDRESS: University Plaza, Brooklyn, NY 11201.

PHONE/FAX: (718) 488-1420/243-0766.

ENROLLMENT: 8,000.

ARENA: Schwartz Athletic Center (1,700).

SCHOOL COLORS: Blue and white.

CONFERENCE: Northeast.

NCAA TOURNAMENT APPEARANCES (2): 1981 and 1984; 0-2 record.

NIT APPEARANCES (9): 1938-39-40-41-42-47-50-68-82; 7-7 record (.500); finished 1st in 1939 and 1941.

CAREER LEADING SCORER: Robert Cole (1,800 points, 1980–83).

CAREER LEADING REBOUNDER: Carey Scurry (1,013, 1983–85; played freshman season in junior college).

NCAA CONSENSUS FIRST-TEAM ALL-AMERICANS (2): Jules Bender (1937) and Irving Torgoff (1939).

LOUISIANA STATE

NICKNAME: Tigers.

ADDRESS: P.O. Box 25095, Baton Rouge, LA 70894-5095.

PHONE/FAX: (504) 388-8226/1861.

ENROLLMENT: 24,750.

ARENA: Pete Maravich Assembly Center (14,164).

SCHOOL COLORS: Purple and gold.

CONFERENCE: Southeastern.

FINAL AP TOP 10 RANKINGS (4): 1953-79-80-81.

NCAA TOURNAMENT APPEARANCES (15): 1953-54-79-80-81-84-85-86-87-88-89-90-91-92-93; 17-18 record (.486); reached Final Four in 1953 (4th), 1981 (4th), and 1986 (T3d).

NIT APPEARANCES (3): 1970-82-83; 2-4 record (.333); finished 4th in 1970.

CAREER LEADING SCORER: Pete Maravich (3,667 points, 1968–70).

CAREER LEADING REBOUNDER: Rudy Macklin (1,276, 1977–81; missed 1978–79 season because of an injury).

NCAA CONSENSUS FIRST-TEAM ALL-AMERICANS (8): Bob Pettit (1954), Pete Maravich (1968, 1969, and 1970), Chris Jackson (1989 and 1990), Shaquille O'Neal (1991 and 1992).

LOUISIANA TECH

NICKNAME: Bulldogs.

ADDRESS: P.O. Box 3166TS, Ruston, LA 71272.

PHONE/FAX: (318) 257-3144/3757.

ENROLLMENT: 10,380.

ARENA: Thomas Assembly Center (8,000).

SCHOOL COLORS: Columbia blue and red.

CONFERENCE: Sun Belt.

FINAL AP TOP 10 RANKINGS (1): 1985.

NCAA TOURNAMENT APPEARANCES (5): 1984-85-87-89-91; 4-5 record (.444).

NIT APPEARANCES (4): 1986-88-90-92; 5-4 record (.556); finished 3d in 1986.

CAREER LEADING SCORER: Mike Green (2,340 points, 1970–73).

CAREER LEADING REBOUNDER: Mike Green (1,575, 1970–73).

LOUISVILLE

NICKNAME: Cardinals.

ADDRESS: Belknap Campus, Louisville, KY 40292.

PHONE/FAX: (502) 852-6581/7401.

ENROLLMENT: 23,000.

ARENA: Freedom Hall (18,865).

SCHOOL COLORS: Red, black, and white.

CONFERENCE: Metro.

FINAL AP TOP 10 RANKINGS (11): 1956-57-67-68-72-75-78-80-83-86-94.

NCAA TOURNAMENT APPEARANCES (24): 1951-59-61-64-67-68-72-74-75-77-78-79-80-81-82-83-84-86-88-89-90- 92-93-94; 43-26 record (.623); reached Final Four in 1959 (4th), 1972 (4th), 1975 (3d), 1980 (1st), 1982 (T3d), 1983 (T3d), and 1986 (1st).

NIT APPEARANCES (12): 1952-53-54-55-56-66-69-70-71-73-76-85; 10-12 record (.455); finished 1st in 1956 and 4th in 1985.

CAREER LEADING SCORER: Darrell Griffith (2,333 points, 1977–80).

CAREER LEADING REBOUNDER: Charlie Tyra (1,617, 1954–57).

NCAA CONSENSUS FIRST-TEAM ALL-AMERICANS (6): Charlie Tyra (1957), Wes Unseld (1967 and 1968), Darrell Griffith (1980), Pervis Ellison (1989), and Clifford Rozier (1994).

LOYOLA OF CHICAGO

NICKNAME: Ramblers.

ADDRESS: 6525 North Sheridan Road, Chicago, IL 60626.

PHONE/FAX: (312) 508-2575/3884.

ENROLLMENT: 15,885.

ARENA: Rosemont Horizon (17,500).

SCHOOL COLORS: Maroon and gold.

CONFERENCE: Midwestern Collegiate

FINAL AP TOP 10 RANKINGS (3): 1963-64-66.

NCAA TOURNAMENT APPEARANCES (5): 1963-64-66-68-85; 9-4 record (.692); reached Final Four in 1963 (1st).

NIT APPEARANCES (4): 1939-49-62-80; 6-4 record (.600); finished 2d in 1939, 2d in 1949, and 3d in 1962.

CAREER LEADING SCORER: Alfredrick Hughes (2,914 points, 1982–85).

CAREER LEADING REBOUNDER: LaRue Martin (1,062, 1970–72).

NCAA CONSENSUS FIRST-TEAM ALL-AMERICANS (1): Jerry Harkness (1963).

LOYOLA MARYMOUNT

NICKNAME: Lions.

ADDRESS: Loyola Boulevard at West 80th Street, Los Angeles, CA 90045-2699.

PHONE/FAX: (310) 338-7643/2703.

ENROLLMENT: 3,900.

ARENA: Albert Gersten Pavilion (4,156).

SCHOOL COLORS: Crimson and Columbia blue.

CONFERENCE: West Coast.

NCAA TOURNAMENT APPEARANCES (5): 1961-80-88-89-90; 5-5 record (.500); regional runner-up in 1990.

NIT APPEARANCES (1): 1986; 1-1 record (.500).

CAREER LEADING SCORER: Hank Gathers (2,490 points, 1988–90; played his freshman season at Southern Cal in 1985–86).

CAREER LEADING REBOUNDER: Jim Haderlein (1,161, 1969–71).

MANHATTAN

NICKNAME: Jaspers.

ADDRESS: Manhattan College Parkway, Riverdale, NY 10471-4098.

PHONE/FAX: (718) 920-0228/543-8802.

ENROLLMENT: 3,700.

ARENA: Draddy Gymnasium (3,000).

SCHOOL COLORS: Kelly green and white.

CONFERENCE: Metro Atlantic Athletic.

NCAA TOURNAMENT APPEARANCES (3): 1956-58-93; 1-4 record (.200).

NIT APPEARANCES (15): 1943-49-53-54-55-57-59-65-66-70-73-74-75-92-94; 6-15 record (.286); finished 4th in 1953.

CAREER LEADING SCORER: Keith Bullock (1,992 points, 1990–93).

CAREER LEADING REBOUNDER: Bill Campion (1,070, 1973–75).

MARQUETTE

NICKNAME: Golden Eagles.

ADDRESS: 1212 West Wisconsin Avenue, Milwaukee, WI 53233.

PHONE/FAX: (414) 288-6980/6519.

ENROLLMENT: 11,030.

ARENA: Bradley Center (18,592).

SCHOOL COLORS: Royal blue and gold.

CONFERENCE: Great Midwest.

FINAL AP TOP 10 RANKINGS (10): 1955-70-71-72-73-74-76-77-78-79.

NCAA TOURNAMENT APPEARANCES (19): 1955-59-61-68-69-71-72-73-74-75-76-77-78-79-80-82-83-93-94; 27-20 record (.574); reached Final Four in 1974 (2d) and 1977 (1st).

NIT APPEARANCES (10): 1956-63-67-70-81-84-85-86-87-90; 14-8 record (.636); finished 3d in 1963, 2d in 1967, and 1st in 1970.

CAREER LEADING SCORER: George Thompson (1,773 points, 1967–69).

CAREER LEADING REBOUNDER: Don Kojis (1,222, 1959–61).

NCAA CONSENSUS FIRST-TEAM ALL-AMERICANS (3): Dean Meminger (1971), Jim Chones (1972), and Butch Lee (1978).

MARSHALL

NICKNAME: Thundering Herd.

ADDRESS: 400 Hal Greer Boulevard, Huntington, WV 25755.

PHONE/FAX: (304) 696-5275/2325.

ENROLLMENT: 12,530.

ARENA: Henderson Center (10,250).

SCHOOL COLORS: Green and white.

CONFERENCE: Southern.

NCAA TOURNAMENT APPEARANCES (5): 1956-72-84-85-87; 0-5 record.

NIT APPEARANCES (4): 1967-68-73-88; 2-5 record (.286); finished 4th in 1967.

CAREER LEADING SCORER: Skip Henderson (2,574 points, 1985–88).

CAREER LEADING REBOUNDER: Charlie Slack (1,916, 1953–56).

MARYLAND

NICKNAME: Terrapins, Terps.

ADDRESS: P.O. Box 295, College Park, MD 20742-0295.

PHONE/FAX: (301) 314-7064/9094.

ENROLLMENT: 21,780.

ARENA: Cole Field House (14,500).

SCHOOL COLORS: Red, white, black, and gold.

CONFERENCE: Atlantic Coast.

FINAL AP TOP 10 RANKINGS (5): 1958-73-74-75-80.

NCAA TOURNAMENT APPEARANCES (11): 1958-73-75-80-81-83-84-85-86-88-94; 15-11 record (.577); regional runner-up in 1973 and 1975.

NIT APPEARANCES (4): 1972-79-82-90; 7-3 record (.700); finished 1st in 1972.

CAREER LEADING SCORER: Len Bias (2,149 points, 1983–86).

CAREER LEADING REBOUNDER: Len Elmore (1,053, 1972–74).

NCAA CONSENSUS FIRST-TEAM ALL-AMERICANS (4): Louis Berger (1932), John Lucas (1975 and 1976), and Len Bias (1986).

MASSACHUSETTS

NICKNAMES: Minutemen, UMass.

ADDRESS: Boyden Building, Mullins Center, Amherst, MA 01003.

PHONE/FAX: (413) 545-2439/1556.

ENROLLMENT: 17,210.

ARENA: William D. Mullins Center (9,493).

SCHOOL COLORS: Maroon and white.

CONFERENCE: Atlantic 10.

FINAL AP TOP 10 RANKINGS (1): 1994.

NCAA TOURNAMENT APPEARANCES (4): 1962-92-93-94; 4-4 record (.500).

NIT APPEARANCES (8): 1970-71-73-74-75-77-90-91; 5-9 record (.357); finished 4th in 1991.

CAREER LEADING SCORER: Jim McCoy (2,374 points, 1989–92).

CAREER LEADING REBOUNDER: Julius Erving (1,049, in 1970 and 1971).

MEMPHIS

NICKNAME: Tigers.

ADDRESS: Athletic Office Building, Memphis, TN 38152.

PHONE/FAX: (901) 678-2337/4134.

ENROLLMENT: 21,500.

ARENA: The Pyramid (20,142).

SCHOOL COLORS: Blue and gray.

CONFERENCE: Great Midwest.

FINAL AP TOP 10 RANKINGS (2): 1982 and 1985.

NCAA TOURNAMENT APPEARANCES (14): 1955-56-62-73-76-82-83-84-85-86-88-89-92-93; 16-14 record (.533); reached Final Four in 1973 (2d) and 1985 (T3d).

NIT APPEARANCES (11): 1957-60-61-63-67-72-74-75-77-90-91; 6-11 record (.353); finished 2d in 1957.

CAREER LEADING SCORER: Keith Lee (2,408 points, 1982–85).

CAREER LEADING REBOUNDER: Keith Lee (1,336, 1982–85).

NCAA CONSENSUS FIRST-TEAM ALL-AMERICANS (2): Keith Lee (1983 and 1985).

MIAMI (FLA.)

NICKNAME: Hurricanes.

ADDRESS: P.O. Box 248167, Coral Gables, FL 33124-0814.

PHONE/FAX: (305) 284-3244/2807.

ENROLLMENT: 13,155.

ARENA: Miami Arena (15,388).

SCHOOL COLORS: Orange, green, and white.

CONFERENCE: Big East.

FINAL AP TOP 10 RANKINGS (1): 1960.

NCAA TOURNAMENT APPEARANCES (1): 1960; 0-1 record.

NIT APPEARANCES (3): 1961-63-64; 1-3 record (.250).

CAREER LEADING SCORER: Rick Barry (2,298 points, 1963–65).

CAREER LEADING REBOUNDER: Rick Barry (1,274, 1963–65).

NCAA CONSENSUS FIRST-TEAM ALL-AMERICANS (1): Rick Barry (1965).

MIAMI (OHIO)

NICKNAME: Redskins.

ADDRESS: 230 Millett Hall, Oxford, OH 45056.

PHONE/FAX: (513) 529-4327/6729.

ENROLLMENT: 16,000.

ARENA: Millett Hall (9,200).

SCHOOL COLORS: Red and white.

CONFERENCE: Mid-American.

NCAA TOURNAMENT APPEARANCES (13): 1953-55-57-58-66-69-71-73-78-84-85-86-92; 3-15 record (.167).

NIT APPEARANCES (3): 1970-93-94; 2-3 record (.400).

CAREER LEADING SCORER: Ron Harper (2,377 points, 1983–86).

CAREER LEADING REBOUNDER: Ron Harper (1,119, 1983–86).

MICHIGAN

NICKNAME: Wolverines.

ADDRESS: 1000 South State Street, Ann Arbor, MI 48109-2201.

PHONE/FAX: (313) 763-1381/747-1188.

ENROLLMENT: 36,845.

ARENA: Crisler Arena (13,562).

SCHOOL COLORS: Maize and blue.

CONFERENCE: Big Ten.

FINAL AP TOP 10 RANKINGS (11): 1964-65-66-74-76-77-85-86-88-89-93.

NCAA TOURNAMENT APPEARANCES (17): 1948-64-65-66-74-75-76-77-85-86-87-88-89-90-92-93-94; 40-16 record (.714); reached Final Four in 1964 (3d), 1965 (2d), 1976 (2d), 1989 (1st), 1992 (2d), and 1993 (2d).

NIT APPEARANCES (5): 1971-80-81-84-91; 10-4 record (.714); finished 1st in 1984.

CAREER LEADING SCORER: Glen Rice (2,442 points, 1986–89).

CAREER LEADING REBOUNDER: Rudy Tomjanovich (1,039, 1968–70).

NCAA CONSENSUS FIRST-TEAM ALL-AMERICANS (5): Cazzie Russell (1965 and 1966), Rickey Green (1977), Gary Grant (1988), and Chris Webber (1993).

MICHIGAN STATE

NICKNAME: Spartans.

ADDRESS: Fourth Floor, Olos Hall, East Lansing, MI 48824-1044.

PHONE/FAX: (517) 355-2271/353-9636.

ENROLLMENT: 39,745

ARENA: Jack Breslin Student Events Center (15,138).

SCHOOL COLORS: Green and white.

CONFERENCE: Big Ten.

FINAL AP TOP 10 RANKINGS (4): 1959-78-79-90.

NCAA TOURNAMENT APPEARANCES (10): 1957-59-78-79-85-86-90-91-92-94; 17-10 record (.630); reached Final Four in 1957 (4th) and 1979 (1st).

NIT APPEARANCES (3): 1983-89-93; 4-4 record (.500); finished 4th in 1989.

CAREER LEADING SCORER: Steve Smith (2,263 points, 1988–91).

CAREER LEADING REBOUNDER: Greg Kelser (1,092, 1976–79).

NCAA CONSENSUS FIRST-TEAM ALL-AMERICANS (1): Earvin "Magic" Johnson (1979).

MIDDLE TENNESSEE STATE

NICKNAME: Blue Raiders.

ADDRESS: Box 20, Murfreesboro, TN 37132.

PHONE/FAX: (615) 898-2450/5626.

ENROLLMENT: 17,385.

ARENA: Hale Arena (11,520).

SCHOOL COLORS: Navy blue and white.

CONFERENCE: Ohio Valley.

NCAA TOURNAMENT APPEARANCES (6): 1975-77-82-85-87-89; 2-6 record (.250).

NIT APPEARANCES (2): 1986 and 1988; 2-2 record (.500).

CAREER LEADING SCORER: Robert Taylor (1,622 points, 1990–93).

CAREER LEADING REBOUNDER: Warren Kidd (1,165, 1990–93).

MINNESOTA

NICKNAME: Golden Gophers.

ADDRESS: 208 Bierman Athletic Building, 516 15th Avenue SE, Minneapolis, MN 55455-0101.

PHONE/FAX: (612) 625-4090/0359.

ENROLLMENT: 39,000.

ARENA: Williams Arena (14,300).

SCHOOL COLORS: Maroon and gold.

CONFERENCE: Big Ten.

FINAL AP TOP 10 RANKINGS (4): 1949-65-73-82.

NCAA TOURNAMENT APPEARANCES (5): 1972-82-89-90-94; 8-5 record (.615); regional runner-up in 1990.

NIT APPEARANCES (6): 1973-80-81-83-92-93; 12-5 record (.706); finished 2d in 1980 and 1st in 1993.

CAREER LEADING SCORER: Mychal Thompson (1,992 points, 1975–78).

CAREER LEADING REBOUNDER: Mychal Thompson (956, 1975–78).

NCAA CONSENSUS FIRST-TEAM ALL-AMERICANS (3): Jim McIntyre (1948), Dick Garmaker (1955), and Mychal Thompson (1978).

MISSISSIPPI

NICKNAME: Rebels.

ADDRESS: Fraternity Row, P.O. Box 217, University, MS 38677.

PHONE/FAX: (601) 232-7241/7006.

ENROLLMENT: 10,705.

ARENA: C. M. "Tad" Smith Coliseum (8,135).

SCHOOL COLORS: Cardinal red and navy blue.

CONFERENCE: Southeastern.

NCAA TOURNAMENT APPEARANCES (1): 1981; 0-1 record.

NIT APPEARANCES (5): 1980-82-83-87-89; 4-5 record (.444).

CAREER LEADING SCORER: John Stroud (2,328 points, 1977–80).

CAREER LEADING REBOUNDER: Walter Actwood (945, 1974–77).

MISSISSIPPI STATE

NICKNAME: Bulldogs.

ADDRESS: P.O. Drawer 5308, Mississippi State, MS 39762.

PHONE/FAX: (601) 325-2703/2563.

ENROLLMENT: 13,650.

ARENA: Humphrey Coliseum (10,000).

SCHOOL COLORS: Maroon and white.

CONFERENCE: Southeastern.

FINAL AP TOP 10 RANKINGS (3): 1959-62-63.

NCAA TOURNAMENT APPEARANCES (2): 1963 and 1991; 1-2 record (.333).

NIT APPEARANCES (3): 1979-90-94; 1-3 record (.250).

CAREER LEADING SCORER: Jeff Malone (2,142 points, 1980–83).

CAREER LEADING REBOUNDER: Bailey Howell (1,277, 1957–59).

NCAA CONSENSUS FIRST-TEAM ALL-AMERICANS (1): Bailey Howell (1959).

MISSOURI

NICKNAME: Tigers.

ADDRESS: Box 677, Hearnes Center, Columbia, MO 65205.

PHONE/FAX: (314) 882-3241/4720.

ENROLLMENT: 23,440.

ARENA: Hearnes Center (13,300).

SCHOOL COLORS: Old gold and black.

CONFERENCE: Big Eight (will be renamed Big 12 in 1997).

FINAL AP TOP 10 RANKINGS (4): 1982-83-89-94.

NCAA TOURNAMENT APPEARANCES (15): 1944-76-78-80-81-82-83-86-87-88-89-90-92-93-94; 12-15 record (.444); regional runner-up in 1944, 1976, and 1994.

NIT APPEARANCES (3): 1972-73-85; 0-3 record.

CAREER LEADING SCORER: Derrick Chievous (2,580 points, 1985–88).

CAREER LEADING REBOUNDER: Doug Smith (1,053, 1988–91).

MONTANA

NICKNAME: Grizzlies.

ADDRESS: Adams Fieldhouse, Missoula, MT 59812.

PHONE/FAX: (406) 243-6899/6859.

ENROLLMENT: 10,615.

ARENA: Dahlberg Arena (9,029).

SCHOOL COLORS: Copper, silver, and gold.

CONFERENCE: Big Sky.

NCAA TOURNAMENT APPEARANCES (3): 1975-91-92; 1-4 record (.200).

NIT APPEARANCES (2): 1985 and 1986; 0-2 record.

CAREER LEADING SCORER: Larry Krystkowiak (2,017 points, 1983–86).

CAREER LEADING REBOUNDER: Larry Krystkowiak (1,105, 1983–86).

MONTANA STATE

Fighting Bobcats

NICKNAME: Bobcats.

ADDRESS: 426 Culbertson Hall, Bozeman, MT 59717.

PHONE/FAX: (406) 994-5133/4102.

ENROLLMENT: 10,400.

ARENA: Worthington Arena (7,287).

SCHOOL COLORS: Blue and gold.

CONFERENCE: Big Sky.

NCAA TOURNAMENT APPEARANCES (2): 1951 and 1986; 0-2 record.

NIT APPEARANCES (1): 1987; 0-1 record.

CAREER LEADING SCORER: Larry Chanay (2,034 points, 1957–60).

CAREER LEADING REBOUNDER: Jack Gillespie (1,011, 1967–69).

NCAA CONSENSUS FIRST-TEAM ALL-AMERICANS (3): John Thompson (1929 and 1930), and Frank Ward (1930).

MURRAY STATE

NICKNAME: Racers.

ADDRESS: Stewart Stadium, Murray, KY 42071.

PHONE/FAX: (502) 762-4270/6814.

ENROLLMENT: 8,190.

ARENA: Racer Arena (5,550).

SCHOOL COLORS: Blue and gold.

CONFERENCE: Ohio Valley.

NCAA TOURNAMENT APPEARANCES (6): 1964-69-88-90-91-92; 1-6 record (.143).

NIT APPEARANCES (5): 1980-82-83-89-94; 2-5 record (.286).

CAREER LEADING SCORER: Jeff Martin (2,484 points, 1986–89).

CAREER LEADING REBOUNDER: Ronald "Popeye" Jones (1,374, 1989–92).

NAVY

NICKNAME: Midshipmen.

ADDRESS: 566 Brownson Road, Ricketts Hall, Annapolis, MD 21402-5000.

PHONE/FAX: (410) 268-6226/269-6779.

ENROLLMENT: 4,200.

ARENA: Alumni Hall (5,710).

SCHOOL COLORS: Navy blue and gold.

CONFERENCE: Patriot.

NCAA TOURNAMENT APPEARANCES (9): 1947-53-54-59-60-85-86-87-94; 8-10 record (.444); regional runner-up in 1947, 1954, and 1986.

NIT APPEARANCES (1): 1962; 0-1 record.

CAREER LEADING SCORER: David Robinson (2,669 points, 1984–87).

CAREER LEADING REBOUNDER: David Robinson (1,314, 1984–87).

NCAA CONSENSUS FIRST-TEAM ALL-AMERICANS (2): Elliott Loughlin (1933), and David Robinson (1987).

NEBRASKA

NICKNAMES: Cornhuskers, Huskers.

ADDRESS: 116 South Stadium, P.O. Box 880123, Lincoln, NE 68588-0123.

PHONE/FAX: (402) 472-2263/2005.

ENROLLMENT: 24,000.

ARENA: Devaney Sports Center (14,302).

SCHOOL COLORS: Scarlet and cream.

CONFERENCE: Big Eight (will be renamed Big 12 in 1997).

NCAA TOURNAMENT APPEARANCES (5): 1986-91-92-93-94; 0-5 record.

NIT APPEARANCES (8): 1967-78-80-83-84-85-87-89; 11-8 record (.579); finished tied for 3d in 1983 and 3d in 1987.

CAREER LEADING SCORER: Dave Hoppen (2,167 points, 1983–86).

CAREER LEADING REBOUNDER: Leroy Chalk (782, 1969–71).

NEW MEXICO

NICKNAME: Lobos.

ADDRESS: South Campus, Albuquerque, NM 87131.

PHONE/FAX: (505) 277-2026/0142.

ENROLLMENT: 25,135.

ARENA: University Arena (18,100).

SCHOOL COLORS: Silver and cherry.

CONFERENCE: Western Athletic.

FINAL AP TOP 10 RANKINGS (1): 1968.

NCAA TOURNAMENT APPEARANCES (6): 1968-74-78-91-93-94; 2-7 record (.222).

NIT APPEARANCES (13): 1964-65-67-73-79-84-85-86-87-88-89-90-92; 13-14 record (.481); finished 2d in 1964 and 4th in 1990.

CAREER LEADING SCORER: Luc Longley (1,769 points, 1988–91).

CAREER LEADING REBOUNDER: Luc Longley (922, 1988–91).

NEW MEXICO STATE

NICKNAME: Aggies.

ADDRESS: Box 3145, Las Cruces, NM 88003-8001.

PHONE/FAX: (505) 646-3929/2425.

ENROLLMENT: 15,495.

ARENA: Pan American Center (13,007).

SCHOOL COLORS: Crimson and white.

CONFERENCE: Big West.

FINAL AP TOP 10 RANKINGS (1): 1970.

NCAA TOURNAMENT APPEARANCES (15): 1952-59-60-67-68-69-70-71-75-79-90-91-92-93-94; 10-17 record (.370); reached Final Four in 1970 (3d).

NIT APPEARANCES (2): 1939 and 1989; 1-2 record (.333).

CAREER LEADING SCORER: Albert "Slab" Jones (1,758 points, 1977–80).

CAREER LEADING REBOUNDER: Sam Lacey (1,265, 1968–70).

NEW ORLEANS

NICKNAME: Privateers.

ADDRESS: Lakefront Arena, New Orleans, LA 70148.

PHONE/FAX: (504) 286-6284, 7027/7240.

ENROLLMENT: 15,570.

ARENA: Kiefer UNO Lakefront Arena (10,000).

SCHOOL COLORS: Royal blue and silver.

CONFERENCE: Sun Belt.

NCAA TOURNAMENT APPEARANCES (3): 1987-91-93; 1-3 record (.250).

NIT APPEARANCES (5): 1983-88-89-90-94; 4-5 record (.444).

CAREER LEADING SCORER: Mel Henderson (1,870 points, 1970–73).

CAREER LEADING REBOUNDER: Ervin Johnson (1,287, 1990–93).

NIAGARA

NICKNAME: Purple Eagles.

ADDRESS: LL O'Shea Hall, Niagara University, NY 14109-2009.

PHONE/FAX: (716) 286-8588/8581.

ENROLLMENT: 3,000.

ARENAS: Niagara Falls Convention Center (6,000) and Gallagher Center (3,200).

SCHOOL COLORS: Purple, white, and gold.

CONFERENCE: Metro Atlantic Athletic.

NCAA TOURNAMENT APPEARANCES (1): 1970; 1-2 record (.333).

NIT APPEARANCES (10): 1950-53-54-55-56-58-61-72-76-87; 8-10 record (.444); finished 3d in 1954 and 2d in 1972.

CAREER LEADING SCORER: Calvin Murphy (2,548 points, 1968–70).

CAREER LEADING REBOUNDER: Alex Ellis (1,533, 1956–58).

NCAA CONSENSUS FIRST-TEAM ALL-AMERICANS (2): Calvin Murphy (1969 and 1970).

NORTH CAROLINA

NICKNAME: Tar Heels.

ADDRESS: P.O. Box 2126, Chapel Hill, NC 27515-2126.

PHONE/FAX: (919) 962-2123/0612.

ENROLLMENT: 23,850.

ARENA: Smith Center (21,572).

SCHOOL COLORS: Carolina blue and white.

CONFERENCE: Atlantic Coast.

FINAL AP TOP 10 RANKINGS (23): 1957-59-61-67-68-69-72-75-76-77-79-81-82-83-84-85-86-87-88-89-91- 93-94.

NCAA TOURNAMENT APPEARANCES (28): 1941-46-57-59-67-68-69-72-75-76-77-78-79-80-81-82-83-84-85-86-87- 88-89-90-91-92-93-94; 63-28 record (.692); reached Final Four in 1946 (2d), 1957 (1st), 1967 (4th), 1968 (2d), 1969 (4th), 1972 (3d), 1977 (2d), 1981 (2d), 1982 (1st), 1991 (T3d), and 1993 (1st).

NIT APPEARANCES (4): 1970-71-73-74; 7-3 record (.700); finished 1st in 1971 and 3d in 1973.

CAREER LEADING SCORER: Phil Ford (2,290 points, 1975–78).

CAREER LEADING REBOUNDER: Sam Perkins (1,167, 1981–84).

NCAA CONSENSUS FIRST-TEAM ALL-AMERICANS (14): George Glamack (1940 and 1941), Lennie Rosenbluth (1957), Larry Miller (1968), Bob McAdoo (1972), Phil Ford (1977 and 1978), James Worthy (1982), Michael Jordan (1983 and 1984), Sam Perkins (1983 and 1984), Kenny Smith (1987), and J. R. Reid (1988).

NORTH CAROLINA STATE

NICKNAME: Wolfpack.

ADDRESS: P.O. Box 8501, Raleigh, NC 27695-7501.

PHONE/FAX: (919) 515-2102/2898.

ENROLLMENT: 26,685.

ARENA: Reynolds Coliseum (12,400).

SCHOOL COLORS: Red and white.

CONFERENCE: Atlantic Coast.

FINAL AP TOP 10 RANKINGS (9): 1950-51-55-56-59-70-73-74-75.

NCAA TOURNAMENT APPEARANCES (17): 1950-51-52-54-56-65-70-74-80-82-83-85-86-87-88-89-91; 27-16 record (.628); reached Final Four in 1950 (3d), 1974 (1st), and 1983 (1st).

NIT APPEARANCES (6): 1947-48-51-76-78-84; 7-6 record (.538); finished 3d in 1947, 3d in 1976, and 2d in 1978.

CAREER LEADING SCORER: Rodney Monroe (2,551 points, 1988–91).

CAREER LEADING REBOUNDER: Ronnie Shavlik (1,598, 1954–56).

NCAA CONSENSUS FIRST-TEAM ALL-AMERICANS (5): Sam Ranzino (1951), Ronnie Shavlik (1956), and David Thompson (1973, 1974, and 1975).

NORTHEASTERN

NICKNAME: Huskies.

ADDRESS: 380 Huntington Avenue, Boston, MA 02215.

PHONE/FAX: (617) 373-2691/3152.

ENROLLMENT: 12,000.

ARENA: Matthews Arena (6,000).

SCHOOL COLORS: Red and black.

CONFERENCE: North Atlantic.

NCAA TOURNAMENT APPEARANCES (7): 1981-82-84-85-86-87-91; 3-7 record (.300).

NIT APPEARANCES: None.

CAREER LEADING SCORER: Reggie Lewis (2,708 points, 1984–87).

CAREER LEADING REBOUNDER: Mark Halsel (1,115, 1981–84).

NORTHERN IOWA

NICKNAME: Panthers.

ADDRESS: UNI-Dome, Cedar Falls, IA 50614.

PHONE/FAX: (319) 273-6354/3602.

ENROLLMENT: 13,110.

ARENA: UNI-Dome (10-20,000).

SCHOOL COLORS: Purple and old gold.

CONFERENCE: Missouri Valley.

NCAA TOURNAMENT APPEARANCES (1): 1990; 1-1 record (.500).

NIT APPEARANCES: None.

CAREER LEADING SCORER: Jason Reese (2,033 points, 1987–90).

CAREER LEADING REBOUNDER: Pete Spoden (1,104, 1961–64).

NORTHWESTERN

NICKNAME: Wildcats.

ADDRESS: 1501 Central Street, Evanston, IL 60201-1699.

PHONE/FAX: (708) 491-7503/8818.

ENROLLMENT: 7,400.

ARENA: Welsh-Ryan Arena (8,117).

SCHOOL COLORS: Purple and white.

CONFERENCE: Big Ten.

NCAA TOURNAMENT APPEARANCES: None.

NIT APPEARANCES (2): 1983 and 1994; 2-2 record (.500).

CAREER LEADING SCORER: Billy McKinney (1,900 points, 1974–77).

CAREER LEADING REBOUNDER: Joe Ruklick (868, 1957–59).

NCAA CONSENSUS FIRST-TEAM ALL-AMERICANS (4): Joe Reiff (1931 and 1933), Otto Graham (1944; also played with Colgate), and Max Morris (1946).

NOTRE DAME

NICKNAME: Fighting Irish.

ADDRESS: Joyce Athletic and Convocation Center, Notre Dame, IN 46556.

PHONE/FAX: (219) 631-7516/7941.

ENROLLMENT: 9,850.

ARENA: Joyce Athletic and Convocation Center (11,418).

SCHOOL COLORS: Gold and blue.

CONFERENCE: Independent (will join Big East in 1996).

FINAL AP TOP 10 RANKINGS (12): 1953-54-58-70-74-76-77-78-79-80-81-86.

NCAA TOURNAMENT APPEARANCES (24): 1953-54-57-58-60-63-65-69-70-71-74-75-76-77-78-79-80-81-85-86-87- 88-89-90; 25-28 record (.472); reached Final Four in 1978 (4th).

NIT APPEARANCES (5): 1968-73-83-84-92; 14-5 record (.737); finished 3d in 1968, 2d in 1973, 2d in 1984, and 2d in 1992.

CAREER LEADING SCORER: Austin Carr (2,560 points, 1969–71).

CAREER LEADING REBOUNDER: Tom Hawkins (1,318, 1957–59).

NCAA CONSENSUS FIRST-TEAM ALL-AMERICANS (17): Moose Krause (1932, 1933, and 1934), John Moir (1936, 1937, and 1938), Paul Nowak (1936, 1937, and 1938), Leo Klier (1944 and 1946), Billy Hassett (1945), Kevin O'Shea (1948), Austin Carr (1971), John Shumate (1974), and Adrian Dantley (1975 and 1976).

OHIO

NICKNAME: Bobcats.

ADDRESS: Convocation Center, Athens, OH 45701-2979.

PHONE/FAX: (614) 593-1298/2420.

ENROLLMENT: 18,500.

ARENA: Convocation Center (13,000).

SCHOOL COLORS: Kelly green and white.

CONFERENCE: Mid-American.

NCAA TOURNAMENT APPEARANCES (10): 1960-61-64-65-70-72-74-83-85-94; 4-11 record (.267); regional runner-up in 1964.

NIT APPEARANCES (2): 1941 and 1969; 3-2 record (.600); finished 2d in 1941.

CAREER LEADING SCORER: Dave Jamerson (2,336 points, 1986–90; missed 1986–87 season because of a knee injury).

CAREER LEADING REBOUNDER: John Deveraux (957, 1981–84).

OHIO STATE

NICKNAME: Buckeyes.

ADDRESS: 410 Woody Hayes Drive, 124 St. John Arena, Columbus, OH 43210-1166.

PHONE/FAX: (614) 292-6861/8547.

ENROLLMENT: 52,180.

ARENA: St. John Arena (13,276).

SCHOOL COLORS: Scarlet and gray.

CONFERENCE: Big Ten.

FINAL AP TOP 10 RANKINGS (9): 1950-60-61-62-63-71-80-91-92.

NCAA TOURNAMENT APPEARANCES (18): 1939-44-45-46-50-60-61-62-68-71-80-82-83-85-87-90-91-92; 31-17 record (.646); reached Final Four in 1939 (2d), 1944 (T3d), 1945 (T3d), 1946 (3d), 1960 (1st), 1961 (2d), 1962 (2d), and 1968 (3d).

NIT APPEARANCES (6): 1979-84-86-88-89-93; 13-6 record (.684); finished 4th in 1979, 1st in 1986, and 2d in 1988.

CAREER LEADING SCORER: Dennis Hopson (2,096 points, 1984–87).

CAREER LEADING REBOUNDER: Jerry Lucas (1,411, 1960–62).

NCAA CONSENSUS FIRST-TEAM ALL-AMERICANS (10): Wes Fesler (1931), Jimmy Hull (1939), Dick Schnittker (1950), Robin Freeman (1956), Jerry Lucas (1960, 1961, and 1962), Gary Bradds (1964), and Jim Jackson (1991 and 1992).

OKLAHOMA

NICKNAME: Sooners.

ADDRESS: 180 West Brooks, Room 235, Norman, OK 73019.

PHONE/FAX: (405) 325-8231/7623.

ENROLLMENT: 24,400.

ARENA: Lloyd Noble Center (10,861).

SCHOOL COLORS: Crimson and cream.

CONFERENCE: Big Eight (will be renamed Big 12 in 1997).

FINAL AP TOP 10 RANKINGS (5): 1984-85-88-89-90.

NCAA TOURNAMENT APPEARANCES (13): 1939-43-47-79-83-84-85-86-87-88-89-90-92; 20-13 record (.606); reached Final Four in 1939 (3d), 1947 (2d), and 1988 (2d).

NIT APPEARANCES (6): 1970-71-82-91-93-94; 9-6 record (.600); finished in tie for 3d in 1982 and 2d in 1991.

CAREER LEADING SCORER: Wayman Tisdale (2,661 points, 1983–85).

CAREER LEADING REBOUNDER: Wayman Tisdale (1,048, 1983–85).

NCAA CONSENSUS FIRST-TEAM ALL-AMERICANS (8): Thomas Churchill (1929), Bud Browning (1935), Allie Paine (1944), Gerald Tucker (1947), Wayman Tisdale (1983, 1984, and 1985), and Stacey King (1989).

OKLAHOMA STATE

NICKNAME: Cowboys.

ADDRESS: Gallagher-Iba Arena, Stillwater, OK 74078.

PHONE/FAX: (405) 744-5749/7754.

ENROLLMENT: 18,500.

ARENA: Gallagher-Iba Arena (6,381).

SCHOOL COLORS: Orange and black.

CONFERENCE: Big Eight (will be renamed Big 12 in 1997).

FINAL AP TOP 10 RANKINGS (4): 1949-51-53-54.

NCAA TOURNAMENT APPEARANCES (13): 1945-46-49-51-53-54-58-65-83-91-92-93-94; 21-12 record (.636); reached Final Four in 1945 (1st), 1946 (1st), 1949 (2d), and 1951 (4th).

NIT APPEARANCES (6): 1938-40-44-56-89-90; 5-7 record (.417); finished 3d in 1938, 3d in 1940, and 4th in 1944.

CAREER LEADING SCORER: Byron Houston (2,374 points, 1989–92).

CAREER LEADING REBOUNDER: Byron Houston (1,190, 1989–92).

NCAA CONSENSUS FIRST-TEAM ALL-AMERICANS (3): Bob Kurland (1944, 1945, and 1946).

OLD DOMINION UNIVERSITY

OLD DOMINION

NICKNAME: Monarchs.

ADDRESS: Athletic Administration Building, Norfolk, VA 23529-0201.

PHONE/FAX: (804) 683-3372/3119.

ENROLLMENT: 16,730.

ARENA: Norfolk Scope (10,253).

SCHOOL COLORS: Slate blue and silver.

CONFERENCE: Colonial Athletic Association.

NCAA TOURNAMENT APPEARANCES (5): 1980-82-85-86-92; 1-5 record (.167).

NIT APPEARANCES (8): 1977-79-81-83-84-88-93-94; 4-8 record (.333).

CAREER LEADING SCORER: Ronnie Valentine (2,204 points, 1977–80).

CAREER LEADING REBOUNDER: Randy Leddy (1,153, 1963–66).

ORAL ROBERTS

NICKNAME: Golden Eagles.

ADDRESS: 7777 South Lewis Avenue, Tulsa, OK 74171.

PHONE/FAX: (918) 495-7100/7123.

ENROLLMENT: 4,515.

ARENA: Mabee Center (10,575).

SCHOOL COLORS: Blue, gold, and white.

OREGON

NICKNAME: Ducks.

ADDRESS: Len Casanova Athletic Center, 2727 Leo Harris Parkway, Eugene, OR 97401-8835.

PHONE/FAX: (503) 346-5488/5449.

ENROLLMENT: 16,400.

ARENA: McArthur Court (10,063).

SCHOOL COLORS: Emerald green and lemon yellow.

CONFERENCE: Pacific-10.

NCAA TOURNAMENT APPEARANCES (4): 1939-45-60-61; 6-3 record (.667); reached Final Four in 1939 (1st).

NIT APPEARANCES (6): 1975-76-77-84-88-90; 5-6 record (.455); finished 3d in 1975.

CAREER LEADING SCORER: Ron Lee (2,085 points, 1973–76).

CAREER LEADING REBOUNDER: Greg Ballard (1,114, 1974–77).

NCAA CONSENSUS FIRST-TEAM ALL-AMERICANS (2): Urgel "Slim" Wintermute (1939) and John Dick (1940).

CONFERENCE: Independent.

NCAA TOURNAMENT APPEARANCES (2): 1974 and 1984; 2-2 record (.500); regional runner-up in 1974.

NIT APPEARANCES (5): 1972-73-75-77-82; 2-5 record (.286).

CAREER LEADING SCORER: Greg Sutton (3,070 points, 1989–91; played freshman season at Langston in 1986–87).

CAREER LEADING REBOUNDER: Eddie Woods (1,365, 1971–74).

OREGON STATE

NICKNAME: Beavers.

ADDRESS: 209 Gill Coliseum, Corvallis, OR 97331.

PHONE/FAX: (503) 737-3720/3072.

ENROLLMENT: 15,550.

ARENA: Gill Coliseum (10,400).

SCHOOL COLORS: Orange and black.

CONFERENCE: Pacific-10.

FINAL AP TOP 10 RANKINGS (5): 1955-64-80-81-82.

NCAA TOURNAMENT APPEARANCES (16): 1947-49-55-62-63-64-66-75-80-81-82-84-85-88-89-90; 12-19 record (.387); reached Final Four in 1949 (4th) and 1963 (4th).

NIT APPEARANCES (3): 1979-83-87; 3-3 record (.500).

CAREER LEADING SCORER: Gary Payton (2,172 points, 1987–90).

CAREER LEADING REBOUNDER: Mel Counts (1,375, 1962–64).

NCAA CONSENSUS FIRST-TEAM ALL-AMERICANS (2): Steve Johnson (1981) and Gary Payton (1990).

PACIFIC

NICKNAME: Tigers.

ADDRESS: 3601 Pacific Avenue, Stockton, CA 95211.

PHONE/FAX: (209) 946-2479/2757.

ENROLLMENT: 4,000.

ARENA: Alex G. Spanos Center (6,150).

SCHOOL COLORS: Orange and black.

CONFERENCE: Big West.

NCAA TOURNAMENT APPEARANCES (4): 1966-67-71-79; 2-5 record (.286); regional runner-up in 1967.

NIT APPEARANCES: None.

CAREER LEADING SCORER: Ron Cornelius (2,065 points, 1978–81).

CAREER LEADING REBOUNDER: Keith Swagerty (1,505, 1965–67).

PENNSYLVANIA

NICKNAME: Quakers.

ADDRESS: 235 South 33d Street, Weightman Hall South, Philadelphia, PA 19104-6322.

PHONE/FAX: (215) 898-6128/1747.

ENROLLMENT: 9,300.

ARENA: Palestra (8,700).

SCHOOL COLORS: Red and blue.

CONFERENCE: Ivy League.

FINAL AP TOP 10 RANKINGS (2): 1971 and 1972.

NCAA TOURNAMENT APPEARANCES (15): 1953-70-71-72-73-74-75-78-79-80-82-85-87-93-94; 13-17 record (.433); reached Final Four in 1979 (4th).

NIT APPEARANCES (1): 1981; 0-1 record.

CAREER LEADING SCORER: Ernie Beck (1,827 points, 1951–53).

CAREER LEADING REBOUNDER: Ernie Beck (1,557, 1951–53).

NCAA CONSENSUS FIRST-TEAM ALL-AMERICANS (3): Joe Schaaf (1929), Howie Dallmar (1945), and Ernie Beck (1953).

PENN STATE

NICKNAME: Nittany Lions.

ADDRESS: 234 Recreation Building, University Park, PA 16802.

PHONE/FAX: (814) 865-1757/863-3165.

ENROLLMENT: 30,500.

ARENA: Rec Hall (6,846); Bryce Jordan Center (16,000) is slated to be ready in 1996.

SCHOOL COLORS: Blue and white.

CONFERENCE: Big Ten.

FINAL AP TOP 10 RANKINGS (1): 1954.

NCAA TOURNAMENT APPEARANCES (6): 1942-52-54-55-65-91; 7-8 record (.467); reached Final Four in 1954 (3d).

NIT APPEARANCES (5): 1966-80-89-90-92; 5-5 record (.500); finished 3d in 1990.

CAREER LEADING SCORER: Jesse Arnelle (2,138 points, 1952–55).

CAREER LEADING REBOUNDER: Jesse Arnelle (1,238, 1952–55).

PEPPERDINE

NICKNAME: Waves.

ADDRESS: 24255 Pacific Coast Highway, Malibu, CA 90263.

PHONE/FAX: (310) 456-4333/4322.

ENROLLMENT: 6,800.

ARENA: Firestone Fieldhouse (3,104).

SCHOOL COLORS: Blue, orange, and white.

CONFERENCE: West Coast.

NCAA TOURNAMENT APPEARANCES (11): 1944-62-76-79-82-83-85-86-91-92-94; 4-12 record (.250).

NIT APPEARANCES (4): 1980-88-89-93; 2-4 record (.333).

CAREER LEADING SCORER: Dane Suttle (1,702 points, 1980–83).

CAREER LEADING REBOUNDER: Dana Jones (1,031, 1991–94).

PITTSBURGH

NICKNAME: Panthers.

ADDRESS: P.O. Box 7436, Pittsburgh, PA 15213.

PHONE/FAX: (412) 648-8240/8248.

ENROLLMENT: 13,500.

ARENAS: Fitzgerald Field House (6,798) and Civic Arena (16,725).

SCHOOL COLORS: Blue and gold.

CONFERENCE: Big East.

FINAL AP TOP 10 RANKINGS (1): 1988.

NCAA TOURNAMENT APPEARANCES (13): 1941-57-58-63-74-81-82-85-87-88-89-91-93; 8-14 record (.364); reached Final Four in 1941 (T3d).

NIT APPEARANCES (6): 1964-75-80-84-86-92; 4-6 record (.400).

CAREER LEADING SCORER: Charles Smith (2,045 points, 1985–88).

CAREER LEADING REBOUNDER: Sam Clancy (1,342, 1978–81).

NCAA CONSENSUS FIRST-TEAM ALL-AMERICANS (6): Chuck Hyatt (1929 and 1930), Don Smith (1933), Claire Cribbs (1934 and 1935), and Don Hennon (1958).

PORTLAND

NICKNAME: Pilots.

ADDRESS: 5000 N. Willamette Boulevard, Portland, OR 97203-5798.

PHONE/FAX: (503) 283-7117/7242.

ENROLLMENT: 2,700.

ARENA: Earle A. Chiles Center (5,000).

SCHOOL COLORS: Purple and white.

CONFERENCE: West Coast.

NCAA TOURNAMENT APPEARANCES (1): 1959; 0-1.

NIT APPEARANCES: None.

CAREER LEADING SCORER: Jose Slaughter (1,940 points, 1979–82).

CAREER LEADING REBOUNDER: Rick Raivio (910, 1977–80).

PRINCETON

NICKNAME: Tigers.

ADDRESS: P.O. Box 71, Jadwin Gymnasium, Princeton, NJ 08544.

PHONE/FAX: (609) 258-3568/4477.

ENROLLMENT: 4,500.

ARENA: Jadwin Gymnasium (7,500).

SCHOOL COLORS: Orange and black.

CONFERENCE: Ivy League.

FINAL AP TOP 10 RANKINGS (1): 1967.

NCAA TOURNAMENT APPEARANCES (18): 1952-55-60-61-63-64-65-67-69-76-77-81-83-84-89-90-91-92; 11-22 record (.333); reached Final Four in 1965 (3d).

NIT APPEARANCES (2): 1972 and 1975; 5-1 record (.833); finished 1st in 1975.

CAREER LEADING SCORER: Bill Bradley (2,503 points, 1963–65).

CAREER LEADING REBOUNDER: Bill Bradley (1,008, 1963–65).

NCAA CONSENSUS FIRST-TEAM ALL-AMERICANS (2): Bill Bradley (1964 and 1965).

PROVIDENCE

NICKNAME: Friars.

ADDRESS: River Avenue, Providence, RI 02918.

PHONE/FAX: (401) 865-2272/2583.

ENROLLMENT: 3,800.

ARENA: Civic Center (13,106).

SCHOOL COLORS: Black and white.

CONFERENCE: Big East.

FINAL AP TOP 10 RANKINGS (3): 1965-73-74.

NCAA TOURNAMENT APPEARANCES (12): 1964-65-66-72-73-74-77-78-87-89-90-94; 11-13 record (.458); reached Final Four in 1973 (4th) and 1987 (T3d).

NIT APPEARANCES (12): 1959-60-61-62-63-67-71-75-76-86-91-93; 26-.. record (.667); finished 4th in 1959, 2d in 1960, 1st in 1961, 1st in 19.. ..a 4th in 1993.

CAREER LEADING SCORER: Jimmy Walker (2,045 points, 1964–67).

CAREER LEADING REBOUNDER: Marvin Barnes (1,592, 1971–74).

NCAA CONSENSUS FIRST-TEAM ALL-AMERICANS (4): Jimmy Walker (1966 and 1967), Ernie DiGregorio (1973), and Marvin Barnes (1974).

PURDUE

NICKNAME: Boilermakers.

ADDRESS: 1790 Mackey Arena, West Lafayette, IN 47907-1790.

PHONE/FAX: (317) 494-3200/5447.

ENROLLMENT: 35,160.

ARENA: Mackey Arena (14,123).

SCHOOL COLORS: Old gold and black.

CONFERENCE: Big Ten.

FINAL AP TOP 10 RANKINGS (6): 1969-84-87-88-90-94.

NCAA TOURNAMENT APPEARANCES (13): 1969-77-80-83-84-85-86-87-88-90-91-93-94; 16-13 record (.552); reached Final Four in 1969 (2d) and 1980 (3d).

NIT APPEARANCES (6): 1971-74-79-81-82-92; 18-5 record (.783); finished 1st in 1974, 2d in 1979, 3d in 1981, and 2d in 1982.

CAREER LEADING SCORER: Rick Mount (2,323 points, 1968–70).

CAREER LEADING REBOUNDER: Joe Barry Carroll (1,148, 1977–80).

NCAA CONSENSUS FIRST-TEAM ALL-AMERICANS (16): Charles Murphy (1929 and 1930), John Wooden (1930, 1931, and 1932), Norman Cottom (1934), Bob Kessler (1936), Jewell Young (1937 and 1938), Terry Dischinger (1961 and 1962), Dave Schellhase (1966), Rick Mount (1969 and 1970), Joe Barry Carroll (1980), and Glenn Robinson (1994).

RHODE ISLAND

NICKNAME: Rams.

ADDRESS: Mackal Fieldhouse, Kingston, RI 02881.

PHONE/FAX: (401) 792-2409/5354.

ENROLLMENT: 12,500.

ARENA: Keaney Gymnasium (4,000).

SCHOOL COLORS: Blue and white.

CONFERENCE: Atlantic 10.

NCAA TOURNAMENT APPEARANCES (5): 1961-66-78-88-93; 3-5 record (.375).

NIT APPEARANCES (8): 1941-42-45-46-79-81-87-92; 5-9 record (.357); finished 4th in 1945 and 2d in 1946.

CAREER LEADING SCORER: Steve Chubin (2,154 points, 1963–66; missed 1964–65 season because he was academically ineligible).

CAREER LEADING REBOUNDER: Art Stephenson (1,033, 1966–68).

NCAA CONSENSUS FIRST-TEAM ALL-AMERICANS (1): Chet Jaworski (1939).

RICE

NICKNAME: Owls.

ADDRESS: P.O. Box 1892, 6100 South Main, Houston, TX 77251-1892.

PHONE/FAX: (713) 527-4034/6019.

ENROLLMENT: 2,600.

ARENA: Autry Court (5,000).

SCHOOL COLORS: Blue and gray.

CONFERENCE: Southwest (will join Western Athletic in 1996).

NCAA TOURNAMENT APPEARANCES (4): 1940-42-54-70; 2-5 record (.286); regional runner-up in 1940 and 1942.

NIT APPEARANCES (3): 1943-91-93; 1-3 record (.250).

CAREER LEADING SCORER: Brent Scott (1,906 points, 1990–93).

CAREER LEADING REBOUNDER: Brent Scott (1,049, 1990–93).

NCAA CONSENSUS FIRST-TEAM ALL-AMERICANS (3): Bob Kinney (1942), William Closs (1943), and William Henry (1945).

RICHMOND

NICKNAME: Spiders.

ADDRESS: Robins Center, Richmond, VA 23173.

PHONE/FAX: (804) 289-8365/8820.

ENROLLMENT: 2,800.

ARENA: Robins Center (9,171).

SCHOOL COLORS: Blue and red.

CONFERENCE: Colonial Athletic Association.

NCAA TOURNAMENT APPEARANCES (5): 1984-86-88-90-91; 5-5 record (.500).

NIT APPEARANCES (4): 1982-85-89-92; 2-4 record (.333).

CAREER LEADING SCORER: John Newman (2,383 points, 1983–86).

CAREER LEADING REBOUNDER: Ken Daniel (1,255, 1953–56).

ROBERT MORRIS

NICKNAME: Colonials.

ADDRESS: Narrows Run Road, Coraopolis, PA 15108-1189.

PHONE/FAX: (412) 262-8314/8557.

ENROLLMENT: 5,500.

ARENA: Charles L. Sewall Center (3,056).

SCHOOL COLORS: Blue and white.

CONFERENCE: Northeast.

NCAA TOURNAMENT APPEARANCES (5): 1982-83-89-90-92; 1-5 record (.167).

NIT APPEARANCES: None.

CAREER LEADING SCORER: Myron Walker (1,965 points, 1991–94).

CAREER LEADING REBOUNDER: Anthony Dickens (751, 1986–90; missed 1986–87 season because of a hip injury).

RUTGERS

NICKNAME: Scarlet Knights.

ADDRESS: P.O. Box 1149, Piscataway, NJ 08855-1149.

PHONE/FAX: (908) 932-4200/3063.

ENROLLMENT: 33,585.

ARENA: Louis Brown Athletic Center (9,000).

SCHOOL COLORS: Scarlet and white.

CONFERENCE: Atlantic 10 (will join Big East in 1996).

FINAL AP TOP 10 RANKINGS (1): 1976.

NCAA TOURNAMENT APPEARANCES (6): 1975-76-79-83-89-91; 5-7 record (.417); reached Final Four in 1976 (4th).

NIT APPEARANCES (9): 1967-69-73-74-77-78-82-90-92; 10-9 record (.526); finished 3d in 1967 and 1978.

CAREER LEADING SCORER: Phil Sellers (2,399 points, 1973–76).

CAREER LEADING REBOUNDER: Phil Sellers (1,115, 1973–76).

NCAA CONSENSUS FIRST-TEAM ALL-AMERICANS (1): Bob Lloyd (1967).

ST. BONAVENTURE

NICKNAME: Bonnies.

ADDRESS: Reilly Center, St. Bonaventure, NY 14778.

PHONE/FAX: (716) 375-2319/2383.

ENROLLMENT: 2,300.

ARENA: Reilly Center (6,000).

SCHOOL COLORS: Brown and white.

CONFERENCE: Atlantic 10.

FINAL AP TOP 10 RANKINGS (4): 1960-61-68-70.

NCAA TOURNAMENT APPEARANCES (4): 1961-68-70-78; 6-6 record (.500); reached Final Four in 1970 (4th).

NIT APPEARANCES (11): 1951-52-57-58-59-60-64-71-77-79-83; 16-12 record (.571); finished 3d in 1952, 4th in 1957, 3d in 1958, 4th in 1960, 3d in 1971, and 1st in 1977.

CAREER LEADING SCORER: Greg Sanders (2,238 points, 1975–78).

CAREER LEADING REBOUNDER: Bob Lanier (1,180, 1968–70).

NCAA CONSENSUS FIRST-TEAM ALL-AMERICANS (3): Tom Stith (1960 and 1961) and Bob Lanier (1970).

ST. FRANCIS (N.Y.)

NICKNAME: Terriers.

ADDRESS: 180 Remsen Street, Brooklyn, NY 11201.

PHONE/FAX: (718) 522-2300/1274.

ENROLLMENT: 1,910.

ARENA: Physical Education Center (1,400).

SCHOOL COLORS: Royal blue, red, and white.

CONFERENCE: Northeast.

NCAA TOURNAMENT APPEARANCES: None.

NIT APPEARANCES (3): 1954-56-63; 3-4 record (.429); finished 4th in 1956.

CAREER LEADING SCORER: Darrwin Purdie (1,613 points, 1986–89).

CAREER LEADING REBOUNDER: Jerome Williams (1,018, 1972–74).

ST. FRANCIS (PA.)

NICKNAME: Red Flash.

ADDRESS: Maurice Stokes PEC, Loretto, PA 15940.

PHONE/FAX: (814) 472-3128/3044.

ENROLLMENT: 1,200.

ARENA: Maurice Stokes Physical Education Center (3,500).

SCHOOL COLORS: Red and white.

CONFERENCE: Northeast.

NCAA TOURNAMENT APPEARANCES (1): 1991; 0-1 record.

NIT APPEARANCES (3): 1954-55-58; 3-4 record (.429); finished 4th in 1955.

CAREER LEADING SCORER: Joe Anderson (2,301 points, 1988–91).

CAREER LEADING REBOUNDER: Maurice Stokes (1,819, 1953–55; rebounding statistics weren't kept in 1951–52).

ST. JOHN'S

NICKNAME: Red Storm.

ADDRESS: 8000 Utopia Parkway, Jamaica, NY 11439.

PHONE/FAX: (718) 990-6367/969-8468.

ENROLLMENT: 19,500.

ARENAS: Alumni Hall (6,008) and Madison Square Garden (18,876).

SCHOOL COLORS: Red and white.

CONFERENCE: Big East.

FINAL AP TOP 10 RANKINGS (8): 1950-51-52-53-69-83-85-86.

NCAA TOURNAMENT APPEARANCES (23): 1951-52-61-67-68-69-73-76-77-78-79-80-82-83-84-85-86-87-88-90-91- 92-93; 23-25 record (.479); reached Final Four in 1952 (2d) and 1985 (T3d).

NIT APPEARANCES (25): 1939-40-43-44-45-46-47-49-50-51-52-53-58-59-60-62-65-66-70-71-72- 74-75-81-89; 41-28 record (.594); finished 4th in 1939, 1st in 1943, 1st in 1944, 3d in 1945, 3d in 1950, 3d in 1951, 2d in 1953, 4th in 1958, 1st in 1959, 2d in 1962, 1st in 1965, 2d in 1970, 4th in 1972, 4th in 1975, and 1st in 1989.

CAREER LEADING SCORER: Chris Mullin (2,440 points, 1982–85).

CAREER LEADING REBOUNDER: George Johnson (1,240, 1975–78).

NCAA CONSENSUS FIRST-TEAM ALL-AMERICANS (3): Harry Boykoff (1943), Chris Mullin (1985), and Walter Berry (1986).

ST. JOSEPH'S

NICKNAME: Hawks.

ADDRESS: 5600 City Avenue, Philadelphia, PA 19131.

PHONE/FAX: (215) 660-1704/1724.

ENROLLMENT: 2,950.

ARENA: Alumni Memorial Fieldhouse (3,200).

SCHOOL COLORS: Crimson and gray.

CONFERENCE: Atlantic 10.

FINAL AP TOP 10 RANKINGS (2): 1965 and 1966.

NCAA TOURNAMENT APPEARANCES (14): 1959-60-61-62-63-65-66-69-71-73-74-81-82-86; 12-18 record (.400); reached Final Four in 1961 (3d).

NIT APPEARANCES (8): 1956-58-64-72-79-80-84-85; 5-9 record (.357); finished 3d in 1956.

CAREER LEADING SCORER: Craig Amos (1,735 points, 1990–93); Bernard Blunt is expected to break the record in 1994–95.

CAREER LEADING REBOUNDER: Cliff Anderson (1,288, 1965–67).

NCAA CONSENSUS FIRST-TEAM ALL-AMERICANS (1): George Senesky (1943).

ST. LOUIS

NICKNAME: Billikens.

ADDRESS: 3672 West Pine Boulevard, St. Louis, MO 63108.

PHONE/FAX: (314) 658-2524/7193.

ENROLLMENT: 11,800.

ARENA: Kiel Center (20,000).

SCHOOL COLORS: Blue and white.

CONFERENCE: Great Midwest.

FINAL AP TOP 10 RANKINGS (4): 1949-51-52-57.

NCAA TOURNAMENT APPEARANCES (3): 1952-57-94; 1-4 record (.200); regional runner-up in 1952.

NIT APPEARANCES (15): 1948-49-51-52-53-55-56-59-60-61-63-65-87-89-90; 18-14 record (.563); finished 1st in 1948, 2d in 1961, 2d in 1989, and 2d in 1990.

CAREER LEADING SCORER: Anthony Bonner (1,972 points, 1987–90).

CAREER LEADING REBOUNDER: Anthony Bonner (1,424, 1987–90).

NCAA CONSENSUS FIRST-TEAM ALL-AMERICANS (2): Ed Macauley (1948 and 1949).

ST. MARY'S

NICKNAME: Gaels.

ADDRESS: P.O. Box 5100, Moraga, CA 94575.

PHONE/FAX: (510) 631-4402/4405.

ENROLLMENT: 4,000.

ARENA: McKeon Pavilion (3,500).

SCHOOL COLORS: Blue and red.

CONFERENCE: West Coast.

NCAA TOURNAMENT APPEARANCES (2): 1959 and 1989; 1-2 record (.333); regional runner-up in 1959.

NIT APPEARANCES: None.

CAREER LEADING SCORER: David Vann (1,738 points, 1979–82).

CAREER LEADING REBOUNDER: Tom Meschery (916, 1959–61).

ST. PETER'S

NICKNAME: Peacocks.

ADDRESS: 2641 Kennedy Boulevard, Jersey City, NJ 07306-5997.

PHONE/FAX: (201) 915-9101/9102.

ENROLLMENT: 3,355.

ARENA: Yanitelli Center (3,200).

SCHOOL COLORS: Blue and white.

CONFERENCE: Metro Atlantic Athletic.

NCAA TOURNAMENT APPEARANCES (1): 1991; 0-1 record.

NIT APPEARANCES (12): 1957-58-67-68-69-75-76-80-82-84-87-89; 5-13 record (.278); finished 4th in 1968.

CAREER LEADING SCORER: Willie Haynes (1,730 points, 1986–89).

CAREER LEADING REBOUNDER: Pete O'Dea (1,033, 1966–68).

SAN DIEGO

NICKNAME: Toreros.

ADDRESS: 5998 Alcala Park, San Diego, CA 92110-2492.

PHONE/FAX: (619) 260-4745/292-0388.

ENROLLMENT: 6,200.

ARENA: USD Sports Center (2,500).

SCHOOL COLORS: Columbia blue, navy, and white.

CONFERENCE: West Coast.

NCAA TOURNAMENT APPEARANCES (2): 1984 and 1987; 0-2.

CAREER LEADING SCORER: Stan Washington (1,472, 1972–74).

CAREER LEADING REBOUNDER: Gus Magee (948, 1967–70).

SAN DIEGO STATE

NICKNAME: Aztecs.

ADDRESS: Men's P.E. Building, Room 114, San Diego, CA 92182.

PHONE/FAX: (619) 594-5547/6541.

ENROLLMENT: 34,800.

ARENA: Peterson Gym (3,800).

SCHOOL COLORS: Scarlet and black.

CONFERENCE: Western Athletic.

NCAA TOURNAMENT APPEARANCES (3): 1975-76-85; 0-3 record.

NIT APPEARANCES (1): 1982; 0-1 record.

CAREER LEADING SCORER: Michael Cage (1,846 points, 1981–84).

CAREER LEADING REBOUNDER: Michael Cage (1,317, 1981–84).

SAN FRANCISCO

NICKNAME: Dons.

ADDRESS: 2130 Fulton, San Francisco, CA 94117-1080.

PHONE/FAX: (415) 666-6161/2929.

ENROLLMENT: 7,000.

ARENA: Memorial Gymnasium (5,300).

SCHOOL COLORS: Green and gold.

CONFERENCE: West Coast.

FINAL AP TOP 10 RANKINGS (5): 1949-55-56-58-77.

NCAA TOURNAMENT APPEARANCES (15): 1955-56-57-58-63-64-65-72-73-74-77-78-79-81-82; 21-13 record (.618); reached Final Four in 1955 (1st), 1956 (1st), and 1957 (3d).

NIT APPEARANCES (4): 1949-50-66-76; 5-3 record (.625); finished 1st in 1949.

CAREER LEADING SCORER: Bill Cartwright (2,116 points, 1976–79).

CAREER LEADING REBOUNDER: Bill Russell (1,606, 1954–56).

NCAA CONSENSUS FIRST-TEAM ALL-AMERICANS (3): Bill Russell (1955 and 1956), and Quintin Dailey (1982).

SAN JOSE STATE

NICKNAME: Spartans.

ADDRESS: 1 Washington Square, San Jose, CA 95192.

PHONE/FAX: (408) 924-1217/1291.

ENROLLMENT: 30,000.

ARENA: The Event Center (5,000).

SCHOOL COLORS: Gold, white, and blue.

CONFERENCE: Big West (will join Western Athletic in 1996).

NCAA TOURNAMENT APPEARANCES (2): 1951 and 1980; 0-2 record.

NIT APPEARANCES (1): 1981; 0-1 record.

CAREER LEADING SCORER: Ricky Berry (1,767 points, 1986–88 after transferring from Oregon State).

CAREER LEADING REBOUNDER: Marv Branstrom (864, 1956–58).

SANTA CLARA

NICKNAME: Broncos.

ADDRESS: Toso Pavilion, Santa Clara, CA 95053.

PHONE/FAX: (408) 554-4661/6942.

ENROLLMENT: 7,800.

ARENA: Toso Pavilion (5,000).

SCHOOL COLORS: Bronco red and white.

CONFERENCE: West Coast.

FINAL AP TOP 10 RANKINGS (1): 1969.

NCAA TOURNAMENT APPEARANCES (8): 1952-53-54-60-68-69-70-87; 9-10 record (.474); reached Final Four in 1952 (4th).

NIT APPEARANCES (4): 1984-85-88-89; 2-4 record (.333).

CAREER LEADING SCORER: Kurt Rambis (1,735 points, 1977–80).

CAREER LEADING REBOUNDER: Dennis Awtrey (1,135, 1968–70).

SETON HALL

NICKNAME: Pirates.

ADDRESS: 400 South Orange Avenue, South Orange, NJ 07079.

PHONE/FAX: (201) 761-9497/9493.

ENROLLMENT: 10,200.

ARENA: Meadowlands Arena (20,029).

SCHOOL COLORS: Blue and white.

CONFERENCE: Big East.

FINAL AP TOP 10 RANKINGS (2): 1953 and 1993.

NCAA TOURNAMENT APPEARANCES (6): 1988-89-91-92-93-94; 12-6 record (.667); reached Final Four in 1989 (2d).

NIT APPEARANCES (10): 1941-51-52-53-55-56-57-74-77-87; 6-12 record (.333); finished 4th in 1941, 4th in 1951, and 1st in 1953.

CAREER LEADING SCORER: Terry Dehere (2,494 points, 1990–93).

CAREER LEADING REBOUNDER: Walter Dukes (1,697, 1951–53).

NCAA CONSENSUS FIRST-TEAM ALL-AMERICANS (2): Bob Davies (1942) and Walter Dukes (1953).

SIENA

NICKNAME: Saints.

ADDRESS: 515 Loudon Road, Loudonville, NY 12211-1462.

PHONE/FAX: (518) 783-2411/2992.

ENROLLMENT: 2,700.

ARENAS: Alumni Recreation Center (4,000) and Knickerbocker Arena (15,500).

SCHOOL COLORS: Green and gold.

CONFERENCE: Metro Atlantic Athletic.

NCAA TOURNAMENT APPEARANCES (1): 1989; 1-1 record (.500).

NIT APPEARANCES (3): 1988-91-94; 6-3 record (.667); finished 3d in 1994.

CAREER LEADING SCORER: Marc Brown (2,284 points, 1988–91).

CAREER LEADING REBOUNDER: Lee Matthews (1,037, 1990–93).

SOUTH ALABAMA

NICKNAME: Jaguars.

ADDRESS: 1107 HPELS Building, Mobile, AL 36688-0002.

PHONE/FAX: (205) 460-7121/7297.

ENROLLMENT: 12,465.

ARENA: Mobile Civic Center (10,200).

SCHOOL COLORS: Red, blue, and white.

CONFERENCE: Sun Belt.

NCAA TOURNAMENT APPEARANCES (4): 1979-80-89-91; 1-4 record (.200).

NIT APPEARANCES (2): 1981 and 1984; 3-2 record (.600).

CAREER LEADING SCORER: Jeff Hodge (2,221 points, 1986–89).

CAREER LEADING REBOUNDER: Terry Catledge (932, 1983–85).

SOUTH CAROLINA

NICKNAME: Gamecocks.

ADDRESS: Rex Enright Athletic Center, 1300 Rosewood Drive, Columbia, SC 29208.

PHONE/FAX: (803) 777-5204/2967.

ENROLLMENT: 26,130.

ARENA: Carolina Coliseum/Frank McGuire Arena (12,401).

SCHOOL COLORS: Garnet and black.

CONFERENCE: Southeastern.

FINAL AP TOP 10 RANKINGS (3): 1970-71-72.

NCAA TOURNAMENT APPEARANCES (5): 1971-72-73-74-89; 4-6 record (.400); never reached regional final.

NIT APPEARANCES (5): 1969-75-78-83-91; 5-5 record (.500).

CAREER LEADING SCORER: Alex English (1,972 points, 1973–76).

CAREER LEADING REBOUNDER: Lee Collins (1,159, 1953–56).

NCAA CONSENSUS FIRST-TEAM ALL-AMERICANS (1): Tom Riker (1972).

SOUTH FLORIDA

NICKNAME: Bulls.

ADDRESS: 4202 East Fowler Avenue, PED 214, Tampa, FL 33620.

PHONE/FAX: (813) 974-4086/5328.

ENROLLMENT: 34,000.

ARENA: Sun Dome (10,411).

SCHOOL COLORS: Green and gold.

CONFERENCE: Metro.

NCAA TOURNAMENT APPEARANCES (2): 1990 and 1992; 0-2 record.

NIT APPEARANCES (4): 1981-83-85-91; 2-4 record (.333).

CAREER LEADING SCORER: Charlie Bradley (2,319 points, 1982–85).

CAREER LEADING REBOUNDER: Hakim Shahid (893, 1987–90).

SOUTHERN

NICKNAME: Jaguars.

ADDRESS: P.O. Box 9942, Baton Rouge, LA 70813.

PHONE/FAX: (504) 771-2601/4400.

ENROLLMENT: 9,500.

ARENA: F. G. Clark Activity Center (7,500).

SCHOOL COLORS: Columbia blue and gold.

CONFERENCE: Southwestern Athletic.

NCAA TOURNAMENT APPEARANCES (6): 1981-85-87-88-89-93; 1-6 record (.143).

NIT APPEARANCES (1): 1990; 0-1 record.

CAREER LEADING SCORER: Frankie Sanders (2,141 points, 1976–78).

CAREER LEADING REBOUNDER: Jervaughn Scales (1,099, 1992–94).

SOUTHERN CAL

NICKNAME: Trojans.

ADDRESS: Heritage Hall, Los Angeles, CA 90089-0602.

PHONE/FAX: (213) 740-8480/7584.

ENROLLMENT: 28,375.

ARENA: Los Angeles Sports Arena (15,509).

SCHOOL COLORS: Cardinal and gold.

CONFERENCE: Pacific-10.

FINAL AP TOP 10 RANKINGS (3): 1961-71-92.

NCAA TOURNAMENT APPEARANCES (9): 1940-54-60-61-79-82-85-91-92; 6-11 record (.353); reached Final Four in 1940 (T3d) and 1954 (4th).

NIT APPEARANCES (3): 1973-93-94; 2-3 record (.400).

CAREER LEADING SCORER: Harold Miner (2,048 points, 1990–92).

CAREER LEADING REBOUNDER: Ron Riley (1,067, 1970–72).

NCAA CONSENSUS FIRST-TEAM ALL-AMERICANS (5): Jerry Nemer (1933), Lee Guttero (1935), Ralph Vaughn (1940), Bill Sharman (1950), and Harold Miner (1992).

SOUTHERN ILLINOIS

NICKNAME: Salukis.

ADDRESS: SIU Arena, Carbondale, IL 62901.

PHONE/FAX: (618) 453-7235/2648.

ENROLLMENT: 24,870.

ARENA: SIU Arena (10,014).

SCHOOL COLORS: Maroon and white.

CONFERENCE: Missouri Valley.

NCAA TOURNAMENT APPEARANCES (3): 1977-93-94; 1-3 record (.250).

NIT APPEARANCES (7): 1967-69-75-89-90-91-92; 6-6 record (.500); finished 1st in 1967.

CAREER LEADING SCORER: Charlie Vaughn (2,088 points, 1959–62).

CAREER LEADING REBOUNDER: Seymour Bryson (1,244, 1956–59).

SOUTHERN METHODIST

NICKNAME: Mustangs.

ADDRESS: SMU Box 216, 6024 Airline, Dallas, TX 75275-0216.

PHONE/FAX: (214) 768-2883/2044.

ENROLLMENT: 5,435.

ARENA: Moody Coliseum (9,007).

SCHOOL COLORS: Red and blue.

CONFERENCE: Southwest (will join Western Athletic in 1996).

FINAL AP TOP 10 RANKINGS (2): 1956 and 1957.

NCAA TOURNAMENT APPEARANCES (10): 1955-56-57-65-66-67-84-85-88-93; 10-12 record (.455); reached Final Four in 1956 (4th).

NIT APPEARANCES (1): 1986; 0-1 record.

CAREER LEADING SCORER: Gene Phillips (1,931 points, 1969–71).

CAREER LEADING REBOUNDER: Jon Koncak (1,169, 1982–85).

NCAA CONSENSUS FIRST-TEAM ALL-AMERICANS (1): Jim Krebs (1957).

SOUTHERN MISSISSIPPI

NICKNAME: Golden Eagles.

ADDRESS: Southern Station, Box 5161, Hattiesburg, MS 39406-5161.

PHONE/FAX: (601) 266-4503/4507.

ENROLLMENT: 13,000.

ARENA: Reed Green Coliseum (8,095).

SCHOOL COLORS: Black and gold.

CONFERENCE: Metro.

NCAA TOURNAMENT APPEARANCES (2): 1990 and 1991; 0-2 record.

NIT APPEARANCES (5): 1981-86-87-88-94; 6-4 record (.600); finished 1st in 1987.

CAREER LEADING SCORER: Nick Revon (2,135 points, 1951–54).

CAREER LEADING REBOUNDER: Clarence Weatherspoon (1,320, 1989–92).

SOUTHWEST MISSOURI STATE

NICKNAME: Bears.

ADDRESS: 901 South National, Springfield, MO 65804.

PHONE/FAX: (417) 836-5402/4868.

ENROLLMENT: 20,235.

ARENA: Hammons Student Center (8,858).

SCHOOL COLORS: Maroon and white.

CONFERENCE: Missouri Valley.

NCAA TOURNAMENT APPEARANCES (5): 1987-88-89-90-92; 1-5 record (.167).

NIT APPEARANCES (2): 1986 and 1991; 3-2 record (.600).

CAREER LEADING SCORER: Daryel Garrison (1,975 points, 1972–75).

CAREER LEADING REBOUNDER: Curtis Perry (1,424, 1967–70).

SOUTHWESTERN LOUISIANA

NICKNAME: Ragin' Cajuns.

ADDRESS: 201 Reinhardt Drive, Lafayette, LA 70506.

PHONE/FAX: (318) 482-6331/6649.

ENROLLMENT: 16,500.

ARENA: Cajundome (12,000).

SCHOOL COLORS: Vermilion and white.

CONFERENCE: Sun Belt.

FINAL AP TOP 10 RANKINGS (2): 1972 and 1973.

NCAA TOURNAMENT APPEARANCES (6): 1972-73-82-83-92-94; 4-7 record (.364).

NIT APPEARANCES (3): 1980-84-85; 6-4 record (.600); finished 4th in 1984.

CAREER LEADING SCORER: Dwight "Bo" Lamar (3,493 points, 1970–73).

CAREER LEADING REBOUNDER: Roy Ebron (1,064, 1971–73).

NCAA CONSENSUS FIRST-TEAM ALL-AMERICANS (2): Dwight "Bo" Lamar (1972 and 1973).

STANFORD

NICKNAME: Cardinal.

ADDRESS: Encina Gym, Stanford, CA 94305.

PHONE/FAX: (415) 723-4418/725-2957.

ENROLLMENT: 13,075.

ARENA: Maples Pavilion (7,500).

SCHOOL COLORS: Cardinal and white.

CONFERENCE: Pacific-10.

NCAA TOURNAMENT APPEARANCES (3): 1942-89-92; 3-2 record (.600); reached Final Four in 1942 (1st).

NIT APPEARANCES (4): 1988-90-91-94; 6-3 record (.667); finished 1st in 1991.

CAREER LEADING SCORER: Todd Lichti (2,336 points, 1986–89).

CAREER LEADING REBOUNDER: Adam Keefe (1,119, 1989–92).

NCAA CONSENSUS FIRST-TEAM ALL-AMERICANS (3): Hank Luisetti (1936, 1937, and 1938).

SYRACUSE

NICKNAME: Orangemen.

ADDRESS: Manley Field House, Syracuse, NY 13244-5020.

PHONE/FAX: (315) 443-2608/2076.

ENROLLMENT: 10,500.

ARENA: Carrier Dome (33,000).

SCHOOL COLORS: Orange and white.

CONFERENCE: Big East.

FINAL AP TOP 10 RANKINGS (10): 1975-77-79-80-86-87-88-89-90-91.

NCAA TOURNAMENT APPEARANCES (21): 1957-66-73-74-75-76-77-78-79-80-83-84-85-86-87-88-89-90-91-92-94; 29-22 record (.569); reached Final Four in 1975 (4th) and 1987 (2d).

NIT APPEARANCES (8): 1946-50-64-67-71-72-81-82; 7-8 record (.467); finished 2d in 1981.

CAREER LEADING SCORER: Derrick Coleman (2,143 points, 1987–90); Lawrence Moten is on a pace to become the all-time leader in 1995.

CAREER LEADING REBOUNDER: Derrick Coleman (1,537, 1987–90).

NCAA CONSENSUS FIRST-TEAM ALL-AMERICANS (3): Dave Bing (1966), Derrick Coleman (1990), Billy Owens (1991).

TEMPLE

NICKNAME: Owls.

ADDRESS: 1900 North Broad Street-109-00, McGonigle Hall-047-00, Philadelphia, PA 19122.

PHONE/FAX: (215) 204-7445/7499.

ENROLLMENT: 33,000.

ARENA: McGonigle Hall (3,900).

SCHOOL COLORS: Cherry and white.

CONFERENCE: Atlantic 10.

FINAL AP TOP 10 RANKINGS (3): 1958-87-88.

NCAA TOURNAMENT APPEARANCES (18): 1944-56-58-64-67-70-72-79-84-85-86-87-88-90-91-92-93-94; 22-18 record (.550); reached Final Four in 1956 (3d) and 1958 (3d).

NIT APPEARANCES (12): 1938-57-60-61-62-66-68-69-78-81-82-89; 13-10 record (.565); finished 1st in 1938, 3d in 1957, and 1st in 1969.

CAREER LEADING SCORER: Mark Macon (2,609 points, 1988–91).

CAREER LEADING REBOUNDER: John Baum (1,042, 1967–69).

NCAA CONSENSUS FIRST-TEAM ALL-AMERICANS (3): Meyer Bloom (1938), Bill Mlkvy (1951) and Guy Rodgers (1958).

TENNESSEE

NICKNAME: Volunteers.

ADDRESS: P.O. Box 15016, 1720 Volunteer Boulevard, Knoxville, TN 37901.

PHONE/FAX: (615) 974-1212/1269.

ENROLLMENT: 26,580.

ARENA: Thompson-Boling Arena (24,535).

SCHOOL COLORS: Orange and white.

CONFERENCE: Southeastern.

FINAL AP TOP 10 RANKINGS (1): 1967.

NCAA TOURNAMENT APPEARANCES (9): 1967-76-77-79-80-81-82-83-89; 5-10 record (.333); never reached regional final.

NIT APPEARANCES (8): 1945-69-71-84-85-88-90-92; 12-8 record (.600); finished 3d in 1969 and 1985.

CAREER LEADING SCORER: Allan Houston (2,801 points, 1990–93).

CAREER LEADING REBOUNDER: Gene Tormohlen (1,113, 1957–59).

NCAA CONSENSUS FIRST-TEAM ALL-AMERICANS (2): Bernard King (1977) and Dale Ellis (1983).

TENNESSEE-CHATTANOOGA

NICKNAME: Moccasins.

ADDRESS: 615 McCallie Avenue, Chattanooga, TN 37403.

PHONE/FAX: (615) 755-4618/4610.

ENROLLMENT: 8,200.

ARENA: UTC Arena (11,218).

SCHOOL COLORS: Navy blue and old gold.

CONFERENCE: Southern.

NCAA TOURNAMENT APPEARANCES (6): 1981-82-83-88-93-94; 1-6 record (.143).

NIT APPEARANCES (4): 1984-85-86-87; 3-4 record (.429).

CAREER LEADING SCORER: Wayne Goldon (2,384 points, 1974–77).

CAREER LEADING REBOUNDER: David Bryan (1,059, 1966–69).

TENNESSEE TECH

NICKNAME: Golden Eagles.

ADDRESS: Box 5057, Cookeville, TN 38505.

PHONE/FAX: (615) 372-3088/6139.

ENROLLMENT: 8,240.

ARENA: Eblen Center (10,152).

SCHOOL COLORS: Purple and gold.

CONFERENCE: Ohio Valley.

NCAA TOURNAMENT APPEARANCES (2): 1958 and 1963; 0-2 record.

NIT APPEARANCES (1): 1985; 0-1 record.

CAREER LEADING SCORER: Earl Wise (2,196 points, 1987–90).

CAREER LEADING REBOUNDER: Jimmy Hagan (1,108, 1958–60).

TEXAS

NICKNAME: Longhorns.

ADDRESS: P.O. Box 7399, Austin, TX 78713.

PHONE/FAX: (512) 471-7437/6040.

ENROLLMENT: 49,250.

ARENA: Frank Erwin Center (16,042).

SCHOOL COLORS: Burnt orange and white.

CONFERENCE: Southwest (will join Big 12, now Big Eight, in 1997).

NCAA TOURNAMENT APPEARANCES (13): 1939-43-47-60-63-72-74-79-89-90-91-92-94; 12-16 record (.429); reached Final Four in 1943 (3d) and 1947 (3d).

NIT APPEARANCES (4): 1948-78-80-86; 6-3 record (.667); finished 1st in 1978.

CAREER LEADING SCORER: Travis Mays (2,279 points, 1987–90).

CAREER LEADING REBOUNDER: LaSalle Thompson (1,027, 1980–82).

NCAA CONSENSUS FIRST-TEAM ALL-AMERICANS (1): Jack Gray (1935).

TEXAS A&M

NICKNAME: Aggies.

ADDRESS: Student Services Building, Room 222, College Station, TX 77843-1228.

PHONE/FAX: (409) 845-5725/0564.

ENROLLMENT: 42,990.

ARENA: G. Rollie White Coliseum (7,500).

SCHOOL COLORS: Maroon and white.

CONFERENCE: Southwest (will join Big 12, now Big Eight, in 1997).

NCAA TOURNAMENT APPEARANCES (6): 1951-64-69-75-80-87; 3-7 record (.300); never reached regional final.

NIT APPEARANCES (5): 1979-82-85-86-94; 4-5 record (.444).

CAREER LEADING SCORER: Vernon Smith (1,778 points, 1978–81).

CAREER LEADING REBOUNDER: Vernon Smith (978, 1978–81).

TEXAS CHRISTIAN

NICKNAME: Horned Frogs.

ADDRESS: TCU Box 32924, Ft. Worth, TX 76129.

PHONE/FAX: (817) 921-7969/7964.

ENROLLMENT: 6,990.

ARENA: Daniel-Meyer Coliseum (7,166).

SCHOOL COLORS: Purple and white.

CONFERENCE: Southwest (will join Western Athletic in 1996).

NCAA TOURNAMENT APPEARANCES (6): 1952-53-59-68-71-87; 5-6 record (.455); regional runner-up in 1968.

NIT APPEARANCES (3): 1983-86-92; 4-3 record (.571).

CAREER LEADING SCORER: Darrell Browder (1,886 points, 1980–83).

CAREER LEADING REBOUNDER: Reggie Smith (966, 1989–92).

TEXAS-EL PASO

NICKNAME: Miners.

ADDRESS: 201 Baltimore, El Paso, TX 79968.

PHONE/FAX: (915) 747-5330/5444.

ENROLLMENT: 17,500.

ARENA: Special Events Center (12,222).

SCHOOL COLORS: Orange, blue, and white.

CONFERENCE: Western Athletic.

FINAL AP TOP 10 RANKINGS (3): 1966-67-84.

NCAA TOURNAMENT APPEARANCES (14): 1963-64-66-67-70-75-84-85-86-87-88-89-90-92; 14-13 record (.519); reached Final Four in 1966 (1st).

NIT APPEARANCES (6): 1965-72-80-81-83-93; 3-6 record (.333).

CAREER LEADING SCORER: Tim Hardaway (1,586 points, 1986–89).

CAREER LEADING REBOUNDER: Jim Barnes (965 in 1963 and 1964).

TEXAS TECH

NICKNAME: Red Raiders.

ADDRESS: P.O. Box 43021, Lubbock, TX 79409-3021.

PHONE/FAX: (806) 742-2770/1970.

ENROLLMENT: 25,000.

ARENA: Lubbock Municipal Coliseum (8,174).

SCHOOL COLORS: Red and black.

CONFERENCE: Southwest (will join Big 12, now Big Eight, in 1997).

NCAA TOURNAMENT APPEARANCES (8): 1954-56-61-62-73-76-85-86; 3-9 record (.250); never reached regional final.

NIT APPEARANCES (1): 1979; 0-1 record.

CAREER LEADING SCORER: Rick Bullock (2,118 points, 1973–76).

CAREER LEADING REBOUNDER: Jim Reed (1,330, 1954–56).

TOLEDO

NICKNAME: Rockets.

ADDRESS: Glass Bowl Stadium, Toledo, OH 43606.

PHONE/FAX: (419) 537-3790/3795.

ENROLLMENT: 24,540.

ARENA: John F. Savage Hall (9,000).

SCHOOL COLORS: Midnight blue and gold.

CONFERENCE: Mid-American.

NCAA TOURNAMENT APPEARANCES (4): 1954-67-79-80; 1-4 record (.200).

NIT APPEARANCES (3): 1942-43-81; 4-4 record (.500); finished 4th in 1942 and 2d in 1943.

CAREER LEADING SCORER: Ken Epperson (2,016 points, 1982–85).

CAREER LEADING REBOUNDER: Ken Epperson (960, 1982–85).

TULANE

NICKNAME: Green Wave.

ADDRESS: James W. Wilson Jr. Center for Athletics, New Orleans, LA 70118.

PHONE/FAX: (504) 865-5506/5512.

ENROLLMENT: 11,485.

ARENA: Fogelman Arena (3,600).

SCHOOL COLORS: Olive green and sky blue.

CONFERENCE: Metro.

FINAL AP TOP 10 RANKINGS (1): 1949.

NCAA TOURNAMENT APPEARANCES (2): 1992 and 1993; 2-2 record (.500).

NIT APPEARANCES (3): 1982-83-94; 3-3 record (.500).

CAREER LEADING SCORER: Anthony Reed (1,896 points, 1990–93).

CAREER LEADING REBOUNDER: Jack Ardon (1,062, 1960–62).

TULSA

NICKNAME: Golden Hurricane.

ADDRESS: 600 South College, Tulsa, OK 74104-3189.

PHONE/FAX: (918) 631-2395/3913.

ENROLLMENT: 4,925.

ARENA: Convention Center (8,659).

SCHOOL COLORS: Old gold, royal blue, and crimson.

CONFERENCE: Missouri Valley (will join Western Athletic in 1996).

FINAL AP TOP 10 RANKINGS (1): 1982.

NCAA TOURNAMENT APPEARANCES (7): 1955-82-84-85-86-87-94; 3-7 record (.300).

NIT APPEARANCES (7): 1953-67-69-81-83-90-91; 5-6 record (.455); finished 1st in 1981.

CAREER LEADING SCORER: Steve Harris (2,272 points, 1982–85).

CAREER LEADING REBOUNDER: Bob Goodall (776, 1958–60).

UCLA

NICKNAME: Bruins.

ADDRESS: J. D. Morgan Center, 405 Hilgard Avenue, Los Angeles, CA 90024.

PHONE/FAX: (310) 206-6831/825-8664.

ENROLLMENT: 35,500.

ARENA: Pauley Pavilion (12,819).

SCHOOL COLORS: Blue and gold.

CONFERENCE: Pacific-10.

FINAL AP TOP 10 RANKINGS (20): 1950-56-64-65-67-68-69-70-71-73-73-74-75-76-77-78-79-81-83-92.

NCAA TOURNAMENT APPEARANCES (30): 1950-52-56-62-63-64-65-67-68-69-70-71-72-73-74-75-76-77-78-79-80- 81-83-87-89-90-91-92-93-94; 68-24 record (.739); reached Final Four in 1962 (4th), 1965 (1st), 1967 (1st), 1968 (1st), 1969 (1st), 1970 (1st), 1971 (1st), 1972 (1st), 1973 (1st), 1974 (3d), 1975 (1st), 1976 (3d), and 1980 (2d).

NIT APPEARANCES (2): 1985 and 1986; finished 1st in 1985.

CAREER LEADING SCORER: Don MacLean (2,608 points, 1989–92).

CAREER LEADING REBOUNDER: Bill Walton (1,370, 1972–74).

NCAA CONSENSUS FIRST-TEAM ALL-AMERICANS (17): Walt Hazzard (1964), Gail Goodrich (1965), Lew Alcindor (1967, 1968, and 1969), Sidney Wicks (1971), Henry Bibby (1972), Bill Walton (1972, 1973, and 1974), Keith Wilkes (1973 and 1974), Dave Meyers (1975), Richard Washington (1976), Marques Johnson (1977), and David Greenwood (1978 and 1979).

UNC CHARLOTTE

NICKNAME: 49ers.

ADDRESS: Highway 49/University Loop, Charlotte, NC 28223.

PHONE/FAX: (704) 547-4937/4918.

ENROLLMENT: 15,560.

ARENA: Independence Arena (9,570).

SCHOOL COLORS: Green and white.

CONFERENCE: Metro.

NCAA TOURNAMENT APPEARANCES (3): 1977-88-92; 3-4 record (.429); reached Final Four in 1977 (4th).

NIT APPEARANCES (3): 1976-89-94; 3-3 record (.500); finished 2d in 1976.

CAREER LEADING SCORER: Henry Williams (2,383 points, 1989–92).

CAREER LEADING REBOUNDER: Cedric Maxwell (1,117, 1974–77).

UNLV

NICKNAME: Runnin' Rebels.

ADDRESS: 4505 Maryland Parkway, Las Vegas, NV 89154.

PHONE/FAX: (702) 895-3207/0989.

ENROLLMENT: 19,430.

ARENA: Thomas & Mack (18,500).

SCHOOL COLORS: Scarlet and gray.

CONFERENCE: Big West will join Western Athletic in 1996).

FINAL AP TOP 10 RANKINGS (8): 1976-77-83-85-87-90-91-92.

NCAA TOURNAMENT APPEARANCES (12): 1975-76-77-83-84-85-86-87-88-89-90-91; 30-11 record (.732); reached Final Four in 1977 (3d), 1987 (T3d), 1990 (1st), and 1991 (T3d).

NIT APPEARANCES (3): 1980-82-93; 4-4 record (.500); finished 4th in 1980.

CAREER LEADING SCORER: Eddie Owens (2,221 points, 1974–77).

CAREER LEADING REBOUNDER: Sidney Green (1,276, 1980–83).

NCAA CONSENSUS FIRST-TEAM ALL-AMERICANS (2): Larry Johnson (1990 and 1991).

UTAH

NICKNAME: Utes.

ADDRESS: Jon Huntsman Center, Salt Lake City, UT 84112.

PHONE/FAX: (801) 581-3510/4358.

ENROLLMENT: 26,600.

ARENA: Jon Huntsman Center (15,000).

SCHOOL COLORS: Crimson and white.

CONFERENCE: Western Athletic.

FINAL AP TOP 10 RANKINGS (4): 1955-60-62-91.

NCAA TOURNAMENT APPEARANCES (16): 1944-45-55-56-59-60-61-66-77-78-79-81-83-86-91-93; 19-19 record (.500); reached Final Four in 1944 (1st), 1961 (4th), and 1966 (4th).

NIT APPEARANCES (10): 1944-47-49-57-58-70-74-87-88-92; 11-9 record (.550); finished 1st in 1947, 2d in 1974, and 3d in 1992.

CAREER LEADING SCORER: Josh Grant (2,000 points, 1989–93; missed most of 1991–92 season because of a knee injury).

CAREER LEADING REBOUNDER: Billy McGill (1,106, 1960–62).

NCAA CONSENSUS FIRST-TEAM ALL-AMERICANS (3): Bill Kinner (1936), Arnie Ferrin (1945), and Billy McGill (1962).

UTAH STATE

NICKNAME: Aggies.

ADDRESS: 700 North & 800 East, Logan, UT 84322.

PHONE/FAX: (801) 797-1361/2615.

ENROLLMENT: 17,435.

ARENA: Smith Spectrum (10,270).

SCHOOL COLORS: Navy blue and white.

CONFERENCE: Big West.

FINAL AP TOP 10 RANKINGS (1): 1960.

NCAA TOURNAMENT APPEARANCES (11): 1939-62-63-64-70-71-75-79-80-83-88; 5-13 record (.278); regional runner-up in 1939 and 1970.

NIT APPEARANCES (4): 1960-67-78-84; 2-4 record (.333); finished 3d in 1960.

CAREER LEADING SCORER: Greg Grant (2,127 points, 1983–86).

CAREER LEADING REBOUNDER: Cornell Green (1,067, 1960–62).

VANDERBILT

NICKNAME: Commodores.

ADDRESS: P.O. Box 120158, Nashville, TN 37212.

PHONE/FAX: (615) 322-4121/343-7064.

ENROLLMENT: 9,300.

ARENA: Memorial Gymnasium (15,317).

SCHOOL COLORS: Black and gold.

CONFERENCE: Southeastern.

FINAL AP TOP 10 RANKINGS (4): 1957-65-66-93.

NCAA TOURNAMENT APPEARANCES (6): 1965-74-88-89-91-93; 5-7 record (.417); regional runner-up in 1965.

NIT APPEARANCES (5): 1983-87-90-92-94; 12-4 record (.750); finished 1st in 1990 and 2d in 1994.

CAREER LEADING SCORER: Phil Cox (1,725 points, 1982–85).

CAREER LEADING REBOUNDER: Clyde Lee (1,223, 1964–66).

NCAA CONSENSUS FIRST-TEAM ALL-AMERICANS (1): Clyde Lee (1966).

VILLANOVA

NICKNAME: Wildcats.

ADDRESS: Villanova, PA 19085-1674.

PHONE/FAX: (215) 519-4120/7323.

ENROLLMENT: 5,950.

ARENAS: DuPont Pavilion (6,500) and Spectrum (18,060).

SCHOOL COLORS: Blue and white.

CONFERENCE: Big East.

FINAL AP TOP 10 RANKINGS (3): 1964-65-69.

NCAA TOURNAMENT APPEARANCES (21): 1939-49-51-55-62-64-69-70-71-72-78-80-81-82-83-84-85-86-88-90-91; 35-21 record (.625); reached Final Four in 1939 (T3d), 1971 (2d), and 1985 (1st).

NIT APPEARANCES (12): 1959-60-63-65-66-67-68-77-87-89-92-94; 19-12 record (.613); finished 4th in 1963, 2d in 1965, 3d in 1966, 3d in 1977, and 1st in 1994.

CAREER LEADING SCORER: Keith Herron (2,170 points, 1975–78).

CAREER LEADING REBOUNDER: Howard Porter (1,317, 1969–71).

NCAA CONSENSUS FIRST-TEAM ALL-AMERICANS (1): Paul Arizin (1950).

VIRGINIA

NICKNAME: Cavaliers.

ADDRESS: P.O. Box 3785, University Hall, Charlottesville, VA 22903.

PHONE/FAX: (804) 982-5500/5525.

ENROLLMENT: 18,075.

ARENA: University Hall (8,457).

SCHOOL COLORS: Orange and blue.

CONFERENCE: Atlantic Coast.

FINAL AP TOP 10 RANKINGS (3): 1981-82-83.

NCAA TOURNAMENT APPEARANCES (12): 1976-81-82-83-84-86-87-89-90-91-93-94; 18-12 record (.600); reached Final Four in 1981 (3d) and 1984 (T3d).

NIT APPEARANCES (7): 1941-72-78-79-80-85-92; 13-5 record (.722); finished 1st in 1980 and 1992.

CAREER LEADING SCORER: Bryant Stith (2,516 points, 1989–92).

CAREER LEADING REBOUNDER: Ralph Sampson (1,511, 1980–83).

NCAA CONSENSUS FIRST-TEAM ALL-AMERICANS (3): Ralph Sampson (1981, 1982, and 1983).

VIRGINIA COMMONWEALTH

NICKNAME: Rams.

ADDRESS: VCU Box 2003, Richmond, VA 23284-2003.

PHONE/FAX: (804) 828-7000/9723.

ENROLLMENT: 22,000.

ARENA: Richmond Coliseum (12,500).

SCHOOL COLORS: Black and gold.

CONFERENCE: Metro.

NCAA TOURNAMENT APPEARANCES (5): 1980-81-83-84-85; 4-5 record (.444).

NIT APPEARANCES (3): 1978-88-93; 2-3 record (.400).

CAREER LEADING SCORER: Len Creech (2,019 points, 1965–69; missed 1967–68 season).

CAREER LEADING REBOUNDER: Lorenza Watson (1,143, 1976–79).

VIRGINIA MILITARY

NICKNAME: Keydets.

ADDRESS: Lexington, VA 24450.

PHONE/FAX: (703) 464-7253/7583.

ENROLLMENT: 1,300.

ARENA: Cameron Hall (5,029).

SCHOOL COLORS: Red, white, and yellow.

CONFERENCE: Southern.

NCAA TOURNAMENT APPEARANCES (3): 1964-76-77; 3-3 record (.500); regional runner-up in 1976.

NIT APPEARANCES: None.

CAREER LEADING SCORER: Gay Elmore (2,423 points, 1983–87; missed majority of 1982–83 season because of leg and wrist injuries).

CAREER LEADING REBOUNDER: Dave Montgomery (1,068, 1975–78).

VIRGINIA TECH

NICKNAME: Hokies.

ADDRESS: Jamerson Athletic Center, Blacksburg, VA 24061-0502.

PHONE/FAX: (703) 231-6725/6984.

ENROLLMENT: 22,235.

ARENA: Cassell Coliseum (9,971).

SCHOOL COLORS: Chicago maroon and burnt orange.

CONFERENCE: Metro.

NCAA TOURNAMENT APPEARANCES (6): 1967-76-79-80-85-86; 4-6 record (.400); regional runner-up in 1967.

NIT APPEARANCES (6): 1966-73-77-82-83-84; 12-5 record (.706); finished 1st in 1973 and 3d in 1984.

CAREER LEADING SCORER: Vernell "Bimbo" Coles (2,484 points, 1987–90).

CAREER LEADING REBOUNDER: Chris Smith (1,508, 1958–61).

WAKE FOREST

NICKNAME: Demon Deacons.

ADDRESS: P.O. Box 7426, Winston-Salem, NC 27109.

PHONE/FAX: (910) 759-5640/5140.

ENROLLMENT: 3,600.

ARENA: Lawrence Joel Coliseum (14,407).

SCHOOL COLORS: Old gold and black.

CONFERENCE: Atlantic Coast.

FINAL AP TOP 10 RANKINGS (1): 1977.

NCAA TOURNAMENT APPEARANCES (12): 1939-53-61-62-77-81-82-84-91-92-93-94; 16-12 record (.571); reached Final Four in 1962 (3d).

NIT APPEARANCES (2): 1983 and 1985; 3-2 record (.600); finished in tie for 3d in 1983.

CAREER LEADING SCORER: Dickie Hemric (2,587 points, 1952–55).

CAREER LEADING REBOUNDER: Dickie Hemric (1,802, 1952–55).

NCAA CONSENSUS FIRST-TEAM ALL-AMERICANS (1): Len Chappell (1962).

WASHINGTON

NICKNAME: Huskies.

ADDRESS: Graves Building, Seattle, WA 98195.

PHONE/FAX: (206) 543-2230/5000.

ENROLLMENT: 34,000.

ARENA: Hec Edmundson Pavilion (7,870).

SCHOOL COLORS: Purple and gold.

CONFERENCE: Pacific-10.

FINAL AP TOP 10 RANKINGS (2): 1952 and 1953.

NCAA TOURNAMENT APPEARANCES (8): 1943-48-51-53-76-84-85-86; 8-9 record (.471); reached Final Four in 1953 (3d).

NIT APPEARANCES (3): 1980-82-87; 3-3 record (.500).

CAREER LEADING SCORER: Christian Welp (2,073 points, 1984–87).

CAREER LEADING REBOUNDER: Doug Smart (1,051, 1957–59).

NCAA CONSENSUS FIRST-TEAM ALL-AMERICANS (2): Hal Lee (1934) and Bob Houbregs (1953).

WASHINGTON STATE

NICKNAME: Cougars.

ADDRESS: Bohler Gym, Room M-8, Pullman, WA 99164-1602.

PHONE/FAX: (509) 335-0270/0267.

ENROLLMENT: 17,500.

ARENA: Friel Court (12,058).

SCHOOL COLORS: Crimson and gray.

CONFERENCE: Pacific-10.

NCAA TOURNAMENT APPEARANCES (4): 1941-80-83-94; 3-4 record (.429); reached Final Four in 1941 (2d).

NIT APPEARANCES (1): 1992; 1-1 record (.500).

CAREER LEADING SCORER: Steve Puidokas (1,894 points, 1974–77).

CAREER LEADING REBOUNDER: Steve Puidokas (992, 1974–77).

WEBER STATE

NICKNAME: Wildcats.

ADDRESS: Wildcat Stadium, Ogden, UT 84408-2702.

PHONE/FAX: (801) 626-6010/6490.

ENROLLMENT: 14,500.

ARENA: Dee Events Center (12,000).

SCHOOL COLORS: Royal purple and white.

CONFERENCE: Big Sky.

NCAA TOURNAMENT APPEARANCES (10): 1968-69-70-71-72-73-78-79-80-83; 4-11 record (.266).

NIT APPEARANCES (1): 1984; 1-1 record (.500).

CAREER LEADING SCORER: Bruce Collins (2,019 points, 1977–80).

CAREER LEADING REBOUNDER: Willie Sojourner (1,143, 1969–71).

WEST VIRGINIA

NICKNAME: Mountaineers.

ADDRESS: P.O. Box 0877, Morgantown, WV 26507-0877.

PHONE/FAX: (304) 293-2821/4105.

ENROLLMENT: 22,710.

ARENA: WVU Coliseum (14,000).

SCHOOL COLORS: Old gold and blue.

CONFERENCE: Atlantic 10 (will join Big East in 1996).

FINAL AP TOP 10 RANKINGS (6): 1952-57-58-59-60-61.

NCAA TOURNAMENT APPEARANCES (17): 1955-56-57-58-59-60-62-63-65-67-82-83-84-86-87-89-92; 11-17 record (.393); reached Final Four in 1959 (2d).

NIT APPEARANCES (11): 1942-45-46-47-68-81-85-88-91-93-94; 12-12 record (.500); finished 1st in 1942, 3d in 1946, 4th in 1947, and 4th in 1981.

CAREER LEADING SCORER: Jerry West (2,309 points, 1958–60).

CAREER LEADING REBOUNDER: Jerry West (1,240, 1958–60).

NCAA CONSENSUS FIRST-TEAM ALL-AMERICANS (3): Rod Hundley (1957) and Jerry West (1959 and 1960).

WESTERN KENTUCKY

NICKNAME: Hilltoppers.

ADDRESS: College Heights, Bowling Green, KY 42101.

PHONE/FAX: (502) 745-4298/3444.

ENROLLMENT: 15,400.

ARENA: E. A. Diddle Arena (11,300).

SCHOOL COLORS: Red and white.

CONFERENCE: Sun Belt.

FINAL AP TOP 10 RANKINGS (6): 1949-50-54-66-67-71.

NCAA TOURNAMENT APPEARANCES (15): 1940-60-62-66-67-70-71-76-78-80-81-86-87-93-94; 14-16 record (.467); reached Final Four in 1971 (3d).

NIT APPEARANCES (11): 1942-43-48-49-50-52-53-54-65-82-92; 8-12 record (.400); finished 2d in 1942, 3d in 1948, and 4th in 1954.

CAREER LEADING SCORER: Jim McDaniels (2,238 points, 1969–71).

CAREER LEADING REBOUNDER: Ralph Crosthwaite (1,309, 1955–59; missed 1955–56 season for disciplinary reasons).

NCAA CONSENSUS FIRST-TEAM ALL-AMERICANS (2): Clem Haskins (1967) and Jim McDaniels (1971).

WESTERN MICHIGAN

NICKNAME: Broncos.

ADDRESS: B 206 Ellsworth Hall, Kalamazoo, MI 49008-5166.

PHONE/FAX: (616) 387-4104/4124.

ENROLLMENT: 26,555.

ARENA: Read Fieldhouse (8,250).

SCHOOL COLORS: Brown and gold.

CONFERENCE: Mid-American.

FINAL AP TOP 10 RANKINGS (1): 1976.

NCAA TOURNAMENT APPEARANCES (1): 1976; 1-1 record (.500).

NIT APPEARANCES (1): 1992; 0-1 record.

CAREER LEADING SCORER: Manny Newsome (1,786 points, 1962–64).

CAREER LEADING REBOUNDER: Paul Griffin (1,008, 1973–76).

WICHITA STATE

NICKNAME: Shockers.

ADDRESS: Campus Box 18, Wichita, KS 67260-0018.

PHONE/FAX: (316) 689-3265/3336.

ENROLLMENT: 15,000.

ARENA: Levitt Arena (10,656).

SCHOOL COLORS: Yellow and black.

CONFERENCE: Missouri Valley.

FINAL AP TOP 10 RANKINGS (2): 1963 and 1964.

NCAA TOURNAMENT APPEARANCES (7): 1964-65-76-81-85-87-88; 6-8 record (.429); reached Final Four in 1965 (4th).

NIT APPEARANCES (7): 1954-62-63-66-80-84-89; 1-7 record (.125).

CAREER LEADING SCORER: Cleo Littleton (2,164 points, 1952–55).

CAREER LEADING REBOUNDER: Xavier McDaniel (1,359, 1982–85).

NCAA CONSENSUS FIRST-TEAM ALL-AMERICANS (2): Dave Stallworth (1964) and Xavier McDaniel (1985).

WILLIAM & MARY

NICKNAME: Tribe.

ADDRESS: P.O. Box 399, Williamsburg, VA 23187.

PHONE/FAX: (804) 221-3368/3412.

ENROLLMENT: 5,300.

ARENA: William & Mary Hall (10,000).

SCHOOL COLORS: Green, gold, and silver.

CONFERENCE: Colonial Athletic Association.

NCAA TOURNAMENT APPEARANCES: None.

NIT APPEARANCES (1): 1983; 0-1 record.

CAREER LEADING SCORER: Chet Giermak (2,052 points, 1947–50).

CAREER LEADING REBOUNDER: Jeff Cohen (1,679, 1958–61).

WISCONSIN

NICKNAME: Badgers.

ADDRESS: 1440 Monroe Street, Madison, WI 53711.

PHONE/FAX: (608) 262-1811/8184.

ENROLLMENT: 40,925.

ARENA: UW Field House (11,500).

SCHOOL COLORS: Cardinal and white.

CONFERENCE: Big Ten.

NCAA TOURNAMENT APPEARANCES (3): 1941-47-94; 5-2 record (.714); reached Final Four in 1941 (1st).

NIT APPEARANCES (3): 1989-91-93; 2-3 record (.400).

CAREER LEADING SCORER: Danny Jones (1,854 points, 1987–90).

CAREER LEADING REBOUNDER: Claude Gregory (904, 1978–81).

NCAA CONSENSUS FIRST-TEAM ALL-AMERICANS (2): Gene Englund (1941) and John Kotz (1942).

WISCONSIN-GREEN BAY

NICKNAME: Phoenix.

ADDRESS: Phoenix Sports Center, 2420 Nicolet Drive, Green Bay, WI 54311-7001.

PHONE/FAX: (414) 465-2145/2357.

ENROLLMENT: 5,000.

ARENA: Brown County Arena (5,800).

SCHOOL COLORS: Red, green, and white.

CONFERENCE: Midwestern Collegiate.

NCAA TOURNAMENT APPEARANCES (2): 1991 and 1994; 1-2 record (.333).

NIT APPEARANCES (2): 1990 and 1992; 1-2 record (.333).

CAREER LEADING SCORER: Tony Bennett (2,285 points, 1989–92).

CAREER LEADING REBOUNDER: Dennis Woelffer (947, 1970–73).

WYOMING

NICKNAME: Cowboys.

ADDRESS: P.O. Box 3414, Fieldhouse-North Addition, Laramie, WY 82071-3414.

PHONE/FAX: (307) 766-2256/2346.

ENROLLMENT: 10,600.

ARENA: Arena Auditorium (15,028).

SCHOOL COLORS: Brown and yellow.

CONFERENCE: Western Athletic.

NCAA TOURNAMENT APPEARANCES (13): 1941-43-47-48-49-52-53-58-67-81-82-87-88; 8-18 record (.308); reached Final Four in 1943 (1st).

NIT APPEARANCES (4): 1968-69-86-91; 5-4 record (.556); finished 2d in 1986.

CAREER LEADING SCORER: Fennis Dembo (2,311 points, 1985–88).

CAREER LEADING REBOUNDER: Reginald Slater (1,197, 1989–92).

NCAA CONSENSUS FIRST-TEAM ALL-AMERICANS (3): Les Witte (1932 and 1934) and Ken Sailors (1943).

XAVIER

NICKNAME: Musketeers.

ADDRESS: 3800 Victory Parkway, Cincinnati, OH 45207-6114.

PHONE/FAX: (513) 745-3416/2825.

ENROLLMENT: 6,375.

ARENA: Cincinnati Gardens (10,400).

SCHOOL COLORS: Blue and white.

CONFERENCE: Midwestern Collegiate (will join Atlantic 10 in 1996).

NCAA TOURNAMENT APPEARANCES (9): 1961-83-86-87-88-89-90-91-93; 5-9 record (.357).

NIT APPEARANCES (5): 1956-57-58-84-94; 10-4 record (.714); finished 1st in 1958.

CAREER LEADING SCORER: Byron Larkin (2,696 points, 1985–88).

CAREER LEADING REBOUNDER: Tyrone Hill (1,380, 1987–90).

YALE

NICKNAMES: Elis, Bulldogs.

ADDRESS: Box 208216, New Haven, CT 06520-8216.

PHONE/FAX: (203) 432-1455/1454.

ENROLLMENT: 5,200.

ARENA: Payne Whitney Gymnasium (3,100).

SCHOOL COLORS: Yale blue and white.

CONFERENCE: Ivy League.

NCAA TOURNAMENT APPEARANCES (3): 1949-57-62; 0-4 record.

NIT APPEARANCES: None.

CAREER LEADING SCORER: Butch Graves (2,090 points, 1981–84).

CAREER LEADING REBOUNDER: Ed Robinson (1,182, 1955–57).

NCAA CONSENSUS FIRST-TEAM ALL-AMERICANS (1): Tony Lavelli (1949).

FORMER MAJOR COLLEGES WITH A CONSENSUS FIRST-TEAM ALL-AMERICAN

Denver: Vince Boryla (1949, after playing the two previous seasons for Notre Dame).

New York University: Sid Tannenbaum (1946 and 1947) and Barry Kramer (1963).

West Texas State: Price Brookfield (1942).

FORMER MAJOR COLLEGES WITH AT LEAST ONE NATIONAL POSTSEASON VICTORY

SCHOOL	NCAA	NIT	CURRENT STATUS
City College of New York	4-2	6-3	Division III
Muhlenberg (Pa.)	0-0	1-4	Division III
New York University	9-9	13-10	Division III
Oklahoma City	8-13	0-2	NAIA
Seattle	10-13	0-2	NAIA
Washington and Jefferson (Pa.)	0-0	2-1	Division III
Wayne State (Mich.)	1-2	0-0	Division II

Note: NYU finished 9th in the final AP poll in 1963, Oklahoma City finished 9th in 1957, and Seattle finished 5th in 1957

16

NCAA AWARDS

Excluding specialty publications, there are six nationally-recognized Player of the Year awards. None of them, however, comes anywhere close to being the equivalent to college football's undisputed most prestigious honor, the Heisman Trophy. The reason for this basketball stalemate? It appears to be twofold: Essentially the same people vote on the major awards (writers or coaches or a combination), and the announcements of the winners are made one after the other right around the Final Four when the games dominate the sports page.

United Press International, on the verge of extinction in recent years, got it all started back in 1955. Four years later, the United States Basketball Writers Association (USBWA), having chosen All-American teams in each of the two previous seasons, added a Player of the Year award to its postseason honors. In recent years, the USBWA award was sponsored by Mercedes and then RCA.

The third oldest of the awards comes from the most dominant wire service, the Associated Press. Perhaps because of its vast network of media outlets, the AP award gets more print and broadcast attention than the other honors. The AP award started in 1961 before affiliating in 1972 with the Commonwealth Athletic Club of Lexington, Kentucky, which was looking for a way to honor Hall of Fame coach Adolph Rupp. The result of their merger is the Rupp Trophy.

The Atlanta Tipoff Club initially was associated with UPI before starting its own Naismith Award in 1969. Six years later, the National Association of Basketball Coaches initiated its award, which was sponsored from the outset by the Eastman Kodak Company. In 1977, the Los Angeles Athletic Club began the Wooden Award, in honor of Hall of Fame UCLA coach John Wooden.

NATIONAL PLAYER OF THE YEAR AWARDS

1955: Tom Gola, La Salle, 6-6, Sr. (24.2 ppg, 19.9 rpg/UPI)
The Explorers (26-5) were runner-ups in the NCAA Tournament.

1956: Bill Russell, San Francisco, 6-9, Sr. (20.6 ppg, 21 rpg, 51.3 FG%/UPI)
The Dons (29-0) captured the NCAA championship after winning all 14 of their conference games by more than 10 points.

1957: Chet Forte, Columbia, 5-9, Sr. (28.9 ppg, 4.5 rpg, 85.2 FT%/UPI)
The Lions (18-6) did not appear in postseason competition after finishing in a tie for third place in the Ivy League.

1958: Oscar Robertson, Cincinnati, 6-5, Soph. (35.1 ppg, 15.2 rpg, 57.1 FG%/UPI)

    The Bearcats (25-3) lost their NCAA Tournament opener after winning the Missouri Valley title (13-1 mark) in their first year in the conference.

1959: Oscar Robertson, Cincinnati, 6-5, Jr. (32.6 ppg, 16.3 rpg, 50.9 FG%/UPI, USBWA)

    The Bearcats (26-4) finished in third place in the NCAA Tournament after compiling a 13-1 Missouri Valley record to win the league title.

1960: Oscar Robertson, Cincinnati, 6-5, Sr. (33.7 ppg, 14.1 rpg, 52.6 FG%/UPI, USBWA)

    The Bearcats (28-2), third-place finisher in the NCAA Tournament, captured their third consecutive Missouri Valley title with a 13-1 record.

1961: Jerry Lucas, Ohio State, 6-8, Jr. (24.9 ppg, 17.4 rpg, 62.3 FG%/AP, UPI, USBWA)

    The Buckeyes (27-1) became the first team in 18 years to go undefeated in Big Ten competition (14-0) before finishing runner-up in the NCAA Tournament.

1962: Jerry Lucas, Ohio State, 6-8, Sr. (21.8 ppg, 17.8 rpg, 61.1 FG%/AP, UPI, USBWA)

    The Buckeyes (26-2) lost in the NCAA Championship Game after becoming the first Big Ten school to win three consecutive undisputed league titles since Wisconsin from 1912 to 1914.

1963: Art Heyman, Duke, 6-5, Sr. (24.9 ppg, 10.8 rpg/AP, UPI, USBWA)

    The Blue Devils (27-3), third-place finisher in the NCAA Tournament, went undefeated (14-0) in ACC competition.

1964: Gary Bradds, Ohio State, 6-8, Sr. (30.6 ppg, 13.4 rpg, 52.4 FG%/AP, UPI)

    The Buckeyes (16-8) did not participate in postseason competition after compiling an 11-3 Big Ten record to finish in a tie for first place with Michigan.

Walt Hazzard, UCLA, 6-2, Sr. (18.6 ppg, 4.7 rpg/USBWA)

    The NCAA champion Bruins (30-0) compiled a 15-0 record in the Athletic Association of Western Universities.

1965: Bill Bradley, Princeton, 6-5, Sr. (30.5 ppg, 11.8 rpg, 53.3 FG%, 88.6 FT%/AP, UPI, USBWA)

    The Tigers (23-6) finished in third place in the NCAA Tournament after winning the Ivy League title with a 13-1 mark.

1966: Cazzie Russell, Michigan, 6-5, Sr. (30.8 ppg, 8.4 rpg, 51.8 FG%, 82.5 FT%/AP, UPI, USBWA)

    The Wolverines (18-8) lost the NCAA Tournament Mideast Regional final after winning the Big Ten title with an 11-3 record.

1967: Lew Alcindor, UCLA, 7-2, Soph. (29 ppg, 15.5 rpg, 66.7 FG%/AP, UPI, USBWA)

    The NCAA champion Bruins (30-0) compiled a 14-0 record in the Pacific-8 Conference.

1968: Elvin Hayes, Houston, 6-8, Sr. (36.8 ppg, 18.9, 54.9 FG%/AP, UPI, USBWA)

    The independent Cougars (31-2) finished in fourth place in the NCAA Tournament.

1969: Lew Alcindor, UCLA, 7-2, Sr. (24 ppg, 14.7 rpg, 63.5 FG%/AP, UPI, USBWA, Naismith)

    The NCAA champion Bruins (29-1) compiled a 13-1 Pacific-8 record.

1970: Pete Maravich, Louisiana State, 6-5, Sr. (44.5 ppg, 5.3 rpg/AP, UPI, USBWA, Naismith)

    The Tigers (22-10), fourth-place finisher in the NIT, posted their highest SEC finish (runner-up with a 13-5 record) since going undefeated in league play in 1954.

1971: Austin Carr, Notre Dame, 6-3, Sr. (38 ppg, 7.4 rpg, 51.7 FG%, 81.1 FT%/AP, UPI, Naismith)

    The independent Irish (20-9) lost in the NCAA Tournament Midwest Regional semifinals.

Sidney Wicks, UCLA, 6-8, Sr. (21.3 ppg, 12.8 rpg, 52.4 FG%/USBWA)

    The NCAA champion Bruins (29-1) went undefeated (14-0) in Pacific-8 competition.

UCLA's Walt Hazzard (left) handles the ball against Duke.

1972: Bill Walton, UCLA, 6-11, Soph. (21.1 ppg, 15.5 rpg, 64.0 FG%/AP, UPI, USBWA, Naismith)

    The NCAA champion Bruins (30-0) compiled an unbeaten record (14-0) in Pacific-8 play.

1973: Bill Walton, UCLA, 6-11, Jr. (20.4 ppg, 16.9 rpg, 65.0 FG%/AP, UPI, USBWA, Naismith)

    The NCAA champion Bruins (30-0) went undefeated (14-0) in Pacific-8 competition for the seventh time in 10 years.

1974: Bill Walton, UCLA, 6-11, Sr. (19.3 ppg, 14.7 rpg, 66.5 FG%/UPI, USBWA, Naismith)

    The Bruins (26-4) finished in third place in the NCAA Tournament after winning the Pacific-8 title with a 12-2 record.

David Thompson, North Carolina State, 6-4, Jr. (26 ppg, 7.9 rpg, 54.7 FG%/AP)

    The Wolfpack (30-1) won the NCAA Tournament after becoming the only school to have back-to-back undefeated records in ACC competition.

1975: David Thompson, North Carolina State, 6-4, Sr. (29.9 ppg, 8.2 rpg, 54.6 FG%/AP, UPI, NABC, USBWA, Naismith)

    The Wolfpack (22-6) did not participate in national postseason play after finishing in a three-way tie for second place in the ACC and losing in the ACC Tournament final.

1976: Scott May, Indiana, 6-7, Sr. (23.5 ppg, 7.7 rpg, 52.7 FG%/AP, UPI, NABC, Naismith)

    The NCAA champion Hoosiers (32-0) captured their fourth consecutive Big Ten title.

Adrian Dantley, Notre Dame, 6-5, Jr. (28.6 ppg, 10.1 rpg, 58.8 FG%/USBWA)

    The independent Irish (23-6) lost in the NCAA Tournament Midwest Regional semifinals.

1977: Marques Johnson, UCLA, 6-7, Sr. (21.4 ppg, 11.1 rpg, 59.1 FG%/AP, UPI, NABC, USBWA, Naismith, Wooden)

The Bruins (24-5) lost in the NCAA Tournament West Regional semifinals after winning the Pacific-8 title with an 11-3 record.

1978: Phil Ford, North Carolina, 6-2, Sr. (20.8 ppg, 52.7 FG%, 81.0 FT%/NABC, USBWA, Wooden)

The Tar Heels (23-8) lost their NCAA Tournament West Regional opener after finishing atop the ACC standings with a 9-3 league record.

Butch Lee, Marquette, 6-2, Sr. (17.7 ppg, 3.1 rpg, 50.6 FG%, 87.9 FT%/AP, UPI, Naismith)

The independent Warriors (24-4) lost their NCAA Tournament Mideast Regional opener.

1979: Larry Bird, Indiana State, 6-9, Sr. (28.6 ppg, 14.9 rpg, 53.2 FG%, 83.1 FT%/AP, UPI, NABC, USBWA, Naismith, Wooden)

The Sycamores (33-1), NCAA Tournament runner-up, became the first Missouri Valley school to go undefeated in league competition (16-0) since Oklahoma A&M went 10-0 in 1948.

1980: Mark Aguirre, DePaul, 6-7, Soph. (26.8 ppg, 7.6 rpg, 54.0 FG%/AP, UPI, USBWA, Naismith)

The independent Blue Demons (26-2) lost their NCAA Tournament opener in the West Regional.

Michael Brooks, La Salle, 6-7, Sr. (24.1 ppg, 11.5 rpg, 52.4 FG%/NABC)

The Explorers (22-9) lost in the first round of the NCAA Tournament Mideast Regional after winning the East Coast Conference Tournament following a third-place finish in the ECC's Eastern Section.

Darrell Griffith, Louisville, 6-4, Sr. (22.9 ppg, 4.8 rpg, 55.3 FG%/Wooden).

The NCAA champion Cardinals (33-3) were undefeated in Metro Conference competition (12-0).

1981: Ralph Sampson, Virginia, 7-4, Soph. (17.7 ppg, 11.5 rpg, 55.7 FG%/AP, UPI, USBWA, Naismith)

The Cavaliers (29-4) lost in the NCAA Tournament national semifinals after winning their first ACC regular-season title with a 13-1 league record.

Danny Ainge, Brigham Young, 6-5, Sr. (24.4 ppg, 4.8 rpg, 51.8 FG%, 82.4 FT%/NABC, Wooden)

The Cougars (25-7) lost the NCAA Tournament East Regional final after finishing in third place in the WAC with a 12-4 league record.

1982: Ralph Sampson, Virginia, 7-4, Jr. (15.8 ppg, 11.4 rpg, 56.1 FG%/AP, UPI, NABC, USBWA, Naismith, Wooden)

The Cavaliers (30-4) lost in the NCAA Tournament Mideast Regional semifinals after tying North Carolina for first place in the ACC with a 12-2 record.

1983: Ralph Sampson, Virginia, 7-4, Sr. (19 ppg, 11.7 rpg, 60.4 FG%/AP, UPI, NABC, USBWA, Naismith, Wooden)

The Cavaliers (29-5) lost the NCAA Tournament West Regional final after tying North Carolina for first place in the ACC with a 12-2 record.

1984: Michael Jordan, North Carolina, 6-6, Jr. (19.6 ppg, 5.3 rpg, 55.1 FG%/AP, UPI, NABC, USBWA, Naismith, Wooden)

The Tar Heels (28-3) lost in the NCAA Tournament East Regional semifinals after becoming the first ACC team to go undefeated in league play (14-0) since North Carolina State in 1974.

1985: Chris Mullin, St. John's, 6-6, Sr. (19.8 ppg, 4.8 rpg, 52.1 FG%, 82.4 FT%/UPI., USBWA, Wooden)

The Redmen (31-4) lost in the NCAA Tournament national semifinals after winning the Big East title with a 15-1 mark.

Patrick Ewing, Georgetown, 7-0, Sr. (14.6 ppg, 9.2 rpg, 62.5 FG%/AP, NABC, Naismith)

The Hoyas (35-3) lost the NCAA Tournament final after finishing runner-up in the Big East standings with a 14-2 record.

1986: Walter Berry, St. John's, 6-8, Jr. (23 ppg, 11.1 rpg, 59.8 FG%/AP, UPI, NABC, USBWA, Wooden)

The Redmen (31-5) lost in the second round of the NCAA Tournament West Regional after tying for first place in the Big East with a 14-2 record.

Johnny Dawkins, Duke, 6-2, Sr. (20.2 ppg, 3.6 rpg, 54.9 FG%, 81.2 FT%/Naismith)

The Blue Devils (37-3) lost in the NCAA Tournament final after compiling a 12-2 ACC record to win their second regular-season league title in 20 years.

1987: David Robinson, Navy, 6-11, Sr. (28.2 ppg, 11.8 rpg, 59.1 FG%/AP, UPI, NABC, USBWA, Naismith, Wooden)

The Midshipmen (26-6) lost in the first round of the NCAA Tournament East Regional after winning the Colonial Athletic Association with a 13-1 mark.

1988: Hersey Hawkins, Bradley, 6-3, Sr. (36.3 ppg, 7.8 rpg, 52.4 FG%, 84.8 FT%/AP, UPI, USBWA)

The Braves (26-5) lost in the first round of the NCAA Tournament Southeast Regional after winning the Missouri Valley title with a 12-2 league record.

Danny Manning, Kansas, 6-10, Sr. (24.8 ppg, 9 rpg, 58.3 FG%/NABC, Naismith, Wooden)

The Jayhawks (27-11) won the NCAA Tournament after finishing in third place in the Big Eight with a 9-5 league record.

1989: Danny Ferry, Duke, 6-10, Sr. (22.6 ppg, 7.4 rpg, 52.2 FG%/UPI, USBWA, Naismith)

The Blue Devils (28-8) lost in the NCAA Tournament national semifinals after finishing in a three-way tie for first in the ACC standings with a 9-5 league record.

Sean Elliott, Arizona, 6-8, Sr. (22.3 ppg, 7.2 rpg, 84.1 FT%/AP, NABC, Wooden)

The Wildcats (29-4) lost in the NCAA Tournament West Regional semifinals after winning the Pacific-10 title with a 17-1 league record.

1990: Lionel Simmons, La Salle, 6-7, Sr. (26.5 ppg, 11.1 rpg, 51.3 FG%/AP, UPI, NABC, USBWA, Naismith, Wooden)

The Explorers (30-2) lost in the second round of the NCAA Tournament East Regional after compiling the best record in the Metro Atlantic Athletic Conference (16-0 in South Division).

1991: Larry Johnson, UNLV, 6-7, Sr. (22.7 ppg, 10.9 rpg, 66.2 FG%, 81.8 FT%/NABC, USBWA, Naismith, Wooden)

The Rebels (34-1) lost in the NCAA Tournament national semifinals after going undefeated (18-0) in the Big West Conference.

Shaquille O'Neal, Louisiana State, 7-1, Soph. (27.6 ppg, 14.7 rpg, 62.8 FG%/UPI)

The Tigers (20-10) lost in the first round of the NCAA Tournament Midwest Regional after tying for first place in the SEC standings with a 13-5 league mark.

1992: Christian Laettner, Duke, 6-11, Sr. (21.5 ppg, 7.9 rpg, 57.5 FG%, 81.5 FT%/AP, NABC, USBWA, Naismith, Wooden)

The Blue Devils (35-2) won the NCAA Tournament after winning the ACC regular-season title with a 14-2 league record.

Jim Jackson, Ohio State, 6-6, Jr. (22.4 ppg, 6.8 rpg, 81.1 FT%/UPI)

The Buckeyes (26-6) lost the NCAA Tournament Southeast Regional final after compiling a 15-3 Big Ten record to win their first undisputed league title since 1971.

1993: Calbert Cheaney, Indiana, 6-7, Sr. (22.4 ppg, 6.4 rpg, 54.9 FG%/AP, UPI, NABC, USBWA, Naismith, Wooden)

The Hoosiers (31-4) lost the NCAA Tournament Midwest Regional final after compiling the best record in Big Ten competition (17-1) since they went undefeated in 1976.

1994: Glenn Robinson, Purdue, 6-8, Jr. (30.3 ppg, 10.1 rpg/AP, UPI, NABC, USBWA, Naismith, Wooden)

The Boilermakers (29-5) lost the NCAA Tournament Southeast Regional final after winning the Big Ten championship with their first winning league record in four years (14-4).

NATIONAL COACH OF THE YEAR AWARDS

1955: Phil Woolpert, San Francisco (28-1 overall record; 12-0 in California Basketball Association/UPI)

The Dons ascended to an NCAA title after absorbing three consecutive losing seasons from 1951 to 1953.

1956: Phil Woolpert, San Francisco (29-0; 14-0 in West Coast Athletic/UPI)

The Dons extended their winning streak to 55 consecutive games en route to another NCAA championship.

1957: Frank McGuire, North Carolina (27-0; 14-0 in ACC/UPI)

The Tar Heels captured their first ACC regular-season championship. They won 22 games by at least nine points.

1958: Tex Winter, Kansas State (22-5; 10-2 in Big Seven/UPI)

The Wildcats won the Big Seven championship one year before entering the NCAA Tournament ranked No. 1 in the country.

1959: Eddie Hickey, Marquette (23-6/USBWA)

The Warriors, after losing more than 10 games in 11 of their 12 previous seasons, had a 22-3 record in Hickey's first year at their helm until dropping three of their last four outings.

Adolph Rupp, Kentucky (24-3; 12-2 in SEC/UPI)

The Wildcats extended their streak of 20-win seasons to 14.

1960: Pete Newell, California (28-2; 11-1 in AAWU/UPI, USBWA)

The Bears' bid to win back-to-back NCAA championships was thwarted by Ohio State in the tourney final.

1961: Fred Taylor, Ohio State (27-1; 14-0 in Big Ten/UPI, USBWA)

The Buckeyes became the first team to go undefeated in Big Ten competition since Illinois in 1943.

1962: Fred Taylor, Ohio State (26-2; 13-1 in Big Ten/UPI, USBWA)

The Buckeyes captured their third of five consecutive Big Ten championships.

1963: Ed Jucker, Cincinnati (26-2; 11-1 in Missouri Valley/UPI, USBWA)

The Bearcats captured their sixth MVC championship in as many seasons as a member of the league.

1964: John Wooden, UCLA (30-0; 15-0 in AAWU/UPI, USBWA)

The Bruins went undefeated to capture their first of 10 NCAA championships.

1965: Dave Strack, Michigan (24-4; 13-1 in Big Ten/UPI)

The Wolverines won their first undisputed Big Ten title since 1948.

Butch van Breda Kolff, Princeton (23-6; 13-1 in Ivy League/USBWA)

The Tigers won their third consecutive conference title before reaching the Final Four.

1966: Adolph Rupp, Kentucky (27-2; 15-1 in SEC/UPI, USBWA)

The Wildcats' only regular-season defeat was at Tennessee before bowing to Texas Western in the NCAA Tournament final.

1967: John Wooden, UCLA (30-0; 14-0 in AAWU/AP, UPI, USBWA)

Only one of the Bruins' last 14 opponents scored more than 16 points.

1968: Guy Lewis, Houston (31-2/AP, UPI, NABC, USBWA)

The Cougars were ranked No. 1 in the country entering the NCAA Tournament.

1969: John Wooden, UCLA (29-1; 13-1 in Pacific-8/AP, UPI, NABC)

The Bruins' lone setback was to Southern Cal, 46-44.

Maury John, Drake (26-5; 13-3 in Missouri Valley/USBWA)

The Bulldogs set a school record for victories just two years after compiling an unsightly 9-16 mark.

1970: John Wooden, UCLA (28-2; 12-2 in Pacific-8/AP, UPI, NABC, USBWA)

The Bruins yielded 87.5 points per game while absorbing both of their losses in a late four-game stretch in league play before recovering.

1971: Al McGuire, Marquette (28-1/AP, UPI, USBWA)

The Warriors entered the NCAA Tournament undefeated before losing by one point to Ohio State.

Jack Kraft, Villanova (23-6/NABC)

The Wildcats reached the Final Four for the first time since 1939.

1972: John Wooden, UCLA (30-0; 14-0 in Pacific-8/AP, UPI, NABC, USBWA)

The Bruins scored at least 105 points in their first seven outings and never look back.

1973: John Wooden, UCLA (30-0; 14-0 in Pacific-8/AP, UPI, USBWA)

The Bruins, going undefeated for the fourth time in 10 years, captured their seventh consecutive NCAA championship.

Gene Bartow, Memphis State (24-6; 12-2 in Missouri Valley/NABC)

The Tigers reached the Final Four for the first time just three years after going 6-20.

1974: Al McGuire, Marquette (26-5/NABC)

The Warriors, with only one senior starter, ranked among the top five in both wire-service polls before finishing runner-up in the NCAA Tournament.

Digger Phelps, Notre Dame (26-3/UPI)

The Fighting Irish, two years after compiling a 6-20 record, won more than 25 games for one of only two times in school history.

Norman Sloan, North Carolina State (30-1; 12-0 in ACC/AP, USBWA)

The Wolfpack won the NCAA Tournament after going undefeated in ACC competition for the second consecutive season.

1975: Bob Knight, Indiana (31-1; 18-0 in Big Ten/AP, UPI, NABC, USBWA)

The Hoosiers were unbeaten until they were eliminated in the NCAA Tournament by Kentucky (92-90).

1976: Bob Knight, Indiana (32-0; 18-0 in Big Ten/AP, USBWA)

The Hoosiers became the last undefeated Division I team.

Johnny Orr, Michigan (25-7; 14-4 in Big Ten/NABC)

The Wolverines reached the NCAA Tournament championship game just three years after compiling a 6-8 league record.

Tom Young, Rutgers (31-2/UPI)

The Scarlet Knights arrived at the Final Four with an undefeated record.

1977: Bob Gaillard, San Francisco (29-2; 14-0 in WCAC/AP, UPI)

The Dons won their first 29 games before bowing to Notre Dame in their regular-season finale and UNLV in the opening round of the playoffs.

Dean Smith, North Carolina (28-5; 9-3 in ACC/NABC)

The Tar Heels reached the Final Four for the fifth time in 11 seasons.

Eddie Sutton, Arkansas (26-2; 16-0 in SWC/USBWA)

The Razorbacks became the first team to go undefeated in SWC competition since SMU in 1956.

1978: Eddie Sutton, Arkansas (32-4; 14-2 in SWC/AP, UPI)

The Razorbacks became the first SWC in 22 years to reach the Final Four.

Ray Meyer, DePaul (27-3/USBWA)

The Blue Demons won more than one NCAA Tournament game for the first time since 1960.

Bill Foster, Duke (27-7; 8-4 in ACC/shared NABC)

The Blue Devils compiled their first winning record in ACC competition since 1971 before making their first NCAA Tournament appearance since 1966.

Abe Lemons, Texas (26-5; 14-2 in SWC/shared NABC)

The NIT champion Longhorns won more than 25 games for the first time in school history.

1979: Bill Hodges, Indiana State (33-1; 16-0 in Missouri Valley/AP, UPI)

The Sycamores reached the championship game in its first NCAA Tournament appearance.

Ray Meyer, DePaul (26-6/NABC)

The Blue Demons reached the Final Four for the first time since 1943.

Dean Smith, North Carolina (23-6; 9-3 in ACC/USBWA)

The Tar Heels won their fourth consecutive ACC regular-season championship.

1980: Ray Meyer, DePaul (26-2/AP, UPI, USBWA)

The Blue Demons' only regular-season defeat was in double overtime at Notre Dame.

Lute Olson, Iowa (23-10; 10-8 in Big Ten/NABC)

The Hawkeyes reached the Final Four for the first time since 1956.

1981: Ralph Miller, Oregon State (26-2; 17-1 in Pacific-10/AP, UPI, shared NABC, USBWA)

The Beavers were undefeated until their regular-season finale.

Jack Hartman, Kansas State (24-9; 9-5 in Big Eight/shared NABC)

The Wildcats won their most games in a season since 1959.

1982: Ralph Miller, Oregon State (25-5; 16-2 in Pacific-10/AP)

The Beavers captured their third consecutive conference crown.

Don Monson, Idaho (27-3; 13-1 in Big Sky/NABC)

The Vandals' victories included decisions by at least 19 points away from home against Washington, Washington State, Iowa State, Oregon State, and Oregon.

Norm Stewart, Missouri (27-4; 12-2 in Big Eight/UPI)

The Tigers captured their third of four consecutive outright Big Eight Conference regular-season championships.

John Thompson, Georgetown (30-7; 10-4 in Big East/USBWA)

The Hoyas reached the Final Four for the first time since 1943.

1983: Lou Carnesecca, St. John's (28-5; 12-4 in Big East/NABC, USBWA)

The Redmen won at least 28 games for the first of three times in four seasons.

Guy Lewis, Houston (31-3; 16-0 in SWC/AP)

The Cougars won 26 consecutive games until they were upset in the NCAA Tournament final.

Jerry Tarkanian, UNLV (28-3; 15-1 in PCAA/UPI)

The Rebels won their first of 10 regular-season conference titles in as many years.

1984: Ray Meyer, DePaul (27-3/AP, UPI)

The Blue Demons, in Meyer's swan song, registered their seventh consecutive season with more than 20 victories.

Marv Harshman, Washington (24-7; 15-3 in Pacific-10/NABC)

The Huskies won their first conference crown since 1953.

Gene Keady, Purdue (22-7; 15-3 in Big Ten/USBWA)

The Boilermakers compiled their 12th consecutive winning league record.

1985: Lou Carnesecca, St. John's (31-4; 15-1 in Big East/UPI, USBWA)

The Redmen captured their lone undisputed conference championship.

Bill Frieder, Michigan (26-4; 16-2 in Big Ten/AP)

The Wolverines won the Big Ten title just two years after compiling a 7-11 league record.

John Thompson, Georgetown (35-3; 14-2 in Big East/NABC)

The Hoyas won at least 30 games for the third time in four seasons.

1986: Eddie Sutton, Kentucky (32-4; 17-1 in SEC/AP, NABC)

Three of the Wildcats' four defeats were by a total of just nine points.

Mike Krzyzewski, Duke (37-3; 12-2 in ACC/UPI)

Kansas State coach Jack Hartman.

The Blue Devils established an ACC record for most victories in a single season.

Dick Versace, Bradley (32-3; 16-0 in Missouri Valley/USBWA)

The Braves won their first NCAA Tournament game in more than 30 years.

1987: John Chaney, Temple (32-4; 17-1 in Atlantic 10/USBWA)

The Owls became the first Atlantic 10 team to win more than 30 games in a single season.

Tom Davis, Iowa (30-5; 14-4 in Big Ten/AP)

The Hawkeyes set a school standard for victories just three years after compiling a losing record.

Bob Knight, Indiana (30-4; 15-3 in Big Ten/Naismith)

The Hoosiers finished among the top three in league standings for the seventh time in eight seasons.

Rick Pitino, Providence (25-9; 10-6 in Big East/NABC)

The Friars reached the Final Four two years after posting an 11-20 record.

John Thompson, Georgetown (29-5; 12-4 in Big East/UPI)

The Hoyas ranked among the top 10 in the final AP poll for one of six times in a nine-year span.

1988: John Chaney, Temple (32-2; 18-0 in Atlantic 10/AP, UPI, NABC, USBWA)

The Owls, leading the nation in field-goal percentage defense, won 32 games for the second consecutive campaign.

Larry Brown, Kansas (27-11; 9-5 in Big Eight/Naismith)

The Jayhawks finished at least four games above .500 in Big Eight play for the fifth time in as many seasons under Brown before becoming the first Big Eight team to win a Final Four game in more than 30 years.

1989: Bob Knight, Indiana (27-8; 15-3 in Big Ten/AP, UPI, USBWA)

The Hoosiers won 21 of 22 games in one stretch.

P. J. Carlesimo, Seton Hall (31-7; 11-5 in Big East/NABC)

The Pirates posted their first winning record in conference competition en route to reaching the NCAA Tournament championship game.

Mike Krzyzewski, Duke (28-8; 9-5 in ACC/Naismith)

The Blue Devils won at least 28 games for the second time in five consecutive seasons.

1990: Jim Calhoun, Connecticut (31-6; 12-4 in Big East/AP, UPI)

The Huskies, after finishing at least four games below .500 in league play the previous seven seasons, tied Syracuse for first place.

Bobby Cremins, Georgia Tech (28-7; 8-6 in ACC/Naismith)

The Yellow Jackets reached the Final Four for the only time in school history.

Jud Heathcote, Michigan State (28-6; 15-3 in Big Ten/NABC)

The Spartans won the Big Ten title just one year after finishing next to last place.

Roy Williams, Kansas (30-5; 11-3 in Big Eight/USBWA)

The Jayhawks reached the Final Four just one year after posting a losing record in league play.

1991: Randy Ayers, Ohio State (27-4; 15-3 in Big Ten/AP, Naismith, USBWA)

The Buckeyes captured their first league title since 1971.

Mike Krzyzewski, Duke (32-7; 11-3 in ACC/NABC)

The Blue Devils ended their streak of eight trips to the Final Four without a national championship.

Rick Majerus, Utah (30-4; 15-1 in WAC/UPI)

The Utes, 32-31 over the previous two years, became the only WAC team ever to win 30 games in a single season.

1992: Perry Clark, Tulane (21-8; 8-4 in Metro/UPI, USBWA)

The Green Wave won a conference title two years after compiling a 4-24 record.

Mike Krzyzewski, Duke (34-2; 14-2 in ACC/Naismith)

The Blue Devils reached the Final Four for the fifth consecutive season.

George Raveling, Southern Cal (24-6; 15-3 in Pacific-10/NABC)

The Trojans won more than 20 games for the first time since 1974.

Roy Williams, Kansas (27-5; 11-3 in Big Eight/AP)

The Jayhawks captured their first outright Big Eight crown since 1986.

1993: Eddie Fogler, Vanderbilt (28-6; 14-2 in SEC/AP, UPI, NABC, USBWA)

The Commodores shattered their school record for most victories in a single season.

Dean Smith, North Carolina (34-4; 14-2 in ACC/Naismith)

The Tar Heels won the NCAA title after reaching the Sweet 16 of the NCAA Tournament for the 13th consecutive season.

1994: Norm Stewart, Missouri (28-4; 14-0 in Big Eight/AP, UPI)

The Tigers became the first undefeated team in Big Eight competition since Kansas in 1971.

Nolan Richardson, Arkansas (31-3; 14-2 in SEC/Naismith, shared NABC)

The NCAA champion Razorbacks reached the 30-win plateau for the third time in five seasons.

Charlie Spoonhour, St. Louis (23-6; 8-4 in Great Midwest/USBWA)

The Billikens participated in the NCAA Tournament for the first time since 1957.

Gene Keady, Purdue (29-5; 14-4 in Big Ten/shared NABC)

The Boilermakers won the Big Ten title after three consecutive non-winning records in conference competition.

NCAA CONSENSUS FIRST-TEAM ALL-AMERICANS

1937–38: Meyer "Mike" Bloom, C, Sr., Temple; Hank Luisetti, F, Sr., Stanford; John Moir, F, Sr., Notre Dame; Paul Nowak, C, Sr., Notre Dame; Fred Pralle, G, Sr., Kansas; Jewell Young, F, Sr., Purdue.

1938–39: Ernie Andres, G, Sr., Indiana; Jimmy Hull, F, Sr., Ohio State; Chet Jaworski, G, Sr., Rhode Island; Irving Torgoff, F, Sr., Long Island; Urgel "Slim" Wintermute, C, Sr., Oregon.

1939–40: Gus Broberg, G-F, Jr., Dartmouth; John Dick, F, Sr., Oregon; George Glamack, C, Jr., North Carolina; Bill Hapac, F, Sr., Illinois; Ralph Vaughn, F, Sr., Southern California.

1940–41: John Adams, F, Sr., Arkansas; Gus Broberg, G-F, Sr., Dartmouth; Howard Engleman, F, Sr., Kansas; Gene Englund, C, Sr., Wisconsin; George Glamack, C, Sr., North Carolina.

1941–42: Price Brookfield, C, Sr., West Texas State; Bob Davies, G, Sr., Seton Hall; Bob Kinney, C, Sr., Rice; John Kotz, F, Jr., Wisconsin; Andy Phillip, F, Soph., Illinois.

1942–43: Ed Beisser, C, Sr., Creighton; Charles Black, F, Soph., Kansas; Harry Boykoff, C, Soph., St. John's; Bill Closs, C, Sr., Rice; Andy Phillip, F, Jr., Illinois; George Senesky, F, Sr., St. Joseph's.

1943–44: Bob Brannum, C, Fr., Kentucky; Audley Brindley, C, Jr., Dartmouth; Otto Graham, F, Sr., Northwestern/Colgate; Leo Klier, F, Jr., Notre Dame; Bob Kurland, C, Soph., Oklahoma A&M; George Mikan, C, Soph., DePaul; Allie Paine, G, Jr., Oklahoma.

1944–45: Howie Dallmar, G, Sr., Penn; Arnie Ferrin, F, Soph., Utah; Wyndol Gray, F, Soph., Bowling Green; Billy Hassett, G, Jr., Notre Dame; Bill Henry, C, Sr., Rice; Walt Kirk, G, Jr., Illinois; Bob Kurland, C, Jr., Oklahoma A&M; George Mikan, C, Jr., DePaul.

1945–46: Leo Klier, F, Sr., Notre Dame; Bob Kurland, C, Sr., Oklahoma A&M; George Mikan, C, Sr., DePaul; Max Morris, F-C, Sr., Northwestern; Sid Tannenbaum, G, Jr., NYU.

1946–47: Ralph Beard, G, Soph., Kentucky; Alex Groza, C, Soph., Kentucky; Ralph Hamilton, F, Sr., Indiana; Sid Tannenbaum, G, Sr., NYU; Gerry Tucker, C, Sr., Oklahoma.

1947–48: Ralph Beard, G, Jr., Kentucky; Ed Macauley, C-F, Jr., St. Louis; Jim McIntyre, C, Jr., Minnesota; Kevin O'Shea, G, Soph., Notre Dame; Murray Wier, G, Sr., Iowa.

1948–49: Ralph Beard, G, Sr., Kentucky; Vince Boryla, F, Sr., Denver; Alex Groza, C, Sr., Kentucky; Tony Lavelli, G, Sr., Yale; Ed Macauley, C-F, Sr., St. Louis.

1949–50: Paul Arizin, F, Sr., Villanova; Bob Cousy, G, Sr., Holy Cross; Dick Schnittker, F, Sr., Ohio State; Bill Sharman, G, Sr., Southern California; Paul Unruh, F, Sr., Bradley.

1950–51: Clyde Lovellette, C, Jr., Kansas; Gene Melchiorre, G, Sr., Bradley; Bill Mlkvy, F, Jr., Temple; Sam Ranzino, F, Sr., North Carolina State; Bill Spivey, C, Jr., Kentucky.

1951–52: Chuck Darling, C, Sr., Iowa; Rod Fletcher, G, Sr., Illinois; Dick Groat, G, Sr., Duke; Cliff Hagan, F, Jr., Kentucky; Clyde Lovellette, C, Sr., Kansas.

1952–53: Ernie Beck, F, Sr., Penn; Walter Dukes, C, Jr., Seton Hall; Tom Gola, C-F, Soph., La Salle; Bob Houbregs, C, Sr., Washington; Johnny O'Brien, G, Sr., Seattle.

1953–54: Tom Gola, C-F, Jr., La Salle; Cliff Hagan, F, Sr., Kentucky; Bob Pettit, C, Sr., Louisiana State; Don Schlundt, C, Jr., Indiana; Frank Selvy, F, Sr., Furman.

1954–55: Dick Garmaker, F, Sr., Minnesota; Tom Gola, C-F, Sr., La Salle; Si Green, G, Jr., Duquesne; Dick Ricketts, F-C, Sr., Duquesne; Bill Russell, C, Jr., San Francisco.

1955–56: Robin Freeman, G, Sr., Ohio State; Si Green, G, Sr., Duquesne; Tom Heinsohn, F, Sr., Holy Cross; Bill Russell, C, Sr., San Francisco; Ron Shavlik, C, Sr., North Carolina State.

1956–57: Wilt Chamberlain, C, Soph., Kansas; Chet Forte, G, Sr., Columbia; Rod Hundley, G-F, Sr., West Virginia; Jim Krebs, C, Sr., Southern Methodist; Lennie Rosenbluth, F, Sr., North Carolina; Charlie Tyra, C, Sr., Louisville.

1957–58: Elgin Baylor, F-C, Jr., Seattle; Bob Boozer, F, Jr., Kansas State; Wilt Chamberlain, C, Jr., Kansas; Don Hennon, G, Jr., Pittsburgh; Oscar Robertson, F, Soph., Cincinnati; Guy Rodgers, G, Sr., Temple.

1958–59: Bob Boozer, F, Sr., Kansas State; Johnny Cox, F, Sr., Kentucky; Bailey Howell, F, Sr., Mississippi State; Oscar Robertson, F, Jr., Cincinnati; Jerry West, F, Jr., West Virginia.

1959–60: Darrall Imhoff, C, Sr., California; Jerry Lucas, C, Soph., Ohio State; Oscar Robertson, F, Sr., Cincinnati; Tom Stith, F, Jr., St. Bonaventure; Jerry West, F, Sr., West Virginia.

1960–61: Terry Dischinger, F, Jr., Purdue; Roger Kaiser, G, Sr., Georgia Tech; Jerry Lucas, C, Jr., Ohio State; Tom Stith, F, Sr., St. Bonaventure; Chet Walker, F, Jr., Bradley.

1961–62: Len Chappell, C, Sr., Wake Forest; Terry Dischinger, F, Sr., Purdue; Jerry Lucas, C, Sr., Ohio State; Billy McGill, C, Sr., Utah; Chet Walker, F, Sr., Bradley.

1962–63: Ron Bonham, F, Jr., Cincinnati; Jerry Harkness, F, Sr., Loyola (Ill.); Art Heyman, F, Sr., Duke; Barry Kramer, F, Jr., NYU; Tom Thacker, F-G, Sr., Cincinnati.

1963–64: Gary Bradds, C, Sr., Ohio State; Bill Bradley, F, Jr., Princeton; Walt Hazzard, G, Sr., UCLA; Cotton Nash, F, Sr., Kentucky; Dave Stallworth, F, Jr., Wichita State.

1964–65: Rick Barry, F, Sr., Miami (Fla.); Bill Bradley, F, Sr., Princeton; Gail Goodrich, G, Sr., UCLA; Fred Hetzel, F-C, Sr., Davidson; Cazzie Russell, G, Jr., Michigan.

1965–66: Dave Bing, G, Sr., Syracuse; Clyde Lee, C, Sr., Vanderbilt; Cazzie Russell, G, Sr., Michigan; Dave Schellhase, F, Sr., Purdue; Jimmy Walker, G, Jr., Providence.

1966–67: Lew Alcindor, C, Soph., UCLA; Clem Haskins, G-F, Sr., Western Kentucky; Elvin Hayes, F-C, Jr., Houston; Bob Lloyd, G, Sr., Rutgers; Wes Unseld, C, Jr., Louisville; Bob Verga, G, Sr., Duke; Jimmy Walker, G, Sr., Providence.

1967–68: Lew Alcindor, C, Jr., UCLA; Elvin Hayes, F-C, Sr., Houston; Pete Maravich, G, Soph., Louisiana State; Larry Miller, F, Sr., North Carolina; Wes Unseld, C, Sr., Louisville.

1968–69: Lew Alcindor, C, Sr., UCLA; Spencer Haywood, F-C, Jr., Detroit; Pete Maravich, G, Jr., Louisiana State; Rick Mount, G, Jr., Purdue; Calvin Murphy, G, Jr., Niagara.

1969–70: Dan Issel, F-C, Sr., Kentucky; Bob Lanier, C, Sr., St. Bonaventure; Pete Maravich, G, Sr., Louisiana State; Rick Mount, G, Sr., Purdue; Calvin Murphy, G, Sr., Niagara.

1970–71: Austin Carr, G, Sr., Notre Dame; Artis Gilmore, C, Sr., Jacksonville; Jim McDaniels, C, Sr., Western Kentucky; Dean Meminger, G, Sr., Marquette; Sidney Wicks, F, Sr., UCLA.

1971–72: Henry Bibby, G, Sr., UCLA; Jim Chones, C, Jr., Marquette; Bo Lamar, G, Jr., Southwestern Louisiana; Bob McAdoo, C, Jr., North Carolina; Ed Ratleff, F-G, Jr., Long Beach State; Tom Riker, C, Sr., South Carolina; Bill Walton, C, Soph., UCLA.

1972–73: Doug Collins, G, Sr., Illinois State; Ernie DiGregorio, G, Sr., Providence; Bo Lamar, G, Sr., Southwestern Louisiana; Ed Ratleff, F-G, Sr., Long Beach State; David Thompson, F, Soph., North Carolina State; Bill Walton, C, Jr., UCLA; Keith Wilkes, F, Jr., UCLA.

1973–74: Marvin Barnes, C, Sr., Providence; John Shumate, C-F, Soph., Notre Dame; David Thompson, F, Jr., North Carolina State; Bill Walton, C, Sr., UCLA; Keith Wilkes, F, Sr., UCLA.

1974–75: Adrian Dantley, F, Soph., Notre Dame; John Lucas, G, Jr., Maryland; Scott May, F, Jr., Indiana; Dave Meyers, F, Sr., UCLA; David Thompson, F, Sr., North Carolina State.

1975–76: Kent Benson, C, Jr., Indiana; Adrian Dantley, F, Jr., Notre Dame; John Lucas, G, Sr., Maryland; Scott May, F, Sr., Indiana; Richard Washington, C-F, Jr., UCLA.

1976–77: Kent Benson, C, Sr., Indiana; Otis Birdsong, G, Sr., Houston; Phil Ford, G, Jr., North Carolina; Rickey Green, G, Sr., Michigan; Marques Johnson, F, Sr., UCLA; Bernard King, F, Jr., Tennessee.

1977–78: Larry Bird, F, Jr., Indiana State; Phil Ford, G, Sr., North Carolina; David Greenwood, F, Jr., UCLA; Butch Lee, G, Sr., Marquette; Mychal Thompson, C, Sr., Minnesota.

1978–79: Larry Bird, F-C, Sr., Indiana State; Mike Gminski, C, Jr., Duke; David Greenwood, F, Sr., UCLA; Earvin "Magic" Johnson, G, Soph., Michigan State; Sidney Moncrief, G-F, Sr., Arkansas.

1979–80: Mark Aguirre, F, Soph., DePaul; Michael Brooks, F, Sr., La Salle; Joe Barry Carroll, C, Sr., Purdue; Darrell Griffith, G, Sr., Louisville; Kyle Macy, G, Sr., Kentucky.

1980–81: Mark Aguirre, F, Jr., DePaul; Danny Ainge, G, Sr., Brigham Young; Steve Johnson, C, Sr., Oregon State; Ralph Sampson, C, Soph., Virginia; Isiah Thomas, G, Soph., Indiana.

1981–82: Terry Cummings, F-C, Jr., DePaul; Quintin Dailey, G, Jr., San Francisco; Eric "Sleepy" Floyd, G, Sr., Georgetown; Ralph Sampson, C, Jr., Virginia; James Worthy, F, Jr., North Carolina.

1982–83: Dale Ellis, F, Sr., Tennessee; Patrick Ewing, C, Soph., Georgetown; Michael Jordan, G, Soph., North Carolina; Keith Lee, C, Soph., Memphis State; Sam Perkins, C, Jr., North Carolina; Ralph Sampson, C, Sr., Virginia; Wayman Tisdale, C-F, Fr., Oklahoma.

1983–84: Patrick Ewing, C, Jr., Georgetown; Michael Jordan, G, Jr., North Carolina; Hakeem Olajuwon, C, Jr., Houston; Sam Perkins, C, Sr., North Carolina; Wayman Tisdale, C-F, Soph., Oklahoma.

1984–85: Johnny Dawkins, G, Jr., Duke; Patrick Ewing, C, Sr., Georgetown; Keith Lee, C, Sr., Memphis State; Xavier McDaniel, F, Sr., Wichita State; Chris Mullin, G-F, Sr., St. John's; Wayman Tisdale, C-F, Jr., Oklahoma.

1989–90 All-American Syracuse forward Derrick Coleman brings down a rebound.

1985–86: Steve Alford, G, Jr., Indiana; Walter Berry, F, Jr., St. John's; Len Bias, F, Sr., Maryland; Johnny Dawkins, G, Sr., Duke; Kenny Walker, F, Sr., Kentucky.

1986–87: Steve Alford, G, Sr., Indiana; Danny Manning, F-C, Jr., Kansas; David Robinson, C, Sr., Navy, Kenny Smith, G, Sr., North Carolina; Reggie Williams, F-G, Sr., Georgetown.

1987–88: Sean Elliott, F, Jr., Arizona; Gary Grant, G, Sr., Michigan; Hersey Hawkins, G, Sr., Bradley; Danny Manning, F-C, Sr., Kansas; J. R. Reid, C, Soph., North Carolina.

1988–89: Sean Elliott, F, Sr., Arizona; Pervis Ellison, C, Sr., Louisville; Danny Ferry, F-C, Sr., Duke, Chris Jackson, G, Fr., Louisiana State, Stacey King, C, Sr., Oklahoma.

1989–90: Derrick Coleman, F, Sr., Syracuse; Chris Jackson, G, Soph., Louisiana State; Larry Johnson, F, Jr., UNLV; Gary Payton, G, Sr., Oregon State; Lionel Simmons, F, Sr., La Salle.

1990–91: Kenny Anderson, G, Soph., Georgia Tech; Jim Jackson, G-F, Soph., Ohio State; Larry Johnson, F, Sr., UNLV; Shaquille O'Neal, C, Soph., Louisiana State; Billy Owens, F, Jr., Syracuse.

1991–92: Jim Jackson, G-F, Jr., Ohio State; Christian Laettner, F-C, Sr., Duke; Harold Miner, G, Jr., Southern California; Alonzo Mourning, C, Sr., Georgetown; Shaquille O'Neal, C, Jr., Louisiana State.

1992–93: Calbert Cheaney, F, Sr., Indiana; Anfernee Hardaway, G, Jr., Memphis State; Bobby Hurley, G, Sr., Duke; Jamal Mashburn, F, Jr., Kentucky; Chris Webber, F, Soph., Michigan.

1993–94: Grant Hill, F-G, Sr., Duke; Jason Kidd, G, Soph., California; Donyell Marshall, F, Jr., Connecticut; Glenn Robinson, F, Jr., Purdue; Clifford Rozier, C-F, Jr., Louisville.

SELECTIONS CITED FOR NCAA CONSENSUS ALL-AMERICAN TEAMS

Christy Walsh Syndicate: 1929 and 1930
College Humor Magazine: 1929–33, 1936
Helms Foundation: 1929–48
Converse Yearbook: 1932–48
Literary Digest Magazine: 1934
Omaha World Newspaper: 1937
Madison Square Garden: 1937–42
Newspaper Enterprises Association: 1938, 1953–63
Colliers (Basketball Coaches): 1939, 1949–56
Pic Magazine: 1942–44
The Sporting News: 1943–46
Argosy Magazine: 1945
True Magazine: 1946 and 1947
Associated Press: 1948–
Look Magazine: 1949–63
United Press International: 1949–
International News Service: 1950–58
National Association of Basketball Coaches: 1957–
United States Basketball Writers Association: 1960–

17

NCAA RECORDS

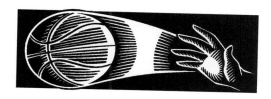

INDIVIDUAL—REGULAR SEASON

SCORING

Most points, game, vs. Division I opponent: 72, Kevin Bradshaw, U.S. International, vs. Loyola Marymount, Jan. 5, 1991.

Most points, game, vs. small-college opponent: 100, Frank Selvy, Furman, vs. Newberry, Feb. 13, 1954 (41 FGs, 18 FTs).

Most points, season: 1,381, Pete Maravich, Louisiana State, 1970 (522 FGs, 337 FTs, 31 games).

Most points, career: 3,667, Pete Maravich, Louisiana State, 1968–70.

Highest scoring average per game, season: 44.5, Pete Maravich, Louisiana State, 1970 (1,381 points in 31 games).

Highest scoring average, career: 44.2, Pete Maravich, Louisiana State, 1968–70 (3,667 points in 83 games).

Most combined points, game, two teammates, vs. Division I opponent: 92, Kevin Brad-shaw (72) and Isaac Brown (20), U.S. International, vs. Loyola Marymount, Jan. 5, 1990.

Most combined points, game, two teammates, vs. non-Division I team: 125, Frank Selvy (100) and Darrell Floyd (25), Furman, vs. Newberry, Feb. 13, 1954.

Most combined points, game, two opposing players on Division I teams: 115, Pete Maravich (64), Louisiana State, and Dan Issel (51), Kentucky, Feb. 21, 1970.

Most games scoring at least 50 points, season: 10, Pete Maravich, Louisiana State, 1970.

Most games scoring at least 50 points, career: 28, Pete Maravich, Louisiana State 1968–70.

Most consecutive games scoring at least 50 points: 3, Pete Maravich, Louisiana State, Feb. 10–15, 1970.

Most games scoring in double figures, career: 132, Danny Manning, Kansas, 1985–88.

Most consecutive games scoring in double figures, career: 115, Lionel Simmons, La Salle, 1987–90.

FIELD GOALS

Most field goals, game: 41, Frank Selvy, Furman, vs. Newberry, Feb. 13, 1954.

Most field goals, season: 522, Pete Maravich, Louisiana State, 1970 (1,168 attempts, 44.7%).

Most field goals, career: 1,387, Pete Maravich, Louisiana State, 1968–70 (3,166 attempts).

Most consecutive field goals, game: 16, Doug Grayson, Kent, vs. North Carolina, Dec. 6, 1967 (18 of 19).

Most consecutive field goals, season: 25, Ray Voelkel, American, 1978 (during nine games, Nov. 24–Dec. 16).

Most field-goal attempts, game: 71, Jay Handlan, Washington & Lee, vs. Furman, Feb. 17, 1951 (made 30).

Most field-goal attempts, season: 1,168, Pete Maravich, Louisiana State, 1970 (522 made).

Most field-goal attempts, career: 3,166, Pete Maravich, Louisiana State, 1968–70 (made 1,387).

Most field goals without a miss, game: 15, Clifford Rozier, Louisville vs. Eastern Kentucky, Dec. 11, 1993..

Highest field-goal percentage, season: 74.6%, Steve Johnson, Oregon State, 1981 (235 of 315).

Highest field-goal percentage, career (min. 400 scored): 68.5%, Stephen Scheffler, Purdue, 1987–90 (408 of 596).

Highest field-goal percentage, career (min. 600 scored): 67.8%, Steve Johnson, Oregon State, 1977–81 (828 of 1,222).

THREE-POINT FIELD GOALS

Most three-point field goals, game: 14, Dave Jamerson, Ohio, vs. Charleston, Dec. 21, 1989 (17 attempts).

Most three-point field goals, season: 158, Darrin Fitzgerald, Butler, 1987 (362 attempts).

Highest three-point field-goal average, season: 5.64, Darrin Fitzgerald, Butler, 1987 (158 in 28 games).

Most three-point field goals, career: 401, Doug Day, Radford, 1990–93 (1,068 attempts).

Highest three-point field-goal average, career (min. 200 made): 4.57, Timothy Pollard, Mississippi Valley State, 1988–89 (256 in 56 games).

Most consecutive three-point field goals, game: 11, Gary Bossert, Niagara, vs. Siena, Jan. 7, 1987.

Most consecutive three-point field goals, season: 15, Todd Leslie, Northwestern, Dec. 1990 (during four games, Dec. 15–28).

Most consecutive games making a three-point field goal, season: 38, Steve Kerr, Arizona, Nov. 27, 1987 to April 2, 1988.

Most consecutive games making a three-point field goal, career: 73, Wally Lancaster, Virginia Tech, Dec. 30, 1986 to Mar. 4, 1989.

Most three-point field-goal attempts, game: 26, Lindsey Hunter, Jackson State, vs. Kansas, Dec. 27, 1992 (11 made).

Most three-point field-goal attempts, season: 362, Darrin Fitzgerald, Butler, 1987 (158 made).

Most three-point field-goal attempts, career: 940, Jeff Fryer, Loyola Marymount, 1987–90 (363 made).

Highest three-point field-goal attempt average per game, season: 12.9, Darrin Fitzgerald, Butler, 1987 (362 in 28 games).

Highest three-point field-goal attempt average per game, career: 7.8, Wally Lancaster, Virginia Tech, 1987–89 (694 in 89 games).

Most three-point field goals without a miss, game: 8, Tomas Thompson, San Francisco, vs. Loyola Marymount, Mar. 7, 1992.

Highest three-point field-goal percentage, season (min. 50 made): 63.4%, Glenn Tropf, Holy Cross, 1988 (52 of 82).

Highest three-point field-goal percentage, career (min. 200 made): 49.7%, Tony Bennett, Wisconsin-Green Bay, 1989–92 (290 of 584).

FREE THROWS

Most free throws, game: 30, Pete Maravich, Louisiana State, vs. Oregon State, Dec. 22, 1969 (31 attempts, 96.8%).

Most free throws, season: 355, Frank Selvy, Furman, 1954 (444 attempts, 80.0%).

Most free throws, career: 905, Dickie Hemric, Wake Forest, 1952–55 (1,359 attempts).

Most consecutive free throws, game: 24, Arlen Clark, Oklahoma State, vs. Colorado, Mar. 7, 1959 (24 of 24).

Most consecutive free throws, season: 64, Joe Dykstra, Western Illinois, 1981–82 (during eight games, Dec. 1–Jan. 4).

Most free-throw attempts, game: 36, Ed Tooley, Brown, vs. Amherst, Dec. 4, 1954 (23 made).

Most free-throw attempts, season: 444, Frank Selvy, Furman, 1954 (355 made).

Most free-throw attempts, career: 1,359, Dickie Hemric, Wake Forest, 1952–55 (905 made).

Most free throws without a miss, game: 24, Arlen Clark, Oklahoma State, vs. Colorado, Mar. 7, 1959.

Highest free-throw percentage, season: 95.9%, Craig Collins, Penn State, 1985 (94 of 98).

Highest free-throw percentage, career (min. 300 scored): 90.9%, Greg Starrick, Kentucky & Southern Ill. 1969–72 (341 of 375).

Highest free-throw percentage, career (min. 2.5 made per game): 92.3%, Dave Hildahl, Portland State, 1979–81 (131 of 142).

REBOUNDS

Most rebounds, game (before 1973): 51, Bill Chambers, William & Mary, vs. Virginia, Feb. 14, 1953.

Most rebounds, game (after 1973): 34, David Vaughn, Oral Roberts, vs. Brandeis, Jan. 8, 1973.

Most rebounds, season (before 1973): 734, Walter Dukes, Seton Hall (734 in 33 games).

Highest rebounding average, season (before 1973): 25.6, Charlie Slack, Marshall (538 in 21 games).

Most rebounds, season (since 1973): 597, Marvin Barnes, Providence (597 in 32 games).

Highest rebounding average, season (since 1973): 20, Kermit Washington, American (511 in 25 games).

Most rebounds, career (3 years): 1,751, Paul Silas, Creighton, 1962–64 (81 games).

Most rebounds, career (4 years): 2,201, Tom Gola, La Salle, 1952–55 (118 games).

Most rebounds, career (since 1973): 1,537, Derrick Coleman, Syracuse, 1987–90 (143 games).

Highest rebounding average, career (min. 800): 22.7, Artis Gilmore, Jacksonville, 1970–71 (1,224 in 54 games).

Highest rebounding average, career (since 1973): 15.2, Glenn Mosley, Seton Hall, 1974–77 (1,263 in 83 games).

ASSISTS

Most assists, game: 22, Tony Fairley, Charleston Southern, vs. Armstrong State, Feb. 9, 1987; Avery Johnson, Southern (La.), vs. Texas Southern, Jan. 25, 1988; and Sherman Douglas, Syracuse, vs. Providence, Jan. 28, 1989.

Most assists, season: 406, Mark Wade, UNLV, 1987 (38 games).

Highest assist average, season: 13.3, Avery Johnson, Southern (La.), 1988 (399 in 30 games).

Most assists, career: 1,076, Bobby Hurley, Duke, 1990–93 (140 games).

Highest average (min. 600 assists), career: 8.91, Avery Johnson, Cameron & Southern (La.), 1985 & 1987–88 (838 in 94 games).

BLOCKED SHOTS

Most blocked shots, game: 14, David Robinson, Navy, vs. N.C.-Wilmington, Jan. 4, 1986; and Shawn Bradley, Brigham Young, vs. Eastern Kentucky, Dec. 7, 1990.

Most blocked shots, season: 207, David Robinson, Navy, 1986 (35 games).

Highest blocked shot average, season: 5.91, David Robinson, Navy, 1986 (207 in 35 games).

Most blocked shots, career: 453, Alonzo Mourning, Georgetown, 1989–92 (120 games).

Highest blocked shot average (min. 200), career: 5.24, David Robinson, Navy, 1986–87 (351 in 67 games).

STEALS

Most steals, game: 13, Mookie Blaylock, Oklahoma, vs. Centenary, Dec. 12, 1987, and vs. Loyola Marymount, Dec. 17, 1988.

Most steals, season: 150, Mookie Blaylock, Oklahoma, 1988 (39 games).

Highest steal average, season: 4.96, Darron Brittman, Chicago State, 1986 (139 in 38 games).

Most steals, career: 376, Eric Murdock, Providence, 1988–91 (117 games).

Highest steal average (min. 200), career: 3.8, Mookie Blaylock, Oklahoma, 1988–89 (281 in 74 games).

TEAM—REGULAR SEASON

SCORING

Most points, one team, one game: 186, Loyola Marymount, vs. U.S. International (140), Jan. 5, 1991.

Most points, two teams, one game: 331, Loyola Marymount (181) vs. U.S. International (150), Jan. 31, 1989.

Most points, one team, one half: 97, Oklahoma, vs. U.S. International, Nov. 29, 1989 (1st half).

Most points, two teams, one half: 172, Loyola Marymount (86) vs. Gonzaga (86), Feb. 18, 1989 (2nd half).

Most points, one team, one season: 4,012, Oklahoma, 1988 (39 games).

Highest scoring average per game, one season: 122.4, Loyola Marymount, 1990 (3,918 points in 32 games).

Highest average scoring margin, one season: 30.3, UCLA, 94.6-64.3, 1972.

Most games with at least 100 points, one season: 28, Loyola Marymount, 1990.

Largest lead before the opponent scores at the start of a game: 32-0, Connecticut, vs. New Hampshire, Dec. 12, 1990.

Largest halftime deficit overcome to win game: 29, Duke (74), vs. Tulane (72), Dec. 30, 1950 (trailed 56-27 at intermission).

Largest deficit before scoring that was overcome to win game: 28, New Mexico State (117), vs. Bradley (109), Jan. 27, 1977 (trailed 28-0 with 13:49 left in the first half).

Fewest points allowed, one team, one game (since 1938): 6, Tennessee (11), vs. Temple, Dec. 15, 1973; Kentucky (75), vs. Arkansas State, Jan. 8, 1945.

Fewest points, two teams, one game (since 1938): 17, Tennessee (11) vs. Temple (6), Dec. 15, 1973.

Widest margin of victory: 97, Southern, La. (154), vs. Patten (57), Dec. 26, 1993.

FIELD GOALS

Most field goals, one team, one game: 74, Houston, vs. Valparaiso, Feb. 24, 1968 (attempted 112, 66.1%).

Most field goals, two teams, one game: 130, Loyola Marymount (67) vs. U.S. International (63), Jan. 31, 1989.

Most field goals, one team, one half: 42, Oklahoma, vs. U.S. International, Nov. 29, 1989 (1st half).

Most field-goal attempts, one team, one game: 147, Oklahoma, vs. U.S. International, Nov. 29, 1989 (made 70).

Most field-goal attempts, two teams, one game: 245, Loyola Marymount (124) vs. U.S. International (121), Jan. 7, 1989.

Fewest field goals, one team, one game (since 1938): 2, Duke, vs. North Carolina State, Mar. 8, 1968 (attempted 11); and Arkansas State, vs. Kentucky, Jan. 8, 1945.

Fewest field-goal attempts, one team, one game (since 1938): 9, Pittsburgh, vs. Penn State, Mar. 1, 1952 (made 3).

Highest field-goal percentage, one team, one game (min. 15 made): 83.3%, Maryland, vs. South Carolina, Jan. 9, 1971 (15 of 18).

Highest field-goal percentage, one team, one game (min. 30 made): 81.4%, New Mexico, vs. Oregon State, Nov. 30, 1985 (35 of 43).

Highest field-goal percentage, one team, one half: 94.1%, North Carolina, vs. Virginia, Jan. 7, 1978 (16 of 17, 2nd half).

Most field goals made and attempted, one team, one season: 1,533, Oklahoma, 1988 (attempted 3,094, 49.5%).

Highest field goals-per-game-percentage, one team, one season: 46.3, UNLV, 1976.

Highest field-goal attempts-per-game percentage, one team, one season: 98.5, Oral Roberts, 1973 (2,659 in 27 games).

Highest field-goal percentage, one team, one season: 57.2%, Missouri, 1980 (936 of 1,635).

THREE-POINT FIELD GOALS

Most three-point field goals, one team, one game: 21, Kentucky, vs. North Carolina, Dec. 27, 1989 (48 attempts); Loyola Marymount, vs. Michigan, Mar. 18, 1990 (40); and UNLV, vs. Nevada, Dec. 8, 1991 (46).

Most three-point field goals, two teams, one game: 33, Temple (19) vs. George Washington (14), Mar. 4, 1992.

Most consecutive three-point field goals made without a miss, one team, one game: 11, Niagara, vs. Siena, Jan. 7, 1987; Eastern Kentucky, vs. N.C.-Asheville, Jan. 14, 1987.

Highest number of different players to score a three-point field goal, one team, one game: 9, Dartmouth, vs. Boston College, Nov. 30, 1993.

Most three-point field-goal attempts, one team, one game: 53, Kentucky, vs. Southwestern Louisiana, Dec. 23, 1989 (15 made).

Most three-point field-goal attempts, two teams, one game: 84, Kentucky (53) vs. Southwestern Louisiana (31), Dec. 23, 1989.

Highest three-point field-goal percentage (min. 10 scored), one team, one game: 90.9%, Duke, vs. Clemson, Feb. 1, 1988 (10 of 11).

Most three-point field goals made and attempted, one team, one season: 317 of 888, Kentucky, 1992.

Highest three-point field goal percentage, one team, one season: 10.04, Kentucky, 1990 (281 3FGM in 28 games).

Highest three-point field-goal attempt percentage, one team, one season: 28.9, Kentucky, 1990 (810 in 28 games).

Highest three-point field-goal percentage (min. 100 scored), one team, one season: 50.8%, Indiana, 1987 (130 of 256).

FREE THROWS

Most free throws, one team, one game: 53, Morehead State, vs. Cincinnati, Feb. 11, 1956 (65 attempts); Miami (Ohio) vs. Central Michigan, Jan. 29, 1992 (64).

Most free throws, two teams, one game: 88, Morehead State (53) vs. Cincinnati (35), Feb. 11, 1956 (attempted 111).

Most free-throw attempts, one team, one game: 79, Northern Arizona, vs. Arizona, Jan. 26, 1953 (made 46).

Most free-throw attempts, two teams, one game: 130, Northern Arizona (79) vs. Arizona (51), Jan. 26, 1953 (made 78).

Most Free Throws Without a Miss (Min. 30 scored), one team, one game: UC Irvine, vs. Pacific, Feb. 21, 1981 (34 of 34); Samford, vs. Central Florida, Dec. 20, 1990 (34 of 34); Marshall, vs. Davidson, Dec. 17, 1979 (31 of 31); Indiana State, vs. Wichita State, Feb. 18, 1991 (31 of 31).

Most free throws without a miss, two teams, one game: Purdue (25-25) vs. Wisconsin (22-22), Feb. 7, 1976 (47 of 47).

Most free throws made and Attempted, one team, one season: 865 of 1,263, Bradley, 1954 (68.5%).

Most free throws per game, one team, one season: 28.9, Morehead State, 1956 (838 in 29 games).

Most consecutive free throws, one team, one season: 49, Indiana State, 1991 (during two games, Feb. 13–Feb. 18).

Highest free-throw attempts-per-game percentage, one team, one season: 41.0, Bradley, 1953 (1,107 attempts in 27 games).

Highest free-throw percentage, one team, one season: 82.2%, Harvard, 1984 (535 of 651).

REBOUNDS

Most rebounds, one team, one game: 108, Kentucky, vs. Mississippi, Feb. 8, 1964.

Most rebounds, two teams, one game: 152, Indiana (95) vs. Michigan (57), Mar. 11, 1961.

Highest rebound margin, one game: 84, Arizona (102), vs. Northern Arizona (18), Jan. 6, 1951.

Most rebounds, one team, one season: 2,074, Houston, 1968 (33 games).

Highest rebound average per game, one team, one season: 70.0, Connecticut, 1955 (1,751 in 25 games).

Highest average rebound margin, one season: 25.0, Morehead State, 1957 (64.3 offense, 39.3 defense).

ASSISTS

Most assists, one team, one game: 41, North Carolina, vs. Manhattan, Dec. 27, 1985; Weber State, vs. Northern Arizona, Mar. 2, 1991.

Most assists, two teams, one game: 65, Dayton (34), vs. Central Florida (31), Dec. 3, 1988.

Most assists, one team, one season: 926, UNLV, 1990 (average of 24.66 per game in 40 games).

BLOCKED SHOTS

Most blocked shots, one team, one game: 20, Iona, vs. Northern Illinois, Jan. 7, 1989.

Most blocked shots, two teams, one game: 29, Rider (17) vs. Fairleigh Dickinson (12), Jan. 9, 1989.

Most blocked shots, one team, one season: 309, Georgetown, 1989 (average of 9.09 per game in 34 games).

STEALS

Most steals, one team, one game: 34, Oklahoma, vs. Centenary, Dec. 12, 1987; Northwestern (La.) State, vs. LeTourneau, Jan. 20, 1992.

Most steals, two teams, one game: 44, Oklahoma (34) vs. Centenary (10), Dec. 12, 1987.

Most steals, one team, one season: 486, Oklahoma, 1988 (39 games).

Highest steals-per-game average, one team, one season: 14.83, Texas-San Antonio, 1991 (430 in 29 games).

PERSONAL FOULS

Most personal fouls, one team, one season: 966, Providence, 1987 (34 games).

Highest personal fouls-per-game percentage, one team, one season: 29.3, Indiana, 1952 (644 in 22 games).

Fewest personal fouls, one team, one season: 253, Air Force, 1962 (average of 11 per game in 23 games).

Most personal fouls, one team, one game: 50, Arizona, vs. Northern Arizona, Jan. 26, 1953.

Most personal fouls, two teams, one game: 84, Arizona (50) vs. Northern Arizona (34), Jan. 26, 1953.

Most players disqualified, one team, one game: 8, St. Joseph's, vs. Xavier, Jan. 10, 1976.

Most players disqualified, two teams, one game: 12, UNLV (6) vs. Hawaii (6), Jan. 19, 1979 (OT); Arizona (7) vs. West Texas State (5), Feb. 14, 1952.

DEFENSE

Lowest scoring average per game allowed, one season (since 1938): 25.7, Oklahoma State (27 games in 1939).

Lowest field goal percentage allowed, one season (since 1978): 36.45, UNLV (628 of 1,723 in 1992).

OVERTIMES

Most overtime periods, one game: 7, Cincinnati (75) at Bradley (73), Dec. 21, 1981.

Most points, one team, one overtime period: 25, Texas A&M, vs. North Carolina, Mar. 9, 1980; Wisconsin-Green Bay, vs. Cleveland State, Feb. 27, 1988; Old Dominion, vs. William & Mary, Feb. 1, 1992.

Most points, two teams, one overtime period: 40, Old Dominion (25) vs. William & Mary (15), Feb. 1, 1992.

Most points, one team, more than one overtime period: 39, Cleveland State, vs. Kent, Dec. 23, 1993 (4 OT).

Most points, two teams, more than one overtime period: 75, Cleveland State (39) vs. Kent (36), Dec. 23, 1993 (4 OT).

Largest winning margin in an overtime game: 18, Nebraska (85), vs. Iowa State (67), Dec. 30, 1949.

Most overtime games, one team, one season: 8, Western Kentucky, 1978 (won 5, lost 3); Portland, 1984 (won 4, lost 4).

Most consecutive overtime games, one team, one season: 4, Jacksonville, 1982 (won 3, lost 1); Illinois State, 1985 (won 3, lost 1); Dayton, 1988 (won 1, lost 3).

GENERAL RECORDS

Most games in a season, one team (since 1947–48): 40, Duke, 1986 (37-3); UNLV, 1990 (35-5).

Most victories, one season: 37, Duke, 1986 (37-3); UNLV, 1987 (37-2).

Most consecutive victories: 88, UCLA, Jan. 30, 1971–Jan. 17, 1974 (ended Jan. 19, 1974 at Notre Dame, 71-70; last UCLA defeat before streak also came at Notre Dame, 89-82).

Most consecutive homecourt victories: 129, Kentucky, Jan. 4, 1943–Jan. 8, 1955 (ended by Georgia Tech, 59-58).

Most consecutive regular-season victories: 76, UCLA, 1971–74 (NCAA, NIT, and CCA tourneys not included).

Most defeats in a season: 28, Prairie View, 1992 (0-28).

Most consecutive defeats: 37, The Citadel, Jan. 16, 1954–Dec. 12, 1955.

Most consecutive homecourt defeats: 32, New Hampshire, Feb. 9, 1988–Feb. 2, 1991 (ended vs. Holy Cross, 72-56).

Most consecutive 20-win seasons: 24, North Carolina, 1971–94.

Most consecutive non-losing seasons: 60, Kentucky, 1928–88 (did not play in 1953).

INDIVIDUAL—NCAA TOURNAMENT

SCORING

Most points, game: 61, Austin Carr, Notre Dame vs. Ohio, Southeast/Mideast Regional, 1st round, 1970.

Most points by two teammates, game: 85, Austin Carr (61) and Collis Jones (24), Notre Dame vs. Ohio, Southeast/Mideast Regional, 1st round, 1970.

Most points by two opposing players, game: 96, Austin Carr (52), Notre Dame, and Dan Issel (44), Kentucky, Southeast/Mideast Regional Semifinal Game, 1970.

Most points, series (three-game minimum): 184, Glen Rice, Michigan, 1989 (6 games).

Highest scoring average, series (three-game minimum): 52.7 (158 points), Austin Carr, Notre Dame, 1970 (3 games).

Most points, career (two-year minimum): 407, Christian Laettner, Duke, 1989-90-91-92 (23 games).

Highest scoring average (min. of 6 games), career (two-year minimum): 41.3 (289 points, Austin Carr, Notre Dame, 1969-70-71 (7 games).

FIELD GOALS

Most field goals made, game: 25, Austin Carr, Notre Dame vs. Ohio, Southeast/Mideast Regional, 1st round, 1970.

Most field-goal attempts, game: 44, Austin Carr, Notre Dame vs. Ohio, Southeast/Mideast Regional, 1st round, 1970.

Most field goals without a miss, game: 11-11, Kenny Walker, Kentucky vs. Western Kentucky, Southeast/Mideast Regional, 2d round, 1986.

Most field goals made, series (three-game minimum): 75, Glen Rice, Michigan, 1989 (6 games).

Most field-goal attempts, series (three-game minimum): 138, Jim McDaniels, Western Kentucky, 1971 (5 games).

Highest field-goal percentage (min. of 5 FGM per game), series (three-game minimum): 78.8% (26-33), Christian Laettner, Duke, 1989 (5 games).

Most field goals, career (two-year minimum): 152, Elvin Hayes, Houston, 1966-67-68 (13 games).

Most field-goal attempts, career (two-year minimum): 310, Elvin Hayes, Houston, 1966-67-68 (13 games).

Highest field-goal percentage (min. of 70 FGM), career (two-year minimum): 68.6% (109-159), Bill Walton, UCLA, 1972-73-74 (12 games).

THREE-POINT FIELD GOALS

Most three-point field goals, game: 11, Jeff Fryer, Loyola Marymount vs. Michigan, West/Far West Regional, 2d round, 1990.

Most three-point field-goal attempts, game: 22, Jeff Fryer, Loyola Marymount vs. Arkansas, Midwest Regional, 1st round, 1989.

Most three-point field goals without a miss, game: 7-7, Sam Cassell, Florida State vs. Tulane, Southeast/Mideast Regional, 2d round, 1993.

Most three-point field goals, series (three-game minimum): 27, Glen Rice, Michigan, 1989 (6 games).

Most three-point field-goal attempts, series (three-game minimum): 65, Freddie Banks, UNLV, 1987 (5 games).

Highest three-point field-goal percentage (min. of 1.5 3FGM per game), series (three-game minimum): 100% (6-6), Ranzino Smith, North Carolina, 1987 (4 games).

Most three-point field goals, career (two-year minimum): 42, Bobby Hurley, Duke, 1990-91-92-93 (20).

Wyoming's Fennis Dembo is tied with Princeton's Bill Bradley for most free throws without a miss in an NCAA tournament game.

Most three-point field-goal attempts, career (two-year minimum): 103, Anderson Hunt, UNLV, 1989-90-91 (15 games).

Highest three-point field-goal percentage (min. of 20 FGM), career (two-year minimum): 65.0% (26-40), William Scott, Kansas State, 1987-88 (5 games).

FREE THROWS

Most free throws made, game: 23, Bob Carney, Bradley vs. Colorado, Midwest Regional Regional Semifinal Game, 1954.

Most free-throw attempts, game: 27, David Robinson, Navy vs. Syracuse, East Regional, 2d round, 1986.

Most free throws without a miss, game: 16-16, Bill Bradley, Princeton vs. St. Joseph's, East

Regional, 1st round, 1963; Fennis Dembo, Wyoming vs. UCLA, West/Far West Regional, 2d round, 1987.

Most free throws made, series (three-game minimum): 55, Bob Carney, Bradley, 1954 (5 games).

Most free-throw attempts, series (three-game minimum): 71, Jerry West, West Virginia, 1959 (5 games).

Most free throws without a miss, series (three-game minimum): 23-23, Richard Morgan, Virginia, 1989 (4 games).

Most free throws made, career (two-year minimum): 142, Christian Laettner, Duke, 1989-90-91-92 (23 games).

Most free-throw attempts, career (two-year minimum): 167, Christian Laettner, Duke, 1989-90-91-92 (23 games).

Highest free-throw percentage (min. of 30 FTM), career (two-year minimum): 95.7% (45-47), LaBradford Smith, Louisville, 1988-89-90 (8 games).

Highest free-throw percentage (min. of 50 FTM), career (two-year minimum): 90.6% (87-96), Bill Bradley, Princeton, 1963-64-65 (9 games); 90.6% (58-64), Steve Alford, Indiana, 1984-86-87 (10 games).

REBOUNDS

Most rebounds, game: 34, Fred Cohen, Temple vs. Connecticut, East Regional Semifinal Game, 1956.

Most rebounds, series (three-game minimum): 97, Elvin Hayes, Houston, 1968 (5 games).

Highest rebound average (min. of 3 games), series (three-game minimum): 23.3 (70 rebounds), Nate Thurmond, Bowling Green, 1963, (3 games).

Most rebounds, career (two-year minimum): 222, Elvin Hayes, Houston, 1966-67-68 (13 games).

Highest rebounding average (min. of 6 games), career (two-year minimum): 19.7 (118 rebounds), John Green, Michigan State, 1957-59 (6 games).

ASSISTS

Most assists, game: 18, Mark Wade, UNLV vs. Indiana, National Semifinal Game, 1987.

Most assists, series (three-game minimum): 61, Mark Wade, UNLV, 1987 (5 games).

Most assists, career (two-year minimum): 145, Bobby Hurley, Duke, 1990-91-92-93 (20 games).

BLOCKED SHOTS

Most blocked shots, game: 11, Shaquille O'Neal, Louisiana State vs. Brigham Young, West/Far West Regional, 1st round, 1992.

Most blocked shots, career (two-year minimum): 37, Alonzo Mourning, Georgetown, 1989-90-91-92 (10 games).

STEALS

Most steals, game: 8, Darrell Hawkins, Arkansas vs. Holy Cross, East Regional, 1st round, 1993; Grant Hill, Duke vs. California, Midwest Regional, 2d round, 1993.

Most steals, series (three-game minimum): 23, Mookie Blaylock, Oklahoma, 1988 (6 games).

Most steals, career (two-year minimum): 32, Mookie Blaylock, Oklahoma, 1988-89 (9 games); Christian Laettner, Duke, 1989-90-91-92 (23 games).

GENERAL RECORDS

Most games played, career (two-year minimum): 23, Christian Laettner, Duke, 1989-90-91-92.

TEAM—NCAA TOURNAMENT

SCORING

Most points, one team, one game: 149, Loyola Marymount, vs. Michigan (115), West/Far West Regional, 2d round, 1990.

Most points, one team, one tournament (three-game minimum): 571, UNLV, 1990 (6 games).

Highest scoring average, one team, one tournament (three-game minimum): 105.8, Loyola Marymount, 1990 (423 points in 4 games).

Most points, two teams, one game: 264, Loyola Marymount (149) vs. Michigan (115), West/Far West Regional, 2d round, 1990.

Fewest points, one team, one game: 20, North Carolina, vs. Pittsburgh (26), East Regional Final Game, 1941.

Largest winning margin, one team, one game: 69, Loyola of Chicago (111) vs. Tennessee Tech (42), Southeast/Mideast Regional, 1st round, 1963.

Most points scored by a losing team, one game: 120, Utah, vs. St. Joseph's (127), National Third Place Game, 1961 (4 OT).

Most players scoring in double figures, one team, one game: 7, Indiana, vs. George Mason, West/Far West Regional, 1st round, 1989; UNLV, vs. Arkansas-Little Rock, West/Far West Regional, 1st round, 1990.

Most players scoring in double figures, two teams, one game: 12, Notre Dame (6) vs. Houston (6), West/Far West Regional, 1st round, 1965.

Most players scoring, one team, one game: 14, Iowa, vs. Santa Clara, West/Far West Regional, 1st round, 1987.

Most players scoring, two teams, one game: 24, Brown (12) vs. Syracuse (12), East Regional, 1st round, 1986; Iowa (14) vs. Santa Clara (10), West/Far West Regional, 1st round, 1987.

Fewest players scoring, one team, one game: 3, Utah State, vs. San Francisco, West/Far West Regional Semifinal Game, 1964.

Fewest players scoring, two teams, one game: 9, Connecticut (4) vs. Temple (5), East Regional, 1st round, 1964; Michigan State (4) vs. Washington (5), Midwest Regional, 1st round, 1986.

FIELD GOALS

Most field goals, one team, one game: 52, Iowa, vs. Notre Dame, Southeast/Mideast Regional, Regional Third Place Game, 1970.

Most field-goal attempts, one team, one tournament (three-game minimum): 442, Western Kentucky, 1971 (5 games).

Most field goals made, two teams, one game: 97, Iowa (52) vs. Notre Dame (45), Southeast/Mideast Regional Third Place Game, 1970.

Fewest field goals, one team, one game: 8, Springfield, vs. Indiana, East Regional, 1st round, 1940.

Most field-goal attempts, one team, one game: 112, Marshall, vs. Southwestern Louisiana, Midwest Regional, 1st round, 1972.

Highest field-goal percentage, one team, one game: 80.0% (28-35), Oklahoma State, vs. Tulane, Southeast/Mideast Regional, 2d round, 1992.

Highest field-goal percentage, one team, one tournament (three-game minimum): 60.4% (113-187), North Carolina, 1975 (3 games).

Lowest field-goal percentage, one team, one game: 12.7% (8-63), Springfield, vs. Indiana, East Regional Semifinal Game, 1940.

THREE-POINT FIELD GOALS

Most three-point field goals, one team, one game: 21, Loyola Marymount, vs. Michigan, West/Far West Regional, 2d round, 1990.

Most three-point field goals made, one team, one tournament (three-game minimum): 56, Loyola Marymount, 1990 (4 games).

Most three-point field goals made, two teams, one game: 27, Wisconsin (15) vs. Missouri (12), West/Far West Regional, 2d round, 1994.

Most three-point field-goal attempts, one team, one game: 41, Loyola Marymount, vs. UNLV, West Regional Final Game, 1990.

Most three-point field-goal attempts, one team, one tournament (three-game minimum): 137, Loyola Marymount, 1990 (4 games).

Most three-point field-goal attempts, two teams, one game: 59, North Carolina A&T (31) vs. Arkansas (28), Midwest Regional, 1st round, 1994; Loyola Marymount (41) vs. UNLV (18), West Regional Final Game, 1990.

Highest three-point field-goal percentage (min. of 7 3FGM), one team, one game: 88.9% (8-9), Kansas State, vs. Georgia, West/Far West Regional, 1st round, 1987.

Highest three-point field-goal percentage (min. of 12 3FGM), one team, one tournament (three-game minimum): 60.9% (14-23), Indiana, 1989 (3 games).

Highest three-point field-goal percentage (min. of 30 3FGM), one team, one tournament (three-game minimum): 51.9% (40-77), Kansas, 1993 (5 games).

FREE THROWS

Most free throws made, one team, one game: 41, Utah, vs. Santa Clara, West/Far West Regional, Regional Third Place Game, 1960; Navy, vs. Syracuse, East Regional, 2d round, 1986.

Most free throws made, one team, one tournament (three-game minimum): 146, Bradley, 1954 (5 games).

Most free throws made, two teams, one game: 69, Morehead State (37) vs. Pittsburgh (32), Southeast/Mideast Regional, 1st round, 1957.

Most free-throw attempts, one team, one game: 55, Texas-El Paso, vs. Tulsa, West/Far West Regional, 1st round, 1985.

Most free-throw attempts, one team, one tournament (three-game minimum): 194, Bradley, 1954 (5 games).

Highest free-throw percentage, one team, one tournament (three-game minimum): 87.0% (47-54), St. John's, 1969 (3 games).

Most free-throw attempts, two teams, one game: 105, Morehead State (53) vs. Iowa (52), Southeast/Mideast Regional Semifinal Game, 1956.

Most free throws without a miss, one team, one game: 22-22, Fordham, vs. South Carolina, East Regional Third Place Game, 1971.

REBOUNDS

Most rebounds, one team, one game: 86, Notre Dame, vs. Tennessee Tech, Southeast/Mideast Regional, 1st round, 1958.

Most rebounds, one team, one tournament (three-game minimum): 306, Houston, 1968 (5 games).

Most rebounds, two teams, one game: 134, Marshall (68) vs. Southwestern Louisiana (66), Midwest Regional, 1st round, 1972.

Largest rebound margin, one team, one game: 42, Notre Dame (86) vs. Tennessee Tech (44), Southeast/Mideast Regional, 1st round, 1958.

ASSISTS

Most assists, one team, one game: 36, North Carolina, vs. Loyola Marymount, West/Far West Regional, 2d round, 1988.

Most assists, one team, one tournament (three-game minimum): 140, UNLV, 1990 (6 games).

Most assists, two teams, one game: 58, UNLV (35) vs. Loyola Marymount (23), West Regional Final Game, 1990.

BLOCKED SHOTS

Most blocked shots, one team, one game: 13, Louisville, vs. Illinois, Midwest Regional Semifinal Game, 1989; Brigham Young, vs. Virginia, West Regional, 1st round, 1991.

Most blocked shots, one team, one tournament (three-game minimum): 33, UNLV, 1990 (6 games).

Most blocked shots, two teams, one game: 18, Iowa (10) vs. Duke (8), East Regional, 2d round, 1992.

STEALS

Most steals, one team, one game: 19, Providence, vs. Austin Peay State, Southeast/Mideast Regional, 2d round, 1987; Connecticut, vs. Boston U., East Regional, 1st round, 1990.

Most steals, one team, one tournament (three-game minimum): 72, Oklahoma, 1988 (6 games).

Most steals, two teams, one game: 28, North Carolina A&T (16) vs. Arkansas (12), Midwest Regional, 1st round, 1994.

PERSONAL FOULS

Most personal fouls, one team, one game: 41, Dayton, vs. Illinois, East Regional Semifinal Game, 1952.

Most personal fouls, one team, one tournament (three-game minimum): 150, Pennsylvania, 1979 (6 games).

Most personal fouls, two teams, one game: 60, Seattle (31) vs. UCLA (29), West/Far West Regional Semifinal Game, 1964.

GENERAL RECORDS

Most players disqualified, one team, one game: 6, Kansas, vs. Notre Dame, Midwest Regional, 1st round, 1975.

Most players used, two teams, one game: 29, Arizona State (15) vs. Loyola Marymount (14), West/Far West Regional, 1st round, 1980.

OVERTIMES

Most overtime periods, one game: 4, Canisius (79) vs. North Carolina State (78), East Regional, 1st round, 1956; St. Joseph's (127) vs. Utah (120), National Third Place Game, 1961.

Most points in overtimes, one team: 38, St. Joseph's, vs. Utah, National Third Place Game, 1961 (4 OT).

Most points in overtimes, two teams: 69, St. Joseph's (38) vs. Utah (31), National Third Place Game, 1961 (4 OT).

Most points, one team, one overtime period: 25, Texas A&M, vs. North Carolina, Midwest Regional, 2d round, 1980 (2d OT).

Most points, two teams, one overtime period: 37, Utah (22) vs. Missouri (15), Midwest Regional, 1st round, 1978.

Largest winning margin in an overtime game: 17, Texas A&M (78) vs. North Carolina (61), Midwest Regional, 2d round, 1980 (2 OT).

Most overtime games, one team, one tournament: 3, Syracuse, 1975.

Louisville's Denny Crum coached two of his teams to NCAA championships.

NCAA TOURNAMENT FINAL FOUR RESULTS

YEAR	CHAMPION (COACH)	SCORE	RUNNER-UP PLACE	THIRD PLACE	FOURTH PLAYER	MOST OUTSTANDING	SITE OF FINALS
1939	Oregon (Howard Hobson)	46-33	Ohio State	*Oklahoma	*Villanova	None selected	Evanston, IL
1940	Indiana (Branch McCracken)	60-42	Kansas	*Duquesne	*Southern Cal	Marvin Huffman, Indiana	Kansas City
1941	Wisconsin (Bud Foster)	39-34	Washington State	*Pittsburgh	*Arkansas	John Kotz, Wisconsin	Kansas City
1942	Stanford (Everett Dean)	53-38	Dartmouth	*Colorado	*Kentucky	Howie Dallmar, Stanford	Kansas City
1943	Wyoming (Everett Shelton)	46-34	Georgetown	*Texas	*DePaul	Ken Sailors, Wyoming	New York City
1944	Utah (Vadal Peterson)	42-40 (OT)	Dartmouth	*Iowa State	*Ohio State	Arnie Ferrin, Utah	New York City
1945	Oklahoma State (Henry Iba)	49-45	New York University	*Arkansas	*Ohio State	Bob Kurland, Okla. State	New York City
1946	Oklahoma State (Henry Iba)	43-40	North Carolina	Ohio State	California	Bob Kurland, Okla. State	New York City
1947	Holy Cross (Doggie Julian)	58-47	Oklahoma	Texas	CCNY	George Kaftan, Holy Cross	New York City
1948	Kentucky (Adolph Rupp)	58-42	Baylor	Holy Cross	Kansas State	Alex Groza, Kentucky	New York City
1949	Kentucky (Adolph Rupp)	46-36	Oklahoma State	Illinois	Oregon State	Alex Groza, Kentucky	Seattle
1950	CCNY (Nat Holman)	71-68	Bradley	N.C. State	Baylor	Irwin Dambrot, CCNY	New York City
1951	Kentucky (Adolph Rupp)	68-58	Kansas State	Illinois	Okla. State	None selected	Minneapolis
1952	Kansas (Phog Allen)	80-63	St. John's	Illinois	Santa Clara	Clyde Lovellette, Kansas	Seattle
1953	Indiana (Branch McCracken)	69-68	Kansas	Washington	Louisiana St.	B.H. Born, Kansas	Kansas City
1954	La Salle (Ken Loeffler)	92-76	Bradley	Penn State	Southern Cal	Tom Gola, La Salle	Kansas City
1955	San Francisco (Phil Woolpert)	77-63	La Salle	Colorado	Iowa	Bill Russell, San Francisco	Kansas City
1956	San Francisco (Phil Woolpert)	83-71	Iowa	Temple	SMU	Hal Lear, Temple	Evanston, IL
1957	North Carolina (Frank McGuire)	54-53 (3 OT)	Kansas	San Francisco	Michigan State	Wilt Chamberlain, Kansas	Kansas City
1958	Kentucky (Adolph Rupp)	84-72	Seattle	Temple	Kansas State	Elgin Baylor, Seattle	Louisville, KY
1959	California (Pete Newell)	71-70	West Virginia	Cincinnati	Louisville	Jerry West, West Virginia	Louisville, KY
1960	Ohio State (Fred Taylor)	75-55	California	Cincinnati	New York Univ.	Jerry Lucas, Ohio State	San Francisco
1961	Cincinnati (Ed Jucker)	70-65 (OT)	Ohio State	St. Joseph's	Utah	Jerry Lucas, Ohio State	Kansas City
1962	Cincinnati (Ed Jucker)	71-59	Ohio State	Wake Forest	UCLA	Paul Hogue, Cincinnati	Louisville, KY
1963	Loyola, Ill. (George Ireland)	60-58 (OT)	Cincinnati	Duke	Oregon State	Art Heyman, Duke	Louisville, KY
1964	UCLA (John Wooden)	98-83	Duke	Michigan	Kansas State	Walt Hazzard, UCLA	Kansas City
1965	UCLA (John Wooden)	91-80	Michigan	Princeton	Wichita State	Bill Bradley, Princeton	Portland, OR
1966	Texas Western (Don Haskins)	72-65	Kentucky	Duke	Utah	Jerry Chambers, Utah	College Park, MD
1967	UCLA (John Wooden)	79-64	Dayton	Houston	North Carolina	Lew Alcindor, UCLA	Louisville, KY
1968	UCLA (John Wooden)	78-55	North Carolina	Ohio State	Houston	Lew Alcindor, UCLA	Los Angeles
1969	UCLA (John Wooden)	92-72	Purdue	Drake	North Carolina	Lew Alcindor, UCLA	Louisville, KY
1970	UCLA (John Wooden)	80-69	Jacksonville	New Mexico St.	St. Bonaventure	Sidney Wicks, UCLA	College Park, MD
1971	UCLA (John Wooden)	68-62	Villanova	Western Ky.	Kansas	Howard Porter, Villanova	Houston
1972	UCLA (John Wooden)	81-76	Florida State	North Carolina	Louisville	Bill Walton, UCLA	Los Angeles
1973	UCLA (John Wooden)	87-66	Memphis State	Indiana	Providence	Bill Walton, UCLA	St. Louis
1974	N.C. State (Norman Sloan)	76-64	Marquette	UCLA	Kansas	David Thompson, N.C. St.	Greensboro, NC
1975	UCLA (John Wooden)	92-85	Kentucky	Louisville	Syracuse	Richard Washington, UCLA	San Diego
1976	Indiana (Bob Knight)	86-68	Michigan	UCLA	Rutgers	Kent Benson, Indiana	Philadelphia
1977	Marquette (Al McGuire)	67-59	North Carolina	UNLV	UNC Charlotte	Butch Lee, Marquette	Atlanta
1978	Kentucky (Joe B. Hall)	94-88	Duke	Arkansas	Notre Dame	Jack Givens, Kentucky	St. Louis
1979	Michigan State (Jud Heathcote)	75-64	Indiana State	DePaul	Penn	Magic Johnson, Mich. St.	Salt Lake City
1980	Louisville (Denny Crum)	59-54	UCLA	Purdue	Iowa	Darrell Griffith, Louisville	Indianapolis
1981	Indiana (Bob Knight)	63-50	North Carolina	Virginia	Louisiana St.	Isiah Thomas, Indiana	Philadelphia
1982	North Carolina (Dean Smith)	63-62	Georgetown	*Houston	*Louisville	James Worthy, N. Carolina	New Orleans
1983	N.C. State (Jim Valvano)	54-52	Houston	*Louisville	*Georgia	Hakeem Olajuwon, Houston	Albuquerque, NM
1984	Georgetown (John Thompson)	84-75	Houston	*Kentucky	*Virginia	Patrick Ewing, Georgetown	Seattle
1985	Villanova (Rollie Massimino)	66-64	Georgetown	*St. John's	*Memphis State	Ed Pinckney, Villanova	Lexington, KY
1986	Louisville (Denny Crum)	72-69	Duke	*Kansas	*Louisiana St.	Pervis Ellison, Louisville	Dallas
1987	Indiana (Bob Knight)	74-73	Syracuse	*Providence	*UNLV	Keith Smart, Indiana	New Orleans
1988	Kansas (Larry Brown)	83-79	Oklahoma	*Arizona	*Duke	Danny Manning, Kansas	Kansas City
1989	Michigan (Steve Fisher)	80-79 (OT)	Seton Hall	*Duke	*Illinois	Glen Rice, Michigan	Seattle
1990	UNLV (Jerry Tarkanian)	103-73	Duke	*Arkansas	*Georgia Tech	Anderson Hunt, UNLV	Denver
1991	Duke (Mike Krzyzewski)	72-65	Kansas	*N. Carolina	*UNLV	Christian Laettner, Duke	Indianapolis
1992	Duke (Mike Krzyzewski)	71-51	Michigan	*Cincinnati	*Indiana	Bobby Hurley, Duke	Minneapolis
1993	North Carolina (Dean Smith)	77-71	Michigan	*Kansas	*Kentucky	Donald Williams, N. Caro.	New Orleans
1994	Arkansas (Nolan Richardson)	76-72	Duke	*Arizona	*Florida	Corliss Williamson, Ark.	Charlotte

*Tied for third position because there was no consolation game.

Most Final Four appearances: UCLA (13), Duke (11), North Carolina (11), Kansas (10), Kentucky (10), Ohio State (8), Indiana (7), Louisville (7), Cincinnati (6), Michigan (6).

Most Final Four victories: UCLA (22), North Carolina (13), Kentucky (12), Duke (11), Indiana (11), Kansas (8), Michigan (8), Cincinnati (7), Ohio State (7).

Most NCAA Tournament appearances: Kentucky (35), UCLA (29), North Carolina (28), Louisville (24), Notre Dame (24), Indiana (23), Kansas (23), St. John's (23), Kansas State (21), Syracuse (21), DePaul (20), Villanova (20).

Most NCAA Tournament victories: North Carolina (63), UCLA (63), Kentucky (61), Duke (56), Indiana (50), Kansas (49), Louisville (43), Michigan (40).

HIT LIST   Here is a look at UCLA's 38-game winning streak in the NCAA Tournament during the Bruins' wonder years when they won nine national championships from 1964 through 1973 before losing to North Carolina State (80-77 in double overtime) at the 1974 Final Four.

1. Seattle, 95-90

2. San Francisco, 76-72

3. Kansas State, 90-84

4. Duke, 98-83

5. Brigham Young, 100-76

6. San Francisco, 101-93

7. Wichita State, 108-89

8. Michigan, 91-80

9. Wyoming, 109-60

10. Pacific, 80-64

11. Houston, 73-58

12. Dayton, 79-64

13. New Mexico State, 58-49

14. Santa Clara, 87-66

15. Houston, 101-69

16. North Carolina, 78-55

17. New Mexico State, 53-38

18. Santa Clara, 90-52

19. Drake, 85-82

20. Purdue, 92-72

21. Long Beach State, 88-65

22. Utah State, 101-79

23. New Mexico State, 93-77

24. Jacksonville, 80-69

25. Brigham Young, 91-73

26. Long Beach State, 57-55

27. Kansas, 68-60

28. Villanova, 68-62

29. Weber State, 90-58

30. Long Beach State, 73-57

31. Louisville, 96-77

32. Florida State, 81-76

33. Arizona State, 98-81

34. San Francisco, 54-39

35. Indiana, 70-59

36. Memphis State, 87-66

37. Dayton*, 111-100

38. San Francisco, 83-60

* Triple overtime.

18

STATISTICAL ODDS & ENDS

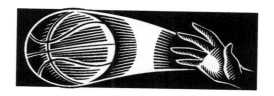

Longest streaks.... 1,000-point scorers.... Coaches who never had a losing record.... Winless teams.... Freshman statistics.... There are an abundance of statistics that just don't fit in anywhere, but are nonetheless valuable to the college basketball fanatic. These are statistics to wow your friends while downing a cold one at the local pub. They can answer a radio trivia question, thereby winning that ever-popular pizza "from our friends at...." They can rekindle memories of your favorite player from alma-mater days gone by. These are the statistical odds and ends of roundball.

PLAYERS WITH MORE THAN 900 POINTS IN EACH OF THREE SEASONS

Oscar Robertson, Cincinnati
1957–58	984 pts.
1958–59	978 pts.
1959–60	1,011 pts.

Pete Maravich, Louisiana State
1967–68	1,138 pts.
1968–69	1,148 pts.
1969–70	1,381 pts.

Larry Bird, Indiana State
1976–77	918 pts.
1977–78	959 pts.
1978–79	973 pts.

PLAYERS WHO AVERAGED MORE THAN 30 POINTS PER GAME IN EACH OF THREE SEASONS

Oscar Robertson, Cincinnati
1957–58	35.1 pts.
1958–59	32.6 pts.
1959–60	33.7 pts.

Pete Maravich, Louisiana State
1967–68	43.8 pts.
1968–69	44.2 pts.
1969–70	44.5 pts.

Freeman Williams, Portland State
1976–77	30.9 pts.
1977–78	38.8 pts.
1978–79	35.9 pts.

PLAYERS WHO AVERAGED 20 OR MORE POINTS PER GAME IN EACH OF FOUR SEASONS

George Dalton, John Carroll
1951–52	20.2 pts.
1952–53	24.8 pts.
1953–54	24.3 pts.
1954–55	23.9 pts.

Dickie Hemric, Wake Forest
1951–52	22.4 pts.
1952–53	24.9 pts.
1953–54	24.3 pts.
1954–55	27.6 pts.

Calvin Natt, Northeast Louisiana
1975–76	20.6 pts.
1976–77	29.0 pts.
1977–78	21.3 pts.
1978–79	24.4 pts.

Michael Brooks, La Salle

1976–77	20.0 pts.
1977–78	24.9 pts.
1978–79	23.3 pts.
1979–80	24.1 pts.

Ronnie Perry, Holy Cross

1976–77	23.0 pts.
1977–78	21.7 pts.
1978–79	25.0 pts.
1979–80	22.9 pts.

Andrew Toney, Southwestern Louisiana

1976–77	21.0 pts.
1977–78	24.5 pts.
1978–79	23.3 pts.
1979–80	26.1 pts.

Harry Kelly, Texas Southern

1979–80	29.0 pts.
1980–81	23.7 pts.
1981–82	29.7 pts.
1982–83	28.8 pts.

Lionel Simmons, La Salle

1986–87	20.3 pts.
1987–88	23.3 pts.
1988–89	28.4 pts.
1989–90	26.5 pts.

Alphonso Ford, Mississippi Valley St.

1989–90	29.9 pts.
1990–91	32.7 pts.
1991–92	27.5 pts.
1992–93	26.0 pts.

Note: Toney, Kelly, Simmons, and Ford are the only players to score more than 600 points in each of four seasons.

PLAYERS WITH AT LEAST 4,000 CAREER POINTS AND REBOUNDS

PLAYER, SCHOOL	YEARS	PTS.	REB.	TOTAL
Tom Gola, La Salle	1952–55	2,462	2,201	4,663
Lionel Simmons, La Salle	1987–90	3,217	1,429	4,646
Elvin Hayes, Houston	1966–68	2,884	1,602	4,486
Dickie Hemric, Wake Forest	1952–55	2,587	1,802	4,389
Oscar Robertson, Cincinnati	1958–60	2,973	1,338	4,311
Joe Holup, George Washington	1953–56	2,226	2,030	4,256
Pete Maravich, Louisiana St.	1968–70	3,667	528	4,195
Harry Kelly, Texas Southern	1980–83	3,066	1,085	4,151
Danny Manning, Kansas	1985–88	2,951	1,187	4,138
Larry Bird, Indiana State	1977–79	2,850	1,247	4,097
Elgin Baylor, CI/Seattle	1956–58	2,500	1,559	4,059
Michael Brooks, La Salle	1977–80	2,628	1,372	4,000

SCHOOLS WITH FOUR TEAMMATES AVERAGING OVER 16 POINTS PER GAME

SCHOOL (SEASON)	PLAYERS (PPG)
Notre Dame (1964–65)	Ron Reed (21) Jay Miller (17.5) Larry Sheffield (17.1) Walt Sahm (16.4)
Oklahoma City (1965–66)	Jerry Wells (27.1) Gary Gray (21.1) Charlie Hunter (19.6) James Ware (16.6)
Loyola Marymount (1987–88)	Hank Gathers (22.5) Bo Kimble (22.2) Mike Yoest (17.6) Corey Gaines (17.4)
Loyola Marymount (1988–89)	Hank Gathers (32.7) Jeff Fryer (22.9) Enoch Simmons (18.7) Bo Kimble (16.8)

SCHOOLS WITH THREE TEAMMATES AVERAGING AT LEAST 20 POINTS PER GAME

SCHOOL (SEASON)	PLAYERS (PPG)
Marshall (1955–56)	Charlie Slack (22.5) Cebe Price (21.2) Paul Underwood (20.2)
Ohio State (1969–70)	Dave Sorenson (24.2) Jim Cleamons (21.6) Jody Finney (20.6)
Loyola Marymount (1989–90)	Bo Kimble (35.3) Hank Gathers (29) Jeff Fryer (22.7)
Georgia Tech (1989–90)	Dennis Scott (27.7) Brian Oliver (21.3) Kenny Anderson (20.6)
Iowa State (1993–94)	Loren Meyer (22.3) Fred Hoiberg (20.2) Julius Michalik (20)

SCHOOLS WITH TWO TEAMMATES AVERAGING AT LEAST 25 POINTS PER GAME

SCHOOL (SEASON)	PLAYERS (PPG)
Mississippi State (1956–57)	Jim Ashmore (28.3) Bailey Howell (25.9)
Oklahoma City (1972–73)	Ozzie Edwards (28.4) Marvin Rich (25.3)
Tennessee (1975–76)	Ernie Grunfeld (25.3) Bernard King (25.2)
Loyola Marymount (1989–90)	Bo Kimble (35.3) Hank Gathers (29)

PLAYERS WITH THE HIGHEST SCORING AVERAGES AS A SENIOR

PLAYER, SCHOOL	SEASON	AVG.
Pete Maravich, Louisiana State	1969–70	44.5
Frank Selvy, Furman	1953–54	41.7
Billy McGill, Utah	1961–62	38.8
Austin Carr, Notre Dame	1970–71	38.0
Kevin Bradshaw, U.S. International	1990–91	37.6
Rick Barry, Miami (Fla.)	1964–65	37.4

PLAYERS WITH THE HIGHEST SCORING AVERAGES AS A JUNIOR

PLAYER, SCHOOL	SEASON	AVG.
Pete Maravich, Louisiana State	1968–69	44.2
Freeman Williams, Portland State	1976–77	38.8
Austin Carr, Notre Dame	1969–70	38.1
Dwight Lamar, Southwestern La.	1971–72	36.3
Richie Fuqua, Oral Roberts	1971–72	36.2

562 ⬤ *ENCYCLOPEDIA OF COLLEGE BASKETBALL*

PLAYERS WITH THE HIGHEST SCORING AVERAGES AS A SOPHOMORE

PLAYER, SCHOOL	SEASON	AVG.
Pete Maravich, Louisiana State	1967–68	43.8
Johnny Neumann, Mississippi	1970–71	40.1
Calvin Murphy, Niagara	1967–68	38.2
Oscar Robertson, Cincinnati	1957–58	35.1
Larry Fogle, Canisius	1973–74	33.4

PLAYERS WITH 1,000 OR MORE POINTS AT TWO DIVISION I SCHOOLS

PLAYER	SCHOOL (POINTS, YEARS)
Jon Manning	Oklahoma City (1,039 points in 1974–75 and 1975–76)
	North Texas State (1,090 points in 1977–78 and 1978–79)
Kenny Battle	Northern Illinois (1,072 points in 1984–85 and 1985–86)
	Illinois (1,112 points in 1987–88 and 1988–89)

Note: Manning is the only player to score more than 40 points for two different schools against Division I opponents—43 for OCU against Tulsa on January 20, 1975, and 41 for North Texas against Baylor on December 4, 1978.

MOST GAMES WITH 40 OR MORE POINTS VS. DIVISION I OPPONENTS

GAMES	PLAYER, SCHOOL (YEARS)
56	Pete Maravich, Louisiana State (1968–70)
21	Oscar Robertson, Cincinnati (1958–60)
21	Austin Carr, Notre Dame (1969–71)
16	Freeman Williams, Portland State (1975–78)
15	Elvin Hayes, Houston (1966–68)
14	Calvin Murphy, Niagara (1968–70)
14	Larry Bird, Indiana State (1977–79)

MOST POINTS FOR TWO TEAMMATES IN SAME GAME

92	Kevin Bradshaw (72) and Isaac Brown (20), U.S. International vs. Loyola Marymount, 12-5-90
91	Randy Woods (46) and Doug Overton (45), La Salle vs. Loyola Marymount, 12-31-90
91	Ronnie Schmitz (51) and Tony Dumas (40), Missouri-Kansas City vs. U.S. International, 3-4-91

MOST POINTS FOR TWO OPPOSING PLAYERS IN SAME GAME

115	Pete Maravich, Louisiana State (64), and Dan Issel, Kentucky (51), 2-21-70
109	Calvin Murphy, Niagara (68), and Bill Smith, Syracuse (41), 12-7-68
108	Chris Jackson, Louisiana State (55), and Gerald Glass, Mississippi (53), 3-4-89
101	Bo Kimble, Loyola Marymount (53), and Gary Payton, Oregon State (48), 12-19-89
100	Johnny Neumann, Mississippi (63), and Al Sanders, Louisiana State (37), 1-30-71

MOST POINTS FOR THREE TEAMMATES IN SAME GAME

120	Randy Woods (46), Doug Overton (45), and Jack Hurd (29), La Salle vs. Loyola Marymount, 12-31-90
118	Brent Price (56), Kermit Holmes (34), and Jeff Webster (28), Oklahoma vs. Loyola Marymount, 12-15-90

MOST PLAYERS WITH 40 OR MORE POINTS IN SAME GAME

3	Doug Spradley, Gonzaga (40), Hank Gathers, Loyola Marymount (40), and Bo Kimble, Loyola Marymount (40), 2-18-89
3	Ronnie Schmitz, UMKC (51), Tony Dumas, UMKC (40), and Kevin Bradshaw, U.S. International (43), 3-4-91

20/20 CLUB

Seven players have averaged at least 20 points and 20 rebounds per game in their careers (minimum of two seasons).

PLAYER	SCHOOL	SEASONS (CAREER AVERAGES)
Walt Dukes	Seton Hall	1952 and 1953 (23.5 ppg, 21.1 rpg)
Bill Russell	San Francisco	1954–56 (20.7 ppg, 20.3 rpg)
Elgin Baylor	College of Idaho and Seattle	1955, 1957, and 1958 (31.3 ppg, 20 rpg)
Paul Silas	Creighton	1962–64 (20.5 ppg, 21.6 rpg)
Julius Erving	Massachusetts	1970 and 1971 (26.3 ppg, 20.2 rpg)
Artis Gilmore	Jacksonville	1970 and 1971 (24.3 ppg, 22.7 rpg)
Kermit Washington	American	1971–73 (20.1 ppg, 20.2 rpg)

MOST POINTS IN A SEASON BY A FRESHMAN

PLAYER, TEAM	YEAR	G.	FG	3FG	FT	PTS.
Chris Jackson, Louisiana St.	1989	32	359	84	163	965
James Williams, Austin Peay	1973	29	360	–	134	854
Wayman Tisdale, Oklahoma	1983	33	338	–	134	810
Mark Aguirre, DePaul	1979	32	302	–	163	767
Harry Kelly, Texas Southern	1980	26	313	–	127	753

HIGHEST SEASON SCORING AVERAGE BY A FRESHMAN

PLAYER, TEAM	YEAR	G.	FG	3FG	FT	PTS.	AVG.
Chris Jackson, Louisiana St. 1989	1989	32	359	84	163	965	30.2
James Williams, Austin Peay St. 1973	1973	29	360	–	134	854	29.4
Harry Kelly, Texas Southern 1980	1980	26	313	–	127	753	29.0
Bernard King, Tennessee 1975	1975	25	273	–	115	661	26.4
Jacky Dorsey, Georgia	1975	25	267	–	112	646	25.8

HIGHEST SEASON FIELD-GOAL PERCENTAGE BY A FRESHMAN

PLAYER, TEAM	YEAR	G.	FG	FGA	PCT.
Sidney Moncrief, Arkansas	1976	28	149	224	66.5
Gary Trent, Ohio	1993	27	194	298	65.1
Ed Pinckney, Villanova	1982	32	169	264	64.0
Jimmy Lunsford, Alabama State	1993	22	142	223	63.7
Cedric Robinson, Nicholls St.	1983	24	146	231	63.2

HIGHEST SEASON THREE-POINT FIELD-GOAL PERCENTAGE BY A FRESHMAN

PLAYER, TEAM	YEAR	G.	3FG	3FGA	PCT.
Jay Edwards, Indiana	1988	23	59	110	53.6
Ross Richardson, LMU	1991	25	61	116	52.6
Lance Barker, Valparaiso	1992	26	61	117	52.1
Ed Peterson, Yale	1989	28	53	104	51.0
Willie Brand, UTA	1988	29	65	128	50.8

MOST THREE-POINT FIELD GOALS IN A SEASON BY A FRESHMAN

PLAYER, TEAM	YEAR	G.	3FG	AVG.
Keith Veney, Lamar	1993	27	106	3.93
Alphonso Ford, Miss. Valley	1990	27	104	3.85
Tony Ross, San Diego State	1987	28	104	3.71
Ronnie Schmitz, UMKC	1990	28	90	3.21
Eddie Benton, Vermont	1993	26	82	3.15

HIGHEST SEASON FREE-THROW PERCENTAGE BY A FRESHMAN

PLAYER, TEAM	YEAR	G.	FT	FTA	PCT.
Jim Barton, Dartmouth	1986	26	65	69	94.2
Steve Alford, Indiana	1984	31	137	150	91.3
Jay Edwards, Indiana	1988	23	69	76	90.8
LaBradford Smith, Louisville	1988	35	143	158	90.5
Mike Waitkus, Brown	1983	26	97	108	89.8

MOST REBOUNDS IN A SEASON BY A FRESHMAN

PLAYER, TEAM	YEAR	G.	REB.
Pete Padgett, Nevada-Reno	1973	26	462
Kenny Miller, Loyola (Ill.)	1988	29	395
Shaquille O'Neal, LSU	1990	32	385
Ralph Sampson, Virginia	1980	34	381
Michael Cage, San Diego State	1981	27	355

HIGHEST SEASON REBOUND AVERAGE BY A FRESHMAN

PLAYER, TEAM	YEAR	G.	REB.	AVG.
Pete Padgett, Nevada-Reno	1973	26	462	17.8
Glenn Mosley, Seton Hall	1974	21	299	14.2
Ira Terrell, SMU	1973	25	352	14.1
Kenny Miller, Loyola (Ill.)	1988	29	395	13.6
Bob Stephens, Drexel	1976	23	307	13.3
Michael Cage, San Diego State	1981	27	355	13.1

MOST ASSISTS IN A SEASON BY A FRESHMAN

PLAYER, TEAM	YEAR	G.	AST.
Bobby Hurley, Duke	1990	38	288
Kenny Anderson, Georgia Tech	1990	35	285
Andre LaFleur, Northeastern	1984	32	252
Orlando Smart, San Francisco	1991	29	237
Chris Corchiani, N.C. State	1988	32	235

HIGHEST SEASON ASSIST AVERAGE BY A FRESHMAN

PLAYER, TEAM	YEAR	G.	AST.	AVG.
Orlando Smart, San Francisco	1991	29	237	8.17
Kenny Anderson, Georgia Tech	1990	35	285	8.14
Taurence Chisholm, Delaware	1985	28	224	8.00
Andre LaFleur, Northeastern	1984	32	252	7.88
Marc Brown, Siena	1988	29	222	7.66
Jason Kidd, California	1993	29	222	7.66

MOST BLOCKED SHOTS IN A SEASON BY A FRESHMAN

PLAYER, TEAM	YEAR	G.	BLK.
Shawn Bradley, Brigham Young	1991	34	177
Alonzo Mourning, Georgetown	1989	34	169
Shaquille O'Neal, LSU	1990	32	115
Dwayne Schintzius, Florida	1987	34	96
Pervis Ellison, Louisville	1986	39	92
Jim McIlvaine, Marquette	1991	28	92

HIGHEST SEASON BLOCKED SHOT AVERAGE BY A FRESHMAN

PLAYER, TEAM	YEAR	G.	BLK.	AVG.
Shawn Bradley, Brigham Young	1991	34	177	5.21
Alonzo Mourning, Georgetown	1989	34	169	4.97
Shaquille O'Neal, LSU	1990	32	115	3.59
Jim McIlvaine, Marquette	1991	28	92	3.29
Derek Stewart, Augusta	1990	28	82	2.93

MOST STEALS IN A SEASON BY A FRESHMAN

PLAYER, TEAM	YEAR	G.	ST.
Nadav Henefeld, Connecticut	1990	37	138
Jason Kidd, California	1993	29	110
Eric Murdock, Providence	1988	28	90
Pat Baldwin, Northwestern	1991	28	90
Clarence Ceasar, LSU	1992	31	90

HIGHEST SEASON STEAL AVERAGE BY A FRESHMAN

PLAYER, TEAM	YEAR	G.	ST.	AVG.
Jason Kidd, California	1993	29	110	3.79
Nadav Henefeld, Connecticut	1990	37	138	3.73
Eric Murdock, Providence	1988	28	90	3.21
Pat Baldwin, Northwestern	1991	28	90	3.21
Jeff Myers, St. Francis (N.Y.)	1993	26	81	3.12

CENTERS OF ATTENTION

A statistical comparison of celebrated college centers sheds some light as to their impact. Here is how ten of the premier pivotmen stack up statistically (winning percentages of their respective schools during their tenures are in parentheses).

STANDOUT CENTER, SCHOOL	COLLEGE CAREER AVERAGES
Lew Alcindor, UCLA (.978)	26.4 ppg, 15.5 rpg, 63.9 FG%
Bill Walton, UCLA (.956)	20.3 ppg, 15.7 rpg, 65.1 FG%
Bill Russell, San Francisco (.899)	20.7 ppg, 20.3 rpg, 51.6 FG%
Hakeem Olajuwon, Houston (.846)	13.3 ppg, 10.7 rpg, 63.9 FG%
Patrick Ewing, Georgetown (.8403)	15.3 ppg, 9.2 rpg, 62.0 FG%
Wilt Chamberlain, Kansas (.840)	29.9 ppg, 18.3 rpg, 47.0 FG%
Ralph Sampson, Virginia (.830)	16.9 ppg, 11.4 rpg, 56.8 FG%
David Robinson, Navy (.809)	21.0 ppg, 10.3 rpg, 61.3 FG%
Alonzo Mourning, Georgetown (.729)	16.7 ppg, 8.6 rpg, 56.6 FG%
Shaquille O'Neal, Louisiana State (.688)	21.6 ppg, 13.5 rpg, 61.0 FG%

WINNERS ALL THE WAY

Six major-college coaches had winning marks in college careers spanning more than 20 years through 1994.

COACH (SEASONS)	CLOSEST TO NON-WINNING RECORD
John Wooden (29)	14-12 with UCLA in 1959–60
Lou Carnesecca (24)	17-12 with St. John's in 1987–88
*Jerry Tarkanian (24)	16-12 with UNLV in 1980–81
Peck Hickman (23)	13-12 with Louisville in 1957–58
Ben Jobe (23)	12-10 with Alabama A&M in 1984–85
Gale Catlett (22)	15-14 with West Virginia in 1979–80

* Tarkanian also compiled seven more winning records in as many seasons for two community colleges in California, where he won five consecutive state championships after notching a 14-13 mark in 1961–62 at Riverside City College to begin his coaching odyssey.

WINNERS FROM THE START

Eight players have been members of teams that won a state high school championship, NCAA Tournament, and NBA title.

PLAYER HIGH SCHOOL	COLLEGE NBA TEAM
Lucius Allen Wyandotte (Kansas City, Mo.), 1965	UCLA, 1967-68 Milwaukee, 1971
Quinn Buckner Thornridge (Phoenix, Ill.), 1971-72	Indiana, 1976 Boston, 1984
Magic Johnson Lansing (Mich.), 1977	Michigan State, 1979 Los Angeles, 1980-82-85-87-88
Jerry Lucas Middletown (Ohio), 1958	Ohio State, 1960 New York, 1973
Rodney McCray Mt. Vernon (N.Y.), 1978-79	Louisville, 1980 Chicago, 1993
Rick Robey Brother Martin (New Orleans, La.), 1974	Kentucky, 1978 Boston, 1981
Billy Thompson Camden (N.J.), 1982	Louisville, 1986 Los Angeles, 1987-88
Milt Wagner Camden (N.J.), 1979	Louisville, 1986 Los Angeles, 1988

Notes: Buckner (1976 in Montreal), Johnson (1992 in Barcelona), and Lucas (1960 in Rome) constitute the unique group that also won an Olympic gold medal. McCray was a member of the 1980 U.S. team that boycotted the XXIInd Olympiad in Moscow after the Soviet Union's invasion of Afghanistan.

COACHES WITH OVER 600 CAREER VICTORIES THROUGH 1993–94

RANK	COACH	WINS
1	Adolph Rupp	876
2	*Dean Smith	800
3	Henry Iba	767
4	Ed Diddle	759
5	Phog Allen	746
6	Ray Meyer	724
7	Ralph Miller	674
8	John Wooden	664
9	Marv Harshman	654
10	*Don Haskins	645
11	*Lefty Driesell	641
12	*Norm Stewart	640
13	*Bob Knight	638
14	Jerry Tarkanian	631
15	Norman Sloan	627
16	*Lou Henson	624
17	*Gene Bartow	616

* Denotes active coaches.

Note: Miller was forced to forfeit 17 of the victories.... Six NCAA Tournament victories for Tarkanian were voided by the NCAA.... Forfeit victories are not included for Knight (two), Henson (two), and Bartow (one).

THE WIN CROWD

Twenty victories in a season has been a benchmark of success. But the parameters have been altered somewhat over the years with the advent of additional games on schedules and more pressure to win.

What would the select group of coaches look like if the standard of undeniable success in a season was increased to 25 triumphs? Here are the 11 major-college coaches with at least eight 25-win campaigns through 1993–94:

COACH (YEARS)	25-WIN SEASONS
*Dean Smith (33)	20
Jerry Tarkanian (24)	12
John Wooden (29)	12
Ed Diddle (42)	11
Hank Iba (41)	10
Adolph Rupp (41)	10
*Jim Boeheim (18)	9
Everett Case (19)	8
*Bob Knight (29)	8
Guy Lewis (30)	8
*Eddie Sutton (24)	8

* Denotes active coaches.

RAGS TO RICHES

Here is a chronological list of the six coaches to go unbeaten in league competition the year after their school posted a losing conference record, since the start of national tournament competition:

SCHOOL (COACH)	UNDEFEATED LEAGUE	CONFERENCE REG.-SEASON	RECORD PREVIOUS SEASON
Iowa (Ralph Miller)			
	Big Ten	14-0 in '70	5-9 in '69 (T8th)
South Alabama (Cliff Ellis)			
	Sun Belt	10-0 in '79	3-7 in '78 (4th)
Northeastern (Jim Calhoun)			
	N. Atlantic	14-0 in '84	4-6 in '83 (6th)
Temple (John Chaney)			
	Atlantic 10	18-0 in '84	5-9 in '83 (E3d)
Loyola Marymount (Paul Westhead)			
	WCC	14-0 in '88	4-10 in '87 (8th)
Missouri (Norm Stewart)			
	Big Eight	14-0 in '94	5-9 in '93 (7th)

DOUBLE DUTY

Only five men have both played for and coached teams in the Final Four.

FINAL FOUR EXPERIENCE

NAME	AS PLAYER	AS HEAD COACH
Vic Bubas	N.C. State (1950)	Duke (1963-64-66)
Dick Harp	Kansas (1940)	Kansas (1957)
Bob Knight	Ohio St. (1960-61-62)	Indiana (1973-76-81-87-92)
Bones McKinney*	North Carolina (1946)	Wake Forest (1962)
Dean Smith	Kansas (1952-53)	N.C. (1967-68-69-72-77-81-82-91-93)

* McKinney played two seasons for North Carolina State prior to World War II military duty.

PICK OF THE LITTER

Nine coaches had compiled more than 25 NCAA Tournament victories through 1994:

COACH, SCHOOL(S)	NCAA WINS	TOURNEY TITLES	FINAL FOURS	FINAL FOUR W-L RECORD
*Dean Smith, North Carolina	56	2	9	8-9 (.471)
John Wooden, UCLA	47	10	12	21-3 (.875)
*Bob Knight, Indiana	40	3	5	7-2 (.778)
*Mike Krzyzewski, Duke	39	2	7	7-5 (.583)
Jerry Tarkanian, Long Beach State/UNLV	37	1	4	3-3 (.500)
*Denny Crum, Louisville	37	2	6	5-5 (.500)
Adolph Rupp, Kentucky	30	4	6	9-2 (.818)
*John Thompson, Georgetown	29	1	3	4-2 (.667)
Guy Lewis, Houston	26	0	5	3-6 (.333)

* Denotes active status.

TRIPLE CROWN

Three coaches have won championships in the NCAA Tournament, NIT, and Summer Olympics.

COACH	NCAA	NIT	OLYMPICS (SITE)
Bob Knight	1976-81-87	1979	1984 (Los Angeles)
Pete Newell	1959	1949	1960 (Rome)
Dean Smith	1982	1971	1976 (Montreal)

Note: Knight and Smith won their NCAA and NIT titles with Indiana and North Carolina, respectively. Newell won the NCAA championship with California after capturing the NIT with San Francisco.

REGAL ROOKIES

Six coaches earned trips to the Final Four in their first college season.

FIRST-YEAR COACH	FINAL FOUR RECORD	TEAM (FINISH)	PREDECESSOR
Ray Meyer	19-5	DePaul '43 (T3d)	Bill Wendt
Gary Thompson	21-9	Wichita State '65 (4th)	Ralph Miller
Denny Crum	26-5	Louisville '72 (4th)	John Dromo
Bill Hodges	33-1	Indiana State '79 (2d)	Bob King
Larry Brown	22-10	UCLA '80 (2d)	Gary Cunningham
Steve Fisher	*6-0	Michigan '89 (1st)	Bill Frieder

* Michigan finished with an overall record of 30-7 after Fisher succeeded Frieder just before the start of the NCAA Tournament.

SCHOOLS WITH FOUR ACTIVE PLAYERS WITH OVER 1,200 POINTS

SEASON	SCHOOL	PLAYERS	GAMES	POINTS
1984–85	Alcorn State	Aaron Brandon	120	1,740
		Michael Phelps	114	1,664
		Tommy Collier	117	1,350
		Eddie Archer	120	1,248
1987–88	Southern Mississippi	Randolph Keys	121	1,626
		Casey Fisher	121	1,599
		Derrick Hamilton	106	1,445
		John White	117	1,331
1990–91	UNLV	Stacey Augmon	145	2,011
		Greg Anthony	138	1,738
		Anderson Hunt*	109	1,632
		Larry Johnson	75	1,617
1990–91	Arkansas	Todd Day*	105	1,895
		Ron Huery	134	1,545
		Lee Mayberry*	105	1,422
		Oliver Miller*	103	1,216

* Denotes juniors.

SCHOOLS WITH FIVE ACTIVE PLAYERS WITH OVER 1,000 POINTS

SEASON	SCHOOL	PLAYERS	GAMES	POINTS
1986–87	Alabama1	Derrick McKey*	99	1,231
		Terry Coner	120	1,214
		Jim Farmer	111	1,197
		Mark Gottfried	126	1,061
		James Jackson	121	1,367
1990–91	East Tennessee State	Keith Jennings	127	1,988
		Greg Dennis	96	1,702
		Calvin Talford*	96	1,386
		Alvin West	126	1,115
		Major Geer	126	1,094
1992–93	Florida State	Doug Edwards	93	1,604
		Sam Cassell	66	1,211
		Rodney Dobard	122	1,058
		Chuck Graham	94	1,055
		Bob Sura**	65	1,055

* Denotes junior eligibility. **Denotes sophomore eligibility.

1. Gottfried and Jackson, transfers from other four-year schools, are listed but neither scored over 1,000 at Alabama. Their point totals include points scored at their previous school—Gottfried played one year at Oral Roberts and Jackson played two seasons at West Texas State. At Alabama, Gottfried scored 854 points and Jackson scored 354.

SCHOOLS WITH THREE OR MORE ACTIVE PLAYERS WITH OVER 1,500 POINTS

SEASON	SCHOOL	PLAYERS	GAMES	POINTS
1985–86	Duke	Johnny Dawkins	133	2,537
		Mark Alarie	133	2,136
		David Henderson	128	1,561
1980–81	Maryland	Albert King	118	2,058
		Ernest Graham	118	1,607
		Greg Manning	118	1,561
1989–90	Pepperdine1	Tom Lewis	114	2,050
		Craig Davis	121	1,619
		Dexter Howard	120	1,546
1989–90	Loyola Marymount2	Hank Gathers	117	2,723
		Bo Kimble	104	2,350
		Jeff Fryer	112	1,922
1990–91	UNLV3	Stacey Augmon	145	2,011
		Greg Anthony	138	1,738
		Anderson Hunt*	109	1,632
		Larry Johnson	75	1,617
1991–92	Arkansas	Todd Day	127	2,395
		Lee Mayberry	139	1,940
		Oliver Miller	137	1,674

* Denotes junior eligibility.

1. Lewis' totals include points scored at USC during his freshman year. His Pepperdine totals were 1,515 points in 87 games.

2. Gathers' totals include points scored at USC in his first season. Gathers' LMU totals are 2,490 points in 89 games. Kimble's totals include points scored at USC in his first season. Kimble's LMU totals are 2,010 points in 76 games.

3. Anthony's totals include points scored at Portland in his freshman year. His UNLV totals are 1,306 points in 110 games.

SCHOOLS WITH TWO ACTIVE PLAYERS WITH OVER 2,000 POINTS

SEASON	SCHOOL	PLAYERS	GAMES	POINTS
1980–81	Lamar	Mike Olliver	122	2,518
		B. B. Davis	119	2,084
1985–86	Duke	Johnny Dawkins	133	2,537
		Mark Alarie	133	2,136
1986–87	Oklahoma	Tim McAlister	136	2,275
		Darryl Kennedy	137	2,097
1989–90	Loyola Marymount	Hank Gathers	117	2,723
		Bo Kimble	104	2,350
1989–90	Texas Southern	Charles Price	116	2,119
		Fred West	118	2,066

Note: The point totals for Gathers (Southern Cal), Kimble (Southern Cal), and Price (Grambling) include freshman year at other schools.

SCHOOLS WITH SEVEN OR MORE PLAYERS WHO WOULD SCORE OVER 1,000 POINTS BEFORE ENDING THEIR MAJOR-COLLEGE CAREERS

SEASON	SCHOOL	PLAYERS	CL.
1977–78	Notre Dame	Dave Batton	Sr.
		Don Williams	Sr.
		Bruce Flowers	Jr.
		Rich Branning	So.
		Kelly Tripucka	Fr.
		Orlando Woolridge	Fr.
		Tracy Jackson	Fr.
1980–81	Wake Forest	Frank Johnson	Sr.
		Guy Morgan	Jr.
		Alvis Rogers	Jr.
		Mike Helms	Jr.
		Jim Johnstone	Jr.
		Danny Young	Fr.
		Anthony Teachey	Fr.
1985–86	Duke	Johnny Dawkins	Sr.
		Mark Alarie	Sr.
		David Henderson	Sr.
		Jay Bilas	Sr.
		Tommy Amaker	Jr.
		Kevin Strickland	So.
		Danny Ferry	Fr.
1986–87	Bucknell	Chris Seneca	Sr.
		Mark Atkinson	Sr.
		Mark Allsteadt	Sr.
		Mike Butts	So.
		Ted Aceto	So.
		Mike Joseph	Fr.
		Greg Leggett	Fr.
1987–88	Pittsburgh	Charles Smith	Sr.
		Demetreus Gore	Sr.
		Jerome Lane	Jr.
		Rod Brookin	So.
		Jason Matthews	Fr.
		Sean Miller	Fr.
		Bobby Martin	Fr.
		Darelle Porter	Fr.
1990–91	West Virginia	Chris Brooks	Sr.
		Tracy Shelton	Jr.
		Chris Leonard	Jr.
		Marsalis Basey	Fr.
		Mike Boyd	Fr.
		Pervires Greene	Fr.
		Ricky Robinson	Fr.

SCHOOLS WITH THREE PLAYERS WHO WOULD SCORE OVER 2,000 POINTS BEFORE ENDING THEIR CAREERS

SEASON	SCHOOL	PLAYERS	CL.
1977–78	Duke	Jim Spanarkel	Jr.
		Mike Gminski	So.
		Gene Banks	Fr.
1978–79	Duke	Jim Spanarkel	Sr.
		Mike Gminski	Jr.
		Gene Banks	So.
1983–84	Oklahoma	Wayman Tisdale	So.
		Tim McAlister	Fr.
		Darryl Kennedy	Fr.
1984–85	Oklahoma	Wayman Tisdale	Jr.
		Tim McAlister	So.
		Darryl Kennedy	So.
1985–86	Oklahoma	Tim McAlister	Jr.
		Darryl Kennedy	Jr.
		Stacey King	Fr.
1985–86	Duke	Johnny Dawkins	Sr.
		Mark Alarie	Sr.
		Danny Ferry	Fr.
1985–86	Southern Cal	Tom Lewis	Fr.
		Hank Gathers	Fr.
		Bo Kimble	Fr.
1986–87	Oklahoma	Tim McAlister	Sr.
		Darryl Kennedy	Sr.
		Stacey King	So.

Note: Neither Gathers, Lewis, nor Kimble remained at USC after their freshman season. Lewis transferred to Pepperdine, while Kimble and Gathers went to Loyola Marymount.

SCHOOLS WITH FIVE OR MORE PLAYERS WITH OVER 2,000 POINTS IN THEIR PLAYING CAREERS

SCHOOL	PLAYERS	YEARS	POINTS
Duke	Johnny Dawkins	83–86	2,537
	Christian Laettner	89–92	2,460
	Mike Gminski	77–80	2,323
	Danny Ferry	86–89	2,155
	Mark Alarie	83–86	2,136
	Gene Banks	78–81	2,079
	Jim Spanarkel	76–79	2,012
North Carolina	Phil Ford	75–78	2,290
	Sam Perkins	81–84	2,133
	Len Rosenbluth	55–57	2,045
	Al Wood	78–81	2,015
	Charlie Scott	68–70	2,007
Oklahoma	Wayman Tisdale	83–85	2,661
	Tim McAlister	84–87	2,275
	Jeff Webster	91–94	2,264
	Darryl Kennedy	84–87	2,097
	Stacey King	86–89	2,008
Tennessee	Allan Houston	90–93	2,801
	Ernie Grunfeld	74–77	2,249
	Tony White	84–87	2,219
	Reggie Johnson	77–80	2,103
	Dale Ellis	80–83	2,065
Villanova	Keith Herron	75–78	2,170
	Doug West	86–89	2,037
	Howard Porter	69–71	2,026
	John Pinone	80–83	2,024
	Bob Schafer	52–55	2,012

SCHOOLS WITH FOUR TEAMMATES WHO COMBINED TO AVERAGE OVER 80 POINTS PER GAME

AVG.	SCHOOL (SEASON)	PLAYERS (AVERAGE)
101.5	Loyola Marymount (1989–90)	Bo Kimble (35.3) Hank Gathers (29) Jeff Fryer (22.7) Terrell Lowery (14.5)
91.1	Loyola Marymount (1989–90)	Hank Gathers (41.7) Jeff Fryer (22.9) Enoch Simmons (18.7) Bo Kimble (16.8)
87.6	Furman (1953–54)	Frank Selvy (41.7) Darrell Floyd (24.3) Fred Fraley (11.8) Ken Deardorff (9.8)
84.4	Oklahoma City (1965–66)	Jerry Wells (27.1) Gary Gray (21.1) Charlie Hunter (19.6) James Ware (16.6)
83.8	Louisiana State (1969–70)	Pete Maravich (44.5) Danny Hester (16.1) Al Sanders (12) Bill Newton (11.2)

SCHOOLS WITH THREE TEAMMATES WHO COMBINED TO AVERAGE OVER 70 POINTS PER GAME

AVG.	SCHOOL (SEASON)	PLAYERS (AVERAGE)
87.0	Loyola Marymount (1989–90)	Bo Kimble (35.3) Hank Gathers (29) Jeff Fryer (22.7)
77.8	Furman (1953–54)	Frank Selvy (41.7) Darrell Floyd (24.3) Fred Fraley (11.8)
74.3	Loyola Marymount (1989–90)	Hank Gathers (32.7) Jeff Fryer (22.9) Enoch Simmons (18.7)
72.6	Louisiana State (1969–70)	Pete Maravich (44.5) Danny Hester (16.1) Al Sanders (12)
70.8	Notre Dame (1970–71)	Austin Carr (37.9) Collis Jones (23.1) Sid Catlett (9.8)

SCHOOLS WITH TWO TEAMMATES WHO COMBINED TO AVERAGE OVER 60 POINTS PER GAME

AVG.	SCHOOL (SEASON)	PLAYERS (AVERAGE)
66.0	Furman (1953–54)	Frank Selvy (41.7) Darrell Floyd (24.3)
64.3	Loyola Marymount (1989–90)	Bo Kimble (35.3) Hank Gathers (29)
61.0	Notre Dame (1970–71)	Austin Carr (37.9) Collis Jones (23.1)
60.6	Louisiana State (1969–70)	Pete Maravich (44.5) Danny Hester (16.1)

SCHOOLS WITH AT LEAST 65 VICTORIES IN TWO SUCCESSIVE SEASONS

SCHOOL (SEASONS)	RECORD
UNLV (1986 and 1987)	70-7
Georgetown (1984 and 1985)	69-6
UNLV (1990 and 1991)	69-6
Duke (1991 and 1992)	66-9
Oklahoma (1988 and 1989)	66-9
UNLV (1987 and 1988)	65-10

SCHOOLS WITH AT LEAST 90 VICTORIES IN THREE SUCCESSIVE SEASONS

SCHOOL (SEASONS)	RECORD
UNLV (1985–87)	98-11
UNLV (1989–91)	98-14
UNLV (1986–88)	98-15
UNLV (1990–92)	95-8
Duke (1990–92)	95-18
Georgetown (1984–86)	93-14
Oklahoma (1988–90)	93-14
UNLV (1988–90)	92-21
Oklahoma (1987–89)	90-19

SCHOOLS WITH MORE THAN 120 VICTORIES IN FOUR SUCCESSIVE SEASONS

SCHOOL (SEASONS)	RECORD
UNLV (1987–90)	129-23
UNLV (1984–87)	127-17
UNLV (1986–89)	127-23
UNLV (1985–88)	126-19
UNLV (1988–91)	126-22
UNLV (1989–92)	124-16
Duke (1989–92)	123-26
Georgetown (1984–87)	122-19
Georgetown (1982–85)	121-23

SCHOOLS WITH MORE THAN 150 VICTORIES IN FIVE SUCCESSIVE SEASONS

SCHOOL (SEASONS)	RECORD
UNLV (1987–91)	163-24
UNLV (1986–90)	162-28
UNLV (1983–87)	155-20
UNLV (1984–88)	155-25
UNLV (1985–89)	155-27
UNLV (1988–92)	152-24
Duke (1988–92)	151-33

SCHOOLS WITH AT LEAST 275 VICTORIES IN 10 SUCCESSIVE SEASONS

SCHOOL (SEASONS)	RECORD
UNLV (1983–92)	307-44
UNLV (1982–91)	301-52
UNLV (1984–93)	300-49
Duke (1985–94)	287-67
UCLA (1967–76)	286-17
UNLV (1981–90)	283-63
Duke (1984–93)	283-71
UCLA (1964–73)	281-15
UCLA (1968–77)	281-21
North Carolina (1980–89)	281-63
UCLA (1965–74)	277-19
UCLA (1966–75)	277-20
UCLA (1969–78)	277-23
North Carolina (1979–88)	275-61

HIGHEST WINNING PERCENTAGE IN TWO SUCCESSIVE SEASONS SINCE 1950–51

SCHOOL (SEASONS)	RECORD	PCT.
UCLA (1972 and 1973)	60-0	1.000
Indiana (1975 and 1976)	63-1	.984
UCLA (1967 and 1968)	59-1	.983
UCLA (1971 and 1972)	59-1	.983
N.C. State (1973 and 1974)	57-1	.983
San Francisco (1955 and 1956)	57-1	.983
UCLA (1964 and 1965)	58-2	.967
UCLA (1968 and 1969)	58-2	.967
UNLV (1991 and 1992)	60-3	.952

HIGHEST WINNING PERCENTAGE IN THREE SUCCESSIVE SEASONS SINCE 1950–51

SCHOOL (SEASONS)	RECORD	PCT.
UCLA (1971–73)	89-1	.989
UCLA (1967–69)	88-2	.978
UCLA (1970–72)	87-3	.967
UCLA (1968–70)	86-4	.956
UCLA (1969–71)	86-4	.956
UCLA (1972–74)	86-4	.956
Indiana (1974–76)	86-6	.935

HIGHEST WINNING PERCENTAGE IN FOUR SUCCESSIVE SEASONS SINCE 1950–51

SCHOOL (SEASONS)	RECORD	PCT.
UCLA (1970–73)	117-3	.975
UCLA (1967–70)	116-4	.967
UCLA (1969–72)	116-4	.967
UCLA (1968–71)	115-5	.958
UCLA (1971–74)	115-5	.958
UCLA (1972–75)	114-7	.942
Cincinnati (1960–63)	110-9	.924

HIGHEST WINNING PERCENTAGE IN FIVE SUCCESSIVE SEASONS SINCE 1950–51

SCHOOL (SEASONS)	RECORD	PCT.
UCLA (1969–73)	146-4	.973
UCLA (1967–71)	145-5	.967
UCLA (1968–72)	145-5	.967
UCLA (1970–74)	143-7	.953
UCLA (1971–75)	143-8	.947

HIGHEST WINNING PERCENTAGE IN 10 SUCCESSIVE SEASONS SINCE 1950–51

SCHOOL (SEASONS)	RECORD	PCT.
UCLA (1964–73)	281-15	.949
UCLA (1967–76)	286-17	.944
UCLA (1965–74)	277-19	.936
UCLA (1966–75)	277-20	.933
UCLA (1968–77)	281-21	.930
UCLA (1969–78)	277-23	.923
UCLA (1970–79)	273-27	.910

HIGHEST NUMBER OF 20-WIN SEASONS SINCE 1950–51

WINS	SCHOOL
32	Kentucky
31	UCLA
29	Louisville
29	North Carolina
27	Duke
24	St. John's
23	North Carolina State
20	Kansas
20	Notre Dame

HIGHEST NUMBER OF 25-WIN SEASONS SINCE 1950–51

WINS	SCHOOL
21	North Carolina
18	UCLA
15	Kentucky
13	UNLV
11	Kansas
11	Duke

HIGHEST NUMBER OF SUCCESSIVE 20-WIN SEASONS SINCE 1950–51

NO.	SEASONS	SCHOOL
24	1971–94	North Carolina
17	1967–83	UCLA
14	1971–84	Louisville
13	1967–79	Marquette
13	1978–90	Georgetown
12	1982–93	UNLV
12	1982–93	Oklahoma
11	1984–94	Duke

HIGHEST NUMBER OF SUCCESSIVE SEASONS WITH 27 OR MORE WINS SINCE 1950–51

NO.	SEASONS	SCHOOL
9	1983–91	UNLV
7	1983–89	North Carolina
7	1967–73	UCLA

UNBEATEN TEAMS SINCE 1937–38

YEAR	SCHOOL	RECORD
1939	Long Island	23-0
1940	Seton Hall	19-0
1944	Army	15-0
1954	Kentucky	25-0
1956	San Francisco	29-0
1957	North Carolina	32-0
1964	UCLA	30-0
1967	UCLA	30-0
1972	UCLA	30-0
1973	North Carolina St.	27-0
1973	UCLA	30-0
1976	Indiana	32-0

ALL-TIME WINLESS SEASONS (AT LEAST 10 GAMES)

YEAR	SCHOOL	RECORD
1992	Prairie View	0-28
1955	The Citadel	0-17
1945	Baylor	0-17
1944	Virginia Military	0-14
1943	Tulsa	0-10
1937	Middle Tenn. State	0-11
1937	William & Mary	0-18
1934	American	0-10
1932	Virginia Military	0-14
1927	St. Louis	0-14
1924	Northwestern	0-16
1918	Dartmouth	0-26
1917	Oregon	0-11
1910	Drake	0-10

NCAA TOURNAMENT CONFERENCE LEADERS THROUGH 1994

RECORDS REFLECT ACTUAL CONFERENCE MEMBERSHIP FOR EACH SEASON, REGARDLESS OF WHETHER SCHOOLS HAVE MOVED TO OTHER CONFERENCES

Most Final Fours

1. Big Ten	33
2. ACC	27
3. Pacific-10	26
4. Big Eight	19
5. MVC and SEC	16

Most Title Games

1. Big Ten	18
2. Pacific-10	16
3. ACC	15
4. Big Eight	9
4. Missouri Valley	9

Most Championships

1. Pacific-10	13
2. Big Ten	9
3. ACC	7
4. SEC	6
5. Missouri Valley	4

Most Victories

1. ACC	212
2. Big Ten	210
3. SEC	133
4. Pacific-10	128
5. Big Eight	125

Best Winning Percentage

1. ACC	.671
2. Big Ten	.644
3. Big East	.624
4. Pacific-10	.595
5. SEC	.568

Most Appearances

1. Big Ten	121
2. ACC	108
3. SEC	100
4. Big Eight	95
5. Pacific-10	90

RECORDS REFLECT CURRENT CONFERENCE MEMBERSHIP REGARDLESS OF WHETHER SCHOOLS' RECORDS ARE FROM WHEN THEY WERE IN OTHER CONFERENCES

Most Final Fours

1. Big Ten	34
2. ACC	30
3. Pacific-10	27
4. Big Eight	24
5. SEC	20

Most Title Games

1. Big Ten	18
2. ACC	17
3. Pacific-10	16
4. Big Eight	12
5. Big East	9

Most Championships

1. Pacific-10	13
2. Big Ten	9
3. ACC	7
4. SEC	6
5. Big Eight	4

Most Victories

1. ACC	226
2. Big Ten	217
3. Big East	175
4. SEC	157
5. Pacific-10	144

Best Winning Percentage

1. ACC	.655
2. Big Ten	.636
3. Pacific-10	.581
4. Big Eight	.562
5. Big East	.543

Most Appearances

1. Big East	141
2. Big Ten	127
3. ACC	122
3. SEC	122
5. Pac-10 & Big 8	105

PERFECT EXAMPLES

Three schools have gone unbeaten in league competition three consecutive seasons since the start of the NCAA Tournament.

SCHOOL (CONFERENCE)	COACH	UNBEATEN IN LEAGUE
Kentucky (SEC)	Adolph Rupp	1947, 1948, and 1949
West Virginia (Southern)	Fred Schaus	1957, 1958, and 1959
UCLA (Pacific-8)	John Wooden	1971, 1972, and 1973

RETURN ENGAGEMENTS

The eight schools that appeared in at least 10 consecutive NCAA Tournaments through 1994:

SCHOOL	NO.	YEARS
North Carolina	20	1975–94
UCLA	15	1967–81
Georgetown	14	1979–92
Duke	11	1984–94
Arizona	10	1985–94
Louisiana State	10	1984–93
Marquette	10	1971–80
Syracuse	10	1983–92

ALL TIED UP IN NOTS

Through 1994, the following 10 Division I schools had never won a regular-season title in their present conference despite membership in a league for more than 25 years:

SCHOOL	CONFERENCE(S)	YEARS
Harvard	Ivy League	64
Mississippi	Southeastern	62
The Citadel	Southern	58
Kent	Mid-American	43
San Jose State	Big West and WCC	42
Washington State	Pacific-10	41
Nebraska	Big Eight	36
Oregon	Pacific-10	34
Texas-Arlington	Southland	30
UC Santa Barbara	Big West and WCC	28

Notes: Nebraska's drought is since the Big Eight went to eight members.... The dry spells for Washington State and Oregon are since the Pacific-10 Conference dropped a divisional format.

GROWTH OF FIELD OF DREAMS

Here is a time frame showing the expansion of the NCAA Tournament field from eight teams to 64 (number of schools classified as Division I at the time are in parentheses for designated years):

PLAYOFF ENTRANTS	YEARS (NUMBER OF DIVISION I SCHOOLS)
8 teams	1939 through 1950 (145 major colleges)
16 teams	1951 (153) and 1952 (156)
22–25 teams	1953 (158) through 1974 (233)
32 teams	1975 (233) through 1978 (254)
40 teams	1979 (257)
48 teams	1980 (261) through 1982 (272)
52 teams	1983 (274)
53 teams	1984 (276)
64 teams	since 1985 (282)

DUNKING FOR DOLLARS

The rapid growth of the NCAA Tournament after television became a key factor and the revenue a school generated are staggering. Each Final Four participant in 1990 received more than $1.47 million, a whopping increase of almost 3,000 percent in just 20 years.

Here is the cumulative payout in five-year increments from 1970 through 1990 to each Final Four school before the NCAA introduced a new revenue-sharing formula, beginning with the 1991 tournament:

YEAR	FINAL FOUR TEAM PAYOUT
1970	$49,576
1975	$133,381
1980	$326,378
1985	$751,899
1990	$1,472,339

THAT'S INCREDIBLE

Three schools won an NCAA Tournament one year after compiling a non-winning record.

CHAMPION, YEAR (W-L)	PREV. SEASON	GAMES IMPROVED
Wisconsin, 1941 (20-3)	5-15	+13
Ohio State, 1960 (25-3)	11-11	+11
Utah, 1944 (22-4)	10-12	+10

RECORDS IN FIRST SEASON OF DIVISION I

Includes schools that moved up to the major-college ranks after the first year of classification in 1948.

UNIVERSITY	YEAR	W	L	PCT.
Md.-Eastern Shore	1974	27	2	.931
Oral Roberts	1972	26	2	.929
Southwestern La.	1972	23	3	.885
Seattle	1953	29	4	.879
Old Dominion	1977	25	4	.862
Long Beach State	1970	24	5	.828
Southern (La.)	1978	23	5	.821
Hawaii	1971	23	5	.821
McNeese State	1974	20	5	.800
Jackson State	1978	19	5	.792
Alabama State	1983	22	6	.786
Alcorn State	1978	22	7	.759
Idaho State	1959	21	7	.750
Memphis State	1956	20	7	.741
Air Force	1958	17	6	.739
S.F. Austin State	1987	22	8	.733
Northeastern	1973	19	7	.731
Georgia Southern	1974	19	7	.731
Va. Commonwealth	1974	17	7	.708
Miami (Fla.)	1949	19	8	.704
Charleston	1992	19	8	.704
New Orleans	1976	18	8	.692
Weber State	1964	17	8	.680
George Mason	1979	17	8	.680
Florida A&M	1979	18	9	.667
Mercer	1974	16	8	.667
Tennessee Tech	1956	14	7	.667
American	1967	16	8	.667
Fairfield	1965	14	7	.667
Morehead State	1956	19	10	.655
UNLV	1970	17	9	.654
James Madison	1977	17	9	.654
Northwestern La.	1977	17	9	.654
Drexel	1974	15	9	.625
Northern Colorado	1974	15	9	.625
Lamar	1970	15	9	.625
Arkansas State	1971	15	9	.625
Abilene Christian	1971	15	9	.625
Massachusetts	1962	15	9	.625
UC Santa Barbara	1964	18	11	.621
Delaware State	1974	18	11	.621
Illinois State	1972	16	10	.615
Northeast La.	1974	16	10	.615
North Carolina A&T	1974	16	10	.615
N.C.-Wilmington	1977	16	10	.615
Texas Southern	1978	16	10	.615
Austin Peay	1964	14	9	.609
Ala.-Birmingham	1980	18	12	.600
Southern Miss.	1969	15	10	.600
Chicago State	1985	16	11	.593
Tenn.-Chattanooga	1978	16	11	.593
Wright State	1988	16	11	.593
Loyola (La.)	1952	20	14	.588
N.C.-Asheville	1987	15	11	.577
San Jose State	1953	15	11	.577
Los Angeles State	1971	15	11	.577
New Mexico State	1951	19	14	.576
Sam Houston State	1987	16	12	.571
Radford	1985	16	12	.571
Kentucky Wesleyan	1957	16	12	.571
East Tenn. State	1959	13	10	.565
East Carolina	1965	12	10	.545
Southern Illinois	1968	13	11	.542
New Mexico	1951	13	11	.542
Cal State Fullerton	1975	13	11	.542
Boise State	1972	14	12	.538
Central Michigan	1974	14	12	.538
West Texas	1951	14	12	.538
Wisc.-Milwaukee	1974	14	12	.538
UNC Charlotte	1973	14	12	.538
Oklahoma City	1951	16	14	.533
Iona	1954	11	10	.524
Corpus Christi	1973	13	12	.520
Wisc.-Green Bay	1982	14	13	.519
Illinois-Chicago	1982	14	13	.519
Southeastern La.	1981	14	13	.519
Western Illinois	1982	14	13	.519
Eastern Illinois	1982	14	13	.519
Gonzaga	1953	15	14	.517

UNIVERSITY	YEAR	W	L	PCT.
Catholic	1977	13	13	.500
Vermont	1962	12	12	.500
St. Peter's	1965	10	10	.500
Texas Tech	1951	14	14	.500
Centenary	1960	12	12	.500
Murray State	1954	15	16	.484
Hofstra	1967	12	13	.480
Tennessee State	1978	11	12	.478
Regis	1962	10	11	.476
Bethune-Cookman	1981	13	15	.464
South Carolina St.	1974	13	15	.464
Mo.-Kansas City	1990	13	15	.464
Southwest Mo. State	1983	13	15	.464
Hardin-Simmons	1951	13	15	.464
San Diego State	1971	12	14	.462
Marist	1982	12	14	.462
Maine	1962	11	13	.458
Fairleigh Dickinson	1968	10	12	.455
Mt. St. Mary's (Md.)	1989	12	15	.444
South Florida	1974	11	14	.440
Md.-Baltimore County	1987	12	16	.429
Coastal Carolina	1987	12	16	.429
Southeast Mo. State	1992	12	16	.429
West Chester	1974	11	15	.423
Howard	1974	11	15	.423
Grambling	1978	10	14	.417
St. Francis (Pa.)	1956	10	14	.417
Northern Illinois	1968	10	14	.417
Texas-El Paso	1951	10	15	.400
Delaware	1958	8	12	.400
Houston	1951	11	17	.393
Cleveland State	1973	9	14	.391
Louisiana Tech	1974	8	13	.381
Ball State	1972	9	15	.375
Rider	1968	9	15	.375
Campbell	1978	9	15	.375
Liberty	1989	10	17	.370
Coppin State	1986	10	17	.370
Southern Utah State	1989	10	18	.357
Central Florida	1985	10	18	.357
Loyola Marymount	1950	9	17	.346
Florida State	1957	9	17	.346
Pacific	1954	9	17	.346
Towson State	1980	9	17	.346
Fresno State	1956	9	17	.346
Middle Tenn. State	1959	9	17	.346
U.S. International	1982	9	18	.333
Western Carolina	1977	8	16	.333
Fla. International	1988	9	19	.321
Portland State	1973	9	19	.321
Texas-Pan American	1969	8	17	.320
UC Irvine	1978	8	17	.320
Jacksonville	1967	8	17	.320
Portland	1954	6	13	.316
Texas-Arlington	1969	8	18	.308
Eastern Michigan	1974	8	18	.308
Texas-San Antonio	1982	8	19	.296
Arizona State	1951	8	19	.296
Northern Arizona	1951	8	19	.296
Northern Iowa	1981	8	19	.296
South Alabama	1972	7	17	.292
Cal State Northridge	1991	8	20	.286
Augusta	1985	8	20	.286
Winthrop	1987	8	20	.286
Central Conn. State	1987	8	21	.276
Providence	1949	7	19	.269
Robert Morris	1977	7	19	.269
Tenn.-Martin	1993	7	19	.269
Hartford	1985	7	21	.250
N.C.-Greensboro	1992	7	21	.250
Evansville*	1978	1	3	.250
Houston Baptist	1974	6	19	.240
Trinity (Tex.)	1971	5	16	.238
Ark.-Little Rock	1979	6	20	.231
Southwest Texas St.	1985	6	20	.231
Stetson	1972	6	20	.231
Monmouth (N.J.)	1984	6	21	.222
Armstrong State	1987	6	22	.214
Nicholls State	1981	6	22	.214
Appalachian State	1974	5	20	.200
Buffalo	1974	5	20	.200
San Diego	1980	5	20	.200
Baptist	1975	4	16	.200
Samford	1973	5	20	.200

Baltimore	1979	4	21	.160
Utica	1982	4	22	.154
Eastern Washington	1984	4	22	.154
Cal St. Sacramento	1992	4	24	.143
North Texas	1958	3	18	.143
New Hampshire	1962	3	20	.130
Wagner	1977	3	21	.125
Miss. Valley State	1980	3	24	.111
Morgan State	1985	3	25	.107
Prairie View	1981	2	22	.083
Pepperdine	1956	2	24	.077
Northeastern Ill.	1991	2	25	.074
Georgia State	1974	1	25	.038

* Evansville's season ended prematurely after a plane crash killed its coach and team.

MOST CONSECUTIVE 20-WIN SEASONS THROUGH 1994

WINS	SCHOOL	YEARS
24	North Carolina	1971–94
14	Kentucky	1945–52, 54–59#
14	Louisville	1971–84
13	Marquette	1967–79
13	UCLA	1967–79
13	Georgetown	1978–90
12	UNLV	1982–93
12	Oklahoma	1982–93
12	Syracuse	1983–94
11	Duke	1984–94
10	Western Kentucky	1934–43
10	North Carolina State	1947–56
9	La Salle	1947–55
9	Louisiana Tech	1984–92
9	Providence	1959–67
9	Arkansas	1977–85

#–Kentucky did not play basketball during the 1953 season.

MOST CONSECUTIVE WINNING SEASONS THROUGH 1994

WINS	SCHOOL	YEARS
46	Louisville	1945–90
46	UCLA	1949–94
38	Kentucky	1928–52, 54–66#
31	St. John's	1923–53
30	Notre Dame	1926–55
30	St. John's	1964–93
30	North Carolina	1965–94
26	Arkansas	1924–49
26	Princeton	1954–79
26	Toledo	1960–85

#–Kentucky did not play basketball during the 1953 season.

MOST CONSECUTIVE NON-LOSING SEASONS (INCLUDES .500 RECORD) THROUGH 1994

WINS	SCHOOL	YEARS
60	Kentucky	1928–52, 54–88# (2 .500 seasons)
47	Louisville	1944–90 (1)
46	UCLA	1949–94
34	Houston	1960–93 (2)
33	Navy	1907–39 (3)
33	Duke	1940–72 (2)
32	Notre Dame	1924–55 (1)
32	Illinois	1929–60 (3)
32	North Carolina	1963–94 (1)
31	St. John's	1923–53
31	Princeton	1954–84 (2)
31	Virginia Tech	1956–86 (2)
30	St. John's	1964–93
26	Arkansas	1924–49
26	Toledo	1960–85

Kentucky did not play basketball during the 1953 season.

TEAMS INELIGIBLE FOR NCAA DIVISION I TOURNAMENT FOR AT LEAST THREE YEARS BECAUSE OF ENFORCEMENT SANCTIONS

(Listed Alphabetically)

Auburn: 1957, 1958, 1959, 1960, 1961, 1980, 1992 (7 years)
Centenary: 1970, 1971, 1973, 1974, 1975, 1976, 1977, 1978 (8)
Cincinnati: 1956, 1979, 1980, 1989 (4)
Clemson: 1976, 1977, 1978 (3)
Florida State: 1969, 1970, 1971 (3)
Illinois: 1968, 1969, 1975, 1991 (4)
Indiana: 1961, 1962, 1963, 1964 (4)
Kansas: 1961, 1962, 1973, 1989 (4)
Kentucky: 1953, 1990, 1991 (3)
Long Beach State: 1974, 1975, 1976 (3)
Louisiana Tech: 1974, 1975, 1976 (3)
Memphis State: 1958, 1959, 1980, 1987 (4)
Minnesota: 1976, 1977, 1978, 1988 (4)
Montana State: 1958, 1960, 1961 (3)
New Mexico State: 1963, 1964, 1973, 1974 (4)
North Carolina State: 1955, 1957, 1958, 1959, 1960, 1973, 1990 (7)
South Carolina: 1967, 1968, 1988 (3)
Texas-Pan American: 1969, 1974, 1975, 1993 (4)
UCLA: 1957, 1958, 1959, 1982 (4)
UNLV: 1978, 1979, 1992 (3)
Western Kentucky: 1973, 1974, 1975 (3)
Wichita State: 1974, 1975, 1982, 1983 (4)

1995 DIVISION I MEN'S TEAMS BY STATE

	NO. OF TEAMS	STATE
1.	20	California
2.	19	New York
	19	Texas
4.	14	North Carolina
	14	Pennsylvania
6.	13	Louisiana
	13	Illinois
	13	Ohio
9.	11	Florida
	11	Virginia
11.	10	Tennessee
12.	9	Maryland
13.	8	South Carolina
	8	Indiana
15.	7	Alabama
	7	New Jersey
17.	6	Kentucky
	6	Mississippi
	6	Michigan
	6	Massachusetts
21.	5	Missouri
	5	Connecticut
	5	Georgia
	5	Utah
25.	4	Wisconsin
	4	District of Columbia
	4	Iowa
	4	Oklahoma
	4	Washington
30.	3	Kansas
	3	Colorado
	3	West Virginia
	3	Arizona
	3	Rhode Island
	3	Idaho
	3	Arkansas
	3	Oregon
38.	2	Delaware
	2	New Mexico
	2	New Hampshire
	2	Nevada
	2	Montana
	2	Nebraska
45.	1	Maine
	1	Hawaii
	1	Vermont
	1	Minnesota
	1	Wyoming
49.	0	Alaska
	0	North Dakota
	0	South Dakota

HOW PLAYING RULES DIFFER

CATEGORY	LEAGUE
Bonus Free Throw	**COLLEGE:** 7th team foul per half* **INTL:** 8th team foul per half **NBA:** 5th team foul per quarter
Game Duration	**COLLEGE:** Two 20-minute halves **INTL:** Two 20-minute halves **NBA:** Four 12-minute quarters
Lane Width at Baseline	**COLLEGE:** 12' (rectangle) **INTL:** 19'8.2" (trapezoid) **NBA:** 16' (rectangle)
Number of Timeouts	**COLLEGE:** Five per game (not including TV timeouts) **INTL.:** Two per half **NBA:** Seven per game
Player Foul Limit	**COLLEGE:** Five personals **INTL.:** Five personals **NBA:** Six personals
Shot Clock	**COLLEGE:** 35 seconds **INTL.:** 30 seconds **NBA:** 24 seconds
Three-Point Distance	**COLLEGE:** 19'9" **INTL.:** 20'6.1" **NBA:** 23'9"

* Beginning with tenth foul per half, player shoots two free throws.

SHOE WARS

Many schools have contracts with sneaker companies to wear their products exclusively. Which companies benefitted the most from Final Four exposure since the playoff field expanded to 64 teams in 1985?

1985: Nike 4 (Georgetown, Memphis State, St. John's, Villanova).
1986: Converse 2 (Louisville, LSU), Adidas 1 (Duke), Puma 1 (Kansas).
1987: Nike 2 (Syracuse, UNLV), Adidas 1 (Indiana), Converse 1 (Provience).
1988: Nike 2 (Arizona, Kansas), Converse 1 (Oklahoma), Adidas 1 (Duke).
1989: Nike 2 (Michigan, Seton Hall), Adidas 1 (Duke), Converse 1 (Illinois).
1990: Nike 2 (Georgia Tech, UNLV), Adidas 1 (Duke), Converse 1 (Arkansas).
1991: Converse 2 (Kansas, North Carolina), Adidas 1 (Duke), Nike 1 (UNLV).
1992: Adidas 2 (Duke, Indiana), Nike 2 (Cincinnati, Michigan).
1993: Converse 3 (Kansas, Kentucky, North Carolina), Nike 1 (Michigan).
1994: Nike 2 (Arizona, Duke), Converse 1 (Arkansas), Reebok 1 (Florida).

Final Four Totals (1985–94): Nike 18, Converse 12, Adidas 8, Puma 1, Reebok 1.

PHOTO CREDITS

Photographs appearing in *Encyclopedia of College Basketball* were received from the following sources:

Bradley University, 240; City College of New York, 360; Dartmouth College, 46; DePaul University, 41, 222; Duke University, 268, 312 (left); Furman University, 67; Georgia Institute of Technology, 100, 254, 257 (right), 295, 391; Indiana University, 179 (left), 235, 269; Jacksonville University, 151; Kansas State University, 541; La Salle University, 68 (left), 363 (right); Louisiana State University, photo by John Titchen, Star Bulletin Photo, 143; Louisiana Tech University, 321 (left), 435, 464; Loyola Marymount University, 253; Marquette University, 184, 186, 190, 301 (bottom), 318, 364; Michigan State University, 193, 194, 384, 395, 403 (right); National Association of Intercollegiate Athletics, 446, 450, 453, 454, 457; Niagara University, 149; North Atlantic Conference, 247; North Carolina State University, 170 (left), 255, 333, 465; North Carolina State University, photo copyright Burnie Batchelor Studio, Inc., 90; North Carolina State University, photo by Simon Griffiths, 370 (top); Northeastern University, photo by J. D. Levine, 339; Oral Roberts University, 156; Oregon

State University, 358; Pennsylvania State University, 68 (right); Princeton University, 411; Providence College, 129, 290, 415; Providence College, photos by Thomas Maguire, Jr. 164, 167; Purdue University, 13, 106, 146, 278, 399; Purdue University, photo copyright Laughead Photographers, 396 (top); Rutgers, The State University of New Jersey, photo by Dean Nathans / *Scarlet Letter*, 179 (right); Rutgers, The State University of New Jersey, photo by F. J. Higgins, 370 (bottom); St. Bonaventure University, 137 (left); St. Joseph's University, 103; St. Louis University, 287; Southeastern Louisiana University, 430; Stanford University, 15, 34, 400; Syracuse University, 297 (bottom), 543; Syracuse University, photo by Stephen Parker 236; Temple University Libraries Photojournalism Collection, 462; United States Military Academy, 350; University of Alabama-Birmingham, 345; University of Arizona, 207, 304, 381 (right); University of California, 275; University of California, Los Angeles (UCLA), 117, 123, 125, 132, 136, 153, 159, 170 (right), 173, 294, 297 (top), 308, 323, 336 (left), 336 (right), 338, 355, 371, 419, 426, 442, 538; University of California, Los Angeles (UCLA), photo by Norm Schindler, 337 (bottom); University of Cincinnati, 89, 266; University of Connecticut, 279, 321 (right), 412; University of Dayton, photo by Ed Morris Photography, 130 (left); University of Denver, 410; University of Florida, 368; University of Houston, 130 (right), 137 (right), 214, 217, 230, 311, 326, 363 (left), 461; University of Idaho, 113; University of Illinois, 375 (bottom), 396 (bottom), 407, 416; University of Iowa, 456; University of Kansas, 2, 80 (right), 80 (left), 244, 337 (top), 353; University of Louisville, 143, 201, 232, 305 (middle), 335, 347, 557; University of Maryland, 375, 417; University of Miami, 120; University of Mississippi, 377, 380, 381 (left); University of Nevada, Las Vegas, 257 (left), 260, 262; University of North Carolina, 409, 432; University of Oklahoma, 226; University of Oregon, 28, 291; University of Tennessee, 177, 182, 215, 305 (top), 312 (right), 317, 388, 394, 406; University of Texas at El Paso, 349; University of Utah, 39, 305 (right); University of Virginia, 330, 390, 438; University of Wisconsin, 403 (left); University of Wyoming, 36, 553; Vanderbilt University, 246; Villanova University, 437; Wake Forest University, 73, 96, 301 (top); West Virginia University, 79, 92; West Virginia University, photo copyright Laughead Photographers, 334; Western Kentucky University, 288; Wichita State University, 110.

School logos appear courtesy of the individual school or conference.

INDEX

This index includes all persons, associations, leagues, and teams appearing in all sections of the encyclopedia except for box scores, individual and team statistics boxes, long lists of names, and material of a general statistical nature. *Italicized numerals* denote references to photos. **Boldfaced numerals** denote an entire section devoted to that subject.

A

AAU. *See* Amateur Athletic Union (AAU)
AAWU. *See* Athletic Association of Western Universities (AAWU)
Abdul-Jabbar, Kareem. *See* Alcindor, Lew
Abdul-Rahmad, Mahdi. *See* Hazzard, Walt
Abdul-Rauf, Mahmoud. *See* Jackson, Chris
Abernethy, Tom, 174
ABFUSA. *See* Amateur Basketball Federation of the United States of America (ABFUSA)
Aces. *See* Evansville
Accounting Hall of Fame, 411
Acre, Mark, 373
Actwood, Walter, 519
Adair, Jerry, 373
Adams, Robert B., 410
Adcock, Joe, 373
Adkins, David, *410*, 410
AFC. *See* American Football Conference (AFC)
African-American coaches, 156, 162, 182

African-American players, issue of, 12, 53, 126–27, 55, 391, 412
Aggies. *See* New Mexico State; Texas A&M; Utah State
Aguirre, Mark, 294, 509, 539
AIAW. *See* Association of Intercollegiate Athletics for Women (AIAW)
Ainge, Danny, 294, 500, 506, 539
Air Force Academy, 75, 503
Akron Goodyears, 320
Akron Pros, 418
Alabama, University of, 75, 129, 134, 249, 503
    in NCAA tournament, 178, 180
Alabama-Birmingham, University of, 211, 503
Alarie, Mark, 232
Alaska-Anchorage, University of, 250
Alcindor, Lew, *125*, 125, 129, 131, *132*, *137*, 141, 151, 161, *294*
    player of the year award, 538
    profile, 294
Alcorn, Gary, 511
Alcorn State, 201, 504
Alford, Sam, 454
Alford, Steve, *235*, 295, 454
All-America Team, 9
All-Border Conference, 27
All-Southwest Conference, 33
All-Yankee Conference, 412

Allen, Bob, 31
Allen, Forrest "Phog," 10, 12, 27, 31, 60, 76, *80*, 365, 368, 455
    profile, 353
Allen, Lucius, 125, 136, 295
Allums, Darrell, 202
Almon, Bill, 374
Alston, Walter, 374
Altman, George, 374
Amaker, Tommy 232
Amateur Athletic Union (AAU), 6, 10, 113, 407, 422, 423, 459
Amateur Basketball Federation of the United States of America, 459
AMCU. *See* Association of Mid-Continent Universities (AMCU)
American Basketball League, 319, 371
American College of Surgeons, 414
American Football Conference (AFC), 395, 397, 401, 402, 403
American League, 15, 38
American Red Cross, 38
American South Conference, 240, 501
American University, 140, 262
Ames, Bob, 410
Ames College, 9
Amherst College, 8
Amling, Warren, 388
Amos, Craig, 527
Andersen, Ladell, 346
Anderson, Cliff, 527
Anderson, Eric, 269
Anderson, Forddy, 354
Anderson, Joe, 526
Anderson, John, 7
Anderson, Ken (football player), 388
Anderson, Kenny (basketball player), 253, *254*, 255, 260, *295*, 295
Anderson, Mitchell, 209
Anderson, Nick, 250
Anderson, Ron, 447
Anderson, W. H., 4
Andreas, Lew, 13, 354
Angell, Emmett, 7
Anteaters. *See* California-Irvine, University of
Anthony, Greg, 260
Antinelli, Al, 59
AP coach of the year awards. *See* National coach of the year awards (1955–94)
AP player of the year awards. *See* National player of the year awards (1955–94)

AP polls. *See* National polls
Archibald, Nate (Tiny), 295, 447
Archibald, Nolan, 410, 446
Ardon, Jack, 532
Arizin, Paul, 50, 52, 53, 225, 295
Arizona, University of, 56, 60, 240, 265, 281
    in NCAA tournament, 179, 250, 269, 274
    profile, 504
Arizona State University, 66, 105, 204, 214, 249
    in NCAA tournament, 205–6
    profile, 504
Arkansas, University of, 33, 38, 49, 205, 220, 232
    in NCAA tournament, 43, 189, 191, 205, 279–81
    profile, 504
Arkansas-Little Rock, University of, 232, 504
Arkansas State University, 42, 279
Army, 8, 12, 39, 40, 152
    profile, 504
Army Athletic Association, 396
Arnelle, Jesse, 67, *68*, 410, 524
Artman, Bob, 25
Ashmore, Jim, 80
Assists leaders (individuals)
    1983–84 – 1988–89, 221, 227, 231, 237, 241, 248
    1989–90 – 1993–94, 256, 261, 267, 273, 280
Associated Press (AP) coach of the year awards. *See* National coach of the year awards (1955–94)
Associated Press (AP) player of the year awards. *See* National player of the year awards (1955–94)
Associated Press (AP) polls. *See* National polls
Associated Press (AP) Women's Basketball Poll, 425
Association of Intercollegiate Athletics for Women (AAWU), 424
Association of Mid-Continent Universities (AMCU), 214, 483
Athletic Association of Western Universities (AAWU), 127, 490, 538
Athletic scholarships (women's), 425
Atkins, Doug, *388*, 388
Atlanta Braves, 375, 376, 380, 384, 385, 387
Atlanta Falcons, 403
Atlanta Hawks, 313, 316, 318, 321, 335, 388, 416
Atlantic Coast Conference (ACC), 66, 103, 125, 134, 145, 167, 173, 188, 199, 204, 217, 222, 225, 235, 275, 281, 290, 347, 348, 350, 352, 355, 360, 390, 429, 433, 435, 438, 467
    tournament, 96, 126, 142, 246, 263, 276
    profile, 469
Atlantic 10 Conference, 182, 220, 290, 346, 347
    profile, 470

Bengals. *See* Idaho State
Bennett, Tony, 483, 535
Benson, Kent, 174, 178, 297
Benton, Eddie, 279
Benton, Jim, 390
Berenson, Senda, 421
Berger, Louis (Bozey), *374,* 374
Berlin Olympic games. *See* Olympics (men's
    basketball team)—1936
Berman, Arnie, 506
Berry, Ricky, 528
Berry, Walter, 297, 539
Bethune-Cookman, 260
Bias, Len, 230, 518, 297
Bibby, Henry, *297,* 297
Big East Conference, 228, 232, 242, 254, 262, 269,
    275, 281, 290, 346, 353, 418, 437, 467
    debut as conference, 199
    profile, 471
    tournament, 236, 246
Big Eight Conference, 53, 84, 108, 115, 156, 235, 242,
    243, 250, 269, 279, 290, 352, 353, 355, 367, 429, 439,
    467
    holiday tournament, 111
    profile, 472
Big Five Hall of Fame, 437
Big Green. *See* Dartmouth
"Big Nasty," 280
Big Nine, 53
Big Red. *See* Cornell
Big Seven Conference, 49, 56, 61, 404, 416, 472, 501
Big Six Conference, 27, 34, 404, 406, 472
Big Sky Conference, 115, 161, 410, 473
Big South Conference, 230, 274, 474
Big Ten Conference, 8, 31, 32, 36, 42, 43, 44, 45, 47,
    56, 67, 71, 75, 100, 105, 122, 146, 157, 172, 177, 179,
    182, 184, 185, 188, 200, 202, 204, 206, 225, 242, 246,
    250, 255, 269, 278, 281, 290, 328, 350, 367, 375, 388,
    391, 394, 395, 396, 401, 405, 406, 407, 414, 416, 429,
    433, 443, 468
    profile, 475
Big 12 Conference, 472
Big West Conference, 145, 265, 369, 476
Biles, Willie, 161
Billikens. *See* St. Louis
Bing, Dave, *297,* 297
Bird, Larry, 145, 182, 193, 194, 289, 459, 514
    player of the year award, 539
    profile, 297
Birdsong, Otis, 183, 275, 298
Bison. *See* Bucknell

Black, Charles, 25, 298
Black, W. O., 4
Black Athletic Clubs, 12
Black Coaches Association (BCA), 199
Black Knights. *See* Army
Blackbirds. *See* Long Island
Blackman, Rolando, 298
Blaik, Red, 396, 399
Blanton, Ricky, 247
Blaylock, Mookie, 240, 243, 447
Blazejowski, Carol, 426, 432
Blazers. *See* Alabama-Birmingham
"The Blind Bomber," 30
Block, John, 125
Blocked shots leaders (individuals)
    1985–86 – 1988–89, 231, 237, 241, 248
    1989–90 – 1993–94, 256, 261, 267, 273, 280
Blue Demons. *See* DePaul
Blue Devils. *See* Duke
Blue Raiders. *See* Middle Tennessee State
Bluejays. *See* Creighton
Blundin, Matt, *390,* 390
Blunt, Bernard, 527
Blye, Sylvester, 100
Bobcats. *See* Montana State; Ohio
Boeheim, Jim, 351, 346
Boilermakers. *See* Purdue
Bond, Phillip, 173
Bonham, Ron, 298
Bonner, Anthony, 254, 527
Bonnies. *See* St. Bonaventure
Bonus shots, 62, 71
Boone, Ron, 447, 298
Booth, Albie, 390
Boozer, Bob, 298
Borcherding, Jim, 388
Border Conference, 56, 57, 419, 501
Bork, George, 390
Born, B. H., 64
Boryla, Vince, 298
Bossert, Gary, 235
Boston Braves, 374, 376, 380, 388
Boston Celtics, 54, 79, 149, 179, 294, 297, 298, 301,
    302, 307, 310, 311, 316, 318, 320, 322, 324, 327, 329,
    331, 337, 338, 361, 376, 378, 448
Boston College, 211, 278, 280, 281, 505
Boston Red Sox, 373, 374, 375, 376, 378, 379, 380,
    382, 384, 385, 386, 387
Boston Redskins, 389
Boswell, Cathy, 433
Boudreau, Lou, 27, *375,* 375

Cain, Carl, 300
Caldwell, Joe, 300
Calhoun, Corky, 154
Calhoun, Jim, 542
California, University of, 10, 12, 91, 422
    in NCAA tournament, 88–89, 96, 275
    profile, 506
California Angels, 374, 378, 384, 386, 388
California Basketball Association, 62, 499
California Collegiate Athletic Association, 408
California-Irvine, University of, 204, 209, 506
California-Los Angeles, University of. *See* UCLA
California-Santa Barbara, University of, 507
California State University, Fullerton, 189, 507
California State University, Long Beach, 154, 163,
    166, 172, 177, 183
Calipari, John, 456
Calloway, Wayne, 412
Calverley, Ernie, 39
Calvin, Mack, 447
Camp Grant, 37, 40
Camp Lejeune, 44
Campbell, Elden, 508
Campbell, Joe, 406
Campion, Bill, 517
Canadian Football League, 389, 394, 398, 402
Canadian Football League Hall of Fame, 390, 402,
    405, 447
Canadian Olympic team (1984), 438
Canisius College, 77, 177, 182, 507
Cann, Howard, 11, 13, 84
Canton Bulldogs, 398
Capua, Joe, 75
Cardwell, Mark, 452
Carey, Bob, 391
Carey, Jim, 448
Cardinal. *See* Stanford
Cardinals. *See* Ball State; Lamar; Louisville
Carlesimo, Pete, 289
Carlesimo, P. J., 289, 541
Carlson, Doc, 11
Carlton, Jerry, 105
Carmichael, Harold, 391
Carnesecca, Lou, 125, 266, 355, 541
Carney, Chuck, 391
Carr, Antoine, 214
Carr, Austin, 149, 151, 300, 522, 538
Carr, M. L., 451, 455
Carrabino, Joe, 512
Carril, Pete, 346
Carroll, Joe Barry, 300, 525

Cartwright, Bill, 300, 527
Casares, Rick, 391
Case, Everett, 88, *90,* 121, 355
Casey, Mike, 149
Cash, James, 129, 412
Cassell, Sam, 272, 447
Cassidy, Ted, 412
Castellani, John, 80
Catholic University, 262
Catledge, Terry, 528
Catlett, Gale, 346, 392
Cavaliers. *See* Virginia
CCNY. *See* City College of New York (CCNY)
Ceballos, Cedric, 447
Centenary College, 134, 151, 161, 166, 172, 177, 182,
    188, 240
Central Arkansas, University of, 455
Central Michigan University, 507
Cerkvenik, Tony, 504
Cerv, Bob, 375
Chalk, Leroy, 520
Chamberlain, Wilt, 53, 76, 79, *80,* 81, 84, 377, 385
    profile, 300
Chambers, Bill, 63
Chambers, Jerry, 127
Chambers, Tom, 300
Championship brackets. *See* National Collegiate
    Athletic Association (NCAA) championship
    brackets
Chanay, Larry, 520
Chandler, Happy, 26
Chaney, Don, *130*
Chaney, John, 347, 541
Chapman, Roosevelt, 223, 509
Chappell, Len, 105, *301,* 301
Charles, Lorenzo, 216
Charleston, University of, 75, 254
Charlotte Hornets, 315, 324, 328
Cheaney, Calbert, *69,* 269, 301, 475, 514, 539
Chicago, University of, 5, 8, 9, 63
Chicago Bears, 382, 388, 389, 390, 391, 392, 393, 394,
    396, 397, 399, 400, 402, 403, 404, 409
Chicago Bulls, 302, 307, 309, 310, 316, 317, 319, 322,
    330, 333, 370, 412, 455
Chicago Cardinals, 400, 402, 404
Chicago Cubs, 374, 375, 378, 380, 383, 384, 385, 386,
    387, 412
Chicago Hornets, 402
Chicago Packers, 296, 301, 316
Chicago Rockets, 397, 402
Chicago Stags, 296, 301, 323, 366

Chicago Staleys, 396

Chicago State University, 230

Chicago Tribune, 47

Chicago White Sox, 373, 374, 376, 378, 379, 380, 382, 384, 386, 387

Chicago Zephyrs, 304, 320

Chievous, Derrick, 520

Childress, Randy, 272

Chilton, Tom, 100

China, 4

Chippewas. *See* Central Michigan

Chones, Jim, 158, *301,* 301

Christian, Jarvis, 214

Christy Walsh Syndicate, 387, 408

Chubin, Steve, 525

Cincinnati, University of, 57, 75, 103, 111, 115, 193, 209, 265
    in NCAA tournament, 89, 97, 101–2, 107–8, 112–13, 126–27, 184
    profile 507

Cincinnati Bengals, 388

Cincinnati Reds, 374, 376, 377, 378, 379, 380, 382, 383, 384, 385, 386, 387

Cincinnati Royals, 295, 298, 304, 306, 311, 313, 319, 328, 333, 339, 384

Citadel, The, 75, 249, 265, 507

City College of New York (CCNY), 7, 11, 12, 13, 15, 16, 57, 285, 286
    in NCAA tournament, 47, 55–56

Civil Rights Restoration Act, 430

Clancy, Sam, 524, 392

Clark, Arlen, 88

Clark, Earl (Dutch), 392

Clark, Mark, 394

Clark, Perry, 542

Clary, Marty, 375

Clay, Dwight, 161, 167

Cleamons, Jim, 147

Clemson Athletic Hall of Fame, 435

Clemson University, 27, 134, 177, 182, 188, 254
    in NCAA tournament, 236
    profile, 507

Cleveland Browns, 388, 389, 390, 391, 392, 393, 395, 399, 401, 402, 403

Cleveland Cavaliers, 299, 300, 301, 303, 306, 315, 319, 323, 327

Cleveland Indians, 374, 375, 378, 379, 380, 381, 382, 383, 385, 386, 387, 388

Cleveland Pipers, 319

Cleveland Rams, 390, 392, 397

Cleveland Rebels, 374

Cleveland Rosenblums, 12

Cleveland State University, 232, 278, 508

Cline, Nancy Lieberman. *See* Lieberman Cline, Nancy

Clinton, Bill, 413, 414, 416

CNN polls. *See* National polls

Coach directory, **345–71**

Coach of the year awards (1955–94), 540–42

Coastal Carolina University, 274

Cody, Josh, 363

Cofield, Bill, 182

Cohen, Fred, 77

Cohen, Jeff, 101, 301, 535

Cohen, Sid, 446

Cole, Robert, 516

Coleman, Derrick, *236,* 238, 301, *543,* 530

Coles, Vernel "Bimbo," 480, 534

Colgate University, 50, 204, 508

College Football Hall of Fame, 388, 389, 390, 391, 392, 393, 394, 395, 396, 397, 398, 399, 400, 401, 404, 406

College Sports Information Directors of America, 502

College World Series, 309

Collegiate Commissioners Association, 288, 297, 350

Collins, Bruce, 534

Collins, Chris, 280

Collins, Craig, 225

Collins, Doug, 156, 280, 301, 513

Collins, Lee, 528

Colonels. *See* Eastern Kentucky

Colonial Athletic Association, 214, 275, 348, 383, 477

Colonials. *See* George Washington; Robert Morris

Colorado, University of, 34, 108, 290, 429, 508

Colorado State University, 508

Columbia College of Pharmacy, 12

Columbia University, 8, 9, 12, 15, 57
    in NCAA tournament, 49, 58
    profile, 508

Combes, Harry, 356

Comey, Dale, *412,* 412

Commission on Intercollegiate Athletics for Women, 424

Commodores. *See* Vanderbilt

Community College League of California, 502

Condie, Lyman, 41

Conference directory, **467–502**

Conferences, formation of, 8

Conley, Gene, 54, 376

Conlin, Ed, 511
Connecticut, University of, 71, 272, 278, 290, 508
   in NCAA tournament, 77
Conner, Jimmy Dan, 174
Connor, George, 392
Connors, Kevin (Chuck), 412
Connors, Mike, 412
The Conquering Heroes, 395
Conradt, Jody, 440, 441, 443
Converse All-American Team, 27
Converse Basketball Yearbook, 43
Converse-Dunkel Ratings, 39–40
Cooley, Denton, 413
Cooper, Michael, 189, 447
Coppin State University, 289
Corbin, Max, 28
Corley, Bill, 57
Cornelius, Ron, 524
Cornell University, 5, 129, 509
Cornhuskers. *See* Nebraska
Corpus Christi NAS, 37
Corzine, Dave, 189, 509
Cosic, Kresimir, 156, 413
Costello, Larry, 63
Cougars. *See* Brigham Young University; Houston;
   Washington State
Coughran, John, 156
Counts, Mel, 523
Cousy, Bob, 49, 54, 55, 301
Cowan, Charlie, 392
Cowboys. *See* Oklahoma State; Wyoming
Cowden, Bill, 35
Cowens, Dave, 149, 511, 302
Cox, Johnny, 302
Cox, Phil, 533
Craig, Roger, 376
Crawford Stanley, Marianne. *See* Stanley, Marianne
   Crawford
Creech, Len, 533
Creighton University, 10, 12, 129, 509
Cremins, Bobby, 145, 274, 374, 542
Cribbs, Claire, 302
Crichton, Michael, 413
Crimson. *See* Harvard
Crimson Tide. *See* Alabama
Crisler, Herbert (Fritz), 392
Crosthwaite, Ralph, 535
Crum, Denny, 157, *347, 347,* 447, *557*
Crusaders. *See* Holy Cross
Culberson, Dick, 42
Cummings, Terry, 302

Cunningham, Billy, 302
Cunningham, Gary, 348
Cuomo, Mario, 410
Curry, Denise, 433
Curtright, Guy, 376
Cyclones. *See* Iowa State

D

Dabney, Mike, 179
Dailey, Quintin, 302
Dallas Chaparrals, 298, 412
Dallas Cowboys, 391, 393, 394, 395, 397, 402, 404,
   406
Dallas Diamonds, 434, 435
Dallas Mavericks, 294, 295, 298, 305, 314, 316, 322,
   327
Dallas Texans, 393
Dallmar, Howie, 35, 172
Daly, Chuck 351
Dampier, Louie, 302
Danforth, Roy, 346
Daniel, Ken, 525
Daniels, Mel, 302
Dantley, Adrian, 303, 462, 538
Danzig, Hal, 506
Dare, Yinka, 156
Darling, Chuck, 303
Dartmouth College, 32, 39, 47, 278
   in NCAA tournament, 33, 35, 40
   profile, 509
Daugherty, Brad, 303
Davidson College, 134, 148, 161, 509
Davies, Bob, 45, 303
Davies, Charles (Chick), 49, 356
Davis, Charlie, 140
Davis, Clarissa, 429
Davis, Ernie, 392
Davis, Glenn, 393
Davis, Lardie, 34
Davis, Larry, 34
Davis, Tom, *456,* 484, 541
Davis, Walter, 166, 303
Davis, Walter (Buddy), 407
Davis & Elkins College, 11
Davis Cup, 408, 409
Davis-Wrightsil, Clarissa, 433
Dawkins, Johnny, 232, 303, 469, 510, 539
Dawson, Len, 393
Day, Todd, 504
Daye, Darren, 202

Dayton, University of, 10, 63, 84, 286, 292
   in NCAA tournament, 131, 169, 223
   profile, 509
Dean, Everett, *34, 35,* 354, 356
Dean, Hal, 413
DeBernardi, Forrest S., 12
DeBusschere, Dave, 107, 303, 510
Decatur Staleys, 396
Dee, Johnny, 75
Dees, Archie, 304
Defensive field goal percentage leaders (team)
   1989–90 – 1990–91, 256, 261
   1993–94, 281
DeHart, Carrick, 507
Dehere, Terry, 471, 528
Dell Basketball Magazine, 379
Delph, Marvin, 191
Delta State University, 424
Dembo, Fennis, 536, *553*
Demon Deacons. *See* Wake Forest
Den Herder, Vern, 393
Dennis, Greg, 510
Denver, University of, 26, 182
Denver Broncos, 399, 400, 405
Denver Nuggets, 309, 314, 333, 419
Denver Rockets, 311
DePaul University, 26, 27, 40, 42, 43, 49, 77, 201, 220, 289, 292
   in NCAA tournament, 189, 202, 205–6, 211
   profile, 509
Detroit, University of. *See* Detroit-Mercy, University of
Detroit Lions, 389, 398, 402, 420
Detroit Mercy, University of, 156, 242, 510
Detroit Pistons, 149, 297, 299, 300, 303, 304, 312, 313, 318, 333, 334, 335, 336, 384
Detroit Tigers, 374, 375, 376, 377, 379, 380, 382, 387
Deveraux, John, 522
DeVries, Ron, 513
Dick, John, 29, 413
Dickens, Anthony, 526
Dickey, Dick, 49
Dickey, Jay, 413
Diddle, Ed, 66, 116, *288,* 356, 365
Didrikson, Babe, 423
DiGregorio, Ernie, 163, *164,* 304
Dischinger, Terry, 105, *106,* 304
Ditka, Mike, 393
Division II, 37, 204, 448–51, 452–57
Division III, 448–51, 452–57
Divisions, creation of, 451

Dobard, Rodney, 272
Dole, Robert J., 413
Dolphins. *See* Jacksonville
Donovan, Anne, 425, 434
Dons. *See* San Francisco
Dooley, Vince, 393
Douglas, James (Buster), 407
Douglas, Leon, 180
Downey, Dave, 111
Downing, Steve, 162
Downs, Raymond, 71, 75
Drake, Bruce, 357, 367
Drake University, 9, 141, 200, 510
"Dream Team," 459, 463
Drexel University, 279
Drexler, Clyde, *214,* 214, 217, 304
Dribble, 5, 9, 10, 12, 423
Driesell, Charles (Lefty), 105, 148, 230, 346, 360
   profile, 348
Driscoll, Terry, 505
Dropo, Walt, 376
Drury, 43
Drysdale, Don, 436
Ducks. *See* Duquesne; James Madison; Oregon
Dudley, Raymond, 503
Dugger, Jack, 393
Duke University, 26, 30, 32, 56, 105, 121, 126, 134, 135, 140, 145, 161, 199, 240, 246, 247, 255, 260, 265, 272, 276
   in NCAA tournament, 116–17, 188, 191, 195–96, 232–33, 242–43, 257, 262–63, 266, 268–70, 274–75, 279–81
   profile, 510
Dukes, Walter, 63, 304, 528
Dukiet, Bob, 201
Duluth Eskimos, 400
Dumars, Joe, 304
Dunk shot, 182
Dunkel, Dick, 396
Dunkel Ratings, 36
Dunkin, Tony, 274, 474
Duquesne University, 15, 17, 26, 49, 55, 134, 142, 286
   profile, 510
Durham, Hugh, 348
Durham, Pat, 508
Durno, Eddie, 413
Dykstra, Joe, 209

E

Eagles. *See* Boston College; Eastern Michigan

Grant, Harvey, 447
Grant, Josh, 533
Grant, Travis "Machine Gun," 452, 454
Grate, Don, 45, 308
Graves, Butch, 536
Graves, Ray, 507
Grayer, Jeff, 514
Grayson, Doug, 129
Great Lakes NTS, 37, 40, 42
Great Midwest Conference, 265, 468, 478
Green, Cornell, 108, 395, 533
Green, Dallas, 377
Green, Litterial, 512
Green, Mike, 517
Green, Rickey, 308
Green, Si, 309
Green, Sidney, 532
Green Bay Packers, 394, 397, 398, 403, 405, 406
Green Wave. *See* Tulane
Greenberg, Mel, 425
Greenwood, David, 309
Greer, Hal, 309
Greer, Hugh, 111, 358
Gregory, Claude, 535
Gregory, George, 12
Grekin, Norm 67, 308
Grentz, Theresa Shank. *See* Shank Grentz, Theresa
Grevey, Kevin, 174
Grey Cup, 406
Grider, Joshua, 453
Griese, Bob, *396*, 396
Griffin, Paul, 535
Griffin, Rod, 309
Griffith, Darrell, 201, *201*, 309, *309*, 517, 539
Grimsley, Lou, 448
Grizzlies. *See* Montana
Groat, Dick, 59, 309, 377
Grooms, Trent, 515
Groza, Alex, 26, 42, 45, 49, 50
    profile, 309
Grubar, Dick, 142
Grunfeld, Ernie, *177*, 177
GTE Academic All-American Hall of Fame, 439
Guilford College, 454
Gulf South Classic, 125
Gulf South Conference, 400, 501
Gulick, Luther, 6
Gunter, Sue, 440
Guziak, Ron, 134
Gwynn, Tony, 378

H

Haderlein, Jim, 517
Haffner, Scott, 249
Hagan, Cliff, 67, 310
Hagan, Jimmy, 531
Hagan, Joe, 26
Hagan, Tom, 140
Halas, George, *396*, 396
Halbrook, Wade "Swede," 67, 71
Halicki, Ed, 378
Hall, Dale, 39, 310, 396
Hall, Joe B., 225, 358, 455
Hall, Ray, 507
Halsel, Mark, 522
Hamilton, Lee H., 415
Hamilton, Leonard, 235
Hamilton, Lowell, 250
Hamilton, Roy, 184
Hamilton, Steve, 79, 378
Hamline College, 5, 50
Hammaker, Atlee, 378
Hampton Institute, 12, 243
Handlan, Jay, 56
Hankins, Cecil, 42
Hankins, Norm, 47
Hankins, Steve, 455
Hankinson, Phil, 154
Hannon, Bill, 59
Hanson, Victor A., 12, 396
Hardaway, Anfernee, 310
Hardaway, Tim, 531
Hardin, Wayne, 396
Hardy, Kevin, 396
Harkness, Jerry, 310
Harlem Globetrotters, 59, 300, 304, 377, 416, 426,
    439, 445, 449, 453
Harmon, Chuck, 378
Harmon, Tom, 396
Harp, Dick, *80, 82*, 352, 367
Harper, Jerilynn, 434
Harper, Jerry, 75, 503
Harper, Ron, 482, 518
Harrell, Billy, 378
Harrick, Jim, 456, 348
Harrington, Tom 88
Harris, Gene, 105
Harris, Janet, 428, 434
Harris, Lucious, 476, 516
Harris, Steve, 532
Harris Stewart, Lusia, 424, 433, 434, 443

International Tennis Hall of Fame, 409
Interracial games, 82, 88
Interstate Intercollegiate Athletic Conference, 390
Invention of basketball, 1–2
IOC. *See* International Olympic Committee (IOC)
Iona College, 129, 514
Iowa, University of, 5, 8, 12, 42, 47, 115, 146, 200, 201, 206, 236, 249, 272, 290
    in NCAA tournament, 77, 201, 206
    profile, 514
Iowa Girls High School Athletic Union, 423
Iowa State University, 9, 54, 79, 235, 279
    in NCAA tournament, 269
    profile, 514
Ireland, George, 361
Irish, Ned, 14, 15, 16
Irving, Drederick, 505
Isaac, Warren, 514
Issel, Dan, 146, 149, 314, 388, 515
Italian League, 434
Ivy League Conference, 7, 32, 39, 56, 79, 84, 172, 201, 346, 414, 445, 467
    profile, 479

J

Jackson, Bo, 373
Jackson, Chris, 247, 314
Jackson, Greg, 455
Jackson, Jim, 314, 539
Jackson, Keith, 242
Jackson, Luke, *450*, 452
Jackson, Mannie, *416*, 416
Jackson, Michael, 221
Jackson, Ray, 265
Jackson, Reggie, 388
Jackson, Ron, 379
Jackson, Tony, 314
Jackson, Willie, 498
Jackson State University, 265
Jacksonville University, 147, 149, 151, 153, 514
Jaguars. *See* South Alabama; Southern
Jakubick, Joe, 220, 489
Jamerson, Dave, 254, 522
James Madison University, 211, 515
Japan, 4
Jaspers. *See* Manhattan
Jaworski, Chester (Chet), 314
Jayhawks. *See* Kansas
Jenkins, Buck, 508
Jennings, Keith "Mister," 262

John, Maury, 540
John Bunn Award, 443
Johnson, Avery, 240, 447
Johnson, Dave, 379
Johnson, Dennis, 314, 447
Johnson, Earvin "Magic," 145, 191, *193*, 193, 194, 428, 459
    profile, 315
Johnson, Eddie, 315
Johnson, Ellis, 57
Johnson, Ervin, 521
Johnson, Evelyn, 428
Johnson, George, 526
Johnson, Gus, *113*, 315, 447
Johnson, John, *146*, 146
Johnson, Johnny, 397
Johnson, Kevin, 315
Johnson, Larry, *260*, 260, 263, 315, 447, 504, 539
Johnson, Marques, 315, 539
Johnson, Rafer, 407
Johnson, Steve, 204, 315
Johnson, Vinnie, 194, 447
Jones, Albert "Slab," 521
Jones, Askia, 279
Jones, Ben, 38
Jones, Billy, 125
Jones, Dana, 524
Jones, Danny, 535
Jones, Ed (Too Tall), 397
Jones, Jeff, 290
Jones, K. C., 72, 77, 316
Jones, Major, 455
Jones, Reggie, 503
Jones, Ronald "Popeye," 520
Jones, Wallace "Wah Wah," 45, 49
Jordan, Eddie, 179
Jordan, Michael, 210, 222, 373, 459
    player of the year award, 539
    profile, 316
Jordan, Ralph (Shug), 398
Josephson, Duane, 380
Jourdet, Lou, 34
Joyner-Kersee, Jackie, 428
Jucker, Ed, 102, 113, 361, 381, 540
"Juco." *See* Junior colleges
Judson, Howie, 380
Julian, Alvin (Doggie), *46*, 47, 361, 364
Jump balls, 151, 172
Junior colleges, 445

K

Kaeding, Jim, 452

Kaeding, Wayne, 452

Kaftan, George, 46, 316

Kaiser, Roger, *100*, 316

Kansas, University of, 8, 10, 25, 27, 34, 84, 161, 233, 250, 265, 275, 286, 429
  in NCAA tournament, 31, 60–61, 64, 81–82, 154, 205–6, 232, 236, 242–43, 262, 268
  profile, 515

Kansas City Athletics, 373, 375, 376, 382, 386, 387

Kansas City Chiefs, 390, 393, 405

Kansas City Kings, 298, 306, 315, 336

Kansas City Royals, 377, 378, 383, 384, 385

Kansas High School Athletic Halls of Fame, 439

Kansas State University (KSU), 10, 49, 57, 60, 84, 108, 111, 115, 127, 242, 279
  in NCAA tournament, 58, 61, 89, 117–18, 184, 205, 243
  profile, 515

Kapp, Joe, 398

Karver, Elliott, 66

Kaufmann, Bob, 454

Kea, Clarence, 516

Keady, Gene, 349, 447, 541, 542

Kean, Henry A., 453

Keaney, Frank, 362

Kearns, Tommy, 81

Keefe, Adam, 530

Keinath, Charles, 8

Kelleher, Ed, 13, 39

Keller, Billy, 142

Keller, Charlie, 380

Keller, John, 447

Kelley, Allen, 64

Kelley, Dean, 64, 316

Kelley, Larry, 398

Kelly, Harry, 210, 214, 275, 316, 496

Kelly, Pam, 435

Kelser, Greg, *194*, 519

Kenna, Edgar, 39

Kennedy, Barbara, 435

Kennedy, Bud, 348

Kennedy, Eugene "Goo," 152

Kennedy, John F., 455

Kent State University. *See* Kent University

Kent University, 129, 278, 515

Kentucky, University of, 26, 40, 42, 43, 45, 53, 54, 55, 62, 64, 66, 71, 75, 82, 84, 86, 108, 115, 121, 125, 129, 140, 161, 177, 220, 221, 225, 249, 254, 265, 275, 278, 286
  in NCAA tournament, 49, 50, 52, 58, 61, 67, 72, 82, 85, 88, 117, 127, 149, 158, 174–75, 188, 191, 196, 217, 222–23, 268–69
  profile, 515

Kentucky Colonels, 302, 307, 314, 335

Keogan, George, 36, 362, 365

Kerr, Steve, 240

Kerwin, Jim, 101

Kessinger, Don, *380, 380, 381*

Keydets. *See* Virginia Military

Kidd, Jason, 275, *275*, 316

Kidd, Warren, 519

Killinger, Glen, 398

Kilmer, Billy, 398

Kimble, Bo, 230, 240, 253, 257, 438

Kindall, Jerry, 380

King, Bernard, 177, *182, 317*, 317

King, Bob, 195

King, Dolly, 12

King, George, 453

King, Jimmy, 265, *269*, 269, 274

King, Reggie, 180, 503

King, Ron, 152

King, Stacey, 317

Kinney, Bob, 317

Kinnick, Nile, 398

Kinsbrunner, Mac, 14

Kirby, Terry, 398

Kirk, Dana, 235

Klier, Leo, 26, 317

Knight, Bob, 56, 125, 152, 163, 174, 179, 281, 540, 541
  profile, 350, *350*

Knoche, Chris, 416

Knoche, E. Henry (Hank), 416

Kodak All-American Team, 425

Kojis, Don, 517

Komives, Howard, 115, 505

Koncak, Jon, 529

Konstanty, Jim, 380

Koonce, Cal, 380

Kosmalski, Len, 168

Kotz, John, 317

Koufax, Sandy, 381

Kraft, Jack, 540

Kramer, Barry, 317

Kramer, Ron, 398

Krause, Ed (Moose), 317

Krebs, Jim, 317

Krystkowiak, Larry, 520
Krzyzewski, Mike, 177, 268, 281, 541, 542
    profile, *350*, 350
Kuester, John, 185
Kundla, John, 27
Kunnert, Kevin, 514
Kupec, C. J., 173
Kurland, Bob, 26, 42, 43, 44, 318
Kytle, Weldon, 508
Kyvallos, Lucille, 440

L

La Salle College, 28, 64, 145, 200, 254, 260, 286, 515
    in NCAA tournament, 67–68, 72–73
Lacey, Edgar, 136
Lacey, Sam, 521
Lacy, Jim, 50
Ladner, Berlin, 134
Lady Magic, 435
Laettner, Christian, 262, 265, 266, 269, 459
    player of the year award, 539
    profile, 318
Lafayette College, 75, 151, 516
LaFleur, Andre, 235
LaGarde, Tommy, 185
Lamar, Dwight "Bo," 156, 157, 318, 494, 530
Lamar University, 194, 516
Lambert, Eugene, 368
Lambert, Ward (Piggy), 31, 43, 362
Landa, Howie, 64
Lane, Jerome, 242
Langer, Ralph, 36
Lanier, Bob, *137*, 140, 149, 318, 526
Lapchick, Joe, 121, 355, 362
Larkin, Byron, 536
LaRusso, Rudy, 84, 509
Laskowski, John, 174
Lattner, John, 399
Lavelli, Tony, 50, 318
Lawrence, Janice, *435*, 435
Lawrence Tech, 47
Layden, Elmer, 399
Layne, Floyd, 55
Leagues, formation of, 8
Lear, Hal, 77, 268
Lebanon Valley College, 64
Leddy, Randy, 523
Lee, Alfred (Butch), 174, 180, 189, *190*, *318*, 318, 539
Lee, Clyde, 319, 533
Lee, Keith, 319, 518

Lee, Ron, 177, *291*, 523
Lehigh University, 516
Lemons, Abe, 135, 540
Lennox, Bennie, 115
Leonard, Bob, 64
Leopards. *See* LaFayette
Leslie, Al, 506
Leslie, Todd, 254
"Lethal Weapon 3," 253, 257
Lever, Fat, 206
Lewis, Bob, 41, 125
Lewis, Guy, *130*, 138, *230*, 232, 363, *363*, 540, 541
Lewis, Raymond, 161
Lewis, Reggie, 223, *339*, 487, 522
Lewis, Tom, 230
Liberty University, 265
Lichti, Todd, 530
Lieberman Cline, Nancy, 426, 434, 435
Lienhard, Bob, 512
Lightfoot, Orlando, 473, 513
Lincoln Memorial University, 32
Lincoln University, 12
Lindeman, Paul, 33
Line, Jim, 49
Linkletter, Art, 416
Linn, George, 71
Lions. *See* Columbia; Loyola Marymount
Lister, Alton, 206
Little Creek NAB, 44
Littleton, Cleo, 59, 535
Litwack, Harry, 161, 363
LIU. *See* Long Island University (LIU)
Lloyd, Bob, 129, 319
Lloyd, Earl, 452
Lloyd, Lewis "Magic," 200
LoBalbo, Al, 152
Lobos. *See* New Mexico
Locke, Tates, 350
Loder, Kevin, 452
Loeffler, Ken, *363*, 363
Lofton, Kenny, *381*, 381
Logan, Dave, 399
Lokar, Marko, 254
Long, John, 510
Long Beach State University, 140, 166, 172, 177, 183, 516
    in NCAA tournament, 154, 163
Long Island University (LIU), 12, 15, 27, 34, 56, 285
    profile, 516
Longest game in history, 209
Longhorns. *See* Texas

Mlkvy, Bill, 56, 59, 323
Moccasins. *See* Tennessee-Chattanooga
Modzelewski, Stan, 323
Moffett, Larry, 184
Moir, John, 324
Molinari, Jim, 456
Molinas, Jack, 57
Monarchs. *See* Old Dominion
Moncrief, Sidney, 183, 191, 324, 504
Monday, Rick, 388
Monroe, Earl "The Pearl," 449, 452
Monroe, Rodney, 521
Monson, Don, 541
Montana, University of, 9, 173, 182, 520
Montana State University, 11, 12, 84, 520
Montgomery, Dave, 534
Montreal Alouettes, 403, 405
Montreal Expos, 374, 383, 384, 385
Montross, Eric, 27, 274, 324
Moore, Billie Jean, 441, 442
Moore, Donald (Dudey), 366
Moore, Jonathan, 511
Moore, Leroy, 405
Morehead State University, 57, 265
Morgan, Ralph, 5, 6, 12, 14
Morgan, Tom, 505
Morgernthaler, Elmore, 43
Morris, Lon, 446
Morris, Max, 42, 324
Morris Harvey College. *See* Charleston, University of
Mortensen, Jesse, 408
Mortimer, Jeff, 377, 382
Morton, John, 249
Moscow Red Army Team, 439
Moss, Perry, 211
Moten, Lawrence, 530
Mount, Rick, 95, 140, 141, 142, *146,* 146, 274, 525
    profile, 324
Mount Holyoke College, 421
Mountain States Conference, 501
Mountain States Intercollegiate Athletic Conference, 501
Mountaineers. *See* West Virginia
Mourning, Alonzo, 265, 324
Mulkey Robertson, Kim, 436
Mullin, Chris, 227, 324, 526, 539
Mullins, Jeff, 117
Mullins, Peter, 64, 408
Murdock, Eric, 262
Murdock, Jackie, 80

Murphy, Calvin 95, 135, 140, 146, *149,* 417, 521
    profile, 324
Murphy, Charles (Stretch), 12, 325
Murphy, Tod, 507
Murphy, Tony, 201
Murray, Lamond, 506
Murray State University, 200, 242, 520
Murrell, Red, 84, 510
Musketeers. *See* Xavier
Musso, George, 400
Mustangs. *See* Southern Methodist
Mutombo, Dikembe, 156

N

NABC. *See* National Association of Basketball Coaches (NABC)
NABC coach of the year awards. *See* National coach of the year awards (1955–94)
NABC player of the year awards. *See* National player of the year awards (1955–94)
NAIA. *See* National Association of Intercollegiate Athletics (NAIA)
Naismith, James, 1–4, *2,* 10, 12, 17, 421, 459
    death of, 30
Naismith coach of the year awards. *See* National coach of the year awards (1955–94)
Naismith Memorial Basketball Hall of Famers
    1959 inductees, 314, 319, 323, 353, 364, 366
    1960–64 inductees, 318, 320, 325,, 327, 333, 339, 357, 360, 363, 364
    1965–69 inductees, 303, 354, 356, 358, 360, 362, 368
    1970–74 inductees, 301, 327, 329, 330, 356, 357, 371
    1975–79 inductees, 295, 296, 300, 308, 310, 319, 328, 331, 337, 363, 364, 365, 366, 368
    1980–84 inductees, 299, 303, 309, 310, 327, 334, 352, 355, 357, 358, 411, 443
    1985–89 inductees, 295, 296, 297, 302, 311, 312, 316, 319, 321, 335, 338, 350, 365, 369, 443
    1990–94 inductees, 295, 296, 305, 314, 336, 350, 355, 364, 371, 432, 434, 436, 443
Naismith player of the year awards. *See* National player of the year awards (1955–94)
Nance, Larry, 325
Nance, Lynn, 455
Nash, Charles (Cotton), 325
Nashville Business College, 423
National Association of Basketball Coaches (NABC), 25, 364, 398, 412, 502, 537

in NCAA tournament, 55, 58–59, 77, 167, 169–70, 185, 195, 216–17, 242

    profile, 521

North Carolina-Wilmington, University of, 230

North Central Conference, 380, 390

North Dallas Forty, 395

North Texas State University, 177, 182

Northeast Conference, 209, 487, 488

Northeastern Illinois University, 254, 272

Northeastern University, 26, 211, 220, 223, 235

    profile, 521

Northern Arizona, University of, 56, 63

Northern Illinois University, 260

Northern Iowa, University of, 255, 522

Northwest College Conference, 8

Northwest College Women's Sports Association, 436

Northwestern University, 39, 43, 75, 115, 146, 194, 254

    profile, 522

Notre Dame, University of, 5, 15, 26, 34, 36, 43, 49, 67, 75, 151, 157, 161, 183, 201, 288

    in NCAA tournament, 67, 149, 194, 196, 232

    profile, 522

Nowak, Henry (Hank), 417, 507

Nowak, Paul, 325

Nowell, Mel, 96

Nuesch, Fred, 502

NYU. *See* New York University (NYU)

O

O'Brien, Eddie, 383

O'Brien, Jim, 281

O'Brien, Johnny, 59, 63, 64, 325, 383

O'Brien, Ralph "Buckshot," 53

O'Conner, Frank (Bucky), 366

O'Connor, Ed, 71

O'Dea, Pete, 527

O'Hanian, Jay Kerkon. *See* Connors, Mike

O'Koren, Mike, 185, 325

O'Neal, Shaquille, 265, 326, 539

O'Neil, Bruce, 351

O'Neil, Dick, 71

O'Neill, E. P., 6

O'Shea, Kevin, 326

Oakland Athletics, 373, 374, 383, 384, 386

Oftring, Frank, 55

Ohio State College Football Hall of Fame, 388

Ohio State University, 5, 25, 29, 55, 79, 105, 115, 151, 179, 281

in NCAA tournament, 43, 44–45, 96–97, 102, 107–8, 153

    profile, 522

Ohio University, 117, 149, 254, 522

Ohio Valley Conference, 50, 154, 161, 356, 489

Oklahoma, University of, 12, 26, 45, 47, 115, 214, 220, 240, 253, 254, 430

    in NCAA tournament, 242–43, 269

    profile, 522

Oklahoma A&M University, 26, 27, 28, 32, 42, 46, 50, 63

    in NCAA tournament, 43, 44–45, 51, 58

Oklahoma City University, 135

Oklahoma State University, 44, 108, 115, 121, 235, 263, 269

    profile, 523

Olajuwon, Hakeem, 156, 212, *217,* 217, 220

    profile, *326,* 326

Old Dominion University, 262, 523

Oldham, John, *288*

Oler, Jim, 511

Oleynick, Frank, 172

Oliphant, Elmer, 401

Oliver, Brian, 253, *257,* 257

Oliver, Newt, 449

Olkowski, June, 437

Olliver, Mike, 516

Olsen, Harold, 25, 366

Olson, Robert (Lute), *207,* 274, 289, 447, 541

    profile, *351,* 351

Olympic boycott, 463

Olympic controversy against USSR, 462

Olympics (men's basketball team), **459–64**

    1904 games, 459

    1912 games, 411

    1924 games, 459

    1928 games, 408, 459

    1932 games, 408

    1936 games, 459, 460

    1948 games, 296, 298, 309, 407, 408, 460

    1952 games, 316, 318, 319, 353, 360, 407, 447, 460

    1956 games, 300, 303, 316, 329, 357, 407, 414, 460–61

    1960 games, 296, 298, 304, 314, 319, 328, 337, 366, 407, 453, 461

    1964 games, 296, 299, 311, 339, 360, 408, 411, 461

    1968 games, 311, 337, 360, 408, 462

    1972 games, 299, 301, 327, 349, 360, 416, 462

    1976 games, 303, 306, 322, 352, 462, 463

    1980 games, 294, 298, 299, 333, 355, 463

Puidokas, Steve, 534
Purdie, Darrwin, 526
Purdue University, 8, 12, 31, 71, 105, 125, 140, 166,
    177, 200, 254, 274, 278
    in NCAA tournament, 141–42, 275
    profile, 525
Purple Eagles. See Niagara

Q

Quakers. See Pennsylvania
Queenan, Daren, 516
Queens College, 424
Quigg, Joe, 81
Quimby, Art, 509
Quinnett, Brian, 235

R

Racers. See Murray State
Radcliff, Jim, 516
Ragin' Cajuns. See Southwestern Louisiana
Rainbow Classic, 276
Rainbows. See Hawaii
Raivio, Rick, 524
Rambis, Kurt, 528
Ramblers. See Loyola of Chicago
Rambling Wreck. See Georgia Tech
Rambo, John, 408
Rams. See Colorado State; Fordham; Rhode Island;
    Virginia Commonwealth
Ramsay, Jack, 102, 103
Ramsey, Frank, 67, 327
Ramsey, Ray, 402
Rankin, Jill, 438
Rankings. See Converse-Dunkel Ratings; Dunkel
    Ratings; National polls; Premo Power Polls
Ranzino, Sam, 58, 327
Rasmussen, Dennis, 384
Rasmussen, Wayne, 402
Ratings. See Converse-Dunkel Ratings; Dunkel
    Ratings; National polls; Premo Power Polls
Ratleff, Ed, 163, 327
Ratterman, George, 43, 403
Raveling, George, 88, 430, 542
Rawlings, Hunter, III, 417
Ray, Don, 288
Raycroft, Joseph E., 4, 9
Rayl, Jimmy, 105, 111
Razorbacks. See Arkansas
Reagan, Ronald, 400

Rebels. See Mississippi
Rebounding leaders (individuals)
    1950–51 – 1953–54, 57, 60, 62, 69
    1954–55 – 1958–59, 72, 76, 81, 85, 90
    1959–60 – 1963–64, 97, 101, 107, 111, 116
    1964–65 – 1968–69, 121, 126, 131, 135, 141
    1969–70 – 1973–74, 147, 152, 157, 162, 168
    1974–75 – 1978–79, 174, 178, 183, 189, 195
    1979–80 – 1983–84, 200, 205, 210, 216, 221
    1984–85 – 1988–89, 227, 231, 237, 241, 248
    1989–90 – 1993–94, 256, 261, 267, 273, 280
Rebounding leaders (teams)
    1954–55 – 1958–59, 72, 76, 81, 85, 90
    1959–60 – 1963–64, 97, 101, 107, 111, 116
    1964–65 – 1968–69, 121, 126, 131, 135, 141
    1969–70 – 1973–74, 147, 152, 157, 162, 168
    1974–75 – 1978–79, 174, 178, 183, 189, 195
    1979–80 – 1983–84, 200, 205, 210, 216, 221
    1984–85 – 1988–89, 227, 231, 237, 241, 248
    1989–90 – 1993–94, 256, 261, 267, 273, 281
Records, NCAA, **545–59**
Recruiting scandal, 428
Red Cross games, 37
Red Flash. See St. Francis (Pa.)
Red Raiders. See Colgate; Texas Tech
Red Storm. See St. John's
Redbirds. See Illinois State
Redskins. See Miami (Ohio)
Reddy, Helen, 425
Reed, Anthony, 532
Reed, Jim, 531
Reed, Ron, 384
Reed, Sykes, 12
Reed, Willis, 452
Reese, Jason, 522
Reeves, Khalid, 281
Referees, 3, 6
Regional third-place games, 177
Rehnquist, Jim ,455
Rehnquist, William, 455
Reid, J. R., 328
Reiff, Joe, 328
Reigel, Bill, 453
Renick, Jesse "Cab," 28
Renko, Steve, 384
Rensselaer Polytechnic Institute, 42
Revon, Nick, 529
Reynolds, Jerry, 227
Rhode Island, University of, 34, 275, 525
Rhode Island State, 39, 42, 43, 49
Rhodes, Lafester, 235

Siebern, Norm, 386, 453
Siebert, Sonny, 386
Siegfried, Larry, 96
Siena College, 63, 250, 528
Sikma, Jack, 452
Silas, C. J. (Pete), 418
Silas, Paul, 105, 331, 509
Simmons, John, 386
Simmons, Lionel, 254, 331, 481, 516, 539
Sinbad. *See* Adkins, David
Singh, Sadat, 12
Six-player basketball, 423
Skyline Conference, 56
Skyline Eight Conference, 501
Skyline Six Conference, 501
Slack, Charlie, 71, 75, 518
Slater, Reginald, 536
Slaughter, Fred, 411
Slaughter, Jose, 524
Sloan, Jerry, 451
Sloan, Norman, 249, *368*, 368, 540
Smart, Doug, 534
Smart, Keith, 236
Smathers, George, 418
Smiley, Jack, 36
Smith, Bev, 438
Smith, Bill, 151
Smith, Charles, 242, 524
Smith, Chris, 509, 534
Smith, Dean, 107, 138, 262, 272, 274, 281, 347, 353,
    355, 419, 462
    coach of the year award, 540, 541, 542
    profile, 352
Smith, Doug, 520
Smith, Elmore, 452, *454*, 454
Smith, George, 369
Smith, Kenny, 332
Smith, Lee, 386
Smith, Michael, 506
Smith, Mike, 510
Smith, Reggie, 531
Smith, Richard, 504
Smith, Robert, 184
Smith, Sam, 185
Smith, Steve (International), 246
Smith, Steve (Michigan State), 519
Smith, Stevin, 504
Smith, Tony, 184
Smith, Vernon (Catfish), 404, 531
Smith College, 421
Smits, Rik, 156, 332

SMU. *See* Southern Methodist University
Smuin, Dick, 41
Snowden, Fred, 162
Sojourner, Mike, 161
Sojourner, Willie, 534
Sooners. *See* Oklahoma
Sophie Newcomb College, 421
Sorenson, Dave, 147
South Alabama, University of, 528
South Carolina, University of, 151, 201, 204, 250,
    528
South Florida, University of, 216, 528
    profile, 492
Southeastern Conference (SEC), 30, 32, 45, 50, 56,
    101, 134, 161, 194, 217, 225, 247, 250, 279, 281, 346,
    351, 352, 358, 368, 374, 393, 406, 409, 427, 428, 434,
    438, 440, 468
Southeastern Louisiana University, 101
Southern Cal. *See* Southern California, University
    of
Southern California, University of, 12, 27, 34, 49,
    79, 88, 125, 129, 131, 140, 154, 216, 230, 254, 286,
    429
    in NCAA tournament, 31, 67–68
    profile, 529
Southern California Intercollegiate Athletic
    Conference, 416
Southern California Junior College Conference,
    385
Southern Conference, 27, 30, 32, 49, 56, 58, 60, 63,
    86, 88, 101, 111, 148, 161, 347, 348, 355, 360, 382,
    387, 400, 404
    profile, 493
Southern Illinois, University of, 134, 214, 529
Southern Intercollegiate Athletic Association, 7,
    493
Southern Methodist University (SMU), 82, 130,
    131, 172, 529
Southern Mississippi, University of, 134, 201, 240,
    274, 278
    profile, 529
Southern University, 274
Southland Conference, 177, 220
Southwest Conference (SWC), 56, 71, 115, 177, 220,
    232, 183, 351, 363, 379, 382, 389, 397, 407, 408, 412,
    413, 429, 433, 440, 494, 501
    profile, 495
Southwest Intercollegiate Athletic Conference, 495
Southwest Missouri State University, 236, 453, 529
Southwestern Athletic Conference (SWAC), 199,
    496

U.S. Basketball Writers Association (USBWA), 153, 379, 411, 420, 436, 439, 440, 441, 443, 502

U.S. Basketball Writers Association (USBWA) coach of the year awards. *See* National coach of the year awards

U.S. Basketball Writers Association (USBWA) player of the year awards. *See* National player of the year awards

U.S. International, 231, 246, 249, 260

U.S. Jones Cup Team, 443

U.S. Military Academy, 12

U.S. Olympic team. *See* Olympics (men's basketball team); Olympics (women's basketball team)

U.S. Select Team, 443

USA Basketball, 431, 459, 502

USA Today polls. *See* National polls

Usilton, Jimmy, 363

Utah, University of, 26, 38, *39*, 50, 75, 108, 121, 286
in NCAA tournament, 40–41, 43, 73, 97, 103, 127
profile, 532

Utah Jazz, 309, 321, 332, 338

Utah Stars, 320

Utah State University, 108, 120, 533

Utes. *See* Utah

Uthoff, Dean, 514

V

Vacendak, Steve, 125

Valenti, Paul, 358

Valentine, Ronnie, 523

Vallely, John 141, 335

Valparaiso University, 279

Valvano, Jim, 129, *255*, 255, *370*, *370*, 370

Van Ackeren, Rev. Maurice E., 419

Van Arsdale, Dick, 335

Van Breda Kolff, Butch, 123, 279, 540

Van Eman, Lanny, 105

Vance, Gene, 36

Vandals. *See* Idaho

Vanderbilt University, 4, 8, 45, 134, 140, 247, 249
profile, 533

VanDerveer, Tara, 429, 430

Vandeweghe, Ernie, 50

Vandeweghe, Kiki, 50, 202

Vann, David, 527

Vaughn, Charlie, 529

Vaughn, David, 161

Vaught, Loy, 250

Veal, Inman (Coot), 387

Veale, Bob, 387

Verga, Bob, 335

Vermillion, Jerry, 512

Vermont, University of, 135, 265, 279

Versace, Dick, 541

Vikings. *See* Cleveland State

Villanova University, 50, 53, 142, 149, 225, 228, 290
in NCAA tournament, 52, 153–54, 211, 225, 232
profile, 533

Vincent, Don, 86

Vinroot, Richard, 419

Virginia, University of, 10, 204, 206, 214, 220, 289, 429
in NCAA tournament, 217, 222, 250
profile, 533

Virginia Commonwealth University, 223, 533

Virginia Military Institute, 533

Virginia Polytechnic Institute and State University, 161, 288, 534

Virginia Squires, 305, 333

Virginia Tech University, 202

Vitale, Dick, 129

Voelkel, Ray, 193

Voigts, Bob, 405

Volunteers. *See* Tennessee

W

WAC. *See* Western Athletic Conference (WAC)

Wacker, Mike, 210

Wade, Bob, 235

Wade, Margaret, 424, 443

Wade, Mark, 238, 235

Wade Trophy, 432, 433, 434, 435, 436, 437, 439, 443

Wagner, Virgil, 405

Wagnon, Dave, 125

Wake Forest University, 44, 63, 105, 134, 140, 162, 270, 272, 276
in NCAA tournament, 102–3, 107, 184
profile, 534

Walk, Neal, 134, 335, 511

Walker, Chet, 336

Walker, Darrell, 447

Walker, Foots, 452

Walker, Jimmy, *129*, 129, 336, 525

Walker, Jimmy (mayor), 15

Walker, Joyce, 439

Walker, Kenny, 223, 336

Walker, Myron, 526

Walker, Rosie, 439

Wallace, Grady, 79

Wilkens, Lenny, *290*, 338
Wilkerson, Bobby, 174, 179
Wilkes, Jamaal. *See* Wilkes, Keith
Wilkes, James, 202
Wilkes, Keith, *170, 170, 338*, 338
Wilkes College, 56
Wilkins, Dominique, 338
Wilkins, Gerald, 447
Wilkinson, Buzz, 66, 71
Wilkinson, Herb, 40
William & Mary, College of, 101, 430, 535
Williams, Charles (Buck), 338
Williams, Donald, 274
Williams, Doug, 454
Williams, Freeman, 182, 188, 275, 338
Williams, Gary, 280
Williams, Henry, 532
Williams, James "Fly," 161, 397
Williams, Jerome, 526
Williams, Joe, 152
Williams, John, 227
Williams, Kenny, 447
Williams, Larry, 185
Williams, Paul, 216
Williams, Ray, 182
Williams, Reggie, 221, 338
Williams, Rob, 211
Williams, Rollie, 366
Williams, Ronnie, 511
Williams, Roy, 275, *353*, 353, 542
Williams, Sam, 206
Williams College, 8, 9
Williamson, Corliss, 280
Williamson, John, 156
Willis, Kevin, 447
Wilson, Bob, 452
Wilson, Clarence, 453
Wilson, George, 339
Wimbledon tennis tournament, 409
Winfield, Dave, 388
Winfrey, Oprah, 414
Winkles, Bobby, 388
Winter, Fred (Tex), 370, 540
Winters, Efrem, 513
Winton, Gary, 504
Wisconsin, University of, 5, 8, 10, 11, 12, 25, 35, 45, 120, 129, 177
   in NCAA tournament, 32–33
   profile, 535
Wisconsin-Green Bay, University of, 535
Wisconsin-Milwaukee, University of, 129

Wise, Dale, 511
Wise, Earl, 531
Wise, Francois, 516
Witte, Les, 339
Wittenberg University, 451
Woelffer, Dennis, 535
Wohl, Dave, 154
Wolf, Ralph, 359
Wolfe, Kenny, 420
Wolfpack. *See* North Carolina State
Wolverines. *See* Michigan
Women's basketball, **421–44**. *See also* Olympics (women's basketball team)
Women's Basketball News Service player of the year award, 435
Women's Professional Basketball League, 434, 436
Women's rights, 422
Women's Sports Foundation Hall of Fame, 443
Women's Sports Foundation player of the year award, 435
Won-lost percentage leaders (teams)
   1967–68 – 1968–69, 135, 141
   1969–70 – 1973–74, 147, 152, 157, 162, 168
   1974–75 – 1978–79, 174, 178, 183, 189, 195
   1979–80 – 1983–84, 200, 205, 210, 216, 221
   1984–85 – 1988–89, 227, 231, 237, 241, 248
   1989–90 – 1993–94, 256, 261, 267, 273, 281
Wood, Al, 206
Wood, Leon, 507
Woodard, Lynette, 426, 439
Wooden, John, 12, *13*, 50, 55, 108, 116, 117, *136*, 136, 137, 161, 166, 172, *173*, 174, 184, 202, 268, 275, 347, 398, 452, 537
   coach of the year award, 540
   coach profile, *371*, 371
   player profile, 339
Wooden coach of the year awards. *See* National coach of the year awards (1955–94)
Wooden player of the year awards. *See* National player of the year awards (1955–94)
Woods, Eddie, 523
Woods, Randy, 260
Woods, Wilbur, 12
Wooldridge, Jim, 455
Woolpert, Phil, 140, 371, 540
Workman, Chuck, 388
Worsley, Larry, 121
Worthy, James, 200, 211, 339
Wothke, Les, 348
Wright Field, 44
Wuycik, Dennis, 151

Wyoming, University of, 40, 115, 216, 268
    in NCAA tournament, 37–38
    profile, 536

X

Xavier University, 84, 115, 287
    in NCAA tournament, 236, 250, 262
    profile, 536

Y

Yale University, 4, 5, 6, 8, 10, 50, 145, 151
    profile, 536
Yankee Conference, 96, 358, 501
Yates, Carlos, 225
Yellow Jackets. *See* Georgia Tech
YMCA's School for Christian Workers, 1
Yoest, Mike, 240
Young, Jewell, 339
Young, Michael, 212, 217
Young, Tom, 262, 540
Youngstown Bears, 374
Yow, Kay, *465*
Yugoslavian Olympic team, 413
Yunkus, Rich, 147, 512

Z

Zags. *See* Gonzaga
Zawoluk, Bob, 53, 61
Zone defenses, 11
Zuppke, Bob, 7, 406

ELDERSBURG

DEC   1996